A SELECT LIBRARY

OF THE

NICENE AND POST-NICENE FATHERS

OF

THE CHRISTIAN CHURCH

EDITED BY

PHILIP SCHAFF, D.D., LL.D.,

PROFESSOR IN THE UNION THEOLOGICAL SEMINARY, NEW YORK,

IN CONNECTION WITH A NUMBER OF PATRISTIC SCHOLARS OF EUROPE AND AMERICA.

VOLUME VIII

SAINT AUGUSTIN:

EXPOSITIONS ON THE BOOK OF PSALMS

TRANSLATED, WITH NOTES AND INDICES

T&T CLARK
EDINBURGH

WM. B. EERDMANS PUBLISHING COMPANY
GRAND RAPIDS, MICHIGAN

British Library Cataloguing in Publication Data

Nicene & Post-Nicene Fathers. — 1st series
1. Fathers of the church
I. Title   II. Schaff, Philip
230'.11   BR60.A62

T&T Clark ISBN 0 567 09397 2

Eerdmans ISBN 0-8028-8105-X

Reprinted, May 1989

PHOTOLITHOPRINTED BY EERDMANS PRINTING COMPANY
GRAND RAPIDS, MICHIGAN, UNITED STATES OF AMERICA

EXPOSITIONS ON THE BOOK OF PSALMS.

BY

SAINT AUGUSTIN,

BISHOP OF HIPPO.

EDITED, WITH BRIEF ANNOTATIONS, AND CONDENSED FROM THE SIX VOLUMES
OF THE OXFORD TRANSLATION,

BY

A. CLEVELAND COXE, D.D.,

EDITOR OF THE ANTE-NICENE FATHERS, ETC.

EDITOR'S PREFACE.

THE delightful task of editing these *Enarrations*, which was what I undertook, became, indeed, a very painful one when the general editor informed me that the whole work must be comprised in a single volume of the series. This allowed but one hundred pages to each one of the six volumes of the Oxford translation. But I felt that my learned friend was right (1) in deciding that St. Augustin's treatment of the Psalms must not be wanting to the series, and (2) that the exposition is so diffuse and digressive, that it readily admits of abridgment, if these exceptional features supply the material for retrenchments. In working out the result, I have " done what I could." I have preserved the African Psalter entire, with as much of the comment as was possible; even so overrunning, at the publishers' cost, the six hundred pages which were all subscribers might expect. The only means of avoiding this was to omit entirely the CXIXth Psalm, an expedient to which I could not consent.

To the primitive believers came the Psalter, like an aftermath, wet with the dews of a new birth as from the womb of the morning. The Spirit had descended upon it anew, as showers upon the mown grass; and it had sprung up afresh, sweeter than before, for the pasture of flocks. The Church received it as full of Christ, as the inheritance of a nobler and truer Israel, for which His coming had illuminated it with a genuine interpretation, painting even its darker and clouded surfaces with the bow of promise, now made the symbol of an everlasting covenant and of all promises fulfilled in Him. Hence the local and temporary meanings of the Psalms were regarded as insignificant. Their Sinaitic comminations and their conformities to the Law were but prophecies which the Jews had voluntarily appropriated by rejecting the Son of David. They were types of what had been fulfilled in their rejected Messiah. The Church received the Psalter from the temple and the synagogue,[1] and adopted it into liturgic use, " with hymns and spiritual songs," all magnifying the crucified and glorified Christ. With the fulfilment of prophecy by the destruction of the Temple and the dispersion of the Jews, everything pertaining to the law was sloughed from its ripened stalk; and the Psalter blossomed with the consummate flowers and fruitage which were its deeper intent, and which had waited so long to be disclosed. The true David had come, and little thought of the typical David was to be entertained: the true Israel was to be seen everywhere, and the dead images of legal rites and symbols were to be interpreted only by the Gospel. To bring out its hidden meanings, the reading and chanting of the Psalter received the accentuation of antiphons and doxologies, and constantly elevated the worshippers into the newness of the spirit out of the oldness of the letter. Thus the whole book breathed a sweetness unknown to the Hebrews, but for which kings and prophets had patiently waited. The name of Jesus disclosed itself in every reference to salvation, and perfumed these sacred odes with a flavour that could come only from " the Root and the Offspring of David." Such

---

[1] See Ante-Nicene Fathers, vol. vii. p. 530 *et seq.*

was the Psalter to the primitive faithful : the walk to Emmaus had opened their eyes to behold the Lord.   To the true interpretation of the Psalms St. Paul had supplied the key, and from the beginning of the Church's institutions we find evidences of the enthusiasm with which the Psalter was appropriated in all the richness of its evangelic import.   The earliest Fathers are full of what the genius of Augustin has embodied in his *Enarrations*, which nobody must confound with works of scientific exegesis.   The author's one idea was widely different from that of modern critics.   His "accommodations" of Scripture, as they would now be called, are part of the system which the Church had received, of which Christ was the Alpha and the Omega, and in which the foreshadowing David was nowhere.[1]   He who comes to this volume with any other conception of its uses will be sadly disappointed.   In the critical study of the Psalms, with all the modern helps, such as Delitzsch and others have so richly supplied, let us not fail to exercise ourselves day and night ; but if, as Christians, we wish to catch the living Spirit that animates the "wheels" or mechanical structure of the Psalms, let us learn from Augustin that indeed in every sense a greater than David, a "greater than Solomon, is here."   The fanciful ingenuity with which our author interweaves the New Testament with the Psalms will at first provoke a smile.   His ideas seem often overstrained and unnatural.   But let us reflect that he is animating the Church of Christ with the true "spirit of prophecy," which is the "testimony of Jesus ; " that his object is to hang Gospel associations upon every stem and twig that come from the root of Jesse, and to wean even the Hebrew Christians from their instinctive references to the Law.   Let us adopt these joint conceptions of the work, and we shall find in it a glorious illustration of the Apostle's assurance, "Ye are not come unto the mount that burned with fire, . . . but unto Mount Sion, and unto the city of the living God, the heavenly Jerusalem, . . . and to Jesus the mediator of the new covenant."

In every way the divine and the student will find this work, even as here presented, a noble introduction to patristic studies.   Let us observe also what it proves.   It gives us the old African Psalter in all its rude and uncouth conceptions of the Septuagint, and teaches us how much we owe to the erudition and labours of St. Jerome.   First of all, the dignity of the Holy Scriptures, and their importance to all Christians, are assumed.   Its historical values are very great : it shows the absolute freedom of the early Church from the corruptions of mediævalism.   The Pentecostal unity of Christendom, the Catholic and Apostolic system as defined in the constitutions of Nicæa and Constantinople, the autonomy of national Churches, the independence of the African Church (illustrated by the personal history of Augustin, who rejected communion with the Bishop of Rome when he stretched his claims beyond seas), and the dogmatic primacy of the patriarch-ate of Carthage in Latin Christendom as the mother of its theology, are assumed in every reflec-tion upon the Donatists, and in the tone and voice of the great preacher himself, to whom the Western Churches owe all that survives their schism and corruptions, even to our own day.   But the ethical and doctrinal teacher will find the charm of these pages, (1) in their correspondence with the evangelical precepts of the Sermon on the Mount, and their freedom from the tainted dis-tinctions and dilutions of modern casuists ; (2) in their perpetual enforcement of the Pauline ideas of justification, harmonized successfully with those of St. James ; (3) in the faithful exhibi-tion of the doctrines of grace ; (4) and in the loyalty to Jesus Christ of every word ; abasing human merit, and presenting Him as "the end of the law for righteousness," with an uncompro-mising tenacity, and a persevering reiteration of this fundamental verity which seems to foresee the gross departure of Western Churches from their original purity, and to "lay an anchor to windward" for their restoration to orthodoxy.

The readers of this volume will need little reference to the innumerable commentaries which have been devoted to the Psalter ; but I must mention the exceptional work of the late erudite J. MASON NEALE, D.D., because it throws light on the liturgical history of the Psalter in the Western

---

[1] Compare 2 Chron. vi. 42, Isa. lv. 3, and Acts xiii. 34.

Churches. The learned commentary of the late Bishop of Lincoln, Dr. Wordsworth, will be found to combine in a remarkable degree, with critical exposition, the Augustinian spirit of devout evangelical associations and elevations.

The editor of this volume blesses God for much spiritual help and comfort afforded by the review of these "songs of our pilgrimage," with which his task has enriched the latest years of that period of our mortality beyond which all is but labour and sorrow.

A. C. C.

May 10, 1888.

NOTE.

It remains to note that I have had the Benedictine edition in the types of Louvain and of Migne constantly at hand, and have referred to them not only in all cases of doubt, but for general refreshment of mind; the epigrammatic beauty and consonance of Augustin's Latin being untranslatable. From the Oxford translations I have rarely departed, and in all important instances have noted the *wherefore* in the margin. It was not the design of this series to give the reader any other than the masterly work of the scholars to whom we owe its appearance. Other instances have been such inconsiderable adaptations as are demanded in the suture of parts dislocated by abridgment. My brief annotations are always bracketed and marked by an initial of my name.

ADVERTISEMENT.

IT seems necessary to give the following outline of the history of this Oxford translation. It was undertaken as part of the great series of original translations which appeared "under the patronage of William, Archbishop of Canterbury, from its commencement, A.D. 1836, until his Grace's departure in peace, A.D. 1848." It proposed to include all the "Fathers of the Holy Catholic Church before the division of the East and West," and this exposition was dedicated as a memorial of Archbishop Howley in the following words: —

"*To the memory of the most reverend father in God, William, Lord Archbishop of Canterbury, Primate of all England, formerly Regius Professor of Divinity in the University of Oxford, this library of ancient bishops, fathers, doctors, martyrs, confessors, of Christ's Holy Catholic Church, undertaken amid his encouragement, and carried on for twelve years under his sanction, until his departure hence in peace, is gratefully and reverently inscribed.*"

The preface to the first volume was by the saintly CHARLES MARRIOTT of Oriel College, with whom I enjoyed some acquaintaince. It is well worth preserving here,[1] and is as follows: —

IN any commentary on a portion of the Old Testament by a writer unacquainted with Hebrew, exact criticism, and freedom from mistake, must not be expected. But the Psalms have been so in the mouth and in the heart of God's people in all languages, that it has been necessary often to find an explanation suitable to imperfect translations. And no doubt it is intended that we should use such explanations for the purpose of edification, when we are unable to be more accurate, though in proving doctrine it is necessary always to remember and allow for any want of acquaintance with the original, or uncertainty with respect to its actual meaning. However, the main scope and bearing of the text is rarely affected by such points as vary in different translations, and the analogy of the faith is sufficient to prevent a Catholic[2] mind from adopting any error in consequence of a text seeming to bear a heterodox meaning. Perhaps the errors of translation in the existing versions may have led the Fathers to adopt rules of interpretation ranging too far from the simple and literal; but having such translations, they could hardly use them otherwise. Meanwhile St. Augustin will be found to excel in the intense apprehension of those great truths which pervade the whole of Sacred Writ, and in the vivid and powerful exposition of what bears upon them. It is hardly possible to read his practical and forcible applications of Holy Scripture, without feeling those truths by the faith of which we ought to live brought home to the heart in a wonderful manner. His was a mind that strove earnestly to solve the great problems of human life, and after exhausting the resources, and discovering the emptiness, of errcneous systems, found truth and rest at last in Catholic Christianity, in the religion of the Bible as expounded by St. Ambrose. And though we must look to his *Confessions* for the full view of all his cravings after real good, and their ultimate satisfaction, yet throughout his works we have the benefit of the earnestnsss with which he sought to feed on the "sincere milk of the word."

His mystical and allegorical interpretation, in spite of occasional mistakes, which belong rather to the translation than to himself, will be found in general of great value. It is to a considerable extent systematic, and the same interpretation of the same symbols is repeated throughout the work, and is indeed often common to him with other Fathers. The "feet" taken for the affections, "clouds" for the Apostles, and many other instances, are of very frequent occurrence. And it is evident that a few such general interpretations must be a great help to those who wish to make an allegorical use of those portions of Holy Scripture which are adapted for it. Nor are they adhered to with such strictness as to deprive the reader of the benefit of other explanations, where it appears that some other metaphor or allegory was intended. Both St. Augustin and St. Gregory acknowledge, and at times impress on their readers, that metaphorical language is used in Holy Scripture with various meanings under the same symbol.

The discourses on the Psalms are not carried throughout on the same plan, but still are tolerably complete as a commentary, since the longer expositions furnish the means of filling out the shorter notices, in thought at least, to the attentive reader of the whole. They were not delivered continuously, nor all at the same place. Occasionally the author is led by the circumstances of the time into long discussions of a controversial character, especially with respect to the Donatists, against whose narrow and exclusive views he urges strongly the prophecies relating to the universality of the Church. Occasionally a Psalm is first reviewed briefly, so as to give a general clew to its interpretation, and then enlarged upon in several discourses.

For the present translation, as far as the first thirty Psalms, the editors are indebted to a friend who conceals his name; for the remainder of the volume, with part of the next which is to appear, to the Rev. J. E. TWEED, M.A., chaplain of Christ Church, Oxford.

C. M.

OXFORD, 1847.

---

[1] Dated Oxford, Feast of St. Augustin of Canterbury, 1847.   [2] *i.e.* Nicene. — C.

After the first two volumes edited by Mr. Tweed of Christ Church, the third volume (carrying the work down to the end of Psalm lxxv.) appeared with this announcement signed by Mr. Marriott: "The whole of it, as well as a few Psalms at the end of the former and the beginning of the following volume, is translated by T. SCRATTON, Esq., M.A., of Christ Church, Oxford." The fifth volume appeared in April, 1853, with the name of the Rev. H. M. WILKINS, M.A., of Merton College, as translator. In December, 1857, came forth the last volume, with the following advertisement from the pen of Dr. Pusey:—

THE first hundred pages of this volume were printed, when it pleased God to withdraw from all further toil our friend, the Rev. C. Marriott, upon whose editorial labours the Library of the Fathers had for some years wholly depended. Full of activity in the cause of truth and religious knowledge, full of practical benevolence, expanding himself, his strength, his paternal inheritance, in works of piety and charity, in one night his labour was closed, and he was removed from active duty to wait in stillness for his Lord's last call. His friends may perhaps rather thankfully wonder that God allowed one, threatened in many ways with severe disease, to labour for Him so long and so variously, than think it strange that He suddenly, and for them prematurely, allowed him thus far to enter into his rest. To those who knew him best, it has been a marvel how, with health so frail, he was enabled in such various ways, and for so many years, to do active good in his generation. Early called, and ever obeying the call, he has been allowed both active duty and an early rest.

This volume, long delayed, has been completed by the Rev. H. WALFORD, Vice-Principal of St. Edmund's Hall. The principal of St. Edmund Hall, Dr. Barrow, has, with great kindness, allowed himself to be referred to in obscure passages.

St. Augustin's Commentary on the Psalms, then, is now, by the blessing of God, completed for the first time in an English garb. Although, as a commentary, it from time to time fails us, because it explains minutely and verbally a translation of Holy Scripture different from and inferior to our own, yet, on this very ground, it is the more valuable when the translations agree. For St. Augustin was so impressed with the sense of the depth of Holy Scripture, that when it seems to him, on the surface, plainest, then he is the more assured of its hidden depth.[1] True to this belief, St. Augustin pressed out word by word of Holy Scripture, and that, always in dependence on the inward teaching of God the Holy Ghost who wrote it, until he had extracted some fulness of meaning from it. More also, perhaps, than any other work of St. Augustin, this commentary abounds in those condensed statements of doctrinal and practical truth which are so instructive, because at once so comprehensive and so accurate.

May He under whose gracious influence this great work was written, be with its readers also, and make it now, as heretofore, a treasure to this portion of His Church.

E. B. P.

ADVENT, 1857.

---

[1] Here Dr. Pusey quotes the saint's preface to Ps. cxix. See p. 560.—C.

CONTENTS.

ST. AUGUSTIN ON THE PSALMS.

PSALM I.

1. "BLESSED is the man that hath not gone away in the counsel of the ungodly" (ver. 1). This is to be understood of our Lord Jesus Christ, the Lord Man.[1] "Blessed is the man that hath not gone away in the counsel of the ungodly," as "the man of earth did,"[2] who consented to his wife deceived by the serpent, to the transgressing the commandment of God. "Nor stood in the way of sinners." For He came indeed in the way of sinners, by being born as sinners are; but He "stood" not therein, for that the enticements of the world held Him not. "And hath not sat in the seat of pestilence." He willed not an earthly kingdom, with pride, which is well taken for "the seat of pestilence;" for that there is hardly any one who is free from the love of rule, and craves not human glory. For a "pestilence" is disease widely spread, and involving all or nearly all. Yet "the seat of pestilence" may be more appropriately understood of hurtful doctrine; "whose word spreadeth as a canker."[3] The order too of the words must be considered: "went away, stood, sat." For he "went away," when he drew back from God. He "stood," when he took pleasure in sin. He "sat," when, confirmed in his pride, he could not go back, unless set free by Him, who neither "hath gone away in the counsel of the ungodly, nor stood in the way of sinners, nor sat in the seat of pestilence."

2. "But his delight is in the law of the Lord, and in His law will he meditate by day and by night (ver. 2). The law is not made for a righteous man,"[4] says the Apostle. But it is one thing to be in the law, another under the law. Whoso is in the law, acteth according to the law; whoso is under the law, is acted upon according to the law: the one therefore is free, the other a slave. Again, the law, which is written and imposed upon the servant, is one thing; the law, which is mentally discerned by him who needeth not its "letter," is another thing. "He will meditate by day and by night," is to be understood either as without ceasing; or "by day" in joy, "by night" in tribulations. For it is said, "Abraham saw my day, and was glad:"[5] and of tribulation it is said, "my reins also have instructed me, even unto the night."[6]

3. "And he shall be like a tree planted hard by the running streams of waters" (ver. 3); that is either Very "Wisdom,"[7] which vouchsafed to assume man's nature for our salvation; that as man He might be "the tree planted hard by the running streams of waters;" for in this sense can that too be taken which is said in another Psalm, "the river of God is full of water."[8] Or, by the Holy Ghost, of whom it is said, "He shall baptize you in the Holy Ghost;"[9] and again, "If any man thirst, let him come unto Me, and drink;"[10] and again, "If thou knewest the gift of God, and who it is that asketh water of thee, thou wouldest have asked of Him, and He would have given thee living water, of which whoso drinketh shall never thirst, but it shall be made in him a well of water springing up into everlasting life."[11] Or, "by the running streams of waters" may be by the sins of the people, because first the waters are called "peoples" in the Apocalypse;[12] and again, by "running stream" is not unreasonably understood "fall," which hath relation to sin. That "tree" then, that is, our Lord, from the running streams of water, that is, from the sinful people's drawing them by the way into the roots of His discipline, will "bring forth fruit," that is, will establish Churches; "in His season," that is, after He hath been glorified by His Resurrection and Ascension into heaven. For then, by the sending of the Holy Ghost to the Apostles, and by the confirming of their faith in Him, and their mission to the world, He made the Churches to "bring forth fruit." "His leaf also shall not fall," that is, His Word shall not be in vain. For, "all flesh is grass, and the glory of man as the flower of grass; the grass withereth,

---

[1] *Homine Dominico*. This term as applied to our Lord, St. Augustin disallows in his *Retractat*. i. 19. [He would not have objected to the expression of our translator, "the Lord Man," as above. It is the adjective *Dominicus* to which he objects, because it is ambiguous, *quasi* Man *of the* Lord. — C.]
[2] 1 Cor. xv. 47.   [3] 2 Tim. ii. 17.   [4] 1 Tim. i. 9.

[5] John viii. 5, 6.   [6] Ps. xvi. 7.   [7] Prov. viii.
[8] Ps. lxv. 9.   [9] Matt. iii. 11.   [10] John vii. 37.
[11] John iv. 10, 14.   [12] Rev. xvii. 15.

and the flower falleth, but the word of the Lord abideth for ever.[1] And whatsoever He doeth shall prosper," that is, whatsoever that tree shall bear; which "all" must be taken of fruit and leaves, that is, deeds and words.

4. "The ungodly are not so," they are not so, "but are like the dust which the wind casteth forth from the face of the earth" (ver. 4). "The earth" is here to be taken as that stedfastness in God, with a view to which it is said, "The Lord is the portion of mine inheritance, yea, I have a goodly heritage."[2] With a view to this it is said, "Wait on the Lord and keep His ways, and He shall exalt thee to inherit the earth."[3] With a view to this it is said, "Blessed are the meek, for they shall inherit the earth."[4] A comparison too is derived hence, for as this visible earth supports and contains the outer man, so that earth invisible the inner man. "From the face of" which "earth the wind casteth forth the ungodly," that is, pride, in that it puffeth him up. On his guard against which he, who was inebriated by the richness of the house of the Lord, and drunken of the torrent stream of its pleasures, saith, "Let not the foot of pride come against me."[5] From this earth pride cast forth him who said, "I will place my seat in the north, and I will be like the Most High."[6] From the face of the earth it cast forth him also who, after that he had consented and tasted of the forbidden tree that he might be as God, hid himself from the Face of God.[7] That his earth has reference to the inner man, and that man[8] is cast forth thence by pride, may be particularly seen in that which is written, "Why is earth and ashes proud? Because, in his life, he cast forth his bowels."[9] For, whence he hath been cast forth, he is not unreasonably said to have cast forth himself.

5. "Therefore the ungodly rise not in the judgment" (ver. 5) : "therefore," namely, because "as dust they are cast forth from the face of the earth." And well did he say that this should be taken away from them, which in their pride they court, namely, that they may judge : so that this same idea is more clearly expressed in the following sentence, "nor sinners in the counsel of the righteous." For it is usual for what goes before,[10] to be thus repeated more clearly. So that by "sinners" should be understood the "ungodly;" what is before "in the judgment," should be here "in the counsel of the righteous." Or if indeed the ungodly are one thing, and sinners another, so that although every ungodly man is a sinner, yet every sinner is not ungodly; "The ungodly rise not in the

judgment," that is, they shall rise indeed, but not that they should be judged, for they are already appointed to most certain punishment. But "sinners" do not rise "in counsel of the just," that is, that they may judge, but peradventure that they may be judged ; so as of these it were said, "The fire shall try every man's work of what sort it is. If any man's work abide, he shall receive a reward. If any man's work shall be burned, he shall then suffer loss : but he himself shall be saved ; yet so as by fire."

6. "For the Lord knoweth the way of the righteous" (ver. 6). As it is said, medicine knows health, but knows not disease, and yet disease is recognised by the art of medicine. In like manner can it be said that "the Lord knoweth the way of the righteous," but the way of the ungodly He knoweth not. Not that the Lord is ignorant of anything, and yet He says to sinners, "I never knew you."[11] "But the way of the ungodly shall perish ;" is the same as if it were said, the way of the ungodly the Lord knoweth not. But it is expressed more plainly that this should be not to be known of the Lord, namely, to "perish ;" and this to be known of the Lord, namely, to "abide ;" so as that to be should appertain to the knowledge of God, but to His not knowing not to be. For the Lord saith, "I AM that I AM," and, "I AM hath sent me."[12]

PSALM II.

1. "Why do the heathen rage, and the people meditate vain things?" (ver. 1). "The kings of the earth have stood up, and the rulers taken counsel together, against the Lord, and against His Christ" (ver. 2). It is said, "why?" as if it were said, in vain. For what they wished, namely, Christ's destruction, they accomplished not ; for this is spoken of our Lord's persecutors, of whom also mention is made in the Acts of the Apostles.[13]

2. "Let us break their bonds asunder, and cast away their yoke from us" (ver. 3). Although it admits of another acceptation, yet is it more fitly understood as in the person of those who are said to "meditate vain things." So that "let us break their bonds asunder, and cast away their yoke from us," may be, let us do our endeavour, that the Christian religion do not bind us, nor be imposed upon us.

3. "He that dwelleth in the heavens shall laugh them to scorn, and the Lord shall have them in derision" (ver. 4). The sentence is repeated ; for "He who dwelleth in the heavens," is afterwards put, "the Lord ;" and for "shall

---

[1] Isa. xl. 6–8.　　[2] Ps. xvi. 5, 6.　　[3] Ps. xxxvii. 34.
[4] Matt. v. 5.　　[5] Ps. xxxvi. 11.　　[6] Isa. xiv. 13, 14.
[7] Gen. iii. 8.　　[8] Oxford mss. "the inner man."
[9] Ecclus. x. 9.　　[10] Oxford mss. "what is darkly said."

[11] Matt. vii. 23.
[12] Exod. iii. 14. [Irenæus, p. 419, vol. i. A. N. F.; also Tertull. p. 682, vol. iii. A. N. F; same series elsewhere. — C.]
[13] Acts iv. 26.

laugh them to scorn," is afterwards put, "shall have them in derision." Nothing of this however must be taken in a carnal sort, as if God either laugheth with cheek, or derideth with nostril; but it is to be understood of that power which He giveth to His saints, that they seeing things to come, namely, that the Name and rule of Christ is to pervade posterity and possess all nations, should understand that those men "meditate a vain thing." For this power whereby these things are foreknown is God's "laughter" and "derision." "He that dwelleth in the heavens shall laugh them to scorn." If by "heavens" we understand holy souls, by these God, as foreknowing what is to come, will "laugh them to scorn, and have them in derision."

4. "Then He shall speak unto them in His wrath, and vex them in His sore displeasure" (ver. 5). For showing more clearly how He will "speak unto them," he added, He will "vex them;" so that "in His wrath," is, "in His sore displeasure." But by the "wrath and sore displeasure" of the Lord God must not be understood any mental perturbation; but the might whereby He most justly avengeth, by the subjection of all creation to His service. For that is to be observed and remembered which is written in the Wisdom of Solomon, "But Thou, Lord of power, judgest with tranquillity, and with great favour orderest us."[1] The "wrath" of God then is an emotion which is produced in the soul which knoweth the law of God, when it sees this same law transgressed by the sinner. For by this emotion of righteous souls many things are avenged. Although the "wrath" of God can be well understood of that darkening of the mind, which overtakes those who transgress the law of God.

5. "Yet am I set by Him as King upon Sion, His holy hill, preaching His decree" (ver. 6). This is clearly spoken in the Person of the very Lord our Saviour Christ. But if Sion signify, as some interpret, beholding, we must not understand it of anything rather than of the Church, where daily is the desire raised of beholding the bright glory of God, according to that of the Apostle, "but we with open face beholding the glory of the Lord."[2] Therefore the meaning of this is, Yet I am set by Him as King over His holy Church; which for its eminence and stability He calleth a mountain. "Yet I am set by Him as King." I, that is, whose "bands" they were meditating "to break asunder," and whose "yoke" to "cast away." "Preaching His decree." Who doth not see the meaning of this, seeing it is daily practised?

6. "The Lord hath said unto me, Thou art My Son, to-day have I begotten Thee" (ver. 7). Although that day may also seem to be prophetically spoken of, on which Jesus Christ was born according to the flesh; and in eternity there is nothing past as if it had ceased to be, nor future as if it were not yet, but present only, since whatever is eternal, always is; yet as "to-day" intimates presentiality, a divine interpretation is given to that expression, "To-day have I begotten Thee," whereby the uncorrupt and Catholic faith proclaims the eternal generation of the Power and Wisdom of God, who is the Only-begotten Son.

7. "Ask of Me, and I shall give Thee the nations for Thine inheritance" (ver. 8). This has at once a temporal sense with reference to the Manhood which He took on Himself, who offered up Himself as a Sacrifice in the stead of all sacrifices, who also maketh intercession for us; so that the words, "ask of Me," may be referred to all this temporal dispensation, which has been instituted for mankind, namely, that the "nations" should be joined to the Name of Christ, and so be redeemed from death, and possessed by God. "I shall give Thee the nations for Thine inheritance," which so possess them for their salvation, and to bear unto Thee spiritual fruit. "And the uttermost parts of the earth for Thy possession." The same repeated, "The uttermost parts of the earth," is put for "the nations;" but more clearly, that we might understand all the nations. And "Thy possession" stands for "Thine inheritance."

8. "Thou shalt rule them with a rod of iron," with inflexible justice, and "Thou shalt break them like a potter's vessel" (ver. 9); that is, "Thou shalt break" in them earthly lusts, and the filthy doings of the old man, and whatsoever hath been derived and inured from the sinful clay. "And now understand, ye kings" (ver. 10). "And now;" that is, being now renewed, your covering of clay worn out, that is, the carnal vessels of error, which belong to your past life, "now understand," ye who now are "kings;" that is, able now to govern all that is servile and brutish in you, able now too to fight, not as "they who beat the air, but chastening your bodies, and bringing them into subjection."[3] "Be instructed, all ye who judge the earth." This again is a repetition; "Be instructed" is instead of "understand;" and "ye who judge the earth" instead of "ye kings." For He signifies the spiritual by "those who judge the earth." For whatsoever we judge, is below us; and whatsoever is below the spiritual man, is with good reason called "the earth;" because it is defiled with earthly corruption.

9. "Serve the Lord with fear;" lest what is

---

[1] Wisd. xii. 18.   [2] 2 Cor. iii. 18.   [3] 1 Cor. ix. 26, 27.

said, "Ye kings and judges of the earth," turn into pride : "And rejoice with trembling" (ver. 11). Very excellently is "rejoice" added, lest "serve the Lord with fear" should seem to tend to misery. But again, lest this same rejoicing should run on to unrestrained inconsiderateness, there is added "with trembling," that it might avail for a warning, and for the careful guarding of holiness. It can also be taken thus, "And now ye kings understand ; " that is, And now that I am set as King, be ye not sad, kings of the earth, as if your excellency were taken from you, but rather "understand and be instructed." For it is expedient for you, that ye should be under Him, by whom understanding and instruction are given you. And this is expedient for you, that ye lord it not with rashness, but that ye "serve the Lord" of all "with fear," and "rejoice" in bliss most sure and most pure, with all caution and carefulness, lest ye fall therefrom into pride.

10. "Lay hold of discipline,[1] lest at any time the Lord be angry, and ye perish from the righteous way" (ver. 12). This is the same as, "understand," and, "be instructed." For to understand and be instructed, this is to lay hold of discipline. Still in that it is said, "lay hold of," it is plainly enough intimated that there is some protection and defence against all things which might do hurt unless with so great carefulness it be laid hold of. "Lest at any time the Lord be angry," is expressed with a doubt, not as regards the vision of the prophet to whom it is certain, but as regards those who are warned ; for they, to whom it is not openly revealed, are wont to think with doubt of the anger of God. This then they ought to say to themselves, let us "lay hold of discipline, lest at any time the Lord be angry, and we perish from the righteous way." Now, how "the Lord be angry" is to be taken, has been said above. And "ye perish from the righteous way." This is a great punishment, and dreaded by those who have had any perception of the sweetness of righteousness ; for he who perisheth from the way of righteousness, in much misery will wander through the ways of unrighteousness.

11. "When His anger shall be shortly kindled, blessed are all they who put their trust in Him ; " that is, when the vengeance shall come which is prepared for the ungodly and for sinners, not only will it not light on those "who put their trust in" the Lord, but it will even avail for the foundation and exaltation of a kingdom for them. For he said not, "When His anger shall be shortly kindled," safe "are all they who put

their trust in Him," as though they should have this only thereby, to be exempt from punishment ; but he said, "blessed ; " in which there is the sum and accumulation of all good things. Now the meaning of "shortly" I suppose to be this, that it will be something sudden, whilst sinners will deem it far off and long to come.

PSALM III.[2]

A PSALM OF DAVID, WHEN HE FLED FROM THE FACE OF ABESSALON HIS SON.

1. The words, "I slept, and took rest ; and rose, for the Lord will take me up," lead us to believe that this Psalm is to be understood as in the Person of Christ ; for they sound more applicable to the Passion and Resurrection of our Lord, than to that history in which David's flight is described from the face of his rebellious son. And, since it is written of Christ's disciples, "The sons of the bridegroom fast not as long as the bridegroom is with them ; "[3] it is no wonder if by his undutiful[4] son be here meant that undutiful[4] disciple who betrayed Him. From whose face although it may be understood historically that He fled, when on his departure He withdrew with the rest to the mountain ; yet in a spiritual sense, when the Son of God, that is the Power and Wisdom of God, abandoned the mind of Judas ; when the Devil wholly occupied him ; as it is written, "The Devil entered into his heart,"[5] may it be well understood that Christ fled from his face ; not that Christ gave place to the Devil, but that on Christ's departure the Devil took possession. Which departure, I suppose, is called a flight in this Psalm, because of its quickness ; which is indicated also by the word of our Lord, saying, "That thou doest, do quickly."[5] So even in common conversation we say of anything that does not come to mind, it has fled from me ; and of a man of much learning we say, nothing flies from him. Wherefore truth fled from the mind of Judas, when it ceased to enlighten him. But Absalom, as some interpret, in the Latin tongue signifies, *Patris pax*, a father's peace. And it may seem strange, whether in the history of the kings, when Absalom carried on war against his father ; or in the history of the New Testament, when Judas was the betrayer of our Lord ; how "father's peace" can be understood. But both in the former place they who read carefully, see that David in that war was at peace with his son, who even with sore grief lamented his death, saying, "O Absalom, my son, would God I had died for thee ! "[6] And in the history of the

---

[1] [This reading is corrected by St. Jerome in his Hebraic Psalter, and our Authorized Version "Kiss the Son" is sustained by the best authorities. See a forcible elucidation in Bishop Wordsworth's *Commentary on Psalms*. Ps. ii.—C.]

[2] [On the place of this Psalm in the *Ordo Psalmorum*, see the important principle laid down by Bishop Wordsworth, in his Introduction to the *Psalms*, p. v.—C.]
[3] Matt. ix. 15.   [4] *Impius.*   [5] John xiii. 27.
[6] 2 Sam. xviii. 33.

New Testament by that so great and so wonderful forbearance of our Lord; in that He bore so long with him as if good, when He was not ignorant of his thoughts; in that He admitted him to the Supper in which He committed and delivered to His disciples the figure of His Body and Blood; finally, in that He received the kiss of peace at the very time of His betrayal; it is easily understood how Christ showed peace to His betrayer, although he was laid waste by the intestine war of so abominable a device. And therefore is Absalom called " father's peace," because his father had the peace, which he had not.

2. "O Lord, how are they multiplied that trouble me!" (ver. 1). So multiplied indeed were they, that one even from the number of His disciples was not wanting, who was added to the number of His persecutors. "Many rise up against me; many say unto my soul, There is no salvation for him in his God" (ver. 2). It is clear that if they had had any idea that He would rise again, assuredly they would not have slain Him. To this end are those speeches, "Let Him come down from the cross, if He be the Son of God;" and again, "He saved others, Himself He cannot save."[1] Therefore, neither would Judas have betrayed Him, if he had not been of the number of those who despised Christ, saying, "There is no salvation for Him in His God."

3. "But Thou, O Lord, art my taker."[2] It is said to God in the nature of man, for the taking of man is, the Word made Flesh. "My glory." Even He calls God his glory, whom the Word of God so took, that God became one with Him. Let the proud learn, who unwillingly hear, when it is said to them, "For what hast thou that thou didst not receive? Now if thou didst receive it, why dost thou glory as if thou hadst not received it?"[3] "And the lifter up of my head" (ver. 3). I think that this should be here taken of the human mind, which is not unreasonably called the head of the soul;[4] which so inhered in, and in a sort coalesced with, the supereminent excellency of the Word taking man, that it was not laid aside by so great humiliation of the Passion.

4. "With my voice have I cried unto the Lord" (ver. 4); that is, not with the voice of the body, which is drawn out with the sound of the reverberation of the air; but with the voice of the heart, which to men speaks not, but with God sounds as a cry. By this voice Susanna was heard;[5] and with this voice the Lord Himself commanded that prayer should be made in closets,[6] that is, in the recesses of the heart noiselessly. Nor would one easily say that prayer is not made with this voice, if no sound of words is uttered from the body; since even when in silence we pray within the heart, if thoughts interpose alien from the mind of one praying, it cannot yet be said, "With my voice have I cried unto the Lord." Nor is this rightly said, save when the soul alone, taking to itself nothing of the flesh, and nothing of the aims of the flesh, in prayer, speaks to God, where He only hears. But even this is called a cry by reason of the strength of its intention. "And He heard me out of His holy mountain." We have the Lord Himself called a mountain by the Prophet, as it is written, "The stone that was cut out without hands grew to the size of a mountain."[7] But this cannot be taken of His Person, unless peradventure He would speak thus, out of myself, as of His holy mountain He heard me, when He dwelt in me, that is, in this very mountain. But it is more plain and unembarrassed, if we understand that God out of His justice heard. For it was just that He should raise again from the dead the Innocent who was slain, and to whom evil had been recompensed for good, and that He should render to the persecutor a meet reward, who repaid Him evil for good. For we read, "Thy justice is as the mountains of God."[8]

5. "I slept, and took rest"[9] (ver. 5). It may be not unsuitably remarked, that it is expressly said, "I," to signify that of His own Will He underwent death, according to that, "Therefore doth My Father love Me, because I lay down My life, that I might take it again. No man taketh it from Me; I have power to lay it down, and I have power to take it again."[10] Therefore, saith He, you have not taken Me as though against My will, and slain Me; but "I slept, and took rest; and rose, for the Lord will take me up." Scripture contains numberless instances of sleep being put for death; as the Apostle says, "I would not have you to be ignorant, brethren, concerning them which are asleep."[11] Nor need we make any question why it is added, "took rest," seeing that it has already been said, "I slept." Repetitions of this kind are usual in Scripture, as we have pointed out many in the second Psalm. But some copies have, "I slept, and was cast into a deep sleep."[12] And different copies express it differently, according to the possible renderings of the Greek words, ἐγὼ δὲ ἐκοιμήθην καὶ ὕπνωσα. Unless perhaps sleeping[13] may be taken of one dying, but

---

[1] Matt. xxvii. 42.   [2] *Susceptor.*   [3] 1 Cor. iv. 7.
[4] [1 Thess. v. 23. See Tertull. vol. iii. p. 450, A. N. F.; also Irenæus, vol. i. p. 386, *ibid.*—C.]
[5] Sus. 44.

[6] Matt. vi. 6.   [7] Dan. ii. 34, 35.
[8] Ps. xxxvi. 6. [See Tertullian, p. 364, A. N. F. vol. iii.—C.]
[9] *Ego dormivi, et somnum cepi.* In the Hebrew, also, *I* is emphatic.
[10] John x. 17, 18.   [11] 1 Thess. iv. 13.
[12] *Dormivi, et soporatus sum.*   [13] *Dormitio.*

sleep [1] of one dead : so that sleeping may be the transition into sleep, as awakening is the transition into wakefulness. Let us not deem these repetitions in the sacred writings empty ornaments of speech. "I slept, and took rest," is therefore well understood as "I gave Myself up to My Passion, and death ensued." "And I rose, for the Lord will take Me up." [2] This is the more to be remarked, how that in one sentence the Psalmist has used a verb of past and future time. For he has said, both "I rose," which is the past, and "will take Me up," which is the future ; seeing that assuredly the rising again could not be without that taking up. But in prophecy the future is well joined to the past, whereby both are signified. Since things which are prophesied of as yet to come in reference to time are future ; but in reference to the knowledge of those who prophesy they are already to be viewed as done. Verbs of the present tense are also mixed in, which shall be treated of in their proper place when they occur.

6. "I will not fear the thousands of people that surround me" (ver. 6). It is written in the Gospels how great a multitude stood around Him as He was suffering, and on the cross. "Arise, O Lord, save me, O my God" (ver. 7). It is not said to God, "Arise," as if asleep or lying down, but it is usual in holy Scripture to attribute to God what He doeth in us; not indeed universally, but where it can be done suitably ; as when He is said to speak, when by His gift Prophets speak, and Apostles, or whatsoever messengers of the truth. Hence that text, "Would you have proof of Christ, who speaketh in me?" [3] For he doth not say, of Christ, by whose enlightening or order I speak ; but he attributes at once the speaking itself to Him, by whose gift he spake.

7. "Since Thou hast smitten all who oppose me without a cause." It is not to be pointed as if it were one sentence, "Arise, O Lord, save me, O my God ; since Thou hast smitten all who oppose me without a cause." For He did not therefore save Him, because He smote His enemies ; but rather He being saved, He smote them. Therefore it belongs to what follows, so that the sense is this ; "Since Thou hast smitten all who oppose me without a cause, Thou hast broken the teeth of the sinners ; " that is, thereby hast Thou broken the teeth of the sinners, since Thou hast smitten all who oppose me. It is forsooth the punishment of the opposers, whereby their teeth have been broken, that is, the words of sinners rending with their cursing the Son of God, brought to nought, as it were to dust ; so

that we may understand "teeth" thus, as words of cursing. Of [4] which teeth the Apostle speaks, "If ye bite one another, take heed that ye be not consumed one of another." [5] The teeth of sinners can also be taken as the chiefs of sinners ; by whose authority each one is cut off from the fellowship of godly livers, and as it were incorporated with evil livers. To these teeth are opposed the Church's teeth, by whose authority believers are cut off from the error of the Gentiles and divers opinions, and are translated into that fellowship which is the body of Christ. With these teeth Peter was told to eat the animals when they had been killed, that is, by killing in the Gentiles what they were, and changing them into what he was himself. Of these teeth too of the Church it is said, "Thy teeth are as a flock of shorn sheep, coming up from the bath, whereof every one beareth twins, and there is not one barren among them." [6] These are they who prescribe rightly, and as they prescribe, live ; who do what is written, "Let your works shine before men, that they may bless your Father which is in heaven." [7] For moved by their authority, they believe God who speaketh and worketh through these men ; and separated from the world, to which they were once conformed, they pass over into the members of the Church. And rightly therefore are they, through whom such things are done, called teeth like to shorn sheep ; for they have laid aside the burdens of earthly cares, and coming up from the bath, from the washing away of the filth of the world by the Sacrament of Baptism, every one beareth twins. For they fulfil the two commandments, of which it is said, "On these two commandments hang all the Law and the Prophets ; " [8] loving God with all their heart, and with all their soul, and with all their mind, and their neighbour as themselves. "There is not one barren among them," for much fruit they render unto God. According to this sense then it is to be thus understood, "Thou hast broken the teeth of the sinners," that is, Thou hast brought the chiefs of the sinners to nought, by smiting all who oppose Me without a cause. For the chiefs according to the Gospel history persecuted Him, whilst the lower people honoured Him.

8. "Salvation is of the Lord ; and upon Thy people be Thy blessing" (ver. 8). In one sentence the Psalmist has enjoined men what to believe, and has prayed for believers. For when it is said, "Salvation is of the Lord," the words are addressed to men. Nor does it follow, "And upon Thy people" be "Thy blessing," in such wise as that the whole is spoken to men, but there is a change into prayer addressed to God Himself, for the very people to whom it

<hr>

[1] Somnus.
[2] [Justin Martyr understands this of Christ and His resurrection. A. N. F. vol. i. p. 175. — C.]
[3] 2 Cor. xiii. 3.

[4] Oxford mss. "De." [5] Gal. v. 15. [6] Sol. Song iv. 2, vi. 6.
[7] Matt. v. 16. [8] Matt. xxii. 40.

was said, " Salvation is of the Lord." What else then doth he say but this? Let no man presume on himself, seeing that it is of the Lord to save from the death of sin ; for, " Wretched man that I am, who shall deliver me from the body of this death? The grace of God through Jesus Christ our Lord." [1] But do Thou, O Lord, bless Thy people, who look for salvation from Thee.

9. This Psalm can be taken as in the Person of Christ another way; which is that whole Christ should speak.[2] I mean by whole, with His body, of which He is the Head, according to the Apostle, who says, " Ye are the body of Christ, and the members." [3] He therefore is the Head of this body; wherefore in another place he saith, " But doing the truth in love, we may increase in Him in all things, who is the Head, Christ, from whom the whole body is joined together and compacted." [4] In the Prophet then at once, the Church, and her Head (the Church founded amidst the storms of persecution throughout the whole world, which we know already to have come to pass), speaks, " O Lord, how are they multiplied that trouble me ! many rise up against me ; " wishing to exterminate the Christian name. " Many say unto my soul, There is no salvation for him in his God." For they would not otherwise hope that they could destroy the Church, branching out so very far and wide, unless they believed that God had no care thereof. " But Thou, O Lord, art my taker ; " in Christ of course. For into that flesh [5] the Church too hath been taken by the Word, " who was made flesh, and dwelt in us ; " [6] for that " In heavenly places hath He made us to sit together with Him." [7] When the Head goes before, the other members will follow ; for, " Who shall separate us from the love of Christ? " [8] Justly then does the Church say, " Thou art my taker. My glory ; " for she doth not attribute her excellency to herself, seeing that she knoweth by whose grace and mercy she is what she is. " And the lifter up of my head," of Him, namely, who, " the First-born from the dead," [9] ascended up into heaven. " With my voice have I cried unto the Lord, and He heard me out of His holy mountain." This is the prayer of all the Saints, the odour of sweetness, which ascends up in the sight of the Lord. For now the Church is heard out of this mountain, which is also her head ; or, out of that justice of God, by which both His elect are set free, and their persecutors punished. Let the people of God also say, " I slept, and took rest ; and rose, for the Lord will take me up ; " that they may be joined, and cleave to their Head.[10] For to this people is it said, " Awake thou that sleepest, and arise from the dead, and Christ shall lay hold on thee." [11] Since they are taken out of sinners, of whom it is said generally, " But they that sleep, sleep in the night." [12] Let them say moreover, " I will not fear the thousands of people that surround me ; " of the heathen verily that compass me about to extinguish everywhere, if they could, the Christian name. But how should they be feared, when by the blood of the martyrs in Christ, as by oil, the ardour of love is inflamed? " Arise, O Lord, save me, O my God." The body can address this to its own Head. For at His rising the body was saved ; who " ascended up on high, led captivity captive, gave gifts unto men." [13] For this is said by the Prophet, in the secret purpose of God,[14] until that ripe harvest [15] which is spoken of in the Gospel, whose salvation is in His Resurrection, who vouchsafed to die for us, shed out our Lord to the earth. " Since Thou hast smitten all who oppose me without a cause, Thou hast broken the teeth of the sinners." Now while the Church hath rule, the enemies of the Christian name are smitten with confusion ; and, whether their curses or their chiefs, brought to nought. Believe then, O man, that " salvation is of the Lord : and," Thou, O Lord, may " Thy blessing " be " upon Thy people."

10. Each one too of us may say, when a multitude of vices and lusts leads the resisting mind in the law of sin, " O Lord, how are they multiplied that trouble me ! many rise up against me." And, since despair of recovery generally creeps in through the accumulation of vices, as though these same vices were mocking the soul, or even as though the Devil and his angels through their poisonous suggestions were at work to make us despair, it is said with great truth, " Many say unto my soul, There is no salvation for him in his God. But Thou, O Lord, art my taker." For this is our hope, that He hath vouchsafed to take the nature of man in Christ. " My glory ; " according to that rule, that no one should ascribe ought to himself. " And the lifter up of my head ; " either of Him, who is the Head of us all, or of the spirit of each several one of us, which is the head of the soul and body. For " the head of the woman is the man, and the head of the man is Christ." [16] But the mind is lifted up, when it can be said already, " With the mind I serve the law of God ; " [17] that the rest of man may be reduced to peaceable submission, when in the resurrection of the flesh

---

[1] Rom. vii. 24, 25.
[2] [On this principle, which rules throughout this commentary, see the author's remark on Ps. xcvi., *infra.* — C.]
[3] 1 Cor. xii. 27.   [4] Eph. iv. 15, 16.   [5] *Homine.*
[6] John i. 14.   [7] Eph. ii. 6.   [8] Rom. viii. 35.
[9] Col. i. 18.

[10] [An Easter antiphon in the Western liturgies. Wordsworth, *apud loc. Commentary on Psalms,* p. 5. — C.]
[11] Eph. v. 14.   [12] 1 Thess. v. 7.
[13] Eph. iv. 8; Ps. lxviii. 18.   [14] *Prædestinatione.*
[15] Matt. ix. 37.   [16] 1 Cor. xi. 3.
[17] Rom. vii. 25.

"death is swallowed up in victory." [1] "With my voice I have cried unto the Lord;" with that most inward and intensive voice. "And He heard me out of His holy mountain;" [2] Him, through whom He hath succoured us, through whose mediation He heareth us. "I slept, and took rest; and rose, for the Lord will take me up." Who of the faithful is not able to say this, when he calls to mind the death of his sins, and the gift of regeneration? "I will not fear the thousands of people that surround me." Besides those which the Church universally hath borne and beareth, each one also hath temptations, by which, when compassed about, he may speak these words, "Arise, O Lord; save me, O my God:" that is, make me to arise. "Since Thou hast smitten all who oppose me without a cause:" it is well in God's determinate [3] purpose said of the Devil and his angels; who rage not only against the whole body of Christ, but also against each one in particular. "Thou hast broken the teeth of the sinners." Each man hath those that revile him, he hath too the prime authors of vice, who strive to cut him off from the body of Christ. But "salvation is of the Lord." Pride is to be guarded against, and we must say, "My soul cleaved after Thee." [4] "And upon Thy people" be "Thy blessing:" that is, upon each one of us.

PSALM IV.

TO THE END, A PSALM SONG TO [5] DAVID.

1. "Christ is the end of the law for righteousness to every one that believeth." [6] For this "end" signifies perfection, not consumption. Now it may be a question, whether every Song be a Psalm, or rather every Psalm a Song; whether there are some Songs which cannot be called Psalms, and some Psalms which cannot be called Songs. But the Scripture must be attended to, if haply "Song" do not denote a joyful theme. But those are called Psalms which are sung to the Psaltery; which the history as a high mystery declares the Prophet David to have used. [7] Of which matter this is not the place to discourse; for it requires prolonged inquiry, and much discussion. Now meanwhile we must look either for the words of the Lord Man [8] after the Resurrection, or of man in the Church believing and hoping on Him.

2. "When I called, the God of my righteousness heard me" (ver. 1). When I called, God heard me, the Psalmist says, of whom is my righteousness. "In tribulation Thou hast enlarged me." Thou hast led me from the straits of sadness into the broad ways of joy. For, "tribulation and straitness is on every soul of man that doeth evil." [9] But he who says, "We rejoice in tribulations, knowing that tribulation worketh patience;" up to that where he says, "Because the love of God is shed abroad in our hearts by the Holy Ghost, which is given unto us;" [10] he hath no straits of heart, they be heaped on him outwardly by them that persecute him. Now the change of person, for that from the third person, where he says, "He heard," he passes at once to the second, where he says, "Thou hast enlarged me;" if it be not done for the sake of variety and grace, it is strange why the Psalmist should first wish to declare to men that he had been heard, and afterwards address Him who heard him. Unless perchance, when he had declared how he was heard, in this very enlargement of heart he preferred to speak with God; that he might even in this way show what it is to be enlarged in heart, that is, to have God already shed abroad in the heart, with whom he might hold converse interiorly. Which is rightly understood as spoken in the person of him who, believing on Christ, has been enlightened; but in that of the very Lord Man, whom the Wisdom of God took, I do not see how this can be suitable. For He was never deserted by It. But as His very prayer against trouble is a sign rather of our infirmity, so also of that sudden enlargement of heart the same Lord may speak for His faithful ones, whom He has personated also when He said, "I was an hungred, and ye gave Me no meat; I was thirsty, and ye gave Me no drink," [11] and so forth. Wherefore here also He can say, "Thou hast enlarged me," for one of the least of His, holding converse with God, whose "love" he has "shed abroad in his heart by the Holy Ghost, which is given unto us." [12] "Have mercy upon me and hear my prayer." Why does he again ask, when already he declared that he had been heard and enlarged? It is for our sakes, of whom it is said, "But if we hope for that we see not, we wait in patience;" [13] or is it, that in him who has believed that which is begun may be perfected?

3. "O ye sons of men, how long heavy in heart" (ver. 2). Let your [14] error, says he, have lasted at least up to the coming of the Son of God; why then any longer are ye heavy in heart? When will ye make an end of crafty

---

[1] 1 Cor. xv. 54.
[2] [Here, for the first time, comes in the word *Selah*, the *Sursum Corda* of the Hebrews. Bishop Wordsworth notes the three *upliftings* which here precede. — C.]
[3] *Præstinatione*.
[4] Ps. lxiii. 8. ἐκολλήθη, Sept.
[5] εἰς τὸ τέλος, ἐν ψαλμοῖς ᾠδὴ τῷ Δαυίδ, Sept.
[6] Rom. x. 4.   [7] 1 Chron. xiii. 8 and xvi. 5.
[8] [Here again, and in all cases (*verba Dominici hominis*), this phrase must be regarded as retracted. "*Ubicunque hoc dixi, dixisse me nollem*," says the great bishop, ed. Migne, vol. i. p. 617. But, as here rendered, it is correct. — C.]

[9] Rom. ii. 9.   [10] Rom. v. 3, 5.   [11] Matt. xxv. 42.
[12] Rom. v. 5.   [13] Rom. viii. 25.
[14] Oxford MSS. "If your."

wiles, if now when the truth is present ye make it not? "Why do ye love vanity, and seek a lie?" Why would ye be blessed by the lowest things? Truth alone, from which all things are true, maketh blessed. For, "vanity is of deceivers, and all is vanity."[1] "What profit hath a man of all his labour, wherewith he laboureth under the sun?" Why then are ye held back by the love of things temporal? Why follow ye after the last things, as though the first, which is vanity and a lie? For you would have them abide with you, which all pass away, as doth a shadow.

4. "And know ye that the Lord hath magnified his Holy One" (ver. 3). Whom but Him, whom He raised up from below, and placed in heaven at His right hand? Therefore doth he chide mankind, that they would turn at length from the love of this world to Him. But if the addition of the conjunction (for he says, "and know ye") is to any a difficulty, he may easily observe in Scripture that this manner of speech is usual in that language, in which the Prophets spoke. For you often find this beginning, "And" the Lord said unto him, "And" the word of the Lord came to him. Which joining by a conjunction, when no sentence has gone before, to which the following one may be annexed, peradventure admirably conveys to us, that the utterance of the truth in words is connected with that vision which goes on in the heart. Although in this place it may be said, that the former sentence, "Why do ye love vanity, and seek a lie?" is as if it were written, Do not love vanity, and seek a lie. And being thus read, it follows in the most direct construction, "and know ye that the Lord hath magnified His Holy One." But the interposition of the *Diapsalma* forbids our joining this sentence with the preceding one. For whether this be a Hebrew word, as some would have it, which means, so be it; or a Greek word, which marks a pause in the psalmody (so as that Psalma should be what is sung in psalmody, but Diapsalma an interval of silence in the psalmody; that as the coupling of voices in singing is called Sympsalma, so their separation Diapsalma, where a certain pause of interrupted continuity is marked): whether I say it be the former, or the latter, or something else, this at least is probable, that the sense cannot rightly be continued and joined, where the Diapsalma intervenes.[2]

5. "The Lord will hear me, when I cry unto Him." I believe that we are here warned, that with great earnestness of heart, that is, with an inward and incorporeal cry, we should implore help of God. For as we must give thanks for enlightenment in this life, so must we pray for rest after this life. Wherefore in the person, either of the faithful preacher of the Gospel, or of our Lord Himself, it may be taken, as if it were written, the Lord will hear you, when you cry unto Him.

6. "Be ye angry, and sin not" (ver. 4). For the thought occurred, Who is worthy to be heard? or how shall the sinner not cry in vain unto the Lord? Therefore, "Be ye angry," saith he, "and sin not." Which may be taken two ways: either, even if ye be angry, do not sin; that is, even if there arise an emotion in the soul, which now by reason of the punishment of sin is not in our power, at least let not the reason and the mind, which is after God regenerated within, that with the mind we should serve the law of God, although with the flesh we as yet serve the law of sin,[3] consent thereunto; or, repent ye, that is, be ye angry with yourselves for your past sins, and henceforth cease to sin. "What you say in your hearts:" there is understood, "say ye:" so that the complete sentence is, "What ye say in your hearts, that say ye;" that is, be ye not the people of whom it is said, "with their lips they honour Me, but their heart is far from Me.[4] In your chambers be ye pricked." This is what has been expressed already "in heart." For this is the chamber, of which our Lord warns us, that we should pray within, with closed doors.[5] But, "be ye pricked," refers either to the pain of repentance, that the soul in punishment should prick itself, that it be not condemned and tormented in God's judgment; or, to arousing, that we should awake to behold the light of Christ, as if pricks were made use of. But some say that not, "be ye pricked," but, "be ye opened," is the better reading; because in the Greek Psalter it is κατανύγητε, which refers to that enlargement of the heart, in order that the shedding abroad of love by the Holy Ghost may be received.

7. "Offer the sacrifice of righteousness, and hope in the Lord" (ver. 5). He says the same in another Psalm, "the sacrifice for God is a troubled spirit."[6] Wherefore that this is the sacrifice of righteousness which is offered through repentance it is not unreasonably here understood. For what more righteous, than that each one should be angry with his own sins, rather than those of others, and that in self-punishment he should sacrifice himself unto God? Or are righteous works after repentance the sacrifice of righteousness? For the interposition of *Diapsalma*[7] not unreasonably perhaps intimates even a transition from the old life to

---

[1] Eccles. i. 2.
[2] [See p. 18, *supra*. Also A. N. F. vol. v. p. 201. St. Augustin seems to have been acquainted with Hippolytus.—C.]

[3] Rom. vii. 25.   [4] Isa. xxix. 13.   [5] Matt. vi. 6.
[6] Ps. li. 17.   [7] [After verse 4.—C.]

the new life: that on the old man being destroyed or weakened by repentance, the sacrifice of righteousness, according to the regeneration of the new man, may be offered to God; when the soul now cleansed offers and places itself on the altar of faith, to be encompassed by heavenly fire, that is, by the Holy Ghost. So that this may be the meaning, "Offer the sacrifice of righteousness, and hope in the Lord;" that is, live uprightly, and hope for the gift of the Holy Ghost, that the truth, in which you have believed, may shine upon you.

8. But yet, "hope in the Lord," is as yet expressed without[1] explanation. Now what is hoped for, but good things? But since each one would obtain from God that good, which he loves; and they are not easy to be found who love interior goods, that is, which belong to the inward man, which alone should be loved, but the rest are to be used for necessity, not to be enjoyed for pleasure; excellently did he subjoin, when he had said, "hope in the Lord" (ver. 6), "Many say, Who showeth us good things?" This is the speech, and this the daily inquiry of all the foolish and unrighteous; whether of those who long for the peace and quiet of a worldly life, and from the frowardness of mankind find it not; who even in their blindness dare to find fault with the order of events, when involved in their own deservings they deem the times worse than these which are past: or, of those who doubt and despair of that future life, which is promised us; who are often saying, Who knows if it's true? or, who ever came from below, to tell us this? Very exquisitely then, and briefly, he shows (to those, that is, who have interior sight), what good things are to be sought; answering their question, who say, "Who showeth us good things?" "The light of Thy countenance," saith he, "is stamped on us, O Lord." This light is the whole and true good of man, which is seen not with the eye, but with the mind. But he says, "stamped on us," as a penny is stamped with the king's image. For man was made after the image and likeness of God,[2] which he defaced by sin: therefore it is his true and eternal good, if by a new birth he be stamped. And I believe this to be the bearing of that which some understand skilfully; I mean, what the Lord said on seeing Cæsar's tribute money, "Render to Cæsar the things that are Cæsar's; and to God the things that are God's."[3] As if He had said, In like manner as Cæsar exacts from you the impression of his image, so also does God: that as the tribute money is rendered to him, so should the soul to God, illumined and stamped with the light of His countenance. (Ver. 7.) "Thou hast put

gladness into my heart." Gladness then is not to be sought without by them, who, being still heavy in heart, "love vanity, and seek a lie;" but within, where the light of God's countenance is stamped. For Christ dwelleth in the inner man,[4] as the Apostle says; for to Him doth it appertain to see truth, since He hath said, "I am the truth."[5] And again, when He spake in the Apostle, saying, "Would you receive a proof of Christ, who speaketh in me?"[6] He spake not of course from without to him, but in his very heart, that is, in that chamber where we are to pray.

9. But men (who doubtless are many) who follow after things temporal, know not to say aught else, than, "Who showeth us good things?" when the true and certain good within their very selves they cannot see. Of these accordingly is most justly said, what he adds next: "From the time of His corn, of wine, and oil, they have been multiplied." For the addition of His, is not superfluous. For the corn is God's: inasmuch as He is "the living bread which came down from heaven."[7] The wine too is God's: for, "they shall be inebriated," he says, "with the fatness of thine house."[8] The oil too is God's: of which it is said, "Thou hast fattened my head with oil." But those many, who say, "Who showeth us good things?" and who see not that the kingdom of heaven is within them: these, "from the time of His corn, of wine, and oil, are multiplied." For multiplication does not always betoken plentifulness, and not, generally, scantiness: when the soul, given up to temporal pleasures, burns ever with desire, and cannot be satisfied; and, distracted with manifold and anxious thought, is not permitted to see the simple good. Such is the soul of which it is said, "For the corruptible body presseth down the soul, and the earthly tabernacle weigheth down the mind that museth on many things."[10] A soul like this, by the departure and succession of temporal goods, that is, "from the time of His corn, wine, and oil," filled with numberless idle fancies, is so multiplied, that it cannot do that which is commanded, "Think on the Lord in goodness, and in simplicity of heart seek Him."[11] For this multiplicity is strongly opposed to that simplicity. And therefore leaving these, who are many, multiplied, that is, by the desire of things temporal, and who say, "Who showeth us good things?" which are to be sought not with the eyes without, but with simplicity of heart within, the faithful man rejoices and says, "In peace, together, I will sleep, and take rest" (ver. 8). For such men justly hope for all manner of estrangement of mind from things

[1] Clause.   [2] Gen. i. 26.   [3] Matt. xxii. 21.

[4] Eph. iii. 16, 17.   [5] John xiv. 6.   [6] 2 Cor. xiii. 3.
[7] John vi. 51.   [8] Ps. xxxvi. 8.   [9] Ps. xxiii. 5.
[10] Wisd. ix. 15.   [11] Wisd. i. 1.

mortal, and forgetfulness of this world's miseries; which is beautifully and prophetically signified under the name of sleep and rest, where the most perfect peace cannot be interrupted by any tumult. But this is not had now in this life, but is to be hoped for after this life. This even the words themselves, which are in the future tense, show us. For it is not said, either, I have slept, and taken rest; or, I do sleep, and take rest; but, "I will sleep, and take rest." Then shall "this corruptible put on incorruption, and this mortal shall put on immortality; then shall death be swallowed up in victory."[1] Hence it is said, "But if we hope for that we see not, we wait in patience."[2]

10. Wherefore, consistently with this, he adds the last words, and says, "Since Thou, O Lord, in singleness hast made me dwell in hope." Here he does not say, wilt make; but, "hast made." In whom then this hope now is, there will be assuredly that which is hoped for. And well does he say, "in singleness." For this may refer in opposition to those many, who being multiplied from the time of His corn, of wine, and oil, say, "Who showeth us good things?" For this multiplicity perishes, and singleness is observed among the saints: of whom it is said in the Acts of the Apostles, "and of the multitude of them that believed, there was one soul, and one heart."[3] In singleness, then, and simplicity, removed, that is, from the multitude and crowd of things, that are born and die, we ought to be lovers of eternity, and unity, if we desire to cleave to the one God and our Lord.

PSALM V.

1. The title of the Psalm is, "For her who receiveth the inheritance." The Church then is signified, who receiveth for her inheritance eternal life through our Lord Jesus Christ; that she may possess God Himself, in cleaving to whom she may be blessed, according to that, "Blessed are the meek, for they shall possess the earth."[4] What earth, but that of which it is said, "Thou art my hope, my portion in the land of the living"?[5] And again more clearly, "The Lord is the portion of mine inheritance and of my cup."[6] And conversely the word Church is said to be God's inheritance according to that, "Ask of Me, and I shall give thee the heathen for thine inheritance."[7] Therefore is God said to be our inheritance, because He feedeth and sustaineth[8] us: and we are said to be God's inheritance, because He ordereth and ruleth us. Wherefore it is the voice of the Church in this Psalm called to her inheritance,

that she too may herself become the inheritance of the Lord.

2. "Hear my words, O Lord" (ver. 1). Being called she calleth upon the Lord; that the same Lord being her helper, she may pass through the wickedness of this world, and attain unto Him. "Understand my cry." The Psalmist well shows what this cry is; how from within, from the chamber of the heart, without the body's utterance,[9] it reaches unto God: for the bodily voice is heard, but the spiritual is understood. Although this too may be God's hearing, not with carnal ear, but in the omnipresence of His Majesty.

3. "Attend Thou to the voice of my supplication;" that is, to that voice, which he maketh request that God would understand: of which what the nature is, he hath already intimated, when he said, "Understand my cry. Attend Thou to the voice of my supplication, my King, and my God" (ver. 2). Although both the Son is God, and the Father God, and the Father and the Son together One God; and if asked of the Holy Ghost, we must give no other answer than that He is God; and when the Father, and the Son, and the Holy Ghost are mentioned together, we must understand nothing else, than One God; nevertheless Scripture is wont to give the appellation of King to the Son. According then to that which is said, "By Me man cometh to the Father,"[10] rightly is it first, "my King;" and then, "my God." And yet has not the Psalmist said, Attend Ye; but, "Attend Thou." For the Catholic faith preaches not two or three Gods, but the Very Trinity, One God. Not that the same Trinity can be together, now the Father, now the Son, now the Holy Ghost, as Sabellius believed: but that the Father must be none but the Father, and the Son none but the Son, and the Holy Ghost none but the Holy Ghost, and this Trinity but One God. Hence when the Apostle had said, "Of whom are all things, by whom are all things, in whom are all things,"[11] he is believed to have conveyed an intimation of the Very Trinity; and yet he did not add, to Them be glory; but, "to Him be glory."

4. "Because I will pray unto Thee (ver. 3). O Lord, in the morning Thou wilt hear my voice." What does that, which he said above, "Hear Thou," mean, as if he desired to be heard immediately? But now he saith, "in the morning Thou wilt hear;" not, hear Thou: and, "I will pray unto Thee;" not, I do pray unto Thee: and, as follows, "in the morning I will stand by Thee, and will see;" not, I do stand by Thee, and do see. Unless perhaps his former prayer marks the invocation itself: but being in

---

[1] 1 Cor. xv. 54. [2] Rom. viii. 25. [3] Acts iv. 32.
[4] Matt. v. 5. [5] Ps. cxlii. 5. [6] Ps. xvi. 5.
[7] Ps. ii. 8. [8] *Continet.*

[9] *Strepitu.* [10] John xiv. 6. [11] Rom. xi. 36.

darkness amidst the storms of this world, he perceives that he does not see what he desires, and yet does not cease to hope, "For hope that is seen, is not hope."¹ Nevertheless, he understands why he does not see, because the night is not yet past, that is, the darkness which our sins have merited. He says therefore, "Because I will pray unto Thee, O Lord;" that is, because Thou art so mighty to whom I shall make my prayer, "in the morning Thou wilt hear my voice." Thou art not He, he says, that can be seen by those, from whose eyes the night of sins is not yet withdrawn: when the night then of my error is past, and the darkness gone, which by my sins I have brought upon myself, then "Thou wilt hear my voice." Why then did he say above not, "Thou wilt hear," but "hear Thou"? Is it that after the Church cried out, "hear Thou," and was not heard, she perceived what must needs pass away to enable her to be heard? Or is it that she was heard above, but doth not yet understand that she was heard, because she doth not yet see by whom she hath been heard; and what she now says, "In the morning Thou wilt hear," she would have thus taken, In the morning I shall understand that I have been heard? Such is that expression, "Arise, O Lord,"² that is, make me arise. But this latter is taken of Christ's resurrection: but at all events that Scripture, "The Lord your God proveth you, that He may know whether ye love Him,"³ cannot be taken in any other sense, than, that ye by Him may know, and that it may be made evident to yourselves, what progress ye have made in His love.

5. "In the morning I will stand by Thee, and will see" (ver. 3). What is, "I will stand," but "I will not lie down"? Now what else is to lie down, but to take rest on the earth, which is a seeking happiness in earthly pleasures? "I will stand by," he says, "and will see." We must not then cleave to things earthly, if we would see God, who is beheld by a clean heart. "For Thou art not a God who hast pleasure in iniquity. The malignant man shall not dwell near Thee, nor shall the unrighteous abide before Thine eyes. Thou hast hated all that work iniquity, Thou wilt destroy all that speak a lie. The man of blood, and the crafty man, the Lord will abominate" (vers. 4–6). Iniquity, malignity, lying, homicide, craft, and all the like, are the night of which we speak: on the passing away of which, the morning dawns, that God may be seen. He has unfolded the reason, then, why he will stand by in the morning, and see: "For," he says, "Thou art not a God who hast pleasure in iniquity." For if He were a God who had pleasure in iniquity, He could be seen even by

the iniquitous, so that He would not be seen in the morning, that is, when the night of iniquity is over.

6. "The malignant man shall not dwell near Thee:" that is, he shall not so see, as to cleave to Thee. Hence follows, "Nor shall the unrighteous abide before Thine eyes." For their eyes, that is, their mind is beaten back by the light of truth, because of the darkness of their sins; by the habitual practice of which they are not able to sustain the brightness of right understanding. Therefore even they who see sometimes, that is, who understand the truth, are yet still unrighteous, they abide not therein through love of those things, which turn away from the truth. For they carry about with them their night, that is, not only the habit, but even the love, of sinning. But if this night shall pass away, that is, if they shall cease to sin, and this love and habit thereof be put to flight, the morning dawns, so that they not only understand, but also cleave to the truth.

7. "Thou hast hated all that work iniquity." God's hatred may be understood from that form of expression, by which every sinner hates the truth. For it seems that she too hates those, whom she suffers not to abide in her. Now they do not abide, who cannot bear the truth. "Thou wilt destroy all that speak a lie." For this is the opposite to truth. But lest any one should suppose that any substance or nature is opposite to truth, let him understand that "a lie" has relation to that which is not, not to that which is. For if that which is be spoken, truth is spoken: but if that which is not be spoken, it is a lie.⁴ Therefore saith he, "Thou wilt destroy all that speak a lie;" because drawing back from that which is, they turn aside to that which is not. Many lies indeed seem to be for some one's safety or advantage, spoken not in malice, but in kindness: such was that of those midwives in Exodus,⁵ who gave a false report to Pharaoh, to the end that the infants of the children of Israel might not be slain.⁶ But even these are praised not for the fact, but for the disposition shown; since those who only lie in this way, will attain in time to a freedom from all lying. For in those that are perfect, not even these lies are found. For to these it is said, "Let there be in your mouth, yea, yea; nay, nay; whatsoever is more, is of evil."⁷ Nor is it without reason written in another place, "The mouth that lieth slayeth the soul:"⁸ lest any should imagine that the perfect and spiritual man ought to lie for this

---

⁴ [Yet on this apparently harmless principle has been built up the art of lying, in the Liguorian casuistry: He who lays his hand on a box or table, and swears "The man is not *here*," speaks a material truth, and hence is judged innocent. See *Theologia Moralis S. Alphons. de Ligorio*, tom. ii. p. 35 *et seqq.*, Paris, ed. 1852.—C.]
⁵ Exod. i. 19.
⁶ See his treatises on lying and against lying.
⁷ Matt. v. 37.
⁸ Wisd. i. 11.

---

¹ Rom. viii. 24.   ² Ps. iii. 7.   ³ Deut. xiii. 3.

temporal life, in the death of which no soul is slain, neither his own, nor another's. But since it is one thing to lie, another to conceal the truth (if indeed it be one thing to say what is false, another not to say what is true), if haply one does not wish to give a man up even to this visible death, he should be prepared to conceal what is true, not to say what is false; so that he may neither give him up, nor yet lie, lest he slay his own soul for another's body. But if he cannot yet do this, let him at all events admit only lies of such necessity, that he may attain to be freed even from these, if they alone remain, and receive the strength of the Holy Ghost, whereby he may despise all that must be suffered for the truth's sake. In fine, there are two kinds of lies, in which there is no great fault,[1] and yet they are not without fault, either when we are in jest, or when we lie that we may do good. That first kind, in jest, is for this reason not very hurtful, because there is no deception. For he to whom it is said knows that it is said for the sake of the jest. But the second kind is for this reason the more inoffensive, because it carries with it some kindly intention. And to say truth, that which has no duplicity, cannot even be called a lie. As if, for example, a sword be intrusted to any one, and he promises to return it, when he who intrusted it to him shall demand it: if he chance to require his sword when in a fit of madness, it is clear it must not be returned then, lest he kill either himself or others, until soundness of mind be restored to him. Here then is no duplicity, because he, to whom the sword was intrusted, when he promised that he would return it at the other's demand, did not imagine that he could require it when in a fit of madness. But even the Lord concealed the truth, when He said to the disciples, not yet strong enough, "I have many things to say unto you, but ye cannot bear them now:"[2] and the Apostle Paul, when he said, "I could not speak unto you as unto spiritual, but as unto carnal."[3] Whence it is clear that it is not blamable, sometimes not to speak what is true. But to say what is false, is not found to have been allowed to the perfect.

8. "The man of blood, and the crafty man, the Lord will abominate." What he said above, "Thou hast hated all that work iniquity, Thou wilt destroy all that speak a lie," may well seem to be repeated here: so that one may refer "the man of blood" to "the worker of iniquity," and "the crafty man" to the "lie." For it is craft, when one thing is done, another pretended. He used an apt word too, when he said, "will abominate." For the disinherited are usually called

abominated. Now this Psalm is, "for her who receiveth the inheritance;" and she adds the exulting joy of her hope, in saying, "But I, in the multitude of Thy mercy, will enter into Thine house" (ver. 7). "In the multitude of mercy:" perhaps he means in the multitude of perfected and blessed men, of whom that city shall consist, of which the Church is now in travail, and is bearing few by few. Now that many men regenerated and perfected, are rightly called the multitude of God's mercy, who can deny; when it is most truly said, "What is man that Thou art mindful of him, or the son of man that Thou visitest him?[4] I will enter into Thine house:" as a stone into a building, I suppose, is the meaning. For what else is the house of God than the Temple of God, of which it is said, "for the temple of God is holy,[5] which temple ye are"? Of which building He is the cornerstone,[6] whom the Power and Wisdom of God coeternal with the Father assumed.

9. "I will worship at Thy holy temple, in Thy fear." "At the temple," we understand as, "near" the temple. For he does not say, I will worship "in" Thy holy temple; but, "I will worship at Thy holy temple." It must be understood too to be spoken not of perfection, but of progress toward perfection: so that the words, "I will enter into Thine house," should signify perfection. But that this may come to a happy issue, "I will" first, he says, "worship at Thy holy temple." And perhaps on this account he added, "in Thy fear;" which is a great defence to those that are advancing toward salvation. But when any one shall have arrived there, in him comes to pass that which is written, "perfect love casteth out fear."[7] For they do not fear Him who is now their friend, to whom it is said, "henceforth I will not call you servants, but friends,"[8] when they have been brought through to that which was promised.

10. "O Lord, lead me forth in Thy justice because of mine enemies" (ver. 8). He has here sufficiently plainly declared that he is on his onward road, that is, in progress toward perfection, not yet in perfection itself, when he desires eagerly that he may be led forth. But, "in Thy justice," not in that which seems so to men. For to return evil for evil seems justice: but it is not His justice of whom it is said, "He maketh His sun to rise on the good and on the evil:" for even when God punishes sinners, He does not inflict His evil on them, but leaves them to their own evil. "Behold," the Psalmist says, "he travailed with injustice, he hath conceived toil, and brought forth iniquity: he hath opened a ditch, and digged it, and hath fallen into the pit which he wrought: his pains shall be turned

---

[1] [Lax language, which has greatly hindered strict conscientiousness in moral teachers. See Meyrick's *Moral and Devotional Theology of Rome*, pp. 68-71, London, 1857. Compare our author, *De Mendacio*, and *Retractations*, ed. Migne, i. pp. 630, 659. — C.]
[2] John xvi. 12. 　　　　[3] 1 Cor. iii. 1.

[4] Ps. viii. 4. 　　　[5] 1 Cor. iii. 17. 　　　[6] Eph. ii. 20.
[7] 1 John iv. 18. 　　　[8] John xv. 15.

on his own head, and his iniquity shall descend on his own pate." [1] When then God punishes, He punishes as a judge those that transgress the law, not by bringing evil upon them from Himself, but driving them on to that which they have chosen, to fill up the sum of their misery. But man, when he returns evil for evil, does it with an evil will: and on this account is himself first evil, when he would punish evil.

11. "Direct in Thy sight my way." Nothing is clearer, than that he here sets forth that time, in which he is journeying onward. For this is a way which is traversed not in any regions of the earth, but in the affections of the heart. "In Thy sight," he says, "direct my way:" that is, where no man sees; who are not to be trusted in their praise or blame. For they can in no wise judge of another man's conscience, wherein the way toward God is traversed. Hence it is added, "for truth is not in their mouth" (ver. 9). To whose judgment of course then there is no trusting, and therefore must we fly within to conscience, and the sight of God. "Their heart is vain." How then can truth be in their mouth, whose heart is deceived by sin, and the punishment of sin? Whence men are called back by that voice, "Wherefore do ye love vanity, and seek a lie?"

12. "Their throat is an open sepulchre." It may be referred to signify gluttony, for the sake of which men very often lie by flattery. And admirably has he said, "an open sepulchre:" for this gluttony is ever gaping with open mouth, not as sepulchres, which, on the reception of corpses, are closed up. This also may be understood hereby, that with lying and blind flattery men draw to themselves those whom they entice to sin; and as it were devour them, when they turn them to their own way of living. And when this happens to them, since by sin they die, those by whom they are led along, are rightly called open sepulchres: for themselves too are in a manner lifeless, being destitute of the life of truth; and they take in to themselves dead men, whom having slain by lying words and a vain heart, they turn unto themselves. "With their own tongues they dealt craftily:" that is, with evil tongues. For this seems to be signified, when he says "their own." For the evil have evil tongues, that is, they speak evil, when they speak craftily. To whom the Lord saith, "How can ye, being evil, speak good things?" [2]

13. "Judge them, O God: let them fall from their own thoughts" (ver. 10). It is a prophecy, not a curse. For he does not wish that it should come to pass; but he perceives what will come to pass. For this happens to them,

not because he appears to have wished for it, but because they are such as to deserve that it should happen. For so also what he says afterwards, "Let all that hope in Thee rejoice," he says by way of prophecy; since he perceives that they will rejoice. Likewise is it said prophetically, "Stir up Thy strength, and come:" [3] for he saw that He would come. Although the words, "Let them fall from their own thoughts," may be taken thus also, that it may rather be believed to be a wish for their good by the Psalmist, whilst they fall from their evil thoughts, that is, that they may no more think evil. But what follows, "drive them out," forbids this interpretation. For it can in no wise be taken in a favourable sense, that one is driven out by God. Wherefore it is understood to be said prophetically, and not of ill will; when this is said, which must necessarily happen to such as chose to persevere in those sins, which have been mentioned. "Let them," therefore, "fall from their own thoughts," is, let them fall by their self-accusing thoughts, "their own conscience also bearing witness," as the Apostle says, "and their thoughts accusing or excusing, in the revelation of the just judgment of God." [4]

14. "According to the multitude of their ungodlinesses drive them out:" that is, drive them out far away. For this is "according to the multitude of their ungodlinesses," [5] that they should be driven out far away. The ungodly then are driven out from that inheritance, which is possessed by knowing and seeing God: as diseased eyes are driven out from the shining of the light, when what is gladness to others is pain to them. Therefore these shall not stand in the morning, [6] and see. And that expression is as great a punishment, as that which is said, "But for me it is good to cleave to the Lord," [7] is a great reward. To this punishment is opposed, "Enter thou into the joy of Thy Lord;" [8] for similar to this expulsion is, "Cast him into outer darkness." [9]

15. "Since they have embittered Thee, O Lord: I am," saith He, "the Bread which came down from heaven;" [10] again, "Labour for the meat which wasteth not;" [11] again, "Taste and see that the Lord is sweet." [12] But to sinners the bread of truth is bitter. Whence they hate the mouth of him that speaketh the truth. These then have embittered God, who by sin have fallen into such a state of sickliness, that the food of truth, in which healthy souls delight, as if it were bitter as gall, they cannot bear.

16. "And let all rejoice that hope in Thee;" those of course to whose taste the Lord is sweet.

---

[1] Ps. vii. 14, 15, 16.   [2] Matt. xii. 34.

[3] Ps. lxxx. 2.   [4] Rom. ii. 15, 16.
[5] It is not possible to preserve in the translation the cognate words, *multitudinem* and *multum*: "hoc est enim secundum *multitudinem* impietatum eorum, ut *multum* expellantur."
[6] Ps. v. 3.   [7] Ps. lxxiii. 28.   [8] Matt. xxv. 21.
[9] Matt. xxv. 30.   [10] John vi. 51.   [11] John vi. 27.
[12] Ps. xxxiv. 8.

"They will exult for evermore, and Thou wilt dwell in them" (ver. 11). This will be the exultation for evermore, when the just become the Temple of God, and He, their Indweller, will be their joy. "And all that love Thy name shall glory in Thee:" as when what they love is present for them to enjoy. And well is it said, "in Thee," as if in possession of the inheritance, of which the title of the Psalm speaks: when they too are His inheritance, which is intimated by, "Thou wilt dwell in them." From which good they are kept back, whom God, according to the multitude of their ungodlinesses, driveth out.

17. "For Thou wilt bless the just man" (ver. 12). This is blessing, to glory in God, and to be inhabited by God. Such sanctification is given to the just. But that they may be justified, a calling goes before: which is not of merit, but of the grace of God. "For all have sinned, and want the glory of God."[1] "For whom He called, them He also justified; and whom He justified, them He also glorified."[2] Since then calling is not of our merit, but of the goodness and mercy of God, he went on to say, "O Lord, as with the shield of Thy good will Thou hast crowned us." For God's good will goes before our good will, to call sinners to repentance. And these are the arms whereby the enemy is overcome, against whom it is said, "Who will bring accusation against God's elect?" Again, "if God be for us, who can be against us? Who spared not His Only Son, but delivered Him up for us all."[3] "For if, when we were enemies, Christ died for us; much more being reconciled, shall we be saved from wrath through Him."[4] This is that unconquerable shield, whereby the enemy is driven back, when he suggests despair of our salvation through the multitude of tribulaions and temptations.

18. The whole contents of the Psalm, then, are a prayer that she may be heard, from the words, "hear my words, O Lord," unto, "my King, and my God." Then follows a view of those things which hinder the sight of God, that is, a knowledge that she[5] is heard, from the words, "because I shall pray unto Thee, O Lord, in the morning Thou wilt hear my voice," unto, "the man of blood and the crafty man the Lord will abominte." Thirdly, she hopes that she, who is to be the house of God, even now begins to draw near to Him in fear, before that perfection which casteth out fear, from the words, "but I in the multitude of Thy mercy," unto, "I will worship at Thy holy temple in Thy fear." Fourthly, as she is progressing and advancing amongst those very things which she feels to hinder her, she prays that she may be assisted within, where no man seeth, lest she be turned aside by evil tongues, for the words, "O Lord, lead me forth in Thy justice because of my enemies," unto, "with their tongues they dealt craftily." Fifthly, is a prophecy of what punishment awaits the ungodly, when the just man shall scarcely be saved; and of what reward the just shall obtain, who, when they were called, came, and bore all things manfully, till they were brought to the end, from the words, "judge them, O God," unto the end of the Psalm.

PSALM VI.

1. "Of the eighth," seems here obscure. For the rest of this title is more clear. Now it has seemed to some to intimate the day of judgment, that is, the time of the coming of our Lord, when He will come to judge the quick and dead. Which coming, it is believed, is to be, after reckoning the years from Adam, seven thousand years: so as that seven thousand years should pass as seven days, and afterwards that time arrive as it were the eighth day. But since it has been said by the Lord, "It is not yours to know the times, which the Father hath put in His own power:"[8] and, "But of the day and that hour knoweth no man, no, neither angel, nor Power, neither the Son, but the Father alone:"[9] and again, that which is written, "that the day of the Lord cometh as a thief,"[10] shows clearly enough that no man should arrogate to himself the knowledge of that time, by any computation of years. For if that day is to come after seven thousand years, every man could learn its advent by reckoning the years. What comes then of the Son's even not knowing this? Which of course is said with this meaning, that men do not learn this by the Son, not that He by Himself doth not know it: according to that form of speech, "the Lord your God trieth you that He may know;"[11] that is, that He may make you know: and, "arise, O Lord;"[12] that is, make us arise. When therefore the Son is thus said not to know this day; not because He knoweth it not, but because He causeth those to know it not, for whom it is not expedient to know it, that is, He doth not show it to them; what does that strange presumption mean, which, by a reckoning up of years, expects the day of the Lord as most certain after seven thousand years?[13]

2. Be we then willingly ignorant of that which the Lord would not have us know: and let us

---

[1] Rom. iii. 23.   [2] Rom. viii. 30.   [3] Rom. viii. 33, 31, 32.
[4] Rom. v. 10.   [5] i.e., the Church.

[6] LXX. ὑπὲρ τῆς ὀγδόης. [See Hippolytus, A. N. F. vol. v. p. 200.—C.]
[7] [The first of the Seven Penitential Psalms, which are Psalms vi., xxxii., xxxviii., li., cii., cxxx., cxliii.—C.]
[8] Acts i. 7.   [9] Mark xiii. 32.   [10] 1 Thess. v. 2.
[11] Deut. xiii. 3.   [12] Ps. iii. 7.
[13] [See *City of God*, this series, vol. ii. p. 426 *et seqq.*—C.]

inquire what this title, " of the eighth," means. The day of judgment may indeed, even without any rash computation of years, be understood by the eighth, for that immediately after the end of this world, life eternal being attained, the souls of the righteous will not then be subject unto times : and, since all times have their revolution in a repetition of those seven days, that peradventure is called the eighth day, which will not have this variety. There is another reason, which may be here not unreasonably accepted, why the judgment should be called the eighth, because it will take place after two generations, one relating to the body, the other to the soul, For from Adam unto Moses the human race lived of the body, that is, according to the flesh : which is called the outward and the old man,[1] and to which the Old Testament was given, that it might prefigure the spiritual things to come by operations, albeit religious, yet carnal. Through this entire season, when men lived according to the body, " death reigned," as the Apostle saith, " even over those that had not sinned." Now it reigned " after the similitude of Adam's transgression," [2] as the same Apostle saith ; for it must be taken of the period up to Moses, up to which time the works of the law, that is, those sacraments of carnal observance, held even those bound, for the sake of a certain mystery, who were subject to the One GOD. But from the coming of the Lord, from whom there was a transition from the circumcision of the flesh to the circumcision of the heart, the call was made, that man should live according to the soul, that is, according to the inner man, who is also called the " new man " [3] by reason of the new birth and the renewing of spiritual conversation. Now it is plain that the number four has relation to the body, from the four well known elements of which it consists, and the four qualities of dry, humid, warm, cold. Hence too it is administered by four seasons, spring, summer, autumn, winter. All this is very well known. For of the number four relating to the body we have treated elsewhere somewhat subtilly, but obscurely : which must be avoided in this discourse, which we would have accommodated to the unlearned. But that the number three has relation to the mind may be understood from this, that we are commanded to love God after a threefold manner, [4] with the whole heart, with the whole soul, with the whole mind : [5] of each of which severally we must treat, not in the Psalms, but in the Gospels : for the present, for proof of the relation of the number three to the mind, I think what has been said

enough. Those numbers then of the body which have relation to the old man and the Old Testament, being past and gone, the numbers too of the soul, which have relation to the new man and the New Testament, being past and gone, a septenary so to say being passed ; because everything is done in time, four having been distributed to the body, three to the mind ; the eighth will come, the day of judgment : which assigning to deserts their due, will transfer at once the saint, not to temporal works, but to eternal life ; but will condemn the ungodly to eternal punishment.

3. In fear of which comdemnation the Church prays in this Psalm, and says, " Reprove me not, O Lord, in Thine anger " (ver. 1). The Apostle too mentions the anger of the judgment ; " Thou treasurest up unto thyself," he says, " anger against the day of the anger of the just judgment of God." [6] In which he would not be reproved, whosoever longs to be healed in this life. " Nor in Thy rage chasten me." " Chasten," seems rather too mild a word ; for it availeth toward amendment. For for him who is reproved, that is, accused, it is to be feared lest his end be condemnation. But since " rage " seems to be more than " anger," it may be a difficulty, why that which is milder, namely, chastening, is joined to that which is more severe, namely, rage. But I suppose that one and the same thing is signified by the two words. For in the Greek θυμὸς, which is in the first verse, means the same as ὀργὴ, which is in the second verse.[7]   But when the Latins themselves too wished to use two distinct words, they looked out for what was akin to " anger," and " rage " [8] was used. Hence copies vary. For in some " anger " is found first, and then " rage : " in others, for " rage," " indignafion " or " choler " is used. But whatever the reading, it is an emotion of the soul urging to the infliction of punishment. Yet this emotion must not be attributed to God, as if to a soul, of whom it is said, " but Thou, O Lord of power, judgest with tranquillity." [9] Now that which is tranquil, is not disturbed. Disturbance then does not attach to God as judge : but what is done by His ministers, in that it is done by His laws, is called His anger. In which anger, the soul, which now prays, would not only not be reproved, but not even chastened, that is, amended or instructed. For in the Greek it is, παιδεύσῃς, that is, instruct. Now in the day of judgment all are " reproved " that hold not the foundation, which is Christ. But they are amended, that is, purged, who " upon this foundation build wood, hay, stubble. For they shall suffer loss, but shall be saved, as by fire." [10]

---

[1] Rom. vi. 6; Eph. iv. 22.   [2] Rom. v. 14.
[3] Col. iii. 10.
[4] [On the tripartite nature of man, see Tertull. A. N. F. vol. iii. pp. 463, 474. — C.]
[5] Deut. vi. 5; Matt. xxii. 37.

[6] Rom. ii. 5.
[7] [Compare Trench on *Synonyms of the New Testament*, p. 178, ed. New York, 1854. — C.]
[8] *Furor.*   [9] Wisd. xii. 18.   [10] 1 Cor. iii. 11, 12, 13, 15.

What then does he pray, who would not be either reproved or amended in the anger of the Lord? what else but that he may be healed? For where sound health is, neither death is to be dreaded, nor the physician's hand with caustics or the knife.

4. He proceeds accordingly to say, "Pity me, O Lord, for I am weak: heal me, O Lord, for my bones are troubled" (ver. 2), that is, the support of my soul, or strength: for this is the meaning of "bones." The soul therefore says, that her strength is troubled, when she speaks of bones. For it is not to be supposed, that the soul has bones, such as we see in the body. Wherefore, what follows tends to explain it, "and my soul is troubled exceedingly" (ver. 3), lest because he mentioned bones, they should be understood as of the body. "And Thou, O Lord, how long?" Who does not see represented here a soul struggling with her diseases; but long kept back by the physician, that she may be convinced what evils she has plunged herself into through sin? For what is easily healed, is not much avoided: but from the difficulty of the healing, there will be the more careful keeping of recovered health. God then, to whom it is said, "And Thou, O Lord, how long?" must not be deemed as if cruel: but as a kind convincer of the soul, what evil she hath procured for herself. For this soul does not yet pray so perfectly, as that it can be said to her, "Whilst thou art yet speaking I will say, Behold, here I am." [1] That she may at the same time also come to know, if they who do turn meet with so great difficulty, how great punishment is prepared for the ungodly, who will not turn to God: as it is written in another place, "If the righteous scarcely be saved, where shall the sinner and ungodly appear?" [2]

5. "Turn, O Lord, and deliver my soul" (ver. 4). Turning herself she prays that God too would turn to her: as it is said, "Turn ye unto Me, and I will turn unto you, saith the Lord." [3] Or is it to be understood according to that way of speaking, "Turn, O Lord," that is, make me turn, since the soul in this her turning feels difficulty and toil? For our perfected turning findeth God ready, as says the Prophet, "We shall find Him ready as the dawn." [4] Since it was not His absence who is everywhere present, but our turning away that made us lose Him; "He was in this world," it is said, "and the world was made by Him, and the world knew Him not." [5] If, then, He was in this world, and the world knew Him not, our impurity doth not endure the sight of Him. But whilst we are turning ourselves, that is, by changing our old life are fashioning our spirit; we feel it hard and

toilsome to be wrested back from the darkness of earthly lusts, to the serene and quiet and tranquillity of the divine light. And in such difficulty we say, "Turn, O Lord," that is, help us, that that turning may be perfected in us, which findeth Thee ready, and offering Thyself for the fruition of them that love Thee. And hence after he said, "Turn, O Lord," he added, "and deliver my soul:" cleaving as it were to the entanglements of this world, and suffering, in the very act of turning, from the thorns, as it were, of rending and tearing desires. "Make me whole," he says, "for Thy pity's sake." He knows that it is not of his own merits that he is healed: for to him sinning, and transgressing a given command, was just condemnation due. Heal me therefore, he says, not for my merit's sake, but for Thy pity's sake.

6. "For in death there is no one that is mindful of Thee" (ver. 5). He knows too that now is the time for turning unto God: for when this life shall have passed away, there remaineth but a retribution of our deserts. [6] "But in hell who shall confess to Thee?" [7] That rich man, of whom the Lord speaks, who saw Lazarus in rest, but bewailed himself in torments, confessed in hell, yea so as to wish even to have his brethren warned, that they might keep themselves from sin, because of the punishment which is not believed to be in hell. Although therefore to no purpose, yet he confessed that those torments had deservedly lighted upon him; since he even wished his brethren to be instructed, lest they should fall into the same. What then is, "But in hell who will confess to Thee?" Is hell to be understood as that place, whither the ungodly will be cast down after the judgment, when by reason of that deeper darkness they will no more see any light of God, to whom they may confess aught? For as yet that rich man by raising his eyes, although a vast gulf lay between, could still see Lazarus established in rest: by comparing himself with whom, he was driven to a confession of his own deserts. It may be understood also, as if the Psalmist calls sin, that is committed in contempt of God's law, death: so as that we should give the name of death to the sting of death, because it procures death. "For the sting of death is sin." [8] In which death this is to be unmindful of God, to despise His law and commandments: so that by hell the Psalmist would mean that blindness of soul which overtakes and enwraps the sinner, that is, the dying. "As they did not think good," the Apostle says,

---

[1] Isa lxv. 24.　　[2] 1 Pet. iv. 18.　　[3] Zech. i. 3.
[4] Hos. vi. 3, LXX.　　[5] John i. 10.

[6] [St. Augustin, whatever he may have imagined of the fire that is to purify at the last day (1 Cor. iii. 13-15), knew nothing of an intermediate purgatory. Compare A. N. F. vol. viii. pp. 239, 390, for apocryphal opinions and a misleading note. Consult (same series) vol. iii. p. 428, and v. p. 222, notes 1 and 7, with p. 223, note 1.—C.]
[7] Luke xvi.　　　　　[8] 1 Cor. xv. 56.

"to retain God in " their "knowledge, God gave them over to a reprobate mind." [1] From this death, and this hell, the soul earnestly prays that she may be kept safe, whilst she strives to turn to God, and feels her difficulties.

7. Wherefore he goes on to say, "I have laboured in my groaning." And as if this availed but little, he adds, "I will wash each night my couch" (ver. 6). That is here called a couch, where the sick and weak soul rests, that is, in bodily gratification and in every worldly pleasure. Which pleasure, whoso endeavours to withdraw himself from it, washes with tears. For he sees that he already condemns carnal lusts; and yet his weakness is held by the pleasure, and willingly lies down therein, from whence none but the soul that is made whole can rise. As for what he says, "each night," he would perhaps have it taken thus: that he who, ready in spirit, perceives some light of truth, and yet, through weakness of the flesh, rests sometime in the pleasure of this world, is compelled to suffer as it were days and nights in an alternation of feeling: as when he says, "With the mind I serve the law of God," he feels as it were day; again when he says, " but with the flesh the law of sin," [2] he declines into night: until all night passeth away, and that one day comes, of which it is said, "In the morning I will stand by Thee, and will see." [3] For then he will stand, but now he lies down, when he is on his couch; which he will wash each night, that with so great abundance of tears he may obtain the most assured remedy from the mercy of God. " I will drench my bed with tears." It is a repetition.[4] For when he says, " with tears," he shows with what meaning he said above, "I will wash." For we take "bed" here to be the same as "couch" above. Although, "I will drench," is something more than, " I will wash : " since anything may be washed superficially, but drenching penetrates to the more inward parts; which here signifies weeping to the very bottom of the heart. Now the variety of tenses which he uses; the past, when he said, "I have laboured in my groaning ; " and the future, when he said, " I will wash each night my couch ; " the future again, "I will drench my bed with tears ; " this shows what every man ought to say to himself, when he labours in groaning to no purpose. As if he should say, It hath not profited when I have done this, therefore I will do the other.

8. "Mine eye is disordered by anger" (ver. 7): is it by his own, or God's anger, in which he maketh petition that he might not be reproved, or chastened? But if anger in that place intimate the day of judgment, how can it be understood now? Is it a beginning of it, that men here suffer pains and torments, and above all the loss of the understanding of the truth ; as I have already quoted that which is said, "God gave them over to a reprobate mind "? [1] For such is the blindness of the mind. Whosoever is given over thereunto, is shut out from the interior light of God : but not wholly as yet, whilst he is in this life. For there is "outer darkness," [5] which is understood to belong rather to the day of judgment ; that he should rather be wholly without God, whosoever whilst there is time refuses correction. Now to be wholly without God, what else is it, but to be in extreme blindness? If indeed God "dwell in inaccessible light," [6] whereinto they enter, to whom it is said, "Enter thou into the joy of thy Lord." [7] It is then the beginning of this anger, which in this life every sinner suffers. In fear therefore of the day of judgment, he is in trial and grief ; lest he be brought to that, the disastrous commencement of which he experiences now. And therefore he did not say, mine eye is extinguished, but, "mine eye is disordered by anger." But if he mean that his eye is disordered by his own anger, there is no wonder either in this. For hence perhaps it is said, "Let not the sun go down upon your wrath ; " [8] because the mind, which, from her own disorder, is not permitted to see God, supposes that the inner sun, that is, the wisdom of God, suffers as it were a setting in her.

9. "I have grown old in all mine enemies." He had only spoken of anger (if it were yet of his own anger that he spoke) : but thinking on his other vices, he found that he was entrenched by them all. Which vices, as they belong to the old life and the old man, which we must put off, that we may put on the new man, [9] it is well said, "I have grown old." But "in all mine enemies," he means, either amidst these vices, or amidst men who will not be converted to God. For these, even if they know them not, even if they bear with them, even if they use the same tables and houses and cities, with no strife arising between them, and in frequent converse together with seeming concord : notwithstanding, by the contrariety of their aims, they are enemies to those who turn unto God. For seeing that the one love and desire this world, the others wish to be freed from this world, who sees not that the first are enemies to the last? For if they can, they draw the others into punishment with them. And it is a great grace, to be conversant daily with their words, and not to depart from the way of God's commandments. For often the mind which is striving to go on to God-ward,

[1] Rom. i. 28.   [2] Rom. vii. 25.   [3] Ps. v. 3.
[4] [St. Augustin was the inventor of what is now called "The Silent Comforter," for the invalid. This Psalm, with the six other Penitential Psalms, he caused to be set up before his dying eyes. See *Vita S. Aug. auctore Possidio*, ed. Migne, vol. i. p. 63. — C.]

[5] Matt. xxv. 30.   [6] 1 Tim. vi. 16.   [7] Matt. xxv. 21, 23.
[8] Eph. iv. 26.   [9] Col. iii. 9, 10.

being rudely handled in the very road, is alarmed; and generally fulfils not its good intent, lest it should offend those with whom it lives, who love and follow after other perishable and transient goods. From such every one that is whole is separated, not in space, but in soul. For the body is contained in space, but the soul's space is her affection.

10. Wherefore after the labour, and groaning, and very frequent showers of tears, since that cannot be ineffectual, which is asked so earnestly of Him, who is the Fountain of all mercies, and it is most truly said, "the Lord is nigh unto them that are of a broken heart:"[1] after difficulties so great, the pious soul, by which we may also understand the Church, intimating that she has been heard, see what she adds: "Depart from me, all ye that work iniquity; for the Lord hath heard the voice of my weeping" (ver. 8). It is either spoken prophetically, since they will depart, that is, the ungodly will be separated from the righteous, when the day of judgment arrives, or, for this time present. For although both are equally found in the same assemblies, yet on the open floor the wheat is already separated from the chaff, though it be hid among the chaff. They can therefore be associated together, but cannot be carried away by the wind together.

11. "For the Lord hath heard the voice of my weeping; The Lord hath heard my supplication; the Lord hath received my prayer" (ver. 9). The frequent repetition of the same sentiments shows not, so to say, the necessities of the narrator, but the warm feeling of his joy. For they that rejoice are wont so to speak, as that it is not enough for them to declare once for all the object of their joy. This is the fruit of that groaning in which there is labour, and those tears with which the couch is washed, and · bed drenched: for, "he that sows in tears, shall reap in joy:"[2] and, "blessed are they that mourn, for they shall be comforted."

12. "Let all mine enemies be ashamed and vexed" (ver. 10). He said above, "depart from me all ye:" which can take place, as it has been explained, even in this life: but as to what he says, "let them be ashamed and vexed," I do not see how it can happen, save on that day when the rewards of the righteous and the punishments of the sinners shall be made manifest. For at present so far are the ungodly from being ashamed, that they do not cease to insult us. And for the most part their mockings are of such avail, that they make the weak to be ashamed of the name of Christ. Hence it is said, "Whosoever shall be ashamed of Me before men, of him will I be ashamed before My Father."[3] But

now whosoever would fulfil those sublime commands, to disperse, to give to the poor, that his righteousness may endure for ever;[4] and selling all his earthly goods, and spending them on the needy, would follow Christ, saying, "We brought nothing into this world, and truly we can carry nothing out; having food and raiment, let us be therewith content;"[5] incurs the profane raillery of those men, and by those who will not be made whole, is called mad; and often to avoid being so called by desperate men, he fears to do, and puts off that, which the most faithful and powerful of all physicians hath ordered. It is not then at present that these can be ashamed, by whom we have to wish that we be not made ashamed, and so be either called back from our proposed journey, or hindered, or delayed. But the time will come when they shall be ashamed, saying as it is written, "These are they whom we had sometimes in derision, and a parable of reproach: we fools counted their life madness, and their end to be without honour: how are they numbered among the children of God, and their lot is among the saints? Therefore have we erred from the way of truth, and the light of rightousness hath not shined into us, nor the sun risen upon us: we have been filled with the way of wickedness and destruction, and have walked through rugged deserts, but the way of the Lord we have not known. What hath pride profited us, or what hath the vaunting of riches brought us? All those things are passed away like a shadow."[6]

13. But as to what he says, "Let them be turned and confounded," who would not judge it to be a most righteous punishment, that they should have a turning unto confusion, who would not have one unto salvation? After this he added, "exceeding quickly." For when the day of judgment shall have begun to be no longer looked for, when they shall have said, "Peace, then shall sudden destruction come upon them."[7] Now whensoever it come, that comes very quickly, of whose coming we give up all expectation; and nothing makes the length of this life be felt but the hope of living. For nothing seems more quick, than all that has already passed in it. When then the day of judgment shall come, then will sinners feel how that all the life which passeth away is not long. Nor will that any way possibly seem to them to have come tardily, which shall have come without their desiring, or rather without their believing. Although it can too be taken in this place thus, that, inasmuch as God has heard, so to say, her groans, and her long and frequent tears, she may be understood to be freed from her sins, and to have tamed every disordered impulse of carnal affection:

[1] Ps. xxxiv. 18.   [2] Ps. cxxvi. 5.
[3] Matt. x. 33; Luke ix. 26.   [4] Ps. cxii. 9.   [5] 1 Tim. vi. 7, 8.   [6] Wisd. v. 3–9.
[7] 1 Thess. v. 3.

as she saith, " Depart from me, all ye that work iniquity, for the Lord hath heard the voice of my weeping : " and when she has had this happy issue, it is no marvel if she be already so perfect as to pray for her enemies. The words then, " Let all mine enemies be ashamed, and vexed," may have this meaning ; that they should repent of their sins, which cannot be effected without confusion and vexation. There is then nothing to hinder us from taking what follows too in this sense, " let them be turned and ashamed," that is, let them be turned to God, and be ashamed that they sometime gloried in the former darkness of their sins ; as the Apostle says, " For what glory had ye sometime in those things of which ye are now ashamed ? " [1] But as to what he added, " exceeding quickly," it must be referred either to the warm affection of her wish, or to the power of Christ ; who converteth to the faith of the Gospel in such quick time the nations, which in their idols' cause did persecute the Church.

PSALM VII.

A PSALM TO DAVID HIMSELF, WHICH HE SUNG TO THE LORD, FOR THE WORDS OF CHUSI, SON OF JEMINI.[2]

1. Now the story which gave occasion to this prophecy may be easily recognised in the second book of Kings.[3] For there Chusi, the friend of king David, went over to the side of Abessalon, his son, who was carrying on war against his father, for the purpose of discovering and reporting the designs which he was taking against his father, at the instigation of Achitophel, who had revolted from David's friendship, and was instructing by his counsel, to the best of his power, the son against the father. But since it is not the story itself which is to be the subject of consideration in this Psalm, from which the prophet hath taken a veil of mysteries, if we have passed over to Christ, let the veil be taken away.[4] And first let us inquire into the signification of the very names, what it means. For there have not been wanting interpreters, who investigating these same words, not carnally according to the letter, but spiritually, declare to us that Chusi should be interpreted silence ; and Gemini, righthanded ; Achitophel, brother's ruin. Among which interpretations, Judas, that traitor, again meets us, that Abessalon should bear his image, according to that interpretation of it as a father's peace ; in that his father was full of thoughts of peace toward him : although he in his guile had war in his heart, as was treated of in the third Psalm. Now as we find in the Gospels that the

disciples of our Lord Jesus Christ are called sons,[5] so in the same Gospels we find they are called brethren also. For the Lord on the resurrection saith, " Go and say to My brethren." [6] And the Apostle calls Him " the first begotten among many brethren." The ruin then of that disciple, who betrayed Him, is rightly understood to be a brother's ruin, which we said is the interpretation of Achitophel. Now as to Chusi, from the interpretation of silence, it is rightly understood that our Lord contended against that guile in silence, that is, in that most deep secret, whereby " blindness happened in part to Israel," [7] when they were persecuting the Lord, that the fulness of the Gentiles might enter in, and " so all Israel might be saved." When the Apostle came to this profound secret and deep silence, he exclaimed, as if struck with a kind of awe of its very depth, " O the depth of the riches of the wisdom and knowledge of God ! how unsearchable are His judgments, and His ways past finding out ! For who hath known the wind of the Lord, or who hath been His counsellor ? " [8] Thus that great silence he does not so much discover by explanation, as he sets forth its greatness in admiration. In this silence the Lord, hiding the sacrament of His adorable passion, turns the brother's voluntary ruin, that is, His betrayer's impious wickedness, into the order of His mercy and providence : that what he with perverse mind wrought for one Man's destruction, He might by providential overruling dispose for all men's salvation. The perfect soul then, which is already worthy to know the secret of God, sings a Psalm unto the Lord, she sings " for the words of Chusi," because she has attained to know the words of that silence : for among unbelievers and persecutors there is that silence and secret. But among His own, to whom it is said, " Now I call you no more servants ; for the servant knoweth not what his lord doeth ; but I have called you friends, for all things that I have heard of My Father I have made known unto you : [9] among His friends, I say, there is not the silence, but the words of the silence, that is, the meaning of that silence set forth and manifested. Which silence, that is, Chusi, is called the son of Gemini, that is, righthanded. For what was done for the Saints was not to be hidden from them. And yet He saith, " Let not the left hand know what the right hand doeth." [10] The perfect soul then, to which that secret has been made known, sings in prophecy " for the words of Chusi," that is, for the knowledge of that same secret. Which secret God at her right hand, that is, favourable [11] and propitious unto her, has

1 Rom. vi. 21.
2 [See Neale's note on this title. *Commentary on the Psalms,* vol. i. p. 131.—C.]
3 2 Sam. xv. 34-37.   4 2 Cor. iii. 16.

5 Matt. ix. 15.   6 John xx. 17.   7 Rom. xi. 25.
8 Rom. xi. 33, 34.   9 John xv. 15.   10 Matt. vi. 3.
11 It is difficult to preserve in translation the double meaning of *dexter* as " righthanded" and "favourable." [We find a corresponding ambiguity, however, in " sinister," as an English word.—C.]

wrought. Wherefore this silence is called the Son of the right hand, which is, "Chusi, the son of Gemini."

2. "O Lord my God, in Thee have I hoped: save me from all them that persecute me, and deliver me" (ver. 1). As one to whom, already perfected, all the war and enmity of vice being overcome, there remaineth no enemy but the envious devil, he says, "Save me from all them that persecute me, and deliver me (ver. 2): lest at any time he tear my soul as a lion." The Apostle says, "Your adversary the devil, as a roaring lion, walketh about, seeking whom he may devour."[1] Therefore when the Psalmist said in the plural number, "Save me from all them that persecute me:" he afterwards introduced the singular, saying, "lest at any time he tear my soul as a lion." For he does not say, lest at any time they tear: he knew what enemy and violent adversary of the perfect soul remained. "Whilst there be none to redeem, nor to save:" that is, lest he tear me, whilst Thou redeemest not, nor savest. For, if God redeem not, nor save, he tears.[2]

3. And that it might be clear that the already perfect soul, which is to be on her guard against the most insidious snares of the devil only, says this, see what follows. "O Lord my God, if I have done this" (ver. 3). What is it that he calls "this"? Since he does not mention the sin by name, are we to understand sin generally? If this sense displease us, we may take that to be meant which follows: as if we had asked, what is this that you say, "this"? He answers, "If there be iniquity in my hands." Now then it is clear that it is said of all sin, "If I have repaid them that recompense me evil" (ver. 4). Which none can say with truth, but the perfect. For so the Lord says, "Be ye perfect, as your Father which is in heaven; who maketh His sun to rise upon the good and the evil, and raineth on the just and the unjust."[3] He then who repayeth not them that recompense evil, is perfect. When therefore the perfect soul prays "for the words of Chusi, the son of Jemini," that is, for the knowledge of that secret and silence, which the Lord, favourable to us and merciful, wrought for our salvation, so as to endure, and with all patience bear, the guiles of this betrayer: as if He should say to this perfect soul, explaining the design of this secret, For thee ungodly and a sinner, that thine iniquities might be washed away by My blood-shedding, in great silence and great patience I bore with My betrayer; wilt not thou imitate me, that thou too mayest not repay evil for evil? Considering

then, and understanding what the Lord has done for him, and by His example going on to perfection, the Psalmist says, "If I have repaid them that recompense me evil:" that is, if I have not done what Thou hast taught me by Thy example: "may I therefore fall by mine enemies empty." And he says well, not, If I have repaid them that do me evil; but, who "recompense." For who so recompenseth, had received somewhat already. Now it is an instance of greater patience, not even to repay him evil, who after receiving benefits returns evil for good, than if without receiving any previous benefit he had had a mind to injure. If therefore he says, "I have repaid them that recompense me evil:" that is, If I have not imitated Thee in that silence, that is, in Thy patience, which Thou hast wrought for me, "may I fall by mine enemies empty." For he is an empty boaster, who, being himself a man, desires to avenge himself on a man; and whilst he openly seeks to overcome a man, is secretly himself overcome by the devil, rendered empty by vain and proud joy, because he could not, as it were, be conquered. The Psalmist knows then where a greater victory may be obtained, and where "the Father which seeth in secret will reward."[4] Lest then he repay them that recompense evil, he overcomes his anger rather than another man, being instructed too by those writings, wherein it is written, "Better is he that overcometh his anger, than he that taketh a city."[5] "If I have repaid them that recompense me evil, may I therefore fall by my enemies empty." He seems to swear by way of execration, which is the heaviest kind of oath, as when one says, If I have done so and so, may I suffer so and so. But swearing in a swearer's mouth is one thing, in a prophet's meaning another. For here he mentions what will really befall men who repay them that recompense evil; not what, as by an oath, he would imprecate on himself or any other.

4. "Let the enemy" therefore "persecute my soul and take it" (ver. 5). By again naming the enemy in the singular number, he more and more clearly points out him whom he spoke of above as a lion. For he persecutes the soul, and if he has deceived it, will take it. For the limit of men's rage is the destruction of the body; but the soul, after this visible death, they cannot keep in their power: whereas whatever souls the devil shall have taken by his persecutions, he will keep. "And let him tread my life upon the earth:" that is, by treading let him make my life earth, that is to say, his food. For he is not only called a lion, but a serpent too, to whom it was said, "Earth shalt thou eat."[6] And to the sinner was

[1] 1 Pet. v. 8.
[2] [This Psalm is the first of those which our author calls *fugitivi*. They are seven, as follows: Psalms xxxiv., lii., liv., lvi., lvii., lix., cxlii. — C.]
[3] Matt. v. 43, 45.

[4] Matt. vi. 6.　　　[5] Prov. xvi. 32.　　　[6] Gen. iii. 14.

it said, " Earth thou art, and into earth shalt thou go." [1] " And let him bring down my glory to the dust." This is that dust which "the wind casteth forth from the face of the earth," [2] to wit, vain and silly boasting of the proud, puffed up, not of solid weight, as a cloud of dust carried away by the wind. Justly then has he here spoken of the glory, which he would not have brought down to dust. For he would have it solidly established in conscience before God, where there is no boasting. " He that glorieth," saith the Apostle, " let him glory in the Lord." [3] This solidity is brought down to the dust, if one through pride despising the secrecy of conscience, where God only proves a man, desires to glory before men. Hence comes what the Psalmist elsewhere says, " God shall bruise the bones of them that please men." [4] Now he that has well learnt or experienced the steps in overcoming vices, knows that this vice of empty glory is either alone, or more than all, to be shunned by the perfect. For that by which the soul first fell, she overcomes the last. " For the beginning of all sin is pride : " and again, " The beginning of man's pride is to depart from God." [5]

5. " Arise, O Lord, in Thine anger " (ver. 6). Why yet does he, who we say is perfect, incite God to anger? Must we not see, whether he rather be not perfect, who, when he was being stoned, said, " O Lord, lay not this sin to their charge "? [6] Or does the Psalmist pray thus not against men, but against the devil and his angels, whose possession sinners and the ungodly are? He then does not pray against him in wrath, but in mercy, whosoever prays that that possession may be taken from him by that Lord "who justifieth the ungodly." [7] For when the ungodly is justified, from ungodly he is made just, and from being the possession of the devil he passes into the temple of God. And since it is a punishment that a possession, in which one longs to have rule, should be taken away from him : this punishment, that he should cease to possess those whom he now possesses, the Psalmist calls the anger of God against the devil. " Arise, O Lord, in Thine anger." " Arise " (he has used it as " appear "), in words, that is, human and obscure ; as though God sleeps, when He is unrecognised and hidden in His secret workings. " Be exalted in the borders of mine enemies." He means by borders the possession itself, in which he wishes that God should be exalted, that is, be honoured and glorified, rather than the devil, while the ungodly are justified and praise God. " And arise, O Lord my God, in the commandment that Thou hast given : " that is, since Thou hast enjoined humility, appear in humility ;

and first fulfil what Thou hast enjoined ; that men by Thy example overcoming pride may not be possessed of the devil, who against Thy commandments advised to pride, saying, " Eat, and your eyes shall be opened, and ye shall be as gods." [8]

6. " And the congregation of the people shall surround Thee." This may be understood two ways. For the congregation of the people can be taken, either of them that believe, or of them that persecute, both of which took place in the same humiliation of our Lord : in contempt of which the multitude of them that persecute surrounded Him ; concerning which it is said, " Why have the heathen raged, and the people meditated vain things? " [9] But of them that believe through His humiliation the multitude so surrounded Him, that it could be said with the greatest truth, " blindness in part is happened unto Israel, that the fulness of the Gentiles might come in : " [10] and again, " Ask of me, and I will give Thee the Gentiles for Thine inheritance, and the boundaries of the earth for Thy possession." [11] " And for their sakes return Thou on high : " that is, for the sake of this congregation return Thou on high : which He is understood to have done by His resurrection and ascension into heaven. For being thus glorified He gave the Holy Ghost, which before His exaltation could not be given, as it is written in the Gospel, " for the Holy Ghost was not yet given, because that Jesus was not yet glorified." [12] Having then returned on high for the sake of the congregation of the people, He sent the Holy Ghost : by whom the preachers of the Gospel being filled, filled the whole world with Churches.

7. It can be taken also in this sense : " Arise, O Lord, in Thine anger, and be exalted in the borders of mine enemies : " that is, arise in Thine anger, and let not mine enemies understand Thee ; so that to " be exalted," should be this, become high,[13] that Thou mayest not be understood ; which has reference to the silence spoken of above. For it is of this exaltation thus said in another Psalm, " And He ascended upon Cherubim, and flew : " and, " He made darkness His secret place." [14] In which exaltation, or concealment, when for their sins' desert they shall not understand Thee, who shall crucify Thee, " the congregation " of believers " shall surround Thee." For in His very humiliation He was exalted, that is, was not understood. So that, " And arise, O Lord my God, in the commandment that Thou hast given : " may have reference to this, that is, when Thou showest Thyself, be high or deep that mine enemies may not un-

1 Gen. iii. 19.   2 Ps. i. 4.   3 1 Cor. i. 31.
4 Ps. liii. 5.   5 Ecclus. x. 13, 12.   6 Acts vii. 60.
7 Rom. iv. 5.

8 Gen. iii. 5.   9 Ps. ii. 1.   10 Rom. xi. 25.
11 Ps. ii. 8.   12 John vii. 39.
13 Altus. Its twofold meaning of " high" and " deep " is not capable of being preserved in translation.
14 Ps. xviii. 10, 11.

derstand Thee. Now sinners are the enemies of the just man, and the ungodly of the godly man. "And the congregation of the people shall surround Thee : " that is, by this very circumstance, that those who crucify Thee understand Thee not, the Gentiles shall believe on Thee, and so " shall the congregation of the people surround Thee." But what follows, if this be the true meaning, has in it more pain, that it begins already to be perceived, than joy that it is understood. For it follows, " and for their sakes return Thou on high," that is, and for the sake of this congregation of the human race, wherewith the Churches are crowded, return Thou on high, that is, again cease to be understood. What then is, " and for their sakes," but that this congregation too will offend Thee, so that Thou mayest most truly foretell and say, " Thinkest Thou when the Son of man shall come, He will find faith on the earth ? " [1] Again, of the false prophets, who are understood to be heretics, He says, " Because of their iniquity the love of many shall wax cold." [2] Since then even in the Churches, that is, in that congregation of peoples and nations, where the Christian name has most widely spread, there shall be so great abundance of sinners, which is already, in great measure, perceived ; is not that famine of the word [3] here predicted, which has been threatened by another prophet also? Is it not too for this congregation's sake, who, by their sins, are estranging from themselves the light of truth, that God returns on high, that is, so that faith, pure and cleansed from the corruption of all perverse opinions, is held and received, either not at all, or by the very few of whom it was said, " Blessed is he that shall endure to the end, the same shall be saved "? [4] Not without cause then is it said, " and for the sake of this " congregation " return Thou on high : " that is, again withdraw into the depth of Thy secrecy, even for the sake of this congregation of the peoples, that hath Thy name, and doeth not Thy deeds.

8. But whether the former exposition of this place, or this last be the more suitable, without prejudice to any one better, or equal, or as good, it follows very consistently, " the Lord judgeth the people." For whether He returned on high, when, after the resurrection, He ascended into heaven, well does it follow, " The Lord judgeth the people : " for that He will come from thence to judge the quick and the dead. Or whether He return on high, when the understanding of the truth leaves sinful Christians, for that of His coming it has been said, " Thinkest thou the Son of Man on His coming will find faith on the earth ? " [1] " The Lord " then " judgeth the

people." What Lord, but Jesus Christ ? " For the Father judgeth no man, but hath committed all judgment unto the Son." [5] Wherefore this soul which prayeth perfectly, see how she fears not the day of judgment, and with a truly secure longing says in her prayer, " Thy kingdom come : judge me," she says, " O Lord, according to my righteousness." In the former Psalm a weak one was entreating, imploring rather the mercy of God, than mentioning any desert of his own : since the Son of God came " to call sinners to repentance." [6] Therefore he had there said, " Save me, O Lord, for Thy mercy's sake ; " [7] that is, not for my desert's sake. But now, since being called he hath held and kept the commandments which he received, he is bold to say, " Judge me, O Lord, according to my righteousness, and according to my harmlessness, that is upon me." This is true harmlessness, which harms not even an enemy. Accordingly, well does he require to be judged according to his harmlessness, who could say with truth, " If I have repaid them that recompense me evil." As for what he added, " that is upon me," it can refer not only to harmlessness, but can be understood also with reference to righteousness ; that the sense should be this, Judge me, O Lord, according to my righteousness, and according to my harmlessness, which righteousness and harmlessness is upon me. By which addition he shows that this very thing, that the soul is righteous and harmless, she has not by herself, but by God who giveth brightness and light. For of this he says in another Psalm, " Thou, O Lord, wilt light my candle." [8] And of John it is said, that " he was not the light, but bore witness of the light." [9] " He was a burning and shining candle." [10] That light then, whence souls, as candles, are kindled, shines forth not with borrowed, but with original, brightness, which light is truth itself. It is then so said, " According to my righteousness, and according to my harmlessness, that is upon me," as if a burning and shining candle should say, Judge me according to the flame which is upon me, that is, not that wherewith [11] I am myself, but that whereby I shine enkindled of thee.

9. " But let the wickedness of sinners be consummated " (ver. 9). He says, " be consummated," be completed, according to that in the Apocalypse, " Let the righteous become more righteous, and let the filthy be filthy still." [12] For the wickedness of those men appears consummate, who crucified the Son of God ; but greater is theirs who will not live uprightly, and hate the precepts of truth, for whom the Son of God was crucified. " Let the wickedness of

[1] Luke xviii. 8.   [2] Matt. xxiv. 12.   [3] Amos viii. 11.
[4] Mark xiii. 13.

[5] John v. 22.   [6] Matt. ix. 13.   [7] Ps. vi. 4.
[8] Ps. xviii. 28.   [9] John i. 8.   [10] John v. 35.
[11] Al. that which.   [12] Rev. xxii. 11.

sinners," then he says, " be consummated," that is, arrive at the height of wickedness, that just judgment may be able to come at once. But since it is not only said, " Let the filthy be filthy still ; " but it is said also, " Let the righteous become more righteous ; " he joins on the words, " And Thou shalt direct the righteous, O God, who searcheth the hearts and reins." How then can the righteous be directed but in secret? when even by means of those things which, in the commencement of the Christian ages, when as yet the saints were oppressed by the persecution of the men of this world, appeared marvellous to men, now that the Christian name has begun to be in such high dignity, hypocrisy, that is pretence, has increased ; of those, I mean, who by the Christian profession had rather please men than God. How then is the righteous man directed in so great confusion of pretence, save whilst God searcheth the hearts and reins ; seeing all men's thoughts, which are meant by the word heart ; and their delights, which are understood by the word reins? For the delight in things temporal and earthly is rightly ascribed to the reins ; for that it is both the lower part of man, and that region where the pleasure of carnal generation dwells, through which man's nature is transferred into this life of care, and deceiving joy, by the succession of the race. God then, searching our heart, and perceiving that it is there where our treasure is, that is, in heaven ; searching also the reins, and perceiving that we do not assent to flesh and blood, but delight ourselves in the Lord, directs the righteous man in his inward conscience before Him, where no man seeth, but He alone who perceiveth what each man thinketh, and what delighteth each. For delight is the end of care ; because to this end does each man strive by care and thought, that he may attain to his delight. He therefore seeth our cares, who searcheth the heart. He seeth too the ends of cares, that is delights, who narrowly searcheth the reins ; that when He shall find that our cares incline neither to the lust of the flesh, nor to the lust of the eyes, nor to the pride of life,[1] all which pass away as a shadow, but that they are raised upward to the joys of things eternal, which are spoilt by no change, He may direct the righteous, even He, the God who searcheth the hearts and reins. For our works, which we do in deeds and words, may be known unto men ; but with what mind they are done, and to what end we would attain by means of them, He alone knoweth, the God who searcheth the hearts and reins.

10. " My righteous help is from the Lord, who maketh whole the upright in heart" (ver. 10). The offices of medicine are twofold, one the curing infirmity, the other the preserving health. According to the first it was said in the preceding Psalm, " Have mercy on me, O Lord, for I am weak ; "[2] according to the second it is said in this Psalm, " If there be iniquity in my hands, if I have repaid them that recompense me evil, may I therefore[3] fall by my enemies empty." For there the weak prays that he may be delivered, here one already whole that he may not change for the worse. According to the one it is there said, " Make me whole for Thy mercy's sake ; " according to this other it is here said, " Judge me, O Lord, according to my righteousness." For there he asks for a remedy to escape from disease ; but here for protection from falling into disease. According to the former it is said, " Make me whole, O Lord, according to Thy mercy : " according to the latter it is said, " My righteous help is from the Lord, who maketh whole the upright in heart." Both the one and the other maketh men whole ; but the former removes them from sickness into health, the latter preserves them in this health. Therefore there the help is merciful, because the sinner hath no desert, who as yet longeth to be justified, " believing on Him who justifieth the ungodly ; "[4] but here the help is righteous, because it is given to one already righteous. Let the sinner then who said, " I am weak," say in the first place, " Make me whole, O Lord, for Thy mercy's sake ;" and here let the righteous man, who said, " If I have repaid them that recompense me evil," say, " My righteous help is from the Lord, who maketh whole the upright in heart." For if he sets forth the medicine, by which we may be healed when weak, how much more that by which we may be kept in health. For if " while we were yet sinners, Christ died for us, how much more being now justified shall we be kept whole from wrath through Him."[5]

11. " My righteous help is from the Lord, who maketh whole the upright in heart." God, who searcheth the hearts and reins, directeth the righteous ; but with righteous help maketh He whole the upright in heart. He doth not as He searcheth the hearts and reins, so make whole the upright in heart and reins ; for the thoughts are both bad in a depraved heart, and good in an upright heart ; but delights which are not good belong to the reins, for they are more low and earthly ; but those that are good not to the reins, but to the heart itself. Wherefore men cannot be so called upright in reins, as they are called upright in heart, since where the thought is, there at once the delight is too ; which cannot be, unless when things divine and eternal are thought of. " Thou hast given," he says, " joy in my heart," when he had said, " The light of Thy countenance

---

[1] 1 John ii. 16.

[2] Ps. vi. 2.   [3] Al. deservedly.   [4] Rom. iv. 5.
[5] Rom. v. 8, 9.

has been stamped on us, O Lord." [1] For although the phantoms of things temporal, which the mind falsely pictures to itself, when tossed by vain and mortal hope, to vain imaginations oftentimes bring a delirious and maddened joy; yet this delight must be attributed not to the heart, but to the reins; for all these imaginations have been drawn from lower, that is, earthly and carnal things. Hence it comes, that God, who searcheth the hearts and reins, and perceiveth in the heart upright thoughts, in the reins no delights, affordeth righteous help to the upright in heart, where [2]heavenly delights are coupled with clean thoughts. And therefore when in another Psalm he had said, " Moreover even to-night my reins have chided me ; " he went on to say as touching help, " I foresaw the Lord alway in my sight, for He is on my right hand, that I should not be moved." [3] Where he shows that he suffered suggestions only from the reins, not delights as well ; for he had suffered these, then he would of course be moved. But he said, " The Lord is on my right hand, that I should not be moved ; " and then he adds, " Wherefore was my heart delighted ; " that the reins should have been able to chide, not delight him. The delight accordingly was produced not in the reins, but there, where against the chiding of the reins God was foreseen to be on the right hand, that is, in the heart.

12. " God the righteous judge, strong [4] (in endurance) and long-suffering " (ver. 11). What God is judge, but the Lord, who judgeth the people ? He is righteous ; who " shall render to every man according to his works." [5] He is strong (in endurance) ; who, being most powerful, for our salvation bore even with ungodly persecutors. He is long-suffering ; who did not immediately, after His resurrection, hurry away to punishment, even those that persecuted Him, but bore with them, that they might at length turn from that ungodliness to salvation : and still He beareth with them, reserving the last penalty for the last judgment, and up to this present time inviting sinners to repentance. " Not bringing in anger every day." Perhaps " bringing in anger " is a more significant expression than being angry (and so we find it in the Greek [6] copies) ; that the anger, whereby He punisheth, should not be in Him, but in the minds of those ministers who obey the commandments of truth through whom orders are given even to the lower ministries, who are called angels of wrath, to punish sin : whom even now the punishment of men delights not for justice' sake, in which they have no pleasure, but for malice' sake. God then doth not " bring in anger every day," that is, He doth not collect His ministers for vengeance every

day. For now the patience of God inviteth to repentance : but in the last time, when men " through their hardness and impenitent heart shall have treasured up for themselves anger in the day of anger, and revelation of the righteous judgment of God, [7] then He will brandish His sword."

13. " Unless ye be converted," He says, " He will brandish His sword " (ver. 12). The Lord Man Himself may be taken to be God's double-edged sword, that is, His spear, which at His first coming He will not brandish, but hideth as it were in the sheath of humiliation : but He will brandish it, when at the second coming to judge the quick and dead, in the manifest splendour of His glory, He shall flash light on His righteous ones, and terror on the ungodly. For in other copies, instead of, " He shall brandish His sword," it has been written, " He shall make bright His spear : " by which word I think the last coming of the Lord's glory most appropriately signified : seeing that is understood of His person, which another Psalm has, " Deliver, O Lord, my soul from the ungodly, [8] Thy spear from the enemies of Thine hand. He hath bent His bow, and made it ready." The tenses of the words must not be altogether overlooked, how he has spoken of "the sword" in the future, " He will brandish ; " of " the bow " in the past, " He hath bent : " and these words of the past tense follow after. [9]

14. " And in it He hath prepared the instruments of death : He hath wrought His arrows for the burning " (ver. 13). That bow then I would readily take to be the Holy Scripture, in which by the strength of the New Testament, as by a sort of string, the hardness of the Old has been bent and subdued. From thence the Apostles are sent forth like arrows, or divine preachings are shot. Which arrows " He has wrought for the burning," arrows, that is, whereby being stricken they might be inflamed with heavenly love. For by what other arrows was she stricken, who saith, " Bring me into the house of wine, place me among perfumes, crowd me among honey, for I have been wounded with love " ? [10] By what other arrows is he kindled, who, desirous of returning to God, and coming back from wandering, asketh for help against crafty tongues, and to whom it is said, " What shall be given thee, or what added to thee against the crafty tongue? Sharp arrows of the mighty, with devastating coals : " [11] that is, coals, whereby, when thou art stricken and set on fire, thou mayest burn with so great love of the kingdom of heaven, as to despise the tongues of all that

---

[1] Ps. iv. 7, 6.　　[2] *Supremæ*.　　[3] Ps. xvi. 7, 8.
[4] *Fortis*.　　[5] Matt. xvi. 27.
[6] μὴ ὀργὴν ἐπάγων, LXX.

[7] Rom. ii. 5.　　　　　　　[8] Ps. xvii. 13.
[9] [So St. Jerome also understood the Hebrew in his strict version. — C.]
[10] Sol. Song ii. 4, 5.　　　　[11] Ps. cxx. 3, 4.

resist thee, and would recall thee from thy purpose, and to deride their persecutions, saying, "Who shall separate me from the love of Christ? shall tribulation, or distress, or persecution, or famine, or nakedness, or peril, or sword? For I am persuaded," he says, "that neither death, nor life, nor angel, nor principality, nor things present, nor things to come, nor power, nor height, nor depth, nor other creature, shall be able to separate me from the love of God, which is in Christ Jesus our Lord." [1] Thus for the burning hath He wrought His arrows. For in the Greek copies it is found thus, "He hath wrought His arrows for the burning." But most of the Latin copies [2] have "burning arrows." But whether the arrows themselves burn, or make others burn, which of course they cannot do unless they burn themselves, the sense is complete.

15. But since he has said that the Lord has prepared not arrows only, but "instruments of death" too, in the bow, it may be asked, what are "instruments of death"? Are they, peradventure, heretics? For they too, out of the same bow, that is, out of the same Scriptures, light upon souls not to be inflamed with love, but destroyed with poison: which does not happen but after their deserts: wherefore even this dispensation is to be assigned to the Divine Providence, not that it makes men sinners, but that it orders them after they have sinned. For through sin reaching them with an ill purpose, they are forced to understand them ill, that this should be itself the punishment of sin: by whose death, nevertheless, the sons of the Catholic Church are, as it were by certain thorns, so to say, aroused from slumber, and make progress toward the understanding of the holy Scriptures. "For there must be also heresies, that they which are approved," he says, "may be made manifest among you:" [3] that is, among men, seeing they are manifest to God. Or has He haply ordained the same arrows to be at once instruments of death for the destruction of unbelievers, and wrought them burning, or for the burning, for the exercising of the faithful? For that is not false that the Apostle says, "To the one we are the savour of life unto life, to the other the savour of death unto death; and who is sufficient for these things?" [4] It is no wonder then if the same Apostles be both instruments of death in those from whom they suffered persecution, and fiery arrows to inflame the hearts of believers.

16. Now after this dispensation righteous judgment will come: of which the Psalmist so speaks, as that we may understand that each man's punishment is wrought out of his own sin, and his iniquity turned into vengeance: that we may not suppose that that tranquillity and ineffable light of God brings forth from Itself the means of punishing sin; but that it so ordereth sins, that what have been delights to man in sinning, should be instruments to the Lord avenging. "Behold," he says, "he hath travailed with injustice." Now what had he conceived, that he should travail with injustice? "He hath conceived," he says, "toil." Hence then comes that, "In toil shalt thou eat thy bread." [5] Hence too that, "Come unto Me all ye that toil and are heavy laden; for My yoke is easy, and My burden light." [6] For toil will never cease, except one love that which cannot be taken away against his will. For when those things are loved which we can lose against our will, we must needs toil for them most miserably; and to obtain them, amid the straitnesses of earthly cares, whilst each desires to snatch them for himself, and to be beforehand with another, or to wrest it from him, must scheme injustice. Duly then, and quite in order, hath he travailed with injustice, who has conceived toil. Now he bringeth forth what, save that with which he hath travailed, although he has not travailed with that which he conceived? For that is not born, which is not conceived; but seed is conceived, that which is formed from the seed is born. Toil is then the seed of iniquity, but sin the conception of toil, that is, that first sin, to "depart from God." [7] He then hath travailed with injustice, who hath conceived toil. "And he hath brought forth iniquity." "Iniquity" is the same as "injustice:" he hath brought forth then that with which he travailed. What follows next?

17. "He hath opened a ditch, and digged it" (ver. 15). To open a ditch is, in earthly matters, that is, as it were in the earth, to prepare deceit, that another fall therein, whom the unrighteous man wishes to deceive. Now this ditch is opened when consent is given to the evil suggestion of earthly lusts: but it is digged when after consent we press on to actual work of deceit. But how can it be, that iniquity should rather hurt the righteous man against whom it proceeds, than the unrighteous heart whence it proceeds? Accordingly, the stealer of money, for instance, while he desires to inflict painful harm upon another, is himself maimed by the wound of avarice. Now who, even out of his right mind, sees not how great is the difference between these men, when one suffers the loss of money, the other of innocence? "He will fall" then "into the pit which

---

[1] Rom. viii. 35, 38, 39.
[2] [Not so the Vulgate nor St. Jerome, which follow the Greek. He refers to the African (old Italic) Psalters. But see Scrivener, p. 307, 2d ed. — C.]
[3] 1 Cor. xi. 19.　　　　[4] 2 Cor. ii. 16.

[5] Gen. iii. 17.　　　[6] Matt. xi. 28, 30.　　　[7] Ecclus. x. 12.

he hath made." As it is said in another Psalm, "The Lord is known in executing judgments; the sinner is caught in the works of his own hands."[1]

18. "His toil shall be turned on his head, and his iniquity shall descend on his pate "(ver. 16). For he had no mind to escape sin: but was brought under sin as a slave, so to say, as the Lord saith, "Whosoever sinneth is a slave."[2] His iniquity then will be upon him, when he is subject to his iniquity; for he could not say to the Lord, what the innocent and upright say, "My glory, and the lifter up of my head."[3] He then will be in such wise below, as that his iniquity may be above, and descend on him; for that it weigheth him down and burdens him, and suffers him not to fly back to the rest of the saints. This occurs, when in an ill regulated man reason is a slave, and lust hath dominion.

19. "I will confess to the Lord according to His justice" (ver. 17). This is not the sinner's confession: for he says this, who said above most truly, "If there be iniquity in my hands:" but it is a confession of God's justice, in which we speak thus, Verily, O Lord, Thou art just, in that Thou both so protectest the just, that Thou enlightenest them by Thyself; and so orderest sinners, that they be punished not by Thine, but by their own malice. This confession so praises the Lord, that the blasphemies of the ungodly can avail nothing, who, willing to excuse their evil deeds, are unwilling to attribute to their own fault that they sin, that is, are unwilling to attribute their fault to their fault. Accordingly they find either fortune or fate to accuse, or the devil, to whom He who made us hath willed that it should be in our power to refuse consent: or they bring in another nature, which is not of God: wretched waverers, and erring, rather than confessing to God, that He should pardon them. For it is not fit that any be pardoned, except he says, I have sinned. He, then, that sees the deserts of souls so ordered by God, that while each has his own given him, the fair beauty of the universe is in no part violated, in all things praises God: and this is not the confession of sinners, but of the righteous. For it is not the sinner's confession when the Lord says, "I confess to Thee, O Lord of heaven and earth, because Thou hast hid these things from the wise, and revealed them to babes."[4] Likewise in Ecclesiasticus it is said, "Confess to the Lord in all His works: and in confession ye shall say this, All the works of the Lord are exceeding good."[5] Which can be seen in this Psalm, if any one with a pious mind, by the Lord's help, distinguish between the rewards of the righteous and the penalties of the sinners, how that in these two the whole creation, which God made and rules, is adorned with a beauty wondrous and known to few. Thus then he says, "I will confess to the Lord according to His justice," as one who saw that darkness was not made by God, but ordered nevertheless. For God said, "Let light be made, and light was made."[6] He did not say, Let darkness be made, and darkness was made: and yet He ordered it. And therefore it is said, "God divided between the light, and the darkness: and God called the light day, and the darkness He called night."[7] This is the distinction, He made the one and ordered it: but the other He made not, but yet He ordered this too. But now that sins are signified by darkness, so is it seen in the Prophet, who says, "And thy darkness shall be as the noon day:"[8] and in the Apostle, who says, "He that hateth his brother is in darkness:"[9] and above all that text, "Let us cast off the works of darkness, and let us put on the armour of light."[10] Not that there is any nature of darkness. For all nature, in so far as it is nature, is compelled to be. Now being belongs to light: not-being to darkness. He then that leaves Him by whom he was made, and inclines to that whence he was made, that is, to nothing, is in this sin endarkened: and yet he does not utterly perish, but he is ordered among the lowest things. Therefore after the Psalmist said, "I will confess unto the Lord:" that we might not understand it of confession of sins, he adds lastly, "And I will sing to the name of the Lord most high." Now singing has relation to joy, but repentance of sins to sadness.

20. This Psalm can also be taken in the person of the Lord Man: if only that which is there spoken in humiliation be referred to our weakness, which He bore.[11]

PSALM VIII.

TO THE END, FOR THE WINE-PRESSES, A PSALM OF DAVID HIMSELF.[12]

1. He seems to say nothing of wine-presses in the text of the Psalm of which this is the title. By which it appears, that one and the same thing is often signified in Scripture by many and various similitudes. We may then take wine-presses to be Churches, on the same principle by which we understand also by a threshing-floor the Church. For whether in the threshing-floor, or in the wine-press, there is nothing else done but the clearing the produce of its covering; which is necessary, both for its first growth

---

[1] Ps. ix. 16.   [2] John viii. 34.   [3] Ps. iii. 3.
[4] Matt. xi. 25.   [5] Ecclus. xxxix. 14, 15, 16.

[6] Gen. i. 3.   [7] Gen. i. 4, 5.   [8] Isa. lviii. 10.
[9] 1 John ii. 11.   [10] Rom. xiii. 12.
[11] [On the continuity of the first seven Psalms, see Bishop Wordsworth's *Commentary*, p. 10. ed. London, 1867. — C.]
[12] See on Ps. lxxxiv. [The octave of Ps. i., and understood by the Fathers of the ascension of Christ. It was probably sung at the Jewish Feast of Tabernacles. — C.]

and increase, and arrival at the maturity either of the harvest or the vintage. Of these coverings or supporters then; that is, of chaff, on the threshing-floor, the corn; and of husks, in the presses, the wine is stripped: as in the Churches, from the multitude of worldly men, which is collected together with the good, for whose birth and adaptating to the divine word that multitude was necessary, this is effected, that by spiritual love they be separated through the operation of God's ministers. For now so it is that the good are, for a time, separated from the bad, not in space, but in affection: although they have converse together in the Churches, as far as respects bodily presence. But another time will come, the corn will be stored up apart in the granaries, and the wine in the cellars. "The wheat," saith he, "He will lay up in garners; but the chaff He will burn with fire unquenchable."[1] The same thing may be thus understood in another similitude: the wine He will lay up in cellars, but the husks He will cast forth to cattle: so that by the bellies of the cattle we may be allowed by way of similitude to understand the pains of hell.

2. There is another interpretation concerning the wine-presses, yet still keeping to the meaning of Churches. For even the Divine Word may be understood by the grape: for the Lord even has been called a Cluster of grapes; which they that were sent before by the people of Israel brought from the land of promise hanging on a staff, crucified as it were.[2] Accordingly, when the Divine Word maketh use of, by the necessity of declaring Himself, the sound of the voice, whereby to convey Himself to the ears of the hearers; in the same sound of the voice, as it were in husks, knowledge, like the wine, is enclosed: and so this grape comes into the ears, as into the pressing machines of the wine-pressers. For there the separation is made, that the sound may reach as far as the ear; but knowledge be received in the memory of those that hear, as it were in a sort of vat; whence it passes into discipline of the conversation and habit of mind, as from the vat into the cellar: where if it do not through negligence grow sour, it will acquire soundness by age. For it grew sour among the Jews, and this sour vinegar they gave the Lord to drink.[3] For that wine, which from the produce of the vine of the New Testament the Lord is to drink with His saints in the kingdom of His Father,[4] must needs be most sweet and most sound.

3. "Wine-presses" are also usually taken for martyrdoms, as if when they who have confessed the name of Christ have been trodden down by the blows of persecution, their mortal remains as husks remained on earth, but their souls flowed forth into the rest of a heavenly habitation. Nor yet by this interpretation do we depart from the fruitfulness of the Churches. It is sung then, "for the wine-presses," for the Church's establishment; when our Lord after His resurrection ascended into heaven. For then He sent the Holy Ghost: by whom the disciples being fulfilled preached with confidence the Word of God, that Churches might be collected.

4. Accordingly it is said, "O Lord, our Lord, how admirarble is Thy Name in all the earth!" (ver. 1). I ask, how is His Name wonderful in all the earth? The answer is, "For Thy glory has been raised above the heavens." So that the meaning is this, O Lord, who art our Lord, how do all that inhabit the earth admire Thee! for Thy glory hath been raised from earthly humiliation above the heavens. For hence it appeared who Thou wast that descendedst, when it was by some seen, and by the rest believed, whither it was that Thou ascendedst.

5. "Out of the mouth of babes and sucklings Thou hast made perfect praise, because of Thine enemies" (ver. 2). I cannot take babes and sucklings to be any other than those to whom the Apostle says, "As unto babes in Christ I have given you milk to drink, not meat."[5] Who were meant by those who went before the Lord praising Him, of whom the Lord Himself used this testimony, when He answered the Jews who bade Him rebuke them, "Have ye not read, out of the mouth of babes and sucklings Thou hast made perfect praise?"[6] Now with good reason He says not, Thou hast made, but, "Thou hast made perfect praise." For there are in the Churches also those who now no more drink milk, but eat meat: whom the same Apostle points out, saying, "We speak wisdom among them that are perfect;"[7] but not by those only are the Churches perfected; for if there were only these, little consideration would be had of the human race. But consideration is had, when they too, who are not as yet capable of the knowledge of things spiritual and eternal, are nourished by the faith of the temporal history, which for our salvation after the Patriarchs and Prophets was administered by the most excellent Power and Wisdom of God, even in the Sacrament of the assumed Manhood, in which there is salvation for every one that believeth; to the end that moved by Its authority each one may obey Its precepts, whereby being purified and "rooted and grounded in love," he may be able to run with Saints, no more now a child in milk, but a young man in meat, "to comprehend the breadth, the length, the height, and depth, to know also the surpassing knowledge of the love of Christ."[8]

---

[1] Luke iii. 17.   [2] Numb. xiii. 23.   [3] John xix. 29.
[4] Matt. xxvi. 29.

[5] 1 Cor. iii. 1, 2.   [6] Matt. xxi. 16.   [7] 1 Cor. ii. 6.
[8] Eph. iii. 17-19.

6. " Out of the mouth of babes and sucklings Thou hast made perfect praise, because of Thine enemies." By enemies to this dispensation, which has been wrought through Jesus Christ and Him crucified, we ought generally to understand all who forbid belief in things unknown,[1] and promise certain knowledge :[2] as all heretics do, and they who in the superstition of the Gentiles are called philosophers. Not that the promise of knowledge is to be blamed ; but because they deem the most healthful and necessary step of faith is to be neglected, by which we must needs ascend to something certain, which nothing but that which is eternal can be. Hence it appears that they do not possess even this knowledge, which in contempt of faith they promise ; seeing that they know not so useful and necessary a step thereof. " Out of the mouth," then " of babes and sucklings Thou hast made perfect praise," Thou, our Lord, declaring first by the Apostle, " Except ye believe, ye shall not understand ; "[3] and saying by His own mouth, " Blessed are they that have not seen, and shall believe."[4] " Because of the enemies : " against whom too that is said, " I confess to Thee, O Lord of heaven and earth, because Thou hast hid these things from the wise, and revealed them unto babes."[5] " From the wise," he saith, not the really wise, but those who deem themselves such. " That Thou mayest destroy the enemy and the defender." Whom but the heretic?[6] For he is both an enemy and a defender, who when he would assault the Christian faith, seems to defend it. Although the philosophers too of this world may be well taken as the enemies and defenders : forasmuch as the Son of God is the Power and Wisdom of God, by which every one is enlightened who is made wise by the truth : of which they profess themselves to be lovers, whence too their name of philosophers ; and therefore they seem to defend it, while they are its enemies, since they cease not to recommend noxious superstitions, that the elements of this world should be worshipped and revered.

7. " For I shall see Thy heavens, the works of Thy fingers " (ver. 3). We read that the law was written with the finger of God, and given through Moses, His holy servant : by which finger of God many understand the Holy Ghost.[7] Wherefore if, by the fingers of God, we are right in understanding these same ministers filled with the Holy Ghost, by reason of this same Spirit which worketh in them, since by them all holy Scripture has been completed for us ; we under-

stand consistently with this, that, in this place, the books of both Testaments are called " the heavens." Now it is said too of Moses himself, by the magicians of king Pharaoh, when they were conquered by him, " This is the finger of God."[8] And what is written, " The heavens shall be rolled up as a book."[9] Although it be said of this æthereal heaven, yet naturally, according to the same image, the heavens of books are named by allegory. " For I shall see," he says, " the heavens, the works of Thy fingers : " that is, I shall discern and understand the Scriptures, which Thou, by the operation of the Holy Ghost, hast written by Thy ministers.

8. Accordingly the heavens named above also may be interpreted as the same books, where he says, " For Thy glory hath been raised above the heavens : " so that the complete meaning should be this, " For Thy glory hath been raised above the heavens ; " for Thy glory hath exceeded the declarations of all the Scriptures :- " Out of the mouth of babes and sucklings Thou hast made perfect praise," that they should begin by belief in the Scriptures, who would arrive at the knowledge of Thy glory : which hath been raised above the Scriptures, in that it passeth by and transcends the announcements of all words and languages. Therefore hath God lowered the Scriptures even to the capacity of babes and sucklings, as it is sung in another Psalm, " And He lowered the heaven, and came down : "[10] and this did He because of the enemies, who through pride of talkativeness, being enemies of the cross of Christ, even when they do speak some truth, still cannot profit babes and sucklings. So is the enemy and defender destroyed, who, whether he seem to defend wisdom, or even the name of Christ, still, from the step of this faith,[11] assaults that truth, which he so readily makes promise of. Whereby too he is convicted of not possessing it ; since by assaulting the step thereof, namely faith, he knows not how one should mount up thereto. Hence then is the rash and blind promiser of truth, who is the enemy and defender, destroyed, when the heavens, the works of God's fingers, are seen, that is, when the Scriptures, brought down even to the slowness of babes, are understood ; and by means of the lowness of the faith of the history, which was transacted in time, they raise them, well nurtured and strengthened, unto the grand height of the understanding of things eternal, up to those things which they establish.[12] For these heavens, that is, these books, are the works of God's fingers ; for by the operation of the Holy Ghost in the Saints they were completed. For they that have regarded their own glory rather than man's salvation, have spoken

---

[1] 1 Cor. ii. 6-10. [2] See " On Profit of Believing."
[3] Isa. vi. 9; Acts xiii. 27-41. [4] John xx. 29. [5] Matt. xi. 25.
[6] See on Ps. cii., and St. Greg. on Job, Intr. § 15.
[7] Exod. xxxi. 18, xxxiv. 28; Deut. ix. 10. [The " arm of the Lord" is understood by the Fathers of the Son: so also the " right hand of the Lord." The " finger " (proceeding from head and hand) is understood of the Holy Spirit. So the Latin hymn, " Dextræ Dei tu Digitus." — C.]

[8] Exod. viii. 19. [9] Isa. xxxiv. 4. See Rev. vi. 14.
[10] Ps. xviii. 9. [11] Al. step of faith.
[12] Oxford MSS. " and establish them in it," for " up," etc.

without the Holy Ghost, in whom are the bowels of the mercy of God.

9. " For I shall see the heavens, the works of Thy fingers, the moon and the stars, which Thou hast ordained." The moon and stars are ordained in the heavens; since both the Church universal, to signify which the moon is often put, and Churches in the several places particularly, which I imagine to be intimated by the name of stars, are established in the same Scriptures, which we believe to be expressed by the word heavens.[1] But why the moon justly signifies the Church, will be more seasonably considered in another Psalm, where it is said, " The sinners have bent their bow, that they may shoot in the obscure moon the upright in heart." [2]

10. " What is man, that Thou art mindful of him? or the son of man, that Thou visitest him?" (ver. 4). It may be asked, what distinction there is between man and son of man. For if there were none, it would not be expressed thus, " man, or son of man," disjunctively. For if it were written thus, " What is man, that Thou art mindful of him, *and* son of man, that Thou visitest him?" it might appear to be a repetition of the word " man." But now when the expression is, " man *or* son of-man," a distinction is more clearly intimated. This is certainly to be remembered, that every son of man is a man; although every man cannot be taken to be a son of man. Adam, for instance, was a man, but not a son of man. Wherefore we may from hence consider and distinguish what is the difference in this place between man and son of man; namely, that they who bear the image of the earthy man, who is not a son of man, should be signified by the name of men; but that they who bear the image of the heavenly Man,[3] should be rather called sons of men; for the former again is called the old man,[4] and the latter the new; but the new is born of the old, since spiritual regeneration is begun by a change of an earthy and worldly life;[5] and therefore the latter is called son of man. " Man " then in this place is earthy, but " son of man " heavenly; and the former is far removed from God, but the latter present with God; and therefore is He mindful of the former, as in far distance from Him; but the latter He visiteth, with whom being present He enlighteneth him with His countenance. For " salvation is far from sinners; " [6] and, " The light of Thy countenance hath been stamped upon us, O Lord." [7] So in another Psalm he saith, that men in conjunction with beasts are made whole together with these beasts, not by any present inward illumination, but by the multiplication of

the mercy of God, whereby His goodness reacheth even to the lowest things; for the wholeness of carnal men is carnal, as of the beasts; but separating the sons of men from those whom being men he joined with cattle, he proclaims that they are made blessed, after a far more exalted method, by the enlightening of the truth itself, and by a certain inundation of the fountain of life. For he speaketh thus: " Men and beasts Thou wilt make whole, O Lord, as Thy mercy hath been multiplied, O God. But the sons of men shall put their trust in the covering of Thy wings. They shall be inebriated with the richness of Thine house, and of the torrent of Thy pleasures Thou shalt make them drink. For with Thee is the fountain of life, and in Thy light shall we see light. Extend Thy mercy to them that know Thee." [8] Through the multiplication of mercy then He is mindful of man, as of beasts; for that multiplied mercy reacheth even to them that are afar off; but He visiteth the son of man, over whom, placed under the covering of His wings, He extendeth mercy, and in His light giveth light, and maketh him drink of His pleasures, and inebriateth him with the richness of His house, to forget the sorrows and the wanderings of his former conversation. This son of man, that is, the new man, the repentance of the old man begets with pain and tears. He, though new, is nevertheless called yet carnal, whilst he is fed with milk; " I would not speak unto you as unto spiritual, but as unto carnal," says the Apostle. And to show that they were already regenerate, he says, " As unto babes in Christ, I have given you milk to drink, not meat." And when he relapses, as often happens, to the old life, he hears in reproof that he is a man; " Are ye not men," he says, " and walk as men?" [9]

11. Therefore was the son of man first visited in the person of the very Lord Man, born of the Virgin Mary. Of whom, by reason of the very weakness of the flesh, which the Wisdom of God vouchsafed to bear, and the humiliation of the Passion, it is justly said, " Thou hast lowered Him a little lower than the Angels " (ver. 5). But that glorifying is added, in which He rose and ascended up into heaven; " With glory," he says, " and with honour hast Thou crowned Him; and hast set Him over the works of Thine hands " (ver. 6). Since even Angels are the works of God's hands, even over Angels we understand the Only-begotten Son to have been set; whom we hear and believe, by the humiliation of the carnal generation and passion, to have been lowered a little lower than the Angels.

12. " Thou hast put," he says, " all things in subjection under His feet." When he says, " all things," he excepts nothing. And that he might

---

[1] [Here is intimated Augustin's idea of the Catholic Church, in which individual national churches hold their own autonomies. — C.]
[2] Ps. xi. 2.   [3] 1 Cor. xv. 49.
[4] Oxford mss. " called man, and the old man."
[5] Eph. iv. 22, 24.   [6] Ps. cxix. 155.   [7] Ps. iv. 6.

[8] Ps. xxxvi. 6-10.   [9] 1 Cor. iii. 1, 2, 3.

not be allowed to understand it otherwise, the Apostle enjoins it to be believed thus, when he says, " He being excepted which put all things under Him." [1]   And to the Hebrews he uses this very testimony from this Psalm, when he would have it to be understood that all things are in such sort put under our Lord Jesus Christ, as that nothing should be excepted.[2]   And yet he does not seem, as it were, to subjoin any great thing, when he says, " All sheep and oxen, yea, moreover, the beasts of the field, birds of the air, and the fish of the sea, which walk through the paths of the sea " (ver. 7).   For, leaving the heavenly excellencies and powers, and all the hosts of Angels, leaving even man himself, he seems to have put under Him the beasts merely ; unless by sheep and oxen we understand holy souls, either yielding the fruit of innocence, or even working that the earth may bear fruit, that is, that earthly men may be regenerated unto spiritual richness.   By these holy souls then we ought to understand not those of men only, but of all Angels too, if we would gather from hence that all things are put under our Lord Jesus Christ.   For there will be no creature that will not be put under Him, under whom the preeminent [3] spirits, that I may so speak, are put. But whence shall we prove that sheep can be interpreted even, not of men, but of the blessed spirits of the angelical creatures on high ?   May we from the Lord's saying that He had left ninety and nine sheep in the mountains, that is, in the higher regions, and had come down for one ? [4]   For if we take the one lost sheep to be the human soul in Adam, since Eve even was made out of his side,[5] for the spiritual handling and consideration of all which things this is not the time, it remains that, by the ninety and nine left in the mountains, spirits not human, but angelical, should be meant.   For as regards the oxen, this sentence is easily despatched ; since men themselves are for no other reason called oxen, but because by preaching the Gospel of the word of God they imitate Angels, as where it is said, " Thou shalt not muzzle the ox that treadeth out the corn." [6]   How much more easily then do we take the Angels themselves, the messengers of truth, to be oxen, when Evangelists by the participation of their title are called oxen ?   " Thou hast put under " therefore, he says, " all sheep and oxen," that is, all the holy spiritual creation ; in which we include that of holy men, who are in the Church, in those winepresses to wit, which are intimated under the other similitude of the moon and stars.[7]

13.   " Yea moreover," saith he, " the beasts of the field." [8]   The addition of " moreover " is by no means idle.   First, because by beasts of the plain may be understood both sheep and oxen : so that, if goats are the beasts of rocky and mountainous regions, sheep may be well taken to be the beasts of the field.   Accordingly had it been written even thus, " all sheep and oxen and beasts of the field ; " it might be reasonably asked what beasts of the plain meant, since even sheep and oxen could be taken as such. But the addition of " moreover " besides, obliges us, beyond question, to recognise some difference or another.   But under this word, " moreover," not only " beasts of the field," but also " birds of the air, and fish of the sea, which walk through the paths of the sea " (ver. 8), are to be taken in.   What is then this distinction? Call to mind the " wine-presses," holding husks and wine ; and the threshing-floor, containing chaff and corn ; and the nets, in which were enclosed good fish and bad ; and the ark of Noah, in which were both unclean and clean animals :[9] and you will see that the Churches for a while, now in this time, unto the last time of judgment, contain not only sheep and oxen, that is, holy laymen and holy ministers, but " moreover beasts of the field, birds of the air, and birds of the sea, that walk through the paths of the sea."   For the beasts of the field were very fitly understood, as men rejoicing in the pleasure of the flesh where they mount up to nothing high, nothing laborious.   For the field is also " the broad way, that leadeth to destruction : " [10] and in a field is Abel slain.[11]   Wherefore there is cause to fear, lest one coming down from the mountains of God's righteousness (" for thy righteousness," he says, " is as the mountains of God " [12]) making choice of the broad and easy paths of carnal pleasure, be slain by the devil. See now too " the birds of heaven," the proud, of whom it is said, " They have set their mouth against the heaven." [13]   See how they are carried on high by the wind, " who say, We will magnify our tongue, our lips are our own, who is our Lord ? " [14]   Behold too the fish of the sea, that is, the curious ; who walk through the paths of the sea, that is, search in the deep after the temporal things of this world : which, like paths in the sea, vanish and perish, as quickly as the water comes together again after it has given room, in their passage, to ships, or to whatsoever walketh or swimmeth.   For he said not merely, who walk the paths of the sea ; but " walk through," he said ; showing the very determined earnestness of those who seek after vain and fleeting things.   Now these three kinds

---

[1] 1 Cor. xv. 27.   [2] Heb. ii. 8.
[3] *Primates.*   [4] Matt. xviii. 12; Luke xv. 4.
[5] Gen. ii. 21, 22.   [6] 1 Cor. ix. 9; 1 Tim. v. 18.
[7] [See p. 27, and p. 30, note 1, *supra*. —C.]

[8] *Campi.*
[9] See on title. Matt. iii. 12, xiii. 47; Gen. vii.8.
[10] Matt. vii. 13.   [11] Gen. iv. 8.
[12] Ps. xxxvi. 6.   [13] Ps. lxxiii. 9.   [14] Ps. xii. 4.

of vice, namely, the pleasure of the flesh, and pride, and curiosity, include all sins. And they appear to me to be enumerated by the Apostle John, when he says, "Love not the world; for all that is in the world is the lust of the flesh, and the lust of the eyes, and the pride of life." [1] For through the eyes especially prevails curiosity. To what the rest indeed belong is clear. And that temptation of the Lord Man was threefold: by food, that is, by the lust of the flesh, where it is suggested, "command these stones that they be made bread:" [2] by vain boasting, where, when stationed on a mountain, all the kingdoms of this earth are shown Him, and promised if He would worship: [3] by curiosity, where, from the pinnacle of the temple, He is advised to cast Himself down, for the sake of trying whether He would be borne up by Angels. [4] And accordingly after that the enemy could prevail with Him by none of these temptations, this is said of him, "When the devil had ended all his temptation." [5] With a reference then to the meaning of the wine-presses, not only the wine, but the husks too are put under His feet; to wit, not only sheep and oxen, that is, the holy souls of believers, either in the laity, or in the ministry; but moreover both beasts of pleasure, and birds of pride, and fish of curiosity. All which classes of sinners we see mingled now in the Churches with the good and holy. May He work then in His Churches, and separate the wine from the husks: let us give heed, that we be wine, and sheep or oxen; not husks, or beasts of the field, or birds of heaven, or fish of the sea, which walk through the paths of the sea. Not that these names can be understood and explained in this way only, but the explanation of them must be according to the place where they are found. For elsewhere they have other meanings. And this rule must be kept to in every allegory, that what is expressed by the similitude should be considered agreeably to the meaning of the particular place: for this is the manner of the Lord's and the Apostles' teaching. Let us repeat then the last verse, which is also put at the beginning of the Psalm, and let us praise God, saying, "O Lord our Lord, how wonderful is Thy name in all the earth!" For fitly, after the matter of the discourse, is the return made to the heading, whither all that discourse must be referred.

PSALM IX.

1. The inscription of this Psalm is, "To the end for the hidden things of the Son, a Psalm of David himself." [6] As to the hidden things of

the Son there may be a question: but since he has not added whose, the very only-begotten Son of God should be understood. For where a Psalm has been inscribed of the son of David,[7] "When," he says, "he fled from the face of Absalom his son;" although his name even was mentioned, and therefore there could be no obscurity as to whom it was spoken of: yet it is not merely said, from the face of son Absalom; but "his" is added. But here both because "his" is not added, and much is said of the Gentiles, it cannot properly be taken of Absalom.[8] For the war which that abandoned one waged with his father, no way relates to the Gentiles, since there the people of Israel only were divided against themselves. This Psalm is then sung for the hidden things of the only-begotten Son of God.[9] For the Lord Himself too, when, without addition, He uses the word Son, would have Himself, the Only-begotten to be understood; as where He says, "If the Son shall make you free, then shall ye be free indeed." [10] For He said not, the Son of God; but in saying merely, Son, He gives us to understand whose Son it is. Which form of expression nothing admits of, save His excellency of whom we so speak, that, though we name Him not, He can be understood. For so we say, it rains, clears up, thunders, and such like expressions; and we do not add *who* does it all; for that the excellency of the doer spontaneously presents itself to all men's minds, and does not want words. What then are the hidden things of the Son? By which expression we must first understand that there are some things of the Son manifest, from which those are distinguished which are called hidden. Wherefore since we believe two advents of the Lord, one past, which the Jews understood not: the other future, which we both hope for; and since the one which the Jews understood not, profited the Gentiles; "For the hidden things of the Son" is not unsuitably understood to be spoken of this advent, in which "blindness in part is happened to Israel, that the fulness of the Gentiles might come in." [11]

For notice of two judgments is conveyed to us throughout the Scriptures, if any one will give heed to them, one hidden, the other manifest. The hidden one is passing now, of which the Apostle Peter says, "The time is come that judgment should begin from the house of the Lord." [12] The hidden judgment accordingly is the pain, by which now each man is either exercised to purification, or warned to conversion, or if he despise the calling and discipline

---

[1] 1 John ii. 15, 16. [2] Matt. iv. 3. [3] Matt. iv. 8, 9.
[4] Matt. iv. 6. [5] Luke iv. 13.
[6] [This title is only conjecturally elucidated by expositors. Here arises the confusion of numbering the Psalms; the Septuagint and Vulgate making the following Psalm all one with this. — C.]

[7] Ps. iii. [8] 2 Sam. xv.
[9] [It is the first of the alphabetical Psalms, which are: Ps. ix., x., xxv., xxxiv., cxi., cxii., cxix., cxlv. Of these, only four are ascribed to David; viz., ix., xxv., xxxiv., and cxlv. — C.]
[10] John viii. 36. [11] Rom. xi. 25. [12] 1 Pet. iv. 17.

of God, is blinded unto damnation. But the manifest judgment is that in which the Lord, at His coming, will judge the quick and the dead, all men confessing that it is He by whom both rewards shall be assigned to the good, and punishments to the evil. But then that confession will avail, not to the remedy of evils, but to the accumulation of damnation. Of these two judgments, the one hidden, the other manifest, the Lord seems to me to have spoken, where He says, "Whoso believeth on Me hath ·passed from death unto life, and shall not come into judgment;"[1] into the manifest judgment, that is. For that which passes from death unto life by means of some affliction, whereby "He scourgeth every son whom He receiveth,"[2] is the hidden judgment. "But whoso believeth not," saith He, "hath been judged already:"[3] that is, by this hidden judgment hath been already prepared for that manifest one. These two judgments we read of also in Wisdom, whence it is written, "Therefore unto them, as to children without the use of reason, Thou didst give a judgment to mock them; But they that have not been corrected by this judgment have felt a judgment worthy of God."[4] Whoso then are not corrected by this hidden judgment of God, shall most worthily be punished by that manifest one. . . .

2. "I will confess unto Thee, O Lord, with my whole heart" (ver. 1). He doth not, with a whole heart, confess unto God, who doubteth of His Providence in any particular: but he who sees already the hidden things of the wisdom of God, how great is His invisible reward, who saith, "We rejoice in tribulations;"[5] and how all torments, which are inflicted on the body, are either for the exercising of those that are converted to God, or for warning that they be converted, or for just preparation of the obdurate unto their last damnation: and so now all things are referred to the governance of Divine Providence, which fools think done as it were by chance and at random, and without any Divine ordering. "I will tell all Thy marvels." He tells all God's marvels, who sees them performed not only openly on the body, but invisibly indeed too in the soul, but far more sublimely and excellently. For men earthly, and led wholly by the eye, marvel more that the dead Lazarus rose again in the body, than that Paul the persecutor rose again in soul.[6] But since the visible miracle calleth the soul to the light, but the invisible enlighteneth the soul that comes when called, he tells all God's marvels, who, by believing the visible, passes on to the understanding of the invisible.

3. "I will be glad and exult in Thee" (ver. 2). Not any more in this world, not in pleasure of bodily dalliance, not in relish of palate and tongue, not in sweetness of perfumes, not in joyousness of passing sounds, not in the variously coloured forms of figure, not in vanities of men's praise, not in wedlock and perishable offspring, not in superfluity of temporal wealth, not in this world's getting, whether it extend over place and space, or be prolonged in time's succession: but, "I will be glad and exult in Thee," namely, in the hidden things of the Son, where "the light of Thy countenance hath been stamped on us, O Lord:"[7] for, "Thou wilt hide them," saith he, "in the hiding place of Thy countenance."[8] He then will be glad and exult in Thee, who tells all Thy marvels. And He will tell all Thy marvels (since it is now spoken of prophetically), "who came not to do His own will, but the will of Him who sent Him."[9]

4. For now the Person of the Lord begins to appear speaking in this Psalm. For it follows, "I will sing to Thy Name, O Most High, in turning mine enemy behind." His enemy then, where was he turned back? Was it when it was said to him, "Get thee behind, Satan"?[10] For then he who by tempting desired to put himself before, was turned behind, by failing in deceiving Him who was tempted, and by availing nothing against Him. For earthly men are behind: but the heavenly man is preferred before, although he came after. For "the first man is of the earth, earthy: the second Man is from heaven, heavenly."[11] But from this stock he came by whom it was said, "He who cometh after me is preferred before me."[12] And the Apostle forgets "those things that are behind, and reaches forth unto those things that are before."[13] The enemy, therefore, was turned behind, after that he could not deceive the heavenly Man being tempted; and he turned himself to earthy men, where he can have dominion. . . . For in truth the devil is turned behind, even in the persecution of the righteous, and he, much more to their advantage, is a persecutor, than if he went before as a leader and a prince. We must sing then to the Name of the Most High in turning the enemy behind: since we ought to choose rather to fly from him as a persecutor, than to follow him as a leader. For we have whither we may fly and hide ourselves in the hidden things of the Son; seeing that "the Lord hath been made a refuge for us."[14]

5. "They will be weakened, and perish from Thy face" (ver. 3). Who will be weakened and perish, but the unrighteous and ungodly? "They will be weakened," while they shall avail

[1] John v. 24.   [2] Heb. xii. 6.   [3] John iii. 18.
[4] Wisd. xii. 25, 26.   [5] Rom. v. 3.
[6] John xi.; Acts ix.

[7] Ps. iv. 6.   [8] Ps. xxxi. 20.   [9] John vi. 38.
[10] Matt. xvi. 23.   [11] 1 Cor. xv. 47.   [12] John i. 15.
[13] Phil. iii. 13.   [14] Ps. xc. 1.

nothing ; "and they shall perish," because the ungodly will not be ; "from the face " of God, that is, from the knowledge of God, as he perished who said," But now I live not, but Christ liveth in me."[1] But why will the ungodly "be weakened and perish from thy face?" "Because," he saith, "Thou hast made my judgment, and my cause : " that is, the judgment in which I seemed to be judged, Thou hast made mine ; and the cause in which men condemned me just and innocent, Thou hast made mine. For such things served[2] Him for our deliverance : as sailors too call the wind theirs, which they take advantage of for prosperous sailing.

6. "Thou satest on the throne Who judgest equity" (ver. 4). Whether the Son say this to the Father, who said also, "Thou couldest have no power against Me, except it were given thee from above,"[3] referring this very thing, that the Judge of men was judged for men's advantage, to the Father's equity and His own hidden things : or whether man say to God, "Thou satest on the throne Who judgest equity," giving the name of God's throne to his soul, so that his body may peradventure be the earth, which is called God's "footstool : "[4] for "God was in Christ, reconciling the world unto Himself : "[5] or whether the soul of the Church, perfect now and without spot and wrinkle,[6] worthy, that is, of the hidden things of the Son, in that "the King hath brought her into His chamber,"[7] say to her spouse, "Thou satest upon the throne Who judgest equity," in that Thou hast risen from the dead, and ascended up into heaven, and sittest at the right hand of the Father : whichsoever, I say, of those opinions, whereunto this verse may be referred, is preferred, it transgresses not the rule of faith.

7. "Thou hast rebuked the heathen, and the ungodly hath perished" (ver. 5). We take this to be more suitably said to the Lord Jesus Christ, than said by Him. For who else hath rebuked the heathen, and the ungodly perished, save He, who after that He ascended up into heaven, sent the Holy Ghost, that, filled by Him, the Apostles should preach the word of God with boldness, and freely reprove men's sins? At which rebuke the ungodly perished ; because the ungodly was justified and was made godly. "Thou hast effaced their name for the world,[8] and for the world's world. The name of the ungodly hath been effaced. For they are not called ungodly who believe in the true God. Now their name is effaced " for the world," that is, as long as the course of the temporal world endures. "And for the world's world." What

is "the world's world," but that whose image and shadow, as it were, this world possesses? For the change of seasons succeeding one another, whilst the moon is on the wane, and again on the increase, whilst the sun each year returns to his quarter, whilst spring, or summer, or autumn, or winter passes away only to return, is in some sort an imitation of eternity. But this world's world is that which abides in immutable eternity. As a verse in the mind, and a verse in the voice ﬤ the former is understood, the latter heard ; and the former fashions the latter ; and hence the former works in art and abides, the latter sounds in the air and passes away. So the fashion of this changeable world is defined by that world unchangeable which is called the world's world. And hence the one abides in the art, that is, in the Wisdom and Power of God : but the other is made to pass in the governance of creation. If after all it be not a repetition, so that after it was said "for the world," lest it should be understood of this world that passeth away, it were added "for the world's world." For in the Greek copies it is thus, εἰς τὸν αἰῶνα, καὶ εἰς τὸν αἰῶνα τοῦ αἰῶνος. Which the Latins have for the most rendered, not, "for the world, and for the world's world ; "[9] but, "for ever, and for the world's world,"[10] that in the words "for the world's world," the words "for ever," should be explained. "The name," then, "of the ungodly Thou hast effaced for ever," for from henceforth the ungodly shall never be. And if their name be not prolonged unto this world, much less unto the world's world.[11]

8. "The swords of the enemy have failed at the end" (ver. 6). Not enemies in the plural, but this enemy in the singular. Now what enemy's swords have failed but the devil's? Now these are understood to be divers erroneous opinions, whereby as with swords he destroys souls. In overcoming these swords, and in bringing them to failure, that sword is employed, of which it is said in the seventh Psalm, "If ye be not converted, He will brandish His sword."[12] And peradventure this is the end, against which the swords of the enemy fail ; since up to it they are of some avail. Now it worketh secretly, but in the last judgment it will be brandished openly. By it the cities are destroyed. For so it follows, "The swords of the enemy have failed at the end : and Thou hast destroyed the cities." Cities indeed wherein the devil rules, where crafty and deceitful counsels hold, as it were, the place of a court, on which supremacy attend as officers and ministers the services of all the members,

---

[1] Gal. ii. 20.   [2] *Militaverunt.*   [3] John xix. 11.
[4] Isa. lxvi. 1.   [5] 2 Cor. v. 19.   [6] Eph. v. 27.
[7] Song of Sol. i. 4.
[8] Or "unto the age," *sæculum.* The meaning of "age," as in our expression "world without end," is the primary one in Latin.

[9] *In sæculum et in sæculum sæculi.* [African Psalter, probably. —C.]
[10] *In æternum et in sæculum sæculi.* [So the Vulgate.—C.]
[11] [Jerome reads: *In sempiternum et jugiter.*—C.]
[12] Ps. vii. 12.

the eyes for curiosity, the ears for lasciviousness, or for whatsoever else is gladly listened to that bears on evil, the hands for rapine or any other violence or pollution soever, and all the other members after this manner serving the tyrannical supremacy, that is, perverse counsels. Of this city the commonalty, as it were, are all soft affections and disturbing emotions of the mind, stirring up daily seditions in a man. So then where a king, where a court, where ministers, where commonalty are found, there is a city. Now again would such things be in bad cities, unless they were first in individual men, who are, as it were, the elements and seeds of cities. These cities He destroys, when on the prince being shut out thence, of whom it was said, "The prince of this world" has been "cast out,"[1] these kingdoms are wasted by the word of truth, evil counsels are laid to sleep, vile affections tamed, the ministries of the members and senses taken captive, and transferred to the service of righteousness and good works: that as the Apostle says, "Sin should no more reign in" our "mortal body,"[2] and so forth. Then is the soul at peace, and the man is disposed to receive rest and blessedness. "Their memorial has perished with uproar:" with the uproar, that is, of the ungodly. But it is said, "with uproar," either because when ungodliness is overturned, there is uproar made: for none passeth to the highest place, where there is the deepest silence, but he who with much uproar shall first have warred with his own vices: or "with uproar," is said, that the memory of the ungodly should perish in the perishing even of the very uproar, in which ungodliness riots.

9. "And the Lord abideth for ever" (ver. 7). "Wherefore" then "have the heathen raged, and the people imagined vain things against the Lord, and against His anointed:"[3] for "the Lord abideth for ever. He hath prepared His seat in judgment, and He shall judge the world in equity." He prepared His seat when He was judged. For by that patience Man purchased heaven, and God in Man profited believers. And this is the Son's hidden judgment. But seeing He is also to come openly and in the sight of all to judge the quick and the dead, He hath prepared His seat in the hidden judgment: and He shall also openly "judge the world in equity:" that is, He shall distribute gifts proportioned to desert, setting the sheep on His right hand, and the goats on His left.[4] "He shall judge the people with justice" (ver. 8). This is the same as was said above, "He shall judge the world in equity." Not as men judge who see not the heart, by whom very often worse men are acquitted than are condemned: but "in

equity" and "with justice" shall the Lord judge, "conscience bearing witness, and thoughts accusing, or else excusing."[5]

10. "And the Lord hath become a refuge to the poor" (ver. 9). Whatsoever be the persecutions of that enemy, who hath been turned behind, what harm shall he do to them whose refuge the Lord hath become? But this will be, if in this world, in which that one has an office of power, they shall choose to be poor, by loving nothing which either here leaves a man while he lives and loves, or is left by him when he dies. For to such a poor man hath the Lord become a refuge, "an Helper in due season, in tribulation." Lo, He maketh poor, for "He scourgeth every son whom He receiveth."[6] For what "an Helper in due season" is, he explained by adding "in tribulation." For the soul is not turned to God, save when it is turned away from this world: nor is it more seasonably turned away from this world, except toils and pains be mingled with its trifling and hurtful and destructive pleasures.

11. "And let them who know Thy Name, hope in Thee" (ver. 10), when they shall have ceased hoping in wealth, and in the other enticements of this world. For the soul indeed that seeketh where to fix her hope, when she is torn away from this world, the knowledge of God's Name seasonably receives. For the mere Name of God hath now been published everywhere: but the knowledge of the name is, when He is known whose name it is. For the name is not a name for its own sake, but for that which it signifies. Now it has been said, "The Lord is His Name."[7] Wherefore whoso willingly submits himself to God as His servant, hath known this name. "And let them who know Thy Name hope in Thee" (ver. 10). Again, the Lord saith to Moses, "I am That I am; and Thou shalt say to the children of Israel, I AM, hath sent me."[8] "Let them" then "who know Thy Name, hope in Thee;" that they may not hope in those things which flow by in time's quick revolution, having nothing but "will be" and "has been." For what in them is future, when it arrives, straightway becomes the past; it is awaited with eagerness, it is lost with pain. But in the nature of God nothing will be, as if it were not yet; or hath been, as if it were no longer: but there is only that which is, and this is eternity. Let them cease then to hope in and love things temporal, and let them apply themselves to hope eternal, who know His name who said, "I am That I am;" and of whom it was said, "I AM hath sent me."[8] "For Thou hast not forsaken them that seek Thee, O Lord." Whoso seek Him, seek no more things transient

---

[1] John xii. 31.　　[2] Rom. vi. 12.　　[3] Ps. ii. 1, 2.
[4] Matt. xxv. 33.

[5] Rom. ii. 15.　　[6] Heb. xii. 6.　　[7] Jer. xxxiii. 2.
[8] Ex. iii. 14.

and perishable; "For no man can serve two masters."[1]

12. "Sing to the Lord, who dwelleth in Sion" (ver. 11), is said to them, whom the Lord forsakes not as they seek Him. He dwelleth in Sion, which is interpreted watching, and which beareth the likeness of the Church that now is; as Jerusalem beareth the likeness of the Church that is to come, that is, the city of Saints already enjoying life angelical; for Jerusalem is by interpretation the vision of peace.[2] Now watching goes before vision, as this Church goes before that one which is promised, the city immortal and eternal. But in time it goes before, not in dignity: because more honourable is that whither we are striving to arrive, than what we practise, that we may attain to arrive; now we practise watching, that we may arrive at vision. But again this same Church which now is, unless the Lord inhabit her, the most earnest watching might run into any sort of error. And to this Church it was said, "For the temple of God is holy, which temple ye are:"[3] again, "that Christ may dwell in the inner man in your hearts by faith."[4] It is enjoined us then, that we sing to the Lord who dwelleth in Sion, that with one accord we praise the Lord, the Inhabitant of the Church. "Show forth His wonders among the heathen." It has both been done, and will not cease to be done.

13. "For requiring their blood He hath remembered" (ver. 12). As if they, who were sent to preach the Gospel, should make answer to that injunction which has been mentioned, "Show forth His wonders among the heathen," and should say, "O Lord, who hath believed our report?"[5] and again, "For Thy sake we are killed all the day long;"[6] the Psalmist suitably goes on to say, That Christians not without great reward of eternity will die in persecution, "for requiring their blood He hath remembered." But why did he choose to say, "their blood"? Was it, as if one of imperfect knowledge and less faith should ask, How will they "show them forth," seeing that the infidelity of the heathen will rage against them; and he should be answered, "For requiring their blood He hath remembered," that is, the last judgment will come, in which both the glory of the slain and the punishment of the slayers shall be made manifest? But let no one suppose "He hath remembered" to be so used, as though forgetfulness can attach to God; but since the judgment will be after a long interval, it is used in accordance with the feeling of weak men, who think God hath forgotten, because He doth not act so speedily as they wish. To such is said

what follows also, "He hath not forgotten the cry of the poor:" that is, He hath not, as you suppose, forgotten. As if they should on hearing, "He hath remembered," say, Then He had forgotten; No, "He hath not forgotten," says the Psalmist, "the cry of the poor."

14. But I ask, what is that cry of the poor, which God forgetteth not? Is it that cry, the words whereof are these, "Pity me, O Lord, see my humiliation at the hands of my enemies"? (ver. 13). Why then did he not say, Pity "us" O Lord, see our humiliation at the hands of "our" enemies, as if many poor were crying; but as if one, Pity "me," O Lord? Is it because One intercedeth for the Saints, "who" first "for our sakes became poor, though He was rich;"[7] and it is He who saith, "Who exaltest me from the gates of death (ver. 14), that I may declare all Thy praises in the gates of the daughter of Sion"? For man is exalted in Him, not that Man only which He beareth, which is the Head of the Church; but whichsoever one of us also is among the other members, and is exalted from all depraved desires; which are the gates of death, for that through them is the road to death. But the joy in the fruition is at once death itself, when one gains what he hath in abandoned wilfulness coveted: for "coveting is the root of all evil:"[8] and therefore is the gate of death, for "the widow that liveth in pleasures is dead."[9] At which pleasures we arrive through desires as it were through the gates of death. But all highest purposes are the gates of the daughter of Sion, through which we come to the vision of peace in the Holy Church. . . . Or haply are the gates of death the bodily senses and eyes, which were opened when the man tasted of the forbidden tree,[10] . . . and are the gates of the daughter of Sion the sacraments and beginnings of faith, which are opened to them that knock, that they may arrive at the hidden things of the Son? . . .

15. Then follows, "I will exult for Thy salvation:" that is, with blessedness shall I be holden by Thy salvation, which is our Lord Jesus Christ, the Power and Wisdom of God. Therefore says the Church, which is here in affliction and is saved by hope, as long as the hidden judgment of the Son is, in hope she says, "I will exult for Thy salvation:" for now she is worn down either by the roar of violence around her, or by the errors of the heathen. "The heathen are fixed in the corruption, which they made" (ver. 15). Consider ye how punishment is reserved for the sinner, out of his own works; and how they that have wished to persecute the Church, have been fixed in that corruption, which they thought to inflict. For they were desiring to

---

[1] Matt. vi. 24.　　[2] See more fully on Ps. li. 18 (Lat. l. 20).
[3] 1 Cor. iii. 17　　[4] Eph. iii. 17.　　[5] Isa. liii. 1.
[6] Ps. xliv. 22.

[7] 2 Cor. viii. 9.　　[8] 1 Tim. vi. 10.　　[9] 1 Tim. v. 6.
[10] Gen. iii. 7.

kill the body, whilst they themselves were dying in soul. "In that snare which they hid, has their foot been taken." The hidden snare is crafty devising. The foot of the soul is well understood to be its love : which, when depraved, is called coveting or lust ; but when upright, love or charity. . . . And the Apostle says, "That being rooted and grounded in love, ye may be able to take in."[1] The foot then of sinners, that is, their love, is taken in the snare, which they hide : for when delight shall have followed on to deceitful dealing, when God shall have delivered them over to the lust of their heart ; that delight at once binds them, that they dare not tear away their love thence and apply it to profitable objects ; for when they shall make the attempt, they will be pained in heart, as if desiring to free their foot from a fetter : and giving way under this pain they refuse to withdraw from pernicious delights. "In the snare" then "which they have hid," that is, in deceitful counsel, "their foot hath been taken," that is, their love, which through deceit attains to that vain joy whereby pain is purchased.

16. "The Lord is known executing judgments" (ver. 16). These are God's judgments. Not from that tranquillity of His blessedness, nor from the secret places of wisdom, wherein blessed souls are received, is the sword, or fire, or wild beast, or any such thing brought forth, whereby sinners may be tormented : but how are they tormented, and how does the Lord do judgment? "In the works," he says, "of his own hands hath the sinner been caught."

17. Here is interposed, "The song of the diapsalma" (ver. 16) : as it were the hidden joy, as far as we can imagine, of the separation which is now made, not in place, but in the affections of the heart, between sinners and the righteous, as of the corn from the chaff, as yet on the floor. And then follows, "Let the sinners be turned into hell" (ver. 17) : that is, let them be given into their own hands, when they are spared, and let them be ensnared in deadly delight. "All the nations that forget God." Because "when they did not think good to retain God in their knowledge, God gave them over to a reprobate mind."[2]

18. "For there shall not be forgetfulness of the poor man to the end" (ver. 18) ; who now seems to be in forgetfulness, when sinners are thought to flourish in this world's happiness, and the righteous to be in travail : but "the patience," saith He, "of the poor shall not perish for ever." Wherefore there is need of patience now to bear with the evil, who are already separated in will, till they be also separated at the last judgment.

19. "Arise, O Lord, let not man prevail" (ver. 19). The future judgment is prayed for : but before it come, "Let the heathen," saith he, "be judged in Thy sight : " that is, in secret ; which is called in God's sight, with the knowledge of a few holy and righteous ones. "Place a lawgiver over them, O Lord." (ver. 20). He seems to me to point out Antichrist : of whom the Apostle says, "When the man of sin shall be revealed."[3] "Let the heathen know that they are men." That they who will be set free by the Son of God, and belong to the Son of Man, and be sons of men, that is, new men, may serve man, that is, the old man the sinner, "for that they are men."

20. And because it is believed that he is to arrive at so great a pitch of empty glory, and he will be permitted to do so great things, both against all men and against the Saints of God, that then some weak ones shall indeed think that God cares not for human affairs, the Psalmist interposing a diapsalma, adds as it were the voice of men groaning and asking why judgment is deferred.[4]

PSALM X.[5]

"Why, O Lord," saith he, "hast Thou withdrawn afar off ?" (ver. 1). Then he who thus inquired, as if all on a sudden he understood, or as if he asked, though he knew, that he might teach, adds, "Thou despisest in due seasons, in tribulations : " that is, Thou despisest seasonably, and causest tribulations to inflame men's minds with longing for Thy coming. For that fountain of life is sweeter to them that have much thirst. Therefore he hints the reason of the delay, saying, "Whilst the ungodly vaunteth himself, the poor man is inflamed" (ver. 2). Wondrous it is and true with what earnestness of good hope the little ones are inflamed unto an upright living by comparison with sinners. In which mystery it comes to pass, that even heresies are permitted to exist ; not that heretics themselves wish this, but because Divine Providence worketh this result from their sins, which both maketh and ordaineth the light ; but ordereth only the darkness, that by comparison therewith the light may be more pleasant, as by comparison with heretics the discovery of truth is more sweet. For so, by this comparison, the approved, who are known to God, are made manifest among men.

1. "They are taken in their thoughts, which they think : " that is, their evil thoughts become chains to them. But how become they chains?

---

[1] Eph. iii. 17, 18.   [2] Rom. i. 28.

[3] 2 Thess. ii. 3.
[4] [For light on this interpretation, see Neale, *Commentary*, p. 160. — C.]
[5] The two Psalms are combined in the Vulgate. But here the verses begin again, treating this as " Ps. x. *secundum Hebræos.*" [And so our English version. — C.]

"For the sinner is praised," saith he, "in the desires of his soul" (ver. 3). The tongues of flatterers bind souls in sin. For there is pleasure in doing those things, in which not only is no reprover feared, but even an approver heard. "And he that does unrighteous deeds is blessed." Hence "are they taken in their thoughts, which they think."

2. "The sinner hath angered the Lord" (ver. 4). Let no one congratulate the man that prospers in his way, to whose sins no avenger is nigh, and an approver is by. This is the greater anger of the Lord. For the sinner hath angered the Lord, that he should suffer these things, that is, should not suffer the scourging of correction. "The sinner hath angered the Lord : according to the multitude of His anger He will not search it out." Great is His anger, when He searcheth not out, when He as it were forgetteth and marketh not sin, and by fraud and wickedness man attains to riches and honours : which will especially be the case in that Antichrist, who will seem to man blessed to that degree, that he will even be thought God.[1] But how great this anger of God is, we are taught by what follows.

3. "God is not in his sight, his ways are polluted in all time" (ver. 5). He that knows what in the soul gives joy and gladness, knows how great an ill it is to be abandoned by the light of truth : since a great ill do men reckon the blindness of their bodily eyes, whereby this light is withdrawn. How great then the punishment he endures, who through the prosperous issue of his sins is brought to that pass, that God is not in his sight, and that his ways are polluted in all time, that is, his thoughts and counsels are unclean ! "Thy judgments are taken away from his face." For the mind conscious of evil, whilst it seems to itself to suffer no punishment, believes that God doth not judge, and so are God's judgments taken away from its face ; while this very thing is great condemnation. "And he shall have dominion over all his enemies." For so is it delivered, that he will overcome all kings, and alone obtain the kingdom ; since too according to the Apostle, who preaches concerning him, "He shall sit in the temple of God, exalting himself above all that is worshipped and that is called God."[2]

4. And seeing that being delivered over to the lust of his own heart, and predestinated to extreme[3] condemnation, he is to come, by wicked arts, to that vain and empty height and rule ; therefore it follows, "For he hath said in his heart, I shall not move from generation to generation without evil" (ver. 6) : that is, my fame and my name will not pass from this generation to the generation of posterity, unless by evil arts I acquire so lofty a principality, that posterity cannot be silent concerning it. For a mind abandoned and void of good arts, and estranged from the light of righteousness, by bad arts devises a passage for itself to a fame so lasting, as is celebrated even in posterity. And they that cannot be known for good, desire that men should speak of them even for ill, provided that their name spread far and wide. And this I think is here meant, "I shall not move from generation to generation without evil." There is too another interpretation, if a mind vain and full of error supposes that it cannot come from the mortal generation to the generation of eternity, but by bad arts : which indeed was also reported of Simon, when he thought that he would gain heaven by wicked arts, and pass from the human generation to the generation divine by magic.[4] Where then is the wonder, if that man of sin too, who is to fill up all the wickedness and ungodliness, which all false prophets have begun, and to do such "great signs ; that, if it were possible, he should deceive the very elect,"[5] shall say in his heart, "I shall not move from generation to generation without evil"?

5. "Whose mouth is full of cursing and bitterness and deceit" (ver. 7). For it is a great curse to seek heaven by such abominable arts, and to get together such earnings for acquiring the eternal seat. But of this cursing his mouth is full. For this desire shall not take effect, but within his mouth only will avail to destroy him, who dared promise himself such things with bitterness and deceit, that is, with anger and insidiousness, whereby he is to bring over the multitude to his side. "Under his tongue is toil and grief." Nothing is more toilsome than unrighteousness and ungodliness : upon which toil follows grief ; for that the toil is not only without fruit, but even unto destruction. Which toil and grief refer to that which he hath said in his heart, "I shall not be moved from generation to generation without evil." And therefore, "under his tongue," not on his tongue, because he will devise these things in silence, and to men will speak other things, that he may appear good and just, and a son of God.

6. "He lieth in ambush with the rich" (ver. 8). What rich, but those whom he will load with this world's gifts? And he is therefore said to lie in ambush with them, because he will display their false happiness to deceive men ; who, when with a perverted will they desire to be such as they, and seek not the good things eternal, will fall into his snares. "That in the dark he may kill the innocent." "In the dark,"[6] I suppose, is said, where it is not easily understood what should be sought, or what avoided.

---

[1] [Compare Hippolytus, A. N. F. vol. v. pp. 205–219. — C.]
[2] 2 Thess. ii. 4.   [3] *Ultima.*
[4] Acts viii. 9.   [5] Matt. xxiv. 24.   [6] *In occultis.*

Now to kill the innocent, is of an innocent to make one guilty.

7. "His eyes look against the poor," for he is chiefly to persecute the righteous, of whom it is said, "Blessed are the poor in spirit, for theirs is the kingdom of heaven"[1] (ver. 9). "He lieth in wait in a secret place, as a lion in his den." By a lion in a den, he means one in whom both violence and deceit will work. For the first persecution of the Church was violent, when by proscriptions, by torments, by murders, the Christians were compelled to sacrifice : another persecution is crafty, which is now conducted by heretics of any kind and false brethren : there remains a third, which is to come by Antichrist, than which there is nothing more perilous ; for it will be at once violent and crafty. Violence he will exert in empire, craft in miracles. To the violence, the word "lion" refers ; to craft, the words "in his den." And these are again repeated with a change of order. "He lieth in wait," he says, "that he may catch the poor ;" this, hath reference to craft : but what follows, "To catch the poor whilst he draweth him," is put to the score of violence. For "draweth" means, he bringeth him to himself by violence, by whatever tortures he can.

8. Again, the two which follow are the same. "In his snare he will humble him," is craft (ver. 10). "He shall decline and fall, whilst he shall have domination over the poor," is violence. For a "snare" naturally points to "lying in wait :" but domination most openly conveys the idea of terror. And well does he say, "He will humble him in his snare." For when he shall begin to do those signs, the more wonderful they shall appear to men, the more those Saints that shall be then will be despised, and, as it were, set at nought : he, whom they shall resist by righteousness and innocence, shall seem to overcome by the marvels that he does. But "he shall decline and fall, whilst he shall have domination over the poor ;" that is, whilst he shall inflict whatsoever punishments he will upon the servants of God that resist him.

9. But how shall he decline, and fall? "For he hath said in his heart, God hath forgotten ; He turneth away His face, that He see not unto the end" (ver. 11). This is declining, and the most wretched fall, while the mind of a man prospers as it were in its iniquities, and thinks that it is spared ; when it is being blinded, and kept for an extreme and timely vengeance : of which the Psalmist now speaks : "Arise, O Lord God, let Thine hand be exalted" (ver. 12) : that is, let Thy power be made manifest. Now he had said above, "Arise, O Lord, let not man prevail, let the heathen be judged in Thy sight :"[2]

that is, in secret, where God alone seeth. This comes to pass when the ungodly have arrived at what seems great happiness to men : over whom is placed a lawgiver, such as they had deserved to have, of whom it is said, "Place a lawgiver over them, O Lord, let the heathen know that they are men."[3] But now after that hidden punishment and vengeance it is said, "Arise, O Lord God, let Thine hand be exalted ;" not of course in secret, but now in glory most manifest. "That Thou forget not the poor unto the end ;" that is, as the ungodly think, who say, "God hath forgotten, He turneth away His face, that He should not see unto the end." Now they deny that God seeth unto the end, who say that He careth not for things human and earthly, for the earth is as it were the end of things ; in that it is the last element, in which men labour in most orderly sort, but they cannot see the order of their labours, which specially belongs to the hidden things of the Son. The Church then labouring in such times, like a ship in great waves and tempests, awaketh the Lord as if He were sleeping, that He should command the winds, and calm should be restored.[4] He says therefore, "Arise, O Lord God, let Thine hand be exalted, that Thou forget not the poor unto the end."

10. Accordingly understanding now the manifest judgment, and in exultation at it, they say, "Wherefore hath the ungodly angered God ?" (ver. 13) ; that is, what hath it profited him to do so great evil? "For he said in his heart, He will not require it." Then follows, "For Thou seest toil and considerest anger, to deliver them into Thine hands" (ver. 14). This sentence looks for distinct explanation, wherein if there shall be error it becomes obscure. For thus has the ungodly said in his heart, God will not require it, as though God regarded toil and anger, to deliver them into His hands ; that is, as though He feared toil and anger, and for this reason would spare them, lest their punishment be too burdensome to Him, or lest He should be disturbed by the storm of anger : as men generally act, excusing themselves of vengeance, to avoid toil or anger.

11. "The poor hath been left unto Thee." For therefore is he poor, that is, hath despised all the temporal goods of this world, that Thou only mayest be his hope. "Thou wilt be a helper to the orphan," that is, to him to whom his father this world, by whom he was born after the flesh, dies, and who can already say, "The world hath been crucified unto me, and I unto the world."[5] For of such orphans God becomes the Father. The Lord teaches us in truth that His disciples do become orphans, to whom He saith, "Call

---

[1] Matt. v. 3.   [2] Ps. ix. 19.   [3] Ps. ix. 20.   [4] Matt. viii. 24–26.   [5] Gal. vi. 14.

no man father on earth." [1] Of which He first Himself gave an example in saying, " Who is my mother, and who my brethren ? " [2] Whence some most mischievous heretics [3] would assert that He had no mother ; and they do not see that it follows from this, if they pay attention to these words, that neither had His disciples fathers. For as He said, " Who is my mother ? " so He taught them, when He said, " Call no man your father on earth."

12. " Break the arm of the sinner and of the malicious " (ver. 15) ; of him, namely, of whom it was said above, " He shall have dominion over all his enemies." He called his power then, his arm ; to which Christ's power is opposed, of which it is said, " Arise, O Lord God, let Thine hand be exalted. His fault shall be required, and he shall not be found because of it ; " [4] that is he shall be judged for his sins, and himself shall perish because of his sin. After this, what wonder if there follow, " The Lord shall reign for ever and world without end ; ye heathen shall perish out of His earth " ? (ver. 16). He uses heathen for sinners and ungodly.

13. " The Lord hath heard the longing of the poor "(ver. 17) : that longing wherewith they were burning, when in the straits and tribulations of this world they desired the day of the Lord. " Thine ear hath heard the preparation of their heart." This is the preparation of the heart, of which it is sung in another Psalm, " My heart is prepared, O God, my heart is prepared : " [5] of which the Apostle says, " But if we hope for what we see not, we do with patience wait for it." [6] Now, by the ear of God, we ought, according to a general rule of interpretation, to understand not a bodily member, but the power whereby He heareth ; and so (not to repeat this often) by whatever members of His are mentioned, which in us are visible and bodily, must be understood powers of operation. For we must not suppose it anything bodily, in that [7] the Lord God hears not the sound of the voice, but the preparation of the heart.

14. " To judge for the orphan and the humble" (ver. 18) : that is, not for him who is conformed to this world, nor for the proud. For it is one thing to judge the orphan, another to judge for the orphan. He judges the orphan even, who condemns him ; but he judges for the orphan, who delivers sentence for him. " That man add not further to magnify himself upon earth." For they are men, of whom it was said, " Place a lawgiver over them, O Lord : let the heathen know that they are men." [8] But he

too, who in this same passage is understood to be placed over them, will be man, of whom it is now said, " That man add not further to magnify himself upon earth : " namely, when the Son of Man shall come to judge for the orphan, who hath put off from himself the old man, and thus, as it were, buried his father.

15. After the hidden things then of the Son, of which, in this Psalm, many things have been said, will come the manifest things of the Son, of which a little has been now said at the end of the same Psalm. But the title is given from the former, which here occupy the larger portion. Indeed, the very day of the Lord's advent may be rightly numbered among the hidden things of the Son, although the very presence of the Lord itself will be manifest. For of that day it is said, that no man knoweth it, neither angels, nor powers, nor the Son of man. [9] What then so hidden, as that which is said to be hidden even to the Judge Himself, not as regards knowledge, but disclosure ? But concerning the hidden things of the Son, even if any one would not wish to understand the Son of God, but of David himself, to whose name the whole Psalter is attributed, for the Psalms we know are called the Psalms of David, let him give ear to those words in which it is said to the Lord, " Have mercy on us, O Son of David : " [10] and so even in this manner let him understand the same Lord Christ, concerning whose hidden things is the inscription of this Psalm. For so likewise is it said by the Angel : " God shall give unto Him the throne of His father David." [11] Nor to this understanding of it is the sentence opposed in which the same Lord asks of the Jews, " If Christ be the Son of David, how then doth he in spirit call Him Lord, saying, The Lord said unto my Lord, Sit Thou on my right hand, until I put Thine enemies under Thy feet." [12] For it was said to the unskilled, who although they looked for Christ's coming, yet expected Him as man, not as the Power and Wisdom of God. He teacheth then, in that place, the most true and pure faith, that He is both the Lord of king David, in that He is the Word in the beginning, God with God, [13] by which all things were made ; and Son, in that He was made to him of the seed of David according to the flesh. For He doth not say, Christ is not David's Son, but if ye already hold that He is his Son, learn how He is his Lord : and do not hold in respect of Christ that He is the Son of Man, for so is He David's Son ; [14] and leave out that He is the Son of God, for so is He David's Lord. [15]

---

[1] Matt. xxiii. 9.   [2] Matt. xii. 48.
[3] [Manichees. See A. N. F. vol. vi. p. 252.—C.]
[4] LXX. var. lect. δι' αὐτήν, " because of it." These words should be marked as part of the text, as some MSS. are pointed.
[5] Ps. lvii. 7.
[6] Rom. viii. 25.   [7] Al. wherewith.   [8] Ps. ix. 20.

[9] Mark xiii. 32.   [10] Matt. xx. 30.
[11] Luke i. 32.   [12] Matt. xxii. 43, 44.
[13] John i. 1.   [14] Rom. i. 3.
[15] [On the " hidden things " compare Isa. xlv. 15 with 1 Pet. i. 10-12.—C.]

PSALM XI.[1]

TO THE END, A PSALM OF DAVID HIMSELF.[2]

1. This title does not require a fresh consideration: for the meaning of, "to the end," has already been sufficiently handled.[3] Let us then look to the text itself of the Psalm, which to me appears to be sung against the heretics,[4] who, by rehearsing and exaggerating the sins of many in the Church, as if either all or the majority among themselves were righteous, strive to turn and snatch us away from the breasts of the one True Mother Church: affirming that Christ is with them, and warning us as if with piety and earnestness, that by passing over to them we may go over to Christ, whom they falsely declare they have. Now it is known that in prophecy Christ, among the many names in which notice of Him is conveyed in allegory, is also called a mountain.[5] We must accordingly answer these people, and say, "I trust in the Lord: how say ye to my soul, Remove into the mountains as a sparrow?" (ver. 1). I keep to one mountain wherein I trust, how say ye that I should pass over to you, as if there were many Christs? Or if through pride you say that you are mountains, I had indeed need to be a sparrow winged with the powers and commandments of God: but these very things hinder my flying to these mountains, and placing my trust in proud men. I have a house where I may rest, in that I trust in the Lord. For even "the sparrow hath found her a house,"[6] and, "The Lord hath become a refuge to the poor."[7] Let us say then with all confidence, lest while we seek Christ among heretics we lose Him, "In the Lord I trust: how say ye to my soul, Remove into the mountains as a sparrow?"

2. "For, lo, sinners have bent the bow, they have prepared their arrows in the quiver, that they may in the obscure moon shoot at the upright in heart" (ver. 2). These be the terrors of those who threaten us as touching sinners, that we may pass over to them as the righteous. "Lo," they say, "the sinners have bent the bow:" the Scriptures, I suppose, by carnal interpretation of which they emit envenomed sentences from them. "They have prepared their arrows in the quiver:" the same words, that is, which they will shoot out on the authority of Scripture, they have prepared in the secret place of the heart. "That they may in the obscure moon[8] shoot at the upright in heart:" that when they see, from the Church's light being obscured by the

multitude of the unlearned and the carnal, that they cannot be convicted, they may corrupt good manners by evil communications.[9] But against all these terrors we must say, "In the Lord I trust."

3. Now I remember that I promised to consider in this Psalm with what suitableness the moon signifies the Church.[10] There are two probable opinions concerning the moon: but of these which is the true, I suppose it either impossible or very difficult for a man to decide. For when we ask whence the moon has her light, some say that it is her own, but that of her globe half is bright, and half dark: and when she revolves in her own orbit, that part wherein she is bright gradually turns towards the earth, so as that it may be seen by us; and that therefore at first her appearance is as if she were horned. . . . According to this opinion the moon in allegory signifies the Church, because in its spiritual part the Church is bright, but in its carnal part is dark: and sometimes the spiritual part is seen by good works, but sometimes it lies hid in the conscience, and is known to God alone, since. in the body alone is it seen by men. . . . But according to the other opinion also the moon is understood to be the Church, because she has no light of her own, but is lighted by the only-begotten Son of God, who in many places of holy Scripture is allegorically called the Sun.[11] Whom certain heretics[12] being ignorant of, and not able to discern Him, endeavour to turn away the minds of the simple to this corporeal and visible sun, which is the common light of the flesh of men and flies, and some they do pervert, who as long as they cannot behold with the mind the inner light of truth, will not be content with the simple Catholic faith; which is the only safety to babes, and by which milk alone they can arrive in assured strength at the firm support of more solid food. Whichever then of these two opinions be the true, the moon in allegory is fitly understood as the Church. Or if in such difficulties as these, troublesome rather than edifying, there be either no satisfaction or no leisure to exercise the mind, or if the mind itself be not capable of it, it is sufficient to regard the moon with ordinary[13] eyes, and not to seek out obscure causes, but with all men to perceive her increasings and fulnesses and wanings; and if she wanes to the end that she may be renewed, even to this rude multitude she sets forth the image of the Church, in which the resurrection of the dead is believed.

4. Next we must enquire, what in this Psalm is meant by "the obscure moon," in which sinners have prepared to shoot at the upright in

---

[1] Lat. X.
[2] [It has been most aptly supposed that this Psalm is based on Lot's escape to the mountain. Gen. xix. 20. The imagery of the Psalm strikingly corresponds with his story. — C.]
[3] See on Ps. iv.   [4] Donatists.   [5] See on Ps. iii. 3.
[6] Ps. lxxxiv. 3.   [7] Ps ix. 9.
[8] [This appears to be from the African Psalter, following the Sept. — C.]

[9] 1 Cor. xv. 33.
[10] [See on Ps. viii. p. 30, *supra.* — C.]
[11] Mal. iv. 2, etc.   [12] Manichees.   [13] *Popularibus.*

heart? For not in one way only may the moon be said to be obscure : for when her monthly course is finished, and when her brightness is interrupted by a cloud, and when she is eclipsed at the full, the moon may be called obscure. It may then be understood first of the persecutors of the Martyrs, for that they wished in the obscure moon to shoot at the upright in heart; whether it be yet in the time of the Church's youth, because she had not yet shone forth in greatness on the earth, and conquered the darkness of heathen superstitions ; or by the tongues of blasphemers and such as defame the Christian name, when the earth was as it were beclouded, the moon, that is, the Church, could not be clearly seen ; or when by the slaughter of the Martyrs themselves and so great effusion of blood, as by that eclipse and obscuration, wherein the moon seems to exhibit a bloody face, the weak were deterred from the Christian name ; in which terror sinners shot out words crafty and sacrilegious to pervert even the upright in heart. And secondly, it can be understood of these sinners, whom the Church contains, because at that time, taking the opportunity of this moon's obscurity, they committed many crimes, which are now tauntingly objected to us by the heretics, whereas their founders are said to have been guilty of them.[1] But howsoever that be which was done in the obscure moon, now that the Catholic name is spread and celebrated throughout the whole world, what concern of mine is it to be disturbed by things unknown? For " in the Lord I trust ; " nor do I listen to them that say to my soul, " Remove into the mountains as a sparrow. For, lo, sinners have bent the bow, that they may in the obscure moon shoot at the upright in heart." Or if the moon seem even [2] now obscure to them, because they would make it uncertain which is the Catholic Church, and they strive to convict her by the sins of those many carnal men whom she contains ; what concern is this to him, who says in truth, " In the Lord I trust "? By which word every one shows that he is himself wheat, and endures the chaff with patience unto the time of winnowing.

5. " In the Lord," therefore, " I trust." Let them fear who trust in man, and cannot deny that they are of man's party, by whose grey hairs they swear ; and when in conversation it is demanded of them, of what communion they are, unless they say that they are of his party, they cannot be recognised. . . . Or perhaps you will say that it is written, " Ye shall know them by their works "?[3] I see indeed marvellous works the daily violences

of the Circumcelliones,[4] with the bishops and presbyters for their leaders, flying about in every direction, and calling their terrible clubs " Israels ; " which men now living daily see and feel. But for the times of Macarius,[5] respecting which they raise an invidious cry,[6] most men have not seen them, and no one sees them now : and any Catholic who saw them could say, if he wished to be a servant of God, " In the Lord I trust.". . .

6. Let the Catholic soul then say, " In the Lord I trust ; how say ye to my soul, Remove into the mountains as a sparrow? For, lo, the sinners have bent the bow, they have prepared their arrows in the quiver, that they may in the obscure moon shoot at the upright in heart : " and from them let her turn her speech to the Lord, and say, " For they have destroyed what Thou hast perfected "[7] (ver. 3). And this let her say not against these only, but against all heretics. For they have all, as far as in them lies, destroyed the praise which God hath perfected out of the mouth of babes and sucklings,[8] when they disturb the little ones with vain and scrupulous questions, and suffer them not to be nourished with the milk of faith. As if then it were said to this soul, why do they say to you, " Remove into the mountains as a sparrow ; " why do they frighten you with sinners, who " have bent the bow, to shoot in the obscure moon at the upright in heart "? She answers, Therefore it is they frighten me, " because they have destroyed what Thou hast perfected." Where but in their conventicles, where they nourish not with milk, but kill with poison the babes and ignorant of the interior light. " But what hath the Just done? "[9] If Macarius, if Cæcilianus, offend you, what hath Christ done to you, who said, " My peace I give unto you, My peace I leave with you ; "[10] which ye with your abominable dissensions have violated? What hath Christ done to you? who with such exceeding patience endured His betrayer, as to give to him, as to the other Apostles, the first Eucharist consecrated [11] with His own hands, and blessed with His own mouth.[12] What hath Christ done to you? who sent this same betrayer, whom He called a devil,[13] who before betraying the Lord could not show good faith even to the Lord's purse,[14] with the other disciples to preach the kingdom of heaven ; [15] that He might show that the gifts of God come to those that with

---

[1] He alludes to the charge of having surrendered the Holy Scriptures, alleged by the Donatists as the ground of their separation. See Ep. 76, § 2, and 105, § 2. " We would prove to you," he says, " that those were rather the betrayers who condemned Cæcilianus (Bishop of Carthage) and his companions on a false charge of betrayal ; " referring to the municipal records. — *Ben.*

[2] So Oxford MSS.   [3] Matt. vii. 16.

[4] [*i.e.*, " *Circum cellas* rusticorum *ientes.*" Concerning these miscreants, see enough in Smith's popular *Student's Ecclesiastical History*, vol. i. p. 250. — C.]

[5] Of the mission of Macarius and Paulus into Africa by Constans, about A.D. 348, and the complaint of persecution, see *S. Optatus*, lib. 3, and St. Augustin. Ep. 44, etc. — *Ben.*

[6] *De quibus invidiam faciunt.*

[7] [Here Jerome reads: *Quia leges dissipatæ sunt: justus quid operatus est ?* — C.]

[8] Ps. viii. 2.

[9] [" Delivered *just Lot.*" 2 Pet. ii. 7; Acts xxii. 14. — C.]

[10] John xiv. 27.   [11] *Confectam.*   [12] Luke xxii. 19, 21.

[13] John vi. 70.   [14] John xii. 6.   [15] Matt. x. 5-7.

faith receive them, though he, through whom they receive them, be such as Judas was.

7. "The Lord is in His holy temple" (ver. 4), yea in such wise as the Apostle saith, "For the temple of God is holy, which" temple "ye are."[1] "Now if any man shall violate the temple of God, him shall God destroy." He violateth the temple of God, who violateth unity : for he "holdeth not the head, from which the whole body fitly joined together and compacted by that which every joint supplieth[2] according to the working after the measure of every part maketh increase of the body to the edifying of itself in love."[3] The Lord is in this His holy temple ; which consisteth of His many members, fulfilling each his own separate duties, by love built up into one building. Which temple he violateth, who for the sake of his own pre-eminence separateth himself from the Catholic society. "The Lord is in His holy temple ; the Lord, His seat is in heaven." If you take heaven to be the just man, as you take the earth to be the sinner, to whom it was said, "Earth thou art, and unto earth shalt thou go;"[4] the words, "The Lord is in His holy temple" you will understand to be repeated, whilst it is said, "The Lord, His seat is in heaven."

8. "His eyes look upon the poor."[5] His to Whom the poor man hath been left, and Who hath been made a refuge to the poor.[6] And therefore all the seditions and tumults within these nets,[7] until they be drawn to shore, concerning which heretics upbraid us to their own ruin and our correction, are caused by those men, who will not be Christ's poor. But do they turn away God's eyes from such as would be so? "For His eyes look upon the poor." Is it to be feared lest, in the crowd of the rich, He may not be able to see the few poor, whom He brings up in safe keeping in the bosom of the Catholic Church? "His eyelids question the sons of men." Here by that rule I would wish to take "the sons of men"[8] of those that from old men have been regenerated by faith. For these, by certain obscure passages of Scripture, as it were the closed eyes of God, are exercised that they may seek : and again, by certain clear passages, as it were the open eyes of God, are enlightened that they may rejoice. And this frequent closing and opening in the holy Books are as it were the eyelids of God ; which question, that is, which try the "sons of men ;" who are neither wearied with

the obscurity of the matter, but exercised ; nor puffed up by knowledge, but confirmed.

9. "The Lord questioneth the righteous and ungodly" (ver. 5). Why then do we fear lest the ungodly should be any hurt to us, if so be they do with insincere heart share the sacraments with us, seeing that He "questioneth the righteous and the ungodly." "But whoso loveth iniquity, hateth his own soul :" that is, not him who believeth God, and putteth not his hope in man, but only his own soul doth the lover of iniquity hurt.

10. "He shall rain snares upon the sinners" (ver. 6). If by clouds are understood prophets generally, whether good or bad, who are also called false prophets : false prophets are so ordered by the Lord God, that by them He may rain snares upon sinners.[9] For no one, but the sinner, falls into a following of them, whether by way of preparation for the last punishment, if he shall choose to persevere in sin ; or to dissuade from pride, if in time he shall come to seek God with a more sincere intent. But if by clouds are understood good and true prophets only ; by these too it is clear that God raineth snares upon sinners, although by them He watereth also the godly unto fruitfulness. "To some," saith the Apostle, "we are the savour of life unto life ; to some the savour of death unto death."[10] For not prophets only, but all who with the word of God water souls, may be called clouds. Who when they are understood amiss, God raineth snares upon sinners ; but when they are understood aright, He maketh the hearts of the godly and believing fruitful. As, for instance, the passage, "and they two shall be in one flesh,"[11] if one interpret it with an eye to lust, He raineth a snare upon the sinner. But if you understand it, as he who says, "But I speak concerning Christ and the Church,"[12] He raineth a shower on the fertile soil. Now both are effected by the same cloud, that is, holy Scripture. Again the Lord says, "Not that which goeth into your mouth defileth you, but that which cometh out."[13] The sinner hears this, and makes ready his palate for gluttony : the righteous hears it, and is guarded against the superstitious distinction in meats. Here then also out of the same cloud of Scripture, according to the several desert of each, upon the sinner the rain of snares, upon the righteous the rain of fruitfulness, is poured.

11. "Fire and brimstone and the blast of the tempest is the portion of their cup." This is their punishment and end, by whom the name of God is blasphemed ; that first they should be wasted by the fire of their own lusts, then by the ill savour of their evil deeds cast off from the company of the blessed, at last carried away

---

[1] 1 Cor iii. 17.
[2] διὰ πάσης ἁφῆς τῆς ἐπιχορηγίας. *Per omnem tactum subministrationis.*
[3] Col. ii. 19; Eph. iv. 16.   [4] Gen. iii. 19.
[5] [Here, too, is a striking correspondence with Gen. xviii. 21: "I will go down and *see.*"—C.]
[6] Ps. x. 14, ix. 9   [7] Matt. xiii. 47.
[8] Cf. S. Aug. Ps. viii. 4, § 10, on the words, "What is *man,* that Thou art mindful of him; or the *son of man,* that Thou visitest him?" and Ps ix. 20, § 19, on the words, "Let the heathen know that they are *men.*"

[9] Matt. xxiv. 24.   [10] 2 Cor. ii. 16.   [11] Eph. v. 31.
[12] Eph. v 32.   [13] Matt. xv. 11.

and overwhelmed suffer penalties unspeakable. For this is the portion of their cup : as of the righteous, "Thy cup inebriating how excellent is it ! for they shall be inebriated with the richness of Thine house."[1] Now I suppose a cup is mentioned for this reason, that we should not suppose that anything is done by God's providence, even in the very punishments of sinners, beyond moderation and measure. And therefore as if he were giving a reason why this should be, he added, "For the Lord is righteous, and hath loved righteousnesses" (ver. 7). The plural not without meaning, but only because he speaks of men, is as that righteousnesses be understood to be used for righteous men. For in many righteous men there seem, so to say, to be righteousnesses, whereas there is one only righteousness of God whereof they all participate. Like as when one face looks upon many mirrors, what in it is one only, is by those many mirrors reflected manifoldly. Wherefore he recurs to the singular, saying, "His face hath seen equity." Perhaps, "His face hath seen equity," is as if it were said, Equity hath been seen in His face, that is, in knowledge of Him. For God's face is the power by which He is made known to them that are worthy. Or at least, "His face hath seen equity," because He doth not allow Himself to be known by the evil, but by the good ; and this is equity.

12. But if any one would understand the moon of the synagogue, let him refer the Psalm to the Lord's passion, and of the Jews say, "For they have destroyed what Thou hast perfected ;"[2] and of the Lord Himself, "But what hath the Just done?" whom they accused as the destroyer of the Law : whose precepts, by their corrupt living, and by despising them, and by setting up their own, they had destroyed, so that the Lord Himself may speak as Man, as He is wont, saying, "In the Lord I trust ; how say ye to my soul, Remove into the mountains as a sparrow?"[3] by reason, that is, of the fear of those who desire to apprehend and crucify Him. Since the interpretation is not unreasonable of sinners wishing to "shoot at the upright in heart,"[4] that is, those who believed in Christ, "in the obscure moon," that is, the Synagogue filled with sinners. To this too the words, "The Lord is in His holy temple ; the Lord, His seat is in heaven,"[5] are suitable ; that is, the Word in Man, or the very Son of Man who is in heaven.[6] "His eyes look upon the poor ;" either on Him whom He assumed as God, or for whom He suffered as Man. "His eyelids question the sons of men." The closing and opening of the eyes, which is probably meant by the word eyelids, we may take to be His death and resurrec-

tion, whereby He tried the sons of men His disciples, terrified at His passion, and gladdened by the resurrection. "The Lord questioneth the righteous and ungodly,"[7] even now from out of Heaven governing the Church. "But whoso loveth iniquity, hateth his own soul." Why it is so, what follows teaches us. For "He shall rain snares upon the sinners : "[8] which is to be taken according to the exposition above given, and so on with all the rest to the end of the Psalm.

PSALM XII.[9]

TO THE END, FOR THE EIGHTH, A PSALM OF DAVID.

1. It has been said on the sixth Psalm,[10] that "the eighth" may be taken as the day of judgment. "For the eighth" may also be taken "for the eternal age ; " for that after the time present, which is a cycle of seven days, it shall be given to the Saints.

2. "Save me, O Lord, for the holy hath failed ; " that is, is not found : as we speak when we say, Corn fails, or, Money fails. "For the truths have been minished from among the sons of men" (ver. 1). The truth is one, whereby holy souls are enlightened : but forasmuch as there are many souls, there may be said in them to be many truths : as in mirrors there are seen many reflections from one face.

3. "He hath talked vanity each man to his neighbour" (ver. 2). By neighbour we must understand every man : for that there is no one with whom we should work evil ; "and the love of our neighbour worketh no evil."[11] "Deceitful lips, with a heart and a heart they have spoken evil things."[12] The repetition, "with a heart and a heart," signifies a double heart.

4. "May the Lord destroy all deceitful lips" (ver. 3). He says "all," that no one may suppose himself excepted : as the Apostle says, "Upon every soul of man that doeth evil, of the Jew first, and of the Greek."[13] "The tongue speaking great things : " the proud tongue.

5. "Who have said, We will magnify our tongue, our lips are our own, who is Lord over us?" (ver. 4). Proud hypocrites are meant, putting confidence in their speech to deceive men, and not submitting themselves to God.

6. "Because of the wretchedness of the needy and the sighing of the poor, now I will arise, saith the Lord"[14] (ver. 5). For so the Lord Himself in the Gospel pitied His people, because they had no ruler, when they could well obey. Whence too it is said in the Gospel, "The har-

---

[1] Ps. xxxvi. 8.   [2] Ps. xi. 3.   [3] Ps. xi. 1.
[4] Ps. xi. 2.   [5] Ps. xi. 4.   [6] John iii. 13.

[7] Ps. xi. 5.   [8] Ps. xi. 6.   [9] Lat. XI.
[10] [A. N. F., vol. i. p. 63, note 2. The world created in seven days; and the Fathers take the eighth to mean the new creation, or "regeneration." Matt. xix. 28, with which compare Acts iii. 21.— C.]
[11] Rom. xiii. 10.   [12] LXX. Al. κακά.   [13] Rom. ii. 9.
[14] [Here the Anglican Psalter is inimitable for rhythm and pathos and for its archaic charm: "Now for the comfortless troubles' sake of the needy, and because of the deep sighing of the poor, I will up, saith the Lord."— C.]

vest is plenteous, but the labourers are few." [1] But this must be taken as spoken in the person of God the Father, who, because of the needy and the poor, that is, who in need and poverty were lacking spiritual good things, vouchsafed to send His own Son. From thence begins His sermon on the mount to Matthew, where He says, " Blessed are the poor in spirit : for theirs is the kingdom of heaven." [2] " I will place in salvation." He does not say what He would place : but, " in salvation," must be understood as, in Christ ; according to that, " For mine eyes have seen Thy salvation." [3] And hence He is understood to have placed in Him what appertains to the taking away the wretchedness of the needy, and the comforting the sighing of the poor. " I will deal confidently in Him : " according to that in the Gospel, " For He taught them as one having authority, and not as their scribes." [4]

7. " The words of the Lord " are " pure words " (ver. 6). This is in the person of the Prophet himself, " The words of the Lord " are " pure words." He says " pure," without the alloy of pretence. For many preach the truth impurely ; [5] for they sell it for the bribe of the advantages of this life. Of such the Apostle says, that they declared Christ not purely. " Silver tried by the fire for the earth." [6] These words of the Lord by means of tribulations approved to sinners. " Purified seven times : " by the fear of God, by godliness, by knowledge, by might, by counsel, by understanding, by wisdom. [7] For seven steps also of beatitude there are, which the Lord goes over, according to Matthew, in the same sermon which He spake on the Mount, " Blessed " are " the poor in spirit, blessed the meek, blessed they that mourn, blessed they which do hunger and thirst after righteousness, blessed the merciful, blessed the pure in heart, blessed the peace-makers." [8] Of which seven sentences, it may be observed how all that long sermon was spoken. For the eighth where it is said, " Blessed " are " they which suffer persecution for righteousness' sake," [9] denotes the fire itself, whereby the silver is proved seven times. And at the termination of this sermon it is said, " For He taught them as one having authority, and not as their scribes." [4] Which refers to that which is said in this Psalm, " I deal confidently in Him."

8. " Thou, O Lord, shalt preserve us, and keep us from this generation to eternity " (ver. 7) : here as needy and poor, there as wealthy and rich.

9. " The ungodly walk in a circle round about " (ver. 8) : that is, in the desire of things temporal, which revolves as a wheel in a repeated circle of seven days ; and therefore they do not arrive at the eighth, that is, at eternity, for which this Psalm is entitled. [10] So too it is said by Solomon, " For the wise king is the winnower of the ungodly, and he bringeth on them the wheel of the wicked. — After Thine height Thou hast multiplied the sons of men." [11] For there is in temporal things too a multiplication, which turns away from the unity of God. Hence " the corruptible body weigheth down the soul, and the earthy tabernacle presseth down the mind that museth upon many things." [12] But the righteous are multiplied " after the height of God," when " they shall go from strength to strength." [13]

PSALM XIII. [14]

UNTO THE END, A PSALM OF DAVID.

1. " For Christ is the end of the law to every one that believeth." [15] " How long, O Lord, wilt Thou forget me unto the end ? " (ver. 1) that is, put me off as to spiritually understanding Christ, who is the Wisdom of God, and the true end of all the aim of the soul. " How long dost Thou turn away Thy face from me ? " As God doth not forget, so neither doth He turn His face away : but Scripture speaks after our manner. Now God is said to turn away His face, when He doth not give to the soul, which as yet hath not the pure eye of the mind, the knowledge of Himself.

2. " How long shall I place counsel in my soul ? " (ver. 2). There is no need of counsel but in adversity. Therefore " How long shall I place counsel in my soul ? " is as if it were said, How long shall I be in adversity? Or at least it is an answer, so that the meaning is this, So long, O Lord, wilt Thou forget me to the end, and so long turn away Thy face from me, until I shall place counsel in mine own soul : so that except a man place counsel in his own soul to work mercy perfectly, God will not direct him to the end, nor give him that full knowledge of Himself, which is " face to face." " Sorrow in my heart through the day ? " How long shall I have, is understood. And " through the day " signifies continuance, so that day is taken for time : from which as each one longs to be free, he has sorrow in his heart, making entreaty to rise to things eternal, and not endure man's day.

3. " How long shall mine enemy be exalted over me ? " either the devil, or carnal habit.

---

[1] Matt. ix. 37.   [2] Matt. v. 3.   [3] Luke ii. 30.
[4] Matt. vii. 29.   [5] Phil. i. 16.
[6] [Or, " from the earth." So St. Jerome. The earthen crucible may be the figure. — C.]
[7] Isa. xi. 2.   [8] Matt. v. 3-9.   [9] Matt. v 10.

[10] [So the Septuagint and Vulgate, " in a cycle." Contrasted by the Fathers with the straightforward march of the (Prov. iv. 18) just. This Psalm was used by the Hebrews on the eighth day, for circumcision. — C.]
[11] Prov. xx. 26. See LXX.   [12] Wisd. ix. 15.
[13] Ps. lxxxiv. 7.
[14] Lat. XII. [Regarded by the critics as a link between Ps. xii. and xiv. — C.]
[15] Rom. x. 4.

4. "Look on me, and hear me, O Lord my God" (ver. 3). "Look on me," refers to what was said, "How long" dost "Thou turn away Thy face from me." "Hear," refers to what was said, "How long wilt Thou forget me to the end? Lighten mine eyes, that I sleep not in death." The eyes of the heart must be understood, that they be not closed by the pleasurable eclipse of sin.

5. "Lest at any time mine enemy say, I have prevailed against him" (ver. 4). The devil's mockery is to be feared. "They that trouble me will exult, if I be moved;" the devil and his angels; who exulted not over that righteous man, Job, when they troubled him; because he was not moved, that is, did not draw back from the stedfastness of his faith.[1]

6. "But I have hoped in Thy mercy" (ver. 5). Because this very thing, that a man be not moved, and that he abide fixed in the Lord, he should not attribute to self: lest when he glories that he hath not been moved, he be moved by this very pride. "My heart shall exult in Thy salvation;" in Christ, in the Wisdom of God. "I will sing[2] to the Lord who hath given me good things;" spiritual good things, not belonging to man's day. "And I will chant[3] to the name of the Lord most high" (ver. 6); that is, I give thanks with joy, and in most due order employ my body, which is the song of the spiritual soul. But if any distinction is to be marked here, "I will sing" with the heart, "I will chant" with my works; "to the Lord," that which He alone seeth, but "to the name of the Lord," that which is known among men, which is serviceable not for Him, but for us.

PSALM XIV.[4]

TO THE END, A PSALM OF DAVID HIMSELF.

1. What "to the end" means, must not be too often repeated. "For Christ is the end of the law for righteousness to every one that believeth;"[5] as the Apostle saith. We believe on Him, when we begin to enter on the good road: we shall see Him, when we shall get to the end. And therefore is He the end.

2. "The fool hath said in his heart, There is no God" (ver. 1). For not even have certain sacrilegious and abominable philosophers, who entertain perverse and false notions of God, dared to say, "There is no God." Therefore it is, hath said "in his heart;" for that no one dares to say it, even if he has dared to think it. "They are corrupt, and become abominable in their affections:" that is, whilst they love this world and love not God; these are the affections which corrupt the soul, and so blind it, that the fool can even say, "in his heart, There is no God. For as they did not like to retain God in their knowledge, God gave them over to a reprobate mind."[6] "There is none that doeth goodness, no not up to one." "Up to one," can be understood either with that one, so that no man be understood: or besides one, that the Lord Christ may be excepted. As we say, This field is up to the sea; we do not of course reckon the sea together with the field. And this is the better interpretation, so that none be understood to have done goodness up to Christ; for that no man can do goodness, except He shall have shown it. And that is true; for until a man know the one God, he cannot do goodness.

3. "The Lord from heaven looked out upon the sons of men, to see if there be one understanding, or seeking after God" (ver. 2). It may be interpreted, upon the Jews; as he may have given them the more honourable name of the sons of men, by reason of their worship of the One God, in comparison with the Gentiles; of whom I suppose it was said above, "The fool hath said in his heart, There is no God," etc. Now the Lord looks out, that He may see, by His holy souls: which is the meaning of, "from heaven." For by Himself nothing is hid from Him.

4. "All have gone out of the way, they have together become useless:" that is, the Jews have become as the Gentiles, who were spoken of above. "There is none that doeth good, no not up to one" (ver. 3), must be interpreted as above. "Their throat is an open sepulchre."[7] Either the voracity of the ever open palate is signified: or allegorically those who slay, and as it were devour those they have slain, into whom they instil the disorder of their own conversation. Like to which with the contrary meaning is that which was said to Peter, "Kill and eat;"[8] that he should convert the Gentiles to his own faith and good conversation. "With their tongues they have dealt craftily." Flattery is the companion of the greedy and of all bad men. "The poison of asps is under their lips." By "poison," he means deceit; and "of asps," because they will not hear the precepts of the law, as asps "will not hear the voice of the charmer;"[9] which is said more clearly in another Psalm. "Whose mouth is full of cursing and bitterness:" this is, "the poison of asps." "Their feet are swift to shed blood." He here shows forth the habit of ill doing. "Destruction and unhappiness" are

---

[1] Job ii. 3.   [2] Cantabo.   [3] Psallam.
[4] Lat. XIII.   [5] Rom. x. 4.
[6] Rom. i. 28.
[7] [Here the author quotes the African Psalter, no doubt, from which the three verses have passed into the Vulgate. They are in the Septuagint, from which St. Paul quotes them (Rom. iii. 13–18); but St. Jerome omits them, as not in the Hebrew of his day. They are, nevertheless, to be found in other parts of the original, and the passage may be compiled from Ps. v. 10, cxl. 3, x. 7, xxxvi. 1; from Prov. i. 16 and Isa. lix. 7 come the clauses, "their feet," etc. — C.]
[8] Acts x. 13.   [9] Ps. lviii. 5.

"in their ways." For all the ways of evil men are full of toil and misery. Hence the Lord cries out, "Come unto Me, all ye that labour and are heavy laden, and I will refresh you. Take My yoke upon you, and learn of Me, for I am meek and lowly in heart. For My yoke is easy and My burden light."[1] "And the way of peace have they not known:" that way, namely, which the Lord, as I said, mentions, in the easy yoke and light burden. "There is no fear of God before their eyes." These do not say, "There is no God;" but yet they do not fear God.

5. "Shall not all, who work iniquity, know?" (ver. 4). He threatens the judgment. "Who devour My people as the food of bread:" that is, daily. For the food of bread is daily food. Now they devour the people, who serve their own ends out of them, not referring their ministry to the glory of God, and the salvation of those over whom they are.

6. "They have not called upon the Lord." For he doth not really call upon Him, who longs for such things as are displeasing to Him. "There they trembled for fear, where no fear was" (ver. 5): that is, for the loss of things temporal. For they said, "If we let Him thus alone, all men will believe on Him; and the Romans will come, and take away both our place and nation."[2] They feared to lose an earthly kingdom, where no fear was; and they lost the kingdom of heaven, which they ought to have feared. And this must be understood of all temporal goods, the loss of which when men fear, they come not to things eternal.

7. "For God is in the just generation." It refers to what went before, so that the sense is, "shall not all they that work iniquity know that the Lord is in the just generation;"[3] that is, He is not in them who love the world. For it is unjust to leave the Maker of the worlds, and "serve the creature more than the Creator."[4] Ye have shamed the counsel of the poor, for the Lord is his hope" (ver. 6): that is, ye have despised the humble coming of the Son of God, because ye saw not in Him the pomp of the world: that they, whom he was calling, should put their hope in God alone, not in the things that pass away.

8. "Who will give salvation to Israel out of Sion?" (ver. 7). Who but He whose humiliation ye have despised? is understood. For He will come in glory to the judgment of the quick and the dead, and the kingdom of the just: that, forasmuch as in that humble coming "blindness hath happened in part unto Israel, that the fulness of the Gentiles might enter in,"[5] in that

other should happen what follows, "and so all Israel should be saved." For the Apostle too takes that testimony of Isaiah, where it is said, "There shall come out of Sion He who shall turn away ungodliness from Jacob:"[6] for the Jews, as it is here, "Who shall give salvation to Israel out of Sion?" "When the Lord shall turn away the captivity of His people, Jacob shall rejoice, and Israel shall be glad."[7] It is a repetition, as is usual: for I suppose, "Israel shall be glad," is the same as, "Jacob shall rejoice."

PSALM XV.[8]

A PSALM OF DAVID HIMSELF.

1. Touching this title there is no question. "O Lord, who shall sojourn in Thy tabernacle?" (ver. 1). Although tabernacle be sometimes used even for an everlasting habitation: yet when tabernacle is taken in its proper meaning, it is a thing of war. Hence soldiers are called tent-fellows,[9] as having their tents together. This sense is assisted by the words, "Who shall sojourn?" For we war with the devil for a time, and then we need a tabernacle wherein we may refresh ourselves. Which specially points out the faith of the temporal Dispensation, which was wrought for us in time through the Incarnation of the Lord. "And who shall rest in Thy holy mountain?" Here perhaps he signifies at once the eternal habitation itself,[10] that we should understand by "mountain" the supereminence of the love of Christ in life eternal.[11]

2. "He who walketh without stain, and worketh righteousness" (ver. 2). Here he has laid down the proposition; in what follows he sets it forth in detail.

3. "Who speaketh the truth in his heart." For some have truth on their lips, and not in their heart. As if one should deceitfully point out a road, knowing that there were robbers there, and should say, If you go this way, you will be safe from robbers; and it should turn out that in fact there were no robbers found there: he has spoken the truth, but not in his heart. For he supposed it to be otherwise, and spoke the truth in ignorance. Therefore it is not enough to speak the truth, unless it be so also in heart. "Who hath practised no deceit in his tongue" (ver. 3). Deceit is practised with the tongue, when one thing is professed with the mouth, another concealed in the breast. "Nor done evil to his neighbour." It is well known that by "neighbour," every man should be un-

---

[1] Matt. xi. 28-30.   [2] John xi. 48.
[3] Thus far the sentence is quoted from the Oxford MSS.
[4] Rom. i. 25.   [5] Rom. xi. 25.

[6] Isa. lix. 20.
[7] [A prophetic *prolepsis* of the Captivity; but stretching forward to the final restoration, in our author's view. — C.]
[8] Lat. XIV.   [9] *Contubernales.*   [10] 2 Cor. v. 1, 2.
[11] [This Psalm is called by some of the Fathers "the Ladder of Jacob," by which the righteous ascend to God. It is the octave of Ps. viii., which is appropriate to the ascension of humanity in Christ. — C.]

derstood. "And hath not entertained slander against his neighbour," that is, hath not readily or rashly given credence to an accuser.

4. "The malicious one hath been brought to nought in his sight"[1] (ver. 4). This is perfection, that the malicious one have no force against a man; and that this be "in his sight;" that is, that he know most surely that the malicious is not, save when the mind turns itself away from the eternal and immutable form[2] of her own Creator to the form of the creature, which was made out of nothing. "But those that fear the Lord, He glorifieth:" the Lord Himself, that is. Now "the fear of the Lord is the beginning of wisdom."[3] As then the things above belong to the perfect, so what he is now going to say belongs to beginners.

5. "Who sweareth unto his neighbour, and deceiveth him not." "Who hath not given his money upon usury, and hath not taken rewards against the innocent" (ver. 5). These are no great things: but he who is not able to do even this, much less able is he to speak the truth in his heart, and to practise no deceit in his tongue, but as the truth is in the heart, so to profess and have it in his mouth, "yea, yea; nay, nay;"[4] and to do no evil to his neighbour, that is, to any man; and to entertain no slander against his neighbour: all which are the virtues of the perfect, in whose sight the malicious one hath been brought to nought. Yet he concludes even these lesser things thus, "Whoso doeth these things shall not be moved for ever:" that is, he shall attain unto those greater things, wherein is great and unshaken stability. For even the very tenses are, perhaps not without cause, so varied, as that in the conclusion above the past tense should be used, but in this the future. For there it was said, "The malicious one hath been brought to nought in his sight:" but here, "shall not be moved for ever."

PSALM XVI.[5]

THE INSCRIPTION OF THE TITLE, OF DAVID HIMSELF.[6]

1. Our King in this Psalm speaks in the character of the human[7] nature He assumed, of whom the royal title at the time of His passion was eminently set forth.

2. Now He saith as follows; "Preserve me, O Lord, for in Thee have I hoped" (ver. 1): "I have said to the Lord, Thou art my God, for Thou requirest not my goods" (ver. 2): for

with my goods Thou dost not look to be made blessed.

3. "To the saints who are on His earth" (ver. 3): to the saints who have placed their hope in the land of the living, the citizens of the heavenly Jerusalem, whose spiritual conversation is, by the anchor of hope, fixed in that country, which is rightly called God's earth; although as yet in this earth too they be conversant in the flesh. "He hath wonderfully fulfilled all My wishes in them." To those saints then He hath wonderfully fulfilled all My wishes in their advancement, whereby they have perceived, how both the humanity of My divinity hath profited them that I might die, and the divinity of the humanity that I might rise again.

4. "Their infirmities have been multiplied"[8] (ver. 4): their infirmities have been multiplied not for their destruction, but that they might long for the Physician. "Afterwards they made haste." Accordingly after infirmities multiplied they made haste, that they might be healed. "I will not gather together their assemblies by blood." For their assemblies shall not be carnal, nor will I gather them together as one propitiated by the blood of cattle.[9] "Nor will I be mindful of their names within My lips." But by a spiritual change what they have been shall be forgotten; nor by Me shall they be any more called either sinners, or enemies, or men; but righteous, and My brethren, and sons of God through My peace.

5. "The Lord is the portion of Mine inheritance, and of My cup" (ver. 5). For together with Me they shall possess the inheritance, the Lord Himself. Let others choose for themselves portions, earthly and temporal, to enjoy: the portion of the Saints is the Lord eternal. Let others drink of deadly pleasures, the portion of My cup is the Lord. In that I say, "Mine," I include the Church: for where the Head is, there is the body also. For into the inheritance will I gather together their assemblies, and by the inebriation of the cup I will forget their old names. "Thou art He who will restore to Me My inheritance:" that to these too, whom I free, may be known "the glory wherein I was with Thee before the world was made."[10] For Thou wilt not restore to Me that which I never lost, but Thou wilt restore to these, who have lost it, the knowledge of that glory: in whom because I am, Thou wilt restore to Me.

6. "The lines have fallen to me in glorious places" (ver. 6). The boundaries of my possession have fallen in Thy glory as it were by lot, like as God is the possession of the Priests and Levites.[11] "For Mine inheritance is glorious

---

[1] [*Malignus* in the Vulgate, which the Anglican Psalter does not follow here. — C.]
[2] *Specie.*   [3] Ps. cxi. 10; Ecclus. i. 14; Prov. i. 7.
[4] Matt. v. 37.   [5] Lat. XV.
[6] ["*Michtam* of David," which Bishop Wordsworth derives from *Catham*, and illustrates by Job xix. 23. — C.]
[7] *Susceptionis humanæ.*

[8] So Oxford MSS.   [9] Isa. i. 11, 12.   [10] John xvii. 5.
[11] Numb. xviii. 20.

to Me." "For Mine inheritance is glorious," not to all, but to them that see; in whom because I am, "it is to Me."

7. "I will bless the Lord, who hath given Me understanding" (ver. 7): whereby this inheritance may be seen and possessed. "Yea moreover too even unto night my reins have chastened Me." Yea besides understanding, even unto death, My inferior part, the assumption of flesh, hath instructed Me, that I might experience the darkness of mortality, which that understanding hath not.

8. "I foresaw the Lord in My sight always" (ver. 8). But coming into things that pass away, I removed not Mine eye from Him who abideth ever, foreseeing this, that to Him I should return after passing through the things temporal. "For He is on My right hand, that I should not be moved." For He favoureth Me, that I should abide fixedly in Him.

9. "Wherefore My heart was glad, and My tongue exulted" (ver. 9). Wherefore both in My thoughts is gladness, and in my words exultation. "Moreover too My flesh shall rest in hope." Moreover too My flesh shall not fail unto destruction, but shall sleep in hope of the resurrection.

10. "For Thou wilt not leave My soul in hell" (ver. 10). For Thou wilt neither give My soul for a possession to those parts below. "Neither wilt Thou grant Thine Holy One to see corruption." Neither wilt Thou suffer that sanctified body, whereby others are to be also sanctified, to see corruption. "Thou hast made known to Me the paths of life" (ver. 11). Thou hast made known through Me the paths of humiliation, that[1] men might return to life, from whence they fell through pride; in whom because I am, "Thou hast made known to Me." "Thou wilt fill Me with joy with Thy countenance." Thou wilt fill them with joy, that they should seek nothing further, when they shall see Thee "face to face;" in whom because I am, "Thou wilt fill Me." "Pleasure is at Thy right hand even to the end." Pleasure is in Thy favour and mercy in this life's journey, leading on even to the end of the glory of Thy countenance.[2]

PSALM XVII.[3]

A PRAYER OF DAVID HIMSELF.

1. This prayer must be assigned to the Person of the Lord, with the addition of the Church, which is His body.

2. "Hear My righteousness, O God, consider My supplication" (ver. 1). "Hearken unto My prayer, not in deceitful lips:" not going forth to Thee in deceitful lips. "Let My judgment from Thy countenance go forth" (ver. 2). From the enlightening of the knowledge of Thee, let Me judge truth. Or at least, let My judgment go forth, not in deceitful lips, from Thy countenance, that is, that I may not in judging utter aught else than I understand in Thee. "Let Mine eyes see equity:" the eyes, of course, of the heart.

3. "Thou hast proved and visited Mine heart in the night-season" (ver. 3). For this Mine heart hath been proved by the visitation of tribulation. "Thou hast examined Me by fire, and iniquity hath not been found in Me." Now not night only, in that it is wont to disturb, but fire also, in that it burns, is this tribulation to be called; whereby when I was examined I was found righteous.

4. "That My mouth may not speak the works of men" (ver. 4). That nothing may proceed out of My mouth, but what relates to Thy glory and praise; not to the works of men, which they do beside Thy will. "Because of the words of Thy lips."[4] Because of the words of Thy peace, or of Thy prophets. "I have kept hard ways." I have kept the toilsome ways of human mortality and suffering.

5. "To perfect My steps in Thy paths" (ver. 5). That the love of the Church might be perfected in the strait ways, whereby she arrives at Thy rest. "That My footsteps be not moved." That the signs of My way, which, like footsteps, have been imprinted on the Sacraments and Apostolical writings, be not moved, that they may mark them who would follow Me. Or at least, that I may still abide fixedly in eternity, after that I have accomplished the hard ways, and have finished My steps in the straits of Thy paths.

6. "I have cried out, for Thou hast heard Me, O God" (ver. 6). With a free and strong effort have I directed My prayers unto Thee: for that I might have this power, Thou hast heard Me when praying more weakly. "Incline Thine ear to Me, and hear My words." Let not Thy hearing forsake My humiliation.

7. "Make Thy mercies marvellous" (ver. 7). Let not Thy mercies be disesteemed, lest they be loved too little.

8. "Who savest them that hope in Thee from such as resist Thy right hand:" from such as resist the favour, whereby Thou favourest Me. "Keep Me, O Lord, as the apple of Thine eye" (ver. 8): which seems very little and minute: yet by it is the sight of the eye directed, whereby the light is distinguished from the darkness; as by Christ's humanity, the divinity of the Judgment[5] distinguishing between the righteous and

---

1 Oxford mss. "that by it."
2 [Compare Acts ii. 25 and xiii. 34.—C.]
3 Lat. XVI.

4 See on Ps. xlv. 2: "the word of grace, the kiss of grace."
5 Al. "the judgment of Godhead."

sinners. "In the covering of Thy wings protect Me." In the defence of Thy love and mercy protect Me. "From the face of the ungodly who have troubled Me" (ver. 9).

9. "Mine enemies have compassed about My soul;" "they have shut up their own fat" (ver. 10). They have been covered with their own gross joy, after that their desire hath been satiated with wickedness. "Their mouth hath spoken pride." And therefore their mouth spoke pride, in saying, "Hail, King of the Jews," [1] and other like words.

10. "Casting Me forth they have now compassed Me about" (ver. 11). Casting Me forth outside the city, they have now compassed Me about on the Cross. "Their eyes they have determined to turn down on the earth." The bent of their heart they have determined to turn down on these earthly things: deeming Him, who was slain, to endure a mighty evil, and themselves, that slew Him, none.

11. "As a lion ready for prey, have they taken Me" (ver. 12). They have taken Me, like that adversary who "walketh about, seeking whom he may devour." [2] "And as a lion's whelp dwelling in secret places." And as his whelp, the people to whom it was said, "Ye are of your father the devil:" [3] meditating on the snares, whereby they might circumvent and destroy the just One.

12. "Arise, O Lord, prevent them, and cast them down" (ver. 13). Arise, O Lord, Thou whom they suppose to be asleep, and regardless of men's iniquities; be they blinded before by their own malice, that vengeance may prevent their deed; and so cast them down.

13. "Deliver My soul from the ungodly." Deliver My soul, by restoring Me after the death, which the ungodly have inflicted on Me. "Thy weapon: from the enemies of Thine hand" (ver. 14). For My soul is Thy weapon, which Thy hand, that is, Thy eternal Power, hath taken to subdue thereby the kingdoms of iniquity, and divide the righteous from the ungodly. This weapon then "deliver from the enemies of Thine hand," that is, of Thy Power, that is, from Mine enemies. "Destroy them, O Lord, from off the earth, scatter them in their life." O Lord, destroy them from off the earth, which they inhabit, scatter them throughout the world in this life, which only they think their life, who [4] despair of life eternal. "And by Thy hidden things their belly hath been filled." Now not only this visible punishment shall overtake them, but also their memory hath been filled with sins, which as darkness are hidden from the light of Thy truth, that they should forget God. "They have been filled with swine's flesh." They have been

filled with uncleanness, treading under foot the pearls of God's words. "And they have left the rest to their babes:" crying out, "This sin be upon us and upon our children." [5]

14. "But I shall appear in Thy righteousness in Thy sight" (ver. 15). But I, Who have not appeared to them that, with their filthy and darkened heart, cannot see the light of wisdom, "shall appear in Thy righteousness in Thy sight." "I shall be satiated, when Thy glory shall be manifested." And when they have been satiated with their uncleanness, that they could not know Me, I shall be satiated, when Thy glory shall be manifested, in them that know Me. In that verse indeed where it is said, "filled with swine's flesh," some copies have, "filled with children:" for from the ambiguity of the Greek [6] a double interpretation has resulted. Now by "children" we understand works; and as by good children, good works, so by evil, evil.

PSALM XVIII. [7]

TO THE END, FOR THE SERVANT OF THE LORD, DAVID HIMSELF.

1. That is, for the strong of hand, Christ in His Manhood. [8] "The words of this song which he spoke to the Lord on the day when he delivered him out of the hands of his enemies, and of the hand of Saul; and he said, On the day when the Lord delivered him out of the hands of his enemies and of the hand of Saul:" namely, the king of the Jews, whom they had demanded for themselves. [9] For as "David" is said to be by interpretation, strong of hand; so "Saul" is said to be demanding. Now it is well known, how that People demanded for themselves a king, and received him for their king, not according to the will of God, but according to their own will.

2. Christ, then, and the Church, that is, whole Christ, the Head and the Body, saith here, "I will love Thee, O Lord, My strength" (ver. 1). I will love Thee, O Lord, by whom I am strong. [10]

3. "O Lord, My stay, and My refuge, and My deliverer" (ver. 2). O Lord, who hast stayed Me, because I sought refuge with Thee: and I sought refuge, because Thou hast delivered Me. "My God is My helper; and I will hope in Him." My God, who hast first afforded me the help of Thy call, that I might be able to hope in Thee. "My defender, and the horn of My salvation, and My redeemer." My defender, because I have not leant upon Myself, lifting up as it were the horn of pride against Thee; but have found Thee a horn indeed, that is, the sure

---

[1] Matt. xxvii. 29.   [2] 1 Pet. v. 8.   [3] John viii. 44.
[4] Al. "because they."

[5] Matt. xxvii. 25.
[6] υἱῶν, ὑῶν, ὑείων, various readings. — Ben.
[7] Lat. XVII.   [8] Secundum Hominem.
[9] 1 Sam. viii. 5.   [10] [2 Sam. xxii. — C.]

height of salvation : and that I might find it, Thou redeemedst Me.

4. "With praise will I call upon the Lord, and I shall be safe from Mine enemies" (ver. 3). Seeking not My own but the Lord's glory, I will call upon Him, and there shall be no means whereby the errors of ungodliness can hurt Me.

5. "The pains of death," that is, of the flesh, have "compassed Me about. And the over-flowings of ungodliness have troubled Me" (ver. 4). Ungodly troubles[1] stirred up for a time, like torrents of rain which will soon sub-side, have come on to trouble Me.

6. "The pains of hell compassed Me about" (ver. 5). Among those that compassed Me about to destroy Me, were pains of envy, which work death, and lead on to the hell of sin. "The snares of death prevented Me." They prevented Me, so that they wished to hurt Me first, which shall afterwards be recompensed unto them. Now they seize unto destruction such men as they have evilly persuaded by the boast of righteousness : in the name but not in the reality of which they glory against the Gentiles.

7. "And in Mine oppression I called upon the Lord, and cried unto My God. And He heard My voice from His holy temple" (ver. 6). He heard from My heart, wherein He dwelleth, My voice. "And My cry in His sight entered into His ears ; " and My cry, which I utter, not in the ears of men, but inwardly before Him Himself, "entered into His ears."

8. "And the earth was moved and trembled" (ver. 7). When the Son of Man was thus glori-fied, sinners were moved and trembled. "And the foundations of the mountains were troubled." And the hopes of the proud, which were in this life, were troubled. "And were moved, for God was wroth with them." That is, that the hope of temporal goods might have now no more establishment in the hearts of men.

9. "There went up smoke in His wrath" (ver. 8). The tearful supplication of penitents went up, when they came to know God's threat-enings against the ungodly. "And fire burneth from His face." And the ardour of love after repentance burns by the knowledge of Him. "Coals were kindled from Him." They, who were already dead, abandoned by the fire of good desire and the light of righteousness, and who remained in coldness and darkness, re-enkindled and enlightened, have come to life again.

10. "And He bowed the heaven, and came down" (ver. 9). And He humbled the just One, that He might descend to men's infirmity. "And darkness under His feet." And the un-

godly, who savour of things earthly, in the darkness of their own malice, knew not Him : for the earth under His feet is as it were His footstool.

11. "And He mounted above the cherubim, and did fly" (ver. 10). And He was exalted above the fulness of knowledge, that no man should come to Him but by love : for "love is the fulfilling of the law."[2] And full soon He showed to His lovers that He is incomprehen-sible, lest they should suppose that He is com-prehended by corporeal imaginations. "He flew above the wings of the winds." But that swiftness, whereby He showed Himself to be incomprehensible, is above the powers of souls, whereon as upon wings they raise themselves from earthly fears into the air of liberty.

12. "And hath made darkness His hiding place" (ver. 11). And hath settled the ob-scurity of the Sacraments, and the hidden hope in the heart of believers, where He may lie hid, and not abandon them. In this darkness too, wherein "we yet walk by faith, and not by sight,"[3] as long as "we hope for what we see not, and with patience wait for it."[4] Round about Him is His tabernacle." Yet they that believe Him turn to Him and encircle Him ; for that He is in the midst of them, since He is equally the friend of all, in whom as in a taber-nacle He at this time dwells. "Dark water in clouds of air." Nor let any one on this account, if he understand the Scripture, imagine that he is already in that light, which will be when we shall have come out of faith into sight : for in the prophets and in all the preachers of the word of God there is obscure teaching.

13. "In respect of the brightness in His sight" (ver. 12) : in comparison with the bright-ness, which is in the sight of His manifestation. "His clouds have passed over." The preach-ers of His word are not now bounded by the confines of Judæa, but have passed over to the Gentiles. "Hail and coals of fire." Reproofs are figured,[5] whereby, as by hail, the hard hearts are bruised : but if a cultivated and genial soil, that is, a godly mind, receive them, the hail's hardness dissolves into water, that is, the terror of the lightning-charged,[6] and as it were frozen, reproof dissolves into satisfying doctrine ; and hearts kindled by the fire of love revive. All these things in His clouds have passed over to the Gentiles.

14. "And the Lord hath thundered from heaven" (ver. 13). And in confidence of the Gospel the Lord hath sounded forth from the heart of the just One. "And the Highest gave His voice ; " that we might entertain it, and in

---

[1] Or, "crowds."

[2] Rom. xiii. 10.　　[3] 2 Cor. v. 7.　　[4] Rom. viii. 25.
[5] Read "full lightning-charged reproofs."
[6] *Fulguratæ.*

the depth of human things, might hear things heavenly.

15. "And He sent out His arrows, and scattered them" (ver. 14). And He sent out Evangelists traversing straight paths on the wings of strength, not in their own power, but His by whom they were sent. And "He scattered them," to whom they were sent, that to some of them they should be "the savour of life unto life, to others the savour of death unto death." [1] "And He multiplied lightnings, and troubled them." And He multiplied miracles, and troubled them.

16. "And the fountains of water were seen. And the fountains of water springing up into everlasting life," [2] which were made in the preachers, were seen. "And the foundations of the round world were revealed" (ver. 15). And the Prophets, who were not understood, and upon whom was to be built the world of believers in the Lord, were revealed. "At Thy chiding, O Lord:" crying out, "The kingdom of God is come nigh unto you." [3] "At the blasting of the breath of Thy displeasure;" saying, "Except ye repent, ye shall all likewise perish." [4]

17. "He hath sent down from on high, and hath fetched Me" (ver. 16): by calling out of the Gentiles for an inheritance "a glorious Church, not having spot, or wrinkle." [5] "He hath taken Me out of the multitude of waters." He hath taken Me out of the multitude of peoples.

18. "He hath delivered Me from My strongest enemies" (ver. 17). He hath delivered Me from Mine enemies, who prevailed to the afflicting and overturning of this temporal life of Mine. "And from them which hate Me; for they are too strong for Me:" as long as I am under them knowing not God.

19. "They have prevented Me in the day of My affliction" (ver. 18). They have first injured Me, in the time when I am bearing a mortal and toilsome body. "And the Lord hath become My stay." And since the stay of earthly pleasure was disturbed and torn up by the bitterness of misery, the Lord hath become My stay.

20. "And hath brought Me forth into a broad place" (ver. 19). And since I was enduring the straits of the flesh, He brought Me forth into the spiritual breadth of faith. "He hath delivered Me, because He desired Me." Before that I desired Him, He delivered Me from My most powerful enemies (who were envious of Me when I once desired Him), and from them that hated Me, because I do desire Him.

21. "And the Lord shall reward Me according to My righteousness" (ver. 20). And the Lord shall reward Me according to the righteousness of My good will, who first showed mercy, before that I had the good will. "And according to the cleanness of My hands He will recompense Me." And according to the cleanness of My deeds He will recompense Me, who hath given Me to do well by bringing Me forth into the broad place of faith.

22. "Because I have kept the ways of the Lord" (ver. 21). That the breadth of good works, that are by faith, and the long-suffering of perseverance should follow after.

23. "Nor have I walked impiously apart from My God." "For all His judgments are [6] in My sight" (ver. 22). "For" with persevering contemplation I weigh "all His judgments," that is, the rewards of the righteous, and the punishments of the ungodly, and the scourges of such as are to be chastened, and the trials of such as are to be proved. "And I have not cast out His righteousness from Me:" as they do that faint under their burden of them, and return to their own vomit.

24. "And I shall be undefiled with Him, and I shall keep Myself from Mine iniquity" (ver. 23).

25. "And the Lord shall reward Me according to My righteousness" (ver. 24). Accordingly not only for the breadth of faith, which worketh by love; but also for the length of perseverance, will the Lord reward Me according to My righteousness. "And according to the cleanness of My hands in the sight of His eyes." Not as men see, but "in the sight of His eyes." For "the things that are seen are temporal; but the things that are not seen are eternal:" [7] whereto the height of hope appertains.

26. "With the holy Thou shalt be holy" (ver. 25). There is a hidden depth also, wherein Thou art known to be holy with the holy, for that Thou makest holy. "And with the harmless Thou shalt be harmless." For Thou harmest no man, but each one is bound by the bands of his own sins. [8]

27. "And with the chosen Thou shalt be chosen" (ver. 26). And by him whom Thou choosest, Thou art chosen. "And with the froward Thou shalt be froward." And with the froward Thou seemest froward: for they say, "The way of the Lord is not right:" [9] and their way is not right.

28. "For Thou wilt make whole the humble people" (ver. 27). Now this seems froward to the froward, that Thou wilt make them whole that confess their sins. "And Thou wilt humble the eyes of the proud." But them that are "ignorant of God's righteousness, and seek to establish their own," [10] Thou wilt humble.

[1] 2 Cor. ii. 16.   [2] John iv. 14.   [3] Luke x. 9.
[4] Luke xiii. 5.   [5] Eph. v. 27.

[6] Oxford MSS. "are always."   [7] 2 Cor. iv. 18.
[8] Prov. v. 22.   [9] Ezek. xviii. 25.   [10] Rom. x. 3.

29. "For thou wilt light My candle, O Lord" (ver. 28). For our light is not from ourselves; but "Thou wilt light my candle, O Lord. O my God, Thou wilt enlighten my darkness." For we through our sins are darkness; but "Thou, O my God, wilt enlighten my darkness."

30. "For by Thee shall I be delivered from temptation" (ver. 29). For not by myself, but by Thee, shall I be delivered from temptation. "And in my God shall I leap over the wall." And not in myself, but in my God shall I leap over the wall, which sin has raised between men and the heavenly Jerusalem.

31. "My God, His way is undefiled" (ver. 30). My God cometh not unto men, except they shall have purified the way of faith, whereby He may come to them; for that "His way is undefiled." "The words of the Lord have been proved by fire." The words of the Lord are tried by the fire of tribulation. "He is the Protector of them that hope in Him." And all that hope not in themselves, but in Him, are not consumed by that same tribulation. For hope followeth faith.

32. "For who is God, but the Lord?" (ver. 31) whom we serve. "And who God, but our God?" And who is God, but the Lord? whom after good service we sons shall possess as the hoped-for inheritance.

33. "God, who hath girded me with strength" (ver. 32). God, who hath girded me that I might be strong, lest the loosely flowing folds of desire hinder my deeds and steps. "And hath made my way undefiled." And hath made the way of love, whereby I may come to Him, undefiled, as the way of faith is undefiled, whereby He comes to me.

34. "Who hath made my feet perfect like harts' feet" (ver. 33). Who hath made my love perfect to surmount the thorny and dark entanglements of this world. "And will set me up on high." And will fix my aim on the heavenly habitation, that "I may be filled with all the fulness of God." [1]

35. "Who teacheth my hands for battle" (ver. 34). Who teacheth me to work for the overthrow of mine enemies, who strive to shut the kingdom of heaven against us. "And Thou hast made mine arms as a bow of steel." And Thou hast made my earnest striving after good works unwearied.

36. "And Thou hast given me the defence of my salvation, and Thy right hand hath held me up" (ver. 35). And the favour of Thy grace hath held me up. "And Thy discipline hath directed me to the end." And Thy correction, not suffering me to wander from the way, hath directed me that whatsoever I do, I refer to that end, whereby I may cleave to Thee. "And this Thy discipline, it shall teach me." And that same correction of Thine shall teach me to attain to that, whereunto it hath directed me.

37. "Thou hast enlarged my steps under me" (ver. 36). Nor shall the straits of the flesh hinder me; for Thou hast enlarged my love, working in gladness even with these mortal things and members which are under me. "And my footsteps have not been weakened." And either my goings, or the marks which I have imprinted for the imitation of those that follow, have not been weakened.

38. "I will follow up mine enemies, and seize them" (ver. 37). I will follow up my carnal affections, and will not be seized by them, but will seize them, so that they may be consumed. "And I will not turn, till they fail." And from this purpose I will not turn myself to rest, till they fail who make a tumult about me.

39. "I will break them, and they shall not be able to stand" (ver. 38): and they shall not hold out against me. "They shall fall under my feet." When they are cast down, I will place before me the loves [2] whereby I walk for evermore.

40. "And Thou hast girded me with strength to the war" (ver. 39). And the loose desires of my flesh hast Thou bound up with strength, that in such a fight I may not be encumbered. "Thou hast supplanted under me them that rose up against me." Thou hast caused them to be deceived, who followed upon me, that they should be brought under me, who desired to be over me.

41. "And thou hast given mine enemies the back to me" (ver. 40). And thou hast turned mine enemies, and hast made them to be a back to me, that is, to follow me. "And Thou hast destroyed them that hate me." But such other of them as have persisted in hatred, Thou hast destroyed.

42. "They have cried out, and there was none to save them" (ver. 41). For who can save them, whom Thou wouldest not save? "To the Lord, and He did not hear them." Nor did they cry out to any chance one, but to the Lord: and He did not judge them worthy of being heard, who depart not from their wickedness.

43. "And I will beat them as small as dust before the face of the wind" (ver. 42). And I will beat them small; for dry they are, receiving not the shower of God's mercy; that borne aloft and puffed up with pride they may be hurried along from firm and unshaken hope, and as it were from the earth's solidity and stability. "As the clay of the streets I will destroy them." In their wanton and loose course along the broad ways of perdition, which many walk, will I destroy them.

---

[1] Ephes. iii. 19.

[2] See p. 37. "The foot of sinners; that is, their love."

44. "Thou wilt deliver Me from the contradictions of the people" (ver. 43). Thou wilt deliver Me from the contradictions of them who said, "If we send Him away, all the world will go after Him."[1]

45. "Thou shalt make Me the head of the Gentiles. A people whom I have not known have served Me." The people of the Gentiles, whom in bodily presence I have not visited, have served Me. "At the hearing of the ear they have obeyed Me" (ver. 44). They have not seen Me with the eye: but, receiving my preachers, at the hearing of the ear they have obeyed Me.

46. "The strange children have lied unto Me." Children, not to be called Mine, but rather strange children, to whom it is rightly said, "Ye are of your father the devil,"[2] have lied unto Me. "The strange children have waxen old" (ver. 45). The strange children, to whom for their renovation I brought the new Testament, have remained in the old man. "And they have halted from their own paths." And like those that are weak in one foot, for holding the old they have rejected the new Testament, they have become halt, even in their old Law, rather following their own traditions, than God's. For they brought frivolous charges of unwashen hands,[3] because such were the paths, which themselves had made and worn by long use, in wandering from the ways of God's commands.

47. "The Lord liveth, and blessed be my God." "But to be carnally minded is death:"[4] for "the Lord liveth, and blessed be my God. And let the God of my salvation be exalted" (ver. 46). And let me not think after an earthly fashion of the God of my salvation; nor look from Him for this earthly salvation, but that on high.

48. "O God, who givest Me vengeance, and subduest the people under Me" (ver. 47). O God, who avengest Me by subduing the people under Me. "My Deliverer from My angry enemies:" the Jews crying out, "Crucify Him, Crucify Him."[5]

49. "From them that rise up against Me Thou wilt exalt Me" (ver. 48). From the Jews that rise up against Me in My passion, Thou wilt exalt Me in My resurrection. "From the unjust man Thou wilt deliver Me." From their unjust rule Thou wilt deliver Me.

50. "For this cause will I confess to Thee among the Gentiles, O Lord" (ver. 49). For this cause shall the Gentiles confess to Thee through Me, O Lord. "And I will sing unto Thy Name." And Thou shalt be more widely known by My good deeds.

51. "Magnifying the salvation of His King" (ver. 50). God, who magnifieth, so as to make wonderful, the salvation, which His Son giveth to believers.[6] "And showing mercy to His Christ:" God, who showeth mercy to His Christ: "To David and to His seed for evermore:" to the Deliverer Himself strong of hand, who hath overcome this world; and to them whom, as believers in the Gospel, He hath begotten for evermore. What things soever are spoken in this Psalm which cannot apply to the Lord Himself personally, that is to the Head of the Church, must be referred to the Church. For whole Christ speaks here, in whom are all His members.

PSALM XIX.[7]

TO THE END, A PSALM OF DAVID HIMSELF.

1. It is a well-known title; nor does the Lord Jesus Christ say what follows, but it is said of Him.

2. "The heavens tell out the glory of God" (ver. 1). The righteous Evangelists, in whom, as in the heavens, God dwelleth, set forth the glory of our Lord Jesus Christ, or the glory wherewith the Son glorified the Father upon earth. "And the firmament showeth forth the works of His hands." And the firmament showeth forth the deeds of the Lord's power, that now made heaven by the assurance of the Holy Ghost, which before was earth by fear.

3. "Day unto day uttereth word" (ver. 2). To the spiritual the Spirit giveth out the fulness of the unchangeable Wisdom of God, the Word which in the beginning is God with God.[8] "And night unto night announceth knowledge." And to the fleshly, as to those afar off, the mortality of the flesh, by conveying faith, announceth future knowledge.

4. "There is no speech nor language, in which their voices are not heard" (ver. 3). In which the voices of the Evangelists have not been heard, seeing that the Gospel was preached in every tongue.

5. "Their sound is gone out into all the earth, and their words to the ends of the world"[9] (ver. 4).

6. "In the sun hath He set His tabernacle." Now that He might war against the powers of temporal error, the Lord, being about to send not peace but a sword on earth,[10] in time, or in manifestation, set so to say His military dwelling, that is, the dispensation of His incarnation. "And He as a bridegroom coming forth out of His chamber" (ver. 5). And He, coming forth

---

[1] John xi. 48, xii. 19.　　[2] John viii. 44.
[3] Matt. xv. 2.　　[4] Rom. viii. 6.
[5] John xix. 6.

[6] [The epigraph of this Psalm in 2 Sam. xxiii. 1-5 seems to connect with Isa. lv. 3, and so with Acts xiii. 34.— C.]
[7] Lat. XVIII.　　[8] John i. 1.
[9] [Rom. x. 18. "And therefore are *we even speaking here,*" says our author in his second homily (omitted) on this Psalm. — C.]
[10] Matt. x. 34.

out of the Virgin's womb, where God was united
to man's nature as a bridegroom to a bride.
" Rejoiced as a giant to run His way." Rejoiced
as One exceeding strong, and surpassing all other
men in power incomparable, not to inhabit, but
to run His way. For, " He stood not in the
way of sinners." [1]

7. "His going forth is from the highest heaven"
(ver. 6). From the Father is His going forth,
not that in time, but from everlasting, whereby
He was born of the Father. "And His meeting is even to the height of heaven." And in
the fulness of the Godhead He meets even to
an equality with the Father.[2] "And there is
none that may hide himself from His heat."
But whereas, "the Word was even made flesh,
and dwelt in us,"[3] assuming our mortality, He
permitted no man to excuse himself from the
shadow of death; for the heat of the Word
penetrated even it.

8. "The law of the Lord is undefiled, converting souls" (ver. 7). The law of the Lord,
therefore, is Himself who came to fulfil the law,
not to destroy it;[4] an undefiled law, "Who did
no sin, neither was guile found in His mouth,"[5]
not oppressing souls with the yoke of bondage,
but converting them to imitate Him in liberty.
"The testimony of the Lord is sure, giving wisdom to babes." "The testimony of the Lord
is sure;" for, "no man knoweth the Father save
the Son, and he to whomsoever the Son will reveal Him,"[6] which things have been hidden from
the wise and revealed to babes;[7] for, "God
resisteth the proud, but giveth grace to the
humble."[8]

9. "The statutes of the Lord are right, rejoicing the heart" (ver. 8). All the statutes of
the Lord are right in Him who taught not what
He did not; that they who should imitate Him
might rejoice in heart, in those things which they
should do freely with love, not slavishly with
fear. "The commandment of the Lord is lucid,
enlightening the eyes." "The commandment
of the Lord is lucid," with no veil of carnal ob-
servances, enlightening the sight of the inner
man.

10. "The fear of the Lord is chaste, enduring
for ever" (ver. 9). "The fear of the Lord;"
not that distressing[9] fear under the law, dread-
ing exceedingly the withdrawal of temporal
goods, by the love of which the soul commits
fornication; but that chaste fear wherewith the
Church, the more ardently she loves her Spouse,
the more carefully does she take heed of offend-
ing Him, and therefore, "perfect love casteth"
not "out" this "fear,"[10] but it endureth for ever.

11. "The judgments of the Lord are true,
justified together." The judgments of Him, who
"judgeth no man, but hath committed all judgment unto the Son,"[11] are justified in truth un-
changeably. For neither in His threatenings nor
His promises doth God deceive any man, nor
can any withdraw either from the ungodly His
punishment, or from the godly His reward. "To
be desired more than gold, and much precious
stone" (ver. 10). Whether it be "gold and
stone itself much," or "much precious," or
"much to be desired;" still, the judgments of
God are to be desired more than the pomp
of this world; by desire of which it is brought
to pass that the judgments of God are not desired, but feared, or despised, or not believed.
But if any be himself gold and precious stone,
that he may not be consumed by fire, but received
into the treasury of God, more than himself does
he desire the judgments of God, whose will he
preferreth to his own. "And sweeter than honey
and the honey comb." And whether one be
even now honey, who, disenthralled already from
the chains of this life, is awaiting the day when
he may come up to God's feast; or whether he
be yet as the honey comb, wrapped about with
this life as it were with wax, not mixed and become one with it, but filling it, needing some
pressure of God's hand, not oppressing but expressing it, whereby from life temporal it may be
strained out into life eternal: to such an one the
judgments of God are sweeter than he himself
is to himself, for that they are "sweeter than
honey and the honey comb."

12. "For Thy servant keepeth them"(ver.11).
For to him who keepeth them not the day of the
Lord is bitter. "In keeping them there is great
reward." Not in any external benefit, but in
the thing itself, that God's judgments are kept, is
there great reward; great because one rejoiceth
therein.

13. "Who understandeth sins?" (ver. 12).
But what sort of sweetness can there be in sins,
where there is no understanding? For who can
understand sins, which close the very eye, to
which truth is pleasant, to which the judgments
of God are desirable and sweet? yea, as darkness
closes the eye, so do sins the mind, and suffer it
not to see either the light, or itself.

14. "Cleanse me, O Lord, from my secret
faults." From the lusts which lie hid in me,
cleanse me, O Lord. "And from the" faults
"of others preserve Thy servant" (ver. 13).
Let me not be led astray by others. For he is
not a prey to the faults of others, who is cleansed
from his own. Preserve therefore from the lusts
of others, not the proud man, and him who
would be his own master, but, Thy servant. "If

---

[1] Ps. i. 1.
[2] Vid. in Psalm lviii (lix. E. V.). *Enarrat.* i. § 10.
[3] John i. 14.　　[4] Matt. v. 17.　　[5] 1 Pet. ii. 22
[6] Matt. xi. 27.　　[7] Luke x. 21.　　[8] Jas. iv. 6
[9] *Pœnalis.*　　[10] 1 John iv. 18.

[11] John v. 22.

they get not the dominion over me, then shall I be undefiled." If neither my own secret sins, nor those of others, get the dominion over me, then shall I be undefiled. For there is no third source of sin, but one's own secret sin, by which the devil fell, and another's sin, by which man is seduced, so as by consenting to make it his own. " And I shall be cleansed from the great offence." What but pride? for there is none greater than apostasy from God, which is " the beginning of the pride of man."¹ And he shall indeed be undefiled, who is free from this offence also; for this is the last to them who are returning to God, which was the first as they departed from Him.

15. "And the words of my mouth shall be pleasing, and the meditation of my heart is always in Thy sight" (ver. 14). The meditation of my heart is not after the vain glory of pleasing men, for now there is pride no more, but in Thy sight alway, who regardest a pure conscience. "O Lord, my Helper, and my Redeemer"² (ver. 15). O Lord, my Helper, in my approach to Thee; for Thou art my Redeemer, that I might set out unto Thee: lest any attributing to his own wisdom his conversion to Thee, or to his own strength his attaining to Thee, should be rather driven back by Thee, who resistest the proud; for he is not cleansed from the great offence, nor pleasing in Thy sight, who redeemest us that we may be converted, and helpest us that we may attain unto Thee.

PSALM XX.³

TO THE END, A PSALM OF DAVID.

1. This is a well-known title; and it is not Christ who speaks; but the prophet speaks to Christ, under the form of wishing, foretelling things to come.⁴

2. "The Lord hear Thee in the day of trouble" (ver. 1). The Lord hear Thee in the day in which Thou saidst, " Father glorify Thy Son."⁵ " The name of the God of Jacob protect Thee." For to Thee belongeth the younger people. Since " the elder shall serve the younger."⁶

3. " Send Thee help from the Holy, and from Sion defend Thee" (ver. 2). Making for Thee a sanctified Body, the Church, from watching⁷ safe, which waiteth when Thou shalt come from the wedding.

4. " Be mindful of all Thy sacrifice " (ver. 3). Make us mindful of all Thy injuries and despiteful treatment, which Thou hast borne for us. " And be Thy whole burnt offering made fat."

And turn the cross, whereon Thou wast wholly offered up to God, into the joy of the resurrection.

5. " *Diapsalma*. The Lord render to Thee according to Thine Heart " (ver. 4). The Lord render to Thee, not according to their heart, who thought by persecution they could destroy Thee; but according to Thine Heart, wherein Thou knewest what profit Thy passion would have.⁸ " And fulfil all Thy counsel." " And fulfil all Thy counsel," not only that whereby Thou didst lay down Thy life for Thy friends,⁹ that the corrupted grain might rise again to more abundance;¹⁰ but that also whereby " blindness in part hath happened unto Israel, that the fulness of the Gentiles might enter in, and so all Israel might be saved."¹¹

6. " We will exult in Thy salvation " (ver. 5). We will exult in that death will in no wise hurt Thee; for so Thou wilt also show that it cannot hurt us either. " And in the name of the Lord our God will we be magnified." And the confession of Thy name shall not only not destroy us, but shall even magnify us.

7. " The Lord fulfil all Thy petitions." The Lord fulfil not only the petitions which Thou madest on earth, but those also whereby Thou intercedest for us in heaven. " Now have I known that the Lord hath saved his Christ" (ver. 6). Now hath it been shown to me in prophecy, that the Lord will raise up His Christ again. " He will hear Him from His holy heaven." He will hear Him not from earth only, where He prayed to be glorified;¹² but from heaven also, where interceding for us at the Right Hand of the Father,¹³ He hath from thence shed abroad the Holy Spirit on them that believe on Him. " In strength is the safety of His right hand." Our strength is in the safety of His favour, when even out of tribulation He giveth help, that " when we are weak, then we may be strong."¹⁴ " For vain is " that " safety of man,"¹⁵ which comes not of His right hand but of His left: for thereby are they lifted up to great pride, whosoever in their sins have secured a temporal safety.

8. " Some in chariots, and some in horses " (ver. 7). Some are drawn away by the ever moving succession of temporal goods; and some are preferred to proud honours, and in them exult: " But we will exult in the name of the Lord our God." But we, fixing our hope on things eternal, and not seeking our own glory, will exult in the name of the Lord our God.

9. " They have been bound, and fallen " (ver. 8). And therefore were they bound by the lust of temporal things, fearing to spare the

¹ Ecclus. x. 12.
² [Here the word is rendered " Redeemer" in the Septuagint, and is the same in the Hebrew as in Job xix. 25.—C.]
³ Lat. XIX.
⁴ [This and the next Psalm are a prelude to the great Psalm of the expiation which is to follow.—C.]
⁵ John xvii. 5 and xii. 28.   ⁶ Gen. xxv. 23; Rom. ix. 12.
⁷ " *Sion*," "beholding," p. 13, ver. 6.

⁸ John xii. 32.   ⁹ John xv. 13.   ¹⁰ John xii. 24.
¹¹ Rom. xi. 25, 26.   ¹² John xvii. 1.   ¹³ Heb. vii. 25.
¹⁴ 2 Cor. xii. 10.   ¹⁵ Ps. lx. 11.

Lord, lest they should lose their place by "the Romans:"[1] and rushing violently on the stone of offence and rock of stumbling, they fell from the heavenly hope: to whom the blindness in part of Israel hath happened, being ignorant of God's righteousness, and wishing to establish their own.[2] "But we are risen, and stand upright." But we, that the Gentile people might enter in, out of the stones raised up as children to Abraham,[3] who followed not after righteousness, have attained to it, and are risen;[4] and not by our own strength, but being justified by faith, we stand upright.

10. "O Lord, save the King:" that He, who in His Passion hath shown us an example of conflict, should also offer up our sacrifices, the Priest raised from the dead, and established in heaven. "And hear us in the day when we shall call on Thee" (ver. 9). And as He now offereth for us, "hear us in the day when we shall call on Thee."

PSALM XXI.[5]

TO THE END, A PSALM OF DAVID HIMSELF.

1. The title is a familiar one; the Psalm is of Christ.[6]

2. "O Lord, the King shall rejoice in Thy strength" (ver. 1). O Lord, in Thy strength, whereby the Word was made flesh, the Man Christ Jesus shall rejoice. "And shall exult exceedingly in Thy salvation." And in that, whereby Thou quickenest all things, shall exult exceedingly.

3. "Thou hast given Him the desire of His soul" (ver. 2). He desired to eat the Passover,[7] and to lay down His life when He would, and again when He would to take it; and Thou hast given it to Him.[8] "And hast not deprived Him of the good pleasure of His lips." "My peace," saith He, "I leave with you:"[9] and it was done.

4. "For Thou hast presented Him with the blessings of sweetness" (ver. 3). Because He had first quaffed the blessing of Thy sweetness, the gall of our sins did not hurt Him. "*Diapsalma*. Thou hast set a crown of precious stone on His Head."[10] At the beginning of His discoursing precious stones were brought, and compassed Him about;[11] His disciples, from whom the commencement of His preaching should be made.

5. "He asked life; and Thou gavest Him:" He asked a resurrection, saying, "Father, glorify

Thy Son;"[12] and Thou gavest it Him, "Length of days for ever and ever" (ver. 4). The prolonged ages of this world which the Church was to have, and after them an eternity, world without end.

6. "His glory is great in Thy salvation" (ver. 5). Great indeed is His glory in the salvation, whereby Thou hast raised Him up again. "Glory and great honour shalt Thou lay upon Him." But Thou shalt yet add unto Him glory and great honour, when Thou shalt place Him in heaven at Thy right hand.

7. "For Thou shalt give Him blessing for ever and ever." This is the blessing which Thou shalt give Him for ever and ever: "Thou shalt make Him glad in joy together with Thy countenance" (ver. 6). According to His manhood, Thou shalt make Him glad together with Thy countenance, which He lifted up to Thee.

8. "For the King hopeth in the Lord." For the King is not proud, but humble in heart, he hopeth in the Lord. "And in the mercy of the Most Highest He shall not be moved" (ver. 7). And in the mercy of the Most Highest His obedience even unto the death of the Cross shall not disturb His humility.

9. "Let Thy hand be found by all Thine enemies." Be Thy power, O King, when Thou comest to judgment, found by all Thine enemies; who in Thy humiliation discerned it not. "Let Thy right hand find out all that hate Thee" (ver. 8). Let the glory, wherein Thou reignest at the right hand of the Father, find out for punishment in the day of judgment all that hate Thee; for that now they have not found it.

10. "Thou shalt make them like a fiery oven:" Thou shalt make them on fire within, by the consciousness of their ungodliness: "In the time of Thy countenance:" in the time of Thy manifestation. "The Lord shall trouble them in His wrath, and the fire shall devour them" (ver. 9). And then, being troubled by the vengeance of the Lord, after the accusation of their conscience, they shall be given up to eternal fire, to be devoured.

11. "Their fruit shalt Thou destroy out of the earth." Their fruit, because it is earthly, shalt Thou destroy out of the earth. "And their seed from the sons of men" (ver. 10). And their works; or, whomsoever they have seduced, Thou shalt not reckon among the sons of men, whom Thou hast called into the everlasting inheritance.

12. "Because they turned evils against Thee." Now this punishment shall be recompensed to them, because the evils which they supposed to hang over them by Thy reign, they turned against Thee to Thy death. "They imagined a

---

[1] John xi. 48.   [2] Rom. xi. 25; Rom. x. 3.
[3] Matt. iii. 9.   [4] Rom. ix. 30.
[5] Lat. XX.   [6] [Prophetic of His ascension.—C.]
[7] Luke xxii. 15.   [8] John x. 18.   [9] John xiv. 27.
[10] [Rev. xix. 12. Our author agrees with the Septuagint and the Vulgate here, as to "precious stone." Jerome gives *coronam obrizam*. Gr. ὄβρυζον.—C.]
[11] Matt. v. 1. [Compare Mal. iii. 17.—C.]

[12] John xvii. 1.

device, which they were not able to establish"
(ver. 11). They imagined a device, saying, "It
is expedient that one die for all:"[1] which they
were not able to establish, not knowing what
they said.

13. "For Thou shalt set them low." For
Thou shalt rank them among those from whom
in degradation and contempt Thou wilt turn
away. "In Thy leavings[2] Thou shalt make ready
their countenance" (ver. 12). And in these
things that Thou leavest, that is, in the desires
of an earthly kingdom, Thou shalt make ready
their shamelessness for Thy passion.

14. "Be Thou exalted, O Lord, in Thy
strength" (ver. 13). Be Thou, Lord, whom in
humiliation they did not discern, exalted in Thy
strength, which they thought weakness. "We
will sing and praise Thy power." In heart and
in deed we will celebrate and make known Thy
marvels.

PSALM XXII.[3]

TO THE END, FOR THE TAKING UP OF THE MORN-
ING, A PSALM OF DAVID.[4]

1. "To the end," for His own resurrection,
the Lord Jesus Christ Himself speaketh.[5] For
in the morning on the first day of the week was
His resurrection, whereby He was taken up, into
eternal life, "Over whom death shall have no
more dominion."[6] Now what follows is spoken
in the person of The Crucified. For from the
head of this Psalm are the words, which He
cried out, whilst hanging on the Cross, sustaining also the person of the old man, whose mortality He bare. For our old man was nailed
together with Him to the Cross.[7]

2. "O God, my God, look upon me, why
hast Thou forsaken[8] me far from my salvation?"
(ver. 1). Far removed from my salvation:
for "salvation is far from sinners."[9] "The words
of my sins." For these are not the words of
righteousness, but of my sins. For it is the old
man nailed to the Cross that speaks, ignorant
even of the reason why God hath forsaken him:
or else it may be thus, The words of my sins are
far from my salvation.

3. "My God, I will cry unto Thee in the day-
time, and Thou wilt not hear" (ver. 2). My
God, I will cry unto Thee in the prosperous circumstances of this life, that they be not changed;
and Thou wilt not hear, because I shall cry unto
Thee in the words of my sins. "And in the
night-season, and not to my folly." And so in

the adversities of this life will I cry to Thee for
prosperity; and in like manner Thou wilt not
hear. And this Thou doest not to my folly, but
rather that I may have wisdom to know what
Thou wouldest have me cry for, not with the
words of sins out of longing for life temporal,
but with the words of turning to Thee for life
eternal.

4. "But Thou dwellest in the holy place, O
Thou praise of Israel" (ver. 3). But Thou
dwellest in the holy place, and therefore wilt not
hear the unclean words of sins. The "praise"
of him that seeth Thee; not of him who hath
sought his own praise in tasting of the forbidden
fruit, that on the opening of his bodily eyes he
should endeavour to hide himself from Thy
sight.

5. "Our Fathers hoped in Thee." All the
righteous, namely, who sought not their own
praise, but Thine. "They hoped in Thee, and
Thou deliveredst them" (ver. 4).

6. "They cried unto Thee, and were saved."
They cried unto Thee, not in the words of sins,
from which salvation is far; and therefore were
they saved. "They hoped in Thee, and were not
confounded" (ver. 5). "They hoped in Thee,"
and their hope did not deceive them. For they
placed it not in themselves.

7. "But I am a worm, and no man" (ver. 6).
But I, speaking now not in the person of Adam,
but I in My own person, Jesus Christ, was born
without human generation in the flesh, that I
might be as man beyond men; that so at least
human pride might deign to imitate My humility.
"The scorn of men, and outcast of the people."
In which humility I was made the scorn of men,
so as that it should be said, as a reproachful
railing, "Be thou His disciple:"[10] and that the
people despise Me.

8. "All that saw Me laughed Me to scorn"
(ver. 7). All that saw Me derided Me. "And
spake with the lips, and shook the head."[11]
And they spoke, not with the heart, but with the
lips.

9. For they shook their head in derision, saying, "He trusted in the Lord, let Him deliver
Him:"[12] "let Him save Him, since He desireth
Him" (ver. 8). These were their words; but
they were spoken "with the lips."

10. "Since Thou art He who drew Me out
of the womb" (ver. 9). Since Thou art He
who drew Me, not only out of that Virgin womb
(for this is the law of all men's birth, that they
be drawn out of the womb), but also out of the
womb of the Jewish nation; by the darkness
whereof he is covered, and not yet born into the
light of Christ, whosoever places his salvation in
the carnal observance of the Sabbath, and of circumcision, and the like. "My hope from My

---

[1] John xi. 50.
[2] [In reliquiis tuis. So Vulgate. — C.]
[3] Lat. XXI.
[4] [This was read on the anniversary of our Lord's passion, as
appears from the (omitted) Second Exposition. — C.]
[5] John xx. 1–17.   [6] Rom. vi. 9.   [7] Rom. vi. 6.
[8] Vid. Ps. xxxvii. § 6 and xliii. § 2, and Enarr. i. Ps. lviii. § 2,
and Ep. 149. [Opp. S. August. ed. Migne, tom. iv. pp. 399, 483,
691, etc. — C.]
[9] Ps. cxix. 155.

[10] John ix. 28.   [11] Matt. xxvii. 39.   [12] Matt. xxvii. 43.

mother's breasts." "My hope," O God, not from the time when I began to be fed by the milk of the Virgin's breasts ; for it was even before ; but from the breasts of the Synagogue, as I have said, out of the womb, Thou hast drawn Me, that I should not suck in the customs of the flesh.

11. "I have been strengthened in Thee from the womb" (ver. 10). It is the womb of the Synagogue, which did not carry Me, but threw Me out : but I fell not, for Thou heldest me. "From My mother's womb Thou art My God." From My mother's womb : My mother's womb did not cause that, as a babe, I should be forgetful of Thee.

12. "Thou art My God," "depart not from Me ; for trouble is hard at hand " (ver. 11). Thou art, therefore, My God, depart not from Me ; for trouble is nigh unto Me ; for it is in My body. "For there is none to help." For who helpeth, if Thou helpest not?

13. "Many calves came about Me." The multitude of the wanton populace came about Me. "Fat bulls closed Me in" (ver. 12). And their leaders, glad at My oppression, "closed Me in."

14. "They opened their mouth upon Me" (ver. 13). They opened their mouth upon Me, not out of Thy Scripture, but of their own lusts. "As a ravening and roaring lion." As a lion, whose ravening is, that I was taken and led ; and whose roaring, "Crucify, Crucify." [1]

15. "I was poured out like water, and all My bones were scattered " (ver. 14). "I was poured out like water," when My persecutors fell : and through fear, the stays of My body, that is, the Church, My disciples were scattered from Me.[2] "My heart became as melting wax, in the midst of my belly." My wisdom, which was written of Me in the sacred books, was, as if hard and shut up, not understood : but after that the fire of My Passion was applied, it was, as if melted, manifested, and entertained in the memory of My Church.

16. "My strength dried up as a potsherd " (ver. 15). My strength dried up by My Passion ; not as hay, but a potsherd, which is made stronger by fire. "And My tongue cleaved to My jaws." And they, through whom I was soon to speak, kept My precepts in their hearts. "And Thou broughtest Me down to the dust of death." And to the ungodly appointed to death, whom the wind casteth forth as dust from the face of the earth,[3] Thou broughtest Me down.

17. "For many dogs came about Me" (ver. 16). For many came about Me barking, not for truth, but for custom. "The council of the malignant came about Me." The council

of the malignant besieged Me.[4] "They pierced My hands and feet." They pierced with nails My hands and feet.

18. "They numbered distinctly all My bones " (ver. 17). They numbered distinctly all My bones, while extended on the wood of the Cross. "Yea, these same regarded, and beheld Me." Yea, these same, that is, unchanged, regarded and beheld Me.

19. "They divided My garments for themselves, and cast the lot upon My vesture "[5] (ver. 18).

20. "But Thou, O Lord, withhold not Thy help far from Me " (ver. 19). But Thou, O Lord, raise Me up again, not as the rest of men, at the end of the world, but immediately. "Look to My defence." "Look," that they in no wise hurt Me.

21. "Deliver My soul from the sword." "Deliver My soul " from the tongue of dissension. "And My only One from the hand of the dog" (ver. 20). And from the power of the people, barking after their custom, deliver My Church.

22. "Save Me from the lion's mouth : " save Me from the mouth of the kingdom of this world : "and my humility from the horns of the unicorns "[6] (ver. 21). And from the loftiness of the proud, exalting themselves to special pre-eminence, and enduring no partakers, save My humility.

23. "I will declare Thy name to My brethren "[7] (ver. 22). I will declare Thy name to the humble,[8] and to My Brethren that love one another as they have been beloved by Me.[9] "In the midst of the Church will I sing of Thee." In the midst of the Church will I with rejoicing preach Thee.

24. "Ye that fear the Lord, praise Him." "Ye that fear the Lord," seek not your own praise, but "praise Him." "All ye seed of Jacob, magnify Him " (ver. 23). All ye seed of him whom the elder shall serve, magnify Him.

25. "Let all the seed of Israel fear Him." Let all who have been born to a new life, and restored to the vision of God "fear Him." "Since He hath not despised, nor disregarded the prayer of the poor man " (ver. 24). Since He hath not despised the prayer, not of him who, crying unto God in the words of sins was loath to overpass a vain life, but the prayer of the poor man, not swollen up with transitory pomps. "Nor hath He turned away His face

---

[1] John xix. 6.   [2] Matt. xxvi. 56.   [3] Ps. i. 4.

[4] These seven words from the Oxford MS.
[5] [The *garments* he elsewhere makes the *sacraments*, his vesture the undivided unity of the Church. See his Second Exposition, here omitted. — C.]
[6] [The original Hebrew seems to me a foreshadowing of the *Romans*, as Peres (Dan. v. 28) points to the Persians. — C]
[7] [Here he makes Part II. to begin; i.e., the triumph over death and the grave. — C.]
[8] Or, " to My Brethren that are humble, and," etc.
[9] John xvii. 6, 21.

from Me." As from him who said, I will cry unto Thee, but Thou wilt not hear. "And when I cried unto Him He heard Me."

26. "With Thee is My praise" (vèr. 25). For I seek not Mine own praise,[1] for Thou art My praise, who dwellest in the holy place ; and, praise of Israel, Thou hearest The Holy One now beseeching Thee. "In the great Church I will confess Thee." In the Church of the whole world "I will confess Thee." "I will offer My vows in the sight of them that fear Him." I will offer the sacraments of My Body and Blood in the sight of them that fear Him.

27. "The poor shall eat, and be filled" (ver. 26). The humble and the despisers of the world shall eat, and imitate Me. For so they will neither desire this world's abundance, nor fear its want. "And they shall praise the Lord, who seek Him." For the praise of the Lord is the pouring out of that fulness. "Their hearts shall live for ever and ever." For that food is the food of the heart.

28. "All the borders of the earth shall remember themselves, and be turned to the Lord" (ver. 27). They shall remember themselves : for, by the Gentiles, born in death and bent on outward things, God had been forgotten ; and then shall all the borders of the earth be turned to the Lord. "And all the kindreds of the nations shall worship in His sight." And all the kindreds of the nations shall worship in their own consciences.

29. " For the kingdom is the Lord's, and He shall rule over the nations" (ver. 28). For the kingdom is the Lord's, not proud men's : and He shall rule over the nations.

30. "All the rich of the earth have eaten, and worshipped"[2] (ver. 29). The rich of the earth too have eaten the Body of their Lord's humiliation, and though they have not, as the poor, been filled even to imitation, yet they have worshipped. "In His sight shall fall all that descend to earth." For He alone seeth how all they fall, who abandoning a heavenly conversation, make choice, on earth, to appear happy to men, who see not their fall.

31. "And My Soul shall live to Him." And My Soul, which in the contempt of this world seems to men as it were to die, shall live, not to itself, but to Him. "And My seed shall serve Him" (ver. 30). And My deeds, or they who through Me believe on Him, shall serve Him.

32. "The generation to come shall be declared to the Lord" (ver. 31). The generation of the New Testament shall be declared to the honour of the Lord. "And the heavens shall declare

His righteousness." And the Evangelists shall declare His righteousness. "To a people that shall be born, whom the Lord hath made." To a people that shall be born to the Lord through faith.

PSALM XXIII.[3]

A PSALM OF DAVID HIMSELF.

1. The Church speaks to Christ : "The Lord feedeth me, and I shall lack nothing" (ver. 1). The Lord Jesus Christ is my Shepherd, "and I shall lack nothing."

2. " In a place of pasture there hath He placed me " (ver. 2). In a place of fresh pasture, leading me to faith,[4] there hath He placed me to be nourished. "By the water of refreshing hath He brought me up." By the water of baptism, whereby they are refreshed who have lost health and strength, hath He brought me up.

3. "He hath converted my soul : He hath led me forth in the paths of righteousness, for His Name's sake " (ver. 3). He hath brought me forth in the narrow ways, wherein few walk, of His righteousness ; not for my merit's sake, but for His Name's sake.

4. "Yea, though I walk in the midst of the shadow of death " (ver. 4). Yea, though I walk in the midst of this life, which is the shadow of death.[5] "I will fear no evil, for Thou art with me." I will fear no evil, for Thou dwellest in my heart by faith : and Thou art now with me, that after the shadow of death I too may be with Thee. "Thy rod and Thy staff, they have comforted me." Thy discipline, like a rod for a flock of sheep, and like a staff for children of some size, and growing out of the natural into spiritual life, they have not been grievous to me ; rather have they comforted me : because Thou art mindful of me.

5. "Thou hast prepared a table in my sight, against them that trouble me " (ver. 5). Now after the rod, whereby, whilst a little one, and living the natural life, I was brought up among the flock in the pastures ; after that rod, I say, when I began to be under the staff, Thou hast prepared a table in my sight, that I should no more be fed as a babe with milk,[6] but being older should take meat, strengthened against them that trouble me. "Thou hast fattened my head with oil." Thou hast gladdened my mind with spiritual joy. "And Thy inebriating cup, how excellent is it !" And Thy cup yielding forgetfulness of former vain delights, how excellent is it !

6. "And Thy mercy shall follow me all the days of my life : " that is, as long as I live in this mortal life, not Thine, but mine. "That I may

---

[1] John viii. 50.
[2] [Here the African Psalter reads, "*divites terræ*," the counterpart of *pauperes* in ver. 26. Would this had been followed in our English, which makes a ludicrous transition in this sublime prophecy. — C.]

[3] Lat. XXII.   [4] *Pascuæ incipientis.*
[5] [Note this very comprehensive comment on the real meaning of the valley. — C.]
[6] 1 Cor. iii. 2.

dwell in the house of the Lord [1] for length of days"
(ver. 6).   Now Thy mercy shall follow me not
here only, but also that I may dwell in the house
of the Lord for ever.

PSALM XXIV.[2]

A PSALM OF DAVID HIMSELF, ON THE FIRST DAY
OF THE WEEK.[3]

1. A Psalm of David himself, touching the
glorifying and resurrection of the Lord, which
took place early in the morning on the first day
of the week, which is now called the Lord's Day.

2. "The earth is the Lord's, and the fulness
thereof, the compass of the world, and all they
that dwell therein" (ver. 1) ; when the Lord,
being glorified, is announced for the believing of
all nations ; and the whole compass of the world
becomes His Church.   "He hath founded it
above the seas."   He hath most firmly established it above all the waves of this world, that
they should be subdued by it, and should not
hurt it.   "And hath prepared it above the
rivers" (ver. 2).   The rivers flow into the sea,
and men of lust lapse into the world : these also
the Church, which, when worldly lusts have been
conquered by the grace of God, hath been prepared by love for the reception of immortality,
subdues.

3. "Who shall ascend into the mount of the
Lord?"   Who shall ascend to the height of the
righteousness of the Lord?   "Or who shall stand
in His holy place?" (ver. 3).   Or who shall abide
in that place, whither He shall ascend,[4] founded
above the seas, and prepared above the rivers?

4. "The innocent of hand, and the pure in
heart" (ver. 4).   Who then shall ascend thither,
and abide there, but the guiltless in deed, and
pure in thought?   "Who hath not received his
soul in vain."   Who hath not reckoned his soul
among things that pass away, but feeling it to be
immortal, hath longed for an eternity stedfast
and unchangeable.   "And hath not sworn in
deceit to his neighbour."   And therefore without
deceit, as things eternal are simple and undeceiv-
ing, hath so behaved himself to his neighbour.

5. "This man shall receive blessing from the
Lord, and mercy from the God of his salvation"[5]
(ver. 5).

6. "This is the generation of them that seek
the Lord" (ver. 6).   For thus are they born that
seek Him.   "Of them that seek the face of the
God of Jacob.[6]   Diapsalma."   Now they seek

the face of God, who gave the pre-eminence to
the younger born.[7]

7. "Take away your gates, ye princes" (ver.
7).   All ye, that seek rule among men, remove,
that they hinder not, the entrances which ye have
made, of desire and fear.   "And be ye lift up,
ye everlasting gates."   And be ye lift up, ye
entrances of eternal life, of renunciation of the
world, and conversion to God.   "And the King
of glory shall come in."   And the King, in whom
we may glory without pride, shall come in :
who having overcome the gates of death, and
having opened for Himself the heavenly places,
fulfilled that which He said, "Be of good cheer,
for I have overcome the world."[8]

8. "Who is this King of glory?"   Mortal
nature is awe-struck in wonder, and asks, "Who
is this King of glory?"   "The Lord strong and
mighty."   He whom thou didst deem weak
and overwhelmed.   "The Lord mighty in battle"
(ver. 8).   Handle the scars, and thou wilt find
them made whole, and human weakness restored to immortality.   The glorifying of the
Lord, which was owing to earth, where It warred
with death, hath been paid.

9. "Take away your gates, ye princes."[9]
Let us go hence straightway into heaven.
Again, let the Prophet's trumpet cry aloud,
"Take away too, ye princes of the air, the gates,
which ye have in the minds of men who
'worship the host of heaven.'"[10]   "And be ye
lift up, ye everlasting gates."   And be ye lift
up, ye doors of everlasting righteousness, of
love, and chastity, through which the soul loveth
the One True God, and goeth not a-whoring
with the many that are called gods.   "And the
King of glory shall come in" (ver. 9).   "And
the King of glory shall come in," that He may
at the right hand of the Father intercede for us.

10. "Who is this King of glory?"   What!
dost thou too, prince of the power of this air,[11]
marvel and ask, "Who is this King of glory?"
"The Lord of powers, He is the King of glory"
(ver. 10).   Yea, His Body now quickened, He
who was tempted marches above thee ; He who
was tempted by the angel, the deceiver, goes
above all angels.   Let none of you put himself
before us and stop our way, that he may be
worshipped as a god by us : neither principality, nor angel, nor power, separateth us from
the love of Christ.[12]   It is good to trust in the
Lord, rather than to trust in a prince ;[13] that he
who glorieth, should glory in the Lord.[14]   These
indeed are powers in the administration of this
world, but "the Lord of powers, He is the King
of glory."

---

[1] [He applies the figures of ver. 5 and here to the Lord's Table, the
chrism (i.e., confirmation), and the Church in time and eternity. — C.]
[2] Lat. XXIII.
[3] [Surely a foretokening of our Sunday. — C.]
[4] Al. "hath ascended."
[5] [Light, resurrection, and sanctification are the glories of the
Lord's Day, and "this man" inherits all this. — C.]
[6] ["God of Jacob." So the Vulgate, after the Septuagint. — C.]

[7] Rom. ix. 12.   [8] John xvi. 33.
[9] [" Ye princes." So Septuagint and Vulgate. — C.]
[10] 2 Kings xvii. 16.   [11] Eph. ii. 2.   [12] Rom. viii. 39.
[13] Ps. cxviii. 9.   [14] 1 Cor. i. 31.

PSALM XXV.[1]

1. Christ speaks, but in the person of the Church: for what is said has reference rather to the Christian People turned unto God.

2. "Unto Thee, O Lord, have I lift up my soul" (ver. 1): with spiritual longing have I lift up the soul, that was trodden down on the earth with carnal longings. "O my God, in Thee I trust, I shall not be ashamed" (ver. 2). O my God, from trusting in myself I was brought even to this weakness of the flesh; and I who on abandoning God wished to be as God, fearing death from the smallest insect, was in derision ashamed for my pride; now, therefore, "in Thee I trust, I shall not be ashamed."

3. "And let not my enemies mock me." And let them not mock me, who by ensnaring me with serpent-like and secret suggestions, and prompting me with "Well done, well done," have brought me down to this. "For all that wait upon Thee shall not be confounded" (ver. 3).

4. "Let them be confounded who do vain things unrighteously." Let them be confounded who act unrighteously for the acquiring things that pass away. "Make Thy ways, O Lord, known to me, and teach me Thy paths" (ver. 4): not those which are broad, and lead the many to destruction;[3] but Thy paths, narrow, and known to few, teach Thou me.

5. "In Thy truth guide me:" avoiding error. "And teach me:" for by myself I know nothing, but falsehood. "For Thou art the God of my salvation; and for Thee have I waited all the day" (ver. 5). For dismissed by Thee from Paradise, and having taken my journey into a far country,[4] I cannot by myself return, unless Thou meetest the wanderer: for my return hath throughout the whole tract of this world's time waited for Thy mercy.

6. "Remember Thy compassions, O Lord" (ver. 6). Remember the works of Thy mercy, O Lord; for men deem of Thee as though Thou hadst forgotten. "And that Thy mercies are from eternity." And remember this, that Thy mercies are from eternity. For Thou never wast without them, who hast subjected even sinful man to vanity indeed, but in hope;[5] and not deprived him of so many and great consolations of Thy creation.

7. "Remember not the offences of my youth and of my ignorance" (ver. 7). The offences of my presumptuous boldness and of my ignorance reserve not for vengeance, but let them be as if forgotten by Thee. "According to Thy mercy, be mindful of me, O God." Be mindful indeed of me, not according to the anger of which I am worthy, but according to Thy mercy which is worthy of Thee. "For Thy goodness, O Lord." Not for my deservings, but for Thy goodness, O Lord.

8. "Gracious and upright is the Lord" (ver. 8). The Lord is gracious, since even sinners and the ungodly He so pitied, as to forgive all that is past; but the Lord is upright too, who after the mercy of vocation and pardon, which is of grace without merit, will require merits meet for the last judgment. "Wherefore He will establish a law for them that fail in the way." For He hath first bestowed mercy to bring them into the way.

9. "He will guide the meek in judgment." He will guide the meek, and will not confound in the judgment those that follow His will, and do not, in withstanding It, prefer their own. "The gentle He will teach His ways" (ver. 9). He will teach His ways, not to those that desire to run before, as if they were better able to rule themselves; but to those who do not exalt the neck, nor lift the heel, when the easy yoke and the light burden is laid upon them.[6]

10. "All the ways of the Lord are mercy and truth" (ver. 10). And what ways will He teach them, but mercy wherein He is placable, and truth wherein He is incorrupt? Whereof He hath exhibited the one in forgiving sins, the other in judging deserts. And therefore "all the ways of the Lord" are the two advents of the Son of God, the one in mercy, the other in judgment. He then attaineth unto Him holding on His ways, who seeing himself freed by no deserts of his own, lays pride aside, and henceforward bewares of the severity of His trial, having experienced the clemency of His help. "To them that seek His testament and His testimonies." For they understand the Lord as merciful at His first advent, and as the Judge at His second, who in meekness and gentleness seek His testament, when with His Own Blood He redeemed us to a new life; and in the Prophets and Evangelists, His testimonies.

11. "For Thy Name's sake, O Lord, Thou wilt be favourable to my sin; for it is manifold" (ver. 11). Thou hast not only forgiven my sins, which I committed before I believed; but also to my sin, which is manifold, since even in the way there is no lack of stumbling, Thou wilt be made favourable by the sacrifice of a troubled spirit.[7]

12. "Who is the man that feareth the Lord?" from which fear he begins to come to wisdom. "He shall establish a law for him in the way, which he hath chosen" (ver. 12). He shall establish a law for him in the way, which in his

---

[1] Lat. XXIV.   [2] [Alphabetical Psalm. — C.]
[3] Matt. vii. 13.   [4] Luke xv. 13.   [5] Rom. viii. 20.
[6] Matt. xi. 30.
[7] [Here our author, as did St. Chrysostom, treats true contrition as completed by pardon, without sacramental absolution. — C.]

freedom he has taken, that he may not sin now with impunity.

13. " His soul shall dwell in good, and his seed shall, by inheritance, possess the earth "(ver. 13). And his work shall possess the stable inheritance of a renewed body.

14. " The Lord is the stay of them that fear Him " (ver. 14). Fear seems to belong to the weak, but the Lord is the stay of them that fear Him. And the Name of the Lord, which hath been glorified throughout the whole world, is a stay to them that fear Him. " And His testament, that it may be manifested unto them." And He maketh His testament to be manifested unto them, for the Gentiles and the bounds of the earth are Christ's inheritance.

15. " Mine eyes are ever unto the Lord ; for He shall pluck my feet out of the snare " (ver. 15). Nor would I fear the dangers of earth, while I look not upon the earth : for He upon whom I look, will pluck my feet out of the snare.

16. " Look upon me, and have mercy upon me ; for I am single and poor " (ver. 16). For I am a single people, keeping the lowliness of Thy single Church, which no schisms or heresies possess.

17. " The tribulations of my heart have been multiplied " (ver. 17). The tribulations of my heart have been multiplied by the abounding of iniquity and the waxing cold of love.[1] " O bring Thou me out of my necessities." Since I must needs bear this, that by enduring unto the end I may be saved, bring Thou me out of my necessities.

18. " See my humility and my travail " (ver. 18). See my humility, whereby I never, in the boast of righteousness, break off from unity ; and my travail, wherein I bear with the unruly ones that are mingled with me. " And forgive all my sins." And, propitiated by these sacrifices, forgive all my sins, not those only of youth and my ignorance before I believed, but those also which, living now by faith, I commit through infirmity, or the darkness of this life.

19. " Consider mine enemies, how they are multiplied " (ver. 19). For not only without, but even within, in the Church's very communion, they are not wanting. " And with an unrighteous hate they hate me." And they hate me who love them.

20. " Keep my soul, and deliver me." Keep my soul, that I turn not aside to imitate them ; and draw me out from the confusion wherein they are mingled with me. " Let me not be confounded, for I have put my trust in Thee " (ver. 20). Let me not be confounded, if haply they rise up against me : for not in myself, but in Thee have I put my trust.

21. " The innocent and the upright have cleaved to me, for I have waited for Thee, O Lord " (ver. 21). The innocent and the upright, not in bodily presence only, as the evil, are mingled with me, but in the agreement of the heart in the same innocence and uprightness cleave to me : for I have not fallen away to imitate the evil ; but I have waited for Thee, expecting the winnowing of Thy last harvest.[2]

22. " Redeem Israel, O God, out of all his troubles " (ver. 22). " Redeem Thy people, O God," whom Thou hast prepared to see Thee, out of his troubles, not those only which he bears without, but those also which he bears within.

PSALM XXVI.[3]

OF DAVID HIMSELF.

1. It may be attributed to David himself, not the Mediator, the Man Christ Jesus, but the whole Church now perfectly established in Christ.

2. " Judge me, O Lord, for I have walked in my innocence " (ver. 1). Judge me, O Lord, for, after the mercy which Thou first showedst[4] me, I have some desert of my innocence, the way whereof I have kept. " And trusting in the Lord I shall not be moved." And yet not even so trusting in myself, but in the Lord, I shall abide in Him.

3. " Prove me, O Lord, and try me " (ver. 2). Lest, however, any of my secret sins should be hid from me, prove me, O Lord, and try me, making me known, not to Thee from whom nothing is hid, but to myself, and to men. " Burn my reins and my heart." Apply a remedial purgation, as it were fire, to my pleasures and thoughts. " For Thy mercy is before mine eyes " (ver. 3). For, that I be not consumed by that fire, not my merits, but Thy mercy, whereby Thou hast brought me on to such a life, is before my eyes. " And I have been pleasing in Thy truth." And since my own falsehood hath been displeasing to me, but Thy truth pleasing, I have myself been pleasing also with it and in it.

4. " I have not sat with the council of vanity " (ver. 4). I have not chosen to give my heart to them who endeavour to provide, what is impossible, how they may be blessed in the enjoyment of things transitory. " And I will not enter in with them that work wickedly." And since this is the very cause of all wickedness, therefore I will not have my conscience hid, with them that work wickedly.

5. " I have hated the congregation of evil doers." But to arrive at this council of vanity, congregations of evil doers are formed, which I have hated. " And I will not sit with the un-

---

[1] Matt. xxiv. 12.

[2] [So the dying Jacob, Gen. xlix. 18. — C.]   [3] Lat. XXV.
[4] Prærogasti.

godly" (ver. 5). And, therefore, with such a council, with the ungodly, I will not sit, that is, I will not place my consent.[1] "And I will not sit with the ungodly."

6. "I will wash mine hands amid the innocent" (ver. 6). I will make clean my works among the innocent: among the innocent will I wash mine hands, with which I shall embrace Thy glorious gifts.[2] "And I will compass Thy altar, O Lord."[3]

7. "That I may hear the voice of Thy praise." That I may learn how to praise Thee. "And that I may declare all Thy wondrous works" (ver. 7). And after I have learnt, I may set forth all Thy wondrous works.

8. "O Lord, I have loved the beauty of Thy house:" of Thy Church. "And the place of the habitation of Thy glory" (ver. 8): where Thou dwellest, and art glorified.

9. "Destroy not my soul with the ungodly" (ver. 9). Destroy not then, together with them that hate Thee, my soul, which hath loved the beauty of Thy house. "And my life with the men of blood." And with them that hate their neighbour. For Thy house is beautified with the two commandments.[4]

10. "In whose hands is wickedness." Destroy me not then with the ungodly and the men of blood, whose works are wicked. "Their right hand is full of gifts" (ver. 10). And that which was given them to obtain eternal salvation, they have converted into the receiving this world's gifts, "supposing that godliness is a trade."[5]

11. "But I have walked in mine innocence: deliver me, and have mercy on me" (ver. 11). Let so great a price of my Lord's Blood avail for my complete deliverance: and in the dangers of this life let not Thy mercy leave me.

12. "My foot hath stood in uprightness." My Love hath not withdrawn from Thy righteousness. "In the Churches I will bless Thee, O Lord" (ver. 12). I will not hide Thy blessing, O Lord, from those whom Thou hast called; for next to the love of Thee I join the love of my neighbour.

PSALM XXVII.[6]

OF DAVID HIMSELF, BEFORE HE WAS ANOINTED.[7]

1. Christ's young soldier speaketh, on his coming to the faith. "The Lord is my light, and my salvation: whom shall I fear?" (ver. 1). The Lord will give me both knowledge of Himself, and salvation: who shall take me from Him?

"The Lord is the Protector of my life: of whom shall I be afraid?" The Lord will repel all the assaults and snares of mine enemy: of no man shall I be afraid.

2. "Whilst the guilty approach unto me to eat up my flesh" (ver. 2). Whilst the guilty come near to recognise and insult me, that they may exalt themselves above me in my change for the better; that with their reviling tooth they may consume not me, but rather my fleshly desires. "Mine enemies who trouble me." Not they only who trouble me, blaming me with a friendly intent, and wishing to recall me from my purpose, but mine enemies also. "They became weak, and fell."[8] Whilst then they do this with the desire of defending their own opinion, they became weak to believe better things, and began to hate the word of salvation, whereby I do what displeases them.

3. "If camps stand together against me, my heart will not fear." But if the multitude of gainsayers conspire to stand together against me, my heart will not fear, so as to go over to their side. "If war rise up against me, in this will I trust" (ver. 3). If the persecution of this world arise against me, in this petition, which I am pondering, will I place my hope.

4. "One have I asked of the Lord, this will I require." For one petition have I asked the Lord, this will I require. "That I may dwell in the house of the Lord all the days of my life" (ver. 4). That as long as I am in this life, no adversities may exclude me from the number of them who hold the unity and the truth of the Lord's faith throughout the world. "That I may contemplate the delight of the Lord." With this end, namely, that persevering in the faith, the delightsome vision may appear to me, which I may contemplate face to face. "And I shall be protected, His temple." And death being swallowed up in victory, I shall be clothed with immortality, being made His temple.[9]

5. "For He hath hidden me in His tabernacle in the day of my evils" (ver. 5). For He hath hidden me in the dispensation of His Incarnate Word in the time of temptations, to which my mortal life is exposed. "He hath protected me in the secret place of His tabernacle." He hath protected me, with the heart believing unto righteousness.

6. "On a rock hath He exalted me." And that what I believed might be made manifest for salvation, He hath made my confession to be conspicuous in His own strength. "And now, lo! He hath exalted mine head above mine enemies" (ver. 6). What doth He reserve for me

---

1 *Placitum non collocabo.*　　2 *Sublimia tua.*
3 [We are "made unto our God, *priests*."—C.]
4 [Matt. xxii. 40.—C.]　　5 1 Tim. vi. 5.
6 Lat. XXVI.
7 [In the Second Exposition he dwells on the spiritual *chrism*, from which the Son of David is called *Christ;* affirms that Christians partake of the same anointing; speaking of confirmation as their sacramental anointing and what it implies.—C.]

8 [A minute prophecy. John xviii. 6.—C.]
9 [The Old Latin of this charming verse seems to have read, "One hope have I desired," etc. See Cyprian, A. N. F. vol. v. p. 501.—C.]

at the last, when even now the body is dead because of sin, lo! I feel that my mind serves the law of God, and is not led captive under the rebellious law of sin? "I have gone about, and have sacrificed in His tabernacle the sacrifice of rejoicing." I have considered the circuit of the world, believing on Christ; and in that for us God was humbled in time, I have praised Him with rejoicing: for with such sacrifice He is well pleased. "I will sing and give praises to the Lord." In heart and in deed I will be glad in the Lord.

7. "Hear my voice, O Lord, wherewith I have cried unto Thee" (ver. 7). Hear, Lord, my interior voice, which with a strong intention I have addressed to Thy ears. "Have mercy upon me, and hear me." Have mercy upon me, and hear me therein.

8. "My heart hath said to Thee, I have sought Thy countenance" (ver. 8). For I have not exhibited myself to men; but in secret, where Thou alone hearest, my heart hath said to Thee; I have not sought from Thee aught without Thee as a reward, but Thy countenance. "Thy countenance, O Lord, will I seek." In this search will I perseveringly persist: for not aught that is common, but Thy countenance, O Lord, will I seek, that I may love Thee freely, since nothing more precious do I find.

9. "Turn not away Thy face from me" (ver. 9): that I may find what I seek. "Turn not aside in anger from Thy servant:" lest, while seeking Thee, I fall in with somewhat else. For what is more grievous than this punishment to one who loveth and seeketh the truth of Thy countenance? "Be Thou my Helper." How shall I find it, if Thou help me not? "Leave me not, neither despise me, O God my Saviour." Scorn not that a mortal dares to seek the Eternal; for Thou, God, dost heal the wound of my sin.

10. "For my father and my mother have left me" (ver. 10). For the kingdom of this world and the city of this world, of which I was born in time and mortality, have left me seeking Thee, and despising what they promised, since they could not give what I seek. "But the Lord took me up." But the Lord, who can give me Himself, took me up.

11. "Appoint me a law, O Lord, in Thy way" (ver. 11). For me then who am setting out toward Thee, and commencing so great a profession, of arriving at wisdom, from fear, appoint, O Lord, a law in Thy way, lest in my wandering Thy rule abandon me. "And direct me in the right path because of mine enemies." And direct me in the right way of its straits. For it is not enough to begin, since enemies cease not until the end is attained.

12. "Deliver me not up unto the souls of them that trouble me" (ver. 12). Suffer not them that trouble me to be satiated with my evils. "For unrighteous witnesses have risen up against me." For there have risen up against me they that speak falsely of me, to remove and call me back from Thee, as if I seek glory of men. "And iniquity hath lied unto itself." Therefore iniquity hath been pleased with its own lie. For me it hath not moved, to whom because of this there hath been promised a greater reward in heaven.

13. "I believe to see the good things of the Lord in the land of the living" (ver. 13). And since my Lord hath first suffered these things, if I too despise the tongues of the dying ("for the mouth that lieth slayeth the soul"[1]), I believe to see the good things of the Lord in the land of the living, where there is no place for falsity.

14. "Wait on the Lord, quit thyself like a man: and let thy heart be strong, yea wait on the Lord" (ver. 14). But when shall this be? It is arduous for a mortal, it is slow to a lover: but listen to the voice, that deceiveth not, of him that saith, "Wait on the Lord." Endure the burning of the reins manfully, and the burning of the heart stoutly. Think not that what thou dost not as yet receive is denied thee. That thou faint not in despair, see how it is said, "Wait on the Lord."[2]

PSALM XXVIII.[3]

OF DAVID HIMSELF.

1. It is the Voice of the Mediator Himself, strong of hand in the conflict of the Passion. Now what He seems to wish for against His enemies, is not the wish of malevolence, but the declaration of their punishment; as in the Gospel,[4] with the cities, in which though He had performed miracles, yet they had not believed on Him, He doth not wish in any evil will what He saith, but predicteth what is impending over them.

2. "Unto Thee, O Lord, have I cried;[5] My God, be not silent from me" (ver. 1). Unto Thee, O Lord, have I cried; My God, separate not the unity of Thy Word from that which as Man I am. "Lest at any time Thou be silent from me: and I shall be like them that go down into the pit." For from this, that the Eternity of Thy Word ceaseth not to unite Itself to Me, it comes that I am not such a man as the rest of men, who are born into the deep misery of this

---

1 Wisd. i. 11.
2 [On the first three verses of this Psalm, see Origen, A. N. F. vol. iv. pp. 333, 575, 649. Compare Cyprian, A. N. F. vol. iv. p. 501.—C.]
3 Lat. XXVII.　　　　　　4 Matt. xi. 20-24.
5 [The Greek and Vulgate omit the epithet of the Hebrew, "My Rock," which is the link with the Psalm foregoing (ver. 5), and the key to other parallels. St. Jerome renders it, *fortis meus*.—C.]

world: where, as if Thou art silent, Thy Word is not recognised. "Hear, O Lord, the voice of my supplication, whilst I pray unto Thee, whilst I hold up my hands to Thy holy temple" (ver. 2). Whilst I am crucified for their salvation, who on believing become Thy holy temple.

3. "Draw not My Soul away with sinners, and destroy me not with them that work iniquity, with them that speak peace with their neighbours" (ver. 3). With them that say unto Me, "We know that Thou art a Master come from God." [1] "But evil in their hearts." But they speak evil in their hearts.

4. "Give unto them according to their works" (ver. 4). Give unto them according to their works, for this is just. "And according to the malice of their affections." [2] For aiming at evil, they cannot discover good. "According to the works of their hands give Thou unto them." Although what they have done may avail for salvation to others, yet give Thou unto them according to the works of their wills. "Pay them their recompense." Because, for the truth which they heard, they wished to recompense deceit; let their own deceit deceive them.

5. "For they have not had understanding in the works of the Lord" (ver. 5). And whence is it clear that this hath befallen them? From this forsooth, "for they have not had understanding in the works of the Lord." This very thing, in truth, hath been, even now, their recompense, that in Him whom they tempted with malicious intent as a Man, they should not recognise God, with what design the Father sent Him in the Flesh. "And the works of His hands." Nor be moved by those visible works, which are laid out before their very eyes. "Thou shalt destroy them, and not build them up." Let them do Me no hurt, nay, nor again in their endeavour to raise engines against My Church, let them aught avail.

6. "Blessed be the Lord, for He hath heard the voice of My prayer" (ver. 6).

7. "The Lord My Helper and My Protector" (ver. 7). The Lord helping Me in so great sufferings, and protecting Me with immortality in My resurrection. "In Him hath My Heart trusted, and I have been helped." "And My Flesh hath flourished again:" that is, and My Flesh hath risen again. "And of my will I will confess unto Him." Wherefore, the fear of death being now destroyed, not by the necessity of fear under the Law, but with a free will with the Law, shall they who believe on Me, confess unto Him; and because I am in them, I will confess.

8. "The Lord is the strength of His people" (ver. 8). Not that people "ignorant of the

righteousness of God, and willing to establish their own." [3] For they thought not themselves strong in themselves: for the Lord is the strength of His people, struggling in this life's difficulties with the devil. "And the protector of the salvation of His Christ." That, having saved them by His Christ, after the strength of war, He may protect them at the last with the immortality of peace.

9. "Save Thy people, and bless Thine inheritance" (ver. 9). I intercede therefore, after My Flesh hath flourished again, because Thou hast said, "Desire of Me, and I will give Thee the heathen for Thine inheritance;" [4] "Save Thy people, and bless Thine inheritance:" for "all Mine are Thine." [5] "And rule them, and set them up even for ever." And rule them in this temporal life, and raise them from hence into life eternal.

PSALM XXIX. [6]

A PSALM OF DAVID HIMSELF, OF THE CONSUMMA-
TION OF THE TABERNACLE.

1. A Psalm of the Mediator Himself, strong of hand, of the perfection of the Church in this world, where she wars in time against the devil.

2. The Prophet speaks, "Bring unto the Lord, O ye Sons of God, bring unto the Lord the young of rams" (ver. 1). Bring unto the Lord yourselves, whom the Apostles, the leaders of the flocks, have begotten by the Gospel. [7] "Bring unto the Lord glory and honour" (ver. 2). By your works let the Lord be glorified and honoured. "Bring unto the Lord glory to His name." Let Him be made known gloriously throughout the world. "Worship the Lord in His holy court." Worship the Lord in your heart enlarged and sanctified. For ye are His regal holy habitation.

3. "The Voice of the Lord is upon the waters" (ver. 3). The Voice of Christ is upon the peoples. "The God of majesty hath thundered." The God of majesty, from the cloud of the flesh, hath awfully preached repentance. "The Lord is upon many waters." The Lord Jesus Himself, after that He sent forth His Voice upon the peoples, and struck them with awe, converted them to Himself, and dwelt in them.

4. "The Voice of the Lord is in power" (ver. 4). The Voice of the Lord now in them themselves, making them powerful. "The Voice of the Lord is in great might." The Voice of the Lord working great things in them.

5. "The Voice of the Lord breaking the cedars" (ver. 5). The Voice of the Lord humbling the proud in brokenness of heart. "The Lord shall break the cedars of Libanus." The Lord by repentance shall break them that are

---

[1] John iii. 2.   [2] *Al. affectationum,* "aims."

[3] Rom x. 3.   [4] Ps ii. 8.   [5] John xvii. 10.
[6] Lat. XXVIII.   [7] 1 Cor. iv. 15.

lifted on high by the splendour of earthly nobility, when to confound them He shall have "chosen the base things of this world,"[1] in the which to display His Divinity.

6. "And shall bruise them as the calf of Libanus" (ver. 6). And when their proud exaltation hath been cut off, He will lay them low after the imitation of His Own humility, who like a calf was led to slaughter[2] by the nobility of this world. "For the kings of the earth stood up, and the rulers agreed together against the Lord, and against His Christ."[3] "And the Beloved is as the young of the unicorns." For even He the Beloved, and the Only One of the Father, "emptied Himself" of His glory; and was made man,[4] like a child of the Jews, that were "ignorant of God's righteousness,"[5] and proudly boasting of their own righteousness as peculiarly theirs.

7. "The Voice of the Lord cutting short the flame of fire" (ver. 7). The Voice of the Lord, without any harm to Himself, passing through all the excited ardour of them that persecute Him, or dividing the furious rage of His persecutors, so that some should say, "Is not this haply the very Christ;" others, "Nay; but He deceiveth the people:"[6] and so cutting short their mad tumult, as to pass some over into His love, and leave others in their malice.

8. "The Voice of the Lord moving the wilderness" (ver. 8). The Voice of the Lord moving to the faith the Gentiles once "without hope, and without God in the world;"[7] where no prophet, no preacher of God's word, as it were, no man had dwelt. "And the Lord will move the desert of Cades." And then the Lord will cause the holy word of His Scriptures to be fully known, which was abandoned by the Jews who understood it not.

9. "The Voice of the Lord perfecting the stags"[8] (ver. 9). For the Voice of the Lord hath first perfected them that overcame and repelled the envenomed tongues.[9] "And will reveal the woods." And then will He reveal to them the darknesses of the Divine books, and the shadowy depths of the mysteries, where they may feed with freedom. "And in His temple doth every man speak of His glory." And in His Church all born again to an eternal hope praise God, each for His own gift, which He hath received from the Holy Spirit.

10. "The Lord inhabiteth the deluge" (ver. 10). The Lord therefore first inhabiteth the deluge of this world in His Saints, kept safely in the Church, as in the ark. "And the Lord shall sit a King for ever." And afterward He will sit reigning in them for ever.

11. "The Lord will give strength to His people"[10] (ver. 11). For the Lord will give strength to His people fighting against the storms and whirlwinds of this world, for peace in this world He hath not promised them.[11] "The Lord will bless His people in peace." And the same Lord will bless His people, affording them peace in Himself; for, saith He, "My peace I give unto you, My peace I leave with you."[12]

PSALM XXX.[13]

TO THE END, THE PSALM OF THE CANTICLE[14] OF THE DEDICATION OF THE HOUSE, OF DAVID HIMSELF.

1. To the end, a Psalm of the joy of the Resurrection, and the change, the renewing of the body to an immortal state, and not only of the Lord, but also of the whole Church. For in the former Psalm the tabernacle was finished, wherein we dwell in the time of war: but now the house is dedicated, which will abide in peace everlasting.

2. It is then whole Christ who speaketh. "I will exalt Thee, O Lord, for Thou hast taken Me up" (ver. 1). I will praise Thy high Majesty, O Lord, for Thou hast taken Me up. "Thou hast not made Mine enemies to rejoice over Me." And those, who have so often endeavoured to oppress Me with various persecutions throughout the world, Thou hast not made to rejoice over Me.

3. "O Lord, My God, I have cried unto Thee, and Thou hast healed Me" (ver. 2). O Lord, My God, I have cried unto Thee, and I no longer bear about a body enfeebled and sick by mortality.

4. "O Lord, Thou hast brought back My Soul from hell, and Thou hast saved Me from them that go down into the pit" (ver. 3). Thou hast saved Me from the condition of profound darkness, and the lowest slough of corruptible flesh.

5. "Sing to the Lord, O ye saints of His." The prophet seeing these future things, rejoiceth, and saith, "Sing to the Lord, O ye saints of His. And make confession of the remembrance of His holiness" (ver. 4). And make confession to Him, that He hath not forgotten the sanctification, wherewith He hath sanctified you, although all this intermediate period belong to your desires.

6. "For in His indignation is wrath" (ver. 5).

---

[1] 1 Cor. i. 28.　　　[2] Isa. liii. 7.　　　[3] Ps. ii. 2.
[4] Phil. ii. 7.　　　[5] Rom. x. 3.　　　[6] John vii. 41, 12.
[7] Eph. ii. 12.
[8] [Jerome's Hebraic version reads, *Vox Domini obstetricans cervas*, which the Authorized English follows. — C.]
[9] Plin. *Hist. Nat.* viii. 32 and xxviii. 9 says, that they bring serpents out of their holes with their breath, and kill and eat them. See S. Greg. *Mor.* xxx. 36.

[10] [This Psalm was referred to Pentecost by the Jews, and to the giving of the law. Heb. xii. :8–21. — C.]
[11] John xvi. 33.　　[12] John xiv. 27.　　[13] Lat. XXIX.
[14] [A *shir*, or "song." So Psalm xviii. = *shirah*, the only two instances in the first division of the Psalter, forty-one Psalms. — C.]

For He hath avenged against you the first sin, for which you have paid by death. "And life in His will." And life eternal, whereunto you could not return by any strength of your own, hath He given, because He so would. "In the evening weeping will tarry." Evening began, when the light of wisdom withdrew from sinful man, when he was condemned to death : from this evening weeping will tarry, as long as God's people are, amid labours and temptations, awaiting the day of the Lord. "And exultation in the morning." Even to the morning, when there will be the exultation of the resurrection, which hath shone forth by anticipation in the morning resurrection of the Lord.

7. "But I said in my abundance, I shall not be moved for ever" (ver. 6). But I, that people which was speaking from the first, said in mine abundance, suffering now no more any want, "I shall not be moved for ever."

8. "O Lord, in Thy will Thou hast afforded strength unto my beauty" (ver. 7). But that this my abundance, O Lord, is not of myself, but that in Thy will Thou hast afforded strength unto my beauty, I have learnt from this, "Thou turnedst away Thy Face from me, and I became troubled ;" for Thou hast sometimes turned away Thy Face from the sinner, and I became troubled, when the illumination of Thy knowledge withdrew from me.

9. "Unto Thee, O Lord, will I cry, and unto my God will I pray" (ver. 8). And bringing to mind that time of my trouble and misery, and as it were established therein, I hear the voice of Thy First-Begotten, my Head, about to die for me, and saying, "Unto Thee, O Lord, will I cry, and unto My God will I pray."

10. "What profit" is there "in My blood, whilst I go down to corruption?" (ver. 9) What profit is there in the shedding of My blood, whilst I go down to corruption? "Shall dust confess unto Thee?" For if I shall not rise immediately, and My body shall become corrupt, "shall dust confess unto Thee?" that is, the crowd of the ungodly, whom I shall justify by My resurrection? "Or declare Thy truth?" Or for the salvation of the rest declare Thy truth?

11. "The Lord hath heard, and had mercy on Me, the Lord hath become My helper." Nor did "He suffer His holy One to see corruption"[1] (ver. 10).

12. "Thou hast turned My mourning into joy to Me" (ver. 11). Whom I, the Church, having received, the First-Begotten from the dead,[2] now in the dedication of Thine house, say, "Thou hast turned my mourning into joy to me. Thou hast put off my sackcloth, and girded me with

gladness." Thou hast torn off the veil of my sins, the sadness of my mortality ; and hast girded me with the first robe, with immortal gladness.

13. "That my glory should sing unto Thee, and I should not be pricked" (ver. 12). That now, not my humiliation, but my glory should not lament, but should sing unto Thee, for that now out of humiliation Thou hast exalted me ; and that I should not be pricked with the consciousness of sin, with the fear of death, with the fear of judgment. "O Lord, my God, I will confess unto Thee for ever." And this is my glory, O Lord, my God, that I should confess unto Thee for ever, that I have nothing of myself, but that all my good is of Thee, who art "God, All in all."[3]

PSALM XXXI.[4]

TO THE END, A PSALM OF DAVID HIMSELF, AN ECSTASY.[5]

1. To the end a Psalm of David Himself, the Mediator strong of hand in persecutions. For the word ecstasy, which is added to the title, signifies a transport of the mind, which is produced either by a panic, or by some revelation. But in this Psalm the panic of the people of God troubled by the persecution of all the heathen, and by the failing of faith throughout the world, is principally seen. But first the Mediator Himself speaks : then the People redeemed by His Blood gives thanks : at last in trouble it speaks at length, which is what belongs to the ecstasy ; but the Person of the Prophet himself is twice interposed, near the end, and at the end.

2. "In Thee, O Lord, have I trusted, let Me not be put to confusion for ever" (ver. 1). In Thee, O Lord, have I trusted, let Me never be confounded, whilst they shall insult Me as one like other men. "In Thy righteousness rescue Me, and deliver Me." And in Thy righteousness rescue Me from the pit of death, and deliver Me out of their company.

3. "Bend down Thine ear unto Me" (ver. 2). Hear Me in My humiliation, nigh at hand unto Me. "Make haste to deliver Me." Defer not to the end of the world, as with all who believe on Me, My separation from sinners. "Be unto Me a God who protecteth Me." Be unto Me God, and Protector. "And a house of refuge, that Thou mayest save Me." And as a house, wherein taking refuge I may be saved.

4. "For Thou art My strength, and My refuge" (ver. 3). For Thou art unto Me My strength to bear My persecutors, and My refuge

---

[3] 1 Cor. xv. 28. [This Psalm was used at Easter and Pentecost. Compare Cyprian, vol. v. p. 525, A. N. F. — C.]
[4] Lat. XXX.
[5] [Borrowed from the Septuagint, where it is anticipated from ver. 22. See p. 70, infra. — C.]

---

[1] Ps. xvi. 10.   [2] Rev. i. 5.

to escape them. "And for Thy Name's sake Thou shalt be My guide, and shalt nourish Me." And that by Me Thou mayest be known to all the Gentiles, I will in all things follow Thy will; and, by assembling, by degrees, Saints unto Me, Thou shalt fulfil My body, and My perfect stature.

5. "Thou shalt bring Me out of this trap, which they have hidden for Me" (ver. 4). Thou shalt bring Me out of these snares, which they have hidden for Me. "For Thou art My Protector."

6. "Into Thy hands I commend My Spirit" (ver. 5). To Thy power I commend My Spirit, soon to receive It back. "Thou hast redeemed Me, O Lord God of truth." Let the people too, redeemed by the Passion of their Lord, and joyful in the glorifying of their Head, say, "Thou hast redeemed me, O Lord God of truth."

7. "Thou hatest them that hold to vanity uselessly" (ver. 6). Thou hatest them that hold to the false happiness of the world. "But I have trusted in the Lord."

8. "I will be glad, and rejoice in Thy mercy:" which doth not deceive me. "For Thou hast regarded My humiliation:" wherein Thou hast subjected me to vanity in hope.[1] "Thou hast saved my soul from necessities" (ver. 7). Thou hast saved my soul from the necessities of fear, that with a free love it may serve Thee.

9. "And hast not shut me up into the hands of the enemy" (ver. 8). And hast not shut me up, that I should have no opening for recovering unto liberty, and be given over for ever into the power of the devil, ensnaring me with the desire of this life, and terrifying me with death. "Thou hast set my feet in a large room." The resurrection of my Lord being known, and mine own being promised me, my love, having been brought out of the straits of fear, walks abroad in continuance, into the expanse of liberty.

10. "Have mercy on me, O Lord, for I am troubled" (ver. 9). But what is this unlooked-for cruelty of the persecutors, striking such dread into me? "Have mercy on me, O Lord." For I am now no more alarmed for death, but for torments and tortures. "Mine eye hath been disordered by anger." I had mine eye upon Thee, that Thou shouldest not abandon me: Thou art angry, and hast disordered it. "My soul, and my belly." By the same anger my soul hath been disturbed, and my memory, whereby I retained what my God hath suffered for me, and what He hath promised me.

11. "For my life hath failed in pain" (ver. 10). For my life is to confess Thee, but it failed in pain, when the enemy had said, Let them be tortured until they deny Him. "And

my years in groanings." The time that I pass in this world is not taken away from me by death, but abides, and is spent in groanings. "My strength hath been weakened by want." I want the health of this body, and racking pains come on me: I want the dissolution of the body, and death forbears to come: and in this want my confidence hath been weakened. "And my bones have been disturbed." And my stedfastness hath been disturbed.

12. "I have been made a reproach above all mine enemies" (ver. 11). All the wicked are my enemies; and nevertheless they for their wickednesses are tortured only till they confess: I then have overpassed their reproach, I, whose confession death doth not follow, but racking pains follow upon it. "And to my neighbours too much." This hath seemed too much to them, who were already drawing near to know Thee, and to hold the faith that I hold. "And a fear to mine acquaintance." And into my very acquaintance I struck fear by the example of my dreadful tribulation. "They that did see me, fled without from me." Because they did not understand my inward and invisible hope, they fled from me into things outward and visible.

13. "I have been forgotten, as one dead from the heart" (ver. 12). And they have forgotten me, as if I were dead from their hearts. "I have become as a lost vessel." I have seemed to myself to be lost to all the Lord's service, living in this world, and gaining none, when all were afraid to join themselves unto me.

14. "For I have heard the rebuking of many dwelling by in a circuit" (ver. 13). For I have heard many rebuking me, in the pilgrimage of this world near me, following the circuit of time, and refusing to return with me to the eternal country. "Whilst they were assembling themselves together against me, they conspired that they might take my soul." That my soul, which should by death easily escape from their power, might consent unto them, they imagined a device, whereby they would not suffer me even to die.

15. "But I have hoped in Thee, O Lord; I have said, Thou art my God" (ver. 14). For Thou hast not changed, that Thou shouldest not save, Who dost correct.

16. "In Thy hands" are "my lots" (ver. 15). In Thy power are my lots. For I see no desert, for which out of the universal ungodliness of the human race Thou hast elected me particularly to salvation. And though there be with Thee some just and secret order in my election, yet I, from whom this is hid, have attained by lot unto my Lord's vesture.[2] "Deliver me from the

---

[1] Rom. viii. 20.

[2] John xix. 24.

hands of mine enemies, and from them that persecute me."

17. "Make Thy Face to shine upon Thy servant" (ver. 16). Make it known to men, who do not think that I belong unto Thee, that Thy Face is bent upon me, and that I serve Thee. "Save me in Thy mercy."

18. "O Lord, let me not be confounded, for I have called upon Thee" (ver. 17). O Lord, let me not be put to shame by those who insult me, for that I have called upon Thee. "Let the ungodly be ashamed, and be brought down to hell." Let them rather who call upon stones be ashamed, and made to dwell with darkness.[1]

19. "Let the deceitful lips be made dumb" (ver. 18). In making known to the peoples Thy mysteries wrought in me, strike with dumb amazement the lips of them that invent falsehood of me. "Which speak iniquity against the Righteous, in pride and contempt." Which speak iniquity against Christ, in their pride and contempt of Him as a crucified man.

20. "How great" is "the multitude of Thy sweetness, O Lord" (ver. 19). Here the Prophet exclaims, having sight of all this, and admiring how manifoldly plenteous is Thy sweetness, O Lord. "Which Thou hast hid for them that fear Thee." Even those, whom Thou correctest, Thou lovest much: but lest they should go on negligently from relaxed security, Thou hidest from them the sweetness of Thy love, for whom it is profitable to fear Thee. "Thou hast perfected it for them that hope in Thee." But Thou hast perfected this sweetness for them that hope in Thee. For Thou dost not withdraw from them what they look for perseveringly even unto the end. "In sight of the sons of men." For it does not escape the notice of the sons of men, who now live no more after Adam, but after the Son of Man. "Thou wilt hide them in the hidden place of Thy Countenance:" which seat Thou shalt preserve for everlasting in the hidden place of the knowledge of Thee for them that hope in Thee. "From the troubling of men." So that now they suffer no more trouble from men.

21. "Thou wilt protect them in Thy tabernacle from the contradiction of tongues" (ver. 20). But here meanwhile whilst evil tongues murmur against them, saying, Who hath known this? or, Who hath come thence? Thou wilt protect them in the tabernacle, that of faith in those things, which the Lord wrought and endured for us in time.

22. "Blessed be the Lord; for He hath made His mercy marvellous, in the city of compassing" (ver. 21). Blessed be the Lord, for after the correction of the sharpest persecutions He hath made His mercy marvellous to all throughout the world, in the circuit of human society.[2]

23. "I said in my ecstasy"[3] (ver. 22). Whence that people again speaking saith, I said in my fear, when the heathen were raging horribly against me. "I have been cast forth from the sight of Thine eyes." For if Thou hadst regard to me, Thou wouldest not suffer me to endure these things. "Therefore Thou heardest, O Lord, the voice of my prayer, when I cried unto Thee." Therefore putting a limit to correction, and showing that I have part in Thy care, Thou heardest, O Lord, the voice of my prayer, when I raised it high[4] out of tribulation.

24. "Love the Lord, all ye His saints" (ver. 23). The Prophet again exhorts, having sight of these things, and saith, "Love the Lord, all ye His saints; for the Lord will require truth." Since "if the righteous shall scarcely be saved, where shall the sinner and the ungodly appear?"[5] "And He will repay them that do exceeding proudly." And He will repay them who even when conquered are not converted, because they are very proud.

25. "Quit you like men, and let your heart be strengthened" (ver. 24): working good without fainting, that ye may reap in due season. "All ye who trust in the Lord:" that is, ye who duly fear and worship Him, trust ye in the Lord.

PSALM XXXII.[6]

TO DAVID HIMSELF ; FOR UNDERSTANDING.

1. To David himself; for understanding; by which it is understood that not by the merits of works, but by the grace of God, man is delivered, confessing his sins.

2. "Blessed are they whose unrighteousness is forgiven, and whose sins are covered" (ver. 1): and whose sins are buried in oblivion. "Blessed is the man to whom the Lord hath not imputed sin, nor is there guile in his mouth" (ver. 2): nor has he in his mouth boastings of righteousness, when his conscience is full of sins.

3. "Because I kept silence, my bones waxed old:" because I made not with my mouth "confession unto salvation,"[7] all firmness in me has grown old in infirmity. "Through my roaring all the day long" (ver. 3): when I was ungodly and a blasphemer, crying against God, as though defending and excusing my sins.

4. "Because day and night Thy Hand was heavy upon me:" because, through the continual punishment of Thy scourges, "I was turned in misery, while a thorn was fixed through me"

---

[1] Umbris socientur.

[2] [Compare Hippolytus, vol. v. p. 202, A. N. F.—C.]
[3] [Elsewhere St. Augustin explains the word "ecstasy" as sometimes = transport, sometimes = panic. See his sermon on this Psalm, usually following this exposition.—C.]
[4] Nimis.   [5] 1 Pet. iv. 18.   [6] Lat. XXXI.
[7] Rom. x. 10.

(ver. 4) : I was made miserable by knowing my misery, being pricked with an evil conscience.

5. "I acknowledged my sin, and my unrighteousness have I not hid:" that is, my unrighteousness have I not concealed.[1] "I said, I will confess against myself my unrighteousness to the Lord:" I said, I will confess, not against God (as in my ungodly crying, when I kept silence), but against myself, my unrighteousness to the Lord. "And Thou forgavest the iniquity of my heart" (ver. 5) ; hearing the word of confession in the heart, before it was uttered with the voice.

6. "For this shall every one that is holy pray unto Thee in an acceptable time:" for this wickedness of heart shall every one that is righteous pray unto Thee. For not by their own merits will they be holy, but by that acceptable time, that is, at His coming, who redeemed us from sin. "Nevertheless in the flood of great waters they shall not come nigh him" (ver. 6): nevertheless, let none think, when the end has come suddenly, as in the days of Noah,[2] that there remaineth a place of confession, whereby he may draw nigh unto God.

7. "Thou art my refuge from the pressures, which have compassed me about:" Thou art my refuge from the pressure of my sins, which hath compassed my heart. "O Thou, my Rejoicing, deliver me from them that compass me about" (ver. 7) : in Thee is my joy: deliver me from the sorrow which my sins bring upon me.

8. *Diapsalma.* The answer of God : "I will give thee understanding, and will set thee in the way in which thou shalt go ;" I will give thee understanding after confession, that thou depart not from the way in which thou shouldest go ; lest thou wish to be in thine own power. "I will fix Mine Eyes upon thee" (ver. 8) : so will I make sure upon thee My Love.

9. "Be not ye like unto horse or mule, which have no understanding :" and therefore would govern themselves. But saith the Prophet, "Hold in their jaws with bit and bridle." Do Thou then, O God, unto them "that will not come nigh Thee" (ver. 9), what man doth to horse and mule, that by scourges Thou make them to bear Thy rule.

10. "Many are the scourges of the sinner : " much is he scourged, who, confessing not his sins to God, would be his own ruler. "But he that trusteth in the Lord, mercy compasseth him about" (ver. 10) ; but he that trusteth in the Lord, and submitteth himself to His rule, mercy shall compass him about.

11. "Be glad in the Lord, and rejoice, ye righteous :" be glad, and rejoice, ye righteous, not in yourselves, but in the Lord. "And glory, all ye that are right in heart" (ver. 11) : and glory in Him, all ye who understand that it is right to be subject unto Him, that so ye may be placed above all things beside.

PSALM XXXIII.[3]

1. "Rejoice in the Lord, O ye righteous :" rejoice, O ye righteous, not in yourselves, for that is not safe ; but in the Lord. "For praise is comely to the upright" (ver. 1) : these praise the Lord, who submit themselves unto the Lord ; for else they are distorted and perverse.

2. "Praise the Lord with harp :" praise the Lord, presenting unto Him your bodies a living sacrifice.[4] "Sing unto Him with the psaltery of ten strings" (ver. 2) : let your members be servants to the love of God, and of your neighbour, in which are kept both the three and the seven commandments.[5]

3. "Sing unto Him a new song :" sing unto Him a song of the grace of faith. "Sing skilfully unto Him·with jubilation" (ver. 3) : sing skilfully unto Him with rejoicing.

4. "For the Word of the Lord is right :" for the Word of the Lord is right, to make you that which of yourselves ye cannot be. "And all His works are done in faith" (ver. 4) : lest any think that by the merit of works he hath arrived at faith, when in faith are done all the works which God Himself loveth.

5. "He loveth Mercy and Judgment :" for He loveth Mercy, which now He showeth first ; and Judgment, wherewith He exacteth that which He hath first shown. "The earth is full of the Mercy of the Lord" (ver. 5) : throughout the whole world are sins forgiven unto men by the Mercy of the Lord.

6. "By the Word of the Lord were the heavens made firm :" for not by themselves, but by the Word of the Lord were the righteous made strong. "And all the strength[6] of them by the Breath of His Mouth" (ver. 6). And all their faith by His Holy Spirit.

7. "He gathereth the waters of the sea together as into a bottle :" He gathereth the people of the world together, to confession of mortified sin, lest through pride they flow too freely. • "He layeth up the deep in storehouses" (ver. 7) : and keepeth in them His secrets for riches.

8. "Let all the earth fear the Lord :" let

---

[1] [Here in our Psalter version is verse 6; not so the Authorized, nor the Vulgate, nor the other versions.—C.]
[2] Matt xxiv. 37-41.

[3] Lat. XXXII. [4] Rom. xii. 1.
[5] See St. Augustin on Faith and Works, § 17, Tr. note h. He takes our first and second as one, dividing the tenth. [Compare St. Augustin, Sermon ix. cap. 5. He is credited with introducing this division into the Western churches. Compare Irenæus (*Adv. Hæres.* ii. 24, § 4, note 9), A. N. F. vol. i. p. 395; also Clement, *Stromata,* A. N. F. vol. ii. p. 512.—C.]
[6] *Virtus.*

every sinner fear, that so he may cease to sin. "Let all the inhabitants of the world stand in awe of Him" (ver. 8): not of the terrors of men, or of any creature, but of Him let them stand in awe.

9. "For He spake, and they were made:" for no other one made those things which are to fear; but He spake, and they were made. "He commanded, and they were created" (ver. 9): He commanded by His Word,[1] and they were created.

10. "The Lord bringeth the counsel of the heathen to nought;" of them that seek not His Kingdom, but kingdoms of their own. "He maketh the devices of the people of none effect:" of them that covet earthly happiness. "And reproveth the counsels of princes" (ver. 10): of them that seek to rule over such peoples.

11. "But the counsel of the Lord standeth for ever;" but the counsel of the Lord, whereby He maketh none blessed but him that submitteth unto Himself, standeth for ever. The thoughts of His Heart to all generations" (ver. 11): the thoughts of His Wisdom are not mutable, but endure to all generations.

12. "Blessed is the nation whose God is the Lord:" one nation is blessed, belonging to the heavenly city, which hath not chosen save the Lord for their God: "And the people whom He hath chosen for His own inheritance" (ver. 12): and which not of itself, but by the gift of God, hath been chosen, that He by possessing it may not suffer it to be uncared for and miserable.

13. "The Lord looketh from Heaven; He beholdeth all the sons of men" (ver. 13). From the souls of the righteous, the Lord looketh mercifully upon all who would rise to newness of life.

14. "From His prepared habitation:" from His habitation of assumed Humanity, which He prepared for Himself. "He looketh upon all the inhabitants of the earth" (ver. 14): He looketh mercifully upon all who live in the flesh, that He may be over them in ruling them.

15. "He fashioneth their hearts singly:" He giveth spiritually to their hearts their proper gifts, so that neither the whole body may be eye, nor the whole hearing;[2] but that one in this manner, another in that manner, may be incorporated with Christ. "He understandeth all their works" (ver. 15). Before Him are all their works understood.

16. "A king shall not be saved by much strength:" he shall not be saved who ruleth his own flesh, if he presume much upon his own strength. "Neither shall a giant be saved by much strength" (ver. 16): nor shall he be

saved whoever warreth against the habit of his own lust, or against the devil and his angels, if he trust much to his own might.

17. "A horse is a deceitful thing for safety:" he is deceived, who thinketh either that through men he gaineth salvation received among men, or that by the impetuosity of his own courage he is defended from destruction. "In the abundance of his strength shall he not be saved" (ver. 17).

18. "Behold, the Eyes of the Lord are upon them that fear Him:" because if thou seek salvation, behold, the love of the Lord is upon them that fear Him. "Upon them that hope in His mercy" (ver. 18): that hope not in their own strength, but in His mercy.

19. "To deliver their souls from death, and to keep them alive in famine" (ver. 19). To give them the nourishment of the Word, and of Everlasting Truth, which they lost while presuming on their own strength, and therefore have not even their own strength, from lack of righteousness.

20. "My soul shall be patient for the Lord:" that hereafter it may be filled with dainties incorruptible, meanwhile, whilst here it remaineth, my soul shall be patient for the Lord. "For He is our Helper and Defender" (ver. 20): our Helper He is, while we endeavour after Him; and our Defender, while we resist the adversary.

21. "For our heart shall rejoice in Him:" for not in ourselves, wherein without Him there is great need; but in Himself shall our heart rejoice. "And we have trusted in His holy Name" (ver. 21); and therefore have we trusted that we shall come to God, because unto us absent hath He sent, through faith, His own Name.

22. "Let Thy mercy, O Lord, be upon us, according as we have hoped in Thee" (ver. 22): let Thy mercy, O Lord, be upon us; for hope confoundeth not, because we have hoped in Thee.

PSALM XXXIV.[3]

A PSALM OF DAVID, WHEN HE CHANGED HIS COUNTENANCE BEFORE ABIMELECH, AND HE SENT HIM AWAY, AND HE DEPARTED.

1. Because there was there a sacrifice after the order of Aaron, and afterwards He of His Own Body and Blood appointed a sacrifice after the order of Melchizedek; He changed then His Countenance in the Priesthood, and sent away the kingdom of the Jews, and came to the Gentiles. What then is, "He affected"?[4] He was full of affection. For what is so full of

---

[1] See De Genesi ad Lit. b. i. §§ 5, 6.
[2] 1 Cor. xii. 17.

[3] Lat. XXXIII.
[4] [1 Sam. xxi. 13. He follows the Septuagint, which differs from the Vulgate. — C.]

affection as the Mercy of our Lord Jesus Christ, who, seeing our infirmity, that He might deliver us from everlasting death, underwent temporal death with such great injury and contumely? "And He drummed:" because a drum is not made, except when a skin is extended on wood; and David drummed, to signify that Christ should be crucified. But, "He drummed upon the doors of the city:" what are "the doors of the city," but our hearts which we had closed against Christ, who by the drum of His Cross hath opened the hearts of mortal men? "And was carried in His Own Hands:" how "carried in His Own Hands"? Because when He commended His Own Body and Blood, He took into His Hands that which the faithful know; and in a manner carried Himself, when He said, "This is My Body."[1] "And He fell down at the doors of the gate;" that is, He humbled Himself. For this it is, to fall down even at the very beginning of our faith. For the door of the gate is the beginning of faith; whence beginneth the Church, and arriveth at last even unto sight: that as it believeth those things which it seeth not, it may deserve to enjoy them, when it shall have begun to see face to face. So is the title of the Psalm; briefly we have heard it; let us now hear the very words of Him that affecteth, and drummeth upon the doors of the city.

2. "I will bless the Lord at all times; His praise shall be ever in my mouth" (ver. 1). So speaketh Christ, so also let a Christian speak; for a Christian is in the Body of Christ; and therefore was Christ made Man, that that Christian might be enabled to be an Angel, who saith, "I will bless the Lord at all times." When shall I "bless the Lord"? When He blesseth thee? When the goods of this world abound? When thou hast great abundance of corn, oil, and wine, of gold and silver, of servants and cattle; when this mortal health remaineth unwounded and sound; when all that are born to thee grow up, nothing is withdrawn by immature death, happiness wholly reigneth in thy house, and all things overflow around thee; then shalt thou bless the Lord? No; but "at all times." Therefore both then, and when according to the time, or according to the scourges of our Lord God, these things are troubled, are taken away, are seldom born to thee, and born pass away. For these things come to pass, and thence followeth penury, need, labour, pain, and temptation. But thou, who hast sung, "I will bless the Lord at all times: His praise shall be ever in my mouth," both when He giveth them, bless; and when He taketh them away, bless. For it is He that giveth, it is He that taketh away: but Himself

from him that blesseth Him He taketh not away.

3. But who is it that blesseth the Lord at all times, except the humble in heart. For very humility taught our Lord in His Own Body and Blood: because when He commendeth His Own Body and Blood, He commendeth His Humility, in that which is written in this history, in that seeming madness of David, which we have passed by, "And his spittle ran down over his beard."[2] When the Apostle was read,[3] Ye heard the same spittle, but running down over the beard. One saith perhaps, What spittle have we heard? Was it not read but now, where the Apostle saith, "The Jews require a sign, and the Greeks seek after wisdom?" But now it was read, "But we preach," saith he, "Christ crucified" (for then He drummed), "unto the Jews a stumbling block, and unto the Greeks foolishness; but unto them which are called, both Jews and Greeks, Christ the Power of God, and the Wisdom of God. Because the Foolishness of God is wiser than men, and the Weakness of God is stronger than men."[4] For spittle signifieth foolishness; spittle signifieth weakness. But if the Foolishness of God is wiser than men, and the Weakness of God is stronger than men; let not the spittle as it were offend thee, but observe that it runneth down over the beard: for as by the spittle, weakness; so by the beard, strength is signified. He covered then His Strength by the body of His Weakness, and that which without was weak, appeared as it were in spittle; but within His Divine Strength was covered as a beard. Therefore humility is commended unto us. Be humble if thou wouldest bless the Lord at all times, and that His praise should be ever in thy mouth. . . .

4. But wherefore doth man bless the Lord at all times? Because he is humble. What is it to be humble? To take not praise unto himself. Who would himself be praised, is proud: who is not proud, is humble. Wouldest thou not then be proud? That thou mayest be humble, say what is here written; "In the Lord shall my soul be praised: the humble shall hear thereof and be glad" (ver. 2). Those then who will not be praised in the Lord, are not humble, but fierce, rough, lifted up, proud. Gentle cattle would the Lord have; be thou the Lord's *jumentum;* that is, be thou humble. He sitteth upon thee, He ruleth thee: fear not lest thou stumble, and fall headlong: that indeed is thy infirmity; but consider Who sitteth upon thee. Thou art an ass's colt, but thou carriest Christ.

---

[1] Matt. xxvi. 26.

[2] 1 Sam. xxi. 13.
[3] [This expression, so frequent in St. Augustin, refers to the Epistle for the day. As the Law and the Prophets in the synagogue, so also the Evangelists and Apostles were read ceremonially in the Church. — C.]
[4] 1 Cor. i. 22-25.

For even He on an ass's colt came into the city; and that beast was gentle. . . . "Be not ye as the horse or as the mule, which have no understanding."[1] For horse and mule sometimes lift up their neck, and by their own fierceness throw off their rider. They are tamed with the bit, with bridle, with stripes, until they learn to submit, and to carry their master. But thou, before thy jaws are bruised with the bridle, be humble, and carry thy Lord : wish not praise for thyself, but praised be He who sitteth upon thee, and say thou, " In the Lord shall my soul be praised; the humble shall hear thereof, and be glad." . . .

5. Now followeth, "O magnify the Lord with me " (ver. 3). Who is this that exhorteth us, that we should magnify the Lord with him? Whoever, Brethren, is in the body of Christ, ought for this to labour, that the Lord may be magnified with him. For he loveth the Lord, whoever he is. And how doth he love Him? So as not to envy his fellow-lover. . . . Let them blush who so love God as to envy others. Abandoned men love a charioteer, and whoever loveth a charioteer or hunter, wisheth the whole people to love with him, and exhorteth, saying, Love with me this pantomime, love with me this or that shame. He calleth among the people that shame may be loved with him ; and doth not a Christian call in the Church, that the Truth of God may be loved with him? Stir up then love in yourselves, Brethren ; and call to every one of yours, and say, "O magnify the Lord with me." Let there be in you that fervour. Wherefore are these things recited and explained? If ye love God, bring quickly to the love of God all who are joined unto you, and all who are in your house ; if the Body of Christ is loved by you, that is, if the unity of the Church, bring them quickly to enjoy, and say, "O magnify the Lord with me."

6. "And let us exalt His Name together."[2] What is, "let us exalt His Name together"? That is, in one. For many copies so have it, " O magnify the Lord with me ; and let us exalt His Name in one."[3] Whether it be said, " together," or "in one," it is the same thing. Therefore bring quickly whom ye can, by exhorting, by transporting,[4] by beseeching, by disputing, by rendering a reason, with meekness, with gentleness. Bring them quickly unto love ; that if they magnify the Lord, they may magnify Him in one. . . .

7. " I sought the Lord, and He heard me " (ver. 4). Where heard the Lord? Within. Where giveth He? Within. There thou prayest, there thou art heard, there thou art blessed.

Thou hast prayed, thou art heard, thou art blessed ; and he knoweth not who standeth by thee : it is all carried on in secret, as the Lord saith in the Gospel, " Enter into thy closet, and when thou hast shut thy door, pray to thy Father which is in secret ; and thy Father which seeth in secret, shall reward thee openly."[5] When therefore thou enterest into thy chamber, thou enterest into thy heart. Blessed are they who rejoice when they enter into their heart, and find therein nought of evil. . . .

8. " I sought the Lord, and He heard me." Who then are not heard, seek not the Lord. Attend, Holy Brethren ;[6] he said not, I sought gold from the Lord, and He heard me ; I sought from the Lord long life, and He heard me ; I sought from the Lord this or that, and He heard me. It is one thing to seek anything from the Lord, another to seek the Lord Himself. " I sought " (saith he) " the Lord, and He heard me." But thou, when thou prayest, saying, Kill that my enemy, seekest not the Lord, but, as it were, makest thyself a judge over thy enemy, and makest thy God an executioner.[7] How knowest thou that he is not better than thou, whose death thou seekest? In that very thing haply he is, that he seeketh not thine. Therefore seek not from the Lord anything without, but seek the Lord Himself, and He will hear thee, and while thou yet speakest, He will say, " Lo, here I am."[8] . . .

9. I have said who was the exhorter, namely, that lover who would not alone embrace what he loveth, and saith, " Approach unto Him, and be ye lightened " (ver. 5). For he saith what he himself proved. For some spiritual person in the Body of Christ, or even our Lord Jesus Christ Himself according to the flesh, the Head exhorting His Own Members, saith ; what? " Approach unto Him, and be ye lightened." Or rather some spiritual Christian inviteth us to approach to our Lord Jesus Christ Himself. But let us approach to Him and be lightened ; not as the Jews approached to Him, that they might be darkened ; for they approached to Him that they might crucify Him : let us approach to Him that we may receive His Body and Blood. They by Him crucified were darkened ; we by eating and drinking The Crucified are lightened. " Approach unto Him, and be· ye lightened." Lo, this is said to the Gentiles. Christ was crucified amid the Jews raging and seeing ; the Gentiles were absent ; lo, they have approached who were in darkness, and they who saw not are lightened. Whereby approach the Gentiles? By following with faith, by longing with the

---

[1] Ps. xxxii. 9.   [2] *In idipsum.*
[3] *In unum.* [In the Septuagint ἐπὶ τὸ αὐτό, as in Acts ii. 1. — C.]
[4] *Al.* "by working."

[5] Matt. vi. 6.
[6] [He makes the same exhortation to a brother bishop who was present : *attendat, Sanctitas Vestra.* — C.]
[7] *Quæstionarium.*   [8] Isa. lxv. 24.

heart, by running with charity. Thy feet are thy charity. Have two feet, be not lame. What are thy two feet? The two commandments of love, of thy God, and of thy Neighbour. With these feet run thou unto God, approach unto Him, for He hath both exhorted thee to run, and hath Himself shed His Own Light, as he hath magnificently and divinely continued.[1] "And your faces shall not be ashamed." "Approach" (saith he) "unto Him, and be ye lightened; and your faces shall not be ashamed." No face shall be ashamed but of the proud. Wherefore? Because he would be lifted up, and when he hath suffered insult, or ignominy, or mischance in this world, or any affliction, he is ashamed. But fear not thou, approach unto Him, and thou shalt not be ashamed. . . .

10. As the Prophet testifieth, "The poor man cried, and the Lord heard him" (ver. 6). He teacheth thee how thou mayest be heard. Therefore art thou not heard, because thou art rich. Lest haply thou say, thou criedst and wast not heard, hear wherefore; "The poor man cried, and the Lord heard him." As poor cry thou, and the Lord heareth. And how shall I cry as poor? By not, if thou hast aught, presuming therefrom upon thy own strength: by understanding that thou art needy; by understanding that so long art thou poor, as thou hast not Him who maketh thee rich. But how did the Lord hear him? "And saved him out of all his troubles." And how saveth He men out of all their troubles? "The Angel of the Lord shall send[2] round about them that fear Him, and shall deliver them" (ver. 7). So it is written, brethren, not as some bad copies have it, "The Lord shall send His Angel round about them that fear Him, and He shall deliver them:" but thus, "The Angel of the Lord shall send round about them that fear Him, and shall deliver them." Whom called He here the Angel of the Lord, who shall send round about them that fear Him, and shall deliver them? Our Lord Jesus Christ Himself is called in Prophecy, the Angel of the great Counsel, the Messenger of the great Counsel;[3] so the Prophets called Him.[4] Even He then, the Angel of the great Counsel, that is, the Messenger, shall send unto them that fear the Lord, and shall deliver them. Fear not then lest thou be hid: wheresoever thou hast feared the Lord, there doth that Angel know thee, who shall send to succour thee, and shall deliver thee.

11. Now will He speak openly of the same Sacrament, whereby He was carried in His Own Hands. "O taste and see that the Lord is good" (ver. 8). Doth not the Psalm now open itself, and show thee that seeming insanity and constant madness, the same insanity and sober inebriety of that David, who in a figure showed I know not what, when in the person of king Achis they said to him, How is it?[5] When the Lord said, "Except a man eat My Flesh and drink My Blood, he shall have no life in him"?[6] And they in whom reigned Achis, that is, error and ignorance, said; what said they? "How can this man give us his flesh to eat?"[7] If thou art ignorant, "Taste and see that the Lord is good:" but if thou understandest not, thou art king Achis: David shall change His Countenance and shall depart from thee, and shall quit thee, and shall depart.[8]

12. "Blessed is the man that trusteth in Him." Why needeth this to be explained at length? Whoever trusteth not in the Lord, is miserable. Who is there that trusteth not in the Lord? He that trusteth in himself. . . .

13. "O fear the Lord, all ye His saints, for there is no want to them that fear Him" (ver. 9). For many therefore will not fear God the Lord, lest they suffer hunger. It is said to them, Defraud not; and they say, Whence can I feed myself? No art can be without imposture; no business can be without fraud. But fraud God punisheth: fear God. But if I should fear God, I shall not have whence to live. "O fear the Lord, all ye His saints, for there is no want to them that fear Him." He promiseth plenty to him that trembleth, and doubteth, lest haply if he should fear God, he should lose things superfluous. The Lord fed thee despising Him, and will He desert thee fearing Him? Attend, and say not, Such an one is rich, and I am poor. I fear the Lord, he by not fearing how much has he gained, and I by fearing am bare! See what follows; "The rich[9] do lack and suffer hunger, but they that seek the Lord shall not want any good thing" (ver. 10). If thou receive it according to the letter, He seemeth to deceive thee, for thou seest that many rich men that are wicked die in their riches, and are not made poor while they live; thou seest them grow old, and come even to the end of life amid great abundance and riches. Thou seest their funeral pomp celebrated with great profusion, the man himself brought rich even to the sepul-

---

[1] So our MSS. and others, as Ed. Ben. says, *magno consensu. Sicut magnifice et divine secutus est.* Ben. however reads, "so that ye may be able magnificently and divinely to follow Him." *Sic, ut magnifice et divine se sequi possitis.* See on Ps. xxii. Exp. ii. § 16. "Gloriously expressed." The word is *magnifice.*
[2] *Immittet.* LXX. παρεμβαλεῖ, "shall encamp."
[3] Isa. ix. 6, LXX.; Mal. iii. 1.
[4] [See Ante-Nicene Fathers, vol. i. p. 223, note 7; also vol. v. p 628, note 2, and *passim.* — C.]

[5] *Al.* "when those wretched ones before king Achis said, How is it?"
[6] John vi. 53.　　[7] John vi. 52.
[8] [Luther's doctrine, and even Calvin's, admits of this language. Rhetorically, even Zwinglians might use the same. For the primitive doctrine see Justin Martyr and Irenæus, A. N. F. vol. i. p. 185, note 6, and 528, note 4. Observe also the fragment (xiii.) on p. 570. — C.]
[9] E. V. "The young lions do lack," etc.

chre, having expired in beds of ivory, his family weeping around; and thou sayest in thy mind, if haply thou knowest some both sins and crimes done by him: I know what things that man hath done; lo, he hath grown old, he hath died in his bed, his friends follow him to the grave, his funeral is celebrated with all this pomp; I know what he hath done; the Scripture has deceived me, and has spoken falsely, where I hear and sing; "The rich do lack and suffer hunger." When was this man in need? when did he suffer hunger? "But they that seek the Lord shall not want any good thing." Daily I rise up to Church, daily I bend the knee, daily I seek the Lord, and have nothing good: this man sought not the Lord, and he hath died in the midst of all these good things! Thus thinking, the snare of offence choketh him; for he seeketh mortal food on the earth, and seeketh not a true reward in heaven, and so he putteth his head into the devil's noose, his jaws are tied close, and the devil holdeth him fast unto evil doing, that so he may imitate the evil men, whom he seeth to die in such plenty.

14. Therefore understand it not so. . . . When thou art filled with spiritual riches, canst thou be poor? And was he therefore rich, because he had a bed of ivory; and art thou poor who hast the chamber of thy heart filled with such jewelry of virtues, justice, truth, charity, faith, endurance? Unfold thy riches, if thou hast them, and compare them with the riches of the rich. But such an one has found in the market mules of great value, and has bought them. If thou couldest find faith to be sold, how much wouldest thou give for that, which God willeth that thou shouldest have gratis, and thou art ungrateful? Those rich then lack, they lack, and what is heavier, they lack bread. . . . For He hath said, "I am the Living Bread which came down from Heaven."[1] And again, "Blessed are they which do hunger and thirst after righteousness: for they shall be filled."[2] "But they that seek the Lord shall not want any good thing:" but what manner of good, I have already said.

15. "Come, ye children, hearken unto me: I will teach you the fear of the Lord" (ver. 11). Ye think,[3] brethren, that I say this: think that David saith it; think that an Apostle saith it; nay think that our Lord Jesus Christ Himself saith it; "Come, ye children, hearken unto Me." Let us hearken unto Him together: hearken ye unto Him through us. For He would teach us; He the Humble, He that drummeth, He that affecteth, would teach us. . . .

16. "What man is he that desireth life, and loveth to see good days?" (ver. 12). He ask-

eth a question. Doth not every one among you answer, I? Is there any man among you that loveth not life, that is, that desireth not life, and loveth not to see good days? Do ye not daily thus murmur, and thus speak; How long shall we suffer these things? Daily are they worse and worse: in our fathers' time were days more joyful, were days better. O if thou couldest ask those same, thy fathers, in like manner would they murmur to thee of their own days. Our fathers were happy, miserable are we, evil days have we: such an one ruled over us, we thought that after his death might some refreshing be given to us; worse things have come: O God, show unto us good days! "What man is he that desireth life, and loveth to see good days?" Let him not seek here good days. A good thing he seeketh, but not in its right place doth he seek it. As, if thou shouldest seek some righteous man in a country, wherein he lived not, it would be said to thee, A good man thou seekest, a great man thou seekest, seek him still, but not here; in vain thou seekest him here, thou wilt never find him. Good days thou seekest, together let us seek them, seek not here. . . . Read the Scriptures. . . .

17. Let not a Christian then murmur, let him see whose steps he followeth: but if he loveth good days, let him hearken unto Him teaching and saying, "Come, ye children, hearken unto Me; I will teach you the fear of the Lord." What wouldest thou? Life and good days. Hear, and do. "Keep thy tongue from evil" (ver. 13). This do. I will not, saith a miserable man, I will not keep my tongue from evil, and yet I desire life and good days. If a workman of thine should say to thee, I indeed lay waste this vineyard, yet I require of thee my reward; thou broughtest me to the vineyard to lop and prune it, I cut away all the useful wood, I will cut short also the very trunks of the vines, that thou have thereon nothing to gather, and when I have done this, thou shalt repay to me my labour. Wouldest thou not call him mad? Wouldest thou not drive him from thy house or ever he put his hand to the knife? Such are those men who would both do evil, and swear falsely, and speak blasphemy against God, and murmur, and defraud, and be drunken, and dispute, and commit adultery, and use charms, and consult diviners, and withal see good days. To such it is said, thou canst not doing ill seek a good reward. If thou art unjust, shall God also be unjust? What shall I do, then? What desirest thou? Life I desire, good days I desire. "Keep thy tongue from evil, and thy lips that they speak no guile," that is, defraud not any, lie not to any.

18. But what is, "Depart from evil"? (ver. 14). It is little that thou injure none, murder

<hr>

[1] John vi. 51.   [2] Matt. v. 6; Luke i. 53; 1 Sam. ii. 5.
[3] Most MSS. "Think," imperative, as in the other clauses.

none, steal not, commit not adultery, do no wrong, speak no false witness; "Depart from evil." When thou hast departed, thou sayest, Now I am safe, I have done all, I shall have life, I shall see good days. Not only saith he, "Depart from evil," but also, "and do good." It is nothing that thou spoil not: clothe the naked. If thou hast not spoiled, thou hast declined from evil; but thou wilt not do good, except thou receive the stranger into thine house. So then depart from evil, as to do good. "Seek peace, and ensue it." He hath not said, Thou shalt have peace here; seek it, and ensue it. Whither shall I ensue it? Whither it hath gone before. For the Lord is our peace, hath risen again, and hath ascended into Heaven. "Seek peace, and ensue it;" because when thou also hast risen, this mortal shall be changed, and thou shalt embrace peace there where no man shall trouble thee. For there is perfect peace, where thou wilt not hunger. . . .

19. "The Eyes of the Lord are upon the righteous:" fear not then; labour; the eyes of the Lord are upon thee. "And His Ears are open unto their prayers" (ver. 15). What wouldest thou more? If an householder in a great house should not hearken to a servant murmuring, he would complain, and say, What hardship do we here suffer, and none heareth us. Canst thou say this of God, What hardships I suffer, and none heareth me? If He heard me, haply, sayest thou, He would take away my tribulation: I cry unto Him, and yet have tribulation. Only do thou hold fast His ways, and when thou art in tribulation, He heareth thee. But He is a Physician, and still hast thou something of putrefaction; thou criest out, but still He cutteth, and taketh not away His Hand, until He hath cut as much as pleaseth Him. For that Physician is cruel who heareth a man, and spareth his wound and putrefaction. How do mothers rub their children in the baths for their health. Do not the little ones cry out in their hands? Are they then cruel because they spare not, nor hearken unto their tears? Are they not full of affection? And yet the children cry out, and are not spared. So our God also is full of charity, but therefore seemeth He not to hear, that He may spare and heal us for everlasting.

20. Haply say the wicked, I securely do evil, because the Eyes of the Lord are not upon me: God attendeth to the righteous, me He seeth not, and whatever I do, I do securely. Immediately added the Holy Spirit, seeing the thoughts of men, and said, "But the Face of the Lord is against them that do evil; to cut off the remembrance of them from the earth" (ver. 16).

21. "The righteous cried, and the Lord heard them, and delivered them out of all their troubles" (ver. 17). Righteous were the Three Children; out of the furnace cried they unto the Lord, and in His praises their flames cooled. The flame could not approach nor hurt the innocent and righteous Children praising God, and He delivered them out of the fire.[1] Some one saith, Lo, truly righteous were those who were heard, as it is written, "The righteous cried, and the Lord heard them, and delivered them out of all their troubles:" but I have cried, and He delivereth me not; either I am not righteous, or I do not[2] the things which He commandeth me, or haply He seeth me not. Fear not: only do what He commandeth; and if He deliver thee not bodily, He will deliver thee spiritually. For He who took out of the fire the Three Children, did He take out of the fire the Maccabees?[3] Did not the first sing hymns in the flames, these last in the flames expire? The God of the Three Children, was not He the God also of the Maccabees? The one He delivered, the other He delivered not. Nay, He delivered both: but the Three Children He so delivered, that even the carnal were confounded; but the Maccabees therefore He delivered not so, that those who persecuted them should go into greater torments, while they thought that they had overcome God's Martyrs. He delivered Peter, when the Angel came unto him being in prison, and said, "Arise, and go forth,"[4] and suddenly his chains were loosed, and he followed the Angel, and He delivered him. Had Peter lost righteousness when He delivered him not from the cross? Did He not deliver him then? Even then He delivered him. Did his long life make him unrighteous? Haply He heard him more at last than at first, when truly He delivered him out of all his troubles. For when He first delivered him, how many things did he suffer afterwards! For thither He sent him at last, where he could have suffered no evil.

22. "The Lord is nigh unto them that have broken their heart; and saveth such as be lowly in spirit" (ver. 18). God is High: let a Christian be lowly. If he would that the Most High God draw nigh unto him, let him be lowly. A great mystery, Brethren. God is above all: thou raisest thyself, and touchest not Him: thou humblest thyself, and He descendeth unto thee. "Many are the troubles of the righteous" (ver. 19): doth He say, "Therefore let Christians be righteous, therefore let them hear My Word, that they may suffer no tribulation? He promiseth not this; but saith, "Many are the troubles of the righteous." Rather, if they be unrighteous they have fewer troubles, if righteous they have many. But after few tribulations, or none, these shall come to tribulation everlasting, whence

---

[1] Dan. iii. 28.　　[2] *Al.* "and do not."　　[3] 2 Macc. vii. 3.
[4] Acts xii. 7.

they shall never be delivered : but the righteous after many tribulations shall come to peace everlasting, where they shall never suffer any evil. "Many are the tribulations of the righteous : but the Lord delivereth him out of all."

23. "The Lord keepeth all their bones : not one of them shall be broken " (ver. 20) : this also, Brethren, let us not receive carnally. Bones are the firm supports of the faithful. For as in flesh our bones give firmness, so in the heart of a Christian it is faith that gives firmness.[1] The patience then which is in faith, is as the bones of the inner man : this is that which cannot be broken. "The Lord keepeth all their bones : not one of them shall be broken." If of our Lord God Jesus Christ he had said this, "The Lord keepeth all the bones of His Son ; not one of them shall be broken ; " as is prefigured of Him also in another place, when the lamb was spoken of that should be slain, and it was said of it, " Neither shall ye break a bone thereof : "[2] then was it fulfilled in the Lord, because when He hung upon the Cross, He expired before they came to the Cross, and found His Body lifeless already, and would not break His legs, that it might be fulfilled which was written.[3] But He gave this promise to other Christians also, "The Lord keepeth all their bones ; not one of them shall be broken." Therefore, Brethren, if we see any Saint suffer tribulation, and haply either by a Physician so cut, or by some persecutor so mangled, that his bones be broken ; let us not say, This man was not righteous, for this hath the Lord promised to His righteous, of whom He said, "The Lord keepeth all their bones ; not one of them shall be broken." Wouldest thou see that He spoke of other bones, those which we called the firm supports of faith, that is, patience and endurance in all tribulations? For these are the bones which are not broken. Hear, and see ye in the very Passion of our Lord, what I say. The Lord was in the middle Crucified ; near Him were two thieves : the one mocked, the other believed : the one was condemned, the other justified : the one had his punishment both in this world, and that which shall be, but unto the other said the Lord, " Verily I say unto thee, To-day shalt thou be with Me in Paradise ; "[4] and yet those who came brake not the bones of the Lord, but of the thieves they brake : as much were broken the bones of the thief who blasphemed, as of the thief who believed. Where then is that which is spoken, "The Lord keepeth all their bones ; not one of them shall be broken"? Lo, unto whom He said, " To-day shalt thou be with Me in Paradise," could He

keep all his bones? The Lord answereth thee : Yea, I kept them : for the firm support of his faith could not be broken by those blows whereby his legs were broken.

24. "The death of sinners is the worst" (ver. 21). Attend, Brethren, for the sake of those things which I said. Truly Great is the Lord, and His Mercy, truly Great is He who gave to us to eat His Body, wherein He suffered such great things, and His Blood to drink. How regardeth He them that think evil and say, "Such an one died ill, by beasts was he devoured : he was not a righteous man, therefore he perished ill ; for else would he not have perished." Is he then righteous who dieth in his own house and in his own bed? This then (sayest thou) it is whereat I wonder ; because I know the sins and the crimes of this same man, and yet he died well ; in his own house, within his own doors, with no injury of travel, with none even in mature [5] age. Hearken, "The death of sinners is worst." What seemeth to thee a good death, is worst if thou couldest see within. Thou seest him outwardly lying on his bed, dost thou see him inwardly carried to hell? Hearken, Brethren, and learn from the Gospel what is the "worst death" of sinners. Were there not two in that age,[6] a rich man who was clothed in purple and fine linen, and fared sumptuously every day ; another a poor man who lay at his door full of sores, and the dogs came and licked his sores, and he desired to be fed with the crumbs which fell from the rich man's table? Now it came to pass that the poor man died (righteous was that poor man), and was carried by Angels into Abraham's bosom. He who saw his body lying at the rich man's door, and no man to bury it, what haply said he? So die he who is my enemy ; and whoever persecutes me, so may I see him. His body is accursed with spitting, his wounds stink ; and yet in Abraham's bosom he resteth.[7] If we are Christians, let us believe : if we believe not, Brethren, let none feign himself a Christian. Faith bringeth us to the end. As the Lord spake these things, so are they. Doth indeed an astrologer [8] speak unto thee, and it is true, and doth Christ speak, and it is false? But by what sort of death died the rich man? What sort of death must it not be in purple and fine linen, how sumptuous, how pompous ! What funeral ceremonies were there ! In what spices was that body buried ! And yet when he was in hell, being in torments, from the finger of that despised poor man he desired one drop of water to be poured upon his burning tongue, and obtained it not. Learn then what meaneth,

---

[1] [" Let us not receive carnally " is language which reflects light upon ver. 8, p. 75, *supra*. Note also what is here said of faith. —C.]
[2] Exod. xii. 46.   [3] John xix. 33.   [4] Luke xxiii. 43.

[5] *Al.* " even at no premature."
[6] *Al.* " in this world."   [7] Luke xvi. 19–22.
[8] *Mathematicus.*

"The death of sinners is worst;" and ask not beds covered with costly garments, and to have the flesh wrapped in many rich things, friends exhibiting a show of lamentation, a household beating their breasts, a crowd of attendants going before and following when the body is carried out, marble and gilded memorials. For if ye ask those things, they answer you what is false, that of many not light sinners, but altogether wicked, the death is best, who have deserved to be so lamented, so embalmed, so covered, so carried out, so entombed. But ask the Gospel, and it will show to your faith the soul of the rich man burning in torments, which was nothing profited by all those honours and obsequies, which to his dead body the vanity of the living did afford.

25. But because there are many kinds of sinners, and not to be a sinner is difficult, or perhaps in this life impossible, he added immediately, of what kind of sinners the death is worst. "And they that hate the righteous one" (saith he) "shall perish." What righteous one, but "Him that justifieth the ungodly"?[1] Whom, but our Lord Jesus Christ, who is also "the propitiation for our sins"?[2] Who then hate Him, have the worst death; because they die in their sins, who are not through Him reconciled to our God. "For the Lord redeemeth the souls of His servants." But according to the soul is death to be understood either the worst or best, not according to bodily either dishonour, or honours which men see. "And none of them which trust in Him shall perish" (ver. 22); this is the manner of human righteousness, that mortal life, however advanced, because without sin it cannot be, in this perisheth not, while it trusteth in Him, in whom is remission of sins. Amen.

PSALM XXXV.[3]

1. . . . The title of it causeth us no delay, for it is both brief, and to be understood not difficult, especially to those nursed in the Church of God. For so it is, "To David himself." The Psalm then is to David himself: now David is interpreted, Strong in hand, or Desirable. The Psalm then is to the Strong in hand, and Desirable, to Him who for us hath overcome death, who unto us hath promised life: for in this is He Strong in hand, that He hath overcome death for us; in this is He Desirable, that He hath promised unto us life eternal. For what stronger than that Hand which touched the bier, and he that was dead rose up?[4] What stronger than that Hand which overcame the world, not armed with steel, but pierced with

wood? Or what more desirable than He, whom not having seen, the Martyrs wished even to die, that they might be worthy to come unto Him? Therefore is the Psalm unto Him: to Him let our heart, to Him our tongue sing worthily: if yet Himself shall deign to give somewhat to sing. . . .

2. "Judge Thou, O Lord" (saith he), "them that hurt me, and fight Thou against them that fight against me" (ver. 1). "If God be for us, who can be against us?"[5] And whereby doth God this for us? "Take hold" (saith he) "of arms and shield, and rise up to my help" (ver. 2). A great spectacle is it, to see God armed for thee. And what is His Shield, what are His Arms? "Lord," in another place saith the man who here also speaketh, "as with the shield of Thy good-will hast Thou compassed us."[6] But His Arms, wherewith He may not only us defend, but also strike His enemies, if we have well profited, shall we ourselves be. For as we from Him have this, that we be armed, so is He armed from us. But He is armed from those whom He hath made, we are armed with those things which we have received from Him who made us. These our arms the Apostle in a certain place calleth, "The shield of Faith, the helmet of Salvation, and the sword of the Spirit, which is the Word of God."[7] He hath armed us with such arms as ye have heard, arms admirable, and unconquered, insuperable and shining; spiritual truly and invisible, because we have to fight also against invisible enemies. If thou seest thine enemy, let thine arms be seen. We are armed with faith in those things which we see not, and we overthrow enemies whom we see not. . . .

3. "Pour forth the weapon, and stop the way against them that persecute me" (ver. 3). Who are they that persecute thee? Haply thy neighbour, or he whom thou hast offended, or to whom thou hast done wrong, or who would take away what is thine, or against whom thou preachest the truth, or whose sin thou rebukest, or whom living ill by thy well living thou offendest. There are indeed even these enemies to us, and they persecute us: but other enemies we are taught to know, those against whom we fight invisibly, of whom the Apostle warneth us, saying, "We wrestle not against flesh and blood,"[8] that is, against men; not against those whom ye see, but against those whom ye see not; "against principalities, against powers, against the rulers of the world, of this darkness." . . . "The whole world lieth in wickedness;"[9] therefore the Apostle explained of what world they were rulers, he said, "of this darkness." The rulers of this world, I say, are the rulers of this darkness. . . .

---

[1] Rom. iv. 5. [2] 1 John ii. 2.
[3] Lat. XXXIV. Delivered upon the occasion of some Council. [He begins by addressing his "fellow-bishops."—C.]
[4] Luke vii. 14.

[5] Rom. viii. 31. [6] Ps. v. 12. [7] Eph. vi. 16, 17. [8] Eph. vi. 12
[9] 1 John v. 19. [Gr. "in the Wicked One."—C.]

4. And what follows? "Let them be confounded and put to shame, that seek after my soul" (ver. 4): for to this end they seek after it, to destroy it. For I would that they would seek it for good ! for in another Psalm he blameth this in men, that there was none who would seek after his soul: "Refuge failed me: there was none that would seek after my soul."[1] Who is this that saith, "There was none that would seek after my soul"?[2] Is it haply He, of whom so long before it was predicted, "They pierced My Hands and My Feet, they numbered all My Bones, they stared and looked upon Me, they have parted My Garments among them, and cast lots for My Vesture"?[3] Now all these things were done before their eyes, and there was none who would seek after His Soul. . . .

5. . . . Many have been confounded to their health: many, put to shame, have passed over from the persecution of Christ to the society of His members with devoted piety; and this would not have been, had they not been confounded and put to shame. Therefore he wished well to them. . . . Let them not go before, but follow; let them not give counsel, but take it. For Peter would go before the Lord, when the Lord spake of His future Passion: he would to Him as it were give counsel for His health. The sick man to the Saviour give counsel for His health ! And what said he to the Lord, affirming that His future Passion? "Be it far from Thee, Lord. Be gracious to Thyself. This shall not be to Thee." He would go before that the Lord might follow; and what said He? "Get thee behind Me, Satan."[4] By going before thou art Satan, by following thou wilt be a disciple. The same then is said to these also, "Let them be turned back and brought to confusion that think evil against me." For when they have begun to follow after, now they will not think evil against me, but desire my good.

6. What of others? For all are not so conquered as to be converted and believe: many continue in obstinacy, many preserve in heart the spirit of going before, and if they exert it not, yet they labour with it, and finding opportunity bring it forth. Of such, what followeth? "Let them be as dust before the wind" (ver. 5). "Not so are the ungodly, not so; but as the dust which the wind driveth away from the face of the earth."[5] The wind is temptation; the dust are the ungodly. When temptation cometh, the dust is raised, it neither standeth nor resisteth. "Let them be as dust before the wind, and let the Angel of the Lord trouble them." "Let their way be darkness and slipping"(ver. 6). A horri-

ble way ! Darkness alone who feareth not? A slippery way alone who avoids not? In a dark and slippery way how shalt thou go? where set foot? These two ills are the great punishments of men: darkness, ignorance; a slippery way, luxury. "And let the Angel of the Lord persecute them;" that they be not able to stand. For any one in a dark and slippery way, when he seeth that if he move his foot he will fall, and there is no light before his feet, haply resolveth to wait until light come; but here is the Angel of the Lord persecuting them. These things he predicted would come upon them, not as though he wished them to happen. Although the Prophet in the Spirit of God so speaketh these things, even as God doth the same, with sure judgment, with a judgment good, righteous, holy, tranquil; not moved with wrath, not with bitter jealousy, not with desire of wreaking enmities, but of punishing wickedness with righteousness; nevertheless, it is a prophecy.

7. But wherefore these so great evils? By what desert? Hear by what desert. "For without cause have they hid for me the corruption of their trap" (ver. 7). For Him that is our Head, observe, the Jews did this: they hid the corruption of their trap. For whom hid they their trap? For Him who saw the hearts of those that hid. But yet was He among them like one ignorant, as though He were deceived, whereas they were in that deceived, that they thought Him to be deceived. For therefore was He as though deceived, living among them, because we among such as they were so to live, as to be without doubt deceived. He saw His betrayer, and chose him the more to a necessary work. By his evil He wrought a great good: and yet among the twelve was he chosen, lest even the small number of twelve should be without one evil. This was an example of patience to us, because it was necessary that we should live among the evil: it was necessary that we should endure the evil, either knowing them or knowing them not: an example of patience He gave thee lest thou shouldest fail, when thou hast begun to live among the evil. And because that School of Christ in the twelve failed not, how much more ought we to be firm, when in the great Church is fulfilled what was predicted of the mixture of the evil. . . .

8. But yet what is to be done? "Without a cause have they hid for me the corruption of their trap." What meaneth, "Without a cause"? I have done them no evil, I have hurt them not at all. "Vainly have they reviled my soul." What is, "Vainly"? Speaking falsely, proving nothing. "Let a trap come upon them which they know not of" (ver. 8). A magnificent retribution, nothing more just ! They have hidden a trap that I might know not: let a trap come

[1] Ps. cxlii. 4.
[2] "Who is," etc. Most mss. read, "That is, who asks, Who is that who is crucified? There is no one that saith, It is haply He," etc.
[3] Ps. xxii. 16-18.   [4] Matt. xvi. 22, 23.   [5] Ps. i. 4.

upon them which they know not of. For I know of their trap. But what trap is coming upon them? That which they know not of. Let us hear, lest haply he speak of that. " Let a trap come upon them, which they know not of." Perhaps that is one which they hid for him, that another which shall come upon themselves. Not so: but what? " The wicked shall be holden with the cords of his own sins." [1] Thereby are they deceived, whereby they would deceive. Thence shall come mischief to them, whence they endeavoured mischief. For it follows, " And let the net which they have hidden catch themselves, and let them fall into their own trap." As if any one should prepare a cup of poison for another, and forgetting should drink it up himself: or as if one should dig a pit, that his enemy might fall thereinto in the darkness; and himself forgetting what he had dug, should first walk that way, and fall into it. . . .

9. This then for the wicked that would hurt me: what for me? " But my soul shall rejoice in the Lord" (ver. 9); as in Him from whom it hath heard, " I am thy salvation;" as not seeking other riches from without; as not seeking to abound in pleasures and good things of earth; but loving freely the true Spouse, not from Him wishing to receive aught that may delight, but Him alone proposing to itself, by whom it may be delighted. For what better than God will be given unto me? God loveth me: God loveth thee. See He hath proposed to thee, Ask what thou wilt.[2] If the emperor should say to thee, Ask what thou wilt, what commands,[3] what dignities,[4] wouldest thou burst forth with! What great things wouldest thou propose to thyself, both to receive and to bestow! When God saith unto thee, Ask what thou wilt, what wilt thou ask? empty thy mind, exert thy avarice, stretch forward as far as possible, and enlarge thy desire: it is not any one, but Almighty God that said, Ask what thou wilt. If of possessions thou art a lover, thou wilt desire the whole earth, that all who are born may be thy husbandmen, or thy slaves. And what when thou hast possessed the whole earth? Thou wilt ask the sea, in which yet thou canst not live. In this greediness the fishes will have the better of thee. But perhaps thou wilt possess the islands. Pass over these also; ask the air, although thou canst not fly; stretch thy desire even unto the heavens, call thine own the sun, the moon, and the stars, because He who made all said, Ask what thou wilt: yet nothing wilt thou find more precious, nothing wilt thou find better, than Himself who made all things. Him seek, who made all things, and in Him and from Him shalt thou have all things which He made.

All things are precious, because all are beautiful; but what more beautiful than He? Strong are they; but what stronger than He? And nothing would He give thee rather than Himself. If aught better thou hast found, ask it. If thou ask aught else, thou wilt do wrong to Him, and harm to thyself, by preferring to Him that which He made, when He would give to thee Himself who made. . . .

" But my soul shall be joyful in the Lord; it shall rejoice in His salvation." The salvation of God is Christ: " For mine eyes have seen Thy salvation." [5]

10. " All my bones shall say, Lord, who is like unto Thee" (ver. 10). Who can speak anything worthily of these words? I think them only to be pronounced, not to be expounded. Why seekest thou this or that? What is like unto thy Lord? Him hast thou before thee. " The unrighteous have declared unto me delights, but not after Thy law, O Lord!" [6] Persecutors have been who have said, Worship Saturn, worship Mercury. I worship not idols (saith he): " Lord, who is like unto Thee? They have eyes, and see not; ears have they, but they hear not." [7] " Lord, who is like unto Thee," who hast made the eye to see, the ear to hear? But I (saith he) worship not idols, for them a workman made. Worship a tree or mountain; did a workman make them also? Here too, Lord, who is like unto Thee? Earthly things are shown unto me; Thou art Creator of the earth. And from these haply they turn to the higher creation, and say to me, Worship the Moon, worship this Sun, who with his light, as a great lamp in the Heavens, maketh the day. Here also I plainly say, " Lord, who is like unto Thee?" The Moon and the Stars Thou hast made, the Sun to rule the day hast Thou kindled, the Heavens hast Thou framed together. There are many invisible things better. But haply here also it is said to me, Worship Angels, adore Angels. And here also will I say, " Lord, who is like unto Thee?" Even the Angels Thou hast created. The Angels are nothing, but by seeing Thee. It is better with them to possess Thee, than by worshipping them to fall from Thee.

11. O Body of Christ, Holy Church, let all thy bones say, " Lord, who is like unto thee?" And if the flesh under persecution hath fallen away, let the bones say, " Lord, who is like unto Thee?" For of the righteous it is said, " The Lord keepeth all their bones; not one of them shall be broken." [8] Of how many righteous have the bones under persecution been broken? Finally, " The just shall live by faith," [9] and " Christ justifieth the ungodly." [10] But how justi-

---

[1] Prov. v. 22.   [2] Matt. vii. 7.   [3] *Tribunatus.*
[4] *Comitivas.* [Part Second begins with ver. 11.—C.]

[5] Luke ii. 30.   [6] Ps. cxix. 85.   [7] Ps. cxv. 5,6.   [8] Ps. xxxiv. 20.
[9] Rom. i. 17.   [P. 78, *supra.*—C.]   [10] Rom. iv. 5.

fieth He any except believing and confessing? "For with the heart man believeth unto righteousness, and with the mouth confession is made unto salvation."[1] Therefore also that thief, although from His theft led to the judge, and from the judge to the cross, yet on the very cross was justified: with his heart he believed, with his mouth he confessed. For neither to a man unrighteous and not already justified, would the Lord have said, "To-day shalt thou be with Me in Paradise,"[2] and yet his bones were broken. For when they came to take down the bodies, by reason of the approaching Sabbath, the Lord was found already dead, and His Bones were not broken.[3] But of those that yet lived, that they might be taken down, the legs were broken, that so from this pain having died, they might be buried. Were then of the one thief, who persisted in his ungodliness on the cross, the bones broken, and not also of the other who with his heart believed, and with his mouth made confession unto salvation? Where then is that which was said, "The Lord keepeth all his bones; not one of them shall be broken;" except that in the Body of the Lord the name of bones is given to all the righteous, the firm in heart, the strong, yielding to no persecutions, no temptations, so as to consent unto evil? . . .

12. "Which deliverest the poor from him that is too strong for him; yea, the poor and needy from him that spoileth him." . . . Who that deliverest, but He who is Strong in hand? Even that David shall deliver the poor from him that is too strong for him. For the devil was too strong for thee, and held thee, because he conquered thee, when thou consentedst unto him. But what hath the Strong in hand done? "No man entereth into a strong man's house, to spoil his goods, except he first bind the strong man."[4] By His own Power, most Holy, most Magnificent, hath He bound the devil by pouring forth the weapon to stop the way against him, that He may deliver the poor and needy, to whom there was no helper.[5] For who is thy helper but the Lord to whom thou sayest, "O Lord, My Strength, and My Redeemer."[6] If thou wilt presume of thy own strength, thereby wilt thou fall, whereof thou hast presumed: if of another's, he would lord it over thee, not succour thee. He then alone is to be sought Who hath redeemed them, and made them free, and hath given His Blood to purchase them, and of His servants hath made them His Brethren. . . .

13. Let then our Head say, "False witnesses did rise up, they laid to My charge things that I knew not" (ver. 11). But let us say to our Head, Lord, what knewest Thou not? Didst Thou indeed know not anything? Didst Thou not know the hearts of them that charged Thee? Didst Thou not foresee their deceits? Didst Thou not give Thyself into their hands knowingly? Hadst Thou not come that Thou mightest suffer by them? What then knewest Thou not? He knew not sin, and thereby He knew not sin, not by not judging, but by not committing. There are phrases of this kind also in daily use, as when thou sayest of any one, He knoweth not to stand, that is, he doth not stand; and, He knoweth not to do good, because he doth not good; and, He knoweth not to do ill, because he doth not ill. . . . What knew not Christ so much, as to blaspheme? Thereof was He called in question by His persecutors, and because He spake truth, He was judged to have spoken blasphemy.[7] But by whom? By them of whom it followeth, "They rewarded Me evil for good, and barrenness to My Soul" (ver. 12). I gave unto them fruitfulness, they rewarded Me barrenness; I gave life, they death; I honour, they dishonour; I medicine, they wounds; and in all these which they rewarded Me, was truly barrenness. This barrenness in the tree He cursed, when seeking fruit He found none.[8] Leaves there were, and fruit there was not: words there were, and deeds there were not. See of words abundance, and of deeds barrenness. "Thou that preachest a man should not steal, stealest: thou that sayest a man should not commit adultery, committest adultery."[9] Such were they who charged Christ with things that He knew not.

14. "But I, when they troubled me, clothed myself with sackcloth, and humbled my soul with fasting, and my prayer shall return into mine own bosom" (ver. 13). . . . Brethren, if for some little space with pious curiosity we lift the veil, and search with the intent eye of the heart the inner part of this Scripture, we find that even this the Lord did. Sackcloth, haply He calleth His mortal flesh. Wherefore Sackcloth? For the likeness of sinful flesh. For the Apostle saith, "God sent His Son in the likeness of sinful flesh, that through sin He might condemn sin in the flesh:"[10] that is, He clothed His Own Son with sackcloth, that through sackcloth[11] He might condemn the goats. Not that there was sin, I say not in the Word of God, but not even in that Holy Soul and Mind of a Man, which the Word and Wisdom of God had so joined to Himself as to be One Person. Nay, nor even in His very Body was any sin, but the likeness of sinful flesh there was in the Lord; because death is not but by sin,[12] and surely that Body was mortal. For

---

[1] Rom. x. 10. [2] Luke xxiii. 43. [3] John xix. 33.
[4] Matt. xii. 29. [5] Ps. lxxii. 12. [6] Ps. xix. 14.

[7] Matt. xxvi. 65. [8] Matt. xxi. 19. [9] Rom. ii. 21, 22.
[10] Rom. viii. 3.
[11] Lat. de cilicio; i.e., sackcloth made of goats' hair. [Acts xvii. 3 and xxi. 39. — C.] Compare Matt. xxv. 32, 33.
[12] Rom. v. 12.

had It not been mortal, It had not died; had It not died, It had not risen again; had It not risen again, It had not showed us an example of eternal life. So then death, which is caused by sin, is called sin; as we say the Greek tongue, the Latin tongue, meaning not the very member of flesh, but that which is done by the member of flesh. For the tongue in our members is one among others, as the eyes, nose, ears, and the rest: but the Greek tongue is Greek words, not that the tongue is words, but that words are by the tongue. . . . So then the sin of the Lord is that which was caused by sin; because He assumed flesh, of the same lump which had deserved death by sin. For to speak more briefly, Mary who was of Adam died for sin,[1] Adam died for sin, and the Flesh of the Lord which was of Mary died to put away sin. With this sackcloth the Lord clothed Himself, and therefore was He not known, because He lay hid under sackcloth. "When they," saith He, "troubled Me, I clothed Myself with sackcloth:" that is, they raged, I lay hid. For had He not willed to lie hid, neither could He have died, since in one moment of time one drop only of His Power, if indeed it is to be called a drop, He put forth, when they wished to seize Him, and at His one question, "Whom seek ye?" they all went back and fell to the ground.[2] Such power could He not have humbled in passion, if He had not lain hid under sackcloth.

15. Again, if we have understood the sackcloth, how understand we the fasting? Wished Christ to eat, when He sought fruit on the tree,[3] and if He had found, would He have eaten? Wished Christ to drink, when He said to the woman of Samaria, "Give Me to drink"?[4] when He said on the Cross, "I thirst"?[5] For what hungered, for what thirsted Christ, but our good works? Because in them that crucified and persecuted Him He had found no good works, He fasted; for they rewarded barrenness to His soul. For what a fast was His, who found barely one thief, whom on the Cross He might taste! For the Apostles had fled, and had hidden themselves in the multitude. And even Peter, who even to the death of his Lord had promised to persevere, had now thrice denied Him, had now wept, and still lay hid in the multitude, still feared lest He should be known. Lastly, having seen Him dead, all of them despaired of their own safety; and despairing He found them, after His resurrection, and when He spake with them, found them grieving and mourning, no longer hoping anything. . . . In great fasting had the Lord

remained, had He not refreshed them that He might feed on them. For He refreshed them, He comforted them, He confirmed them, and into His Own Body converted them. In this manner then was our Lord also in fasting.

16. "And My prayer shall return into Mine Own Bosom." In the bosom of this verse is plainly a great depth, and may the Lord grant that it be fathomable by us. For in the "bosom" a secret is understood. And we ourselves, Brethren, are here well admonished to pray within our own bosom, where God seeth, where God heareth, where no human eye penetrateth, where none seeth but He who succoureth; where Susanna prayed, and her voice, though it was not heard by men, yet by God was heard.[6] . . . We read also that in the mount Jesus prayed alone,[7] we read that He passed the night in prayer,[8] even at the time of His Passion.[9] What then? "And My prayer shall return into Mine Own Bosom." I know not what better to understand concerning the Lord: take meanwhile what now occurs;[10] perhaps something better will occur hereafter, either to me or to some better: "My prayer shall return into Mine Own Bosom:" this I understand to be said, because in His Own Bosom He had the Father. "For God was in Christ reconciling the world unto Himself."[11] In Himself He had Him to whom He prayed. He was not far from Him, for Himself had said, "I am in the Father, and the Father in Me."[12] But because prayer rather belongeth to very Man (for according as Christ is the Word, He prayeth not, but heareth prayer; and seeketh not to be succoured for Himself, but with the Father succoureth all): what is, "My prayer shall return into Mine Own Bosom," but in Me My Manhood invoketh in Me My Godhead.

17. "As a Neighbour, as our Brother, so I pleased Him: as one mourning and sorrowful, so I humbled myself" (ver. 14). Now looketh He back to His Own Body: let us now look to this. When we rejoice in prayer, when our mind is calmed, not by the world's prosperity, but by the light of Truth: (who perceiveth this light, knoweth what I say, and he seeth and acknowledgeth what is said, "As a Neighbour, as our Brother, so I pleased Him") : even then our soul pleaseth God, not placed afar off, for, "In Him," saith one, "we live and move and have our being,"[13] but as a Brother, as a Neighbour, as a Friend. But if it be not such that it can so rejoice, so shine, so approach, so cleave unto Him, and seeth itself far off thence, then let it do what followeth, "As one mourning and

---

[1] ["All, *without one exception*, were dead in sins." See (*City of God*, book xx. cap. 6) vol ii. p. 425, *supra*. Mary is not excepted by any of the Fathers; and the Latin Fathers, the last of whom is St. Bernard, unanimously ascribe to Christ the only immaculate conception. — C.]

[2] John xviii. 4, 6.　　[3] Mark xi. 13.　　[4] John iv. 7.

[5] John xix. 28. [On *assimilation*, compare p. 86, n. 2. — C.]

[6] Susanna i. 35, 44.　　　　　　[7] Matt. xiv. 23.

[8] Luke vi. 12.　[9] Matt. xxvi. 36; Mark xiv. 35; Luke xxii. 41.

[10] [A significant hint of the improvised character of many of the saint's expositions. — C.]

[11] 2 Cor. v. 19.　　[12] John xiv. 10.　　[13] Acts xvii. 28.

sorrowful, so I humbled Myself. As our Brother, so I pleased Him," said He, drawing near; "As one mourning and sorrowful, so I humbled Myself," said He, removed and set afar off. . . . Did not Peter draw near, when he said, "Thou art the Christ, the Son of the Living God"? And yet the same man became afar off by saying, "Be it far from Thee, Lord; this shall not be unto Thee." Lastly, what said He, his Neighbour, as it were, to him drawing near? "Blessed art thou, Simon, Barjona." To him afar off, as it were, and unlike, what said He? "Get thee behind Me, Satan."[1] To him drawing near, "Flesh and blood," saith He, "hath not revealed it unto thee, but My Father, which is in Heaven." His Light is shed over thee, in His Light thou shinest. But when having become afar off, he spake against the Lord's Passion, which should be for our Salvation, "Thou savourest not," said He, "the things that be of God, but those that be of men." One rightly placing together both of these saith in a certain Psalm, "I said in my ecstasy, I am cast off from before Thine Eyes."[2] In my ecstasy, would he not have said, had he not drawn near; for ecstasy is the transporting of the mind. He poured over himself his own soul, and drew near unto God; and through some cloud and weight of the flesh being again cast down to earth, and recollecting where he had been, and seeing where he was, he said, "I am cast off from before Thine Eyes." This then, "As a Neighbour, as our Brother, so I pleased Him," may He grant to be done in us; but when that is not, let even this be done, "As one mourning and sorrowful, so I humbled myself."

18. And against Me they rejoiced, and gathered themselves together"[3] (ver. 15), against Me only: they rejoicing, I sorrowful. But we heard just now in the Gospel, "Blessed are they that mourn."[4] If they are blessed that mourn, miserable are they that laugh. "Against Me they rejoiced, and gathered themselves together: scourges were gathered together against Me, and they knew not."[5] Because they laid to My charge things that I knew not, they also knew not Whom they charged.

19. "They tempted Me, and mocked Me with mocking"[6] (ver. 16). That is, they derided Me, they insulted Me; this of the Head, this of the Body. Consider, Brethren, the glory of the Church which now is; remember its past dishonours, remember how once were Christians

everywhere put to flight, and wherever found, mocked, beaten, slain, exposed to beasts, burned, men rejoicing against them. As it was to the Head, so it is also to the Body. For as it was to the Lord on the Cross, so has it been to His Body in all that persecution which was made but now: nor even now cease the persecutions of the same. Wherever men find a Christian, they are wont to insult, to persecute, to deride him, to call him dull, senseless, of no spirit, of no knowledge. Do they what they will, Christ is in Heaven: do they what they will, He hath honoured His punishment, already hath He fixed His Cross in the foreheads of all; the ungodly is permitted to insult, to rage he is not permitted; but yet from that which the tongue uttereth, is understood what he beareth in his heart: "They gnashed upon Me with their teeth."

20. "Lord, when wilt Thou look on? Rescue My Soul from their deceits, My Darling from the lions" (ver. 17). For to us the time is slow; and in our person is this said, "When wilt Thou look on?" that is, when shall we see vengeance upon those who insult us? When shall the Judge, overcome by weariness, hear the widow?[7] But our Judge, not from weariness, but from love, delayeth our salvation; from reason, not from need; not that He could not even now succour us, but that the number of us all may be filled up even to the end. And yet out of our desire, what do we say? "Lord, when wilt Thou look on? Rescue My Soul from their deceits, My Darling from the lions:" that is, My Church from raging powers.

21. Lastly, wouldest thou know what is that Darling? Read the words following: "I will confess unto Thee, O Lord, in the great Congregation; in a weighty[8] people will I praise Thee" (ver. 18). Truly saith He, "I will confess unto Thee:" for confession is made in all the multitude, but not in all is God praised: the whole multitude heareth our confession,[9] but not in all the multitude is the praise of God. For in all the whole multitude, that is, in the Church which is spread abroad in the whole world, is chaff, and wheat: the chaff flieth, the wheat remaineth; therefore, "in a weighty people will I praise Thee." In a weighty people, which the wind of temptation carries not away, in such is God praised. For in the chaff He is ever blasphemed. . . .

22. "Let not them that are Mine enemies wrongfully rejoice over Me:" for they rejoice over Me because of My chaff. "Who hate Me without a cause;" that is, whom I never hurt;

---

[1] Matt. xvi. 16–23.   [2] Ps. xxxii. 22. [See p. 70, *supra*.]
[3] E. V. "But in mine adversity they rejoiced and gathered themselves together."
[4] Matt. v. 5.
[5] E. V. "Yea, the abjects gathered themselves together against me, and I knew it not."
[6] E. V. "They did tear Me and ceased not:" 16. "With hypocritical mockers in feasts, they gnashed upon Me with their teeth." The words here omitted are mentioned on Ps. lvii. — *Ben.*

[7] Luke xviii. 3.   [8] Latin, "in populo *gravi*."
[9] [The recitation of the Creed, perhaps; but in the ancient Church the confession of sin, also, was public. Bingham, b. xviii. cap. 3. — C.]

"winking with their eyes" (ver. 19): that is, pretending hypocrites, "For they spake indeed peace to Me" (ver. 20). What is, "winking with their eyes"? Declaring by their looks, what they carry not in their heart. And who are these "winking with their eyes"? "For they spake indeed peace to Me; and with wrath devised craftily." "Yea they opened their mouth wide against Me" (ver. 21). First winking with their eyes, those lions sought to ravish and devour; first fawning they spake peace, and then with wrath devised craftily. What peace spake they? "Master, we know that Thou acceptest not man's person, and teachest the way of God in truth. Is it lawful to give tribute unto Cæsar, or not?" They spake indeed peace unto Me. What then? Didst not Thou know them, and deceived they Thee, winking with their eyes? Truly He knew them; therefore said He, "Why tempt ye Me, ye hypocrites?"[1] Afterward, "they opened their mouth wide against Me," crying, "Crucify Him, Crucify Him!"[2] and said, Aha, Aha, our eyes have seen it." This, when they insulted Him, "Aha, Aha, Prophesy unto us, Thou Christ."[3] As their peace was pretended when they tempted Him concerning the money, so now insulting was their praise. "They said, Aha, Aha, our eyes have seen it" (ver. 21): that is, Thy deeds, Thy miracles. This Man is the Christ. "If He be the Christ, let Him come down from the Cross, and we will believe Him. He saved others, Himself He cannot save."[4] "Our eyes have seen it." This is all whereof He boasted Himself, when "He called Himself the Son of God."[5] But the Lord was hanging patient upon the Cross: His power had He not lost, but He showed His patience. For what great thing was it for Him to come down from the Cross, who could afterward rise again from the sepulchre? But He seems to have yielded to His insulters; and this, beloved, that having risen again He should show Himself to His own, and not to them, and this is a great mystery; for His resurrection signified the New Life, but the New Life is known to His friends, not to His enemies.

23. "This Thou hast seen, O Lord; keep not silence" (ver. 22). What is, "keep not silence"? Judge Thou. For of judgment is it said in a certain place,[6] "I have kept silence; shall I keep silence for ever?" And of the delaying of judgment it is said to the sinner, "These things hast thou done, and I kept silence;" "Thou thoughtest that I was altogether such an one as thyself."[7] How keepeth He silence, who speaketh by the Prophets, who speaketh with His own mouth in the Gospel, who speaketh by the Evangelists, who speaketh by us, when we speak the truth? What then? He keepeth silence from judgment, not from precept, not from doctrine. But this His judgment the Prophet in a manner invoketh, and predicteth: "Thou hast seen, O Lord: keep not silence;" that is, Thou wilt not keep silence, needs must that Thou wilt judge. "O Lord, be not far from Me." Until Thy judgment come, be not far from Me, as Thou hast promised, "Lo, I am with you alway, even unto the end of the world."

24. "Arise, Lord, and attend to My judgment" (ver. 23). To what judgment? That Thou art in tribulation; that Thou art tormented with labours and pains? Do not even many wicked men suffer the same? To what judgment? Therefore art Thou righteous, because Thou sufferest these things? No: but what? "To My judgment." What followeth? "Attend to My judgment; even to My cause, My God, and My Lord." Not to My punishment, but to My cause: not to that which the robber hath in common with Me, but to that whereof is said, "Blessed are they which are persecuted for righteousness' sake."[8] For this cause is distinguished. For punishment is equal to good and bad. Therefore Martyrs, not the punishment, but the cause maketh, for if punishment made Martyrs, all the mines would be full of Martyrs, every chain would drag Martyrs, all that are executed with the sword would be crowned. Therefore let the cause be distinguished; let none say, because I suffer, I am righteous. Because He who first suffered, suffered for righteousness' sake, therefore He added a great exception, "Blessed are they which are persecuted for righteousness' sake." For many having a good cause do persecution, and many having a bad cause suffer persecution. For if persecution could not be done rightly, it had not been said in a certain Psalm, "Whoso privily slandereth his neighbour, him did I persecute."[9] . . . Let none then say, I suffer persecution: let him not sift the punishment, but prove the cause: lest if he prove not the cause, he be numbered with the ungodly. Therefore how watchfully, how excellently hath This Man recommended Himself, "O Lord, attend to My judgment," not to My punishments; "even to My cause, My God, and My Lord."

25. "Judge me, O Lord, according to My righteousness" (ver. 24); that is, attend to My cause. Not according to My punishment, but "according to My righteousness, O Lord, My God," that is, according to this judge Thou Me. "And let them not rejoice over Me;" that is, Mine enemies.

[1] Matt. xxii. 16–18.　　[2] Luke xxiii. 21.　　[3] Matt. xxvi. 68.
[4] Matt. xxvii. 42; Luke xxiii. 35.　　[5] John xix. 7.
[6] Isa. xlii. 14, Sept.　　[7] Ps. l. 21.

[8] Matt. v. 10.　　　　　[9] Ps. ci. 5.

26. "Let them not say in their heart, Aha, aha, so would we have it" (ver. 25); that is, We have done what we could,[1] we have slain him, we have taken him away. "Let them not say:" show them that they have done nothing. "Let them not say, We have swallowed him up." Whence say those Martyrs, "If the Lord had not been on our side, then they had swallowed us up quick."[2] What is, "had swallowed us up"? Had passed into their own body. For that thou swallowest up, which thou passest into thy own body. The world would swallow thee up; swallow thou the world, pass it into thy own body : kill and eat. As it was said to Peter, "Kill and eat;"[3] do thou kill in them what they are, make them what thou art. But if they on the other hand persuade thee to ungodliness, thou art swallowed up by them. Not when they persecute thee art thou swallowed up by them, but when they persuade thee to be what they are. "Let them not say, We have swallowed him up." Do thou swallow up the body of Pagans. Why the body of Pagans? It would swallow thee up. Do thou to it, what it would to thee. Therefore perhaps that calf, being ground to powder, was cast into the water and given to the children of Israel to drink,[4] that so the body of ungodliness might be swallowed up by Israel. "Let them be ashamed and brought to confusion together that rejoice at mine hurt : let them be clothed with shame and dishonour" (ver. 26) ; so that we may swallow up them ashamed and brought to confusion. "Who speak evil against me :" let them be ashamed, let them be brought to confusion.

27. What sayest thou now, the Head with the Members? "Let them shout for joy and be glad that favour My righteous cause :" who cleave to My Body. Yea, let them say "continually, Let the Lord be magnified, which hath pleasure in the prosperity of His servant" (ver. 27). "And my tongue shall speak of Thy righteousness, and of Thy praise all the day long" (ver. 28). And whose tongue endureth to speak the praise of God all the day long? See now I have made a discourse something longer ; ye are wearied. Who endureth to praise God all the day long? I will suggest a remedy, whereby thou mayest praise God all the day long if thou wilt. Whatever thou dost, do well, and thou hast praised God. When thou singest an hymn, thou praisest God, but what doth thy tongue, unless thy heart also praise Him? Hast thou ceased from singing hymns, and departed, that thou mayest refresh thyself? Be not drunken, and thou hast praised God. Dost thou go away to sleep? Rise not to do evil, and thou hast praised God. Dost thou transact business? Do no wrong, and thou hast praised God. Dost thou till thy field? Raise not strife, and thou hast praised God. In the innocency of thy works prepare thyself to praise God all the day long.

PSALM XXXVI.[5]

1. . . . "The ungodly hath said in himself that he will sin : there is no fear of God before his eyes" (ver. 1). Not of one man, but of a race of ungodly men he speaketh, who fight against their own selves, by not understanding, that so they may live well ; not because they cannot, but because they will not. For it is one thing, when one endeavours to understand some thing, and through infirmity of flesh cannot ; as saith the Scripture[6] in a certain place, "For the corruptible body presseth down the soul, and the earthly tabernacle weigheth down the mind that museth upon many things ;" but another when the human heart acts mischievously against itself, so that what it could understand, if it had but good will thereto, it understandeth not, not because it is difficult, but because the will is contrary. But so it is when men love their own sins, and hate God's Commandments. For the Word of God is thy adversary, if thou be a friend to thy ungodliness ; but if thou art an adversary to thy ungodliness, the Word of God is thy friend, as well as the adversary of thy ungodliness. . . .

2. "For he hath wrought deceitfully in His sight" (ver. 2). In whose sight? In His, whose fear was not before the eyes of him that did work deceitfully. "To find out his iniquity, and hate it." He wrought so as not to find it. For there are men who as it were endeavour to seek out their iniquity, and fear to find it ; because if they should find it, it is said to them, Depart from it : this thou didst before thou knewest ; thou didst iniquity being in ignorance ; God giveth pardon : now thou hast discovered it, forsake it, that to thy ignorance pardon may easily be given ; and that with a clear face thou mayest say to God, "Remember not the sins of my youth, and of my ignorance."[7] Thus he seeketh it, thus he feareth lest he find it ; for he seeketh it deceitfully. When saith a man, I knew not that it was sin? When he hath seen that it is sin, and ceaseth to do the sin, which he did only because he was ignorant : such an one in truth would know his sin, to find it out, and hate it. But now many "work deceitfully to find out their iniquity :" they work not from their heart to find it out and hate it. But because in the very search after iniquity, there is

---

[1] Al. "We have done it, we have prevailed" (potuimus).
[2] Ps. cxxiv. 1–3.   [3] Acts x. 13.   [4] Exod. xxxii. 20.

[5] Lat. XXXV.
[6] Wisd. ix. 15. [Here cited as Scripture, but only deutero-canonical (as St. Jerome testifies), illustrating the Law and the Prophets, but not of authority in itself. — C.]
[7] Ps. xxv. 7.

deceit, in the finding it there will be defence of it. For when one hath found his iniquity, lo now it is manifest to him that it is iniquity. Do it not, thou sayest. And he who wrought deceitfully to find it out, now he hath found, hateth it not; for what saith he? How many do this! Who is there that doth it not? And will God destroy them all? Or at least he saith this: if God would not these things to be done, would men live who commit the same? Seest thou that thou didst work deceitfully to find out thy iniquity? For if not deceitfully but sincerely thou hadst wrought, thou wouldest now have found it out, and hated it; now thou hast found it out, and thou defendest it; therefore thou didst work deceitfully, when thou soughtest it.

3. "The words of his mouth are iniquity and deceit: he would not understand, that he might do good" (ver. 3). Ye see that he attributeth that to the will: for there are men who would understand and cannot, and there are men who would not understand, and therefore understand not. "He would not understand, that he might do good."

4. "He hath meditated iniquity on his bed." What said He, "On his bed?" (ver. 4). "The ungodly hath said in himself, that he will sin:" what above he said, in himself, that here he said, "On his bed." Our bed is our heart: there we suffer the tossing of an evil conscience; and there we rest when our conscience is good. Whoso loveth the bed of his heart, let him do some good therein. There is our bed, where the Lord Jesus Christ commands us to pray. "Enter into thy chamber, and shut thy door." [1] What is, "Shut thy door?" Expect not from God such things as are without, but such as are within; "and thy Father which seeth in secret, shall reward thee openly." Who is he that shutteth not the door? He who asketh much from God such things, and in such wise directeth all his prayers, that he may receive the goods that are of this world. Thy door is open, the multitude seeth when thou prayest. What is it to shut thy door? To ask that of God, which God alone knoweth how He giveth. What is that for which thou prayest, when thou hast shut the door? What "eye hath not seen, nor ear heard, nor hath entered into the heart of man." [2] And haply it hath not entered into thy very bed, that is, into thy heart. But God knoweth what He will give: but when shall it be? When the Lord shall be revealed, when the Judge shall appear. . . .

5. "He hath set himself in every way that is not good." What is, "he hath set himself"? He hath sinned perseveringly. Whence also of a certain pious and good man it is said, "He

hath not stood in the way of sinners." [3] As this "hath not stood," so that "hath set himself." "But wickedness hath he not hated." There is the end, there the fruit: if a man cannot but have wickedness, let him at least hate it. For when thou hatest it, it scarcely occurs to thee to do any wickedness. For sin is in our mortal body, but what saith the Apostle? "Let not sin reign in your mortal body, that ye should obey it in the lusts thereof." [4] When beginneth it not to be therein? When that shall be fulfilled in us which he saith, "When this corruptible shall have put on incorruption, and this mortal shall have put on immortality." [5] Before this come to pass, there is a delighting in sin in the body, but greater is the delighting and the pleasure in the Word of Wisdom, in the Commandment of God. Overcome sin and the lust thereof. Sin and iniquity do thou hate, that thou mayest join thyself to God, who hateth it as well as thou. Now being joined in mind unto the Law of God, in mind thou servest the Law of God. And if in the flesh thou therefore servest [6] the law of sin, [7] because there are in thee certain carnal delightings, then will there be none when thou shalt no longer fight. It is one thing not to fight, and to be in true and lasting peace; another to fight and overcome; another to fight and to be overcome; another not to fight at all, but to be carried away. . . .

6. "Thy mercy, O Lord, is in the heavens, and Thy truth reacheth even unto the clouds" (ver. 5). I know not what Mercy of Him he meaneth, which is in the heavens. For the Mercy of the Lord is also in the earth. Thou hast it written, "The earth is full of the Mercy of the Lord." [8] Of what Mercy then speaketh He, when He saith, "Thy Mercy, O Lord, is in the heavens"? The gifts of God are partly temporal and earthly, partly eternal and heavenly. Whoso for this worshippeth God, that he may receive those temporal and earthly goods, which are open to all, is still as it were like the brutes: he enjoyeth indeed the Mercy of God, but not that which is excepted, which shall not be given, save only to the righteous, to the holy, to the good. What are the gifts which abound to all? "He maketh His sun to rise on the evil and on the good, and sendeth rain on the just and on the unjust." [9] Who hath not this Mercy of God, first that he hath being, that he is distinguished from the brutes, that he is a rational animal, so as to understand God; secondly, that he enjoys this light, this air, rain, fruits, diversity of seasons, and all the earthly comforts, health of body, the affection of friends, the safety of his

---

[3] Ps. i. 1.   [4] Rom. vi. 12.   [5] 1 Cor. xv. 54.
[6] i.e., "art subject to it," not "obeyest it." He is not here speaking of actual wilful sin, but of motions toward sin to which the man does not consent. [Concupiscence, art. ix. Angl. XXXIX. Articles. — C.]
[7] Rom. vii. 25.   [8] Ps. xxxiii. 5.   [9] Matt. v. 45.

---

[1] Matt. vi. 6.   [2] Isa. lxiv. 4; 1 Cor. ii. 9.

family? All these are good, and they are God's gifts. . . .

7. But this man rightly understood what mercy he should pray for from God. "Thy Mercy, O Lord, is in the Heavens; and Thy Truth reacheth even to the clouds." That is, the Mercy which Thou givest to Thy Saints, is Heavenly, not earthly; is Eternal, not temporal. And how couldest Thou declare it unto men? Because "Thy Truth reacheth even unto the clouds." For who could know the Heavenly Mercy of God, unless God should declare it unto men? How did He declare it? By sending His truth even unto the clouds. What are the clouds? The Preachers of the Word of God. . . . Truth reached even to the clouds: therefore unto us could be declared the Mercy of God, which is in Heaven and not in earth. And truly, Brethren, the clouds are the Preachers of the Word of Truth. When God threateneth through His Preachers, He thunders through the clouds. When God worketh miracles through His Preachers, He lightneth through the clouds, He terrifieth through the clouds, and watereth by the rain. Those Preachers, then, by whom is preached the Gospel of God, are the clouds of God. Let us then hope for Mercy, but for that which is in the Heavens.

8. "Thy Righteousness is like the mountains of God: Thy Judgments are a great deep" (ver. 6). Who are the mountains of God? Those who are called clouds, the same are also the mountains of God. The great Preachers are the mountains of God. And as when the sun riseth, he first clothes the mountains with light, and thence the light descends to the lowest parts of the earth: so our Lord Jesus Christ, when He came, first irradiated the height of the Apostles, first enlightened the mountains, and so His Light descended to the valley of the world. And therefore saith He in a certain Psalm, "I lifted up mine eyes unto the mountains, from whence cometh my help."[1] But think not that the mountains themselves will give thee help: for they receive what they may give, give not of their own. And if thou remain in the mountains, thy hope will not be strong: but in Him who enlighteneth the mountains, ought to be thy hope and presumption. Thy help indeed will come to thee through the mountains, because the Scriptures are administered to thee through the mountains, through the great Preachers of the Truth: but fix not thy hope in them. Hear what He saith next following: "I lifted up mine eyes unto the mountains, from whence cometh my help." What then? Do the mountains give thee help? No; hear what follows, "My help cometh from the Lord, which made Heaven and earth."[2]

Through the mountains cometh help, but not from the mountains. From whom then? "From the Lord, which made Heaven and earth." . . .

9. "Thy Judgments are like the great abyss." The abyss he calleth the depth of sin, whither every one cometh by despising God; as in a certain place it is said, "God gave them over to their own hearts' lusts, to do the things which are not convenient."[3] . . . Because then they were proud and ungrateful, they were held worthy to be delivered up to the lusts of their own hearts, and became a great abyss, so that they not only sinned, but also worked craftily, lest they should understand their iniquity, and hate it. That is the depth of wickedness, to be unwilling to find it out and to hate it. But how one cometh to that depth, see; "Thy Judgments are the great abyss." As the mountains are by the Righteousness of God,[4] who through His Grace become great: so also through His Judgments come they unto the depth, who sink lowest. By this then let the mountains delight thee, by this turn away from the abyss, and turn thyself unto that, of which it is said, "My help cometh from the Lord." But whereby? "I have lifted up mine eyes unto the mountains." What meaneth this? I will speak plainly.[5] In the Church of God thou findest an abyss, thou findest also mountains; thou findest there but few good, because fhe mountains are few, the abyss broad; that is, thou findest many living ill after the wrath of God, because they have so worked that they are delivered up to the lusts of their own heart; so now they defend their sins and confess them not; but say, Why? What have I done? Such an one did this, and such an one did that. Now will they even defend what the Divine Word reproves. This is the abyss. Therefore in a certain place[6] saith the Scripture (hear this abyss), "The sinner when he cometh unto the depth of sin despiseth." See, "Thy Judgments are like the great abyss." But yet not art thou a mountain; not yet art thou in the abyss; fly from the abyss, tend towards the mountains; but yet remain not on the mountains. "For thy help cometh from the Lord, which made Heaven and earth."

10. Because he said, Thy Mercy is in the Heavens, that it may be known to be also on earth, he said, "O Lord, Thou savest man and beast,[7] as Thy Mercy is multiplied, O God" (ver. 7). Great is Thy Mercy, and manifold is Thy Mercy, O God; and that showest Thou both to man and beast. For from whom is the saving of men? From God. Is not the saving of beasts also from God? For He who made

---

[1] Ps. cxxi. 1.   [2] Ps. cxxi. 2.

[3] Rom. i. 28.
[4] Al. "The Righteousness of God is like the mountains."
[5] Latinè.   [6] Prov. xviii. 3.
[7] [In Vulgate and Septuagint this is included in verse 6. The English Version agrees with the text as here connected.—C.]

man, made also beasts; He who made both, saveth both; but the saving of beasts is temporal. But there are who as a great thing ask this of God, which He hath given to beasts. "Thy Mercy, O God, is multiplied," so that not only unto men, but unto beasts also is given the same saving which is given to men, a carnal and temporal saving.

11. Have not men then somewhat reserved with God, which beasts deserve not, and whereunto beasts arrive not? They have evidently. And where is that which they have. "The children of men put their trust under the shadow of Thy wings." Attend, my Beloved, to this most pleasant sentence: "Thou savest man and beast." First, he spake of "man and beast," then of "the children of men;" as though "men" were one, "the children of men" other. Sometimes in Scripture children of men is said generally of all men, sometimes in some proper manner, with some proper signification, so that not all men are understood; chiefly when there is a distinction. For not without reason is it here put; "O Lord, Thou savest man and beast: but the children of men;" as though setting aside the first, he keepeth separate the children of men. Separate from whom? Not only from beasts, but also from men, who seek from God the saving of beasts, and desire this as a great thing. Who then are the children of men? Those who put their trust under the shadow of His wings. For those men together with beasts rejoice in possession, but the children of men rejoice in hope: those follow after present goods with beasts, these hope for future goods with Angels. . . .

12. "They shall be satiated[1] with the fulness of Thy House" (ver. 8). He promiseth us some great thing. He would speak it, and He speaketh it not. Can He not, or do not we receive it? I dare, my Brethren, to say, even of holy tongues and hearts, by which Truth is declared to us, that it can neither be spoken, which they declared, nor even thought of. For it is a great thing, and ineffable; and even they saw through a glass darkly, as saith the Apostle, "For now we see through a glass darkly; but then face to face."[2] Lo, they who saw through a glass darkly, thus burst forth. What then shall we be, when we shall see face to face? That with which they travailed in heart, and could not with their tongue bring forth, that men might receive it. For what necessity was there that he should say, "They shall be satiated with the fulness of Thy House"? He sought a word whereby to express from human things what he would say; and because he saw that men drowning themselves in drunkenness receive indeed wine without measure, but lose their senses, he saw what to say; for when shall have been received that ineffable joy, then shall be lost in a manner the human soul, it shall become Divine, and be satiated with the fulness of God's House. Wherefore also in another Psalm it is said, "Thy cup inebriating, how excellent is it!"[3] With this cup were the Martyrs satiated when going to their passion, they knew not their own. What so inebriated as not to know a wife weeping, not children, not parents? They knew them not they thought not that they were before their eyes. Wonder not: they were inebriated Wherewith were they so? Lo, they had received a cup wherewith they were satiated Wherefore he also gives thanks to God, saying "What shall I render unto the Lord for all His benefits towards me? I will take the cup of Salvation, and call upon the Name of the Lord." Therefore, Brethren of men," let us be "children and let us trust under the shadow of His wings and be satiated with the fulness of His House As I could, I have spoken; and as far as I can I see; and how far I see, I cannot speak. "And of the torrent of Thy Pleasure shalt Thou give them to drink." A torrent we call water coming with a flood. There will be a flood of God's Mercy to overflow and inebriate those who now put their trust under the shadow of His wings. What is that Pleasure? As it were a torrent inebriating the thirsty. Let him then who thirsts now, lay up hope: whoso thirsts now, let him have hope; when inebriated, he shall have possession: before he have possession, let him thirst in hope. "Blessed are they which do hunger and thirst after righteousness, for they shall be filled."[6]

13. With what fountain then wilt thou be overflowed, and whence runneth such a torrent of His Pleasure? "For with Thee," saith he, "is the fountain of Life." What is the fountain of Life, but Christ? He came to thee in the flesh, that He might bedew thy thirsty lips: He will satisfy thee trusting, who bedewed thee thirsting. "For with Thee is the fountain of Life; in Thy Light shall we see light" (ver. 9). Here a fountain is one thing, light another: there not so. For that which is the Fountain, the same is also Light: and whatever thou wilt thou callest It, for It is not what thou callest It: for thou canst not find a fit name: for It remaineth not in one name. If thou shouldest say, that It is Light only, it would be said to thee, Then without cause am I told to hunger

[1] [I cannot but change the word "drunken" here for one more decent and equally faithful. But note "sober inebriety," p. 75, supra.—C.]
[2] 1 Cor. xiii. 12.
[3] Ps. xxiii. 5, LXX.   [4] Ps. cxvi. 12, 13.
[5] [To spiritualize inebriation seems a difficult task; but as in heraldry we introduce the boar and the serpent for other qualities than their filth and their venom, so here the suggestion is explained by a reference to Acts ii. 13-18 and Eph. v. 18, 19.—C.]
[6] Matt. v. 6.

and thirst, for who is there that eateth light? It is said to me plainly, directly, "Blessed are the pure in heart: for they shall see God." [1] If It is Light, my eyes must I prepare. Prepare also lips; for That which is Light is also a Fountain: a Fountain, because It satisfieth the thirsty: Light, because It enlighteneth the blind. Here sometimes, light is in one place, a fountain in another. For sometimes fountains run even in darkness; and sometimes in the desert thou sufferest the sun, findest no fountain: here then can these two be separated: there thou shalt not be wearied, for there is a Fountain; there thou shalt not be darkened, for there is Light.

14. "Show forth Thy Mercy unto them that know Thee; Thy Righteousness to them that are of a right heart" (ver. 10). As I have said, Those are of a right heart who follow in this life the Will of God. The will of God is sometimes that thou shouldest be whole, sometimes that thou shouldest be sick. If when thou art whole God's Will be sweet, and when thou art sick God's Will be bitter; thou art not of a right heart. Wherefore? Because thou wilt not make right thy will according to God's Will, but wilt bend God's Will to thine. That is right, but thou art crooked: thy will must be made right to That, not That made crooked to thee; and thou wilt have a right heart. It is well with thee in this world; be God blessed, who comforteth thee: it goeth hardly with thee in this world; be God blessed, because He [2] chasteneth and proveth thee; and so wilt thou be of a right heart, saying, "I will bless the Lord at all times: His Praise shall be ever in my mouth." [3]

15. "Let not the foot of pride come against me" (ver. 11). But now he said, The children of men shall put their trust under the shadow of Thy wings: they shall be satiated with the fulness of Thy House. When one hath begun to be plentifully overflowed with that Fountain, let him take heed lest he grow proud. For the same was not wanting to Adam, the first man: but the foot of pride came against him, and the hand of the sinner removed him, that is, the proud hand of the devil. As he who seduced him, said of himself, "I will sit in the sides of the north;" [4] so he persuaded him, by saying, "Taste, and ye shall be as gods." [5] By pride then have we so fallen as to arrive at this mortality. And because pride had wounded us, humility maketh us whole. God came humbly, that from such great wound of pride He might heal man. He came, for "The Word was made Flesh, and dwelt among us." [6] He was taken by the Jews; He was reviled of them. Ye heard when the Gospel was read, what they said,

and to Whom they said, "Thou hast a devil:" [7] and He said not, Ye have a devil, for ye are still in your sins, and the devil possesseth your hearts. He said not this, which if He had said, He had said truly: but it was not meet that He should say it, lest He should seem not to preach Truth, but to retort evil speaking. He let go what He heard as though He heard it not. For a Physician was He, and to cure the madman had He come. As a Physician careth not what he may hear from the madman; but how the madman may recover and become sane; nor even if he receive a blow from the madman, careth he; but while he to him giveth new wounds, he cureth his old fever: so also the Lord came to the sick man, to the madman came He, that whatever He might hear, whatever He might suffer, He should despise; by this very thing teaching us humility, that being taught by humility, we might be healed from pride: from which he here prayeth to be delivered, saying, "Let not the foot of pride come against me; neither let the hand of the sinner remove me." For if the foot of pride come, the hand of the sinner removeth. What is the hand of the sinner? The working of him that adviseth ill. Hast thou become proud? Quickly he corrupteth thee who adviseth ill. Humbly fix thyself in God, and care not much what is said to thee. Hence is that which is elsewhere spoken, "From my secret sins cleanse Thou me; and from others' sins also keep Thy servant." [8] What is, "From my secret sins"? "Let not the foot of pride come against me." What is, "From other men's sins also keep Thy servant"? "Let not the hand of the wicked remove me." Keep that which is within, and thou shalt not fear from without.

16. But wherefore so greatly fearest thou this? Because it is said, "Thereby have fallen all that work iniquity" (ver. 12); so that they have come into that abyss of which it is said, "Thy judgments are like the great abyss:" so that they have come even to that deep wherein sinners who despise have fallen. "Have fallen." Whereby did they first fall? By the foot of pride. Hear the foot of pride. "When they knew God, they glorified Him not as God." Therefore came against them the foot of pride, whereby they came into the depth. "God gave them over to their own hearts' lusts, to do those things which are not convenient." [9] The root of sin, and the head of sin feared he who said, "Let not the foot of pride come against me." Wherefore said he, "the foot"? Because by walking proudly man deserted God, and departed from Him. His foot, called he his

[1] Matt. v. 6, 8.　　[2] Al. "Who."　　[3] Ps. xxxiv. 1.
[4] Isa. xiv. 13.　　[5] Gen. iii. 5.
[6] John i. 34.

[7] John viii. 48. [This was then the Gospel for the day, or one of the Lessons. — C.]
[8] Ps. xix. 12, 13.　　[9] Rom. i. 21-24.

affection. "Let not the foot of pride come against me : let not the hand of the wicked remove me : " that is, let not the works of the wicked remove me from Thee, that I should wish to imitate them. But wherefore said he this against pride, " Thereby have fallen all that work iniquity "? Because those who now are ungodly, have fallen by pride. Therefore when the Lord would caution His Church, He said, " It shall watch thy head, and thou shall watch [1] his heel." [2] The serpent watcheth when the foot of pride may come against thee, when thou mayest fall, that he may cast thee down. But watch thou his head : the beginning of all sin is pride.[3] " Thereby have fallen all that work iniquity : they are driven out, and are not able to stand." He first, who in the Truth stood not, then, through him, they whom God sent out of Paradise. Whence he, the humble, who said that he was not worthy to unloose His shoe's latchet, is not driven out, but standeth and heareth Him, and rejoiceth greatly because of the Bridegroom's voice ; [4] not because of his own, lest the foot of pride come against him, and he be driven out, and be not able to stand. . . .

PSALM XXXVII.[5]

On the First Part of the Psalm.

1. With terror do they hear of the coming of the last day, who will not be secure by living well : and who fain would live ill, long. But it was for useful purposes that God willed that day to remain unknown ; that the heart may be ever ready to expect that of which it knows it is to come, but knows not when it is to come. Seeing, however, that our Lord Jesus Christ was sent to us to be our " Master," [6] He said, that " of the day not even the Son of Man knew," [7] because it was not part of His office as our Master that through Him it should become known to us. For indeed the Father knoweth nothing that the Son knoweth not ; since that is the Very Knowledge of the Father Itself, which is His Wisdom ; now His Son, His Word, is " His Wisdom." But because it was not for our good to know that, which however was known to Him who came indeed to teach us, though not to teach us that which it was not good for us to know, He not only, as a Master, taught us something, but also, as a Master, left something

untaught. For, as a Master, He knew how both to teach us what was good for us, and not to teach us what was injurious. Now thus, according to a certain form of speech, the Son [8] is said not to know what He does not teach : that is, in the same way that we are daily in the habit of speaking, He is said not to know what He causes us not to know.[9] . . .

2. This it is that disturbs you who are a Christian ; that you see men of bad lives prospering, and surrounded with abundance of things like these ; you see them sound in health, distinguished with proud honours ; you see their family unvisited by misfortune ; the happiness of their relatives, the obsequious attendance of their dependants, their most commanding influence, their life uninterrupted by any sad event ; you see their characters most profligate, their external resources most affluent ; and your heart says that there is no Divine judgment ; that all things are carried to and fro by accidents, and blown about in disorderly and irregular motions. For if God, thou sayest, regarded human affairs, would his iniquity flourish, and my innocence suffer? Every sickness of the soul hath in Scripture its proper remedy. Let him then whose sickness is of that kind that he says in his heart things like these, let him drink this Psalm by way of potion. . . .

3. " Be not envious because of evil-doers, neither be envious against the workers of iniquity " (ver. 1). " For they shall soon wither like the grass, and shall fade like the herbs of the meadow" (ver. 2). That which to thee seemeth long, is " soon " in the sight of God. Conform [10] thou thyself to God ; and it will be " soon " to thee. That which he here calls " grass," that we understand by the " herbs of the meadow." They are some worthless things, occupying the surface only of the ground, they have no depth of root. In the winter then they are green ; but when the summer sun shall begin to scorch, they will wither away. For now it is the season of winter. Thy glory doth not as yet appear. But if thy love hath but a deep root, like that of many trees during winter, the frost passes away, the summer (that is, the Day of Judgment) will come ; then will the greenness of the grass wither away. Then will the glory of the trees appear. " For ye " (saith the Apostle) " are dead," [11] even as trees seem to be in winter, as it were dead, as it were withered. What is our hope then, if we are dead ? The root is within ; where our root is, there is our life also, for there our love is fixed. " And your life is hid with Christ in God." [11] When shall he

---

[1] Lat. *observabit.* [2] Gen. iii. 15. [3] Ecclus. x. 13.
[4] John i. 27, iii. 29.
[5] Lat. XXXVI. This is a sermon which was delivered at Carthage, as well as the two following. It should be noticed that in the life of St. Fulgentius, c. 3, we are told that, " having some time before resolved with himself to renounce the world, he was so roused and moved by St. Augustin's exposition of this Psalm that he determined to make his vow public, and earnestly desired to adopt the religious habit." — *Ben*
[6] *Magister Magisterio.* Master, in sense of teacher or guide ; Καθηγητης, in Matt. xxiii. 8, being in the Latin translated " *Magister*," as in English, " Master."
[7] Mark xiii. 32.

[8] *Al.* " Son of Man," as below.
[9] [Here he enlarges : but our common use of the word " ignore " sufficiently explains the use here. We *ignore* what it is needless to say. — C.]
[10] *Subjunge.* [11] Col. iii. 3.

wither who is thus rooted? But when will our spring be? When our summer? When will the honour of foliage clothe us around, and the fulness of fruit make us rich? When shall this come to pass? Hear what follows: "When Christ, who is our life, shall appear, then shall ye also appear with Him in glory." And what then shall we do now? "Be not envious because of the evil-doers, neither be envious against the workers of iniquity. For they shall soon wither like the grass, and fade like the herb of the meadow."

4. What shouldest thou do then? "Trust in the Lord" (ver. 3). For they too trust, but not "in the Lord." Their hope is perishable. Their hope is short-lived, frail, fleeting, transitory, baseless. "Trust thou in the Lord." "Behold," thou sayest, "I do trust; what am I to do?"

"And do good." Do not do that evil which thou beholdest in those men, who are prosperous in wickedness. "Do good, and dwell in the land." Lest haply thou shouldest be doing good without "dwelling in the land." For it is the Church that is the Lord's land. It is her whom He, the Father, the tiller of it, waters and cultivates. For there are many that, as it were, do good works, but yet, in that they do not "dwell in the land," they do not belong to the husbandman. Therefore do thou thy good, not outside of the land, but do thou "dwell in the land." And what shall I have?

"And thou shalt be fed in its riches." What are the riches of that land? Her riches are her Lord! Her riches are her God! He it is to whom it is said, "The Lord is the portion of mine inheritance, and of my cup." [1] In a late discourse we suggested to you, dearly beloved, that God is our possession, [2] and that we are at the same time God's possession. Hear how that He is Himself the riches of that land.

"Delight thyself in the Lord" (ver. 4). As if thou hadst put the question, and hadst said, "Show me the riches of that land, in which thou biddest me dwell, he says, "Delight thyself in the Lord."

5. "And He shall give thee the desires of thine heart." Understand in their proper signification, [3] "the desires of thine heart." Distinguish the "desires of thine heart" from the desires of thy flesh; distinguish as much as thou canst. It is not without a meaning that it is said in a certain Psalm, "God is" (the strength) "of mine heart." For there it says in what follows: "And God is my portion for ever." For instance: One labours under bodily blind-ness. He asks that he may receive his sight. Let him ask it; for God does that too, and gives those blessings also. But these things are asked for even by the wicked. This is a desire of the flesh. One is sick, and prays to be made sound. From the point of death he is restored to health. That too is a desire of the flesh, as are all of such a kind. What is "the desire of the heart"? As the desire of the flesh is to wish to have one's eyesight restored, to enable him, that is, to see that light, which can be seen by such eyes; so "the desire of the heart" relates to a different sort of light. For, "Blessed are the pure in heart, for they shall see God. Delight thou thyself in the Lord; and He shall give thee the desires of thine heart."

6. "Behold" (you say), "I do long after it, I do ask for it, I do desire it. Shall I then accomplish it?" No. Who shall then? "Reveal thy way unto the Lord: trust also in Him, and He shall bring it to pass" (ver. 5). Mention to Him what thou sufferest, mention to Him what thou dost desire. For what is it that thou sufferest? "The flesh lusteth against the spirit, and the spirit against the flesh." [4] What is it then that thou dost desire? "Wretched man that I am! Who shall deliver me from the body of this death?" [5] And because it is He "Himself" that "will bring it to pass," when thou shalt have "revealed thy ways unto Him;" hear what follows: "The grace of God through Jesus Christ our Lord." What is it then that He is to bring to pass, since it is said, "Reveal thy way unto Him, and He will bring it to pass"? What will He bring to pass?

"And He shall bring forth thy righteousness as the light" (ver. 6). For now, "thy righteousness" is hid. Now it is a thing of faith; not yet of sight. You believe something that you may do it. You do not yet see that in which you believe. But when thou shalt begin to see that, which thou didst believe before, "thy righteousness will be brought forth to the light," because it is thy faith that was [6] thy righteousness. For "the just lives by faith."

7. "And He shall bring forth thy judgment as the noon-day." That is to say, "as the clear light." It was too little to say, "as the light." For we call it "light" already, even when it but dawns: we call it light even while the sun is rising. But never is the light brighter than at mid-day. Therefore He will not only "bring forth thy righteousness as the light," but "thy judgment shall be as the noon-day." For now dost thou make thy "judgment" to follow Christ. This is thy purpose: this is thy choice: this is thy "judgment." . . .

8. "What should I do then?" Hear what

---

[1] Ps. xvi. 5.
[2] See Disc. 2 (omitted) on Ps. 33, delivered at Carthage in the Church of St. Cyprian.
[3] *Signanter accipe.*

[4] Gal. v. 17. [5] Rom. vii. 24. [6] *Al.* "shall be."

thou shouldest do. "Submit thee to the Lord, and entreat Him" (ver. 7). Be this thy life, to obey His commandments. For this is to submit thee to Him ; and to entreat Him until He give thee what He hath promised. Let good works "continue ; "[1] let prayer "continue." For "men ought always to pray, and not to faint."[2] Wherein dost thou show that thou art "submitted to Him"? In doing what He hath commanded. But haply thou dost not receive thy wages as yet, because as yet thou art not able. For He is already able to give them ; but thou art not already able to receive them. Exercise thou thyself in works. Labour in the vineyard ; at the close of the day crave thy wages. "Faithful is He" who brought thee into the vineyard. "Submit thee to the Lord, and entreat Him."

9. "See! I do so; I do 'submit to the Lord, and I do entreat.' But what do you think? That neighbour of mine is a wicked man, living a bad life, and prosperous! His thefts, adulteries, robberies, are known to me. Lifted up above every one, proud, and raised on high by wickedness, he deigns not to notice me. In these circumstances, how shall I hold out with patience?" This is a sickness; drink, by way of remedy. "Fret not thyself because of him who prospereth in his way." He prospereth, but it is "in his way :" thou sufferest, but it is in God's way! His portion is prosperity on his way, misery on arriving at its end : yours, toil on the road, happiness in its termination. "The Lord knoweth the way of the righteous ; and the way of the ungodly shall perish."[3] Thou walkest those ways which "the Lord knoweth," and if thou dost suffer toil in them, they do not deceive thee. The "way of the ungodly" is but a transitory happiness ; at the end of the way the happiness is at an end also. Why? Because that way is "the broad road ; " its termination leads to the pit of hell. Now, thy way is narrow ; and "few there be" that enter in through it :[4] but into how ample a field it comes at the last, thou oughtest to consider. "Fret not thyself at him who prospereth in his way ; because of the man who bringeth wicked devices to pass."

"Cease from anger, and forsake wrath" (ver. 8). Wherefore art thou wroth? Wherefore is it that, through that passion and indignation, thou dost blaspheme, or almost blaspheme? Against "the man who bringeth wicked devices to pass, cease from anger, and forsake wrath." Knowest thou not whither that wrath tempts thee on? Thou art on the point of saying unto God, that He is unjust. It tends to that. "Look! why is that man prosperous, and this

man in adversity?" Consider what thought it begets : stifle the wicked notion. "Cease from anger, and forsake wrath : " so that now returning to thy senses, thou mayest say, "Mine eye is disturbed because of wrath."[5] What eye is that, but the eye of faith? To the eye of thy faith I appeal.[6] Thou didst believe in Christ : why didst thou believe? What did He promise thee? If it was the happiness of this world that Christ promised thee, then murmur against Christ ; yes ! murmur against Him, when thou seest the wicked flourishing. What of happiness did He promise? What, save in the Resurrection of the Dead? But what in this life? That which was His portion. His portion, I say! Dost thou, servant and disciple, disdain what thy Lord, what thy Master bore? . . .

"For evil-doers shall be cut off" (ver. 9). "But I see their prosperity." Believe Him who saith, "they shall be cut off ; " Him who seeth better than thou, since His eye anger cannot cloud. "For evil-doers shall be cut off. But those that wait upon the Lord," — not upon any one that can deceive them ; but verily on Him who is the Truth itself, — "But those that wait upon the Lord, they shall inherit the land." What "land," but that Jerusalem, with the love of which whosoever is inflamed, shall come to peace at the last.

10. "But how long is the sinner to flourish? How long shall I have to endure?" Thou art impatient ;[7] that which seems long to thee, will soon come to pass. It is infirmity makes that seem long, which is really short, as is found in the case of the longings of sick men. Nothing seems so long as the mixing of the potion for him when athirst. For all that his attendants are making all speed, lest haply the patient be angry ; "When will it be done? (he cries). When will it be drest? When will it be served?" Those who are waiting upon you are making haste, but your infirmity fancies that long which is being done with expedition. Behold ye, therefore, our Physician complying with the infirmity of the patient, saying, "How long shall I have to endure? How long will it be?"

"Yet a little while, and the sinner shall not be " (ver. 10). Is it certainly among sinners, and because of the sinner, that thou murmurest? "A little while, and he shall not be." Lest haply because I said, "They that wait upon the Lord, they shall inherit the land," thou shouldest think that waiting to be of very long duration. Wait "a little while," thou shalt receive without end what thou waitest for. A little while, a moderate space. Review the years from Adam's time up to this day ; run through the Scriptures. It is almost yesterday that he fell from Paradise !

---

[1] *Perseveret*, alluding to a word in the portion omitted. Matt. xxiv. 13.
[2] Luke xviii. 1. [3] Ps. i. 6. [4] Matt. vii. 13, 14.

[5] Ps. vi. 7. [6] *Interrogo*. [7] *Festinas*.

So many ages have been measured out, and unrolled.[1] Where now are the past ages? Even so, however, shall the few which remain, pass away also. Hadst thou been living throughout all that time, since Adam was banished from Paradise up to this present day, thou wouldest certainly see that the life, which had thus flown away, had not been of long duration. But how long is the duration of each individual's life? Add any number of years you please : prolong old age to its longest duration : what is it? Is it not but a morning breeze? Be it so, however, that the Day of Judgment is far off, when the reward of the righteous and of the unrighteous is to come : your last day at all events cannot be far off. Make thyself ready against this ! For such as thou shall have departed from this life, shalt thou be restored to the other. At the close of that short life, you will not yet be, where the Saints shall be, to whom it shall be said, " Come, ye blessed of My Father : inherit the kingdom prepared for you from the beginning of the world." [2] You will not yet be there? Who does not know that? But you may already be there, where that beggar, once " covered with sores," was seen at a distance, at rest, by that proud and unfruitful " rich man " in the midst of his torments.[3] Surely laid in that rest thou waitest in security for the Day of Judgment, when thou art to receive again a body, to be changed so as to be made equal to an Angel. How long then is that for which we are impatient, and are saying, " When will it come? Will it tarry long?" This our sons will say hereafter, and our sons' sons will say too ; and, though each one of these in succession will say this same thing, that " little while" that is yet to be, passes away, as all that is already past hath passed away already ! O thou sick one ! " Yet a little while, and the sinner shall not be. Yea, thou shalt diligently consider his place, and thou shalt not find him." . . .

11. " But the meek shall inherit the land " [4] (ver. 11). That land is the one of which we have often spoken, the holy Jerusalem, which is to be released from these her pilgrimages, and to live for ever with God, and on God. Therefore, " They shall inherit the land." What shall be their delight? " And they shall delight themselves in the abundance of peace." Let the ungodly man delight himself here in the multitude of his gold, in the multitude of his silver, in the multitude of his slaves, in the multitude, lastly, of his baths, his roses, his intoxicating wines, his most sumptuous and luxurious banquets. Is this the power thou enviest? Is this the glory that delights thee? Would not his fate be worthy to be deplored, even if he were to be so for ever? What shall be thy delights? " And they shall delight themselves in the abundance of peace." Peace shall be thy gold. Peace shall be thy silver. Peace shall be thy lands. Peace shall be thy life, thy God Peace. Peace shall be to thee whatsoever thou dost desire. . . .

On the Second Part of the Psalm.[5]

1. Then follow these words : " The wicked plotteth against the just, and gnasheth upon him with his teeth " (ver. 12) : " But the Lord shall laugh at him " (ver. 13). At whom? Surely at the sinner, " gnashing upon " the other " with his teeth." But wherefore shall the Lord " laugh at him "? " For He foreseeth that his day is coming." He seems indeed full of wrath, while, ignorant of the morrow that is in store for him, he is threatening the just. But the Lord beholds and " foresees his day." " What day?" That in which " He will render to every man according to his works." For he is " treasuring up unto himself wrath against the day of wrath, and revelation of the just judgment of God." [6] But it is the Lord that foresees it ; thou dost not foresee it. It hath been revealed to thee by Him who foresees it. Thou didst not know of the " day of the unrighteous," in which he is to suffer punishment. But He who knows it hath revealed it to thee. It is a main part of knowledge to join thyself to Him who hath knowledge. He hath the eyes of knowledge : have thou the eyes of a believing mind. That which God " sees," be thou willing to believe. For the day of the unjust, which God foresees, will come. What day is that? The day for all vengeance ! For it is necessary that vengeance should be taken upon the ungodly, that vengeance be taken upon the unjust, whether he turn, or whether he turn not. For if he shall turn from his ways, that very thing, that his " injustice is come to an end," is the infliction of vengeance. . . .

2. " The wicked have drawn out the sword, and have bent their bow, to cast down the poor and needy, and to slay such as be of upright heart " (ver. 14). " Their weapon shall enter into their own heart " (ver. 15). It is an easy thing for his weapon, that is, his sword, to reach thy body, even as the sword of the persecutors reached the body of the Martyrs, but when the body had been smitten, " the heart " remained unhurt ; but his heart who " drew out the sword

---

[1] [Few consider how very short is the span of all human history. Daily we read of men and women who live a *hundred* years. Eighteen such lives go back to the age of Christ and His Apostles. Official lives of *fifty* years are not uncommon, and six-and-thirty such cover the entire Christian era. — C.]
[2] Matt. xxv. 34.   [3] Luke xvi. 20, 23.
[4] [Comp. St. Matt. v. 5. The earlier Fathers believed in the " regeneration " of this earth. See A. N. F. vol. i. 240, 435, and (Apocryphal Revelation) viii. 584, vii. 218, 254, iv. 211, 212, 218, and conversely, 274, 275. Our author, after sharing this early opinion, gave it up, and founded a new school. — C.]

[5] Preached at another time.   [6] Rom. ii. 6, 5.

against" the body of the just did not clearly remain unhurt. This is attested by this very Psalm. It saith, Their weapon, that is, "Their sword shall," not go into their body, but, "their weapon shall go into their own heart." They would fain have slain him in the body. Let them die the death of the soul. For those whose bodies they sought to kill, the Lord hath freed from anxiety, saying, "Fear not them who kill the body, but cannot kill the soul." [1] . . .

3. "And their bows shall be broken." What is meant by, "And their bows shall be broken"? Their plots shall be frustrated. For above He had said, "The wicked have drawn out the sword and bent their bows." By the "drawing out of the sword" he would have understood open hostility; but by the "bending of the bow," secret conspiracies. See! His sword destroys himself, and his laying of snares is frustrated. What is meant by frustrated? That it does no mischief to the righteous. How then, for instance (you ask), did it do no mischief to the man, whom it thus stripped of his goods, whom it reduced to straitened circumstances by taking away his possessions? He has still cause to sing, "A little that a righteous man hath, is better than great riches of the ungodly" (ver. 16).

4. . . . "For the arms of the wicked shall be broken" (ver. 17). Now by "their arms" is meant their power. What will he do in hell? Will it be what the rich man had to do, he who was wont "to fare sumptuously" in the upper world, and in hell "was tormented"? [2] Therefore their arms shall be broken; "but the Lord upholdeth the righteous." How does He "uphold" them? What saith He unto them? Even what is said in another Psalm, "Wait on the Lord, be of good courage; and let thine heart be strengthened. Wait, I say, on the Lord." [3] What is meant by this, "Wait on the Lord"? Thou sufferest but for a time; thou shalt rest for ever: thy trouble is short; thy happiness is to be everlasting. It is but for "a little while" thou art to sorrow; thy joy shall have no end. But in the midst of trouble does thy "foot" begin to "slip"? The example even of Christ's sufferings is set before thee. Consider what He endured for thee, in whom no cause was found why He should endure it? How great soever be thy sufferings, thou wilt not come to those insults, those scourgings, to that robe of shame, to that crown of thorns, and last of all to that Cross, which He endured; because that is now removed from the number of human punishments. [4] For though under the ancients criminals were crucified, in the present day no one is crucified. It was honoured, and it came to an end. It came to an end as a punishment; it is continued in glory. It hath removed from the place of execution to the foreheads of Emperors. He who hath invested His very sufferings with such honour, what doth He reserve for His faithful servants? . . .

5. But observe whether that was fulfilled in his case which the Psalm now speaks of. "The Lord strengtheneth the righteous. — Not only so" (saith that same Paul, whilst suffering many evils), "but we glory in tribulations also: knowing that tribulation worketh patience, and patience experience; and experience hope; but hope maketh not ashamed, because the love of God is shed abroad in our hearts by the Holy Ghost, which is given unto us." [5] Justly is it said by him, now righteous, now "strengthened." As therefore those who persecuted him did no harm to him, when now "strengthened," so neither did he himself do any harm to those whom he persecuted. "But the Lord," he saith, "strengtheneth the righteous." . . .

6. Therefore "the Lord does strengthen the righteous." In what way does He strengthen them? "The Lord knoweth the ways [6] of the spotless ones" (ver. 18). When they suffer ills, they are believed to be walking ill ways by those who are ignorant, by those who have not knowledge to discern "the ways of the spotless ones." He who "knoweth those ways," knoweth by what way to lead His own, "them that are gentle," in the right way. Whence in another Psalm he said, "The meek shall He guide in judgment; them that are gentle will He teach His way." [7] How, think you, was that beggar, who lay covered with sores before the rich man's door, [8] spurned by the passers by! How did they, probably, close their nostrils and spit at him! The Lord, however, knew how to reserve [9] Paradise for him. How did they, on the other hand, desire for themselves the life of him who was "clad in purple and fine linen, and fared sumptuously every day!" [10] But the Lord, who foresaw that man's "day coming," knew the torments, the torments without end, that were in store for him. Therefore "The Lord knoweth the ways of the upright."

7. "And their inheritance shall be for ever" (ver. 18). This we hold by faith. Doth the Lord too know it by faith? The Lord knoweth those things with as clear a manifestation, as we cannot speak of even when we shall be made equal to the Angels. For the things that shall be manifest to us, shall not be equally manifest to us as they are now to Him, who is incapable of change. Yet even of us ourselves what is

---

[1] Matt. x. 28.　　[2] Luke xvi. 19, 23.　　[3] Ps. xxvii. 14.
[4] [Sozomen, b. i. cap. 8. This author tells us that Constantine made this change, dictated alike by reverence and humanity. — C.]

[5] Rom. v. 3-5.　　[6] E. V. and Vulgate, "days."
[7] Ps. xxv. 9.　　[8] Luke xvi. 20.
[9] *Al.* "knew that Paradise was in store."　　[10] Luke xvi. 19.

said? "Beloved, now are we the sons of God: and it doth not yet appear what we shall be: but we know that, when He shall appear, we shall be like Him, for we shall see Him as He is."[1] There is therefore surely some blissful vision reserved for us; and if it can be now in some measure conceived, "darkly and through a glass,"[2] yet cannot we in any way express in language the ravishing beauty of that bliss, which God reserves for them that fear Him, which He consummates in those that hope in Him, It is for that destination that our hearts are being disciplined in all the troubles and trials of this life. Wonder not that it is in trouble that thou art disciplined for it. It is for something glorious that thou art being disciplined. Whence comes that speech of the now strengthened righteous man: "The sufferings of this present time are not worthy to be compared to the glory which shall be revealed in us"?[3] What is that promised glory to be, but to be made equal to the Angels and to see God? How great a benefit doth he bestow on the blind man, who makes his eyes sound so as to be able to see the light of this life. . . . What reward then shall we give unto that Physician who restores soundness to our inward eyes, to enable them to see a certain eternal Light, which is Himself? . . .

8. "They shall not be ashamed in the evil time" (ver. 19). In the day of trouble, in the day of distress, they shall not be "ashamed," as he is ashamed whose hope deceives him. Who is the man that is "ashamed"? He who saith, "I have not found that which I was in hopes of." Nor undeservedly either; for thou didst hope it from thyself or from man, thy friend. But "cursed is he that putteth his trust in man."[4] Thou art ashamed, because thy hope hath deceived thee; thy hope that was set on a lie. For "every man is a liar."[5] But if thou dost place thy hopes on thy God, thou art not made "ashamed." For He in whom thou hast put thy trust, cannot be deceived.[6] Whence also the man whom we mentioned just above, the now "strengthened" righteous man, when fallen on an evil time, on the day of tribulation, what saith he to show that he was not "ashamed"? "We glory in tribulation; knowing that tribulation worketh patience, and patience experience, and experience hope; but hope maketh not ashamed." Whence is it that hope "maketh not ashamed"? Because it is placed on God. Therefore follows immediately, "Because the love of God is spread in our hearts by the Holy Spirit, which is given unto us."[7] The Holy Spirit hath been given to us already: how should He deceive us, of

whom we possess such an "earnest" already? "They shall not be ashamed in the evil time, and in the days of famine they shall be satisfied." . . .

9. "For the wicked shall perish. But the enemies of the Lord, when they shall begin to glory, and to be lifted up, immediately shall consume away utterly, even as the smoke" (ver. 20). Recognise from the comparison itself the thing which he intimates. Smoke, breaking forth from the place where fire has been, rises up on high, and by the very act of rising up, it swells into a large volume: but the larger that volume is, the more unsubstantial does it become; for from that very largeness of volume, which has no foundation or consistency, but is merely loose, shifting and evanescent, it passes into air, and dissolves; so that you perceive its very largeness to have been fatal to it. For the higher it ascends, the farther it is extended, the wider the circumference which it spreads itself over, the thinner, and the more rare and wasting and evanescent does it become. "But the enemies of the Lord, when they shall begin to glory, and to be lifted up, immediately shall consume away utterly even as the smoke." Of such as these was it said, "As Jannes and Jambres withstood Moses, so do these also resist the Truth; men of corrupt minds, reprobate concerning the faith."[8] But how is it that they resist the Truth, except by the vain inflation of their swelling pride, while they raise themselves up on high, as if great and righteous persons, though on the point of passing away into empty air? But what saith he of them? As if speaking of smoke, he says, "They shall proceed no farther, for their folly shall be manifest unto all men, even as theirs also was." . . .

10. "The wicked borroweth, and payeth not again" (ver. 20). He receiveth, and will not repay. What is it he will not repay? Thanksgiving. For what is it that God would have of thee, what doth He require of thee, except that He may do thee good? And how great are the benefits which the sinner hath received, and which he will not repay! He hath received the gift of being; he hath received the gift of being a man; and of a being highly distinguished above the brutes; he hath received the form of a body, and the distinction of the senses in the body, eyes for seeing, ears for hearing, the nostrils for smelling, the palate for tasting, the hands for touching, and the feet for walking; and even the very health and soundness of the body. But up to this point we have these things in common even with the brute; he hath received yet more than this; a mind capable of understanding, capable of Truth, capable of distinguishing right from wrong; capable of seeking after, of longing for,

---

[1] 1 John iii. 2.   [2] 1 Cor. xiii. 12.   [3] Rom. viii. 18.
[4] Jer. xvii. 5.   [5] Ps. cxvi. 11.   [6] *Al.* "deceive."
[7] Rom. v. 3-5.   [8] 2 Tim. iii. 8.

its Creator, of praising Him, and fixing itself upon Him. All this the wicked man hath received as well as others; but by not living well, he fails to repay that which he owes. Thus it is, "the wicked borroweth, and payeth not again:" he will not requite Him from whom he hath received; he will not return thanks; nay, he will even render evil for good, blasphemies, murmuring against God, indignation. Thus it is that he "borroweth, and payeth not again; but the righteous showeth mercy, and lendeth" (ver. 21). The one therefore hath nothing; the other hath. See, on the one side, destitution: see, on the other, wealth. The one receiveth and "payeth not again:" the "other showeth mercy, and lendeth:" and he hath more than enough. What if he is poor? Even so he is rich; do you but look at his riches with the eyes of Religion. For thou lookest at the empty chest; but dost not look at the conscience, that is full of God. . . .

11. "For such as shall bless Him[1] shall inherit the land" (ver. 23), that is,[2] they shall possess that righteous One: the only One who both is truly righteous, and maketh righteous: who both was poor in this world, and brought great riches to it, wherewith to make those rich whom He found poor. For it is He who hath enriched the hearts of the poor with the Holy Spirit; and having emptied out their souls by confession of sins, hath filled them with the richness of righteousness: He who was able to enrich the fisherman, who, by forsaking his nets, spurned what he possessed already, but sought to draw up what he possessed not. For "God hath chosen the weak things of the world to confound the things which are mighty."[3] And it was not by an orator that He gained to Himself the fisherman; but by the fisherman that He gained to Himself the orator; by the fisherman that He gained the Senator; by the fisherman that He gained the Emperor. For "such as shall bless Him shall inherit the land;" they shall be fellow-heirs with Him, in that "land of the living," of which it is said in another Psalm, "Thou art my hope, my portion in the land of the living."[4] . . .

12. Observe what follows: "The steps of a good man are ordered by the Lord; and he delighteth in His way" (ver. 23). That man may himself "delight in the Lord's way," his steps are ordered by the Lord Himself. For if the Lord did not order the steps of man, so crooked are they naturally, that they would always be going through crooked paths, and by pursuing crooked ways, would be unable to return again. He however came, and called us, and redeemed us, and shed His blood; He hath given this ransom; He hath done this good, and suffered these evils.

Consider Him in what He hath done, He is God! Consider Him in what He hath suffered, He is Man! Who is that God-Man? Hadst not thou, O man, forsaken God, God would not have been made Man for thee! For that was too little for thee to requite, or for Him to bestow, that He had made thee man; unless He Himself should become Man for thee also. For it is He Himself that hath "ordered our steps;" that we should "delight in His way." . . .

13. Now if man were to be through the whole of his life in toil, and in sufferings, in pain, in tortures, in prison, in scourgings, in hunger, and in thirst, every day and every hour through the whole length of life, to the period of old age, yet the whole life of man is but a few days. That labour being over, there is to come the Eternal Kingdom; there is to come happiness without end; there is to come equality with the Angels; there is to come Christ's inheritance, and Christ, our "joint Heir,"[5] is to come. How great is the labour, for which thou receivest so great a recompense? The Veterans who serve in the wars, and move in the midst of wounds for so many years, enter upon the military service from their youth, and quit it in old age: and to obtain a few days of repose in their old age, when age itself begins to weigh down those whom the wars do not break down, how great hardships do they endure; what marches, what frosts, what burning suns; what privations, what wounds, and what dangers! And while suffering all these things, they fix their thoughts on nothing but those few days of repose in old age, at which they know not whether they will ever arrive. Thus it is, the "steps of a good man are ordered by the Lord, and he delighteth in His way." This is the point with which I commenced. If thou dost "delight in the way" of Christ, and art truly a Christian (for he is a Christian indeed who does not despise the way of Christ, but "delighteth in" following Christ's "way" through His sufferings), do not thou go by any other way than that by which He Himself hath also gone. It appears painful, but it is the very way of safety; another perhaps is delightful, but it is full of robbers. "And he delighteth in His way."

14. "Though he fall, he shall not be utterly cast down; for the Lord upholdeth his hand" (ver. 24). See what it is "to delight in" Christ's "way." Should it happen that he suffers some tribulation; some forfeiture of honour, some affliction, some loss, some contumely, or all those other accidents incident to mankind frequently in this life, he sets the Lord before him, what kind of trials He endured! and, "though he fall he shall not be utterly cast down, for the

---

[1] E. V. "such as be blessed."
[2] *Scilicet, Ben.* Conj. for *sicut.*   [3] 1 Cor. i. 27.
[4] Ps. cxlii. 5.

[5] Rom. viii. 17.

Lord upholdeth his hand," because He has suffered before him. For what shouldest thou fear, O man, whose steps are ordered so, that thou shouldest "delight in the way of the Lord"? What shouldest thou fear? Pain? Christ was scourged. Shouldest thou fear contumelies? He was reproached with, "Thou hast a devil," [1] who was Himself casting out the devils. Haply thou fearest faction, and the conspiracy of the wicked. Conspiracy was made against Him. Thou canst not make clear the purity of thy conscience in some accusation, and sufferest wrong and violence, because false witnesses are listened to against thee. False witness was borne against Him first, not only before His death, but also after His resurrection. . . . .

On the Third Part of the Psalm. [2]

1. "I have been young, and now am old; yet have I not seen the righteous forsaken, nor his seed begging bread" (ver. 25).

If it is spoken but in the person of one single individual, how long is the whole life of one man? And what is there wonderful in the circumstance, that a single man, fixed in some one part of the earth, should not, throughout the whole space of his life, being so short as man's life is, have ever seen "the righteous forsaken, nor his seed begging bread," although he may have advanced from youth to age. It is not anything worthy of marvel; for it might have happened, that before his lifetime there should have been some "righteous man seeking bread;" it might have happened, that there had been some one in some other part of the earth not where he himself was. Hear too another thing, which makes an impression upon us. Any single one among you (look you) who has now grown old, may perhaps, when looking back upon the past course of his life, he turns over in his thoughts the persons whom he has known, not find any instance of a righteous man begging bread, or of his seed begging bread, suggest itself to him; but nevertheless he turns to the inspired Scriptures, and finds that righteous Abraham was straitened, and suffered hunger in his own country, and left that land for another; he finds too that the son of the very same man, Isaac, removed to other countries in search of bread, for the same cause of hunger. And how will it be true to say, "I have never seen the righteous forsaken, nor his seed begging bread"? And if he finds this true in the duration of his own life, he finds it is otherwise in the inspired writings, which are more trustworthy than human life is.

2. What are we to do then? Let us be seconded by your pious attention, so that we may discern the purpose of God in these verses of the Psalm, what it is He would have us understand by them. For there is a fear, lest any unstable person, not capable of understanding the Scriptures spiritually, should appeal to human instances, and should observe the virtuous servants of God to be sometimes in some necessity, and in want, so as to be compelled to beg bread: should particularly call to mind the Apostle Paul, who says, "In hunger and thirst; in cold and nakedness;" [3] and should stumble thereat, saying to himself, "Is that certainly true [4] which I have been singing? Is that certainly true, which I have been sounding forth in so devout a voice, standing in church? 'I have never seen the righteous forsaken, nor his seed begging bread.'" Lest he should say in his heart, "Scripture deceives us;" and all his limbs should be paralyzed to good works: and when those limbs within him, those limbs of the inner man, shall have been paralyzed (which is the more fearful paralysis), he should henceforth leave off from good works, and say to himself, "Wherefore do I do good works? Wherefore do I break my bread to the hungry, and clothe the naked, and take home to mine house him who hath no shelter, [5] putting faith in that which is written? 'I have never seen the righteous forsaken, nor his seed begging bread;' whereas I see so many persons who live virtuously, yet for the most part suffering from hunger. But if perhaps I am in error in thinking the man who is living well, and the man who is living ill, to be both of them living well, and if God knows him to be otherwise; that is, knows him, whom I think just, to be unjust, what am I to make of Abraham's case, who is commended by Scripture itself as a righteous person? What am I to make of the Apostle Paul, who says, 'Be ye followers of me, even as I also am of Christ.'[6] What? that I should myself be in evils such as he endured, 'In hunger and thirst, in cold and nakedness'?" [3]

3. Whilst therefore he thus thinks, and whilst his limbs are paralyzed to the power of good works, can we, my brethren, as it were, lift up the sick of the palsy; and, as it were, "lay open the roof" of this Scripture, and let him down before the Lord.[7] For you observe that it is obscure. If obscure therefore, it is covered. And I behold a certain patient paralytic in mind, and I see this roof, and am convinced that Christ is concealed beneath the roof. Let me, as far as I am able, do that which was praised in those who opened the roof, and let down the sick of the palsy before Christ; that He might say unto him, "Son, be of good cheer, thy sins be forgiven

---

1 John vii. 20, viii. 48.   2 On another day.

3 2 Cor. xi. 27.   4 Al. vanum, "Is it not false."
5 Isa. lviii. 7.   6 1 Cor. xi. 1.
7 Luke v. 19.

thee."[1] For it was so that He made the inner man whole of his palsy, by loosing his sins, by binding fast his faith. . . .

4. But who is "the righteous" man, who "hath never been seen forsaken, nor his seed begging bread"? If you understand what is meant by "bread," you understand who is meant by him. For the "bread" is the Word of God, which never departs from the righteous man's mouth. . . . See now if "holy meditation doth 'keep thee'" in the rumination of this bread, then "hast thou never seen the righteous forsaken, nor his seed begging bread."

5. "He is always merciful, and lendeth" (ver. 26). "Fœneratur" is used in Latin indeed, both for him who lendeth, and for him who borroweth. But in this passage the meaning is more plain, if we express it by "fœnerat." What matters it to us, what the grammarians please to rule? It were better for us to be guilty of a barbarism, so that ye understand, than that in our propriety of speech ye be left unprovided. Therefore, that "righteous man is all day merciful, and (fœnerat) lendeth." Let not the lenders of money on usury, however, rejoice. For we find it is a particular kind of lender that is spoken of, as it was a particular kind of bread; that we may, in all passages, "remove the roof," and find our way to Christ. I would not have you be lenders of money on usury; and I would not have you be such for this reason, because God would not have you. . . . Whence does it appear that God would not have it so? It is said in another place, "He that putteth not out his money to usury."[2] And how detestable, odious, and execrable a thing it is, I believe that even usurers themselves know. Again, on the other hand, I myself, nay rather our God Himself, bids thee be an usurer, and says to thee, "Lend unto God." If thou lendest to man, hast thou hope? and shalt thou not have hope, if thou lendest to God? If thou hast lent thy money on usury to man, that is, if thou hast given the loan of thy money to one, from whom thou dost expect to receive something more than thou hast given, not in money only, but anything, whether it be wheat, or wine, or oil, or whatever else you please, if you expect to receive more than you have given, you are an usurer, and in this particular are not deserving of praise, but of censure. "What then," you say, "am I to do, that I may 'lend' profitably?" Consider what the usurer does. He undoubtedly desires to give a less sum, and to receive a larger; do thou this also; give thou a little, receive much. See how thy principal grows, and increases! Give

"things temporal," receive "things eternal:" give earth, receive heaven! And perhaps thou wouldest say, "To whom shall I give them?" The self-same Lord, who bade thee not lend on usury, comes forward as the Person to whom thou shouldest lend on usury! Hear from Scripture in what way thou mayest "lend unto the Lord." "He that hath pity on the poor, lendeth unto the Lord."[3] For the Lord wanteth not aught of thee. But thou hast one who needs somewhat of thee: thou extendest it to him; he receives it. For the poor hath nothing to return to thee, and yet he would himself fain requite thee, and finds nothing wherewith to do it: all that remains in his power is the good-will that desires to pray for thee. Now when the poor man prays for thee, he, as it were, says unto God, "Lord, I have borrowed this; be Thou surety for me." Then, though you have no bond on the poor man to compel his repayment, yet you have on a sponsible security. See, God from His own Scriptures saith unto thee; "Give it, and fear not; I repay it. It is to Me thou givest it." In what way do those who make themselves sureties for others, express themselves? What is it that they say? "I repay it: I take it upon myself. It is to me you are giving it." Do we then suppose that God also says this, "I take it on Myself. It is unto me thou givest it"? Assuredly, if Christ be God, of which there is no doubt, He hath Himself said, "I was an hungred, and ye gave Me meat."[4] And when they said unto Him, "When saw we Thee hungry?"[5] that He might show Himself to be the Surety for the poor, that He answers for all His members, that He is the Head, they the members, and that when the members receive, the Head receiveth also; He says, "Inasmuch as ye have done it to one of the least of these that belong to Me, ye have done it unto Me."[6] Come, thou covetous usurer, consider what thou hast given; consider what thou art to receive. Hadst thou given a small sum of money, and he to whom thou hadst given it were to give thee for that small sum a great villa, worth incomparably more money than thou hadst given, how great thanks wouldest thou render, with how great joy wouldest thou be transported! Hear what possession He to whom thou hast been lending bestows. "Come, ye blessed of My Father, receive"[7] — What? The same that they have given? God forbid! What you gave were earthly things, which, if you had not given them, would have become corrupted on earth. For what could you have made of them, if you had not given them? That which on earth would have been lost, has been preserved in heaven. Therefore what we

[1] Luke v. 20.
[2] Ps. xv. 5. [This intricate subject is nowhere more ably handled than by M. Huet in his *Règne Social du Christianisme*, cap. ix. p. 317, Paris, 1853. — C.]

[3] Prov. x. 17.   [4] Matt. xxv. 35.   [5] Matt. xxv. 37.
[6] Matt. xxv. 40.   [7] Matt. xxv. 34.

are to receive is that which hath been preserved. It is thy desert that hath been preserved, thy desert hath been made thy treasure. For consider what it is that thou art to receive. Receive — "the kingdom prepared for you from the foundation of the world." On the other hand, what shall be their sentence, who would not "lend"? "Go ye into everlasting fire, prepared for the devil and his angels."[1] And what is the kingdom which we receive called? Consider what follows: "And these shall go into everlasting burning; but the righteous into life eternal."[2] Make interest for this; purchase this. Give your money on usury to earn this. You have Christ throned in heaven, begging on earth. We have discovered in what way the righteous lendeth. "He is alway merciful, and lendeth."

6. "And his seed is blessed." Here too let not any carnal notion suggest itself. We see many of the sons of the righteous dying of hunger; in what sense then will his seed be blessed? His seed is that which remains of him afterwards; that wherewith he soweth here, and will hereafter reap. For the Apostle says, "Let us not be weary in well-doing; for in due season we shall reap if we faint not. As we have therefore time," he says, "let us do good unto all men."[3] This is that "seed" of thine which shall "be blessed." You commit it to the earth, and gather ever so much more; and dost thou lose it in committing it to Christ? See it expressly termed "seed" by the Apostle, when he was speaking of alms. For this he saith; "He which soweth sparingly, shall reap also sparingly; and he which soweth in blessings,[4] shall also reap in blessings."[5] . . .

7. Observe therefore what follows, and be not slothful. "Depart from evil, and do good" (ver. 27). Do not think it to be enough for thee to do, if thou dost not strip the man who is already clothed. For in not stripping the man who is already clothed, thou hast indeed "departed from evil:" but do not be barren, and wither. So choose not to strip the man who is clothed already, as to clothe the naked. For this is to "depart from evil, and to do good." And you will say, "What advantage am I to derive from it?" He to whom thou lendest has already assured thee of what He will give thee. He will give thee everlasting life. Give to Him, and fear not! Hear too what follows: "Depart from evil, and do good, and dwell for evermore." And think not when thou givest that no one sees thee, or that God forsakes thee, when haply after thou hast given to the poor, and some loss,

or some sorrow for the property thou hast lost, should follow, and thou shouldest say to thyself, "What hath it profited me to have done good works? I believe God doth not love the men who do good." Whence comes that buzz, that subdued murmur among you, except that those expressions are very common? Each one of you at this present moment recognises these expressions, either in his own lips, or on those of his friend. May God destroy them; may He root out the thorns from His field; may He plant "the good seed," and "the tree bearing fruit"! For wherefore art thou afflicted, O man, that thou hast given some things away to the poor, and hast lost certain other things? Seest thou not that it is what thou hast not given, that thou hast lost? Wherefore dost thou not attend to the voice of thy God? Where is thy faith? wherefore is it so fast asleep? Wake it up in thy heart. Consider what the Lord Himself said unto thee, while exhorting thee to good works of this kind: "Provide yourselves bags which wax not old; a treasure in the heavens that faileth not, where no thief approacheth."[6] Call this to mind therefore when you are lamenting over a loss. Wherefore dost thou lament, thou fool of little mind, or rather of unsound mind? Wherefore didst thou lose it, except that thou didst not lend it to Me? Wherefore didst thou lose it? Who has carried it off? Thou wilt answer, "A thief." Was it not this, that I forewarned thee of? that thou shouldest not lay it up where the thief could approach? If then he who has lost anything, grieves, let him grieve for this, that he did not lay it up there, whence it could not be lost.

8. "For the Lord loveth judgment, and forsaketh not His Saints" (ver. 28). When the Saints suffer affliction, think not that God doth not judge, or doth not judge righteously. Will He, who warns thee to judge righteously, Himself judge unrighteously? He "loveth judgment, and forsaketh not His Saints." But (think) how[7] the "life" of the Saints is "hid with Him," in such a manner, that who now suffer trouble on earth, like trees in the wintertime, having no fruit and leaves, when He, like a newly-risen sun, shall have appeared, that which before was living in their root, will show itself forth in fruits. He does then "love judgment, and doth not forsake His Saints." . . .

9. "But the unrighteous shall be punished; the seed of the wicked shall be cut off." Just as the "seed of the" other "shall be blessed," so shall the "seed of the wicked be cut off." For the "seed" of the wicked is the works of the wicked. For again, on the other hand, we

[1] Matt. xxv. 41.   [2] Matt. xxv. 46.   [3] Gal. vi. 9, 10.
[4] *In benedictionibus* (ἐπ' εὐλογίαις), Rec. text; E. V. "bountifully."
[5] 2 Cor. ix. 6.

[6] Luke xii. 33.
[7] *Quomodo.* — Ben. *Quò modò. Quòd modò,* "that now," gives a better sense, or, *quo modo,* "in such sort that."

find the son of the wicked man flourish in the world, and sometimes become righteous, and flourish in Christ. Be careful therefore how thou takest it; that thou mayest remove the covering, and make thy way to Christ.[1] Do not take the text in a carnal sense; for thou wilt be deceived. But "the seed of the wicked" — all the works of the wicked — "will be cut off:" they shall have no fruit. For they are effective indeed for a short time; afterwards they shall seek for them, and shall not find the reward of that which they have wrought. For it is the expression of those who lose what they have wrought, that text which says, "What hath pride profited us, or what good hath riches with our vaunting brought us? All those things are passed away like a shadow."[2] "The seed of the wicked," then, "shall be cut off."

10. "The righteous shall inherit the land" (ver. 29). Here again let not covetousness steal on thee, nor promise thee some great estate; hope not to find there, what you are commanded to despise in this world. That "land" in the text, is a certain "land of the living," the kingdom of the Saints. Whence it is said: "Thou art my hope, my portion in the land of the living."[3] For if thy life too is the same life as that there spoken of, think what sort of "land" thou art about to inherit. That is "the land of the living;" this the land of those who are about to die: to receive again, when dead, those whom it nourished when living. Such then as is that land, such shall the life itself be also: if the life be for ever, "the land" also is to be thine "for ever." And how is "the land" to be thine "for ever"?

"And they shall dwell therein" (it says) "for ever." It must therefore be another land, where "they are to dwell therein for ever." For of this land (of this earth) it is said, "Heaven and earth shall pass away."[4]

11. "The mouth of the righteous speaketh wisdom" (ver. 30). See here is that "bread." Observe with what satisfaction this righteous man feedeth upon it; how he turns wisdom over and over in his mouth. "And his tongue talketh of judgment."

"The law of his God is in his heart" (ver. 31). Lest haply thou shouldest think him to have that on his lips, which he hath not in his heart, lest thou shouldest reckon him among those of whom it is said, "This people honour Me with their lips, but their heart is far from Me."[5] And of what use is this to him?

"And none of his steps shall slide." The "word of God in the heart" frees from the snare; the "word of God in the heart" delivers from the evil way; "the word of God in the

heart" delivers from "the slippery place."[6] He is with thee, Whose word departeth not from thee. Now what evil doth he suffer, whom God keepeth? Thou settest a watchman in thy vineyard, and feelest secure from thieves; and that watchman may sleep, and may himself fall, and may admit a thief. But "He who keepeth Israel shall neither slumber nor sleep."[7] "The law of his God is in his heart, and none of his steps shall slide." Let him therefore live free from fear; let him live free from fear even in the midst of the wicked; free from fear even in the midst of the ungodly. For what evil can the ungodly or unrighteous man do to the righteous? Lo! see what follows.

"The wicked watcheth the righteous, and seeketh to slay him" (ver. 32). For he says, what it was foretold in the book of Wisdom that he should say, "He is grievous unto us, even to behold; for his life is not like other men's."[8] Therefore he "seeks to slay him." What? Doth the Lord, who keepeth him, who dwelleth with him, who departeth not from his lips, from his heart, doth He forsake him? What then becomes of what was said before: "And He forsaketh not His Saints"?[9]

12. "The wicked therefore watcheth the righteous, and seeketh to slay him. But the Lord will not leave him in his hands" (ver. 33). Wherefore then did He leave the Martyrs in the hands of the ungodly? Wherefore did they do unto them "whatsoever they would"?[10] Some they slew with the sword; some they crucified; some they delivered to the beasts; some they burnt by fire; others they led about in chains, till wasted out by a long protracted decay. Assuredly "the Lord forsaketh not His Saints." He will not "leave him in his hands." Lastly, wherefore did He leave His own Son in "the hands of the ungodly"? Here also, if thou wouldest have all the limbs of thy inner man made strong, remove the covering of the roof, and find thy way to the Lord. Hear what another Scripture, foreseeing our Lord's future suffering at the hands of the ungodly, saith. What saith it? "The earth is given into the hands of the wicked."[11] What is meant by "earth" being "given into the hands of the ungodly"? The delivering of the flesh into the hands of the persecutors. But God did not leave "His righteous One"[12] there: from the flesh, which was taken captive, He leads forth the soul unconquered. . . .

"The Lord will not leave him in his hand, nor condemn him when there shall be judgment for him" (ver. 33). Some copies have it, "and when He shall judge him, there shall be judg-

---

[1] Luke v. 19.   [2] Wisd. v. 8, 9.   [3] Ps. cxlii. 5.
[4] Matt. xxiv. 35.   [5] Isa. xxix. 13.

[6] *Labina. Lubricus locus.* Isidor.   [7] Ps. cxxi. 4.
[8] Wisd. ii. 15.   [9] Ps. xxxvii. 28.   [10] Matt. xvii. 12.
[11] Job ix. 24.   [12] Ps. xvi. 10.

ment for him." "For him," however, means when sentence is passed upon him. For we can express ourselves so as to say to a person, "Judge for me," i.e. "hear my cause." When therefore God shall begin to hear the cause of His righteous servant, since "we must all" be presented "before the tribunal of Christ," and stand before it to receive every one "the things he hath done in this body,"[1] whether good or evil, when therefore he shall have come to that Judgment, He will not condemn him; though he may seem to be condemned in this present life by man. Even though the Proconsul may have passed sentence on Cyprian,[2] yet the earthly seat of judgment is one thing, the heavenly tribunal is another. From the inferior tribunal he receives sentence of death; from the superior one a crown, "Nor will He condemn him when there shall be judgment for him." . . .

13. "Wait on the Lord" (ver. 34). And while I am waiting upon Him, what am I to do?—"and keep His ways." And if I keep them, what am I to receive? "And He shall exalt thee to inherit the land." "What land"? Once more let not any estate suggest itself to your mind:— the land of which it is said, "Come, ye blessed of My Father, inherit the kingdom prepared for you from the foundation of the world."[3] What of those who have troubled us, in the midst of whom we have groaned, whose scandals we have patiently endured, for whom, while they were raging against us, we have prayed in vain? What will become of them? What follows? "When the wicked are cut off, thou shalt see it." . . .

"I have seen the ungodly lifted up on high, and rising above the cedars of Libanus" (ver. 35). And suppose him to be "lifted up on high;" suppose him to be towering above the "rest;" what follows?

"I passed by, and, lo, he was not! I sought him, and his place could nowhere be found!" (ver. 36). Why was he "no more, and his place nowhere to be found"? Because thou hast "passed by." But if thou art yet carnally-minded, and that earthly prosperity appears to thee to be true happiness, thou hast not yet "passed by" him; thou art either his fellow, or thou art below him; go on, and pass him; and when thou hast made progress, and hast passed by him, thou observest him by the eye of faith; thou seest his end, thou sayest to thyself, "Lo! he who so swelled before, is not!" just as if it were some smoke that thou wert passing near to. For this too was said above in this very Psalm, "They shall consume and fade away as the smoke."[4] . . .

14. "Keep innocency" (ver. 37); keep it even as thou usedst to keep thy purse, when thou wert covetous; even as thou usedst to hold fast that purse, that it might not be snatched from thy grasp by the thief, even so "keep innocency," lest that be snatched from thy grasp by the devil. Be that thy sure inheritance, of which the rich and the poor may both be sure. "Keep innocency." What doth it profit thee to gain gold, and to lose innocence?

"Keep innocency, and take heed unto the thing which is right." Keep thou thine eyes "right," that thou mayest see "the thing which is right;" not perverted, wherewith thou lookest upon the wicked; not distorted, so that God should appear to thee distorted and wrong, in that He favours the wicked, and afflicts the faithful with persecutions. Dost thou not observe how distorted thy vision is? Set right thine eyes, and "behold the thing that is right." What "thing that is right"?. Take no heed of things present. And what wilt thou see?

"For there is a remainder for the man that maketh peace."[5] What is meant by "there is a remainder"? When thou art dead, thou shalt not be dead. This is the meaning of "there is a remainder." He will still have something remaining to him, even after this life, that is to say, that "seed," which "shall be blessed." Whence our Lord saith, "He that believeth on Me, though he die, yet shall he live;"[6]—"seeing there is a remainder for the man that maketh peace."

15. "But the transgressors shall be destroyed in the self-same thing"[7] (ver. 38). What is meant by, "in the self-same thing"? It means for ever: or all together in one and the same destruction.

"The remainder of the wicked shall be cut off." Now there is "(a remainder) for the man that maketh peace:" they therefore who are not peace-makers[8] are ungodly. For, "Blessed are the peace-makers: for they shall be called the children of God."[9]

16. "But the salvation of the righteous is of the Lord, and He is their strength in the time of trouble" (ver. 39). "And the Lord shall help them, and deliver them; He shall deliver them from the sinners"[10] (ver. 40). At present therefore let the righteous bear with the sinner; let the wheat bear with the tares; let the grain bear with the chaff: for the time of separation will come, and the good seed shall be set apart from that which is to be consumed with fire.[11] The one will be consigned to the garner, the other to "everlasting burning;" for it was for

---

[1] 2 Cor. v. 10.   [2] [See A. N. F. vol. V. p. 273.—C.]
[3] Matt. xxv. 34.   [4] Ps. xxxvii. 20.

[5] E. V. "For the end of that man is peace."   [6] John xi. 25.
[7] *In id ipsum.*   [8] The Donatists.   [9] Matt. v. 9.
[10] St. Augustin omits, "because they trust in Him." Vulgate has, *quia speraverunt in eo.*
[11] Matt. xiii. 30.

this reason that the just and the unjust were at the first together; that the one should lay a stumbling-block, [1] that the other should be proved; that afterwards the one should be condemned, the other receive a crown. . . .

PSALM XXXVIII.[2]

A PSALM TO DAVID HIMSELF, ON THE REMEMBRANCE OF THE SABBATH.

1. What doth this recollection of the Sabbath mean? What is this Sabbath? For it is with groaning that he "calls it to recollection." You have both heard already when the Psalm was read, and you will now hear it when we shall go over it, how great is his groaning, his mourning, his tears, his misery. But happy he who is wretched after this manner! Whence the Lord also in the Gospel[3] called some who mourn blessed. "How should he be blessed if he is a mourner? How blessed, if he is miserable?" Nay rather, he would be miserable, if he were not a mourner. Such an one then let us understand here too, calling the Sabbath to remembrance (viz.), some mourner or other: and would that we were ourselves that "some one or other"! For there is here some person sorrowing, groaning, mourning, calling the Sabbath to remembrance. The Sabbath is rest. Doubtless he was in some disquietude, who with groaning was calling the Sabbath to remembrance. . . .

2. "O Lord, rebuke me not in Thine indignation; neither chasten me in Thy hot displeasure" (ver. 1). For it will be that some shall be chastened in God's "hot displeasure," and rebuked in His "indignation." And haply not all who are "rebuked" will be "chastened;" yet are there some that are to be saved in the chastening.[4] So it is to be indeed, because it is called "chastening," [5] but yet it shall be "so as by fire." But there are to be some who will be "rebuked," and will not be "corrected." For he will at all events "rebuke" [6] those to whom He will say, "I was an hungred, and ye gave me no meat." [7] . . . "Neither chasten me in Thy hot displeasure;" so that Thou mayest cleanse me in this life, and make me such, that I may after that stand in no need of the cleansing fire, for those "who are to be saved, yet so as by fire." [8] Why? Why, but because they "build upon the foundation, wood, stubble, and hay." Now they should build on it, "gold, silver, and precious stones;" [9] and should have nothing to fear from either fire: not only that which is to consume the ungodly for ever, but

also that which is to purge those who are to escape through [10] the fire. For it is said, "he himself shall be saved, yet so as by fire." And because it is said, "he shall be saved," that fire is thought lightly of. For all that, though we should be "saved by fire," yet will that fire be more grievous than anything that man can suffer in this life whatsoever.[11] . . .

3. Now on what ground does this person pray that he may not be "rebuked in indignation, nor chastened in hot displeasure"? (He speaks) as if he would say unto God, "Since the things which I already suffer are many in number, I pray Thee let them suffice;" and he begins to enumerate them, by way of satisfying God; offering what he suffers now, that he may not have to suffer worse evils hereafter.

4. "For Thine arrows stick fast in me, and Thy hand presseth me sore" (ver. 2). "There is no soundness in my flesh, from the face of Thine anger" (ver. 3). He has now begun telling these evils, which he is suffering here: and yet even this already was from the wrath of the Lord, because it was of the vengeance of the Lord. "Of what vengeance?" That which He took upon Adam. For think not that punishment was not inflicted upon him, or that God had said to no purpose, "Thou shalt surely die;" [12] or that we suffer anything in this life, except from that death which we earned by the original sin. . . . Whence then do His "arrows stick fast in" him? The very punishment, the very vengeance, and haply the pains both of mind and of body, which it is necessary for us to suffer here, these he describes by these self-same "arrows." For of these arrows holy Job also made mention,[13] and said that the arrows of the Lord stuck fast in him, whilst he was labouring under those pains. We are used, however, to call God's words also arrows; but could he grieve that he should be struck by these? The words of God are arrows, as it were, that inflame love, not pain. . . . We may then understand the "arrows sticking fast," thus: Thy words are fixed fast in my heart; and by those words themselves is it come to pass, that I "called the Sabbath to remembrance:" and that very remembrance of the Sabbath, and the non-possession of it at present, prevents me from rejoicing at present; and causes me to acknowledge that there "is neither health in my very flesh," neither ought it to be so called when I compare this sort of soundness to that soundness which I am to possess in the

---

[1] Most MSS. "should stumble."   [2] Lat. XXXVII.
[3] Matt. v. 4.
[4] *Futuri sunt in emendatione quidam salvi.*
[5] *Emendatio* (alluding to *emendes* in the Latin of v. 1).
[6] *Utique arguet.*   [7] Matt. xxv. 42.
[8] 1 Cor. iii. 15.   [9] 1 Cor. iii. 12.

[10] *Per.*
[11] [See Augustin's ideas as to a *possible* meaning of the text 1 Cor. iii. 11-15 in vol. ii. this series, p. 474. He there propounds, *as a conjecture merely*, a purification of some souls in the intermediate state, which he does not care to reject. It is not his own theory; he says, "I do not contradict; *possibly* it is true." He thus proves there was no *dogma* of any sort of purgatory in his day, and even this theory is entirely inconsistent with the dogma as expounded in the Trent Catechism. — C.]
[12] Gen. ii. 17.   [13] Job vi. 4.

cverlasting rest; where "this corruptible shall put on incorruption, and this mortal shall put on immortality," [1] and see that in comparison with that soundness this present kind is but sickness.

5. "Neither is there any rest in my bones, from the face of my sin." It is commonly enquired, of what person this is the speech; and some understand it to be Christ's, on account of some things which are here said of the Passion of Christ; to which we shall shortly come; and which we ourselves shall acknowledge to be spoken of His Passion. But how could He who had no sin, say, "There is no rest in my bones, from the face of my sin." ... For if we were to say that they are not the words of Christ, those words, "My God, My God, why hast Thou forsaken Me?" [2] will also not be the words of Christ. For there too you have, "My God, My God, why hast Thou forsaken Me?" "The words of mine offences are far from my health." Just as here you have, "from the face of my sins," so there also you have, "the words of my offences." And if Christ is, for all that, without "sin," and without "offences," we begin to think those words in the Psalm also not to be His. And it is exceedingly harsh and inconsistent that that Psalm should not relate to Christ, where we have His Passion as clearly laid open as if it were being read to us out of the Gospel. For there we have, "They parted My garments among them, and cast lots upon My vesture." [3] Why should I mention that the first verse of that Psalm was pronounced by the Lord Himself while hanging on the Cross, with His own mouth, saying, "My God, My God, why hast Thou forsaken Me?" What did He mean to be inferred from it, but that the whole of that Psalm relates to Him, seeing He Himself, the Head of His Body, pronounced it in His own Person? Now when it goes on to say, "the words of mine offences," it is beyond a doubt that they are the words of Christ. Whence then come "the sins," but from the Body, which is the Church? Because both the Head and the Body of Christ are speaking. Why do they speak as if one person only? Because "they twain," as He hath said, "shall be one flesh." [4] "This" (says the Apostle) "is a great mystery; but I speak concerning Christ and the Church." ... For why should He not say, "my sins," who said, "I was an hungred, and ye gave Me no meat; I was thirsty, and ye gave Me no drink; I was a stranger, and ye took Me not in. I was sick and in prison, and ye visited Me not." [5] Assuredly the Lord was not in prison. Why should He not say this, to whom when it was said, "When saw we Thee a hungred, and athirst, or in prison; and did not minister unto Thee?" He replied, that He spake thus

in the person of His Body. "Inasmuch as ye did it not unto one of the least of Mine, ye did it not unto Me." [6] Why should He not say, "from the face of my sins," who said to Saul, "Saul, Saul, why persecutest thou Me," [7] who, however, being in Heaven, now suffered from no persecutors? But just as, in that passage, the Head spake for the Body, so here too the Head speaks the words of the Body; whilst you hear at the same time the accents of the Head Itself also. Yet do not either, when you hear the voice of the Body, separate the Head from it; nor the Body, when you hear the voice of the Head: because "they are no more twain, but one flesh." [8]

6. "There is no soundness in my flesh from the face of thine anger." But perhaps God is unjustly angry with thee, O Adam; unjustly angry with thee, O son of man; because now brought to acknowledge that thy punishment, now that thou art a man that hath been placed in Christ's Body, thou hast said, "There is no soundness in my flesh from the face of Thine anger." Declare the justice of God's anger: lest thou shouldest seem to be excusing thyself, and accusing Him. Go on to tell whence the "anger" of the Lord proceeds. "There is no soundness in my flesh from the face of Thine anger; neither is there any rest in my bones." He repeats what he said before, "There is no soundness in my flesh;" for, "There is no rest in my bones," is equivalent to this. He does not however repeat "from the face of Thine anger;" but states the cause of the anger of God. "There is no rest in my bones from the face of my sins."

7. "For mine iniquities have lifted up my head; and are like a heavy burden too heavy for me to bear" (ver. 4). Here too he has placed the cause first, and the effect afterwards. What consequence followed, and from what cause, he has told us. "Mine iniquities have lift up mine head." For no one is proud but the unrighteous man, whose head is lifted up. He is "lifted up," whose "head is lifted up on high" against God. You heard when the lesson of the Book of Ecclesiasticus was read: "The beginning of pride is when a man departeth from God." [9] He who was the first to refuse to listen to the Commandment, "his head iniquity lifted up" against God. And because his iniquities have lifted up his head, what hath God done unto him? They are "like a heavy burden, too heavy for me to bear"! It is the part of levity to lift up the head, just as if he who lifts up his head had nothing to carry. Since therefore that which admits of being lifted up is light, it receives a weight by which it may be weighed down. For "his mischief returns upon his own head, and his violent dealing comes

---

[1] 1 Cor. xv. 53.　　[2] Ps. xxii. 1.　　[3] Ps. xxii. 18.
[4] Gen. ii. 24.　　[5] Matt. xxv. 42, 43.

[6] Matt. xxv. 44, 45.　　[7] Acts ix. 4.　　[8] Matt. xix. 6.
[9] Ecclus. x. 12. [Note "as a Lesson:" part of Divine Service. — C.]

down upon his own pate."[1] "They are like a heavy burden, too heavy for me to bear."

8. "My wounds stink and are corrupt" (ver. 5). Now he who has wounds is not perfectly sound. Add to this, that the wounds "stink and are corrupt." Wherefore do they "stink"? Because they are "corrupt:" now in what way this is explained in reference to human life, who doth not understand? Let a man but have his soul's sense of smelling sound, he perceives how foully sins stink. The contrary to which stink of sin, is that savour of which the Apostle says, "We are the sweet savour of Christ unto God, in every place, unto them which be saved."[2] But whence is this, except from hope? Whence is this, but from our "calling the Sabbath to remembrance"? For it is a different thing that we mourn over in this life, from that which we anticipate in the other. That which we mourn over is *stench*, that which we reckon upon is *fragrance*. Were there not therefore such a perfume as that to invite us, we should never call the Sabbath to remembrance.[3] But since, by the Spirit, we have such a perfume, as to say to our Betrothed, "Because of the savour of Thy good ointments we will run after Thee;"[4] we turn our senses away from our own unsavouri-nesses, and turning ourselves to Him, we gain some little breathing-time. But indeed, unless our evil deeds also did smell rank in our nostrils, we should never confess with those groans, "My wounds stink and are corrupt." And wherefore? "from the face of my foolishness."[5] From the same cause that he said before, "from the face of my sins;" from that same cause he now says, "from the face of my foolishness."

9. "I am troubled, I am bowed down even unto the end" (ver. 6). Wherefore was he "bowed down"? Because he had been "lifted up." If thou art "humble, thou shalt be ex-alted;" if thou exaltest thyself, thou shalt be "bowed down;" for God will be at no loss to find a weight wherewith to bow thee down. . . . Let him groan on these things; that he may receive the other; let him "call the Sabbath to remembrance," that he may deserve to arrive at it. For that which the Jews used to celebrate was but a sign. Of what thing was it the sign? Of that which he calls to remembrance, who saith, "I am troubled, and am bowed down even unto the end." What is meant by even "unto the end"? Even to death.

"I go mourning all the day long." "All day long," that is, "without intermission." By "all the day long," he means, "all my life long." But from what time hath he known it? From the time that he began to "call the Sabbath to remembrance." For so long as he "calls to remembrance" what he no longer possesses, wouldest thou not have him "go mourning"? "All the day long have I gone mourning."

10. "For my soul is filled with illusions, and there is no soundness in my flesh" (ver. 7). Where there is the whole man, there is soul and flesh both. The "soul is filled with illusions;" the *flesh* hath "no soundness." What does there remain that can give joy? Is it not meet that one should "go mourning"? "All the day long have I gone mourning." Let mourning be our portion, until our soul be divested of its illusions; and our body be clothed with soundness. For true soundness is no other than immortality. How great however are the soul's illusions, were I even to attempt to express, when would the time suffice me? For whose soul is not subject to them? There is a brief particular that I will remind you of, to show how our soul is filled with illusions. The presence of those illusions sometimes scarcely permits us to pray. We know not how to think of material objects without images, and such as we do not wish, rush in upon the mind; and we wish to go from this one to that, and to quit that for another. And sometimes you wish to return to that which you were thinking of before, and to quit that which you are now thinking of; and a fresh one presents itself to you; you wish to call up again what you had forgotten; and it does not occur to you; and another comes in-stead which you would not have wished for. Where meanwhile was the one that you had forgotten? For why did it afterwards occur to you, when it had ceased to be sought after; whereas, while it was being sought for, innumer-able others, which were not desired, presented themselves instead of it? I have stated a fact briefly; I have thrown out a kind of hint or suggestion to you, brethren, taking up which, you may yourselves suggest the rest to your-selves, and discover what it is to mourn over the "illusions" of our "soul." He hath received therefore the punishment of illusion; he hath forfeited Truth. For just as illusion is the soul's punishment, so is Truth its reward. But when we were set in the midst of these illusions, the Truth Itself came to us, and found us over-whelmed by illusions, took upon Itself our flesh, or rather took flesh from us; that is, from the human race. He manifested himself to the eyes of the Flesh, that He might "by faith" heal those to whom He was going to reveal the Truth hereafter, that Truth might be manifested to the now healed eye. For He is Himself "the Truth,"[6] which He promised unto us at that time, when His Flesh was to be seen by the eye, that the foundation might be laid of that Faith,

---

[1] Ps. vii. 16. [2] 2 Cor. ii. 15. [3] [Isa. lviii. 13. — C.]
[4] Song of Sol. i. 3, 4. [5] Ps. xxxviii. 5. [6] John xiv. 6.

of which the Truth was to be the reward. For it was not Himself that Christ showed forth on earth; but it was His Flesh that He showed. For had He showed Himself, the Jews would have seen and known Him; but had they "known Him, they would never have crucified the Lord of Glory."[1] But perhaps His disciples saw Him, when they said unto Him, "Show us the Father, and it sufficeth us;"[2] and He, to show that it was not Himself that had been seen by them, added: "Have I been so long with you, and have ye not known Me, Philip? He that seeth Me, seeth the Father also."[3] If then they saw Christ, wherefore did they yet seek for the Father? For if it were Christ whom they saw, they would have seen the Father also. They did not therefore yet see Christ, who desired that the Father should be shown unto them. To prove that they did not yet see Him, hear that, in another place, He promised it by way of reward, saying, "He who loveth Me, keepeth My commandments; and whoso loveth Me, shall be loved of My Father; and I will love Him, and" (as if it were said to Him, "what wilt Thou give unto him, as Thou lovest him?" He saith), "I will manifest Myself unto him."[4] If then He promises this by way of a reward unto them that love Him, it is manifest that the vision of the Truth, promised to us, is of such a nature, that, when we have seen it, we shall no longer say, "My soul is filled with illusions."

11. "I am become feeble,[5] and am bowed down greatly" (ver. 8). He who calls to mind the transcendent height of the Sabbath, sees how "greatly" he is himself "bowed down." For he who cannot conceive what is that height of rest, sees not where he is at present. Therefore another Psalm hath said, "I said in my trance, I am cast out of the sight of Thine eyes."[6] For his mind being taken up thither,[7] he beheld something sublime; and was not yet entirely there, where what he beheld was; and a kind of flash, as it were, if one may so speak, of the Eternal Light having glanced upon him, when he perceived that he was not yet arrived at this, which he was able after a sort to understand, he saw where he himself was, and how he was cramped and "bowed down" by human infirmities. And he says, "I said in my trance, I am cast out of the sight of Thine eyes." Such is that certain something which I saw in my trance, that thence I perceive how far off I am, who am not already there. He was already there who said that he was "caught up into the third Heaven, and there heard unspeakable words, which it is not lawful for a man to utter."[8] But he was recalled to us, in order that, as requiring to be made perfect, he might first mourn his infirmity, and afterwards be clothed with might. Yet encouraged for the ministration of his office by having seen somewhat of those things, he goes on saying, "I heard unspeakable words, which it is not lawful for a man to utter."[9] Now then what use is it for you to ask, either of me or of any one, the "things which it is not lawful for man to utter." If it was not lawful for him to utter them, to whom is it lawful to hear them? Let us however lament and groan in Confession; let us own where we are; let us "call the Sabbath to remembrance," and wait with patience for what He has promised, who hath, in His own Person also, showed forth an example of patience to us. "I am become feeble, and bowed down greatly."

12. "I have roared with the groaning of my heart."[10] You observe the servants of God generally interceding with groaning; and the reason of it is asked, and there is nothing apparent, but the groaning of some servant of God, if indeed it does find its way at all to the ears of a person placed near him. For there is a secret groaning, which is not heard by man: yet if the thought of some strong desire has taken so strong hold of the heart, that the wound of the inner man finds expression in some uttered exclamation, the reason of it is asked; and a man says to himself, "Perhaps this is the cause of his groaning;" and, "Perhaps this or that hath befallen him." Who can determine, but He in whose Eyes and Ears he groaned? Therefore he says, "I roared with the groaning of mine heart;" because if men ever hear a man's groanings, they for the most part hear but the groaning of the flesh; they do not hear him who groans "with the groaning of his heart." Some one hath carried off his goods; he "roareth," but not "with the groaning of his heart:" another because he has buried his son, another his wife; another because his vineyard has been injured by a hailstorm; another because his cask has turned sour; another because some one hath stolen his beast; another because he has suffered some loss; another because he fears some man who is his enemy: all these "roar" with the "groaning of the flesh." The servant of God, however, because he "roareth" from the recollection of the Sabbath, where the Kingdom of God is, which flesh and blood shall not possess, says, "I have roared with the groaning of my heart."

13. And who observed and noticed the cause of his groaning? "All my desire is before Thee" (ver. 9). For it is not before men who

---

[1] 1 Cor. ii. 10.　　[2] John xiv. 8.　　[3] John xiv. 9.
[4] John xiv. 21.
[5] St. Augustin, *infirmatus;* E. V. "troubled;" Prayer Book, "feeble;" Vulgate, *afflictus.*
[6] Ps. xxxi. 22.　　[7] *Assumpta mente.*

[8] 2 Cor. xii. 2, 4.　　[9] 2 Cor. xii. 4.
[10] *Rugiebam a gemitu cordis mei.* E. V. "by reason of the disquietness."

cannot see the heart, but it is before Thee that all my desire is open! Let your desire be before Him; and "the Father, who seeth in secret, shall reward thee." [1] For it is thy heart's desire that is thy prayer; and if thy desire continues uninterrupted, thy prayer continueth also. For not without a meaning did the Apostle say, "Pray without ceasing." [2] Are we to be "without ceasing" bending the knee, prostrating the body, or lifting up our hands, that he says, "Pray without ceasing"? Or if it is in this sense that we say that we "pray," this, I believe, we cannot do "without ceasing." There is another inward kind of prayer without ceasing, which is the desire of the heart. Whatever else you are doing, if you do but long for that Sabbath, you do not cease to pray. If you would never cease to pray, never cease to long after it. The continuance of thy longing is the continuance of thy prayer. You will be ceasing to speak, if you cease to long for it. Who are those who have ceased to speak? They of whom it is said, "Because iniquity shall abound, the love of many shall wax cold." [3] The freezing of charity is the silence of the heart; the burning of charity is the cry of the heart. If love continues still, you are still lifting up your voice; if you are always lifting up your voice, you are always longing after something; if always longing for something absent, you are calling "the Sabbath rest to remembrance." And it is important you should understand too before whom the "roaring of thine heart" is open. Now then consider what sort of desires those should be, that are before the eyes of God. Should it be the desire for the death of our enemy? a thing which men flatter themselves they lawfully wish for? For sometimes we pray for what we ought not. Let us consider what they flatter themselves they pray for lawfully! For they pray that some person may die, and his inheritance come to them. But let those too, who pray for the death of their enemies, hear the Lord saying, "Pray for your enemies." [4] Let them not pray for this, that their enemies may die; but rather pray for this, that they may be reclaimed; then will their enemies be dead; for from the time that they are reclaimed, henceforth they will be enemies no longer. "And all my desire is before Thee." What if we suppose that our desire is before Him, and that yet that very "groaning" is not before Him? How can that be, since our desire itself finds its expression in "groaning"? Therefore follows, "And my groaning is not hid from Thee."

From Thee indeed it is not hid; but from many men it is hid. The servant of God sometimes seems to be saying in humility, "And my groaning is not hid from Thee." Sometimes also he seems to smile. Is then that longing dead in his heart? If however there is the desire within, there is the "groaning" also. It does not always find its way to the ears of man; but it never ceases to sound in the ears of God.

14. "My heart is troubled" (ver. 10). Wherefore is it troubled? "And my courage hath failed me." Generally something comes upon us on a sudden; the "heart is troubled;" the earth quakes; thunder is sent from Heaven; a formidable attack is made upon us, or a horrible sound heard. Perhaps a lion is seen on the road; the "heart is troubled." Perhaps robbers lie in wait for us; the "heart is troubled:" we are filled with a panic fear; from every quarter something excites anxiety. Wherefore? Because "my courage hath failed me." For what would be feared, did that courage still remain unmoved? Whatever bad tidings were brought, whatever threatened us, whatever sound was heard, whatever were to fall, whatever appeared horrible, would inspire no terror. But whence that trouble? "My courage faileth me." Wherefore hath my courage failed me? "The light of mine eyes also is gone from me." Thus Adam also could not see "the light of his eyes." For the "light of his eyes" was God Himself, whom when he had offended, he fled to the shade, and hid himself among the trees of Paradise.[5] He shrunk in alarm from the face of God: and sought the shelter of the trees; thenceforth among the trees he had no more "the light of his eyes," at which he had been wont to rejoice. . . .

15. "My lovers;" why should I henceforth speak of my enemies? "My lovers and my neighbours drew nigh, and stood over against me" (ver. 11). Understand this that he saith, "Stood over against me." For if they stood over against me, they fell against themselves. "My lovers and my neighbours drew nigh and stood over against me."[6] Let us now recognise the words of the Head speaking; now let our Head in His Passion begin to dawn upon us. Yet again when the Head begins to speak, do not sever the Body from it. If the Head would not separate itself from the words of the Body, should the Body dare to separate itself from the sufferings of the Head? Do thou suffer in Christ's suffering: for Christ, as it were, sinned in thy infirmity. For just now He spoke of thy sins, as if speaking in His own Person, and called them His own. . . . To those who wished to be near His exaltation, yet thought not of His humility, He answered and said to them, "Can ye drink of the cup that I shall drink of?" [7] Those sufferings of the Lord then are

[1] Matt. vi. 6.　　[2] 1 Thess. v. 17.　　[3] Matt. xxiv. 12.
[4] Matt. v. 44.

[5] Gen. iii 8.　　[6] E. V. "and my friends stand aloof."
[7] Matt. xx. 22.

our sufferings also : and were each individual to serve God well, to keep faith truly, to render to each their dues, and to conduct himself honestly among men, I should like to see if he does not suffer even that which Christ here details in the account of His Passion. "My lovers and my neighbours drew nigh, and stood over against me."

16. "And my neighbours stood afar off " Who were the "neighbours" that drew nigh, and who were those who stood afar off? The Jews were "neighbours" because "near kinsmen," they drew near even when they crucified Him : the Apostles also were His "neighbours ; " and they also "stood afar off," that they might not have to suffer with Him. This may also be understood thus : "My friends," that is, those who feigned themselves "My friends : " for they feigned themselves His friends, when they said, "We know that Thou teachest the way of God in truth ; "[1] when they wished to try Him, whether tribute ought to be paid to Cæsar ; when He convinced them out of their own mouth, they wished to seem to be His friends. "But He needed not that any should testify of man, for He Himself knew what was in man ; "[2] so that when they spoke unto Him words of friendship, He answered them, "Why tempt ye Me, ye hypocrites?"[3] "My friends and my neighbours" then "drew near and stood over against me, and my neighbours stood afar off." You understand what I said. I called those neighbours who "drew nigh," and at the same time "stood afar off." For they "drew nigh" in the body, but "stood afar off" in their heart. Who were in the body so near to Him as those who lifted Him on the Cross? Who in heart so far off as those who blasphemed Him? Hear this sort of distance described by the Prophet Isaiah ; observe this nearness and distance at one and the same time. "This people honours Me with their lips : " behold, with their body they draw near ; "but their heart is far from Me."[4] The same persons are at the same time "near" and "afar off" also : with their lips they are near, in heart afar off. However, because the Apostles also stood afar off, through fear, we understand it more simply and properly of them ; so that we mean by it, that some drew near, and others stood afar off ; since even Peter, who had followed more boldly than the rest, was still so far off, that being questioned and alarmed, he thrice denied the Lord, with whom he had promised to "be ready to die." Who afterwards that, from being afar off, he might be made to draw nigh, heard after the resurrection the question, "Lovest thou Me?" and said, "I love Thee ; "[5] and by so saying was brought "nigh," even as by denying Him, he

had become "far off ; " till with the threefold confession of love, he had put away from him his threefold denial. "And my neighbours stood afar off."

17. "They also that sought after my soul were preparing violence against me " (ver. 12). It is now plain who "sought after His soul ; " viz. those who had not His soul, in that they were not in His Body. They who were "seeking after His soul," were far removed from His soul ; but they were "seeking it" to destroy it. For His soul may be "sought after" in a right way also. For in another passage [6] He finds fault with some persons, saying, "There is no man to care for My soul." He finds fault with some for not seeking after His soul ; and again, with others for seeking after it. Who is he that seeketh after His soul in the right way? He who imitates His sufferings. Who are they that sought after His soul in the wrong way? Even those who "prepared violence against Him," and crucified Him.

18. He goes on : "Those who sought after My faults had spoken vanity." What is, "sought after My faults"? They sought after many things, and found them not. Perhaps He may have meant this : "They sought for criminal charges against me." For they sought for somewhat to say against Him, and "they found not."[7] For they were seeking to find evil things to say of "the Good ; " crimes of the Innocent ; When would they find such things in Him, who had no sin? But because they had to seek for sins in Him who had no sin, it remained for them to invent that which they could not find. Therefore, "those who sought after My faults have spoken vanity," i.e., untruth, "and imagined deceit all the day long ; " that is, they meditated treachery without intermission. You know how atrocious false-witness was borne against the Lord, before He suffered. You know how atrocious false-witness was borne against Him, even after His resurrection. For those soldiers who watched His sepulchre of whom Isaiah spake, "I will appoint the wicked for His burial"[8] (for they were wicked men, and would not speak the truth, and being bribed they disseminated a lie), consider what "vanity" they spake. They also were examined, and they said, "While we slept, His disciples came and stole Him away."[9] This it is, "to speak vanity." For if they were sleeping, how could they know what had been done?

19. He saith then, "But I as a deaf man heard not" (ver. 13). He who replied not to what He heard, did, as it were, not hear them. "But I as a deaf man heard not. And I was as

[1] Matt. xxii. 16.   [2] John ii. 25.   [3] Matt. xxii. 18.
[4] Isa. xxix. 13.   [5] John xxi. 15.

[6] Ps. cxlii. 4.   [7] Matt. xxvi 60.
[8] Isa. liii. 9. St Augustin, *Ponam malos pro sepulturâ ejus.*
Vulgate, *Dabit impios,* etc.
[9] Matt. xxviii. 13.

a dumb man that openeth not his mouth." And he repeats the same things again.

"And I became as a man that heareth not, and in whose mouth are no reproofs" (ver. 14). As if He had nothing to say unto them, as if He had nothing wherewith to reproach them. Had He not already reproached them for many things? Had He not said many things, and also said, "Woe unto you, Scribes and Pharisees,"[1] and many things besides? Yet when He suffered, He said none of these things; not that He had not what to say, but He waited for them to fulfil all things, and that all the prophecies might be fulfilled of Him, of whom it had been said, "And as a sheep before her shearer is dumb, so openeth He not His mouth."[2] It behoved Him to be silent in His Passion, though not hereafter to be silent in Judgment. For He had come to be judged, then, who was hereafter coming to judge; and who was for this reason to come with great power to judge, that He had been judged in great humility.

20. "For in Thee, O Lord, do I hope; Thou wilt hear, O Lord, my God" (ver. 15). As if it were said to Him, "Wherefore openedst thou not thy mouth? Wherefore didst Thou not say, 'Refrain'? Wherefore didst Thou not rebuke the unrighteous, while hanging on the Cross?" He goes on and says, "For in Thee, O Lord, do I hope; Thou, O Lord my God, wilt hear." He warns you what to do, should tribulation haply befall. For you seek to defend yourself, and perhaps your defence is not listened to by any one. Then are you confounded, as if you had lost your cause; because you have none to defend or to bear testimony in your favour. "Keep" but your "innocence" within, where no one can pervert thy cause. False-witness has prevailed against you before men. Will it then prevail before God, where your cause has to be pleaded? When God shall be Judge, there shall be no other witness than your own conscience. In the presence of a just judge, and of your own conscience, fear nothing but your own cause. If you have not a bad cause, you will have no accuser to dread; no false-witness to confute, nor witness to the truth to look for. Do but bring into court a good conscience, that you may say, "For in Thee, O Lord, do I hope; Thou, O Lord my God, wilt hear."

21. "For I said, Let not mine enemies ever rejoice over me. And when my feet slip, they magnify themselves against me" (ver. 16). Again He returns to the infirmity of His Body: and again the Head takes heed of Its "feet." The Head is not in such a manner in Heaven, as to forsake what It has on earth; He evidently sees and observes us. For sometimes, as is the way of this life, our feet are "turned aside," and they slip by falling into some sin; there the tongues of the enemy rise up with the bitterest malignity. From this then we discern what they really had in view, even while they kept silence. Then they speak with an unsparing harshness; rejoicing to have discovered what they ought to have grieved for. "And I said, Lest at any time my adversaries should rejoice over me." I said this indeed; and yet it was perhaps for my correction that Thou hast caused them to "magnify themselves against me, when my feet slipped;" that is to say, when I stumbled, they were elated, and said many things. For pity, not insult, was due from them to the weak; even as the Apostle speaks: "Brethren, if a man be overtaken in a fault, ye which are spiritual restore such an one in the spirit of meekness;" and he combines the reason why: "considering thyself also, lest thou also be tempted."[3] Not such as these were the persons of whom He speaks: "And when my feet slipped, they rejoiced greatly against me;" but they were such as those of whom He says elsewhere: "They that hate me will rejoice if I fall."

22. "For I am prepared for the scourges" (ver. 17). Quite a magnificent expression; as if He were saying, "It was even for this that I was born; that I might suffer." For He was not to be born,[4] but from Adam, to whom the scourge is due. But sinners are in this life sometimes not scourged at all, or are scourged less than their deserts: because the wickedness of their heart is given over as already desperate. Those, however, for whom eternal life is prepared, must needs be scourged in this life: for that sentence is true: "My son, faint not under the chastening of the Lord, neither be weary when thou art rebuked of Him."[5] "For whom the Lord loveth He chasteneth, and scourgeth every son whom He receiveth."[6] Let not mine enemies therefore insult over me; let "them not magnify themselves;" and if my Father scourgeth me, "I am prepared for the scourge;" because there is an inheritance in store for me. Thou wilt not submit to the scourge: the inheritance is not bestowed upon thee. For "every son" must needs be scourged. So true it is that "every son" is scourged, that He spared not even Him who had no sin. For "I am prepared for the scourges."

23. "And my sorrow is continually before me." What "sorrow" is that? Perhaps, a sorrow for my scourge. And, in good truth, my brethren, in good truth, let me say unto you, men do mourn for their scourges, not for the causes on account of which they are scourged. Not such was the person here. Listen, my brethren: If

---

[1] Matt. xxiii. 13.   [2] Isa. liii. 7.

[3] Gal. vi. 1.   [4] *Al.* "He would not suffer."
[5] Prov. iii. 11.   [6] Heb. xii. 6.

any person suffers any loss, he is more ready to say, "I did not deserve to suffer it," than to consider why he suffered it, mourning the loss of money, not mourning over that of righteousness. If thou hast sinned, mourn for the loss of thy inward treasure. Thou hast nothing in thy house, but perhaps thou art still more empty in heart; but if thine heart is full of its Good, even thy God, why dost thou not say, "The Lord gave, the Lord hath taken away; as it pleased the Lord was it done. Blessed be the Name of the Lord."[1] Whence then was it that He was grieving? Was it for the "scourging" wherewith He was scourged? God forbid. "And my sorrow"(says He) "is continually before me." And as if we were to say, "What sorrow? whence comes that sorrow?" he says: "For I declare mine iniquity; and I will have a care for my sin" (ver. 18). See here the reason for the sorrow! It is not a sorrow occasioned by the scourge; not one for the remedy, not for the wound. For the scourge is a remedy against sins. Hear, brethren; We are Christians, and yet if any one's son dies, he mourns for him; but does not mourn for him if he sins. It is then, when he sees him sinning, that he ought to make mourning for him, to lament over him. It is then he should restrain him, and give him a rule to live by; should impose a discipline upon him: or if he has done so, and the other has not taken heed, then was the time when he ought to have been mourned over; then he was more fatally dead whilst living in luxury, than when, by death, he brought his luxury to its close: at that time, when he was doing such things in thine house, he was not only "dead, but he stank also."[2] These things were worthy to be lamented, the others were such as might well be endured; those, I say, were tolerable, these worthy to be mourned over. They were to be mourned over in the same way that you have heard this person mourn over them: "For I declare mine iniquity. I will have a care for my sin." Be not free from anxiety when you have confessed your sin, as if always able to confess thy sin, and to commit it again. Do thou "declare thine iniquity in such a manner, as to have a care for thy sin." What is meant by "having a care of thy sin"? To have a care of thy wound. If you were to say, "I will have a care of my wound," what would be meant by it, but I will do my endeavour to have it healed. For this is "to have a care for one's sin," to be ever struggling, ever endeavouring, ever exerting one's self, earnestly and zealously, to heal one's wound. Behold! thou art from day to day mourning over thy sins; but perhaps thy tears indeed flow, but thy hands are unemployed. Do

alms, redeem[3] thy sins, let the poor rejoice of thy bounty, that thou also mayest rejoice of the Grace of God. He is in want; so art thou in want also: he is in want at thy hands; so art thou also in want at God's hand. Dost thou despise one who needs thy aid; and shall God not despise thee when thou needest His? Do thou therefore supply the needs of him who is in want of thine aid; that God may supply thy needs within.[4] This is the meaning of, "I will have a care for my sin." I will do all that ought to be done, to blot out and to heal my sin. "And I will have a care for my sin."

24. "But mine enemies live" (ver. 19). They are well off: they rejoice in worldly prosperity, while I am suffering, and "roaring with the groaning of my heart." In what way do His enemies "live," in that He hath said of them already, that they have "spoken vanity"? Hear in another Psalm also: "Whose sons are as young plants; firmly rooted." But above He had said, "Whose mouth speaketh vanity. Their daughters polished after the similitude of a temple: their garners full bursting forth more and more; their cattle fat, their sheep fruitful, multiplying in their streets; no hedge falling into ruin; no cry in their streets."[5] "Mine enemies" then "live." This is their life; this life they praise; this they set their hearts upon: this they hold fast to their own ruin. For what follows? They pronounce "the people that is in such a case" blessed. But what sayest thou, who "hast a care for thy sin"? What sayest thou, who "confessest thine iniquity"? He says, "Blessed is the people whose God is the Lord."[6]

"But mine enemies live, and are strengthened against me, and they that hate me wrongfully are multiplied." What is "hate me wrongfully"? They hate me, who wish their good, whereas were they simply requiting evil for evil, they would not be righteous; were they not to requite with good the good done to them, they would be ungrateful: they, however, who "hate wrongfully," actually return evil for good. Such were the Jews; Christ came unto them with good things; they requited Him evil for good. Beware, brethren, of this evil; it soon steals[7] upon us. Let no one of you think himself to be far removed from the danger, because we said, "Such were the Jews." Should a brother, wishing your good, rebuke you, and you hate him, you are like them. And observe, how easily, how soon it is produced; and avoid an evil so great, a sin so easily committed.

25. "They also that render evil for good, were speaking evil of me, because I have pursued the thing that is just" (ver. 20). There-

[1] Job i. 21.   [2] John xi. 39.

[3] *Fiant, redimantur*.   [4] *Al.* "fill thine inward parts."
[5] Ps. cxliv. 12–14.   [6] Ps. cxliv. 15.   [7] *Cito subintrat*.

fore was it that I was requited evil for good. What is meant by "pursued after the thing that is just"? Not forsaken it. That you might not always understand *persecutio* in a bad sense, He means by *persecutus* pursued after, thoroughly followed. "Because I have followed the thing that is just." Hear also our Head crying with a lamentable voice in His Passion: "And they cast Me forth, Thy Darling, even as a dead man in abomination." [1] Was it not enough that He was "dead"? wherefore "in abomination" also? Because He was crucified. For this death of the Cross was a great abomination in their eyes, as they did not perceive that it was spoken in prophecy, "Cursed is every one that hangeth on a tree." [2] For He did not Himself bring death; but He found it here, propagated from the curse of the first man; and this same death of ours, which had originated in sin, He had taken upon Himself, and hung on the Tree. Lest therefore some persons should think (as some of the Heretics think), that our Lord Jesus Christ had only a false body of flesh; and that the death by which He made satisfaction on the Cross was not a real death, the Prophet notices this, and says, "Cursed is every one that hangeth on a tree." He shows then that the Son of God died a true death, the death which was due to mortal flesh: lest if He were not "accursed," you should think that He had not truly died. But since that death was not an illusion, but had descended from that original stock, which had been derived from the curse, when He said, "Ye shall surely die:" [3] and since a true death assuredly extended even to Him, that a true life might extend itself to us, the curse of death also did extend to Him, that the blessing of life might extend even unto us. "And they cast Me forth, Thy Darling, even as a dead man in abomination."

26. "Forsake me not, O Lord; O my God, depart not from me" (ver. 21). Let us speak in Him, let us speak through Him (for He Himself intercedeth for us), and let us say, "Forsake me not, O Lord my God." And yet He had said, "My God! My God! why hast Thou forsaken Me?" [4] and He now says, "O My God, depart not from Me." If He does not forsake the body, did He forsake the Head? Whose words then are these but the First Man's? To show then that He carried about Him a true body of flesh derived from him, He says, "My God, My God, why hast Thou forsaken Me?" God had not forsaken Him. If He does not forsake Thee, who believest in Him, could the Father, the Son, and the Holy Ghost, One God, forsake Christ? But He had transferred to Himself the person of the First Man. We know by

the words of an Apostle, that "our old man is crucified with Him." [5] We should not, however, be divested of our old nature, had He not been crucified "in weakness." For it was to this end that He came, that we may be renewed in Him, because it is by aspiration after Him, and by following the example of His suffering, that we are renewed. Therefore that was the cry of infirmity; that cry, I mean, in which it was said, "Why hast Thou forsaken Me?" Thence was it said in that passage above, "the words of mine offences." As if He were saying, These words are transferred to My Person from that of the sinner.

27. "Depart not from me. Make haste to help me, Lord of my salvation" (ver. 22). This is that very "salvation," Brethren, concerning which, as the Apostle Peter saith, "Prophets have enquired diligently," [6] and though they have enquired diligently, yet have not found it. But they searched into it, and foretold of it; while we have come and have found what they sought for. And see, we ourselves too have not as yet received it; and after us shall others also be born, and shall find, what they also shall not receive, and shall pass away, that we may, all of us together, receive the "penny of salvation in the end of the day," with the Prophets, the Patriarchs, and the Apostles. For you know that the hired servants, or labourers, were taken into the vineyard at different times; yet did they all receive their wages on an equal footing. [7] Apostles, then, and Prophets, and Martyrs, and ourselves also, and those who will follow us to the end of the world, it is in the End itself that we are to receive everlasting salvation; that beholding the face of God, and contemplating His Glory, we may praise Him for ever, free from imperfection, free from any punishment of iniquity, free from every perversion of sin: praising Him; and no longer longing after Him, but now clinging to Him for whom we used to long to the very end, and in whom we did rejoice, in hope. For we shall be in that City, where God is our Bliss, God is our Light, God is our Bread, God is our Life; whatever good thing of ours there is, at being absent from which we now grieve, we shall find in Him. In Him will be that "rest," which when we "call to remembrance" now, we cannot choose but grieve. For that is the "Sabbath" which we "call to remembrance;" in the recollection of which, so great things have been said already; and so great things ought to be said by us also, and ought never to cease being said by us, not with our lips indeed, but in our heart: for therefore do our lips cease to speak, that we may cry out with our hearts. [8]

---

[1] A few MSS. of LXX. note this to be added here.
[2] Deut. xxi. 23.   [3] Gen. ii. 17.   [4] Matt. xxvii. 46.

[5] Rom. vi. 6.   [6] 1 Pet. i. 10.   [7] Matt. xx. 9.
[8] [Heb. iv. 9. The Sabbath that "remaineth" is the only Sabbath our author sees in this Psalm.—C.]

PSALM XXXIX.[1]

1. The title of this Psalm, which we have just chanted and proposed to discuss, is, "On the end, for Idithun, a Psalm for David himself." Here then we must look for, and must attend to, the words of a certain person who is called Idithun; and if each one of ourselves may be Idithun, in that which he sings he recognises himself, and hears himself speak. For thou mayest see who was called Idithun, according to the ancient descent of man; let us, however, understand what this name is translated, and seek to comprehend the Truth in the translation of the word. According therefore to what we have been able to discover by enquiry in those names which have been translated from the Hebrew tongue into the Latin, by those who study the sacred writings, Idithun being translated is "over-leaping them." Who then is this person "over-leaping them"? or who those whom he hath "over-leaped"? . . . For there are some persons, yet clinging to the earth, yet bowed down to the ground, yet setting their hearts on what is below, yet placing their hopes in things that pass away, whom he who is called "over-leaping them" hath "over-leaped."

2. You know that some of the Psalms are entitled, "Songs of Degrees;" and in the Greek it is obvious enough what the word ἀναβαθμῶν means. For ἀναβαθμοὶ are degrees (or steps) of them that ascend, not of them that descend. The Latin, not being able to express it strictly, expresses it by the general term; and in that it called them "steps," left it undetermined, whether they were "steps" of persons ascending or descending. But because there is no "speech or language where their voices are not heard among them,"[2] the earlier language explains the one which comes after it: and what was ambiguous in one is made certain in another. Just then as there the singer is some one who is "ascending," so here is it some one who is "over-leaping." . . . Let this Idithun come still to us; let him "over-leap" those whose delight is in things below, and take delight in these things, and let him rejoice in the Word of the Lord; in the delight of the law of the Most High. . . .

3. "I said, I will take heed to my ways, that I sin not with my tongue" (ver. 1). . . . For it is not without reason that the tongue is set in a moist place, but because it is so prone to slip.[3] Perceiving therefore how hard it was for a man to be under the necessity of speaking, and not to say something that he will wish unsaid, and filled with disgust at these sins, he seeks to avoid the like. To this difficulty is he exposed who is seeking to "leap beyond." . . . Although I have "leaped beyond" the pleasures of earth, although the fleeting [4] passions for things temporal ensnare me not, though now I despise these things below, and am rising up to better things than these, yet in these very better things the satisfaction of knowledge in the sight of God is enough for me. Of what use is it for me to speak what is to be laid hold of, and to give a handle to cavillers? Therefore, "I said, I will take heed to my ways, that I sin not with my tongue. I keep my mouth with a bridle." Wherefore is this? Is it on account of the religious, the thoughtful, the faithful, the holy ones? God forbid! These persons hear in such a manner, as to praise what they approve; but as for what they disapprove, perhaps, among much that they praise they rather excuse than cavil at it; on account of what persons then dost thou "take heed to thy ways," and place a guard on thy lips "that thou mayest not sin with thy tongue"? Hear: it is, "While the wicked standeth over against me." It is not "by me" that he takes up his station, but "against me." Why? . . . Even the Lord Himself says, "I have yet many things to say unto you, but ye cannot bear them now."[5] And the Apostle, "I could not speak unto you as unto spiritual, but as unto carnal."[6] Yet not as to persons to be despaired of, but as to those who still required to be nourished. For he goes on to say, "As babes in Christ, I have fed you with milk, and not with meat; for hitherto ye were not able." Well, tell it unto us even now. "Neither yet now are ye able."[7] Be not therefore impatient to hear that which as yet thou art not capable of; but grow that thou mayest be "able to bear it." It is thus we address the little one, who yet requires to be fed with kindly milk[8] in the bosom of Mother Church, and to be rendered meet for the "strong meat" of the Lord's Table. But what can I say even of that kind to the sinner, who "taketh his stand against me," who either thinks or pretends himself capable of what he "cannot bear;" so that when I say anything unto him, and he has failed to comprehend it, he should not suppose that it was not he that had failed to comprehend, but I who had broken down. Therefore because of this sinner, who "taketh up his stand against me, I keep my mouth as it were with a bridle."

4. "I became deaf, and was humbled, I held my peace from good" (ver. 2). For this person, who is "leaping beyond," suffers some difficulty in a certain stage to which he hath already attained; and he desires to advance beyond, even from thence, to avoid this difficulty. I was afraid of committing a sin; so that I spoke not; that I imposed on myself the necessity of silence: for I had spoken thus, "I will take heed

---

[1] Lat. XXXVIII.   [2] Ps. xix. 3.
[3] Non frustra in udo est, nisi quia facile labitur.
[4] Volatici.   [5] John xvi. 12.   [6] 1 Cor. iii. 1.
[7] 1 Cor. iii. 2.   [8] Pio lacte.

to my ways, that I may not sin with my tongue." Whilst I was too much afraid of saying anything wrong, I kept silence from all that is good. For whence could I say good things, except that I heard them? "It is Thou that shalt make me to hear of joy and gladness." [1] And the "friend of the bridegroom standeth and heareth Him, and rejoiceth on account of the bridegroom's voice," [2] not his own. That he may speak true things, he hears what he is to say. For it is he that "speaketh a lie," that "speaketh of his own." [3] . . . When therefore I had "put a bridle," as it were, "on my lips;" and constrained myself to silence, because I saw that everywhere speech was dangerous, then, says he, that came to pass upon me, which I did not wish, "I became deaf, and was humbled;" not humbled myself, but was humbled; "and I held my peace even from good." Whilst afraid of saying any evil, I began to refrain from speaking what is good: and I condemned my determination; for "I was holding my peace even from what is good."

"And my sorrow was stirred up again" (ver. 2). Inasmuch as I had found in silence a kind of respite from a certain "sorrow," that had been inflicted upon me by those who cavilled at my words, and found fault with me: and that sorrow that was caused by the cavillers, had ceased indeed; but when "I held my peace even from good, my sorrow was stirred up again." I began to be more grieved at having refrained from saying what I ought to have said, than I had before been grieved by having said what I ought not. "And my sorrow was stirred up again. [4]

5. "And while I was musing, the fire burned" (ver. 3). . . . I reflected on the words of my Lord, "Thou wicked and slothful servant, thou oughtest to have put My money to the exchangers, and I at My coming should receive it again with usury." [5] And that which follows may God avert from those who are His stewards! Bind him hand and foot, and let him be cast into outer darkness;" [6] the servant, who was not a waster of his master's goods, so as to destroy them, but was slothful in laying them out to improve them. What ought they to expect, who have wasted them in luxury, if they are condemned who through slothfulness have kept them? "As I was musing, the fire burned." And as he was in this state of wavering suspense, between speaking and holding his peace, between those who are prepared to cavil and those who are anxious to be instructed, . . . in this state of suspense, he prays for a better place, a place different from this his present

stewardship, in which man is in such difficulty and in such danger, and sighing after a certain "end," when he was not to be subject to these things, when the Lord is to say to the faithful dispenser, "Enter thou into the joy of thy Lord," [7] he says, "Then spake I with my tongue." In this fluctuation, in the midst of these dangers and these difficulties, because, that in consequence of the abundance of offences "the love of many is waxing cold," [8] although the law of the Lord inspires delight, in this fluctuation then, (I say), "then spake I with my tongue." To whom? not to the hearer whom I would fain instruct; but to Him who heareth and taketh heed also, by whom I would fain be instructed myself. "I spake with my tongue" to Him, from whom I inwardly hear whatever I hear that is good or true. — What saidst thou?

"Lord, make me to know mine end" (ver. 4). For some things I have passed by already; and I have arrived at a certain point, and that to which I have arrived is better than that from which I have advanced to this; but yet there remains a point, which has to be left behind. For we are not to remain here, where there are trials, offences, where we have to bear with persons who listen to us and cavil at us. "Make me to know mine end;" the end, from which I am still removed, not the course which is already before me.

6. The "end" he speaks of, is that which the Apostle fixed his eye upon, in his course; and made confession of his own infirmity, perceiving in himself a different state of things from that which he looked for elsewhere. For he says, "Not that I have already attained, or am already perfect. Brethren, I count not myself to have apprehended." [9] And that you might not say, "If the Apostle hath not apprehended, have I apprehended? If the Apostle is not perfect, am I perfect?" . . .

7. "And the number of my days, what it is." I ask of "the number of my days, what it is." I can speak of "number" without number, and understand "number without number," in the same sense as "years without years" may be spoken of. For where there are years, there is a sort of "number" at all events, also. But yet, "Thou art the same, and Thy years shall not fail." [10] "Make me to know the number of my days;" but "to know what it is." What then? that number in which thou art, think you that it "is" not? Assuredly, if I weigh the matter well, it has no being; if I linger behind, it has a sort of being; if I rise above it, it has none. If, shaking off the trammels of these things, I contemplate things above, if I compare things that pass away with those that endure, I see

---

[1] Ps. li. 8.   [2] John iii. 29.   [3] John viii. 44.
[4] He omits, "My heart became hot within me."
[5] Matt. xxv. 26, 27.   [6] Matt. xxv. 30.

[7] Matt. xxv. 27.   [8] Matt. xxiv. 12.   [9] Phil. iii. 12, 13.
[10] Ps. cii. 27.

what has a true being, and what rather seems to be, than really is. Should I say that these days of mine "are;" and shall I rashly apply this word so full of meaning to this course of things passing away? To such a degree have I my own self almost ceased to "be, failing" as I am in my weakness, that He escaped from my memory, who said, "I AM HE THAT IS."[1] Hath then any number of days any existence? In truth it hath, and it is "number without end." . . . Everything is swept on by a series of moments, fleeting by, one after the other; there is a torrent of existences ever flowing on and on; a "torrent,"[2] of which He "drank in the way," who hath now "lift up His Head." These days then have no true being; they are gone almost before they arrive; and when they are come, they cannot continue; they press upon one another, they follow the one the other, and cannot check themselves in their course. Of the past nothing is called back again; what is yet to be, is expected as something to pass away again: it is not as yet possessed, whilst as yet it is not arrived; it cannot be kept when once it has arrived. He asks then concerning "the number of his days, which is;" not that which is "not:" and (which confounds me by a still greater and more perplexing difficulty) at once "is," and "is not." We can neither say that that "is," which does not continue; nor that it "is not," when it has come and is passing. It is that absolute "IS," that true "IS," that "IS" in the true sense of the word, that I long for; that "IS;" which "is" in that "Jerusalem" which is "the Bride" of my Lord;[3] where there will not be death, there will not be failing; there will be a day that passeth not away, but continueth: which has neither a yesterday to precede it, nor a to-morrow pressing close upon it.[4] This "number of my days, which is," this (I say), "make Thou me to know."

8. "That I may know what is wanting to me." For while I am struggling here, "this" is wanting unto me: and so long as it is wanting unto me, I do not call myself perfect. So long as I have not received it, I say, "not that I have already attained, either am already perfect; but I am pressing towards the prize of God's high calling."[5] This let me receive as the prize of my running the race! There will be a certain resting-place, to terminate my course; and in that resting-place there will be a Country, and no pilgrimage, no dissension, no temptation. Make me then to know "this number of my days, which is, that I may know what is wanting unto me;" because I am not there yet; lest I should be made proud of what I already am, that "I

may be found in Him, not having mine own righteousness."[6] . . .

9. "Behold, thou hast made my days old"[7] (ver. 5). For these days are "waxing old." I long for new days "that never shall wax old," that I may say, "Old things have passed away; behold, things are become new."[8] Already new in hope; then in reality. For though, in hope and in faith, made new already, how much do we even now do after our old nature! For we are not so completely "clothed upon" with Christ, as not to bear about with us anything derived from Adam. Observe that Adam is "waxing old" within us, and Christ is being "renewed" in us. "Though our outward man is perishing, yet is our inward man being renewed day by day."[9] Therefore, while we fix our thoughts on sin, on mortality, on time, that is hastening by, on sorrow, and toil, and labour, on stages of life following each other in succession, and continuing not, passing on insensibly from infancy even to old age; whilst, I say, we fix our eyes on these things, let us see here "the old man," the "day that is waxing old;" the Song that is out of date; the Old Testament;[10] when however we turn to the inner man, to those things that are to be renewed in place of these which are to be changed, let us find the "new man," the "new day," the "new song," the "New Testament;" and that "newness," let us so love, as to have no fears of its "waxing old." . . . This man, therefore, who is hasting forward to those things which are new, and "reaching forward to those things which are before," says, "Lord, make me to know mine end, and the number of my days, which really is, that I may know what is wanting unto me." See he still drags with him Adam; and even so he is hasting unto Christ. "Behold," saith he, "thou hast made my days old." It is those days that are derived from Adam, those days, I say, that thou hast made old. They are waxing old day by day: and so waxing old, as to be at some day or other consumed also. "And my substance is as nothing before Thee."[11] "Before Thee, O Lord, my substance is as nothing." "Before Thee;" who seest this; and I too, when I see it, see it only when "before Thee." When "before men" I see it not. For what shall I say? What words shall I use to show, that that which I now am is nothing in comparison of That which truly "IS"? But it is within that it is said;[12] it is within that it is felt, so far as it is felt. "Before Thee, O Lord," where Thine eyes are; and not where the eyes of men are. And where Thine eyes are, what is the state of things? "That which I am is as nothing."

---

[1] Exod. iii. 14.   [2] E. V. Ps. cx. 7, "the brook."
[3] Rev. xxi. 9.   [4] Rev. xxi. 25.
[5] Phil. iii. 12, 14.

[5] Phil. iii. 9.   [6] E. V. "as an *hand-breadth*."
[7] 2 Cor. v. 17.   [8] 2 Cor. iv. 16.
[9] Alluding to παλαιούμενον, Heb. viii. 13.   [10] Ps. cxxxix. 16.
[11] *Al.* "learned."

10. "But, verily, every man living is altogether vanity." "But, verily." For what was he saying above? Behold, I have already "leaped beyond" all mortal things, and despised things below, have trampled under foot the things of earth, have soared upwards to the delights of the law of the Lord, I have been afloat in the dispensation of the Lord,[1] have yearned for that "End" which Itself is to know no end, have yearned for the number of my days that truly "is," because the number of days like these hath no real being. Behold, I am already such a one as this; I have already overleaped so much; I am longing for those things which abide. "But verily," in the state in which I am here, so long as I am here, so long as I am in this world, so long as I bear mortal flesh, so long as the life of man on earth is a trial, so long as I sigh among causes of offence, as long as while I "stand" I am in "fear lest I fall,"[2] as long as both my good and my ill hangs in uncertainty, "every man living is altogether vanity." . . .

11. "Albeit man walketh in the Image"[3] (ver. 6). In what "Image," save that of Him who said, "Let Us make man in Our Image, after Our Likeness."[4] "Albeit man walks in the Image." For the reason he says "albeit," is, that this is some great thing. And this "albeit" is followed by "nevertheless," that the "albeit" which you have already heard, should relate to what is beyond the sun; but this "nevertheless," which is to follow, to what is "under the sun," and that the one should relate to the Truth, the other to "vanity." "Albeit," then, "that man walketh in the Image, nevertheless he is disquieted in vain." Hear the cause of his "disquieting," and see if it be not a vain one; that thou mayest trample it under foot, that thou mayest "leap beyond it," and mayest dwell on high, where that "vanity" is not. What "vanity" is that? "He heapeth up riches, and knoweth not for whom he may be gathering them together." O infatuated vanity! "Blessed is the man that maketh the Lord his trust, and hath not respected vanities, nor lying deceits."[5] To you indeed, O covetous man, to you I seem to be out of my senses, these words appear to you to be "old wives' tales." For you, a man of great judgment, and of great prudence, to be sure, are daily devising methods of acquiring money, by traffic, by agriculture, by eloquence perhaps, by making yourself learned in the law, by warfare, perhaps you even add that of usury. Like a shrewd man as you are, you leave nothing untried, whereby you may

pile coin on coin; and may store it up[6] more carefully in a place of secrecy. You plunder others; you guard against the plunderer; you are afraid lest you should yourself suffer the wrong, that you yourself do; and even what you do suffer, does not correct you. . . . Examine your own heart, and that prudence of yours, which leads you to deride me, to think me out of my senses for saying these things: and tell me now, "You are heaping up treasures; for whom are you gathering them together?" I see what you would tell me; as if what you would say had not occurred to the person described here; you will say, I am keeping them for my children? This is the voice of parental affection; the excuse of injustice. "I am keeping them" (you say) "for my children." So then you are keeping them for your children, are you? Did not Idithun then know this? Assuredly he did; but he reckoned it one of the things of the "old days," that have waxed old, and therefore he despised it: because he was hastening on to the new "days." . . .

12. For He, "by whom all things were made,"[7] hath built "mansions" for all of us: thither He would have that which we have go before us; that we may not lose it[8] on earth. When, however, you have kept them on earth, tell me for whom you are to "gather them together"? You have children: add one more to their number; and give something to Christ also. "He is disquieted in vain."

13. "And now" (ver. 7). "And now," saith this Idithun, — looking back on a certain "vain" show, and looking up to a certain Truth, standing midway where he has something beyond him, and something also behind him, having below him the place from which he took his spring, having above him that toward which he has stretched forth; — "And now," when I have "over-leaped" some things, when I have trampled many things under foot, when I am no longer captivated by things temporal; even now, I am not perfect, "I have not yet apprehended."[9] "For it is by hope that we are saved; but hope that is seen is not hope; for what a man seeth, why doth he yet hope for? But if we hope for that we see not, then do we with patience wait for it."[10] Therefore he says: "And now what wait I for? Is it not for the Lord?"[11] He is my expectation, who hath given

---

[1] i.e., in the high doctrine, p. 114; but some MSS. ap. Ben. and ours, *Fluctuavi in dispensatione munerum* (or *nummorum*) *Dominicorum:* "I have wavered in the dispensing of the Lord's gifts (or moneys)." A better sense, see p. 113.
[2] Job iii. 25.   [3] E. V. "in a vain show."
[4] Gen. i. 26.   [5] Ps. xl. 4.

[6] Text, *castigetur.* Four MSS have *congregetur*, one *collocetur*; three *cartigetur*, on which word there is a gloss. *Cartigare est in chartâ propter memoriam aliquid scribere; usitatius de usurariis dicitur.* Nine MSS. *castigetur*, as Martial, *Et cujus laxas arca flagellat opes*, and the Juriconsults *flagellare annonam*, for "to shut up."—*Ben.* *Flagellare annonam*, however, seems rather to mean to "drive up the prices," and perhaps *arca flagellat* may be the lid striking the heaped contents, thus affording no parallel. However, it may be to "keep it from peeping out." Oxf. MSS. *cartigetur.*
[7] Col. i. 16.   [8] *Hoc*, qu. *hic*, "here."
[9] Phil. iii. 13.   [10] Rom. viii. 24, 25.
[11] E. V. "And now, Lord, what wait I for," etc.

me all those things, that I might despise them. He will give unto me Himself also, even He who is above all, and "by whom all things were made,"[1] and by whom I was made amongst all; even He, the Lord, is my Expectation! You see Idithun, brethren, you see in what way he waiteth for Him! Let no man therefore call himself perfect here; he deceives and imposes upon himself; he is beguiling himself, he cannot have perfection here, and what avails it that he should lose humility? . . .

"And my substance is ever before Thee." Already advancing, already tending towards Him, and to some extent already beginning to "be," still (he says[2]) "my substance is ever before Thee." Now that other substance is also before men. You have gold, silver, slaves, estates, trees, cattle, servants. These things are visible even to men. There is a certain "substance that is ever before Thee."

14. "Deliver me from all my transgressions" (ver. 8). I have "over-leaped" a great deal of ground, a very great deal of ground already; but, "If we say that we have no sin, we deceive ourselves, and the Truth is not in us."[3] I have "over-leaped" a great deal: but still do I "beat my breast," and say, "Forgive us our debts, as we forgive our debtors."[4] Thou therefore art "my expectation!" my "End." For "Christ is the end of the Law unto righteousness, unto every man that believeth."[5] From all mine offences:" not only from those, that I may not relapse into those which I have already "over-leaped;" but from all, without exception, of those on account of which I now beat my breast, and say, "Forgive us our debts." "Deliver me from all mine offences:" me being thus minded, and holding fast what the Apostle said, "As many of us as be perfect, let us be thus minded."[6] For at the time that he said that he was not "already perfect," he then immediately goes on and says, "As many of us as be perfect, let us be thus minded." . . . Art thou then, O Apostle, not perfect, and are we perfect? But hath it escaped you, that he did just now call himself "perfect"? For he does not say, "As many of you as are perfect, be ye thus minded;" but "As many of us as be perfect, let us be thus minded;" after having said a little before, "Not that I have already attained; either am already perfect." In no other way then can you be perfect in this life, than by knowing that you cannot be perfect in this life. This then will be your perfection, so to have "over-leaped" some things, as to have still some point to which you are hastening on: so as to have something remaining, to which you will have to leap on, when everything else

has been passed by. It is such faith as this that is secure; for whoever thinks that he has already attained, is "exalting himself," so as to be "abased" hereafter.[7] . . .

15. "Thou hast made me the reproach of the foolish." Thou hast so willed it, that I should live among those, and preach the Truth among those, who love vanity; and I cannot but be a laughing-stock to them. "For we have been made a spectacle unto this world, and unto angels, and unto men:"[8] to angels who praise, to men who censure, us; or rather to angels, some of whom praise, some of whom are censuring us: and to men also, some of whom are praising, and some censuring us. . . . Both the one and the other are arms to us: the one "on the right hand," the other "on the left:" arms however they are both of them; both of these kinds of arms, both those "on the right hand," and those "on the left;" both those who praise, and those who censure; both those who pay us honour, and those who heap dishonour upon us; with both these kinds I contend against the devil; with both of these I smite him; I defeat him with prosperity, if I be not corrupted by it; by adversity, if I am not broken in spirit by it.

16. "I became dumb;[9] and I opened not my mouth" (ver. 9). But it was to guard against "the foolish man," that "I became dumb, and opened not my mouth." For to whom should I tell what is going on within me? "For I will hear what the Lord God will speak in me;[10] for He will speak peace unto His people."[11] But "There is no peace," saith the Lord, "to the wicked."[12] "I was dumb, and opened not my mouth; because it is Thou that madest me." Was this the reason that thou openedst not thy mouth, "because God made thee"? That is strange; for did not God make thy mouth, that thou shouldest speak? "He that planted the ear, doth He not hear? He that formed the eye, doth He not see?"[13] God hath given thee a mouth to speak with; and dost thou say, "I was dumb, and opened not my mouth, because Thou madest me"? Or does the clause, "Because Thou madest me," belong to the verse that follows? "Remove Thy stroke away from me" (ver. 10). Because it is "Thou that hast made me," let it not be Thy pleasure to destroy me utterly; scourge, so that I may be made better, not so that I faint; beat me, so that I may be[14] beaten out to a greater length and breadth, not so that I may be ground to powder. "By the heaviness of Thy hand I fainted in in corrections." That is, I "fainted" while Thou wast correcting me. And what is meant by "correcting" me? except what follows.

---

[1] Col. i. 16. [2] Oxf. MSS. inquit. [3] 1 John i. 8.
[4] Matt. vi. 12. [5] Rom. x. 4. [6] Phil. iii. 15.
[7] Luke xviii. 14. [8] 1 Cor. iv. 9. [9] Or, "deaf."
[10] Augustin and Vulgate, quid loquatur in me.
[11] Ps. lxxxv. 8. [12] Isa. xlviii. 22. [13] Ps. xciv. 9.
[14] Ut producar, non ut comminuar.

17. "Thou with rebukes hast chastened man for iniquity; Thou hast made my life to consume away like a spider" (ver. 11). There is much that is discerned by this Idithun; by every one who discerns as he does; who overleaps as he does. For he says, that he has fainted in God's corrections; and would fain have the stroke removed away from him, "because it is He who made him." Let Him renew me, who also made me; let Him who created me, create me anew. But yet, Brethren, do we suppose that there was no cause for his fainting, so that he wishes to be "renewed," to be "created anew"? It is "for iniquity," saith he, "that Thou hast chastened man." All this, my having fainted, my being weak, my "crying out of the deep," all of this is because of "iniquity;" and in this Thou hast not condemned, but hast "chastened" me. "Thou hast chastened man for sin." Hear this more plainly from another Psalm: "It is good for me that Thou hast afflicted me, that I might learn Thy righteousness."[1] I have been "afflicted," and at the same time "it is good for me;" it is at once a punishment, and an act of favour. What hath He in store for us after punishment is over, who inflicts punishment itself by way of favour? For He it is of whom it was said, "I was brought low, and He made me whole:" and, "It is good for me that Thou hast afflicted me, that I might learn Thy righteousness."[2] "Thou chastenest man for iniquity." And that which is written, "Thou formest my grief in teaching me,"[3] could only be said unto God by one who was "leaping beyond" his fellows; "Thou formest my grief in teaching me;" Thou makest, that is to say, a lesson for me out of my sorrow. It is Thou that formest that very grief itself; Thou dost not leave it unformed, but formest it; and that grief, that has been inflicted by Thee, when formed, will be a lesson unto me, that I may be set free by Thee. For the word *finges* is used in the sense of "forming," as it were moulding, my grief; not in the sense of "feigning" it; in the same way that *fingit* is applied to the artist, in the same sense that *figulus* is derived from *fingere*. Thou therefore "hast chastened man for iniquity." I see myself in afflictions; I see myself under punishment; and I see no unrighteousness in Thee. If I therefore am under punishment, and if there is no unrighteousness with Thee, it remains that Thou must have been "chastening man for iniquity."

18. And by what means hast Thou "chastened" him? Tell us, O Idithun, the manner of thy chastening; tell us in what way thou hast been "chastened." "And Thou hast made my life consume like a spider." This is the chastening! What consumes away sooner than the spider? I speak of the creature itself; though what can be more liable to "consume away" than the spider's webs? Observe too how liable to decay is the creature itself. Do but set your finger lightly upon it, and it is a ruin: there is nothing at all more easily destroyed. To such a state hast Thou brought my life, by chastening me "because of iniquity." When chastening makes us weak, there is a kind of strength that would be a fault. . . . It was by a kind of strength that man offended, so as to require to be corrected by weakness: for it was by a certain "pride" that he offended; so as to require to be chastened by humility. All proud persons call themselves strong men. Therefore have many "come from the East and the West," and have attained "to sit down with Abraham, and Isaac, and Jacob, in the kingdom of Heaven."[4] Wherefore was it that they so attained? Because they would not be strong. What is meant by "would not be strong"? They were afraid to presume of their own merits. They did not "go about to establish their own righteousness," that they might "submit themselves to the righteousness of God."[5] . . . Behold! you are mortal; and you bear about you a body of flesh that is corrupting away: "And ye shall fall like one of the princes. Ye shall die like men,"[6] and shall fall like the devil[7] What good does the remedial discipline of mortality do you? The devil is proud, as not having a mortal body, as being an angel. But as for you, who have received a mortal body, and to whom even this does no good, so as to humble you by so great weakness, you shall "fall like one of the princes." This then is the first grace of God's gift, to bring us to the confession of our infirmity, that whatever good we can do, whatever ability we have, we may be that in Him; that "He that glorieth, may glory in the Lord."[8] "When I am weak," saith he, "then am I strong."[9]

19. "But surely every man living disquieteth himself in vain." He returns to what he mentioned a little before. Although he be improving here, yet for all that, "every man living disquieteth himself in vain;" forasmuch as he lives in a state of uncertainty. For who has any assurance even of his own goodness? "He is disquieted in vain." Let him "cast upon the Lord the burden"[10] of his care; let him cast upon Him whatever causes him anxiety. "Let Him sustain thee;" let Him keep thee. For on this earth what is there that is certain, except death?

---

[1] Ps. cxix. 71. *Justificationes.*   [2] Ps. cxvi. 6, cxix. 71. [3] Ps. xliv. 20. Qui fingis *dolorem* in præcepto (Vulgate, *laborem*); E. V. "which *frameth mischief by a law.*"

[4] Matt. viii. 11.   [5] Rom. x. 3.   [6] Ps. lxxxii. 7. [7] [Dan. x. 13. "Princes" understood of angels. Then, Isa. xiv. 12. So Shaks.: "He falls like Lucifer," etc. — C.] [8] 1 Cor. i. 31.   [9] 2 Cor. xii. 10.   [10] Ps. lv. 22.

Consider the whole sum of all the good or the ill of this life, either those belonging to righteousness, or those belonging to unrighteousness; what is there that is certain here, except death? Have you been advancing in goodness? You know what you are to-day; what you will be to-morrow, you know not! Are you a sinner? you know what you are to-day; what you will be to-morrow, you know not! You hope for wealth; it is uncertain whether it will fall to your lot. You hope to have a wife; it is uncertain whether you will obtain one, or what sort of one you will obtain. You hope for sons: it is uncertain whether they will be born to you. Are they born? it is uncertain whether they will live: if they live, it is uncertain whether they will grow up in virtue, or whether they will fall away. Whichever way you turn, all is uncertain, death alone is certain. Art thou poor? It is uncertain whether thou wilt grow rich. Art thou unlearned? It is uncertain whether thou wilt become learned. Art thou in feeble health, it is uncertain whether thou wilt regain thy strength. Art thou born? It is certain that thou wilt die: and in this certainty of death itself, the day of thy death is uncertain. Amidst these uncertainties, where death alone is certain, while even of that the hour is uncertain, and while it alone is studiously guarded against, though at the same time it is in no way to be escaped, "every man living disquieteth himself in vain." . . .

20. "Hear my prayer, O Lord" (ver. 12). Whereof shall I rejoice? Whereof should I groan? I rejoice on account of what is past, I groan longing for these which are not yet come. "Hear my prayer, and give ear unto my cry. Hold not Thy peace at my tears." For do I now no longer weep, because I have already "passed by," have "left behind" so great things as these? "Do I not weep much the more?" For, "He that increaseth knowledge, increaseth sorrow."[1] The more I long for what is not here, do I not so much the more groan for it until it comes? do I not so much the more weep until it comes? . . .

21. "For I am a sojourner with Thee." But with whom am I a "sojourner"? When I was with the devil, I was a "sojourner;" but then I had a bad host and entertainer; now, however, I am with Thee; but I am a "sojourner" still. What is meant by a sojourner? I am a "sojourner" in the place from which I am to remove; not in the place where I am to dwell for ever. The place where I am to abide for ever, should be rather called my home. In the place from which I am to remove I am a "sojourner;" but yet it is with my God that I am

a sojourner, with whom I am hereafter to abide, when I have reached my home. But what home is that to which you are to remove from this estate of a sojourner? Recognise that home, of which the Apostle speaks, "We have an habitation of God, an house not made with hands, eternal in the Heavens."[2] If this house is eternal in the Heavens, when we have come to it, we shall not be sojourners any more. For how should you be a sojourner in an eternal home? But here, where the Master of the house is some day to say to you, "Remove," while you yourself know not when He will say it, be thou in readiness. And by longing for your eternal home, you will be keeping yourself in readiness for it. And be not angry with Him, because He gives thee notice to remove, when He Himself pleases. For He made no covenant with thee, nor did He bind Himself by any engagement; nor didst thou enter upon the tenancy of this house on a certain stipulation for a definite term: thou art to quit, when it is its Master's pleasure. For therefore is it that you now dwell there free of charge. "For I am a sojourner with Thee, and a stranger." Therefore it is there is my country: it is there is my home. "I am a sojourner with Thee, and a stranger." Here too is understood "with Thee." For many are strangers with the devil: but they who have already believed and are faithful, are, it is true, "strangers" as yet, because they have not yet come to that country and to that home: but still they are strangers with God. For so long as we are in the body, we are strangers from the Lord, and we desire, whether we are strangers, or abiding here, "we may be accepted with Him."[3] I am a "sojourner with Thee; and a stranger, as all my fathers were." If then I am as all my fathers were, shall I say that I will not remove, when they have removed? Am I to lodge here on other terms, than those on which they lodged here also? . . .

22. "Grant me some remission, that I may be refreshed before I go hence" (ver. 13). Consider well, Idithun, consider what knots those are which thou wouldest have "loosed" unto thee, that thou mightest be "refreshed before thou goest hence." For thou hast certain fever-heats from which thou wouldest fain be refreshed, and thou sayest, "that I may be refreshed," and "grant me a remission." What should He remit, or loosen unto thee, save that difficulty under which, and in consequence of which, thou sayest, "Forgive us our debts. Grant me a remission before I go hence, and be no more." Set me free from my sins, "before I go hence," that I may not go hence with my

---

[1] Eccles. i. 18.　　[2] 2 Cor. v. 1.　　[3] 2 Cor. v. 9.

sins. Remit them unto me, that I may be set at rest in my conscience, that it may be disburthened of its feverish anxiety, the anxiety with which "I am sorry for my sin. Grant me a remission, that I may be refreshed" (before everything else), "before I go hence, and be no more." For if thou grantest me not a "remission, that I may be refreshed," I shall "go and be no more." "Before I go" thither, where if I go, I shall thenceforth "be no more. Grant me a remission, that I may be refreshed." A question has suggested itself, how he will be no more. . . . What is meant then by "shall be no more," unless Idithun is alluding to what is true "being," and what is not true "being." For he was beholding with the mind, with which he could do so, with the "mind's eye," by which he was able to behold it, that end, which he had desired to have shown unto him, saying, "Lord, make me to know mine end." He was beholding "the number of his days, which truly is ; " and he observed that all that is below, in comparison of that true being, has no true being. For those things are permanent ; these are subject to change ; mortal, and frail, and the eternal suffering, though full of corruption, is for this very reason not to be ended, that it may ever be being ended without end. He alluded therefore to that realm of bliss, to the happy country, to the happy home, where the Saints are partakers of eternal Life, and of Truth unchangeable ; and he feared to "go" where that is not, where there is no true being ; longing to be there, where "Being" in the highest sense is ! It is on account of this contrast then, while standing midway between them, he says, "Grant me a remission, that I may be refreshed before I go hence and be no more." For if Thou "grantest me not a remission" of my sins, I shall go from Thee unto all eternity ! And from whom shall I go to all eternity ? From Him who said, I AM HE THAT AM : from Him who said, "Say unto the children of Israel, I AM hath sent me unto you." [1] He then who goes from Him, in the contrary direction, goes to non-existence. . . .

PSALM XL.[2]

1. Of all those things which our Lord Jesus Christ has foretold, we know part to have been already accomplished, part we hope will be accomplished hereafter. All of them, however, will be fulfilled, because He is "the Truth" who speaks them, and requires of us to be as "faithful," as He Himself speaks them faithfully. . . .

2. Let us say then what this Psalm says. "I waited patiently for the Lord" (ver. 1). I waited patiently for the promise of no mere

mortal who can both deceive and be himself deceived : I waited for the consolation of no mere mortal, who may be consumed by sorrow of his own, before he gives me comfort. Should a brother mortal attempt to comfort me, when he himself is in sorrow likewise ? Let us mourn in company ; let us weep together, let us "wait patiently" together, let us join our prayers together also. Whom did I wait for but for the Lord ? The Lord, who though He puts off the fufilment of His promises, yet never recalls them ? He will make it good ; assuredly He will make it good, because He has made many of His promises good already : and of God's truth we ought to have no fears, even if as yet He had made none of them good. Lo ! let us henceforth think thus, "He has promised us everything ; He has not as yet given us possession of anything ; He is a sponsible Promiser ; a faithful Paymaster : do you but show yourself a dutiful exactor of what is promised ; and if you be "weak," if you be one of the little ones, claim the promise of His mercy. Do you not see tender [3] lambs striking their dams' teats with their heads, in order that they may get their fill of milk ? . . . "And He took heed unto me, and heard my cry." He took heed to it, and He heard it. See thou hast not waited in vain. His eyes are over thee. His ears turned towards thee. For, "the eyes of the Lord are upon the righteous, and His ears are open unto their cry." [4] What then ? Did He not see thee, when thou usedst to do evil and to blaspheme Him ? What then becomes of what is said in that very Psalm, "The face of the Lord is upon them that do evil" ? [5] But for what end ? "That He may cut off the remembrance of them from the earth." Therefore, even when thou wert wicked, He "took heed of thee ; " but He "took no heed to thee." [6] So then to him who "waited patiently for the Lord," it was not enough to say, "He took heed of me, He says, "He took heed to me ; " that is, He took heed by comforting me, that He might do me good. What was it that He took heed to ? "and He heard my cry."

3. And what hath He accomplished for thee ? What hath He done for thee ? "He brought me up also out of a horrible pit, out of the miry clay, and set my feet upon a rock, and established my goings" (ver. 2). He hath given us great blessings already : and still He is our debtor ; but let him who hath this part of the debt repaid already, believe that the rest will be also, seeing that he ought to have believed even before he received anything. Our Lord has employed facts themselves to persuade us, that He is a faithful promiser, a liberal giver. What then

---

[1] Ex. iii. 14.　　　　　[2] Lat. XXXIX.

[3] Al. "very small."　　　　[4] Ps. xxxiv. 15.
[5] Ps. xxxiv. 16. E. V. "against." Lat. Vulgate, super.
[6] Attendebat te; sed non attendebat tibi.

has He already done? "He has brought me out of a horrible pit." What horrible pit is that? It is the depth of iniquity, from the lusts of the flesh, for this is meant by "the miry clay."[1] Whence hath He brought thee out? Out of a certain deep, out of which thou criedst out in another Psalm, "Out of the deep have I called unto Thee, O Lord."[2] And those who are already "crying out of the deep," are not absolutely in the lowest deep: the very act of crying is already lifting them up. There are some deeper in the deep, who do not even perceive themselves to be in the deep. Such are those who are proud despisers, not pious entreaters for pardon; not tearful criers for mercy: but such as Scripture thus describes. "The sinner[3] when he comes into the depth of evil despiseth."[4] For he is deeper in the deep, who is not satisfied with being a sinner, unless instead of confessing he even defends his sins. But he who has already "cried out of the deep," hath already lifted up his head in order that he might "cry out of the deep," has been heard already, and has been "brought out of the horrible pit, and out of the mire and clay." He already has faith, which he had not before; he has hope, which he was before without; he now walks in Christ, who before used to go astray in the devil. For on that account it is that he says, "He hath set my feet upon a rock, and established my goings." Now "that Rock was Christ."[5] Supposing that we are "upon the rock," and that our "goings are ordered," still it is necessary that we continue to walk; that we advance to something farther. For what did the Apostle Paul say when now upon the Rock, when his "goings had now been established"? "Not as though I had already attained, either were already perfect: Brethren, I count not myself to have apprehended."[6] What then has been done for thee, if thou hast not apprehended? On what account dost thou return thanks, saying, "But I have obtained mercy"?[7] Because his goings are now established, because he now walks on the Rock? . . . Therefore, when he was saying, "I press forward toward the prize of my high calling," because "his feet were now set on the Rock," and "his goings were ordered," because he was now walking on the right way, he had something to return thanks for; something to ask for still; returning thanks for what he had received already, while he was claiming that which still remained due. For what things already received was he giving thanks? For the remission of sins, for the illumination of faith; for the strong support of hope, for the fire of charity. But in what respects had he still a claim of debt on the Lord? "Henceforth," he says, "there is laid up for me a crown of righteousness." There is therefore something due me still. What is it that is due? "A crown of righteousness, which the Lord, the righteous Judge, shall give me at that day." He was at first a loving Father to "bring him forth from the horrible pit;" to forgive his sins, to rescue him from "the mire and clay;" hereafter he will be a "righteous Judge," requiting to him walking rightly, what He promised; to him (I say), unto whom He had at the first granted that power to walk rightly. He then as a "righteous Judge" will repay; but whom will he repay? "He that endureth unto the end, the same shall be saved."[8]

4. "And He hath put a new song in my mouth." What new song is this? "Even a hymn unto our God" (ver. 3). Perhaps you used to sing hymns to strange gods; old hymns, because they were uttered by the "old man," not by the "new man;" let the "new man" be formed, and let him sing a "new song;" being himself made "new," let him love those "new" things by which he is himself made new. For what is more Ancient than God, who is before all things, and is without end and without beginning? He becomes "new" to thee, when thou returnest to Him; because it was by departing from Him, that thou hadst become old; and hadst said, "I have waxed old because of all mine enemies."[9] We therefore utter "a hymn unto our God;" and the hymn itself sets us free. "For I will call upon the Lord to praise Him, and I will be safe from all mine enemies." For a hymn is a song of praise. Call on God to "praise" Him, not to find fault with Him. . . .

5. If haply any one asks, what person is speaking in this Psalm? I would say briefly, "It is Christ." But as ye know, brethren, and as we must say frequently, Christ sometimes speaks in His own Person, in the Person of our Head. For He Himself is "the Saviour of the Body."[10] He is our Head; the Son of God, who was born of the Virgin, suffered for us, "rose again for our justification," sitteth "at the right hand of God," to "make intercession for us:"[11] who is also to recompense to the evil and to the good, in the judgment, all the evil and the good that they have done. He deigned to become our Head; to become "the Head of the Body," by taking of us that flesh in which He should die for us; that flesh which He also raised up again for our sakes, that in that flesh He might place before us an instance of the resurrection; that we might learn to hope for

---

[1] Or thus, "What horrible pit is that? It is the depth of iniquity. From the lusts of the flesh, for this is meant by the 'miry clay.'"
[2] Ps. cxxx. 1.
[3] Eng. Vers. "When the wicked cometh, then cometh also contempt."
[4] Prov. xviii. 3.
[5] 1 Cor. x. 4.   [6] Phil. iii. 12, 13.   [7] 1 Tim. i. 13.
[8] Matt. x. 22.   [9] Ps. vi. 7.   [10] Eph. v. 23.
[11] Rom. viii. 34.

that of which we heretofore despaired, and might henceforth have our feet upon the rock, and might walk in Christ. He then sometimes speaks in the name of our Head ; sometimes also He speaks of us who are His members. For both when He said, " I was an hungred, and ye gave Me meat," [1] He spoke on behalf of His members, not of Himself: and when He said, " Saul, Saul, why persecutest thou Me ? " [2] the Head was crying on behalf of its members : and yet He did not say, " Why dost thou persecute My members ? " but, " Why persecutest thou Me ? " If He suffers in us, then shall we also be crowned in Him. Such is the love of Christ. What is there can be compared to this ? This is the thing on account of which " He hath put a hymn in our mouth," and this He speaks on behalf of His members.

6. " The just shall see, and shall fear, and shall trust in the Lord." " The just shall see." Who are the just ? The faithful ; because it is " by faith that the just shall live." [3] For there is in the Church this order, some go before, others follow ; and those who go before make themselves " an example " to those who follow ; and those who follow imitate those who go before. But do those then follow no one, who exhibit themselves as an ensample to them that come after ? If they follow no one at all, they will fall into error. These persons then must themselves also follow some one, that is, Christ Himself. . . . " The just," therefore, " shall see, and shall fear." They see a narrow way on the one hand ; on the other side, " a broad road : " on this side they see few, on the other many. But thou art a just man ; count them not, but weigh them ; bring " a just balance," not a " deceitful " one : because thou art called just. " The just shall see, and fear," applies to thee. Count not therefore the multitudes of men that are filling the " broad ways," that are to fill the circus to-morrow ; celebrating with shouts the City's Anniversary, [4] while they defile the City itself by evil living. Look not at them ; they are many in number ; and who can count them ? But there are a few travelling along the narrow road. Bring forth the balance, I say. Weigh them ; see what a quantity of chaff you lift up on the one side, against a few grains of corn on the other. Let this be done by " the just," the " believers," who are to follow. And what shall they who precede do ? Let them not be proud, let them not " exalt themselves ; " let them not deceive those who follow them. How may they deceive those who follow them ? By promising them salvation in themselves. What then ought those who follow to do ? " The just shall see, and fear : and shall trust in the Lord ; " not in

those who go before them. But indeed they fix their eyes on those who go before them, and follow and imitate them ; but they do so, because they consider from Whom they have received the grace to go before them ; and because they trust in Him. [5] Although therefore they make these their models, they place their trust in Him from whom the others have received the grace whereby they are such as they are. " The just shall see it, and fear, and shall trust in the Lord." Just as in another Psalm, " I lift up mine eyes unto the hills," [6] we understand by hills, all distinguished and great spiritual persons in the Church ; great in solidity, not by swollen inflation. By these it is that all Scripture hath been dispensed unto us ; they are the Prophets, they are the Evangelists ; they are sound Doctors : to these " I lift up mine eyes, from whence shall come my help." And lest you should think of mere human help, he goes on to say, " My help cometh from the Lord, which made heaven and earth. The just shall see it, and fear, and shall trust in the Lord." . . .

7. " Blessed is that man that maketh the name of the Lord his trust, and hath not respected vanities or lying madnesses " (ver. 4). Behold the way by which thou wouldest fain have gone. Behold the " multitude that fill the Broad way." [7] It is not without reason " that " road leads to the amphitheatre. It is not without reason it leads to Death. The " broad way " leads unto death, [8] its breadth delights for time : its end is straitness to all eternity. Aye ; but the multitudes murmur ; the multitudes are rejoicing together ; the multitudes are hastening along ; the multitudes are flocking together ! Do not thou imitate them ; do not turn aside after them : they are " vanities, and lying madnesses." Let the Lord thy God be thy hope. Hope for nothing else from the Lord thy God ; but let the Lord thy God Himself be thine hope. For many persons hope to obtain from God's hands riches, and many perishable and transitory honours ; and, in short, anything else they hope to obtain at God's hands, except only God Himself. But do thou seek after thy God Himself : nay, indeed, despising all things else, make thy way unto Him ! Forget other things, remember Him. Leave other things behind, and " press forward " [9] unto Him. Surely it is He Himself, who set thee right, when turned away from the right path ; who, now that thou art set in the right path, guides thee aright, who guides thee to thy destination. Let Him then be thy hope, who both guides thee, and guides thee to thy destination. Whither does worldly covetous-

---

[1] Matt. xxv. 35. [2] Acts ix. 4.
[3] Hab. ii. 4. [4] *Civitatis Natalem.*

[5] [A clear exposition of the Catholic (Nicene) doctrine concerning the merits of the saints. — C.]
[6] Ps. cxxi. 1. [7] A street perhaps so named.
[8] Matt. vii. 13. [9] Phil. iii. 14.

ness lead thee? And to what point does it conduct thee at the last? Thou didst at first desire a farm; then thou wouldest possess an estate; thou wouldest shut out thy neighbours; having shut them out, thou didst set thy heart on the possessions of other neighbours; and didst extend thy covetous desires till thou hadst reached the shore: arriving at the shore, thou covetest the islands: having made the earth thine own, thou wouldest haply seize upon heaven. Leave thou all thy loves. He who made heaven and earth is more beautiful than all.

8. "Blessed is the man that maketh the name of the Lord his hope, and who hath not regarded vanities and lying madnesses." For whence is it that "madness" is called "lying"? Insanity is a lying thing, even as it is sanity that sees the Truth. For what thou seest as good things,[1] thou art deceived; thou art not in thy sound senses: a violent fever has driven thee to frenzy: that which thou art in love with is not a reality. Thou applaudest the charioteer; thou cheerest the charioteer; thou art madly in love with the charioteer. It is "vanity;" it is "a lying madness." "It is 'not'" (he cries). "Nothing can be better; nothing more delightful." What can I do for one in a state of high fever? Pray ye for such persons, if you have any feelings of compassion in you. For the physician himself also in a desperate case generally turns to those in the house, who stand around weeping; who are hanging on his lips to hear his opinion of the patient who is sick and in danger. The physician stands in a state of doubt: he sees not any good to promise; he fears to pronounce evil, lest he should excite alarm. He devises a thoroughly modest sentence: "The good God can do all things. Pray ye for him." Which then of these madmen shall I check? Which of them will listen to me? Which of them would not call us miserable? Because they suppose us to have lost great and various pleasures, of which they are madly fond, in that we are not as madly in love with them as they are: and they do not see that they are "lying" pleasures. . . . "And hath not respected vanities, and lying madnesses." "Such a one has won," he cries; "he harnessed such and such a horse," he proclaims aloud. He would fain be a kind of diviner; he aspires to the honours of divination by abandoning the fountain of Divinity; and he frequently pronounces an opinion, and is frequently mistaken. Why is this? Even because they are "lying madnesses." But why is it that what they say sometimes comes true? That they may lead astray the foolish ones; that by loving the semblance of truth there, they may fall into the snare of falsehood: let them be left behind, let them be "given over," let them be "cut off." If they were members of us, they must be mortified. "Mortify," he says, "your members which are upon the earth."[2] Let our God be our hope. He who made all things, is better than all! He who made what is beautiful, is more beautiful than all that is such. He who made whatever is mighty, is Himself mightier. He who made whatever is great, is Himself greater. He will be unto you everything that you love. Learn in the creature to love the Creator; and in the work Him who made it. Let not that which has been made by Him detain thine affections, so that thou shouldest lose Him by whom thou thyself wert made also. "Blessed," then, "is the man that maketh the Name of the Lord his trust, and hath not respected vanities and lying madnesses." . . .

9. We will give him other sights in exchange for such sights as these. And what sights shall we present to the Christian, whom we would fain divert from those sights? I thank the Lord our God; He in the following verse of the Psalm hath shown us what sights we ought to present and offer to spectators who would fain have sights to see? Let us now suppose him to be weaned from the circus, the theatre, the amphitheatre; let him be looking after, let him by all means be looking after, some sight to see; we do not leave him without a spectacle. What then shall we give in exchange for those? Hear what follows.

"Many, O Lord my God, are the wonderful works which Thou hast made" (ver. 5). He used to gaze at the "wonderful works" of man; let him now contemplate the wonderful works of God. "Many are the wonderful works" that God "has made." Why are they become vile in his eyes? He praises the charioteer guiding four horses; running all of them without fault and without stumbling. Perhaps the Lord has not made such "wonderful works" in things spiritual. Let him control lust,[3] let him control cowardice,[4] let him control injustice, let him control imprudence, I mean, the passions which falling into excess produce those vices; let him control these and bring them into subjection, and let him hold the reins, and not suffer himself to be carried away; let him guide them the way he himself would have them go; let him not be forced away whither he would not. He used to applaud the charioteer, he himself shall be applauded for his own charioteering; he used to call out that the charioteer should be invested with a dress of honour; he shall himself be clothed with immortality. These are the spectacles, these the sights that God exhibits to us. He cries out of heaven, "My eyes are upon you.

---

[1] MSS. want *putas*; with it, the sense is, "What you see, you think to be good things."

[2] Col. iii. 5.   [3] *Luxuriam*.   [4] *Ignaviam*.

Strive, and 'I will' assist you; triumph, and I will crown you."

"And in Thy thought there is none that is like unto Thee." Now then look at the actor! For the man hath by dint of great pains learnt to walk upon a rope; and hanging there he holds thee hanging in suspense. Turn to Him who exhibits spectacles far more wonderful. This man hath learned to walk upon the rope; but hath he caused another to walk on the sea? Forget now thy theatre; behold our Peter; not a walker on the rope, but, so to speak, a walker on the sea.[1] And do thou also walk on other waters (though not on those on which Peter walked, to symbolize a certain truth), for this world is a sea. It hath a deleterious bitterness; it hath the waves of tribulations, the tempests of temptations; it hath men in it who, like fish, delight in their own ruin, and prey upon each other; walk thou here, set thou thy foot on this. Thou wouldest see sights; be thyself a "spectacle." That thy spirit may not sink, look on Him who goes before thee, and says, "We have been made a spectacle unto this world, and unto angels, and unto men."[2] Tread thou on the waters; suffer not thyself to be drowned in the sea. Thou wilt not go there, thou wilt not "tread it under foot," unless it be His bidding, who was Himself the first to walk upon the sea. For it was thus that Peter spoke. "If Thou art, bid me come unto Thee on the waters."[3] And because "He was," He heard him when praying; He granted his wish to him when expressing his desire; He raised him up when sinking. These are the "wonderful works" that the "Lord hath made." Look on them; let faith be the eye of him who would behold them. And do thou also likewise; for although the winds alarm thee, though the waves rage against thee, and though human frailty may have inspired thee with some doubt of thy salvation, thou hast it in thy power to "cry out," thou mayest say "Lord, I perish."[4] He who bids thee walk there, suffers thee not to perish. For in that thou now walkest "on the Rock," thou fearest not even on the sea! If thou art without "the Rock," thou must sink in the sea; for the Rock on which thou must walk is such an one as is not sunk in the sea.

10. Observe then the "wonderful works" of God. "I have declared, and have spoken; they are multiplied beyond number." There is "a number," there are some over and above the number. There is a fixed number that belongs to that heavenly Jerusalem. For "the Lord knoweth them that are His;"[5] the Christians that fear Him, the Christians that believe, the Christians that keep the commandments, that

walk in God's ways, that keep themselves from sins; that if they fall confess: they belong to "the number." But are they the only ones? There are also some "beyond the number." For even if they be but a few (a few in comparison of the numbers of the larger majority), with how great numbers are our Churches filled, crowded up to the very walls; to what a degree do they annoy each other by the pressure, and almost choke each other by their overflowing numbers. Again, out of these very same persons, when there is a public spectacle,[6] there are numbers flocking to the amphitheatre; these are over and above "the number." But it is for this reason that we say this, that they may be in "the number." Not being present, they do not hear this from us; but when ye have gone from hence, let them hear it from you. "I have declared," he says, "and have spoken." It is Christ who speaks. "He hath declared it," in His own Person, as our Head. He hath Himself declared it by His members. He Himself hath sent those who should "declare" it; He Himself hath sent the Apostles. "Their sound is gone out into all lands, and their words unto the ends of the world."[7] How great the number of believers that are gathered together; how great the multitudes that flock together; many of them truly converted, many but in appearance: and those who are truly converted are the minority; those who are so but in appearance are the majority: because "they are multiplied beyond the number."

11. . . . . These are the "wonderful works" of God; these are the "thoughts" of God, to which "no man's thoughts are like;" that the lover of sight-seeing may be weaned from curiosity:[8] and with us may seek after those more excellent, those more profitable things, in which, when he shall have attained unto them, he will rejoice. . . .

12. "Sacrifice and offering Thou didst not desire" (ver. 6), saith the Psalm to God. For the men of old time, when as yet the true Sacrifice, which is known to the faithful, was foreshown in figures, used to celebrate rites that were figures of the reality that was to be hereafter; many of them understanding their meaning; but more of them in ignorance of it. For the Prophets and the holy Patriarchs understood what they were celebrating; but the rest of the "stiff-necked people" were so carnal, that what was done by them was but to symbolize the things that were to come afterwards; and it came to pass,[9] when that first sacrifice was abolished; when the burnt-offerings of "rams, of

---

[1] *Mariambulum.*   [2] 1 Cor. iv. 9.   [3] Matt. xiv. 28.
[4] Matt. xiv 30.   [5] 2 Tim. ii. 19.

[6] *Munus.*   [7] Ps. xix. 4.
[8] *Al.* "may be drawn to curiosity."
[9] *Et venit*   Some MSS. *en venit veritas,* "Lo, the Truth came," which makes easier sense.

goats, and of calves," and of other victims, had been abolished, "God did not desire them." Why did God not desire them? And why did He at the first desire them? Because all those things were, as it were, the words of a person making a promise; and the expressions conveying a promise, when the thing that they promise is come, are no longer uttered. . . . Those sacrifices then, as being but expressions of a promise, have been abrogated. What is that which has been given as its fulfilment? That "Body;" which ye know; which ye do not all of you know; which, of you who do know it, I pray God all may not know it unto condemnation. Observe the time when it was said; for the person is Christ our Lord, speaking at one time for His members, at another in His own person. "Sacrifice and offering," said He, "Thou didst not desire." What then? Are we left at this present time without a sacrifice? God forbid! "But a Body hast Thou perfected for me."[1] It was for this reason that Thou didst not desire the others; that Thou mightest "perfect" this; before Thou "perfectedst" this, Thou didst desire the others. The fulfilment of the promise has done away with the words that express the promise. For if they still hold out a promise, that which was promised is not yet fulfilled. This was promised by certain signs; the signs that convey the promise are done away; because the Substance that was promised is come. We are in this "Body." We are partakers of this "Body." We know that which we ourselves receive; and ye who know it not yet, will know it bye and bye; and when ye come to know it, I pray ye may not receive it unto condemnation.[2] "For he that eateth and drinketh unworthily, eateth and drinketh damnation unto himself."[3] "A Body" hath been "perfected" for us; let us be made perfect in the Body.

13. "Burnt-offerings also for sin hast Thou not required." "Then said I, Lo, I come!" (ver. 7). It is time that what "was promised should come;" because the signs, by means of which they were promised, have been put away. And indeed, Brethren, observe these put away; those fulfilled. Let the Jewish nation at this time show me their priest, if they can! Where are their sacrifices? They are brought to an end;[4] they are put away now. Should we at that time have rejected them?[5] We do reject them now; because, if you chose to celebrate them now, it were unseasonable;[6] unfitting at the time; incongruous. You are still making promises; I have already received! There has remained to them a certain thing for them to celebrate; that

they might not remain altogether without a sign. . . . In such a case then are they; like Cain with his mark. The sacrifices, however, which used to be performed there, have been put away; and that which remained unto them for a sign like that of Cain, hath by this time been fulfilled; and they know it not. They slay the Lamb; they eat the unleavened bread. "Christ has been sacrificed for us, as our Passover."[7] Lo, in the sacrifice of Christ, I recognise the Lamb that was slain! What of the unleavened bread? "Therefore," says he, "let us keep the feast; not with old leaven, neither with the leaven of wickedness" (he shows what is meant by "old;" it is "stale" flour; it is sour), "but in the unleavened bread of sincerity and truth."[8] They have continued in the shade; they cannot abide the Sun of Glory. We are already in the light of day. We have "the Body" of Christ, we have the Blood of Christ. If we have a new life, let us "sing a new song, even a hymn unto our God."[9] "Burnt offerings for sin Thou didst not desire. Then said I, Lo, I come!"

14. "In the head [10] of the Book it is written of me, that I should fulfil Thy will: O my God, I am willing, and Thy Law is within my heart" (ver. 8). Behold! He turns His regards to His members. Behold! He hath Himself "fulfilled the will" of the Father. But in what "beginning [10] of a Book" is it written of Him? Perhaps in the beginning of this Book of Psalms. For why should we seek far for it, or examine into other books for it? Behold! It is written in the beginning of this Book of Psalms! "His will is in the Law of the Lord;"[11] that is, "'O my God, I am willing,' and 'Thy Law is within my heart;'" that is the same as, "And in His Law doth he meditate day and night."

15. "I have well declared Thy righteousness in the great congregation" (ver. 9). He now addresses His members. He is exhorting them to do what He has already done. He has "declared;" let us declare also. He has suffered; let us "suffer with Him." He has been glorified; we shall be "glorified with Him."[12] "I have declared Thy righteousness in the great congregation." How great an one is that? In all the world. How great is it? Even among all nations. Why among all nations? Because He is "the Seed of Abraham, in whom all nations shall be blessed."[13] Why among all nations? "Because their sound hath gone forth into all lands."[14] "Lo! I will not refrain my lips, O Lord, and that Thou knowest." My lips speak; I will not "refrain" them from speaking. My lips indeed sound audibly in the ears of men; but "Thou knowest" mine heart. "I will not re-

---

[1] Corpus perfecisti, Augustin; aures perfecisti, Vulgate; corpus aptasti, Heb. x. 5, Vulgate.
[2] Judicium. So Vulgate. [3] 1 Cor. xi. 29.
[4] Perierunt. [5] Reprobaremus. [6] Intemporale.

[7] 1 Cor. v. 7. [8] 1 Cor. v. 8. [9] Supra, ver. 3.
[10] Capite. [11] Ps. i. 2. [12] Rom. viii. 17.
[13] Gen. xxii. 18. [14] Ps. xix. 4.

frain my lips, O Lord ; that Thou knowest." It is one thing that man heareth ; another that God "knoweth." That the "declaring" of it should not be confined to the lips alone, and that it might not be said of us, "Whatsoever things they say unto you, do ; but do not after their works ; "[1] or lest it should be said to the people, "praising God with their lips, but not with their heart," "This people honoureth Me with their lips, but their heart is far from Me ; "[2] do thou make audible confession with thy lips ; draw nigh with thine heart also.[3] "For with the heart man believeth unto righteousness ; but with the mouth confession is made unto salvation."[4] In case like unto which that thief was found, who, hanging on the Cross with the Lord, did on the Cross acknowledge the Lord. Others had refused to acknowledge Him while working miracles ; this man acknowledged Him when hanging on the Cross. That thief had every other member pierced through ; his hands were fastened by the nails ; his feet were pierced also ; his whole body was fastened to the tree ; the body was not disengaged in its other members ; the heart and the tongue were disengaged ;[5] "with the heart" he "believed ; with the tongue" he made "confession." "Remember me, O Lord," he said, "when Thou comest into Thy kingdom." He hoped for the coming of his salvation at a time far remote ; he was content to receive it after a long delay ; his hope rested on an object far remote. The day, however, was not postponed ! The answer was, "This day shalt thou be with Me in Paradise."[6] Paradise hath happy trees ! This day hast thou been with Me on "the Tree" of the Cross. This day shalt thou be with Me on "the Tree" of Salvation. . . .

16. "I have not hid my[7] righteousness within my heart" (ver. 10). What is meant by "my righteousness"? My faith. For, "the just shall live by faith."[8] As suppose the persecutor under threat of punishment, as they were once allowed to do, puts you to the question, "What art thou? Pagan or Christian?" "A Christian." That is his "righteousness." He believeth ; he "lives by faith." He doth not "hide his righteousness within his heart." He has not said in his heart, "I do indeed believe in Christ ; but I will not tell what I believe to this persecutor, who is raging against me, and threatening me. My God knoweth that inwardly, within my heart, I

do believe. He knoweth that I renounce Him not." Lo ! you say that you have this inwardly within your heart ! What have you upon your lips? "I am not a Christian." Your lips bear witness against your heart. "I have not hid my righteousness within my heart." . . .

17. "I have declared Thy Truth and Thy Salvation." I have declared Thy Christ. This is the meaning of, "I have declared Thy Truth and Thy Salvation." How is "Thy Truth" Christ? "I am the Truth."[9] How is Christ "His Salvation"? Simeon recognised the infant in His Mother's hands in the Temple, and said, "For mine eyes have seen Thy Salvation."[10] The old man recognised the little child ; the old man having himself "become a little child"[11] in that infant, having been renewed by faith. For he had received an oracle from God ; and it said this, "The Lord had said unto him, that he was not to depart out of this life, until he had seen the "Salvation of God." This "Salvation of God" it is a good thing to have shown unto men ; but let them cry, "Show us Thy mercy, O Lord, and grant us Thy Salvation." . . .

18. "I have not concealed Thy mercy and Thy Truth from the great congregation." Let us be there ; let us also be numbered among the members of this Body : let us not keep back "the mercy" of the Lord, and "the Truth" of the Lord. Wouldest thou hear what "the mercy of the Lord" is? Depart from thy sins ; He will forgive thy sins. Wouldest thou hear what "the truth" of the Lord is? Hold fast righteousness. Thy righteousness shall receive a crown. For mercy is announced to you now ; "Truth" is to be shown unto thee hereafter. For God is not merciful in such a way as not to be just, nor just in such a way as not to be merciful. Does that mercy seem to thee an inconsiderable one? He will not impute unto thee all thy former sins : thou hast lived ill up to this present day ; thou art still living ; this day live well ; then thou wilt not "conceal" this "mercy." If this is meant by "mercy," what is meant by "truth"? . . .

19. "Remove not Thou Thy mercies far from me, O Lord" (ver. 11). He is turning his attention to the wounded members. Because I have not "concealed Thy mercy and Thy Truth from the great congregation," from the Unity of the Universal Church, look Thou on Thy afflicted members, look on those who are guilty of sins of omission, and on those who are guilty of sins of commission : and withhold not Thou Thy mercies. "Thy mercy and Thy Truth have continually preserved me." I should not dare to turn from my evil way, were I not assured of remission ;

---

[1] Matt. xxiii. 3.   [2] Isa. xxix. 31.
[3] Sona labiis, propinqua corde. [Audible confession, in the great congregation, was the primitive discipline. But St. Chrysostom, who teaches the like discipline, urges to private penitence before God as all-sufficient. Hom. xxxi. In Hebr. tom. xii. p. 216, ed. Migne. — C.]
[4] Rom. x. 10.
[5] Corpus illud non vacabat cæteris membris ; lingua vacabat et cor.
[6] Luke xxiii. 42, etc.
[7] E. V. "Thy." So Vulgate also, tuam.
[8] Hab. ii. 4 ; Rom. i. 17.

[9] John xiv. 6.
[10] Luke ii. 30.
[11] Factus in puero puer. He alludes to Matt. xviii. 3, "Except ye be converted, and become as little children."

I could not endure so as to persevere, if I were not assured of the fulfilment of Thy promise. . . .

"Innumerable evils have compassed me about" (ver. 12). Who can number sins? Who can count his own sins, and those of others? A burden under which he was groaning, who said, "Cleanse Thou me from my secret faults; and from the faults of others, spare Thou Thy servant, O Lord." [1] Our own are too little; those "of others" are added to the burden. I fear for myself; I fear for a virtuous brother, I have to bear with a wicked brother; and under such burthen what shall we be, if God's mercy were to fail? "But Thou, Lord, remove not afar off." Be Thou near unto us! To whom is the Lord near? "Even" unto them that "are of a broken heart." [2] He is far from the proud: He is near to the humble. "For though the Lord is high, yet hath He respect unto the lowly." [3] But let not those that are proud think themselves to be unobserved: for the things that are high, He "beholdeth afar off." He "beheld afar off" the Pharisee, who boasted himself; He was near at hand to succour the Publican, who made confession.[4] The one extolled his own merits, and concealed his wounds; the other boasted not of his merits, but laid bare his wounds. He came to the Physician; he knew that he was sick, and that he required to be made whole; he "dared not lift up his eyes to Heaven: he smote upon his breast." He spared not himself, that God might spare him; he acknowledged himself guilty, that God might "ignore" the charge against him. He punished himself, that God might free him from punishment. . . .

20. "Mine iniquities have taken hold upon me, so that I could not see." There is a something for us "to see;" what prevents us so that we see it not? Is it not iniquity? From beholding this light [5] your eye is prevented perhaps by some humour penetrating into it; perhaps by smoke, or dust, or by something else that has been thrown into it: and you have not been able to raise your wounded eye to contemplate this light of day. What then? Will you be able to lift up your wounded heart unto God? Must it not be first healed, in order that thou mayest see? Do you not show your pride, when you say, "First let me see, and then I will believe"? Who is there who says this? For who that would fain see, says, "Let me see, and then I will believe"? I am about to manifest the Light unto thee; or rather the Light Itself would fain manifest Itself to thee! To whom? It cannot manifest Itself to the blind. He does not see. Whence is it that he seeth not? It is that the eye is clogged by the multitude of sins. . . .

21. "They are more than the hairs of my head." He subjects the number of the "hairs of his head" to calculation. Who is there can calculate the number of the hairs of his head? Much less can he tell the number of his sins, which exceed the number of the hairs of his head. They seem to be minute; but they are many in number. You have guarded against great ones; you do not now commit adultery, or murder; you do not plunder the property of others; you do not blaspheme; and do not bear false witness; those are the weightier kind of sins. You have guarded against great sins, what are you doing about your smaller ones? You have cast off the weight; beware lest the sand overwhelm you. "And my heart hath forsaken me." What wonder if thine heart is forsaken by thy God, when it is even "forsaken" by itself? What is meant by "faileth me," "forsaketh me"? Is not capable of knowing itself. He means this: "My heart hath forsaken me." I would fain see God with mine heart, and cannot from the multitude of my sins: that is not enough; mine heart does not even know itself. For no one thoroughly knows himself: let no one presume upon his own state. Was Peter able to comprehend with his own heart the state of his own heart, who said, "I will be with Thee even unto death"? [6] There was a false presumption in the heart; there was lurking in that heart at the same time a real fear: and the heart was not able to comprehend the state of the heart. Its state was unknown to the sick heart itself: it was manifest to the physician. That which was foretold of him was fulfilled. God knew that in him which he knew not in himself: because his heart had forsaken him, his heart was unknown to his heart.

22. "Be pleased, O Lord, to deliver me" (ver. 13). As if he were saying, "'If Thou wilt, Thou canst make me clean.' [7] Be pleased to deliver me. O Lord, look upon me to help me." Look,[8] that is, on the penitent members, members that lie in pain, members that are writhing under the instruments of the surgeon; but still in hope.

23. "Let them be ashamed and confounded together that seek after my soul to destroy it" (ver. 14). For in a certain passage he makes an accusation, and says, "I looked upon my right hand, and beheld; and there was no man who sought after my soul;" [9] that is, there was no man to imitate Mine example. Christ in His Passion is the Speaker. "I looked on my right hand," that is, not on the ungodly Jews, but on Mine own right hand, the Apostles, — "and there was no man who sought after My soul." So thoroughly was there no man to "seek after

---

[1] Ps. xix. 12.　　　[2] Ps. xxxiv. 18; Isa. lvii. 15.
[3] Ps. cxxxviii. 6.　　　[4] Luke xviii. 9–14.
[5] Natural light.

[6] Luke xxii. 33.　　　[7] Matt. viii. 2.
[8] Oxf. mss. repeat *respice*.　　　[9] Ps. cxlii. 4.

My soul," that he who had presumed on his own strength, "denied My soul." But because a man's soul is sought after in two ways, either in order that you may enjoy his society; or that you may persecute him; therefore he here speaks of others, whom he would have "confounded and ashamed," who are "seeking after his soul." But lest you should understand it in the same way as when he complains of some who did not "seek after his soul," He adds, "to destroy it ; " that is, they seek after my soul in order to my death. . . .

24. "Let them be turned backward [1] and put to shame that wish me evil." "Turned backwards." Let us not take this in a bad sense. He wishes them well; and it is His voice, who said from the Cross, "Father, forgive them ; for they know not what they do." [2] Wherefore then doth he say to them, that they should return "backwards"? Because they who before were proud, so that they fell, are now become humble, so that they may rise again. For when they are before, they are wishing to take precedence of their Lord ; to be better than He ; but if they go behind Him, they acknowledge Him to be better than they ; they acknowledge that He ought to go before ; that He should precede,[3] they follow. Thence He thus rebukes Peter giving Him evil counsel. For the Lord, when about to suffer for our salvation, also foretold what was to happen concerning that Passion itself; and Peter says, "Be it far from Thee," [4] "God forbid it!" "This shall not be!" He would fain have gone before his Lord ; would have given counsel to his Master! But the Lord, that He might make him not go before Him, but follow after Him, says, "Get thee behind, Satan!" It is for this reason He said "Satan," because thou art seeking to go before Him, whom thou oughest to follow ; but if thou art behind, if thou follow Him, thou wilt henceforth not be "Satan." What then? "Upon this Rock I will build My Church." [5] . . .

25. "Let them speedily bear away their own confusion, that say unto me, Well done! Well done!" [6] (ver. 15). They praise you without reason. "A great man! A good man! A man of education and of learning ; but why a Christian?" They praise those things in you which you should wish not to be praised ; they find fault with that at which you rejoice. But if perhaps you say, "What is it you praise in me, O man? That I am a virtuous man? A just man? If you think this, Christ made me this ; praise Him." But the other says, "Be it far from you. Do yourself no wrong! You yourself made yourself

such." "Let them be confounded who say unto me, Well done! Well done!" And what follows?

"Let all those that seek Thee, O Lord, rejoice and be glad" (ver. 16). Those who "seek" not me, but "Thee ;" who say not to me, "Well done! Well done!" but see me "glory in Thee," if I have anything whereof to glory ; for "he who glories, let him glory in the Lord." [7] "Let all those who seek Thee, Lord, rejoice and be glad."

"And say continually, the Lord be magnified." For even if the sinner becometh righteous, thou shouldest give the glory to "Him who justifieth the ungodly." [8] Whether therefore it be a sinner, let Him be praised who calls him to forgiveness ; or one already walking in the way of righteousness, let Him be praised who calls him to receive the crown! Let the Name of the Lord be magnified continually by "such as love Thy salvation."

"But I" (ver. 17). I for whom they were seeking evil, I whose "life they were seeking, that they might take it away." But turn thee to another description of persons. But I to whom they said, "Well done! Well done!" "I am poor and needy." There is nothing in me that may be praised as mine own. Let Him rend my sackcloth in sunder, and cover me with His robe. For, "Now I live, not I myself ; but Christ liveth in me." [9] If it is Christ that "liveth in thee," and all that thou hast is Christ's, and all that thou art to have hereafter is Christ's also ; what art thou in thyself? "I am poor and needy." Now I am not rich, because I am not proud. He was rich who said, "Lord, I thank Thee that I am not as other men are ; " [10] but the publican was poor, who said, "Lord, be merciful to me a sinner!" The one was belching from his fulness ; the other from want was crying piteously, "I am poor and needy!" And what wouldest thou do, O poor and needy man? Beg at God's door ; "Knock, and it shall be opened unto thee." [11] — "As for me, I am poor and needy. Yet the Lord careth for me." — "Cast thy care upon the Lord, and He shall bring it to pass." [12] What canst thou effect for thyself by taking care? what canst thou provide for thyself? Let Him who made thee "care for thee." He who cared for thee before thou wert, how shall He fail to have a care of thee, now that thou art what He would have thee be? For now thou art a believer, now thou art walking in the "way of righteousness." Shall not He have a care for thee, who "maketh His sun rise on the good and on the evil, and sendeth rain on the just and on the unjust"? [13] . . .

---

[1] E. V. "driven backwards." Text, *convertantur.*
[2] Luke xxiii. 34. [3] *Priorem.* [4] Matt. xvi. 22.
[5] Matt. xvi. 18.
[6] E. V. "Let them be desolate for a reward of their shame, that say unto me, Aha! Aha!"

[7] 1 Cor. i. 31. [8] Rom. iv. 5. [9] Gal. ii. 20.
[10] Luke xviii. 11. [11] Matt. vii. 7. [12] Ps. lv. 22.
[13] Matt. v. 45.

"Thou art my Help, and my Deliverer; make no tarrying, O my God" (ver. 17). He is calling upon God, imploring Him, fearing lest he should fall away: "Make no tarrying." What is meant by "make no tarrying"? We lately read concerning the days of tribulation: "Unless those days should be shortened, there should no flesh be saved."[1] The members of Christ — the Body of Christ extended everywhere — are asking of God, as one single person, one single poor man, and beggar! For He too was poor, who "though He was rich, yet became poor, that ye through His poverty might be made rich."[2] It is He that maketh rich those who are the true poor;[3] and maketh poor those who are falsely rich. He crieth unto Him; "From the end of the earth I cried unto Thee, when my heart was in heaviness." There will come days of tribulations, and of greater tribulations; they will come even as the Scripture speaks: and as days advance, so are tribulations increased also. Let no one promise himself what the Gospel doth not promise. . . .

PSALM XLI.[4]

TO THE PEOPLE, ON THE FEAST OF THE MARTYRS.

1. The solemn day of the Martyrs hath dawned; therefore to the glory of the Passion of Christ, the Captain of Martyrs, who spared not Himself, ordering His soldiers to the fight; but first fought, first conquered, that their fighting He might encourage by His example, and aid with His majesty, and crown with His promise: let us hear somewhat from this Psalm pertaining to His Passion. I commend unto you oftentimes, nor grieve I to repeat, what for you is useful to retain, that our Lord Jesus Christ speaketh often of Himself, that is, in His own Person, which is our Head; often in the person of His Body, which are we and His Church; but so that the words sound as from the mouth of one, that we may understand the Head and the Body to consist together in the unity of integrity, and not be separated the one from the other; as in that marriage whereof it is said, "They two shall be one flesh."[5] If then we acknowledge two in one flesh, let us acknowledge two in one voice. First, that which responding to the reader[6] we have sung, though it be from the middle of the Psalm, from that I will take the beginning of this Sermon.

"Mine enemies speak evil of Me, When He shall die, then shall His Name perish" (ver. 5). This is the Person of our Lord Jesus Christ:

but see if herein are not understood the members also. This was spoken also when our Lord Himself walked in the flesh here on earth. . . . When they saw the people go after Him, they said, "When He shall die, then shall His Name perish;" that is, when we have slain Him, then shall His Name be no more in the earth, nor shall He seduce any, being dead; but by that very slaying of Him shall men understand, that He was but a man whom they followed, that there was in Him no hope of salvation, and shall desert His Name, and it shall no more be. He died, and His Name perished not, but His Name was sown as seed: He died, but He was a grain, which dying, the corn immediately sprang up.[7] When glorified then was our Lord Jesus Christ, began they much more, and much more numerously to trust in Him; then began His members to hear what the Head had heard. Now then our Lord Jesus Christ being in heaven set down, and Himself in us labouring on earth, still spake His enemies, "When He shall die, then shall His Name perish." For hence stirred up the devil persecutions in the Church to destroy the Name of Christ. Unless haply ye think, brethren, that those Pagans, when they raged against Christians, said not this among themselves, "to blot out the Name of Christ from the earth." That Christ might die again, not in the Head, but in His Body, were slain also the Martyrs. To the multiplying of the Church availed the Holy Blood poured forth, to help Its seminating came also the death of the Martyrs. "Precious in the sight of the Lord is the death of His Saints."[8] More and more were the Christians multiplied, nor was it fulfilled which spake the enemies, "When He shall die, then shall His Name perish." Even now also is it spoken. Down sit the Pagans, and compute them the years, they hear their fanatics[9] saying, A time shall come when Christians shall be none, and those idols must be worshipped as before they were worshipped: still say they, "When He shall die, then shall His Name perish." Twice conquered, now the third time be wise! Christ died, His Name has not perished: the Martyrs died, multiplied more is the Church, groweth through all nations the Name of Christ. He who foretold of His own Death, and of His Resurrection, He who foretold of His Martyrs' death, and of their crown, He Himself foretold of His Church things yet to come, if truth He spake twice, has He the third time lied? Vain then is what ye be-

---

[1] Matt. xxiv 22.   [2] 2 Cor. viii. 9.
[3] Compare Matt. v. 3, "Blessed are the poor in spirit," and Luke vi. 20, "Blessed be ye poor."
[4] Lat. XL.   [5] Gen. ii. 24; Eph. v. 31.
[6] [He begins with the "Antiphon;" i.e., a verse selected from the Psalm as expressing the chief thought of the Psalmist or the spirit of the festival. This was interjected, at set places, in response to the reader. — C.]

[7] John xii. 24.   [8] Ps. cxvi. 15.
[9] In the *City of God*, b. xviii. c. 53, 54, he mentions that the heathens had some Greek verses, in the form of an oracle, to the effect that the magical arts of Peter had prevailed to procure divine worship to Christ for 365 years, after which it was to terminate. This period, he says, if computed from the first Pentecost after the Resurrection, would expire in the consulship of Honorius and Eutychianus, A.D. 398. The next year, which ought to have seen paganism re-established, was marked by the demolition of idols by imperial authority. — Ben. [See vol. ii. p. 394, this series. — C.]

lieve against Him ; better is it that ye believe in Him, that ye may " understand upon the needy and poor One ; " [1] that " though He was rich, yet for your sakes He became poor, that ye through His poverty might be rich." [2] . . .

2. " Blessed is he that understandeth upon the needy and poor One : in the evil day shall the Lord deliver him " (ver. 1). For the evil day will come : will thou, nill thou, come it will : the Day of Judgment will come upon thee, an evil day if thou " understand not the needy and poor." For what now thou wilt not believe, shall be made manifest in the end. But neither shalt thou escape, when it shall be made manifest, because thou believest not, when it is kept secret. Invited art thou, what thou seest not to believe, lest when thou see, thou be put to the blush. " Understand then upon the needy and poor One," that is, Christ : understand in Him the hidden riches, whom poor thou seest. " In Him are hid all the treasures of wisdom and knowledge." [3] For thereby in the evil day shall He deliver thee, in that He is God : but in that He is man, and that which in Him is human hath raised to life, and changed for the better, He hath lifted (thee [4]) to heaven. But He who is God, who would have one person in man and with man, could neither decrease nor increase, neither die nor rise again. He died out of man's infirmity, but God dieth not. . . . But as we rightly say, Such a man died, though his soul dieth not ; so we rightly say, Christ died, though His Divinity dieth not. Wherefore died ? Because needy and poor. Let not His death offend thee, and avert thee from beholding His Divinity. " Blessed is he that understandeth upon the needy and poor One." Consider also the poor, the needy, the hungry and thirsty, the naked, the sick, the prisoners ; understand also upon such poor, for if upon such thou understand, thou understandest upon Him who said, " I was an hungred, I was thirsty, I was a stranger, naked, sick, in prison ; " [5] so in the evil day shall the Lord deliver thee. . . .

3. " And deliver him not into the hand of his enemy " (ver. 2). The enemy is the devil. Let none think of a man his enemy, when he hears these words. Haply one thought of his neighbour, of him who had a suit with him in court, of him who would take from him his own possession, of him who would force him to sell to him his house. Think not this ; but that enemy think of, of whom said the Lord, " an enemy hath done this." [6] For He it is who suggests that for things earthly he be worshipped, for overthrow the Christian Name this enemy cannot. For he hath seen himself conquered by the fame and praises of Christ, he hath seen, whereas he slew Christ's Martyrs, that they are crowned, he triumphed over. He hath begun to be unable to persuade men that Christ is nought ; and because by reviling Christ, he now with difficulty deceives, by lauding Christ, he endeavours to deceive. Before this what said he ? Whom worship ye ? A Jew, dead, crucified, a man of no moment, who could not even from himself drive away death. When after His Name he saw running the whole human race, saw that in the Name of the Crucified temples are thrown down, idols are broken, sacrifices abolished ; and that all these things predicted in the Prophets are considered by men, by men with wonder astonished, and closing now their hearts against the reviling of Christ ; he clothes himself with praise of Christ, and begins to deter from the faith in another manner. Great is the law of Christ, powerful is that law, divine, ineffable ! but who fulfilleth it ? In the name of our Saviour,[7] " tread upon the lion and the dragon." [8] By reviling openly roared the lion ; by lauding craftily lurks the dragon. Let them come to the faith, who doubted ; and not say, Who fulfilleth it ? If on their own strength they presume, they will not fulfil it. Presuming on the grace of God let them believe, presuming (on it) let them come ; to be aided come, not to be judged. So live all the faithful in the Name of Christ, each one in his degree fulfilling the commands of Christ, whether married, or celibates and virgins, they live as much as God granteth them to live ; neither presume they in their own strength, but know that in Him they ought to glory. . . .

4. " The Lord help him " (ver. 3). But when ? Haply in heaven, haply in the life eternal, that so it remain to worship the devil for earthly needs, for the necessities of this life. Far be it ! Thou hast " promise of the life that now is, and of that which is to come." [9] He came unto thee on earth, by Whom were made heaven and earth. Consider then what He saith, " The Lord help him, on his bed of pain." The bed of pain is the infirmity of the flesh ; lest thou shouldest say, I cannot hold, and carry, and tie up my flesh ; thou art aided that thou mayest. The Lord help thee on thy bed of pain. Thy bed did carry thee, thou carriedst not thy bed, but wast a paralytic inwardly ; He cometh who saith to thee, " Take up thy bed, and go thy way into thy house." [10] " The Lord help him on his bed of pain." Then to the Lord Himself He turneth, as though it were asked,[11] Why then, since the Lord helpeth us, suffer we such great ills in this life, such great scandals, such great labours, such disquiet from the flesh

[1] Ps. xli. 1.   [2] 2 Cor. viii 9.   [3] Col. ii. 3.
[4] Or " It," reading as Ben. Oxf. mss. have " not in that He is Man: and that which in Him was human, in thee He will raise again, and change to better, and lift to heaven." The future, " shall lift," is probably right. Ed. Ben. gives no various readings here; our mss. vary somewhat.
[5] Matt. xxv. 35, 36.   [6] Matt. xiii. 28.

[7] Oxf. mss. " It is fulfilled in the Name," etc.   [8] Ps xci. 13.
[9] 1 Tim. iv. 8.   [10] Mark ii. 11.   [11] Al. " he complained."

and the world? He turneth to God, and as though explaining to us the counsel of His healing, He saith, "Thou hast turned all his bed in his infirmity." By the bed is understood anything earthly. Every soul that is infirm in this life seeketh for itself somewhat whereon to rest, because intensity of labour, and of the soul extended toward God, it can hardly endure perpetually, somewhat it seeketh on earth whereon to rest, and in a manner with a kind of pausing to recline, as are those things which innocent ones love. . . . The innocent man resteth in his house, his family, his wife, his children; in his poverty, his little farm, his orchard planted with his own hand, in some building fabricated with his own study; in these rest the innocent. But yet God willing us not to have love but of life eternal, even with these, though innocent delights, mixeth bitterness, that even in these we may suffer tribulation, and so He turneth all our bed in our infirmity. "Thou hast turned all his bed in his infirmity." Let him not then complain, when in these things which he hath innocently, he suffereth some tribulations. He is taught to love the better, by the bitterness of the worse; lest going a traveller to his country, he choose the inn instead of his own home.

5. But why this? Because He "scourgeth every son whom He receiveth."[1] Why this? Because to men sinning was it said, "In the sweat of thy face shalt thou eat bread."[2] Therefore because all these chastisements, in which all our bed is turned in our infirmity, man ought to acknowledge that he suffers for sin; let him turn himself, and say what follows: "I said, Lord, be merciful unto me; heal my soul, for I have sinned against Thee" (ver. 4). O Lord, by tribulations do Thou exercise me; to be scourged Thou judgest every son whom Thou wilt receive, who sparedst not even the Only-Begotten. He indeed without sin was scourged; but I say, "I have sinned against Thee." . . .

6. "Mine enemies speak evil of Me, When He shall die, then shall His Name perish" (ver. 5). Of this we have already spoken,[3] and from this began.

7. "And entered in[4] to see" (ver. 6). What Christ suffered, that suffereth also the Church; what the Head suffered, that suffer also the Members. "For the disciple is not above his Master, nor the servant above his Lord."[5] . . .

If to Christ's Members thou belongest, come within, cling to the Head. Endure the tares if thou art wheat, endure the chaff if thou art grain.[6] Endure the bad fish within the net if thou art a good fish. Wherefore before the time of win-

nowing dost thou fly away? Wherefore before the time of harvest, dost thou root up the corn also with thyself? Wherefore before thou art come to the shore, hast thou broken the nets? "They go abroad, and tell it."

8. "All mine enemies whisper against Me unto the same thing" (ver. 7). Against Me all unto the same thing. How much better with me unto the same thing, than against me[7] "unto the same thing." What is, "Against me unto the same thing"? With one counsel, with one conspiring. Christ then speaketh unto thee, Ye consent against Me, consent ye to Me: why against Me? wherefore not with Me? That same thing if ye had always had, ye had not divided you into schisms. For, saith the Apostle, "I beseech you, brethren, that ye all speak the same thing, and that there be no division among you."[8] "All mine enemies whisper against Me unto the same thing:" against Me do they "devise evil to Me." To themselves rather, for "they have gathered iniquity to themselves;" but therefore to Me, because by their intention they are to be weighed: for not because to do nothing was in their power, to do nothing was in their will. For the devil lusted to extinguish Christ, and Judas would slay Christ; yet Christ slain and rising again, we are made alive, but to the devil and to Judas is rendered the reward of their evil will, not of our salvation. . . . The intention wherewith they spake, not what they spake, did He consider, who related that they spake evil of Him, "Against Me they devised evil to Me." And what evil to Christ, to the Martyrs what evil? All hath God turned to good.

9. "An ungodly word do they set forth against Me" (ver. 8). What sort of ungodly word? Listen to the Head Itself. "Come, let us kill Him, and the inheritance shall be ours."[9] Fools! How shall the inheritance be yours? Because ye killed Him? Lo! ye even killed Him; yet shall not the inheritance be yours. "Shall not He that sleepeth add this also, that He rise again"? When ye exulted that ye had slain Him, He slept; for He saith in another Psalm, "I slept." They raged and would slay Me; "I slept." If I had not willed, I had not even slept. "I slept," because "I have power to lay down My life, and I have power to take it again."[10] "I laid Me down and slept, and rose up again."[11] Rage then the Jews; be "the earth given into the hands of the wicked,"[12] be the flesh left to the hands of persecutors, let them on wood suspend it, with nails transfix it, with a spear pierce it. "Shall He that sleepeth, not add this, that He rise up again?" Where-

---

[1] Heb. xii. 6.   [2] Gen. iii. 19.
[3] [On the Antiphon, p. 128, *supra.* — C.]
[4] *Al.* "if they entered in."   [5] Matt. x. 24.
[6] Matt. xiii. 30.

[7] "Than," etc., added from Oxf. MSS.
[8] 1 Cor. i. 10.   [9] Mark xii. 7.   [10] John x. 18.
[11] Ps. iii. 5.   [12] Job ix. 24.

fore slept He? Because "Adam is the figure of Him that was to come." [1] And Adam slept, when out of his side was made Eve.[2] Adam in the figure of Christ, Eve in the figure of the Church; whence she was called "the mother of all living." [3] When was Eve created? While Adam slept. When out of Christ's side flowed the Sacraments of the Church? While He slept upon the Cross. . . .

10. "The man of My peace, in whom I trusted, which did eat of My bread, hath enlarged his heel against Me" (ver. 9): hath raised up his foot against Me: would trample upon Me. Who is this man of His peace? Judas. And in him did Christ trust, that He said, "in whom I trusted"? Did He not know him from the beginning? Did He not before he was born know that he would be? Had He not said to all His disciples, "I have chosen you twelve, and one of you is a devil"?[4] How then trusted He in him, but that He is in His Members, and that because many faithful trusted in Judas, the Lord transferred this to Himself? . . . "The man of My peace, in whom I trusted, which did eat of My bread." How showed He him in His Passion? By the words of His prophecy: by the sop He marked Him out, that it might appear said of him, "Which did eat of My bread." [5] Again, when he came to betray Him, He granted him a kiss,[6] that it might appear said of him, "The man of My peace."

11. "But Thou, O Lord, be merciful unto Me" (ver. 10). This is the person of a servant, this is the person of the needy and poor: for, [7] "Blessed is he that understandeth upon the needy and poor One." See, as it was spoken, "Be merciful unto Me, and raise Me up, and I will requite them," so is it done. For the Jews slew Christ, lest they should lose their place.[8] Christ slain, they lost their place. Rooted out of the kingdom were they, dispersed were they. He, raised up, requited them tribulation, He requited them unto admonition, not yet unto condemnation. For the city wherein the people raged, as a ramping and a roaring lion, crying out, "Crucify Him, Crucify Him," [9] the Jews rooted out therefrom, hath now Christians, by not one Jew is inhabited.[10] There is planted the Church of Christ, whence were rooted out the thorns of the synagogue. For truly this fire blazed "as the fire of thorns." [11] But the Lord was as a green tree. This said

Himself, when certain women mourned Christ as dying. . . . " For if they do these things in a green tree, what shall be done in a dry?" When can a green tree be consumed by the fire of thorns? For they blazed as fire among thorns. Fire consumeth thorns, but whatsoever green tree it is applied to, is not easily kindled. . . . Yet lest ye think that God the Father of Christ could raise up Christ, that is, the Flesh of His Son, and that Christ Himself, though He be the Word equal with the Father, could not raise up His own Flesh; hear out of the Gospel, "Destroy this temple, and in three days I will raise it up." [12] "But," said the Evangelist (lest even after this we should doubt), " He spake of the temple of His Body. Raise Me up, and I will requite them."

12. "By this I know that Thou favourest Me, that Mine enemies shall not triumph over Me" (ver. 11.) Because the Jews did triumph, when they saw Christ crucified; they thought that they had fulfilled their will to do Him hurt: the fruits of their cruelty they saw in effect, Christ hanging on the Cross: they shook their heads, saying, "If Thou be the Son of God, come down from the Cross." [13] He came not down, who could; His Potency He showed not, but patience taught. For if, on their saying these things, He had come down from the Cross, He would have seemed as it were to yield to them insulting, and not being able to endure reproach, would have been believed conquered: more firm remained He upon the Cross, than they insulting; fixed was He, they wavering. For therefore shook they their heads, because to the true Head they adhered not. He taught us plainly patience. For mightier is that which He did, who would not do what the Jews challenged. For much mightier is it to rise from the sepulchre, than to come down from the Cross. "That Mine enemies shall not triumph over Me." They triumphed then at that time. Christ rose again, Christ was glorified. Now see they in His Name the human race converted: now let them insult, now shake the head: rather now let them fix the head, or if they shake the head, in wonder and admiration let them shake. . . .

13. " But as for Me, Thou upholdest Me, because of Mine innocence " (ver. 12). Truly innocence; integrity without sin, requiting without debt, scourging without desert. " Thou upholdest Me because of Mine innocence, and hast made Me strong in Thy sight for ever." Thou hast made Me strong for ever, Thou madest Me weak for a time: Thou hast made Me strong in Thy sight, Thou madest Me weak in sight of men. What then? Praise to Him, glory to Him. " Blessed be the Lord God of Israel."

---

[1] Rom. v. 14.   [2] Gen. ii. 21.   [3] Gen. iii. 20.
[4] John vi. 70.   [5] John xiii. 26.   [6] Matt. xxvi. 49.
[7] [He recurs to ver. 1. — C.]   [8] John xi. 48.
[9] Luke xxiii. 21.
[10] [Circa A.D. 400. Very noteworthy. Till the middle of our century only three hundred were permitted to dwell there; now nearly twenty thousand are said to inhabit Jerusalem. Is it a sign? Luke xxi. 24. — C.]
[11] Ps. cxviii. 12.

[12] John ii. 19.   [13] Matt. xxvii. 39, 40.

For He is the God of Israel, our God, the God of Jacob, the God of the younger son, the God of the younger people. Let none say, Of the Jews said He this, I am not Israel; rather the Jews are not Israel. For the elder son, he is the elder people reprobated; the younger, the people beloved. "The elder shall serve the younger:"[1] now is it fulfilled: now, brethren, the Jews serve us, they are as our satchellers,[2] we studying, they carry our books. Hear wherein the Jews serve us, and not without reason. . . . With them are the Law and the Prophets, in which Law, and in which Prophets, Christ is preached. When we have to do with Pagans, and show this coming to pass in the Church of Christ, which before was predicted of the Name of Christ, of the Head and Body of Christ, lest they think that we have forged these predictions, and from things which have happened, as though they were future, had made them up, we bring forth the books of the Jews. The Jews forsooth are our enemies, from an enemy's books convince we the adversary.[3] . . . If any enemy clamour and say, "Ye for yourselves have forged prophecies;" be the books of the Jews brought forth, because the elder shall serve the younger. Therein let them read those predictions, which now we see fulfilled; and let us all say, "Blessed be the Lord God of Israel, from everlasting to everlasting, and all the people shall say, So be it, So be it."

PSALM XLII.[4]

1. We have undertaken the exposition of a Psalm corresponding to your own "longings," on which we propose to speak to you. For the Psalm itself begins with a certain pious "longing;" and he who sings so, says, "Like as the hart desireth the water-brooks, so longeth my soul after Thee, O God" (ver. 1). Who is it then that saith this? It is ourselves, if we be but willing! And why ask, who it is other than thyself, when it is in thy power to be the thing which thou art asking about? It is not however one individual, but it is "One Body;" but "Christ's Body is the Church."[5] Such "longing" indeed is not found in all who enter the Church: let all however who have "tasted" the sweetness "of the Lord,"[6] and who own in Christ that for which they have a relish, think that they are not the only ones; but that there are such seeds scattered throughout "the field" of the Lord, this whole earth: and that there is a certain Christian unity, whose voice thus speaks, "Like as the hart desireth the water-brooks, so longeth my soul after Thee, O God." And indeed it is not ill understood as the cry of those, who being as yet Catechumens,[7] are hastening to the grace of the holy Font. On which account too this Psalm is ordinarily[8] chanted on those occasions, that they may long for the Fountain of remission of sins, even "as the hart for the water-brooks." Let this be allowed; and this meaning retain its place in the Church; a place both truthful and sanctioned by usage.[9] Nevertheless, it appears to me, my brethren, that such "a longing" is not fully satisfied even in the faithful in Baptism: but that haply, if they know where they are sojourning, and whither they have to remove from hence, their "longing" is kindled in even greater intensity.

2. The title then of it is, "On the end: a Psalm for understanding for the sons of Korah." We have met with the sons of Korah in other titles of Psalms:[10] and remember to have discussed and stated already the meaning of this name. Yet we must even now take notice of this title in such a way, that what we have said already should be no prejudice against our saying it again: for all were not present in every place where we said it. Now Korah may have been, as indeed he was, a certain definite person; and have had sons, who might be called "the sons of Korah;" let us however search for the secret of which this is the sacrament, that this name may bring to light the mystery with which it is pregnant. For there is some great mystery in the matter that the name "sons of Korah" is given to Christians. Why "sons of Korah"? They are "sons of the bridegroom, sons of Christ."[11] Why then does "Korah" stand for Christ? Because "Korah" is equivalent to "Calvaria." . . . Therefore, the "sons of the bridegroom," the sons of His Passion, the sons redeemed by His Blood, the sons of His Cross, who bear on their forehead that which His enemies erected on Calvary, are called "the sons of Korah;" to them is this Psalm sung as a Psalm for "understanding." Let then our "understanding" be roused: and if the Psalm be sung to us, let us follow it with our "understanding." . . . Run to the brooks; long after the water-brooks. "With God is the fountain of Life;" a "fountain" that shall never be dried up: in His "Light" is a Light that shall never be darkened. Long thou for this light: for a certain fountain, a certain light, such as thy bodily eyes know not; a light to see which the inward eye must be prepared; a fountain, to drink of which the inward thirst is to be kindled. Run to the fountain; long for the fountain; but do it not anyhow, be not satisfied

---

[1] Gen. xxv. 13.   [2] *Capsarii.*
[3] [Notably with reference to the book of Daniel. See Pusey on *Daniel the Prophet*, p. viii. preface, and 1-8, ed Oxford, 1864. — C.]
[4] Lat. XLI.   [5] Col. i. 24.   [6] Ps. xxxiv. 8.

[7] [See Bingham, b. x. cap. 2. Catechised in Lent, to be baptized at Easter. See the treatise on *Faith and Works*. — C.]
[8] *Solenniter.*   [9] *Et veracem et solennem.*
[10] Later Psalms had been treated before.
[11] Matt. ix. 15. *Filii sponsi*, Lat.

with running like any ordinary animal; run thou "like the hart." What is meant by "like the hart"? Let there be no sloth in thy running; run with all thy might: long for the fountain with all thy might. For we find in "the hart" an emblem of swiftness.

3. But perhaps Scripture meant us to consider in the stag not this point only, but another also. Hear what else there is in the hart. It destroys serpents,[1] and after the killing of serpents, it is inflamed with thirst yet more violent; having destroyed serpents, it runs to "the water-brooks," with thirst more keen than before. The serpents are thy vices, destroy the serpents of iniquity; then wilt thou long yet more for "the Fountain of Truth." Perhaps avarice whispers in thine ear some dark counsel, hisses against the word of God, hisses against the commandment of God. And since it is said to thee, "Disregard this or that thing," if thou prefer working iniquity to despising some temporal good, thou choosest to be bitten by a serpent, rather than destroy it. Whilst, therefore, thou art yet indulgent to thy vice, thy covetousness or thy appetite, when am I to find in thee "a longing" such as this, that might make thee run to the water-brooks? . . .

4. There is another point to be observed in the hart. It is reported of stags . . . that when they either wander in the herds, or when they are swimming to reach some other parts of the earth, that they support the burdens of their heads on each other, in such a manner as that one takes the lead, and others follow, resting their heads upon him, as again others who follow do upon them, and others in succession to the very end of the herd; but the one who took the lead in bearing the burden of their heads, when tired, returns to the rear, and rests himself after his fatigue by supporting his head just as did the others; by thus supporting what is burdensome, each in turn, they both accomplish their journey, and do not abandon each other. Are they not a kind of "harts" that the Apostle addresses, saying, "Bear ye one another's burdens, and so fulfil the Law of Christ"?[2] . . .

5. "My soul is athirst for the living God" (ver. 2). What I am saying, that "as the hart panteth after the water-brooks, so longs my soul after Thee, O God," means this, "My soul is athirst for the living God." For what is it athirst? "When shall I come and appear before God?" This it is for which I am athirst, to "come and to appear before Him." I am athirst in my pilgrimage, in my running; I shall be filled on my arrival. But "When shall I come?" And this, which is soon in the sight of God, is late to our "longing."[3] "When

shall I come and appear before God?" This too proceeds from that "longing," of which in another place comes that cry, "One thing have I desired of the Lord; that will I seek after; that I may dwell in the house of the Lord all the days of my life." Wherefore so? "That I may behold" (he saith) "the beauty of the Lord."[4] "When shall I come and appear before the Lord?" . . .

6. "My tears have been my meat day and night, while they daily say unto me, Where is thy God?" (ver. 3). My tears (he saith) have been not bitterness, but "my bread." Those very tears were sweet unto me: being athirst for that fountain, inasmuch as I was not as yet able to drink of it, I have eagerly made my tears my meat. For he said not, "My tears became my drink," lest he should seem to have longed for them, as for "the water-brooks:" but, still retaining that thirst wherewith I burn, and by which I am hurried away towards the water-brooks, "My tears became my meat," whilst I am not yet there.[5] And assuredly he does but the more thirst for the water-brooks from making his tears his meat. . . . "And they daily say unto me, Where is thy God?" For if a Pagan should say this to me, I cannot retort it upon him, saying, "Where is thine?" inasmuch as he points with his finger to some stone, and says, "Lo, there is my God!" When I have laughed at the stone, and he who pointed to it has been put to the blush, he raises his eyes from the stone, looks up to heaven, and perhaps says, pointing his finger to the Sun, "Behold there my God! Where, I pray, is your God?" He has found something to point out to the eyes of the flesh; whereas I, on my part, not that I have not a God to show to him, cannot show him what he has no eyes to see. For he indeed could point out to my bodily eyes his God, the Sun; but what eyes hath he to which I might point out the Creator of the Sun? . . .

7. "I thought on these things, and poured out my soul above myself"[6] (ver. 4). When would my soul attain to that object of its search, which is "above my soul," if my soul were not to "pour itself out above itself"? For were it to rest in itself, it would not see anything else beyond itself; and in seeing itself, would not, for all that, see God. Let then my insulting enemies now say, "Where is thy God?" aye, let them say it! I, so long as I do not "see," so long as my happiness is postponed, make my tears my "bread day and night." Let them

---

[1] [See p. 67, *supra.* — C.]   [2] Gal. vi. 2.
[3] *Citius Deo, tardum desiderio.*

[4] Ps. xxvii. 4.   [5] *Differor.*
[6] *Super me;* Vulgate, *in me.* Compare Aristotle, *Eth.* ix. 9: νοοῦμεν ὅτι νοοῦμεν· τὸ δ' αἰσθάνεσθαι ἢ νοεῖν, ὅτι αἰσθανόμεθα ἢ νοοῦμεν, [ἐστι τὸ αἰσθάνεσθαι ἢ νοεῖν] ὅτι ἐσμέν· τὸ γὰρ εἶναι ἦν τὸ αἰσθάνεσθαι ἢ νοεῖν, κ. τ. λ. "By the exercise of the powers of sensation and of thought, we become *conscious* of the exercise of those powers of sensation and of thought, and thereby conscious of our own being, for being is implied in the exercise of the powers of *thought* and sensation."

still say, "Where is thy God?" I seek my God in every corporeal nature, terrestrial or celestial, and find Him not: I seek His Substance in my own soul, and I find it not, yet still I have thought on these things, and wishing to "see the invisible things of my God, being understood by the things made,"[1] I have poured forth my soul above myself, and there remains no longer any being for me to attain to, save my God. For it is "there" is the "house of my God." His dwelling-place is above my soul; from thence He beholds me; from thence He created me; from thence He directs me and provides for me; from thence he appeals to[2] me, and calls me, and directs me; leads me in the way, and to the end of my way.[3] . . .

8. For when I was "pouring out my soul above myself," in order to reach my God, why did I do so? "For I will go into the place of Thy Tabernacle." For I should be in error were I to seek for my God without "the place of His tabernacle." "For I will go into the place of Thy wonderful tabernacle, even unto the house of God."

"I will go," he says, "into the place of the wonderful tabernacle, even unto the house of God!" For there are already many things that I admire in "the tabernacle." See how great wonders I admire in the tabernacle! For God's tabernacle on earth is the faithful; I admire in them the obedience of even their bodily members: that in them "Sin does not reign so that they should obey its lusts; neither do they yield their members instruments of unrighteousness unto sin; but unto the living God in good works."[4] I admire the sight of the bodily members warring in the service of the soul that serves God. . . . And wonderful though the tabernacle be, yet when I come to "the house of God," I am even struck dumb with astonishment. Of that "house" he speaks in another Psalm, after he had put a certain abstruse and difficult question to himself (viz., why is it that it generally goes well with the wicked on earth, and ill with the good?), saying, "I thought to know this; it is too painful for me, until I go into the sanctuary of God, and understand of the last things."[5] For it is there, in the sanctuary of God, in the house of God, is the fountain of "understanding." There he "understood of the last things;" and solved the question concerning the prosperity of the unrighteous, and the sufferings of the righteous. How does he solve it? Why, that the wicked, when reprieved here, are reserved for punishments without end; and the good when they suffer here, are being tried in order that they may in the end obtain the inheritance. And it was in the sanctuary of God that he understood this, and "understood

of the last things." . . . For he tells us of his progress, and of his guidance thither; as if we had been saying, "You are admiring the tabernacle here on earth; how came you to the sanctuary of the house of God?" he says, "In the voice of joy and praise; the sound of keeping holiday." Here, when men keep festival simply for their own indulgence, it is their custom to place musical instruments, or to station a chorus of singers,[6] before their houses, or any kind of music that serves and allures to wantonness. And when these are heard, what do we passers by say? "What is going on here?" And we are told in answer, that it is some festival. "It is a birthday that is being celebrated" (say they), "there is a marriage here;" that those songs may not appear out of place, but the luxurious indulgence[7] may be excused by the festive occasion. In the "house of God" there is a never-ending festival: for there it is not an occasion celebrated once, and then to pass away.[8] The angelic choir makes an eternal "holiday:" the presence of God's face, joy that never fails. This is a "holiday" of such a kind, as neither to be opened by any dawn, nor terminated by any evening. From that everlasting perpetual festivity, a certain sweet and melodious strain strikes on the ears of the heart, provided only the world do not drown the sounds. As he walks in this tabernacle, and contemplates God's wonderful works for the redemption of the faithful, the sound of that festivity charms his ears, and bears the "hart" away to "the water-brooks."

9. But seeing, brethren, so long as "we are at home in this body, we are absent from the Lord;"[9] and "the corruptible body presseth down the soul, and the earthly tabernacle weigheth down the mind that museth on many things;"[10] even though we have some way or other dispersed the clouds, by walking as "longing" leads us on, and for a brief while have come within reach of that sound, so that by an effort we may catch something from that "house of God," yet through the burden, so to speak, of our infirmity, we sink back to our usual level, and relapse to our ordinary state.[11] And just as there we found

---

[1] Rom. i. 20.   [2] *Excitat.*   [3] *Ducit . . . perducit.*
[4] Rom. vi. 12, 13.   [5] Ps. lxxiii. 16, 17.

[6] *Symphoniacos.* [7] *Luxuria.* Most MSS. *lætitia,* "the mirth."
[8] *Non enim aliquid ibi celebratur et transit.*
[9] 2 Cor. v. 6.   [10] Wisd. ix. 15.
[11] Compare Wordsworth's *Excursion,* "Despondency Corrected," p. 120: —
    "'Tis a thing impossible to frame
    Conceptions equal to the soul's desires,
    And the most difficult of tasks to *keep*
    Heights which the soul is competent to gain.
    Man is of *dust;* ethereal hopes are his,
    Which, when they should sustain themselves aloft,
    Want due consistence; like a pillar of smoke
    That with majestic energy from earth
    Rises, but having reach'd the thinner air
    Melts and dissolves, and is no longer seen."
Compare also p. 122: —
    "Alas! the endowment of immortal power
    Is match'd unequally with custom, time,
    And domineering faculties of sense
    In all . . . in most with superadded foes," etc.

cause for rejoicing, so here there will not be wanting an occasion for sorrow. For that hart that made "tears" its "bread day and night," borne along by "longing to the water-brooks" (that is, to the spiritual delights of God), "pouring forth his soul above himself," that he may attain to what is "above" his own soul, walking towards "the place of the wonderful tabernacle, even unto the house of God," and led on by the sweetness of that inward spiritual [1] sound to feel contempt for all outward things, and be borne on to things spiritual, is but a mortal man still; is still groaning here, still bearing about the frailty of flesh, still in peril in the midst of the "offences" [2] of this world. He therefore glances back to himself,[3] as if he were coming from that world; and says to himself, now placed in the midst of these sorrows, comparing these with the things, to see which he had entered in there, and after seeing which he had come forth from thence;

"Why art thou cast down, O my soul, and why dost thou disquiet me?" (ver. 5). Lo, we have just now been gladdened by certain inward delights: with the mind's eye we have been able to behold, though but with a momentary glance, something not susceptible of change: why dost thou still "disquiet me, why art thou" still "cast down"? For thou dost not doubt of thy God. For now thou art not without somewhat to say to thyself, in answer to those who say, "Where is thy God?" I have now had the perception of something that is unchangeable; why dost thou disquiet me still?

"Hope in God." Just as if his soul was silently replying to him, "Why do I disquiet thee, but because I am not yet there, where that delight is, to which I was, as it were, rapt for a moment?[4] Am I already 'drinking' from this 'fountain' with nothing to fear?" . . . Still "Hope in God," is his answer to the soul that disquiets him, and would fain account for her disquiet from the evils with which this world abounds. In the mean while dwell in hope: for "hope that is seen is not hope; but if we hope for that we see not, then do we with patience wait for it."[5]

10. "Hope in God." Why "hope"? "For I will confess unto Him." What wilt thou "confess"? "My God is the saving health of my countenance." [6] My "health" (my salvation) cannot be from myself; this it is that I will say, that I will "confess." It is my God that is "the saving health of my countenance." For to account for his fears, in the midst of those

things, which he now knows, having come after a sort to the "understanding" of them,[7] he has been looking behind him again in anxiety, lest the enemy be stealing upon him: he cannot yet say, "I am made whole every whit." For having but "the first-fruits of the Spirit, we groan within ourselves; waiting for the adoption, to wit, the redemption of the body." [8] When that "health" (that salvation) is perfected in us, then shall we be living in the house of God for ever, and praising for ever Him to whom it was said, "Blessed are they that dwell in Thy house, they will be praising Thee world without end." [9] This is not so yet, because the salvation which is promised, is not as yet in being; but it is "in hope" that I confess unto God, and say, "My God is the saving health of my countenance." For it is "in hope" that "we are saved; but hope that is seen, is not hope." . . .

11. "My soul is disquieted on account of myself" [10] (ver. 6). Is it disquieted on account of God? It is on my own account it is disquieted. By the Unchangeable it was revived; it is by the changeable it is disquieted. I know that the righteousness of God remaineth; whether my own will remain stedfast, I know not. For I am alarmed by the Apostle's saying, "Let him that thinketh he standeth, take heed lest he fall." [11] Therefore since "there is no soundness in me for myself," there is no hope either for me of myself. "My soul is disquieted on account of myself." . . . "Therefore I remember Thee, O Lord, from the land of Jordan, and from the little hill of Hermon." From whence did I remember thee? From the "little hill," and from the "land of Jordan." Perhaps from Baptism, where the remission of sins is given. For no one runs to the remission of sins, except he who is dissatisfied with himself; no one runs to the remission of sins, but he who confesses himself a sinner; no one confesses himself a sinner, except by humbling himself before God. Therefore it is from "the land of Jordan I have remembered thee, and from the hill;" observe, not "of the great hill," that thou mayest make of the "little hill" a great one: for "whoso exalteth himself shall be abased, and whoso humbleth himself shall be exalted." If you would also ask the meanings of the names, Jordan means "their descent." Descend then, that thou mayest be "lifted up:" be not lifted up, lest thou be cast down. "And the little hill of Hermon." Hermon means "anathematizing." Anathematize thyself, by being displeased with thyself; for if thou art pleased with thyself, God will be displeased with thee. Because then God gives us all good things, because He Himself is good, not because we are worthy of it; because He is merciful, not because

---

[1] *Intelligibilis*, answering to the Greek νοητοῦ.
[2] Matt. xviii. 7.
[3] . . . *Inter scandala Respexit ergo ad se.*
[4] *Per transitum.*　　　　　[5] Rom. viii. 24, 25.
[6] E. V. "I shall yet give Him thanks for the help of His countenance."

[7] *Utcunque intellecta cognoscit.*　　　[8] Rom. viii. 23.
[9] Ps. lxxxiv. 4.　　[10] E. V. "within."　　[11] 1 Cor. x 12.

we have in anything deserved it; it is from "the land of Jordan, and from Hermon," that I remember thee. And because he so remembers with humility, he shall earn his exaltation to fruition,[1] for he is not "exalted" in himself, who "glories in the Lord."

12. "Deep calleth unto deep with the voice of thy water-spouts"[2] (ver. 7). I may perhaps finish the Psalm, aided as I am by your attention, whose fervour I perceive. As for your fatigue in hearing, I am not greatly solicitous, since you see me also, who speak, toiling in the heat of these exertions.[3] Assuredly it is from your seeing me labouring, that you labour with me: for I am labouring not for myself, but for you. "Deep calleth unto deep with the voice of thy water-spouts." It was God whom he addressed, who "remembered him from the land of Jordan and Hermon." It was in wonder and admiration he spake this: "Abyss calleth unto abyss with the voice of Thy water-spouts." What abyss is this that calls, and to what other abyss? Justly, because the "understanding"[4] spoken of is an "abyss." For an "abyss" is a depth that cannot be reached or comprehended; and it is principally applied to a great body of water. For there is a "depth," a "profound," the bottom of which cannot be reached by sounding. Furthermore, it is said in a certain passage.[5] "Thy judgments are a mighty abyss," Scripture meaning to suggest that the judgments of God are incomprehensible. What then is the "abyss" that calls, and to what other "abyss" does it call? If by "abyss" we understand a great depth, is not man's heart, do you not suppose, "an abyss"? For what is there more profound than that "abyss"? Men may speak, may be seen by the operations of their members, may be heard speaking in conversation: but whose thought is penetrated, whose heart seen into? What he is inwardly engaged on, what he is inwardly capable of,[6] what he is inwardly doing or what purposing, what he is inwardly wishing to happen, or not to happen, who shall comprehend? I think an "abyss" may not unreasonably be understood of man, of whom it is said elsewhere, "Man shall come to a deep heart, and God shall be exalted."[7] If man then is an "abyss," in what way doth "abyss" call on "abyss"? Does man "call on" man as God is called upon? No, but "calls on" is equivalent to "calls to him." For it was said of a certain person, he calls on death;[8] that is, lives in such a way as to be inviting death; for there is no man at all who puts up a prayer, and calls expressly on death: but men by evil-living invite

death. "Deep[9] calls on deep," then, is, "man calls to man." Thus is it wisdom is learnt, and thus faith, when "man calls to man." The holy preachers of God's word call on the "deep:" are they not themselves "a deep" also? . . .

13. "Deep calleth to deep with the voice of Thy water-spouts." I, who tremble all over, when my soul was disquieted on account of myself, feared greatly on account of Thy "judgments." . . . Are those judgments slight ones? They are great ones, severe, hard to bear; but would they were all. "Deep calls to deep with the voice of Thy water-spouts," in that Thou threatenest, Thou sayest, that there is another condemnation in store even after those sufferings. "Deep calls on deep with the voice of Thy water-spouts." "Whither then shall I go from Thy presence? And whither shall I flee from Thy Spirit?" seeing that deep calls to deep, and after those sufferings severer ones are to be dreaded.

14. "All Thy overhangings[10] and Thy waves are come upon me." The "waves" in what I already feel, the "overhangings" in that Thou denouncest. All my sufferings are Thy waves; all Thy denouncements of judgments are Thy "overhangings." In the "waves" that deep "calleth;" in the "overhangings" is the other "deep" which it "calls to." In this that I suffer are all Thy waves; in the severer punishment that Thou threatenest, all Thy "overhangings" are come unto me. For He who threatens does not let His judgments fall upon us, but keeps them suspended over us.[11] But inasmuch as Thou sittest at liberty, I have thus spoken unto my soul. "Hope in God: for I will confess unto Him. My God is the saving health of my countenance." The more numerous my sufferings, the sweeter will be Thy mercy.

15. Therefore follows: "The Lord will commend His loving-kindness in the day-time; and in the night-time will He declare it"[12] (ver. 8). In tribulation no man has leisure to hear: attend, when it is well with you; hear, when it is well with you; learn, when you are in tranquillity, the discipline of wisdom, and store up the word of God as you do food. For in tribulation every one must be profited by what he heard in the time of security. For in prosperity God "commends to thee His mercy," in case thou serve Him faithfully, for He frees thee from tribulation; but it is "in the night" only that He "declares" His mercy to thee, which He "commended" to thee by day. When tribulation shall actually come, He will not leave thee destitute of His help; He will show thee

---

1 *Exaltatus perfrui merebitur.*
2 *Cataractarum.*   3 *Ita in his laboribus sudare.*
4 In the title of the Psalm.   5 Ps. xxxvi. 6, 7.
6 "Quid intus *gerat*, quid possit."   7 Ps. lxiv. 6, 7.
8 Wisd. i. 16.

9 *Abyssum invocat.*
10 *Suspensiones;* Vulgate, *excelsa;* E. V. "billows."
11 *Non premit sed suspendit.* Perhaps his idea is rather, "suspends us over the abyss."
12 E. V. "In the night-time His song shall be with me."

that which He commended to thee in the day-time is true. For it is written in a certain passage, "The mercy of the Lord is seasonable[1] in the time of affliction, as clouds of rain in the time of drought." "The Lord hath commended His loving-kindness in the day-time, and in the night will He declare it." He does not show that He is thine Helper, unless tribulation come, from whence thou must be rescued by Him who promised it to thee "in the day-time." Therefore we are warned to be like "the ant." For just as worldly prosperity is signified by "the day," adversity by the night, so again in another way worldly prosperity is expressed by "the summer," adversity by the winter. And what is it that the ant does? She lays up in summer what will be useful to her in winter. Whilst therefore it is summer, whilst it is well with you, whilst you are in tranquillity, hear the word of the Lord. For how can it be that in the midst of these tempests of the world, you should pass through the whole of that sea, without suffering? How could it happen? To what mortal's lot has it fallen? If even it has been the lot of any, that very calm is more to be dreaded. "The Lord hath commended His loving-kindness in the day-time, and in the night-time will He declare it." . . . "There is with me prayer unto the God of my life." This I make my business here; I who am the "hart thirsting and longing for the water-brooks," calling to mind the sweetness of that strain, by which I was led on through the tabernacle even to the house of God; whilst this "corruptible body presseth down the soul,"[2] there is yet with me "prayer unto the God of my life." For in order to making supplication unto God, I have not to buy aught from places beyond the sea; or in order that He may hear me, have I to sail to bring from a distance frankincense and perfumes, or have I to bring "calf or ram from the flock." There is "with me prayer to the God of my life." I have within a victim to sacrifice; I have within an incense to place on the altar; I have within a sacrifice wherewith to propitiate my God. "The sacrifice of God is a troubled spirit." What sacrifice of a "troubled spirit" I have within, hear.

16. "I will say unto God, Thou art my lifter up. Why hast Thou forgotten me?" (ver. 9). For I am suffering here, even as if Thou hadst forgotten me. But Thou art trying me, and I know that Thou dost but put off, not take utterly from me, what Thou hast promised me. But yet, "Why hast Thou forgotten me?" So cried our Head also, as if speaking in our name. "My God, my God, why hast Thou forsaken me?"[3] I will say unto God, "Thou art my lifter up; why hast Thou forgotten me?"

17. "Why hast Thou rejected me?"[4] "Rejected" me, that is to say, from that height of the apprehension of the unchangeable Truth. "Why hast Thou rejected me?" Why, when already longing for those things, have I been cast down to these, by the weight[5] and burden of my iniquity? This same voice in another passage said, "I said in my trance"[6] (i.e., in my rapture, when he had seen some great thing or other), "I said in my trance, I am cast out of the sight of Thine eyes." For he compared these things in which he found himself, to those toward which he had been raised; and saw himself cast out far "from the sight of God's eyes," as he speaks even here, "Why hast Thou rejected me? Why go I mourning, while mine enemy troubleth me, while he breaketh my bones?" Even he, my tempter, the devil; while offences are everywhere on the increase, because of the abundance of which "the love of many is waxing cold."[7] When we see the strong members of the Church generally giving way to the causes of offence, does not Christ's body say, "The enemy breaketh my bones"? For it is the strong members that are "the bones;" and sometimes even those that are strong sink under their temptations. For whosoever of the body of Christ considers this, does he not exclaim, with the voice of Christ's Body, "Why hast Thou rejected me? Why go I mourning, while mine enemy troubleth me, while he breaketh my bones?"

You may see not my flesh merely, but even my "bones." To see those who were thought to have some stability, giving way under temptations, so that the rest of the weak brethren despair when they see those who are strong succumbing; how great, my brethren, are the dangers!

18. "They who trouble me cast me in the teeth." Again that voice! "While they say daily unto me, Where is thy God?" (ver. 10). And it is principally in the temptations of the Church they say this, "Where is thy God?" How much was this cast in the teeth of the Martyrs! Those men so patient and courageous for the name of Christ, how often was it said to them, "Where is your God?" "Let Him deliver you, if He can." For men saw their torments outwardly; they did not inwardly behold their crowns! "They who trouble me cast me in the teeth, while they say daily unto me, Where is thy God?" And on this account, seeing "my soul is disquieted on account of myself," what else should I say unto it than those words:

"Why art thou cast down, O my soul; and why dost thou disquiet me?" (ver. 11). And, as

---

[1] Ecclus. xxxv. 26. Ὡραῖον ἔλεος; Vulgate, *Speciosa misericordia.*
[2] Wisd. ix. 15.
[3] Matt. xxvii. 46; Ps. xxii. 1.

[4] *Ut quid me repulisti.* Neither in the Vulgate nor in our version.
[5] *Gravedine.*
[6] *In ecstasi meâ.* Ps. xxxi. 22. E. V. "in my haste."
[7] Matt. xxiv. 12.

it seems to answer, "Wouldest thou not have me disquiet thee, placed as I am here in so great evils? Wouldest thou have me not disquiet thee, panting as I am after what is good, thirsting and labouring as I am for it?" What should I say, but,

"Hope thou in God; for I will yet confess unto Him" (ver. 11). He states the very words of that confession; he repeats the grounds on which he fortifies his hope. "He is the health of my countenance, and my God."

PSALM XLIII.[1]

1. This Psalm is a short one; it satisfies the mental cravings of the hearers, without imposing too severe a trial on the hunger of those fasting.[2] Let our soul feed upon it; our soul, which he who sings in this Psalm, speaks of as "cast down;" cast down, I suppose, either in consequence of some fast, or rather in consequence of some hunger he was in. For fasting is a voluntary act; being an-hungered is an involuntary thing. That which is an-hungered, is the Church, is the Body of Christ: and that "Man" who is extended throughout the whole world, of which the Head is above, the limbs below: it is His voice which ought by this time to be perfectly known, and perfectly familiar, to us, in all the Psalms; now chanting joyously, now sorrowing; now rejoicing in hope, now sighing at its actual state, even as if it were our own. We need not then dwell long on pointing out to you, who is the speaker here: let each one of us be a member of Christ's Body; and he will be speaker here. . . .

2. "Judge me, O Lord, and separate my cause from the ungodly nation" (ver. 1). I do not dread Thy judgment, because I know Thy mercy. "Judge me, O God," he cries. Now, meanwhile, in this state of pilgrimage, Thou dost not yet separate my place, because I am to live together with the "tares" even to the time of the "harvest:" Thou dost not as yet separate my rain from theirs; my light from theirs: "separate my cause." Let a difference be made between him who believes in Thee, and him who believes not in Thee. Our infirmity is the same; but our consciences not the same: our sufferings the same; but our longings not the same. "The desire of the ungodly shall perish,"[3] but as to the desire of the righteous, we might well doubt, if He were not "sure" who promised. The object of our desires is He Himself, who promiseth: He will give us Himself, because He has already given Himself to us; He will give Himself in His immortality to us then immortal, even because He gave Himself in His mortality to us when mortal. . . .

3. And since patience is needful in order to endure, until the harvest, a certain distinction without separation,[4] if we may so speak (for they are together with us, and therefore not yet separated; the tares however being still tares, and the corn still corn, and therefore they are already distinct); since then a kind of strength[5] is needful, which must be implored of Him who bids us to be strong, and without whose making us strong, we should not be what He bids us to be; of Him who said, "He that endures unto the end shall be saved,"[6] lest the soul's powers should be impaired in consequence of her ascribing any strength to herself, he subjoins immediately,

"For Thou, O God, art my strength: why hast Thou cast me off, and why go I mourning, while the enemy harasseth me?" (ver. 2). I go mourning: the enemy is harassing me with daily temptations: inspiring either some unlawful love, or some ungrounded cause of fear; and the soul that fights against both of them, though not taken prisoner by them, yet being in danger from them, is contracted with sorrow, and says unto God, "Why?"

Let her then ask of Him, and hear "Why?" For she is in the Psalm enquiring the cause of her dejection; saying, "Why hast Thou cast me off? and why go I mourning?" Let her hear from Isaiah; let the lesson which has just been read, suggest itself to her. "The spirit shall go forth from me, and every breath have I made. For iniquity have I a little afflicted him; I hid my face from him, and he departed from me sorrowful in the ways of his heart."[7] Why then didst thou ask, "Why hast Thou cast me off, and why go I mourning?" Thou hast heard, it was "for iniquity." "Iniquity" is the cause of thy mourning; let "Righteousness" be the cause of thy rejoicing! Thou wouldest sin; and yet thou wouldest fain not suffer; so that it was too little for thee to be thyself unrighteous, without also wishing Him to be unrighteous, in that thou wouldest fain not be punished by Him. Consider a speech of a better kind in another Psalm. "It is good for me that Thou hast humbled me, that I might learn Thy righteousnesses."[8] By being lifted up, I had learned my own iniquities; let me by being "humbled," learn "Thy righteousnesses." "Why go I mourning, while the enemy harasses me?" Thou complainest of the enemy. It is true he does harass thee; but it was thou didst "give place"[9] to him. And even now there is a course open to thee; choose the course of prudence; admit thy King, shut the tyrant out.

---

4. But in order that she may do this, hear what she says, what she supplicates, what she prays for. Pray thou for what thou hearest; pray for it when thou hearest it; let these words be the voice of us all: "O send out Thy Light and Thy Truth. They have led me, and brought me on unto Thy holy hill, and into Thy Tabernacles" (ver. 3). For that very "Light" and "Truth" are indeed two in name; the reality expressed is but One. For what else is the "Light" of God, except the "Truth" of God? Or what else is the "Truth" of God, except the "Light" of God? And the one Person of Christ is both of these. "I am the Light of the world: he that believeth on Me, shall not walk in darkness." "I am the Way, the Truth, and the Life." [1] He is Himself "the Light:" He is Himself "the Truth." Let Him come then and rescue us, and "separate at once our cause from the ungodly nation; let Him deliver us from the deceitful and unjust man," let him separate the wheat from the tares, for at the time of harvest He will Himself send His Angels, that they may "gather out of His kingdom all things that offend," [2] and cast them into flaming fire, while they gather together the corn into the garner. He will send out His "Light," and His "Truth;" for that they have already "brought us and led us to His holy hill, and into His Tabernacles." We possess the "earnest;" [3] we hope for the prize. "His holy Hill" is His holy Church. It is that mountain which, according to Daniel's vision, [4] grew from a very small "stone," till it crushed the kingdoms of the earth; and grew to such a size, that it "filled the face of the earth." This is the "hill," from which he tells us that his prayer was heard, who says, "I cried unto the Lord with my voice, and He heard me out of His holy hill." [5] Let no one of those that are without that mountain, hope to be heard unto eternal life. For many are heard in their prayers for many things. Let them not congratulate themselves [6] on being heard; the devils were heard in their prayer, that they might be sent into the swine. Let us desire to be heard unto eternal life, by reason of our longing, through which we say, "Send out Thy Light and Thy Truth." [7] That is a "Light" which requires the eye of the heart. For "Blessed" (He saith) "are the pure in heart, for they shall see God." [8] We are now on His Hill, that is, in His Church, and in His Tabernacle. The "tabernacle" is for persons sojourning; the house, for those dwelling in one community. [9] The tabernacle is also for those who are both from home, and also in a state of warfare. When

thou hearest of a tabernacle, form a notion of a war; guard against an enemy. But what shall the house be? "Blessed are they that dwell in Thine house: they will be alway praising Thee." [10]

5. Now then that we have been led on even to "the Tabernacle," and are placed on "His holy Hill," what hope do we carry with us? "Then will I go in unto the Altar of God" (ver. 4). For there is a certain invisible Altar on high, which the unrighteous man approaches not. To that Altar he alone draws nigh, who draws nigh to this one without cause to fear. There he shall find his Life, who in this one "separates his cause." "And I will go in unto the Altar of God." From His holy Hill, and from His Tabernacle, from His Holy Church, I will go in unto the Altar of God on High. What manner of Sacrifice is there? He himself who goeth in is taken for a burnt-offering. "I will go in unto the Altar of God." What is the meaning of what he says, "The Altar of my God"? "Unto God, who makes glad my youth." Youth signifies newness: just as if he said, "Unto God, who makes glad my newness." It is He who makes glad my newness, who hath filled my old estate [11] with mourning. For now "I go mourning" in oldness, then shall "I stand," exulting in newness!

"Yea, upon the harp will I praise Thee, O God my God." What is the meaning of "praising on the harp," and praising on the psaltery? For he does not always do so with the harp, nor always with the psaltery. These two instruments of the musicians have each a distinct meaning of their own, worthy of our consideration and notice. They are both borne in the hands, and played by the touch; and they stand for certain bodily works of ours. Both are good, if one knows how to play the psaltery, [12] or to play the harp. [13] But since the psaltery is that instrument which has the shell [14] (i.e. that drum, that hollow piece of wood, by straining on which [15] the chords resound) on the upper part of it, whereas the harp has that same concave sounding-board on the lower part, there is to be a distinction made between our works, when they are "upon the harp," when "on the psaltery:" both however are acceptable to God, and grateful to His ear. When we do anything according to God's Commandments, obeying His commands and hearkening to Him, that we may fulfil His injunctions, when we are active and not passive, it is the psaltery that is playing. For so also do the Angels: for they have nothing to suffer. But when we suffer anything of tribulation, of trials, of offences on this earth (as we suffer only from the inferior part of ourselves; i.e. from the fact that we are mortal, that we owe somewhat of tribulation to our

---

[1] John viii. 12, xiv. 6.　　　　[2] Matt. xiii. 41.
[3] *Pignus.*　　[4] Dan. ii. 35.　　[5] Ps. iii. 4.
[6] *Sibi plaudant.*　　[7] Matt. viii. 31, 32.　　[8] Matt. v. 8.
[9] *Cohabitantium.*

[10] Ps. lxxxiv. 4.　　[11] *Vetustatem.*　　[12] *Psallere.*
[13] *Citharizare.*　　[14] *Testudinem.*　　[15] *Cui innitentes.*

original cause,[1] and also from the fact of our suffering much from those who are not "above ") ; this is " the harp." For there rises a sweet strain from that part of us which is " below : " we " suffer," and we strike the psaltery,[2] or shall I rather say we sing and we strike the harp. . . .

6. And again, in order that he may draw the sound from that sounding-board below, he addresses his soul : he says, " Why art thou sorrowful, O my soul, and why dost thou disquiet me?" (ver. 5). I am in tribulations, in weariness,[3] in mourning, "Why dost thou disquiet me, O my soul?" Who is the speaker, to whom is he speaking? That it is the soul to which he is speaking, everybody knows : for it is obvious : the appeal is addressed to it directly : "Why art thou sorrowful, O my soul, and why dost thou disquiet me?" The question is as to the speaker. It is not the flesh addressing the soul, surely, since the flesh cannot speak without the soul. For it is more appropriate for the soul to address the flesh, than for the flesh to address the soul. . . . We perceive then that we have a certain part, in which is "the image of God ; " viz. the mind and reason.[4] It was that same mind that prayed for " God's Light " and " God's Truth." It is the same mind by which we apprehend[5] right and wrong : it is by the same that we discern truth from falsehood. It is this same that we call " understanding ; " which " understanding," indeed, is wanting to the brutes. And this " understanding " whoever neglects in himself, and holds it in less account than the other parts of his nature, and casts it off, just as if he had it not, is addressed in the Psalm, " Be ye not as the horse and the mule, which have no understanding."[6] It is our " understanding " then that is addressing our soul. The latter is withered away from tribulations, worn out in anguish,[7] made " sorrowful " in temptations, fainting in toils. The mind, catching a glimpse of Truth above, would fain rouse her spirits, and she says, "Why art thou sorrowful, O my soul?" . . .

7. These expressions, brethren, are safe ones : but yet be watchful in good works. Touch " the psaltery," by obeying the Commandments ; touch the harp, by patiently enduring your sufferings. You have heard from Isaiah, " Break thy bread to the hungry ; "[8] think not that fasting by itself is sufficient. Fasting chasteneth thine own self : it does not refresh others. Thy distress will profit thee, if thou affordest comfort[9] to others. See, thou hast denied thyself ; to whom wilt thou give that of which thou hast deprived thyself? Where wilt thou bestow what thou hast denied thyself? How many poor may be filled[10] by the breakfast[11] we[12] have this day given up? Fast in such a way that thou mayest rejoice, that thou hast breakfasted, while another has been eating ; fast on account of thy prayers, that thou mayest be heard in them. For He says in that passage, "Whilst thou art yet speaking I will say, Here I am,"[13] provided thou wilt with cheerful mind " break thy bread to the hungry." For generally this is done by men reluctantly and with murmurs, to rid themselves of the wearisome importunity of the beggar, not to refresh the bowels of him that is needy. But it is " a cheerful giver " that " God loves."[14] If thou givest thy bread reluctantly, thou hast lost both the bread, and the merit of the action. Do it then from the heart : that He " who seeth in secret,"[15] may say, " whilst thou art yet speaking, Here I am." How speedily are the prayers of those received, who work righteousness ! And this is man's righteousness in this life, fasting, alms, and prayer. Wouldest thou have thy prayer fly upward to God? Make for it those two wings of alms and fasting. Such may God's " Light " and God's " Truth " find us, that He may find us without cause for fear, when He comes to free us from death, who has already come to undergo death for us. Amen.

PSALM XLIV.[16]

1. This Psalm is addressed " to the sons of Korah," as its title shows. Now Korah is equivalent to the word baldness ;[17] and we find in the Gospel that our Lord Jesus Christ was crucified in " the place of a skull."[18] It is clear then that this Psalm is sung to the " sons of His ' Passion.' " Now we have on this point a most certain and most evident testimony from the Apostle Paul ; because that at the time when the Church was suffering under the persecutions of the Gentiles, he quoted from hence a verse, to insert by way of consolation, and encouragement to patience. For that which he inserted in his Epistle, is said here : " For Thy sake are we killed all the day long ; we are counted as sheep for the slaughter."[19] Let us then hear in this Psalm the voice of the Martyrs ; and see how good is the cause which the voice of the Martyrs pleads, saying, " For Thy sake," etc. . . .

2. The title then is not simply " To the sons of Korah," but, " For understanding, to the sons of Korah." This is the case also with that Psalm, the first verse of which the Lord Himself

---

[1] Prima nostra causa. He seems to mean our original from Adam.
[2] Psallimus.   [3] Al. " anguishes."
[4] T. Aquin. Prolog ad. I. II. Per imaginem Dei significatur (sicut Damascen. dicit), intellectuale, et arbitrio liberum ; et per se potestativum.
[5] Capimus.   [6] Ps. xxxii. 9.
[7] Some mss. languoribus.   [8] Isa. lviii. 7.
[9] Latitudinem.

[10] Saginare.   [11] Prandium.   [12] Al. "you."
[13] Isa. lviii. 9 and lxv. 24.   [14] 2 Cor. ix. 7.
[15] Matt. vi. 6.   [16] Lat. XLIII.   [17] Calvitium.
[18] Matt. xxvii. 33. Calvariæ.   [19] Rom. viii. 36.

uttered on the Cross : " My God, My God, look
upon Me ; why hast Thou forsaken Me ? "[1] For
" transferring us in a figure "[2] to what He was
saying, and to His own Body (for we are also
" His Body," and He is our " Head "), He
uttered from the Cross not His own cry, but
ours. For God never "forsook" Him : nor did
He Himself ever depart from the Father ; but
it was in behalf of us that He spake this : " My
God, My God, why hast thou forsaken Me ? "
For there follows, " Far from My health are the
words of My offences : " and it shows in whose
person He said this ; for sin could not be
found in Him. . . .

3. " O God, we have heard with our ears ;
our fathers have told us the work that Thou
didst in their days, and in the days of old "
(ver. 1). Wondering wherefore, in these days,
He has seemingly forsaken those whom it was
His will to exercise in sufferings, they recall the
past events which they have heard of from their
fathers ; as if they said, It is not of these things
that we suffer, that our fathers told us ! For in
that other Psalm also, He said this, " Our fathers trusted in Thee ; they trusted, and Thou
didst deliver them. But I am a worm and no
man ; a reproach of men, and the outcast of the
people." [3] They trusted, and Thou didst deliver
them ; have I then hoped, and hast Thou
forsaken me ? And have I believed upon
Thee in vain ? And is it in vain that my name
has been written in Thy Book,[4] and Thy name has
been inscribed on me ? What our fathers told
us was this :

" Thy hand destroyed the nations ; and Thou
plantedst them : Thou didst weaken the peoples, and cast them out " (ver. 2). That is to
say : " Thou didst drive out ' the peoples ' from
their own land, that Thou mightest bring
' them ' in, and plant them ; and mightest by
Thy mercy stablish their kingdom." These are
the things that we heard from our fathers. But
perhaps it was because they were brave, were
men of battle, were invincible, were well-disci-
plined, and warlike, that they could do these
things. Far from it. This is not what our
fathers told us ; this is not what is contained in
Scripture. But what does it say, but what follows ?

" For they gat not the land in possession by
their own sword, neither did their own arm save
them ; but Thy right hand, and Thine arm, and
the light of Thy countenance " (ver. 3). Thy
" right hand " is Thy Power : Thine " arm " is
Thy Son Himself.[5] And " the light of Thy countenance." What means this, but that Thou

wert present with them, in miracles of such a
sort that Thy presence was perceived. For
when God's presence with us appears by any
miracle, do we see His face with our own eyes ?
No. It is by the effect of the miracle He intimates to man His presence. In fact, what do
all persons say, who express wonder at facts of
this description ? " I saw God present." " But
Thy right hand, and Thine arm, and the light
of Thy countenance ; because Thou pleasedst in
them : " [6] i.e. didst so deal with them, that Thou
wert well-pleasing in them : that whoso considered how they were being dealt with, might
say, that " God is with them of a truth ; " and it
is God that moves [7] them.

4. " What ? Was He then other than now
He is ? " Away with the supposition. For what
follows ?

" Thou art Thyself [8] my King and my God."
(ver. 4). " Thou art Thyself ; " for Thou art not
changed. I see that the times are changed ;
but the Creator of times is unchanged. " Thou
art Thyself my King and my God." Thou art
wont to guide me : to govern me, to save me.
" Thou who commandest salvation unto Jacob."
What is, " Thou who commandest "? Even
though in Thine own proper Substance and Nature, in which Thou art whatsoever Thou art,
Thou wast hid from them ; and though Thou
didst not converse with the fathers in that which
Thou art in Thyself, so that they could see Thee
" face to face," yet by any created being whatsoever " Thou commandest salvation unto Israel." For that sight of Thee " face to face " is
reserved for those set free in the Resurrection.
And the very " fathers " of the New Testament
too, although they saw Thy mysteries revealed,
although they preached the secret things so revealed to them, nevertheless said that they themselves saw but " in a glass, darkly," but that
" seeing face to face "[9] is reserved to a future
time, when what the Apostle himself speaks of
shall have come. " When Christ our life shall
appear, then shall ye also appear with Him in
glory." [10] It is against that time then that vision
" face to face " is reserved for you, of which
John also speaks : " Beloved, we are now the
sons of God : and it doth not yet appear what
we shall be. We know that, when He shall appear, we shall be like Him ; for we shall see
Him as He is." [11] Although then at that time
our fathers saw Thee not as Thou art, " face to
face," although that vision is reserved against
the resurrection, yet, even though they were
Angels who presented themselves, it is Thou,
" Who commandest salvation unto Jacob."
Thou art not only present by Thine own Self ;

[1] Ps. xxii. 1.   [2] 1 Cor. iv. 6.   [3] Ps. xxii. 4–6.
[4] Ps. xl. 7.
[5] [So Cyprian, A. N. F. vol. v. p. 516; also others *passim*.
—C.]

[6] *Complacuisti in eis.*   [7] *Agit.*
[8] " Tu es *Ipse*."   [9] 1 Cor. xiii. 12.   [10] Col. iii. 4.
[11] 1 John iii. 2.

but by whatsoever created being Thou didst appear, it is Thou that dost " command " by them, that which Thou doest by Thine own Self in order to the salvation of Thy servants : but that which they do whom Thou " commandest " it, is done to procure the salvation of Thy servants. Since then Thou art Thyself " my King and my God, and Thou commandest salvation unto Jacob," wherefore are we suffering these things?

5. But perhaps it is only what is past that has been described to us : but nothing of the kind is to be hoped for by us for the future. Nay indeed, it is still to be hoped for. " Through Thee will we winnow away [1] our enemies " (ver. 5). Our fathers then have declared to us a work that Thou didst " in their days, and in the days of old," that Thy hand destroyed the Gentiles : that Thou " didst cast out the peoples ; and didst plant them." Such was the past ; but what is to be hereafter? " Through Thee we shall winnow away our enemies." A time will come, when all the enemies of Christians will be winnowed away like chaff, be blown like dust, and be cast off from the earth. . . . Thus much of the future. " I will not trust in my bow," even as our fathers did not in " their sword. Neither shall my sword help me " (ver. 6).

6. " For Thou hast saved us from our enemies " (ver. 7). This too is spoken of the future under the figure of the past. But this is the reason that it is spoken of as if it were past, that it is as certain as if it were past. Give heed, wherefore many things are expressed by the Prophets as if they were past ; whereas it is things future, not past facts that are the subject of prophecy. For the future Passion of our Lord Himself was foretold : [2] and yet it says, " They pierced My hands and My feet. They told all My bones ;" not, " They shall pierce," and " shall tell." " They looked and stared upon Me ;" not " They shall look and stare upon Me." " They parted My garments among them." It does not say, " They shall part " them. All these things are expressed as if they were past, although they were yet to come : because to God things to come also are as certain as if they were past. . . . It is for this reason, in consequence of their certainty, that those things which are yet future, are spoken of as if past. This it is then that we hope. For it is, " Thou hast saved us from our enemies, and hast put them to shame that hated us."

7. " In God will we boast [3] all the day long " (ver. 8). Observe how he intermingles words expressive of a future time, that you may perceive that what was spoken of before as in past time was foretold of future times. " In God

will we boast all day long ; and in Thy name will we confess for ever." [4] What is, " We shall boast "? What, " We shall confess "? That Thou hast " saved us from our enemies ;" that Thou art to give us an everlasting kingdom : that in us are to be fulfilled the words, " Blessed are they that dwell in Thine house : they will be always praising Thee." [5]

8. Since then we have the certainty that these things are to be hereafter, and since we have heard from our fathers that those we spoke of were in time past, what is our state at present? " But now Thou hast cast us off, and put us to shame " (ver. 9). Thou hast " put us to shame " not before our own consciences, but in the sight of men. For there was a time when Christians were persecuted ; when in every place they were outcasts, when in every place it used to be said, " He is a Christian ! " as if it conveyed an insult and reproach. Where then is He, " our God, our King," who " commands salvation unto Jacob"? Where is He who did all those works, which " our fathers have told us "? Where is He who is hereafter to do all those things which He revealed unto us by His Spirit? Is He changed? No. These things are done in order to " understanding, for the sons of Korah." For we ought to " understand " something of the reason, why He has willed we should suffer all these things in the mean time. What " all things "? " But now Thou hast cast us off and put us to shame : and goest not forth, O God, in our powers." [6] We go forth to meet our enemies, and Thou goest not forth with us. We see them : they are very strong, and we are without strength. Where is that might of Thine? Where Thy " right hand," and Thy power? [7] Where the sea dried up, and the Egyptian pursuers overwhelmed with the waves? Where Amalek's resistance subdued by the sign of the Cross? [8] " And Thou, O God, goest not forth in our powers."

9. " Thou hast turned us away backward in presence of our enemies " (ver. 10), so that they are, as it were, before ; we, behind ; they are counted as conquerors, we as conquered. " And they which hate us spoiled for themselves." What did they " spoil " but ourselves?

10. " Thou has given us like sheep appointed for meat, and hast scattered us among the nations " (ver. 11). We have been " devoured " by " the nations." Those persons are meant, who, through their sufferings, have by process of assimilation, becomes part of the " body " of the Gentile world. For the Church mourns over

---

[1] Vulgate, *ventilabimus*. [To which St. Jerome's Hebraic Psalter adheres. — C.]
[2] Ps. xxii. 16–18.
[3] *Laudabimur*.

[4] [Here is the *Diapsalma* in the Septuagint; and in St. Jerome, following the Hebrew. — C.]
[5] Ps. lxxxiv. 4.
[6] Or " hosts," *virtutibus*.
[7] *Virtus*.
[8] Exod. xvii. 12.

them, as over members of her body, that have been devoured.[1]

11. "Thou hast sold Thy people for no price" (ver. 12). For we see whom Thou hast made over; what Thou hast received, we have not seen. "And there was no multitude in their jubilees."[2] For when the Christians were flying before the pursuit of enemies, who were idolaters, were there then held any congregations and "jubilees" to the honour of God? Were those Hymns chanted in concert from the Churches of God, that are wont to be sung in concert in time of peace, and to be sounded in a sweet accord of the brotherhood in the ears of God?

12. "Thou madest us a reproach to our neighbours; a scorn and a derision to them that are round about us" (ver. 13). "Thou madest us a similitude[3] among the heathen" (ver. 14). What is meant by a "similitude"? It is when men in imprecating a curse make a "similitude" of his name whom they detest. "So mayest thou die;" "So mayest thou be punished!" What a number of such reproaches were then uttered! "So mayest thou be crucified!" Even in the present day there are not wanting enemies of Christ (those very Jews themselves), against whom whensoever we defend Christ, they say unto us, "So mayest thou die as He did." For they would not have inflicted that kind of death had they not an intense horror of dying by such a death: or had they been able to comprehend what mystery was contained in it. When the ointment is applied to the eyes of the blind man, he does not see the eye-salve in the physician's hand. For the very Cross was made for the benefit even of the persecutors themselves. Hereby they were healed afterwards; and they believed in Him whom they themselves had slain. "Thou madest us a similitude among the heathen; a shaking of the head among the peoples," a "shaking of the head" by way of insult. "They spake with their lips, they shook the head."[4] This they did to the Lord: this to all His Saints also, whom they were able to pursue, to lay hold of, to mock, to betray, to afflict, and to slay.

13. "My shame is continually before me; and the confusion of my face has covered me" (ver. 15). "For the voice of him that reproacheth and blasphemeth" (ver. 16): that is to say, from the voice of them that insult over me, and

who make it a charge against me that I worship Thee, that I confess Thee! and who make it a charge against me that I bear that name by which all charges against me shall be blotted out. "For the voice of him that reproacheth and blasphemeth," that is, of him that speaketh against me. "By reason of the enemy and the persecutor." And what is the "understanding" conveyed here? Those things which are told us of the time past, will not be done in our case:[5] those which are hoped for, as to be hereafter, are not as yet manifest. Those which are past, as the leading out of Thy people with great glory from Egypt; its deliverance from its persecutors; the guiding of it through the nations, the placing of it in the kingdom, whence the nations had been expelled. What are those to be hereafter? The leading of the people out of this Egypt of the world, when Christ, our "leader" shall appear in His glory: the placing of the Saints at His right hand; of the wicked at His left; the condemnation of the wicked with the devil to eternal punishment; the receiving of a kingdom from Christ with the Saints to last for ever.[6] These are the things that are yet to be: the former are what are past. In the interval, what is to be our lot? Tribulations! "Why so?" That it may be seen with respect to the soul that worships God, to what extent it worships God; that it may be seen whether it worships Him "freely" from whom it received salvation "freely." . . . What hast thou given unto God? Thou wert wicked, and thou wert redeemed! What hast thou given unto God? What is there that thou hast not "received" from Him "freely"? With reason is it named "grace," because it is bestowed (*gratis*, i.e.) freely.[7] What is required of thee then is this, "that thou too shouldest worship "Him freely;" not because He gives thee things temporal, but because He holds out to thee things eternal. . . .

14. "All this is come upon us; yet have we not forgotten Thee" (ver. 17). What is meant by, "have not forgotten Thee"? "Neither have we behaved ourselves frowardly in Thy covenant."

"Our heart has not turned back; and Thou hast turned aside our goings out of Thy way" (ver. 18). See here is "understanding," in that "our heart has not gone back;" that we have not "forgotten Thee, have not behaved frowardly in Thy covenant;" placed as we are in great tribulations, and persecutions of the Gentiles. "Thou hast turned aside our goings out of Thy way." Our "goings" were in the pleasures of the world; our "goings" were in the midst of temporal prosperities. Thou hast taken "our

---

[1] Conversely, in like manner the Fathers (so under Ps. iii. ver. 7) often explain, "Rise, Peter, kill, and eat," and passages where the preachers of the Gospel are represented by beasts of prey. See p. 16, *supra*, between notes 5 and 6. [A fanciful rendering, perhaps; but the *assimilation* of unclean Gentiles, and their identification with the clean body of the Church, is strikingly illustrated by it. — C.]

[2] [St Augustin's Psalter has *jubilationibus*. — C.] For which Vulgate, *commutationibus*.

[3] E. V. "by-word."

[4] Ps. xxii. 7. E. V. "They shoot out the lips," etc.

[5] *In nobis.*

[6] Matt. xxv. 34. St. Augustin, Ser. xviii. 4.

[7] Rom. xi. 6.

goings out of Thy way ; " and hast shown us [1] how "strait and narrow is the way that leadeth unto life." [2] What is meant by, "hast turned aside our goings out of Thy way"? It is as if He said, "Ye are placed in the midst of tribulation; ye are suffering many things; ye have already lost many things that ye loved in this life : but I have not abandoned you on the way, the narrow way that I am teaching you. Ye were seeking "broad ways." What do I tell you? This is the way we go to everlasting life; by the way ye wish to walk, ye are going to death. How "broad and wide is the road that leads to destruction: and " how "many there be that find it ! How strait and narrow the way that leadeth unto life, and " how "few there be " that walk therein ! [3] Who are the few? They who patiently endure tribulations, patiently endure temptations; who in all these troubles do not "fall away : " who do not rejoice in the word "for a season " only; and in the time of tribulation fade away, as on the sun's arising; but who have the "root " of "love," according to what we have lately heard read in the Gospel. [4] . . .

15. "For Thou hast brought us low in the place of infirmity " [5] (ver. 18) : therefore Thou wilt exalt us in the place of strength. "And the shadow of death has covered us " (ver. 19). For this mortality of ours is but the "shadow " of death. The true death is condemnation with the devil.

16. "If we have forgotten the Name of our God." Here is the "understanding " of the "sons of Korah." "And stretched out our hands to a strange God " (ver. 20). "Shall not God search this out? For He knoweth the secrets of the heart " (ver. 21). He "knows," and yet He "searches them out "? If He knows the secrets of the heart, what do the words, "Shall not God search it out," do there? He "knows " it in Himself; He "searches it out " for our sakes. For it is for this reason God sometimes "searches a thing out; " and speaks of that becoming known to Himself, which He is Himself making known to thee. He is speaking of His own work, not of His knowledge. We commonly say, "A gladsome day," when it is fine. Yet is it the day itself that experiences delight? No : we speak of the day as gladsome, because it fills us with delight. And we speak of a "sullen sky." Not that there is any such feeling in the clouds, but because men are affected with sullenness at the sight of such an appearance of the skies, it is called sullen for

this reason, that it makes us sullen. So also God is said to "know " when He causes us to know. God says to Abraham, "Now I know that thou fearest God." [6] Did He then not know it before then? But Abraham did not know himself till then : for it was in that very trial he came to know himself. . . . And God is said to "know " that which He had caused him to know. Did Peter know himself, when he said to the Physician, "I will be with Thee even unto death?" [7] The Physician had felt his pulse, [8] and knew what was going on within His patient's soul : the patient knew it not. The crisis [9] of trial came ; and the Physician approved the correctness of His opinion : the sick man gave up his presumption. Thus God at once "knows " it and "searches it out." "He knows it already. Why does He 'search it out'?" For thy sake : that thou mayest come to know thine own self, and mayest return thanks to Him that made thee. "Shall not God search it out?"

17. "For, for Thy sake we are killed all the day long : we are counted as sheep for the slaughter " (ver. 22). For you may see a man being put to death; you do not know why he is being put to death. God knoweth this. The thing in itself is hid. But some one will say to me, "See, he is detained in prison for the name of Christ, he is a confessor for the name of Christ." Why do not [10] heretics also confess the name of Christ, and yet they do not die for His sake? Nay more ; let me say it, in the Catholic Church itself, do you think there either are, or have been wanting persons such as would suffer for the sake of glory among men? Were there no such persons, the Apostle would not say, "Though I give my body to be burned, and have not charity, it profiteth me nothing." [11] He knew therefore that there might be some persons, who did this not from "charity," but out of vainglory. It is therefore hid from us; God alone sees this; we cannot see it. He alone can judge of this, who "knoweth the secrets of the heart." "For," for Thy sake "are we killed all the day long; we are counted as sheep for the slaughter." I have already mentioned that from hence the Apostle Paul had borrowed a text [12] for the encouragement of the Martyrs : that they might not "faint in the tribulations " undergone by them for the name of Christ. [13]

18. "Awake ; why sleepest Thou, O Lord?" (ver. 23). Who is addressed, and who is the speaker? Would not he be more correctly said to *sleep* and slumber, [14] who speaks such words as these? He replies to you, I know what I am saying : I know that "He that keepeth Israel

---

[1] Oxf. MSS. "hast showed us a way. What way? How," etc. He seems to mean that God has removed such ways as men like from the path of His Saints, and given them narrow ways. St. Ambrose takes it as a complaint of difficulties, so great that we cannot perfectly keep to the right way. E. V. "Neither have our steps declined from Thy way," rightly continuing the negative.
[2] Matt. vii. 14.   [3] Matt. vii. 13, 14.
[4] Matt. xiii. 6, 20, 21.
[5] E. V. "broken us in the place of dragons."

[6] Gen. xxii. 12.   [7] Luke xxii. 33.   [8] *Inspecta vena.*
[9] *Accessio.*   [10] Oxf. MSS. om. "not."   [11] 1 Cor. xiii. 3.
[12] *Testimonium posuisse.* Rom. viii. 36. [Also Rom. v. 3; Eph. iii. 13. — C.]
[13] [See p. 140, note 19. — C.]   [14] *Halare.*

doth not sleep : " [1] but yet the Martyrs cry, "Awake ; why sleepest Thou, O Lord ? " O Lord Jesus, Thou wast slain ; Thou didst "sleep" in Thy Passion ; to us Thou hast now "awaked" from sleep. For "we" know that Thou hast now "awaked" again. To what purpose hast Thou awaked and risen again ? The Gentiles that persecute us, think Thee to be dead ; do not believe Thee to have risen again. "Arise Thou" then to them also ! "Why sleepest Thou," though not to us, yet to them ? For if they already believed Thee to have risen again, could they persecute us who believe in Thee ? But why do they persecute ? "Destroy, slay so and so, whoever have believed in Thee, such an one, who died an ill death !" As yet to them "Thou sleepest ; " arise to them, that they may perceive that Thou hast "awaked" again ; and may be at rest. Lastly, it has come to pass, while the Martyrs die, and say these things ; while they sleep, and "awaken" Christ, truly dead in their sleepings, Christ has, in a certain sense, risen again in the Gentiles ; i.e. it becomes believed, that He has risen again ; so by degrees they themselves, becoming converted to Christ by believing, collected a numerous body : such as the persecutors dreaded ; and the persecutions have come to an end. Why ? Because Christ, who before was *asleep* to them, as not believing, hath risen in the Gentiles. "Arise, and cast us not off for ever ! "

19. "Wherefore hidest Thou Thy face : " as if Thou wert not present ; as if thou hadst forgotten us ? "And forgettest our misery and trouble ? " (ver. 24).

20. "For our soul is bowed down to the dust" (ver. 25). Where is it bowed down ? "To the dust : " i.e. *dust* persecutes us. They persecute us, of whom Thou hast said, "The ungodly are not so ; but are like the dust, which the wind driveth away from the face of the earth." [2] "Our belly hath cleaved to the earth." He seems to me to have expressed the punishment of the extreme of humiliation, in which, when any one prostrates himself, "his belly cleaveth to the earth." For whosoever is humbled so as to be on his knees, has yet a lower degree of humiliation to which he can come : but he who is so humbled, that his "belly cleaveth to the ground," there is no farther humiliation for him. Should one wish to do still farther, it will, after that point, be not bowing him down, but crushing him. Perhaps then he may have meant this : We are "bowed down very low" in this dust ; there is no farther point to which humiliation can go. Humiliation has now reached its highest point : let mercy then come also. . . .

21. "Arise, O Lord, help us" (ver. 26). And indeed, dearly beloved, He has arisen and helped us. For when he awaked (i.e. when He arose again, and became known to the Gentiles) on the cessation of persecutions, even those who had cleaved to the earth were raised up from the earth, and on performing penance,[3] have been restored to Christ's body, feeble and imperfect though they were : so that in them was fulfilled the text, "Thine eyes did see my substance yet being imperfect ; and in Thy book shall they all be written." [4]

"Arise, O Lord, help us, and redeem us for Thy Name's sake ; " that is to say, freely ; for Thy Name's sake, not for the sake of my merits : because Thou hast vouchsafed to do it, not because I am worthy that Thou shouldest do it unto me. For this very thing, that "we have not forgotten Thee ; " that "our heart hath not gone back ; " that we "have not stretched out our hands to any strange god ; " how should we have been able to achieve, except with Thy help ? How should we have strength for it, except through Thy appealing to us within, exhorting us, and not forsaking us ? Whether then we suffer in tribulations, or rejoice in prosperities, redeem Thou us, not for our merits, but for Thy Name's sake.

PSALM XLV.[5]

1. This Psalm, even as we ourselves have been singing with gladness together with you, we would beg you in like manner to consider with attention together with us. For it is sung of the sacred Marriage-feast ; of the Bridegroom and the Bride ; of the King and His people ; of the Saviour and those who are to be saved. . . . His sons are we, in that we are the "children of the Bridegroom ; " and it is to us that this Psalm is addressed, whose title has the words, "For the sons of Korah, for the things that [6] shall be changed."

2. Why need I explain what is meant by, "for the things that shall be changed " ? Every one who is himself "changed," recognises the meaning of this. Let him who hears this, "for the things that shall be changed," consider what was before, and what is now. And first let him see the world itself to be changed, lately worshipping idols, now worshipping God ; lately serving things that they themselves made, now serving Him by whom they themselves were made. Observe at what time the words, "for the things that shall be changed," were said. Already by this time the Pagans that are left are in dread of the "changed" state of things : and those who will not suffer themselves to be

---

[3] [A debased rendering of our author's words, *agentes pœnitentiam ;* for the primitive discipline exacted true contrition. See Chrysos. *Hom.* xxi. p. 215, vol. xii. ed. Migne. The "attrition" of the Trent Catechism is indeed a perfunctory "performance." — C.]

[4] Ps. cxxxix. 16.   [5] Lat. XLIV

[6] Some copies have *qui* for " those (persons) that."

---

[1] Ps. cxxi. 4.   [2] Ps. i. 4.

"changed" see the churches full; the temples deserted; see crowds here, and there solitude! They marvel at the things so changed; let them read that they were foretold; let them lend their ears to Him who promised it; let them believe Him who fulfils that promise. But each one of us, brethren, also undergoes a change from "the old" to "the new men:" from an infidel to a believer: from a thief to a giver of alms: from an adulterer to a man of chastity; from an evil-doer to a doer of good. To us then be sung the words, "for the things that shall be changed;" and so let the description of Him by whom they were changed, begin.

3. For it goes on, "For the things that shall be changed, to the sons of Korah for understanding; a song for the beloved." For that "beloved" One was seen by His persecutors, but yet not for "understanding." For "had they known Him, they would never have crucified the Lord of Glory."[1] In order to this "understanding," other eyes were required by Him when He said, "He that seeth Me, seeth My Father also."[2] Let the Psalm then now sound of Him, let us rejoice in the marriage-feast, and we shall be with those of whom the marriage is made,[3] who are invited to the marriage; and the very persons invited are the Bride herself. For the Church is "the Bride," Christ the Bridegroom. There are commonly spoken by balladists[4] certain verses to Bridegrooms and Brides, called *Epithalamia*.[5] Whatever is sung there, is sung in honour of the Bride and Bridegroom. Is there then no Bridechamber[6] in that marriage-feast to which we are invited? Whence then does another Psalm say, "He hath set up His tabernacle in the Sun; and He is even as a bridegroom coming out of his chamber." The nuptial union is that of "the Word," and the flesh. The Bridechamber of this union, the Virgin's womb. For the flesh itself was united to the Word: whence also it is said, "Henceforth they are not twain, but one flesh."[7] The Church was assumed unto Him out of the human race: so that the Flesh itself, being united to the Word, might be the Head of the Church: and the rest who believe, members of that Head. . . .

4. "Mine heart hath uttered a good word"[8] (ver. 1). Who is the speaker? The Father, or the Prophet? For some understand it to be the Person of the Father, which says, "Mine heart

hath uttered a good word," intimating to us a certain unspeakable generation.[9] Lest you should haply think something to have been taken unto Him, out of which God should beget the Son (just as man takes something to himself out of which he begets children, that is to say, an union of marriage,[10] without which man cannot beget offspring), lest then you should think that God stood in need of any nuptial union, to beget "the Son," he says, "Mine heart uttered a good word."[11] This very day thine heart, O man, begets a counsel, and requires no wife: by the counsel, so born of thine heart, thou buildest something or other, and before that building subsists, the design subsists;[12] and that which thou art about to produce, exists already in that by which thou art going to produce it; and thou praisest the fabric that as yet is not existing, not yet in the visible form of a building, but on the projecting of a design: nor does any one else praise thy design, unless either thou showest it to him, or he sees what thou hast done. If then by the Word "all things were made,"[13] and the Word is of God, consider the fabric reared by the Word, and learn from that building to admire His counsels! What manner of Word is that by which heaven and earth were made;[14] and all the splendour of the heavens; all the fertility of the earth; the expanse of the sea; the wide diffusion of air; the brightness of the constellations; the light of sun and moon? These are visible things: rise above these also; think of the Angels, "Principalities, Thrones, Dominions, and Powers."[15] All were made by Him. How then were these good things made? Because there was "uttered forth 'a good Word,'" by which they were to be made. . . .

5. It proceeds: "I speak of the things which I have made unto the King." Is the Father still speaking? If the Father is still speaking, let us enquire how this also can be understood by us, consistently with the true Catholic Faith, "I speak of the things that I have made unto the King." For if it is the Father speaking of His own works to His Son, our "King," what works is the Father to speak of to the Son, seeing that all the Father's works were made by the Son's agency? Or, in the words, "I speak of My works unto the King," does the word, "I speak," itself signify the generation of the Son?

---

[1] 1 Cor. ii. 8.   [2] John xiv. 9.
[3] *Qui fiunt nuptiæ* (omitted in some MSS.).
[4] *Scholasticis;* MSS. *scolasticis* = "scholars," or perhaps *scoliasticis*, "ballad-mongers." — *Ben.*
[5] "Songs of the Bridechamber."
[6] *Thalamus.* Ps. xix. 5, so Vulgate.
[7] Matt. xix. 5. [For this point in the theology of the Incarnation, see A. N. F. vol. vii. p. 367, *Athanas. Creed*, part ii. — C.]
[8] *Eructavit verbum bonum.* [See Justin Martyr, vol. i. p. 213, A. N. F., and Cyprian, vol. v. p. 516, A. N. F., and so *passim.* — C.]

[9] *Nativitatem.*   [10] *Conjugium.*
[11] [Confusion comes to the human mind by arguing from humanity up to God. His is the only true generative process: the production of a Son by man is not to be considered in process, but in product only. This product is of one substance with the human (though divine). The undivided substance of the Divine Father is the one substance of the Son, by eternal generation. — C.]
[12] So *all* MSS. *antequam stet, stat consilium,* acc. to Ben., which however reads *antequam stet in opere, stat in consilio.* "That building, before it subsists in construction, subsists in design." On the meaning of *Verbum* see St. Aug. on *John* i. 1. St. Ath. on *Nic. Def.* c. 4, and Disc. i. against Ar. c. 6.
[13] John i. 3.   [14] Heb. xi. 3.   [15] Col. i. 16.

I fear whether this can ever be made intelligible to those slow of comprehension : I will nevertheless say it. Let those who can follow me, do so : lest if it were left unsaid, even those who can follow should not be able. We have read where it is said in another Psalm, "God hath spoken once." [1] So often has He spoken by the Prophets, so often by the Apostles, and in these days by His Saints, and does He say, "God has spoken once "? How can He have spoken but "once," except with reference to His "Word"? [2] But as the "Mine heart hath uttered a good Word," [3] was understood by us in the other clause of the generation of the Son, it seems that a kind of repetition is made in the following sentence, so that the "Mine heart hath uttered a good Word," which had been already said, is repeated in what He is now saying, "I speak." For what does "I speak" mean? "I utter a Word." And whence but from His heart, from His very inmost, does God utter the Word? You yourself do not speak anything but what you bring forth from your "heart," this word of yours which sounds once and passes away, is brought forth from no other place : and do you wonder that God "speaks" in this manner? But God's "speaking" is eternal. You are speaking something at the present moment, because you were silent before : or, look you, you have not yet brought forth your word ; but when you have begun to bring it forth, you as it were "break silence ; " and bring into being a word, that did not exist before. It was not so God begat the "Word." God's "speaking" is without beginning, and without end : and yet the "Word" He utters is but "One." Let Him utter another, if what He has spoken shall have passed away. But since He by whom it is uttered abideth, and That which is uttered abideth ; and is uttered but once, and has no end, that very "once" too is said without beginning, and there is no second speaking, because that which is said once, does not pass away. The words, "Mine heart hath uttered a good Word," then, are the same thing with, "I speak of the things which I have made unto the King." Why then, "I speak of the things which I have made"? Because in the Word Itself are all the works of God. For whatever God designed to make in the creation already existed in "the Word ; " and would not exist in the reality, had it not existed in the Word, [4] just as with you the thing would not exist in the building, had it not existed in your design : even as it is said in the Gospel : "That which was made in Him was life." [5] That which was made then was in existence ; but it had its existence in the Word : and

all the works of God existed there, and yet were not as yet "works." "The Word" however already was, as this "Word was God, and was with God : " and was the Son of God, and One God with the Father. "I speak of the things I have made unto the King." Let him hear Him "speaking," who apprehends "the Word : " and let him see together with the Father the Everlasting Word ; in whom exist even those things that are yet to come : in whom even those things that are past have not passed away. These "works" of God are in "the Word," as in the Word, as in the Only-Begotten, as in the "Word of God."

6. What follows then? "My tongue is the pen of a writer writing rapidly." What likeness, my brethren, what likeness, I ask, has the "tongue" of God with a transcriber's pen? What resemblance has "the rock" to Christ? [6] What likeness does the "lamb" bear to our Saviour, [7] or what "the lion" to the strength of the Only-Begotten? [8] Yet such comparisons have been made ; and were they not made, we should not be formed to a certain extent by these visible things to the knowledge of the "Invisible One." So then with this mean simile of the pen ; let us not compare it to His excellent greatness, so let us not reject it with contempt. For I ask, why He compares His "tongue" to "the pen of a writer writing rapidly"? But how swiftly soever the transcriber writes, still it is not comparable to that swiftness of which another Psalm says, "His word runneth very swiftly." [9] But it appears to me (if human understanding may presume so far) that this too may be understood as spoken in the Person of the Father : "My tongue is the pen of a writer." Inasmuch as what is spoken by the "tongue," sounds once and passes away, what is written, remains ; seeing then that God uttereth "a Word," and the Word which is uttered does not sound once and pass away, but is uttered and yet continues, God chose rather to compare this to words written than to sounds. But what He added, saying, "of one writing swiftly," stimulates the mind unto "understanding." Let it however not slothfully rest here, thinking of transcribers, [10] or thinking of some kind of quick shorthand writers : if it be this it sees in the passage, it will be resting there. Let it think swiftly what is the meaning of that word "swiftly." The "swiftly" of God is such that nothing exceeds in swiftness. For in writings letter is written after letter ; syllable after syllable ; word after word : nor do we pass to the second except when the first is written out. But there nothing can exceed the swiftness, where there are not several words ; and yet there is not anything

---

[1] Ps. lxii. 11.   [2] Heb. i. 1, 2.   [3] Heb. i. 3, 4, 5.
[4] Nec esset in rebus, nisi esset in verbo.
[5] John i. 3, 4.

[6] 1 Cor. x. 4.   [7] John i. 29.   [8] Rev. v. 5.
[9] Ps. cxlvii. 15.   [10] Antiquarios.

omitted: since in the One are contained all things.

7. Lo! now then that Word, so uttered, Eternal, the Co-eternal Offspring of the Eternal, will come as "the Bridegroom;" "Fairer than the children of men" (ver. 2). "Than the children of men." I ask, why not than the Angels also? Why did he say, "than the children of men," except because He was Man? Lest you should think "the Man Christ"[1] to be any ordinary man, he says, "Fairer than the children of men." Even though Himself "Man," He is "fairer than the children of men;" though among the children of men, "fairer than the children of men:" though of the children of men, "fairer than the children of men." "Grace is shed abroad on Thy lips." "The Law was given by Moses. Grace and Truth came by Jesus Christ."[2] . . .

8. There have not been wanting those who preferred understanding all the preceding passage also of the Prophet's own person; and would have even this verse, "Mine heart hath uttered forth a good word," understood as spoken by the Prophet, supposed to be uttering a hymn. For whoever utters a hymn to God, his heart is, as it were, "uttering forth a good word," just as his heart who blasphemes God, is uttering forth an evil word. So that even by what follows, " I speak of the things which I have made[3] unto the King," he meant to express that man's chief work was but to praise God. To Him it belongs to satisfy thee, by His beauty; to thee to praise Him with thanksgiving. . . .

9. "My tongue is the pen of a writer writing quickly." There have been persons who have understood the Prophet to have been describing in this manner what he was writing; and therefore to have compared his tongue to "the pen of a writer writing quickly:" but that he chose to express himself in the words "writing quickly," to signify, that he was writing of things which were to come "quickly;" that "writing quickly" should be understood to be equivalent to "writing things that are quick;" i.e. writing things that would not long tarry. For God did not tarry long to manifest Christ. How quickly is that perceived to have rolled by, which is acknowledged to be already past! Call to mind the generations before thee; thou wilt find that the making of Adam is but a thing of yesterday. So do we read that all things have gone on from the very beginning:[4] they were therefore done "quickly." The day of Judgment also will be here "quickly." Do thou anticipate its "quick" coming. It is to come "quickly;" do thou become converted yet more "quickly." The Judge's face will appear: but observe thou what

the Prophet says, "Let us come before" (let us "prevent") "His face with confession."[5]

10. "Gird Thy sword upon Thy thigh, O most Mighty" (ver. 3). What is meant by "Thy sword, but "Thy word"? It was by that sword He scattered His enemies; by that sword he divided the son from the father, "the daughter from the mother, the daughter-in-law from the mother-in-law." We read these words in the Gospel, "I came not to send peace, but a sword."[6] And, "In one house shall five be divided against each other; three against two, and two against three;"[7] i.e. "the father against the son, the daughter against the mother, the daughter-in-law against the mother-in-law." By what "sword," but that which Christ brought, was this division wrought? And indeed, my brethren, we see this exemplified daily. Some young man is minded to give himself up to God's service; his father is opposed to it; they are "divided against each other:" the one promises an earthly inheritance, the other loves an heavenly; the one promises one thing, the other prefers another. The father should not think himself wronged: God alone is preferred to him. And yet he is at strife[8] with the son, who would fain give himself to God's service. But the spiritual sword is mightier to separate them, than the ties of carnal nature to bind them together. This happens also in the case of a mother against her daughter; still more also in that of a daughter-in-law against a mother-in-law. For sometimes in one house mother-in-law and daughter-in-law are found orthodox and heretical respectively. And where that sword is forcibly felt,[9] we do not dread the repetition of Baptism. Could daughter be divided against mother; and could not daughter-in-law be divided against mother-in law? . . .

11. What does he mean to express by the "thigh"? The flesh. Whence those words, "A prince shall not depart from Judah; and a lawgiver from his thighs"?[10] Did not Abraham himself (to whom was promised the seed in which "all the nations of the earth were to be blessed"), when he sent his servant to seek and to bring home a wife for his son, being by faith fully persuaded, that in that, so to speak, contemptible seed was contained the great Name;[11] that is, that the Son of God was to come of the seed of Abraham, out of all the

---

[1] 1 Tim. ii. 5.   [2] John i. 17.   [3] *Lit.* "my works."
[4] 2 Pet. iii. 4.

[5] Ps. xcv. 2.   [6] Matt. x. 34.
[7] Luke xii. 52.   [8] *Litigat.*
[9] *Recipitur.* He seems to mean that the Catholic daughter-in-law who receives the word of Christ is sure not to submit to heretical baptism. [On which compare Cyprian's teaching, A. N. F. vol. v. pp. 376-385, etc. — C.]
[10] Gen. xlix. 10. E. V "from between his feet."
[11] "In illâ veluti humilitate *seminis* esse magnitudinem Nominis." [The promise (Gen. iii. 15) dignified the loins of Isaac (Gen. xvii. 19) as with the Incarnation in its germ. Hence this mysterious form of oath was an oath by the Promised Seed (Gal. iii. 16). St. Paul quotes "the promises" (not one text only), and honours the Septuagint, which gives what he makes so emphatic in Gen. xii. 7, xv. 18, and xxii. 18. — C.]

children of men; did not he, I say, cause his servant to swear unto him in this manner, saying, "Put thy hand under my thigh,"[1] and so swear; as if he had said, "Put thy hand on the altar, or on the Gospel, or on the Prophet, or on any holy thing." "Put" (he says) "thy hand under my thigh;" having full confidence, not ashamed of it as unseemly, but understanding therein a truth. "With Thy beauty and Thy glory." Take to Thee that righteousness, in which Thou art at all times beautiful and glorious. "And speed on, and proceed prosperously, and reign" (ver. 4). Do we not see it so? Is it not already come to pass? He has "sped on; has proceeded prosperously, and He reigns;" all nations are subdued unto Him. What a thing was it to see that "in the Spirit," of which same thing it is now in our power to experience in the reality! At the time when these words were said, Christ did not yet "reign" thus; had not yet sped on, nor "proceeded prosperously." They were then being preached, they have now been fulfilled: in many things we have God's promise fulfilled already; in some few we have to claim its fulfilment yet.

12. "Because of truth, meekness, and righteousness." Truth was restored unto us, when "the Truth sprung out of the earth: and Righteousness looked out from heaven."[2] Christ was presented to the expectation of mankind, that in Abraham's Seed "all nations should be blessed." The Gospel has been preached. It is "the Truth." What is meant by "meekness"? The Martyrs have suffered; and the kingdom of God has made much progress from thence, and advanced throughout all nations; because the Martyrs suffered, and neither "fell away," nor yet offered resistance; confessing everything, concealing nothing; prepared for everything, shrinking from nothing. Marvellous "meekness"! This did the body of Christ, by its Head it learned. He was first "led as a sheep to the slaughter, and as a lamb before his shearer is dumb, even so opened not His mouth;"[3] meek to that degree, that while hanging on the Cross, He said, "Father, forgive them, for they know not what they do."[4] Why because of "righteousness"? He will come also to judge, and to "render to every man according to his works." He spake "the truth;" He patiently endured unrighteousness: He is to bring "righteousness" hereafter.

13. "And Thy right hand shall lead Thee on marvellously." We shall be guided on by His right hand: He by His own. For He is God, we mortal men. He was led on by His own right hand; i.e. by His own power. For the power which the Father hath, He hath also; the Father's immortality He hath also: He hath the Father's Divinity, the Father's Eternity, the Father's Power.[5] Marvellously will His right hand lead Him on, performing the works of God; undergoing human sufferings, overthrowing the evil wills[6] of men by His own goodness. Even now, He is being led on even to places where as yet He is not; and it is His own right hand that is leading Him on. For that is leading Him thither which He has Himself bestowed upon His Saints. "Thy right hand shall lead Thee on marvellously."

14. "Thine arrows are sharp, are most powerful" (ver. 5); words that pierce the heart, that kindle love. Whence in the Song of Songs it is said, "I am wounded with love."[7] For she speaks of being "wounded with love;" that is, of being in love, of being inflamed with passion, of sighing for the Bridegroom, from whom she received the arrow of the Word. "Thine arrows are sharp, are most powerful;" both piercing, and effective; "sharp, most powerful." "The peoples shall fall under Thee." Who have "fallen"? They who were "wounded" have also "fallen." We see the nations subdued unto Christ; we do not see them "fall." He explains where they "fall," viz. "in the heart." It was there they lifted themselves up against Christ, there they "fall" down before Christ. Saul was a blasphemer of Christ: he was then lifted up, he prays to Christ, "he is fallen," he is prostrate before Him: the enemy of Christ is slain, that the disciple of Christ may live! By an arrow launched from heaven, Saul (not as yet Paul, but still Saul), still lifted up, still not yet prostrate, is wounded in "the heart:" he received the arrow, he fell "in heart." For though he fell prostrate on his face, it was not there that he fell down in heart:[8] but it was there where he said aloud, "Lord, what dost Thou bid me do?"[9] But just now thou wert going to bind the Christians, and to bring them to punishment: and now thou sayest unto Christ, "What dost Thou bid me do?" O arrow sharp and most mighty, by whose stroke "Saul" fell, so as to become "Paul." As it was with him, so was it also with "the peoples;" consider the nations, observe their subjection unto Christ. "The peoples" (then) "shall fall under Thee in the heart of the King's enemies;" that is, in the heart of Thine enemies. For it is Him that he calls King, Him that he recognises as King. "The peoples shall fall under Thee in the heart of the King's enemies." They were "enemies" before; they have been stricken by thine arrows: they have fallen before Thee. Out of enemies they have been made

---

[1] Gen. xxiv. 2.　　[2] Ps. lxxxv. 11.　　[3] Isa. liii. 7.
[4] Luke xxiii. 34.

[5] *Virtutem.*　　[6] *Malitias.*　　[7] Song of Sol. ii. 5.
[8] *In corde,* editions not in MSS.　　[9] Acts ix. 6.

friends : the enemies are dead, the friends survive. This is the meaning of, " for those which shall be changed." We are seeking to " understand" each single word, and each separate verse ; yet so far only are we to seek for their " understanding," as to leave no one to doubt that they are spoken of Christ.

15. " Thy throne, O God, is for ever and ever" (ver. 6). Because God has " ' blessed Thee ' for ever," on account of the " grace poured over Thy lips." Now the throne of the Jewish Kingdom was a temporal one ; belonging to those who were under the Law, not to those who were under " grace : " He came to " redeem those who were under the Law," and to place them under " Grace." His " Throne is for ever and ever." Why? for that first throne of the Kingdom was but a temporal one : whence then have we a " throne for ever and ever "? Because it is God's throne. O divine Attribute of Eternity !¹ for God could not have a temporal throne. " Thy throne, O God, is for ever and ever — a sceptre of direction is the sceptre of Thy Kingdom." " The sceptre of direction" is that which directs mankind : they were before crooked, distorted ; they sought to reign for themselves : they loved themselves, loved their own evil deeds : they submitted not their own will to God ; but would fain have bent God's will to conformity with their own lusts. For the sinner and the unrighteous man is generally angry with God, because it rains not !² and yet would have God not be angry with himself, because he is profligate.³ And it is pretty much for this very reason that men daily sit, to dispute against God : " This is what He ought to have done : this He has not well done." Thou forsooth seest what thou doest ; He knows not what He does ! It is thou that art crooked ! His ways are right. When wilt thou make the crooked coincide with the straight? It cannot be made to coincide with it.⁴ Just as if you were to place a crooked stick on a level pavement ; it does not join on to it ; it does not cohere ; it does not fit into the pavement. The pavement is even in every part : but that is crooked ; it does not fit into that which is level. The will of God then is " equal," thine own is " crooked : " it is because thou canst not be conformed unto it, that it seems " crooked " unto thee : rule thou thyself by it ; seek not to bend it to thine own will : for thou canst not accomplish it ; that is at all times " straight " ! Wouldest thou abide in Him? " Correct thou thyself ; " so will the sceptre of Him who rules thee, be unto thee " a rule of direction." Thence is He also called King,⁵ from " ruling." For

that is no " ruler " that does not correct.⁶ Hereunto is our King a King of " right ones." ⁷ Just as He is a Priest (*Sacerdos*) by sanctifying us, so is He our King, our Ruler, by " ruling " us. . . .

16. Thou hast loved righteousness, and hated iniquity" (ver. 7). See there " the rod of direction " described. " Thou hast loved righteousness, and hated iniquity." Draw near to that " rod ; " let Christ be thy King : let Him " rule " thee with that rod, not crush thee with it. For that rod is " a rod of iron ; " an inflexible rod.⁸ " Thou shalt rule them with a rod of iron : and break them in pieces like a potter's vessel." ⁹ Some He rules ; others He " breaks in pieces : " He " rules " them that are spiritual : He " breaks in pieces " them that are carnal. . . . Would He so loudly declare that He was about to smite thee, if He wished to smite thee? He is then holding back His hand from the punishment of thine offences ; but do not thou hold back. Turn thou thyself to the punishment of thine offences : for unpunished offences cannot be : punishment therefore must be executed either by thyself, or by Him : do thou then plead guilty, that He may reprieve thee. Consider an instance in that penitential Psalm : " Hide Thy face from my sins." ¹⁰ Did he mean " from me "? No : for in another passage he says plainly, " Hide not Thy face from me." " Turn " then " Thy face from my sins." I would have Thee not see my sins. For God's " seeing " is animadverting upon. Hence too a Judge is said to " animadvert " ¹¹ on that which he punishes ; i.e. to turn his mind on it, to bend it thereon, even to the punishment of it, inasmuch as he is the Judge. So too is God a Judge. " Turn Thou Thy face from my sins." But thou thyself, if thou wouldest have God turn " His face " from them, turn not thine own face from them. Observe how he proposes this to God in that very Psalm : " I acknowledge," he says, " my transgression, and my sin is ever before me." ¹² He would fain have that which he wishes to be ever before his own eyes, not be before God's eyes. Let no one flatter himself with fond hopes of God's mercy. His sceptre is " a sceptre of righteousness." Do we say that God is not merciful? What can exceed His mercy, who shows such forbearance to sinners ; who takes no account of the past in all that turn unto Him? So love thou Him for His mercy, as still to wish that He should be truthful. For mercy cannot strip Him of His attribute of justice : nor justice of that of mercy. Meanwhile during

---

¹ *O æternitatis divinitas.*   ² *Quia non pluit.*
³ *Quia fluit.*   ⁴ *Collineari.*
⁵ *Rex, a regendo.*

⁶ *Non autem regit qui non corrigit.*
⁷ *Rectorum.*
⁸ *Hæc est tota virga. Al. tuta,* " This is a safe rod."
⁹ Ps. ii. 9.   ¹⁰ Ps. li. 9.
¹¹ *Animum advertere.*
¹² Ps. li. 3.

the time that He postpones thy punishment, do not thou postpone it.

17. "Therefore, God, Thy God, hath anointed Thee." It was for this reason that He anointed thee, that thou mightest love righteousness, and hate iniquity. And observe in what way he expresses himself. "Therefore, God, Thy God, hath anointed Thee:" i.e. "God hath anointed Thee, O God." "God" is "anointed" by God. For in the Latin it is thought to be the same case of the noun repeated: in the Greek however there is a most evident distinction; one being the name of the Person addressed; and one His who makes the address, saying, "God hath anointed Thee." "O God, Thy God hath anointed Thee," just as if He were saying, "Therefore hath Thy God, O God, anointed Thee." Take it in that sense, understand it in that sense; that such is the sense is most evident in the Greek. Who then is the God that is "anointed" by God? Let the Jews tell us; these Scriptures are common to us and them. It was God, who was anointed by God: you hear of an "Anointed" one; understand it to mean "Christ." For the name of "Christ" comes from "chrism;" this name by which He is called "Christ" expresses "unction:" nor were kings and prophets anointed in any kingdom, in any other place, save in that kingdom where Christ was prophesied of, where He was anointed, and from whence the Name of Christ was to come. It is found nowhere else at all: in no one nation or kingdom. God, then, was anointed by God; with what oil was He anointed, but a spiritual one? For the visible oil is in the sign, the invisible oil is in the mystery; [1] the spiritual oil is within. "God" then was "anointed" for us, and sent unto us; and God Himself was man, in order that He might be "anointed:" but He was man in such a way as to be God still. He was God in such a way as not to disdain to be man. "Very man and very God;" in nothing deceitful, in nothing false, as being everywhere true, everywhere "the Truth" itself. God then is man; and it was for this cause that "God" was "anointed," because God was Man, and became "Christ."

18. This was figured in Jacob's placing a stone at his head, and so sleeping. [2] The patriarch Jacob had placed a stone at his head: sleeping with that stone at his head, he saw heaven opened, and a ladder from heaven to earth, and Angels ascending and descending; [3] after this vision he awaked, anointed the stone, and departed. In that "stone" he understood Christ;

for that reason he anointed it. Take notice what it is whereby Christ is preached. What is the meaning of that anointing of a stone, especially in the case of the Patriarchs who worshipped but One God? It was however done as a figurative act: and he departed. For he did not anoint the stone, and come to worship there constantly, and to perform sacrifice there. It was the expression of a mystery; not the commencement of sacrilege. And notice the meaning of "the stone." "The Stone which the builders refused, this is become the head of the corner." [4] Notice here a great mystery. The "Stone" is Christ. Peter calls Him "a living Stone, disallowed indeed of men, but chosen of God." [5] And the stone is set at "the head," because "Christ is the Head of the man." [6] And "the stone" was anointed, because "Christ" was so called from His being anointed. And in the revelation of Christ, the ladder from earth to heaven is seen, or from heaven to earth, and the Angels ascending and descending. What this means, we shall see more clearly, when we have quoted the testimony from the Lord Himself in the Gospel. You know that Jacob is the same as Israel. For when he wrestled with the Angel, and "prevailed," and had been blest by Him over whom he prevailed, his named was changed, so that he was called "Israel;" just as the people of Israel "prevailed" [7] against Christ, so as to crucify Him, and nevertheless was (in those who believed in Christ) blest by Him over whom it prevailed. But many believed not; hence the halting of Jacob. Here we have at once, blessing and halting. Blessing on those who became believers; for we know that afterward many of that people did believe: Halting on the other hand in those who believed not. And because the greater part believed not, and but few believed, therefore that a halting might be produced, He touched "the breadth [8] of his thigh." [9] What is meant by the breadth of the thigh? The great multitude of his descendants. [10] . . .

19. "God, Thy God, hath anointed Thee." We have been speaking of God, who was "anointed;" i.e. of Christ. The name of Christ could not be more clearly expressed than by His being called "God the Anointed." In the same way in which He was "beautiful before the children of men," so is He here "anointed with the oil of gladness above His fellows." Who then are His "fellows"? The children of men; for that He Himself (as the Son of Man) became partaker of their mortality in order to make them partakers of His Immortality.

---

[1] *Al.* "The visible oil is for a sign of the oil invisible, for it is in a sacrament." [The use of oil in confirmation, designed to teach this, operated to conceal it rather; the *material chrism* absorbing the spiritual idea. — C]
[2] Gen. xxviii. 11-18.
[3] [With which he subjoins a reference to John i. 51. — C.]

[4] Ps. cxviii. 22.   [5] 1 Pet. ii. 4.   [6] 1 Cor. xi. 3.
[7] Luke xxiii. 23.
[8] *Lat. tudinem ;* but Vulgate, *nervum.*   [9] Gen. xxxii. 25.
[10] *Multitudo generis.*

20. "Out of Thy garments is the smell of myrrh, amber, and cassia" (ver. 8). Out of Thy garments is perceived the smell of fragrant odours. By His garments are meant His Saints, His elect, His whole Church, which he shows forth, as His garment, so to speak; His robe "without spot and wrinkle,"[1] which on account of its spots He has "washed" in His blood; on account of its "wrinkles" extended on His Cross. Hence the sweet savour which is signified by certain perfumes there mentioned. Hear Paul, that "least of the Apostles" (that "hem of that garment," which the woman with the issue of blood touched, and was healed), hear him saying: "We are a sweet savour of Christ, in every place, both in them that are saved, and in them that perish."[2] He did not say, "We are a sweet savour in them that are saved, and a foul savour in them that are lost:" but, as far as relates to ourselves, "we are a sweet savour both in them that are saved, and in them that perish." . . . They who loved him were saved by the odour of "sweet savour;" they who envied him, perished by means of that "sweet savour." To them that perished then he was not a foul "savour," but a "sweet savour." For it was for this very reason they the more envied him, the more excellent that grace was which reigned in him: for no man envies him who is unhappy. He then was glorious in the preaching of God's Word, and in regulating his life according to the rule of that "rod of direction;" and he was loved by those who loved Christ in him, who followed after and pursued the odour of sweet savour; who loved the friend of the bridegroom: that is to say, by the Bride Herself, who says in the Song of Songs,[3] "We will run after the sweet savour of thy perfumes." But the others, the more they beheld him invested with the glory of the preaching of the Gospel, and of an irreproachable life, were so much the more tortured with envy, and found that sweet savour prove death to them.

21. "Out of thy ivory palaces, whereby kings' daughters have made Thee glad." Choose whichever you please, "ivory" palaces, or "magnificent," or "royal" palaces, it is out of these that the kings' daughters have made Christ glad. Would you understand the spiritual sense of "ivory palaces"? Understand by them the magnificent houses, and tabernacles of God, the hearts of the Saints; and by these self-same "kings" those who rule their flesh; who bring into subjection to themselves the rebellious commonalty of human affections, who chastise the body, and reduce it to bondage: for it is from these that the daughters of kings have made Him glad. For all the souls that have been born through their preaching and evangelizing are "daughters of kings:" and the Churches, as the daughters of Apostles, are daughters of kings. For He is "King of kings;" they themselves kings, of whom it was said, "Ye shall sit upon twelve thrones, judging the twelve tribes of Israel."[4] They preached the "Word of Truth;" and begat Churches not for themselves, but for Him. . . . Therefore as "raising up seed[5] to their brother," to as many as they begat, they gave the name not of "Paulians" or "Petrians," but of "Christians." Observe whether that sense is not wakefully kept[6] in these verses. For when he said, "out of the ivory palaces, he spake of mansions royal, ample, honourable, peaceful, like the heart of the Saints; he added, "Whereby the kings' daughters have made Thee glad in Thine honour." They are indeed daughters of kings, daughters of thine Apostles, but still "in Thine honour:" for they raised up seed to their brother. Hence Paul, when he saw those whom he had raised up unto his Brother, running after his own name, exclaimed, "Was Paul crucified for you?"[7] . . . No; for he says, "Or were ye baptized in the name of Paul?"

"The daughters of kings have made Thee glad in Thine honour." Keep, hold fast this "in Thine honour." This is meant by having "a wedding garment;" seeking His honour, His glory. Understand moreover by "kings' daughters" the cities, which were founded by kings, and have received the faith: and out of the ivory palaces (palaces rich, the proud, the lifted up). "Kings' daughters have made Thee glad in Thine honour;" in that they sought not the honour of their founders, but have sought Thine honour. Show me at Rome a temple of Romulus held in so great honour as I can show you the Monument of Peter.[8] In Peter, who is honoured but He who died for us? For we are followers of Christ, not followers of Peter. And even if we were born from the brother of Him that is dead, yet are we named after the name of Him who is dead.[9] We were begotten by the one, but begotten to the other. Behold, Rome, Carthage, and several other cities are the daughters of kings, and yet have they "made glad the King in His honour:" and all these make up one single Queen.

22. What a nuptial song! Behold in the midst of songs full of rejoicing, comes forth the Bride herself. For the Bridegroom was coming. It was He who was being described: it was on Him all our attention was fixed.

[1] Eph. v. 27.　[2] 2 Cor. ii. 14, 15.　[3] Sol. Song i. 3, Lat.
[4] Matt. xix. 28.
[5] Oxf. MSS. add, "for the Brother's name's sake."
[6] Vigilat.　[7] 1 Cor. i. 13.
[8] Memoriam Petri. [The first basilica of St. Peter, on the Vatican, is attributed to Constantine. —C.]
[9] Deut. xxv. 26.

"Upon Thy right hand did stand the Queen" (ver. 9). She which stands on the left is no Queen. For there will be one standing on "the left" also, to whom it will be said, "Go into everlasting fire."[1] But she shall stand on the right hand, to whom it will be said, "Come, ye blessed of My Father, inherit the kingdom prepared for you from the foundation of the world."[2] On Thy right hand did stand the Queen, "in a vesture of gold, clothed about with divers colours." What is the vesture of this Queen? It is one both precious, and also of divers colours: it is the mysteries of doctrine in all the various tongues: one African, one Syrian, one Greek, one Hebrew, one this, and one that; it is these languages that produce the divers colours of this vesture.[3] But just as all the divers colours of the vesture blend together in the one vesture, so do all the languages in one and the same faith. In that vesture, let there be diversity, let there be no rent. See we have "understood" the divers colours of the diversity of tongues; and the vesture to refer to unity: but in that diversity itself, what is meant by the "gold"? Wisdom itself. Let there be any diversity of tongues you please, but there is but one "gold" that is preached of: not a different gold, but a different form of that gold. For it is the same Wisdom, the same doctrine and discipline that every language preaches. In the languages there is diversity; gold in the thoughts.

23. The Prophet addresses this Queen (for he delights in singing to her), and moreover each one of us, provided, however, we know where we are, and endeavour to belong to that body, and do belong to it in faith and hope, being united in the membership of Christ.[4] For it is us whom he addresses, saying, "Hearken, O daughter, and behold" (ver. 10), as being one of the "Fathers" (for they are "daughters of kings"), although it be a Prophet, or although it be an Apostle[5] that is addressing her; addressing her, as a daughter, for we are accustomed to speak in this way, "Our fathers the Prophets, our fathers the Apostles;" if we address them as "fathers," they may address us as children: and it is one father's voice addressing one daughter. "Hearken, O daughter, and see." "Hear" first; afterward "see." For they came to us with the Gospel; and that has been preached to us, which as yet we do not see, and which on hearing of it we believed, which by believing it, we shall come to see: even as the Bridegroom Himself speaks in the Prophet, "A people whom I have not known served me. In the hearing of me with the ear it obeyed

me."[6] What is meant by on "hearing of me with the ear"? That they did not "see." The Jews saw Him, and crucified Him; the Gentiles saw Him not, and believed. Let the Queen who comes from the Gentiles come in "the vesture of gold, clothed with divers colours;"[7] let her come from among the Gentiles clad in all languages, in the unity of Wisdom: let it be said unto her, "Hearken, O daughter, and see." If thou wilt not hear, thou shalt not "see." . . .

"And incline thine ear." It is not enough to "hearken;" hearken with humility: bow down thine ear. "Forget also thine own people, and thy father's house." There was a certain "people," and a certain house of thy father, in which thou wast born, the people of Babylon, having the devil for thy king. Whencesoever the Gentiles came, they came from their father the devil; but they have renounced their sonship to the devil. "Forget also thine own people, and thy father's house." He, in making thee a sinner, begat thee loathsome: the Other, in that "He justifies the ungodly,"[8] begetteth thee again in beauty.

24. "For the King hath greatly desired thy beauty" (ver. 11). What "beauty" is that, save that which is His own work? "Greatly desired the beauty"—Of whom? Of her the sinner, the unrighteous, the ungodly, such as she was with her "father," the devil, and among her own "people"? No, but hers of whom it is said, "Who is this that cometh up made white?"[9] She was not white then at the first, but was "made" white afterwards. For "though your sins shall be as scarlet, I will make them white as snow."[10] "The king has greatly desired thy beauty." What King is this? "For He is the Lord thy God."[11] Now consider whether thou oughtest not to forego that thy father, and thy own people, and to come to this King, who is thy God? Thy God is "thy King," thy "King" is also thy Bridegroom. Thou weddest to thy King, who is thy God: being endowed by Him, being adorned by Him; redeemed by Him, and healed by Him. Whatever thou hast, wherewith to be pleasing to Him, thou hast from Him.

25. "And the daughters of Tyre shall worship Him with gifts" (ver. 12). It is that selfsame "King, who is thy God," that the daughters of Tyre shall worship with gifts. The daughters of Tyre are the daughters of the Gentiles; the part standing for the whole. Tyre, a city bordering on this country, where the prophecy was delivered, typified the nations that were to believe in Christ. Thence came that

---

[1] Matt. xxv. 41.   [2] Matt. xxv. 34.
[3] [Hence the beauty of a Liturgy is not that it should be in (Latin) one language, but in the many tongues of the many nations, confessing one faith. A. N. F. vol. vii. p. 533.—C.]
[4] Uniti in membris Christ.
[5] Al. "and thus a Prophet addresses her, and thus an Apostle addresses her."

[6] Ps. xviii. 43, 44.
[7] Ben. "with truth." Oxf. mss. varietate.   [8] Rom. iv. 5.
[9] Sol. Song viii. 5. Dealbata; or, Vulgate, deliciis affluens.
[10] Isa. i. 18.
[11] [With the Septuagint our author omits et adora cum. The text of the Vulgate here, and that of St. Augustin and of Jerome's Hebraic Psalter, differ widely.—C.]

Canaanitish woman, who was at first called "a dog;" for that ye may know that she was from thence, the Gospel speaks thus. "He departed into the parts of Tyre and Sidon, and behold a woman of Canaan came out of the same coasts," with all the rest that is related there. She who at first, at the house of her "father," and among her "own people," was but "a dog," who by coming to, and crying after that "King," was made beautiful by believing in Him, what did she obtain to hear? "O woman, great is thy faith." [1] "The King has greatly desired thy beauty. And the daughters of Tyre shall worship with gifts." [2] With what gifts? Even so would this King be approached, and would have His treasuries filled: and it is He Himself who has given us that wherewith they may be filled, and may be filled [3] by you. Let them come (He says) and "worship Him with gifts." What is meant by "with gifts"? . . . "Give alms, and all things are clean unto you." Come with gifts to Him that saith, "I will have mercy rather than sacrifice." [4] To that Temple that existed aforetime as a shadow of that which was to come, they used to come with bulls, and rams, and goats, with every different kind of animal for sacrifice: that with that blood one thing should be done, and another be typified by it. Now that very blood, which all these things used to figure, hath come: the King Himself hath come, and He Himself would have your "gifts." What gifts? Alms. For He Himself will judge hereafter, and will Himself hereafter account "gifts" to certain persons. "Come" (He says), "ye blessed of My Father." Why? "I was an hungred, and ye gave Me meat," [5] etc. These are the gifts with which the daughters of Tyre worship the King; for when they said, "When saw we Thee?" He who is at once above and below (whence those "ascending" and "descending" are spoken of [6]), said, "Inasmuch as ye have done it unto one of the least of Mine, ye have done it unto Me." [7]

26. . . . "The rich among the people shall entreat Thy face." Both they who shall entreat that face, and He whose face they will entreat, are all collectively but one Bride, but one Queen, mother and children belonging all together unto Christ, belonging unto their Head. . . .

27. "All the glory of her, the King's daughter, is from within " (ver. 13). Not only is her robe, outwardly, "of gold, and of divers colours;" but He who loved her beauty, knew her to be also beautiful within. [8] What are those inward charms? [9] Those of conscience. It is there Christ sees; it is there Christ loves her: it is there He addresses her, there punishes, there crowns. Let then thine alms be done in secret; for "all the glory of her, the King's daughter, is from within." "With fringes of gold, clothed with divers colours" (ver. 14). Her beauty is from within; yet in the "fringes of gold " is the diversity of languages: the beauty of doctrine. What do these avail, if there be not that beauty "from within"? "The virgins shall be brought unto the King after her." It has been fulfilled indeed. The Church has believed; the Church has been formed throughout all nations. And to what a degree do virgins now seek to find favour in the eyes of that King! Whence are they moved to do so? Even because the Church preceded them. "The virgins shall be brought unto the King after her. Her near kinswomen [10] shall be brought unto Thee." For they that are brought unto Him are not strangers, but her "near kinswomen," that belong to her. And because he had said, "unto the King," he says, turning the discourse to Him, "her near kinswomen shall be brought unto Thee."

28. "With gladness and rejoicing shall they be brought and shall be led into the Temple of the King" (ver. 15). The "Temple of the King " is the Church itself: it is the Church itself that enters into "the Temple of the King." Whereof is that Temple constructed? Of the men who enter the Temple? Who but God's "faithful" ones are its "living stones"? [11] "They shall be led into the Temple of the King." For there are virgins without the Temple of the King, the nuns among the heretics: [12] they are virgins, it is true; but what will that profit them, unless they be led into the "Temple of the King"? The "Temple of the King " is in unity: the "Temple of the King " is not ruinous, is not rent asunder, is not divided. The cement [13] of those living stones is "charity."

29. "Instead of thy fathers, children are born to thee" (ver. 16). Nothing can be more manifest. Now consider the "Temple of the King " itself, for it is on its behalf he speaks, on account of the unity of the body that is spread throughout all the world: for those very persons who have chosen to be virgins, cannot find favour with the King unless they be led into the Temple of the King. "Instead of thy fathers, are thy children born to thee." It was the Apostles begat thee: they were "sent:" they were the preachers: they are "the fathers."

---

1 Matt. xv. 21-28.
2 " They shall worship Him with gifts." [A truly Punic outburst, and full of point for the Carthaginians. A. N. F. vol. iii. p. 3.—C.]
3 Or, " and let them be filled." *Al.* " and they are filled."
4 Hos. vi. 6; Matt. ix. 13.
5 Matt. xxv. 34, 35.
6 Gen. xxviii. 12. See § 18. John i. 51.
7 Matt. xxv. 40.

8 [*Omnis gloria filiæ regis intrinsecus* is Jerome's version of the Hebrew; preferable, certainly, to the tame idea of modern critics, that " within " means " (*intus domum*) *within* the palaces." —C.]
9 *Interiora pulcritudinis.* 10 *Proximæ.* 11 1 Pet. ii. 4.
12 *Hæreticæ sanctimoniales.* 13 *Junctura.*

But was it possible for them to be with us in the body for ever? Although one of them said, " I desire to depart, and to be with Christ, which is far better : to abide in the flesh is necessary for your sakes." It is true he said this, but how long was it possible for him to remain here? Could it be till this present time, could it be to all futurity? Is the Church then left desolate by their departure? God forbid. " Instead of thy fathers, children have been born to thee." What is that? The Apostles were sent to thee as " fathers," instead of the Apostles sons have been born to thee : there have been appointed Bishops. For in the present day, whence do the Bishops, throughout all the world, derive their origin? The Church itself calls them fathers ; the Church itself brought them forth, and placed them on the thrones of " the fathers." Think not thyself abandoned then, because thou seest not Peter, nor seest Paul : seest not those through whom thou wert born. Out of thine own offspring has a body of " fathers " been raised up to thee. " Instead of thy fathers, have children been born to thee." Observe how widely diffused is the " Temple of the King," that " the virgins that are not led to the Temple of the King," may know that they have nothing to do with that marriage. " Thou shalt make them princes [1] over all the earth." This is the Universal Church : her children have been made " princes over all the earth : " her children have been appointed instead of the " fathers." Let those who are cut off own the truth of this, let them come to the One Body : let them be led into the Temple of the King. God hath established His Temple everywhere : hath laid everywhere " the foundations of the Prophets and Apostles." [2] The Church has brought " forth sons ; " has made them " instead of her fathers" to be " princes over all the earth."

30. " They shall be mindful of thy name in every generation and generation ; therefore shall the peoples confess unto [3] Thee " (ver. 17). What does it profit then to " confess " indeed, and yet to confess out of " the Temple "? What does it profit to pray, and yet not to pray on the Mount? " I cried," says he, " unto the Lord with my voice : and He heard me out of His holy hill." [4] Out of what " hill "? Out of that of which it is said, " A city set upon a hill cannot be hid." [5] Of what " hill "? Out of that hill which Daniel saw " grow out of a small stone, and break all the kingdoms of the earth ; and cover all the face of the earth." [6] There let him pray, who hopes to receive : there let him ask,

who would have his prayer heard : there let him confess, who wishes to be pardoned. " Therefore shall the peoples confess unto thee for ever, world without end." For in that eternal life it is true indeed there will no longer be the mourning over sins : but yet in the praises of God by that everlasting City which is above, there will not be wanting a perpetual confession of the greatness of that happiness. For to that City itself, to which another Psalm [7] sings, " Glorious things are spoken of thee, O City of God," to her who is the very Bride of Christ, the very Queen, a " King's daughter, and a King's consort ; " . . . the peoples shall for this very cause confess even to herself ; the hearts of all, now enlightened by perfect charity, being laid bare, and made manifest, that she may know the whole of herself most completely, who here is, in many parts of her, unknown to herself. . . .

PSALM XLVI.[8]

1. It is called, " A Psalm, to the end, for the sons of Korah, for things secret." Secret is it then ; but He Himself, who in the place of Calvary was crucified, ye know, hath rent the veil,[9] that the secrets of the temple might be discovered. Furthermore since the Cross of our Lord was a key, whereby things closed might be opened ; let us trust that He will be with us, that these secrets may be revealed. What is said, " To the end," always ought to be understood of Christ. For " Christ is the end of the law for righteousness to every one that believeth." [10] But The End He is called, not because He consumeth, but because He perfecteth. For ended call we the food which is eaten, and ended the coat which is woven, the former to consumption, the latter to perfection. Because then we have not where to go farther when we have come to Christ, Himself is called the end of our course. Nor ought we to think, that when we have come to Him, we ought to strive any further to come also to the Father. For this thought Philip also, when he said to Him, " Lord, show us the Father, and it sufficeth us." When he said, " It sufficeth us," he sought the end of satisfaction and perfection. Then said He, " Have I been so long time with you, and hast thou not known Me, Philip : he that hath seen Me, hath seen the Father." [11] In Him then have we the Father, because He is in the Father,

---

[1] [Not worldly princes, but spiritual chiefs and leaders of the flock. — C.]
[2] Eph. ii. 20.　　[3] E. V. " praise Thee."　　[4] Ps. iii. 4.
[5] Matt. v. 14.　　[6] Dan. ii. 34, 35.

[7] Ps. lxxxvii. 3.
[8] Lat. XLV. [In his exordium the Saint recurs to his favourite idea as follows : " Korah is interpreted ' Baldness,' and that our Lord, since in the ' place of the Bald skull ' [Matt. xxvii 33] He was crucified, hath drawn unto Him many ; like that corn of wheat, which except it die, should abide alone ; and that those who are drawn unto Him are called sons of Korah [John xii. 24, 32]. Thus much in the mystery. There were indeed some sons of Korah at the time when this was first sung [1 Chron. xxvi. 1], but to us ought the Spirit to give life, not the letter to be a veil " [2 Cor. iii. 6] — C.]
[9] Matt. xxvii. 51.　　[10] Rom. x. 4.　　[11] John xiv. 8, 9.

and the Father in Him, and He and His Father are One.[1]

2. " Our God is a refuge and strength " (ver. 1). There are some refuges wherein is no strength, whereto when any fleeth, he is more weakened than strengthened. Thou fleest, for example, to some one greater in the world, that thou mayest make thyself a powerful friend ; this seemeth to thee a refuge. Yet so great are this world's uncertainties, and so frequent grow the ruins of the powerful day by day, that when to such refuge thou art come, thou beginnest to fear more than ever therein. . . . Our refuge is not such, but our refuge is strength. When thither we have fled, we shall be firm.

3. " A helper in tribulations, which find us out too much." Tribulations are many, and in every tribulation unto God must we flee ; whether it be a tribulation in our estate, or in our body's health, or about the peril of those dearest to us, or any other thing necessary to the sustaining of this life, refuge ought there to be none at all to a Christian man, other than his Saviour, other than his God, to whom when he has fled, he is strong. For he will not in himself be strong, nor will he to himself be strength, but He will be his strength, who has become his refuge. But, dearly beloved, among all tribulations of the human soul is no greater tribulation than the consciousness of sin. For if there be no wound herein, and that be sound within man which is called conscience, wherever else he may suffer tribulation, thither will he flee, and there find God. . . . Ye see, dearly beloved, when trees are cut down and proved by the carpenters, sometimes in the surface they seem as though injured and rotten ; but the carpenter looks into the inner marrow as it were of the tree, and if within he find the wood sound, he promises that it will last in a building ; nor will he be very anxious about the injured surface, when that which is within he declares sound. Furthermore, to man anything more inward than conscience is not found ; what then profits it, if what is without is sound, and the marrow of conscience has become rotton ? These are close and vehement overmuch, and as this Psalm saith, too great tribulations ; yet even in these the Lord hath become a helper by forgiving sin. For the consciences of the ungodly hateth nothing save indulgence ; for if one saith he hath great tribulations, being a confessed debtor to the treasury, when he beholdeth the narrowness of his estate, and seeth that he cannot be solvent ; if on account of the distrainers every year hanging over him, he saith that he suffereth great tribulations, and doth not breathe freely except in hope of indulgence, and that in things

earthly ;[2] how much more the debtor of penalties out of the abundance of sins : when shall he pay what he owes out of his evil conscience, when if he pay, he perisheth ? For to pay this debt, is to undergo the penalties. Remaineth then that of His indulgence, we may be secure, yet so that, indulgence received, we return not again to contract debts. . . .

4. Now then, such security received, what say they ? " Therefore will not we fear, when the earth shall be confounded " (ver. 2). Just before anxious, suddenly secure ; out of too great tribulations set in great tranquillity. For in them Christ was sleeping, therefore were they tossed : Christ awoke (as but now we heard out of the Gospel), He commanded the winds, and they were still.[3] Since Christ is in each man's heart by faith, it is signified to us, that his heart as a ship in this world's tempest is tossed, who forgetteth his faith : as though Christ sleeping it is tossed, but Christ awaking cometh tranquillity. Nay, the Lord Himself, what said He ? " Where is your faith ? "[4] Christ aroused, aroused up faith, that what had been done in the ship, might be done in their hearts. " A helper in tribulations, which found us[5] out too much." He caused that therein should be great tranquillity.

5. See what tranquillity : " Therefore will not we fear when the earth shall be confounded, and the mountains shall be carried into the heart of the sea." Then we shall find not fear. Let us seek mountains carried, and if we can find, it is manifest that this is our security. The Lord truly said to His disciples, " If ye have faith as a grain of mustard seed, ye shall say to this mountain, Be Thou removed, and be Thou cast into the sea, and it shall be done."[6] Haply " to this mountain," He said of Himself ; for He is called a Mountain : " It shall come to pass in the last days, that the mountain of the Lord shall be manifest."[7] But this Mountain is placed above other mountains ; because the Apostles also are mountains, supporting this Mountain. Therefore followeth, " In the last days the Mountain of the Lord shall be manifest, established in the top of the mountains." Therefore passeth It the tops of all mountains, and on the top of all mountains is It placed ; because the mountains are preaching The Mountain. But the sea signifieth this world, in comparison of which sea, like earth seemed the nation of the Jews. For it was not covered over with the bitterness of idolatry, but, like dry land, was surrounded with the bitterness of the Gentiles as with sea. It was to be, that the earth be confounded, that is, that nation of

---

[1] John x. 30, 38.

[2] Many MSS. " of earthly princes."　　[3] Matt. viii. 24-26.
[4] Luke viii. 25.　　[5] Al. " them."
[6] Matt. xvii. 20, xxi. 21.　　[7] Isa. ii. 2.

the Jews; and that the mountains be carried into the heart of the sea, that is, first that great Mountain established in the top of the mountains. For He deserted the nation of the Jews, and came among the Gentiles. He was carried from the earth into the sea. Who carrying Him? The Apostles, to whom He had said, "If ye have faith as a grain of mustard seed, ye shall say to this mountain, Be thou removed, and be thou cast into the sea, and it shall be done:" that is, through your most faithful preaching it shall come to pass, that this mountain, that is, I Myself, be preached among the Gentiles, be glorified among the Gentiles, be acknowledged among the Gentiles, and that be fulfilled which was predicted of Me, "A people whom I have not known shall serve Me."[1] . . .

6. "The waters thereof roared, and were troubled" (ver. 3): when the Gospel was preached, "What is this? He seemeth to be a setter forth of strange gods:"[2] this the Athenians; but the Ephesians, with what tumult would they have slain the Apostles, when in the theatre, for their goddess Diana, they made such an uproar, as to be shouting, "Great is Diana of the Ephesians!"[3] Amidst which waves and roaring of the sea, feared not they who to that refuge had fled. Nay, the Apostle Paul would enter in to the theatre, and was kept back by the disciples, because it was necessary that he should still abide in the flesh for their sakes. But yet, "the waters thereof roared, and were troubled: the mountains shook at the mightiness thereof." Whose might? The sea's? or rather God's, of whom was said, "refuge and strength, a helper in tribulations, which have found us out too much?" For shaken were the mountains, that is, the powers of this world. For one thing are the mountains of God, another the mountains of the world: the mountains of the world, they whose head is the devil, the mountains of God, they whose Head is Christ. But by these mountains were shaken those mountains. Then gave they their voices against Christians, when the mountains were shaken, the waters roaring; for the mountains were shaken, and there was made a great earthquake, with quaking of the sea. But against whom this? Against the City founded upon a rock. The waters roar, the mountains shake, the Gospel being preached. What then, the City of God? Hear what followeth.

7. "The streams of the river make glad the City of God" (ver. 4). When the mountains shake, when the sea rages, God deserteth not His City, by the streams of the river. What are these streams of the river? That overflowing of the Holy Spirit, of which the Lord said, "If

any man thirst, let him come unto Me, and drink. He that believeth on Me, out of his bosom[4] shall flow rivers of living water."[5] These rivers then flowed out of the bosom[4] of Paul, Peter, John, the other Apostles, the other faithful Evangelists. Since these rivers flowed from one river, many "streams of the river make glad the City of God." For that ye might know this to be said of the Holy Spirit, in the same Gospel next said the Evangelist, "But this spake He of the Spirit, which they that were to believe on Him should receive. For the Holy Ghost was not yet given, because that Jesus was not yet glorified."[6] Jesus being glorified after His Resurrection, glorified after His Ascension, on the day of Pentecost came the Holy Spirit, and filled the believers,[7] who spake with tongues, and began to preach the Gospel to the Gentiles. Hence was the City of God made glad, while the sea was troubled by the roaring of its waters, while the mountains were confounded, asking what they should do, how drive out the new doctrine, how root out the race of Christians from the earth. Against whom? Against the streams of the river making glad the City of God. For thereby showed He of what river He spake; that He signified the Holy Spirit, by "the streams of the river make glad the City of God." And what follows? "The Most High hath sanctified His tabernacle:" since then there followeth the mention of Sanctification, it is manifest that these streams of the river are to be understood of the Holy Spirit, by whom is sanctified every godly soul believing in Christ, that it may be made a citizen of the City of God.

8. "God is in the midst of her: she shall not be moved"(ver. 5). Let the sea rage, the mountains shake; "God is in the midst of her: she shall not be moved." What is, "in the midst of her"? That God stands in any one place, and they surround Him who believe in Him? Then is God circumscribed by place; and broad that which surroundeth, narrow that which is surrounded? God forbid. No such thing imagine of God, who is contained in no place, whose seat is the conscience of the godly: and so is God's seat in the hearts of men, that if man fall from God, God in Himself abideth, not falleth like one not finding where to be. For rather doth He lift up thee, that thou mayest be in Him, than so lean upon thee, as if thou withdraw thyself, to fall. Himself if He withdraw, fall wilt thou: thyself if thou withdraw, fall will not He. What then is, "God is in the midst of her"? It signifieth that God is equal to all, and accepteth not persons. For as that which

---

[1] Ps. xviii. 43.　　[2] Acts xvii. 18.　　[3] Acts xix. 34.

[4] ["Belly," English version. But I have not hesitated to substitute a word more literal in fact, which relieves the text of a ludicrous profanation. — C.]
[5] John vii. 37, 38.　　[6] John vii. 39.　　[7] Acts ii. 1, 2.

is in the middle has equal distances to all the boundaries, so God is said to be in the middle, because He consulteth equally for all. "God is in the midst of her: she shall not be moved." Wherefore shall she not be moved? Because God is in the midst of her. He is "the Helper in tribulations that have found us out too much. God shall help her with His Countenance." What is, "with His Countenance"? With manifestation of Himself. How manifests God Himself, so as that we see His Countenance? I have already told you; ye have learned God's Presence; we have learned it through His works. When from Him we receive any help so that we cannot at all doubt that it was granted to us by the Lord, then God's Countenance is with us.

9. "The heathen are troubled" (ver. 6). And how troubled? why troubled? To cast down the City of God, in the midst whereof is God? To overthrow the tabernacle sanctified, which God helpeth with His Countenance? No: with a wholesome trouble are the heathen now troubled. For what followeth? "And the kingdoms are bowed." Bowed, saith He, are the kingdoms; not now erected that they may rage, but bowed that they may adore. When were the kingdoms bowed? When that came to pass which was predicted in another Psalm, "All kings shall fall down before Him, all nations shall serve Him."[1] What cause made the kingdoms to bow? Hear the cause. "The Most High gave His Voice, and the earth was moved." The fanatics[2] of idolatry, like frogs in the marshes, clamoured, the more tumultuously, the more sordidly, in filth and mire. And what is the brawling of frogs to the thunder of the clouds? For out of them "the Most High gave His Voice, and the earth was moved:" He thundered out of His clouds. And what are His clouds? His Apostles, His preachers, by whom He thundered in precepts, lightened in miracles. The same are clouds who are also mountains: mountains for their height and firmness, clouds for their rain and fruitfulness. For these clouds watered the earth, of which it was said, "The Most High gave His Voice, and the earth was moved." For it is of those clouds that He threateneth a certain barren vineyard, whence the mountains were carried into the heart of the sea; "I will command," saith He, "the clouds that they rain no rain upon it."[3] This was fulfilled in that which I have mentioned, when the mountains were carried into the heart of the sea; when it was said, "It was necessary that the word of God should have been spoken first to you; but seeing ye put it from you, we turn to the Gentiles;"[4] then was fulfilled, "I will command the clouds that they

rain no rain upon it." The nation of the Jews hath just so remained as a fleece dry upon the ground. For this, ye know, happened in a certain miracle, the ground was dry, the fleece only was wet, yet rain in the fleece appeared not.[5] So also the mystery of the New Testament appeared not in the nation of the Jews. What there was the fleece, is here the veil. For in the fleece was veiled the mystery. But on the ground, in all the nations open lieth Christ's Gospel; the rain is manifest, the Grace of Christ is bare, for it is not covered with a veil. But that the rain might come out of it, the fleece was pressed. For by pressure they from themselves excluded Christ, and the Lord now from His clouds raineth on the ground, the fleece hath remained dry. But of them then "the Most High gave His Voice," out of those clouds; by which Voice the kingdoms were bowed and worshipped.

10. "The Lord of Hosts is with us; the God of Jacob is our taker up" (ver. 7). Not any man, not any power, not, in short, Angel, or any creature either earthly or heavenly, but "the Lord of Hosts is with us; the God of Jacob is our taker up." He who sent Angels, came after Angels, came that Angels might serve Him, came that men He might make equal to Angels. Mighty Grace! If God be for us, who can be against us? "The Lord of Hosts is with us." What Lord of Hosts is with us? "If" (I say) "God be for us, who can be against us? He that spared not His own Son, but delivered Him up for us all; how hath He not with Him also freely given[6] us all things."[7] Therefore be we secure, in tranquillity of heart nourish we a good conscience with the Bread of the Lord. "The Lord of Hosts is with us; the God of Jacob is our taker up." However great be thy infirmity, see who taketh thee up. One is sick, a physician is called to him. His own taken-up, the Physician calleth the sick man. Who hath taken him up? Even He. A great hope of salvation; a great Physician hath taken him up. What Physician?[8] Every Physician save He is man: every Physician who cometh to a sick man, another day can be made sick, beside Him. "The God of Jacob is our taker up." Make thyself altogether as a little child, such as are taken up by their parents. For those not taken up, are exposed; those taken up are nursed. Thinkest thou God hath so taken thee up, as when an infant thy mother took thee up? Not so, but to eternity. For thy voice is in that Psalm, "My father and my mother forsake me, but the Lord hath taken me up."[9]

---

[1] Ps. lxxii. 11.   [2] *Arreptitii.*   [3] Isa. v. 6.
[4] Acts xiii. 46.

[5] Judg. vi. 36-40.   [6] So Vulgate.   [7] Rom. viii. 31, 32.
[8] Oxf. mss. add, "hath taken him up? What Physician?"
[9] Ps. xxvii. 10.

11. "Come and see the works of the Lord" (ver. 8). Now of this taking up, what hath the Lord done? Consider the whole world, come and see. For if thou comest not, thou seest not; if thou seest not, thou believest not; if thou believest not, thou standest afar off: if thou believest thou comest, if thou believest thou seest. For how came we to that mountain? Not on foot? Is it by ship? Is it on the wing? Is it on horses? For all that pertain to space and place, be not concerned, trouble not thyself, He cometh to thee. For out of a small stone He hath grown, and become a great mountain, so that He hath filled all the face of the earth. Why then wouldest thou by land come to Him, who filleth all lands? Lo, He hath already come: watch thou. By growing He waketh even sleepers; if yet there is not in them so deep sleep, as that they be hardened even against the mountain coming; but they hear, "Awake, thou that sleepest, and arise from the dead, and Christ shall give thee light."[1] For it was a great thing for the Jews to see the stone. For the stone was yet small: and small they deservedly despised it, and despising they stumbled, and stumbling they were broken; remains that they be ground to powder. For so was it said of the stone, "Whosoever shall fall upon that stone shall be broken; but on whomsoever it shall fall, it will grind him to powder."[2] It is one thing to be broken, another to be ground to powder. To be broken is less than to be ground to powder: but none grindeth He coming exalted, save whom He brake lying low. For now before His coming He lay low before the Jews, and they stumbled at Him, and were broken; hereafter shall He come in His Judgment, glorious and exalted, great and powerful, not weak to be judged, but strong to judge, and grind to powder those who were broken stumbling at Him. For "A stone of stumbling and a rock of offence,"[3] is He to them that believe not. Therefore, brethren, no wonder if the Jews acknowledged not Him, whom as a small stone lying before their feet they despised. They are to be wondered at, who even now so great a mountain will not acknowledge. The Jews at a small stone by not seeing stumbled; the heretics stumble at a mountain. For now that stone hath grown, now say we unto them, Lo, now is fulfilled the prophecy of Daniel, "The stone that was small became a great mountain, and filled the whole earth."[4] Wherefore stumble ye at Him, and go not rather up to Him? Who is so blind as to stumble at a mountain? Came He to thee that thou shouldest have whereat to stumble, and not have whereto to go up? "Come ye, and let us go up to the mountain of the Lord."[5] Isaiah saith this: "Come ye, and let us go up." What is, "Come ye, and let us go up"? "Come ye," is, Believe ye. "Let us go up," is, Let us profit.[6] But they will neither come, nor go up, nor believe, nor profit. They bark against the mountain. Even now by so often stumbling on Him they are broken, and will not go up, choosing always to stumble. Say we to them, "Come ye, and see the works of the Lord:" what "prodigies He hath set forth through the earth." Prodigies are called, because they portend something, those signs of miracles which were done when the world believed. And what thereafter came to pass, and what did they portend?

12. "He maketh wars to cease unto the end of the earth" (ver. 9). This not yet see we fulfilled: yet are there wars, wars among nations for sovereignty; among sects, among Jews, Pagans, Christians, heretics, are wars, frequent wars, some for the truth, some for falsehood contending. Not yet then is this fulfilled, "He maketh wars to cease unto the end of the earth;" but haply it shall be fulfilled. Or is it now also fulfilled? In some it is fulfilled; in the wheat it is fulfilled, in the tares it is not yet fulfilled. What is this then, "He maketh wars to cease unto the end of the earth"? Wars He calleth whereby it is warred against God. But who warreth against God? Ungodliness. And what to God can ungodliness do? Nothing. What doth an earthen vessel dashed against the rock, however vehemently dashed? With so much greater harm to itself it cometh, with how much the greater force it cometh. These wars were great, frequent were they. Against God fought ungodliness, and earthen vessels were dashed in pieces, even men by presuming on themselves, by too much prevailing by their own strength. This is that, the shield whereof Job also named concerning one ungodly. "He runneth against God, upon the stiff neck of his shield."[7] What is, "upon the stiff neck of his shield"? Presuming too much upon his own protection. Were they such who said, "God is our refuge and strength, a Helper in tribulations which have found us out too much"? or in another Psalm, "For I will not trust in my bow, neither shall my sword save me."[8] When one learneth that in himself he is nothing, and help in himself has none, arms in him are broken in pieces, wars are made to cease. Such wars then destroyed that Voice of the Most High out of His holy clouds, whereby the earth was moved, and the kingdoms were bowed. These wars hath He made to cease unto the end of the earth. "He shall break the bow, and

---

[1] Eph. v. 14.　　　[2] Luke xx. 18.　　　[3] 1 Pet. ii. 8.
[4] Dan. ii. 35.
[5] Isa. ii. 3.
[6] Oxf. MSS. add, "*come, and let us go up,* believe, and let us profit."
[7] Job xv. 26.　　　[8] Ps. xliv. 6.

dash in pieces the arms, and burn the shield with fire." Bow, arms, shield, fire.[1] The bow is plots; arms, public warfare; shields, vain presuming of self-protection: the fire wherewith they are burned, is that whereof the Lord said, "I am come to send fire on the earth;"[2] of which fire saith the Psalm, "There is nothing hid from the heat thereof."[3] This fire burning, no arms of ungodliness shall remain in us, needs must all be broken, dashed in pieces, burned. Remain thou unharmed, not having any help of thine own; and the more weak thou art, having no arms thine own, the more He taketh thee up, of whom it is said, "The God of Jacob is our taker up." . . . But when God taketh us up, doth He send us away unarmed? He armeth us, but with other arms, arms Evangelical, arms of truth, continence, salvation, faith, hope, charity. These arms shall we have, but not of ourselves: but the arms which of ourselves we had, are burnt up: yet if by that fire of the Holy Spirit we are kindled, whereof it is said, "He shall burn the shields with fire;" thee, who didst wish to be powerful in thyself, hath God made weak, that He may make thee strong in Him, because in thyself thou wast made weak.

13. What then followeth? "Be still." To what purpose? "And see that I am God" (ver. 10). That is, Not ye, but I am God. I created, I create anew; I formed, I form anew; I made, I make anew. If thou couldest not make thyself, how canst thou make thyself anew? This seeth not the contentious tumult of man's soul; to which contentious tumult is it said, "Be still." That is, restrain your souls from contradiction. Do not argue, and, as it were, arm against God. Else yet live thy arms, not yet burned up with fire. But if they are burned, "Be still;" because ye have not wherewith to fight. But if ye be still in yourselves, and from Me seek all, who before presumed on yourselves, then shall ye "see that I am God." "I will be exalted among the heathen, I will be exalted in the earth." Just before I said, by the name of earth is signified the nation of the Jews, by the name of sea the other nations. The mountains were carried into the heart of the sea; the nations are troubled, the kingdoms are bowed; the Most High gave His Voice, and the earth was moved. "The Lord of Hosts is with us, the God of Jacob is our taker up" (ver. 11). Miracles are done among the heathen, full filled is the faith of the heathen; burned are the arms of human presumption. Still are they, in tranquillity of heart, to acknowledge God the Author of all their gifts. And after this glorifying, doth He yet desert the people of the Jews? of which saith the Apostle, "I say unto you, lest ye should be wise in your own conceits; that blindness in part is happened unto Israel, until the fulness of the Gentiles be come in."[4] That is, until the mountains be carried hither, the clouds rain here, the Lord here bows the kingdoms with His thunder, "until the fulness of the Gentiles be come in." And what thereafter? "And so all Israel shall be saved." Therefore, here too observing the same order, "I will be exalted" (saith He) "among the heathen, I will be exalted in the earth;" that is, both in the sea, and in the earth, that now might all say what followeth: "the God of Jacob is our taker up."

PSALM XLVII.[5]

1. The title of the Psalm goeth thus. "To the end: for the sons of Korah: a Psalm of David himself." These sons of Korah have the title also of some other Psalms, and indicate a sweet mystery, insinuate a great Sacrament: wherein let us willingly understand ourselves, and let us acknowledge in the title us who hear, and read, and as in a glass set before us behold who we are. The sons of Korah, who are they?[6] . . . Haply the sons of the Bridegroom. For the Bridegroom was crucified in the place of Calvary. Recollect the Gospel,[7] where they crucified the Lord, and ye will find Him crucified in the place of Calvary. Furthermore, they who deride His Cross, by devils, as by beasts, are devoured. For this also a certain Scripture signified. When God's Prophet Elisha was going up, children called after him mocking, "Go up thou bald head, Go up thou bald head:" but he, not so much in cruelty as in mystery, made those children to be devoured by bears out of the wood.[8] If those children had not been devoured, would they have lived even till now? Or could they not, being born mortal, have taken off by a fever? But so in them had no mystery been shown, whereby posterity might be put in fear. Let none then mock the Cross of Christ. The Jews were possessed by devils, and devoured; for in the place of Calvary, crucifying Christ, and lifting on the Cross, they said as it were with childish sense, not understanding what they said, "Go up, thou bald head." For what is, "Go up"? "Crucify Him, Crucify Him."[9] For childhood is set before us to imitate humility, and childhood is set before us to beware of foolishness. To imitate humility, childhood was set before us by the Lord, when He called children to Him,[10] and because they were kept from Him, He said, "Suffer them to come unto Me, for of such is the Kingdom of Heaven."[11] The

---

[4] Rom. xi. 25.   [5] Lat. XLVI.
[6] Numb. xvi. 1.   [See p. 155, note 8, *supra.*— C.]
[7] Matt. xxvii. 33.   [8] 2 Kings ii. 23, 24.   [9] Luke xxiii. 21.
[10] Matt. xviii. 2.   [11] Matt. xix. 14.

example of childhood is set before us to beware of foolishness by the Apostle, "Brethren, be not children in understanding:" and again he proposeth it to imitate, "Howbeit in malice be ye children, that in understanding ye may be men."[1] "For the sons of Korah" the Psalm is sung; for Christians then is it sung. Let us hear it as sons of the Bridegroom, whom senseless children crucified in the place of Calvary. For they earned to be devoured by beasts; we to be crowned by Angels. For we acknowledge the humility of our Lord, and of it are not ashamed. We are not ashamed of Him called in mystery "the bald" (*Calvus*), from the place of Calvary. For on the very Cross whereon He was insulted, He permitted not our forehead to be bald; for with His own Cross He marked it. Finally, that ye may know that these things are said to us, see what is said.

2. "O clap your hands, all ye nations" (ver. 1). Were the people of the Jews all the nations? No, but blindness in part is happened to Israel, that senseless children might cry, "Calve," "Calve;" and so the Lord might be crucified in the place of Calvary, that by His Blood shed He might redeem the Gentiles, and that might be fulfilled which saith the Apostle, "Blindness in part is happened unto Israel, until the fulness of the Gentiles be come in."[2] Let them insult, then, the vain, and foolish, and senseless, and say, "Calve," "Calve;" but ye redeemed by His Blood which was shed in the place of Calvary, say, "O clap your hands, all ye nations;" because to you hath come down the Grace of God. "O clap your hands." What is "O clap"? Rejoice. But wherefore with the hands? Because with good works. Do not rejoice with the mouth while idle with the hands. If ye rejoice, "clap your hands." The hands of the nations let Him see, who joys hath deigned to give them. What is, the hands of the nations? The acts of them doing good works. "O clap your hands, all ye nations: shout unto God with the voice of triumph." Both with voice and with hands. If with the voice only it is not well, because the hands are slow; if only with the hands it is not well, because the tongue is mute. Agree together must the hands and tongue. Let this confess, these work. "Shout unto God with the voice of triumph."

3. "For the Lord Most High is terrible" (ver. 2). The Most High in descending made like one ludicrous, by ascending into Heaven is made terrible. "A great King over all the earth." Not only over the Jews; for over them also He is King. For of them also the Apostles believed, and of them many thousands of men sold their

goods, and laid the price at the Apostles' feet,[3] and in them was fulfilled what in the title of the Cross was written, "The King of the Jews."[4] For He is King also of the Jews. But "of the Jews" is little.[5] "O clap your hands, all ye nations: for God is the King of all the earth." For it sufficeth not Him to have under Him one nation: therefore such great price gave He out of His side, as to buy the whole world.

4. "He hath subdued the people under us, and the nations under our feet" (ver. 3). Which subdued, and to whom? Who are they that speak? Haply Jews? Surely, if Apostles; surely, if Saints. For under these God hath subdued the people and the nations, that to-day are they honoured among the nations, who by their own citizens earned to be slain: as their Lord was slain by His citizens, and is honoured among the nations; was crucified by His own, is adored by aliens, but those by a price made His own. For therefore bought He us, that aliens from Him we might not be. Thinkest thou then these are the words of Apostles, "He hath subdued the people under us, and the nations under our feet"? I know not. Strange that Apostles should speak so proudly, as to rejoice that the nations were put under their feet, that is, Christians under the feet of Apostles. For they rejoice that we are with them under the feet of Him who died for us. For under Paul's feet ran they, who would be of Paul, to whom He said, "Was Paul crucified for you?"[6] What then here, what are we to understand? "He hath subdued the people under us, and the nations under our feet." All pertaining to Christ's inheritance are among "all the nations," and all not pertaining to Christ's inheritance are among "all the nations:" and ye see so exalted in Christ's Name is Christ's Church, that all not yet believing in Christ lie under the feet of Christians. For what numbers now run to the Church; not yet being Christians, they ask aid of the Church;[7] to be succoured by us temporally they are willing, though eternally to reign with us as yet they are unwilling. When all seek aid of the Church, even they who are not yet in the Church, hath He not "subdued the people under us, and the nations under our feet"?

5. "He hath chosen an inheritance for us, the excellency[8] of Jacob, whom He loved" (ver. 4). A certain beauty of Jacob He hath chosen for our inheritance. Esau and Jacob were two brothers; in their mother's womb both struggled, and by this struggle their mother's bowels were shaken; and while they two were yet therein, the younger was elected and preferred to the

---

[1] 1 Cor. xiv. 20.　　　[2] Rom. xi. 25.

[3] Acts iv. 34.　　[4] Matt. xxvii. 37.　　[5] [Isa. xlix. 6. — C.]
[6] 1 Cor. i. 13.
[7] [See (A. N. F. vol. v. p. 563) the noble charities of early Christians. — C.]
[8] *Speciem.*

elder, and it was said, "Two peoples are in thy womb, and the elder shall serve the younger." [1] Among all nations is the elder, among all nations the younger; but the younger is in good Christians, elect, godly, faithful; the elder in the proud, unworthy, sinful, stubborn, defending rather than confessing their sins: as was also the very people of the Jews, "being ignorant of God's righteousness, and going about to establish their own righteousness." [2] But for that it is said, "The elder shall serve the younger;" it is manifest that under the godly are subdued the ungodly, under the humble are subdued the proud. Esau was born first, and Jacob was born last; but he who was last born, was preferred to the first-born, who through gluttony lost his birthright. So thou hast it written, [3] He longed for the pottage, and his brother said to him, If thou wilt that I give it thee, give me thy birthright. He loved more that which carnally he desired, than that which spiritually by being born first he had earned: [4] and he laid aside his birthright, that he might eat lentils. But lentils we find to be the food of the Egyptians, for there it abounds in Egypt. Whence is so magnified the lentil of Alexandria, that it comes even to our country, as if here grew no lentil. Therefore by desiring Egyptian food he lost his birthright. So also the people of the Jews, of whom it is said, "in their hearts they turned back again into Egypt." [5] They desired in a manner the lentil, and lost their birthright.

6. "God is gone up with jubilation " (ver. 5). Even He our God, the Lord Christ, is gone up with jubilation; "the Lord with the sound of a trumpet." "Is gone up:" whither, save where we know? Whither the Jews followed Him not, even with their eyes. For exalted on the Cross they mocked Him, ascending into Heaven they did not see Him. "God hath gone up with jubilation." What is jubilation, but admiration of joy which cannot be expressed in words? As the disciples in joy admired, seeing Him go into Heaven, whom they had mourned dead; truly for the joy, words sufficed not: remained to jubilate what none could express. There was also the voice of the trumpet, the voice of Angels. For it is said, "Lift up thy voice like a trumpet." Angels preached the ascension of the Lord: they saw the Disciples, their Lord ascending, tarrying, admiring, confounded, nothing speaking, but in heart jubilant: and now was the sound of the trumpet in the clear voice of the Angels, "Ye men of Galilee, why stand ye gazing up into Heaven? this is Jesus." [6] As if they knew not that it was the same Jesus. Had they not just before seen Him before them? Had they not heard Him speaking with them? Nay, they not

only saw the figure of Him present, but handled also His limbs. Of themselves then knew they not, that it was the same Jesus? But they being by very admiration, from joy of jubilation, as it were transported in mind, the Angels said, "that same is Jesus." As though they said, If ye believe Him, this is that same Jesus, whom crucified, your feet stumbled, whom dead and buried, ye thought your hope lost. Lo, this is the same Jesus. He hath gone up before you, "He shall so come in like manner as ye have seen Him go into Heaven." His Body is removed indeed from your eyes, but God is not separated from your hearts: see Him going up, believe on Him absent, hope for Him coming; but yet through His secret Mercy, feel Him present. For He who ascended into Heaven that He might be removed from your eyes, promised unto you, saying, "Lo, I am with you always, even unto the end of the world." [7] Justly then the Apostle so addressed us, "The Lord is at hand; be careful for nothing." [8] Christ sitteth above the Heavens; the Heavens are far off, He who there sitteth is near. . . .

7. "Sing praises to our God, sing praises" (ver. 6). Whom as Man mocked they, who from God were alienated. "Sing praises to our God." For He is not Man only, but God. Man of the seed of David, [9] God the Lord of David, of the Jews having flesh. "Whose" (saith the Apostle) "are the fathers, of whom as concerning the flesh Christ came." [10] Of the Jews then is Christ, but according to the flesh. But who is this Christ who is of the Jews according to the flesh? "Who is over all, God blessed for ever." God before the flesh, God in the flesh, God with the flesh. Nor only God before the flesh, but God before the earth whence flesh was made; nor only God before the earth whereof flesh was made, but even God before the Heaven which was first made; God before the day which was first made; God before Angels; the same Christ is God: for "In the beginning was the Word, and the Word was with God, and the Word was God." [11]

8. "For God is the King of all the earth" (ver. 7). What? And before was He not God of all the earth? Is He not God of both heaven and earth, since by Him surely were all things made? Who can say that He is not his God? But not all men acknowledged Him their God; and where He was acknowledged, there only, so to say, He was God. "In Judah is God known." [12] Not yet was it said to the sons of Korah, "O clap your hands, all ye nations." For that God known in Judah, is King of all the earth: now by all He is acknowledged, for that is fulfilled which Isaiah saith, "He is thy God who hath

---

[1] Gen. xxv. 23.   [2] Rom. x. 3.   [3] Gen. xxv. 30–34.
[4] *Meruerat.*   [5] Acts vii. 39.   [6] Acts i. 11.

[7] Matt. xxviii. 20.   [8] Phil. iv. 5, 6.   [9] Rom. i. 3.
[10] Rom. ix. 5.   [11] John i. 1.   [12] Ps. lxxvi. 1.

delivered thee, the God of the whole earth shall He be called." [1] "Sing ye praises with understanding." He teacheth us and warneth us to sing praises with understanding, not to seek the sound of the ear, but the light of the heart. The Gentiles, whence ye were called that ye might be Christians, adored gods made with hands, and sang praises to them, but not with understanding. If they had sung with understanding, they had not adored stones. When a man sensible sang to a stone insensible, did he sing with understanding? But now, brethren, we see not with our eyes Whom we adore, and yet correctly [2] we adore.[3] Much more is God commended to us, that with our eyes we see Him not. If with our eyes we saw Him, haply we might despise. For even Christ seen, the Jews despised; unseen, the Gentiles adored.

9. "God shall reign over all nations" (ver. 8). Who reigned over one nation, "shall reign" (saith He) "over all nations." When this was said, God reigned over one nation. It was a prophecy, the thing was not yet shown. Thanks be to God, we now see fulfilled what before was prophesied. A written promise God sent unto us before the time, the time fulfilled He hath repaid us. "God shall reign over all nations," is a promise. "God sitteth upon His Holy Seat." What then was promised to come, now being fulfilled, is acknowledged and held. "God sitteth upon His Holy Seat." What is His Holy Seat? Haply saith one, The Heavens, and he understandeth well. For Christ hath gone up,[4] as we know, with the Body, wherein He was crucified, and sitteth at the right hand of the Father; thence we expect Him to come to judge the quick and the dead.[5] "God sitteth upon His Holy Seat." The Heavens are His Holy Seat. Wilt thou also be His Seat? think not that thou canst not be; prepare for Him a place in thy heart. He cometh, and willingly sitteth. The same Christ is surely "the Power of God, and the Wisdom of God:"[6] and what saith the Scripture of Wisdom Herself? The soul of the righteous is the seat of Wisdom.[7] If then the soul of the righteous is the seat of Wisdom, be thy soul righteous, and thou shalt be a royal seat of Wisdom. And truly, brethren, all men who live well, who act well, converse in godly charity, doth not God sit in them, and Himself command? Thy soul obeyeth God sitting in it, and itself commandeth the members. For thy soul commandeth thy members, that so may move the foot, the hand, the eye, the ear, and itself commandeth the members as

its servants, but yet itself serveth its Lord sitting within. It cannot well rule its inferior, unless its superior it have not disdained to serve.

10. "The princes of the peoples are gathered together unto the God of Abraham" (ver. 9). The God of Abraham, and the God of Isaac, and the God of Jacob.[8] True it is, God said this, and thereupon the Jews prided themselves, and said, "We are Abraham's children;"[9] priding themselves in their father's name, carrying his flesh, not holding his faith; by seed cleaving to Him, in manners degenerating. But the Lord, what said He to them so priding themselves? "If ye are Abraham's children, do the works of Abraham." [10] Again . . . "The princes of the peoples:" the princes of the nations: not the princes of one people, but the princes of all people have "gathered together unto the God of Abraham." Of these princes was that Centurion too, of whom but now when the Gospel was read ye heard. For he was a Centurion having honour and power among men, he was a prince among the princes of the peoples. Christ coming to him, he sent his friends to meet Him, nay unto Christ truly passing over to him he sent his friends, and asked that He would heal his servant who was dangerously sick. And when the Lord would come, he sent to Him this message : "I am not worthy that Thou shouldest enter under my roof, but say in a word only, and my servant shall be healed." "For I also am a man set under authority, having under me soldiers." [11] See how he kept his rank ! first he mentioned that he was under another, and afterwards that another was under him. I am under authority, and I am in authority; both under some I am, and over some I am. . . . As though he said, If I being set under authority command those who are under me, Thou who art set under no man's authority, canst not Thou command Thy creature, since all things were made by Thee, and without Thee was nothing made. "Say," then, said he, "in a word, and my servant shall be healed. For I am not worthy that Thou shouldest enter under my roof." . . . Admiring at his faith, Jesus reprobates the Jews' misbelief. For sound to themselves they seemed, whereas they were dangerously sick, when their Physician not knowing they slew. Therefore when He reprobated, and repudiated their pride, what said he? "I say unto you, that many shall come from the east and west," not belonging to the kindred of Israel: many shall come to whom He said, " O clap your hands, all ye nations;" "and shall sit down with Abraham, and Isaac, and Jacob, in the kingdom of heaven." Abraham begat them not of his own flesh; yet shall they come and

---

[1] Isa. liv. 5.
[2] *Correcti.* MS. Vat. ap. Ben. *corde recti*, "right in heart."
[3] [The adoration of the Host was unknown to the ancient Church. — C.]
[4] Acts i. 2.   [5] 2 Tim. iv. 1.   [6] 1 Cor. i. 24.
[7] Wisd. vii. 27.

[8] Exod. iii. 6.   [9] John viii. 33.   [10] John viii. 39.
[11] Luke vii. 6, 7.

sit down with him in the kingdom of heaven, and be his sons. Whereby his sons? Not as born of his flesh, but by following his faith. "But the children of the kingdom," that is, the Jews, "shall be cast into outer darkness, there shall be weeping and gnashing of teeth." [1] They shall be condemned to outer darkness who are born of the flesh of Abraham, and they shall sit down with him in the kingdom of heaven, who have imitated Abraham's faith.

11. And what they who belonged to the God of Abraham? "For the mighty gods of the earth are greatly lifted up." They who were gods, the people of God, the vineyard of God, whereof it is said, "Judge betwixt Me and My vineyard," [2] shall go into outer darkness, shall not sit down with Abraham, and Isaac, and Jacob, are not gathered unto the God of Abraham. Wherefore? "For the mighty gods of the earth;" they who were mighty gods of the earth, presuming upon earth. What earth? Themselves; for every man is earth. For to man was it said, "Dust thou art, and unto dust shalt thou return." [3] But man ought to presume upon God, and thence to hope for help, not from himself. For the earth raineth not upon itself, nor shineth for itself; but as the earth from heaven expecteth rain and light, so man from God ought to expect mercy and truth. They then, "the mighty gods of the earth, were greatly lifted up," that is, greatly prided themselves: they thought no physician necessary for themselves, and therefore remained in their sickness, and by their sickness were brought down even to death. The natural branches were broken off that the humble wild olive tree might be grafted in.[4] Hold we fast then, brethren, humility, charity, godliness: since we are called, on their proving reprobate, even by their example let us fear to pride ourselves.

PSALM XLVIII.[5]

1. The title of this Psalm is, "A song of praise, to the sons of Korah, on the second day of the week." Concerning this what the Lord deigneth to grant receive ye like sons of the firmament. For on the second day of the week, that is, the day after the first which we call the Lord's day, which also is called the second week-day, was made the firmament of Heaven.[6] . . . The second day of the week then we ought not to understand but of the Church of Christ: but the Church of Christ in the Saints, the Church of Christ in those who are written in Heaven, the Church of Christ in those who to this world's temptations yield not. For they are worthy of the name of "firmament." The Church of Christ, then, in those who are strong, of whom saith the Apostle, "We that are strong ought to bear the infirmities of the weak," [7] is called the firmament. Of this it is sung in this Psalm. Let us hear, acknowledge, associate, glory, reign. For Her called firmament, hear also in the Apostolic Epistles, "the pillar and firmament [8] of the truth." [9] . . .

2. "Great is the Lord, and greatly to be praised" (ver. 1). . . . That is, "in the city of our God, in His holy mountain." This is the city set upon an hill, which cannot be hid: this is the candle which is not hidden under a bushel,[10] to all known, to all proclaimed. Yet are not all men citizens thereof, but they in whom "great is the Lord, and greatly to be praised." What then is that city: let us see whether perhaps, since it is said, "In the city of our God, in His holy mountain," we ought not to enquire for this mountain where also we may be heard. . . . What then is that mountain, brethren? One is it with great care to be enquired for, with great solicitude investigated, with labour also to be occupied and ascended. But if in any part of the earth it is, what shall we do? Shall we go abroad out of our own country, that to that mountain we may arrive? Nay, then we are abroad, when in it we are not. For that is our city, if we are members of the King, who is the head of the same city. . . . For there was a certain corner-stone contemptible, whereat the Jews stumbled,[11] cut out of a certain mountain without hands, that is, coming of the kingdom of the Jews without hands, because human operation went not with Mary of whom was born Christ.[12] But if that stone, when the Jews stumbled thereat, had remained there, thou hadst not had whither to ascend. But what was done? What saith the prophecy of Daniel? What but that the stone grew, and became a great mountain? How great? So that it filled the whole face of the earth.[13] By growing, then, and by filling the whole face of the earth, that mountain came to us. Why then seek we the mountain as though absent, and not as being present ascend to it; that in us the Lord may be "great, and greatly to be praised"?

3. Further, . . . when he had said, "in the city of our God, in His holy mountain," what added he? "Spreading abroad the joys of the whole earth, the mountains of Sion" (ver. 2). Sion is one mountain, why then "mountains"? Is it that to Sion belonged also those which came from the other side, so as to meet together on the Corner Stone, and become two walls, as it were two mountains, one of the circumcision, the other of the uncircumcision; one of the

---

[1] Matt. viii. 12. [2] Isa. v. 3. [3] Gen. iii. 19.
[4] Rom. xi. 17. [5] Lat. XLVII. [6] Gen. i. 6-8.
[7] Rom. xv. 1. [8] E. V. "ground." [9] 1 Tim. iii. 15.
[10] Matt. v. 14, 15. [11] Rom. ix. 32. [12] Matt. i. 16.
[13] Dan. ii. 35.

Jews, the other of the Gentiles: no longer adverse, although diverse, because from different sides, now in the corner not even diverse. "For He is our peace, who hath made both one."[1] The same Corner Stone "which the builders rejected, is become the Head Stone of the corner."[2] The mountain hath joined in itself two mountains; one house there is, and two houses; two, because coming from different sides; one, because of the Corner Stone, wherein both are joined together. Hear also this, "the mountains of Sion: the sides of the North are the city of the great King." . . . See the Gentiles; "the sides of the North:" the sides of the North are joined to the city of the great King. The North is wont to be contrary to Sion: Sion forsooth is in the South, the North over against the South. Who is the North, but He who said, "I will sit in the sides of the North, I will be like the Most High"?[3] The devil had held dominion over the ungodly, and possessed the nations serving images, adoring demons; and all whatsoever there was of human kind anywhere throughout the world, by cleaving to Him, had become North. But since He who binds the strong man, taketh away his goods,[4] and maketh them His own goods; men delivered from infidelity and superstition of devils, believing in Christ, are fitted on to that city, have met in the corner that wall that cometh from the circumcision, and that was made the city of the great King, which had been the sides of the North. Therefore also in another Scripture is it said, "Out of the North come clouds of golden colour: great is the glory and honour of the Almighty."[5] For great is the glory of the physician, when from being despaired of the sick recovers. "Out of the North come clouds," and not black clouds, not dark clouds, not lowering, but "of golden colour." Whence but by grace illumined through Christ? See, "the sides of the North are the city of the great King." . . .

4. Let the Psalm then follow, and say, "God shall be known in her houses." Now in her "houses," because of the mountains, because of the two walls, because of the two sons. "God shall be known in her houses," but he commendeth grace, therefore he added, "when He shall take her up." For what would that city have been, unless He had taken her up? Would it not immediately have fallen, unless it had such foundation? For "other foundation can no man lay than that is laid, which is Jesus Christ."[6] Let none then glory in his own merits; but "he that glorieth, let him glory in the Lord."[7] . . . The Lord then hath taken up this city, and is known therein, that is, His grace is known in that city: for whatever that city hath, which glorieth in the Lord, it hath not of itself. For because of this it is said, "What hast thou that thou didst not receive?"[8]

5. "For, lo, the kings of the earth are gathered together" (ver. 3). Behold now those sides of the North, see how they come, see how they say, "Come ye, and let us go up to the mountain of the Lord: and He will teach us His way, and we will walk in it."[9] "And have come together in one." In what one, but that "corner-stone"?[10] "They saw it, and so they marvelled" (ver. 4). After their marvelling at the miracles and glory of Christ, what followed? "They were troubled, they were moved" (ver. 5), "trembling took hold upon them." Whence took trembling hold upon them, but from the consciousness of sins? Let them run then, kings after a king; kings, let them acknowledge the King. Therefore saith He elsewhere, "Yet have I been set by Him a King upon His holy hill of Sion."[11] . . . A King then was heard of, set up in Sion, to Him were delivered possessions even to the uttermost parts of the earth. Kings behoved to fear lest they should lose the kingdom, lest the kingdom be taken from them. As wretched Herod feared, and for the Child slew the children.[12] But fearing to lose his kingdom, he deserved not to know the King. Would that he too had adored the King with the Magi: not by ill-seeking the kingdom, slain the Innocents, and perished guilty. For as concerning him, he destroyed the Innocents: but as for Christ, even a Child, the children dying for Him did He crown. Therefore behoved kings to fear when it was said, "Yet have I been set a King by Him upon His holy hill of Sion," and inheritance to the uttermost parts of the earth shall He give Him, who set Him up King. . . . Thence also this is said to them, "Understand now therefore, O ye kings: be instructed, ye judges of the earth. Serve the Lord with fear, and rejoice unto Him with trembling."[13] And what did they? "There pains as of a woman in travail." What are the pains "as of a woman in travail," but the pangs of a penitent? See the same conception of pain and travail: "Of Thy fear" (saith Isaiah) "we have conceived, we have travailed of the Spirit of salvation."[14] So then the kings conceived from the fear of Christ, that by travailing they brought forth salvation by believing on Him whom they had feared. "There pains as of a woman in travail:" when of travail thou hearest, expect a birth. The old man travaileth, but the new man is born.

---

[1] Eph. ii. 14.   [2] Ps. cxviii. 22.   [3] Isa. xiv. 13, 14.
[4] Matt. xii. 29.   [5] Job xxxvii. 22.   [6] 1 Cor. iii. 11.
[7] 1 Cor. i. 31.

[8] 1 Cor. iv. 7.   [9] Isa ii. 3.   [10] Eph. ii. 20.
[11] Ps. ii. 6.   [12] Matt. ii. 16.
[13] Ps. ii. 10, 11.
[14] Isa. xxvi. 17, 18.

6. " With a strong wind Thou shalt break the ships of Tarshish " (ver. 6). Briefly understood, this is, Thou shalt overthrow the pride of the nations. But where in this history is mentioned the overthrowing of the pride of the nations? Because of "the ships of Tarshish." Learned men have enquired for Tarshish a city, that is, what city was signified by this name: and to some it has seemed that Cilicia is called Tarshish, because its metropolis is called Tarsus. Of which city was the Apostle Paul, being born in Tarsus of Cilicia.[1] But some have understood by it Carthage, being haply sometimes so named, or in some language so signified. For in the Prophet Isaiah it is thus found : " Howl, ye ships of Carthage." [2] But in Ezekiel [3] by some interpreters the word is translated Carthage, by some Tarshish : and from this diversity it can be understood that the same which was called Carthage, is called Tharsus. But it is manifest, that in the beginning of its reign Carthage flourished with ships, and so flourished, that among other nations they excelled in trafficking and navigation. For when Dido, flying from her brother, escaped to the parts of Africa, where she built Carthage, the ships which had been prepared for commerce in his country she had taken with her for her flight, the princes of the country consenting to it ; and the same ships also when Carthage was built failed not in traffic. And hence that city became too proud, so that justly by its ships may be understood the pride of the nations, presuming on things uncertain, as on the breath of the winds. Now let none presume on full sails, and on the seeming fair state of this life, as of the sea. Be our foundation in Sion : there ought we to be stablished, not to be " carried about with every wind of doctrine." [4] Whoso then by the uncertain things of this life had been puffed up, let them be overthrown, and be all the pride of the nations subjected to Christ, who shall " with a strong wind break all the ships of Tarshish : " not of any city, but of " Tarshish." How " with a strong wind "? With very strong fear. For so all pride feared Him that shall judge, as on Him humble to believe, lest Him exalted it should fear.

7. " As we have heard, so have we seen " (ver. 7). Blessed Church ! at one time thou hast heard, at another time thou hast seen. She heard in promises, seeth in performance : heard in Prophecy, seeth in the Gospel. For all things which are now fulfilled were before prophesied. Lift up thine eyes then, and stretch them over the world ; see now His " inheritance

even to the uttermost parts of the earth : " [5] see now is fulfilled what was said, " All kings shall fall down before Him : all nations shall serve Him : " [6] see fulfilled what was said, " Be Thou exalted, O God, above the heavens, and Thy glory above all the earth." [7] See Him whose feet and hands were pierced with nails, whose bones hanging on the tree were counted, upon whose vesture lots were cast : [8] see reigning whom they saw hanging ; see sitting in Heaven [9] whom they despised walking on earth : see thus fulfilled, " All the ends of the earth shall remember, and turn to the Lord, and all the kindreds of the nations shall worship before Him." Seeing all this, exclaim with joy, " As we have heard, so have we seen." Justly the Church herself is so called out of the Gentiles. . . . They to whom the Prophets were not sent, first heard and understood the Prophets : they who first heard not, afterwards hearing marvelled. They remained behind to whom they were sent, carrying books, understanding not the truth : having the tables of the Testament, and not holding the inheritance. But we, . . . " As we have heard, so have we seen." And where hearest thou ? where seest thou ? " In the city of the Lord of Hosts, in the city of our God. God hath founded it for ever." Let not heretics insult, divided into parties, let them not exalt themselves who say, " Lo, here is Christ, or lo, there." [10] Whoso saith, " Lo, here is Christ, or lo, there," inviteth to parties. Unity God promised. The kings are gathered together in one, not dissipated through schisms. But haply that city which hath held the world, shall sometime be overthrown ? Far be the thought ! " God hath founded it for ever." If then God hath founded it for ever, why fearest thou lest the firmament should fall?

8. " We have received Thy mercy, O God, in the midst of Thy people " (ver. 8). Who have received, and where received ? Hath not the same Thy people received Thy mercy. If Thy people hath received Thy mercy, how then, " in the midst of Thy people " ? As if they who received were one party, they in the midst of whom they received another. A great mystery, but yet well known. When hence also, that is, out of these verses, hath been extracted and brought forth what ye know, it will be not ruder, but sweeter. Now forsooth all are reckoned the people of God, who carry His Sacraments, but not all belong to His Mercy. All forsooth receiving the Sacrament of the Baptism of Christ, are called Christians, but not all live worthily of that Sacrament. There are some of whom saith the Apostle, " Having a form of godliness, but denying the power thereof." [11] Yet on account of

---

[1] Acts xxi. 39.
[2] So LXX.; Heb. *Tarshish*. Isa. xxiii 1.
[3] Ezek. xxxviii. 13. [Note the author's interest in all that bears upon his own field of labour. — C.]
[4] Eph. iv. 14.

[5] Ps. ii. 8. [6] Ps. lxxii. 11. [7] Ps. cviii. 5.
[8] Matt. xxvii. 35. [9] Matt. xxvi. 64. [10] Matt. xxiv. 23.
[11] 2 Tim. iii. 5.

this form of godliness they are named among God's people. As to the floor, until the corn is threshed, belongs not the wheat only, but the chaff. But will it also belong to the garner? In the midst then of an evil people is a good people, which hath received the Mercy of God. He liveth worthily of the Mercy of God who heareth, and holdeth, and doeth what the Apostle saith, "We beseech you that ye receive not the Grace of God in vain." [1] Whoso then receiveth not the Grace of God in vain, the same receiveth not only the Sacrament, but also the Mercy of God as well. . . . So those who have the Sacraments, and have not good manners, are both said to be of God, and not of God; are both said to be His, and to be strangers: His because of His own Sacraments, strangers because of their own vice. So also strange daughters: [2] daughters, because of the form of godliness; strange, because of their loss of virtue. Be the lily there; let it receive the Mercy of God: hold fast the root of a good flower, be not ungrateful for soft rain coming from heaven. Be thorns ungrateful, let them grow by the showers: for the fire they grow, not for the garner. In the midst of Thy people not receiving Thy mercy, we have received Thy mercy. For " He came unto His own, and His own received Him not," yet, in the midst of them, " as many as received Him, to them gave He power to become the sons of God." [3] . . . .

9. For when he had said, " We have received Thy mercy in the midst of Thy people," he signified that there is a people not receiving the mercy of God, in the midst of whom some do receive the mercy of God: and then lest it should occur to men that there are so few, as to be nearly none, how did He console them in the words following? " According to Thy Name, O God, so is Thy praise unto the ends of the earth" (ver. 9). What is this? . . . That is, as Thou art known through all the earth, so Thou art also praised through all the earth, nor are there wanting who now praise Thee through all the earth. But they praise Thee who live well. For, " According to Thy Name, O God, so is Thy praise," not in a part, but " unto the ends of the earth." " Thy right hand is full of righteousness." That is, many are they also who shall stand at Thy right hand. Not only shall they be many who shall stand at Thy left hand, but there also shall be a full heap set at Thy right hand.

10. " Let mount Zion rejoice, and the daughters of Judah be glad, because of Thy judgments, O Lord" (ver. 10). O mount Zion, O daughters of Judah, ye labour now among tares, among chaff, among thorns ye labour: yet be

glad because of God's judgments. God erreth not in judgment. Live ye separate, though separate ye were not born; not vainly hath a voice gone forth from your mouth and heart, " Destroy not my soul with sinners, nor my life with bloody men." [4] He shall winnow with such art, carrying in His hand a fan, that not one grain of wheat shall fall into the heap of chaff prepared to be burned, nor one beard of chaff pass to the heap to be laid up in the garner. [5] Be glad, O ye daughters of Judæa, because of the judgments of God that erreth not, and do not yet judge rashly. To you let it belong to collect, to Him let it belong to separate. But think not that the " daughters of Judah " are Jews. Judah is confession; all the sons of confession are all the sons of Judah. For " salvation is of the Jews," [6] is nothing else than that Christ is of the Jews. This saith also the Apostle, " He is not a Jew which is one outwardly; neither is that circumcision which is outward in the flesh : but he is a Jew which is one inwardly, and circumcision is that of the heart, in the spirit, and not in the letter, whose praise is not of men, but of God." [7] Be such a Jew; glory in the circumcision of the heart, though thou hast not the circumcision of the flesh. Let the daughters of Judah be glad, because of Thy judgments, O Lord.

11. " Walk about Zion, and embrace her " (ver. 11). Be it said to them who live ill, in the midst of whom is the people, which hath received the mercy of God. In the midst of you is a people living well, " Walk about Zion." But how? " embrace her." Not with scandals, but with love go round about her: that so those who live well in the midst of you ye may imitate, and by imitation of them, be incorporate with Christ, whose members they are. " Walk about Zion, go round about her : speak in the towers thereof." In the height of her bulwarks, set forth the praises thereof.

12. " Set your hearts upon her might " (ver. 12). Not that ye may have the form of godliness, deny the power thereof, [8] but, " upon her might set your hearts. Speak ye in her towers." What is the might of this city? Whoso would understand the might of this city, let him understand the force of love. That is a virtue which none conquereth. Love's flame no waves of the world, no streams of temptation, extinguish. Of this it is said, " Love is strong as death." [9] For as when death cometh, it cannot be resisted; by whatever arts, whatever medicines, you meet it; the violence of death can none avoid who is born mortal; so against the violence of love can the world do nothing. For from the contrary the similitude is made of

---

[1] 2 Cor. vi. 1.　　[2] Cant. ii. 2.　　[3] John i. 11, 12.

[4] Ps. xxvi. 9.　　[5] Matt. iii. 12.　　[6] John iv. 22.
[7] Rom. ii. 28, 29.　　[8] 2 Tim. iii. 5.　　[9] Cant. viii. 6.

death; for as death is most violent to take away, so love is most violent to save. Through love many have died to the world, to live to God; by this love inflamed, the martyrs, not pretenders, not puffed up by vain-glory, not such as they of whom it is written, "Though I give my body to be burned, and have not charity, it profiteth me nothing,"[1] but men whom truly a love of Christ and of the truth led on to this passion; what to them were the temptations of the tormentors? Greater violence had the eyes of their weeping friends, than the persecutions of enemies. For how many were held by their children, that they might not suffer? to how many did their wives fall upon their knees, that they might not be left widows? How many have their parents forbidden to die, as we know and read in the Passion of the Blessed Perpetua![2] All this was done; but tears, however great, and with whatever force flowing, when did they extinguish the ardour of love? This is the might of Sion, to whom elsewhere it is said, "Peace be within thy walls, and prosperity within thy palaces."[3]

13. What here understand we, "Set your hearts upon her might, and distribute her houses"? That is, distinguish house from house. Do not confound. For there is a house having the form of godliness, and not having godliness; but there is a house having both form and godliness. Distribute, confound not. But then ye distribute and confound not, when ye "set your hearts upon her might;" that is, when through love ye are made spiritual. Then ye will not judge rashly, then ye will see that the evil harms not the good as long as we are in this floor. "Distribute her houses." There can be also another understanding. The two houses, one coming of the circumcision, one of the uncircumcision, it is commanded the Apostles to distribute. For when Saul was called, and made the Apostle Paul, agreeing in unity with his fellow Apostles, he so with them determined, that they should go to the circumcision, he to the uncircumcision. By that dispensation of their Apostleship, they distributed the houses of the city of the great King; and meeting in the corner, divided the Gospel in dispensation, in love united it. And truly this is rather to be understood; for it followeth and showeth that it is here said to the preachers, "distribute her houses: that ye may tell it to the generation following:" that is, that even to us, who were to come after them, their dispensation of the Gospel should reach: For not for those only they laboured, with whom they lived in the earth; nor

the Lord for those Apostles only to whom He deigned to show Himself alive after His Resurrection, but for us also. For to them He spake, and signified us when He spake, "Lo, I am with you alway, even to the end of the world."[4] Were they then to be here alway, even to the end of the world? Also He said, "Neither pray I for these alone, but for them also which shall believe on Me through their word."[5] Therefore He considereth us, because He suffered on account of us. Justly then it is said, "That ye may tell it to the generation following."

14. Tell what? "For this is God, even our God" (ver. 13). The earth was seen, the earth's Creator was not seen; the flesh was held, God in the flesh was not acknowledged. For the flesh was held by those from whom had been taken the same flesh, for of the seed of Abraham was the Virgin Mary. At the flesh they stayed, the Divinity they did not understand. O Apostles, O mighty city, preach thou on the towers, and say, "This is God, even our God." So, even so as He was despised, as He lay a stone before the feet of the stumbling, that He might humble the hearts of the confessing; even so, "This is God, even our God." Certainly He was seen, as was said, "Afterward did He show Himself upon earth, and conversed with men."[6] "This is God, even our God." He is also Man, and who is there will know Him? "This is God, even our God." But haply for a time as the false gods. For because they can be called gods, but cannot be so, for a time they are even called so. For what saith the Prophet, or what warneth He to be said to them? This shall ye say to them, "The gods that have not made the heavens and the earth, even they shall perish from the earth, and from those that are under the heavens."[7] He is not such a god: for our God is above all gods. Above all what gods? "For all the gods of the nations are idols, but the Lord made the heavens."[8] The same then is our God. "This is God, even our God." For how long? "For ever and ever: He shall rule us for ever." If He is our God, He is also our King. He protecteth us, being our God, lest we die; He ruleth us, being our King, lest we fall. But by ruling us He doth not break us; for whom He ruleth not, He breaketh. "Thou shalt rule them," saith He, "with a rod of iron, and dash them in pieces like a potter's vessel."[9] But there are whom He ruleth not; these He spareth not, as a potter's vessel dashing them in pieces. By Him then let us wish to be ruled and delivered, "for He is our God for ever and ever, and He shall rule us for ever."

---

[1] 1 Cor. xiii. 3.
[2] Ruinart. Acta Martyrum, p. 86, which supports the reading adopted from the Oxford MSS. Ben. has, "How many parents did their sons forbid." [See A. N. F. vol. iii., p. 700.—C.]
[3] Ps. cxxii. 7.

[4] Matt. xxviii. 20.   [5] John xvii. 20.
[6] Baruch iii. 37.
[7] Jer. x. 11.
[8] Ps. xcvi. 5.
[9] Ps. ii. 9.

PSALM XLIX.[1]

The First Part.

1. . . . "Hear ye these things, all ye nations" (ver. 1). Not then you only who are here. For of what power is our voice so to cry out, as that all nations may hear? For Our Lord Jesus Christ hath proclaimed it through the Apostles, hath proclaimed it in so many tongues that He sent; and we see this Psalm, which before was only repeated in one nation, in the Synagogue of the Jews, now repeated throughout the whole world, throughout all Churches; and that fulfilled which is here spoken of, "Hear ye these words, all ye nations." . . . Of whom ye are: "With ears ponder, all ye that dwell in the world." This He seemeth to have repeated a second time, lest to have said "hear," before, were too little. What I say, he saith, "hear, with ears ponder," that is, hear not cursorily. What is, "with ears ponder"? It is what the Lord said, "he that hath ears to hear, let him hear:"[2] for as all who were in His presence must have had ears, what ears did He require save those of the heart, when He said, "he that hath ears to hear, let him hear"? The same ears also this Psalm doth smite. "With ears ponder, all ye that dwell in the world." Perhaps there is here some distinction. We ought not indeed to narrow our view, but there is no harm in explaining even this view of the sense. Perhaps there is some difference between the saying, "all nations," and the saying, "all ye that dwell in the world." For perchance he would have us understand the expression, "dwell in," with a further meaning, so as to take all nations for all the wicked, but the dwellers of the world all the just. For he doth inhabit who is not held fast: but he that is occupied is inhabited, and doth not inhabit. Just as he doth possess whatever he hath, who is master of his property: but a master is one who is not held in the meshes of covetousness: while he that is held fast by covetousness is the possessed, and not the possessor. . . .

2. Therefore let even the ungodly hear: "Hear ye this, all ye nations." Let the just also hear, who have not heard to no purpose, and who rather rule the world than are ruled by the world: "with ears ponder, all ye that dwell in the world."

3. And again he saith, "both all ye earthborn, and sons of men" (ver. 2). The expression "earthborn" he doth refer to sinners; the expression "sons of men" to the faithful and righteous. Ye see then that this distinction is observed. Who are the "earthborn"? The children of the earth. Who are the children of the earth? They who desire earthly inheritances.

Who are the "sons of men"? They who appertain to the Son of Man. We have already before explained this distinction to your Sanctity,[3] and have concluded that Adam was a man, but not the son of man; that Christ was the Son of Man, but was God also. For whosoever pertain to Adam, are "earthborn:" whosoever pertain to Christ, are "sons of men." Nevertheless, let all hear, I withhold my discourse from no one. If one is "earthborn," let him hear, because of the judgment: another is a "son of man," let him hear for the kingdom's sake. "The rich and poor together." Again, the same words are repeated. The expression "rich" refers to the "earthborn;" but the word "poor" to the "sons of men." By the "rich" understand the proud, by the "poor" the humble. . . . He saith in another Psalm, "The poor shall eat and be satisfied."[4] How hath he commended the poor? "The poor shall eat and be satisfied." What eat they? That Food which the faithful know. How shall they be satisfied? By imitating the Passion of their Lord, and not without cause receiving their recompense. "The poor shall eat and be satisfied, and they shall praise the Lord who seek Him." What of the rich? Even they eat. But how eat they? "All the rich upon the earth have eaten and worshipped."[5] He said not, "Have eaten and are satisfied;" but, "have eaten and worshipped." They worship God indeed, but they will not display brotherly humaneness. These eat and worship; those eat and are filled: yet both eat. Of the eater what he eateth is required: let him not be forbidden by the distributor to eat, but let him be admonished to fear him who doth require his account. Let these words then be heard by sinners and righteous, nations, and those who inhabit the world, "earthborn and sons of men, the rich and the poor together:" not divided, not separated. That is for the time of the harvest to do, the hand of the winnower will effect that.[6] Now together let rich and poor hear, let goats and sheep feed in the same pasture, until He come who shall separate the one on His right hand, the other on His left.[7] Let them all hear together the teacher, lest separated from one another they hear the voice of the Judge.

4. And what is it they are now to hear? "My mouth shall speak of wisdom, and the meditation of my heart understanding" (ver. 3). And this repetition is perhaps made, lest perchance if he had said only "my mouth," thou shouldest suppose that one spake to thee who had understanding but in his lips. For many have understanding in their lips, but have not in their heart, of whom the Scripture saith, "This people honoureth me with their lips, but their heart

---

1 Lat. XLVIII. [From a sermon preached before a bishop.]
2 Matt. xi. 15.

3 On Ps. viii.   4 Ps. xxii. 26.   5 Ps. xxii. 29.
6 Matt. iii. 12.   7 Matt. xxv. 32.

is far from me." [1] What saith he then who speaketh to thee? when he hath said, "My mouth shall speak of wisdom," in order that thou mayest know that what is poured forth from the mouth floweth from the bottom of the heart, he hath added, "And the meditation of my heart of understanding."

5. "I will incline mine ear to the parable, I will show my proposition upon the harp" (ver. 4). . . . And why "to a parable"? Because "now we see through a glass darkly," [2] as saith the Apostle; "whilst we are at home in the body, we are absent from the Lord." [3] For our vision is not yet that face to face, where there are no longer parables, where there no longer are riddles and comparisons. Whatever now we understand we behold through riddles. A riddle is a dark parable which it is hard to understand. Howsoever a man may cultivate his heart and apply himself to apprehend mysteries, so long as we see through the corruption of this flesh, we see but in part. . . . But as He was seen by those who believed, and by those who crucified Him, when He was judged; so will He be seen, when He shall have begun to be judge, both by those whom He shall condemn, and by those whom He shall crown. But that vision of divinity, which He hath promised to them that love Him, when He saith, "He that loveth Me shall be loved of My Father, and he that loveth Me keepeth My commandments, and I will love him, and will manifest Myself to him:" [4] this the ungodly shall not see. This manifestation is in a certain way familiar: He keepeth it for His own, He will not show it to the ungodly. Of what sort is the vision itself? Of what sort is Christ? Equal to the Father. Of what sort is Christ? "In the beginning was the Word, and the Word was with God, and the Word was God." [5] For this vision we sigh now, and groan so long as we sojourn here; to this vision we shall be brought home at the last, this vision now we see but darkly. If then we see now darkly, let us "incline our ear to the parable," and then let us "show our proposition upon the harp:" [6] let us hear what we say, do what we enjoin.

6. And what hath he said? "And wherefore shall I fear in the evil day? The iniquity of my heel shall compass me" (ver. 5). He beginneth something obscurely. Therefore he ought the rather to fear if the iniquity of his heel shall compass him. Nay, for let not man fear, he saith, who hath not power to escape. For example, he who feareth death, what shall he do to escape death? Let him tell me how

he is to escape what Adam oweth, he who is born of Adam. But let him consider that he is born of Adam, and hath followed Christ, and ought to pay what Adam oweth, and obtain what Christ hath promised. Therefore, he who feareth death can no wise escape: but he who feareth the damnation which the ungodly shall hear, "Go ye into everlasting fire," [7] hath an escape. Let him not fear then. For why should he fear? Will the iniquity of his heel compass him? If then he avoid "the iniquity of his heel," and walk in the ways of God, he shall not come to the evil day: the evil day, the last day, shall not be evil to him. . . . Now while they live, let them take heed to themselves, let them put away iniquity from their heel: let them walk in that way, let them walk in the way of which He saith Himself, "I am the way, the truth, and the life:" [8] and let them not fear in the evil day, for He giveth them safety who became "The Way." Therefore let them avoid the iniquity of their heel. With the heel a man slippeth. Let your Love observe. What was said by God to the Serpent? "She shall mark thy head, and thou shalt mark her heel." [9] The devil marketh thy heel, in order that when thou slippest he may overthrow thee. He marketh thy heel, do thou mark his head. What is his head? The beginning of an evil suggestion. When he beginneth to suggest evil thoughts, then do thou thrust him away before pleasure ariseth, and consent followeth; and so shalt thou avoid his head, and he shall not grasp thy heel. But wherefore said He this to Eve? Because through the flesh man doth slip. Our flesh is an Eve within us. "He that loveth his wife," he saith, "loveth himself." What meaneth "himself"? He continueth, and saith, "For no man ever yet hath hated his own flesh." [10] Because then the devil would make us slip through the flesh, just as he made that man Adam to slip, through Eve; Eve is bidden to mark the head of the devil, because the devil marketh her heel. [11] "If then the iniquity of our heel shall compass us, why fear we in the evil day," since being converted to Christ we are able not to do iniquity; and there will be nothing to compass us, and we shall joy and not sorrow in the last day?

7. But who are they whom the "iniquity of their heel shall compass"? "They who trust in their virtue," [12] and in the abundance of their riches do glory" (ver. 6). Therefore such sins

---

[1] Isa. xxix. 13.   [2] 1 Cor. xiii. 12.   [3] 2 Cor. v. 6.
[4] John xiv. 21.   [5] John i. 1.
[6] [He explains "the harp" elsewhere as the body, used by the soul "as the harper useth the harp"; and see p. 139, *supra*. — C.]

[7] Matt. xxv. 41.   [8] John xiv. 6.
[9] Gen. iii. 15. ["She shall mark," etc. So the Vulgate, but not in the older editions. The Septuagint is conclusive as to the ancient exposition of the Jews, for the *neuter* (σπέρμα) had a masculine pronoun (αὐτός) as nominative to the verb. So Jerome, *Dominus noster conteret Satanam*. It is noteworthy that our author attaches no such force to his reading as Mariolatry demands. — C.]
[10] Eph. v. 28, 29.
[11] [See Hippolytus, A. N. F. vol. v. p. 166. — C.]
[12] Or, "might" (*virtute*).

will I avoid, and the "iniquity of my heel" shall never compass me. What is avoiding such sins? Let us not trust in our own virtue, let us not glory in the abundance of our own riches, but let us glory in Him who hath promised to us, being humble, exaltation, and hath threatened condemnation to men exalted; and then iniquity of our heel shall never compass us.

8. There are some who rely on their friends, others rely on their virtue, others on their riches. This is the presumption of mankind which relieth not on God. He hath spoken of virtue, he hath spoken of riches, he speaketh of friends. "Brother redeemeth not,[1] shall man redeem?" (ver. 7). Dost thou expect that man shall redeem thee from the wrath to come? If brother redeem thee not, shall man redeem thee? Who is the brother, who if He hath not redeemed thee, no man will redeem? It is He who said after His resurrection, "Go, tell My brethren."[2] Our Brother He hath willed to be: and when we say to God, "Our Father," this is manifested in us. For he that saith to God, "Our Father;" saith to Christ, "Brother."[3] Therefore let him that hath God for his Father and Christ for his Brother, not fear in the evil day. "For the iniquity of his heel shall not compass him;" for he relieth not on his virtue, nor glorieth in the abundance of his riches, nor vaunteth himself cf his powerful friends. Let him rely on Him who died for him, that he might not die eternally: who for his sake was humbled, in order that he might be exalted; who sought him ungodly, in order that He might be sought by him faithful. Therefore if He redeem not, shall man redeem? Shall any man redeem, if the Son of man redeem not? If Christ redeem not, shall Adam redeem? "Brother redeemeth not, shall man redeem?"[4]

9. "He shall not give to God his propitiation, and the price of the redemption of his soul" (ver. 8). He trusteth in his virtue, and in the abundance of his riches doth glory, who "shall not give to God his propitiation:" that is, satisfaction whereby he may prevail with God for his sins: "nor the price of the redemption of his soul," who relieth on his virtue, and on his friends, and on his riches. But who are they that give the price of the redemption of their souls? They to whom the Lord saith, "Make to yourselves friends of the Mammon of unrighteousness, that they may receive you into everlasting habitations."[5] They give the price of the redemption of their soul who cease not to do almsdeeds. So those whom the Apostle chargeth by Timothy

he would not have to be proud, lest they should glory in the abundance of their riches. Lastly, what they possessed he would not have to grow old in their hands: but that something should be made of it to be for the price of the redemption of their souls. For he saith, "Charge them that are rich in this world, that they be not highminded: nor trust in uncertain riches, but in the living God, who giveth us richly all things to enjoy."[6] And as if they had said, "What shall we then make of our riches?" he continueth, "Let them be rich in good works, ready to distribute, willing to communicate,"[7] and they will not lose that. How know we? Hear what followeth. "Let them lay up for themselves a good foundation against the time to come, that they may lay hold on the true life."[8] So shall they give the price of the redemption of their soul. And our Lord counselleth this: "Make for yourselves bags which wax not old, a treasure in the heavens that faileth not, where thief approacheth not, neither moth corrupteth."[9] God would not have thee lose thy wealth, but He hath given thee counsel to change the place thereof. Let your love understand. Suppose thy friend were just now to enter thy house, and find thou hadst placed thy store of grain in a damp place, and he knew the natural proneness of grain to decay, which thou perchance knewest not, he would give thee counsel of this sort, saying, "Brother, thou art losing what with great toil thou hast gathered, thou hast placed it in a damp place, in a few days this grain will decay." "And what am I to do, brother?" "Raise it into a higher place." Thou wouldest hearken to thy friend suggesting that thou shouldest raise grain from a lower to a higher chamber, and dost thou not hearken to Christ charging thee to lift thy treasure from earth to heaven, where not what thou keepest in store may be paid to thee, but that thou mayest keep in store·earth, mayest receive heaven, mayest keep in store things mortal, mayest receive things everlasting, that while thou lendest Christ to receive at thy hands but a small loan upon earth, He may repay thee a great recompense in Heaven? Nevertheless, they whom "the iniquity of their heel shall compass," because they trust in their virtue, and in the abundance of their riches do glory, and rely on human friends who are able to help them in nothing, "shall not give to God their propitiation, and the price of the redemption of their souls."

10. And what hath he said of such a man? "Yea, he hath laboured for ever, and shall live till the end" (ver. 9). His labour shall be without end, his life shall have an end. Wherefore saith he, "He shall live till the end"? Because

---

[1] Oxf. MSS. "hath not redeemed," and so through the paragraph.
[2] Matt. xxviii. 10.
[3] See on St. John, Hom. xxi. § 3.
[4] [The Latin versions do not divide into verses such as our author seems to have made.—C.]
[5] Luke xvi. 9.

[6] 1 Tim. vi. 17.　　[7] 1 Tim. vi. 18.　　[8] 1 Tim. vi. 19.
[9] Luke xii. 33.

such men think life to be nought but daily enjoyments. So when many poor and needy men of our times, unstable, and not looking to what God doth promise them for their labours, see rich men in daily feastings, in the splendour and glitter of gold and of silver, they say what? "These are the only people;[1] they really live!" This is a saying, be it said no longer: we both warn you, and it remains to warn you, that it be said by fewer persons than it would be said, if we had not warned you. For we do not presume to say that we so say these words, as that it be not said, but that it be said by fewer persons: for it will be said even unto the end of the world. It is too little that he saith, "he liveth;" he addeth and saith, he thundereth, thinkest thou that he alone liveth? Let him live! his life will be ended: because he giveth not the price of the redemption of his soul, his life will end, his labour will not end. "He laboured for ever, and shall live till the end." How shall he live till the end? As he lived that was "clothed with purple and fine linen, and fared sumptuously every day,"[2] who, being proud and puffed up, spurned the man full of sores lying before his gate, whose sores the dogs licked, and who longed for the crumbs which fell from his table. What did those riches profit him? Both changed places: the one was borne from the rich man's gate into Abraham's bosom, the other from his rich feasts was cast into the fire; the one was in peace, the other burned; the one was sated, the other thirsted; the one had laboured till the end, but he lived for ever; the other had lived till the end, but he laboured for ever. And what did it profit the rich man, who asked, while lying in torments in hell, that a drop of water should be poured upon his tongue from the finger of Lazarus, saying, "For I am burning here in this flame,"[3] and it was not granted to him? One longed for the drop from the finger, as the other had for the crumbs from the rich man's table; but the labour of the one is ended, and the life of the other is ended: the labour of this is for ever, the life of that is for ever. We who labour perchance here on the earth, have not our life here: and shall not be so placed hereafter, for our life shall be Christ for ever: while they who "will" have their life here, shall labour for ever and live till the end.

11. "For he shall not see death, though he shall have seen wise men dying" (ver. 10). The man who laboured for ever and shall live till the end, "shall not see death, though he shall have seen wise men dying." What is this? He shall not comprehend what death is, whenever he shall have seen wise men dying. For he saith to himself, "this fellow, for all he was wise and

dwelled with wisdom and worshipped God with piety, is he not dead? Therefore I will enjoy myself while I live; for if they that are wise in other respects, could do anything, they would not have died." Just as the Jews saw Christ hanging on the Cross and despised Him, saying, "If this Man were the Son of God, He would come down from the Cross:"[4] not seeing what death is. If they had seen what death is; if they had seen, I say.[5] He died for a time, that He might live again for ever: they lived for a time, that they might die for ever. But because they saw Him dying, they saw not death, that is to say, they understood not what was very death. What say they even in Wisdom? "Let us condemn Him with a most shameful death, for by His own sayings He shall be respected;"[6] for if he is indeed the Son of God, He will deliver Him from the hands of His adversaries: He will not suffer His Son to die, if He is truly His Son. But when they saw themselves insulting Him upon the Cross, and Him not descending from the Cross, they said, He was indeed but a Man. Thus was it spoken: and surely He could have come down from the Cross, He that could rise again from the tomb: but He taught us to bear with those who insult us; He taught us to be patient of the tongues of men, to drink now the cup of bitterness, and afterwards to receive everlasting salvation. . . .

12. "The imprudent and unwise shall perish together." Who is "the imprudent"? He that looketh not out for himself for the future. Who is "the unwise"? He that perceiveth not in what evil case he is. But do thou perceive in what evil case thou art now, and look out that thou be in a good case for the future. By perceiving in what evil case thou art, thou wilt not be unwise: by looking out for thyself for the future, thou wilt not be imprudent. Who is that looketh out for himself? That servant to whom his master gave what he should expend, and afterwards said to him, "Thou canst not be my steward, give an account of thy stewardship;" and who answered, "What shall I do? I cannot dig, to beg I am ashamed;"[7] had, nevertheless, by even his master's goods made to himself friends, who might receive him when he was put out of his stewardship. Now he cheated his master in order that he might get to himself friends to receive him: fear not thou lest thou be cheating, the Lord Himself exhorteth thee to do so: He saith Himself to thee, "Make to thyself friends of the mammon of unrighteousness."[8] Perhaps what thou hast got, thou hast gotten of

1 *Soli sunt isti.*   2 Luke xvi. 19.   3 Luke xvi. 24.

4 Matt. xxvii. 40, 42.   5 *Al.* "if they had seen themselves."
6 Wisd. ii. 20. [The Jews, *even in their own book* of Wisdom, show what they did to "the Just One." The whole passage is so remarkable, that we need not wonder at the esteem in which this book was held by the Fathers. St. James (v. 6) seems to refer to this passage. — C.]
7 Luke xvi. 1, 2, etc.   8 Luke xvi. 9.

unrighteousness: or perhaps this very thing is unrighteousness, that thou hast and another hath not, thou aboundest and another needeth. Of this mammon of unrighteousness, of these riches which the unrighteous call riches, make to thyself friends, and thou shalt be prudent: thou art gaining for thyself, and art not cheating. For now thou seemest to lose it. Wilt thou lose it if thou place it in a treasury? For boys, my brethren, no sooner find some money, wherewith to buy something, than they put it in a money-box,[1] which they open not until afterwards: do they, because they see not what they have got, on that account lose it? Fear not: boys put in a money-box, and are secure: dost thou place it in the hand of Christ, and fear? Be prudent, and provide for thyself against the future in Heaven. Be therefore prudent, copy the ant, as saith the Scripture:[2] "Store in summer, lest thou hunger in winter;" the winter is the last day, the day of tribulation; the winter is the day of offences and of bitterness: gather what may be there for thee for the future: but if thou doest not so, thou wilt perish both imprudent and unwise.

13. But that rich man[3] too died, and a like funeral was made for him. See to what men have brought themselves: they regard not what a wicked life he led while he lived, but what pomp followed him when he died! O happy he, whom so many lament! But the other lived in such sort, that few lament. For all ought to lament a man living so sadly. But there is the funeral train; he is received in a costly tomb, he is wound in costly robes, he is buried in perfumes and spices. Secondly, what a monument he hath! How marbled! Doth he live in that same monument? He is therein dead. Men deeming these to be good things, have strayed from God, and have not sought the true good things, and have been deceived with the false. To this end see what followeth. He who gave not the price of the redemption of his soul, who understood not death, because he saw wise men dying, he became imprudent and unwise, in order that he might die with them. And how shall they perish, who "shall leave their riches to aliens"? . . .

14. But do those same aliens indeed serve them who are called their own? Hear in what they serve them, observe how they are ridiculed: why hath he said, "to strangers"? Because they can do them no good. Nevertheless, wherein do they seem to themselves to do good? "And their tombs shall be their house for ever" (ver. 11). Now because these tombs are erected, the tombs are a house. For often thou hearest a rich man saying, I have a house of marble

which I must quit, and I think not for myself of an eternal house, where I shall alway be. When he thinketh to make for himself a monument of marble or of sculpture, he is deeming as it were of an eternal house: as if therein this rich man would abide! If he would abide there, he would not burn in hell. We must consider that the place where the spirit of an evil doer abideth, is not where the mortal body is laid: but "their tombs shall be their house for ever. Their dwelling places are from generation to generation." "Dwelling places" are wherein they abode for a season: "house" is wherein they will abide as it were for ever, that is to say, their tombs. Thus they leave their dwelling places, where they abode while they lived, to their families, and they pass as it were to everlasting houses, to their tombs. What profit to them are "their dwelling places, from generation to generation"? Now suppose a generation and generation are sons, grandsons there will be, and great grandsons; what do their dwelling places, what do they profit them? What? Hear: "they shall invoke their names in their lands." What is this? They shall take bread and wine to their tombs, and there they shall invoke the names of the dead. Dost thou consider how loudly was invoked the name of the rich man after his death, when men drank them drunk at his monument, and there came down not one drop upon his own burning tongue? Men minister to their own belly, not to the ghosts of their friends. The souls of the dead nothing doth reach, but what they have done of themselves while alive: but if they have done nought of themselves while alive, nothing doth reach them dead. But what do the survivors? They will but "invoke their names in their lands."

15. "And man though he was in honour perceived not, he was compared to the beasts without sense, and was made like to them" (ver. 12). . . . They ought, on the contrary, to have made ready for themselves an eternal house in good works, to have made ready for themselves everlasting life, to have sent before them expenditure, to have followed their works, to have ministered to a needy companion, to have given to him with whom they were walking, not to have despised Christ covered with sores before their gate, who hath said, "Inasmuch as ye have done it unto one of the least of these My brethren, ye have done it unto Me."[4] However, "man being in honour hath not understood." What is, "being in honour"? Being made after the image and likeness of God, man is preferred to beasts. For God hath not so made man as He made a beast: but God hath made man for beasts to minister to: is it to his strength then, and not to his

---

[1] *Thesaurario.*　　[2] Prov. vi. 8, xxx. 25.　　[3] Luke xvi. 22.　　[4] Matt. xxv. 40.

understanding? Nay. But he "understood not;" and he who was made after the image of God, "is compared to the beasts without sense, and is made like unto them." Whence it is said elsewhere, "Be ye not like to horse and mule, in which there is no understanding."[1]

16. "This their own way is an offence to them" (ver. 13). Be it an offence to them, not to thee. But when will it be so to thee too? If thou thinkest such men to be blessed. If thou perceivest that they be not blessed, their own way will be an offence to themselves; not to Christ, not to His Body, not to His members. "And afterwards they shall bless with their mouth." What meaneth, "Afterwards they shall bless with their mouth"? Though they have become such, that they seek nothing but temporal goods, yet they become hypocrites: and when they bless God, with lips they bless, and not with heart. Christians like these, when to them eternal life is commended, and they are told, that in the name of Christ they ought to be despisers[2] of riches, do make grimaces in their hearts: and if they dare not do it with open face, lest they blush, or lest they should be rebuked by men, yet they do it in heart, and scorn; and there remaineth in their mouth blessing, and in their heart cursing.

The Second Part.

1. "Like sheep laid in hell, death is their shepherd" (ver. 14). Whose? Of those whose way is a stumbling-block to themselves. Whose? Of those who mind only things present, while they think not of things future: of those who think not of any life, but of that which must be called death. Not without cause, then, like sheep in hell, have they death to their shepherd. What meaneth, "they have death to their shepherd"? For is death either some thing or some power? Yea, death is either the separation of the soul from the body, or a separation of the soul from God,[3] and that indeed which men fear is the separation of the soul from the body: but the real death, which men do not fear, is the separation of the soul from God. And ofttimes when men fear that which doth separate the soul from the body, they fall into that wherein the soul is separated from God. This then is death. But how is "death their shepherd"? If Christ is life, the devil is death. But we read in many places in Scripture, how that Christ is life. But the devil is death, not because he is himself death, but because through him is death. For whether that (death) wherein Adam fell was given man to drink by the persuasion of him: or whether that wherein the soul is separated from the body, still they have him for the author thereof, who first falling through pride envied him who stood,

and overthrew him who stood with an invisible death, in order that he might have to pay[4] the visible death. They who belong to him have death to their shepherd: but we who think of future immortality, and not without reason do wear the sign of the Cross of Christ on the forehead, have no shepherd but life. Of unbelievers death is the shepherd, of believers life is the shepherd. If then in hell are the sheep, whose shepherd is death, in heaven are the sheep, whose shepherd is life. What then? Are we now in heaven? In heaven we are by faith. For if not in heaven, where is the "Lift up your heart"? If not in heaven, whence with the Apostle Paul, "For our conversation is in heaven"?[5] In body we walk on earth, in heart we dwell in heaven. We dwell there, if thither we send anything which holdeth us there. For no one dwelleth in heart, save where thought is: but there his thought is, where his treasure is. He hath treasured on earth, his heart doth not withdraw from earth: he hath treasured in heaven, his heart from heaven doth not come down: for the Lord saith plainly, "Where thy treasure is, there will thy heart be also."[6]

2. They, then, whose shepherd is death, seem to flourish for a time, and the righteous to labour: but why? Because it is yet night. What meaneth, it is night? The merits of the righteous appear not, and the felicity of the unrighteous hath, as it were, a name. So long as it is winter, grass appeareth more verdant than a tree. For grass flourisheth through the winter, a tree is as it were dry through the winter: when in summer time the sun hath come forth with greater heat, the tree, which seemed dry through the winter, is bursting with leaves, and putteth forth fruits, but the grass withereth: thou wilt see the honour of the tree, the grass is dried. So also now the righteous labour, before that summer cometh. There is life in the root, it doth not yet appear in the branches. But our root is love. And what saith the Apostle? That we ought to have our root above, in order that life may be our shepherd, because our dwelling ought not to quit heaven, because in this earth we ought to walk as if dead; so that living above, below we may be dead; not so as that being dead above, we may live below. . . . Our labour shall appear in the morning, and there shall be fruit in the morning: so that they that now labour shall hereafter reign, and they that now boast them and are proud, shall hereafter be brought under. For what followeth? "Like sheep laid in hell, death is their shepherd; and the righteous shall reign over them in the morning."

3. Endure thou the night, yearn for the morning. Think not because the night hath

---

[1] Ps. xxxii. 9.   [2] Most MSS. "there should be a despising."
[3] Oxf. MSS. add, "or a separation of the soul from God."

[4] Al. "destroy him with the visible death."
[5] Philip. iii. 20.   [6] Matt. vi. 12.

life, the morning too hath not life. Doth then he that sleepeth live, and he that riseth live not? Is not he that sleepeth more like death?[1] And who are they that sleep? They whom the Apostle Paul rouseth, if they choose but to awake. For to certain he saith, "Awake, thou that sleepest, and arise from the dead, and Christ shall give thee light."[2] They then that are lightened by Christ watch now, but the fruit of their watchings appeareth not yet: in the morning it shall appear, that is, when doubtful things of this world shall have passed away. For these are very night: for do they not appear to thee like darkness? . . . But they on whom men have trampled, and who were ridiculed for believing, shall hear from Life Itself, whom they have for shepherd, "Come, ye blessed of My Father, receive the kingdom which was prepared for you from the foundation of the world." Therefore the righteous "shall reign over them," not now, but "in the morning." Let no one say, Wherefore am I a Christian? I rule no one,[3] I would rule the wicked. Be not in haste, thou shalt reign, but "in the morning." "And the help of them shall grow old in hell from their glory." Now they have glory, in hell they shall grow old. What is "the help of them"? Help from money, help from friends, help from their own might. But when a man shall be dead, "in that day shall perish all his thoughts."[4] How great glory he seemed to have among men, while he lived, so great oldness and decay of punishments shall he have, when he shall be dead in hell.

4. "Nevertheless, God shall redeem my soul" (ver. 15). Behold the voice of one hoping in the future: "Nevertheless, God shall redeem my soul."[5] Perhaps it is the voice of one still wishing to be relieved from oppression. Some one is in prison, he saith, "God shall redeem my soul:" some one is in bond, "God shall redeem my soul:" some one is suffering peril by sea, is being tossed by waves and raging tempests, what saith he? "God shall redeem my soul." They would be delivered for the sake of this life. Not such is the voice of this man. Hear what followeth: "God shall redeem my soul from the hand of hell, when He shall have received me." He is speaking of this redemption, which Christ now showeth in Himself. For He hath descended into hell, and hath ascended into heaven. What we have seen in the Head we have found in the Body. For what we have believed in the Head, they that have seen, have themselves told us, and by themselves we have seen: "For we are" all

"one body."[6] But are they better that hear, we worse to whom it hath been told? Not so saith The Life Itself, Our Shepherd Himself. For He rebuketh a certain disciple of His, doubting and desiring to handle His scars, and when he had handled the scars and had cried out, saying, "My Lord and my God,"[7] seeing His disciple doubting, and looking to the whole world about to believe, "Because thou hast seen Me," He saith, "thou hast believed: blessed are they that see not, and believe." "But God shall redeem my soul from the land of hell, when He hath received me." Here then what? Labour, oppression, tribulation, temptation: expect nothing else. Where joy? In future hope. . . .

5. . . . Perchance thy heart saith, Wretch that I am, I suppose to no purpose I have believed, God doth not regard things human. God therefore doth awaken us: and He saith what? "Fear not, though a man have become rich" (ver. 16). For why didst thou fear, because a man hath become rich? Thou didst fear that thou hadst believed to no purpose, that perchance thou shouldest have lost the labour for thy faith, and the hope of thy conversion: because perchance there hath come in thy way gain with guilt, and thou couldest have been rich, if thou hadst seized upon that same gain with the guilt, and neededst not have laboured; and thou, remembering what God hath threatened, hast refrained from guilt, and hast contemned the gain: thou seest another man that hath made gain by guilt, and hath suffered no harm; and thou fearest to be good. "Fear not," saith the Spirit of God to thee, "though a man shall have become rich." Wouldest thou not have eyes but for things present? Things future He hath promised, who hath risen again; peace in this world, and repose in this life, He hath not promised. Every man doth seek repose; a good thing he is seeking, but not in the proper region thereof he is seeking it. There is no peace in this life; in Heaven hath been promised that which on earth we are seeking: in the world to come hath been promised that which in this world we are seeking.

6. "Fear not, though a man be made rich, and though the glory of his house be multiplied." Wherefore "fear not"? "For when he shall die, he shall not receive anything" (ver. 17). Thou seest him living, consider him dying. Thou markest what he hath here, mark what he taketh with him. What doth he take with him? He hath store of gold, he hath store of silver, numerous estates, slaves: he dieth, these remain, he knoweth not for whom. For though he leaveth them for whom he will, he keepeth them not for whom he will. For many

---

[1] Or, "a dead person."
[2] Eph. v. 14.
[3] Most MSS. omit, "I rule no one." See Ser. 72, ad. Fr. in Erem.
[4] Ps. cxlvi. 4.　　[5] [Compare ver. 7, p. 171, *supra.* — C.]
[6] Rom. xii. 5.　　　　[7] John xx. 28.

have gained even what was not left them, and many have lost what was left them. All these things then remain, and he taketh with him what? Perhaps some one saith, He taketh that with him in which he is wound, and that which is expended upon him for a costly and marble tomb. to erect a monument, this he taketh with him. I say, not even this. For these things are presented to him without his feeling them. If thou deckest a man sleeping and not awake, he hath the decorations with him on the couch: perhaps the decorations are resting upon the body of him as he lieth, and perhaps he seeth himself in tatters during sleep. What he feeleth is more to him than what he feeleth not. Though even this when he shall have awaked will not be: yet to him sleeping, that which he saw in sleep was more than that which he felt not. Why then, brethren, should [1] men say to themselves, Let money be spent at my death: why do I leave my heirs rich? Many things will they have of mine, let me too have something of my own for my body. What shall a dead body have? what shall rotting flesh have? what shall flesh not feeling have? If that rich man had anything, whose tongue was dry, then man hath something of his own. My brethren, do we read in the Gospel, that this rich man appeared in the fire with all-silken and fine-linen coverings? Was he of such sort in hell as he was in feastings at table? When he thirsted and desired a drop, all those things were not there. Therefore man carrieth not with him anything, nor doth the dead take with him that which the burial taketh. For where feeling is, there is the man; where is no feeling, the man is not. There lieth fallen the vessel which contained the man, the house which held the man. The body let us call the house, the spirit let us call the inhabitant of the house. The spirit is tormented in hell: what doth it profit him, that the body lieth in spices and perfumes, wound in costly linens? just as if the master of the house should be sent into banishment, and thou shouldest garnish the walls of his house. He in banishment is in need, and doth faint with hunger, he scarce findeth to himself one hovel where he may snatch a sleep, and thou sayest, "Happy is he, for his house hath been garnished." Who would not judge that thou wast either jesting or wast mad? Thou dost garnish the body, the spirit is tormented. Give something to the spirit, and ye have given something to the dead man. But what wilt thou give him, when he desired one drop, and received not? For the man scorned to send before him anything. Wherefore scorned? "because this their way is a stumbling-block to them." [2] He minded not any

but the present life, he thought not but how he might be buried, wound in costly vestments. His soul was taken from him, as the Lord saith: "Thou fool, this night thy soul shall be taken from thee, and whose shall those things be which thou hast provided?" [3] And that is fulfilled which this Psalm saith: "Fear not, though a man be made rich, and though the glory of his house be multiplied: for when he shall die he shall not receive anything, nor shall his glory descend together with him."

7. Let your love observe: "For his soul shall be blessed in his life" (ver. 18). As long as he lived he did well for himself. This all men say, but say falsely. It is a blessing from the mind of the blesser, not from the truth itself. For what sayest thou? Because he ate and drank, because he did what he chose, because he feasted sumptuously, therefore he did well with himself. I say, he did ill for himself. Not I say, but Christ. He did ill for himself. For that rich man, when he feasted sumptuously every day, was supposed to do well with himself: but when he began to burn in hell, then that which was supposed to be well was found to be ill. For what he had eaten with men above,[4] he digested in hell beneath. Unrighteousness I mean, brethren, on which he used to feast. He used to eat costly banquets with the mouth of flesh, with his heart's mouth he used to eat unrighteousness. What he ate with his heart's mouth with men above, this he digested amid those punishments in the places beneath. And verily he had eaten for a time, he digested ill for everlasting. Is then unrighteousness eaten? perhaps some one saith: what is it that he saith? Unrighteousness eaten? It is not I that say: hear the Scripture: "As a sour grape is vexation to the teeth, and smoke to the eyes, so is unrighteousness to them that use it." [5] For he that shall have eaten unrighteousness, that is, he that shall have had unrighteousness wilfully, shall not be able to eat righteousness. For righteousness is bread. Who is bread? "I am the living bread which came down from heaven." [6] Himself is the bread of our heart. . . . Is then even righteousness eaten? If it were not eaten, the Lord would not have said, "Blessed are they which do hunger and thirst after righteousness." [7] Therefore "since his soul shall be blessed in life," in life it "shall" be blessed, in death it shall be tormented. . . .

8. "He shall confess to Thee, when Thou shalt have done him good." Be not of such sort, brethren: see ye how that to this end we say these words, to this end we sing, to this end we treat, to this end toil — do not these things. Your business doth prove you: sometimes in

---

[1] Oxf. mss. "do."   [2] Ps. xlix. 13.

[3] Luke xii. 20.   [4] Apud superos.   [5] Prov. x. 26.
[6] John vi. 51.   [7] Matt. v. 6.

your business ye hear the truth, and ye blaspheme. The Church ye blaspheme. Wherefore? Because ye are Christians. "If so it be, I betake myself to Donatus's party: I will be a heathen."[1] Wherefore? Because thou hast eaten bread, and the teeth are in pain. When thou sawest the bread itself, thou didst praise; thou beginnest to eat, and the teeth are in pain; that is, when thou wast hearing the Word of God thou didst praise: when it is said to thee, "Do this," thou blasphemest: do not so ill: say this, "The bread is good, but I cannot eat it." But now if thou seest with the eyes, thou praisest: when thou beginnest to close the teeth, thou sayest, "Bad is this bread, and like him that made it." So it cometh to pass that thou confessest to God, when God doeth thee good: and thou liest when thou singest, "I will alway bless God, His praise is ever in my mouth."[2] How alway? If alway gain, alway He is blessed: if sometime there is loss, He is not blessed, but blasphemed. Forsooth thou blessest alway, forsooth His praise is ever in thy mouth! Thou wilt be such as just now he describeth: "He will confess to Thee, when Thou shalt have done him good."

9. "He shall enter even unto the generations of his fathers" (ver. 19): that is, he shall imitate his fathers. For the unrighteous, that now are, have brothers, have fathers. Unrighteous men of old, are the fathers of the present; and they that are now unrighteous, are the fathers of unrighteous posterity: just as the fathers of the righteous, the righteous of old, are the fathers of the righteous that now are; and they that now are, are the fathers of them that are to be. The Holy Spirit hath willed to show that righteousness is not evil when men murmur against her: but these men have their father from the beginning, even to the generation of their fathers. Two men Adam begat, and in one was unrighteousness, in one was righteousness: unrighteousness in Cain, righteousness in Abel.[3] Unrighteousness seemed to prevail over righteousness, because Cain unrighteous slew Abel righteous[4] in the night. Is it so in the morning? Nay, "but the righteous shall reign over them in the morning."[5] The morning shall come, and it shall be seen where Abel is, and where Cain. So all men who are after Cain, and so all who are after Abel, even unto the end of the world. "He shall enter even unto the generations of his fathers: even to eternity he shall not see light." Because even when he was here, he was in darkness, taking pleasure in false goods, and not loving real goods: even so he shall go hence

into hell: from the darkness of his dreams the darkness of torments shall receive him. Therefore, "even to eternity he shall not see light."

But wherefore this? What he hath written in the middle of the Psalm,[6] the same also he hath writ at the end: "Man, though he was in honour, understood not, was compared to the beasts without sense, and was made like to them" (ver. 20). But ye, brethren, consider that ye be men made after the image and likeness of God. The image[7] of God is within, is not in the body; is not in these ears which ye see, and eyes, and nostrils, and palate, and hands, and feet; but is made nevertheless:[8] wherein is the intellect, wherein is the mind, wherein the power of discovering truth, wherein is faith, wherein is your hope, wherein your charity, there God hath His Image: there at least ye perceive and see that these things pass away; for so he hath said in another Psalm, "Though man walketh in an image, yet he is disquieted in vain: he heapeth up treasures, and knoweth not for whom he shall gather them."[9] Be not disquieted, for of whatsoever kind these things be, they are transitory, if ye are men who being in honour understand. For if being men in honour ye understand not, ye are compared to the beasts without sense, and are made like to them.

PSALM L.[10]

1. How much availeth the Word of God to us for the correction of our life, both regarding His rewards to be expected, and His punishments to be feared, let each one measure[11] in himself; and let him put his conscience without deceit before His eyes, and not flatter himself in a danger so great: for ye see that even our Lord God Himself doth flatter no one: though He comforteth us by promising His blessings, and by strengthening our hope; yet them that live ill and despise His word He assuredly spareth not. Let each one examine himself, while it is time, and let him see where he is, and either persevere in good, or be changed from evil. For as he saith in this Psalm, not any man whatever nor any angel whatever, but, "The Lord, the God of gods, hath spoken" (ver. 1). But in speaking, He hath done what? "He hath called the earth from the rising of the sun unto the going down." He that "hath called the world from the rising of the sun unto the going down," is Our Lord and Saviour Jesus Christ, "the Word made Flesh,"[12] in order that He might dwell in us. Our Lord Jesus Christ then

---

[1] Those who became Donatists declared themselves not yet Christians, in order to be rebaptized.
[2] Ps. xxxiv. 1.　　[3] 1 John iii. 12.　　[4] Gen. iv. 8.
[5] Ps. xlix. 14.

[6] Ps. xlix. 12.　　[7] Gen. i. 26.　　[8] Most MSS. "made a mind."
[9] Ps. xxxix. 6.
[10] Lat. XLIX. From a sermon to the people.
[11] Some MSS. "meditate."　　[12] John i. 14.

is the "God of gods;" because by Himself were all things made, and without Himself was nothing made. The Word of God, if He is God, is truly the God of gods; but whether He be God the Gospel answereth, "In the beginning was the Word, and the Word was with God, and the Word was God." [1] And if all things were made by Himself, as He saith in the sequel, then if any were made gods, by Himself were they made. For the one God was not made, and He is Himself alone truly God. But Himself the only God, Father and Son and Holy Ghost, is one God.

2. But then who are those gods, or where are they, of whom God is the true God? Another Psalm saith, "God hath stood in the synagogue of gods, but in the midst He judgeth gods." [2] As yet we know not whether perchance any gods be congregated in heaven, and in their congregation, for this is "in the synagogue," God hath stood to judge. See in the same Psalm those to whom he saith, "I have said, Ye are gods, and children of the Highest all; but ye shall die like men, and fall like one of the princes." [3] It is evident then, that He hath called men gods, that are deified of His Grace, not born of His Substance. For He doth justify, who is just through His own self, and not of another; and He doth deify who is God through Himself, not by the partaking of another. But He that justifieth doth Himself deify, in that by justifying He doth make sons of God. "For He hath given them power to become the sons of God." [4] If we have been made sons of God, we have also been made gods: but this is the effect of Grace adopting, not of nature generating. For the only Son of God, God, and one God with the Father, Our Lord and Saviour Jesus Christ, was in the beginning the Word, and the Word with God, the Word God. The rest that are made gods, are made by His own Grace, are not born of His Substance, that they should be the same as He, but that by favour they should come to Him, and be fellow-heirs with Christ. For so great is the love in Him the Heir, that He hath willed to have fellow-heirs. What covetous man would will this, to have fellow-heirs? But even one that is found so to will, will share with them the inheritance, the sharer having less himself, than if he had possessed alone: but the inheritance wherein we are fellow-heirs of Christ, is not lessened by multitude of possessors, nor is it made narrower by the number of fellow-heirs: but is as great for many as it is for few, as great for individuals as for all. "See," saith the Apostle, "what love God hath bestowed upon us, that we should be called, and be, the sons of God." [5] And in

another place, "Dearly beloved, we are the sons of God, and it doth not yet appear what we shall be." We are therefore in hope, not yet in substance. "But we know," he saith, "that when He shall have appeared, we shall be like Him, for we shall see Him as He is." [6] The Only Son is like Him by birth, we like by seeing. For we are not like in such sort as He, who is the same as He is by whom He was begotten: for we are like, not equal: He, because equal, is therefore like. We have heard who are the gods that being made are justified, because they are called the sons of God: and who are the gods that are not Gods, to whom the God of gods is terrible? For another Psalm saith, "He is terrible over all gods." [7] And as if thou shouldest enquire, what gods? He saith, "For all the gods of the nations are devils." To the gods of the nations, to the devils, terrible: to the gods made by Himself, to sons, lovely. Furthermore, I find both of them confessing the Majesty of God, both the devils confessed Christ, and the faithful confessed Christ. "Thou art Christ, the Son of the living God," [8] said Peter. "We know who Thou art, Thou art the Son of God," [9] said the devils. A like confession I hear, but like love I find not; nay even here love, there fear. To whom therefore He is lovely, the same are sons; to whom He is terrible, are not sons; to whom He is lovely, the same He hath made gods; those to whom He is terrible He doth prove not to be gods. For these are made gods, those are reputed gods: these Truth maketh gods, those error doth so account.

3. "The God," therefore, "of gods, the Lord hath spoken" [10] (ver. 1). Hath spoken many ways. By Angels He hath Himself spoken, by Prophets He hath Himself spoken, by His own mouth He hath Himself spoken, by His faithful He doth Himself speak, by our lowliness, when we say anything true, He doth Himself speak. See then, by speaking diversely, many ways, by many vessels, by many instruments, yet He doth Himself sound everywhere, by touching, moulding, inspiring: see what He hath done. For "He hath spoken, and hath called the world." What world? Africa, perhaps! for the sake of those that say, the Church of Christ is the portion of Donatus. Africa indeed alone He hath not called, but even Africa He hath not severed. For He that "hath called the world from the rising of the sun unto the going down," leaving out no parts that He hath not called, in His calling hath found Africa. Let it rejoice therefore in unity, not pride itself in division. We say well, that the voice of the God of gods hath come even into Africa, hath not stayed in Africa.

---

[1] John i. 1.   [2] Ps. lxxxii. 1.   [3] Ps. lxxxii. 6, 7.
[4] John i. 12.   [5] 1 John iii. 1.

[6] 1 John iii. 2.   [7] Ps. xcvi. 4.   [8] Matt. xvi 16.
[9] Mark iii. 11; Luke iv. 41.   [10] Vid. Heb. i. 1.

For " He hath called the world from the rising of the sun unto the going down." There is no place where may lurk the conspiracies of heretics, they have no place wherein they may hide themselves under the shadow of falsehood; for " there is none that can hide himself from the heat thereof." [1] He that hath called the world, hath called even the whole world: He that hath called the world, hath called as much as He hath formed. Why do false christs and false prophets rise up against me? why is it that they strive to ensnare me with captious words, saying, " Lo! here is Christ, Lo! He is there! " [2] I hear not them that point out portions: the God of gods hath pointed out the whole : " He" that " hath called the world from the rising of the sun unto the going down," hath redeemed the whole; but hath condemned them that lay false claim to [3] portions.

4. But we have heard the world called from the rising of the sun unto the going down: whence doth He begin to call, who hath called? This thing also hear ye: " Out of Sion is the semblance of His beauty" (ver. 2). Evidently the Psalm doth agree with the Gospel, which saith, " Throughout all nations, beginning at Jerusalem." [4] Hear, " Throughout all nations : " He hath called the world from the rising of the sun unto the going down." Hear, " Beginning at Jerusalem : " " Out of Sion is the semblance of His beauty." Therefore, " He hath called the world from the rising of the sun unto the going down," agreeth with the words of the Lord, who saith, " It behoved Christ to suffer, and to rise from the dead the third day; and that repentance and remission of sins should be preached in His Name throughout all nations." [5] For all nations are from the rising of the sun unto the going down. But that, " Out of Sion is the semblance of His beauty," that thence beginneth the beauty of His Gospel, that thence He began to be preached, being " beautiful in form beyond the sons of men," [6] agreeth with the words of the Lord, who saith, " Beginning at Jerusalem." New things are in tune with old, old things with new : the two Seraphim say to one another, " Holy, holy, holy, Lord God of Sabaoth." [7] The two Testaments are both in tune, and the two Testaments have one voice : let the voice of the Testaments in tune be heard, not that of pretenders disinherited. This thing then hath the God of gods done, " He hath called the world from the rising of the sun unto the going down, His semblance going before out of Sion." For in that place were His disciples,[8] who received the Holy Ghost sent from heaven on the fiftieth day after His resurrection. Thence the Gospel, thence the preaching, thence the whole world filled, and that in the Grace of Faith.

5. For when the Lord Himself had come, because He came to suffer, He came hidden : and though He was strong in Himself, He appeared in the flesh weak. For He must needs appear in order that He might not be perceived ; be despised, in order that He might be slain. There was semblance of glory in divinity, but it lay concealed in flesh. " For if they had known, they would never have crucified the Lord of glory." [9] So then He walked hidden among the Jews, among His enemies, doing marvels, suffering ills, until He was hanged on the tree, and the Jews seeing Him hanging both despised Him the more, and before the Cross wagging their heads they said, " If He be the Son of God, let Him come down from the Cross." [10] Hidden then was the God of gods, and He gave forth words more out of compassion for us than out of His own majesty. For whence, unless assumed from us, were those words, " My God, My God, why hast Thou forsaken me?" [11] But when hath the Father forsaken the Son, or the Son the Father? Are not Father and Son one God? Whence then, " My God, My God, why hast Thou forsaken Me," save that in the Flesh of infirmity there was acknowledged the voice of a sinner? For as He took upon Him the likeness of the flesh of sin,[12] why should He not take upon Him the voice of sin? Hidden then was the God of gods, both when He walked among men, and when He hungered, and when He thirsted, and when fatigued He sat, and when with wearied body He slept, and when taken, and when scourged, and when standing before the judge, and when He made answer to him in his pride, " Thou couldest have no power against Me, except it had been given thee from above ; " [13] and while led as a victim " before His shearer He opened not His mouth," [14] and while crucified, and while buried, He was always hidden God of gods. What took place after He rose again? The disciples marvelled, and at first believed not, until they touched and handled.[15] But flesh had risen, because flesh had been dead : Divinity which could not die, even still lay hid in the flesh of Him rising. Form could be seen, limbs held, scars handled : the Word by whom all things were made, who doth see? who doth hold? who doth handle? And yet " the Word was made flesh, and dwelled among us." [16] And Thomas, that was holding Man, understood God as he was able. For when he had handled the scars, he cried out,

---

[1] Ps. xix. 6.   [2] Matt. xxiv. 23.   [3] *Calumniantes.*
[4] Luke xxiv. 47.   [5] Luke xxiv. 46, 47.   [6] Ps. xlv. 2.
[7] Isa. vi. 3.   [8] Acts i. 4.

[9] 1 Cor. ii. 8.   [10] Matt. xxvii. 39, 40.
[11] Ps. xxii. 1; Matt. xxvii. 46.   [12] Rom. viii. 3.
[13] John xix. 11.   [14] Isa. liii. 7.
[15] Luke xxiv. 37-40.   [16] John i. 14.

"My Lord, and my God." Yet the Lord was showing that form, and that flesh, which they had seen upon the Cross, which had been laid in the sepulchre. He stayed with them forty days. . . . But what was said to Thomas handling? "Because thou hast seen, thou hast believed; blessed are they that see not, and believe." [1] We are foretold. That world called from the rising of the sun unto the going down seeth not, and believeth. Hidden then is the God of gods, both to those among whom He walked, and to those by whom He was crucified, and to those before whose eyes He rose, and to us who believe on Him in heaven sitting, whom we have not seen on earth walking. But even if we were to see, should we not see that which the Jews saw and crucified? It is more, that not seeing we believe Christ to be God, than that they seeing deemed Him only to be man. They in a word by thinking evil slew, we by believing well are made alive.

6. What then, brethren? This God of gods, both then hidden, and now hidden, shall He ever be hidden? Evidently not: hear what followeth: "God shall come manifest" (ver. 3). He that came hidden, shall come manifest. Hidden He came to be judged, manifest He shall come to judge: hidden He came that He might stand before a judge, manifest He shall come that He may be judge even of judges: "He shall come manifest, and shall not be silent." But why? Is He now silent? And whence are all the words that we say? whence those precepts? whence those warnings? whence that trumpet of terror? He is not silent, and is silent: is not silent from warning, is silent from avenging: is not silent from precept, is silent from judgment. For He suffereth sinners daily doing evil things, not caring for God, not in their conscience, not in heaven, not in earth: all these things escape Him not, and universally He doth admonish all; and whenever He chastiseth any on earth, it is admonition, not yet condemnation. He is silent then from judgment, He is hidden in heaven, as yet He intercedeth for us: He is long-suffering to sinners, not putting forth His wrath, but awaiting penitence. He saith in another place : "I have held my peace, shall I always hold my peace?" [2] When then He shall not hold His peace, "God shall come manifest." What God? "Our God." And the God Himself, who is our God: for he is not God, who is not our God. For the gods of the nations are devils: the God of Christians is very God. Himself shall come, but "manifest," not still to be mocked, not still to be buffeted and scourged: He shall come, but "manifest," not still to be smitten with a reed

upon the head, not still to be crucified, slain, buried: for all these things God being hidden hath willed to suffer. "He shall come manifest, and shall not be silent."

7. But that He shall come to judgment, the following words teach. "Fire shall go before Him." [3] Do we fear? Be we changed, and we shall not fear. Let chaff fear the fire: what doth it to gold? What thou mayest do is now in thy power, so thou mayest not experience, for want of being corrected, that which is to come even against thy will. For if we might so bring it about, brethren, that the day of judgment should not come; I think that even then it were not for us to live ill. If the fire of the day of judgment were not to come, and over sinners there impended only separation from the face of God, in whatever affluence of delights they might be, not seeing Him by whom they were created, and separated from that sweetness of His ineffable [4] countenance, in whatever eternity and impunity of sin, they ought to bemoan themselves. But what shall I say, or to whom shall I say? This is a punishment to lovers, not to despisers. They that have begun to feel in any degree the sweetness of wisdom and truth, know what I say, how great a punishment it is to be only separated from the face of God: but they that have not tasted that sweetness, if not yet they yearn for the face of God, let them fear even fire; let punishments terrify those, whom rewards win not. Of no value to thee is what God promiseth, tremble at what He threateneth. The sweetness of His presence shall come ; thou art not changed, thou art not awakened, thou sighest not, thou longest not: thou embracest thy sins and the delights of thy flesh, thou art heaping stubble to thyself, the fire will come. "Fire shall burn in His presence." This fire will not be like thy hearth-fire, into which nevertheless, if thou art compelled to thrust thy hand, thou wilt do whatsoever he would have thee who doth threaten this alternative. If he say to thee, "write against the life [5] of thy father, write against the lives of thy children, for if thou do not, I thrust thy hand into thy fire : " thou wilt do it in order that thy hand be not burned, in order that thy member be not burned for a time, though it is not to be ever in pain. Thine enemy threateneth then but so light an evil, and thou doest evil; God threateneth eternal evil, and doest thou not good? To do evil not even menaces should compel thee : from doing good not even menaces should deter thee. But by the menaces of God, by menaces of everlasting fire, thou art dissuaded from evil, invited to good. Wherefore doth it grieve thee, except because thou believest not? Let each one then

---

[1] John xx. 29.   [2] Isa. xlii. 14.   [3] Ps. xcvii. 3.   [4] Oxf. MSS. "ineffable sweetness of His."   [5] Head.

examine his heart, and see what faith doth [1] hold there. If we believe a judgment to come, brethren, let us live well. Now is time of mercy, then will be time of judgment. No one will say, "Call me back to my former years." Even then men will repent, but will repent in vain : now let there be repentance, while there is fruit of repentance ; now let there be applied to the roots of the tree a basket of dung,[2] sorrow of heart, and tears ; lest He come and pluck up by the roots. For when He shall have plucked up, then the fire is to be looked for. Now, even if the branches have been broken, they can again be grafted in : [3] then, "every tree which bringeth not forth good fruit, shall be cut down, and shall be cast into the fire." [4] " Fire shall burn in His presence."

8. "And a mighty tempest round about Him " (ver. 3). "A mighty tempest," in order to winnow so great a floor. In this tempest shall be that winnowing whereby from the saints shall be put away everything impure, from the faithful every unreality ; from godly men and them that fear the Word of God, every scorner and every proud man. For now a sort of mixture doth lie there, from the rising of the sun unto the going down. Let us see then how He will do that is to come, what He will do with that tempest which "shall be a mighty tempest round about Him." Doubtless this tempest is to make a sort of separation. It is that separation which they waited not for, who brake the nets, before they came to land.[5] But in this separation there is made a sort of distinction between good men and bad men. There be some that now follow Christ with lightened shoulders without the load of the world's cares, who have not heard in vain, " If thou wilt be perfect, go and sell all that thou hast, and give to the poor, and thou shalt have treasure in heaven : and come, follow Me ; " [6] to which sort is said, "Ye shall sit upon twelve thrones, judging the twelve tribes of Israel." [7] Some then shall be judging with the Lord : but others to be judged, but to be placed on the right hand. For that there will be certain judging with the Lord, we have most evident testimony, which I have but now quoted : " Ye shall sit upon twelve thrones, judging the twelve tribes of Israel." . . .

9. But what the Lord did after His resurrection, signified what is to be to us after our resurrection, in that number of the kingdom of heaven, where shall be no bad man. . . . Lastly, those seven thousand of whom reply was made to Elias, " I have left me seven thousand men that have not bowed knees before Baal," [8] far exceed that number of fishes. Therefore the hundred and fifty-three fishes [9] doth not alone express just such a number of saints, but Scripture doth express the whole number of saints and righteous men by so great a number for a particular reason ; to wit, in order that in those hundred and fifty-three all may be understood that pertain to the resurrection to eternal life. For the Law hath ten commandments : [10] but the Spirit of Grace, through which alone the Law is fulfilled,[11] is called sevenfold. The number then must be examined, what mean ten and seven : ten in commandments, seven in the grace of the Holy Spirit : by which grace the commandments are fulfilled. Ten then and seven contain all that pertain to the resurrection, to the right hand, to the kingdom of heaven, to life eternal, that is, they that fulfil the Law by the Grace of the Spirit, not as it were by their own work or their own merit. But ten and seven, if thou countest from one unto seventeen, by adding all the numbers by steps, so that to one thou mayest add two, add three, add four, that they may become ten, by adding five that they may become fifteen, by adding six that they may become twenty-one, by adding seven that they may become twenty-eight, by adding eight that they may become thirty-six, by adding nine that they may become forty-five, by adding ten that they may become fifty-five, by adding eleven that they may become sixty-six, by adding twelve that they may become seventy-eight, by adding thirteen that they may become ninety-one, by adding fourteen that they may become one hundred and five, by adding fifteen that they may become one hundred and twenty, by adding sixteen that they may become one hundred and thirty-six, by adding seventeen, make up one hundred and fifty-three, thou wilt find a vast number of all saints to belong to this number of a few fishes. In like manner then as in five virgins, countless virgins ; as in five brethren of him that was tormented in hell, thousands of the people of the Jews ; as in the number of one hundred and fifty-three fishes, thousands of thousands of saints : so in twelve thrones, not twelve men, but great is the number of the perfect.[12]

10. But I see what is next required of us ; in like manner as in the case of the five virgins, a reason was given why many should belong to five, and why to those five many Jews, and why to a hundred and fifty-three many perfect — to show why and how to the twelve thrones not twelve men, but many belong. What mean the twelve thrones, which signify all men every-

---

9 John xxi. 11.   10 Deut. iv. 13.   11 Isa. xi. 2, 3.
12 [That there is ground for all this regard to numbers, fanciful though it seems, has been demonstrated. See Dan. viii. 13; also note 1, p. 514, vol. ii. A. N. F. Compare margin of our English Version on the text of Daniel; Heb. *Palmoni*, " the Wonderful Numberer." See Dr. Mahan's " Palmoni," Ed. New York, 1863. — C.]

---

1 *Al.* " he doth."   2 Luke xiii. 8.   3 Rom. xi. 19.
4 Matt. iii. 10.   5 Luke v. 6.   6 Matt. xix. 21.
7 Matt. xix. 28.   8 1 Kings xix. 18.

where that have been enabled to be so perfect as they must be perfect, to whom it is said, "Ye shall sit over the twelve tribes of Israel"?[1] And why do all men everywhere belong to the number twelve? Because the very "everywhere" which we say, we say of the whole world: but the compass of lands is contained in four particular quarters, East, West, South, and North: from all these quarters they being called in the Trinity and made perfect in the faith and precept of the Trinity, — seeing that three times four are twelve, ye perceive wherefore the saints belong to the whole world; they that shall sit upon twelve thrones to judge the twelve tribes of Israel, since the twelve tribes of Israel, also, are the twelve tribes of the whole of Israel. For like as they that are to judge are from the whole world, so also they that are to be judged are from the whole world. The Apostle Paul of himself, when he was reproving believing laymen, because they referred not their causes to the Church, but dragged them with whom they had matters before the public, said, "Know ye not that we shall judge Angels?"[2] See after what sort He hath made Himself judge: not only himself, but also all that judge aright in the Church.

11. Since then it is evident, that many are to judge with the Lord, but that others are to be judged, not however on equality, but according to their deserts; He will come with all His Angels,[3] when before Him shall be gathered all nations, and among all the Angels are to be reckoned those that have been made so perfect, that sitting upon twelve thrones they judge the twelve tribes of Israel. For men are called Angels: the Apostle saith of himself, "As an angel of God ye received me."[4] Of John Baptist it is said, "Behold, I send My Angel before Thy face, that shall prepare Thy way before Thee."[5] Therefore, coming with all Angels, together with Him He shall have the Saints also. For plainly saith Isaias also, "He shall come to judgment with the elders of the people."[6] Those "elders of the people," then, those but now named Angels, those thousands of many men made perfect coming from the whole world, are called Heaven. But the others *are called* earth, yet fruitful. Which is the earth that is fruitful? That which is to be set on the right hand, unto which it shall be said, "I was an hungred, and ye gave Me to eat:"[7] truly fruitful earth in which the Apostle doth joy, when they sent to him to supply his necessities: "Not because I ask a gift," he saith, "but I require fruit."[8] And he giveth thanks, saying, "Because at length ye have budded forth again to be thoughtful for

me."[9] He saith, "Ye have budded forth again," as to trees which had withered away with a kind of barrenness. Therefore the Lord coming to judgment (that we may now hear the Psalm, brethren), He will do what? "He will call the heaven from above" (ver. 4). The heaven, all the Saints, those made perfect that shall judge, them He shall call from above, to be sitters with Him to judge the twelve tribes of Israel. For how shall "He call the heaven from above," when the heaven is always above? But those that He here calleth heaven, the same elsewhere He calleth heavens. What heavens? That tell out the glory of God: for, "The heavens tell out the glory of God:"[10] whereof is said, "Into all the earth their sound hath gone forth, and into the ends of the world their words." For see the Lord severing in judgment: "He shall call the heaven from above and the earth, to sever His people." From whom but from evil men? Of whom here afterwards no mention is made, now as it were condemned to punishment. See these good men, and distinguish. "He shall call the heaven from above, and the earth, to sever His people." He calleth the earth also, not however to be associated, but to be dissociated. For at first He called them together, "when the God of gods spake and called the world from the rising of the sun unto the going down," He had not yet severed: those servants had been sent to bid to the marriage,[11] who had gathered good and bad. But when the God of gods shall come manifest and shall not keep silence, He shall so call the "heaven from above" that it may judge with Him. For what the heaven is, the heavens themselves are; just as what the earth is, the lands themselves, just as what the Church is, the Churches themselves: "He shall call the heaven from above, and the earth, to sever His people." Now with the heaven He severeth the earth, that is, the heaven with Him doth sever the earth. How doth He sever the earth? In such sort that He setteth on the right hand some, others on the left. But to the earth severed, He saith what? "Come, ye blessed of My Father, receive the kingdom which was prepared for you from the beginning of the world. For I was an hungred, and ye gave me to eat," and so forth. But they say, "When saw we Thee an hungred?" And He, "Inasmuch as ye have done it unto one of the least of Mine, ye have done it unto Me."[12] "He shall call therefore the heaven from above, and the earth, to sever His people."

12. "Gather to Him His righteous" (ver. 5). The voice divine and prophetic, seeing future things as if present doth exhort the Angels gathering. For He shall send His Angels, and before

---

[1] Matt. xix. 28. [2] 1 Cor. vi. 3. [3] Matt. xxv. 31.
[4] Gal. iv. 14. [5] Mal. iii. 1; Matt. xi. 10.
[6] Isa. iii. 14. [7] Matt. xxv. 35. [8] Phil. iv. 17.

[9] Phil. iv. 10. [10] Ps. xix. 1. [11] Matt. xxii. 3.
[12] Matt. xxv. 34, etc.

Him shall be gathered all nations.[1] Gather to Him His righteous. What righteous men save those that live of faith and do works of mercy? For those works are works of righteousness. Thou hast the Gospel : " Beware of doing your righteousness before men to be seen of them."[2] And as if it were inquired, What righteousness? " When therefore thou doest alms," He saith. Therefore alms He hath signified to be works of righteousness. Those very persons gather for His righteous : gather those that have had compassion on the " needy," that have considered the needy and poor : [3] gather them, " The Lord preserve them, and make them to live ; " " Gather to Him His righteous : who order His covenant above sacrifices : " that is, who think of His promises above those things which they work. For those things are sacrifices, God saying, " I will have mercy more than sacrifice."[4] " Who keep His covenant more than sacrifice."

13. " And the Heaven shall declare His righteousness " (ver. 6). Truly this righteousness of God to us the " heavens have declared," the Evangelists have foretold. Through them we have heard that some will be on the right hand, to whom the Householder saith, " Come, ye blessed of My Father, receive. [5] Receive what? " A kingdom." In return for what thing? " I was an hungred, and ye gave Me to eat." What so valueless, what so earthly, as to break bread to the hungry? At so much is valued the kingdom of heaven. " Break thy bread to the hungry, and the needy without covering bring into thy house ; if thou seest one naked, clothe him."[6] If thou hast not the means of breaking bread, hast not house into which thou mayest bring, hast not garment wherewith thou mayest cover : give a cup of cold water,[7] cast two mites into the treasury.[8] As much the widow doth buy with two mites, as Peter buyeth, by leaving the nets,[9] as Zacchæus buyeth by giving half his goods.[10] Of so much worth is all that thou hast. " The heavens shall declare His righteousness, for God is Judge." Truly judge not confounding but severing. For " the Lord knoweth them that are His."[11] Even if grains lie hid in the chaff, they are known to the husbandman. Let no one fear that he is a grain even among the chaff; the eyes of our winnower are not deceived. Fear not lest that tempest, which shall be round about Him, should confound thee with chaff. Certainly mighty will be the tempest ; yet not one grain will it sweep from the side of the corn to the chaff : because not any rustic with three-pronged fork, but God, Three in One, is Judge. And the heavens shall

declare His righteousness : for God is Judge. Let heavens go, let the heavens tell, into every land let their sound go out, and unto the ends of the world their words : [12] and let that body say, " From the ends of the world unto Thee have I cried, when my heart was in heaviness." [13] For now mingled it groaneth, divided it shall rejoice. Let it cry then and say, " Destroy not my soul with ungodly men, and with men of blood my life." [14] He destroyeth not together, because God is Judge. Let it cry to Him and say, " Judge me, O Lord, and sever my cause from the nation unholy : " [15] let it say, He shall do it : there shall be gathered to Him His righteous ones. He hath called the earth that He may sever His people.

14. " Hear, my people, and I will speak to thee " (ver. 7). He shall come and shall not keep silence ; see how that even now, if ye hear, He is not silent. Hear, my people, and I will speak to thee. For if thou hearest not, I will not speak to thee. " Hear, and I will speak to thee." For if thou hearest not, even though I shall speak, it will not be to thee. When then shall I speak to thee? If thou hearest. When hearest thou? If thou art my people. For, " Hear, my people : " thou hearest not if thou art an alien people. " Hear, my people, and I will speak to thee : Israel, and I will testify to thee." . . . For " Thy God," is properly said to that man whom God doth keep more as one of His family, as though in His household, as though in His peculiar : " Thy God am I." What wilt thou more? Requirest thou a reward from God, so that God may give thee something ; so that what He hath given thee may be thine own? Behold God Himself, who shall give, is thine own. What richer than He? Gifts thou wast desiring, thou hast the Giver Himself. " God, thy God, I am."

15. What He requireth of man, let us see ; what tribute our God, our Emperor and our King doth enjoin us ; since He hath willed to be our King, and hath willed us to be His province? Let us hear His injunctions. Let not a poor man tremble beneath the injunction of God : what God enjoineth to be given to Himself, He doth Himself first give that enjoineth : be ye only devoted. God doth not exact what He hath not given, and to all men hath given what He doth exact. For what doth He exact? Let us hear now : " I will not reprove thee because of thy sacrifices " (ver. 8). I will not say to thee, Wherefore hast thou not slain for me a fat bull? why hast thou not selected the best he-goat from thy flock? Wherefore doth that ram amble among thy sheep, and is not laid upon mine altar? I will not say, Examine thy fields and thy pen [16]

---

[1] Matt. xxv. 32.   [2] Matt. vi. 1.   [3] Ps. xli. 1.
[4] Hos. vi. 6; Matt. ix. 13.   [5] Matt. xxv. 34.
[6] Isa. lviii. 7.   [7] Matt. x. 42.   [8] Mark xii. 42.
[9] Matt. iv. 20.   [10] Luke xix. 8.   [11] 2 Tim. ii. 19.
[12] Ps. xix. 4.   [13] Ps. lxi. 2.   [14] Ps. xxvi. 9.
[15] Ps. xxvi. 1.   [16] Curte.

and thy walls, seeking what thou mayest give Me. "I will not reprove thee because of thy sacrifices." What then : Dost Thou not accept my sacrifices? "But thy holocausts are always in My sight" (ver. 9). Certain holocausts concerning which it is said in another Psalm, "If Thou hadst desired sacrifice, I would surely have given, with holocausts Thou wilt not be delighted : "[1] and again he turneth himself, "Sacrifice to God is a troubled spirit, a heart broken and humbled God doth not despise."[2] Which be then holocausts that He despiseth not? Which holocausts that are always in His sight? "Kindly, O Lord," he saith, "deal in Thy good will with Sion, and be the walls of Jerusalem builded, then shalt Thou accept the sacrifice of righteousness, oblations, and holocausts." He saith that certain holocausts God will accept. But what is a holocaust? A whole consumed with fire : *causis* is burning, *holon* is whole : but a "holocaust" is a whole consumed with fire. There is a certain fire of most burning love : be the mind inflamed with love, let the same love hurry off the limbs to its use, let it not allow them to serve cupidity, in order that we may wholly glow with fire of divine love that will offer to God a holocaust. Such "holocausts of thine are in My sight always."

16. As yet that Israel perchance doth not understand what are the holocausts thereof which He hath in His sight always, and is still thinking of oxen, of sheep, of he-goats : let it not so think : "I will not accept calves of thy house." Holocausts I named ; at once in mind and thought to earthly flocks thou wast running, therefrom thou wast selecting for Me some fat thing : "I will not accept calves of thy house." He is foretelling the New Testament, wherein all those sacrifices have ceased. For they were then foretelling a certain Sacrifice which was to be, with the Blood whereof we should be cleansed. "I will not accept calves of thy house, nor he-goats of thy flocks."

17. "For mine are all the beasts of the wood" (ver. 10). Why should I ask of thee what I have made? Is it more thine, to whom I have given it to possess, than Mine, who have made it? "For mine are all the beasts of the wood." But perchance that Israel saith, The beasts are God's, those wild beasts which I enclose not in my pen, which I bind not to my stall ; but this ox and sheep and he-goat— these are mine own. "Cattle on the mountain, and oxen."[3] Mine are those which thou possessest not, Mine are these which thou possessest. For if thou art My servant, the whole of thy property is Mine. For it cannot be, that that is the property of the master which the servant hath gotten to himself, and yet that not be the property of the Master which the Master Himself hath created for the servant. Therefore Mine are the beasts of the wood which thou hast not taken ; Mine are also the cattle on the mountains which are thine, and the oxen which are at thy stall : all are Mine own, for I have created them.

18. "I know all the winged creatures of heaven" (ver. 11). How doth He know? He hath weighed them, hath counted. Which of us knoweth all the winged creatures of heaven? But even though to some man God give knowledge of all the winged creatures of heaven, He doth not Himself know in the same manner as He giveth man to know. One thing is God's knowledge, another man's : in like manner as there is one possession of God's, another of man's : that is, God's possessing is one thing, man's another. For what thou possessest thou hast not wholly in thy power, or else thy ox, so long as it liveth, is in thy power ; so as that it either die not, or be not to be fed. With whom there is the highest power, there is highest and most secret cognition. Let us ascribe this to God, while praising God. Let us not dare to say, How knoweth God? Do not, I pray you, brethren, of me expect this, that I should unfold to you, how God doth know : this only I say, He doth not so know as a man, He doth not so know as an Angel : and how He knoweth I dare not say, because also I cannot ken. One thing, nevertheless, I ken, that even before all the winged creatures of heaven were, God knew that which He was to create. What is that knowledge? O man, thou beginnest to see, after that thou hadst been formed, after that thou hadst received sense of seeing. These fowls sprung of the water at the word of God, saying, "Let the waters bring forth fowls."[4] Whereby did God know the things which He commanded the water to bear forth? Now surely He knew what He had created, and before He created He knew. So great then is the knowledge of God, so that with Himself they were in a certain ineffable manner before they were created : and of thee doth He expect to receive what He had, before He created? "I know all the winged creatures of heaven," which thou to Me canst not give. The things which thou wast about to slay for Me, I know all : not because I made I know, but in order that I might make. "And the beauty of the field is with Me." The fairness of the field, the abundance of all things engendering upon earth, "is with Me," He saith. How with Him? Were they so, even before they were made? Yea, for with Him were all things to come, and

with Him are all things by-gone : things to come in such sort, that there be not withdrawn from Him all things by-gone. With Him are all things by a certain cognition of the ineffable wisdom of God residing in the Word, and the [1] Word Himself is all things. Is not the beauty of the field in a manner with Him, inasmuch as He is everywhere, and Himself hath said, "Heaven and earth I fill"? [2] What with Him is not, of whom it is said, "If I shall have ascended into heaven, Thou art there ; and if I shall have descended into hell, Thou art present"? [3] With Him is the whole : but it is not so with Him as that He doth suffer any contamination from those things which He hath created, or any want of them. For with thee, perchance, is a pillar near which thou art standing, and when thou art weary, thou leanest against it. Thou needest that which is with thee, God needeth not the field which is with Him. With Him is field, with Him beauty of earth, with Him beauty of heaven, with Him all winged creatures, because He is Himself everywhere. And wherefore are all things near Him? Because even before that all things were, or were created, to Him were known all things.

19. Who can explain, who expound that which is said to Him in another Psalm, "For my goods Thou needest not"? [4] He hath said that He needeth not from us any necessary thing. "If I shall be hungry, I will not tell thee" (ver. 12). He that keepeth Israel shall neither hunger nor thirst, nor be weary, nor fall asleep.[5] But, lo ! according to thy carnality I speak : because thou wilt suffer hunger when thou hast not eaten, perhaps thou thinkest even God doth hunger that He may eat. Even though He shall be hungry, He telleth not thee : all things are before Him, whence He will He taketh what is needful for Him. These words are said to convince little understanding ; not that God hath declared His hunger. Though for our sake this God of gods deigned even to hunger. He came to hunger, and to fill ; He came to thirst, and give drink ; He came to be clothed with mortality, and to clothe with immortality ; He came poor, to make rich. For He lost not His riches by taking to Him our poverty, for, "In him are all the treasures of wisdom and knowledge hidden." [6] "If I shall be hungry, I will not tell thee. For Mine is the whole world, and the fulness thereof." Do not then labour to find what to give Me, without whom I have what I will.

20. Why then dost still think of thy flocks? "Shall I eat the flesh of bulls, or shall I drink the blood of he-goats?" (ver. 13). Ye have heard what of us He requireth not, who willeth to enjoin us somewhat. If of such things ye were thinking, now withdraw your thoughts from such things : think not to offer God any such thing. If thou hast a fat bull, kill for the poor : let them eat the flesh of bulls, though they shall not drink the blood of he-goats. Which, when thou shalt have done, He will account it to thee, that hath said, "If I shall be hungry, I will not tell thee :" and He shall say to thee, "I was hungry, and thou gavest Me to eat." [7] "Shall I eat the flesh of bulls, or shall I drink the blood of he-goats?"

21. Say then, Lord our God, what dost Thou enjoin thy people, Thy Israel? "Immolate to God the sacrifice of praise" (ver. 14). Let us also say to Him, "In me, O God, are thy vows, which I will render of praise to Thee." I had feared lest Thou mightest enjoin something which would be out of my power, which I was counting to be in my pen, and but now perchance it had been taken away by a thief. What dost Thou enjoin me? "Immolate to God the sacrifice of praise." Let me revert to myself, wherein I may find what I may immolate : let me revert to myself ; in myself may I find immolation of praise : be Thy altar my conscience. We are without anxiety, we go not into Arabia in quest of frankincense : [8] not any bags of covetous dealer do we sift : God requireth of us the sacrifice of praise. Zacchæus had this sacrifice of praise in his patrimony ; [9] the widow had it in her bag ; [10] some poor host or other hath had it in his jar : another neither in patrimony, nor in bag, nor in jar, hath had anything, had it wholly in his heart : salvation was to the house of Zacchæus ; and more this poor widow cast in than those rich men : this man, that doth offer a cup of cold water, shall not lose his reward : [11] but there is even "peace on earth to men of good will." [12] "Immolate to God the sacrifice of praise." O sacrifice gratuitous, by grace given ! I have not indeed bought this to offer, but Thou hast given : for not even this should I have had. And this is the immolation of the sacrifice of praise, to render thanks to Him from whom thou hast whatever of good thou hast, and by whose mercy is forgiven thee whatsoever of evil of thine thou hast. "Immolate to God the sacrifice of praise : and render to the Highest thy prayers." With this odour the Lord is well pleased.[13]

22. "And call thou upon Me in the day of thy tribulation : and I will draw thee forth, and thou shalt glorify Me" (ver. 15). For thou

---

[1] Or, "In (or with) the Word Himself are all things."
[2] Jer. xxiii. 24.   [3] Ps. cxxxix. 8.   [4] Ps. xvi. 2.
[5] Ps. cxxi. 4.   [6] Col. ii. 3.

[7] Matt. xxv. 35.
[8] [A. N. F. (Tertullian), vol. iii. p. 67, and (Irenæus) vol. i. p. 484, note 9.—C.]
[9] Luke xix. 8.   [10] Mark xii. 42.   [11] Matt. x. 42.
[12] Luke ii. 14.
[13] [A. N. F. vol. vii. p. 553, note 6.—C.]

oughtest not to rely on thy powers, all thy aids are deceitful. "Upon Me call thou in the day of tribulation : I will draw thee forth, and thou shalt glorify Me." For to this end I have allowed the day of tribulation to come to thee : because perchance if thou wast not troubled, thou wouldest not call on Me : but when thou art troubled, thou callest on Me ; when thou callest upon Me, I will draw thee forth ; when I shall draw thee forth, thou shalt glorify Me, that thou mayest no more depart from Me. A certain man had grown dull and cold in fervour of prayer, and said, "Tribulation and grief I found, and on the Name of the Lord I called."[1] He found tribulation as it were some profitable thing ; he had rotted in the slough of his sins ; now he had continued without feeling, he found tribulation to be a sort of caustic and cutting. "I found," he saith, "tribulation and grief, and on the Name of the Lord I called." And truly, brethren, tribulations are known to all men. Behold those afflictions that abound in mankind ; one afflicted with loss bewaileth ; another smitten with bereavement mourneth ; another exiled from country grieveth and desireth to return, deeming sojourning intolerable ; another's vineyard is hailed upon, he observeth his labours and all his toil spent in vain. When can a human being not be made sad ? An enemy he findeth in a friend. What greater misery in mankind ? These things all men do deplore and grieve at, and these are tribulations : in all these they call upon the Lord, and they do rightly. Let them call upon God, He is able either to teach how it must be borne, or to heal it when borne. He knoweth how not to suffer us to be tried above that we are able to bear.[2] Let us call upon God even in those tribulations : but these tribulations do find us ; as in another Psalm is written, "Helper in tribulations which have found us too much :"[3] there is a certain tribulation which we ought to find. Let such tribulations find us : there is a certain tribulation which we ought to seek and to find. What is that ? The above-named felicity in this world, abundance of temporal things : that is not indeed tribulation, these are the solaces of our tribulation. Of what tribulation ? Of our sojourning. For the very fact that we are not yet with God, the very fact that we are living amid trials and difficulties, that we cannot be without fear, is tribulation : for there is not that peace which is promised us. He that shall not have found this tribulation in his sojourning, doth not think of going home to his father-land. This is tribulation, brethren. Surely now we do good works, when we deal bread to the hungry, home to the stranger, and the like : tribulation even this is.

For we find pitiful objects upon whom we show pity ; and the pitiful case of pitiful objects maketh us compassionate. How much better now would it be with thee in that place, where thou findest no hungry man whom thou mayest feed, where thou findest no stranger whom thou mayest take in, no naked man whom thou mayest cover, no sick man whom thou mayest visit, no litigant whom thou mayest set at one ! For all things in that place are most high, are true, are holy, are everlasting. Our bread in that place is righteousness, our drink there is wisdom, our garment there is immortality, our house is everlasting in the heavens, our stedfastness[4] is immortality : doth sickness come over? Doth weariness weigh down to sleep ? No death, no litigation : there peace, quiet, joy, righteousness. No enemy hath entrance, no friend falleth away. What is the quiet there ? If we think and observe where we are, and where He that cannot lie hath promised that we are to be, from His very promise we find in what tribulation we are. This tribulation none findeth, but he that shall have sought it. Thou art whole, see if thou art miserable ; for it is easy for him that is sick to find himself miserable : when thou art whole, see if thou art miserable ; that thou art not yet with God. "Tribulation and grief I found, and on the Name of the Lord I called."[5] "Immolate," therefore, "to God the sacrifice of praise." Praise Him promising, praise Him calling, praise Him exhorting, praise Him helping : and understand in what tribulation thou art placed. Call upon (Him), thou shalt be drawn forth, thou shalt glorify, shalt abide.

23. But see what followeth, my brethren. For now some one or other, because God had said to him, "Immolate to God the sacrifice of praise," and had enjoined in a manner this tribute, did meditate to himself and said, I will rise daily, I will proceed to Church, I will say one hymn at matins, another at vespers, a third or fourth in my house, daily I do sacrifice the sacrifice of praise, and immolate to my God. Well thou doest indeed, if thou doest this : but take heed, lest now thou be careless, because now thou doest this : and perchance thy tongue bless God, and thy life curse God. O my people, saith to thee the God of gods, the Lord that spake, "calling the earth from the rising of the sun unto the setting," though yet thou art placed amid the tares,[6] "Immolate the sacrifice of praise to thy God, and render to Him thy prayers :" but take heed lest thou live ill, and chant well. Wherefore this ? For, "Unto the sinner, saith God, why dost thou tell out My judgments, and takest My Covenant in thy mouth?" (ver. 16). Ye see, brethren, with

---

[1] Ps. cxvi. 4. [2] 1 Cor. x. 13. [3] Ps. xlvi. 1. [4] *Firmitas* (perhaps "health"). [5] Matt. xiii. 25

what trembling we say these words. We take the Covenant of God in our mouth, and we preach to you the instruction and judgment of God. And what saith God to the sinner? "Why dost thou?" Doth He then forbid preachers that be sinners? And where is that, " What they say do, but what they do, do not "?[1] Where is that, " Whether in truth or on occasion Christ be preached "?[2] But these words were said, lest they should fear that hear, from whomsoever it be that they hear: not that they should be without care that speak good words, and do evil deeds. Now therefore, brethren, ye are without care: if ye hear good words ye hear God,[3] through whomsoever it be that ye may hear. But God would not dismiss without reproof them that speak: lest with their speaking alone, without care for themselves they should slumber in evil life, and say to themselves, " For God will not consign us to perdition, through whose mouth He has willed that so many good words should be spoken to His people." Nay, but hear what thou speakest, whoever thou art that speakest: and thou that wilt be heard thyself, first hear thyself; and speak what a certain man doth speak in another Psalm,[4] " I will hear what in me speaketh the Lord God, for He shall speak peace to His people." What am I then, that hear not what in me He speaketh, and will that other hear what through me He speaketh? I will hear first, will hear, and chiefly I will hear what speaketh in me the Lord God, for He shall speak peace to His people. Let me hear, and " chasten my body, and to servitude subject it, lest perchance to others preaching, myself be found a cast-away."[5] " Why dost thou tell out my judgments?" Wherefore to thee what profiteth not thee? He admonisheth him to hear: not to lay down preaching, but to take up obedience. " But thou, why dost thou take My Covenant in thy mouth?"

24. " But thou hatest instruction " (ver. 17). Thou hatest discipline. When I spare, thou singest and praisest: when I chasten, thou murmurest: as though, when I spare, I am thy God: and, when I chasten, I am not thy God. " I rebuke and chasten those whom I love."[6] " But thou hatest instruction: and hast thrown My sayings behind thee." The words that are said through thee, thou throwest behind thee. " And thou hast thrown My sayings behind thee: " to a place where they may not be seen by thee, but may load thee. " And thou hast thrown My sayings behind thee."

25. " If thou sawest a thief, thou didst consent unto him, and with adulterers thou didst make thy portion " (ver. 18). Lest perchance thou shouldest say, I have not committed theft, I have not committed adultery. What if he pleased thee that hath committed? Hast thou not with the very pleasing consented? Hast thou not by approval made thy portion with him that hath committed? For this is, brethren, to consent with a thief, and to make with an adulterer thy portion: for even if thou committest not, and approvest what is committed, thou art an accessory in the deed: for " the sinner is praised in the longings of his soul, and he that doeth iniquity shall be blessed."[7] Thou doest not evil things, thou praisest evil-doers. For is this a small evil? " Thou didst make thy portion with adulterers."

26. " Thy mouth hath abounded in malice, and thy tongue hath embraced deceit " (ver. 19). Of the malevolence and deceit, brethren, of certain men he speaketh, who by adulation, though they know what they hear to be evil, yet lest they offend those from whom they hear, not only by not reproving but by holding their peace do consent.[8] Too little is it, that they do not say, Thou hast done evil: but they even say, Thou hast done even well: and they know it to be evil: but their mouth aboundeth in malice, and their tongue embraceth deceit. Deceit is a sort of guile in words, of uttering one thing, thinking another. He saith not, thy tongue hath committed deceit or perpetrated deceit, but in order to point out to thee a kind of pleasure taken in the very evil doing, He hath said, " Hath embraced." It is too little that thou doest it, thou art delighted too; thou praisest openly, thou laughest to thyself. Thou dost push to destruction a man heedlessly putting forth his faults, and knowing not whether they be faults: thou that knowest it to be a fault, sayest not, " Whither art thou rushing? " If thou wert to see him heedlessly walk in the dark, where thou knewest a well to be, and wert to hold thy peace, of what sort wouldest thou be? wouldest thou not be set down for an enemy of his life?[9] And yet if he were to fall into a well, not in soul[10] but in body he would die. He doth fall headlong into his vices, he doth expose before thee his evil doings: thou knowest them to be evil, and praisest and laughest to thyself. Oh that at length he were to be turned to God at whom thou laughest, and whom thou wouldest not reprove, and that he were to say, " Let them be confounded that say to me, Well, well."[11]

27. " Sitting against thy brother thou didst detract " (ver. 20). And this " sitting " doth belong to that whereof he hath spoken above in,

---

[1] Matt. xxiii. 3.   [2] Philip. i. 18.
[3] *Al.* " They are of God."   [4] Ps. lxxxv. 8.
[5] 1 Cor. ix. 27.   [6] Rev. iii. 19.

[7] Ps. x. 3.
[8] MSS. Bodl. and Ex Coll. " lest they offend those from whom they hear, not only by reproof but by silence, think it not enough that they do not say."
[9] *Anima.*   [10] *Anima.*   [11] Ps. xl. 15.

" hath embraced." For he that doeth anything while standing or passing along, doth it not with pleasure : but if he for this purpose sitteth, how much leisure doth he seek out to do it ! That very evil detraction thou wast making with diligence, thou wast making sitting ; thou wouldest thereon be wholly engaged ; thou wast embracing thy evil, thou wast kissing thy craftiness. " And against thy mother's son thou didst lay a stumbling-block." Who is " mother's son"? Is it not brother? He would repeat then the same that he had said above, " thy brother." Hath he intimated that any distinction must be perceived by us? Evidently, brethren, I think a distinction must be made. Brother against brother doth detract, for example's sake, as though for instance one strong, and now a doctor and scholar of some weight, doth detract from his brother, one perchance that is teaching well and walking well : but another is weak, against him he layeth a stumbling-block by detracting from the former. For when the good are detracted from by those that seem to be of some weight and to be learned, the weak fall upon the stumbling-block, who as yet know not how to judge. Therefore this weak one is called " mother's son," not yet father's, still needing milk, and hanging on the breast. He is borne as yet in the bosom of his mother the Church, he is not strong enough to draw near to the solid food of his Father's table, but from the mother's breast he draweth sustenance, unskilled in judging, inasmuch as yet he is animal and carnal. " For the spiritual man judgeth all things," [1] but " the animal man perceiveth not those things which are of the Spirit of God ; for they are foolishness to him." [2] To such men saith the Apostle, " I could not speak unto you as unto spiritual, but as unto carnal, as to babes in Christ I gave you milk to drink, not meat ; for ye were not able, but not even now are ye able." [3] A mother I have been to you : as is said in another place, " I became a babe among you, even as a nurse cherishing her own children." [4] Not a nurse nursing children of others, but a nurse cherishing her own children. For there are mothers who when they have borne give to nurses : they that have borne cherish not their children, because they have given them to be nursed ; [5] but those that cherish, cherish not their own, but those of others : but he himself had borne, he was himself cherishing, to no nurse did commit what he had borne ; for he had said, " Of whom I travail again until Christ be formed in you." [6] He did cherish them, and gave milk.

But there were some as it were learned and spiritual men who detracted from Paul. " His letters indeed, say they, are weighty and powerful ; but the presence of his body weak, and speech contemptible : " [7] he saith himself in his Epistle, that certain his detractors had said these words. They were sitting, and were detracting against their brother, and against that their mother's son, to be fed with milk, they were laying a stumbling-block. " And against thy mother's son thou didst lay a stumbling-block."

28. " These things hast thou done, and I held my tongue " (ver. 21). Therefore the Lord our God shall come, and shall not keep silence. Now, " These things hast thou done, and I held my tongue." What is, " I held my tongue"? From vengeance I have desisted, my severity I have deferred, patience to thee I have prolonged, thy repentance I have long looked for. . . . " Thou hast imagined iniquity, that I shall be like unto thee ; " Thou hast [8] imagined that I shall be like unto thee, while thou wilt not be like unto Me. For, " Be ye," he saith, " perfect, even as your Father, which is in the heavens, who maketh His sun to rise on the good and evil." [9] Him thou wouldest not copy, who giveth good things even to evil men, insomuch that sitting thou dost detract even from good men. " I will reprove thee," when " God manifest shall come, our God, and shall not keep silence," " I will reprove thee." And what to thee shall I do in reproving thee? what to thee shall I do? Now thyself thou seest not, I will make thee see thyself. Because if thou shouldest see thyself, and shouldest displease thyself, thou wouldest please Me : but because not seeing thyself thou hast pleased thyself, thou wilt displease both Me and thyself ; Me when thou shalt be judged ; thyself when thou shalt burn. But what to thee shall I do? He saith. " I will set thee before thy face." For why wouldest thou escape thyself? At thy back thou art to thyself, thou seest not thyself : I make thee see thyself : what behind thy back thou hast put, before thy face will I put ; thou shalt see thy uncleanness, not that thou mayest amend, but that thou mayest blush. . . .

29. But, " understand these things, ye that forget God " (ver. 22). See how He crieth, and keepeth not silence, spareth [10] not. Thou hadst forgotten the Lord, [11] didst not think of thy evil life. Perceive thou how thou hast forgotten the Lord. " Lest at length He seize like a lion, and there be none to deliver." What is " like a lion "? Like a brave one, like a mighty one, like him whom none can withstand. To this he made reference when he said, " Lion." For it is used

---

[1] 1 Cor. ii. 15. [2] 1 Cor. ii. 14. [3] 1 Cor. iii. 1, 2.
[4] 1 Thess. ii. 7.
[5] [See Jer. Taylor's remarkable sermon on " The Nursing of Children by their Mothers, after the Example of the Blessed Virgin," vol. i. 38, Bungay ed. of Heber's edition. — C.]
[6] Gal. iv. 19.

[7] 2 Cor. x. 10. [8] Oxf. MS. rep. " Thou hast," etc.
[9] Matt. v. 48, 45. [10] Some MSS. " When He spareth."
[11] Oxf. MSS. " God."

for praise, it is used also for showing evil. The devil hath been called lion: " Your adversary," He saith, "like a roaring lion, goeth about seeking whom He may devour." [1] May it not be that whereas he hath been called lion because of savage fierceness, Christ hath been called Lion for wondrous mightiness? And where is that, "The Lion hath prevailed of the tribe of Judah?" [2] . . .

30. "Sacrifice of praise shall glorify Me" (ver. 23). How shall "sacrifice of praise glorify Me"? Assuredly sacrifice of praise doth no wise profit evil men, because they take Thy Covenant in their mouth, and do damnable things that displease Thine eyes. Straightway, he saith, even to them this I say, "Sacrifice of praise shall glorify Me." For if thou livest ill and speakest good words, not yet dost thou praise: but again, if, when thou beginnest to live well, to thy merits thou dost ascribe thy living well, not yet dost thou praise. . . . Therefore the Publican went down justified, rather than that Pharisee. Therefore hear ye that live well, hear ye that live ill: "Sacrifice of praise shall glorify Me." No one offereth Me this sacrifice, and is evil. I say not, Let there not offer Me this any one that is evil; but no one doth offer Me this, that is evil. For he that praiseth, is good: because if he praiseth, he doth also live well, because if he praiseth, not only with tongue he praiseth, but life also with tongue doth agree.

31. "And there is the way whereby I will show him the salvation of God." In sacrifice of praise "is the way." What is "the salvation of God"? Christ Jesus. And how in sacrifice of praise to us is shown Christ? Because Christ with grace came to us. These words saith the Apostle: " But I live, now not I, but Christ liveth in me: but that in flesh I live, in faith I live of the Son of God, who loved me, and gave Himself for me." [3] Acknowledge then sinners, that there would not need physician, if they were whole.[4] For Christ died for the ungodly.[5] When then they acknowledge their ungodlinesses, and first copy that Publican, saying, " Lord, be merciful to me a sinner: " [6] show wounds, beseech Physician: and because they praise not themselves, but blame themselves, — " So that he that glorieth, not in himself but in the Lord may glory," [7] — they acknowledge the cause of the coming of Christ, because for this end He came, that He might save sinners: for " Jesus Christ came," he saith, " into this world to save sinners; of whom I am chief." [8] Further, those Jews, boasting of their work, thus the same Apostle doth rebuke, in saying, that they to grace belonged not, who to their merits and their works

thought that reward was owing.[9] He therefore that knoweth himself to belong to grace, doth know what is Christ and what is Christ's, because he needeth grace. If grace it is called, *gratis* it is given; if *gratis* it is given, not any merits of thine have preceded that it should be given. . . .

PSALM LI.[10]

1. Neither must this multitude's throng be defrauded, nor their infirmity burthened. Silence we ask, and quiet, in order that our voice, after yesterday's labour, be able with some little vigour to last out. It must be believed, that your love hath met together in greater numbers to-day for nothing else, but that ye may pray for those whom an alien and perverse inclination doth keep away. For we are speaking neither of heathens nor of Jews, but of Christians: nor of those that are yet Catechumens, but of many that are even baptized, from the Laver of whom ye do no wise differ, and yet to their heart ye are unlike. For to-day how many brethren of ours we think of, and deplore their going unto vanities and lying insanities, to the neglect of that to which they have been called. Who, if in the very circus from any cause they chance to be startled, do immediately cross themselves,[11] and stand bearing It on the forehead, in the very place, from whence they had withdrawn, if they had borne It in heart. God's mercy must be implored, that He may give understanding for condemning these things, inclination to flee them, and mercy to forgive. Opportunely, then, of Penitence a Psalm to-day has been chanted. Speak we even with the absent: there will be to them for our voice your memory. Neglect not the wounded and feeble, but that ye may more easily make whole, whole ye ought to abide. Correct by reproving, comfort by addressing, set an example by living well, He will be with them that hath been with you. For now that ye have overpassed these dangers, the fountain of God's mercy is not closed. Where ye have come they will come; where ye have passed they will pass. A grievous thing it is indeed, and exceeding perilous, nay ruinous, and for certain a deadly thing, that witting they sin. For in one way to these vanities doth he run that despiseth the voice of Christ; in another way, he that knoweth from what he is fleeing. But that not even of such men we ought to despair, this Psalm doth show.

2. For there is written over it the title thereof, "A Psalm of David himself, when there came to him Nathan the prophet, when he went in unto Bersabee." Bersabee was a woman, wife of

[1] 1 Pet. v. 8.   [2] Rev. v. 5.   [3] Gal. ii. 20.
[4] Matt. ix. 12.   [5] Rom. v. 6.   [6] Luke xviii. 13.
[7] 1 Cor. i. 31.   [8] 1 Tim. i. 15.

[9] Gal. v. 4.
[10] From a sermon to the people of Carthage. See below, § 11.
[11] [On the sign of the Cross, see (Tertullian) A. N. F. vol. iii. p. 104; also vol. vii. (Lactant.) p. 130, note 3. — C.]

another. With grief indeed we speak, and with trembling; but yet God would not have to be hushed what He hath willed to be written. I will say then not what I will, but what I am obliged; I will say not as one exhorting to imitation, but as one instructing you to fear. Captivated with this woman's beauty, the wife of another, the king and prophet David, from whose seed according to the flesh the Lord was to come,[1] committed adultery with her. This thing in this Psalm is not read, but in the title thereof it appeareth; but in the book of Kings[2] it is more fully read. Both Scriptures are canonical, to both without any doubt by Christians credit must be given. The sin was committed, and was written down. Moreover her husband in war he caused to be killed: and after this deed there was sent to him Nathan the prophet;[3] sent by the Lord, to reprove him for so great an outrage.

3. What men should beware of, we have said; but what if they shall have fallen they should imitate, let us hear. For many men will to fall with David, and will not to rise with David. Not then for falling is the example set forth, but if thou shalt have fallen for rising again. Take heed lest thou fall. Not the delight of the younger be the lapse of the elder, but be the fall of the elder the dread of the younger. For this it was set forth, for this was written, for this in the Church often read and chanted: let them hear that have not fallen, lest they fall; let them hear that have fallen, that they may rise. So great a man's sin is not hushed, is proclaimed in the Church. There men hear that are ill hearers, and seek for themselves countenance for sinning: they look out for means whereby they may defend what they have made ready to commit, not how they may beware of what they have not committed, and they say to themselves, If David, why not I too? Thence that soul is more unrighteous, which, forasmuch as it hath done it because David did, therefore hath done worse than David. I will say this very thing, if I shall be able, more plainly. David had set forth to himself none for a precedent as thou hast: he had fallen by lapse of concupiscence, not by the countenance of holiness: thou dost set before thine eyes as it were a holy man, in order that thou mayest sin: thou dost not copy his holiness, but dost copy his fall. Thou[4] dost love that in David, which in himself David hated: thou makest thee ready to sin, thou inclinest to sin: in order that thou mayest sin thou consultest the book of God: the Scriptures of God for this thou hearest, that thou mayest do what displeaseth God. This did not David; he was reproved by a Prophet, he stumbled not over a Prophet. But others hearing to their health, by the fall of a strong man measure their

weakness: and desiring to avoid what God condemneth, from careless looking do restrain their eyes. Them they fix not upon the beauty of another's flesh, nor make themselves careless with perverse simpleness; they say not, "With good intent I have observed, of kindness I have observed, of charity I have long looked." For they set before themselves the fall of David, and they see that this great man for this purpose hath fallen, in order that little men may not be willing to look on that whereby they may fall. For they restrain their eyes from wantonness, not readily do they join themselves in company, they do not mingle with strange women, they raise not complying eyes to strange balconies, to strange terraces. For from afar David saw her with whom he was captivated.[5] Woman afar, lust near. What he saw was elsewhere, in himself that whereby he fell. This weakness of the flesh must be therefore minded, the words of the Apostle recollected, "Let not sin therefore reign in your mortal body."[6] He hath not said, let there not be; but, "let there not reign." There is sin in thee, when thou takest pleasure; there reigneth, if thou shalt have consented. Carnal pleasure, especially if proceeding unto unlawful and strange objects, is to be bridled, not let loose: by government to be tamed, not to be set up for government. Look and be without care, if thou hast nothing whereby thou mayest be moved. But thou makest answer, "I contain with strong resolution." Art thou any wise stronger than David?[7]

4. He admonisheth, moreover, by such an example, that no one ought to lift himself up in prosperous circumstances. For many fear adverse circumstances, fear not prosperous circumstances. Prosperity is more perilous to soul than adversity to body. First, prosperity doth corrupt, in order that adversity may find something to break. My brethren, stricter watch must be kept against felicity. Wherefore, see ye after what manner the saying of God amid our own felicity doth take from us security: "Serve ye," He saith, "the Lord in fear, and exult unto Him with trembling."[8] In exultation, in order that we may render thanks; in trembling, lest we fall. This sin did not David, when he was suffering Saul for persecutor.[9] When holy David was suffering Saul his enemy, when he was being vexed by his persecutions, when he was fleeing through divers places, in order that he might not fall into his hands, he lusted not for her that was another's, he slew not husband after committing adultery with wife. He was in the infirmity of his tribulation so much the more intimate with God as

---

[1] Rom. i. 3.   [2] 2 Sam. xi. 2-17.   [3] 2 Sam. xii. 1.
[4] Al. " Love this in David which in himself David hated not."

[5] 2 Sam. xi. 2.   [6] Rom. vi. 12.
[7] [Compare the author's Confessions, vol. i. of this series, pp. 126, 153, 154, and book viii. passim. — C.]
[8] Ps. ii. 11.   [9] 1 Sam. xxiv. 5, xxvi. 9.

he seemed more miserable. Something useful is tribulation; useful the surgeon's lancet rather than the devil's temptation. He became secure when his enemies were overthrown, pressure was removed, swelling grew out. This example therefore doth avail to this end, that we should fear felicity. "Tribulation," he saith, "and grief I found, and on the name of the Lord I called." [1]

5. But it was done; I would say these words to those that have not done the like, in order that they should watch to keep their uncorruptness, and that while they take heed how a great one has fallen, they that be small should fear. But if any that hath already fallen heareth these words, and that hath in his conscience any evil thing; to the words of this Psalm let him advert; let him heed the greatness of the wound, but not despair of the majesty of the Physician. Sin with despair is certain death. Let no one therefore say, If already any evil thing I have done, already I am to be condemned: God pardoneth not such evil things, why add I not sins to sins? I will enjoy this world in pleasure, in wantonness, in wicked cupidity: now hope of amendment having been lost, let me have even what I see, if I cannot have what I believe. This Psalm then, while it maketh heedful those that have not believed, so doth not will them that have fallen to be despaired of. Whoever thou art that hast sinned, and hesitatest to exercise penitence [2] for thy sin, despairing of thy salvation, hear David groaning. To thee Nathan the prophet hath not been sent, David himself hath been sent to thee. Hear him crying, and with him cry: hear him groaning, and with him groan; hear him weeping, and mingle tears; hear him amended, and with him rejoice. If from thee sin could not be excluded, be not hope of pardon excluded. There was sent to that man Nathan the prophet, observe the king's humility.[3] He rejected not the words of him giving admonition, he said not, Darest thou speak to me, a king? An exalted king heard a prophet, let His humble people hear Christ.

6. Hear therefore these words, and say thou with him: "Have pity upon me, O God, after Thy great mercy" (ver. 1). He that imploreth great mercy, confesseth great misery. Let them seek a little mercy of Thee, that have sinned in ignorance: "Have pity," he saith, "upon me, after Thy great mercy." Relieve a deep wound after Thy great healing. Deep is what I have, but in the Almighty I take refuge. Of my own so deadly wound I should despair, unless I could find so great a Physician. "Have pity upon me, O God, after Thy great mercy: and after the multitude of Thy pities, blot out my iniquity." What he saith, "Blot out my iniquity," is this, "Have pity upon me, O God." And what he saith, "After the multitude of Thy pities," is this, "After Thy great mercy." Because great is the mercy, many are the mercies; and of Thy great mercy, many are Thy pityings. Thou dost regard mockers to amend them, dost regard ignorant men to teach them, dost regard men confessing to pardon. Did he this in ignorance? A certain man had done some, aye many evil things he had done; "Mercy," he saith, "I obtained, because ignorant I did it in unbelief." [4] This David could not say, "Ignorant I did it." For he was not ignorant how very evil a thing was the touching of another's wife, and how very evil a thing was the killing of the husband, who knew not of it, and was not even angered. They obtain therefore the mercy of the Lord that have in ignorance done it; and they that have knowing done it, obtain not any mercy it may chance, but "great mercy."

7. "More and more wash me from mine unrighteousness" (ver. 2). What is, "More and more wash"? One much stained. More and more wash the sins of one knowing. Thou that hast washed off the sins of one ignorant. Not even thus is it to be despaired of Thy mercy. "And from my delinquency purge Thou me." According to the manner in which He is physician, offer a recompense. He is God, offer sacrifice. What wilt thou give that thou mayest be purged? For see upon whom thou callest; upon a Just One thou callest. He hateth sins, if He is just; He taketh vengeance upon sins, if He is just; thou wilt not be able to take away from the Lord God His justice: entreat mercy, but observe the justice: there is mercy to pardon the sinner, there is justice to punish the sin. What then? Thou askest mercy; shall sin unpunished abide? Let David answer, let those that have fallen answer, answer with David, and say, No, Lord, no sin of mine shall be unpunished; I know the justice of Him whose mercy I ask: it shall not be unpunished, but for this reason I will not that Thou punish me, because I punish my sin: for this reason I beg that Thou pardon, because I acknowledge.

8. "For mine iniquity I acknowledge, and my delinquency is before me ever" (ver. 3). I have not put behind my back what I have done, I look not at others, forgetful of myself, I pretend not to pull out a straw from my brother's eye, when there is a beam in my eye; [5] my sin is before me, not behind me. For it was behind me when to me was sent the Prophet, and set before me the parable of the poor man's sheep.[6] For saith Nathan the Prophet to David, "There

---

[1] Ps. cxvi. 3, 4.
[2] [Here I have corrected the feeble translation, "do penance," which is unjust to the author's entire system of thought. See *Confessions*, book viii. vol. i. this series. — C.]
[3] *Al.* "The pride of royalty."

[4] 1 Tim. i. 13.   [5] Matt. vii. 5.   [6] 2 Sam. xii. 1, 2, etc.

was a certain rich man having very many sheep; but a poor man his neighbour had one little ewe sheep, which in his bosom and of his own food he was feeding: there came a stranger to the rich man, nothing from his flock he took, for the little ewe sheep of the poor man his neighbour he lusted; her he slew for the stranger: what doth he deserve?" But the other being angry doth pronounce sentence: then the king, evidently knowing not wherein he had been taken,[1] declared the rich man deserving of death, and that the sheep be restored fourfold. Most sternly and most justly. But his sin was not yet before him, behind his back was what he had done: his own iniquity he did not yet acknowledge, and therefore another's he did not pardon. But the Prophet, being for this purpose sent, took from his back the sin, and before his eyes placed it, so that he might see that sentence so stern to have been pronounced against himself. For cutting and healing his heart's wound, he made a lancet of his tongue. . . .

9. "Against Thee alone have I sinned, and before Thee an evil thing have I done" (ver. 4). What is this? For before men was not another's wife debauched and husband slain? Did not all men know what David had done?[2] What is, "Against Thee alone have I sinned, and before Thee an evil thing have I done." Because Thou alone art without sin. He is a just punisher that hath nothing in Him to be punished; He is a just reprover that hath nothing in Him to be reproved. "That thou mayest be justified in Thy sayings, and conquer when Thou art judged." To whom he speaketh, brethren, to whom he speaketh, is difficult to understand. To God surely he speaketh, and it is evident that God the Father is not judged. What is, "And conquer when Thou art judged"? He seeth the future Judge to be judged, one just by sinners to be judged, and therein conquering, because in Him was nothing to be judged. For alone among men could truly say the God-Man, "If ye have found in Me sin, say."[3] But perchance there was what escaped men, and they found not what was really there, but was not manifest. In another place[4] He saith, "Behold there cometh the Prince of the world," being an acute observer of all sins; "Behold," He saith, "there cometh the Prince of this world," with death afflicting sinners, presiding over death: for, "By the malice of the devil death came into the world."[5] "Behold," He saith, "there cometh the Prince of the world:" — He said these words close upon His Passion: — "and in Me he shall find nothing," nothing of sin, nothing worthy of death, nothing worthy of condemna-

tion. And as if it were said to Him, Why then dost Thou die? He continueth and saith, "But that all men may know that I do the will of My Father; arise, let us go hence." I suffer, He saith, undeserving, for men deserving, in order that them I may make deserving of My Life, for whom I undeservedly suffer their death. To Him then, having no sin, saith on the present occasion the Prophet David, "Against Thee only have I sinned, and before Thee an evil thing have I done, that Thou mayest be justified in Thy sayings, and conquer when Thou art judged." For Thou overcomest all men, all judges; and he that deemeth himself just, before Thee is unjust: Thou alone justly judgest, having been unjustly judged, That hast power to lay down Thy life, and hast power again to take it.[6] Thou conquerest, then, when Thou art judged. All men Thou overcomest, because Thou art more than men, and by Thee were men made.

10. "For, behold, in iniquities I was conceived" (ver. 6). As though he were saying, They are conquered that have done what thou, David, hast done: for this is not a little evil and little sin, to wit, adultery and man-slaying. What of them that from the day that they were born of their mother's womb, have done no such thing? even to them dost thou ascribe some sins, in order that He may conquer all men when He beginneth to be judged. David hath taken upon him the person of mankind, and hath heeded the bonds of all men, hath considered the offspring of death, hath adverted to the origin of iniquity, and he saith, "For, behold, in iniquities I was conceived." Was David born of adultery; being born of Jesse,[7] a righteous man, and his own wife? What is it that he saith himself to have been in iniquity conceived, except that iniquity is drawn from Adam? Even the very bond of death, with iniquity itself is engrained? No man is born without bringing punishment, bringing desert of punishment. A Prophet saith also in another place,[8] "No one is clean in Thy sight, not even an infant, whose life is of one day upon earth." For we know both by the Baptism of Christ that sins are loosed, and that the Baptism of Christ availeth the remission of sins. If infants are every way innocent, why do mothers run with them when sick to the Church?[9] What by that Baptism, what by that remission is put away? An innocent one I see that rather weeps than is angry. What doth Baptism wash off? what doth that Grace loose? There is loosed the offspring of sin. For if that infant could speak to thee, it would say, and if it had the understanding which David had, it would answer thee, Why

1 *Al.* "he was captive," or, "was held captive."
2 2 Sam. xi. 4, 15.   3 John viii. 46.   4 John xiv. 30.
5 Wisd. ii. 24.

6 John x. 18.
8 Job xiv. 5, LXX.

7 1 Sam. xvi. 18.
9 Against the Pelagians.

heedest thou me, an infant? Thou dost not indeed see my actions: but I in iniquity have been conceived, "And in sins hath my mother nourished me in the womb."

Apart from this bond of mortal[1] concupiscence was Christ born without a male, of a virgin conceiving by the Holy Ghost. He cannot be said to have been conceived in iniquity, it cannot be said, In sins His mother nourished Him in the womb, to whom was said, "The Holy Ghost shall come upon thee, and the Virtue of the Highest shall overshadow thee."[2] It is not therefore because it is sin to have to do with wives that men are conceived in iniquity, and in sins nourished in the womb by their mother; but because that which is made is surely made of flesh deserving punishment.[3] For the punishment of the flesh is death, and surely there is in it liability to death itself. Whence the Apostle spoke not of the body as if to die, but as if dead: "The body indeed is dead," he saith, "because of sin, but the Spirit is life because of righteousness."[4] How then without bond of sin is born that which is conceived and sown of a body dead because of sin? This chaste operation in a married person hath not sin, but the origin of sin draweth with it condign punishment. For there is no husband that, because he is an husband, is not subject to death, or that is subject to death for any other reason but because of sin. For even the Lord was subject to death, but not on account of sin: He took upon Him our punishment, and so looseth our guilt. With reason then, "In Adam all die, but in Christ shall all be made alive."[5] For, "Through one man," saith the Apostle, "sin hath entered into this world, and through sin death, and so hath passed unto all men, in that all have sinned."[6] Definite is the sentence: "In Adam," he saith, "all have sinned." Alone then could such an infant be innocent, as hath not been born of the work of Adam.

11. "For, behold, truth Thou hast loved: uncertain and hidden things of Thy wisdom, Thou hast manifested to me" (ver. 6). That is, Thou hast not left unpunished even the sins of those whom Thou dost pardon. "Truth Thou hast loved:" so mercy Thou hast granted first,[7] as that Thou shouldest also preserve truth. Thou pardonest one confessing, pardonest, but only if he punisheth himself: so there are preserved mercy and truth: mercy because man is set free; truth, because sin is punished. "Uncertain and hidden things of Thy wisdom Thou hast manifested to me." What "hidden things"? What "uncertain things"? Because God pardoneth even such. Nothing is so hidden, nothing so uncertain.[8] For this uncertainty the Ninevites repented, for they said, though after the threatenings of the Prophet, though after that cry, "Three days and Nineve shall be overthrown:"[9] they said to themselves, Mercy must be implored; they said in this sort reasoning among themselves, "Who knoweth whether God may turn for the better His sentence, and have pity?"[10] It was "uncertain," when it is said, "Who knoweth?" on an uncertainty they did repent,[11] certain mercy they earned: they prostrated them in tears, in fastings, in sackcloth and ashes they prostrated them, groaned, wept, God spared. Nineve stood: was Nineve overthrown? One way indeed it seemeth to men, and another way it seemed to God. But I think that it was fulfilled that the Prophet had foretold. Regard what Nineve was, and see how it was overthrown; overthrown in evil, builded in good; just as Saul the persecutor was overthrown, Paul the preacher builded.[12] Who would not say that this city, in which we now are, was happily overthrown, if all those madmen, leaving their triflings,[13] were to run together to the Church with contrite heart, and were to call upon God's mercy for their past doings? Should we not say, Where is that Carthage? Because there is not what there was, it is overthrown: but if there is what there was not, it is builded. So is said to Jeremiah, "Behold, I will give to thee to root up, to dig under, to overthrow, to destroy," and again, "to build, and to plant."[14] Thence is that voice of the Lord, "I will smite and I will heal."[15] He smiteth the rottenness of the deed, He healeth the pain of the wound. Physicians do thus when they cut; they smite and heal; they arm themselves in order to strike, they carry steel, and come to cure. But because great were the sins of the Ninevites, they said, "Who knoweth?" This uncertainty had God disclosed to His servant David. For when he had said, before the Prophet standing and convicting him, "I have sinned:" straightway he heard from the Prophet, that is, from the Spirit of God which was in the Prophet, "Thy sin is put away from thee."[16] "Uncertain and hidden things" of His wisdom He manifested to him.[17]

12. "Thou shalt sprinkle me," he saith, "with hyssop, and I shall be cleansed" (ver. 7). Hyssop we know to be a herb humble but heal-

---

[1] So most mss. Ben. "carnal," but see below.
[2] Luke i. 35.
[3] [The mother need not be conceived of as sinning in her passive relations to an act which is undefiled in itself (Heb. xiii. 4); but she is a sinner like all mortals, and in that estate of sinfulness her offspring is begotten and nourished in the womb. So he argues. — C.]
[4] Rom. viii. 10.   [5] 1 Cor. xv. 22.   [6] Rom. v. 12.
[7] Prærogasti.

[8] i.e., as His mercy is to us beforehand.
[9] Jonah iii. 4.   [10] Jonah iii. 9.
[11] [Here the translator has "did penance," which has no meaning at all apart from ecclesiastical discipline, to which the men of Nineve were certainly not subjected. — C.]
[12] Acts ix. 4.   [13] [See p. 166, note 3, supra. — C.]
[14] Jer. i. 10.   [15] Deut. xxxii. 39.   [16] 2 Sam. xii. 13.
[17] [The English Version is not sustained by Jerome, whose rendering is (happier than that so beautifully expounded by our author), absconditum et arcanum sapietatiæ manifestasti. — C.]

ing: to the rock it is said to adhere with roots. Thence in a mystery the similitude of cleansing the heart has been taken. Do thou also take hold, with [1] the root of thy love, on thy Rock: be humble in thy humble God, in order that thou mayest be exalted in thy glorified God. Thou shalt be sprinkled with hyssop, the humility of Christ shall cleanse thee. Despise not the herb, attend to the efficacy of the medicine. Something further I will say, which we are wont to hear from physicians, or to experience in sick persons. Hyssop, they say, is proper for purging the lungs. In the lung is wont to be noted pride: for there is inflation, there breathing. It was said of Saul the persecutor as of Saul the proud, that he was going to bind Christians, breathing slaughter:[2] he was breathing out slaughter, breathing out blood, his lung not yet cleansed. Hear also in this place one humbled, because with hyssop purged: "Thou shalt wash me," that is, shalt cleanse me: "and above snow I shall be whitened." "Although," he saith, "your sins shall have been like scarlet, like snow I will whiten."[3] Out of such men Christ doth present to Himself a vesture without spot and wrinkle.[4] Further, His vesture on the mount, which shone forth like whitened snow,[5] signified the Church cleansed from every spot of sin.

13. But where is humility from hyssop? Hear what followeth: "To my hearing Thou shalt give exultation and gladness, and bones humbled shall exult" (ver. 8). I will rejoice in hearing Thee, not in speaking against Thee. Thou hast sinned, why defendest thou thyself? Thou wilt speak: suffer thou; hear, yield to divine words, lest thou be put to confusion, and be still more wounded: sin hath been committed, be it not defended: to confession let it come, not to defence. Thou engagest thyself as defender of thy sin, thou art conquered: no innocent patron hast thou engaged, thy defence is not profitable to thee. For who art thou that defendest thyself? Thou art meet to accuse thyself. Say not, either, "I have done nothing;" or, "What great thing have I done?" or, "Other men as well have done." If in doing sin thou sayest thou hast done nothing, thou wilt be nothing, thou wilt receive nothing: God is ready to give indulgence, thou closest the door against thyself: He is ready to give, do not oppose the bar of defence, but open the bosom of confession. "To my hearing Thou shalt give exultation and gladness." . . .

14. "Turn Thou away Thy face from my sins, and all mine iniquities blot out" (ver. 9). For now bones humbled exult, now with hyssop cleansed, humble I have become. "Turn Thou away Thy face," not from me, but "from my sins." For in another place praying he saith, "Turn not away Thy face from me." [6] He that would not that God's face be turned away from himself, would that God's face be turned away from his sins. For to sin, when God turneth not Himself away, he adverteth: if he adverteth, he animadverteth. "And all mine iniquities blot out." He is busied [7] with that capital sin: he reckoneth on more, he would have all his iniquities to be blotted out: he relieth on the Physician's hand, on that "great mercy," upon which he hath called in the beginning of the Psalm: "All mine iniquities blot out." God turneth away His face, and so blotteth out; by "turning away" His face, sins He blotteth out. By "turning towards," He writeth them. Thou hast heard of Him blotting out by turning away, hear of Him by turning towards, doing what? "But the countenance of the Lord is upon men doing evil things, that He may destroy from the earth the remembrance of them:"[8] He shall destroy the remembrance of them,[9] not by "blotting out their sins." But here he doth ask what? "Turn away Thy face from my sins." Well he asketh. For he himself doth not turn away his face from his *own* sins, saying, "For my sin I acknowledge." With reason thou askest and well askest, that God turn away from thy sin, if thou from thence dost not turn away thy face: but if thou settest thy sin at thy back, God doth there set His face. Do thou turn sin before thy face, if thou wilt that God thence turn away His face; and then safely thou askest, and He heareth.

15. "A clean heart create in me, O God" (ver. 10). "Create" — he meant [10] to say, "as it were *begin* something new." But, because repentant he was praying (that had committed some sin, which before he had committed, he was more innocent), after what manner he hath said "create" he showeth. "And a right spirit renew in my inner parts." By my doing, he saith, the uprightness of my spirit hath been made old and bowed. For he saith in another Psalm, "They have bowed my soul."[11] And when a man doth make himself stoop unto earthly lusts, he is "bowed" in a manner, but when he is made erect for things above, upright is his heart made, in order that God may be good to him. For, "How good is the God of Israel to the upright of heart!"[12] Moreover, brethren, listen. Sometimes God in this world chastiseth for his sin him that He pardoneth in the world to come. For even to David himself, to whom it had been already said by the Prophet,

---

[1] Oxf. MSS. *radice.*   [2] Acts ix. 1.   [3] Isa. i. 18.
[4] Eph. v. 27.   [5] Matt. xvii. 2.

[6] Ps. xxvii. 9.
[7] *Satagit.* Oxf. MSS. *Sategit,* "he hath done enough for."
[8] Ps. xxxiv. 16.
[9] Oxf. MSS. add, *perdet de terrâ memoriam eorum.*
[10] So MSS. Ben. "He meant not," but "as it were" seems to meet the difficulty.
[11] Ps. lvii. 6.   [12] Ps. lxxiii. 1.

"Thy sin is put away," [1] there happened certain things which God had threatened for that very sin.[2] For his son Abessalom against him waged bloody war, and many ways humbled his father.[3] He was walking in grief, in the tribulation of his humiliation, so resigned to God, that, ascribing to Him all that was just, he confessed that he was suffering nothing undeservedly, having now an heart upright, to which God was not displeasing. A slanderous person and one throwing in his teeth harsh curses [4] he patiently heard, one of the soldiers on the opposite side, that were with his unnatural son. And when he was heaping curses upon the king, one of the companions of David, enraged, would have gone and smitten him; but he is kept back by David. And he is kept back how? For that he said, God sent him to curse me. Acknowledging his guilt he embraced his penance, seeking glory not his own, praising the Lord in that good which he had, praising the Lord in that which he was suffering, "blessing the Lord alway, ever His praise was in his mouth." [5] Such are all the upright in heart: not those crooked persons who think themselves upright and God crooked: who when they do any evil thing, rejoice; when they suffer any evil thing, blaspheme; nay, if set in tribulation and scourging, they say from their distorted heart, "O God, what have I done to Thee?" Truly it is because they have done nothing to God, for they have done all to themselves. "And an upright spirit, renew in my inner parts."

16. "Cast me not forth from Thy face" (ver. 11). Turn away Thy face from my sins: and "cast me not forth from Thy face." Whose face he feareth, upon the face of the Same he calleth. "And Thy Holy Spirit take not away from me." For in one confessing there is the Holy Spirit. Even now, to the gift of the Holy Spirit it belongeth, that what thou hast done displeaseth thee. The unclean spirit sins do please; the Holy One they displease. Though then thou still implore pardon, yet thou art joined to God on the other part, because the evil thing that thou hast committed displeaseth thee: for the same thing displeaseth both thee and Him. Now, to assail thy fever, ye are two, thou and the Physician. For the reason that there cannot be confession of sin and punishment of sin in a man of himself: when one is angry with himself, and is displeasing to himself, then it is not without the gift of the Holy Spirit, nor doth he say, Thy Holy Spirit give to me, but, "Take not away from me."

17. "Give back to me the exultation of Thy salvation" [6] (ver. 12). "Give back" what I had; what by sinning I had lost: to wit, of Thy Christ. For who without Him can be made whole? Because even before that He was Son of Mary, "In the beginning He was the Word, and the Word was with God, and the Word was God;" [7] and so, by the holy fathers a future dispensation of flesh taken upon Him, was looked for; [8] as is believed by us to have been done. Times are changed, not faith. "And with Principal Spirit confirm me." Some have here understood the Trinity in God, Itself God; the dispensation of Flesh being excepted therefrom: since it is written, "God is a Spirit." [9] For that which is not body, and yet is, seemeth to exist in such sort as that it is spirit. Therefore some understand here the Trinity spoken of: "In upright Spirit," the Son; in "Holy Spirit," Holy Ghost; in "Principal Spirit," Father.[10] It is not any heretical opinion, therefore, whether this be so, or whether "upright Spirit" He would have to be taken of man himself (when He saith, "An upright spirit renew in my inner parts"), which I have bowed and distorted by sinning, so that in that case the Holy Spirit be Himself the Principal Spirit: which also he would not have to be taken away from him, and thereby would have himself to be confirmed therein.

18. But see what he annexeth: "With Principal Spirit," he saith, "confirm Thou me." Wherein "confirm"? Because Thou hast pardoned me, because I am secure, that what Thou hast forgiven is not to be ascribed, on this being made secure and with this grace confirmed, therefore I am not ungrateful. But I shall do what? "I would teach unrighteous men Thy ways" (ver. 13). Being *myself* of the unrighteous [11] (that is, one that was myself an unrighteous man, now no longer unrighteous; the Holy Spirit not having been taken away from me, and I being confirmed with Principal Spirit). "I would teach unrighteous men Thy ways." What ways wilt thou teach unrighteous men? "And ungodly men to Thee shall be converted." If David's sin is counted for ungodliness, let not ungodly men despair of themselves, forasmuch as God hath spared an ungodly man; but let them take heed that to Him they be converted, that His ways they learn. But if David's deed is not counted for ungodliness, but this is properly call ungodliness, namely, to apostatize from God, not to worship one God, or never to have worshipped, or to have forsaken, Him whom one did worship, then what he saith hath the force of superabundance, "And ungodly men shall to Thee be converted." So full art thou of the fatness of mercy, that for those converted to Thee, not only sinners of any

---

[1] 2 Sam. xii. 13.　　　[2] [Compare 2 Sam. xii. 10. — C.]
[3] 2 Sam. xv. 10.　　　[4] 2 Sam. xvi. 10.　　　[5] Ps. xxxiv. 1.
[6] *Salutaris tui.*

[7] John i. 1.　　　[8] [*Credebatur.* — C.]　　　[9] John iv. 24.
[10] Jerome on the Epist. to Gal. iv. 6.
[11] *Ex iniquo.* Oxf. mss. *ex iniquus.*

sort, but even ungodly, there is no cause for despair. Wherefore? That believing on Him that justifieth an ungodly man, their faith may be counted for righteousness.[1]

19. "Deliver me from bloods, O God, God of my health" (ver. 14). The Latin translator hath expressed, though by a word not Latin, yet an accuracy from the Greek.[2] For we all know that in Latin, *sanguines* (bloods) are not spoken of, nor yet *sanguina* (bloods in the neuter), nevertheless because the Greek translator hath thus used the plural number, not without reason, but because he found this in the original language the Hebrew, a godly translator hath preferred to use a word not Latin, rather than one not exact. Wherefore then hath he said in the plural number, "From bloods"? In many bloods, as in the origin of the sinful flesh, many sins he would have to be understood. The Apostle having regard to the very sins which come of the corruption of flesh and blood, saith, "Flesh and blood shall not possess the kingdom of God."[3] For doubtless, after the true faith of the same Apostle, that flesh shall rise again and shall itself gain incorruption, as He saith Himself, "This corruptible must put on incorruption, and this mortal put on immortality."[4] Because then this corruption is of sin, by the name thereof sins are called. In like manner as both that morsel of flesh and member which playeth in the mouth when we articulate words is called a tongue, and that is called a tongue which by the tongue is made, so we call one tongue the Greek, another the Latin; for the flesh is not diverse, but the sound. In the same manner, then, as the speech which is made by the tongue is called a tongue; so also the iniquity which is made by blood is called blood. Heeding, then, his many iniquities, as[5] in the expression above,[6] "And all my iniquities blot out," and ascribing them to the corruption of flesh and blood, "Free me," he saith, "from bloods:" that is, free me from iniquities, cleanse me from all corruption. . . . Not yet is the substance, but certain hope. "And my tongue shall exult of Thy righteousness."

20. "O Lord, my lips Thou shalt open, and my mouth shall tell of Thy praise" (ver. 15). "Thy praise," because[7] I have been created: "Thy praise," because sinning I have not been forsaken: "Thy praise," because I have been admonished to confess: "Thy praise," because in order that I might be secured I have been cleansed.

21. "Because if Thou hadst willed sacrifice, I would have given it surely" (ver. 16). David was living at that time when sacrifices of victim animals were offered to God, and he saw these times that were to be. Do we not perceive ourselves in these words? Those sacrifices were figurative, foretelling the One Saving Sacrifice. Not even we have been left without a Sacrifice to offer to God. For hear what he saith, having a concern for his sin, and wishing the evil thing which he hath done to be forgiven him: "If Thou hadst willed," he saith, "sacrifice, I would have given it surely. With holocausts Thou wilt not be delighted." Nothing shall we therefore offer? So shall we come to God? And whence shall we propitiate Him? Offer; certainly in thyself thou hast what thou mayest offer. Do not from without fetch frankincense,[8] but say, "In me are, O God, Thy vows, which I will render of praise to Thee."[9] Do not from without seek cattle to slay, thou hast in thyself what thou mayest kill. "Sacrifice to God is a spirit troubled, a heart contrite and humbled God despiseth not" (ver. 17). Utterly he despiseth bull, he-goat, ram: now is not the time that these should be offered. They were offered when they indicated something, when they promised something; when the things promised come, the promises are taken away. "A heart contrite and humbled God despiseth not." Ye know that God is high: if thou shalt have made thyself high, He will be from thee; if thou shalt have humbled thyself, He will draw near to thee.

22. See who this is: David as one man was seeming to implore; see ye here our image and the type of the Church.

"Deal kindly, O Lord, in Thy good will with Sion" (ver. 18). With this Sion deal kindly. What is Sion? A city holy. What is a city holy? That which cannot be hidden, being upon a mountain established. Sion in prospect, because it hath prospect of something which it hopeth for. For Sion is interpreted "prospect," and Jerusalem, "vision of peace." Ye perceive then yourselves to be in Sion and in Jerusalem, if being sure ye look for hope that is to be, and if ye have peace with God. "And be the walls of Jerusalem builded." "Deal kindly, O Lord, in Thy good will with Sion, and be the walls of Jerusalem builded." For not to herself let Sion ascribe her merits: do Thou with her deal kindly, "Be the walls of Jerusalem builded:" be the battlements of our immortality laid, in faith and hope and charity.

23. "Then Thou shalt accept the sacrifice of righteousness" (ver. 19). But now sacrifice for iniquity, to wit, a spirit troubled, and a heart humbled; then the sacrifice of righteousness, praises alone. For, "Blessed they that dwell in Thy house, for ever and ever they shall praise Thee:"[10] for this is the sacrifice of righteousness.

---

[1] Rom. iv. 5. [2] [ἐξ αἱμάτων, Sept. — C.] [3] 1 Cor. xv. 50.
[4] 1 Cor. xv. 53. [5] Some mss. *ut.* [6] Ps. li. 9.
[7] Most mss. "whereby" throughout.

[8] [So Lactantius, A. N. F. vol. vii. p. 193, note 1, and the whole chapter. — C.]
[9] Ps. lvi. 12.   [10] Ps. lxxxiv. 4.

"Oblations and holocausts." What are "holocausts"? A whole victim by fire consumed. When a whole beast was laid upon the altar with fire to be consumed, it was called a holocaust. May divine fire take us up whole, and that fervour catch us whole. What fervour? "Neither is there that hideth himself from the heat thereof." [1] What fervour? That whereof speaketh the Apostle : "In spirit fervent." [2] Be not merely our soul taken up by that divine fire of wisdom, but also our body; that [3] it may earn their immortality; so be it lifted up for a holocaust, that death be swallowed into victory. "Oblations and holocausts." "Then shall they lay upon thine altar calves." Whence "calves"? What shall He therein choose? Will it be the innocence of the new age, or necks freed from the yoke of the law? . . .

PSALM LII. [4]

1. The title of the Psalm hath : "At the end, understanding of David, when there came Doeg the Edomite and told Saul, David hath come into the house of Abimelech:" whereas we read that he had come into the house of Achimelech. And it may chance that we do not unreasonably suppose, that because of the similarity of a name and the difference of one syllable, or rather of one letter, the titles have been varied. In the manuscripts, however, of the Psalms, when we looked into them, rather Abimelech we have found than Achimelech. And since in another place thou hast a most evident Psalm, intimating not a dissimilarity of name, but an utterly different name; when, for instance, David changed his face before King Achish, not before king Abimelech, and he sent him away, and he departed : and yet the title of the Psalm is thus written, "When he changed his countenance in the presence of Abimelech" [5] — the very change of name maketh us the rather intent upon a mystery, lest thou shouldest pursue the quasi-facts of history, and despise the sacred veilings. . . .

2. Observe ye two kinds of men ; the one of men labouring, the other of those among whom they labour : the one of men thinking of earth, the other of heaven : the one of men weighing down their heart unto the deep, the other of men with Angels their heart conjoining : the one trusting in earthly things, wherein this world aboundeth, the other confiding in heavenly things, which God, who lieth not, hath promised. But mingled are these kinds of men. We see now the citizen of Jerusalem, citizen of the kingdom of heaven, have some office upon earth : to wit, one weareth purple, is a Magistrate, is Ædile, is Proconsul, is Emperor, doth direct the earthly republic : but he hath his heart above, if he is a Christian, if he is a believer, if he is godly, if he is despising those things wherein he is, and trusteth in that wherein he is not yet. Of which kind was that holy woman Esther, who, though she was wife of a king, incurred the danger of interceding for her countrymen : and when she was praying before God, where she could not lie, in her prayer said, that her royal ornaments were to her but as the cloth of a menstruous woman. [6] Despair we not then of the citizens of the kingdom of heaven, when we see them engaged in any of Babylon's matters, doing something earthly in republic earthly : nor again let us forthwith congratulate all men that we see doing matters heavenly ; because even the sons of pestilence sit sometimes in the seat of Moses, of whom is said, "What things they say, do ye : but what things they do, do not : for they say, and do not." [7] Those, amid earthly things, lift up heart unto heaven, these, amid heavenly words, trail heart upon earth. But there will come time of winnowing, when both are to be severed with greatest diligence, in order that no grain may pass over unto the heap of chaff that is to be burned, that not one single straw may pass over to the mass that is to be stored in the barn. [8] So long as then now it is mingled, hear we thence our voice, that is, voice of the citizens of the kingdom of heaven (for to this we ought to aspire, to bear with evil men here, rather than be borne with by good men) : and let us conjoin ourselves to this voice, both with ear and with tongue, and with heart and work. Which if we shall have done, we are here speaking in those things which we hear. Let us therefore speak first of the evil body of kingdom earthly.

3. "Why doth he glory in malice that is mighty?" (ver. 1). Observe, my brethren, the glorying of malignity, the glorying of evil men. Where is glorying? "Why doth he glory in malice that is mighty?" That is, he that in malice is mighty, why doth he glory? There is need that a man be mighty, but in goodness, not in malice. Is it any great thing to glory in malice? To build a house doth belong to few men, any ignorant man you please can pull down. To sow wheat, to dress the crop, to wait until it ripen, and in that fruit on which one has laboured to rejoice, doth belong to few men : with one spark any man you please can burn all the crop. To breed an infant, when born to feed him, to educate, to bring him on to youth's estate, is a great task : to kill him in one moment of time any one you please is able. Therefore those things which are done for destruction,

---

[1] Ps. xix. 6.　　　　[2] Rom. xii. 11.
[3] Mss. omit *ut*, "also let our body earn," etc.
[4] Lat. LI.　　　　[5] Ps. xxxiii. tit.

[6] Esth. xiv. 16.　　　[7] Matt. xxiii. 3.　　　[8] Matt. iii. 12.

are most easily done. "He that glorieth, let him glory in the Lord : " [1] he that glorieth, let him glory in goodness. Thou gloriest, because thou art mighty in evil. What art thou about to do, O mighty man, what art thou about to do, boasting thyself much? Thou art about to kill a man : this thing also a scorpion, this also one fever, this also a poisonous fungus can do. To this is thy mightiness reduced, that it be made equal to a poisonous fungus? This therefore do the good citizens of Jerusalem, who not in malice but in goodness glory : firstly, that not in themselves, but in the Lord they glory. Secondly, that those things which make for edification they earnestly do, and do such things as are strong to abide : but things which make for destruction they may do, for the discipline of men advancing, not for the oppression of the innocent. To this mightiness then that earthly body being compared, why may it not hear out of these words, "Why doth he glory in malice that is mighty?"

4. "In iniquity the whole day upon injustice hath thy tongue thought" (ver. 2) : that is, in the whole of time, without weariness, without intermission, without cessation. And when thou doest not, thou thinkest; so that when anything of evil is away from thy hands, from thy heart it is not away ; either thou doest an evil thing, or while thou canst not do, thou sayest an evil thing, that is, thou evil-speakest : or when not even this thou canst do, thou willest and thinkest an evil thing. "The whole day," then, that is, without intermission. We expect punishment to this man. Is he to himself a small punishment? Thou threatenest him : thou, when thou threatenest him, wilt send him whither? Unto evil? Send him away unto himself. In order that thou mayest vent much rage, thou art going to give him into the power of beasts : unto himself he is worse than beasts. For a beast can mangle his body : of himself he cannot leave his heart whole. Within, against himself he doth rage of himself, and dost thou from without seek for stripes? Nay, pray God for him, that he may be set free from himself. Nevertheless in this Psalm, my brethren, there is not a prayer for evil men, or against evil men, but a prophecy of what is to result to evil men. Think not therefore that the Psalm of ill-will saith anything : for it is said in the spirit of prophecy.

5. There followeth then what? All thy might and all thy thought of iniquity all the day, and meditation of malignity in thy tongue without intermission, hath performed what, done what? "As with a sharp razor thou hast done deceit" (ver. 3). See what do evil men to Saints, they scrape their hair. What is it that I have said? If there be such citizens of Jerusalem, that hear the voice of their Lord, of their King, saying, "Fear not them which kill the body, but are not able to kill the soul : " that hear the voice which but now from the Gospel hath been read, "What doth it profit a man, if he shall gain the whole world, and of himself make wreck : " [2] they despise all present good things, and above all life itself. And what is Doeg's razor to do to a man on this earth meditating on the kingdom of heaven, and about to be in the kingdom of heaven, having with him God, and about to abide with God? What is that razor to do? Hair it is to scrape, it is to make a man bald. And this belongeth to Christ, who in the Place of a Skull was crucified. [3] It maketh also the son of Core, which is interpreted baldness. [4] For this hair signifieth a superfluity of things temporal. Which hairs indeed are not made by God superfluously on the body of men, but for a sort of ornament : yet because without feeling they are cut off, they that cleave to the Lord with their heart, so have these earthly things as they have hair. But sometimes even something of good with "hair" is wrought, when thou breakest bread to the hungry, the poor without roof thou bringest into thy house ; if thou shalt have seen one naked, thou coverest him : [5] lastly, the Martyrs themselves also imitating the Lord, blood for the Church shedding, hearing that voice, "As Christ laid down His life for us, so also ought we also to lay down for the brethren," [6] in a certain way with their hair did good to us, that is, with those things which that razor can lop off or scrape. But that therefore even with the very hair some good can be done, even that woman a sinner intimated, who, when she had wept over the feet of the Lord, with her hair wiped what with tears she wetted. [7] Signifying what? That when thou shalt have pitied any one, thou oughtest to relieve him also if thou canst. For when thou hast pity, thou sheddest as it were tears : when thou relievest, thou wipest with hair. And if this to any one, how much more to the feet of the Lord. The feet of the Lord are what? The holy Evangelists, whereof is said, "How beautiful are the feet of them that tell of peace, that tell of good things ! " [8] Therefore like a razor let Doeg whet his tongue, let him whet deceit as much as he may : he will take away superfluous temporal things ; will he take away necessary things everlasting?

6. "Thou hast loved malice above benignity" (ver. 4). Before thee was benignity ; herself thou shouldest have loved. For thou wast not going to expend anything, nor wast thou going

---

[2] Matt. xvi. 26.   [3] Matt. xxvii. 33.   [4] 1 Chron. vi. 22.
[5] Isa. lviii. 7.   [6] 1 John iii. 16.   [7] Luke vii. 38.
[8] Isa. lii. 7; Rom. x. 15.

to fetch something to love by a distant voyage. Benignity is before thee, iniquity before thee : compare and choose. But perchance thou hast an eye wherewith thou seest malignity, and hast no eye wherewith thou seest benignity. Woe to the iniquitous heart. What is worse, it doth turn away itself, that it may not see what it is able to see. For what of such hath been said in another place? "He would not understand that he might do good."[1] For it is not said, he could not : but "he would not," he saith, "understand that he might do good," he closed his eyes from present light. And what followeth? "Of iniquity he hath meditated in his bed;" that is, in the inner secrecy of his heart. Some reproach of this kind is heaped upon this Doeg the Edomite, a malignant body, a motion of earth, not abiding, not heavenly. "Thou hast loved malignity above benignity." For wilt thou know how an evil man doth see both, and the former he doth rather choose, from the other doth turn himself away? Wherefore doth he cry out when he suffereth anything unjustly? Wherefore doth he then exaggerate as much as he can the iniquity, and praise benignity, censuring him that hath wrought in him malignity above benignity? Be he then a rule to himself for seeing : out of himself he shall be judged. Moreover, if he do what is written, "Thou shalt love thy neighbour as thyself;"[2] and, "Whatsoever good things ye will that men should do unto you, these also do ye do unto them : "[3] at home he hath means of knowing, because what on himself he will not have to be done, he ought not to do to another. "Thou hast loved malice above benignity." Iniquitously, inordinately, perversely thou wouldest raise water above oil :[4] the water will be sunk, the oil will remain above. Thou wouldest under darkness place a light : the darkness will be put to flight, the light will remain. Above heaven thou wouldest place earth, by its weight the earth will fall into its place. Thou therefore wilt be sunk by loving malice above benignity. For never will malice overcome benignity. "Thou hast loved malice above benignity : iniquity more than to speak of equity." Before thee is equity, before thee is iniquity : one tongue thou hast, whither thou wilt thou turnest it : wherefore then rather to iniquity and not to equity? Food of bitterness dost thou not give to thy belly, and food of iniquity dost thou give to thy malignant tongue? As thou choosest whereon to live, so choose what thou mayest speak. Thou preferrest iniquity to equity, and preferrest malice to benignity ; thou indeed preferrest, but above what can ever be but benignity and equity? But thou, by placing thyself in a manner upon those things which it is

necessary should go beneath, wilt not make them to be above good things, but thou with them wilt be sunk unto evil things.

7. Because of this there followeth in the Psalm, "Thou hast loved all words of sinking under" (ver. 5). Rescue therefore thyself, if thou canst, from sinking under. From shipwreck thou art fleeing, and dost embrace lead ! If thou wilt not sink, catch at a plank, be borne on wood, let the Cross carry thee through. But now because thou art a Doeg the Edomite, a "motion," and "of earth," thou doest what? "Thou hast loved all words of sinking-under, a tongue deceitful." This hath preceded, words of sinking-under have followed a tongue deceitful. What is a tongue deceitful? A minister of guile is a tongue deceitful, of men bearing one thing in heart, another thing from mouth bringing forth. But in these is overthrowing, in these sinking under.

8. "Wherefore God shall destroy thee at the end" (ver. 6) : though now thou seemest to flourish like grass in the field before the heat of the sun. For, "All flesh is grass, and the brightness of man as the bloom of grass : the grass hath withered, and the bloom hath fallen down : but the word of the Lord abideth for everlasting."[5] Behold that to which thou mayest bind thyself, to what[6] "abideth for everlasting." For if to grass, and to the bloom of grass, thou shalt have bound thyself, since the grass shall wither, and the bloom shall fall down, "God shall destroy thee at the end : " and if not now, certainly at the end He shall destroy, when that winnowing shall have come, and the heap of chaff from the solid grain shall have been separated.[7] Is not the solid grain for the barns, and the chaff for the fire? Shall not the whole of that Doeg stand at the left hand, when the Lord is to say, "Go ye into fire everlasting, which hath been prepared for the devil and his angels"?[8] Therefore "God shall destroy at the end : shall pluck thee out, and shall remove thee from thy dwelling." Now then this Doeg the Edomite is in a dwelling : "But a servant abideth not in the house for ever."[9] Even he worketh something of good, even if not with his doings, at least with the words of God, so that in the Church, when he "seeketh his own,"[10] he would say, at least, those things which are of Christ. "But He shall remove thee from thy dwelling." "Verily, verily, I say unto you, they have received their reward."[11] "And thy root from the land of the living." Therefore in the land of the living we ought to have root. Be our root there. Out of sight is the root : fruits may be seen, root cannot be seen. Our root is our love, our

---

[1] Ps. xxxvi. 4.   [2] Matt. xxii. 39.   [3] Matt. vii. 12.
[4] See S. Chrys. on 1 Thess. Hom. xi.

[5] Isa. xl. 6–8.   [6] Al. "to the Word that."
[7] Matt. iii. 12, xiii. 40.   [8] Matt. xxv. 41.   [9] John viii. 35.
[10] Phil. ii. 21.   [11] Matt. vi. 2.

fruits are our works : it is needful that thy works proceed from love, then is thy root in the land of the living.   Then shall be rooted up that Doeg, nor any wise shall he be able there to abide, because neither more deeply there hath he fixed a root : [1] but it shall be with him in like manner as it is with those seeds on the rock, which even if a root they throw out, yet, because moisture they have not, with the risen sun forthwith do wither.   But, on the other hand, they that fix a root more deeply, hear from the Apostle what ?   "I bow my knees for you to the Father of our Lord Jesus Christ, that ye may be in love rooted and grounded."   And because there now is root, "That ye may be able," he saith, "to comprehend what is the height, and breadth, and length, and depth : to know also the super-eminent knowledge of the love of Christ, that ye may be filled unto all the fulness of God." [2] Of such fruits so great a root is worthy, being so single, so budding, for buddings so deeply grounded.   But truly this man's root shall be rooted up from the land of the living.

9.   "And the just shall see, and shall fear ; and over him they shall laugh" (ver. 7). Shall fear when ?   Shall laugh when ?   Let us therefore understand, and make a distinction between those two times of fearing and laugh-ing, which have their several uses.   For so long as we are in this world, not yet must we laugh, lest hereafter we mourn.   We have read what is reserved at the end for this Doeg, we have read, and because we understand and believe, we see but fear.   This, therefore, hath been said, "The just shall see, and shall fear."   So long as we see what will result at the end to evil men, wherefore do we fear ?   Because the Apostle hath said, "In fear and trembling work out your own salvation : " [3] because it hath been said in a Psalm, [4] "Serve the Lord in fear, and exult unto Him with trembling."   Wherefore "with fear" ? "Wherefore let him that thinketh himself to stand, see that he fall not." [5]   Wherefore "with trembling" ?   Because he saith in another place : "Brethren, if a man shall have been overtaken in any delinquency, ye that are spiritual instruct such sort in the spirit of gentleness ; heeding thyself, lest thou also be tempted." [6]   Therefore, the just that are now, that live of faith, so see this Doeg, what to him is to result, that never-theless they fear also for themselves : for what they are to-day, they know ; what to-morrow they are to be, they know not.   Now, therefore, "The just shall see, and they shall fear."   But when shall they laugh ?   When iniquity shall have passed over ; when it shall have flown over ; as now to a great degree hath flown over the time uncertain ; when shall have been put

to flight the darkness of this world, wherein now we walk not but by the lamp of the Scriptures, and therefore fear as though in night.   For we walk by prophecy ; whereof saith the Apostle Peter, "We have a more sure prophetic word, to which giving heed ye do well, as to a lamp shining in a dark place, until the day shine, and the day-star arise in your hearts." [7]   So long then as by a lamp we walk, it is needful that with fear we should live.   But when shall have come our day, that is, the manifestation of Christ, whereof the same Apostle saith, "When Christ shall have appeared, your life, then ye also shall appear with Himself in glory," [8] then the just shall laugh at that Doeg. . . .

10. But what shall they then say that shall laugh ?   "And over him they shall laugh ; and shall say, Behold a man that hath not set God for his helper" (ver. 8).   See ye the body earthly !   "As much as thou shalt have, so great shalt thou be," is a proverb of covetous men, of grasping men, of men oppressing the inno-cent, of men seizing upon other men's goods, of men denying things entrusted to their care. Of what sort is this proverb ?   "As much as thou shalt have, so great shalt thou be ; " that is, as much as thou shalt have had of money, as much as thou shalt have gotten, by so much the more mighty shalt thou be.   "Behold a man that hath not set God for his helper, but hath trusted in the multitude of his riches."   Let not a poor man, one perchance that is evil, say, I am not of this body.   For he hath heard the Prophet saying, "He hath trusted in the multi-tude of his riches : " forthwith if he is poor, he heedeth his rags, he hath observed near him perchance a rich man among the people of God more richly apparelled, and he saith in his heart, Of this man he speaketh ; doth he speak of me ?   Do not thence except thyself, do not separate thyself, unless thou shalt have seen and feared, in order that thou mayest hereafter laugh.   For what doth it profit thee, if thou dost want means, and thou burnest with cu-pidity ?   When our Lord Jesus Christ to that rich man that was grieved, and that was depart-ing from Him, had said, "Go, sell all that thou hast, and give to the poor, and thou shalt have treasure in heaven, and come follow Me : " [9] and great hopelessness for rich men foretold, so that He said, more easily could a camel pass through the eye of a needle, than a rich man enter into the kingdom of Heaven, [10] were not forthwith the disciples grieved, saying with themselves, "Who shall be able to be saved ?"   Therefore when they were saying, "Who shall be able to be saved ?" did they think of the few rich men, did there escape them so great a multitude of

[1] Matt xiii. 5.   [2] Eph. iii. 14, 17-19.   [3] Phil. ii. 12.
[4] Ps. ii. 11.   [5] 1 Cor. x. 12.   [6] Gal. vi. 1.

[7] 2 Pet. i. 19.   [8] Col. iii. 4.
[9] Matt. xix. 21.   [10] Matt. xix. 24.

poor men? Could they not say to themselves, If it is hard, aye an impossible thing, that rich men should enter into the kingdom of heaven, as it is impossible that a camel should enter through the eye of a needle, let all poor men enter into the kingdom of heaven, be the rich alone shut out? For how few are the rich men? But of poor men are thousands innumerable. For not the coats are we to look upon in the kingdom of heaven; but for every one's garment shall be reckoned the effulgence of righteousness: there shall be therefore poor men equal to Angels of God, clothed with the stoles of immortality, they shall shine as the sun in the kingdom of their Father: what reason is there for us about a few rich men to be concerned, or distressed? This thought not the Apostles; but when the Lord had spoken this, " It is easier for a camel to go through the eye of a needle, than for a rich man to enter into the kingdom of heaven:" they saying to themselves, " Who shall be able to be saved," meant what? Not means, but desires; for they saw even poor men themselves, even if not having money, yet to have covetousness. And that ye may know, that not money in a rich man, but covetousness is condemned, attend to what I say; Thou observest that rich man standing near thee, and perchance in him is money, and is not covetousness; in thee is not money, and is covetousness. A poor man full of sores, full of woe, licked by dogs, having no help, having no morsel, not having perchance a mere garment, was borne by the Angels unto Abraham's bosom.[1] Ho! being a poor man, art thou glad now; for are even sores by thee to be desired? Is not thy patrimony soundness? There is not in this Lazarus the merit of poverty, but that of godliness. For thou seest who was borne up, thou seest not whither he was borne up. Who was borne up by Angels? A poor man, full of woe, full of sores. Whither was he borne up? Unto Abraham's bosom. Read the Scriptures, and thou shalt find Abraham to have been a rich man.[2] In order that thou mayest know, that not riches are blamed; Abraham had much gold, silver, cattle, household, was a rich man, and unto his bosom Lazarus, a poor man, was borne up. Unto bosom of rich man, poor man: are not rather both unto God rich men, both in cupidity poor men? . . .

11. Therefore that man having been condemned that " hath trusted in the multitude of his riches, and hath prevailed in his vanity:" for what more vain, than he that thinketh coin more to avail than God? Therefore that man having been condemned that said, blessed of the people to whom these things are: thou that sayest,

" Blessed the people of whom is the Lord their own God," dost think of thyself what? dost hope for thyself what? " But I;" now at length hear that body: " But I am like an olive, fruit-bearing in the house of God " (ver. 9). Not one man speaketh, but that olive fruit-bearing, whence have been pruned the proud branches, and the humble wild olive graffed in.[3] " Like an olive, fruit-bearing in the house of God, I have trusted in the mercy of God." He did what? " In the multitude of his riches: " therefore his root shall be plucked out from the land of the living. " But I," because " like an olive, fruit-bearing in the house of God," the root whereof is nourished, is not rooted out, " have trusted in the mercy of God." But perchance now? For even herein men err sometimes. God indeed they worship, and are not now like to that Doeg: but though on God they rely, it is for temporal things nevertheless; so that they say to themselves, I worship my God, who will make me rich upon earth, who to me will give sons, who to me will give a wife. Such things indeed giveth none but God, but God would not have Himself for the sake of such things to be loved. For to this end oftentimes those things He giveth even to evil men, in order that some other thing good men of Him may learn to seek. In what manner then sayest thou, " I have trusted in the mercy of God "? Perchance for obtaining temporal things? Nay but, " For everlasting and world without end." The expression, " For everlasting," he willed to repeat by adding, " world without end," in order that by there repeating he might affirm how rooted he was in the love of the kingdom of heaven, and in the hope of everlasting felicity.

12. " I will confess to Thee for ever, because Thou hast done " (ver. 10). " Hast done what?" Doeg Thou hast condemned, David Thou hast crowned. " I will confess to Thee for ever, because Thou hast done." Great confession, " Because thou hast done "! " Hast done " what? except these very things which above have been spoken of, that like an olive fruit-bearing in the house of God, I should trust in the mercy of God for everlasting and world without end? Thou hast done: an ungodly man cannot justify himself. But who is He that justifieth? " Believing," he saith, " on Him " that justifieth " the ungodly."[4] " For what hast thou which thou hast not received? But if thou hast received, why dost thou glory as if thou hast not received, as if of thyself thou hast? "[5] Be it far from me that I should so glory, saith he, that is opposed against Doeg, that beareth with Doeg upon earth, until he remove from his dwelling, and be rooted up from the land of the living. I glory not as if I have not received, but in God I glory. " And

---

[1] Luke xvi. 22.　　　[2] Gen. xiii. 2.　　　[3] Rom. xi. 17.　　　[4] Rom. iv. 5.　　　[5] 1 Cor. iv. 7.

I will confess to Thee because Thou hast done," that is, because Thou hast done not according to my merits, but according to Thy mercy. But I have done what? If thou recollectest, " Before, I was a blasphemer, and a persecutor, and injurious." But thou, what hast thou done? " But mercy I have obtained, because ignorant I did it." [1] " I will confess to Thee for ever, because Thou hast done."

13. " And I will look for Thy name, for it is pleasant." Bitter is the world, but Thy name is pleasant. Even if certain sweet things are in the world, yet with bitterness they are digested. Thy name is preferred, not only for greatness but also for pleasantness. " For unjust men have told to me their delights, but it is not as Thy law, O Lord." [2] For if there were nothing sweet to the Martyrs, they would not have suffered with equanimity so great bitterness of tribulations. Their bitterness by any one was experienced, their sweetness easily could no one taste. The name of God therefore is pleasant to men loving God above all pleasantnesses. " I will look for Thy name, for it is pleasant." And to what dost Thou prove that it is pleasant? Give me a palate to which it is pleasant. Praise honey as much as thou art able, exaggerate the sweetness thereof with what words thou shalt have the power: a man knowing not what honey is, unless he shall have tasted, what thou sayest knoweth not. Therefore the rather to the proof the Psalm inviting thee saith what? " Taste and see that sweet is the Lord." [3] Taste thou wilt not, and thou sayest, Is it pleasant? What is pleasant? If thou hast tasted, in thy fruit be it found, not in words alone, as it were only in leaves, lest by the curse of the Lord, to wither like that fig-tree [4] thou shouldest deserve. " Taste," he saith, " and see, that sweet is the Lord." Taste and see: then ye shall see, if ye shall have tasted. But to a man not tasting, how provest thou? By praising the pleasantness of the name of God, whatsoever things thou shalt have said are words: something else is taste. The words of His praise there hear even the ungodly, but none taste how sweet it is, but the Saints. Further, a man discerning the sweetness of the name of God, and wishing to unfold and wishing to show the same, and not finding persons to whom he may unfold it; for to the Saints there is no need that he show it, because they even of themselves taste and know, but the ungodly cannot discern what they will not taste: doth, I say, what, because of the sweetness of the name of God? He hath borne him forthwith away from the crowds of the ungodly. " And I will look," he saith, " for Thy name, for it is pleasant, in the sight of Thy Saints." Pleasant is Thy name, but not in the sight of the ungodly. I know how sweet a thing it is, but it is to them that have tasted.

PSALM LIII.[5]

1. Of this Psalm we undertake to treat with you, as far as the Lord supplieth us. A brother biddeth us [6] that we may have the will, and prayeth that we may have the power. If anything in haste perchance I shall have passed over, He that even to us deigneth to give what we shall be enabled to say, will supply it in you. The title of it is: " At the end, for Maeleth, understanding to David himself." " For Maeleth," as we find in interpretations of Hebrew names, seemeth to say, For one travailing, or in pain. But who there is in this world that travaileth and is in pain, the faithful acknowledge, because thereof they are. Christ here travaileth, Christ here is in pain: the Head is above, the members below. For one not travailing nor in pain would not say, " Saul, Saul, why persecutest thou me?" [7] Him, with whom when persecuting He was travailing, being converted, He made to travail. For he also was himself afterwards enlightened, and grafted on those members which he used to persecute; being pregnant with the same love, he said, " My little children, of whom again I travail, until Christ be formed in you." [8] For the members therefore of Christ, for His Body which is the Church,[9] for that same One Man, that is, for that very unity, whereof Head is above, this Psalm is sung. . . . Who are they, then, amid whom we travail and groan, if in the Body of Christ we are, if under Him, the Head, we live, if amongst His members we are counted? Who they are, hear ye.

2. " The unwise man hath said in his heart, There is no God " (ver. 1). Such sort is it of men amid whom is pained and groaneth the Body of Christ. If such is this sort of men, of not many do we travail; as far as seemeth to occur to our thoughts, very few there are; and a difficult thing it is to meet with a man that saith in his heart, " There is no God; " [10] nevertheless, so few there are, that, fearing amid the many to say this, in their heart they say it, for that with mouth to say it they dare not. Not much then is that which we are bid to endure, hardly is it found: uncommon is that sort of men that say in their heart, " There is no God." But, if it be examined in another sense, is not that found to be in more men, which we supposed to be in men few and uncommon, and almost in none? Let them come forth into the midst that live evil lives, let us look into the doings of profligate,

[1] 1 Tim. i. 13. [2] Ps. cxix. 85. [3] Ps. xxxiv. 8.
[4] Matt. xxi. 19.

[5] Lat. LII. From a sermon preached to the people at the request of some one, perhaps of a bishop. — Ben.
[6] Al. " Bid us, brethren, . . . pray for us."
[7] Acts ix. 4. [8] Gal. iv. 19. [9] Col. i. 24.
[10] Ps. xiv. 1.

daring, and wicked men, of whom there is a great multitude; who foster day by day their sins, who, their acts having been changed into habit, have even lost sense of shame: this is so great a multitude of men, that the Body of Christ, set amid them, scarce dareth to censure that which it is not constrained to commit, and deemeth it a great matter for itself that the integrity of innocence be preserved in not doing that which now, by habit, either it doth not dare to blame, or if it [1] shall have dared, there breaketh out the censure and recrimination of them that live evil lives, more readily than the free voice of them that live good lives. And those men are such as say in their heart, "There is no God." Such men I am confuting. Whence confuting? That their doings please God, they judge. He doth not therefore affirm, "some say," but "The unwise man hath said in his heart, There is no God." Which men do so far believe there is a God, that the same God they judge with what they do to be pleased. But if thou being wise dost perceive, how "the unwise man hath said in his heart, There is no God," if thou give heed, if thou understand, if thou examine; he that thinketh that evil doings please God, Him he doth not think to be God. For if God is, He is just; if He is just, injustice displeaseth Him, iniquity displeaseth. But thou, when thou thinkest that iniquity pleaseth Him, dost deny God. For if God is one Whom iniquity displeaseth, but God seemeth not to thee to be one whom iniquity displeaseth, and there is no God but one whom iniquity displeaseth, then when thou sayest in thy heart, God doth countenance my iniquities, thou sayest nothing else than, "There is no God."

3. Let us advert also to that sense, which concerning Christ our Lord Himself, our Head Himself, doth present itself. For when Himself in form of a servant [2] appeared on earth, they that crucified Him said, "He is not God." Because Son of God He was, truly God He was. But they that are corrupted and have become abominable said what? "He is not God:" let us slay Him, "He is not God." Thou hast the voice of these very men in the book of Wisdom.[3] For after there had gone before the verse, "The unwise man hath said in his heart, There is no God;" as if reasons were required why the unwise man could say this, he hath subjoined, "Corrupted they are, and abominable have become in their iniquities" (ver. 2). Hear ye those corrupted men. "For they have said with themselves, not rightly thinking:"[4] corruption beginneth with evil belief, thence it proceedeth to depraved morals, thence to the most flagrant iniquities, these are the grades. But what with

themselves said they, thinking not rightly? "A small thing and with tediousness is our life."[5] From this evil belief followeth that which also the Apostle hath spoken of, "Let us eat and drink, for to-morrow we shall die."[6] But in the former passage more diffusely luxury itself is described: "Let us crown us with roses, before they be withered; in every place let us leave the tokens of our gladness."[7] After the more diffuse description of that luxury, what followeth? "Let us slay the poor just man:"[8] this is therefore saying, "He is not God." Soft words they seemed but now to say: "Let us crown us with roses, before they be withered." What more delicate, what more soft? Wouldest thou expect, out of this softness, Crosses, swords? Wonder not, soft are even the roots of brambles; if any one handle them, he is not pricked: but that wherewith thou shalt be pricked from thence hath birth. "Corrupted," therefore, are those men, "and abominable have become in their iniquities." They say, "If Son of God He is, let Him come down from the Cross."[9] Behold them openly saying, "He is not God." . . .

4. "The Lord from Heaven hath looked forth upon the sons of men, that He might see if there is one understanding and seeking after God" (ver. 3). What is this? "Corrupted they are," all these that say, "There is no God"? And what? Did it escape God, that they were become such? Or indeed to us would their inward thought be opened, except by Him it were told? If then He understood, if then He knew, what is this which hath been said, "that He might see"? For the words are of one inquiring, of one not knowing. "God from Heaven hath looked forth," etc. And as though He had found what He sought by looking upon, and by looking down from Heaven, He giveth sentence: "All men have gone aside, together useless they have become: there is not one that doeth good, not so much as one" (ver. 4). Two questions arise somewhat difficult: for if God looketh out from Heaven, in order that He may see if there is one understanding or seeking after God; there stealeth upon an unwise man the thought, that God knoweth not all things. This is one question: what is the other? If there is not one that doeth good, is not so much as one; who is he that travaileth amid bad men? The former question then is solved as followeth: ofttimes the Scripture speaketh in such manner, that what by the gift of God a creature doth, God is said to do. . . . For hence has been said the following also, "For the Spirit searcheth all things, even the depth of God;"[10] not because He that knoweth all things searcheth, but because to thee hath been given the Spirit,

---

[1] So Oxf. MSS. (ausum); Ben. ausus, "one."　　[2] Phil. ii. 7.
[3] Wisd. ii. 18-20. [See p. 172, supra.—C.]　　[4] Wisd. ii. 1.
[5] Wisd. ii. 1.　　[6] 1 Cor. xv. 32.　　[7] Wisd. ii. 8, 9.
[8] Wisd. ii. 10.　　[9] Matt. xxvii. 40.　　[10] 1 Cor. ii. 10.

which maketh thee also to search: and that which by His own gift thou doest, He is said to do; because without Him thou wouldest not do it: therefore God is said to do, when thou doest. . . . And because this by the gift of God thou doest, God from heaven is "looking forth upon the sons of men." The former question then, according to our measure, thus hath been solved.

5. What is that which looking forth we acknowledge? What is that which looking forth God acknowledgeth? What (because here He giveth it) doth He acknowledge? Hear what it is; that "All have gone aside, together useless they have become: there is not one that doeth good, there is not so much as one." What then is that other question, but the same whereof a little before I have made mention? If, "There is not one that doeth good, is not so much as one," no one remaineth to groan amid evil men. Stay, saith the Lord, do not hastily give judgment. I have given to men to do well; but of Me, He saith, not of themselves: for of themselves evil they are: sons of men they are, when they do evil; when well, My sons. For this thing God doth, out of sons of men He maketh sons of God: because out of Son of God He hath made Son of Man. See what this participation is: there hath been promised to us a participation of Divinity: He lieth that hath promised, if He is not first made partaker of mortality. For the Son of God hath been made partaker of mortality, in order that mortal man may be made partaker of divinity. He that hath promised that His good is to be shared with thee, first with thee hath shared thy evil: He that to thee hath promised divinity, showeth in thee love. Therefore take away that men are sons of God, there remaineth that they are sons of men: "There is none that doeth good, is not so much as one."

6. "Shall not all know that work iniquity, that devour My people for the food of bread"? (ver. 5). . . . There is therefore here a people of God that is being devoured. Nay, "There is not one that doeth good, there is not so much as one." We reply by the rule above. But this people that is devoured, this people that suffereth evil men, this that groaneth and travaileth amid evil men, now out of sons of men have been made sons of God: therefore are they devoured. For, "The counsel of the needy man thou hast confounded, because the Lord is his hope."[1] For ofttimes, in order that the people of God may be devoured, this very thing in it is despised, that it is the people of God. I will pillage, he saith, and despoil; if he is a Christian, what will he do to me? . . . But what

followeth? "I will convince thee, and will set thee before thy face." Thou wilt not now know so as thou shouldest be displeasing to thyself, thou shalt know so as thou mayest mourn. For God cannot but show to the unrighteous their iniquity. If He is not to show, who will they be that are to say, "What hath profited us pride, and what hath boasting of riches bestowed upon us?"[2] For then shall they know, that now will not know. "Shall not all know?" etc. Why hath He added, "for the food of bread"? As it were as bread, they eat My people. For all other things which we eat, we can eat now these, now those; not always this vegetable, not always this flesh, not always these apples: but always bread. What is then, "Devour My people for the food of bread"? Without intermission, without cessation they devour.

7. "On God they have not called." He is comforting the man that groaneth, and chiefly by an admonition, lest by imitating evil men, who ofttimes prosper, they delight in evil doing. There is kept for thee that which to thee hath been promised: their hope is present, thine is future, but theirs is transient, thine sure; theirs false, thine true. For they "upon God have not called." Do not daily such men ask of God? They do "not" ask of God. Give heed, if I am able to say this by the aid of God Himself. God gratuitously will have Himself to be worshipped, gratuitously will have Himself to be loved, that is chastely to be loved; not Himself to be loved for the reason that He giveth anything besides Himself, but because He giveth Himself. He then that calleth upon God in order that He may be made rich, on God doth not call: for upon that He calleth which to himself he willeth to come. . . . But now thou wouldest have coffer full, and conscience void: God filleth not coffer, but breast. What do outward riches profit thee, if inward need presseth thee? Therefore those men that for the sake of worldly comforts, that for the sake of earthly good things, that for the sake of present life and earthly felicity, call upon God, do not call upon God.

8. For this reason what followeth concerning them? "There have they feared with fear, where there was no fear" (ver. 6). For is there fear, if a man lose riches? There is no fear there, and yet in that case men are afraid. But if a man lose wisdom, truly there is fear, and in that case he is not afraid. . . . Thou hast feared to give back money, and hast willed to lose fidelity. The Martyrs took not away property of other persons, but even their own they despised that they might not lose fidelity: and it was too little to lose money, when they were

---

[1] Ps. xiv. 6.　　　　　　[2] Wisd. v. 8.

proscribed; they took also their life when they suffered: they lost life, in order that unto everlasting life they might find it.[1] Therefore there they feared, where they ought to have been afraid. But they that of Christ have said, "He is not God," have there feared where was no fear. For they said, "If we shall have let Him go, there will come the Romans, and will take away from us both place and kingdom."[2] O folly and imprudence saying in its heart, "He is not God"! Thou hast feared to lose earth, thou hast lost Heaven: thou hast feared lest there should come the Romans, and take away from thee place and kingdom! Could they take away from thee God? What then remaineth? what but that thou confess, that thou hast willed to keep, and by keeping ill hast lost? For thou hast lost both place and nation by slaying Christ. For ye did will rather to slay Christ, than to lose place; and ye have lost place, and nation, and Christ. In fearing, they have slain Christ: but wherefore this? "For God hath scattered the bones of them that please men."[3] Willing to please men, they feared to lose their place. But Christ Himself, of whom they said, "He is not God," willed rather to displease such men, as they were: sons of men, not sons of God, He willed rather to displease. Thence were scattered their bones, His bones no one hath broken. "They were confounded, for God hath despised them." In very deed, brethren, as far as regardeth them, great confusion hath come to them. In the place where they crucified the Lord, whom for this cause they crucified, that they might not lose both place and nation, the Jews are not. "God," therefore, "hath despised them:" and yet in despising He warned them to be converted. Let them now confess Christ, and say, He is God, of whom they said, "He is not God." Let them return to the inheritance of their fathers, to the inheritance of Abraham, of Isaac, and of Jacob, let them possess with these very persons life eternal: though they have lost life temporal. Wherefore this? Because out of sons of men have been made sons of God. For so long as they remain, and will not, there is not one that doeth good, there is not so much as one. "They were confounded, for God hath despised them." And as though to these very persons He were turned, He saith, "Who shall give out of Sion salvation to Israel?" (ver. 7). O ye fools, ye revile, insult, buffet, besmear with spittings, with thorns ye crown, upon the Cross ye lift up; whom? "Who shall give out of Sion salvation to Israel?" Shall not That Same of whom ye have said, "He is not God"? "In God's turning away the captivity of His people." For there turneth away the captivity

of His people, no one but He that hath willed to be a captive in your own hands. But what men shall understand this thing? "Jacob shall exult, and Israel shall rejoice." "Israel;" the true Jacob, and the true Israel, that younger, to whom the elder was servant,[4] shall himself exult, for he shall himself understand.

PSALM LIV.[5]

1. The title of this Psalm hath fruit in the prolixity thereof, if it be understood: and because the Psalm is short, let us make up our not having to tarry over the Psalm by tarrying over the title. For upon this dependeth every verse which is sung. If any one, therefore, observe that which on the front of the house is fixed, secure he will enter; and, when he shall have entered, he will not err. For this on the post itself is prominently marked, namely, in what manner within he may not be in error. The title thereof standeth thus: "At the end, in hymns, understanding to David himself, when there came the Ziphites, and said to Saul, Behold, is not David hidden with us?" That Saul was persecutor of the holy man David, very well we know: that Saul was bearing the figure of a temporal kingdom, not to life but to death belonging, this also to your Love we remember to have imparted. And also that David himself was bearing the figure of Christ, or of the Body of Christ, ye ought both to know and to call to mind, ye that have already learned.[6] What then of the Ziphites? There was a certain village, Ziph, whereof the inhabitants were Ziphites, in whose country David had hidden himself, when Saul would find and slay him. These Ziphites then, when they had learned this, betrayed him to the king his persecutor, saying, "Behold, is not David hidden with us?" Of no good to them indeed was their betrayal, and to David himself of no harm. For their evil disposition was shown: but Saul not even after their betrayal could seize David; but rather in a certain cave in that very country, when into his hands Saul had been given to slay, David spared him, and that which he had in his power he did not.[7] But the other was seeking to do that which he had not in his power. Let them that have been Ziphites take heed: let us see those whom to us the Psalm presenteth to be understood by the occasion of those same men.

2. If we inquire then by what word is translated Ziphites, we find, "Men flourishing." Flourishing then were certain enemies to holy David, flourishing before him hiding. We may find them in mankind, if we are willing to under-

[1] Matt. x. 39.   [2] John xi. 48.
[3] E. V. "that encamp against thee."

[4] Gen. xxv. 23.
[5] Lat. LIII.   From a sermon to the people.
[6] See exposition upon Ps. lii. §§ 1, 2.   [7] 1 Sam. xxiv. 4.

'stand the Psalm. Let us find here at first David hiding, and we shall find his adversaries flourishing. Observe David hiding: "For ye are dead," saith the Apostle to the members of Christ, "and your life is hid with Christ in God." [1] These men, therefore, that are hiding, when shall they be flourishing? "When Christ," he saith, "your life, shall have appeared, then ye also with Him shall appear in glory." [2] When these men shall be flourishing, then shall be those Ziphites withering. For observe to what flower their glory is compared: "All flesh is grass, and the honour of flesh as the flower of grass." [3] What is the end? "The grass hath withered, and the flower hath fallen off." Where then shall be David? See what followeth: "But the Word of the Lord abideth for ever." . . .

3. These men sometimes are observed of the weak sons of light, and their feet totter, when they have seen evil men in felicity to flourish, and they say to themselves, "Of what profit to me is innocence? What doth it advantage me that I serve God, that I keep His commandments, that I oppress no one, from no one plunder anything, hurt no one, that what I can I bestow? behold, all these things I do, and they flourish, I toil." But why? Wouldest thou also wish to be a Ziphite? They flourish in the world, wither in judgment, and after withering, into fire everlasting shall be cast: wouldest thou also choose this? Art thou ignorant of what He hath promised thee, who to thee hath come, what in Himself here He displayed? If the flower of the Ziphites were to be desired, would not Himself thy Lord also in this world have flourished? Or indeed was there wanting to Him the power to flourish? Nay but here He chose rather amid the Ziphites to hide, and to say to Pontius Pilate, as if to one being himself also a flower of the Ziphites, and in suspicion about His kingdom, "My kingdom is not of this world." [4] Therefore here He was hidden: and all good men are hidden here, because their good is within, it is concealed, in the heart it is, where is faith, where charity, where hope, where their treasure is. Do these good things appear in the world? Both these good things are hidden, and the reward of these good things is hidden. . . .

4. "O God, in Thy name make me safe, and in Thy virtue judge me" (ver. 1). Let the Church say this, hiding amid the Ziphites. Let the Christian body say this, keeping secret the good of its morals, expecting in secret the reward of its merits, let it say this: "In Thy virtue [5] judge me." Thou hast come, O Christ, humble Thou hast appeared, despised Thou hast been, scourged hast been, crucified hast been, slain hast been; but, on the third day hast risen, on the fortieth day into Heaven hast ascended: Thou sittest at the right hand of the Father, and no one seeth: Thy Spirit thence Thou hast sent, which men that were worthy have received; fulfilled with Thy love, the praise of that very humility of Thine throughout the world and nations they have preached: Thy name I see to excel among mankind, but nevertheless as weak to us hast Thou been preached. For not even did that Teacher of the Gentiles say, that among us he knew anything, "Save Christ Jesus, and Him crucified;" [6] in order that of Him we might choose the reproach, rather than the glory of the flourishing Ziphites. Nevertheless, of Him he saith what? "Although He died of weakness, yet He liveth of the power [7] of God." He came then that He might die of weakness, He is to come that He may judge in the power of God: but through the weakness of the Cross His name hath been illustrious. Whosoever shall not have believed upon the name made illustrious through weakness, shall stand in awe at the Judge, when He shall have come in power. But, lest He that once was weak, when He shall have come strong, with that fan send us to the left hand; may He "save us in His name, and judge us in His virtue." For who so rash as to have desired this, as to say to God, for instance "Judge me"? Is it not wont to be said to men for a curse, "God judge thee"? So evidently it is a curse, if He judge thee in His virtue; and shall not have saved thee in His name: but when in name precedent He shall have saved thee, to thy health in virtue consequent He shall judge. Be thou without care: that judgment shall not to thee be punishment, but dividing. For in a certain Psalm [8] thus is said: "Judge me, O God, and divide my cause from the nation unholy." . . .

5. "O God, hearken to my prayer, in Thy ears receive the words of my mouth" (ver. 2). . . . To Thee may my prayer attain, driven forth and darted out from the desire of Thy eternal blessings: to Thy ears I send it forth, aid it that it may reach, lest it fall short in the middle of the way, and fainting as it were it fall down. But even if there result not to me now the good things which I ask, I am secured nevertheless that hereafter they will come. For even in the case of transgressions a certain man is said to have asked of God, and not to have been hearkened to for his good. For privations of this world had inspired him to prayer, and being set in temporal tribulations he had wished that temporal tribulations should pass away, and there should return the flower of grass; and he saith, "My God, my God, why hast Thou forsaken me?" [9] The very voice of Christ it is, but for

---

[1] Col. iii. 3. [2] Col. iii. 4. [3] Isa. xl. 6.
[4] John xviii. 36. [5] [i.e., power or strength. — C.]
[6] 1 Cor. ii. 2. [7] Virtute. [8] Ps. xliii. 1.
[9] Ps. xxii. 1.

His members' sake. "The words," he saith, "of my transgressions I have cried to Thee throughout the day, and Thou hast not hearkened : and by night, and not for the sake of folly to me : " that is, "and by night I have cried, and Thou hast not hearkened ; and nevertheless in this very thing that Thou hast not hearkened, it is not for the sake of folly to me that Thou hast not hearkened, but rather for the sake of wisdom that Thou hast not hearkened, that I might perceive what of Thee I ought to ask. For those things I was asking which to my cost perchance I should have received." Thou askest riches, O man ; how many have been overset through their riches ? Whence knowest thou whether to thee riches may profit ? Have not many poor men more safely been in obscurity ; having become rich men, so soon as they have begun to blaze forth, they have been a prey to the stronger ? How much better they would have lain concealed, how much better they would have been unknown, that have begun to be inquired after not for the sake of what they were, but for the sake of what they had ! In these temporal things therefore, brethren, we admonish and exhort you in the Lord, that ye ask not anything as if it were a thing settled, but that which God knoweth to be expedient for you. For what is expedient for you, ye know not at all. Sometimes that which ye think to be for you is against you, and that which ye think to be against you is for you. For sick ye are ; do not dictate to the physician the medicines he may choose to set beside you. If the teacher of the Gentiles, Paul the Apostle, saith, "For what we should pray for as we ought, we know not," [1] how much more we ? Who nevertheless, when he seemed to himself to pray wisely, namely, that from him should be taken away the thorn of the flesh, the angel of Satan, that did buffet him, in order that he might not in the greatness of the revelations be lifted up, heard from the Lord what ? Was that done which he wished ? Nay,[2] in order to that being done which was expedient, he heard from the Lord, I say, what ? "Thrice," he saith, "I besought the Lord that He would take it from me ; and He said to me, My Grace sufficeth for thee : for virtue in weakness is made perfect." [3] Salve to the wound I have applied ; when I applied it I know, when it should be taken away I know. Let not a sick man draw back from the hands of the physician, let him not give advice to the physician. So it is with all these things temporal. There are tribulations ; if well thou worshippest God, thou wilt know that He knoweth what is expedient for each man : there are prosperities ; take the more heed, lest these same corrupt thy soul, so

that it withdraw from Him that hath given these things. . . .

6. "For aliens have risen up against me" (ver. 3). What "aliens" ? Was not David himself a Jew of the tribe of Judah ? But the very place Ziph belonged to the tribe of Judah ; it was of the Jews. How then "aliens" ? Not in city, not in tribe, not in kindred, but in flower.[4] . . . But see the Ziphites, see them for a time flourishing. With reason "alien" sons. Thou amid the Ziphites hiding saidst what ? "Blessed the people whereof the Lord is its God." Out of this affection this prayer [5] is being sent forth into the ears of the Lord, when it is said, "for aliens have risen up against me."

7. "And mighty men have sought after my soul." For in a new manner, my brethren, they would destroy the race of holy men, and the race of them that abstain from hoping in this world, all they that have hope in this world. Certainly commingled they are, certainly together they live. Very much to one another are opposed these two sorts : the one of those that place no hope but in things secular, and in temporal felicity, and the other of those that do firmly place their hope in the Lord God. And though concordant are these Ziphites, do not much trust to their concord : temptations are wanting ; when there shall have come any temptation, so as that a person may be reproved for the flower of the world, I say not to thee he will quarrel with the Bishop, but not even to the Church Herself will he draw near, lest there fall any part of the grass.[6] Wherefore have I said these words, brethren ? Because now gladly ye all hear in the name of Christ, and according as ye understand, so ye shout out at the word ; ye would not indeed shout at it unless ye understood.[7] This your understanding ought to be fruitful. But whether it is fruitful, temptation doth try ; lest suddenly when ye are said to be ours, through temptation ye be found aliens, and it be said, "Aliens have risen up against me, and mighty men have sought my soul." Be not that said which followeth, "They have not set forth God before their face." For when will he set God before his face, before whose eyes there is nought but the world ? namely, how he may have coin upon coin, how flocks may be increased, how barns may be filled, how it may be said to his soul, "Thou hast many good things, be merry, feast, take thy fill." Doth he set before his face Him, that unto one so boasting and so blooming with the flower of the Ziphites saith, "Fool" (that is, "man not understanding,"

---

[1] Rom. viii. 26.　　　[2] "Nay" not in MSS.　　　[3] 2 Cor. xii. 8, 9.

[4] [Jas. i. 10, 11. He seems to bear this text in mind in these comments. — C.]
[5] [i.e., this Psalm. — C.]
[6] [Isa. xl. 6. Note 5, p. 199, *supra*. — C.]
[7] [They seem to have applauded, or shouted *Amen*. So, also, often when Chrysostom preached. — C.]

" man unwise "), " this night shall be taken from thee thy soul; all these things which thou hast prepared, whose shall they be?"[1]

8. "For behold, God helpeth me" (ver. 4). Even themselves know not themselves, amid whom I am hiding. But if they too were to set God before their face, they would find in what manner God helpeth me. For all holy men are helped by God, but within, where no one seeth. For in like manner as the conscience of ungodly men is a great punishment, so a great joy is the very conscience of godly men. "For our glory this is," saith the Apostle, "the testimony of our conscience."[2] In this within, not in the flower of the Ziphites without, doth glory that man that now saith, "For behold God helpeth me." Surely though afar off are to be those things which He promiseth, this day have I a sweet and present help; to-day in my heart's joy I find that without cause certain say, "Who doth show to us good things? For there is signed upon us the light of Thy countenance, O Lord, Thou hast put pleasantness into my heart."[3] Not into my vineyard, not into my flock, not into my cask, not into my table, but " into my heart." "For behold God helpeth me." How doth He help thee? "And the Lord is the lifter up of my soul."

9. "Turn away evil things unto mine enemies" (ver. 5). So however green they are, so however they flourish, for the fire they are being[4] reserved. "In Thy virtue destroy Thou them." Because to wit they flourish now, because to wit they spring up like grass:[5] do not thou be a man unwise and foolish, so that by giving thought to these things thou perish for ever and ever. For, "Turn Thou away evil things unto mine enemies." For if thou shalt have place in the body of David Himself, in His virtue He will destroy them. These men flourish in the felicity of the world, perish in the virtue of God. Not in the same manner as they flourish, do they also perish: for they flourish for a time, perish for everlasting: flourish in unreal good things, perish in real torments. "In Thy strength destroy," whom in Thy weakness Thou hast endured.

10. "Voluntarily I will sacrifice to Thee" (ver. 6). Who can even understand this good thing of the heart, at another's speaking thereof, unless in himself he hath tasted it? What is, "Voluntarily I will sacrifice to Thee"? . . . For what sacrifice here shall I take, brethren? or what worthily shall I offer to the Lord for His mercy? Victims shall I seek from flock of sheep, ram shall I select, for any bull in the herds shall I look out, frankincense indeed from the land of the Sabæans shall I bring? What

shall I do? What offer; except that whereof He speaketh, "Sacrifice of praise shall honour Me"?[6] Wherefore then "voluntarily"? Because truly I love that which I praise. I praise God, and in the self-same praise I rejoice: in the praise of Himself I rejoice, at whom being praised, I blush not. For He is not praised in the same manner as by those who love the theatrical follies is praised either by a charioteer, or a hunter, or actor of any kind, and by their praisers, other praisers are invited, are exhorted, to shout together: and when all have shouted, ofttimes, if their favourite is overcome, they are all put to the blush. Not so is our God: be He praised with the will, loved with charity: let it be gratuitous (or voluntary) that He is loved and that He is praised. What is "gratuitous"? Himself for the sake of Himself, not for the sake of something else. For if thou praisest God in order that He may give thee something else, no longer freely dost thou love God. Thou wouldest blush, if thy wife for the sake of riches were to love thee, and perchance if poverty should befall thee, should begin to think of adultery. Seeing that therefore thou wouldest be loved by thy partner freely, wilt thou for anything else love God? What reward art thou to receive of God, O covetous man? Not earth for thee, but Himself He keepeth, who made heaven and earth. "Voluntarily I will sacrifice to Thee:" do it not of necessity. For if for the sake of anything else thou praisest God, out of necessity thou praisest. . . . These things also which He hath given, because of the Giver are good things. For He giveth entirely, He giveth these temporal things: and to certain men to their good, to certain men to their harm, after the height and depth of His judgments. . . . "Voluntarily I will sacrifice to Thee." Wherefore "voluntarily"? Because *gratis.* What is *gratis?* "And I will confess to Thy name, O Lord, for it is a good thing:" for nothing else, but because a "good thing" it is. Doth he say, "I will confess to Thy name, O Lord," because Thou givest me fruitful manors, because Thou givest me gold and silver, because Thou givest me extended riches, abundant money, most exalted dignity? Nay. But what? "For it is a good thing." Nothing I find better than Thy name.

11. "For out of all tribulation Thou hast delivered me" (ver. 7). For this cause I have perceived how good a thing is Thy name: for if this I were able before tribulations to acknowledge, perchance for me there had been no need of them. But tribulation hath been applied for admonition, admonition hath redounded to Thy praise. For I should not have understood

---

[1] Luke xii. 20.   [2] 2 Cor. i. 12.   [3] Ps. iv. 6, 7.
[4] *Al.* "let them be."   [5] Ps. xcii. 7.   [6] Ps. l. 23.

where I was, except of my weakness I had been admonished. "Out of all tribulations," therefore, "Thou hast delivered me. And upon mine enemies mine eye hath looked back:" upon those Ziphites "mine eye hath looked back." Yea, their flower I have passed over in loftiness of heart, unto Thee I have come, and thence I have looked back upon them, and have seen that "All flesh is grass, and all the glory of man as the flower of grass:"[1] as in a certain place is also said, "I have seen the ungodly man to be exalted and raised up like[2] the cedars of Lebanon: I passed by, and, lo! he was not."[3] Wherefore "he was not"? Because thou hast passed by. What is, "because thou hast passed by"? Because not to no purpose hast thou heard "Lift up thy heart;" because not on earth, where thou wouldest have rotted, thou hast remained; because thou hast lifted thy soul to God, and thou hast mounted beyond the cedars of Lebanon, and from that elevation hast observed: and "Lo! he was not;" and thou hast sought him, and there hath not been found place for him. No longer is labour before thee; because thou hast entered into the sanctuary of God, and hast understood for the last things.[4] So also here thus he concludeth. "And upon mine enemies mine eye hath looked back." This do ye therefore, brethren, with your souls; lift up your hearts, sharpen the edge of your mind, learn truly to love God, learn to despise the present world, learn voluntarily to sacrifice the offerings of praise; to the end that, mounting beyond the flower of the grass, ye may look back upon your enemies.

PSALM LV.[5]

1. Of this Psalm the title is: "At the end, in hymns, understanding to David himself." What the "end" is, we will briefly call to your recollection, because ye have known it. "For the end of the Law is Christ, for righteousness unto every man believing."[6] Be the attention therefore directed unto the End, directed unto Christ. Wherefore is He called the end? Because whatever we do, to Him we refer it, and when to Him we shall have come home, more to ask we shall not have. For there is an end spoken of which doth consume, there is an end spoken of which doth make perfect. In one sense, for instance, we understand it, when we hear, there is ended the food which was in eating; and in another sense we understand it, when we hear, there is ended the vesture which was in weaving: in each case we hear, there is

ended; but the food so that it no longer is, the vesture so that it is perfected. Our end therefore ought to be our perfection, our perfection Christ. For in Him we are made perfect, because of Himself the Head, the Members are we. And he hath been spoken of as "the End of the Law," because without Him no one doth make perfect the Law. When therefore ye hear in the Psalms, "At the end," — for many Psalms are thus superscribed, — be not your thought upon consuming, but upon consummation.

2. "In hymns:" in praises. For whether we are troubled and are straitened, or whether we rejoice and exult, He is to be praised, who both in tribulations doth instruct, and in gladness doth comfort. For the praise of God from the heart and mouth of a Christian man ought not to depart; not that he may be praising in prosperity, and speaking evil in adversity; but after the manner that this Psalm doth prescribe, "I will speak good of the Lord in every time, alway the praise of Him is in my mouth." Thou dost rejoice; acknowledge a Father indulging: thou art troubled; acknowledge a Father chastening. Whether He indulge, or whether He chasten, He is instructing one for whom He is preparing an inheritance.

3. What then is, "Understanding to David himself"? David indeed was, as we know, a holy prophet, king of Israel, son of Jesse:[7] but because out of his seed there came for our salvation after the flesh the Lord Jesus Christ,[8] often under that name He is figured, and David instead of Christ is in a figure set down, because of the origin of the Flesh of the Same. For after some sort He is Son of David, after some sort He is the Lord of David; Son of David after the flesh, Lord of David after the divinity. For if by Him have been made all things,[9] by Him also David himself hath been made, out of whose seed He came to men. Moreover, when the Lord had questioned the Jews, whose Son they affirmed Christ to be, they made answer, "David's:" where the Lord chides the Jews, when they said that He was the Son of David.[10] He saw that they had stayed at the flesh, and had lost sight of the divinity; and He reproveth them by propounding a question: "How then doth David himself in spirit call Him Lord, 'The Lord hath said unto my Lord.' . . . If then He in spirit calleth Him Lord, how is He is Son?"[11] A question He propounded; His being Son He denied not. Ye have heard "Lord;" say ye how He is his "Son:" ye have heard "Son;" say how He is "Lord." This question the Catholic Faith solveth. How "Lord"? Because "In the beginning was the Word, and the Word was with

---

[1] Isa. xl. 6.
[2] Oxf. MSS. "above."
[3] Ps. xxxvii. 35, 36.
[4] Ps. lxxiii. 16, 17.
[5] Lat. LIV. From a sermon to the people, wherein he is discoursing of enduring evil men, and disputing against the Donatists.
[6] Rom. x. 4.
[7] 2 Sam. xxiii. 1.
[8] Rom. i. 3.
[9] John i. 3.
[10] Oxf. MSS. add 16 words ending here.
[11] Matt. xxii. 43–45.

God, and the Word was God." [1] How " Son "? Because " The Word was made flesh, and dwelt among us." [2] Because then David in a figure is Christ, but Christ, as we have often reminded your Love, is both Head and Body; neither ought we to speak of ourselves as alien from Christ, of whom we are members, nor to count ourselves as if we were any other thing: because " The two shall be in one flesh." [3] " This is a great Sacrament," saith the Apostle, " but I speak in regard of Christ and the Church." [4] Because then whole Christ is " Head and Body; " when we hear, " Understanding to David himself," understand we ourselves also in David. Let the members of Christ understand, and Christ in His members understand, and the members of Christ in Christ understand : because Head and Members are one Christ. The Head was in heaven, and was saying, " Why dost thou persecute Me ? " [5] We with Him are in heaven through hope, Himself is with us on earth through love. Therefore " understanding to David himself." Be we admonished when we hear, and let the Church understand : for there belongeth to us great diligence to understand in what evil we now are, and from what evil we desire to be delivered, remembering the Prayer of the Lord, where at the end we say, " Deliver us from evil." [6] Therefore amid many tribulations of this world, this Psalm complaineth somewhat of understanding. He lamenteth not with it, who hath not understanding. But furthermore, dearly beloved, we ought to remember, that after the image of God we have been made, and that not in any other part than in the understanding itself. For in many things by beasts we are surpassed : but when a man knoweth himself to have been made after the image of God,[7] therein something in himself he acknowledgeth to be more than hath been given to dumb animals. But on consideration of all those things which a man hath, he findeth himself in this thing peculiarly distinguished from a dumb animal, in that he hath himself an understanding. Whence certain men despising in themselves that peculiar and especial thing which from their Maker they had received, the Maker Himself reproveth, saying, " Do not become like horse and mule, in which there is no understanding." [8] . . .

4. " Hear Thou, O God, my entreaty, and despise not my prayer : give heed unto me, and hearken unto me " (ver. 1). Of one earnest, anxious, of one set in tribulation, are these words. He is praying, suffering many things, from evil yearning to be delivered : it remaineth that we hear in what evil he is, and when he beginneth to speak, let us acknowledge there ourselves to

be ; in order that the tribulation being shared, we may conjoin prayer. " I have been made sad in my exercise, and have been troubled " (ver. 2). Where made sad, where troubled? " In my exercise," he saith. Of evil men, whom he suffereth, he hath made mention, and the same suffering of evil men he hath called his " exercise." Think ye not that without profit there are evil men in this world, and that no good God maketh of them. Every evil man either on this account liveth that he may be corrected, or on this account liveth that through him a good man may be exercised. O that therefore they that do now exercise us would be converted, and together with us be exercised ! Nevertheless, so long as they are such as to exercise, let us not hate them : because in that wherein any one of them is evil, whether unto the end he is to persevere, we know not ; and ofttimes when to thyself thou seemest to have been hating an enemy, thou hast been hating a brother, and knowest not. The devil and his angels in the holy Scriptures have been manifested to us, that for fire everlasting they have been destined. Of them only must amendment be despaired of. . . . Therefore since this rule of Love for thee is fixed, that imitating the Father thou shouldest love an enemy : for, He saith, " love your enemies : " [9] in this precept how wouldest thou be exercised, if thou hadst no enemy to suffer? Thou seest then that he profiteth thee somewhat : and let God sparing evil men profit thee, so that thou show mercy : because perchance thou too, if thou art a good man, out of an evil man hast been made a good man : and if God spared not evil men, not even thou wouldest be found to return thanks. May He therefore spare others, that hath spared thee also. For it were not right, when thou hadst passed through, to close up the way of godliness.

5. Whence then doth this man pray, set among evil men, with whose enmities he was being exercised? Why saith he, " I have been made sad in my exercise, and have been troubled "? While he is extending his love so as to love enemies, he hath been affected with disgust, being bayed at all around by the enmities of many men, by the frenzy of many, and under a sort of human infirmity he hath sunk. He hath seen himself now begin to be pierced through with an evil suggestion of the devil, to bring on hatred against his enemies : wrestling against hatred in order to perfect love herself, in the very fight, and in the wrestling, he hath been troubled. For there is his voice in another Psalm, " Mine eye hath been troubled, because of anger." And what followeth there? " I have waxen old among all mine enemies." [10] As if in storm and waves he were beginning to sink, like

---

[1] John i. 1.   [2] John i. 14.   [3] Gen. ii. 24.
[4] Eph. v. 32.   [5] Acts ix. 4.   [6] Matt. vi. 13.
[7] Gen. i. 26.   [8] Ps. xxxii. 9.

[9] Luke vi. 27.   [10] Ps. vi. 7.

Peter.[1] For he doth trample the waves of this world, that loveth enemies. Christ on the sea was walking fearless, from whose heart there could not by any means be taken away the love of an enemy, who hanging on the Cross did say, "Father, forgive them, for they know not what they do."[2] Peter too would walk. He as Head, Peter as Body: because, "Upon this rock," He saith, "I will build My Church."[3] He was bidden to walk, and he was walking by the Grace of Him bidding, not by his own strength. But when he saw the wind mighty, he feared; and then he began to sink, being troubled in his exercise. By what mighty wind? "By the voice of the enemy, and by the tribulation of the sinner" (ver. 3). Therefore, in the same manner as he cried out on the waves, "Lord, I perish, save me,"[1] a similar voice from this man hath preceded, "Hearken unto me." Wherefore? For what sufferest thou? Of what dost thou groan? "I have been made sad in my exercise." To be exercised indeed among evil men Thou hast set me, but too much they have risen up, beyond my powers: calm Thou one troubled, stretch forth a hand to one sinking. "For they have brought down upon me iniquity, and in anger they were shadowing me." Ye have heard of waves and winds: one as it were humbled they were insulting, and he was praying: on every side against him with the roar of insult they were raging, but he within was calling upon Him whom they did not see. . . .

6. But this man being troubled and made sad was praying, his eye being disturbed as it were on account of anger.[4] But the anger of a brother if it shall have been inveterate is then hatred. Anger doth trouble the eye, hatred doth quench it: anger is a straw, hatred is a beam. Sometimes thou hatest and chidest an angry man: in thee is hatred, in him whom thou chidest anger: with reason to thee is said, "Cast out first the beam from thine own eye, and so thou shalt see to cast out the straw from thy brother's eye."[5] For that ye may know how much difference there is between anger and hatred: day by day men are angry with their sons, show me them that hate their[6] sons! This man being troubled was praying even when made sad, wrestling against all revilings of all revilers; not in order that he might conquer any one of them by giving back reviling, but that he might not hate any one of them. Hence he prayeth, hence asketh: "From the voice of the enemy and from the tribulation of the sinner." "My heart hath been troubled in me" (ver. 4). This is the same as elsewhere hath been said, "Mine eye because of anger hath been troubled."[4] And if eye hath been troubled, what followeth? "And fear of death hath fallen upon me." Our life is love: if life is love, death is hatred. When a man hath begun to fear lest he should hate him that he was loving, it is death he is fearing; and a sharper death, and a more inward death, whereby soul is killed, not body. Thou didst mind a man raging against thee; what was he to do, against whom thine own Lord had given thee security, saying, "Fear not them that kill the body"?[7] He by raging killeth body, thou by keeping hatred hast killed soul; and he the body of another, thou thine own soul. "Fear," therefore, "of death hath fallen upon me."

7. "Fearfulness and trembling have come upon me, and darkness hath covered me" (ver. 5). "And I have said," "He that hateth his brother, is in darkness until now."[8] If love is light, hatred is darkness. And what saith to himself one set in that weakness and troubled in that exercise? "Who shall give me wings as to a dove, and I shall fly and shall rest?" (ver. 6). Either for death he was wishing, or for solitude he was longing. So long, he saith, as this is the work with me, as this command is given me, that I should love enemies, the revilings of these men, increasing and shadowing me, do derange mine eye, perturb my sight, penetrate my heart, slay my soul. I could wish to depart, but [9] weak I am, lest by abiding I should add sins to sins: or at least may I be separated for a little space from mankind, lest my wound suffer from frequent blows, in order that when it hath been made whole it may be brought back to the exercise. This is what takes place, brethren, and there ariseth ofttimes in the mind of the servant of God a longing for solitude, for no other reason than because of the multitude of tribulations and scandals, and he saith, "Who shall give me wings?" Doth he find himself without wings, or rather with bound wings? If they are wanting, be they given; if bound, be they loosed; because even he that looseth a bird's wings, either giveth, or giveth back to it its wings. For it had not as though its own them, wherewith it could not fly. Bound wings make a burden. "Who," he saith, "shall give me wings as to a dove, and I shall fly and shall rest?" Shall rest, where? I have said there are two senses here: either, as saith the Apostle, "To be dissolved and to be with Christ, for it is by far the best thing."[10] . . . Even he that amended cannot be, is thine, either by the fellowship of the human race, or ofttimes by Church Communion; he is within, what wilt thou do? whither wilt go? whither separate thyself, in order that these things thou mayest not suffer? But go to him,

---

[1] Matt. xiv. 30.　　[2] Luke xxiii. 34.　　[3] Matt. xvi. 18.
[4] Ps. vi. 7.　　[5] Matt. vii. 5.
[6] Oxf. mss. "him that hateth."

[7] Matt. x. 28.　　[8] 1 John ii. 9, 11.
[9] Oxf. mss. "for as much as."
[10] Philip. i. 23.

speak, exhort, coax, threaten, reprove. I have done all things, whatever powers I had I have expended and have drained, nothing I see have I prevailed; all my labour hath been spent out, sorrow hath remained. How then shall my heart rest from such men, except I say, "Who shall give me wings?" "As to a dove," however, not as to a raven. A dove seeketh a flying away from troubles, but she loseth not love. For a dove as a type of love is set forth, and in her the plaint is loved. Nothing is so fond of plaints as a dove: day and night she complaineth, as though she were set here where she ought to complain. What then saith this lover? Revilings of men to bear I am unable, they roar, with frenzy are carried away, are inflamed with indignation, in anger they shadow [1] me; to do good to them I am unable; O that I might rest somewhere, being separated from them in body, not in love; lest in me there should be troubled love itself: with my words and my speech no good can I do them, by praying for them perchance I shall do good. These words men say, but ofttimes they are so bound, that to fly they are not able. For perchance they are not bound with any birdlime, but are bound by duty. But if they are bound with care and duty, and to leave it are unable, let them say, "I was wishing to be dissolved and to be with Christ, for it is by far the best thing: to abide in the flesh is necessary because of you." [2] A dove bound back by affection, not by cupidity, was not able to fly away because of duty to be fulfilled, not because of little merit. Nevertheless a longing in heart must needs be; nor doth any man suffer this longing, but he that hath begun to walk in that narrow way: [3] in order that he may know that there are not wanting to the Church persecutions, even in this time, when a calm is seen in the Church, at least with respect to those persecutions which our Martyrs have suffered. But there are not wanting persecutions, because a true saying is this, "All that will godly to live in Christ, shall suffer persecution." [4] . . .

8. "Behold I have gone afar fleeing, and have abode in the desert" (ver. 7). In what desert? Wherever thou shalt be, there will gather them together other men, the desert with thee they will seek, will attach themselves to thy life, thou canst not thrust back the society of brethren: there are mingled with thee also evil men; still exercise is thy due portion, "Behold I have gone afar, and have abode in the desert." In what desert? It is perchance in the conscience, whither no man entereth, where no one is with thee, where thou art and God. For if in the desert, in any place, what wilt thou do with men gathering themselves together? For thou wilt

not be able to be separated from mankind, so long as among men thou livest. [5] . . .

9. "I was looking for him that should save me from weakness of mind and tempest" (ver. 8). Sea there is, tempest there is: nothing for thee remaineth but to cry out, "Lord, I perish." [6] Let Him stretch forth hand, who doth the waves tread fearlessly, let Him relieve thy dread, let Him confirm in Himself thy security, let Him speak to thee within, and say to thee, "Give heed to Me, what I have borne:" an evil brother perchance thou art suffering, or an enemy without art suffering; which of these have I not suffered? There roared without Jews, within a disciple was betraying. There rageth therefore tempest, but He doth save men from weakness of mind, and tempest. Perchance thy ship is being troubled, because He in thee is sleeping. The sea was raging, the bark wherein the disciples were sailing was being tossed; but Christ was sleeping: at length it was seen by them that among them was sleeping the Ruler [7] and Creator of winds; they drew near and awoke Christ; [8] He commanded [9] the winds, and there was a great calm. With reason then perchance thy heart is troubled, because thou hast forgotten Him on whom thou hast believed: beyond endurance thou art suffering, because it hath not come into thy mind what for thee Christ hath borne. If unto thy mind cometh not Christ, He sleepeth: awake Christ, recall faith. For then in thee Christ is sleeping, if thou hast forgotten the sufferings of Christ: then in thee Christ is watching, if thou hast remembered the sufferings of Christ. But when with full heart thou shalt have considered what He hath suffered, wilt not thou too with equanimity endure? and perchance rejoicing, because thou hast been found in some likeness of the sufferings of thy King. When therefore on these things thinking thou hast begun to be comforted and to rejoice, He hath arisen, He hath commanded the winds; therefore there is a great calm. "I was looking for Him that should save me from weakness of mind and tempest."

10. "Sink, O Lord, and divide the tongues of them" (ver. 9). He is referring to men troubling him and shadowing him, and he hath wished this thing not of anger, brethren. They that have wickedly lifted up themselves, for them it is expedient that they be sunk. They that have wickedly conspired, it is expedient for them that their tongues should be divided: to good let them consent, and let their tongues agree together. But if to one purpose [10] there were a whispering against me, [11] he saith, all mine ene-

[1] Adumbrant.   [2] Philip. i. 23, 24.   [3] Matt. vii. 14.
[4] 2 Tim. iii. 12.

[5] [Professor Cooke's Scientific Culture, pp. 291, 292. New York, 1885. — C.]
[6] Matt. xiv. 30.   [7] Imperator.   [8] Matt. viii. 24, 25.
[9] Imperavit.   [10] In idipsum.   [11] Ps. xli. 7.

mies, let them lose their " one purpose " in evil, divided be the tongues of them, let them not with themselves agree together. "Sink, O Lord, and divide the tongues of them." Wherefore "sink"? Because themselves they have lifted up. Wherefore "divide"? Because for an evil thing they have united. Recollect that tower of proud men made after the deluge : what said the proud men? Lest we perish in a deluge, let us make a lofty tower.[1] In pride they were thinking themselves to be fortified, they builded up a lofty tower, and the Lord divided the tongues of them. Then they began not to understand one another ; hence arose the beginning of many tongues. For before, one tongue there was : but one tongue for men agreeing was good, one tongue for humble men was good : but when that gathering together did into a union of pride fall headlong, God spared them ; even though He divided the tongues, lest by understanding one another they should make a destructive unity. Through proud men, divided were the tongues ; through humble Apostles, united were the tongues. Spirit of pride dispersed tongues, Spirit Holy united tongues. For when the Holy Spirit came upon the disciples, with the tongues of all men they spake,[2] by all men they were understood : tongues dispersed, into one were united. Therefore if still they rage and are Gentiles, it is expedient for them divided to have their tongues. They would have one tongue ; let them come to the Church ; because even among the diversity of tongues of flesh, one is the tongue in faith of heart.

11. "For I have seen iniquity and contradiction in the city." With reason this man was seeking the desert, for he saw iniquity and contradiction in the city. There is a certain city turbulent : the same it was that was building a tower, the same was confounded and called Babylon, the same through innumerable nations dispersed :[3] thence is gathered the Church into the desert of a good conscience. For he saw contradiction in the city. "Christ cometh."— "What Christ?" thou contradictest.— "Son of God."— "And hath God a Son?" thou contradictest.— "He was born of a virgin, suffered, rose again."— "And whence is it possible for this to be done?" thou contradictest.— Give heed at least to the glory of the Cross itself. Now on the brow of kings that Cross hath been fixed, over which enemies insulted. The effect hath proved the virtue.[4] It hath subdued the world, not with steel, but with wood. The wood of the Cross deserving of insults hath seemed to enemies, and before the wood itself standing they were wagging the head, and saying, "If Son of God He is, let Him come down from the Cross."[5] He was stretching forth His hands to a people unbelieving and contradicting. For if just he is that of faith liveth,[6] unjust he is that hath not faith. By that which here he saith "iniquity," I understand unbelief. The Lord therefore was seeing in the city iniquity and contradiction, and was stretching forth His hands to a people unbelieving and contradicting : and nevertheless waiting for these same, He was saying, "Father, forgive them, for they know not what they do."[7] Even now indeed there rage the remnant of that city, even now they contradict. From the brows of all men now He is stretching forth hands to the remnant unbelieving and contradicting.

12. "Day and night there will compass it upon the walls thereof iniquity, and labour."[8] "Upon the walls thereof ;" upon the fortifications thereof, holding as it were the heads thereof, the noble men thereof. If that noble man were a Christian, not one would remain a pagan ! Ofttimes men say, "no one would remain a pagan, if he were a Christian." Ofttimes men say, "If he too were made a Christian, who would remain a pagan?" Because therefore not yet they are made Christians, as if walls they are of that city unbelieving and contradicting. How long shall these walls stand? Not always shall they stand. The Ark is going around the walls of Jericho : there shall come a time at the seventh going round of the Ark, when all the walls of the city unbelieving and contradicting shall fall.[9] Until it come to pass, this man is being troubled in his exercise ; and enduring the remains of men contradicting, he would choose wings for flying away, would choose the rest of the desert. Yea let him continue amid men contradicting, let him endure menaces, drink revilings, and look for Him that will save him from weakness of mind and tempest : let him look upon the Head, the pattern for his life,[10] let him be made calm in hope, even if he is troubled in fact. "Day and night there will compass it upon the walls thereof iniquity ; and labour in the midst thereof and injustice." And for this reason labour is there, because iniquity is there : because injustice is there, therefore also labour is there. But let them hear him stretching forth hands. "Come unto Me, all ye that labour."[11] Ye cry, ye contradict, ye revile : He on the contrary, "Come unto Me, all ye that labour," in your pride, and ye shall rest in My humility. "Learn of Me," He saith, "for meek I am and humble in heart, and ye shall find rest unto your souls."[12] For whence do they labour, but because they are not meek and humble in

---

[1] Gen. xi. 4.   [2] Acts ii. 4.
[3] Gen. xi. 9.
[4] Nearly all MSS. " By effect prove the virtue." — Ben.

[5] Matt. xxvii. 40.   [6] Rom. i. 17.
[7] Luke xxiii. 34.   [8] Oxf. MSS. omit " and labour."
[9] Josh. vi. 5.   [10] Or, " way."
[11] Matt. xi. 28.   [12] Matt. xi. 29.

heart? God humble was made, let man blush to be proud.

13. "There hath not failed from the streets thereof usury and deceit" (ver. 11). Usury and deceit are not hidden at least, because they are evil things, but in public they rage. For he that in his house doth any evil thing, however for his evil thing doth blush: "In the streets thereof usury and deceit." Money-lending[1] even hath a profession, Money-lending also is called a science; a corporation is spoken of, a corporation as if necessary to the state, and of its profession it payeth revenue; so entirely indeed in the streets is that which should have been hidden. There is also another usury worse, when thou forgivest not that which to thee is owed; and the eye is disturbed in that verse of the prayer, "Forgive us our debts — as we too forgive our debtors."[2] For what there wilt thou do, when thou art going to pray, and coming to that same verse? An insulting word thou hast heard: thou wouldest exact the punishment of condemnation. Do but consent to exact just so much as thou hast given, thou usurer of injuries! With the fist thou hast been smitten, slaying thou seekest. Evil usury! How wilt thou go to prayer? If thou shalt have left praying, which way wilt thou come round unto the Lord? Behold thou wilt say: "Our Father which art in heaven, hallowed be Thy Name, Thy kingdom come, Thy will be done, as in heaven so on earth." Thou wilt say, "Our daily bread give us to-day." Thou wilt come to, "Forgive us our debts, as we also forgive our debtors."[3] Even in that evil city let there abound these usuries; let them not enter the walls where the breast is smitten! What wilt thou do? because there thou and that verse are[4] in the midst? Petitions for thee hath a heavenly Lawyer composed.[5] He that knew what used there to be done, said to thee, "Otherwise thou shalt not obtain." "Verily, verily, I say unto you, that if ye shall have forgiven men sins, they shall be forgiven you; but if ye shall not have forgiven sins unto men, neither will your Father forgive you."[6] Who saith this? He that knoweth what there is being done, in the place whereat thou art standing to make request. See how Himself hath willed to be thy Advocate; Himself thy Counsellor,[7] Himself the Assessor of the Father, Himself thy Judge hath said, "Otherwise thou shalt not receive." What wilt thou do? Thou wilt not receive, unless thou shalt speak; wilt not receive if falsely thou shalt speak. Therefore either thou must do and speak, or else what thou askest thou wilt not earn; because

they that this do not do, are in the midst of those evil usuries. Be they engaged therein, that yet do idols either adore or desire: do not thou, O people of God, do not thou, O people of Christ, do not thou the Body of Him the Head! Give heed to the bond[8] of thy peace, give heed to the promise of thy life. For what doth it profit thee, that thou exactest for injuries which thou hast endured? doth vengeance refresh thee? Therefore, over the evil of another shalt thou rejoice? Thou hast suffered evil; pardon thou; be not ye two.[9] . . .

14. "For if an enemy had upbraided me" (ver. 12). And indeed above he was "troubled in his exercise" by the voice of the enemy and by the tribulation of the sinner, perhaps being placed in that city, that proud city that was building a tower, which was "sunk,"[10] that divided might be the tongues: give heed to his inward groaning because of perils from false brethren. "For if an enemy had upbraided me, I would have undergone it assuredly, and if he that did hate me had over me spoken great words," that is, through pride had on me trampled, did magnify himself above me, did threaten me all in his power: "I would hide myself assuredly from him." From him that is abroad, thou wouldest hide thyself where? Amid those that are within. But now see whether anything else remaineth, but that thou seek solitude. "But thou," he saith, "man of one mind, my guide and my friend" (ver. 13). Perchance sometimes good counsel thou hast given, perchance sometimes thou hast gone before me, and some wholesome advice thou hast given me: in the Church of God together we have been. "But thou, . . . that together with me didst take sweet morsels" (ver. 14). What are the sweet morsels? Not all they that are present know: but let them not be soured that do know, in order that they may be able to say to them that as yet know not: "Taste ye and see, how sweet is the Lord."[11] "In the House of God we have walked with consent." Whence then dissension? Thou that wast within, hast become one without. He hath walked with me in the House of God with consent: another house hath he set up against the House of God. Wherefore hath that been forsaken, wherein we have walked with consent?[12] wherefore hath that been deserted, wherein together we did take sweet morsels?

15. "Let there come death upon them, and let them go down unto Hell living" (ver. 15). How hath he cited and hath made us call to mind that first beginning of schism, when in that first people of the Jews certain proud men

---

1 *Fœnus.* [See note 2, p. 99, *supra.* —C.]
2 Matt. vi. 12. So Oxf. mss. 3 Matt. vi. 9-12.
4 Oxf. mss. "Where thou and that verse are there."
5 See Tract. 7, On the Gospel of St. John, § 11.
6 Matt. vi. 14. 7 *Jurisperitus; i.e.,* lawyer.

8 *Vinculum.* 9 *i.e.,* evil men.
10 MSS. *submersa* (not *subversa*), alluding to ver. 9. — Ben.
11 Ps. xxxiv. 8. 12 Against the Donatists.

separated themselves, and would without have sacrificed? A new death upon them came: the earth opened herself, and swallowed them up alive.[1] "Let there come," he saith, "death upon them, and let them go down into Hell living." What is "living"? knowing that they are perishing, and yet perishing. Hear of living men perishing and being swallowed up in a gulf of the earth, that is, being swallowed up in the voraciousness of earthly desires.[2] Thou sayest to a man, What aileth thee, brother? Brethren we are, one God we invoke, in one Christ we believe, one Gospel we hear, one Psalm we sing, one Amen we respond, one Hallelujah we sound, one Easter we celebrate: why art thou without and I am within? Ofttimes one straitened, and perceiving how true are the charges which are made, saith, May God requite our ancestors! Therefore alive he perisheth. In the next place thou continuest and thus givest warning. At least let the evil of separation stand alone, why dost thou adjoin thereto that of rebaptism? Acknowledge in me what thou hast; and if thou hatest me, spare thou Christ in me. And this evil thing doth frequently and very greatly displease them. . . . Because they themselves have the Scriptures in their hands, and know well by daily reading how the Church Catholic through the whole world is so spread, that in a word all contradiction is void; and that there cannot be found any support for their schism they know well: therefore unto the lower places living they go down, because the evil which they do, they know evil to be. But the former a fire of divine indignation consumed. For being inflamed with desire of strife, from their evil leaders they would not depart. There came upon fire a fire, upon the heat of dissension the heat of consuming. "For naughtiness is in their lodgings, in the midst of them." "In their lodgings,"[3] wherein they tarry and pass away. For here they are not alway to be: and nevertheless in defence of a temporal animosity they are fighting so fiercely. "In their lodgings is iniquity; in the midst of them is iniquity:" no part of them is so near the middle of them as their heart.

16. "Therefore to the Lord I have cried out" (ver. 16). The Body of Christ and the oneness of Christ in anguish, in weariness, in uneasiness, in the tribulation of its exercise, that One Man, Oneness in One Body set, when He was wearying His soul in crying out from the ends of the earth; saith, "From the ends of the earth to Thee I have cried out, when My heart was being vexed."[4] Himself one, but a oneness[5] that One! and Himself one, not in one place one, but from the ends of the earth is crying as one. How from the ends of the earth should

there cry one, except in many there were one? "I to the Lord have cried out." Rightly do thou cry out to the Lord, cry not to Donatus: lest for thee he be instead of the Lord a lord, that under the Lord would not be a fellow-servant.

17. "In evening, in morning, at noon-day I will recount and will tell forth, and He shall hearken to my voice"[6] (ver. 18). Do thou proclaim glad tidings, keep not secret that which thou hast received, "in evening" of things gone by, "in morning" of things to be, at "noon-day" of things ever to be. Therefore to that which he saith "in evening" belongeth that which he recounteth: to that which he saith, "in morning," belongeth that which he telleth forth: to that which he saith "at noon-day," belongeth that wherein his voice is hearkened to. For the end is at noon-day; that is to say, whence there is no going down unto setting. For at noon-day there is light full high, the splendour of wisdom, the fervour of love. "In evening and in morning and at noon-day." "In evening," the Lord on the Cross; "in morning," in Resurrection; "at noon-day," in Ascension. I will recount in evening the patience of Him dying, I will tell forth in morning the life of Him rising, I will pray that He hearken at noon-day sitting at the right hand of the Father. He shall hearken to my voice, That intercedeth for us.[7] How great is the security of this man. How great the consolation, how great the refuge "from weakness of mind and tempest," against evil men, against ungodly men both without and within, and in the case of those that are without though they had been within.

18. Therefore, my Brethren, those that in the very congregation of these walls ye see to be rebellious men, proud, seeking their own, lifted up; not having a zeal for God that is chaste, sound, quiet, but ascribing to themselves much; ready for dissension, but not finding opportunity; are the very chaff of the Lord's floor.[8] From hence these few men the wind of pride hath dislodged: the whole floor will not fly, save when He at the last shall winnow. But what shall we do, save with this man sing, with this man pray, with this man mourn and say securely, "He shall redeem in peace my soul" (ver. 18). Against them that love not peace: "in peace He shall redeem my soul." "Because with those that hated peace I was peace-making."[9] "He shall redeem in peace my soul, from those that draw near to me." For from those that are afar from me, it is an easy case: not so soon doth he deceive me that saith, Come, pray to an idol: he is very far from

---

[1] Num. xvi. 31.   [2] Against the Donatists.
[3] *Hospitiis.*   [4] Ps. lxi. 2.   [5] *Unitas.*

[6] [Acts ii. 15, iii. 1, x. 3, x. 9. The Apostles observed the "hours of prayer;" and they survive, theoretically, in the liturgies of Christendom. A. N. F. vol. iii. p. 689.—C.]
[7] Rom. viii. 34.   [8] Matt. iii. 12.   [9] Ps. cxx. 6, 7.

me. Art thou a Christian? A Christian, he saith. Out of a neighbouring place he is my adversary, he is at hand. "He shall redeem in peace my soul, from those that draw near to me: for in many things they were with me." Wherefore have I said, "draw near to me"? Because "in many things they were with me." In this verse two propositions occur. "In many things they were with me." Baptism we had both of us, in that they were with me: the Gospel we both read, they were in that with me: the festivals of martyrs we celebrated, they were there with me: Easter's solemnity we attended, they were there with me. But not entirely with me: in schism not with me, in heresy not with me. In many things with me, in few things not with me. But in these few things wherein not with me, there is no profit to them of the many things wherein they were with me. For see, brethren, how many things hath recounted the Apostle Paul: one thing, he hath said, if it shall have been wanting, in vain are those things. "If with the tongues of men and of angels I shall speak," he saith, "if I have all prophecy, and all faith, and all knowledge; if mountains I shall remove, if I shall bestow all my goods upon the poor, if I shall deliver my body even so that it be burned."[1] How many things he hath enumerated! To all these many things let there be wanting one thing, charity; the former in number are more, the latter in weight is greater. Therefore in all Sacraments they are with me, in one charity not with me: "In many things they were with me." Again, by a different expression: "For in many things they were with me." They that themselves have separated from me, with me they were, not in few things, but in many things. For throughout the whole world few are the grains, many are the chaffs. Therefore he saith what? In chaff with me they were, in wheat with me they were not. And the chaff is nearly related to the wheat, from one seed it goeth forth, in one field is rooted, with one rain is nourished, the same reaper it suffereth, the same threshing sustaineth, the same winnowing awaiteth, *but* not into one barn entereth.

19. "God will hear me, and He shall humble them That is before ages" (ver. 19). For they rely on some leader or other of theirs that hath begun but yesterday. "He shall humble them That is before ages." For even if with reference to time Christ is of Mary the Virgin, nevertheless before ages: "In the beginning He is the Word, and the Word with God, and the Word God."[2] "He shall humble them That is before ages. For to them is no changing:" of them I "speak to whom is no changing." He knew of some to persevere, and in the perseverance of their own

wickedness to die. For we see them, and to them is no changing: they that die in that same perverseness, in that same schism, to them is no changing. God shall humble them, shall humble them in damnation, because they are exalted in dissension. To them is no changing, because they are not changed for the better, but for the worse: neither while they are here, nor in the resurrection. For all we shall rise again, but[3] not all shall be changed. Wherefore? Because "To them is no changing: and they have not feared God." . . .

20. "He stretcheth forth His hand in requiting" (ver. 20). "They have polluted His Testament." Read the testament which they have polluted: "In thy seed shall be blessed all nations."[4] Thou against these words of the Testator sayest what? The Africa of holy Donatus hath alone deserved this grace, in him hath remained the Church of Christ. Say at least the Church of Donatus. Wherefore addest thou, of Christ? Of whom it is said, "In thy seed shall be blessed all nations." After Donatus wilt thou go? Set aside Christ, and then secede. See therefore what followeth: "They have polluted His Testament." What Testament? To Abraham have been spoken the promises, and to his seed. The Apostle saith, "Nevertheless, a man's testament confirmed no one maketh void, or superaddeth to: to Abraham have been spoken the promises, and to his seed. He saith not, And to seeds, as if in many; but as if in one, And to thy Seed, which is Christ."[5] In this Christ, therefore, what Testament hath been promised? "In thy seed shall be blessed all nations." Thou that hast given up the unity of all nations, and in a part hast remained, hast polluted His Testament. . . .

21. "And His heart hath drawn near" (ver. 22). Of whom do we understand it, except of Him, by the anger of whom they have been divided? How "hath his heart drawn near"? In such sort, that we may understand His will. For by heretics hath been vindicated the Catholic Church, and by those that think evil have been proved those that think well. For many things lay hid in the Scriptures: and when heretics had been cut off, with questions they troubled the Church of God: then those things were opened which lay hid, and the will of God was understood.[6] Thence is said in another Psalm, "In order that they might be excluded that have been proved with silver."[7] For let them be excluded, He hath said, let them come forth, let them appear. Whence even in silver-working men are called "excluders," that is, pressers out

---

[3] E. V. omits "not." [1] Cor. xv. 51.
[4] Gen. xii. 3, xxvi. 4.   [5] Gal. iii. 15, 16.
[6] [Scripture is the rule of faith. See Tertull. vol. iii. p. 265, A. N F., and hereafter in this series, Vincent of Lerins, *passim*. — C.]
[7] Ps. lxviii. 30.

[1] 1 Cor. xiii. 1-3.   [2] John i. 1.

of form from the sort of confusion of the lump. Therefore many men that could understand and expound the Scriptures very excellently, were hidden among the people of God : but they did not declare the solution of difficult questions, when no reviler again urged them. For was the Trinity perfectly treated of before the Arians snarled thereat? Was repentance perfectly treated of before the Novatians opposed? So not perfectly of Baptism was it treated, before rebaptizers removed outside [1] contradicted ; nor of the very oneness of Christ were the doctrines clearly stated which have been stated, save after that this separation began to press upon the weak : in order that they that knew how to treat of and solve these questions (lest the weak should perish vexed with the questions of the ungodly), by their discourses and disputations should bring out unto open day the dark things of the Law.[2] . . . This obscure sense see in what manner the Apostle bringeth out into light ; " It is needful," he saith, " that also heresies there be, in order that men proved may be made manifest among you." [3] What is " men proved "? Proved with silver, proved with the word. What is " may be made manifest "? May be brought out.[4] Wherefore this? Because of heretics. So therefore these also " have been divided because of the anger of His countenance, and His heart hath drawn near."

22. " His discourses have been softened above oil, and themselves are darts " (ver. 21). For certain things in the Scriptures were seeming hard, while they were obscure ; when explained, they have been softened. For even the first heresy in the disciples of Christ, as it were from the hardness of His discourse arose. For when He said, " Except a man shall have eaten My flesh and shall have drunk My blood, he shall not have life in himself : " they, not understanding, said to one another, " Hard is this discourse, who can hear it?" Saying that, " Hard is this discourse," they separated from Him : He remained with the others, the twelve. When they had intimated to Him, that by His discourse they had been scandalized, " Will ye also," He saith, " choose to go?" Then Peter : " Thou hast the Word of life eternal : to whom shall we go?"[5] Attend, we beseech you, and ye little ones learn godliness. Did Peter by any means at that time understand the secret of that discourse of the Lord? Not yet he understood : but that good were the words which he understood not, godly he believed. Therefore if hard is a discourse, and not yet is understood, be it hard to

an ungodly man, but to thee be it by godliness softened : for whenever it is solved, it both will become for thee oil, and even unto the bones it will penetrate.

23. Furthermore, just as Peter, after their having been scandalized by the hardness, as they thought, of the discourse of the Lord, even then said, " to whom shall we go?" so he hath added, " Cast upon the Lord thy care, and He shall Himself nourish thee up " (ver. 22). A little one thou art, not yet thou understandest the secret things of words : perchance from thee the bread is hidden, and as yet with milk thou must be fed :[6] be not angry with the breasts : they will make thee fit for the table, for which now little fitted thou art. Behold by the division of heretics many hard things have been softened : His discourses that were hard have been softened above oil, and they are themselves darts. They have armed men preaching the Gospel : and the very discourses are aimed at the breast of every one that heareth, by men instant in season and out of season : by those discourses, by those words, as though by arrows, hearts of men unto the love of peace are smitten. Hard they were, and soft they have been made. Being softened they have not lost their virtue, but into darts have been converted. . . . Upon the Lord cast thyself. Behold thou wilt cast thyself upon the Lord, let no one put himself in the place of the Lord. " Cast upon the Lord thy care." . . .

24. But to the others what? " But Thou, O God, shalt bring them down unto the pit of corruption " (ver. 23). The pit of corruption is the darkness of sinking under. When blind leadeth blind, they both fall into a ditch.[7] God bringeth them down into the pit of corruption, not because He is the author of their own guilt, but because He is Himself the judge of their iniquities. " For God hath delivered them unto the desires of their heart."[8] For they have loved darkness, and not light ; they have loved blindness, and not seeing. For behold the Lord Jesus hath shone out to the whole world, let them sing in unity with the whole world : " For there is not one that can hide himself from the heat of Him."[9] But they passing over from the whole to a part, from the body to a wound, from life to a limb cut off, shall meet with what, but going into the pit of corruption?

25. " Men of bloods and of deceitfulness." Men of bloods, because of slayings he calleth them : and O that they were corporal and not spiritual slayings. For blood from the flesh going forth, is seen and shuddered at : who seeth the blood of the heart in a man rebaptized? Those deaths require other eyes. Although even about these visible deaths Circumcelliones armed

---

[1] Foris positi.
[2] [That is, not by new ideas incorporated with old truth, but by collecting into focus the testimony of all recognised doctors of the Church as to the true meaning and intent of Holy Scripture. This is development as distinguished from corruption. — C.]
[3] 1 Cor. xi. 19.   [4] Excludantur.   [5] John vi. 53, etc.

[6] 1 Cor. iii. 1.   [7] Matt. xv. 14.   [8] Rom. i. 24.
[9] Ps. xix. 6.

everywhere remain not quiet. And if we think of these visible deaths, there are men of bloods. Give heed to the armed man, whether he is a man of peace and not of blood. If at least a club only he were to carry, well ; but he carrieth a sling, carrieth an axe, carrieth stones, carrieth lances ; and carrying these weapons, wherever they may they scour, for the blood of innocent men they thirst.[1] Therefore even with regard to these visible deaths there are men of bloods. But even of them let us say, O that such deaths alone they perpetrated, and souls they slew not. These that are men of bloods and of deceit, let them not suppose that we thus wrongly understand men of bloods, of them that kill souls : they themselves of their Maximianists[2] have so understood it. For when they condemned them, in the very sentence of their Council they have set down these words : "Swift are the feet of them to shed the blood" (of the proclaimers[3]), "tribulation and calamity are in the ways of them, and the way of peace they have not known."[4] This of the Maximianists they have said. But I ask of them, when have the Maximianists shed the body's blood ; not because they too would not shed, if there were so great a multitude as could shed, but because of the fear in their minority rather they have suffered somewhat from others, than have themselves at any time done any such thing. Therefore I question the Donatist and say : In thy Council thou hast set down of the Maximianists, "Swift are the feet of them to shed blood." Show me one of whom the Maximianists have hurt so much as a finger ! What other thing to me is he to answer, than that which I say ? They that have separated themselves from unity,[5] and who slay souls by leading astray, spiritually, not carnally, do shed blood. Very well thou hast expounded, but in thy exposition acknowledge their own deeds. "Men of bloods and of deceitfulness." In guile is deceitfulness, in dissimulation, in seduction. What therefore of those very men that have been divided because of the anger of His countenance ? They are themselves men of bloods and of deceit.

26. But of them he saith what? "They shall not halve their days." What is, "They shall not halve their days"? They shall not make progress as much as they think : within the time which they expect, they shall perish. For he is that partridge, whereof hath been said, "In the

half of his days they shall leave him, and in his last days he shall be an unwise one."[6] They make progress, but for a time. For what saith the Apostle? "But evil men and seducers shall make progress for the worse, themselves erring, and other men into error driving."[7] But "a blind man leading a blind man, together into a ditch they fall."[8] Deservedly they fall "into the pit of corruption." What therefore saith he? They shall make progress for the worse : not however for long. For a little before he hath said, "But further they shall not make progress :"[9] that is, "shall not halve their days." Let the Apostle proceed and tell wherefore : "For the madness of them shall be manifest to all men, as also was that of the others." "But I in Thee will hope, O Lord." But deservedly they shall not halve their days, because in man they have hoped. But I from days temporal have reached unto day eternal. Wherefore? Because in Thee I have hoped, O Lord.

PSALM LVI.[10]

1. Just as when we are going to enter into any house, we look on the title to see whose it is and to whom it belongeth, lest perchance inopportunely we burst into a place whereunto we ought not ; and again, in order that we may not through timidity withdraw from that which we ought to enter : as if in a word we were to read, These estates belong to such an one or to such an one : so on the lintel of this Psalm we have inscribed, "At the end, for the people that from holy men were put afar off, to David himself, at the inscription of the Title, when the Allophyli held him in Gath."[11] Let us therefore take knowledge of the people that from holy men were put afar off at the inscription of the Title. For this doth belong to that David whom now ye know how to understand spiritually. For there is here commended to our notice no other than He of whom hath been said, "The end of the Law is Christ for righteousness to every man believing."[12] Therefore when thou hearest "at the end," unto Christ give heed, lest tarrying in the way thou arrive not at the end. . . .

2. Who are then the people that from holy men were put afar off at the inscription of the Title? Let the Title itself declare to us that people. For there was written a certain title at the Passion of the Lord, when the Lord was crucified : there was in that place a Title inscribed in Hebrew, in Greek, and in Latin, "The King of the Jews ;"[13] in three tongues as

---

1 [What but *Circumcelliones* were the perpetrators of the Bartholomew massacres, of the *Dragonnades*, of the awful butcheries under Alva? — C.]

2 See on Ps. xxxvi.

3 The word *annuntiatorum* is omitted in some copies. It is not in the sentence of the Synod of Bagai, as given in the fourth book against Crescontius, c. 4 — Ben.

4 Ps. xiv. 7, Vulg. and Angl. ; also Rom. iii. 15-17.

5 [How fearfully this comes home to those who separated themselves from the Nicene unity under lead of Nicholas and his Decretals, in the ninth age! (John xiii. 30.) The "Dark Ages" instantly settled upon the Church. See A. N. F. vol. viii. p. 642. — C.]

6 Jer. xvii. 11.　　7 2 Tim. iii. 13.　　8 Matt. xv. 14.

9 2 Tim. iii. 9.

10 Lat. LV. A discourse to the people of Carthage. A Paris MS. has the title, "*Incipit Carthagine Sermo habitus in Basilicâ Restitutâ, Feriâ V. de Psalmo LV.— Ben.*

11 1 Sam. xxi. 10.　　12 Rom. x. 4.　　13 John xix. 19.

though by three witnesses the Title was confirmed : because "in the mouth of two or three
witnesses shall stand every word." [1] . . .

3. What therefore meaneth that which to
the title itself still belongeth, namely, that "the
Allophyli held him in Geth "? Geth was a certain city of the *Allophyli*,[2] that is, of *strangers*,
to wit, of people afar from holy men. All they
that refuse Christ for King become strangers.
Wherefore strangers are they made? Because
even that vine, though by Him planted, when it
had become sour what heard it? "Wherefore
hast thou been turned into sourness, O alien
vine?"[3] It hath not been said, My vine : because if Mine, sweet ; if sour, not Mine ; if not
Mine, surely alien. "There held him," then,
"Allophyli in Geth." We find indeed, brethren, David himself, son of Jesse, king of Israel,
to have been in a strange land among the Allophyli, when he was sought by Saul, and was
in that city and with the king of that city,[4] but
that there he was detained we read not.
Therefore our David, the Lord Jesus Christ out
of the seed of that David, not alone they held,
but there hold Him still Allophyli in Geth. Of
Geth we have said that it is a city. But the
interpretation of this name, if asked for, signifieth "press." . . . How therefore here is He
held in Geth? Held in a winepress is His Body,
that is, His Church. What is, in a winepress?
In pressings. But in a winepress fruitful is the
pressing. A grape on the vine sustaineth no
pressing, whole it seemeth, but nothing thence
floweth : it is thrown into a winepress, is trodden, is pressed ; harm seemeth to be done to
the grape, but this harm is not barren ; nay, if
no harm had been applied, barren it would have
remained.

4. Let whatsoever holy men therefore that
are suffering pressing from those that have been
put afar off from the saints, give heed to this
Psalm, let them perceive here themselves, let
them speak what here is spoken, that suffer
what here is spoken of. . . . Private enmities
therefore let no one think of, when about to
hear the words of this Psalm : "Know ye that
for us the wrestling is not against flesh and
blood, but against princes and powers, and
spiritual things of wickedness,"[5] that is, against
the devil and his angels ; because even when
we suffer men that annoy us, he is instigating,
he is inflaming, as it were his vessels he is
moving. Let us give heed therefore to two enemies, him whom we see, and him whom we see
not ; man we see, the devil we see not ; man
let us love, of the devil beware ; for man pray,
against the devil pray, and let us say to God,

"Have pity on me, O Lord, for man hath trodden me down" (ver. 1). Fear not because
man hath trodden thee down : have thou wine,
a grape thou hast become in order that thou
shouldest be trodden. "All day long warring he hath troubled me," every one that hath
been put afar off from the saints. But why
should not here be understood even the devil
himself? Is it because mention is made of
"man "?[6] doth therefore the Gospel err, because
it hath said, "A man that is an enemy hath
done this "?[7] But by a kind of figure may he
also be called a man,[8] and yet not be a man.
Whether therefore it was him whom he that
said these words was beholding, or whether it
was the people and each one that was put afar
off from holy men, through which kind the
devil troubleth the people of God, who cleave
to holy men, who cleave to the Holy One,
who cleave to the King, at the title of which
King being indignant they were as though beat-
en back, and put afar off : let him say, "Have
pity on me, O Lord, for man hath trodden me
down : " and let him faint not in this treading
down, knowing Him on whom he is calling,
and by whose example he hath been made
strong. The first cluster in the winefat pressed
is Christ. When that cluster by passion was
pressed out,[9] there flowed that whence "the cup
inebriating is how passing beautiful !"[10] Let His
Body likewise say, looking upon its Head,
"Have pity on me, O Lord, for man hath trodden me down : all day long warring he hath
troubled me." "All day long," at all times.
Let no one say to himself, There have been
troubles in our fathers' time, in our time there
are not. If thou supposest thyself not to have
troubles, not yet hast thou begun to be a Christian. And where is the voice of the Apostle,
"But even all that will live godly in Christ,
persecutions shall suffer." [11] If therefore thou
sufferest not any persecution for Christ, take
heed lest not yet thou hast begun godly to
live in Christ. But when thou hast begun
godly to live in Christ, thou hast entered into
the winepress ; make ready thyself for pressings : but be not thou dry, lest from the pressing
nothing go forth.

5. "Mine enemies have trodden me down all
day long" (ver. 2). They that have been put
afar off from holy men, these are mine enemies.
All day long : already it hath been said, "From
the height [12] of the day." What meaneth, "from
the height of the day"? Perchance it is a high
thing to understand. And no wonder, because

---

[1] Matt. xviii. 16 ; Deut. xix. 15.
[2] The usual name of the Philistines in LXX. and Vulgate.
[3] Jer. ii. 21.　　　[4] 1 Sam. xxi. 10.　　　[5] Eph. vi. 12.

[6] So MSS. edd. "because he is not called man."
[7] Matt. xiii. 28.
[8] [Angels are so called. Dan. ix. 21, Acts x. 26. Compare Mark
xvi. 5 ; Rev. xix. 10 ; also this vol. p. 117, note 7, *supra*. — C.]
[9] Isa. lxiii. 3.　　[10] Ps. xxiii. 5.　　[11] 2 Tim. iii. 12.
[12] Or, "depth."

the height of the day it is. For perchance they for this reason have been put afar off from holy men, because they were not able to penetrate the height of the day, whereof the Apostles are twelve shining hours. Therefore they that crucified Him, as if man, in the day have erred. But why have they suffered darkness, so that they should be put afar off from holy men? Because on high the day was shining, Him in the height hidden they knew not. "For if they had known, never the Lord of Glory would they have crucified."[1] . . .

6. "For many men that war against me, shall fear" (ver. 3). Shall fear when? When the day shall have passed away, wherein they are high. For for a time high they are, when the time of their height is finished they will fear. "But I in Thee will hope, O Lord." He saith not, "But I will not fear:" but, "Many men, that war against me, shall fear." When there shall have come that day of Judgment, then "shall mourn for themselves all the tribes of the earth."[2] When there shall have appeared the sign of the Son of Man in heaven, then secure shall be all holy men. For that thing shall come which they hoped for, which they longed for, the coming whereof they prayed for: but to those men no place for repentance shall remain, because in that time wherein fruitful might have been repentance, their heart they hardened against a warning Lord. Shall they too raise up a wall against a judging God? The godliness of this man do thou indeed acknowledge, and if in that Body thou art, imitate him. When he had said, "Many men, that war against me, shall fear:" he did not continue, "But I will not fear;" lest to his own powers ascribing his not fearing, he too should be amid high temporal things, and through pride temporal he should not deserve to come to rest everlasting: rather he hath made thee to perceive whence he shall not fear. "But I," he saith, "in thee will hope, O Lord:" he hath not spoken of his confidence: but of the cause of his confidence. For if I shall not fear, I may also by hardness of heart not fear, for many men by too much pride fear nothing. . . .

7. "In God I will praise my discourses, in God I have[3] hoped: I will not fear what flesh doeth to me" (ver. 4). Wherefore? Because in God I will praise my discourses. If in thyself thou praisest thy discourses: I say not that thou art not to fear; it is impossible that thou have not to fear. For thy discourses either false thou wilt have, and therefore thine own, because false: or if thy discourses shall be true, and thou shalt deem thyself not to have them from God, but of thyself to speak; true they will be, but thou wilt be false: but if thou shalt have known

that thou canst say nothing true in the wisdom of God, in the faith of the Truth, save that which from Him thou hast received, of whom is said, "For what hast thou which thou hast not received?"[4] Then in God thou art praising thy discourses, in order that in God thou mayest be praised by the discourses of God. . . . "In God I have hoped, I will not fear what flesh doeth to me." Wast thou not the same that a little before wast saying, "Have pity on me, O Lord, for man hath trodden me down; all day long warring he hath troubled me"?[5] How therefore here, "I will not fear what flesh doeth to me"? What shall he do to thee? Thou thyself a little before hast said, "Hath trodden me down, hath troubled me." Nothing shall he do, when these things he shall do? He hath had regard to the wine which floweth from treading, and hath made answer, Evidently he hath trodden down, evidently hath troubled; but what to me shall he do? A grape I was, wine I shall be: "In God I have hoped, I will not fear what flesh doeth to me."

8. "All day long my words they abhorred" (ver. 5). Thus they are, ye know. Speak truth, preach truth, proclaim Christ to the heathen, proclaim the Church to heretics, proclaim to all men salvation: they contradict, they abhor my words. But when my words they abhor, whom think ye they abhor, save Him in whom I shall praise my discourses? "All day long my words they abhorred." Let this at least suffice, let them abhor words, no farther let them proceed, censure, reject! Be it far from them! Why should I say this? When words they reject, when words they hate, those words which from the fount of truth flow forth, what would they do to him through whom the very words are spoken? what but that which followeth, "Against me all the counsels of them are for evil?" If the bread itself they hate, how spare they the basket wherein it is ministered? "Against me all the counsels of them are for evil." If so even against the Lord Himself, let not the Body disdain that which hath gone before in the Head, to the end that the Body may cleave to the Head. Despised hath been thy Lord, and wilt thou have thyself be honoured by those men that have been put afar off from holy men? Do not for thyself wish to claim that which in Him hath not gone before. "The disciple is not greater than his Master; the servant is not greater than his Lord. If the Master of the family they have called Beelzebub, how much more them of His household?"[6] Against me all the counsels of them are for evil."

9. "They shall sojourn, and shall hide" (ver. 6). To sojourn is to be in a strange land.

---

[1] 1 Cor. ii. 8.   [2] Matt. xxiv. 30.   [3] Or, "will hope," mss.   [4] 1 Cor. iv. 7.   [5] Ps. lvi. 1.   [6] Matt. x. 24, 25.

Sojourners is a term used of those then that live in a country not their own. Every man in this life is a foreigner : in which life ye see that with flesh we are covered round, through which flesh the heart cannot be seen. Therefore the Apostle saith, " Do not before the .time judge anything, until the Lord come, and He shall enlighten the hidden things of darkness, and shall manifest the thoughts of the heart ; and then praise shall be to each one from God." [1] Before that this be done, in this sojourning of fleshly life every one carrieth his own heart, and every heart to every other heart is shut. Furthermore, those men of whom the counsels are against this man for evil, " shall sojourn, and shall hide : " because in this foreign abode they are, and carry flesh, they hide guile in heart ; whatsoever of evil they think, they hide. Wherefore? Because as yet this life is a foreign one. Let them hide ; that shall appear which they hide, and they too will not be hidden. There is also in this hidden thing another interpretation, which perchance will be more approved of. For out of those men that have been put afar off from holy men, there creep in certain false brethren, and they cause worse tribulations to the Body of Christ ; because they are not altogether avoided as if entirely aliens. . . . Not even those men nevertheless let us fear, brethren : " I will not fear what flesh doeth to me." Even if they sojourn, even if they go in, even if they feign, even if they hide, flesh they are : do thou in the Lord hope, nothing to thee shall flesh do. But he bringeth in tribulation, bringeth in treading down. There is added wine, because the grape is pressed : thy tribulation will not be unfruitful : another seeth thee, imitateth thee : because thou also in order that thou mightest learn to bear such a man, to thy Head hast looked up, that first cluster, unto whom there hath come in a man that he might see, hath sojourned, and hath hidden, to wit, the traitor Judas. All men, therefore, that with false heart go in, sojourning and hiding, do not thou fear : the father of these same men, Judas, with thy Lord hath been : and He indeed knew him ; although Judas the traitor was sojourning and hiding, nevertheless, the heart of him was open to the Lord of all : [2] knowingly He chose one man, whereby He might give comfort to thee that wouldest not know whom thou shouldest avoid. For He might have not chosen Judas, because He knew Judas : for He saith to His disciples, " Have not I chosen you twelve, and one out of you is a devil? " [3] Therefore even a devil was chosen. Or if chosen he was not, how is it that He hath chosen twelve, and not rather eleven? Chosen even he is, but for another purpose. Chosen were eleven for the

work of probation, chosen one for the work of temptation.[4] Whence could He give an example to thee, that wouldest not know what men thou shouldest avoid as evil, of what men thou shouldest beware as false and artificial, sojourning and hiding, except He say to thee, Behold, with Myself I have had one of those very men ! There hath gone before an example, I have borne, to suffer I have willed that which I knew, in order that to thee knowing not I might give consolation. That which to Me he hath done, the same he will do to thee also : in order that he may be able to do much, in order that he may make much havoc, he will accuse, false charges he will allege. . . .

10. " These same men shall mark my heel." For they shall sojourn and hide in such sort, that they may mark where a man slippeth. Intent they are upon the heel, to see when a slip may chance to be made ; in order that they may detain the foot for a fall, or trip up the foot for a stumble ; certes that they may find that which they may accuse. And what man so walketh, that nowhere he slippeth? For example, how speedily is a slip made even in tongue? For it is written, " Whosoever in tongue stumbleth not, the same is a perfect man." [5] What man I pray would dare himself to call or deem perfect? Therefore it must needs be that every one slip in tongue. But let them that shall sojourn and shall hide, carp at all words, seeking somewhere to make snares and knotty false accusations, wherein they are themselves entangled before those whom they strive to entangle : in order that they may themselves be taken and perish before that they catch other men in order to destroy them. . . . Whatever good thing I have said, whatever true thing I have said, of God I have said it, and from God have said it : whatever other thing perchance I have said, which to have said I ought not, as a man I have said, but under God I have said. He that strengtheneth one walking, doth menace one straying, forgive one acknowledging, recalleth the tongue, recalleth him that slipped. . . . Attend thou unto the discourses of him whom thou blamest, whether perchance he may teach thee something to thy health. And what, he saith, shall he be able to teach to my health, that hath so slipped in word? This very thing perchance he is teaching thee to thy health, that thou be not a carper at words, but a gatherer of precepts. " As my soul hath undergone." I speak of that which I have undergone. He was speaking as one experienced : " As my soul hath undergone. They shall sojourn and hide." Let my soul undergo all men, men without barking, men within hiding, let it undergo. From without

---

[1] 1 Cor. iv. 5.　　　[2] Oxf. mss. " guilty before the Lord."
[3] John vi. 70.

[4] [See A N. F. vol. i. pp. 40, 117, 153, 157, vi. 207. — C.]
[5] Jas. iii. 2.

coming, like a river cometh temptation : on the Rock let it find thee, let it strike against, not throw thee down ; the house hath been founded upon a Rock.[1] Within he is, he shall sojourn and hide : suppose chaff is near thee, let there come in the treading of oxen, let there come in the roller of temptations ; thou art cleansed, the other is crushed.

11. "For nothing Thou shalt save them" (ver. 7). He hath taught us even for these very men to pray. However "they shall sojourn and hide," however deceitful they be, however dissemblers and liers in wait they be ; do thou pray for them, and do not say, Shall God amend even such a man, so evil, so perverse? Do not despair : give heed to Him whom thou askest, not him for whom thou askest. The greatness of the disease seest thou, the might of the Physician seest thou not? "They shall sojourn and hide : as my soul hath undergone." Undergo, pray : and there is done what? "For nothing Thou shalt save them." Thou shalt make them safe so as that nothing to Thee it may be, that is, so that no labour to Thee it may be. With men they are despaired of, but Thou with a word dost heal ; Thou wilt not toil in healing, though we are astounded in looking on. There is another sense in this verse, "For nothing Thou shalt save them : " with not any merits of their going before Thou shalt save them. . . .They shall not bring to Thee he-goats, rams, bulls, not gifts and spices shall they bring Thee in Thy temple, not anything of the drink-offering of a good conscience do they pour thereon ; all in them is rough, all foul, all to be detested : and though they to Thee bring nothing whereby they may be saved ; "For nothing Thou shalt save them," that is, with the free gift of Thy Grace. . . .

12. "In anger the peoples Thou shalt bring down." Thou art angry and dost bring down, dost rage and save, dost terrify and call. Thou fillest with tribulations all things, in order that being set in tribulations men may fly to Thee, lest by pleasures and a wrong security they be seduced. From Thee anger is seen, but that of a father. A father is angry with a son, the despiser of his injunctions : being angry with him he boxeth him, striketh, pulleth the ear, draggeth with hand, leadeth to school. How many men have entered, how many men have filled the House of the Lord, in the anger of Him brought down, that is, by tribulations terrified and with faith filled? For to this end tribulation stirreth up ; in order to empty the vessel which is full of wickedness, so as that it may be filled with grace.

13. "O God, my life I have told out to

Thee " (ver. 8). For that I live hath been Thy doing, and for this reason I tell out my life to Thee. But did not God know that which He had given? What is that which thou tellest out to Him? Wilt thou teach God? Far be it. Therefore why saith he, "I have told out to Thee "? Is it perchance because it profiteth Thee that I have told out my life? And what doth it profit God? To the advantage of God it doth profit. I have told out to God my life, because that life hath been God's doing. In like manner as his life Paul the Apostle did tell out, saying, "I that before was a blasphemer and a persecutor and injurious," he shall tell out his life. "But mercy I have obtained."[2] He hath told out his life, not for himself, but for Him : because he hath told it out in such sort, that in Him men believe, not for his own advantages, but for the advantages of Him. . . . "O God, my life I have told out to Thee. Thou hast put my tears in Thy sight." Thou hast hearkened to me imploring Thee. "As also in Thy promise." Because as Thou hadst promised this thing, so Thou hast done. Thou hast said Thou wouldest hearken to one weeping. · I have believed, I have wept, I have been hearkened unto ; I have found Thee merciful in promising, true in repaying.

14. "Turned be mine enemies backward" (ver. 9). This thing to these very men is profitable, no ill to these men he is wishing. For to go before they are willing, therefore to be amended they are not willing. Thou warnest thine enemy to live well, that he amend himself : he scorneth, he rejecteth thy word : "Behold him that adviseth me ; behold him from whom I am to hear the commandments whereby I shall live !" To go before thee he willeth, and in going before is not amended. He mindeth not that thy words are not thine, he mindeth not that thy life to God thou tellest out, not to thyself. In going before therefore he is not amended : it is a good thing for him that he be turned backward, and follow him whom to go before he willed. The Lord to His disciples was speaking of His Passion that was to be. Peter shuddered, and saith, "Far be it, O Lord ; "[3] he that a little before had said, "Thou art the Christ, Son of the living God," having confessed God, feared for Him to die, as if but a man. But the Lord who so came that He might suffer (for we could not otherwise be saved unless with His blood we were redeemed), a little before had praised the confession of Peter. . . . But immediately when the Lord beginneth to speak of His Passion, he feared lest He should perish by death, whereas we ourselves should perish unless He died ; and he saith, "Far be it, O Lord,

---

[1] Matt. vii. 25. [2] 1 Tim. i. 13. [3] Matt. xvi. 22.

this thing shall not be done." And the Lord, to him to whom a little before He had said, "Blessed thou art, and upon this Rock I will build my Church," saith, "Go back behind, Satan, an offence thou art to Me." Why therefore "Satan" is he, that a little before was "blessed," and a "Rock"? "For thou savourest not the things which are of God," He saith, "but those things which are of man." [1] A little before *he savoured* the things which are of God: because "not flesh and blood hath revealed to thee, but My Father which is in the Heavens." When in God he was praising his discourse, not Satan but Peter, from *petra :* but when of himself and out of human infirmity, carnal love of man, which would be for an impediment to his own salvation, and that of the rest, Satan he is called. Why? Because to go before the Lord he willed, and earthly counsel to give to the heavenly Leader. "Far be it, O Lord, this thing shall not be done." Thou sayest, "Far be it," and thou sayest, "O Lord:" surely if Lord He is, in power He doeth: if Master He is, He knoweth what He doeth, He knoweth what He teacheth. But thou willest to lead thy Leader, teach thy Master, command thy Lord, choose for God: much thou goest before, go back behind. Did not this too profit these enemies? "Turned be Mine enemies backward;" but let them not remain backward. For this reason let them be turned backward, lest they go before; but so that they follow, not so that they remain.

15. "In whatsoever day I shall have called upon Thee, behold I have known that my God art Thou" (ver. 9). A great knowledge. He saith not, "I have known that God Thou art:" but, "that *my* God art Thou." For thine He is, when thee He succoureth: thine He is, when thou to Him art not an alien. Whence is said, "Blessed the people of whom is the Lord the God of the same." [2] Wherefore "of whom is"? For of whom is He not? Of all things indeed God He is: but of those men the God peculiarly He is said to be, that love Him, that hold Him, that possess Him, that worship Him, as though belonging to His own House: the great family of Him are they, redeemed by the great blood of the Only Son. How great a thing hath God given to us, that His own we should be, and He should be ours! But in truth foreigners afar have been put from holy men, sons alien they are. See what of them is said in another Psalm : "O Lord, deliver me," he saith, "from the hand of alien sons, of whom the mouth hath spoken vanity, and the right hand of them is a right hand of iniquity." [3] . . .

16. Let us therefore love God, brethren, purely

and chastely. There is not a chaste heart, if God for reward it worshippeth. How so? Reward of the worship of God shall not we have? We shall have evidently, but it is God Himself whom we worship. Himself for us a reward shall be, because "we shall see Him as He is." [4] Observe that a reward [5] thou shalt obtain. . . . I will tell you, brethren : in these human alliances consider a chaste heart, of what sort it is towards God : certainly human alliances are of such sort, that a man doth not love his wife, that loveth her because of her portion : a woman her husband doth not chastely love, that for these reasons loveth him, because something he hath given, or because much he hath given. Both a rich man is a husband, and one that hath become a poor man is a husband. How many men proscribed, by chaste wives have been the more beloved! Proved have been many chaste marriages by the misfortunes of husbands : that the wives might not be supposed to love any other object more than their husband, not only have they not forsaken, but the more have they obeyed. If therefore a husband of flesh freely is loved, if chastely he is loved; and a wife of flesh freely is loved, if chastely she is loved; in what manner must God be loved, the true and truth-speaking Husband of the soul, making fruitful unto the offspring of everlasting life, and not suffering us to be barren? Him, therefore, so let us love, as that any other thing besides Himself be not loved : and there takes place in us that which we have spoken of, that which we have sung, because even here the voice is ours : "In whatsoever day I shall have called upon Thee, behold, I have known that my God art Thou." This is to call upon God, freely to call upon Him. Furthermore, of certain men hath been said what? "Upon the Lord they have not called." [6] The Lord they seemed as it were to call unto themselves; and they besought Him about inheritances, about increasing money, about lengthening this life, about the rest of temporal things : and concerning them the Scripture saith what? "Upon the Lord they have not called." Therefore there followeth what? "There they have feared with fear, where there was no fear." What is, "where there was no fear"? Lest money should be stolen from them, lest anything in their house should be made less; lastly, lest they should have less of years in this life, than they hoped for themselves : but there have they trembled with fear, where there was no fear. . . . "In God I will praise the word, in the Lord I will praise the discourse" (ver. 10) : "in God I have hoped, I will not fear what man doeth unto me"

---

[1] Matt. xvi. 23.   [2] Ps. cxliv. 15.   [3] Ps. cxliv. 11.

[4] 1 John iii. 2.
[5] *Al.* "what reward."
[6] Ps. xiv. 4.

(ver. 11). Now this is the very sense which above [1] hath been repeated.

17. "In me, O God, are Thy vows, which I will render of praise to Thee" (ver. 12). "Vow ye, and render to the Lord your God." [2] What vow, what render? Perchance those animals which were offered at the altars aforetime? No such thing offer thou: in thyself is what thou mayest vow and render. From the heart's coffer bring forth the incense of praise; from the store of a good conscience bring forth the sacrifice of faith. Whatsoever thing thou bringest forth, kindle with love. In thyself be the vows, which thou mayest render of praise to God. Of what praise? For what hath He granted thee? "For Thou hast rescued my soul from death" (ver. 13). This is that very life which he telleth out to Him: "O God, my life I have told out to Thee." [3] For I was what? Dead. Through myself I was dead: through Thee I am what? Alive. Therefore "in me, O God, are Thy vows, which I will render of praise to Thee." Behold I love my God: no one doth tear Him from me: that which to Him I may give, no one doth tear from me, because in the heart it is shut up. With reason is said with that former confidence, "What should man do unto me?" [4] Let man rage, let him be permitted to rage, be permitted to accomplish that which he attempteth: what is he to take away? Gold, silver, cattle, men servants, maid servants, estates, houses, let him take away all things: doth he by any means take away the vows, which are in me, which I may render of praise to God? The tempter was permitted to tempt a holy man, Job; [5] in one moment he took away all things: whatever of possessions he had had, he carried off: took away inheritance, slew heirs; and this not little by little, but in a crowd, at one blow, at one swoop, so that all things were on a sudden announced: when all was taken away, alone there remained Job, but in him were vows of praise, which he might render to God, in him evidently there were: the coffer of his holy breast the thieving devil had not rifled, full he was of that wherefrom he might sacrifice. Hear what he had, hear what he brought forth: "The Lord hath given, the Lord hath taken away; as hath pleased the Lord, so hath been done: be the name of the Lord blessed." [6] O riches interior, whither thief doth not draw near! God Himself had given that whereof He was receiving; He had Himself enriched him with that whereof to Him he was offering that which He loved. Praise from thee God requireth, thy confession God requireth. But from thy field wilt thou give anything? He hath Himself rained in order that thou mayest have.

From thy coffer wilt thou give anything? He hath Himself put in that which thou art to give. What wilt thou give, which from Him thou hast not received? "For what hast thou which thou hast not received?" [7] From the heart wilt thou give? He too hath given faith, hope, and charity: this thou must bring forth: this thou must sacrifice. But evidently all the other things the enemy is able to take away against thy will; this to take away he is not able, unless thou be willing. These things a man will lose even against his will: and wishing to have gold, will lose gold; and wishing to have house, will lose house: faith no one will lose, except him that shall have despised her.

18. "Because Thou hast rescued my soul from death, mine eyes from tears, and my feet from slipping: that I may be pleasing before God in the light of the living" (ver. 13). With reason he is not pleasing to alien sons, that are put afar off from holy men, because they have not the light of the living, whence they may see that which to God is pleasing. "Light of the living," is light of the immortal, light of holy men. He that is not in darkness, is pleasing in the light of the living. A man is observed, and the things which belong to him; no one knoweth of what sort he is: God seeth of what sort he is. Sometimes even the devil himself he escapeth; except he tempt, he findeth not: just as concerning that man of whom just now I have made mention: . . . "Doth Job by any means worship God for nought?" [8] For this was true light, this the light of the living, that *gratis* he should worship God. God saw in the heart of His servant His gratuitous worship. For that heart was pleasing in the sight of the Lord in the light of the living: the devil's sight he escaped, because in darkness he was. God admitted the tempter, not in order that He might Himself know that which He did know, but in order that to us to be known and imitated He might set it forth. Admitted was the tempter; he took away everything, there remained the man bereft of possessions, bereft of family, bereft of children, full of God. A wife certainly was left. [9] Merciful do ye deem the devil, that he left him a wife? He knew through whom he had deceived Adam. . . . With wound smitten from head even unto feet, whole nevertheless within, he made answer to the woman tempting, out of the light of the living, out of the light of his heart: "thou hast spoken as though one of the unwise women," [10] that is, as though one that hath not the light of the living. For the light of the living is wisdom, and the darkness of unwise men is folly. Thou hast spoken as though one of the unwise women: my flesh thou seest, the light of my heart thou seest not. For she then might more have loved her husband, if the inte-

---

[1] Ps. lvi. 4, p. 220, *supra.*　　　[2] Ps. lxxvi. 11.
[3] Ps. lvi. 8, p. 222, *supra.*　　　[4] Ps. lvi. 11.
[5] Job i. 12.　　　[6] Job i. 21.

[7] 1 Cor. iv. 7.　　　[8] Job i. 9.　　　[9] Job ii. 9.
[10] Job ii. 10.

rior beauty she had known, and had beheld the place where he was beautiful before the eyes of God : because in Him were vows which he might render of praise to God.   How entirely the enemy had forborne to invade that patrimony ! How whole was that which he was possessing, and that because of which yet more to be possessed he hoped for, being to go on " from virtues unto virtue." [1]   Therefore, brethren, to this end let all these things serve us, that God *gratis* we love, in Him hope always, neither man nor devil fear.   Neither the one nor the other doeth anything, except when it is permitted : permitted for no other reason can it be, except because it doth profit us.   Let us endure evil men, let us be good men : because even we have been evil.   Even as nothing [2] God shall save men, of whom we dare to despair.   Therefore of no one let us despair, for all men whom we suffer let us pray, from God let us never depart.   Our patrimony let Him be, our hope let Him be, our safety let Him be.   He is Himself here a comforter, there a remunerator, everywhere Maker-alive, and of life the Giver, not of another life, but of that whereof hath been said, " I am the Way, and the Truth, and the Life : " [3] in order that both here in the light of faith, and there in the light of sight, as it were in the light of the living, in the sight of the Lord we may be pleasing.

PSALM LVII. [4]

1. We have heard in the Gospel just now, brethren, how loveth us our Lord and Saviour Jesus Christ, God with the Father, Man with us, out of our own selves, now at [5] the right hand of the Father ; ye have heard how much He loveth us. . . .

2. Because then this Psalm is singing of the Passion of the Lord, see what is the title that it hath : " at the end."   The end is Christ. [6]   Why hath He been called end ?   Not as one that consumeth, but one that consummateth. . . .

3. " At the end, corrupt not, for David himself, for the inscription of the title ; when he fled from the face of Saul into a cavern."   We referring to holy Scripture, do find indeed how holy David, that king of Israel, from whom too the Psalter of David hath received the name thereof, had suffered for persecutor Saul the king of his own people, as many of you know that have either read or have heard the Scriptures. King David had then for persecutor Saul : and whereas the one was most gentle, the other most ferocious : the one mild, the other envious ; the one patient, the other cruel ; the one beneficent, the other ungrateful : he endured

him with so much mildness, that when he had gotten him into his hands, him he touched not, hurt not. [7] . . . What reference hath this to Christ ? If all things which then were being done, were figures of things future, we find there Christ, and by far in the greatest degree.   For this, " corrupt not for the inscription of the title," I see not how it belongeth to that David.   For not any " title " was inscribed over David himself which Saul would " corrupt."   But we see in the Passion of the Lord that there had been written a title, " King of the Jews : " [8] in order that this title might put to the blush these very men, seeing that from their King they withheld not their hands.   For in them Saul was, in Christ David was.   For Christ, as saith the Apostolic Gospel, is, as we know, as we confess, of the seed of David after the flesh ; [9] for after the Godhead He is above David, above all men, above heaven and earth, above angels, above all things visible and invisible. . . . And because already it had been sung through the Holy Spirit, " Unto the end, corrupt not, for the inscription of the title : " Pilate answered them, " What I have written, I have written : " [10] why do ye suggest to me falsehood ?   I corrupt not truth.

4. What therefore is, " When he fled from the face of Saul into a cavern " ?   Which thing indeed the former David also did : but because in him we find not the inscription of the title, in the latter let us find the flight into the cavern. [11] For that cavern wherein David hid himself did figure somewhat.   But wherefore hid he himself ?   It was in order that he might be concealed and not be found.   What is to be hidden in a cavern ?   To be hidden in earth.   For he that fleeth into a cavern, with earth is covered so that he may not be seen.   But Jesus did carry earth, flesh which He had received from earth : and in it He concealed Himself, in order that by Jews He might not be discovered as God.   " For if they had known, never the Lord of glory would they have crucified." [12]   Why therefore the Lord of glory found they not ?   Because in a cavern He had hidden Himself, that is, the flesh's weakness to their eyes He presented, but the Majesty of the Godhead in the body's clothing, as though in a hiding-place of the earth, He hid. . . . But wherefore even unto death willed He to be patient ?   It was in order that He might flee from the face of Saul into a cavern.   For a cavern may be understood as a lower part of the earth.   And certainly, as is manifest and certain to all, His Body in a Tomb was laid, which was cut in a Rock.   This Tomb therefore was the Cavern ; thither He fled from the face of Saul.

---

[1] Ps. lxxxiv. 7.   [2] *Pro nihilo.*
[3] John xiv. 6.   [4] Lat. LVI.   Sermon to the Commonalty.
[5] *Circa.*   [6] Rom. x. 4.

[7] 1 Sam. xxiv. 4, 7.   [8] Matt. xxvii. 37 ; John xix. 19.
[9] Rom. i. 3 ; Matt. i. 1.   [10] John xix 22.
[11] 1 Sam. xxiv. 3.   [12] 1 Cor. ii. 8.

For so long the Jews did persecute Him, even until He was laid in a cavern. Whence prove we that so long they persecuted Him, until therein He was laid? Even when dead, and, on the Cross hanging, with lance they wounded Him.[1] But when shrouded, the funeral celebrated, He was laid in a cavern, no longer had they anything which to the Flesh they might do. Rose therefore the Lord again out of that cavern unhurt, uncorrupt, from that place whither He had fled from the face of Saul: concealing Himself from ungodly men, whom Saul prefigured, but showing Himself to His members. For the members of Him rising again by His members were handled: for the members of Him, the Apostles, touched Him rising again and believed;[2] and behold nothing profited the persecution of Saul. Hear we therefore now the Psalm; because concerning the title thereof enough we have spoken, as far as the Lord hath deigned to give.

5. "Have pity on me, O God, have pity on me, for in Thee hath trusted my Soul" (ver. 1). Christ in the Passion saith, "Have pity on Me, O God." To God, God saith, "Have pity on Me!" He that with the Father hath pity on thee, in thee crieth, "Have pity on Me." For that part of Him which is crying, "Have pity on Me," is thine: from thee this He received, for the sake of thee, that thou shouldest be delivered, with Flesh He was clothed. The flesh itself crieth: "Have pity on Me, O God, have pity on me:" Man himself, soul and flesh. For whole Man did the Word take upon Him, and whole Man the Word became. Let it not therefore be thought that there Soul was not, because the Evangelist thus saith: "The Word was made flesh, and dwelled in us."[3] For man is called flesh, as in another place saith the Scripture, "And all flesh shall see the salvation of God."[4] Shall anywise flesh alone see, and shall Soul not be there? . . . Thou hearest the Master praying, learn thou to pray. For to this end He prayed, in order that He might teach how to pray: because to this end He suffered, in order that He might teach how to suffer; to this end He rose again, in order that He might teach thou to hope for rising again. "And in the shadow of Thy wings I will hope, until iniquity pass over." This now evidently whole Christ doth say: here is also our voice. For not yet hath passed over, still rife is iniquity. And in the end our Lord Himself said there should be an abounding of iniquity: "And since iniquity shall abound, the love of many shall wax cold; but he that shall have persevered unto the end, the same shall be saved."[5] But who shall persevere even unto the end, even until in-

iquity pass over? He that shall have been in the Body of Christ, he that shall have been in the members of Christ, and from the Head shall have learned the patience of persevering. Thou passest away, and behold passed are thy temptations; and thou goest into another life whither have gone holy men, if holy thou hast been. Into another life have gone Martyrs; if Martyr thou shalt have been, thou also goest into another life. Because "thou" hast passed away hence, hath by any means iniquity therefore passed away? There are born other unrighteous men, as there die some unrighteous men. In like manner therefore as some unrighteous men die and others are born: so some just men go, and others are born. Even unto the end of the world neither iniquity will be wanting to oppress, nor righteousness to suffer. . . .

6. "I will cry to God most high" (ver. 2). If most high He is, how heareth He thee crying? Confidence hath been engendered by experience: "to God," he saith, "who had done good to me." If before that I was seeking Him, He did good to me, when I cry shall He not hearken to me? For good to us the Lord God hath done in sending to us our Saviour Jesus Christ, that He might die for our offences, and rise again for our justification.[6] For what sort of men hath He willed His Son to die? For ungodly men. But ungodly men were not seeking God, and have been sought of God. For He is Most High in such sort, as that not far from Him is our misery and our groaning: because "near is the Lord to them that have bruised the heart."[7] "God that hath done good to me."

7. "He hath sent from heaven and hath saved me" (ver. 3). Now the Man Himself, now the Flesh Itself, now the Son of God after His partaking of ourselves, of Him it is manifest, how He was saved, and hath sent from heaven the Father and hath saved Him, hath sent from heaven, and hath raised Him again: but in order that ye may know, that also the Lord Himself hath raised again Himself; both truths are written in Scripture, both that the Father hath raised Him again, and that Himself Himself hath raised again. Hear ye how the Father hath raised Him again: the Apostle saith, "He hath been made," he saith, "obedient unto death, even the death of the Cross: wherefore God also hath exalted Him, and hath given Him a name which is above every name."[8] Ye have heard of the Father raising again and exalting the Son; hear ye how that He too Himself His flesh hath raised again. Under the figure of a temple He saith to the Jews, "Destroy this Temple, and in three days I will raise it up."[9] But the Evangelist hath explained to us what it

---

[1] John xix. 34. [2] Luke xxiv. 39. [3] John i. 14. [4] Isa. xl. 5, lii. 10; Luke iii. 6. [5] Matt. xxiv. 12. [6] Rom. iv. 25. [7] Ps. xxxiv. 18. [8] Phil. ii. 8, 9. [9] John ii. 19.

was that He said: "But this," he saith, "He spake of the Temple of His Body." Now therefore out of the person of one praying, out of the person of a man, out of the person of the flesh, He saith, "He hath saved me. He hath given unto reproach those that trampled on me." Them that have trampled on Him, that over Him dead have insulted, that Him as though man have crucified, because God they perceived not, them He hath given unto reproach. See ye whether it has not been so done. The thing we do not believe as yet to come, but fulfilled we acknowledge it. The Jews raged against Christ, they were overbearing against Christ. Where? In the city of Jerusalem. For where they reigned, there they were puffed up, there their necks they lifted up. After the Passion of the Lord thence they were rooted out; and they lost the kingdom, wherein Christ for King they would not acknowledge. In what manner they have been given unto reproach, see ye: dispersed they have been throughout all nations, nowhere having a settlement, nowhere a sure abode. But for this reason still Jews they are, in order that our books they may carry to their confusion. For whenever we wish to show Christ prophesied of, we produce to the heathen these writings. And lest perchance men hard of belief should say that we Christians have composed these books, so that together with the Gospel which we have preached we have forged the Prophet, through whom there might seem to be foretold that which we preach: by this we convince them; namely, that all the very writings wherein Christ hath been prophesied are with the Jews, all these very writings the Jews have. We produce documents from enemies, to confound other enemies. In what sort of reproach therefore are the Jews? A document the Jew carrieth, wherefrom a Christian may believe. Our librarians they have become, just as slaves are wont behind their masters to carry documents, in such sort that these faint in carrying, those profit by reading.[1] Unto such a reproach have been given the Jews: and there hath been fulfilled that which so long before hath been foretold, "He hath given unto reproach those that trampled on me." But how great a reproach it is, brethren, that this verse they should read, and themselves being blind should look upon their mirror! For in the same manner the Jews appear in the holy Scripture which they carry, as appeareth the face of a blind man in a mirror: by other men it is seen, by himself not seen.

8. Thou wast inquiring perhaps when he said, "He hath sent from heaven and hath saved me." What hath He sent from heaven? Whom hath He sent from heaven? An Angel hath He sent, to save Christ, and through a servant is the Lord saved? For all Angels are creatures [2] serving Christ. For obedience there might have been sent Angels, for service they might have been sent, not for succour: as is written, "Angels ministered unto Him,"[3] not like men merciful to one indigent, but like subjects to One Omnipotent. What therefore "hath He sent from heaven, and hath saved me"? Now we hear in another verse what from heaven He hath sent. "He hath sent from heaven His mercy and His truth."[4] For what purpose? "And hath drawn out my soul from the midst of the lions' whelps."[5] "Hath sent," he saith, "from heaven His mercy and His truth:" and Christ Himself saith, "I am Truth." There was sent therefore Truth, that it should draw out my soul hence from the midst of the lions' whelps: there was sent mercy. Christ Himself we find to be both mercy and truth; mercy in suffering with us, and truth in requiting us. . . . Who are the lions' whelps? That lesser[6] people, unto evil deceived, unto evil led away by the chiefs of the Jews: so that these are lions, those lions' whelps. All roared, all slew. For we are to hear even here the slaying of these very men, presently in the following verses of this Psalm.

9. "And hath drawn out," he saith, "my soul from the midst of the lions' whelps" (ver. 4). Why sayest thou, "And hath drawn out my soul"? For what hadst thou suffered, that thy soul should be drawn out? "I have slept troubled." Christ hath intimated His death. . . .

10. Whence "troubled"? Who troubling? Let us see in what manner he brandeth an evil conscience upon the Jews, wishing to excuse themselves of the slaying of the Lord. For to this end, as the Gospel speaketh, to the judge they delivered Him, that they might not themselves seem to have killed Him. . . . Let us question Him, and say, since Thou hast slept troubled, who have persecuted Thee? who have slain Thee? was it perchance Pilate, who to soldiers gave Thee, on the Tree to be hanged, with nails to be pierced? Hear who they were, "Sons of men" (ver. 5). Of them He speaketh, whom for persecutors He suffered. But how did they slay, that steel bare not? They that sword drew not, that made no assault upon Him to slay; whence slew they? "Their teeth are arms and arrows, and their tongue a sharp sword." Do not consider the unarmed hands, but the mouth armed: from thence the sword proceeded, wherewith Christ was to be slain: in like manner also as from the mouth of Christ, that wherewith the Jews were to be slain. For He hath a sword twice whetted:[7] and rising again He hath smit-

---

[1] [See p. 132, note 3, *supra*. — C.]

[2] Lat. "a creature."　　[3] Matt. iv. 11.　　[4] Ps. lvii. 3.
[5] Ps. lvii. 4.　　[6] *Minutus*.　　[7] Rev. i. 16.

ten them, and hath severed from them those whom He would make His faithful people. They an evil sword, He a good sword : they evil arrows, He good arrows. For He hath Himself also arrows good, words good, whence He pierceth the faithful heart, in order that He may be loved. Therefore of one kind are their arrows, and of another kind their sword. "Sons of men, their teeth are arms and arrows, and their tongue a sharp sabre." Tongue of sons of men is a sharp sabre, and their teeth arms and arrows. When therefore did they smite, save when they clamoured, "Crucify, crucify"?[1]

11. And what have they done to Thee, O Lord ? Let the Prophet here exult! For above, all those verses the Lord was speaking : a Prophet indeed, but in the person of the Lord, because in the Prophet is the Lord. . . . "Be exalted," he saith, "above the Heavens, O God" Man on the Cross, and above the Heavens, God. Let them continue on the earth raging, Thou in Heaven be judging. Where are they that were raging? where are their teeth, the arms and arrows? Have not "the stripes of them been made the arrows of infants"? For in another place a Psalm[2] this saith, desiring to prove them vainly to have raged, and vainly unto frenzies to have been driven headlong : for nothing they were able to do to Christ when for the time crucified, and afterwards when He was rising again, and in Heaven was sitting. How do infants make to themselves arrows? Of reeds?[3] But what arrows? or what powers? or what bows? or what wound? "Be Thou exalted above the Heavens, O God, and above all the earth Thy glory" (ver. 6). Wherefore exalted above the Heavens, O God? Brethren, God exalted above the Heavens we see not, but we believe : but above all the earth His glory to be not only we believe, but also see. But what kind of madness heretics are afflicted with, I pray you observe. They being cut off from the bond of the Church of Christ, and to a part holding, the whole losing, will not communicate with the whole earth, where is spread abroad the glory of Christ.[4] But we Catholics are in all the earth, because with all the world we communicate, wherever the Glory of Christ is spread abroad.[5] For we see that which then was sung, now fulfilled. There hath been exalted above the Heavens our God, and above all the earth the Glory of the Same. O heretical insanity ! That which thou seest not thou believest with me, that which thou seest thou deniest : thou believest with me in Christ exalted above the Heavens, a thing

which we see not ; and deniest His Glory over all the earth, a thing which we see.

12. . . . Let your Love see the Lord speaking to us, and exhorting us by His example : "A trap[6] they have prepared for My feet, and have bowed down My Soul" (ver. 7). They wished to bring It down as if from Heaven, and to the lower places to weigh It down : "They have bowed My Soul : they have digged before My face a pit and themselves have fallen into it." Me have they hurt, or themselves? Behold He hath been exalted above the Heavens, God, and behold above all the earth the Glory of the Same : the kingdom of Christ we see, where is the kingdom of the Jews? Since therefore they did that which to have done they ought not, there hath been done in their case that which to have suffered they ought : themselves have dug a ditch, and have fallen into it. For their persecuting Christ, to Christ did no hurt, but to themselves did hurt. And do not suppose, brethren, that themselves alone hath this befallen. Every one that prepareth a pit for his brother, it must needs be that himself fall into it. . . .

13. But the patience of good men with preparation of heart accepteth the will of God : and glorieth in tribulations, saying that which followeth : "Prepared is my heart, O God, I will sing and play" (ver. 8). What hath he done to me? He hath prepared a pit, my heart is prepared. He hath prepared pit to deceive, shall I not prepare heart to suffer? He hath prepared pit to oppress, shall I not prepare heart to endure? Therefore he shall fall into it, but I will sing and play. Hear the heart prepared in an Apostle, because he hath imitated his Lord : "We glory," he saith, "in tribulations : because tribulation worketh patience : patience probation, probation hope, but hope maketh not ashamed : because the love of God is shed abroad in our hearts through the Holy Spirit, which hath been given to us."[7] He was in oppressions, in chains, in prisons, in stripes, in hunger and thirst, in cold and nakedness,[8] in every wasting of toils and pains, and he was saying, "We glory in tribulations." Whence, but that prepared was his heart? Therefore he was singing and playing.

14. "Rise up, my glory" (ver. 9). He that had fled from the face of Saul into a cavern, saith, "Rise up, my glory :" glorified be Jesus after His Passion. "Rise up, psaltery and harp." He calleth upon what to rise? Two organs I see : but Body of Christ one I see, one flesh hath risen again, and two organs have risen. The one organ then is the psaltery, the other the harp. Organs[9] is the word used for

---

[1] Matt. xxvii. 22; John xix. 6.
[2] [Vulgate and Septuagint, Ps. lxiv. 7.—C.]
[3] *Cannæ.* [4] Against the Donatists.
[5] [This comes home with terrible import to that portion of the Church which has made itself the whole Church with a novel creed, and broken communion with the Easterns.—C.]

[6] *Muscipulam.* [7] Rom. v. 3. [8] 2 Cor. xi. 27.
[9] *Organa.*

all instruments of musicians. Not only is that called an organ, which is great, and blown into with bellows ;[1] but whatsoever is adapted to playing and is corporeal, whereof for an instrument the player maketh use, is said to be an organ. But distinguished from one another are these organs.[2] . . . What therefore do these two organs figure to us? For Christ the Lord our God is waking up His psaltery and His harp ; and He saith, " I will rise up at the dawn." I suppose that here ye now perceive the Lord rising. We have read thereof in the Gospel :[3] see the hour of the Resurrection. How long through shadows was Christ being sought? He hath shone, be He acknowledged ; " at the dawn" He rose again. But what is psaltery? what is harp? Through His flesh two kinds of deeds the Lord hath wrought, miracles and sufferings : miracles from above have been, sufferings from below have been. But those miracles which He did were divine ; but through Body He did them, through flesh He did them. The flesh therefore working things divine, is the psaltery : the flesh suffering things human is the harp. Let the psaltery sound, let the blind be enlightened, let the deaf hear, let the paralytics be braced to strength, the lame walk, the sick rise up, the dead rise again ; this is the sound of the Psaltery. Let there sound also the harp, let Him hunger, thirst, sleep, be held, scourged, derided, crucified, buried. When therefore thou seest in that Flesh certain things to have sounded from above, certain things from the lower part, one flesh hath risen again, and in one flesh we acknowledge both psaltery and harp. And these two kinds of things done have fulfilled the Gospel, and it is preached in the nations : for both the miracles and the sufferings of the Lord are preached.

15. Therefore there hath risen psaltery and harp in the dawn, and he confesseth to the Lord ; and saith what? " I will confess to Thee among the peoples, O Lord, and will play to Thee among the nations : for magnified even unto the Heavens hath been Thy mercy, and even unto the clouds Thy truth " (ver. 10). Heavens above clouds, and clouds below heavens : and nevertheless to this nearest heaven belong clouds. But sometimes clouds rest upon the mountains, even so far in the nearest air are they rolled. But a Heaven above there is, the habitations of Angels, Thrones, Dominions, Principalities, Powers. This therefore may perchance seem to be what should have been said : " Unto the Heavens Thy truth, and even unto the clouds

Thy mercy." For in Heaven Angels praise God, seeing the very form of truth, without any darkness of vision, without any admixture of unreality : they see, love, praise, are not wearied. There is truth : but here in our own misery surely there is mercy. For to a miserable one must be rendered mercy. For there is no need of mercy above, where is no miserable one. I have said this because that it seemeth as though it might have been more fittingly said, " Magnified even unto the Heavens hath been Thy truth, and even unto the clouds Thy mercy." For " clouds " we understand to be preachers of truth, men bearing that flesh in a manner dark, whence God both gleameth in miracles, and thundereth in precepts.[4] . . . Glory to our Lord, and to the Mercy of the Same, and to the Truth of the Same, because neither hath He forsaken by mercy to make us blessed through His Grace, nor defrauded us of truth : because first Truth veiled in flesh came to us and healed through His flesh the interior eye of our heart, in order that hereafter face to face we may be able to see It.[5] Giving therefore to Him thanks, let us say with the same Psalm the last verses, which sometime since too I have said, " Be Thou exalted above the Heavens, O God, and above all the earth Thy glory " (ver. 11). For this to Him the Prophet said so many years before ; this now we see ; this therefore let us also say.

PSALM LVIII.[6]

1. The words which we have sung must be rather hearkened to by us, than proclaimed. For to all men as it were in an assemblage of mankind, the Truth crieth, " If truly indeed justice ye speak, judge right things, ye sons of men " (ver. 1). For to what unjust man is it not an easy thing to speak justice? or what man if questioned about justice, when he hath not a cause, would not easily answer what is just? Inasmuch as the hand of our Maker in our very hearts hath written this truth, " That which to thyself thou wouldest not have done, do not thou to another."[7] Of this truth, even before that the Law was given, no one was suffered to be ignorant, in order that there might be some rule whereby might be judged even those to whom Law had not been given.[8] But lest men should complain that something had been wanting for them, there hath been written also in tables that

---

[1] [Of which see a primitive example in Parker's *Glossary of Architecture* (vol. i. p. 264), Oxford, 1845. The use of organs in churches is very modern. The Greeks exclude them still. St. Thomas Aquinas testifies their non-use in the Latin churches in the thirteenth century. — C.]
[2] [See p. 139, *supra*. — C.]	[3] Mark xvi. 2.

[4] [Ps. xxxvi. p. 88, § 7, *supra*. — C.]	[5] 1 Cor. xiii. 12.
[6] Lat. LVII. Sermon to the Commonalty, wherein everywhere he confuteth the Donatists.
[7] Tob. iv. 15.
[8] [Matt. vii. 12. The quotation from the father of Tobias shows this maxim, negative in its form, and reflecting the Mosaic law, which " made nothing perfect." It was probably Noahic, and was therefore known to Gentilism, as *e.g.* to Confucius. The glory of " the Golden Rule " is not merely that it gives a positive form to this law : Christ made it the energetic and characteristic principle of His Church towards humanity, and of all Christians towards all men. — C.]

which in their hearts they read not. For it was not that they had it not written, but read it they would not. There hath been set before their eyes that which in their conscience to see they would be compelled; and as if from without the voice of God were brought to them, to his own inward parts hath man been thus driven, the Scripture saying, "For in the thoughts of the ungodly man there will be questioning."[1] Where questioning is, there is law. But because men, desiring those things which are without, even from themselves have become exiles, there hath been given also a written law: not because in hearts it had not been written, but because thou wast a deserter from thy heart, thou art seized by Him that is everywhere, and to thyself within art called back. Therefore the written law, what crieth it, to those that have deserted the law written in their hearts?[2] "Return ye transgressors to the heart."[3] For who hath taught thee, that thou wouldest have no other man draw near thy wife? Who hath taught thee, that thou wouldest not have a theft committed upon thee? Who hath taught thee, that thou wouldest not suffer wrong, and whatever other thing either universally or particularly might be spoken of? For many things there are, of which severally if questioned men with loud voice would answer, that they would not suffer. Come, if thou art not willing to suffer these things, art thou by any means the only man? dost thou not live in the fellowship of mankind? He that together with thee hath been made, is thy fellow; and all men have been made after the image of God,[4] unless with earthly covetings they efface that which He hath formed. That which therefore to thyself thou wilt not have to be done, do not thou to another. For thou judgest that there is evil in that, which to suffer thou art not willing: and this thing thou art constrained to know by an inward law; that in thy very heart is written. Thou wast doing somewhat, and there was a cry raised in thy hands: how art thou constrained to return to thy heart when this thing thou sufferest in the hands of others? Is theft a good thing? No! I ask, is adultery a good thing? All cry, No! Is man-slaying a good thing? All cry, that they abhor it. Is coveting the property of a neighbour a good thing? No! is the voice of all men. Or if yet thou confessest not, there draweth near one that coveteth thy property: be pleased to answer what thou wilt have. All men therefore, when of these things questioned, cry that these things are not good. Again, of doing kindnesses, not only of not hurting, but also of conferring and distributing, any hungry soul is questioned thus: "thou sufferest hunger, another man hath bread, and there is abundance with him beyond

sufficiency, he knoweth thee to want, he giveth not: it displeaseth thee when hungering, let it displease thee when full also, when of another's hungering thou shalt have known. A stranger wanting shelter cometh into thy country, he is not taken in: he then crieth that inhuman is that city, at once among barbarians he might have found a home. He feeleth the injustice because he suffereth; thou perchance feelest not, but it is meet that thou imagine thyself also a stranger; and that thou see in what manner he will have displeased thee, who shall not have given that, which thou in thy country wilt not give to a stranger." I ask all men. True are these things? True. Just are these things? Just. But hear ye the Psalm. "If truly therefore justice ye speak, judge right things, ye sons of men." Be it not a justice of lips, but also of deeds. For if thou actest otherwise than thou speakest, good things thou speakest, and ill thou judgest. . . .

2. But now to the present case let us come, if ye please. For the voice is that sweet voice, so well known to the ears of the Church, the voice of our Lord Jesus Christ, and the voice of His Body, the voice of the Church toiling, sojourning upon earth, living amid the perils of men speaking evil and of men flattering. Thou wilt not fear a threatener, if thou lovest not a flatterer. He therefore, of whom this is the voice, hath observed and hath seen, that all men speak justice. For what man doth dare not to speak it, lest he be called unjust? When, therefore, as though he were hearing the voices of all men, and were observing the lips of all men, he cried out to them, "If truly indeed justice ye speak,"—if not falsely justice ye speak, if not one thing on lips doth sound, whilst another thing is concealed in hearts,—"judge right things, ye sons of men." Hear out of the Gospel His own voice, the very same as is in this Psalm: "Hypocrites," saith the Lord to the Pharisees, "how are ye able good things to speak, when ye are evil men?" "Either make the tree good, and the fruit thereof good: or make the tree evil, and the fruit thereof evil."[5] Why wilt thou whiten thee, wall of mud? I know thy inward parts, I am not deceived by thy covering: I know what thou holdest forth, I know what thou coverest. "For there was no need for Him, that any one to Him should bear testimony of man: for He knew Himself what was in man."[6] For He knew what was in man, who had made man, and who had been made Man, in order that He might seek man. . . .

3. But now ye do what? Why these things to you do I speak? "Because in heart iniquities ye work on earth" (ver. 2). Iniquities per-

---

[1] Wisd. i. 9.   [2] Rom. ii. 15.   [3] Isa. xlvi. 8.
[4] Gen. i. 26.

[5] Matt. xii. 33, 34.   [6] John ii. 25.

chance in heart alone? Hear what followeth: both their heart hands do follow, and their heart hands do serve, the thing is thought of, and it is done; or else it is not done, not because we would not, but because we could not, WHATEVER THOU WILLEST AND CANST NOT, FOR DONE GOD DOTH COUNT IT. "For in heart Iniquities ye work on earth." What next? "Iniquities your hands knit together." What is, "knit together"? From sin, sin, and to sin, sin, because of sin. What is this? A theft a man hath committed, a sin it is: he hath been seen, he seeketh to slay him by whom he hath been seen: there hath been knit together sin with sin: God hath permitted him in His hidden judgment to slay that man whom he hath willed to slay: he perceiveth that the thing is known, he seeketh to slay a second also; he hath knit together a third sin: while these things he is planning, perchance that he may not be found out, or that he may not be convicted of having done it, he consulteth an astrologer; there is added a fourth sin: the astrologer answereth perchance with some hard and evil responses, he runneth to a soothsayer, that expiation may be made; the soothsayer maketh answer that he is not able to expiate: a magician is sought. And who could enumerate those sins which are knit together with sins? "Iniquities your hands do knit together." So long as thou knittest together, thou bindest sin upon sin. Loose thyself from sins. But I am not able, thou sayest. Cry to Him. "Unhappy man I, who shall deliver me from the body of this death?"[1] For there shall come the Grace of God, so that righteousness shall be thy delight, as much as thou didst delight in iniquity; and thou, a man that out of bonds hast been loosed, shalt cry out to God, "Thou hast broken asunder my bonds."[2] "Thou hast broken asunder my bonds," is what else but, "Thou hast remitted my sins"? Hear why chains they are: the Scripture maketh answer, "with the chains of his sins each one is bound fast."[3] Not only bonds, but chains[4] also they are. Chains are those which are made by twisting in: that is, because with sins sins thou wast knitting together...

4. "Alienated are sinners from the womb, they have gone astray from the belly, they have spoken false things" (ver. 3). And when iniquity they speak, false things they speak; because deceitful is iniquity: and when justice they speak, false things they speak; because one thing with mouth they profess, another thing in heart they conceal. "Alienated are sinners from the womb." What is this? Let us search more diligently: for perhaps he is saying this, because God hath foreknown men that are

to be sinners even in the wombs of their mothers.[5] For whence when Rebecca was yet pregnant, and in womb was bearing twins, was it said, "Jacob I have loved, but Esau I have hated"?[6] For it was said, "The elder shall serve the younger." Hidden at that time was the judgment of God: but yet from the womb, that is, from the very origin, alienated are sinners. Whence alienated? From truth. Whence alienated? From the blessed country, from the blessed life. Perchance alienated they are from the very womb. And what sinners have been alienated from the womb? For what men would have been born, if therein they had not been held? Or what men to-day would be alive to hear these words to no purpose, unless they were born? Perchance therefore sinners have been alienated from a certain womb, wherein that charity was suffering pains, which speaketh through the Apostle, "Of whom again I am in labour, until Christ be formed in you."[7] Expect thou therefore; be formed: do not to thyself ascribe a judgment which perchance thou knowest not. Carnal thou art as yet, conceived thou hast been: from that very time when thou hast received the name of Christ, by a sort of sacrament thou hast been born in the bowels of a mother. For not only out of bowels a man is born, but also in bowels. First he is born in bowels, in order that he may be able to be born of bowels. Wherefore it hath been said even to Mary, "For that which is born in thee, is of the Holy Spirit."[8] Not yet of Her It had been born, but already in Her It had been born. Therefore there are born within the bowels of the Church certain little ones, and a good thing it is that being formed they should go forth, so that they drop not by miscarriage. Let the mother bear thee, not miscarry. If patient thou shalt have been, even until thou be formed, even until in thee there be the sure doctrine of truth, the maternal bowels ought to keep thee. But if by thy impatience thou shalt have shaken the sides of thy mother, with pain indeed she expelleth thee out, but more to thy loss than to hers.

5. For this reason therefore have they gone astray from the belly, because "they have spoken false things"? Or rather have they not for this reason spoken false things, because they have gone astray from the belly? For in the belly of the Church truth abideth. Whosoever from this belly of the Church separated shall have been, must needs speak false things: must needs, I say, speak false things; whoso either conceived would not be, or whom when conceived the

---

[1] Rom. vii. 24.　　　[2] Ps. cxvi. 16.　　　[3] Prov. v. 22.
[4] Criniculi.

[5] Gen. xxv. 23. [Here foreknowledge precedes predestination. See Clement, vol. ii. p. 497, A. N. F. — C.]
[6] Mal. i. 2; Rom. ix. 13.　　　[7] Gal. iv. 19.
[8] Matt. i. 20; Luke i. 35.

mother hath expelled. Thence heretics exclaim against the Gospel (to speak in preference of those whom expelled we lament). We repeat to them: behold Christ hath said, "It behoved Christ to suffer, and from the dead to rise again the third day."[1] I acknowledge there our Head, I acknowledge there our bridegroom: acknowledge thou also with me the Bride. . . .

6. "Indignation to them after the similitude of a serpent" (ver. 4). A great thing ye are to hear. "Indignation to them after the similitude of a serpent." As if we had said, What is that which thou hast said? there followeth, "As if of a deaf asp." Whence deaf? "And closing its ears." Therefore deaf, because it closeth its ears. "And closing its ears." "Which will not hearken to the voice of men charming, and of the medicine medicated by the wise man" (ver. 5). As we have heard, because even men speak who have learned it with such research as they were able, but nevertheless it is a thing which the Spirit of God knoweth much better than any men. For it is not to no purpose that of this he hath spoken, but because it may chance that true is even that which we have heard of the asp. When the asp beginneth to be affected by the Marsian charmer, who calleth it forth with certain peculiar incantations, hear what it doeth. . . . Give heed what is spoken to thee for a simile's sake, what is noted thee for avoidance.[2] So therefore here also there hath been given a certain simile derived from the Marsian, who maketh incantation to bring forth the asp from the dark cavern; surely into light he would bring it: but it loving its darkness, wherein coiled up it hideth itself, when it will not choose to come forth, nevertheless refusing to hear those words whereby it feeleth itself to be constrained, is said to press one ear against the ground, and with its tail to stop up the other, and therefore as much as possible escaping those words, it cometh not forth to the charmer. To this as being like, the Spirit of God hath spoken of certain persons hearing not the Word of God, and not only not doing, but altogether, that they may not do it, refusing to hear.

7. This thing hath been done even in the first times of the faith. Stephen the Martyr was preaching the Truth, and to minds as though dark, in order to bring them forth into light, was making incantation: when he came to make mention of Christ, whom they would not hear at all, of them the Scripture saith what? of them relateth what? "They shut," he saith, "their ears."[3] But what they did afterwards, the narrative of the passion of Stephen doth publish. They were not deaf, but they made themselves deaf. . . . For this thing they did at the point where Christ was named. The indignation of these men was as

the indignation of a serpent. Why your ears do ye shut? Wait, hear, and if ye shall be able, rage. Because they chose not to do aught but rage, they would not hear. But if they had heard, perchance they would have ceased to rage. The indignation of them was as the indignation of a serpent. . . .

8. "God hath broken utterly the teeth of them in their own mouth" (ver. 6). Of whom? Of them to whom indignation is as the similitude of a serpent, and of an asp closing up its ears, so that it heareth not the voice of men charming, and of medicine medicated by the wise man. The Lord hath done to them what? "Hath broken utterly the teeth of them in their own mouth." It hath been done, this at first hath been done, and now is being done. But it would have sufficed, my brethren, that it should have been said, "God hath broken utterly the teeth of them." The Pharisees would not hear the Law, would not hear the precepts of truth from Christ, being like to that serpent and asp. For in their past sins they took delight, and present life they would not lose, that is, joys earthly for joys heavenly. . . . What is, "in their own mouth"? In such sort, that with their own mouth against themselves they should make declaration: He hath compelled them with their mouth against themselves to give sentence. They would have slandered Him, because of the tribute:[4] He said not, "It is lawful to pay tribute," or, "It is not lawful to pay tribute." And He willed to break utterly their teeth, wherewith they were gaping in order to bite; but in their own mouth He would do it. If He said, Let there be paid to Cæsar tribute, they would have slandered Him, because He had spoken evil to the nation of the Jews, by making it a tributary. For because of sin they were paying tribute, having been humbled, as to them in the Law had been foretold. We have Him, say they, a maligner of our nation, if He shall have bidden us to pay tribute: but if He say, Do not pay, we have Him for saying that we should not be under allegiance to Cæsar. Such a double noose as it were to catch the Lord they laid. But to whom had they come? To Him that knew how to break utterly the teeth of them in their own mouth. "Show to Me the coin,"[5] He saith. Why tempt ye Me, ye hypocrites?" Of paying tribute do ye think? To do justice are ye willing? the counsel of justice do ye seek? "If truly justice ye speak, judge right things, ye sons of men." But now because in one way ye speak, in another way judge, hypocrites ye are: "Why tempt ye Me, ye hypocrites?" Now I will break utterly your teeth in your mouth: "show to Me the coin." And they showed it to Him. And He saith not, it is Cæsar's: but asketh

---

[1] Luke xxiv. 46.   [2] So p. 133.   [3] Acts vii. 57.   [4] Matt. xxii. 17, 18.   [5] Matt. xxii. 19.

Whose it is? in order that their teeth in their own mouth might be utterly broken. For on His inquiring, of whom it had the image and inscription, they said, of Cæsar. Even now the Lord shall break utterly the teeth of them in their own mouth. Now ye have made answer, now have been broken utterly your teeth in your mouth. "Render unto Cæsar the things which are of Cæsar, and unto God the things which are of God."[1] Cæsar seeketh his image; render it: God seeketh His image; render it. Let not Cæsar lose from you his coin: let not God lose in you His coin. And they found not what they might answer. For they had been sent to slander Him: and they went back, saying, that no one to Him could make answer. Wherefore? Because broken utterly had been the teeth of them in their own mouth. Of that sort is also the following: "In what power doest Thou these things? I also will ask of you one question, answer me."[2] And He asked them of John, whence was the Baptism of John, from heaven, or of men? so that whatever they might answer might tell against themselves. . . .

9. The Lord displeased that Pharisee, who to dinner had bidden Him, because a woman that was a sinner drew near to His feet, and he murmured against Him, saying, "If this man were a prophet, He would know what woman drew near to His feet."[3] O thou that art no prophet, whence knowest thou that He knew not what woman drew near to His feet? Because indeed He kept not the purifying of the Jews, which outwardly was as it were kept in the flesh, and was afar from the heart, this thing he suspected of the Lord. And in order that I may not speak at length on this point, even in his mouth He willed to break utterly the teeth of him. For He set forth to him: "A certain usurer had two debtors, one was owing five hundred pence, the other fifty: both had not wherewithal to pay, he forgave both. Which loved him the more?"[4] To this end the one asketh, that the other may answer: to this end he answereth, that the teeth of him in his mouth may be broken utterly. . . .

10. "The jaw-bones of lions the Lord hath broken utterly."[5] Not only of asps. What of asps? Asps treacherously desire to throw in their venom, and scatter it, and hiss. Most openly raged the nations, and roared like lions. "Wherefore have raged the nations, and the peoples meditated empty things?"[6] When they were lying in wait for the Lord. Is it lawful to give tribute to Cæsar, or is it not lawful?[7] Asps they were, serpents they were, broken utterly were the teeth of them in their own mouth.

Afterwards they cried out, "Crucify, Crucify."[8] Now is there no tongue of asp, but roar of lion. But also "the jaw-bones of lions the Lord hath broken utterly." Perchance here there is no need of that which he hath not added, namely, "in the mouth of them." For men lying in wait with captious questions, were forced to be conquered with their own answer: but those men that openly were raging, were they by any means to be confuted with questions? Nevertheless, even their jaw-bones were broken utterly: having been crucified, He rose again, ascended into heaven, was glorified as the Christ, is adored by all nations, adored by all kings. Let the Jews now rage, if they are able. We have also in the case of heretics this as a warning and precedent, because themselves also we find to be serpents with indignation made deaf, not choosing to hear the "medicine medicated by the wise man:" and in their own mouth the Lord hath broken utterly the teeth of them. . . .

11. "They shall be despised like water running down" (ver. 7). Be not terrified, brethren, by certain streams, which are called torrents: with winter waters they are filled up; do not fear: after a little it passeth by, that water runneth down; for a time it roareth, soon it will subside: they cannot hold long. Many heresies now are utterly dead: they have run in their channels as much as they were able, have run down, dried are the channels, scarce of them the memory is found, or that they have been. "They shall be despised like water running down." But not they alone; the whole of this age for a time is roaring, and is seeking whom it may drag along. Let all ungodly men, all proud men resounding against the rocks of their pride as it were with waters rushing along and flowing together, not terrify you, winter waters they are, they cannot alway flow: it must needs be that they run down unto their place, unto their end. And nevertheless of this torrent of the world the Lord hath drunk. For He hath suffered here, the very torrent He hath drunk, but in the way He hath drunk, but in the passage over: because in way of sinners He hath not stood.[9] But of Him saith the Scripture what? "Of the torrent in the way He shall drink, therefore He shall lift up His Head;"[10] that is, for this reason glorified He hath been, because He hath died; for this reason hath risen again, because He hath suffered. . . .

12. "Like wax melted they shall be taken away" (ver. 8). For thou wast about to say, all men are not so made weak, like myself, in order that they may believe: many men do persevere in their evil, and in their malice. And of the same fear thou nothing: "Like wax melted

[1] Matt. xxii. 21. [2] Matt. xxi. 23, 24; Mark xi. 28, 29.
[3] Luke vii. 39. [4] Luke vii. 41, 42. [5] Ps. lviii. 6.
[6] Ps. ii. 1.
[7] Matt. xxii. 17.

[8] Matt. xxvii. 23; John xix. 6. [9] Ps. i. 1.
[10] Ps. cx. 7.

they shall be taken away." Against thee they shall not stand, they shall not continue : with a sort of fire of their own lusts they shall perish. For there is here a kind of hidden punishment,[1] of it the Psalm is about to speak now, to the end of it. There are but a few verses ; be attentive. There is a certain punishment future, fire of hell, fire everlasting. For future punishment hath two kinds : either of the lower places it is, where was burning that rich man, who was wishing for himself a drop of water to be dropped on his tongue off the finger of the poor man, whom before his gate he had spurned, when he saith, "For I am tormented in this flame."[2] And the second is that at the end, whereof they are to hear, that on the left hand are to be set : "Go ye into fire everlasting, that hath been prepared for the devil and his angels."[3] Those punishments shall be manifest at that time, when we shall have departed out of this life, or when at the end of the world men shall have come to the resurrection of the dead. Now therefore is there no punishment, and doth God suffer sins utterly unpunished even unto that day? There is even here a sort of hidden punishment, of the same he is treating now... . . We see nevertheless sometimes with these punishments just men to be afflicted, and to these punishments unjust men to be strangers : for which reason did totter the feet of him that afterwards rejoicing saith, "How good is the God of Israel to men right in heart ! But my own feet have been almost shaken, because I have been jealous in the case of sinners, beholding the peace of sinners."[4] For he had seen the felicity of evil men, and well-pleased he had been to be an evil man, seeing evil men to reign, seeing that it was well with them, that they abounded in plenty of all things temporal, such as he too, being as yet but a babe, was desiring from the Lord : and his feet did totter, even until he saw what at the end is either to be hoped for or to be feared. For he saith in the same Psalm, "This thing is a labour before me, until I enter into the sanctuary of God, and understand unto the last things."[5] It is not therefore the punishments of the lower places, not the punishments of that fire everlasting after the resurrection, not those punishments which as yet in this world are common to just men and unjust men, and ofttimes more heavy are those of just men than those of unjust men ; but some punishment or other of the present life the Spirit of God would recommend to our notice. Give heed, hear ye me about to speak of that which ye know : but a more sweet thing it is when it is declared in a Psalm, which, before it was declared, was deemed obscure. For behold I bring forth that which already ye knew : but because these things are brought forth from a place where ye have never yet seen them, it cometh to pass that even known things, as if they were new things, do delight you. Hear ye the punishment of ungodly men : "Like wax," he saith, "melted they shall be taken away." I have said that through their lusts this thing to them is done. Evil lust is like a burning and a fire. Doth fire consume a garment, and doth not the lust of adultery consume the soul? Of meditated adultery when the Scripture was speaking it saith, "Shall one bind fire in his bosom, and his garments shall he not burn up?"[6] Thou bearest in thy bosom live coals ; burned through is thy vest ; thou bearest in thought adultery, and whole then is thy soul? But these punishments few men do see : therefore them the Spirit of God doth exceedingly recommend to our notice. Hear the Apostle saying, "God hath given them up unto the lusts of their heart."[7] Behold, the fire from the face of which like wax they are melting. For they loose themselves from a certain continence of chastity ; therefore even these same men, going unto their lusts, as loose and melting are spoken of. Whence melting? whence loose? From the fire of lusts. "God hath given them up unto the lusts of their heart, so that they do those things which beseem not, being filled full of all iniquity." . . .

13. "There hath fallen upon them fire, and they have not seen the sun." Ye see in what manner he speaketh of a certain punishment of darkening. "Fire hath fallen upon them," fire of pride, a smoky fire, fire of lust, fire of wrath. How great a fire is it? He upon whom it shall have fallen, shall not see the sun. Therefore hath it been said, "Let not the sun go down upon your wrath."[8] Therefore, brethren, fire of evil lust fear ye, if ye will not melt like wax, and to perish from the face of God. For there falleth upon you that fire, and the sun ye shall not see. What sun? Not that which together with thee see both beasts and insects, and good men and evil men : because "He maketh His sun to rise upon good men and evil men."[9] But there is another sun, whereof those men are to speak, "And the sun hath not risen to us, passed away are all those things as it were a shadow. Therefore we have strayed from the way of truth, and the light of righteousness hath not shone to us, and the sun hath not risen to us."[10] . . .

14. "Before that the bramble [11] bringeth forth your thorns : as though living, as though in anger, it shall drink them up" (ver. 9). What is the bramble? Of prickly plants it is a kind, upon which there are said to be certain of the closest thorns. At first it is a herb ; and while it is a herb, soft and fair it is : but thereon there

---

[1] Hidden punishment of sinners.　　[2] Luke xvi. 24.
[3] Matt. xxv. 41.　　[4] Ps. lxxiii. 1-3.　　[5] Ps. lxxiii. 16, 17.
[6] Prov. vi. 27.　　[7] Rom. i. 24.　　[8] Eph. iv. 26.
[9] Matt. v. 45.　　[10] Wisd. v. 6.　　[11] *Rhamnus.*

are nevertheless thorns to come forth. Now therefore sins are pleasant, and as it were they do not prick. A herb is the bramble; even now nevertheless there is a thorn. "Before that the bramble bringeth forth thorns:" is before that of miserable delights and pleasures the evident tortures come forth. Let them question themselves that love any object, and to it cannot attain; let them see if they are not racked with longing: and when they have attained to that which unlawfully they long for, let them mark if they are not racked with fear. Let them see therefore here their punishments; before that there cometh that resurrection, when in flesh rising again they shall not be changed. "For all we shall rise again, but not [1] all we shall be changed."[2] For they shall have the corruption of the flesh wherein to be pained, not that wherein to die: otherwise even those pains would be ended. Then the thorns of that bramble, that is, all pains and piercings of tortures shall be brought forth. Such thorns as they shall suffer that are to say, "These are they whom sometimes we had in derision:"[3] thorns of the piercing of repentance, but of one too late and without fruit like the barrenness of thorns. The repentance of this time is pain healing: repentance of that time is pain penal. Wouldest thou not suffer those thorns? here be thou pierced with the thorns of repentance; in such sort that thou do that which hath been spoken of, "Turned I have been in sorrow, when the thorn was piercing:[4] my sin I have known, and mine iniquity I have not covered: I have said, I will declare against me my shortcoming to the Lord, and Thou hast remitted the ungodliness of my heart."[5] Now do so, now be pierced through, be there not in thee done that which hath been said of certain execrable men, "They have been cloven asunder, and have not been pierced through."[6] Observe them that have been cloven asunder and have not been pierced through.[7] Ye see men cloven asunder, and ye see them not pierced through. Behold beside the Church they are, and it doth not repent them, so as they should return whence they have been cloven asunder. The bramble hereafter shall bring forth their thorns. They will not now have a healing piercing through, they shall have hereafter one penal. But even now before that the bramble produceth thorns, there hath fallen upon them fire, that suffereth them not to see the sun, that is, the wrath of God is drinking up them while still living: fire of evil lusts, of empty honours,

of pride, of their covetousness: and whatsoever is weighing them down, that they should not know the truth, so that they seem not to be conquered, so that they be not brought into subjection even by truth herself. For what is a more glorious thing, brethren, than to be brought in subjection and to be overcome by truth? Let truth overcome thee willing: for even unwilling she shall of herself overcome thee. . . .

15. As yet the punishments of the lower places have not come, as yet fire everlasting hath not come: let him that is growing in God compare himself now with an ungodly man, a blind heart with an enlightened heart: compare ye two men, one seeing and one not seeing in the flesh. And what so great thing is vision of the flesh? Did Tobias by any means have fleshly eyes?[8] His own son had, and he had not; and the way of life a blind man to one seeing did show. Therefore when ye see that punishment, rejoice, because in it ye are not.

Therefore saith the Scripture, "The just man shall rejoice when he shall have seen vengeance" (ver. 10). Not that future punishment; for see what followeth: "his hands he shall wash in the blood of the sinner." What is this? Let your love attend. When man-slayers are smitten, ought anywise innocent men to go thither and wash their hands? But what is, "in the blood of the sinner he shall wash his hands"? When a just man seeth the punishment of a sinner, he groweth himself; and the death of one is the life of another. For if spiritually blood runneth from those that within are dead, do thou, seeing such vengeance, wash therein thy hands; for the future more cleanly live. And how shall he wash his hands, if a just man he is? For what hath he on his hands to be washed, if just he is? "But the just man of faith shall live."[9] Just men therefore he hath called believers: and from the time that thou hast believed, at once thou beginnest to be called just. For there hath been made a remission of sins. Even if out of that remaining part of thy life some sins are thine, which cannot but flow in, like water from the sea into the hold; nevertheless, because thou hast believed, when thou shalt have seen him that altogether is turned away from God to be slain in that blindness, there falling upon him that fire so that he see not the sun — then do thou that now through faith seest Christ, in order that thou mayest see in substance (because the just man liveth of faith), observe the ungodly man dying, and purge thyself from sins. So thou shalt wash in a manner thy hands in the blood of the sinner.

16. "And a man shall say, If therefore there is fruit to a just man" (ver. 10). Behold, before that there cometh that which is promised, before

---

[1] So several early writers and MSS. But the balance of authority as well as the sense is in favour of the received reading.
[2] 1 Cor. xv. 51.   [3] Wisd. v. 3.
[4] Or, "being made to pierce."   [5] Ps. xxxii. 5.
[6] Ps. xxxv. 15. These words are in the Vulgate, for "they did tear me, and ceased not;" but St. Augustin does not notice them in his comment on the Psalm.
[7] Against the Donatists.

[8] Tob. iv. 3-19.   [9] Rom. i. 17.

that there is given life everlasting, before that ungodly men are cast forth into fire everlasting, here in this life there is fruit to the just man. What fruit? " In hope rejoicing, in tribulation enduring."[1] What fruit to the just man? " We glory in tribulations, knowing that tribulation worketh patience, but patience probation, but probation hope : but hope confoundeth not : because the love of God is shed abroad in our hearts through the Holy Spirit, that hath been given to us."[2] Doth he rejoice that is a drunk-ard ; and doth he not rejoice that is just? In love there is fruit to a just man. Miserable the one, even when he maketh himself drunken : blessed the other, even when he hungereth and thirsteth. The one wine-bibbing doth gorge, the other hope doth feed. Let him see therefore the punishment of the other, his own rejoicing, and let him think of God. He that hath given even now such joy of faith, of hope, of charity, of the truth of His Scriptures, what manner of joy is He making ready against the end? In the way thus He feedeth, in his home how shall He fill him? " And a man shall say, If therefore there is fruit to the just man." Let them that see believe, and see, and perceive. Rejoice shall the just man when he shall have seen vengeance. But if he hath not eyes whence he may see vengeance, he will be made sad, and will not be amended by it. But if he seeth it, he seeth what difference there is between the darkened eye of the heart, and the eye enlightened of the heart : between the cool-ness of chastity and the flame of lust, between the security of hope and the fear there is in crime. When he shall have seen this, let him separate himself, and wash his hands in the blood of the same. Let him profit by the comparison, and say, " Therefore there is fruit to the just man : therefore there is a God judging them in the earth." Not yet in that life, not yet in fire eter-nal, not yet in the lower places, but here in earth. . . .

17. If somewhat too prolix we have been, par-don us. We exhort you in the name of Christ, to meditate profitably on those things which ye have heard. Because even to preach the truth is nought, if heart from tongue dissenteth ; and to hear the truth nothing profiteth, if a man upon the rock build not. He that buildeth upon a Rock, is the same that heareth and doeth :[3] but he that heareth and doeth not, buildeth upon sand : he that neither heareth nor doeth, build-eth nothing. . . .

PSALM LIX.[4]

The First Part.

1. As the Scripture is wont to set mysteries of the Psalms on the titles, and to deck the brow of a Psalm with the high announcement of a Mystery,[5] in order that we that are about to go in may know (when as it were upon the door-post we have read what within is doing) either of whom the house is, or who is the owner of that estate : so also in this Psalm there hath been written a title, of a title. For it hath, " At the end, corrupt not for David himself unto the inscription of the title." This is that which I have spoken of, title of Title. For what the inscription of this title is, which to be corrupted he forbiddeth, the Gospel to us doth indicate. For when the Lord was being crucified, a title by Pilate was inscribed and set, " King of the Jews,"[6] in three tongues, Hebrew, Greek, and Latin :[7] which tongues in the whole world mostly do prevail. . . . Therefore " corrupt not " is most proper and prophetic : since indeed even those Jews made suggestion at that time to Pilate, and said, " Do not write King of the Jews, but write, that Himself said that He was King of the Jews : "[8] for this title, say they, hath established Him King over us. And Pilate, " What I have written, I have written." And there was fulfilled, " corrupt not."

2. Nor is this the only Psalm which hath an inscription of such sort, that the Title be not cor-rupted. Several Psalms thus are marked on the face, but however in all the Passion of the Lord is foretold. Therefore here also let us perceive the Lord's Passion, and let there speak to us Christ, Head and Body. So always, or nearly always, let us hear the words of Christ from the Psalm, as that we look not only upon that Head, the one mediator between God and man, the Man Christ Jesus.[9] . . . But let us think of Christ, Head and whole Body, a sort of entire Man. For to us is said, " But ye are the Body of Christ and members,"[10] by the Apostle Paul. If therefore He is Head, we Body ; whole Christ is Head and Body. For sometimes thou findest words which do not suit the Head, and unless thou shalt have attached them to the Body, thy understanding will waver : again thou findest words which are proper for the Body, and Christ nevertheless is speaking. In that place we must have no fear lest a man be mistaken : for quickly he pro-ceedeth to adapt to the Head, that which he seeth is not proper for the Body. . . .

3. Let us hear, therefore, what followeth : " When Saul sent and guarded his house in or-der that he might kill him." This though not to the Cross of the Lord, yet to the Passion of the Lord doth belong. For Crucified was Christ, and dead, and buried. That sepulchre was therefore as it were the house : to guard which the government of the Jews sent, when guards were set to the sepulchre of Christ.[11] There is

---

[1] Rom. xii. 12. [2] Rom. v. 3–5. [3] Matt. vii. 24.
[4] Lat. LVIII. Delivered after the discovery of the error of Pelagius.

[5] *Sacramenti.* [6] Matt. xxvii. 37. [7] John xix. 20.
[8] John xix. 21. [9] 1 Tim. ii. 5. [10] 1 Cor. xii. 27.
[11] Matt. xxvii. 66.

indeed a story in the Scripture of the Reigns, of the occasion when Saul sent to guard the house in order that he might kill David.[1] . . . But in like manner as Saul effected not his purpose of slaying David : so this could not the government of the Jews effect, that the testimony of guards sleeping should avail more than that of Apostles watching. For what were the guards instructed to say? We give to you, they say, as much money as ye please ; and say ye, that while ye were sleeping there came His disciples, and took Him away. Behold what sort of witnesses of falsehood against truth and the Resurrection of Christ, His enemies, through Saul figured, did produce. Enquire, O unbelief, of sleeping witnesses, let them reply to thee of what was done in the tomb. Who, if they were sleeping, whence knew it? If watching, wherefore detained they not the thieves? Let him say therefore what followeth.

4. " Deliver me from mine enemies, my God, and from men rising up upon me, redeem Thou me " (ver. 1). There hath been done this thing in the flesh of Christ, it is being done in us also. For our enemies, to wit the devil and his angels, cease not to rise up upon us every day, and to wish to make sport of our weakness and our frailness, by deceptions, by suggestions, by temptations, and by snares of whatsoever sort to entangle us, while on earth we are still living. But let our voice watch unto God, and cry out in the members of Christ, under the Head that is in heaven, " Deliver me from mine enemies, my God, and from men rising up upon me, redeem Thou me."

5. " Deliver me from men working iniquity, and from men of bloods, save Thou me " (ver. 2). They indeed were men of bloods, who slew the Just One, in whom no guilt they found : they were men of bloods, because when the foreigner washed his hands, and would have let go Christ, they cried, " Crucify, Crucify :"[2] they were men of bloods, on whom when there was being charged the crime of the blood of Christ, they made answer, giving it to their posterity to drink, " His blood be upon us and upon our sons."[3] But neither against His Body did men of bloods cease to rise up; for even after the Resurrection and Ascension of Christ, the Church suffered persecutions, and she indeed first that grew out of the Jewish people, of which also our Apostles were. There at first Stephen was stoned,[4] and received that of which he had his name. For Stephanus doth signify a crown. Lowly stoned but highly crowned. Secondly, among the Gentiles rose up kingdoms of Gentiles, before that in them was fulfilled that which had been foretold, " There shall

adore Him all the kings of the earth, all nations shall serve Him : "[5] and there roared the fierceness of that kingdom against the witnesses of Christ : there was shed largely and frequently the blood of Martyrs : wherewith when it had been shed, being as it were sown, the field of the Church more productively put forth, and filled the whole world as we now behold. From these therefore, men of bloods, is delivered Christ, not only Head, but also Body. From men of bloods is delivered Christ, both from them that have been, and from them that are, and from them that are to be ; there is delivered Christ, both He that hath gone before, and He that is, and He that is to come. For Christ is the whole Body of Christ ; and whatsoever good Christians that now are, and that have been before us, and that after us are to be, are an whole Christ, who is delivered from men of bloods ; nor is this voice void, " And from men of bloods save Thou me."

6. " For behold they have hunted my soul. . . . There have rushed upon me strong men " (ver. 3). We must not however pass on from these strong men : diligently we must trace who are the strong men rising up. Strong men, upon whom but upon weak men, upon powerless men, upon men not strong? And praised nevertheless are the weak men, and condemned are the strong men. If it would be perceived who are strong men, at first the devil himself the Lord hath called a strong man : " No one," He saith, " is able to go into the house of a strong man, and to carry off his vessels, unless first he shall have bound the strong man."[6] He hath bound therefore the strong man with the chains of His dominion : and his vessels He hath carried off, and His own vessels hath made them. For all unrighteous men were vessels of the devil. . . . But there are among mankind certain strong men of a blameable and damnable strength, that are confident indeed, but on temporal felicity. That man doth not[7] seem to you to have been strong, of whom now from the Gospel[8] hath been read : how his estate brought forth abundance of fruits, and he being troubled, hit upon the design of rebuilding, so that, having pulled down his old barns, he should construct new ones more capacious, and, these having been finished, should say to his soul, " Thou hast many good things, soul, feast, be merry, be filled." . . . There are also other men men strong, not because of riches, not because of the powers of the body, not because of any temporally pre-eminent power of station, but relying on their righteousness. This sort of strong men must be guarded against, feared, repulsed, not imitated : of men relying, I say, not on

---

[1] 1 Sam. xix. 11.   [2] Matt. xxvii. 23.   [3] Matt. xxvii. 25.   [5] Ps. lxxi. 11.   [6] Matt. xii. 29.
[4] Acts vii. 58.   [7] Perhaps " doth not that man."   [8] Luke xii. 16.

body, not on means, not on descent, not on honour; for all such things who would not see to be temporal, fleeting, falling, flying? but relying on their own righteousness. . . . "Wherefore," say they, doth your Master eat with publicans and sinners?[1] O ye strong men, to whom a Physician is not needful! This strength to soundness belongeth not, but to insanity. For even than men frenzied nothing can be stronger, more mighty they are than whole men: but by how much greater their powers are, by so much nearer is their death. May God therefore turn away from our imitation these strong men. . . . The same are therefore the strong men, that assailed Christ, commending their own justice. Hear ye these strong men: when certain men of Jerusalem were speaking, having been sent by them to take Christ, and not daring to take Him (because when he would, then was He taken, that truly was strong): Why therefore, say they, "could ye not take Him?" And they made answer, "No one of men did ever so speak as He." And these strong men, "Hath by any means any one of the Pharisees believed on Him, or any one of the Scribes, but this people knowing not the Law?"[2] They preferred themselves to the sick multitude, that was running to the Physician: whence but because they were themselves strong? and what is worse, by their strength, all the multitude also they brought over unto themselves, and slew the Physician of all. . . .

7. What next? "Neither iniquity is mine, nor sin mine, O Lord" (ver. 4). There have rushed on indeed strong men on their own righteousness relying, they have rushed on, but sin in me they have not found. For truly those strong men, that is, as it were righteous men, on what account would they be able to persecute Christ, unless it were as if a sinner? But, however, let them look to it how strong they be, in the raging of fever not in the vigour of soundness: let them look to it how strong they be, and how as though just against an unrighteous man they have raged.[3] But, however, "neither iniquity is mine, nor sin mine, O Lord. Without iniquity I did run, and I was guided." Those strong men therefore could not follow me running: therefore a sinner they have deemed me, because my steps they have not seen.

8. "Without iniquity I did run, and was guided; rise up to meet me, and see." To God is said this. But why? If He meet not, is He unable to see? It is just as if thou wast walking in a road, and from afar by some one

thou couldest not be recognised, thou wouldest call to him and wouldest say, Meet me, and see how I am walking; for when from afar thou espiest me, my steps thou art not able to see. So also unless God were to meet, would He not see how without iniquity he was guided, and how without sin he was running? This interpretation indeed we can also accept, namely, "Rise up to meet me," as if "help me." But that which he hath added, "and see," must be understood as, make it to be seen that I run, make it to be seen that I am guided: according to that figure wherein this also hath been said to Abraham, "Now I know that thou fearest God."[4] God saith, "Now I know:" whence, but because I have made thee to know? For unknown to himself every one is before the questioning of temptation: just as of himself Peter[5] in his confidence was ignorant, and by denying learned what kind of powers he had, in his very stumbling he perceived that it was falsely he had been confident: he wept, and in weeping he earned profitably to know what he was, and to be what he was not. Therefore Abraham when tried, became known to himself: and it was said by God, "Now I know," that is, now I have made thee to know. In like manner as glad is the day because it maketh men glad; and sad is bitterness because it maketh sad one tasting thereof: so God's seeing is making to see. "Rise up, therefore," he saith, "to meet me, and see" (ver. 5). What is, "and see"? And help me, that is, in those men, in order that they may see my course, may follow me; let not that seem to them to be crooked which is straight, let not that seem to them to be curved which keepeth the rule of truth.

9. Something else I am admonished to say in this place of the loftiness of our Head Himself: for He was made weak even unto death, and He took on Him the weakness of flesh, in order that the chickens of Jerusalem He might gather under His wings, like a hen showing herself weak with her little ones.[6] For have we not observed this thing in some bird at some time or other, even in those which build nests before our eyes, as the house-sparrows, as swallows, so to speak, our annual guests, as storks, as various sorts of birds, which before our eyes build nests, and hatch eggs, feed chickens, as the very doves which daily we see; and some bird to become weak with her chickens, have we not known, have we not looked upon, have we not seen? In what way doth a hen experience this weakness? Surely a known fact I am speaking of, which in our sight is daily taking place. How her voice groweth hoarse, how her whole body is made languid? The wings droop, the feathers are

---

[1] Matt. ix. 11.   [2] John vii. 45–49.
[3] Oxf. MSS. "and how far they were righteous and raging against one unrighteous" (*et quam justi contra iniquum sævierint*). The common reading is scarcely grammatical.

[4] Gen. xxii. 12.   [5] Matt. xxvi. 35–69.   [6] Matt. xxiii. 37.

loosened, and thou seest around the chickens some sick thing, and this is maternal love which is found as weakness. Why was it therefore, but for this reason, that the Lord willed to be as a Hen, saying in the Holy Scripture, " Jerusalem, Jerusalem, how often have I willed to gather thy sons, even as a hen her chickens under her wings, and thou hast not been willing." But He hath gathered all nations, like as a hen her chickens. . . .

10. " And Thou, Lord God of virtues, God of Israel." Thou God of Israel, that art thought to be but God of one nation, which worshippeth Thee, when all nations worship idols, Thou God of Israel, " Give heed unto the visiting all nations." Fulfilled be that prophecy wherein Isaiah in Thy person speaketh to Thy Church, Thy holy City, that barren one of whom many more are the sons of Her forsaken than of her that hath a husband. To Her indeed hath been said, " Rejoice, thou barren, that bearest not," [1] etc., more than of the Jewish nation which hath a Husband, which hath received the Law, more than of that nation which had a visible king. For thy king is hidden, and more sons to thee there are by a hidden Bridegroom. . . . The Prophet addeth, "Enlarge the place of Thy tabernacle, and Thy [2] courts fix thou : there is no cause for thee to spare, extend further thy cords, and strong stakes set thou again and again on the right and on the left." [3] Upon the right keep good men, on the left keep evil men,[4] until there come the fan : [5] occupy nevertheless all nations ; bidden to the marriage be good men and evil men, filled be the marriage with guests ; [6] it is the office of servants to bid, of the Lord to sever. " Cities which had been forsaken Thou shalt inhabit : " [7] forsaken of God, forsaken of Prophets, forsaken of Apostles, forsaken of the Gospel, full of demons. For Thou shalt prevail ; and blush not because abominable Thou hast been. Therefore though there have risen up upon thee strong men, blush not : when against the name of Christ laws were enacted, when ignominy and infamy it was to be a Christian. " Blush not because abominable Thou hast been : for confusion for everlasting Thou shalt forget, of the ignominy of Thy widowhood Thou shalt not be mindful." . . .

11. " Have not pity upon all men that work iniquity." Here evidently He is terrifying. Whom would He not terrify? What man falling back upon his own conscience would not tremble? Which even if to itself it is conscious of godliness, strange if it be not in some sort conscious of iniquity. For whosoever doeth sin, also doeth iniquity.[8] " For if Thou shalt have marked iniquities, O Lord, what man shall abide it ? " [9] And nevertheless a true saying it is, and not said to no purpose, and neither is nor will it be possible to be void, " Have not pity upon all men that work iniquity." But He had pity even upon Paul, who at first as Saul wrought iniquity. For what good thing did he, whence he might deserve of God? Did he not hate His Saints unto death? [10] did he not bear letters from the chief of the priests, to the end that wheresoever he might find Christians, to punishment he should hurry them? When bent upon this, when thither proceeding, breathing and panting slaughter, as the Scripture testified of him, was he not from Heaven with a mighty voice summoned, thrown down, raised up ; blinded, lightened ; slain, made alive ; destroyed, restored? In return for what merit? Let us say nothing ; himself rather let us hear : " I that before have been," he saith, " a blasphemer, and persecutor ; and injurious, but mercy I have obtained." [11] Surely "Thou wouldest not have pity upon all men that work iniquity : " this in two ways may be understood : either that in fact not any sins doth God leave unpunished ; or that there is a sort of iniquity, on the workers whereof God hath indeed no pity.

12. All iniquity, be it little or great, punished must needs be, either by man himself repenting, or by God avenging. For even he that repenteth punisheth himself. Therefore, brethren, let us punish our own sins, if we seek the mercy of God. God cannot have mercy on all men working iniquity as if pandering to sins, or not rooting out sins. In a word, either thou punishest, or He punisheth. . . .

13. But let us see now another way in which this sentence may be understood. There is a certain iniquity, on the worker whereof it cannot be that God have mercy. Ye enquire, perchance, what that is? It is the defending of sins. When a man defendeth his sins, great iniquity he worketh : that thing he is defending which God hateth. And see how perversely, how iniquitously. Whatever of good he hath done, to himself he would have it to be ascribed ; whatever of evil, to God. For in this manner men defend sins in the person of God, which is a worse sin. . . . Therefore thou defendest thy sin in such sort, that thou layest blame on God. So the guilty is excused, so that the Judge may be charged. However on men working iniquity God hath no pity at all.

14. " Let them be converted at the evening " (ver. 6). Of certain men he is speaking that were once workers of iniquity, and once darkness, being converted in the evening. What is, " in the evening "? Afterward. What is " at the even-

[1] Isa. liv. 1.   [2] " Hangings " some MSS.   [3] Isa. liv. 2.
[4] Matt. xxv. 33.   [5] Matt. iii. 12.   [6] Matt. xxii. 9.
[7] Isa. liv. 3.   [8] 1 John iii. 4.

[9] Ps. cxxx. 3.   [10] Acts ix. 1.   [11] 1 Tim. i. 13.

ing"? Later. For before, before that they crucified Christ, they ought to have acknowledged their Physician. Wherefore, when He had been crucified — rising again, into Heaven ascending — after that He sent His Holy Spirit, wherewith were fulfilled they that were in one house, and they began to speak with the tongues of all nations, there feared the crucifiers of Christ; they were pricked through with their consciences, they besought counsel of safety from the Apostles, they heard, "Repent, and be baptized each one of you in the name of our Lord Jesus Christ, and your sins shall be remitted unto you." [1] After the slaying of Christ, after the shedding of the blood of Christ, remitted are your sins. . . . "Let these be converted," therefore, they also "at evening." Let them yearn for the grace of God, perceive themselves to be sinners; let those strong men be made weak, those rich men be made poor, those just men acknowledge themselves sinners, those lions be made dogs. "Let them be converted at evening, and suffer hunger as dogs. And they shall go around the city." What city? That world, which in certain places the Scripture calleth "the city of standing round:" [2] that is, because in all nations everywhere the world had encompassed the one nation of Jews, where such words were being spoken, and it was called "the city of standing round." Around this city shall go those men, now having become hungry dogs. In what manner shall they go around? By preaching. Saul out of a wolf was made a dog at evening, that is, being late converted by the crumbs of his Lord, in His grace he ran, and went around the city. [3]

15. "Behold, themselves shall speak in their mouth, and a sword is on the lips of them" (ver. 7). Here is that sword twice whetted, whereof the Apostle saith, "And the sword of the Spirit, which is the Word of God." [4] Wherefore twice whetted? Wherefore, but because smiting out of both Testaments? With this sword were slain those whereof it was said to Peter, "Slay, and eat." [5] "And a sword is on the lips of them. For who hath heard?" They all speak in their mouth, "Who hath heard?" That is, they shall be wroth with men that are slow to believe. They that a little before were even themselves unwilling to believe, do feel disgust from men not believing. And truly, brethren, so it is. Thou seest a man slow before he is made a Christian; thou criest to him daily, hardly he is converted: suppose him to be converted, and then he would have all men to be Christians, and wondereth that not yet they are. It hath chanced out to him at

evening to have been converted: but because he hath been made hungering like a dog, he hath also on his lips a sword; he saith, "Who hath heard?" What is, "Who hath heard?" "Who hath believed our hearing, and to whom hath the arm of the Lord been revealed?" [6] "For who hath heard?" The Jews believe not: they have turned them to the nations, and have preached. The Jews did not believe; and nevertheless through believing Jews the Gospel went around the city, and they said, "For who hath heard?" "And Thou, Lord, shalt deride them" (ver. 8). All nations are to be Christian, and ye say, "Who hath heard?" What is, "shalt deride them"? "As nothing Thou shalt esteem all nations." Nothing for Thee it shall be; because a most easy thing it will be for all nations to believe in Thee.

16. "My strength to Thee I will keep" (ver. 9). For those strong men have fallen for this reason; because their strength to Thee they have not kept: that is, they that upon me have risen up and rushed, on themselves have relied. But I "my strength to Thee will keep:" because if I withdraw, I fall; if I draw near, stronger I am made. For see, brethren, what there is in a human soul. It hath not of itself light, hath not of itself powers: but all that is fair in a soul, is virtue and wisdom: but it neither is wise for itself, nor strong for itself, nor itself is light to itself, nor itself is virtue to itself. There is a certain origin and fountain of virtue, there is a certain root of wisdom, there is a certain, so to speak, if this also must be said, region of unchangeable truth: from this the soul withdrawing is made dark, drawing near is made light. [7] "Draw near to Him, and be made light:" because by withdrawing ye are made dark. Therefore, "my strength, I will keep to Thee:" not from Thee will I withdraw, not on myself will I rely. "My strength, to Thee I will keep: because, O God, my lifter up [8] Thou art." For where was I, and where am I? Whence hast Thou taken me up? What iniquities of mine hast Thou remitted? Where was I lying? To what have I been raised up? I ought to have remembered these things: because in another Psalm is said, "For my father and my mother have forsaken me, but the Lord hath taken me unto Him." [9]

17. "My God, the mercy of Him shall [10] come before me" (ver. 10). Behold what is, "My strength, to Thee I will keep:" on myself I will in no ways at all rely. For what good thing have I brought, that thou shouldest have mercy on me, and shouldest justify me? What in me hast Thou found, save sins alone? Of Thine there is nothing else but the nature which Thou

---

[1] Acts ii. 38.
[2] E. V. "strong city." Ps. xxxi. 21, lx. 9, cviii. 10.
[3] Acts ix. 1, 20.   [4] Eph. vi. 17.   [5] Acts x. 13.

[6] Isa. liii. 1.   [7] Ps. xxxiv. 5.   [8] Or, "taker up."
[9] Ps. xxvii. 10.   [10] Or, "prevent."

hast created : the other things are mine own evil things which Thou hast blotted out. I have not first risen up to Thee, but to awake me Thou hast come : for " His mercy shall come before me." Before that anything of good I shall do, " His mercy shall come before me." What answer here shall the unhappy Pelagius make? " My God hath shown to me among mine enemies " (ver. 11). How great mercy He hath put forth concerning me, among mine enemies He hath showed. Let one gathered compare himself with men forsaken, and one elect with men rejected : let the vessel of mercy compare itself with the vessels of wrath ; and let it see how out of one lump God hath made one vessel unto honour, another unto dishonour.

" For so God, willing to show wrath, and to manifest His power, hath brought in, in much patience, the vessels of wrath, which have been perfected unto perdition."[1] And wherefore this? " In order that He might make known His riches upon the vessels of mercy." If therefore vessels of wrath He hath brought in, wherein He might make known His riches upon the vessels of mercy, most rightly hath been said, " His mercy shall come before me : My God hath showed to me among mine enemies : " that is, however great mercy He hath had concerning me, to me He hath showed it among these men concerning whom He hath not had mercy. For unless the debtor be in suspense, he is less grateful to him by whom the debt hath been forgiven. " My God hath showed to me among mine enemies."

18. But of the enemies themselves what? " Slay them not, lest sometime they forget Thy law." He is making request for his enemies, he is fulfilling the commandment. . . . Slay not them of whom the sins Thou slayest. But what is it to be slain? To forget the law of the Lord. It is real death, to go into the pit of sin ; this indeed may be also understood of the Jews. Why of the Jews, " Slay not them, lest sometime they forget Thy law "? Those very enemies of mine, that have slain me, do not Thou slay. Let the nation of the Jews remain : certes conquered it hath been by the Romans, certes effaced is the city of them, Jews are not admitted into their city, and yet Jews there are. For all those provinces by the Romans have been subjugated. Who now can distinguish the nations in the Roman empire the one from the other, inasmuch as all have become Romans and all are called Romans? The Jews nevertheless remain with a mark ; nor in such sort conquered have they been, as that by the conquerors they have been swallowed up. Not without reason is there that Cain, on whom, when he had slain his brother, God set a mark in order that no one should slay him.[2] This is the mark which the Jews have : they hold fast by the remnant of their law, they are circumcised, they keep Sabbaths, they sacrifice the Passover ; they eat unleavened bread. These are therefore Jews, they have not been slain, they are necessary to believing nations. Why so? In order that He may show to us among our enemies His mercy. " My God hath shown to me in mine enemies." He showeth His mercy to the wild-olive grafted on branches that have been cut off because of pride. Behold where they lie, that were proud, behold where thou hast been grafted, that didst lie : and be not thou proud, lest thou shouldest deserve to be cut off.

19. " Scatter them abroad in Thy virtue " (ver. 11). Now this thing hath been done : throughout all nations there have been scattered abroad the Jews, witnesses of their own iniquity and our truth. They have themselves writings, out of which hath been prophesied Christ, and we hold Christ. And if sometime perchance any heathen man shall have doubted, when we have told him the prophecies of Christ, at the clearness whereof he is amazed, and wondering hath supposed that they were written by ourselves, then out of the copies of the Jews we prove, how this thing so long time before had been foretold. See after what sort by means of our enemies we confound other enemies. " Scatter them abroad in Thy virtue : " take away from them " virtue," take away from them their strength. " And bring them down, my protector, O Lord." " The transgressions of their mouth, the discourse of their lips : and let them be taken in their pride : and out of cursing and lying shall be declared consummations, in the anger of consummation, and they shall not be " (ver. 12). Obscure words these are, and I fear lest they be not well instilled. . . .

The Second Part.

1. For, behold, the Jews are enemies, whom this Psalm seemeth to imply ; the law of God they hold, and therefore of them hath been said, " Slay not them, lest sometime they forget Thy law : " in order that the nation of Jews might remain, and by it remaining the number of Christians might increase. Throughout all nations they remain certainly, and Jews they are, nor have they ceased to be what they were : that is, this nation hath not so yielded to Roman institutions, as to have lost the form of Jews ; but hath been subjected to the Romans so as that it still retaineth its own laws ; which are the laws of God. But what in their case hath been done? " Ye tithe mint and cummin, and have

---

[1] Rom. ix. 22. [2] Gen. iv. 15.

forsaken the weightier matters of the law, mercy, and judgment, straining a gnat, but swallowing a camel."[1] This to them the Lord saith. And in truth so they are; they hold the law, hold the Prophets; read all things, sing all things: the light of the Prophets therein they see not, which is Christ Jesus. Not only Him now they see not, when he is sitting in Heaven: but not even at that time saw they Him, when among them humble He was walking, and they were made guilty by shedding the blood of the Same; but not all. This even to-day we commend to the notice of your Love. Not all: because many of them were turned to Him whom they slew, and by believing on Him, they obtained pardon even for the shedding of His blood: and they have given an example for men; how they ought not to despair that sin of whatsoever kind would be remitted to them, since even the killing of Christ was remitted to them confessing. . . .

2. What in them wilt Thou slay? The Crucify, Crucify,[2] which they cried out, not them that cried out. For they willed to blot out, cut off, destroy Christ: but Thou, by raising to life Christ, whom they willed to destroy, dost slay the "transgressions of their mouth, the discourse of their lips." For in that He whom they cried out should be destroyed, liveth, they are taken with dread: and that He whom on earth they despised, in heaven is adored by all nations, they wonder: thus are there slain the transgressions of them, and the discourse of their lips. What is, "let them be taken in their pride"? Because to no purpose have strong men rushed on, and it hath fallen out to them as it were to think themselves to have done somewhat, and they have prevailed against the Lord. They were able to crucify a man, weakness might prevail and virtue[3] be slain; and they thought themselves somewhat, as it were strong men, as it were mighty men, as it were prevailing, as it were a lion prepared for prey, as it were fat bulls, as of them in another place he maketh mention: "Fat bulls have beset me."[4] But what have they done in the case of Christ? Not life, but death they have slain. . . . And what now hath come to pass in those men that have been converted? For it was told to them that He whom they slew rose again. They believed Him to have risen again, because they saw that He, being in Heaven, thence sent the Holy Spirit, and filled those that on Him believed; and they found themselves to have condemned nought, and to have done nought. Their doing issued in emptiness, the sin remained. Because therefore the doing was made void, but the sin remained upon the doers; they were taken in their pride, they saw themselves under their iniquity.[5] It remained therefore for them to confess the sin, and for Him to pardon, that had given Himself up to sinners, and to forgive His death, having been slain by men dead, and making alive men dead. They were taken therefore in their pride.

3. "And out of cursing and lying shall be declared consummations, in anger of consummation, and they shall not be." This too with difficulty is understood, to what is joined the "and they shall not be." What shall they not be? Let us therefore examine the context above: when they shall have been taken in their pride, "there shall be declared out of cursing and lying consummations." What are consummations? Perfections: for to be consummated, is to be perfected. One thing it is to be consummated, another thing to be consumed. For a thing is consummated which is so finished as that it is perfected: a thing is consumed which is so finished that it is not. Pride would not suffer a man to be perfected, nothing so much hindereth perfection. For let your Love attend a little to what I am saying; and see an evil very pernicious, very much to be guarded against. What sort of evil do ye think it is? How long could I enlarge upon how much evil there is in pride? The devil on that account alone is to be punished. Certes he is the chief of all sinners: certes he is the tempter to sin: to him is not ascribed adultery, not winebibbing, not fornication, not the robbing of others' goods: by pride alone he fell. And since pride's companion is envy, it must needs be that a proud man should envy. . . . In a word, all vices in evil-doings are to be feared, pride in well-doings is more to be feared. It is no wonder, then, that so humble is the Apostle, as to say, "When I am made weak, then I am strong."[6] For lest he should himself be tempted by this sin, what sort of medicine doth he say was applied to him against swelling by the Physician, who knew what He was healing? "Lest by the greatness," he saith, "of the revelations I should be exalted, there was given to me a thorn of my flesh, the angel of Satan, to buffet me: wherefore thrice the Lord I besought, that it should depart from me: and He said to me, My grace is sufficient for thee, for virtue in weakness is made perfect."[7] See what the consummations are. An Apostle, the teacher of Gentiles, father of the faithful through the Gospel, received a thorn of the flesh whereby he might be buffeted. Which of us would dare to say this, unless he had not been ashamed to confess this? For if we shall have said that Paul had not suffered this; while to him as it were honour we give, a liar we make him. But be-

---

[1] Matt. xxiii. 23, 24.   [2] Matt. xxvii. 23; John xix. 5.
[3] Or, "strength."   [4] Ps. xxii. 12.
[5] Acts i. 9, ii. 4, 37.   [6] 2 Cor. xii. 10.   [7] 2 Cor. xii. 7–9.

cause truthful he is, and truth he hath spoken; it behoveth us to believe that there was given to him an angel of Satan, lest by the greatness of the revelations he should be exalted. Behold how much to be feared is the serpent of pride. . . .

4. What is, "in the anger of consummation shall be declared consummations"? There is an anger of consummation, and there is an anger of consuming. For every vengeance of God is called anger: sometimes God avengeth, to the end that He may make perfect; sometimes He avengeth, to the end that He may condemn. How doth He avenge, to the end that He may make perfect? "He scourgeth every son whom He receiveth."[1] How doth He avenge, to the end that He may condemn? When He shall have set ungodly men on the left hand, and shall have said to them, "Go ye into fire everlasting, that hath been prepared for the devil and his angels."[2] This is the anger of consuming, not that of consummation. But "there shall be declared consummations in the anger of consummation;" it shall be preached by the Apostles, that "where sin hath abounded, grace shall much more abound,"[3] and the weakness of man hath belonged to the healing of humility. Those men thinking of this, and finding out and confessing their iniquities, "shall not be." "Shall not be" what? In their pride.

5. "And they shall know how God shall have dominion of Jacob, and of the ends of the earth" (ver. 13). For before they thought themselves just men, because the Jewish nation had received the Law, because it had kept the commandments of God: it is proved to them that it hath not kept them, since in the very commandments of God Christ it perceived not, because "blindness in part has happened to Israel."[4] Even the Jews themselves see that they ought not to despise the Gentiles, of whom they deemed as of dogs and sinners. For just as alike they have been found in iniquity, so alike they will attain unto salvation. "Not only to Jews," saith the Apostle, "but also even to Gentiles."[5] For to this end the Stone which the builders set at nought, hath even been made for the Head of the corner,[6] in order that two in itself It might join: for a corner doth unite two walls. The Jews thought themselves exalted and great: of the Gentiles they thought as weak, as sinners, as the servants of demons, as the worshippers of idols, and yet in both was there iniquity. Even the Jews have been proved sinners; because "there is none that doeth good, there is not even so much as one:"[7] they have laid down their pride, and have not envied the salvation of the Gentiles, because they have known their own and their weakness to be alike: and in the Corner Stone being united, they have together worshipped the Lord. . . .

6. "They shall be converted at evening" (ver. 14): that is, even if late, that is, after the slaying of our Lord Jesus Christ: "They shall be converted at evening: and hereafter they shall suffer hunger as dogs." But "as dogs," not as sheep or calves: "as dogs," as Gentiles, as sinners; because they too have known their sin that thought themselves righteous. . . . It is a good thing therefore for a sinner to be humbled; and no one is more incurable than he that thinketh himself whole. "And they shall go around the city." Already we have explained "city;"[8] it is the "city of standing round;" all nations.

7. "They shall be scattered abroad in order that they may eat" (ver. 15); that is, in order that they may gain others, in order that into their Body they may change believers. "But if they shall not be filled, they shall murmur." Because above also he had spoken of the murmur of them, saying, "For who hath heard?" "And Thou, O Lord," he saith, "shalt deride them, saying, Who hath heard?"[9] Wherefore? Because, as nothing Thou shalt count all nations. Let the Psalm be concluded. See ye the Corner[10] exulting, now with both walls rejoicing. The Jews were proud, humbled they have been; Gentiles were despairing, raised up they have been: let them come to the Corner, there let them meet, there run together, there find the kiss of peace; from different parts let them come, but with differing not come, those of Circumcision, these of uncircumcision. Far apart were the walls, but before that to the Corner they came: but in the Corner let them hold themselves, and now let the whole Church from both walls, say what? "But I will sing of Thy power, and I will exult in the morning of Thy mercy" (ver. 16). In the morning when temptations have been overcome, in the morning when the night of this world shall have passed away; in the morning when no longer the lyings in wait of robbers and of the devil and of his angels we dread, in the morning when no longer by the lamp of prophecy we walk, but Himself the Word of God as it were a Sun we contemplate. "And I will exult in the morning of Thy mercy." With reason in another Psalm is said, "In the morning I will stand by Thee, and I will meditate."[11] With reason also of the Lord Himself the Resurrection was at dawn, that there should be fulfilled that which hath been said in another Psalm, "In the evening shall tarry weeping, and in the morning exultation."[12] For at even the disciples mourned our Lord Jesus

1 Heb. xii. 6.   2 Matt. xxv. 41.   3 Rom. v. 20.
4 Rom. xi. 25.   5 Rom. ii. 10.   6 Ps. cxviii. 22.
7 Ps. xiv. 3.

8 See p. 240, note 2.   9 Ps. lix. 7.
10 Eph. ii. 20.   11 Ps. v. 3.   12 Ps. xxx. 5.

Christ as dead, at dawn at Him rising again they exulted. "For Thou hast become my taker up, and my refuge in the day of my tribulation."

8. "My Helper, to Thee I will play, because Thou, O God, art my taker up" (ver. 17). What was I, unless Thou didst succour? How much despaired of was I, unless Thou didst heal? Where was I lying, unless Thou didst come to me? Certes with a huge wound I was endangered, but that wound of mine did call for an Almighty Physician. To an Almighty Physician nothing is incurable. . . . Lastly, thinking of all good things whatsoever we may have, either in nature or in purpose, or in conversion itself, in faith, in hope, in charity, in good morals, in justice, in fear of God; all these to be only by His gifts, he hath thus concluded: "My God is my mercy." He being filled with the good things of God hath not found what he might call his God, save "his mercy." O name, under which no one must despair! If thou say, my salvation, I perceive that He giveth salvation; if thou say, my refuge, I perceive that thou takest refuge in Him; if thou say, my strength, I perceive that He giveth to thee strength: "my mercy," is what? All that I am is of Thy mercy. . . .

PSALM LX.[1]

1. David the king was one man, but not one man he figured; sometimes to wit he figured the Church of many men consisting, extended even unto the ends of the earth: but sometimes One Man he figured, Him he figured that is Mediator of God and men, the Man Christ Jesus.[2] In this Psalm therefore, or rather in this Psalm's title, certain victorious actions of David are spoken of: . . . "To the end, in behalf of those men that shall be changed unto the title's inscription, unto teaching for David himself, when he burned up Mesopotamia in Syria, and Syria Sobal, and turned Joab, and smote Edom, in the valley of salt-pits twelve thousand." We read of these things in the books of the Reigns,[3] that all those persons whom he hath named, were defeated by David, that is, Mesopotamia in Syria, and Syria Sobal, Joab,[4] Edom. These things were done, and just as they were done, so there they have been written, so they are read: let him read that will. Nevertheless, as the Prophetic Spirit in the Psalms' titles is wont to depart somewhat from the expression of things done, and to say something which in history is not found, and hence rather to admonish us that titles of this kind have been written not that we may know things done,

but that things future may be prefigured. . . . But here this thing is inserted for this especial reason, that there it is not written[5] that he burned up Mesopotamia in Syria, and Syria Sobal. But now let us begin to examine these things after the significations of things future, and to bring out the dimness of shadows into the light of the word.

2. What is "to the end" ye know. For "the end of the law is Christ."[6] Those that are changed ye know. For who but they that do pass from old life into new? . . . "For ye were sometime darkness, but now light in the Lord."[7] But they are changed "into the title's inscription," . . . who into the kingdom of Christ do pass over from the kingdom of the devil. It is well that they are changed unto this title's inscription. But they are changed, as followeth, "unto teaching." He added, "for David himself unto teaching:" that is, are changed not for themselves, but for David himself, and are changed unto teaching. . . . When therefore would Christ have changed us, unless He had done that which He spake of, "Fire I have come to send into the world"?[8] If therefore Christ came to send into the world fire, to wit to its health and profit, we must inquire not how He is to send the world into fire, but how into the world fire. Inasmuch as therefore He came to send fire into the world, let us inquire what is Mesopotamia which was burned up, what is Syria Sobal? The interpretations therefore of the names let us examine according to the Hebrew language, wherein first this Scripture was written. Mesopotamia[9] they say is interpreted, "exalted calling." Now the whole world by calling hath been exalted, Syria[10] is interpreted "lofty." But she which was lofty, burned up hath been and humbled. Sobal is interpreted "empty antiquity." Thanks to Christ that hath burned her. Whenever old bushes are burned up, green places succeed; and more speedily and more plentifully, and more fully green, fresh ones spring out, when fire hath gone before them to the burning up of the old. Let not therefore the fire of Christ be feared, hay it consumeth. "For all flesh is hay, and all the glory of man as flower of hay."[11] He burneth up therefore those things with that fire. "And turned Joab." Joab is interpreted enemy. There was turned an enemy, as thou wilt understand it. If turned unto flight, the devil it is: if converted to the faith, a Christian it is. How unto flight? From the heart of a Christian: "The Prince of this world," He saith, "now hath been cast out."[12] But how can a Christian turned to the Lord be an enemy turned? Because he hath become a believer that had been an enemy. "Smote Edom." Edom is interpreted "earthly." That earthly one ought

[1] Lat. LIX. Sermon preached to the people a little while after the exposition of the former Psalm.
[2] 1 Tim. ii. 5.   [3] *Vide* 2 Sam. viii.
[4] He seems to take "Joab" as in the accusative, as though it were not the name of David's officer, but of some conquered nation.
[5] *i.e.*, elsewhere.   [6] Εἰς τὸ τέλος, LXX. Rom. x. 4.
[7] Eph. v. 8.   [8] Luke xii. 49.   [9] Aram Naharaim.
[10] Aram.   [11] Isa. xl. 6.   [12] John xii. 31.

to be smitten. For why should one live earthly, that ought to live heavenly? There hath been slain therefore life earthly, let there live life heavenly. "For as we have borne the image of the earthly, let us bear also the image of Him that is from Heaven." [1] See it slain: "Mortify your members which are upon earth." [2] But when he had smitten Edom, he smote "twelve thousand in the valley of salt-pits." Twelve thousand is a perfect number, to which perfect number also the number of the twelve Apostles is ascribed: for not to no purpose is it, but because through the whole world was to be sent the Word. But the Word [3] of God, which is Christ, is in clouds, that is, in the preachers of truth. But the world of four parts doth consist. The four parts thereof are exceeding well known to all, and often in the Scriptures they are mentioned: they are the same as the name of the four winds, East, West, North, and South. To all these four parts was sent the Word, so that in the Trinity all might be called. The number twelve four times three do make. With reason therefore twelve thousand [4] earthly things were smitten, the whole world was smitten: for from the whole world was chosen out the Church, mortified from earthly life. Why "in the valley of salt-pits"? A valley is humility: salt-pits signify savour. For many men are humbled, but emptily and foolishly, in empty oldness they are humbled. One suffereth tribulation for money, suffereth tribulation for temporal honour, suffereth tribulation for the comforts of this life; he is to suffer tribulation and to be humbled: why not for the sake of God? why not for the sake of Christ? why not for the savour of salt? Knowest thou not that to thee hath been said, "Ye are the salt of earth," and, "If the salt shall have been spoiled, for no other thing will it be of use, but to be cast out"? [5] A good thing it is therefore wisely to be humbled. Behold now are not heretics being humbled? Have not laws been made even by men to condemn them, against whom divine laws do reign, which even before had condemned them? Behold they are humbled, behold they are put to flight, behold persecution they suffer, but without savour; for folly, for emptiness. For now the salt hath been spoiled: therefore it hath been cast out, to be trodden down of men. We have heard the title of the Psalm, let us hear also the words of the Psalm.

3. "God, Thou hast driven us back, and hast destroyed us" (ver. 1). Is that David speaking that smote, that burned up, that defeated, and not they to whom He did these things, that is to say, their being smitten and driven back, that were evil men, and again their being made alive

and returning in order that they might be good men? That destruction indeed that David made, strong of hand, our Christ, whose figure that man was bearing; He did those things, He made this destruction with His sword and with His fire: for both He brought into this world. Both "Fire I am come to send into the world," [6] thou hast in the Gospel: and "A sword I have come to send into the earth," [7] thou hast in the Gospel. He brought in fire, whereby might be burned up Mesopotamia in Syria, and Syria Sobal: He brought in a sword whereby might be smitten Edom. Now again this destruction was made for the sake of "those that are changed unto the title's inscription." Hear we therefore the voice of them: to their health smitten they were, being raised up let them speak. Let them say, therefore, that are changed into something better, changed unto the title's inscription, changed unto teaching for David himself; let them say, "Thou hast had mercy upon us." Thou hast destroyed us, in order that Thou mightest build us; Thou hast destroyed us that were ill builded, hast destroyed empty oldness; in order that there may be a building unto a new man, building to abide for everlasting. . . .

4. "Thou hast moved the earth, and hast troubled it" (ver. 2). How hath the earth been troubled? In the conscience of sinners. Whither go we? Whither flee we, when this sword hath been brandished, "Repent, for near hath drawn the kingdom of Heaven"? [8] "Heal the crushings [9] thereof, for moved it hath been." Unworthy it is to be healed, if moved it hath not been: but thou speakest, preachest, threatenest us with God, of coming judgment holdest not thy peace, of the commandment of God thou warnest, from these things thou abstainest not; and he that heareth, if he feareth not, if he is not moved, is not worthy to be healed. Another heareth, is moved, is stung, smiteth the breast, sheddeth tears. . . .

5. The first labour is, that thou shouldest be displeasing to thyself, that sins thou shouldest battle out, that thou shouldest be changed into something better: the second labour, in return for thy having been changed, is to bear the tribulations and temptations of this world, and amid them to hold on even unto the end. Of these things therefore when he was speaking, while pointing out such things, he addeth what? "Thou hast shown to Thy people hard things" (ver. 3): to Thy people now, made tributary after the victory of David. "Thou hast shown to Thy people hard things." Wherein? In persecutions which the Church of Christ hath endured, when so much blood of martyrs was spilled. "Thou hast given us to drink of the

---

[1] 1 Cor. xv. 49.   [2] Col. iii. 5.
[3] Ezek. xxxvii. 9.   [4] [See p. 181, note 12, *supra.* — C.]
[5] Matt. v. 13.

[6] Luke xii. 49.   [7] Matt. x. 34.
[8] Matt. iii. 2.   [9] *Contritiones.*

wine of goading." "Of goading" is what? Not of killing. For it was not a killing that destroyeth, but a medicine that smarteth.[1] "Thou hast given us to drink of the wine of goading."

6. Wherefore this? "Thou hast given to men fearing Thee, a sign that they should flee from the face of the bow" (ver. 4). Through tribulations temporal, he saith, Thou hast signified to Thine own to flee from the wrath of fire everlasting. For, saith the Apostle Peter, "Time it is that Judgment begin with the House of God."[2] And exhorting the Martyrs to endurance, when the world should rage, when slaughters should be made at the hands of persecutors, when far and wide blood of believers should be spilled, when in chains, in prisons, in tortures, many hard things Christians should suffer, in these hard things, I say, lest they should faint, Peter saith to them, "Time it is that Judgment begin with the House of God," etc.[3] What therefore is to be in the Judgment? The bow is bended, still in menacing posture it is, not yet in aiming. And see what there is in the bow: is there not an arrow to be shot forward? The string however is stretched back in a contrary direction to that in which it is going to be shot; and the more the stretching thereof hath gone backward, with the greater swiftness it starteth forward. What is it that I have said? The more the Judgment is deferred, with so much the greater swiftness it is to come. Therefore even for temporal tribulations to God let us render thanks, because He hath given to His people a sign, "that they should flee from the face of the bow:" in order that His faithful ones having been exercised in tribulations temporal, may be worthy to avoid the condemnation of fire everlasting, which is to find out all them that do not believe these things.

7. "That Thy beloved may be delivered: save me with Thy right hand, and hearken unto me" (ver. 5). With Thy right hand save me, Lord: so save me as that at the right hand I may stand. Not any safety temporal I require, in this matter Thy Will be done. For a time what is good for us we are utterly ignorant: for "what we should pray for as we ought we know not:"[4] but "save me with Thy right hand," so that even if in this time I suffer sundry tribulations, when the night of all tribulations hath been spent, on the right hand I may be found among the sheep, not on the left hand among the goats.[5] "And hearken unto me." Because now I am deserving that which Thou art willing to give; not "with the words of my transgressions" I am crying through the day, so that Thou hearken not, and "in the night so that Thou hearken not,"[6] and

that not for folly to me," but truly for my warning, by adding savour from the valley of salt-pits, so that in tribulation I may know what to ask: but I ask life everlasting; therefore hearken unto me, because Thy right hand I ask. . . .

8. "God hath spoken in His Holy One" (ver. 6). . . . In what Holy One of His? "God was in Christ reconciling the world to Himself."[7] In that Holy One, of whom elsewhere ye have heard, "O God, in the Holy One is Thy way."[8] "I will rejoice and will divide Sichima, . . . and the valley of tabernacles I will measure out." Sichima is interpreted shoulders. But according to history, Jacob returning from Laban his father-in-law with all his kindred, hid the idols in Sichima[9] which he had from Syria, where for a long time he had dwelled, and at length was coming from thence. But tabernacles he made there because of his sheep and herds, and called the place Tabernacles.[10] And these I will divide, saith the Church. What is this, "I will divide Sichima"? If to the story where the idols were hidden is the reference, the Gentiles it signifieth; I divide the Gentiles. I divide, is what? "For not in all men is there faith."[11] I divide, is what? Some will believe, others will not believe. . . . The shoulders are divided, in order that their sins may burthen some men, while others may take up the burden of Christ. For godly shoulders He was requiring when He said, "For My yoke is gentle, and My burden is light."[12] Another burden oppresseth and loadeth thee, but Christ's burden relieveth thee: another burden hath weight, Christ's burden hath wings. For even if thou pull off the wings from a bird, thou dost remove a kind of weight; and the more weight thou hast taken away, the more on earth it will abide. She that thou hast chosen to disburden lieth there: she flieth not, because thou hast taken off a weight: let there be given back the weight, and she flieth. Such is Christ's burden; let men carry it, and not be idle: let them not be heeded that will not bear it; let them bear it that will, and they shall find how light it is, how sweet, how pleasant, how ravishing unto Heaven, and from earth how transporting. . . . Perchance because of the sheep of Jacob, "the valley of Tabernacles" is to be understood of the nation of the Jews, and the same is divided: for they have passed from thence that have believed, the rest have remained without.

9. "Mine is Galaad" (ver. 7). These names are read in the Scriptures of God. Galaad hath the voice of an interpretation of its own and of a great Mystery: for it is interpreted "the heap of testimony." How great a heap of testimony in the Martyrs? "Mine is Galaad," mine is a heap of testimony, mine are the true Martyrs.

[1] Lit. "burneth."   [2] 1 Pet. iv. 17.
[3] 1 Pet. iv. 18.   He quotes the whole passage.
[4] Rom. viii. 26.   [5] Matt. xxv. 33.   [6] Ps. xxii. 2.

[7] 2 Cor. v. 19.   [8] Ps. lxxvii. 13.   [9] Gen. xxxv. 4.
[10] *Succoth.*   [11] 2 Thess. iii. 2.   [12] Matt. xi. 30.

. . . Then meanly esteemed was the Church among men, then reproach on Her a Widow was being thrown, because Christ's She was, because the sign of the Cross on her brow She was wearing: not yet was there honour, censure there was then: when therefore not honour, but censure there was, then was made a heap of witness; and through the heap of witness was the Love of Christ enlarged; and through the enlargement of the Love of Christ, were the Gentiles possessed. There followeth, "And mine is Manasses;" which is interpreted forgotten. For to Her had been said, "Confusion for everlasting Thou shalt forget, and of the reproach of Thy widowhood Thou shalt not be mindful." [1] There was therefore a confusion of the Church once, which now hath been forgotten: for of Her confusion and of the "reproach" of Her widowhood now She is not mindful. For when there was a sort of confusion among men, a heap of witness was made. Now no longer doth any even remember that confusion, when it was a reproach to be a Christian, now no one remembereth, now all have forgotten, now "Mine is Manasses, and Ephraim the strength of My head." Ephraim is interpreted fruitfulness. Mine, he saith, is fruitfulness, and this fruitfulness is the strength of My Head. For My Head is Christ. And whence is fruitfulness the strength of Him? Because unless a grain were to fall into the earth, it would not be multiplied, alone it would remain.[2] Fall then to earth did Christ in His Passion, and there followed fruit-bearing in the Resurrection. He was hanging and was being despised: the grain was within, it had powers to draw after it all things. How in a grain do numbers of seeds lie hid, something abject it appeareth to the eyes, but a power[3] turning into itself matter and bringing forth fruit is hidden; so in Christ's Cross virtue[4] was hidden, there appeared weakness. O mighty grain! Doubtless weak is He that hangeth, Doubtless before Him that people did wag the head, Doubtless they said, "If Son of God He is, let Him come down from the Cross."[5] Hear the strength of Him: that which is a weak thing of God, is stronger than men.[6] With reason so great fruitfulness hath followed: it is mine, saith the Church.

10. "Juda is my king: Moab the pot of my hope" (ver. 7). What Juda? He that is of the tribe of Juda. What Juda, but He to whom Jacob himself said, "Juda, thy brethren shall praise thee"?[7] What therefore should I fear, when Juda my king saith, "Fear not them that kill the body"?[8] Moab the pot of my hope." Wherefore "pot"? Because tribulation. Where-

fore "of my hope"? Because there hath gone before Juda my king. . . . Moab is perceived in the Gentiles. For that nation was born of sin,[9] that nation was born of the daughters of Lot, who lay with their father drunken, abusing a father. Better were it to have remained barren, than thus to have become mothers. But this was a kind of figure of them that abuse the law. For do not heed that law in the Latin language is of the feminine gender: in Greek of the masculine gender it is: but whether it be of the feminine gender in speaking, or of the masculine, the expression maketh no difference to the truth. For law hath rather a masculine force, because it ruleth, is not ruled. But moreover, the Apostle Paul saith what? "Good is the law, if any one use it lawfully."[10] But those daughters of Lot unlawfully used their father. But in the same manner as good works begin to grow when a man useth well the law: so arise evil works, when a man ill useth the law. Furthermore, they ill using their father, that is, ill using the law, engendered the Moabites, by whom are signified evil works. Thence the tribulation of the Church, thence the pot boiling up. Of this pot in a certain place of prophecy is said, "A pot heated by the North wind."[11] Whence but by the quarters of the devil, who hath said, "I will set my seat at the North"?[12] The chiefest tribulations therefore arise against the Church from none except from those that ill use the law. . . .

11. "Into Idumæa I will stretch out my shoe" (ver. 8). The Church speaketh, "I will come through even unto Idumæa." Let tribulations rage, let the world boil with offences, even unto those very persons that lead an earthly life (for Idumæa is interpreted earthly), even unto those same, "even unto Idumæa, I will stretch out my shoe." Of what thing the shoe except of the Gospel? "How beautiful the feet of them that tell of peace, that tell of good things,"[13] and "the feet shod unto the preparation of the Gospel of peace."[14] . . . In these times we see, brethren, how many earthly men do perpetrate frauds for the sake of gain, for frauds perjuries; on account of their fears they consult fortune-tellers, astrologers: all these men are Edomites, earthly; and nevertheless all these men adore Christ, under His own shoe they are; now even unto Idumæa is stretched out His shoe. "To Me Allophyli have been made subject." Who are "Allophyli"? Men of other race, not belonging to My race.[15] They "have been made subject," because many men adore Christ, and are not to reign with Christ.

12. "Who will lead Me down into the city of standing round?" (ver. 9). What is the city

[1] Isa. liv. 4.　　　[2] John xii. 24.　　　[3] Vis.
[4] Virtus.　　　[5] Matt. xxvii. 40.　　　[6] 1 Cor. i. 25.
[7] Gen. xlix. 8.　　　[8] Matt. x. 28.
[9] Gen. xix. 37.　　　[10] 1 Tim. i. 8.　　　[11] Jer. i. 13.
[12] Isa. xiv. 13.　　　[13] Rom. x. 15.　　　[14] Eph. vi. 15.
[15] [See Ps. lvi. p. 219, supra. — C.]

of standing round? If ye remember already, I have made mention thereof in another Psalm,[1] wherein hath been said, "And they shall go around the city." For the city of standing round is the compassing around of the Gentiles, which compassing around of the Gentiles in the middle thereof had the one nation of the Jews, worshipping one God : the rest of the compassing around of the Gentiles to idols made supplication, demons they did serve. And mystically it was called the city of standing round ; because on all sides the Gentiles had poured themselves around, and had stood around that nation which did worship one God. . . . "Who will lead me down even unto Idumæa?"

13. "Wilt not Thou, O God, that hast driven us back? And wilt not Thou, O God, march forth in our powers?" (ver. 10). Wilt not Thou lead us down, that hast driven us back? But wherefore "hast driven us back"? Because Thou hast destroyed us.[2] Wherefore hast destroyed us? Because angry Thou hast been, and hast had pity on us. Thou therefore wilt lead down, that hast driven back ; Thou, O God, that wilt not march forth in our powers, wilt lead down. What is, "wilt not march forth in our powers"? The world is to rage, the world is to tread us down, there is to be a heap of witnesses, builded of the spilled blood of martyrs, and the raging heathen are to say, "Where is the God of them?"[3] Then "Thou wilt not march forth in our powers : " against them Thou wilt not show Thyself, Thou wilt not show Thy power, such as Thou hast shown in David, in Moses, in Joshua the son of Nun, when to their might the Gentiles yielded, and when the slaughter had been ended, and the great laying waste repaired, into the land which Thou promisedst Thou leddest in Thy people. This thing then Thou wilt not do, "Thou wilt not march forth in our powers," but within Thou wilt work. What is, "wilt not march forth"? Wilt not show Thyself. For indeed when in chains the Martyrs were being led along, when they were being shut up in prison, when they were being led forth to be mocked, when to the beasts they were exposed,[4] when they were being smitten with the sword, when with fire they were being burned, were they not despised as though forsaken, as though without helper? In what manner was God working within? in what manner within was He comforting? in what manner to these men was He making sweet the hope of life everlasting? in what manner was He not forsaking the hearts of them, where the man was dwelling[5] in silence, well if good, ill if evil? Was He then by any means forsaking, because

He was not marching forth in the powers[6] of them? By not marching forth in the powers of them, did He not the more lead down the Church even unto Idumæa, lead down the Church unto the city of standing around? For if the Church chose to war and to use the sword, She would seem to be fighting for life present : but because she was despising life present, therefore there was made a heap of witness for the life that shall be.

14. Thou therefore, O God, that wilt not march forth in our powers, "Give to us aid from tribulation, and vain is the safety of man " (ver. 11). Go now they that salt have not, and desire safety temporal for their friends, which is empty oldness. " Give to us aid : " from thence whence Thou wast supposed to forsake, thence succour. "In God we will do valour,[7] and Himself to nothing shall bring down our enemies " (ver. 12). We will not do valour with the sword, not with horses, not with breastplates, not with shields, not in the mightiness of an army, not abroad. But where? Within, where we are not seen. Where within? "In God we will do virtue : " and as if abjects, and as if trodden down, men as if of no consideration we shall be, but "Himself to nothing shall bring down our enemies." In a word, this thing hath been done to our enemies. Trodden down have been the Martyrs : by suffering, by enduring, by persevering even unto the end, in God they have done valour. Himself also hath done that which followeth : to nothing He hath brought down the enemies of them. Where are now the enemies of the Martyrs, except perchance that now drunken men with their cups do persecute those whom at that time frenzied men did use with stones to persecute?

PSALM LXI.[8]

1. The title of it doth not detain us. For it is "Unto the end, in hymns, to David himself. "In hymns," to wit in praises. "Unto the end," to wit unto Christ. . . . But the voice in this Psalm (if we are among the members of Him, and in the Body, even as upon His exhortation we have the boldness to trust) we ought to acknowledge to be our own, not that of any foreigner. But I have not so called it our own, as if it were of those only that are now in presence ; but our own, as being of us that are throughout the whole world, that are from the East even unto the West. And in order that ye may know it thus to be our voice, He speaketh here as if one Man : but He is not One Man ; but even as One, the Unity is speaking. But in Christ we all are one man : because of this One

[1] *Vide* Ps. lix. 6, p. 240, *supra*.   [2] Ps. lx. 1.
[3] Ps. lxxix. 10.   [4] *Subrigebantur.*
[5] Oxf. mss. "dwelleth."
[6] Or, " hosts" (*virtutibus*).   [7] *Virtutem.*
[8] Lat. LX. Sermon to the Commonalty.

Man the Head is in Heaven, and the members are yet toiling on earth: and because they are toiling see what He saith.[1]

2. "Hearken, O God, to my supplication, give heed to my prayer" (ver. 1). Who saith? He, as if One. See whether one: "From the ends of the earth to Thee I have cried, while my heart was being vexed" (ver. 2). Now therefore not one: but for this reason one, because Christ is One, of whom all we are the members. For what one man crieth from the ends of the earth? There crieth not from the ends of the earth any but that inheritance, of which hath been said to the Son Himself, "Demand of Me, and I will give to Thee the nations for Thine inheritance, and for Thy possession the boundaries of the earth."[2] This therefore Christ's possession, this Christ's inheritance, this Christ's Body, this Christ's one Church, this the Unity which we are, is crying from the ends of the earth. . . . But wherefore have I cried this thing? "While my heart was being vexed." He showeth himself to be throughout all nations in the whole round world, in great glory, but in great tribulation. For our life in this sojourning cannot be without temptation: because our advance is made through our temptation, nor does a man become known to himself unless tempted, nor can he be crowned except he shall have conquered, nor can he conquer except he shall have striven, nor can he strive except he shall have experienced an enemy, and temptations. This Man therefore is being vexed, that from the ends of the earth is crying, but nevertheless He is not forsaken. For ourselves who are His Body He hath willed to prefigure also in that His Body wherein already He hath both died and hath risen again, and into Heaven hath ascended, in order that whither the Head hath gone before, thither the members may be assured that they shall follow. Therefore us He did transfer by a figure into Himself, when He willed to be tempted of Satan.

3. But now there was read in the Gospel, how the Lord Jesus Christ in the wilderness was being tempted of the devil.[3] Christ entirely was tempted of the devil. For in Christ thou wast being tempted, because Christ of thee had for Himself flesh, of Himself for thee salvation; of thee for Himself death, of Himself for thee life; of thee for Himself revilings, of Himself for thee honours; therefore of thee for Himself temptation, of Himself for thee victory. If in Him tempted we have been, in Him we overcome the devil. . . . "On the Rock Thou hast exalted me." Now therefore here we perceive who is crying from the ends of the earth. Let us call to mind the Gospel: "Upon this Rock I will build My Church."[4] Therefore She crieth from the ends of the earth, whom He hath willed to be builded upon a Rock. But in order that the Church might be builded upon the Rock, who was made the Rock? Hear Paul saying: "But the Rock was Christ."[5] On Him therefore builded we have been. For this reason that Rock whereon we have been builded,[6] first hath been smitten with winds, flood, rain, when Christ of the devil was being tempted. Behold on what firmness He hath willed to stablish thee. With reason our voice is not in vain, but is hearkened unto: for on great hope we have been set: "On the Rock Thou hast exalted me." . . .

4. "Thou hast led me down, because Thou hast been made my hope: a tower of strength from the face of the enemy" (ver. 3). My heart is vexed, saith that Unity from the ends of the earth, and I toil amid temptations and offences: the heathen envy, because they have been conquered; the heretics lie in wait, hidden in the cloak of the Christian name: within in the Church itself the wheat suffereth violence from the chaff: amid all these things when my heart is vexed, I will cry from the ends of the earth. But there forsaketh me not the Same that hath exalted me upon the Rock, in order to lead me down even unto Himself, because even if I labour, while the devil through so many places and times and occasions lieth in wait against me, He is to me a tower of strength, to whom when I shall have fled for refuge, not only I shall escape the weapons of the enemy, but even against him securely I shall myself hurl whatever darts I shall please. For Christ Himself is the tower, Himself for us hath been made a tower from the face of the enemy, who is also the Rock whereon hath been builded the Church. Art thou taking heed that thou be not smitten of the devil? Flee to the Tower; never to that tower will the devil's darts follow thee: there thou wilt stand protected and fixed. But in what manner shalt thou flee to the Tower? Let not a man, set perchance in temptation, in body seek that Tower, and when he shall not have found it, be wearied, or faint in temptation. Before thee is the Tower: call to mind Christ, and go into the Tower.[7] . . .

5. "A sojourner I will be in Thy tabernacle even unto ages" (ver. 4). Ye see how he, of whom we have spoken, is he that crieth. Which of us is a sojourner even unto ages? For a few days here we live, and we pass away: for sojourners here we are, inhabitants in Heaven we shall be. Thou art a sojourner in that place where thou art to hear the voice of the Lord

---

[1] Or, "they say," mss.   [2] Ps. ii. 8.   [3] Matt. iv. 1.

[4] Matt. xvi. 18.
[5] 1 Cor. x. 4. [Rhetorically he may say this of Cephas; but as of Peter's confession elsewhere, so here, *dogmatically* he understands only Christ. Compare p. 223, *supra*.—C.]
[6] Matt. vii. 24.   [7] [Zech. ix. 12.—C.]

thy God, "Remove." For from that Home everlasting in the Heavens no one will bid thee to remove. Here therefore a sojourner thou art. Whence also is said in another Psalm, "A sojourner I am with Thee and a stranger, as all my fathers were."[1] Here therefore sojourners we are; there the Lord shall give to us mansions everlasting: "Many are," He saith, "the mansions in My Father's house."[2] Those mansions not as though to sojourners He will give, but as though to citizens to abide for everlasting. Here however, brethren, because for no small time the Church was to be on this earth, but because here shall be the Church even unto the end of the world:[3] therefore here He hath said, "A dweller I will be in Thy tabernacle even unto ages."[4] . . . Well, of a few days thou wouldest choose that the temptations should be: but how would She gather together all Her sons, unless for a long time She were to be here, unless even unto the end She were to be prolonged? Do not envy the rest of mankind that hereafter shall be: do not, because thou hast already passed over, wish to cut down the bridge of mercy:[5] be it here even for ever. And what of temptations, which needs must abound, by how much the more offences come? For Himself saith, "Because iniquity hath abounded, the love of many shall wax cold."[6] But that Church, which crieth from the ends of the earth, is in these circumstances whereof he speaketh in continuation. "But he that shall have persevered even unto the end, the same shall be saved." But whence shalt thou persevere? . . . "I shall be covered up in the veiling of Thy wings." Behold the reason why we are in safety amid so great temptations, until there come the end of the world, and ages everlasting receive us; namely, because we are covered up in the veiling of His Wings. There is heat in the world, but there is a great shade under the wings of God.

6. "For Thou, O God, hast hearkened to my prayer" (ver. 5). What prayer? That wherewith he beginneth: "Hearken, O God, to my supplication." . . . "Thou hast given inheritance to men fearing Thy name." Let us continue therefore in the fear of God's name: the eternal Father deceiveth us not. Sons labour, that they may receive the inheritance of their parents, to whom when dead they are to succeed: are we not labouring to receive an inheritance from that Father, to whom not dying we succeed; but together with Him in the very inheritance for everlasting are to live?

7. "Days upon days of the King Thou shalt add to the years of Him" (ver. 6). This is therefore the King of whom we are the members. A King Christ is, our Head, our King. Thou hast given to Him days upon days; not only those days in that time that hath end, but days upon those days without end. "I will dwell," he saith, "in the house of the Lord, for length of days."[7] Wherefore for length of days, but because now is the shortness of days? For everything which hath an end, is short: but of this King are days upon days, so that not only while these days pass away, Christ reigneth in His Church, but the Saints shall reign together with Him in those days which have no end. . . . For years of God have been also spoken of: "But Thou art the very Same, and Thy years shall not fail."[8] In the same manner as years, so days, so one day. Whatsoever thou wilt thou sayest of eternity. Whatever thou wilt thou sayest for this reason, because whatever thou shalt have said, it is too little that thou hast said. For thou must needs say somewhat, to the end that there may be something whereby thou mayest meditate on that which cannot be told. "Even unto the day of generation and of generation." Of this generation and of the generation that shall be: of this generation which is compared to the moon, because as the moon is new, waxeth, is full, waneth, and vanisheth, so are these mortal generations; and of the generation wherein we are born anew by rising again, and shall abide for everlasting with God, when now no longer we are like the moon, but like that of which saith the Lord, "Then the righteous shall shine like the sun in the kingdom of their Father."[9] For the moon by a figure in the Scriptures is put for the mutability of this mortal state. . . .

8. "He shall abide for everlasting in the sight of God" (ver. 7); according to what, or because of what? "His mercy and truth who shall seek for Him?" He saith also in another place, "All the ways of the Lord are mercy and truth, to men seeking His testament and His testimonies."[10] Large is the discourse of truth and mercy, but shortness we have promised. Briefly hear ye what is truth and mercy: because no small thing is that which hath been said, "All the ways of the Lord are mercy and truth." Mercy is spoken of, because our merits God regarded not, but His own goodness, in order that He might forgive us all our sins, and might promise life everlasting: but truth is spoken of, because He faileth not to render those things which He hath promised. Let us acknowledge it here, and let us do it; so that, just as to us God hath shown forth His mercy and His truth, mercy in forgiving our sins, truth in showing forth His promises; so also, I say, let us execute mercy and truth, mercy concerning the weak,

---

[1] Ps. xxxix. 12.   [2] John xiv. 2.
[3] Sæculi.   [4] Sæcula.
[5] Many omit "of mercy." [6] Matt. xxiv. 12.
[7] Ps. xxvii. 4.   [8] Ps. cii. 27.   [9] Matt. xiii. 43.
[10] Ps. xxv. 10.

concerning the needy, concerning even our enemies; truth in not sinning, and in not adding
sin upon sin. . . . Who is therefore he that
doeth this, save one out of those few, of whom
is said, "He that shall have continued unto the
end, the same shall be saved"? With reason here
also "His mercy and truth who shall seek for
Him?" Why is there "for Him"? "Who shall
seek," would be sufficient. Why hath he added,
"for Him," but because many men seek to learn
His mercy and truth in His books? And when
they have learned, for themselves they live, not
for Him;[1] their own things they seek, not the
things which are of Jesus Christ:[2] they preach
mercy and truth, and do not mercy and truth.
But by preaching it, they know it: for they
would not preach it, unless they knew it. But
he that loveth God and Christ, in preaching the
mercy and truth of the Same, doth himself seek
her for Him, not for himself: that is, not in
order that himself may have by this preaching
temporal advantages, but in order that he may
do good to His members, that is, His faithful
ones, by ministering with truth of that which he
knoweth: in order that he that liveth, no longer
for himself may live, but for Him that for all
men hath died.[1]

9. "So I will play music to Thy name, that
I may render my vows from day unto day" (ver.
8). If thou playest music to the name of God,
play not for a time. Wilt thou for ever play?
wilt thou for everlasting play? Render to Him
thy vows from day unto day. What is, render
to Him thy vows from day unto day? From
this day unto that day. Continue to render
vows in this day, until thou come to that day:
that is, "He that shall have continued even unto
the end, the same shall be saved."[3]

PSALM LXII.[4]

1. The title of it is, "Unto the end, in behalf
of Idithun, a Psalm to David himself." I
recollect that already[5] to you hath been explained what Idithun is. . . . Let us see how
far he hath leaped over, and whom he hath
"leaped over," and in what place, though he
hath leaped over certain men, he is situate,
whence as from a kind of spiritual and secure
position he may behold what is below. . . . He
being set, I say, in a certain fortified place,
doth say, "Shall not my soul be subject to
God?" (ver. 1). For he had heard, "He that
doth exalt himself shall be humbled; and he
that humbleth himself shall be exalted:"[6] and
fearful lest by leaping over he should be proud,

not elated by those things which were below,
but humble because of Him that was above; to
envious men, as it were threatening to him a
fall, who were grieved that he had leaped over,
he hath made answer, "Shall not my soul be
subject to God?" . . . "For from Himself is
my salvation." "For Himself is my God and my
salvation, my taker up, I shall not be moved
more"(ver. 2). I know who is above me, I know
who stretcheth forth His mercy to men that
know Him, I know under the coverings of whose
wings I should hope: "I shall not be moved
more." . . .

2. Therefore, down from the higher place
fortified and protected, he, to whom the Lord
hath been made a refuge, he, to whom is God
Himself for a fortified place,[7] hath regard to
those whom he hath leaped over, and looking
down upon them speaketh as though from a
lofty tower: for this also hath been said of Him,
"A Tower of strength from the face of the
enemy:"[8] he giveth heed therefore to them, and
saith, "How long do ye lay upon a man?" (ver.
3). By insulting, by hurling reproaches, by laying wait, by persecuting, ye lay upon a man
burthens, ye lay upon a man as much as a
man can[9] bear: but in order that a man may
bear, under him is He that hath made man. If
to a man ye look, "slay ye, all of you." Behold, lay upon, rage, "slay ye, all of you." "As
though a wall bowed down, and as a fence
smitten against;" lean against, smite against, as
if going to throw down. And where is, "I shall
not be moved more"? But wherefore? "I
shall not be moved more." Because Himself is
God my Saving One, my taker up, therefore ye
men are able to lay burdens upon a man; can
ye anywise lay upon God, who protecteth man?
"Slay ye, all of you." What is that size of body in
one man so great as that he may be slain by all?
But we ought to perceive our person, the person
of the Church, the person of the Body of Christ.
For one Man with His Head and Body is Jesus
Christ, the Saviour of the Body and the Members of the Body: two in one Flesh,[10] and in one
voice, and in one passion, and, when iniquity
shall have passed over, in one rest. The sufferings therefore of Christ are not in Christ alone;
nay, there are not any save in Christ. For if
Christ thou understandest to be Head and Body,
the sufferings of Christ are not, save in Christ:
but if Christ thou understand of Head alone,
the sufferings of Christ are not in Christ alone. For
if the sufferings of Christ are in Christ alone, to
wit in the Head alone; whence saith a certain
member of Him, Paul the Apostle, "In order
that I may supply what are wanting of the oppressions of Christ in my flesh"?[11] If therefore

---

[1] 2 Cor. v. 15.　　　　　　[2] Philip. ii. 21.
[3] Matt. xxiv. 13.
[4] Lat. LXI. Sermon to the people.
[5] On Ps. xxxix. p. 113, *supra*.　　[6] Matt. xxiii. 12.

[7] Ps. xc. 1.　　[8] Ps. lxi. 3.　　[9] Some MSS. "cannot."
[10] Gen. ii. 24; Eph. v. 31.　　[11] Col. i. 24.

in the members of Christ thou art, whatsoever man thou art that art hearing these words, whosoever thou art that dost hear these words (but however, thou dost hear, if in the members of Christ thou art) : whatsoever thing thou sufferest from those that are not in the members of Christ, was wanting to the sufferings of Christ. Therefore it is added because it was wanting ; thou fillest up the measure, thou causest it not to run over : thou sufferest so much as was to be contributed out of thy sufferings to the whole suffering of Christ, that hath suffered in our Head, and doth suffer in His members, that is, in our own selves.   Unto this our common republic, as it were each of us according to our measure payeth that which we owe, and according to the powers which we have, as it were a quota[1] of sufferings we contribute.   The storehouse[2] of all men's sufferings will not be completely made up, save when the world shall have been ended. . . . That whole City therefore is speaking, from the blood of righteous Abel even to the blood of Zacharias.[3]   Thence also hereafter from the blood of John, through the blood of the Apostles, through the blood of Martyrs, through the blood of the faithful ones of Christ, one City speaketh, one man saith, " How long do ye lay upon a man ?   Slay ye, all of you."   Let us see if ye efface, let us see if ye extinguish, let us see if ye remove from the earth the name thereof, let us see if ye peoples do not meditate of empty things,[4] saying, " When shall She die, and when shall perish the name of Her ? "[5]   " As though She were a wall bowed down, and a fence smitten against,"[6] lean ye against Her, smite against Her. Hear from above :[7] " My taker up, I shall not be moved more : " for as though a heap of sand I have been smitten against that I might fall, and the Lord hath taken me up.

3. " Nevertheless, mine honour they have thought to drive back " (ver. 4).   Conquered while they slay men yielding, by the blood of the slain multiplying the faithful, yielding to these and no longer being able to kill ; " Nevertheless, mine honour they have thought to drive back." Now because a Christian cannot be killed, pains are taken that a Christian should be dishonoured. For now by the honour of Christians the hearts of ungodly men are tortured : now that spiritual Joseph, after his selling by his brethren, after his removal from his home into Egypt as though into the Gentiles, after the humiliation of a prison,[8] after the made-up tale of a false witness, after that there had come to pass that which of him was said, " Iron passed through the soul of him : "[9] now he is honoured, now he is not made subject

to brethren selling him, but corn he supplieth to them hungering.[10]   Conquered by his humility and chastity, uncorruptness, temptations, sufferings, now honoured they see him, and his honour they think to check. . . . Is it all against one man, or one man against all ; or all against all, or one against one?   Meanwhile, when he saith, " ye lay upon a man," it is as it were upon one man : and when he saith, " Slay all ye," it is as if all men were against one man : but nevertheless it is also all against all, because also all are Christians, but in One.   But why must those divers errors hostile to Christ be spoken of as all together?   Are they also one?   Truly them also as one I dare to speak of : because there is one City and one city, one People and one people, King and king.   One City and one city is what?   Babylon one, Jerusalem one.   By whatsoever other mystical names besides She is called, yet One City there is and one city ; over this the devil is king, over that Christ is King. . . .

4. Give heed, brethren, give heed, I entreat you.   For it delighteth me yet to speak a few words to you of this beloved City.   For " most glorious things of Thee have been spoken, City of God."[11]   And, " if I forget Thee, O Jerusalem, let mine own right hand forget me."[12]   For dear is the one Country, and truly but one Country, the only Country : besides Her whatsoever we have, is a sojourning in a strange land.   I will say therefore that which ye may acknowledge, that of which ye may approve : I will call to your minds that which ye know, I will not teach that which ye know not.   " Not first," saith the Apostle, " that which is spiritual, but that which is natural,[13] afterwards that which is spiritual."[14] Therefore the former city is greater by age, because first was born Cain, and afterwards Abel :[15] but in these the elder shall serve the younger.[16] The former greater by age, the latter greater in dignity.   Wherefore is the former greater by age?   Because " not first that which is spiritual, but that which is natural."[14]   Wherefore is the latter greater in dignity?   Because " the elder shall serve the younger."[16] . . . Cain first builded a city, and in that place he builded where no city was.   But when Jerusalem was being builded, it was not builded in a place where there was not a city, but there was a city at first which was called Jebus, whence the Jebusites.   This having been captured, overcome, made subject, there was builded a new city, as though the old were thrown down ; and it was called Jerusalem,[17] vision of peace, City of God.   Each one therefore that is born of Adam, not yet doth belong to Jerusalem : for he beareth with him

---

[1] *Canonem.*   [2] *Pariatoria.*   [3] Matt. xxiii. 35.
[4] Ps. ii. 1.   [5] Ps. xli. 5.   [6] Ps. cxviii. 13.
[7] § 1, p. 251, *supra.*
[8] Gen. xxxvii. 36, xxxix. 20.   [9] Ps. cv. 18.

[10] Gen. xlii. 5.   [11] Ps. lxxxvii. 3.   [12] Ps. cxxxvii. 5.
[13] Or, " animal."   [14] 1 Cor. xv. 46.   [15] Gen. iv. 1, 2.
[16] Gen. xxv. 23.   [17] Josh. xviii. 28.

the offshoot[1] of iniquity, and the punishment of sin, having been consigned to death, and he belongeth in a manner to a sort of old city. But if he is to be in the people of God; his old self will be thrown down, and he will be builded up new. For this reason therefore Cain builded a city where there was not a city. For from mortality and from naughtiness every one setteth out, in order that he may be made good hereafter. "For as by the disobedience of one man many were made sinners, so by the obedience of One Man many shall be made just."[2] And all we in Adam do die:[3] and each one of us of Adam was born. Let him pass over to Jerusalem, he shall be thrown down old, and shall be builded new. As though to conquered Jebusites, in order that there may be builded up Jerusalem, is said, "Put ye off the old man, and put on the new."[4] And now to them builded in Jerusalem, and shining by the light of Grace, is said, "Ye have been sometime darkness, but now light in the Lord."[5] The evil city therefore from the beginning even unto the end doth run on, and the good City by the changing of evil men is builded up. And these two cities are meanwhile mingled, at the end to be severed; against each other mutually in conflict, the one for iniquity, the other for the truth. And sometimes this very temporal mingling bringeth it to pass that certain men belonging to the city Babylon, do order matters belonging to Jerusalem, and again certain men belonging to Jerusalem, do order matters belonging to Babylon. Something difficult I seem to have propounded. Be ye patient, until it be proved by examples. "For all things" in the old people, as writeth the Apostle, "in a figure used to befall them: but they have been written for our amendment, upon whom the end of the world hath come."[6] Regard therefore that people as also set to intimate an after people; and see then what I say. There were great[7] kings in Jerusalem: it is a known fact, they are enumerated, are named. They all were, I say, wicked citizens of Babylon, and they were ordering matters of Jerusalem: all men from thence to be dissevered at the end, to no one but to the devil do belong. Again we find citizens of Jerusalem to have ordered certain matters belonging to Babylon. For those three children, Nabuchodonosor, overcome by a miracle, made the ministers of his kingdom, and set them over his Satraps; and so there were ordering the matters of Babylon citizens of Jerusalem.[8] Observe now how this is being fulfilled and done in the Church, and in these times. ... Every earthly commonwealth, sometime

assuredly to perish, whereof the kingdom is to pass away, when there shall come that kingdom, whereof we pray, "Thy kingdom come;"[9] and whereof hath been foretold, "And of His kingdom shall be no end:"[10] an earthly commonwealth, I say, hath our citizens conducting the affairs of it. For how many faithful, how many good men, are both magistrates in their cities, and are judges, and are generals, and are counts, and are kings? All that are just and good men, having not anything in heart but the most glorious things, which of Thee have been said, City of God.[11] And as if they were doing bond-service[12] in the city which is to pass away, even there by the doctors of the Holy City they are bidden to keep faith with those set over them, "whether with the king as supreme, or with governors as though sent by God for the punishment of evil men, but for the praise of good men:[13]" or as servants, that to their masters they should be subject,[14] even Christians to Heathens, and the better should keep faith with the worse, for a time to serve, for everlasting to have dominion. For these things do happen until iniquity do pass away.[15] Servants are commanded to bear with masters unjust and capricious: the citizens of Babylon are commanded to be endured by the citizens of Jerusalem, showing even more attentions, than if they were citizens of the same Babylon, as though fulfilling the precept, "He that shall have exacted of thee a mile, go with him other twain."[16] ...

5. "I have run in thirst."[17] For they were rendering evil things for good things:[18] for them was I thirsting: mine honour they thought to drive back: I was thirsting to bring them over into my body. For in drinking what do we, but send into our members liquor that is without, and suck it into our body? Thus did Moses in that head of the calf.[19] The head of the calf is a great sacrament.[20] For the head of the calf was the body of ungodly men, in the similitude of a calf eating hay,[21] seeking earthly things: because all flesh is hay.[22] ... And what now is more evident, than that into that City Jerusalem, of which the people Israel was a type, by Baptism men were to be made to pass over? Therefore in water it was scattered, in order that for drink it might be given. For this even unto the end this man thirsteth; he runneth and thirsteth. For many men He drinketh, but never will He be without thirst. For thence is, "I thirst, woman, give Me to drink."[23] That Samaritan

---

[1] *Traducem.*   [2] Rom. v. 19.   [3] 1 Cor. xv. 22.
[4] Col. iii. 9, 10; Eph. iv. 22, 24.   [5] Eph. v. 8.
[6] 1 Cor. x. 11.   [7] *Magni.* Ben. conj. *Mali,* "evil."
[8] Dan. ii. 48, iii. 30.

[9] Matt. vi. 10.   [10] Luke i. 33.   [11] Ps. lxxxvii. 3.
[12] *Angariam.*   [13] 1 Pet. ii. 13, 14.   [14] Eph. vi. 5.
[15] Ps. lvii. 1.   [16] Matt. v. 41.
[17] Thus Septuagint; E. V. "Their delight is in lies."
[18] Ps. xxxv. 12.   [19] Exod. xxxii. 10.
[20] [The non-technical use of this word, here and elsewhere, by our author must be noted. Just so the Anglican Church speaks of matrimony as a sacrament, while jealously guarding the two which are sacraments, κατ' ἐξοχὴν. — C.]
[21] Ps. cvi. 20.   [22] Isa. xl. 6.   [23] John iv. 7.

woman at the well found the Lord thirsting, and by Him thirsting she was filled: she first found Him thirsting, in order that He might drink her believing. And when He was on the Cross, " I thirst,"[1] He said, although they gave not to Him that for which He was thirsting. For for themselves He was thirsting: but they gave vinegar, not new wine, wherewith are filled up the new bottles, but old wine, but old to its loss.[2] For old vinegar also is said of the old men, of whom hath been said, " For to them is no changing; "[3] namely, that the Jebusites should be overthrown, and Jerusalem be builded.[4]

6. So also the Head of this body even unto the end from the beginning runneth in thirst. And as if to Him were being said, Why in thirst? what is wanting to Thee, O Body of Christ, O Church of Christ? in so great honour, in so great exaltation, in so great height also even in this world established, what is wanting to Thee? There is fulfilled that which hath been foretold of thee, " There shall adore Him all kings of the earth, all nations shall serve Him."[5] . . . They that at Jerusalem's festivals fill up the Churches, at Babylon's festivals fill up the theatres: and for all they serve, honour, obey Her — not only those very persons that bear the Sacraments of Christ, and hate the commandments of Christ, but also they, that bear not even the mere Sacraments, Heathen though they be, Jews though they be, — they honour, praise, proclaim, " but with their mouths they were blessing." I heed not the mouth, He knoweth that hath instructed me, " with their heart they were cursing." In that place they were cursing, where " mine honour they thought to drive back."

7. What dost Thou, O Idithun, Body of Christ, leaping over them? What dost Thou amid all these things? What wilt Thou? wilt faint? wilt Thou not persevere even unto the end? wilt Thou not hearken, " He that shall have persevered even unto the end, the same shall be saved,"[6] though for that iniquity aboundeth, the love of many shall wax cold?[7] And where is it that Thou hast leaped over them? where is it that Thy conversation is in Heaven?[8] But they cleave unto earthly things, as though earthborn they mind the earth, and are earth, the serpent's food.[9] What dost thou amid these things? . . . " Nevertheless, to God my soul shall be made subject" (ver. 5). And who would endure so great things, either open wars, or secret lyings-in-wait? Who would endure so great things amid open enemies, amid false brethren? Who would endure so great things? Would a man? and if a man would, would a man of himself? I have not so leaped over that

I should be lifted up, and fall: " To God my soul shall be made subject: for from Himself is my patience." What patience is there amid so great scandals, except that " if for that which we do not see we hope, through patience we look for it"?[10] There cometh my pain, there will come my rest also; there cometh my tribulation, there will come my cleansing also. For doth gold glitter in the furnace of the refiner? In a necklace it will glitter, in an ornament it will glitter: let it suffer however the furnace, in order that being cleansed from dross it may come into light. This is the furnace, there is there chaff, there gold, there fire, into this bloweth the refiner: in the furnace burneth the chaff, and the gold is cleansed; the one into ashes is turned, of dross the other is cleansed. The furnace is the world, the chaff unrighteous men, the gold just men; the fire tribulation, the refiner God: that which therefore the refiner willeth I do; wherever the Maker setteth me I endure it. I am commanded to endure, He knoweth how to cleanse. Though there burn the chaff to set me on fire, and as if to consume me; that into ashes is burned, I of dross am cleansed. Wherefore? Because " to God my soul shall be made subject: for from Himself is my patience."

8. " For Himself is my God and My Saving One, my Taker up, I will not remove hence " (ver. 6). Because " Himself is my God," therefore He calleth me: " and my Saving One," therefore He justifieth me: " and my Taker up," therefore He glorifieth me. For here I am called and am justified, but there I am glorified; and from thence where I am glorified, " I will not remove." For a sojourner I am with Thee on earth as all my fathers were. Therefore from my lodging I shall remove, from my Heavenly home I shall not remove. " In God is my salvation and my glory " (ver. 7). Saved I shall be in God, glorious I shall be in God: for not only saved, but also glorious, saved, because a just man I have been made out of an ungodly man, by Him justified;[11] but glorious, because not only justified, but also honoured. For " those whom He hath predestined, those also He hath called."[12] Calling them, what hath He done here? " Whom He hath called, the same also He hath justified; but whom He hath justified, the same also He hath glorified." Justification therefore to salvation belongeth, glorifying to honour. How glorifying to honour belongeth, it is not needful to discuss. How justification belongeth to salvation, let us seek some proof. Behold there cometh to mind out of the Gospel: there were some who to themselves were seeming to be just men, and they were finding fault with the Lord because He

---

1 John xix. 28.   2 Matt. ix. 17.   3 Ps. lv. 19.
4 2 Sam. v. 9.   5 Ps. lxxii. 11.   6 Matt. x. 22.
7 Matt. xxiv. 12.   8 Philip. iii. 20.   9 Gen. iii. 14.

10 Rom. viii. 25.   11 Rom. iv. 2.   12 Rom. viii. 30.

admitted to the feast sinners, and with publicans and sinners was eating; to such men therefore priding themselves, strong men of earth very much lifted up, much glorying of - their own soundness, such as they counted it, not such as they had, the Lord answered what? "They that are whole need not a Physician, but they that are sick." [1] Whom calleth He whole, whom calleth He sick? He continueth and saith, " I have not come to call just men, but sinners unto repentance." [2] He hath called therefore " the whole " just men, not because the Pharisees were so, but because themselves they thought so to be ; and for this reason were proud, and grudged sick men a physician, and being more sick than those, they slew the Physician. He hath called whole, however, righteous men, sick, the sinners. My being justified therefore, saith that man that leapeth over, from Himself I have : my being glorified, from Himself I have : " For God is my salvation and my glory." " My salvation," so that saved I am : " my glory," so that honoured I am. This thing hereafter : now what? " God of my help, and my hope is in God ; " until I attain unto perfect justification and salvation. " For by hope we are saved : but hope which is seen, is not hope." [3] . . .

9. " Hope ye in Him, all the council of the people " (ver. 8). Imitate ye Idithun, leap over your enemies ; men fighting against you, stopping up your way, men hating you, leap ye over : " Hope in Him all the council of the people : pour out before Him your hearts : " . . . By imploring, by confessing, by hoping. Do not keep back your hearts within your hearts : " Pour out before Him your hearts." That perisheth not which ye pour out. For He is my Taker up. If He taketh up, why fearest thou to pour out? " Cast upon the Lord thy care, and hope in Him." [4] What fear ye amid whisperers, slanderers hateful to God, [5] where they are able openly assailing, where they are unable secretly lying in wait, falsely praising, truly at enmity, amid them what fear ye? " God is our Helper." Do they anywise equal God? Are they anywise stronger than He? " God is our Helper," be ye without care. " If God is for us, who is against us?" [6] " Pour out before Him your hearts," by leaping over unto Him, by lifting up your souls : " God is our helper." . . . " Nevertheless, vain are the sons of men, and liars are the sons of men in the balances, in order that they may deceive, being at one because of vanity " (ver. 9). Certainly many men there are : behold there is that one man, that one man that was cast forth from the multitude of guests. [7] They conspire, they all seek things temporal, and they that are carnal

things carnal, and for the future they hope them, whosoever do hope : even if because of variety of opinions they are in division, nevertheless because of vanity they are at one. Divers indeed are errors and of many forms, and the kingdom against itself divided shall not stand : [8] but alike in all is the will vain and lying, belonging to one king, with whom into fire everlasting it is to be thrown headlong [9]—" these men because of vanity are at one." And for them see how He thirsteth, see how He runneth in thirst.

10. He turneth therefore Himself to them, thirsting for them : " Do not hope in iniquity " (ver. 10). For my hope is in God. Ye that will not draw near and pass over, " do not hope in iniquity." For I that have leapt over, my hope is in God ; and is there anywise iniquity with God? [10] This thing let us do, that thing let us do, of that thing let us think, thus let us adjust our lyings in wait ; " Because of vanity being at one." Thou thirstest : they that think of those things against thee are given up by those whom thou drinkest, " Do not hope in vanity." Vain is iniquity, nought is iniquity, mighty is nothing save righteousness. Truth may be hidden for a time, conquered it cannot be. Iniquity may flourish for a time, abide it cannot. " Do not hope upon iniquity : and for robbery be not covetous." Thou art not rich, and wilt thou rob? What findest thou? What losest thou? O losing gains ! Thou findest money, thou losest righteousness. " For robbery be not covetous." . . . Therefore, vain sons of men, lying sons of men, neither rob, nor, if there flow riches, set heart upon them : no longer love vanity, and seek lying. For " blessed is the man who hath the Lord God for his hope, and who hath not had regard unto vanities, and lying follies." [11] Ye would deceive, ye would commit a fraud, what bring ye in order that ye may cheat. Deceitful balances. For " lying," he saith, " are the sons of men in the balances," in order that they may cheat by bringing forth deceitful balances. By a false balance ye beguile men looking on : know ye not that one is he that weigheth, Another He that judgeth of the weight? He seeth not, for whom thou weighest, but He seeth that weigheth thee and him. Therefore neither fraud nor robbery covet ye any longer, nor on those things which ye have set your hope : [12] I have admonished, have foretold, saith this Idithun.

11. What followeth? " Once hath God spoken, these two things I have heard, that power is of God (ver. 11), and to Thee, O Lord, is mercy, for Thou shalt render to each one after his works " (ver. 12). . . . " Once hath God spoken." What sayest thou, Idithun? If thou that hadst leapt over them art saying, " Once He hath

---

[1] Matt. ix. 13.　　[2] Matt. ix. 12.　　[3] Rom. viii. 24.
[4] Ps lv. 22.　　[5] Rom. i. 29, 30.　　[6] Rom. viii. 31.
[7] Matt. xxii. 11.

[8] Matt. xii. 25.　　[9] Matt. xxv. 41.　　[10] Rom. ix. 14.
[11] Ps. xl. 4.　　[12] Luke xii. 15.　St. Augustin, *habet.*

spoken;" I turn to another Scripture and it saith to me, "In many quarters and in many ways formerly God hath spoken to the fathers in the prophets."[1] What is, "Once hath God spoken"? Is He not the God that in the beginning of mankind spake to Adam?[2] Did not the Selfsame speak to Cain, to Noe, to Abraham, to Isaac, to Jacob, to all the Prophets, and to Moses?[3] One man Moses was, and how often to him spake God? Behold even to one man, not once but ofttimes God hath spoken. Secondly, He hath spoken to the Son when standing here, "Thou art My beloved Son."[4] God hath spoken to the Apostles, He hath spoken to all the Saints, even though not with voice sounding through the cloud, nevertheless in the heart where He is Himself Teacher.[5] What is therefore, "Once hath God spoken"? Much hath that man leapt over in order to arrive at that place, where once God hath spoken. Behold briefly I have spoken to your Love. Here among men, to men ofttimes, in many ways, in many quarters, through creatures of many forms God hath spoken: by Himself once God hath spoken, because One Word God hath begotten. . . . For it could not be but that God did Himself know that which by the Word He made:[6] but if that which He made He knew, in Him there was that which was made before it was made. For if in Him was not that which was made before it was made, how knew He that which He made? For thou canst not say that God made things He knew not. God therefore hath known that which He hath made. And how knew He before He made, if there cannot be known any but things made? But by things made there cannot be known any but things previously made, by thee, to wit, who art a man made in a lower place, and set in a lower place: but before that all these things were made, they were known by Him by whom they were made, and that which He knew He made. Therefore in that Word by which He made all things, before that they were made, were all things; and after they have been made there are all things; but in one way here, in another there, in one way in their own nature wherein they have been made, in another in the art by which they have been made. Who could explain this? We may endeavour: go ye with Idithun, and see.

12. . . . For even the Lord saith, "Many things I have to say to you, but ye cannot bear them now."[7] What is therefore, "These two things I have heard"? These two things which to you I am about to say not of myself to you I say, but what things I have heard I say. "Once hath God spoken:" One Word hath He, the Only-begotten God. In that Word are all things, because by the Word were made all things. One Word hath He, "in whom all the treasures of wisdom and knowledge are hidden."[8] One Word He hath, "once hath God spoken." "These two things," which to you I am about to say, these I have heard: not of myself I speak, not of myself I say: to this belongeth the "I have heard."[9] But the friend of the Bridegroom standeth and heareth Him, that he may speak the truth. For he heareth Him, lest by speaking a lie, of his own he should speak:[10] lest thou shouldest say, Who art thou that sayest this thing to me? whence dost thou say this to me? I have heard these two things, and I that speak to thee that I have heard these two things, am one who also doth know that once God hath spoken. Do not despise a hearer saying to thee certain two things for thee so necessary; him, I say, that by leaping over the whole creation hath attained unto the Only-begotten Word of God, where he hath learned that "once God hath spoken."

13. Let him therefore now say certain two things. For greatly to us belong these two things. "For power is of God, and to Thee, O Lord, is mercy." Are these the two things, power and mercy? These two evidently: perceive ye the power of God, perceive ye the mercy of God. In these two things are contained nearly all the Scriptures. Because of these two things are the Prophets, because of these two, the Patriarchs, because of these the Law, because of these Himself our Lord Jesus Christ, because of these the Apostles, because of these all the preaching and spreading of the word of God in the Church, because of these two, because of the power of God, and His mercy. His power fear ye, His mercy love ye. Neither so on His mercy rely, as that His power ye despise: nor so the power fear ye, as that of mercy ye despair. With Him is power, with Him mercy. This man He humbleth, and that man He exalteth:[11] this man He humbleth with power, that man He exalteth in mercy. "For if God, willing to show wrath and to prove His power, hath in much patience borne with the vessels of wrath, which have been perfected unto perdition[12]"— thou hast heard of power: inquire for mercy— "and that He might make known," He saith, "His riches unto the vessels of mercy." It belongeth therefore to His power to condemn unjust men. And to Him who would say, What hast thou done? "For thou, O man, who art thou that should make answer to God?"[13] Fear therefore and tremble at His power: but hope for His mercy. The devil is a sort of power; ofttimes however he wisheth to hurt, and is not

1 Heb. i. 1.   2 Gen. iii. 17.   3 Gen. iv. 6, etc.
4 Matt. iii. 17.   5 Magister.   6 John i. 3.
7 John xvi. 12.

8 Col. ii. 3.   9 John viii. 26.   10 John viii. 44.
11 Ps. lxxv. 7.   12 Rom. ix. 22.   13 Rom. ix. 20.

able, because that power is under power. For if the devil could hurt as much as he would; no one of just men would remain, nor could any one of the faithful be on earth. The same through his vessels smiteth against, as it were, a wall bowed down: but he only smiteth against, so far as he receiveth power. But in order that the wall may not fall, the Lord will support: for He that giveth power to the tempter, doth Himself to the tempted extend mercy. For according to measure the devil is permitted to tempt. And, "Thou wilt give us to drink in tears in a measure."[1] Do not therefore fear the tempter permitted to do somewhat: for thou hast a most merciful Saviour. So much he is permitted to tempt as is profitable for thee, that thou mayest be exercised, mayest be proved; in order that by thyself thou mayest be found out, that knowest not thyself. For where, or from whence, ought we to be secure, except by this power and mercy of God? After that Apostolic saying, "Faithful is God, that doth not suffer you to be tempted above that which ye are able."[2] . . . Fear not the enemy: so much he doeth as he hath received power to do, Him fear thou that hath the chief power: Him fear, that doeth as much as He willeth, and that doeth nothing unjustly, and whatever He shall have done, is just. We might suppose something or other to be unjust: inasmuch as God hath done it, believe it to be just.

14. Therefore, thou sayest, if any one slay an innocent man, doeth he justly or unjustly? Unjustly certainly. Wherefore doth God permit this? . . . The counsel of God to tell to thee, O man, I am not able: this thing however I say, both that the man hath done unjustly that hath slain an innocent person, and that it would not have been done unless God permitted it: and though the man hath done unjustly, yet God hath not unjustly permitted this. Let the reason lie concealed in that person whoever it be, for whose sake thou art moved, whose innocence doth much move thee. For to thee speedily I might make answer. He would not have been slain unless he were guilty: but thou thinkest him innocent. I might speedily say this to thee. For thou couldest not examine his heart, sift his deeds, weigh his thoughts, so that thou couldest say to me, unjustly he was slain. I might easily therefore make answer: but there is forced upon my view a certain Just One, without dispute just, without doubt just, who had no sin, slain by sinners, betrayed by a sinner; Himself Christ the Lord, of whom we cannot say that He hath any iniquity, for "those things which He robbed not He paid,"[3] is made an objection to my answer. And why should I speak of Christ?

"With thee I am dealing," thou sayest. And I with thee. About Him thou proposest a question, about Him I am solving the question. For therein the counsel of God we know, which except by His own revealing we should not know: so that when thou shalt have found out that counsel of God, whereby He hath permitted His innocent Son to be slain by unjust men, and such a counsel as pleaseth thee, and such a counsel as cannot displease thee, if thou art just, thou mayest believe that in other things also by His counsel God doeth the same, but it escaped thee. Ah! brethren, need there was of the blood of a just one to blot out the handwriting of sins; need there was of an example of patience, of an example of humility; need there was of the Sign of the Cross to beat down the devil and his angels; need for us there was of the Passion of our Lord; for by the Passion of the Lord redeemed hath been the world. How many good things hath the Passion of the Lord done! And yet the Passion of this Just One would not have been, unless unrighteous men had slain the Lord. What then? is this good thing which to us hath been granted by the Lord's Passion to be ascribed to the unjust slayers of Christ? Far be it. They willed, God permitted. They guilty would have been, even if only they had willed it: but God would not have permitted it, unless just it had been. . . . Accordingly, my brethren, both Judas the foul traitor to Christ, and the persecutors of Christ, malignant all, ungodly all, unjust all, are to be condemned all: and nevertheless the Father His own proper Son hath not spared, but for the sake of us all He hath delivered Him up.[4] Order if thou art able; distinguish if thou art able (these things): render to God thy vows, which thy lips have uttered: see what the unjust hath here done, what the Just One. The one hath willed, the Other hath permitted: the one unjustly hath willed, the Other justly hath permitted. Let unjust will be condemned, just permission be glorified. For what evil thing hath befallen Christ, in that Christ hath died? Both evil were they that evil willed to do, and yet nothing of evil did He suffer on whom they did it. Slain was mortal flesh, slaying death by death, giving a lesson of patience, sending before an example of Resurrection. How great good things of the Just One were wrought by the evil things of the unjust! This is the great mystery[5] of God: that even a good thing which thou doest He hath Himself given it to thee, and by thy evil He doeth good Himself. Do not therefore wonder, God permitteth, and in judgment permitteth: He permitteth, and in measure, number, weight, He permitteth. With Him is not iniquity:[6] do

[1] Ps. lxxx. 5.   [2] 1 Cor. x. 13.   [3] Ps. lxix. 4.

[4] Rom. viii. 32.
[5] Magnum, Al. regnum, "the royal power."   [6] Rom. ix. 14.

thou only belong to Him ; on Himself thy hope set thou, let Himself be thy Helper, thy Salvation : in Him be there the fortified place, the tower of strength,[1] thy refuge let Himself be, and He will not suffer thee to be tempted above that which thou art able to bear, but will make with the temptation also an escape, that thou mayest be able to support it :[2] so that His suffering thee to bear temptation, be His power ; His suffering not any more on thee to be done than thou art able to bear, be His mercy : " for power is of God, and to Thee, O Lord, is mercy, because Thou wilt render to each one after his works."

15. That thirst of the Church, would fain drink up that man also whom ye see.[3] At the same time also, in order that ye may know how many in the mixed multitude of Christians with their mouth do bless, and in their heart curse, this man having been a Christian and a believer returneth as a penitent, and being terrified by the power of the Lord, turneth him to the mercy of the Lord. For having been led astray by the enemy when he was a believer, long time he hath been an astrologer, led astray, leading astray, deceived, deceiving, he hath allured, hath beguiled, many lies he hath spoken against God, That hath given to men power of doing that which is good, and of not doing that which is evil. He used to say, that one's own will did not adultery, but Venus ; one's own will did not manslaying, but Mars ; and God did not what is just, but Jupiter ; and many other blasphemous things, and not light ones. From how many Christians do ye think he hath pocketed money? How many from him have bought a lie, to whom we used to say, " Sons of men, how long are ye dull of heart, wherefore love ye vanity, and seek a lie"?[4] Now, as of him must be believed, he hath shuddered at his lie, and being the allurer of many men, he hath perceived at length that by the devil he hath himself been allured, and he turneth to God a penitent. We think, brethren, that because of great fear of heart it hath come to pass. For what must we say? If out of a heathen an astrologer were converted, great indeed would be the joy : but nevertheless it might appear, that, if he had been converted, he was desiring the clerical office in the Church. A penitent he is, he seeketh not anything save mercy alone. He must be recommended therefore both to your eyes and hearts. Him whom ye see in hearts love ye, with eyes guard ye. See ye him, mark ye him, and whithersoever he shall have gone his way, to the rest of the brethren that now are not here, point him out : and such diligence is mercy ; lest that leader astray drag back[5] his heart and take it by storm.

Guard ye him, let there not escape you his conversation, his way : in order that by your testimony it may be proved to us that truly to the Lord he hath been turned. For report will not be silent about his life, when to you he is thus presented both to be seen and to be pitied. Ye know in the Acts of the Apostles how it is written, that many lost men, that is, men of such arts, and followers of naughty doctrines, brought unto the Apostles all their books ; and there were burned so many volumes, that it was the writer's task to make a valuation of them, and write down the sum of the price.[6] This truly was for the glory of God, in order that even such lost men might not be despaired of by Him that knew how to seek that which had been lost. Therefore this man had been lost, is now sought, found,[7] led hither, he bringeth with him books to be burned, by which he had been to be burned, so that when these have been thrown into the fire, he may himself pass over into a place of refreshment. Know ye that he, brethren, once knocked at the Church door before Easter :[8] for before Easter he began to ask of the Church Christ's medicine. But because the art wherein he had been practised is of such sort as that it was suspected of lying and deceit, he was put off that he might not tempt ; at length however he was admitted, that he might not more dangerously be tempted. Pray for him through Christ. Straightway to-day's prayer pour out for him to the Lord our God. For we know and are sure, that your prayer effaceth all his impieties. The Lord be with you.

PSALM LXIII.[9]

1. This psalm hath the title, " For David himself, when he was in the desert of Idumæa." By the name of Idumæa is understood this world. For Idumæa was a certain nation of men going astray, where idols were worshipped. In no good sense is put this Idumæa. If not in a good sense it is put, it must be understood that this life, wherein we suffer so great toils, and wherein to so great necessities we are made subject, by the name of Idumæa is signified.[10] Even here is a desert where there is much thirst, and ye are to hear the voice of One now thirsting in the desert. But if we acknowledge ourselves as thirsting, we shall acknowledge ourselves as drinking also. For he that thirsteth in this world, in the world to come shall be satisfied, according to the Lord's saying, " Blessed are they that hunger and thirst after righteousness,

---

[1] Ps. lxi. 3.   [2] 1 Cor. x. 13.
[3] When an astrologer was pointed out among the people about him, he added *this*.
[4] Ps. iv. 2.   [5] *Al.* " return to."

[6] Acts xix. 19.   [7] Luke xv. 32.
[8] [A glimpse of the ancient discipline The public confession of the man is made through the bishop. Bingham, *Antiquities*, etc., b. xxi. cap. 1, § 12 *et seq.* — C.]
[9] Lat. LXII. Sermon to the Commonalty.
[10] 1 Sam. xxi. 7. See on "the Edomite," p. 199.

for the same shall be satisfied."[1] Therefore in this world we ought not to love fulness. Here we must thirst, in another place we shall be filled. But now in order that we may not faint in this desert, He sprinkleth upon us the dew of His word, and leaveth us not utterly to dry up, so that there should not be in our case any seeking of us again, but that we may so thirst as that we may drink. But in order that we may drink, with somewhat of His Grace we are sprinkled: nevertheless we thirst. And what saith our soul to God?

2. "God, my God, unto Thee from the light I watch" (ver. 1). What is to watch? It is, not to sleep. What is to sleep? There is a sleep of the soul; there is a sleep of the body. Sleep of body we all ought to have : because if sleep of body is not taken, a man fainteth, the body itself fainteth. For our frail body cannot long sustain a soul watching and on the stretch on active works ; if for a long time the soul shall have been intent on active pursuits, the body being frail and earthly holdeth her not, sustaineth her not for ever in activity, and fainteth and falleth. Therefore God hath granted sleep to the body, whereby are recruited the members of the body, in order that they may be able to sustain the soul watching. But of this let us take heed, namely, that our soul herself sleep not: for evil is the sleep of the soul. Good is the sleep of the body, whereby is recruited the health of the body. But the sleep of the soul is to forget her God. Whatsoever soul shall have forgotten her God, sleepeth. Therefore the Apostle saith to certain persons that forgot their God, and being as it were in sleep, did act the follies of the worship of idols — the Apostle, I say, saith to certain persons, "Rise, thou that sleepest, and rise up from the dead, and Christ shall enlighten thee."[2] Was the Apostle waking up one sleeping in body? Nay, but he was waking a soul sleeping, inasmuch as he was waking her, in order that she might be lightened by Christ. Therefore as to these same watchings saith this man, "God, my God, unto Thee from the light I watch." For thou wouldest not watch of thyself, unless there should arise thy Light, to wake thee from sleep. For Christ lighteneth souls, and maketh them to watch : but if His light He taketh away, they slumber. For for this cause to Him there is said in another Psalm, "Lighten mine eyes, that I may never slumber in death."[3] . . .

3. "My soul hath thirsted for Thee" (ver. 2). Behold that desert of Idumæa. See how here he thirsteth : but see what good thing is here, "Hath thirsted for Thee." For there are they that thirst, but not for God. For every one

that willeth anything to be granted to him, is in the heat of longing ; the longing itself is the thirst of the soul. And see ye what[4] longings there are in the hearts of men : one longeth for gold, another longeth for silver, another longeth for possessions, another inheritance, another abundance of money, another many herds, another a wife, another honours, another sons. Ye see those longings, how they are in the hearts of men. All men are inflamed with longing, and scarce is found one to say, "My soul hath thirsted for Thee." For men thirst for the world : and perceive not themselves to be in the desert of Idumæa, where their souls ought to thirst for God. . . .

4. Wisdom therefore must be thirsted after, righteousness must be thirsted after. With it we shall not be satisfied, with it we shall not be filled, save when this life shall have been ended, and we shall have come to that which God hath promised. For God hath promised equality with Angels :[5] and now the Angels thirst not as we do, they hunger not as we do ; but they have the fulness of truth, of light, of immortal wisdom. Therefore blessed they are, and out of so great blessedness, because they are in that City, the Heavenly Jerusalem, afar from whence we now are sojourning in a strange land, they observe us sojourners, and they pity us, and by the command of the Lord they help us, in order that to this common country sometime we may return, and there with them sometime with the Lord's fountain of truth and eternity we may be filled. Now therefore let our soul thirst : whence doth our flesh also thirst, and this in many ways? "In many ways for Thee," he saith, "my flesh also." Because to our flesh also is promised Resurrection. As to our soul is promised blessedness, so also to our flesh is promised resurrection. . . . For if God hath made us that were not, is it a great thing for Him to make again us that were? Therefore let not this seem to you to be incredible, because ye see dead men as it were decaying, and passing into ashes and into dust. Or if any dead man be burned, or if dogs tear him in pieces, do ye think that from this he will not rise again? All things which are dismembered, and into a sort of dust do decay, are entire with God. For into those elements of the world they pass, whence at first they have come, when we were made : we do not see them ; but yet God will bring them forth, He knoweth whence, because even before we were, He created us from whence He knew. Such a resurrection of the flesh therefore to us is promised, as that, although it be the same flesh that now we carry[6] which is to rise again, yet it hath not

[1] Matt. v. 6.   [2] Eph. v. 14.   [3] Ps. xiii. 3.

[4] *Quanta.*   [5] Luke xx. 36.
[6] [The same as to identity (*i.e.*, of continuity), not the same as to material. But see Tertullian, vol. iii. 562. — C.]

the corruption which now it hath. For now because of the corruption of frailty, if we eat not, we faint and are hungry; if we drink not, we faint and are thirsty; if long time we watch, we faint and sleep; if long time we sleep, we faint, therefore we watch. . . . Secondly, see how without any standing is our flesh: for infancy passeth away into boyhood, and thou seekest infancy, and infancy is not, for now instead of infancy is boyhood: again this same also passeth into youth, thou seekest boyhood and findest not: the young man becometh a middle-aged man, thou seekest the young man and he is not: the middle-aged man becometh an old man, thou seekest a middle-aged man and findest not: and an old man dieth, thou seekest an old man and findest not: our age therefore standeth not still: everywhere is weariness, everywhere faintness, everywhere corruption. Observing what a hope of resurrection God promiseth to us, in all those our manifold faintings we thirst for that incorruption: and so our flesh manifoldly doth thirst for God.

5. Nevertheless, my brethren, the flesh of a good Christian and a believer even in this world for God doth thirst: for if the flesh hath need of bread, if it hath need of water, if it hath need of wine, if it hath need of money, if this flesh hath need of a beast, from God it ought to seek it, not from demons and idols and I know not what powers of this world. For there are certain who when they suffer hunger in this world, leave God and ask Mercury or ask Jove to give unto them, or her whom they call "Heavenly," [1] or any the like demons: not for God their flesh thirsteth. But they that thirst for God, [2] everywhere ought to thirst for Him, both soul and flesh: for to the soul also God giveth His bread, that is the Word of Truth: and to the flesh God giveth the things which are necessary, for God hath made both soul and flesh. For the sake of thy flesh thou askest of demons: hath God made the soul, and the demons made the flesh? He that hath made the soul, the Same hath made the flesh also: He that hath made both of them, the Same feedeth both of them. Let either part of us thirst for God, and after labour manifold let either simply be filled.

6. But where thirsteth our soul, and our flesh manifoldly, not for any one but for Thee, O Lord, that is our God? it thirsteth where? "In a land desert, and without way, and without water." Of this world we have spoken, the same is Idumæa, this is the desert of Idumæa, whence the Psalm hath received its title. "In a land desert." Too little it is to say "desert," where no man dwelleth; it is besides, both "without way, and without water." O that the same desert had even a way: O that into this a man running, even knew where he might thence get forth! . . . Evil is the desert, horrible, and to be feared: and nevertheless God hath pitied us, and hath made for us a way in the desert, Himself our Lord Jesus Christ: [3] and hath made for us a consolation in the desert, in sending to us preachers of His Word: and hath given to us water in the desert, by fulfilling with the Holy Spirit His preachers, in order that there might be created in them a well of water springing up unto life everlasting. [4] And, lo! we have here all things, but they are not of the desert. . . .

7. "Thus in a holy thing I have appeared to Thee, that I might see Thy power and Thy glory" (ver. 3). . . . Unless a man first thirst in that desert, that is in the evil wherein he is, he never arriveth at the good, which is God. But "I have appeared to Thee," he saith, "in a holy thing." Now in a holy thing is there great consolation. "I have appeared to Thee," is what? In order that Thou mightest see me: and for this reason Thou hast seen me, in order that I might see Thee. "I have appeared to Thee, that I might see." He hath not said, "I have appeared to Thee, that Thou mightest see:" but, "I have appeared to Thee, that I might see Thy power and Thy glory." Whence also the Apostle, "But now," he saith, "knowing God, nay, having been known of God." [5] For first ye have appeared to God, in order that to you God might be able to appear. "That I might see Thy power and Thy glory." In truth in that forsaken place, that is, in that desert, if as though from the desert a man striveth to obtain enough for his sustenance, he will never see the power of the Lord, and the glory of the Lord, but he will remain to die of thirst, and will find neither way, nor consolation, nor water, whereby he may endure in the desert. But when he shall have lifted up himself to God, so as to say to Him out of all his inward parts, "My soul hath thirsted for Thee; how manifoldly for Thee also my flesh!" lest perchance even the things necessary for the flesh of others he ask, and not of God, or else long not for that resurrection of the flesh, which God hath promised to us: when, I say, he shall have lifted up himself, he will have no small consolations.

8. . . . But ye have heard but now when the Gospel was being read in what terms He hath notified His Majesty: "I and My Father are One." [6] Behold how great a Majesty and how

---

[1] Ed. Ben. refers to Tertullian, *Apol.* xxiii., where *Virgo Cœlestis* is represented as "promising rain," and St. Augustin, *De Civ. Dei*, ii. 4, where the same goddess is mentioned as worshipped together with Berecynthia, the mother of the gods. [An intimation of the lingerings of heathenism, now *Paganism*, the religion of Rustics. But how easily this *Virgo Cœlestis* became a new idolatry among Christians is here illustrated. Compare Coleridge's paraphrase of Schiller, "The fair humanities of old religion," etc.—C.]
[2] Oxf. mss. *Deo.*

[3] John xiv. 6.   [4] John iv. 14.   [5] Gal. iv. 9.
[6] John x. 30.

great an Equality with the Father hath come down to the flesh because of our infirmity. Behold how greatly beloved we have been, before that we loved God. If before that we loved God, so much by Him we were beloved, as that His Son, Equal with Himself, He made a Man for our sake, what doth He reserve for us now loving Him? Therefore many men think it to be a very small thing that the Son of God hath appeared on earth; because they are not in the Holy One, to them hath not appeared the power of the Same and the glory of the Same: that is, not yet have they a heart made holy, whence they may perceive the eminence of that virtue, and may render thanks to God, nor that to which for their own sakes so great an One came, unto what a nativity, unto what a Passion, they are not able to see, His glory and His power.[1]

9. "For better is Thy mercy than[2] lives." Many are the lives of men, but one life God promiseth: and He giveth not this to us as if for our merits but for His mercy. . . . For what is so just a thing as that a sinner should be punished? Though a just thing it be that a sinner should be punished, it hath belonged to the mercy of Him not to punish a sinner but to justify him, and of a sinner to make a just man, and of an ungodly man to make a godly man. Therefore "His mercy is better than lives." What lives? Those which for themselves men have chosen. One hath chosen for himself a life of business, another a country life, another a life of usury, another a military life; one this, another that. Divers are the lives, but "better is Thy" life "than" our "lives." . . . "My lips shall praise Thee." My lips would not praise Thee, unless before me were to go Thy mercy. By Thy gift Thee I praise, through Thy mercy Thee I praise. For I should not be able to praise God, unless He gave me to be able to praise Him.

10. "So I will speak good of Thee in my life, and in Thy name I will lift up my hands" (ver. 5). Now in my life which to me Thou hast given, not in that which I have chosen after the world with the rest among many lives, but that which Thou hast given to me through Thy mercy, that I should praise Thee. "So I will speak good of Thee in my life." What is "so"? That to Thy mercy I may ascribe my life wherein Thee I praise, not to my merits. "And in Thy name I will lift up my hands." Lift up therefore hands in prayer. Our Lord hath lifted up for us His hands on the Cross, and stretched out were His hands for us, and therefore were His hands stretched out on the Cross, in order that our hands might be stretched out unto good works: because His Cross hath brought us mercy. Behold, He hath lifted up hands, and

hath offered for us Himself a Sacrifice to God, and through that Sacrifice have been effaced all our sins. Let us also lift up our hands to God in prayer: and our hands being lifted up to God shall not be confounded, if they be exercised in good works. For what doth he that lifteth up hands? Whence hath it been commanded that with hands lifted up we should pray to God? For the Apostle saith, "Lifting up pure hands without anger and dissension."[3] It is in order that when thou liftest up hands to God, there may come into thy mind thy works. For whereas those hands are lifted up that thou mayest obtain that which thou wilt, those same hands thou thinkest in good works to exercise, that they may not blush to be lifted up to God. "In thy name I will lift up my hands." Those are our prayers in this Idumæa, in this desert, in the land without water and without way, where for us Christ is the Way,[4] but not the way of this earth.

11. . . . Already our fathers are dead, but God liveth: here we could not always have fathers, but there we shall alway have one living Father, when we have our father-land. . . . What sort of country is that? But thou lovest here riches. God Himself shall be to thee thy riches. But thou lovest a good fountain. What is more passing clear than that wisdom? What more bright? Whatsoever is an object of love here, in place of all thou shalt have Him that hath made all things, "as though with marrow and fatness my soul should be filled: and lips of exultation shall praise Thy name." In this desert, in Thy name I will lift up my hands: let my soul be filled as though with marrow and fatness, "and my lips with exultation shall praise Thy name." For now is prayer, so long as there is thirst: when thirst shall have passed away, there passeth away praying and there succeedeth praising. "And lips of exultation shall praise Thy name."

12. "If I have remembered Thee upon my bed, in the dawnings I did meditate on thee" (ver. 7): because Thou hast become my helper" (ver. 8). His "bed" he calleth his rest. When any one is at rest, let him be mindful of God; when any one is at rest, let him not by rest be dissolved, and forget God: if mindful he is of God when he is at rest, in his actions on God he doth meditate. For the dawn he hath called actions, because every man at dawn beginneth to do something. What therefore hath he said? If therefore I was not mindful on my bed, in the dawn also I did not meditate on Thee. Can he that thinketh not of God when he is at leisure, in his actions think of God? But he that is mindful of Him when he

---

[1] The construction here seems imperfect.   [2] Lat. "above."   [3] 1 Tim. ii. 8.   [4] John xiv. 6.

is at rest, on the Same doth meditate when he is doing, lest in action he should come short. Therefore he hath added what? "Because Thou has become my helper." For unless God aid our good works, they cannot be accomplished by us. And worthy things we ought to work: that is, as though in the light, since by Christ showing the way we work. Whosoever worketh evil things, in the night he worketh, not in the dawn; according to the Apostle, saying, "They that are drunken, in the night are drunken; and they that sleep, in the night do sleep; let us that are of the day, be sober." [1] He exhorteth us that after the day we should walk honestly: "As in the day, honestly let us walk." [2] And again, "Ye," he saith, "are sons of light, and sons of day; we are not of night nor of darkness." [3] Who are sons of night, and sons of darkness? They that work all evil things. To such a degree they are sons of night, that they fear lest the things which they work should be seen. . . . No one therefore in the dawn worketh, except him that in Christ worketh. But he that while at leisure is mindful of Christ, on the Same doth meditate in all his actions, and He is a helper to him in a good work, lest through his weakness he fail. "And in the covering of Thy wings I will exult." I am cheerful in good works, because over me is the covering of Thy wings. If thou protect me not, forasmuch as I am a chicken, the kite will seize me. For our Lord Himself saith in a certain place to that Jerusalem, a certain city, where He was crucified: "Jerusalem," He saith, "Jerusalem, how often I have willed to gather thy sons, as though a hen her chickens, and thou wouldest not." [4] Little ones we are: therefore may God protect us under the shadow of His wings. What when we shall have grown greater? A good thing it is for us that even then He should protect us, so that under Him the greater, alway we be chickens. For alway He is greater, however much we may have grown. Let no one say, let Him protect me while I am a little one: as if sometime he would attain to such magnitude, as should be self-sufficient. Without the protection of God, nought thou art. Alway by Him let us desire to be protected: then alway in Him we shall have power to be great, if alway under Him little we be. "And in the covering of Thy wings I will exult."

13. "My soul hath been glued on behind Thee" (ver. 9). See ye one longing, see ye one thirsting, see ye how he cleaveth to God. Let there spring up in you this affection. If already it is sprouting, let it be rained upon and grow: let it come to such strength, that ye also may say from the whole heart, "My soul hath been glued

on behind Thee." Where is that same glue? The glue itself is love. Have thou love, wherewith as with glue thy soul may be glued on behind God. Not with God, but behind God; that He may go before, thou mayest follow. For he that shall have willed to go before God, by his own counsel would live, and will not follow the commandments of God. Because of this even Peter was rebuked, when he willed to give counsel to Christ, who was going to suffer for us. . . . "Far be it from Thee, O Lord, be Thou merciful to Thyself." And the Lord, "Go back behind Me, Satan: for thou savourest not the things which are of God, but the things which are of men." [5] Wherefore, the things which are of men? Because to go before Me thou desirest, go back behind Me, in order that thou mayest follow me: so that now following Christ he might say, "My soul hath been glued on behind Thee." With reason he addeth, "Me Thy right hand hath taken up." This Christ hath said in us: that is in the Man [6] which He was bearing for us, which He was offering for us, He hath said this. The Church also said this in Christ, she saith it in her Head: for she too hath suffered here great persecutions, and by her individual members even now she suffereth. . . .

14. "But themselves in vain have sought my soul. They shall go unto the lower places of the earth" (ver. 9). Earth they were unwilling to lose, when they crucified Christ: into the lower places of the earth they have gone. What are the lower places of the earth? Earthly lusts. Better it is to walk upon earth, than by lust to go under earth. For every one that in prejudice of his salvation desireth earthly things, is under the earth: because earth he hath put before him, earth upon himself he hath put, and himself beneath he hath laid. They therefore fearing to lose earth, said what of the Lord Jesus Christ, when they saw great multitudes go after Him, forasmuch as He was doing wonderful things? "If we shall have let Him go alive, there will come the Romans, and will take away from us both place and nation." [7] They feared to lose earth, and they went under the earth: there befell them even what they feared. For they willed to kill Christ, that they might not lose earth; and earth they therefore lost, because Christ they slew. For when Christ had been slain, because the Lord Himself had said to them, "The kingdom shall be taken from you, and shall be given up to a nation doing righteousness:" [8] there followed them great calamities of persecutions: there conquered them Roman emperors, and kings of the nations: they were shut out from

---

[1] 1 Thess. v. 7, 8.   [2] Rom. xiii. 13.   [3] 1 Thess. v. 5.
[4] Matt. xxiii. 37.

[5] Matt. xvi. 22, 23.
[6] He does not mean by this phrase to attribute a twofold *personality* to our Lord, as appears from his *Retractations on Ps.* i. 1.
[7] John xi. 48.   [8] Matt. xxi. 43.

that very place where they crucified Christ, and now that place is full of Christian praisers: it hath no Jew, it hath been cleared of the enemies of Christ, it hath been fulfilled with the praisers of Christ. Behold, they have lost at the hands of the Romans the place, because Christ they slew, who to this end slew, that they might not lose the place at the hands of the Romans. Therefore, "They shall enter into the lower places of the earth."

15. "They shall be delivered unto the hands of the sword" (ver. 10). In truth, thus it hath visibly befallen them, they have been taken by storm by enemies breaking in. "Portions of foxes they shall be." Foxes he calleth the kings of the world, that then were when Judæa was conquered. Hear in order that ye may know and perceive, that those he calleth foxes. Herod the king the Lord Himself hath called a fox. "Go ye," He saith, "and tell that fox." [1] See and observe, my brethren: Christ as King they would not have, and portions of foxes they have been made. For when Pilate the deputy governor in Judæa slew Christ at the voices of the Jews, he said to the same Jews, "Your King shall I crucify?" [2] Because He was called King of the Jews, and He was the true King. And they rejecting Christ said, "We have no king but Cæsar." They rejected a Lamb, chose a fox: deservedly portions of foxes they were made.

16. "The King in truth," [3] is so written, because they chose a fox, a King in truth they would not have. "The King in truth:" that is, the true King, to whom the title was inscribed, when He suffered. For Pilate set this title inscribed over His Head, "The King of the Jews," in the Hebrew, Greek, and Latin tongues: in order that all they that should pass by might read of the glory of the King, and the infamy of the Jews themselves, who, rejecting the true King, chose the fox Cæsar. "The King in truth shall rejoice in God. . . . "Stopped up is the mouth of men speaking unjust things." No one dareth now openly to speak against Christ, now all men fear Christ. "For stopped up is the mouth of men speaking unjust things." When in weakness the Lamb was, even foxes were bold against the Lamb. There conquered the Lion of the tribe of Judah,[4] and the foxes were silenced.

PSALM LXIV.[5]

1. Though chiefly the Lord's Passion is noticed in this Psalm, neither could the Martyrs have been strong, unless they had beheld Him, that first suffered; nor such things would they have endured in suffering, as He did, unless they had hoped for such things in the Resurrection as He had showed of Himself: but your Holiness [6] knoweth that our Head is our Lord Jesus Christ, and that all that cleave unto Him are the members of Him the Head. . . . And let no one say, that now-a-days in tribulation of passions we are not. For alway ye have heard this fact, how in those times the whole Church together as it were was smitten against, but now through individuals she is tried. Bound indeed is the devil, that he may not do as much as he could, that he may not do as much as he would: nevertheless, he is permitted to tempt as much as is expedient for men advancing. It is not expedient for us to be without temptations: nor should we beseech God that we be not tempted, but that we be not "led into temptation." [7]

2. Say we, therefore, ourselves also: "Hearken, O God, to my prayer, while I am troubled; from fear of the enemy deliver my soul" (ver. 1). Enemies have raged against the Martyrs: for what was that voice of Christ's Body praying? For this it was praying, to be delivered from enemies, and that enemies might not have power to slay them. Were they not therefore hearkened to, because they were slain; and hath God forsaken His servants of a contrite heart, and despised men hoping in Him? Far be it. For "who hath called upon God, and hath been forsaken; who hath hoped in Him, and hath been deserted by Him?" [8] They were hearkened to therefore, and they were slain; and yet from enemies they were delivered. Others being afraid gave consent, and lived, and yet the same by enemies were swallowed up. The slain were delivered, the living were swallowed up. Thence is also that voice of thanksgiving, "Perchance alive they would have swallowed us up." [9] . . . Therefore for this prayeth the voice of the Martyrs, "From fear of the enemy deliver Thou my soul:" not so that the enemy may not slay me, but that I may not fear an enemy slaying. For that to be fulfilled in the Psalm the servant prayeth, which but now in the Gospel the Lord was commanding. What but now was the Lord commanding? "Fear not them that kill the body, but the soul are not able to kill; but Him rather fear ye, that hath power to kill both body and soul in the hell of fire." [10] And He repeated, "Yea, I say unto you, fear Him." [11] Who are they that kill the body? Enemies. What was the Lord commanding? That they should not be feared. Be prayer offered, therefore, that He may grant what He hath commanded. "From fear of the enemy deliver my soul." Deliver

---

[1] Luke xiii. 32.   [2] John xix. 15.   [3] *Rex vero.*
[4] Rev. v. 5.
[5] Lat. LXIII. Sermon to the Commonalty while keeping the festival of the holy Martyrs.

[6] [Preached in the presence of a bishop, thus addressed. — C.]
[7] Matt. vi. 13.   [8] Ecclus. ii. 10.   [9] Ps. cxxiv. 3.
[10] Matt. x. 28.   [11] Luke xii. 5.

me from fear of the enemy, and make me submit to the fear of Thee. I would not fear him that killeth the body, but I would fear Him that hath power to kill both body and soul in the hell of fire. For not from fear would I be free: but from fear of the enemy being free, under fear of the Lord a servant.

3. "Thou hast protected me from the gathering together of malignants, and from the multitude of men working iniquity" (ver. 2). Now upon Himself our Head let us look. Like things many Martyrs have suffered: but nothing doth shine out so brightly as the Head of Martyrs; in Him rather let us behold what they have gone through. Protected He was from the multitude of malignants, God protecting Himself, the Son Himself and the Manhood [1] which He was carrying protecting His flesh: because Son of Man He is, and Son of God He is; Son of God because of the form of God, Son of Man because of the form of a servant: having in His power to lay down His life: and to take it again.[2] To Him what could enemies do? They killed body, soul they killed not. Observe. Too little therefore it were for the Lord to exhort the Martyrs with word, unless He had enforced it by example. Ye know what a gathering together there was of malignant Jews, and what a multitude there was of men working iniquity. What iniquity? That wherewith they willed to kill the Lord Jesus Christ. "So many good works," He saith, "I have shown to you, for which of these will ye to kill Me?" [3] He endured all their infirm,[4] He healed all their sick, He preached the Kingdom of Heaven, He held not His peace at their vices, so that these same should have been displeasing to them, rather than the Physician by whom they were being made whole: for all these His remedies being ungrateful, like men delirious in high fever raving at the physician, they devised the plan of destroying Him that had come to heal them; as though therein they would prove whether He were indeed a man, that could die, or were somewhat above men, and would not suffer Himself to die. The word of these same men we perceive in the wisdom of Solomon: "with death most vile," say they, "let us condemn Him; let us question Him, for there will be regard in the discourses of Him; for if truly Son of God He is, let Him deliver Him." [5] Let us see therefore what was done.

4. "For they have whet like a sword their tongues" (ver. 3). Which saith another Psalm also, "Sons of men; their teeth are arms and arrows, and their tongue is a sharp sword." [6] Let not the Jews say, we have not killed Christ. For to this end they gave Him to Pilate the judge, in order that they themselves might seem as it were guiltless of His death. . . . But if he is guilty because he did it though unwillingly, are they innocent who compelled him to do it? By no means. But he gave sentence against Him, and commanded Him to be crucified: and in a manner himself killed Him; ye also, O ye Jews, killed Him. Whence did ye kill Him? With the sword of the tongue: for ye did whet your tongues. And when did ye smite, except when ye cried out, "Crucify, Crucify"? [7]

5. But on this account we must not pass over that which hath come into mind, lest perchance the reading of the Divine Scriptures should disquiet any one. One Evangelist saith that the Lord was crucified at the sixth hour,[8] and another at the third hour: [9] unless we understand it, we are disquieted. And when the sixth hour was already beginning, Pilate is said to have sat on the judgment-seat: and in reality when the Lord was lifted up upon the tree, it was the sixth hour. But another Evangelist, looking unto the mind of the Jews, how they wished themselves to seem guiltless of the death of the Lord, by his account proveth them guilty, saying, that the Lord was crucified at the third hour. But considering all the circumstance of the history, how many things might have been done, when before Pilate the Lord was being accused, in order that He might be crucified; we find that it might have been the third hour, when they cried out, "Crucify, Crucify." Therefore with more truth they killed at the time when they cried out. The ministers of the magistrate at the sixth hour crucified, the transgressors of the law at the third hour cried out: that which those did with hands at the sixth hour, these did with tongue at the third hour. More guilty are they that with crying out were raging, than they that in obedience were ministering. This is the whole of the Jews' sagacity, this is that which they sought as some great matter. Let us kill and let us not kill: so let us kill, as that we may not ourselves be judged to have killed.

6. "They have bended the bow, a bitter thing, in order that they may shoot in secret One unspotted" (ver. 4). The bow he calleth lyings in wait. For he that with sword fighteth hand to hand, openly fighteth: he that shooteth an arrow deceiveth, in order to strike. For the arrow smiteth, before it is foreseen to come to wound. But whom could the lyings in wait of the human heart escape? Would they escape our Lord Jesus Christ, who had no need that any one should bear witness to Him of man? "For Himself knew what was in man," [10] as the Evangelist testifieth. Nevertheless, let us hear them, and look upon them in their doings as if

---

[1] *Homine.* See on Ps. i. *Retrs.*   [2] John x. 18.
[3] John x. 32.   [4] Oxf. MSS. "infirmities."
[5] Wisd. ii. 20, 18.   [6] Ps. lvii. 4.

[7] Luke xxiii. 21.   [8] John xix. 14.   [9] Mark xv. 25.
[10] John ii. 25.

the Lord knew not what they devise. The expression he used, "They have bended the bow," is the same as, "in secret:" as if they were deceiving by lyings in wait. For ye know by what artifices they did this, how with money they bribed a disciple that clave to Him, in order that He might be betrayed to them,[1] how they procured false witnesses; with what lyings in wait and artifices they wrought, "in order that they might shoot in secret One unspotted." Great iniquity! Behold from a secret place there cometh an arrow, which striketh One unspotted, who had not even so much of spot as could be pierced with an arrow. A Lamb indeed He is unspotted, wholly unspotted, alway unspotted; not one from whom spots have been removed, but that hath contracted not any spots. For He hath made many unspotted by forgiving sins, being Himself unspotted by not having sins. "Suddenly they shall shoot Him, and shall not fear." O heart hardened, to wish to kill a Man that did raise the dead! "Suddenly:" that is, insidiously, as if unexpectedly, as if not foreseen. For the Lord was like to one knowing not, being among men knowing not what He knew not and what He knew: yea, knowing not that there was nothing that He knew not, and that He knew all things, and to this end had come in order that they might do that which they thought they did by their own power.

7. "They have confirmed to themselves malignant discourse" (ver. 5). There were done so great miracles, they were not moved, they persisted in the design of the evil discourse. He was given up to the judge: the judge trembleth, and they tremble not that have given Him up to the judge: trembleth power, and ferocity trembleth not: he would wash his hands, and they stain their tongues. But wherefore this? "They have confirmed to themselves malignant discourse." How many things did Pilate, how many things that they might be restrained! What said he? what did he? But "they have confirmed to themselves malignant discourse: Crucify, crucify."[2] The repetition is the confirmation of the "malignant discourse." Let us see in what manner "they have confirmed to themselves malignant discourse." "Your King shall I crucify?" They said, "We have no king but Cæsar alone."[3] He was offering for King the Son of God: to a man they betook themselves: worthy were they to have the one, and not have the Other. "I find not anything in this Man," saith the judge, "wherefore He is worthy of death."[4] And they that "confirmed malignant discourse," said, "His blood be upon us and upon our sons."[5] "They confirmed malignant discourse," not to the Lord, but to "themselves."

For how not to themselves when they say, "Upon us and upon our sons"? That which therefore they confirmed, to themselves they confirmed: because the same voice is elsewhere, "They dug before my face a ditch, and fell into it." Death killed not the Lord, but He death: but them iniquity killed, because they would not kill iniquity. . . .

8. "They told, in order that they might hide traps: they said, Who shall see them?" (ver. 5). They thought they would escape Him, whom they were killing, that they would escape God. Behold, suppose Christ was a man, like the rest of men, and knew not what was being contrived for Him: doth God also know not? O heart of man! wherefore hast thou said to thyself, Who seeth me? when He seeth that hath made thee? "They said, Who shall see them?"[6] God did see, Christ also was seeing: because Christ is also God. But wherefore did they think that He saw not? Hear the words following.

9. "They have searched out iniquity, they have failed, searching searchings" (ver. 6): that is, deadly and acute designs. Let Him not be betrayed by us, but by His disciple: let Him not be killed by us, but by the judge: let us do all, and let us seem to have done nothing. . . .

10. But what befell them? "They failed searching searchings." Whence? Because he saith, "Who shall see them?" that is, that no one saw[7] them. This they were saying, this among themselves they thought, that no one saw them. See what befalleth an evil soul: it departeth from the light of truth, and because itself seeth not God, it thinketh that itself is not seen by God. . . .

11. For what followeth? "There shall draw near a man and a deep heart." They said, Who shall see us? They failed in searching searchings, evil counsels. There drew near a man to those same counsels, He suffered Himself to be held as a man. For He would not have been held except He were man, or have been seen except He were man, or have been smitten except He were man, or have been crucified or have died except He were man. There drew near a man therefore to all those sufferings, which in Him would have been of no avail except He were Man. But if He were not Man, there would not have been deliverance for man. There hath drawn near a Man "and a deep heart," that is, a secret "heart:" presenting before human faces Man, keeping within God: concealing the "form of God," wherein He is equal with the Father,[8] and presenting the form of a servant, wherein He is less than the Father. For Himself hath spoken of both: but one thing there is which He saith in the form of God,

---

[1] Matt. xxvi. 14, 15.　　[2] Luke xxiii. 21.　　[3] John xix. 15.
[4] Luke xxiii. 14, 20, 22.　　[5] Matt. xxvii. 25.
[6] *Eas* (the traps). Oxf. MSS. "us."
[7] Oxf. MSS. "will see."　　[8] Philip. ii. 6.

another thing in the form of a servant. He hath said in the form of God, "I and the Father are one :" [1] He hath said in the form of a servant, "For the Father is greater than I." [2] Whence in the form of God saith He, "I and the Father are one "? . . .

12. "Arrows of infants have been made the strokes of them " (ver. 7). Where is that savageness? where is that roar of the lion, of the people roaring and saying, " Crucify, Crucify "? [3] Where are the lyings in wait of men bending the bow? Have not "the strokes of them been made the arrows of infants "? Ye know in what manner infants make to themselves arrows of little canes. What do they strike, or whence do they strike? What is the hand, or what the weapon? what are the arms, or what the limbs?

13. "And the tongues of them have been made weak upon them" (ver. 8). Let them whet now their tongues like a sword, let them confirm to themselves malignant discourse. Deservedly to themselves they have confirmed [4] it, because " the tongues of them have been made weak upon them." Could this be strong against God? "Iniquity," he saith, "hath lied to itself ;" [5] "their tongues have been made weak upon them." Behold, the Lord hath risen, that was killed. . . . What thinkest thou of Him who from the cross came not down, and from the tomb rose again? What therefore did they effect? But even if the Lord had not risen again, what would they have effected, except what the persecutors of the martyrs have also effected? For the Martyrs have not yet risen again, and nevertheless they have effected nothing ; of them not yet rising again we are now celebrating the nativities. Where is the madness of their raging? To what did they bring those their searchings, in which searchings they failed, so that even, when the Lord was dead and buried, they set guards at the tomb? For they said to Pilate, "That deceiver ;" by this name the Lord Jesus Christ was called, for the comfort of His servants when they are called deceivers ; they say therefore to Pilate, "That deceiver said when yet living, After three days I will rise again :" [6] . . . They set for guards soldiers at the sepulchre. At the earth quaking, the Lord rose again : such miracles were done about the sepulchre, that even the very soldiers that had come for guards were made witnesses, if they chose to tell the truth : but the same covetousness which had led captive a disciple, the companion of Christ, led captive also the soldier that was guard of the sepulchre. We give you, they say, money ; [7] and say ye, while yourselves were sleeping there came His disciples, and took Him

away. . . . Sleeping witnesses ye adduce : truly thou thyself hast fallen asleep, that in searching such devices hast failed. If they were sleeping, what could they see? if nothing they saw, how are they witnesses? But " they failed in searching searchings : " failed of the light of God, failed in the very completion of their designs : when that which they willed, nowise they were able to complete, surely they failed. Wherefore this? Because " there drew near a Man and a deep heart, and God was exalted." . . .

14. "And every man feared " (ver. 9). They that feared not, were not even men. " Every man feared ; " that is, every one using reason to perceive the things which were done. Whence they that feared not, must rather be called cattle, rather beasts savage and cruel. A lion ramping and roaring is that people as yet. But in truth every man feared : that is, they that would believe, that trembled at the judgment to come. " And every man feared : and they declared the works of God." . . . "And every man hath feared : and they have declared the works of God, and His doings they have perceived." What is, " His doings they have perceived "? Was it, O Lord Jesu Christ, that Thou wast silent, and like a sheep for a victim wast being led, and didst not open before the shearer Thy mouth, [8] and we thought Thee to be set in smiting and in grief, [9] and knowing how to bear weakness ? [10] Was it that Thou wast hiding Thy beauty, O Thou beautiful in form before the sons of men ? [11] Was it that Thou didst not seem to have beauty nor grace ? [12] Thou didst bear on the Cross men reviling and saying, " If Son of God He is, let Him come down from the Cross." [13] . . . This thing they, that would have had Him come down from the Cross, perceived not : but when He rose again, and being glorified ascended into Heaven, they perceived the works of God.

15. "The just man shall rejoice in the Lord " (ver. 10). Now the just man is not sad. For sad were the disciples at the Lord's being crucified ; overcome with sadness, sorrowing they departed, they thought they had lost hope. He rose again, even when appearing to them He found them sad. He held the eyes of two men that walked in the way, so that by them he was not known, and He found them groaning and sighing, and He held them until He had expounded the Scriptures, and by the same Scriptures had shown that so it ought to have been done as it was done. [14] For He showed in the Scriptures, how after the third day it behoved the Lord to rise again. [15] And how on the third day would He have risen again, if from the Cross He had come down? . . . Therefore let us all rejoice in the Lord,

---

1 John x. 30.　　2 John xiv. 28.　　3 Luke xxiii. 21; John xix. 6.
4 Or, strengthened.　　5 Ps. xlvii. 12, Vulgate.
6 Matt. xxvii. 63.　　7 Matt. xxviii. 12, 13.

8 Isa. liii. 7.　　9 Isa. liii. 4.　　10 Isa. liii. 3.
11 Ps. xlv. 2.　　12 Isa. liii. 2.　　13 Matt. xxvii. 40.
14 Luke xxiv. 16, etc.　　15 Luke xxiv. 46.

let us all after the faith be ONE JUST MAN, and let us all in one Body hold One Head, and let us rejoice in the Lord, not in ourselves : because our Good is not ourselves to ourselves, but He that hath made us. Himself is our good to make us glad. And let no one rejoice in himself, no one rely on himself, no one despair of himself : let no one rely on any man, whom he ought to bring in to be the partner of his own hope, not the giver of the hope.

16. Now because the Lord hath risen again, now because He hath ascended into Heaven, now because He hath showed that there is another life, now because it is evident that His counsels, wherein He lay concealed in deep heart, were not empty, because to this end That Blood was shed to be the price of the redeemed ; now because all things are evident, because all things have been preached, because all things have been believed, under the whole of heaven, "the just man shall rejoice in the Lord, and shall hope in Him ; and all men shall be praised that are right in heart." . . . God is displeasing to thee, and thou art pleasing to thyself, of perverted and crooked heart thou art : and this is the worse, that the heart of God thou wouldest correct by thy heart, to make Him do what thou wilt have, whereas thou oughtest to do what He willeth. What then ? Thou wouldest make crooked the heart of God which alway is right, according to the depravity of thy own heart ? How much better to correct thy heart by the rectitude of God ? Hath not thy Lord taught thee this, of Whose Passion but now were we speaking ? Was He not bearing thy weakness, when He said, "Sad is My soul even unto death "?[1] Was He not figuring thyself in Himself, when He was saying, "Father, if it be possible, let there pass from Me this cup "?[2] For the hearts of the Father and of the Son were not two and different : but in the form of a servant He carried thy heart, that He might teach it by His example. Now behold trouble found out as it were another heart of thine, which willed that there should pass away that which was impending : but God would not. God consenteth not to thy heart, do thou consent to the heart of God.

17. What followeth ? If "there shall be praised all men right in heart," there shall be condemned the crooked in heart. Two things are set before thee now, choose while there is time. . . . If of crooked heart thou hast become, there will come that Judgment, there will appear all the reasons on account of which God doeth all these things : and thou that wouldest not in this life correct thy heart by the rectitude of God, and prepare thyself for the right hand, where "there shall be praised all men right in heart," wilt

be on the left, where at that time thou shalt hear, "Go ye into fire everlasting, that hath been prepared for the devil and his angels."[3] And will there be then time to correct the heart ? Now therefore correct, brethren, now correct. Who doth hinder ? Psalm is chanted, Gospel is read, Reader crieth, Preacher crieth ; long-suffering is the Lord ; thou sinnest, and He spareth ; still thou sinnest, still He spareth, and still thou addest sin to sin. How long is God long-suffering ? Thou wilt find God just also. We terrify because we fear ; teach us not to fear, and we terrify no more. But better it is that God teach us to fear, than that any man teach us not to fear. . . . Thou bringest forth grain, barn expect thou ; bringest forth thorns, fire expect thou. But not yet hath come either the time of the barn or the time of the fire : now let there be preparation, and there will not be fear. In the name of Christ both we who speak are living, and ye to whom we speak are living : for amending our plan, and changing evil life into a good life, is there no place, is there no time ? Can it not, if thou wilt, be done to-day ? Can it not, if thou wilt, be now done ? What must thou buy in order to do it, what specifics[4] must thou seek ? To what Indies must thou sail ? What ship prepare ? Lo, while I am speaking, change the heart ; and there is done what so often and so long while is cried out for, that it be done, and which bringeth forth everlasting punishment if it be not done.

PSALM LXV.[5]

1. The voice of holy prophecy must be confessed in the very title of this Psalm. It is inscribed, "Unto the end, a Psalm of David, a song of Jeremiah and Ezekiel, on account of the people of transmigration when they were beginning to go forth." How it fared with our fathers[6] in the time of the transmigration to Babylon, is not known to all, but only to those that diligently study the Holy Scriptures, either by hearing or by reading. For the captive people Israel from the city of Jerusalem was led into slavery unto Babylon.[7] But holy Jeremiah prophesied, that after seventy years the people would return out of captivity, and would rebuild the very city Jerusalem, which they had mourned as having been overthrown by enemies. But at that time there were prophets in that captivity of the people dwelling in Babylon, among whom was also the prophet Ezekiel. But that people was waiting until there should be fulfilled the

---

[1] Matt. xxvi. 38.   [2] Matt. xxvi. 39.

[3] Matt. xxv. 41.
[4] *Symplasia*, probably meaning "compounds;" older edition, *emplastra;* Oxf. and some other MSS., *Templa Asiæ*, "Temples of Asia."
[5] Lat. LXIV. Sermon to the Commonalty.
[6] [The student of the Ante-Nicene Fathers will remember similar references to the Hebrew faithful as *our* fathers. — C.]
[7] 2 Kings xxiv. 14.

space of seventy years, according to the prophecy of Jeremiah.[1] It came to pass, when the seventy years had been completed, the temple was restored which had been thrown down: and there returned from captivity a great part of that people. But whereas the Apostle saith, "these things in figure happened unto them, but they have been written for our sakes, upon whom the end of the world hath come:"[2] we also ought to know first our captivity, then our deliverance: we ought to know the Babylon wherein we are captives, and the Jerusalem for a return to which we are sighing. For these two cities, according to the letter, in reality are two cities. And the former Jerusalem indeed by the Jews is not now inhabited. For after the crucifixion of the Lord vengeance was taken upon them with a great scourge, and being rooted up from that place where, with impious licentiousness being infuriated, they had madly raged against their Physician, they have been dispersed throughout all nations, and that land hath been given to Christians: and there is fulfilled what the Lord had said to them, "Therefore the kingdom shall be taken away from you, and it shall be given to a nation doing justice."[3] But when they saw great multitudes then following the Lord, preaching the kingdom of Heaven, and doing wonderful things, the rulers of that city said, "If we shall have let Him go, all men will go after Him, and there shall come the Romans, and shall take from us both place and nation."[4] That they might not lose their place, they killed the Lord; and they lost it, even because they killed. Therefore that city, being one earthly, did bear the figure of a certain city everlasting in the Heavens: but when that which was signified began more evidently to be preached, the shadow, whereby it was being signified, was thrown down: for this reason in that place now the temple is no more, which had been constructed for the image of the future Body of the Lord. We have the light, the shadow hath passed away: nevertheless, still in a kind of captivity we are: "So long as we are," he saith, "in the body, we are sojourning afar from the Lord."[5]

2. And see ye the names of those two cities, Babylon and Jerusalem. Babylon is interpreted confusion, Jerusalem vision of peace. Observe now the city of confusion, in order that ye may perceive the vision of peace; that ye may endure that, sigh for this. Whereby can those two cities be distinguished? Can we anywise now separate them from each other? They are mingled, and from the very beginning of mankind mingled they run on unto the end of the world. Jerusalem received beginning through Abel, Babylon through Cain: for the buildings of the cities were afterwards erected. That Jerusalem in the land of the Jebusites was builded: for at first it used to be called Jebus,[6] from thence the nation of the Jebusites was expelled, when the people of God was delivered from Egypt, and led into the land of promise. But Babylon was builded in the most interior regions of Persia, which for a long time raised its head above the rest of nations. These two cities then at particular times were builded, so that there might be shown a figure of two cities begun of old, and to remain even unto the end in this world, but at the end to be severed. Whereby then can we now show them, that are mingled? At that time the Lord shall show, when some He shall set on the right hand, others on the left. Jerusalem on the right hand shall be, Babylon on the left. . . . Two loves make up these two cities: love of God maketh Jerusalem, love of the world maketh Babylon. Therefore let each one question himself as to what he loveth: and he shall find of which he is a citizen: and if he shall have found himself to be a citizen of Babylon, let him root out cupidity, implant charity: but if he shall have found himself a citizen of Jerusalem, let him endure captivity, hope for liberty. . . . Now therefore let us hear of, brethren, hear of, and sing of, and long for, that city whereof we are citizens. And what are the joys which are sung of to us? In what manner in ourselves is formed again the love of our city, which by long sojourning we had forgotten? But our Father hath sent from thence letters to us, God hath supplied to us the Scriptures, by which letters there should be wrought in us a longing for return: because by loving our sojourning, to enemies we had turned our face, and our back to our fatherland. What then is here sung?

3. "For Thee a hymn is meet, O God, in Sion" (ver. 1). That fatherland is Sion: Jerusalem is the very same as Sion; and of this name the interpretation ye ought to know. As Jerusalem is interpreted vision of peace, so Sion *Beholding*,[7] that is, vision and contemplation. Some great inexplicable sight to us is promised: and this is God Himself that hath builded the city. Beauteous and graceful the city, how much more beauteous a Builder it hath! "For Thee a hymn is meet, O God," he saith. But where? "In Sion:" in Babylon it is not meet. For when a man beginneth to be renewed, already with heart in Jerusalem he singeth, with the Apostle saying, "Our conversation is in the Heavens."[8] For "in the flesh though walking," he saith, "not after the flesh we war."[9] Already in longing we are there, already hope into that land, as it were an anchor, we have sent before,

---

[1] Jer. xxv. 11, xxix. 10. [2] 1 Cor. x. 11. [3] Matt. xxi. 43.
[4] John xi. 48. [5] 2 Cor. v. 6.
[6] Josh. xviii. 28. [7] *Speculati*. [8] Philip. iii. 20.
[9] 2 Cor. x. 3.

lest in this sea being tossed we suffer shipwreck. In like manner therefore as of a ship which is at anchor, we rightly say that already she is come to land, for still she rolleth, but to land in a manner she hath been brought safe in the teeth of winds and in the teeth of storms ; so against the temptations of this sojourning, our hope being grounded in that city Jerusalem causeth us not to be carried away upon rocks. He therefore that according to this hope singeth, in that city singeth : let him therefore say, " For Thee a hymn is meet, O God, in Sion." . . .

4. "And to Thee shall there be paid a vow in Jerusalem." Here we vow, and a good thing it is that there we should pay. But who are they that here do vow and pay not? They that persevere not even unto the end [1] in that which they have vowed. Whence saith another Psalm, "Vow ye, and pay ye unto the Lord your God : " [2] and, "to Thee shall it be paid in Jerusalem." For there shall we be whole, that is, entire in the resurrection of just men : there shall be paid our whole vow, not soul alone, but the very flesh also, no longer corruptible, because no longer in Babylon, but now a body heavenly and changed. What sort of change is promised? " For we all shall rise again," saith the Apostle, " but we shall not [3] all be changed. . . . Where is, O death, thy sting? " [4] For now while there begin in use the first-fruits of the mind, from whence is the longing for Jerusalem, many things of corruptible flesh do contend against us, which will not contend, when death shall have been swallowed up in victory. Peace shall conquer, and war shall be ended. But when peace shall conquer, that city shall conquer which is called the vision of peace. On the part of death therefore shall be no contention. Now with how great a death do we contend ! For thence are carnal pleasures, which to us even unlawfully do suggest many things : to which we give no consent, but nevertheless in giving no consent we contend. . . .

5. "Hearken," he saith, "to my prayer, unto Thee every flesh shall come " (ver. 2). And we have the Lord saying, that there was given to Him "power over every flesh." [5] That King therefore began even now to appear, when there was being said, "Unto Thee every flesh shall come." "To Thee," he saith, "every flesh shall come." Wherefore to Him shall "every " flesh come? Because flesh He hath taken to Him. Whither shall there come every flesh? He took the first-fruits thereof out of the womb of the Virgin ; and now that the first-fruits have been taken to Him, the rest shall follow, in order that the holocaust may be completed. Whence then

" every flesh "? Every man. And whence every man? Have all been foretold, as going to believe in Christ? Have not many ungodly men been foretold, that shall be condemned also? Do not daily men not believing die in their own unbelief ? After what manner therefore do we understand, " Unto Thee every flesh shall come "? By " every flesh " he hath signified, " flesh of every kind : " out of every kind of flesh they shall come to Thee. What is, out of every kind of flesh ? Have there come poor men, and have there not come rich men ? Have there come humble men, and not come lofty men ? Have there come unlearned men, and not come learned men ? Have there come men, and not come women ? Have there come masters, and not come servants ? Have there come old men, and not come young men ; or have there come young men, and not come youths ; or have there come youths, and not come boys ; or have there come boys, and have there not been brought infants ? In a word, have there come Jews [6] (for thence were the Apostles, thence many thousands of men at first betraying, afterwards believing [7]), and have there not come Greeks ; or have there come Greeks, and not come Romans ; or have there come Romans, and not come Barbarians ? And who could number all nations coming to Him, to whom hath been said, " Unto Thee every flesh shall come " ?

6. " The discourses of unjust men have prevailed over us, and our iniquities Thou shalt propitiate " [8] (ver. 3). . . . Every man, in whatsoever place he is born, of that same land or region or city learneth the language, is habituated to the manners and life of that place. What should a boy do, born among Heathens, to avoid worshipping a stone, inasmuch as his parents have suggested that worship? from them the first words he hath heard, that error with his milk he hath sucked in ; and because they that used to speak were elders, and the boy that was learning to speak was an infant, what could the little one do but follow the authority of elders, and deem that to be good which they recommended? Therefore nations that are converted to Christ afterwards, and taking to heart the impieties of their parents, and saying now what the prophet Jeremias himself said, " Truly a lie our fathers have worshipped, vanity which hath not profited them " [9] — when, I say, they now say this, they renounce the opinions and blasphemies of their unjust parents. . . . There have led us away men teaching evil things, citizens of Babylon they have made us, we have left the Creator, have adored the creature : have left Him by whom we were made, have adored that which we ourselves

[6] Oxf. mss. "have there not come Jews (for, etc.), or have there come Jews and not come Greeks," etc.
[7] Acts ii. 41.
[8] *Propitiaberis*. One mss. here, and many below, *propitiabis*.
[9] Jer. xvi. 19.

[1] Matt. xxiv. 13.   [2] Ps. lxxvi. 11.
[3] " Not " is wanting in our text.
[4] 1 Cor. xv. 51, etc.   [5] John xvii. 2.

have made. For "the discourses of unjust men have prevailed over us : " but nevertheless they have not crushed us. Wherefore? "Our impieties Thou shalt propitiate," is not said except to some priest offering somewhat, whereby impiety may be expiated and propitiated. For impiety is then said to be propitiated, when God is made propitious to the impiety. What is it for God to be made propitious to impiety? It is, His becoming forgiving, and giving pardon. But in order that God's pardon may be obtained, propitiation is made through some sacrifice. There hath come forth therefore, sent from God the Lord, One our Priest; He took upon Him from us that which He might offer to the Lord ; we are speaking of those same first-fruits of the flesh from the womb of the Virgin. This holocaust He offered to God. He stretched out His hands on the Cross, in order that He might say, "Let My prayer be directed as incense in Thy sight, and the lifting up of My hands an evening sacrifice." [1] As ye know, the Lord about eventide hung on the Cross : [2] and our impieties were propitiated; otherwise they had swallowed us up : the discourses of unjust men had prevailed over us; there had led us astray preachers of Jupiter, and of Saturn, and of Mercury : "the discourses of ungodly men had prevailed over us." But what wilt Thou do? "Our impieties Thou wilt propitiate." Thou art the priest, Thou the victim ; Thou the offerer, Thou the offering. [3] . . .

7. "Blessed is he whom Thou hast chosen, and hast taken to Thee" (ver. 4). Who is he that is chosen by Him and taken to Him? Was any one chosen [4] by our Saviour Jesu Christ, or was Himself after the flesh, because He is man, chosen and taken to Him? . . . Or hath not rather Christ Himself taken to Him some blessed one, and the same whom He hath taken to Him is not spoken of in the plural number but in the singular? For one man He hath taken to Him, because unity He hath taken to Him. Schisms He hath not taken to Him, heresies He hath not taken to Him : a multitude they have made of themselves, there is not one to be taken to Him. But they that abide in the bond of Christ and are the members of Him, make in a manner one man, of whom saith the Apostle, "Until we all arrive at the acknowledging of the Son of God, unto a perfect man, unto the measure of the age of the fulness of Christ." [5] Therefore one man is taken to Him, to which the Head is Christ ; because "the Head of the man is Christ." [6] The same is that blessed man that "hath not departed in the counsel of ungodly men," [7] and the like things which there are spoken of : the same

is He that is taken to Him. He is not without us, in His own members we are, under one Head we are governed, by one Spirit we all live, one fatherland we all long for. . . . And to us He will give what? "He shall inhabit," he saith, "in Thy courts." Jerusalem, that is, to which they sing that begin to go forth from Babylon : "He shall inhabit in Thy courts : we shall be filled with the good things of Thy House." What are the good things of the House of God? Brethren, let us set before ourselves some rich house, with what numerous good things it is crowded, how abundantly it is furnished, how many vessels there are there of gold and also of silver ; how great an establishment of servants, how many horses and animals, in a word, how much the house itself delights us with pictures, marble, ceilings, pillars, recesses, chambers : — all such things are indeed objects of desire, but still they are of the confusion of Babylon. Cut off all such longings, O citizen of Jerusalem, cut them off ; if thou wilt return, let not captivity delight thee. But hast thou already begun to go forth? Do not look back, do not loiter on the road. Still there are not wanting foes to recommend thee captivity and sojourning : no longer let there prevail against thee the discourses of ungodly men. For the House of God long thou, and for the good things of that House long thou : but do not long for such things as thou art wont to long for either in thy house, or in the house of thy neighbour, or in the house of thy patron. . . .

8. "Thy holy Temple is marvellous in righteousness" (ver. 5). These are the good things of that House. He hath not said, Thy holy Temple is marvellous in pillars, marvellous in marbles, marvellous in gilded ceilings ; but is "marvellous in righteousness." Without thou hast eyes wherewith thou mayest see marbles, and gold : within is an eye wherewith may be seen the beauty of righteousness. If there is no beauty in righteousness, why is a righteous old man loved? What bringeth he in body that may please the eyes? Crooked limbs, brow wrinkled, head blanched with gray hairs, dotage everywhere full of plaints. But perchance because thine eyes this decrepit old man pleaseth not, thine ears he pleaseth : with what words? with what song? Even if perchance when a young man he sang well, all with age hath been lost. Doth perchance the sound of his words please thine ears, that can hardly articulate whole words for loss of teeth? Nevertheless, if righteous he is, if another man's goods he coveteth not, if of his own that he possesseth he distributeth to the needy, if he giveth good advice, and soundly judgeth, if he believeth the entire faith, if for his belief in the faith he is ready to expend even those very shattered limbs, for many Martyrs are

---

[1] Ps. cxli. 2.
[2] Matt. xxvii. 46.
[3] Heb. ix. 7.
[4] Oxf. MSS. "taken and chosen."
[5] Eph. iv. 13.
[6] 1 Cor. xi. 3.
[7] Ps. i. 1.

even old men; why do we love him? What
good thing in him do we see with the eyes of
the flesh? Not any. There is therefore a kind
of beauty in righteousness, which we see with the
eye of the heart, and we love, and we kindle
with affection: how much men found to love in
those same Martyrs, though beasts tare their
limbs! Is it possible but that when blood was
staining all parts, when with the teeth of mon-
sters their bowels gushed out, the eyes had nothing but objects to shudder at? What was there
to be loved, except that in that hideous spectacle
of mangled limbs, entire was the beauty of righteousness? These are the good things of the
House of God, with these prepare thyself to be
satisfied. . . . "Blessed they which hunger and
thirst after righteousness, for they shall be filled."[1]
"Thy holy Temple is marvellous in righteousness." And that same temple, brethren, do not
imagine to be aught but yourselves. Love ye
righteousness, and ye are the Temple of God.

9. "Hearken to us, O God, our Saviour"
(ver. 5). He hath disclosed now Whom he
nameth as God. The "Saviour" specially is the
Lord Jesus Christ. It hath appeared now more
openly of Whom he had said, "Unto Thee every
flesh shall come."[2] That One Man that is
taken unto Him into the Temple of God, is both
many and is One. In the person of One he hath
said, "Hearken, O God, i.e., to my hunger:"[3]
and because the same One of many is composed, now he saith, "Hearken to us, O God,
our Saviour." Hear Him now more openly
preached: "Hearken to us, O God, our Saviour,
the Hope of all the ends of the earth and in the
sea afar." Behold wherefore hath been said,
"Unto Thee every flesh shall come." From
every quarter they come. "Hope of all the
ends of the earth," not hope of one corner, not
hope of Judæa alone, not hope of Africa alone,
not hope of Pannonia, not hope of East or of
West: but "Hope of all the ends of the earth,
and in the sea afar:" of the very ends of the
earth. "And in the sea afar:" and because in
the sea, therefore afar. For the sea by a figure
is spoken of this world, with saltness bitter, with
storms troubled; where men of perverse and
depraved appetites have become like fishes devouring one another. Observe the evil sea,
bitter sea, with waves violent, observe with what
sort of men it is filled. Who desireth an inheritance except through the death of another? Who
desireth gain except by the loss of another?
By the fall of others how many men wish to be
exalted? How many, in order that they may
buy, desire for other men to sell their goods?
How they mutually oppress, and how they that
are able do devour! And when one fish hath

devoured, the greater the less, itself also is
devoured by some greater. . . . Because evil
fishes that were taken within the nets they said
they would not endure; they themselves have
become more evil than they whom they said[4]
they could not endure. For those nets did take
fishes both good and evil. The Lord saith,
"The kingdom of Heaven is like to a sein cast
into the sea, which gathereth of every kind,
which, when it had been filled, drawing out, and
sitting on the shore, they gathered the good into
vessels, but the evil they cast out: so it shall
be," He saith, "in the consummation of the
world."[5] He showeth what is the shore, He
showeth what is the end of the sea. "The
angels shall go forth, and shall sever the evil
from the midst of the just, and shall cast them
into the furnace of fire: there shall be weeping
and gnashing of teeth." Ha! ye citizens of
Jerusalem that are within the nets, and are good
fishes; endure the evil, the nets break ye not:
together with them ye are in a sea, not together
with them will ye be in the vessels. For "Hope"
He is "of the ends of the earth," Himself is
Hope "also in the sea afar." Afar, because
also in the sea.

10. "Preparing mountains in His strength"
(ver. 6). Not in their strength. For He hath
prepared great preachers, and those same He
hath called mountains; humble in themselves,
exalted in Him. "Preparing mountains in His
strength." What saith one of those same
mountains? "We ourselves in our own selves
have had the answer of death, in order that in
ourselves we should not trust, but in God that
raiseth the dead."[6] He that in himself doth
trust, and in Christ trusteth not, is not of those
mountains which He hath prepared in His
strength. "Preparing mountains in His strength:
girded about in power." "Power," I understand: "girded about," is what? They that
put Christ in the midst, "girded about" they
make Him, that is on all sides begirt. We all
have Him in common, therefore in the midst
He is: all we gird Him about that believe in
Him: and because our faith is not of our
strength, but of His power; therefore girded
about He is in His power; not in our own
strength.

11. "That troublest the bottom of the sea"
(ver. 7). He hath done this: it is seen what
He hath done. For He hath prepared mountains in His strength, hath sent them to preach:
girded about He is by believers in power: and
moved is the sea, moved is the world, and it
beginneth to persecute His saints. "Girded
about in power: that troublest the bottom of
the sea." He hath not said, that troublest the

---

[1] Matt. v. 6.　　[2] Ps. lxv. 2.　　[3] Ps. lxv. 4.　　[4] Al. "pretended."　　[5] Matt. xiii. 47-49.　　[6] 2 Cor. i. 9.

sea; but "the bottom of the sea." The bottom of the sea is the heart of ungodly men. For just as from the bottom more thoroughly all things are stirred, and the bottom holdeth firm all things: so whatsoever hath gone forth by tongue, by hands, by divers powers for the persecution of the Church, from the bottom hath gone forth. For if there were not the root of iniquity in the heart, all those things would not have gone forth against Christ. The bottom He troubled, perchance in order that the bottom He might also empty: for in the case of certain evil men He emptied the sea from the bottom, and made the sea a desert place. Another Psalm saith this, "That turneth sea into dry land." [1] All ungodly and heathen men that have believed were sea, have been made land; with salt waves at first barren, afterwards with the fruit of righteousness productive. "That troublest the bottom of the sea: the sound of its waves who shall endure?" "Who shall endure," is what? What man shall endure the sound of the waves of the sea, the behests of the high powers of the world? But whence are they endured? Because He prepareth mountains in His strength. In that therefore which he hath said "who shall" endure? he saith thus: We ourselves of our own selves should not be able to endure those persecutions, unless He gave strength.

12. "The nations shall be troubled" (ver. 8). At first they shall be troubled: but those mountains prepared in the strength of Christ, are they troubled? Troubled is the sea, against the mountains it dasheth: the sea breaketh, unshaken the mountains have remained. "The nations shall be troubled, and all men shall fear." Behold now all men fear: they that before have been troubled do now all fear. The Christians feared not, and now the Christians are feared. All that did persecute do now fear. For He hath overcome that is girded about with power, to Him hath come every flesh in such sort, that the rest by their very minority do now fear. And all men shall fear, that inhabit the ends of the earth, because of Thy signs. For miracles the Apostles wrought, and thence all the ends of the earth have feared and have believed. "Outgoings in morning and in evening Thou shall delight:" that is, Thou makest delightful. Already in this life what is there being promised to us? There are outgoings in morning, there are outgoings in evening. By the morning he signifieth the prosperity of the world, by the evening he signifieth the trouble of the world. . . . At first when he was promising gain, it was morning to thee: but now evening draweth on, sad thou hast become. But He that hath given thee an outgoing in the

morning, will give one also in the evening. In the same manner as thou hast contemned the morning of the world by the light of the Lord, so contemn the evening also by the sufferings of the Lord, in saying to thy soul, What more will this man do to me, than my Lord hath suffered for me? May I [2] hold fast justice, not consent to iniquity. Let him vent his rage on the flesh, the trap will be broken, and I will fly to my Lord, that saith to me, "Do not fear them that kill the body, but the soul are not able to kill." [3] And for the body itself He hath given security, saying, "A hair of your head shall not perish." [4] Nobly here he hath set down, " Thou wilt delight outgoings in morning and in evening." For if thou take not delight in the very outgoing, thou wilt not labour to go out thence. Thou runnest thy head into the promised gain, if thou art not delighted with the promise of the Saviour. And again thou yieldest to one tempting and terrifying, if thou find no delight in Him that suffered before thee, in order that He might make an outgoing for thee.

13. "Thou hast visited the earth, and hast inebriated it" (ver. 9). Whence hast inebriated the earth? "Thy cup inebriating how glorious it is!" [5] "Thou hast visited the earth, and hast inebriated it." Thou hast sent Thy clouds, they have rained down the preaching of the truth, inebriated is the earth. "Thou hast multiplied to enrich it." Whence? "The river of God is filled with water." What is the river of God? The people of God. The first people was filled with water, wherewith the rest of the earth might be watered. Hear Him promising water: " If any man thirst, let him come to Me and drink: he that believeth on Me, rivers of living water from his belly shall flow:" [6] if rivers, one river also; for in respect of unity many are one. Many Churches and one Church, many faithful and one Bride of Christ: so many rivers and one river. Many Israelites believed, and were fulfilled with the Holy Spirit; from thence they were scattered abroad through the nations, they began to preach the truth, and from the river of God that was filled with water, was the whole earth watered. "Thou hast prepared food for them: because thus is Thy preparing." Not because they have deserved of Thee, whom Thou hast forgiven sins: the merits of them were evil, but Thou for Thy mercy's sake, "because thus is Thy preparing," thus " Thou hast prepared food for them."

14. "The furrows thereof inebriate Thou" (ver. 10). Let there be made therefore at first furrows to be inebriated: let the hardness of our breast be opened with the share of the word of God, "The furrows thereof inebriate Thou: multiply the generations thereof." We see, they

---

[1] Ps. lxvi. 6.

[2] Oxf. MSS. and old ed. "that I may."   [3] Matt. x. 28.
[4] Luke xxi. 18.   [5] Ps. xxiii. 5.   [6] John vii. 37, 38.

believe, and by them believing other men believe, and because of those others believe ; and it is not sufficient for one man, that having become himself a believer, he should gain one. So is multiplied seed too : a few grains are scattered, and fields spring up. " In the drops thereof it shall rejoice, when it shall rise up." That is, before it be perchance enlarged to the bulk of a river, " when it shall rise up, in its drops," that is, in those meet for it, " it shall rejoice." For upon those that are yet babes, and upon the weak, are dropped some portions of the sacraments, because they cannot receive the fulness of the truth. Hear in what manner he droppeth upon babes, while they are rising up, that is, in their recent rising having small capacities : the Apostle saith, " To you I could not speak as if to spiritual, but as if to carnal, as if to babes in Christ." [1] When he saith, " to babes in Christ," he speaketh of them as already risen up, but not yet meet to receive that plenteous wisdom, whereof he saith, " Wisdom we speak among perfect men." [2] Let it rejoice in its drops, while it is rising up and is growing, when strengthened it shall receive wisdom also : in the same manner as an infant is fed with milk, and becometh fit for meat, and nevertheless at first out of that very meat for which it was not fit, for it milk is made.

15. " Thou shalt bless the crown of the year of Thy goodness" (ver. 11). Seed is now sowing, that which is sown is growing, there will be the harvest too. And now over the seed the enemy hath sown tares ; and there have risen up evil ones among the good, false Christians, having like leaf, but not like fruit. For those are properly called tares,[3] which spring up in the manner of wheat, for instance darnel, for instance wild oats, and all such as have the first leaf the same. Therefore of the sowing of the tares thus saith the Lord : " There hath come an enemy, and hath sown over them tares ; " [4] but what hath he done to the grain? The wheat is not choked by the tares, nay, through endurance of the tares the fruit of the wheat is increased. For the Lord Himself said to certain workmen desiring to root up the tares, " Suffer ye both to grow unto the harvest." [5] . . . Conquer the devil, and thou wilt have a crown. " Thou shalt bless the crown of the year of Thy goodness." Again he maketh reference to the goodness of God, lest any one boast of his own merits. " Thy plains shall be filled with abundance."

16. " The ends of the desert shall grow fat, and the hills shall be encircled with exultation " (ver. 12). Plains, hills, ends of the desert, the same are also men. Plains, because of the equality : because of equality, I say, from thence just peoples have been called plains. Hills, because of lifting up : because God doth lift up in Himself those that humble themselves. Ends of the desert are all nations. Wherefore ends of the desert? Deserted they were, to them no Prophet had been sent : they were in like case as is a desert where no man passeth by. No word of God was sent to the nations : to the people Israel alone the Prophets preached. We came to the Lord ; [6] the wheat believed among that same people of the Jews. For He said at that time to the disciples, " Ye say, far off is the harvest : look back, and see how white are the lands to harvest." There hath been therefore a first harvest, there will be a second in the last age. The first harvest was of Jews, because there were sent to them Prophets proclaiming a coming Saviour. Therefore the Lord said to His disciples, " See how white are the lands to harvest : " [7] the lands, to wit, of Judæa. " Other men," He saith, " have laboured, and into their labours ye have entered." [8] The Prophets laboured to sow, and ye with the sickle have entered into their labours. There hath been finished therefore the first harvest, and thence, with that very wheat which then was purged, hath been sown the round world ; so that there ariseth another harvest, which at the end is to be reaped. In the second harvest have been sown tares, now here there is labour. Just as in that first harvest the Prophets laboured until the Lord came : so in that second harvest the Apostles laboured, and all preachers of the truth labour, even until at the end the Lord send unto the harvest His Angels. Aforetime, I say, a desert there was, " but the ends of the desert shall grow fat." Behold where the Prophets had given no sound, the Lord of the Prophets hath been received, " The ends of the desert shall grow fat, and with exultation the hills shall be encircled."

17. " Clothed have been the rams of the sheep " (ver. 13) : " with exultation " must be understood. For with what exultation the hills are encircled, with the same are clothed the rams of the sheep. Rams are the very same as hills. For hills they are because of more eminent grace ; rams, because they are leaders of the flocks. . . . " They shall shout : " thence they shall abound with wheat, because they shall shout. What shall they shout? " For a hymn they shall say." For one thing it is to shout against God, another thing to say a hymn ; one thing to shout iniquities, another thing to shout the praises of God. If thou shout in blasphemy, thorns thou hast brought forth : if thou shoutest in a hymn, thou aboundest in wheat.

---

[1] 1 Cor. iii. 1.   [2] 1 Cor. ii. 6.   [3] *Zizania.*
[4] Matt. xiii. 25.   [5] Matt. xiii. 30.

[6] *Ventum est ad Dominum;* al. *a Domino,* " The Lord came."
[7] John iv. 35.
[8] John iv. 38.

PSALM LXVI.[1]

1. This Psalm hath on the title the inscription, "For the end, a song of a Psalm of Resurrection." When ye hear "for the end," whenever the Psalms are repeated, understand it "for Christ:" the Apostle saying, "For the end of the law is Christ, for righteousness to every one believing." [2] In what manner therefore here Resurrection is sung, ye will hear, and whose Resurrection it is, as far as Himself deigneth to give and disclose. For the Resurrection we Christians know already hath come to pass in our Head, and in the members it is to be. The Head of the Church is Christ,[3] the members of Christ are the Church. That which hath preceded in the Head, will follow in the Body. This is our hope ; for this we believe, for this we endure and persevere amid so great perverseness of this world, hope comforting us, before that hope becometh reality. . . . The Jews did hold the hope of the resurrection of the dead : and they hoped that themselves alone would rise again to a blessed life because of the work of the Law, and because of the justifications of the Scriptures, which the Jews alone had, and the Gentiles had not. Crucified was Christ, "blindness in part happened unto Israel, in order that the fulness of the Gentiles might enter in : " [4] as the Apostle saith. The resurrection of the dead beginneth to be promised to the Gentiles also that believe in Jesus Christ, that He hath risen again. Thence this Psalm is against the presumption and pride of the Jews, for the comfort of the Gentiles that are to be called to the same hope of resurrection.

2. . . . Thence he beginneth, " Be joyful in God." Who? "Every land" (ver. 1). Not therefore Judæa alone. See, brethren, after what sort is set forth the universality of the Church in the whole world spread abroad : and mourn ye not only the Jews, who envied the Gentiles that grace, but still more for heretics wail ye. For if they are to be mourned, that have not been gathered together, how much more they that being gathered together have been divided? " Jubilate in God every land." What is "jubilate"? Into the voice of rejoicings break forth if ye cannot into that of words. For "jubilation" is not of words, but the sound alone of men rejoicing is uttered, as of a heart labouring and bringing forth into voice the pleasure of a thing imagined which cannot be expressed. " Be joyful in God every land : " let no one jubilate in a part : let every land be joyful, let the Catholic Church jubilate. The Catholic Church embraceth the whole : whosoever holdeth a part and from the whole is cut off, should howl, not jubilate.

3. " But play ye to His name " (ver. 2).

What hath he said? By you "playing" let His name be blessed. But what it is to "play"? To play is also to take up an instrument which is called a psaltery, and by the striking and action of the hands to accompany voices. If therefore ye jubilate so that God may hear ; play also something that men may both see and hear : but not to your own name. . . . For if for the sake of yourselves being glorified ye do good works, we make the same reply as He made to certain of such men, " Verily I say unto you, they have received their reward : " [5] and again, " Otherwise no reward ye will have with your Father that is in Heaven." [6] Thou wilt say, ought I, then, to hide my works, that I do them not before men? No. But what saith He? " Let your works shine before men." In doubt then I shall remain. On one side Thou sayest to me, " Take heed that ye do not your righteousness before men : " on the other side Thou sayest to me, " Let your good works shine before men ; " what shall I keep? what do? what leave undone? A man can as well serve two masters commanding different things as one commanding different things. I command not, saith the Lord, different things. The end observe, for the end sing : with what end thou doest it, see thou. If for this reason thou doest it, that thou mayest be glorified, I have forbidden it : but if for this reason, that God may be glorified, I have commanded it. Play therefore, not to your own name, but to the name of the Lord your God. Play ye, let Him be lauded : live ye well, let Him be glorified. For whence have ye that same living well? If for everlasting ye had had it, ye would never have lived ill ; if from yourselves ye had had it, ye never would have done otherwise than have lived well. " Give glory to His praise." Our whole attention upon the praise of God he directeth, nothing for us he leaveth whence we should be praised. Let us glory thence the more, and rejoice : to Him let us cleave, in Him let us be praised. Ye heard when the Apostle was being read, " See ye your calling, brethren, how not many wise after the flesh, not many mighty, not many noble, but the foolish things of the world God hath chosen to confound the wise." [7] . . . But the Lord chose afterwards orators also ; but they would have been proud, if He had not first chosen fishermen ; He chose rich men ; but they would have said that on account of their riches they had been chosen, unless at first He had chosen poor men : He chose Emperors afterwards ; but better is it, that when an Emperor hath come to Rome, he should lay aside his crown, and weep at the monument of a fisherman, than that a fisherman should weep at the monument of an Emperor. "For the weak things of the world God hath chosen to confound the strong," etc.[1] . . . And what followeth? The Apostle hath concluded, "That there might not glory before God any flesh." See ye how from us He hath taken away, that He might give glory : hath taken away ours, that He might give His own ; hath taken away empty, that He might give full ; hath taken away insecure, that He might give solid. . . .

4. "Say ye to God, How to be feared are Thy works !" (ver. 3). Wherefore to be feared and not to be loved? Hear thou another voice of a Psalm : "Serve ye the Lord in fear, and exult unto Him with trembling."[2] What meaneth this? Hear the voice of the Apostle : "With fear," he saith, "and trembling, your own salvation work ye out."[3] Wherefore with fear and trembling? He hath subjoined the reason : "for God it is that worketh in you both to will and to work according to good will."[4] If therefore God worketh in thee, by the Grace of God thou workest well, not by thy strength. Therefore if thou rejoicest, fear also : lest perchance that which was given to a humble man be taken away from a proud one. . . . Brethren, if against the Jews of old, cut off from the root of the Patriarchs, we ought not to exalt ourselves, but rather to fear and say to God, "How to be feared are Thy works : " how much less ought we not to exalt ourselves against the fresh wounds of the cutting off ! Before there had been cut off Jews, graffed in Gentiles ; from the very graft there have been cut off heretics ; but neither against them ought we to exalt ourselves ; lest perchance he deserve to be cut off, that delighteth to revile them that are cut off. My brethren, a bishop's voice, however unworthy, hath sounded to you :[5] we pray you to beware, whosoever ye are in the Church, do not revile them that are not within ; but pray ye rather, that they too may be within. For God is able again to graft them in.[6] Of the very Jews the Apostle said this, and it was done in their case. The Lord rose again, and many believed : they perceived not when they crucified, nevertheless afterwards they believed in Him, and there was forgiven them so great a transgression. The shedding of the Lord's blood was forgiven the manslayers, not to say, God-slayers : "for if they had known, the Lord of glory they never would have crucified."[7] Now to the manslayers hath been forgiven the shedding of the blood of Him innocent : and that same blood which through madness they shed, through grace they have drunk. . . . O fulness of Gentiles, say thou to God, "How to

be feared are Thy works !" and so rejoice thou as that thou mayest fear, be not exalted above the branches cut off.

5. "In the multitude of thy power Thine enemies shall lie to Thee." For this purpose he saith, "to Thee thine enemies shall lie," in order that great may be Thy power. What is this? With more attention hearken. The power of our Lord Jesus Christ most chiefly appeared in the Resurrection, from whence this Psalm hath received its title. And rising again, He appeared to His disciples.[8] He appeared not to His enemies, but to His disciples. Crucified He appeared to all men, rising again to believers : so that afterwards also he that would might believe, and to him that should believe, resurrection might be promised. Many holy men wrought many miracles ; no one of them when dead did rise again : because even they that by them were raised to life, were raised to life to die. . . . Because therefore the Jews might say, when the Lord did miracles, Moses hath done these things, Elias hath done, Eliseus hath done them : they might for themselves say these words, because those men also did raise to life dead men, and did many miracles : therefore when from Him a sign was demanded, of the peculiar sign making mention which in Himself alone was to be, He saith, "This generation crooked and provoking[9] seeketh a sign, and a sign shall not be given to it, except the sign of Jonas the Prophet : for as Jonas was in the belly of the whale three days and three nights, so shall be also the Son of Man in the heart of the earth three days and three nights."[10] In what way was Jonas in the belly of the whale? Was it not so that afterwards alive he was vomited out? Hell[11] was to the Lord what the whale was to Jonas. This sign peculiar to Himself He mentioned, this is the most mighty sign. It is more mighty to live again after having been dead, than not to have been dead. The greatness of the power of the Lord as He was made Man, in the virtue of the Resurrection doth appear. . . .

6. Observe also the very lie of the false witnesses in the Gospel, and see how it is about Resurrection. For when to the Lord had been said, "What sign showest Thou to us, that Thou doest these things?"[12] besides that which He had spoken about Jonah[13] through another similitude of this same thing also He spake, that ye might know this peculiar sign had been especially pointed out : "Destroy this Temple," He saith, "and in three days I will raise it up." And they said, "In forty and six years was builded this temple, and wilt Thou in three

---

[1] 1 Cor. i. 27.　　[2] Ps. ii. 11.　　[3] Philip. ii. 12.
[4] Philip. ii. 13.
[5] Some Oxf. MSS. "My brethren, however their voice soundeth toward you."
[6] Rom. xi. 23.　　[7] 1 Cor. ii. 8.

[8] Acts x. 40.
[9] *Americans*, etc.; most MSS." evil and adulterous."
[10] Matt. xii. 39, 40.
[11] [*i e.*, Hades, Sheol. — C.]　　[12] John ii. 18.
[13] Matt. xii. 39.

days raise it up?"[1] And the evangelist explaining what it was, "But this," he saith, "spake Jesus of the Temple of His Body."[2] Behold this His power He said He would show to men in the same thing as that from whence He had given the similitude of a Temple, because of His flesh, which was the Temple of the Divinity hidden within. Whence the Jews outwardly saw the Temple, the Deity dwelling within they saw not. Out of those words of the Lord false witnesses made up a lie to say against Him, out of those very words wherein He mentioned His future Resurrection, in speaking of the Temple. For false witnesses, when they were asked what they had heard Him say, alleged against Him : "We heard Him saying, I will destroy this Temple, and after three days I will raise it up."[3] "After three days I will raise up," they had heard : "I will destroy," they had not heard : but had heard "destroy ye." One word they changed and a few letters, in order to support their false testimony. But for whom changest thou a word, O human vanity, O human weakness? For the Word, the Unchangeable, dost thou change a word? Thou changest thy word, dost thou change God's Word? . . . Wherefore said they that Thou hadst said, "I will destroy ;" and said not that which Thou saidest, "destroy ye"? It was, as it were, in order that they might defend themselves from the charge of destroying the Temple without cause. For Christ, because He willed it, died : and nevertheless ye killed Him. Behold we grant you, O ye liars, Himself destroyed the Temple. For it hath been said by the Apostle, "That loved me, and gave up Himself for me."[4] It hath been said of the Father, "That His own Son spared not, but gave Him up for us all."[5] . . . By all means be it that Himself destroyed the Temple, Himself destroyed that said, "Power I have to lay down My Soul,[6] and power I have again to take it : no one taketh it from Me, but I Myself lay it down from Me, and again I take it."[7] Be it that Himself hath destroyed the Temple in His Grace, in your malice. "In the multitude of Thy power thine enemies shall lie to Thee." Behold they lie, behold they are believed, behold Thou art oppressed, behold Thou art crucified, behold Thou art insulted, behold head is wagged at Thee, "If Son of God He is, let Him come down from the Cross."[8] Behold when Thou wilt, life Thou layest down, and with lance in the side art pierced, and Sacraments from Thy side flow forth ;[9] Thou art taken down from the Tree, wound in linens, laid in the sepulchre, there are set guards lest Thy disciples take Thee away ;

there cometh the hour of Thy Resurrection, earth is shaken, tombs are cloven, Thou risest again in secret, appearest openly. Where then are those liars? Where is the false testimony of evil will? Have not Thine enemies in the multitude of Thy power lied to Thee?

7. Give them also those guards at the Tomb, let them recount what they have seen, let them take money and lie too.[10] . . . They too were added to the lie of the enemies : increased was the number of liars, that increased might be the reward of believers. Therefore they lied, "in the multitude of Thy power" they lied : to confound liars Thou hast appeared to men of truth, and Thou hast appeared to those men of truth whom Thou hast made men of truth.

8. Let Jews remain in their lies : to Thee, because in the multitude of Thy power they lied, let there be done that which followeth, "Let every land worship Thee, and play to Thee, play to Thy name, O Most Highest" (ver. 4). A little before, Most Lowly, now Most Highest : Most Lowly in the hands of lying enemies ; Most Highest above the head of praising Angels. O ye Gentiles, O most distant nations, leave lying Jews, come confessing. "Come ye, and see the works of the Lord : terrible in counsels above the sons of men" (ver. 5). Son of Man indeed He too hath been called, and verily Son of Man He became : very Son of God in the form of God ;[11] very Son of Man in form of a servant : but do not judge of that form by the condition of others alike : "terrible" He is "in counsels above the sons of men." Sons of men took counsel to crucify Christ, being crucified He blinded the crucifiers. What then have ye done, sons of men, by taking keen counsels against your Lord, in whom was hidden Majesty, and to sight shown weakness? Ye were taking counsels to destroy, He to blind and save ; to blind proud men, to save humble men : but to blind those same proud men, to the end that, being blinded they might be humbled, being humbled might confess, having confessed might be enlightened. "Terrible in counsels above the sons of men." Terrible indeed. Behold blindness in part to Israel hath happened :[12] behold the Jews, out of whom was born Christ, are without : behold the Gentiles, that were against Judæa, in Christ are within. "Terrible in counsels above the sons of men."

9. Wherefore what hath He done by the terror of His counsel? He hath turned the sea into dry land. For this followeth, "That hath turned the sea into dry land" (ver. 6). A sea was the world, bitter with saltness, troubled with tempest, raging with waves of persecutions, sea it was : truly into dry land the sea hath been

---

[1] John ii. 19, 20. [2] John ii. 21.
[3] Matt. xxvi. 61; Mark xiv. 58; John ii. 19
[4] Gal. ii. 20. [5] Rom. viii. 32. [6] Or, "life."
[7] John x. 18. [8] Matt. xxvii. 49. [9] John xix. 34.

[10] Matt. xxviii. 12. [11] Philip. ii. 6. [12] Rom. xi. 25.

turned, now there thirsteth for sweet water the world that with salt water was filled. Who hath done this? He "that hath turned the sea into dry land." Now the soul of all the Gentiles saith what? "My soul is as it were land without water to Thee."[1] "That hath turned the sea into dry land. In the river they shall pass over on foot." Those same persons that have been turned into dry land, though they were before sea, "in the river on foot shall pass over." What is the river? The river is all the mortality of the world. Observe a river: some things come and pass by, other things that are to pass by do succeed. Is it not thus with the water of a river, that from earth springeth and floweth? Every one that is born must needs give place to one going to be born: and all this order of things rolling along is a kind of river. Into this river let not the soul greedily throw herself, let her not throw herself, but let her stand still. And how shall she pass over the pleasures of things doomed to perish? Let her believe in Christ, and she will pass over on foot: she passeth over with Him for Leader, on foot she passeth over.

10. "There we will be joyous in Him." O ye Jews, of your own works boast ye: lay aside the pride of boasting of yourselves, take up the Grace of being joyous in Christ. For therein we will be joyous, but not in ourselves: "there we will be joyous in Him." When shall we joy? When we shall have passed over the river on foot. Life everlasting is promised, resurrection is promised, there our flesh no longer shall be a river: for a river it is now, while it is mortality. Observe whether there standeth still any age. Boys desire to grow up; and they know not how by succeeding years the span of their life is lessened. For years are not added to but taken from them as they grow: just as the water of a river alway draweth near, but from the source it withdraweth. And boys desire to grow up that they may escape the thraldom of elders; behold they grow up, it cometh to pass quickly, they arrive at youth: let them that have emerged from boyhood retain, if they are able, their youth: that too passeth away. Old age succeedeth:[2] let even old age be everlasting; with death it is removed. Therefore a river there is[3] of flesh that is born. This river of mortality, so that it doth not by reason of concupiscence of things mortal undermine and carry him away, he easily passeth over, that humbly, that is on foot, passeth over, He being leader that first hath passed over, that of the flood in the way even unto death hath drunk, and therefore hath lifted up the head.[4] Passing over therefore on foot that river, that is, easily passing over that mortality that glideth along, "there we will be joyous in Him." But now in what save in Him, or in the hope of Him? For even if we are joyous now, in hope we are joyous; but then in Him we shall be joyous. And now in Him, but through hope: "but then face to face."[5] "There we will be joyous in Him."

11. In whom? "In Him that reigneth in His virtue for everlasting" (ver. 7). For what virtue have we? and is it everlasting? If everlasting were our virtue, we should not have slipped, should not have fallen into sin, we should not have deserved penal mortality. He, of His good pleasure, took up that whereunto our desert threw us down.[6] "That reigneth in His virtue for everlasting." Of Him partakers let us be made, in whose virtue we shall be strong, but He in His own. We enlightened, He a light enlightening: we, being turned away from Him, are in darkness; turned away from Himself He cannot be. With the heat of Him we are warmed; from whence withdrawing we had grown cold, to the Same drawing near again we are warmed. Therefore let us speak to Him that He may keep us in His virtue, because "in Him we will be joyous that reigneth in His virtue for everlasting."

12. But this thing is not granted to believing Jews alone. . . . "The eyes of Him do look upon the Gentiles." And what do we? The Jews will murmur; the Jews will say, "what He hath given to us, the same to them also; to us Gospel, to them Gospel; to us the Grace of Resurrection, and to them the Grace of Resurrection; doth it profit us nothing that we have received the Law, and that in the justifications of the Law we have lived, and have kept the commandments of the fathers? Nothing will it avail? The same to them as to us." Let them not strive, let them not dispute. "Let not them that are bitter be exalted in their own selves."[7] O flesh miserable and wasting, art thou not sinful? Why crieth out thy tongue? Let the conscience be listened to. "For all men have sinned, and need the glory of God."[8] Know thyself, human weakness. Thou didst receive the Law, in order that a transgressor also of the Law thou mightest be:[9] for thou hast not kept and fulfilled that which thou didst receive. There hath come to thee because of the Law, not the justification which the Law enjoineth, but the transgression which thou hast done. If therefore there hath abounded sin, why enviest thou Grace more abounding. Be not bitter, for "let not them that are bitter be

---

[1] Ps. cxliii. 6.
[2] Oxf. mss. add, "Let even old age succeed for everlasting, let," etc.
[3] Oxf. mss. "is the mortality."

[4] Ps. cx. 7.   [5] 1 Cor. xiii. 12.   [6] Gen. iii. 17, etc.
[7] [See on Ps. lxix. ver. 10, *infra.* — C.]
[8] Rom. iii. 23.   [9] Rom. v. 20.

exalted in their own selves." He seemeth in a manner to have uttered a curse in "Let not them that are bitter be exalted;" yea, be they exalted, but not "in themselves." Let them be humbled in themselves, exalted in Christ. For, "he that humbleth himself shall be exalted; and he that exalteth himself shall be humbled."[1] "Let not them that are bitter be exalted in their own selves."

13. "Bless our God, ye nations" (ver. 8). Behold, there have been driven back they that are bitter, reckoning hath been made with them: some have been converted, some have continued proud. Let not them terrify you that grudge the Gentiles Gospel Grace: now hath come the Seed of Abraham, in whom are blessed all nations.[2] Bless ye Him in whom ye are blessed, "Bless our God, ye nations: and hear ye the voice of His praise." Praise not yourselves, but praise Him. What is the voice of His praise? That by His Grace we are whatever of good we are. "Who hath set my Soul unto life" (ver. 9). Behold the voice of his praise: "Who hath set my Soul unto life." Therefore in death she was: in death she was, in thyself. Thence it is that ye ought not to have been exalted in yourselves. Therefore in death she was, in thyself: where will it be in life, save in Him that said, "I am the Way, the Truth, and the Life"?[3] Just as to certain believers the Apostle saith, "Ye were sometime darkness, but now light in the Lord."[4] . . . "And hath not given unto motion my feet." He hath set my Soul unto life, He guideth the feet that they stumble not, be not moved and given unto motion; He maketh us to live, He maketh us to persevere even unto the end, in order that for everlasting we may live. . . .

14. "For thou hast proved us, O God; Thou hast fired us as silver is fired" (ver. 10). Hast not fired us like hay, but like silver: by applying to us fire, Thou hast not turned us into ashes, but Thou hast washed off uncleanness, "Thou hast fired us, as silver is fired." And see in what manner God is wroth against them, whose Soul He hath set unto life. "Thou hast led us into a trap:" not that we might be caught and die, but that we might be tried and delivered from it. "Thou hast laid tribulations upon our back." For having been to ill purpose lifted up, proud we were: having been to ill purpose lifted up, we were bowed down, in order that being bowed down, we should be lifted up for good. "Thou hast laid tribulations on our back:" "Thou hast set men over our heads" (ver. 11). All these things the Church hath suffered in sundry and divers persecutions: She hath suffered this in Her individual members, even now doth suffer it. For there is not one, that in this life

could say that he was exempt from these trials. Therefore there are set even men over our heads: we endure those whom we would not, we suffer for our betters those whom we know to be worse. But if sins be wanting, a man is justly superior: but by how much there are more sins, by so much he is inferior. And it is a good thing to consider ourselves to be sinners, and thus endure men set over our heads: in order that we also to God may confess that deservedly we suffer. For why dost thou suffer with indignation that which He doeth who is just? "Thou hast laid tribulations upon our back: Thou hast set men over our heads." God seemeth to be wroth, when He doeth these things: fear not, for a Father He is, He is never so wroth as to destroy. When ill thou livest, if He spareth, He is more angry. In a word, these tribulations are the rods of Him correcting, lest there be a sentence from Him punishing. . . .

15. "We have passed through fire and water." Fire and water are both dangerous in this life. Certainly water seemeth to extinguish fire, and fire seemeth to dry up water. Thus also these are the trials, wherein aboundeth this life. Fire burneth, water corrupteth: both must be feared, both the burning of tribulation and the water of corruption. Whenever there is adversity, and anything which is called unhappiness in this world, there is as it were fire: whenever there is prosperity, and the world's plenty floweth about one, there is as it were water. See that fire burn thee not, nor water corrupt. . . . Hasten not to the water: through fire pass over to the water, that thou mayest pass over the water also. Therefore also in the mystic rites,[5] and in catechising and in exorcising,[6] there is first used fire. For whence ofttimes do the unclean spirits cry out, "I burn," if that is not fire? But after the fire of Exorcism we come to Baptism: so that from fire to water, from water unto refreshment. But as in the Sacraments, so it is in the temptations of this world: the straitness of fear draweth near first, in place of fire; afterwards fear being removed, we ought to be afraid lest worldly happiness corrupt. But when the fire hath not made thee burst, and when thou hast not sunk in the water, but hast swum out; through discipline thou passest over to rest, and passing over through fire and water, thou art led forth into a place of refreshment. For of those things whereof the signs are in the Sacraments, there are the very realities in that perfection of life everlasting. . . . But we are not torpid there, but we rest: nor though it be called heat, shall we be hot there, but we shall be fervent in spirit. Observe that same heat in another Psalm: "nor is there any one that hideth himself from the

---

[1] Matt. xxiii. 12.　[2] Gen. xii. 3.
[3] John xiv. 6.　[4] Eph. v. 8.
[5] *Sacramentis.*
[6] Exorcism before Baptism.

heat thereof." [1]　What saith also the Apostle? "In spirit fervent." [2]　Therefore, "we have gone over through fire and water: and Thou hast led us forth into a cool place."

16. Observe how not only concerning a cool place, but neither of that very fire to be desired he hath been silent: "I will enter into Thy House in holocausts" (ver. 13). What is a holocaust? A whole sacrifice burned up, but with fire divine. For a sacrifice is called a holocaust, when the whole is burned. One thing are the parts of sacrifices, another thing a holocaust: when the whole is burned and the whole consumed by fire divine, it is called a holocaust: when a part, a sacrifice. Every holocaust indeed is a sacrifice: but not every sacrifice a holocaust. Holocausts therefore he is promising, the Body of Christ is speaking, the Unity of Christ is speaking, "I will enter into Thy House in holocausts." All that is mine let Thy fire consume, let nothing of mine remain to me, let all be Thine. But this shall be in the Resurrection of just men, "when both this corruptible shall be clad in incorruption, and this mortal shall be clad in immortality: then shall come to pass that which hath been written, ' Death is swallowed up in victory.'" [3] Victory is, as it were, fire divine: when it swalloweth up our death also, it is a holocaust. There remaineth not anything mortal in the flesh, there remaineth not anything culpable in the spirit: the whole of mortal life shall be consumed, in order that in life everlasting it may be consummated, that from death we may be preserved in life.[4] These therefore will be the holocausts. And what shall there be "in the holocausts"?

17. "I will render to Thee my vows, which my lips have distinguished" (ver. 14). What is the distinction in vows? This is the distinction, that thyself thou censure, Him thou praise: perceive thyself to be a creature, Him the Creator: thyself darkness, Him the Enlightener, to whom thou shouldest say, "Thou shalt light my lamp, O Lord my God, Thou shalt enlighten my darkness." [5] For whenever thou shalt have said, O soul, that from thyself thou hast light, thou wilt not distinguish. If thou wilt not distinguish, thou wilt not render distinct vows. Render distinct vows, confess thyself changeable, Him unchangeable: confess thyself without Him to be nothing, but Himself without thee to be perfect; thyself to need Him, but Him not to need thee. Cry to Him, "I have said to the Lord, My God art Thou, for my good things Thou needest not." [6] Now though God taketh thee to Him for a holocaust, He groweth not, He is not increased, He is not richer, He be-

cometh not better furnished: whatsoever He maketh of thee for thy sake, is the better for thee, not for Him that maketh. If thou distinguishest these things, thou renderest the vows to thy God which thy lips have distinguished.

18. "And my mouth hath spoken in my tribulation." How sweet ofttimes is tribulation, how necessary! In that case what hath the mouth of the same spoken in his tribulation? "Holocausts marrowed I will offer to Thee" (ver. 15). What is "marrowed"? Within may I keep Thy love, it shall not be on the surface, in my marrow it shall be that I love Thee. For there is nothing more inward than our marrow: the bones are more inward than the flesh, the marrow is more inward than those same bones. Whosoever therefore on the surface loveth God, desireth rather to please men, but having some other affection within, he offereth not holocausts of marrow: but into whosesoever marrow He looketh, him He receiveth whole. "With incense and rams." The rams are the rulers of the Church: the whole Body of Christ is speaking: this is the thing which he offereth to God. Incense [7] is what? Prayer. "With incense and rams." For especially the rams do pray for the flocks. "I will offer to Thee oxen with he-goats." Oxen we find treading out corn, and the same are offered to God. The Apostle hath said, that of the preachers of the Gospel must be understood that which hath been written, "Of the ox treading out corn the mouth thou shalt not muzzle. Doth God care for oxen?" [8] Therefore great are those rams, great the oxen. What of the rest, that perchance are conscious of certain sins, that perchance in the very road have slipped, and, having been wounded, by penitence are being healed? Shall they too continue, and to the holocausts shall they not belong? Let them not fear, he hath added he-goats also. "I will offer to Thee oxen with he-goats." By the very yoking are saved the he-goats; of themselves they have no strength, being yoked to bulls they are accepted. For they have made friends of the mammon of iniquity, that the same may receive them into everlasting tabernacles.[9] Therefore those he-goats shall not be on the left, because they have made to themselves friends of the mammon of iniquity. But what he-goats shall be on the left? They to whom shall be said, "I hungered, and ye gave me not to eat: " [10] not they that have redeemed their sins by almsdeeds.

19. "Come ye, hear, and I will tell, all ye that fear God" (ver. 16). Let us come, let us hear, what he is going to tell, "Come ye, hear, and I will tell." But to whom, "Come ye, and hear"?

---

[1] Ps. xix. 6.　　[2] Rom. xii. 11.
[3] 1 Cor. xv. 54.　[4] Oxf. mss. add, "that from," etc.
[5] Ps. xviii. 28.　[6] Ps. xvi. 2.

[7] [See (A. N. F. vol. vi. p. 528) Arnobius on incense. — C.]
[8] 1 Cor. ix. 9; Deut. xxv. 4.　　[9] Luke xvi. 9.
[10] Matt. xxv. 42.

"All ye that fear God." If God ye fear not, I will not tell. It is not possible that it be told to any where the fear of God is not. Let the fear of God open the ears, that there may be something to enter in, and a way whereby may enter in that which I am going to tell. But what is he going to tell? "How great things He hath done to my soul." Behold, he would tell: but what is he going to tell? Is it perchance how widely the earth is spread, how much the sky is extended, and how many are the stars, and what are the changes of sun and of moon? This creation fulfilleth its course: but they have very curiously sought it out, the Creator thereof have not known.[1] This thing hear, this thing receive, "O ye that fear God, how great things He hath done to my soul:" if ye will, to yours also. "How great things He hath done to my soul." "To Him with my mouth I have cried" (ver. 17). "And this very thing, he saith, hath been done to his soul; that to Him with his mouth he should cry, hath been done, he saith, to his soul. Behold, brethren, Gentiles we were, even if not in ourselves, in our parents. And what saith the Apostle? "Ye know, when Gentiles ye were, to idols without speech how ye went up, being led."[2] Let the Church now say, "how great things He hath done to my soul." "To Him with my mouth I have cried." I a man to a stone was crying, to a deaf stock I was crying, to idols deaf and dumb I was speaking: now the image of God hath been turned to the Creator thereof. I that was "saying to a stock, My father thou art; and to a stone, Thou hast begotten me:"[3] now say, "Our Father, which art in Heaven."[4] . . . "To Him with my mouth I have cried, and I have exalted Him under my tongue." See how in secret He would be uncorrupt that offereth marrowed holocausts. This do ye, brethren, this imitate, so that ye may say, "Come ye, see how great things He hath done to my soul." For all those things of which he telleth, by His Grace are done in our soul. See the other things of which he speaketh.

20. "If I have beheld iniquity in my heart, may not the Lord hearken" (ver. 18). Consider now, brethren, how easily, how daily men blushing for fear of men do censure iniquities; He hath done ill, He hath done basely, a villain the fellow is: this perchance for man's sake he saith. See whether thou beholdest no iniquity in thy heart, whether perchance that which thou censurest in another, thou art meditating to do, and therefore against him dost exclaim, not because he hath done it, but because he hath been found out. Return to thyself, within be to thyself a judge. Behold in thy hid chamber, in the very inmost recess of the heart, where thou and He that seeth are alone, there let iniquity be displeasing to thee, in order that thou mayest be pleasing to God. Do not regard it, that is, do not love it, but rather despise it, that is, contemn it, and turn away from it. Whatever pleasing thing it hath promised to allure thee to sin; whatever grievous thing it hath threatened, to drive thee on to evil doing; all is nought, all passeth away: it is worthy to be despised, in order that it may be trampled upon; not to be eyed lest it be accepted.[5] . . .

21. "Therefore God hath hearkened to me" (ver. 19). Because I have not beheld iniquity in my heart. "And He hath listened to the voice of my prayer." "Blessed be my God, that hath not thrust away my supplication and His mercy from me" (ver. 20). Gather the sense from that place, where he saith, "Come ye, hear, and I will tell you, all ye that fear God, how great things He hath done to my soul:"[6] he hath both said the words which ye have heard, and at the end thus he hath concluded: "Blessed be my God, that hath not thrust away my supplication and His mercy from me." For thus there arriveth at the Resurrection he that speaketh, where already we also are by hope: yea both it is we ourselves, and this voice is ours. So long therefore as here we are, this let us ask of God, that He thrust not from us our supplication, and His mercy, that is, that we pray continually, and He continually pity. For many become feeble in praying, and in the newness of their own conversion pray fervently, afterwards feebly, afterwards coldly, afterwards negligently: as if they have become secure. The foe watcheth: thou sleepest. The Lord Himself hath given commandment in the Gospel, how "it behoveth men always to pray and not to faint."[7] And he giveth a comparison from that unjust judge, who neither feared God, nor regarded man, whom that widow daily importuned to hear her; and he yielded for weariness, that was not influenced by pity: and the naughty judge saith to himself, "Though neither God I fear, nor men I regard, even because of the weariness which this widow daily putteth upon me, I will hear her cause, and will avenge her." And the Lord saith, "If a naughty judge hath done this, shall not your Father avenge His chosen, that to Him do cry day and night? Yea, I say unto you, He shall make judgment of them speedily." Therefore let us not faint in prayer. Though He putteth off what He is going to grant, He putteth it not away: being secure of His promise, let us not faint in praying, and this is by His goodness. Therefore he hath said, "Blessed is my God, that hath not thrust away my supplication and His mercy from me."

[1] Wisd. xiii. 1.   [2] 1 Cor. xii. 2.
[3] Jer. ii. 27.   [4] Matt. vi. 9.

[5] Here followeth in the Oxf. ed. a part in brackets, "which is omitted in some good MSS. — Ben."
[6] Ps. lxvi. 16.   [7] Luke xviii. 1, etc.

When thou hast seen thy supplication "not thrust away from thee," be secure, that His mercy hath not been thrust away from thee.

PSALM LXVII.[1]

1. Your Love remembereth, that in two Psalms,[2] which have been already treated of, we have stirred up our soul to bless the Lord, and with godly chant have said, "Bless thou, O my soul, the Lord." If therefore we have stirred up our soul in those Psalms to bless the Lord, in this Psalm is well said, "May God have pity on us, and bless us" (ver. 1). Let our soul bless the Lord, and let God bless us. When God blesseth us, we grow, and when we bless the Lord, we grow, to us both are profitable. He is not increased by our blessing, nor is He lessened by our cursing. He that curseth the Lord, is himself lessened : he that blesseth the Lord, is himself increased. First, there is in us the blessing of the Lord, and the consequence is that we also bless the Lord. That is the rain, this the fruit. Therefore there is rendered as it were fruit to God the Husbandman, raining upon and tilling us. Let us chant these words with no barren devotion, with no empty voice, but with true heart. For most evidently God the Father hath been called a Husbandman.[3] The Apostle saith, "God's husbandry ye are, God's building ye are."[4] In things visible of this world, the vine is not a building, and a building is not a vineyard : but we are the vineyard of the Lord, because He tilleth us for fruit ; the building of God we are, since He who tilleth us, dwelleth in us. And what saith the same Apostle? "I have planted, Apollos hath watered, but the increase God hath given. Therefore neither he that planteth is anything, nor he that watereth, but He that giveth the increase, even God."[5] He it is therefore that giveth the increase. Are those perchance the husbandmen? For a husbandman he is called that planteth, that watereth : but the Apostle hath said, "I have planted, Apollos hath watered." Do we enquire whence himself hath done this? The Apostle maketh answer, "Yet not I, but the Grace of God with me."[6] Therefore whithersoever thou turn thee, whether through Angels, thou wilt find God thy Husbandman ; whether through Prophets, the Same is thy Husbandman ; whether through Apostles, the very Same acknowledge to be thy Husbandman. What then of us? Perchance we are the labourers of that Husbandman, and this too with powers imparted by Himself, and by Grace granted by Himself. . . .

2. "Lighten His countenance upon us." Thou wast perchance going to enquire, what is "bless us"? In many ways men would have themselves to be blessed of God : one would have himself to be blessed, so that he may have a house full of the necessary things of this life ; another desireth himself to be blessed, so that he may obtain soundness of body without flaw ; another would have himself to be blessed, if perchance he is sick, so that he may acquire soundness ; another longing for sons, and perchance being sorrowful because none are born, would have himself to be blessed so that he may have posterity. And who could number the divers wishes of men desiring themselves to be blessed of the Lord God? But which of us would say, that it was no blessing of God, if either husbandry should bring him fruit, or if any man's house should abound in plenty of things temporal, or if the very bodily health be either so maintained that it be not lost, or, if lost, be regained? . . .

3. "Every soul that is blessed is simple," [7] not cleaving to things earthly nor with glued wings grovelling, but beaming with the brightness of virtues, on the twin wings of twin love doth spring into the free air ; and seeth how from her is withdrawn that whereon she was treading, not that whereon she was resting, and she saith securely, "The Lord hath given, the Lord hath taken away ; as it hath pleased the Lord, so hath been done : be the name of the Lord blessed." . . . But let not perchance any weak man say, when shall I be of so great virtue, as was holy Job? The mightiness of the tree thou wonderest at, because but now thou hast been born: this great tree, whereat thou wonderest, under the branches and shade whereof thou coolest thyself, hath been a switch. But dost thou fear lest there be taken away from thee these things, when such thou shalt have become? Observe that they are taken away from evil men also. Why therefore dost thou delay conversion? That which thou fearest when good to lose, perchance if evil thou wilt lose still. If being good thou shalt have lost them, there is by thee the Comforter that hath taken them away : the coffer is emptied of gold ; the heart is full of faith : without, poor thou art, but within, rich thou art : thy riches with thee thou carriest, which thou wouldest not lose, even if naked from shipwreck thou shouldest escape. Why doth not the loss, that perchance, if evil, thou wilt lose, find thee good? forasmuch as thou seest evil men also suffer loss? But with greater loss they are stricken : empty is the house, more empty the conscience is. Whatsoever evil man shall have lost these things, hath nothing to hold by without, hath nothing

[1] Lat. LXVI.   Sermon to the Commonalty.
[2] Ps. ciii., civ.   [3] John xv. 1.   [4] 1 Cor. iii. 9.
[5] 1 Cor. iii. 6, 7.   [6] 1 Cor. xv. 10.

[7] Prov. xi. 25, LXX.

within whereon he may rest. He fleeth when he hath suffered loss from the place where before the eyes of men with the display of riches he used to vaunt himself; now in the eyes of men to vaunt himself he is not able: to himself within he returneth not, because he hath nothing. He hath not imitated the ant, he hath not gathered to himself grains, while it was summer.[1] What have I meant by, while it was summer? While he had quietude of life, while he had this world's prosperity, when he had leisure, when happy he was being called by all men, his summer it was. He should have imitated the ant, he should have heard the Word of God, he should have gathered together grains, and he should have stored them within. There had come the trial of tribulation, there had come upon him a winter of numbness, tempest of fear, the cold of sorrow, whether it were loss, or any danger to his safety, or any bereavement of his family; or any dishonour and humiliation; it was winter; the ant falleth back upon that which in summer she hath gathered together; and within in her secret store, where no man seeth, she is recruited by her summer toils. When for herself she was gathering together these stores in summer, all men saw her: when on these she feedeth in winter, no one seeth. What is this? See the ant of God, he riseth day by day, he hasteneth to the Church of God, he prayeth, he heareth lection, he chanteth hymn, he digesteth that which he hath heard, with himself[2] he thinketh thereon, he storeth within grains gathered from the threshing-floor. They that providently hear those very things which even now are being spoken of, do thus, and by all men are seen to go forth to the Church, go back from Church, to hear sermon, to hear lection, to choose a book, open and read it: all these things are seen, when they are done. That ant is treading his path, carrying and storing up in the sight of men seeing him. There cometh winter sometime, for to whom cometh it not? There chanceth loss, there chanceth bereavement: other men pity him perchance as being miserable, who know not what the ant hath within to eat, and they say, miserable he whom this hath befallen, or what spirits, dost thou think, hath he whom this hath befallen? how afflicted is he? He measureth by himself, hath compassion according to his own strength; and thus he is deceived: because the measure wherewith he measureth himself, he would apply to him whom he knoweth not. . . . O sluggard, gather in summer while thou art able; winter will not suffer thee to gather, but to eat that which thou shalt have gathered. For how many men so suffer tribulation, that there is no opportunity either to read anything, or to hear anything, and they obtain

no admittance, perchance, to those that would comfort them. The ant hath remained in her nest, let her see if she hath gathered anything in summer, whereby she may recruit herself in winter.

4. . . . There is a double interpretation, both must be given: "lighten," he saith, "Thy face upon us," show to us Thy countenance. For God doth not ever light His countenance, as if ever it had been without light: but He lighteth it upon us, so that what was hidden from us, is opened to us, and that which was, but to us was hidden, is unveiled upon us, that is, is lightened. Or else surely it is, "Thy image lighten upon us:" so that he said this, in "lighten Thy countenance upon us:" Thou hast imprinted Thy countenance upon us; Thou hast made us after Thine image and Thy likeness,[3] Thou hast made us Thy coin; but Thine image ought not in darkness to remain: send a ray of Thy wisdom, let it dispel our darkness, and let there shine in us Thy image; let us know ourselves to be Thine image, let us hear what hath been said in the Song of Songs, "If Thou shalt not have known Thyself, O Thou fair one among women."[4] For there is said to the Church, "If Thou shalt not have known Thyself." What is this? If Thou shalt not have known Thyself to have been made after the image of God. O Soul of the Church, precious, redeemed with the blood of the Lamb immaculate, observe of how great value Thou art, think what hath been given for Thee. Let us say, therefore, and let us long that He "may lighten His face upon us." We wear His face: in like manner as the faces of emperors are spoken of, truly a kind of sacred face is that of God in His own image: but unrighteous men know not in themselves the image of God. In order that the countenance of God may be lightened upon them, they ought to say what? "Thou shalt light my candle, O Lord my God, Thou shalt light my darkness."[5] I am in the darkness of sins, but by the ray of Thy wisdom dispelled be my darkness, may Thy countenance appear; and if perchance through me it appeareth somewhat deformed, by Thee be there reformed that which by Thee hath been formed.

5. "That we may know on earth Thy way" (ver. 2). "On earth," here, in this life, "we may know Thy way." What is, "Thy way"? That which leadeth to Thee. May we acknowledge whither we are going, acknowledge where we are as we go; neither in darkness we can do. Afar Thou art from men sojourning, a way to us Thou hast presented, through which we must return to Thee. "Let us acknowledge on earth Thy way." What is His way wherein we have desired, "That we may know on earth Thy

---

[1] Prov. vi. 6, xxx. 25.　　　[2] Or, "at home."　　　[3] Gen. i. 26.　　　[4] Song of Sol. i. 8.　　　[5] Ps. xviii. 28.

way"? We are going to enquire this ourselves, not of ourselves to learn it. We can learn of it from the Gospel: "I am the Way,"[1] the Lord saith: Christ hath said, "I am the Way." But dost thou fear lest thou stray? He hath added, "And the Truth." Who strayeth in the Truth? He strayeth that hath departed from the Truth. The Truth is Christ, the Way is Christ: walk therein. Dost thou fear lest thou die before thou attain unto Him? "I am the Life: I am," He saith, "the Way and the Truth and the Life." As if He were saying, "What fearest thou? Through Me thou walkest, to Me thou walkest, in Me thou restest." What therefore meaneth, "We may know on earth Thy Way," but "we may know on earth Thy Christ"? But let the Psalm itself reply: lest ye think that out of other Scriptures there must be adduced testimony, which perchance is here wanting: by repetition he hath shown what signified, "That we may know on earth Thy Way:" and as if thou wast inquiring, "In what earth, what way?" "In all nations Thy Salvation." In what earth, thou art inquiring? Hear: "In all nations." What way art thou seeking? Hear: "Thy Salvation." Is not perchance Christ his Salvation? And what is that which the old Symeon hath said, that old man, I say, in the Gospel, preserved full of years even unto the infancy of the Word?[2] For that old man took in his hands the Infant Word of God. Would He that in the womb deigned to be, disdain to be in the hands of an old man? The Same was in the womb of the virgin, as was in the hands of the old man, a weak infant both within the bowels, and in the old man's hand, to give us strength, by whom were made all things; and if all things, even His very mother. He came humble, He came weak, but clothed with a weakness to be changed into strength,[3] because "though He was crucified of weakness, yet He liveth of the virtue of God,"[4] the Apostle saith. He was then in the hands of an old man. And what saith that old man? Rejoicing that now he must be loosed from this world, seeing how in his own hand was held He by whom and in whom his Salvation was upheld; he saith what? "Now Thou lettest go," he saith, "O Lord, Thy servant in peace, for mine eyes have seen Thy Salvation."[5] Therefore, "May God bless us, and have pity on us; may He lighten His countenance upon us, that we may know on earth Thy Way!" In what earth? "In all nations?" What Way? "Thy Salvation."

6. What followeth because the Salvation of God is known in all nations? "Let the peoples confess to Thee, O God" (ver. 3); "confess to Thee," he saith, "all peoples." There standeth forth a heretic, and he saith, In Africa I[6] have peoples: and another from another quarter, And I in Galatia have peoples. Thou in Africa, he in Galatia: therefore I require one that hath them everywhere. Ye have indeed dared to exult at that voice, when ye heard, "Let the peoples confess to Thee, O God." Hear the following verse, how he speaketh not of a part: "Let there confess to Thee all peoples." Walk ye in the Way together with all nations; walk ye in the Way together with all peoples, O sons of peace, sons of the One Catholic Church,[7] walk ye in the Way, seeing as ye walk. Wayfarers do this to beguile their toil. Sing ye in this Way; I implore you by that Same Way, sing ye in this Way: a new song sing ye, let no one there sing old ones: sing ye the love-songs of your fatherland, let no one sing old ones. New Way, new wayfarer, new song. Hear thou the Apostle exhorting thee to a new song: "Whatever therefore is in Christ is a new creature; old things have passed away, behold they have been made new." A new song sing ye in the way, which ye have learned "on the earth." In what earth? "In all nations." Therefore even the new song doth not belong to a part. He that in a part singeth, singeth an old song: whatever he please to sing, he singeth an old song, the old man singeth: divided he is, carnal he is. Truly in so far as carnal he is, so far he is old; and in so far as he is spiritual, so far new. See what saith the Apostle: "I could not speak to you as if to spiritual, but as if to carnal."[8] Whence proveth he them carnal? "For while one saith, I am of Paul; but another, I of Apollos: are ye not," he saith, "carnal?"[9] Therefore in the Spirit a new song sing thou in the safe way. Just as wayfarers sing, and ofttimes in the night sing. Awful round about all things do sound, or rather they sound not around, but are still around; and the more still the more awful; nevertheless, even they that fear robbers do sing.[10] How much more safely thou singest in Christ! That way hath no robber, unless thou by forsaking the way fallest in the hands of a robber. . . . Why fear ye to confess, and in your confession to sing a new song together with all the earth; in all the earth, in Catholic peace, dost thou fear to confess to God, lest He condemn thee that hast confessed? If having not confessed thou liest concealed, having confessed thou wilt be condemned. Thou fearest to confess, that by not confessing canst not be concealed: thou

---

[1] John xiv. 6.　　　[2] Luke ii. 30.
[3] Oxf. MSS. add "into strength."　　　[4] 2 Cor. xiii. 4.
[5] Luke ii. 29, 30.

[6] Oxf. MSS. "I too."
[7] [i.e., the Nicene communion, in which Rome and Constantinople had co-equal dignities,—primacies of honour only, based on synodical concession to imperial capitals. On which see A. N. F. vol. viii. pp. 601-605, and pp. 641-644.— C.]
[8] 1 Cor. iii. 1.　　　[9] 1 Cor. iii. 4.
[10] [Coram latrone viator. Juv. Sat. x. 22. — C.]

wilt be condemned if thou hast held thy peace, that mightest have been delivered, by having confessed. " O God, confess to Thee all peoples."

7. And because this confession leadeth not to punishment, he continueth and saith, " Let the nations rejoice and exult " (ver. 4). If robbers after confession made do wail before man, let the faithful after confessing before God rejoice. If a man be judge, the torturer and his fear exact from a robber a confession : yea sometimes fear wringeth out confession, pain extorteth it : and he that waileth in tortures, but feareth to be killed if he confess, supporteth tortures as far as he is able : and if he shall have been overcome by pain, he giveth his voice for death. Nowise therefore is he joyful ; nowise exulting : before he confesseth the claw teareth[1] him ; when he hath confessed, the executioner leadeth him along a condemned felon : wretched in every case. But " let the nations rejoice and exult." Whence ? Through that same confession. Why ? Because good He is to whom they confess : He exacteth confession, to the end that He may deliver the humble ; He condemneth one not confessing, to the end that He may punish the proud. Therefore be thou sorrowful before thou confessest ; after having confessed exult, now thou wilt be made whole. Thy conscience had gathered up evil humours, with boil it had swollen, it was torturing thee, it suffered thee not to rest : the Physician applieth the fomentations of words,[2] and sometimes He lanceth it, He applieth the surgeon's knife by the chastisement of tribulation : do thou acknowledge the Physician's hand, confess thou, let every evil humour go forth and flow away in confession : now exult, now rejoice, that which remaineth will be easy to be made whole. . . . " Let the nations rejoice and exult, for Thou judgest the peoples in equity." And that unrighteous men may not fear, he hath added, " and the nations on the earth Thou directest." Depraved were the nations and crooked were the nations, perverse were the nations ; for the ill desert of their depravity, and crookedness and perverseness, the Judge's coming they feared : there cometh the hand of the same, it is stretched out mercifully to the peoples, they are guided in order that they may walk the straight way ; why should they fear the Judge to come, that have first acknowledged Him for a Corrector ? To His hand let them give up themselves, Himself guideth the nations on the earth. But guided nations are walking in the Truth, are exulting in Him, are doing good works ; and if perchance there cometh in any water (for on sea they are sailing) through the very small holes, through the crevices into the hold, pumping it out by good works, lest by more and more coming it accumulate, and sink the ship, pumping it out daily, fasting, praying, doing almsdeeds, saying with pure heart, " Forgive us our debts, as also we forgive our debtors "[3] — saying such words walk thou secure, and exult in the way, sing in the way. Do not fear the Judge : before thou wast a believer, thou didst find a Saviour. Thee ungodly He sought out that He might redeem, thee redeemed will He forsake so as to destroy ? " And the nations on earth Thou directest."

8. He exulteth, rejoiceth, exhorteth, he repeateth those same verses in exhortation.[4] " The earth hath given her fruit " (ver. 6). What fruit ? " Let all peoples confess to Thee." Earth it was, of thorns it was full ; there came the hand of One rooting them up, there came a calling by His majesty and mercy, the earth began to confess ; now the earth giveth her fruit. Would she give her fruit unless first she were rained on ? Would she give her fruit, unless first the mercy of God had come from above ? Let them read to me, thou sayest, how the earth being rained upon gave her fruit. Hear of the Lord raining upon her : " Repent, for the kingdom of heaven is at hand."[5] He raineth, and that same rain is thunder ; it terrifieth : fear thou Him thundering, and receive Him raining. Behold, after that voice of a thundering and raining God, after that voice let us see something out of the Gospel itself. Behold that harlot of ill fame in the city burst into a strange house into which she had not been invited by the host, but by One invited she had been called ;[6] called[7] not with tongue, but by Grace. The sick woman knew that she had there a place, where she was aware that her Physician was sitting at meat. She has gone in, that was a sinner ; she dareth not draw near save to the feet : she weepeth at His feet, she washeth with tears, she wipeth with hair, she anointeth with ointment. Why wonderest thou ? The earth hath given her fruit. This thing, I say, came to pass by the Lord raining there through His own mouth ; there came to pass the things whereof we read in the .Gospel ; and by His raining through His clouds, by the sending of the Apostles and by their preaching the truth, the earth more abundantly hath given her fruit, and that crop now hath filled the round world.

9. The fruit of the earth was first in Jerusalem. For from thence began the Church : there came there the Holy Spirit, and filled full the holy men gathered together in one place ; miracles were done, with the tongues of all men they spake.[8] They were filled full of the Spirit of God, the

---

[1] *Exarat ungula*, perhaps the torture referred to in πλευρὰς καταξαίνοντες. S. Chrys. on *Stat.* Hom. xx. § 3, tr. p. 329.
[2] So Ben.: Oxf. MSS. *ferramenta verborum*, "the instruments of words."

[3] Matt. vi. 12.   [4] " Let the people confess," etc., ver. 5.
[5] Matt. iii. 2.   [6] Luke vii. 37.
[7] Oxf. MSS. repeat *vocata*.   [8] Acts ii. 1, 4.

people were converted that were in that place, fearing and receiving the divine shower, by confession they brought forth so much fruit, that all their goods they brought together into a common stock, making distribution to the poor, in order that no one might call anything his own, but all things might be to them in common, and they might have one soul and one heart unto God.[1] For there had been forgiven[2] them the blood which they had shed, it had been forgiven them by the Lord pardoning, in order that now they might even learn to drink that which they had shed. Great in that place is the fruit: the earth hath given her fruit, both great fruit, and most excellent fruit. Ought by any means that earth alone to give her fruit? "May there bless us God, our God, may there bless us God" (ver. 7). Still may He bless us: for blessing in multiplication is wont most chiefly and properly to be perceived. Let us prove this in Genesis; see the works of God: God made light,[3] and God made a division between light and darkness: the light He called day, and the darkness He called night. It is not said, He blessed the light. For the same light returneth and changeth by days and nights. He calleth the sky the firmament between waters and waters: it is not said, He blessed the sky: He severed the sea from the dry land, and named both, the dry land earth, and the gathering together of the waters sea: neither here is it said, God blessed. . . .

10. How should we will that *to us* He come? By living well, by doing well. Let not things past please us; things present not hold us; let us not "close the ear" as it were with tail,[4] let us not press down the ear on the ground; lest by things past we be kept back from hearing, lest by things present we be entangled and prevented from meditating on things future; let us reach forth unto those things which are before, let us forget things past.[5] And that for which now we toil, for which now we groan, for which now we sigh, of which now we speak, which in part, however small soever, we perceive, and to receive are not able, we shall receive, we shall thoroughly enjoy in the resurrection of the just. Our youth shall be renewed as an eagle's,[6] if only our old man we break[7] against the Rock of Christ. Whether those things be true, brethren, which are said of the serpent, or those which are said of the eagle, or whether it be rather a tale of men than truth, truth is nevertheless in the Scriptures, and not without reason the Scriptures have spoken of this: let us do whatever it signifieth, and not toil to discover how far that is true. Be thou such an one, as that thy youth may be able

to be renewed as an eagle's. And know thou that it cannot be renewed, except thine old man on the Rock shall have been broken off: that is, except by the aid of the Rock, except by the aid of Christ, thou wilt not be able to be renewed. Do not thou because of the pleasantness of the past life be deaf to the word of God: do not by things present be so held and entangled, as to say, I have no leisure to read, I have no leisure to hear. This is to press down the ear upon the ground. Do thou therefore not be such an one: but be such an one as on the other side thou findest, that is, so that thou forget things past, unto things before reach thyself out, in order that thine old man on the Rock thou mayest break off. And if any comparisons shall have been made for thee, if thou hast found them in the Scriptures, believe: if thou shalt not have found them spoken of except by report, do not very much believe them.[8] The thing itself perchance is so, perchance is not so. Do thou profit by it, let that comparison avail for thy salvation. Thou art unwilling to profit by this comparison, by some other profit, it mattereth not provided thou do it: and, being secure, wait for the Kingdom of God, lest thy prayer quarrel with thee. For, O Christian man, when thou sayest, Thy Kingdom come, how sayest thou, "Thy kingdom come"?[9] Examine thy heart: see, behold, "Thy kingdom come:" He crieth out to thee, "I come:" dost thou not fear? Often we have told Your Love: both to preach the truth is nothing, if heart from tongue dissent: and to hear the truth is nothing, if fruit follow not hearing. From this place exalted as it were we are speaking to you: but how much we are beneath your feet in fear, God knoweth, who is gracious to the humble; for the voices of men praising do not give us so much pleasure as the devotion of men confessing, and the deeds of men now righteous. And how we have no pleasure but in your advances, but by those praises how much we are endangered, He knoweth, whom we pray to deliver us from all dangers, and to deign to know and crown us together with you, saved from every trial, in His Kingdom.

PSALM LXVIII.[10]

1. Of this Psalm, the title seemeth not to need operose discussion: for simple and easy it appeareth. For thus it standeth: "For the end, for David himself a Psalm of a Song." But in many Psalms already we have reminded you what is "at the end: for the end of the Law is Christ for righteousness to every man believing:"[11] He is the end which maketh perfect, not that

---

[1] Acts iv. 32.　　　[2] Or, "given."　　　[3] Gen. i. 3.
[4] Ps. lviii. 4.　[See p. 232, *supra.*—C.]　　[5] Philip. iii. 13.
[6] Ps. ciii. 5.
[7] On Ps. ciii. 5, *infra*, he says that the eagle is said to break off an excessive growth of the beak against a rock.

[8] [The rule concerning the phœnix and other illustrations which, as such, were current among the Fathers. — C.]
[9] Matt. vi. 10.　　[10] Lat. LXVII.　　[11] Rom. x. 4.

which consumeth or destroyeth. Nevertheless, if any one endeavoureth to inquire, what meaneth, "a Psalm of a Song:" why not either " Psalm " or " Song," but both ; or what is the difference between Psalm of Song, and Song of Psalm, because even thus of some Psalms the titles are inscribed : he will find perchance something which we leave for men more acute and more at leisure than ourselves. . . .

2. " Let God rise up, and let His enemies be scattered " (ver. 1). Already this hath come to pass, Christ hath risen up, "who is over all things, God blessed for ever,"[1] and His enemies have been dispersed through all nations, to wit, the Jews ; in that very place, where they practised their enmities, being overthrown in war; and thence through all places dispersed : and now they hate, but fear, and in that very fear they do that which followeth, "And let them that hate Him flee from His face." The flight indeed of the mind is fear. For in carnal flight, whither flee they from the face of Him who everywhere showeth the efficacy[2] of His presence? " Whither shall I depart," saith he, " from Thy Spirit, and from Thy face whither shall I flee ? "[3] With mind, therefore, not with body, they flee ; to wit, by being afraid, not by being hidden ; and not from that face which they see not, but from that which they are compelled to see. For the face of Him hath His presence in His Church been called. . . .

3. " As smoke faileth, let them fail " (ver. 2). For they lifted up themselves from the fires of their hatred unto the vapouring of pride, and against Heaven setting their mouth, and shouting, " Crucify, Crucify,"[4] Him taken captive they derided, Him hanging they mocked : and being soon conquered by that very Person against whom they swelled victorious, they vanished away. " As wax melteth from the face of fire, so let sinners perish from the face of God." Though perchance in this passage he hath referred to those men, whose hard-heartedness in tears of penitence is dissolved : yet this also may be understood, that he threateneth future judgment ; because though in this world like smoke, in lifting up themselves, that is, in priding themselves, they have melted away, there will come to them at the last final damnation, so that from His face they will perish for everlasting, when in His own glory He shall have appeared, like fire, for the punishment of the ungodly, and the light of the righteous.

4. " Lastly, there followeth, " And let just men be joyous, and exult in the sight of God, let them delight in gladness " (ver. 3). For then shall they hear, " Come, ye blessed of My Father, receive ye the kingdom."[5] " Let them be joy-

ous," therefore, that have toiled, " and exult in the sight of God." For there will not be in this exultation, as though it were before men, any empty boasting ; but (it will be) in the sight of Him who unerringly looketh into that which He hath granted. " Let them delight in gladness : " no longer exulting with trembling,[6] as in this world, so long as " human life is a trial upon earth." [7] Secondly, he turneth himself to those very persons to whom he hath given so great hope, and to them while here living he speaketh and exhorteth : " Sing ye to God, psalm ye to His name " (ver. 4). Already on this subject in the exposition of the Title we have before spoken that which seemed meet. He singeth to God, that liveth to God : He psalmeth to His name, that worketh unto His Glory. In singing thus, in psalming thus, that is, by so living, by so working, " a way make ye to Him," he saith, " that hath ascended above the setting." A way make ye to Christ : so that through the beautiful feet of men telling good tidings,[8] the hearts of men believing many have a way opened to Him. For the Same is He that hath ascended above the " setting : " either because the new life of one turned to Him receiveth Him not, except the old life shall have set by his renouncing this world, or because He ascended above the setting, when by rising again He conquered the downfall of the body. " For The Lord is His name." Which if they had known, the Lord of glory they never would have crucified.[9]

5. " Exult ye in the sight of Him," O ye to whom hath been said, " Sing ye to God, psalm ye to the name of Him, a way make ye to Him that hath ascended above the setting," also " exult in the sight of Him : " as if " sorrowful, yet alway rejoicing." [10] For while ye make a way to Him, while ye prepare a way whereby He may come and possess the nations, ye are to suffer in the sight of men many sorrowful things. But not only faint not, but even exult, not in the sight of men, but in the sight of God. " In hope rejoicing, in tribulation enduring : "[11] " exult ye in the sight of Him." For they that in the sight of men trouble you, " shall be troubled by the face of Him, the Father of orphans and Judge of widows " (ver. 5). For desolate they suppose them to be, from whom ofttimes by the sword of the Word of God [12] both parents from sons, and husbands from wives, are severed : but persons destitute and widowed have the consolation " of the Father of orphans and Judge of widows : " they have the consolation of Him that say to Him, " For my father and my mother have forsaken me, but the Lord hath taken up

---

[1] Rom. ix. 5. [2] *Effectum.* [3] Ps. cxxxix. 6.
[4] John xix. 6. [5] Matt. xxv. 34.
[6] Ps. ii. 11. [7] Job vii. 1, LXX. [8] Isa. lii. 7.
[9] 1 Cor. ii. 8. [10] 2 Cor. vi. 10. [11] Rom. xii. 12.
[12] Matt. x. 34.

me :" [1] and they that have hoped in the Lord, continuing in prayers by night and by day : [2] by whose face those men shall be troubled when they shall have seen themselves prevail nothing, for that the whole world hath gone away after Him.[3] For out of those orphans and widows, that is, persons destitute of partnership in this world's hope, the Lord for Himself doth build a Temple : whereof in continuation he saith, "The Lord is in His holy place."

6. For what is His place he hath disclosed, when he saith, "God that maketh to dwell men of one mood in a house" (ver. 6) : men of one mind, of one sentiment : this is the holy place of the Lord. For when he had said, "The Lord is in His holy place : " as though we were inquiring in what place, since He is everywhere wholly, and no place of corporal space containeth Him ; forthwith he hath subjoined somewhat, that we should not seek Him apart from ourselves, but rather being of one mood dwelling in a house, we should deserve that He also Himself deign to dwell among us. This is the holy place of the Lord, the thing that most men seek to have, a place where in prayer they may be hearkened unto. . . . For as in a great house of a man, the Lord thereof doth not abide in every place whatsoever, but in some place doubtless more private and honourable : so God dwelleth not in all men that are in His house (for He dwelleth not in the vessels of dishonour), but His holy place are they whom "He maketh to dwell of one mood," or "of one manner, in a house." For what are called τρόποι in Greek, by both *modi* and *mores* (moods and manners), in Latin may be interpreted. Nor hath the Greek writer, "Who maketh to dwell," but only "maketh to dwell." "The Lord," then, "is in His holy place." . . .

7. But to prove that by His Grace He buildeth to Himself this place, not for the sake of the merits preceding of those persons out of whom He buildeth it, see what followeth : "Who leadeth forth men fettered, in strength." For He looseth the heavy bonds of sins, wherewith they were fettered so that they could not walk in the way of the commandments : but He leadeth them forth "in strength," which before His Grace they had not. "Likewise men provoking that dwell in the tombs : " that is, every way dead, taken up with dead works. For these men provoke Him to anger by withstanding justice : for those fettered men perchance would walk, and are not able, and are praying of God that they may be able, and are saying to Him, "From my necessities lead me forth." [4] By whom being heard, they give thanks, saying, "Thou hast broken asunder my bonds." [5] But

these provoking men that dwell in the tombs, are of that kind, which in another passage the Scripture pointeth out, saying, "From a dead man, as from one that is not, confession perisheth." [6] Whence there is this saying, "When a sinner shall have come into the depth of evil things, he despiseth." [7] For it is one thing to long for, another thing to fight against righteousness : one thing from evil to desire to be delivered, another thing one's evil doings to defend rather than to confess : both kinds nevertheless the Grace of Christ leadeth forth in strength. With what strength, but that wherewith against sin even unto blood they are to strive ? For out of each kind are made meet persons, whereof to construct His holy place ; those being loosened, these being raised to life. For even of the woman, whom Satan had bound for eighteen years, by His command He loosed the bonds ; [8] and Lazarus' death by His voice He overcame.[9] He that hath done these things in bodies, is able to do more marvellous things in characters, and to make men of one mood to dwell in a house : "leading forth men fettered in strength, likewise men provoking that dwell in the tombs." [10]

8. "O God, when Thou wentest forth before Thy people" (ver. 7). His going forth is perceived, when He appeareth in His works. But He appeareth not to all men, but to them that know how to spy out His works. For I do not now speak of those works which are conspicuous to all men, Heaven and earth and sea and all things that in them are ; but the works whereby He leadeth forth men fettered in strength, likewise men provoking that dwell in the tombs, and maketh them of one manner to dwell in a house. Thus He goeth forth before His people, that is, before those that do perceive this His Grace. Lastly, there followeth, "When Thou wentest by in the desert, the earth was moved" (ver. 8). A desert were the nations, which knew not God : a desert they were, where by God Himself no law had been given, where no Prophet had dwelled, and foretold the Lord to come. "When," then, "Thou wentest by in the desert," when Thou wast preached in the nations ; "the earth was moved," to the faith earthly men were stirred up. But whence was it moved ? "For the heavens dropped from the face of God." Perchance here some one calleth to mind that time, when in the desert God was going over before His people, before the sons of Israel, by day in the pillar of cloud, by night in the brightness of fire ; [11] and determineth that thus it is that "the heavens dropped from the face of God," for manna He rained upon His people : [12] that the same thing also is that which

---

[1] Ps. xxvii. 10.   [2] 1 Tim. v. 5.   [3] John xii. 19.
[4] Ps. xxv. 17.   [5] Ps. cxvi. 16.

[6] Ecclus. xvii. 28.   [7] Prov. xviii. 3.   [8] Luke xiii. 16.
[9] John. xi. 43.   [10] Ps. lxviii. 6.   [11] Exod. xiii. 21.
[12] Exod. xvi. 15.

followeth, "Mount Sina from the face of the God of Israel," [1] "with voluntary rain severing God to Thine inheritance" (ver. 9), namely, the God that on Mount Sina spake to Moses, when He gave the Law, so that the manna is the voluntary rain, which God severed for His inheritance, that is, for His people; because them alone He so fed, not the other nations also: so that what next he saith, "and it was weakened," is understood of the inheritance being itself weakened; for they murmuring, fastidiously loathed the manna, longing for victuals of flesh, and those things on which they had been accustomed to live in Egypt.[2] . . . Lastly, all those men in the desert were stricken down, nor were any of them except two found worthy to go into the land of promise.[3] Although even if in the sons of them that inheritance be said to have been perfected, we ought more readily to hold to a spiritual sense. For all those things in a figure did happen to them;[4] until the day should break, and the shadows should be removed.[5]

9. May then the Lord be open to us that knock; and may the secret things of His mysteries, as far as Himself vouchsafeth, be disclosed. For in order that the earth might be moved to the Truth when into the desert of the Gentiles the Gospel was passing, "the Heavens dropped from the face of God." These are the Heavens, whereof in another Psalm is sung, "The Heavens are telling forth the glory of God."[6] . . . So here also, "the Heavens dropped;" but "from the face of God." For even these very persons have been "saved through faith, and this not of themselves, but God's gift it is, not of works, lest perchance any man should be lifted up. For of Himself we are the workmanship,"[7] "that maketh men of one mood to dwell in a house."[8]

10. But what is that which followeth, "Mount Sina from the face of the God of Israel"? Must there be understood "dropped;" so that what he hath called by the name of Heavens, the same he hath willed to be understood under the name of Mount Sina also; just as we said that those are called mountains, which were called Heavens? Nor in this sense ought it to move us that He saith "mountain," not mountains, while in that place they were called "Heavens," not Heaven: for in another Psalm also after it had been said, "The Heavens are telling forth the glory of God:"[6] after the manner of Scripture repeating the same sense in different words, subsequently there is said, "And the firmament telleth the works of His hands."[6] First he said "Heavens," not "Heaven:" and yet afterwards not "firmaments," but "firma-

ment." For God called the firmament Heaven,[9] as in Genesis hath been written. Thus then Heavens and Heaven, mountains and mountain, are not a different thing, but the very same thing: just as Churches many, and the One Church, are not a different thing, but the very same thing. Why then "Mount Sina, which gendereth unto bondage"?[10] as saith the Apostle. . Is perchance the Law itself to be understood in Mount Sina, as that which "the Heavens dropped from the face of God," in order that the earth might be moved? And is this the very moving of the earth, when men are troubled, because the Law they cannot fulfil? But if so it is, this is the voluntary rain, whereof in confirmation he saith, "Voluntary rain God severing to Thine inheritance:" because "He hath not done so to any nation, and His judgment He hath not manifested to them."[11] God therefore set apart this voluntary rain to His inheritance because He gave the Law. And "there was made weak," either the Law, or the inheritance. The Law may be understood to have been made weak, because it was not fulfilled; not that of itself it is weak, but because it maketh men weak, by threatening punishment, and not aiding through grace. For also the very word the Apostle hath used, where he saith, "For that which was impossible of the Law, wherein it was made weak through the flesh:"[12] willing to intimate that through the Spirit it is fulfilled: nevertheless, itself he hath said is made weak, because by weak men it cannot be fulfilled. But the inheritance, that is, the people, without any doubt is understood to have been made weak by the giving to them of the Law. For "the Law came in, that transgression might abound."[13] But that which followeth, "But Thou hast made it perfect," to the Law is thus referred, forasmuch as it is made perfect, that is, is fulfilled after that which the Lord saith in the Gospel, "I have not come to annul the Law, but to fulfil."[14] . . . There is in these words yet another sense: which seemeth to me more to approve itself. For much more in accordance with the context, grace itself is understood to be the voluntary rain,[15] because with no preceding merits of works it is given gratis.[16] "For if grace, no longer of works: otherwise grace no longer is grace."[17] . . . "But to humble men He giveth grace."[18] And it was made weak, but Thou hast made it perfect:" because "virtue in weakness is perfected."[19] Some copies indeed, both Latin and Greek, have not "Mount Sina;" but, "from the face of the God of Sina, from the face of the God of Israel." That is, "The Heavens dropped from the face

---

[1] Ps. lxviii. 8. [2] Numb. xi. 5, 6. [3] Numb. xiv. 23, 34.
[4] 1 Cor. x. 11. [5] Sol. Song ii. 17. [6] Ps. xix. 1.
[7] Eph. ii. 8-10. [8] Ps. lxviii. 6.

[9] Gen. i. 8. [10] Gal. iv. 24. [11] Ps. cxlvii. 20.
[12] Rom. viii. 3. [13] Rom. v. 20. [14] Matt. v. 17.
[15] Grace the voluntary rain.
[16] [See p. 189, supra. — C.] [17] Rom. xi. 6.
[13] Jas. iv. 6. [19] 2 Cor. xii. 9.

of God:" and, as if enquiry were made of what God, "from the face of the God," he saith, "of Sina, from the face of the God of Israel," that is, from the face of the God that gave the Law to the people of Israel. Why then "the Heavens dropped from the face of God," from the face of this God, but because thus was fulfilled that which had been foretold, "Blessing He shall give that hath given the Law"?[1] The Law whereby to terrify a man that relieth on human powers; blessing, whereby He delivereth a man that hopeth in God. Thou then, O God, hast made perfect Thine inheritance; because it is made weak in itself, in order that it may be made perfect by Thee.

11. "Thine animals shall dwell therein" (ver. 10). "Thine," not their own; to Thee subject, not for themselves free; for Thee needy, not for themselves sufficient. Lastly, he continueth, "Thou hast prepared in Thine own sweetness for the needy, O God." "In Thine own sweetness," not in his meetness. For the needy he is, for he hath been made weak, in order that he may be made perfect: he hath acknowledged himself indigent, that he may be replenished. This is that sweetness, whereof in another place is said, "The Lord shall give sweetness, and our land shall give her fruit:"[2] in order that a good work may be done not for fear, but for love; not for dread of punishment, but for love of righteousness. For this is true and sound freedom. But the Lord hath prepared for one wanting, not for one abounding, whose reproach is that poverty: of which sort in another place is said, "Reproach to these men that abound, and contempt to proud men."[3] For those he hath called proud, whom he hath called them that abound.

12. "The Lord shall give the Word" (ver. 11): to wit, food for His animals which shall dwell therein. But what shall these animals work to whom He shall give the word? What but that which followeth? "To them preaching the Gospel in much virtue." With what virtue, but with that strength wherein He leadeth forth men fettered? Perchance also here he speaketh of that virtue, wherewith in preaching the Gospel they wrought wondrous signs. Who then "shall give the Word to men preaching the Gospel with much virtue"? "The King," he saith, "of the virtues of the Beloved" (ver. 12). The Father therefore is King of the virtues of the Son. For the Beloved, when there is not specified any person that is beloved, by a substitution of name, of the Only Son is understood. Is not the Son Himself King of His virtues, to wit of the virtues serving Himself? Because with much virtue the King of Virtues shall give the Word to men preaching the Gospel, of Whom

it hath been said, "The Lord of Virtues, He is the King of Glory?"[4] But his not having said King of Virtues, but "King of the Virtues of the beloved," is a most usual expression in the Scriptures, if any one observe: which thing chiefly appeareth in those cases where even the person's own name is already expressed, so that it cannot at all be doubted that it is the same person of whom something is said. Of which sort also is that which in the Pentateuch in many passages is found: "And Moses did it, as the Lord commanded Moses." He said not that which is usual in our expressions, And Moses did, as the Lord commanded him; but, "Moses did as the Lord commanded Moses," as if one person were the Moses whom He commanded, and another person the Moses who did, whereas it is the very same. In the New Testament such expressions are most difficult to find.[5] . . . "The King," therefore, "of the virtues of the Beloved," thus may be understood, as if it were to be said, the King of His virtues, because both King of Virtues is Christ, and the Beloved is the very same Christ. However, this sense hath not so great urgency, as that no other can be accepted: because the Father also may be understood as King of the virtues of His Beloved Son, to whom the Beloved Himself saith, "All Mine are Thine, and Thine Mine."[6] But if perchance it is asked, whether God the Father of the Lord Jesus Christ can be called King also, I know not whether any one would dare to withhold this name from Him in the passage where the Apostle saith, "But to the King of ages, immortal, invisible, the only God."[7] Because even if this be said of the Trinity itself, therein is also God the Father. But if we do not carnally understand, "O God, Thy Judgment to the King give Thou, and Thy justice to the Son of the King:"[8] I know not whether anything else hath been said than, "to Thy Son." King therefore is the Father also. Whence that verse of this Psalm, "King of the virtues of the Beloved," in either way may be understood. When therefore he had said, "The Lord shall give the Word to men preaching the Gospel with much virtue:" because virtue itself by Him is ruled, and serveth Him by whom it is given; the Lord Himself, he saith, who shall give the Word to men preaching the Gospel with much virtue, is the King of the virtues of the Beloved.

13. In the next place there followeth, "Of the Beloved, and of the beauty of the House to divide the spoils." The repetition belongeth to eulogy.[9] . . . But whether it be repeated, or

---

[1] Ps. lxxxiv. 6 (al. lxxxiii. 8). Vulgate nearly so.
[2] Ps. lxxxv. 12.　　[3] Ps. cxxiii. 4.

[4] Ps. xxiv. 10.　　[5] Rom. i. 3, 4.　　[6] John xvii. 10.
[7] 1 Tim. i. 17.　　[8] Ps. lxxii. 1.
[9] He adds: "This repetition all the copies have not, and the more careful mark it with a star put before it, which marks are called asterisks, whereby they would have to be noted, that there are not in the Septuagint Version, but there are in the Hebrew, those words which are distinguished by such marks."

whether it be received as spoken once, the word which hath been set down, namely, "Beloved,"[1] I suppose that thus must be understood that which followeth, "and of the beauty of a house to divide the spoils;" as if there were said, "Chosen even to divide the spoils of the beauty of a house," that is, Chosen even for dividing the spoils. For beautiful Christ hath made His House, that is, the Church, by dividing to Her spoils: in the same manner as the Body is beautiful in the distribution of the members. "Spoils" moreover those are called that are stripped off from conquered foes. What this is the Gospel adviseth us in the passage where we read, "No one goeth into the house of a strong man to spoil his vessels, unless first he shall have bound the strong man."[2] Christ therefore hath bound the devil with spiritual bonds, by overcoming death, and by ascending from Hell above the Heavens: He hath bound him by the Sacrament of His Incarnation, because though finding nothing in Him deserving of death, yet he was permitted to kill: and from him so bound He took away his vessels as though they were spoils. For he was working in the sons of disobedience,[3] of whose unbelief he made use to work his own will. These vessels the Lord cleansing by the remission of sins, sanctifying these spoils wrested from the foe laid prostrate and bound, these He hath divided to the beauty of His House; making some apostles, some prophets, some pastors and doctors,[4] for the work of the ministry, for the building up of the Body of Christ. For as the body is one, and hath many members, and though all the members of the body are many, the body is one: so also is Christ.[5] "Are all Apostles? Are all Prophets? Are all Powers? Have all the gifts of healings? Do all speak with tongues? Do all interpret?"[6] "But all these things worketh one and the same Spirit, dividing to each one his own gifts, as He willeth."[7] And such is the beauty of the house, whereto the spoils are divided, that a lover thereof with this fairness being enkindled, crieth out, "O Lord, I have loved the grace of Thy House."[8]

14. Now in that which followeth, he turneth himself to address the members themselves, whereof the beauty of the House is composed, saying, "If ye sleep in the midst of the lots,[9] wings of a dove silvered, and between the shoulders thereof in the freshness of gold" (ver. 13). First, we must here examine the order of the words, in what manner the sentence is ended; which certainly awaiteth, when there is said, "If ye sleep:" secondly, in that which

he saith, namely, "wings of dove silvered," whether in the singular number it must be understood as being, "of this wing"[10] thereof, or in the plural as, "these wings."[11] But the singular number the Greek excludeth, where always in the plural we read it written. But still it is uncertain whether it be these wings; or whether, "O ye wings," so as that he may seem to speak to the wings themselves. Whether therefore by the words which have preceded, that sentence be ended, so that the order is, "The Lord shall give the Word to men preaching the Gospel with much virtue, if ye sleep in the midst of the lots, O ye wings of a dove silvered:" or by these which follow, so that the order is, "If ye sleep in the midst of the lots, the wings of a dove silvered with snow shall be whitened in Selmon:" that is, the wings themselves shall be whitened, if ye sleep in the midst "of the lots:" so that he may be understood to say this to them that are divided to the beauty of the House, as it were spoils; that is, if ye sleep in the "midst of the lots," O ye that are divided to the beauty of the House, "through the manifestation of the Spirit unto profit,"[12] so that "to one indeed is given through the Spirit the word of wisdom, to another the word of knowledge," etc., if then ye sleep in the midst of the lots, then the wings of a dove silvered with snow shall be whitened in Selmon. It may also be thus: "If ye being the wings of a dove silvered, sleep in the midst of the lots, with snow they shall be whitened in Selmon," so as that those men be understood who through grace receive remission of sins. Whence also of the Church Herself, is said in the Song of Songs, "Who is She that goeth up whitened?" For this promise of God is held out through the Prophet, saying, "If your sins shall have been like scarlet, like snow I will whiten them." It may also thus be understood, so that in that which hath been said, "wings of a dove silvered," there be understood, ye shall be, so that this is the sense, O ye that like as it were spoils to the beauty of the house are divided, if ye sleep in the "midst of the lots," wings of a dove silvered ye shall be: that is, into higher places ye shall be lifted up, adhering however to the bond of the Church. For I think no other dove silvered can be better perceived here, than that whereof hath been said, "One is My dove."[13] But silvered She is because with divine sayings she hath been instructed: for the sayings of the Lord in another place are called "silver with fire refined, purged sevenfold."[14] Some great good thing therefore it is, to sleep in the midst of the lots, which some would have to be the Two Testaments, so that to "sleep in the midst of the

[1] *Dilecti*, which signifies a love of choice.
[2] Matt. xii. 29.   [3] Eph. ii. 2.   [4] Eph. iv. 11.
[5] 1 Cor. xii. 12.   [6] 1 Cor. xii. 29. [7] 1 Cor. xii. 11.
[8] Ps. xxvi. 8.
[9] [Ἐὰν κοιμηθῆτε ἀναμέσον τῶν κλήρων, κ.τ.λ., Sept.: *si dormiatis inter medios cleros*, Vulgate; *Inter medios terminos*, Jerome. — C.]

[10] *Hujus pennæ*.   [11] *Hæ pennæ*.   [12] 1 Cor. xii. 7.
[13] Song of Sol. vi. 9.
[14] Ps. xii. 6.

lots "¹ is to rest on the authority of those Testaments, that is, to acquiesce in the testimony of either Testament: so that whenever anything out of them is produced and proved, all strife is ended in peaceful acquiescence. . . .

15. "Between the shoulders," however. This is indeed a part of the body, it is a part about the region of the heart, at the hinder parts however, that is, at the back: which part of that dove silvered he saith is "in the greenness of gold," that is, in the vigour of wisdom, which vigour I think cannot be better understood than by love. But why on the back, and not on the breast? Although I wonder in what sense this word is put in another Psalm, where there is said, "Between His shoulders He shall overshadow thee, and under His wings thou shalt hope:"² forasmuch as under wings there cannot be overshadowed anything but what shall be under the breast. And in Latin, indeed, "between the shoulders," perchance in some degree of both parts may be understood, both before and behind, that we may take shoulders to be the parts which have the head betwixt them; and in Hebrew perchance the word is ambiguous, which may in this manner also be understood: but the word that is in the Greek, μετάφρενα, signifieth not anything but at the back, which is "between the shoulders." Is there for this reason there the greenness of gold, that is, wisdom and love, because in that place there are in a manner the roots of the wings? or because in that place is carried that light burden? For what are even the wings themselves, but the two commandments of love, whereon hangeth the whole Law and the Prophets?³ what is that same light burden, but that same love⁴ which in these two commandments is fulfilled? For whatever thing is difficult in a commandment, is a light thing to a lover. Nor on any other account is rightly understood the saying, "My burden is light,"⁵ but because He giveth the Holy Spirit, whereby love is shed abroad in our hearts,⁶ in order that in love we may do freely that which he that doeth in fear doeth slavishly; nor is he a lover of what is right, when he would prefer, if so be it were possible, that what is right should not be commanded.

16. It may also be required, when it hath not been said, if ye sleep in the lots, but "in the midst of the lots;" what this is, "in the midst of the lots." Which expression indeed, if more exactly it were translated from the Greek, would signify, "in the midst between the lots,"⁷ which is in no one of the interpreters I have read: therefore I suppose, that what hath been said

signifieth much the same, to wit the expression, "in the midst of the lots." Hence therefore what seemeth to me I will explain. Ofttimes this word is wont to be used for uniting and pacifying one thing and another, that they may not mutually disagree: as when God is establishing His covenant⁸ between Himself and His people, this word the Scripture useth; for instead of that expression which is in Latin between Me and you, the Greek hath, in the midst of Me and you. So also of the sign of Circumcision, when God speaketh to Abraham, He saith, "There shall be a testament between Me and thee and all thy seed:"⁹ which the Greek hath, in the midst of Me and thee, and the midst of thy seed. Also when He was speaking to Noe of the bow in the clouds to establish a sign,¹⁰ this word very often He repeateth: and that which the Latin copies have, between Me and you, or between Me and every living soul, and whatever suchlike expressions there are used, is found in the Greek to be, in the middle of Me and you, which is ἀνὰ μέσον. David also and Jonathan establish a sign between them,¹¹ that they may not disagree with a difference of thought: and that which in Latin is expressed, between both, in the middle of both, the Greek hath expressed in the same word, which is ἀνὰ μέσον. But it was best that in this passage of the Psalms our translators said not, "among the lots," which expression is more suited to the Latin idiom; but, "in the midst of the lots," as though "in the midst between the lots," which rather is the reading in the Greek, and which is wont to be said in the case of those things which ought to have a mutual consent. . . . But why in the "lots"¹² the Testaments should be perceived, though this word is Greek, and the Testament is not so named, the reason is, because through a testament is given inheritance, which in Greek is called κληρονομία, and an heir κληρονόμος. Now κλῆρος in Greek is the term for lot, and lots according to the promise of God are called those parts of the inheritance which were distributed to the people.¹³ Whence the tribe of Levi was commanded not to have lot among their brethren, because they were sustained by tithes from them. For, I think, they that have been ordained in the grades of the Ecclesiastical Ministry have been called both Clergy and Clerks, because Matthias by lot was chosen, who we read was the first that was ordained by the Apostles.¹⁴ Henceforth, because of inheritance which is given by testament, as though by that which is made that which maketh, by the name of "lots" the Testaments themselves are signified.

---

¹ *Inter medios cleros.*   ² Ps. xci. 4.
³ Matt. xxii. 40.   ⁴ Charitas.   ⁵ Matt. xi 30.
⁶ Rom. v. 5.
⁷ *Inter medium clerorum.* The other might mean, between or among the middlemost lots.

⁸ *Testamentum.*   ⁹ Gen. xvii. 4, 7.   ¹⁰ Gen. ix. 12.
¹¹ 1 Sam. xx. 42.   ¹² *Cleros.*   ¹³ Numb. xviii. 20.
¹⁴ Acts i. 26.

17. Nevertheless, to me here another sense also occurreth, if I mistake not, to be preferred; understanding by *cleri* the inheritances themselves: so that, whereas the inheritance of the Old Testament, although in a shadow significant of the future, is earthly felicity; but the inheritance of the New Testament is everlasting immortality; to "sleep in the midst of the lots" is not too earnestly now to seek the former, and still patiently to look for the latter. . . . And because so well they have slept, on them, as it were on wings now flieth, and with praises is exalted, the Church: to wit, the Dove silvered, in order that by this fame of theirs, posterity having been invited to imitate them, while in like manner the rest also sleep, there may be added wings whereby even unto the end of the world sublimely she may be preached.

18. "While He that is above the heavens[1] distinguisheth kings over Her, with snow they shall be made white in Selmon" (ver. 14). While He "above the heavens," He that ascended over all heavens that He might fulfil all things, "while He distinguisheth kings over Her," that is, over that same "Dove silvered." For the Apostle continueth and saith, and "He hath Himself given some for Apostles, and some Prophets, and some Evangelists, and some Pastors and Teachers."[2] For what other reason is there to distinguish kings over Her, save for the work of the Ministry, for the edification of the Body of Christ: when she is indeed Herself the Body of Christ? But they are called kings from ruling: and what more than the lusts of the flesh, that sin may not reign in their mortal body to obey the desires thereof, that they yield not their members instruments of iniquity unto sin, but yield themselves to God, as though from the dead living, and their members instruments of righteousness to God?[3] For thus shall the kings be distinguished from foreigners, because they draw not the yoke with unbelievers: secondly, in a peaceful manner being distinguished from one another by their proper gifts. For not all are Apostles, or all Prophets, or all Teachers, or all have gifts of healings, or all with tongues do speak, or all interpret.[4] "But all these things worketh one and the same Spirit, dividing proper gifts to each one as He willeth."[5] In giving which Spirit He that is above the Heavens distinguisheth kings over the Dove silvered. Of which Holy Spirit, when, sent to His Mother full of grace, the Angel was speaking, to her enquiring in what manner it could come to pass that she was announced as going to bear, seeing she knew not a man:[6] . . . he saith, "The Holy Spirit shall come over upon thee, and the virtue of the Most Highest shall overshadow thee," that is, shall make a shadow for thee, "wherefore that Holy Thing which shall be born of thee, shall be called the Son of God."[7] That "shadow" again is understood of a defence against the heat of carnal lusts: whence not in carnal concupiscence, but in spiritual belief, the Virgin conceived Christ. But the shadow consisteth of light and body: and further, The "Word" that "was in the beginning,"[8] that true Light,[9] in order that a noonday shadow might be made for us; "the Word," I say, "was made Flesh, and dwelled in us."[10] . . .

19. But this mountain he calleth the "mountain of God, a mountain fruitful, a mountain full of curds" (ver. 15), or "a mountain fat." But here what else would he call fat but fruitful? For there is also a mountain called by that name, that is to say, Selmon. But what mountain ought we to understand by "the mountain of God, a mountain fruitful, a mountain full of curds," but the same Lord Christ? Of whom also another Prophet saith, "There shall be manifest in the last times the mountain of the Lord prepared on the top of the mountains"?[11] He is Himself the "Mountain full of curds,"[12] because of the babes to be fed with grace as though it were with milk;[13] a mountain rich to strengthen and enrich them by the excellence of the gifts; for even the milk itself whence curd is made, in a wonderful manner signifieth grace; for it floweth out of the overflowing of the mother's bowels, and of a sweet compassion unto babes freely it is poured forth. But in the Greek the case is doubtful, whether it be the nominative or the accusative: for in that language mountain is of the neuter gender, not of the masculine: therefore some Latin translators have not translated it, "unto the Mountain of God," but, "the Mountain of God." But I think, "unto Selmon the Mountain of God," is better, that is, "unto" the Mountain of God which is called Selmon: according to the interpretation which, as we best could, we have explained above.

20. Secondly, in the expression, "Mountain of God, Mountain full of curds," Mountain "fruitful," let no one dare from this to compare the Lord Jesus Christ with the rest of the Saints, who are themselves also called mountains of God. . . . For there were not wanting men to call Him, some John Baptist, some Elias, some Jeremias, or one of the Prophets;[14] He turneth to them and saith, "Why do ye imagine[15] mountains full of curds, a mountain," he saith, "wherein it hath pleased God to dwell therein"? (ver. 16).

[7] Luke i. 35.   [8] John i. 1.   [9] John i. 9.
[10] John i. 14.   [11] Isa. ii. 2.   [12] *Incaseatus.*
[13] 1 Cor. iii. 1.   [14] Matt. xvi. 14.
[15] *Suspicamini.*

[1] *Supercælestis.*   [2] Eph. iv. 11.   [3] Rom. vi. 12, 13.
[4] 1 Cor. xii. 29, 30.   [5] 1 Cor. xii. 11.   [6] Luke i. 34.

"Why do ye imagine?"[1] For as they are a light, because to themselves also hath been said, "Ye are the Light of the world,"[2] but something different hath been called "the true Light which enlighteneth every man."[3] so they are mountains; but far different is the Mountain "prepared on the top of the mountains."[4] These mountains therefore in bearing that Mountain are glorious: one of which mountains saith, "but from me far be it to glory, save in the Cross of our Lord Jesus Christ, through whom to me the world hath been crucified, and I to the world:"[5] so that "he hath glorieth, not in himself, but in the Lord may glory."[6] "Why" then "do ye imagine mountains full of curds," that "Mountain wherein it hath pleased God to dwell therein"? Not because in other men He dwelleth not, but because in them through Him. "For in Him dwelleth all the fulness of the Godhead,"[7] not in a shadow, as in the temple made by king Solomon,[8] but "bodily," that is, solidly and truly. . . . "For there is One God, and One Mediator of God and men, the Man Christ Jesus,"[9] Mountain of mountains, as Saint of saints. Whence He saith, "I in them and Thou in Me."[10] "Why then do ye imagine mountains full of curds, the mountain wherein it hath pleased God to dwell in Him?" For those mountains full of curds that Mountain the Lord shall inhabit even unto the end, that something they may be to whom He saith, "for without Me nothing ye are able to do."[11]

21. Thus cometh to pass that also which followeth: "The Chariot of God is of ten thousands manifold:" or "of tens of thousands manifold:" or, "ten times thousand times manifold" (ver. 17). For one Greek word, which hath there been used, μυριοπλάσιον, each Latin interpreter hath rendered as best he could, but in Latin it could not be adequately expressed: for a thousand with the Greeks is called χίλια, but μυριάδες are a number of tens of thousands: for one μυριὰς are ten thousands. Thus a vast number of saints and believers, who by bearing God become in a manner the chariot[12] of God, he hath signified under this name. By abiding in and guiding this, He conducteth it, as though it were His Chariot, unto the end, as if unto some appointed place. For, "the beginning is Christ; secondly, that are of Christ, at the appearing of Him; then the end."[13] This is Holy Church: which is that which followeth, "thousands of men rejoicing." For in hope they are joyful, until they be conducted unto the end, which now they look for through patience.[14] For

admirably, when he had said, "Thousands of men rejoicing:" immediately he added, "The Lord is in them." That we may not wonder why they rejoice, "The Lord is in them." For through many tribulations we must needs enter into the kingdom of God,[15] but, "The Lord is in them." Therefore even if they are as it were sorrowful, yet alway rejoicing,[16] though not now in that same end, to which they have not yet come, yet in hope they are rejoicing, and in tribulation patient: for, "The Lord is in them, in Sina in the holy place." In the interpretations of Hebrew names, we find Sina interpreted commandment: and some other interpretations it has, but I think this to be more agreeable to the present passage. For giving a reason why those thousands rejoice, whereof the Chariot of God doth consist, "The Lord," he saith, "is in them, in Sina in the holy place:" that is, the Lord is in them, in the commandment; which commandment is holy, as saith the Apostle: "Therefore the law indeed is holy, and the commandment is holy, and just, and good."[17] . . .

22. In the next place, turning his address to the Lord Himself, "Thou hast gone up," he saith, "on high, Thou hast led captivity captive, Thou hast received gifts in men" (ver. 18). Of this the Apostle thus maketh mention, thus expoundeth in speaking of the Lord Christ: "But unto each one of us," he saith, "is given grace after the measure of the giving of Christ: for which cause he saith, He hath gone up on high, He hath led captive captivity, He hath given gifts to men."[18] . . . And let it not move us that the Apostle making mention of that same testimony saith not, "Thou hast received gifts in men;" but, "He hath given gifts unto men." For he with Apostolic authority hath spoken thus according to the faith that the Son is God with the Father. For in respect of this He hath given gifts to men, sending to them the Holy Spirit, which is the Spirit of the Father and of the Son. But forasmuch as the self-name Christ is understood in His Body which is the Church, wherefore also His members are His saints and believers, whence to them is said, "But ye are the Body of Christ, and the members,"[19] doubtless He hath Himself also received gifts in men. Now Christ hath gone up on high, and sitteth at the right hand of the Father:[20] but unless He were here also on the earth, He would not thence have cried, "Saul, Saul, why persecutest thou me?"[21] When the Same saith Himself, "Inasmuch as to one of My least ye have done it, to Me ye have done it:"[22] why do we doubt that He receiveth in His members, the gifts which the members of Him receive?

---

[1] Or, "look up to."　　[2] Matt. v. 14.　　[3] John i. 9.
[4] Isa. ii. 2.　　[5] Gal. vi. 14.　　[6] 1 Cor. i. 31.
[7] Col. ii. 9.　　[8] 1 Kings viii. 27.　　[9] 1 Tim. ii. 5.
[10] John xvii. 23.　　[11] John xv. 5.
[12] See St. Macarius, *Hom.* 1　　　[13] 1 Cor. xv. 23, 24.
[14] Rom. xii. 12.

[15] Acts xiv. 22.　　[16] 2 Cor. vi. 10.　　[17] Rom. vii. 12.
[18] Eph. iv. 7, 8.　　[19] 1 Cor. xii. 27.　　[20] Mark xvi. 19.
[21] Acts ix. 4.　　[22] Matt. xxv. 40.

23. But what is, "Thou hast led captivity captive"? Is it because He hath conquered death, which was holding captive those over whom it reigned? Or hath he called men themselves captivity, who were being held captive under the devil? Which thing's mystery even the title of that Psalm[1] doth contain, to wit, "when the house was being builded after the captivity:" that is, the Church after the coming in of the Gentiles. Calling therefore those very men who were being held captive a captivity, as when "the service"[2] is spoken of there are understood those that serve also, that same captivity he saith by Christ hath been led captive. For why should not captivity be happy, if even for a good purpose men may be caught? Whence to Peter hath been said, "From henceforth thou shalt catch men."[3] Led captive therefore they are because caught, and caught because subjugated, being sent under that gentle yoke,[4] being delivered from sin whereof they were servants, and being made servants of righteousness[5] whereof they were children. Whence also He is Himself in them, that hath given gifts to men, and hath received gifts in men. And thus in that captivity, in that servitude, in that chariot, under that yoke, there are not thousands of men lamenting, but thousands of men rejoicing. For the Lord is in them, in Sina, in the holy place.[6] . . .

24. But what next doth he adjoin? "For they that believe not to dwell" (ver. 18): or, as some copies have, "For not believing to dwell:" for what else are men not believing, but they that believe not? To whom this hath been said, is not easy to perceive. For as though a reason were being given of the above words, when it had been said, "Thou hast led captivity captive, Thou hast received gifts in men:" there hath been added in continuation, "for they that believe not to dwell," that is, not believing that they should dwell. What is this? Of whom saith he this? Did that captivity, before it passed into a good captivity, show whence it was an evil captivity? For through not believing they were possessed by the enemy, "that worketh in the sons of unbelief: among whom ye were sometime, while ye were living among them."[7] By the gifts therefore of His grace, He that hath received gifts in men, hath led captive that captivity. For they believed not that they should dwell. For faith hath thence delivered them, in order that now believing they may dwell in the House of God, even they too becoming the House of God, and the Chariot of God, consisting of thousands of men rejoicing.

25. Whence he that was singing of these things,

in the Spirit foreseeing them, even he too being fulfilled with joy hath burst forth[8] a hymn, saying, "The Lord God is blessed, blessed is the Lord God from day unto day" (ver. 19). Which some copies have, "by day daily," because the Greeks have it thus, ἡμέραν καθ᾽ ἡμέραν: which more exactly would be expressed by, "by day daily." Which expression I think signifieth the same as that which hath been said, to wit, "from day unto day." For daily this He doeth even unto the end, He leadeth captive captivity, receiving gifts in men.

26. And because He leadeth that chariot unto the end, He continueth and saith, "A prosperous journey there shall make for us the God of our healths, our God, the God of making men safe" (ver. 20). Highly is grace here commended. For who would be safe, unless He Himself should make whole? But that it might not occur to the mind, Why then do we die, if through His grace we have been made safe? immediately he added below, "and the Lord's is the outgoing of death:" as though he were saying, Why are thou indignant, O lot of humanity, that thou hast the outgoing of death? Even thy Lord's outgoing was no other than that of death. Rather therefore be comforted than be indignant: for even "the Lord's is the outgoing of death." "For by hope we have been saved: but if that which we see not we hope for, through patience we wait for it."[9] Patiently therefore even death itself let us suffer, by the example of Him, who though by no sin He was debtor to death, and was the Lord, from whom no one could take away life, but Himself laid it down of Himself, yet had Himself the outgoing of death.

27. "Nevertheless, God shall break in pieces the heads of His enemies, the scalp of hair of men walking on in their transgressions" (ver. 21): that is, too much exalting themselves, being too proud in their transgressions: wherein at least they ought to be humble, saying, "O Lord, be Thou merciful to me a sinner."[10] But He shall break in pieces their heads: for he that exalteth himself shall be humbled.[11] And thus though even of the Lord be the outgoing of death: nevertheless the same Lord, because He was God, and died after the flesh of His own will, not of necessity, "shall[12] break in pieces the heads of His enemies:" not only of those who mocked and crucified Him, and wagged their heads, and said, "If Son of God He is, let Him come down from the Cross;"[13] but also of all men lifting up themselves against His doctrine, and deriding His death as though it were of a man. For that very same One of whom hath been said, "Others He saved, Himself He can-

---

[1] See Title Ps. xcv., Vulgate.   [2] Militia.
[3] Luke v. 10.   [4] Matt. xi. 30.   [5] Rom. vi. 18.
[6] Ps. lxviii. 17. He adds: "with which sense agreeth another interpretation also, whereby Sina is interpreted 'measure.'"
[7] Eph. ii. 2.

[8] Eructavit.   [9] Rom. viii. 24, 25.   [10] Luke xviii. 13.
[11] Luke xviii. 14.   [12] Oxf. MSS. "did."
[13] Matt xxvii. 40.

not save," [1] is the "God of our healths," and is the "God of saving men : " but for an example of humility and of patience, and to efface the handwriting of our sins, He even willed that the outgoing of death should be His own, that we might not fear that death, but rather this from which He hath delivered us through that. Nevertheless, though mocked and dead, "He shall break [2] in pieces the heads of His enemies," of whom He saith, "Raise Thou me up, and I shall render to them : " [3] whether it be good things for evil things, while to Himself He subdueth the heads of them believing, or whether just things for unjust things, while He punisheth the heads of them proud. For in either way are shattered and broken the heads of enemies, when from pride they are thrown down, whether by humility being amended, or whether unto the lowest depths of hell being hurled.

28. "The Lord hath said, Out of Basan I will be turned " (ver. 22) : or, as some copies have, "Out of Basan I will turn." For He turneth that we may be safe, of whom above hath been said, "God of our healths, and God of saving men." [4] For to Him elsewhere also is said, "O God of virtues, turn Thou us, and show Thy face, and safe we shall be." [5] Also in another place, "Turn us, O God of our healths." [6] But he hath said, "Out of Basan I will turn." Basan is interpreted confusion. What is then, I will turn out of confusion, but that there is confounded because of his sins, he that is praying of the mercy of God that they may be put away? Thence it is that the Publican dared not even to lift up his eyes to Heaven : [7] so, on considering himself, was he confounded ; but he went down justified,[8] because "the Lord hath said, Out of Basan I will turn." Basan is also interpreted drought : and rightly the Lord is understood to turn out of drought, that is, out of scarcity. For they that think themselves to be in plenty, though they be famished ; and full, though they be altogether empty ; are not turned. . . . "I will turn unto the deep of the sea." If, "I will turn," why, "unto the deep of the sea"? Unto Himself indeed the Lord turneth, when savingly He turneth, and He is not surely Himself the deep of the sea. Doth perchance the Latin expression deceive us, and hath there been put "unto the deep," for a translation of what signifieth "deeply"? For He doth not turn Himself : but He turneth those that in the deep of this world lie sunk down with the weight of sins, in that place where one that is turned saith, "From the depths I have cried to Thee, O Lord." [9] But if it is not, "I will turn," but, "I will be turned unto the deep

of the sea ; " our Lord is understood to have said, how by His own mercy He was turned even unto the deep of the sea, to deliver even those that were sinners in most desperate case. Though in one Greek copy I have found, not, "unto the deep," but "in the depths," that is, ἐν βυθοῖς : which strengtheneth the former sense, because even there God turneth to Himself men crying from the depths. And even if He be understood Himself there to be turned, to deliver such sort also, it is not beside the purpose : and so then He turneth, or else to deliver them is so turned, that His foot is stained in blood. Which to the Lord Himself the Prophet speaketh : "That Thy foot may be stained in blood" (ver. 23) : that is, in order that they themselves who are turned to Thee, or to deliver whom Thou art turned, though in the deep of the sea by the burden of iniquity they may have been sunk, may make so great proficiency by Thy Grace (for where there hath abounded sin, there hath superabounded grace [10]), that they may become Thy foot among Thy members, to preach Thy Gospel, and for Thy name's sake drawing out a long martyrdom, even unto blood they may contend. For thus, as I judge, more meetly is perceived His foot stained in blood.

29. Lastly, he addeth, "The tongue of Thy dogs out of enemies by Himself," calling those very same that had been about to strive for the faith of the Gospel, even dogs, as though barking for their Lord. Not those dogs, whereof saith the Apostle, "Beware of dogs : " [11] but those that eat of the crumbs which fall from the table of their masters. For having confessed this, the woman of Canaan merited to hear, "O woman, great is thy faith, be it done to thee as thou wilt." [12] Dogs commendable, not abominable ; observing fidelity towards their master, and before his house barking against enemies. Not only "of dogs" he hath said, but "of Thy dogs : " nor are their teeth praised, but their tongue is : for it was not indeed to no purpose, not without a great mystery, that Gedeon was bidden to lead those alone, who should lap the water of the river like dogs ; [13] and of such sort not more than three hundred among so great a multitude were found. In which number is the sign of the Cross because of the letter T, which in the Greek numeral characters signifieth three hundred. Of such dogs in another Psalm also is said, "They shall be turned at even, and hunger they shall suffer as dogs." [14] For even some dogs have been reproved by the Prophet Isaiah, not because they were dogs, but because they knew not how to bark, and loved to sleep.[15] In which place indeed he hath shown, that if they had watched and barked for their Lord,

[1] Matt. xxvii. 42.   [2] Oxf. mss. " breaketh."
[3] Ps. xli. 10.   [4] Ps. lxviii. 19.   [5] Ps. lxxx. 19.
[6] Ps. lxxxv. 4.   [7] Luke xviii. 13.   [8] Luke xviii. 14.
[9] Ps. cxxx. 1.

[10] Rom. v. 20.   [11] Philip. iii. 2.   [12] Matt. xv. 27, 28.
[13] Judg. vii. 5.   [14] Ps. lix. 14.   [15] Isa. lvi. 10.

they would have been praiseworthy dogs: just as they are praised, of whom is said, "The tongue of Thy dogs." . . .

30. "There have been seen Thy steps, O God" (ver. 24). The steps are those wherewith Thou hast come through the world, as though in that chariot Thou wast going to traverse the round world; which chariot of clouds He intimateth to be His holy and faithful ones in the Gospel, where He saith, "From this time[1] ye shall see the Son of Man coming in the clouds."[2] Leaving out that coming wherein He shall be Judge of quick and dead,[3] "From this time," He saith, "ye shall see the Son of Man coming in clouds." These "Thy steps have been séen," that is, have been manifested, by the revealing the grace of the New Testament. Whence hath been said, "How beautiful are the feet of them that proclaim peace, that proclaim good things!"[4] For this grace and those steps were lying hid in the Old Testament: but when there came the fulness of time, and it pleased God to reveal His Son,[5] that He might be proclaimed among the Gentiles, "there were seen Thy steps, O God: the steps of my God, of the[6] King who is in the holy place." In what holy place, save in His Temple? "For the Temple of God is holy," he saith, "which ye are."[7]

31. But in order that those steps might be seen, "there went before princes conjoined with men psalming, in the midst of damsels players on timbrels" (ver. 25). The princes are the Apostles: for they went before, that the peoples might come in multitudes. "They went before" proclaiming the New Testament: "conjoined with men psalming," by whose good works that were even visible, as it were with instruments of praise, God was glorified. But those same princes are "in the midst of damsels players on timbrels," to wit, in an honourable ministry: for thus in the midst are ministers set over new Churches; for this is "damsels:" with flesh subdued praising God; for this is "players on timbrels," because timbrels are made of skin dried and stretched.

32. Therefore, that no one should take these words in a carnal sense, and by these words should conceive in his mind certain choral bands of wantonness, he continueth and saith, "In the Churches bless ye the Lord" (ver. 26): as though he were saying, wherefore, when ye hear of damsels, players on timbrels, do ye think of wanton pleasures? "In the Churches bless ye the Lord." For the Churches are pointed out to you by this mystic intimation: the Churches are the damsels, with new grace decked: the Churches are the players on the timbrels, with chastened flesh being spiritually tuneful. "In the Churches," then, "bless ye the Lord God from the wells of Israel." For from thence He first chose those whom He made wells. For from thence were chosen the Apostles; and they first heard, "He that shall have drunk of the water that I shall give him, shall never thirst, but there shall be made in him a well of water springing unto life everlasting."[8]

33. "There is Benjamin the younger in a trance" (ver. 27). There is Paul the last of the Apostles, who saith, "For even I am an Israelite, out of the seed of Abraham, out of the tribe of Benjamin."[9] But evidently "in a trance," all men being amazed at a miracle so great as that of his calling. For a trance is the mind's going out: which thing sometimes chanceth through fear; but sometimes through some revelation, the mind suffering separation from the corporal senses, in order that that which is to be represented may be represented to the spirit. Whence even thus may be understood that which here hath been written, namely, "in a trance;" for when to that persecutor there had been said[10] from Heaven, "Saul, Saul, why persecutest thou me:"[11] there being taken from him the light of the eyes of flesh, he made answer to the Lord, whom in spirit he saw, but they that were with him heard the voice of him replying, though seeing no one to whom he was speaking. Here also the trance may be understood to be that one of his, whereof he himself speaking, saith, that he knew a man caught up even unto the third Heaven; but whether in the body, or whether out of the body, he knew not:[12] but that he being caught up into Paradise, heard ineffable words, which it was not lawful for a man to speak. "Princes of Juda the leaders of them, princes of Zabulon, princes of Nephthalim." Since he is indicating the Apostles as princes, wherein is even "Benjamin the younger in a trance," in which words that Paul is indicated no one doubteth; or when under the name of princes there are indicated in the Churches all men excelling and most worthy of imitation: what mean these names of the tribes of Israel? . . . For the names are Hebrew: whereof Juda is said to be interpreted confession, Zabulon habitation of strength, Nephthalim my enlargement. All which words do intimate to us the most proper princes of the Church, worthy of their leadership, worthy of imitation, worthy of honours. For the Martyrs in the Churches hold the highest place, and by the crown of holy worth they do excel. But however in martyrdom the first thing is confession,

---

[1] *A modo.*　　　[2] Mark xiii. 26.　　　[3] 2 Tim. iv. 1.
[4] Rom. x. 15.　　　[5] Gal. iv. 4.　　　[6] Oxf. mss. "my."
[7] 1 Cor. iii. 17.

[8] John iv. 14.　　　[9] Philip. iii. 5.
[10] Oxf. mss. "He was about to say."　　　[11] Acts ix. 4.
[12] 2 Cor. xii. 2.

and for this is next put on strength to endure whatsoever shall have chanced; then after all things have been endured, straits being ended, breadth followeth in reward. It may also thus be understood; that whereas the Apostle chiefly commendeth these three things, faith, hope, love;[1] confession is in faith, strength in hope, breadth in love. For of faith the substance is, that with the heart men believe unto righteousness, but with the mouth confession be made unto salvation.[2] But in sufferings of tribulations the thing itself is sorrowful, but the hope is strong. For, "if that which we see not we hope for, through patience we wait for it."[3] But breadth the shedding abroad of love in the heart doth give. For "love perfected casteth out fear:" which fear "hath torment,"[4] because of the straits of the soul. . . .

34. "Command, O God, Thy Virtue" (ver. 28). For one is our Lord Jesus Christ, through whom are all things,[5] and we in Him, of whom we read that He is "the Virtue of God and the Wisdom of God."[6] But how doth God command His Christ, save while He commendeth Him? For "God commendeth His love in us, in that while yet we were sinners, for us Christ died."[7] "How hath He not also with Him given to us all things?"[8] "Command, O God, Thy Virtue: confirm, O God, that which Thou hast wrought in us." Command by teaching, confirm by aiding.

35. "From Thy Temple in Jerusalem, to Thee kings shall offer presents" (ver. 29). Jerusalem, which is our free mother,[9] because the same also is Thy holy Temple: from that Temple then, "to Thee kings shall offer presents." Whatever kings be understood, whether kings of the earth, or whether those whom "He that is above the heavens distinguisheth over the dove silvered;" "to Thee kings shall offer presents." And what presents are so acceptable[10] as the sacrifices of praise? But there is a noise against this praise, from men bearing the name of Christian, and having diverse opinions. Be there done that which followeth, "Rebuke Thou the beasts of the cane"[11] (ver. 30). For both beasts they are, since by not understanding they do hurt: and beasts of the cane they are, since the sense of the Scriptures they wrest according to their own misapprehension. For in the cane the Scriptures are as reasonably perceived, as language in tongue, according to the mode of expression whereby the Hebrew or the Greek or the Latin tongue is spoken of, or the like; that is to say, by the efficient cause the thing which is being effected is implied. Now

it is usual in the Latin language for writing to be called style, because with the *stilus* it is done: so then cane also, because with a cane it is done. The Apostle Peter saith, that "men unlearned and unstable do wrest the Scriptures to their own proper destruction:"[12] these are the beasts of the cane, whereof here is said, "Rebuke Thou the beasts of the cane."

36. Concerning these also is that which followeth, "The congregation of bulls amid the cows of the peoples, in order that there may be excluded they that have been tried with silver."[13] Calling them bulls because of the pride of a stiff and untamed neck: for he is referring to heretics. But by "the cows of the peoples," I think souls easily led astray must be understood, because easily they follow these bulls. For they lead not astray entire peoples, among whom are men grave and stable; whence hath been written, "In a people grave I will praise Thee:"[14] but only the cows which they may have found among those peoples. "For of these are they that steal into houses, and lead captive silly women laden with sins, who are led with divers lusts, alway learning, and at the knowledge of the truth never arriving."[15] . . . For, "may be excluded," hath been said, meaning, may appear, may stand forth: as he saith, "may be made manifest." Whence also, in the art of the silversmith, they are called *exclusores*, who out of the shapelessness of the lump are skilled to mould the form of a vessel. For many meanings of the holy Scriptures are concealed, and are known only to a few of singular intelligence, and are never vindicated so suitably and acceptably as when our diligence to make answer to heretics constraineth us. For then even they that neglect the pursuits of learning, shaking off their slumber, are stirred up to a diligent hearing, in order that their opponents may be refuted. In a word, how many senses of holy Scriptures concerning Christ as God have been vindicated against Photinus, how many concerning Christ as man against Manichæus, how many concerning the Trinity against Sabellius, how many concerning the Unity of the Trinity against Arians, Eunomians, Macedonians? How many concerning the Catholic Church in the whole world spread abroad, against Donatists, and Luciferians, and others, whoever they be, that with like error dissent from the truth: how many against the rest of heretics, whom to enumerate or mention were too long a task, and for the present work unnecessary? . . . Of whom, as it were bulls, that is, not subject to the peaceful and gentle yoke of discipline, the Apostle maketh mention, in the place where he hath said that such an one

1 1 Cor. xiii. 13. 2 Rom. x. 10. 3 Rom. viii. 25.
4 1 John iv. 18. 5 1 Cor. viii. 6. 6 1 Cor. i. 24.
7 Rom. v. 8. 8 Rom. viii. 32. 9 Gal. iv. 26.
10 Oxf. MSS. "more acceptable than."
11 Or, "pen" (of cane), *calami*.

12 2 Pet. iii. 16. 13 See on Ps. lv. p. 216, note 7.
14 Ps. xxxv. 18. 15 2 Tim. iii. 6, 7.

must be chosen for the Episcopate as is "able to exhort in sound doctrine and to convince the gainsayers. For there are many unruly;"[1] these are bulls with uplifted neck, impatient of plough and yoke: vain-talkers and leaders astray of minds; which minds this Psalm hath intimated under the name of cows. . . .

37. "There shall come ambassadors out of Egypt, Ethiopia shall prevent the hands of Him" (ver. 31). Under the name of Egypt or of Ethiopia, he hath signified the faith of all nations, from a part the whole: calling the preachers of reconciliation ambassadors. "For Christ," he saith, "we have an embassy, God as it were exhorting through us: we beseech you for Christ to be reconciled to God."[2] Not then of the Israelites alone, whence the Apostles were chosen, but also from the rest of the nations that there should be preachers of Christian peace, in this manner hath been mystically prophesied. But by that which he saith, "shall prevent the hands of Him," he saith this, shall prevent the vengeance of Him: to wit, by turning to Him, in order that their sins may be forgiven, lest by continuing sinners they be punished. Which thing also in another Psalm is said, "Let us come before[3] the face of Him in confession."[4] As by hands he signifieth vengeance, so by face, revelation and presence, which will be in the Judgment. Because then, by Egypt and Ethiopia he hath signified the nations of the whole world; immediately he hath subjoined, "to God (are) the kingdoms of the earth." Not to Sabellius, not to Arius, not to Donatus, not to the rest of the bulls stiff-necked, but "to God (are) the kingdoms of the earth." But the greater number of Latin copies, and especially the Greek, have the verses so punctuated, that there is not one verse in these words, "to God the kingdoms of the earth," but, "to God," is at the end of the former verse, and so there is said, "Ethiopia shall come before the hands of her to God," and then there followeth in another verse, "Kingdoms of the earth, sing ye to God, psalm ye to the Lord" (ver. 32). By which punctuation, doubtless to be preferred by the agreement of many copies, and those deserving of credit, there seemeth to me to be implied faith which precedeth works: because without the merits of good works through faith the ungodly is justified, just as the Apostle said, "To one believing in Him that justifieth the ungodly, his faith is counted for righteousness:"[5] in order that afterwards faith itself through love may begin to work. For those alone are to be called good works,[6] which are done through love of God. But these faith must needs go before, so that from thence these

may begin, not from these this. . . . This is faith, whereof to the Church Herself is said in the Song of Songs, "Thou shalt come and shalt pass hence from the beginning of faith."[7] For She hath come[8] like the chariot of God in thousands of men rejoicing, having a prosperous course, and She hath passed over from this world to the Father: in order that there may come to pass in Her that which the Bridegroom Himself saith, who hath passed hence from this world to the Father,[9] "I will that where I am, these also may be with Me:"[10] but from the beginning of faith. Because then in order that good works may follow, faith doth precede; and there are not any good works, save those which follow faith preceding: nothing else seemeth to have been meant in, "Ethiopia shall come before the hands of her to God," but, Ethiopia shall believe in God. For thus she "shall come before the hands of her," that is, the works of her. Of whom, except of Ethiopia herself? For this in the Greek is not ambiguous: for the word "of her"[11] there in the feminine gender most clearly hath been put down. And thus nothing else hath been said than "Ethiopia shall come before her hands to God," that is, by believing in God she shall come before her works. For, "I judge," saith the Apostle, "that a man is justified through faith without the works of the Law. Is He God of the Jews only? Is He not also of the Gentiles?"[12] So then Ethiopia, which seemeth to be the utmost limit of the Gentiles, is justified through faith, without the works of the Law. . . . For the expression in Greek, χείρα αὐτῆς, which most copies have, both of "hand of her" and "her own hand" may be understood: but that which is uncommon in the Greek copies, χειρὰς αὐτῆς, by both "hands of her" and "her own[13] hands," in Latin may be expressed.

38. Henceforward, as if through prophecy all things had been discoursed of which now we see fulfilled, he exhorteth to the praise of Christ, and next He foretelleth His future Advent. "Kingdoms of earth, sing ye to God, psalm ye to the Lord: psalm ye to God, who hath ascended above the Heaven of Heavens to the East" (ver. 33). Or, as some copies have it, "who hath ascended above the Heaven of Heaven to the East." In these words he preceiveth not Christ, who believeth not His Resurrection and Ascension. But hath not "to the East," which he hath added, expressed the very spot; since in the quarters of the East is where He rose again, and whence He ascended? Therefore above the Heaven of Heaven He

---

[1] Tit. i. 9, 10. [2] 2 Cor. v. 20. [3] Or, "prevent."
[4] Ps. xcv. 2. [5] Rom. iv. 5. [6] *Sola bona opera.*

[7] Cant. iv. 8, LXX. E. V. "the top of Amana."
[8] Oxf. MSS. "shall come," "shall pass." [9] John xiii. 1.
[10] John xvii. 24. [11] Lat. *ejus*, of him or her.
[12] Rom. iii. 28, etc. [13] *Suas.*

sitteth at the right hand of the Father. This is what the Apostle saith, "the Same is He that hath ascended above all Heavens." [1] For what of Heavens doth remain after the Heaven of Heaven? Which also we may call the Heavens of Heavens, just as He hath called the firmanent Heaven: [2] which Heaven, however, even as Heavens we read of, in the place where there is written, "and let the waters which are above the Heavens praise the name of the Lord." [3] And forasmuch as from thence He is to come,[4] to judge quick and dead, observe what followeth: "behold, He shall give His voice, the voice of power." [5] He that like a lamb before the shearer of Him was without voice,[6] "behold shall give His voice," and not the voice of weakness, as though to be judged; but "the voice of power," as though going to judge. For God shall not be hidden, as before, and in the judgment of men not opening His mouth; but "God shall come manifest, our God, and He shall not be silent." [7] Why do ye despair, ye unbelieving men? Why do ye mock? What saith the evil servant? "My Lord delayeth to come." [8] "Behold, He shall give His voice, the voice of power."

39. "Give ye glory to God, above Israel is the magnificence of Him" (ver. 34). Of whom saith the Apostle, "Upon the Israel of God." [9] For "not all that are out of Israel, are Israelites:" [10] for there is also an Israel after the flesh. Whence he saith, "See ye Israel after the flesh." [11] "For not they that are sons of the flesh, are sons of God, but sons of promise are counted for a seed." [12] Therefore at that time when without any intermixture of evil men His people shall be, like a heap purged by the fan,[13] like Israel in whom guile is not,[14] then most pre-eminent "above Israel" shall be "the magnificence" of "Him: and the virtue of Him in the clouds." For not alone He shall come to judgment, but with the elders of His people: [15] to whom He hath promised that they shall sit upon thrones to judge,[16] who even shall judge angels.[17] These be the clouds.

40. Lastly, lest of anything else the clouds be understood, he hath in continuation added, "Wonderful is God in His saints, the God of Israel" (ver. 35). For at that time even most truly and most fully there shall be fulfilled the name Israel itself, which is one "seeing God:" for we shall see Him as He is.[18] "He Himself shall give virtue [19] and strength to His people, blessed be God:" to His people now frail and weak. For "we have this treasure in earthen vessels." [20]

But then by a most glorious changing even of our bodies, "He Himself shall give virtue and strength to His people." For this body is sown in weakness, shall rise in virtue.[21] He Himself then shall give the virtue which in His own flesh He hath sent before, whereof the Apostle saith, "the power of His Resurrection." [22] But strength whereby shall be destroyed the enemy death.[23] Now then of this long and difficultly understood Psalm we have at length by His own aid made an end. "Blessed be God. Amen."

PSALM LXIX.[24]

1. We have been born into this world, and added to the people of God, at that period wherein already the herb from a grain of mustard seed hath spread out its branches; wherein already the leaven, which at first was contemptible, hath leavened three measures,[25] that is, the whole round world repeopled by the three sons of Noe: [26] for from East and West and North and South shall come they that shall sit down with the Patriarchs,[27] while those shall have been driven without, that have been born of their flesh and have not imitated their faith. Unto his glory then of Christ's Church our eyes we have opened; and that barren one, for whom joy was proclaimed and foretold, because she was to have more sons than she that had the husband,[28] her we have found to be such an one as hath forgotten the reproaches and infamy of her widowhood: and so we may perhaps wonder when we chance to read in any prophecy the words of Christ's humiliation, or our own. And it may be, that we are less affected by them; because we have not come at that time when these things were read with zest, in that tribulation abounded. But again if we think of the abundance of tribulations, and observe the way wherein we are walking (if indeed we do walk in it), how narrow it is, and how through straits and tribulations it leadeth unto rest everlasting,[29] and how that very thing which in human affairs is called felicity, is more to be feared than misery; since indeed misery ofttimes doth bring out of tribulation a good fruit, but felicity doth corrupt the soul with a perverse security, and giveth place for the Devil the Tempter — when, I say, we shall have judged prudently and rightly, as the salted victim [30] did, that "human life upon earth is trial," [31] and that no one is at all secure, nor ought to be secure, until he be come to that country, whence no one that is a friend goeth forth, into which no one that is an enemy is

---

1 Eph. iv. 10.
2 Gen. i. 8.
3 Ps. cxlviii. 4.
4 Acts i. 11.
5 *Virtutis.*
6 Isa. liii. 7.
7 Ps. l. 3.
8 Luke xii. 45.
9 Gal. vi. 16.
10 Rom. ix. 6.
11 1 Cor. x. 18.
12 Rom. ix. 8.
13 Matt. iii. 12.
14 John i. 47.
15 Isa. iii. 14.
16 Matt. xix. 28.
17 1 Cor. vi. 3.
18 1 John iii. 2.
19 Or, " power."
20 2 Cor. iv. 7.

21 1 Cor. xv. 43.
22 Philip. iii. 10.
23 1 Cor. xv. 26.
24 Lat. LXVIII.
25 Matt. xiii. 31, 33; Luke xiii. 19, 21.
26 Gen. ix. 19.
27 Matt. viii. 11.
28 Isa. liv. 1; Gal. iv. 27.
29 Matt. vii. 14.
30 *Salita victima ;* most copies have *psallit hæc victima.* — Ben. [Mark ix. 4. — C.]
31 Job vii. 1, LXX.

admitted, even now in the very glory of the Church we acknowledge the voices of our tribulation : and being members of Christ, subject to our Head in the bond of love, and mutually supporting one another, we will say from the Psalms, that which here we have found the Martyrs said, who were before us ; that tribulation is common to all men from the beginning even unto the end. . . .

2. The Title of the Psalm is : "Unto the end, in behalf of those that shall be changed, to David himself." Now of the change for the better hear thou ; for change either is for the worse or for the better. . . . That we have been changed then for the worse, to ourselves let us ascribe : that for the better we are changed, let us praise God. "For those," then, "that shall be changed," this Psalm is. But whence hath this change been made but by the Passion of Christ? The very word Pascha in Latin is interpreted passage. For Pascha [1] is not a Greek word but a Hebrew. It soundeth indeed in the Greek language like Passion, because πάσχειν signifieth to suffer : but if the Hebrew expression be examined, it pointeth to something else. Pascha doth intimate passage. Of which even John the Evangelist hath admonished us, who (just before the Passion when the Lord was coming to the supper wherein He set forth the Sacrament of His Body and Blood) thus speaketh : "But when there had come the hour, wherein Jesus was to pass from this world to the Father." [2] He hath expressed then the "passage" of the Pascha. But unless He passed Himself hence to the Father, who came for our sake, how should we have been able to pass hence, who have not come down for the sake of taking up anything, but have fallen? But He Himself fell not ; He but came down, in order that He might raise up him that had fallen. The passage therefore both of Him and of us is hence to the Father, from this world to the kingdom of Heaven, from life mortal to life everlasting, from life earthly to life heavenly, from life corruptible to life incorruptible, from intimacy with tribulations to perpetual security. Accordingly, "In behalf of them that shall be changed," the Psalm's title is. The cause therefore of our change, that is, the very Passion of the Lord and our own voice in tribulations in the text of the Psalm let us observe, let us join in knowing, join in groaning, and in hearing, in joint-knowing, joint-groaning, let us be changed, in order that there may be fulfilled in us the Title of the Psalm, " In behalf of them that shall be changed."

3. "Save me, O God, for the waters have entered in even unto my soul" (ver. 1). That grain is despised now, that seemeth to give forth humble words. In the garden it is buried, though the world will admire the greatness of the herb, of which herb the seed was despised by the Jews. For in very deed observe ye the seed of the mustard, minute, dull coloured, altogether despicable, in order that therein may be fulfilled that which hath been said, We have seen Him, and He had neither form nor comeliness.[3] But He saith, that waters have come in even unto His soul ; because those multitudes, which under the name of waters He hath pointed out, were able so far to prevail as to kill Christ. . . . Whence then doth He so cry out, as though He were suffering something against His will, except because the Head doth prefigure the Members? For He suffered because He willed : but the Martyrs even though they willed not ; for to Peter thus He foretold his passion : "When thou shalt be old," He saith, "another shall gird thee, and lead thee whither thou wilt not." [4] For though we desire to cleave to Christ, yet we are unwilling to die : and therefore willingly or rather patiently we suffer, because no other passage is given us, through which we may cleave to Christ. For if we could in any other way arrive at Christ, that is, at life everlasting, who would be willing to die? For while explaining our nature, that is, a sort of association of soul and body, and in these two parts a kind of intimacy of gluing and fastening together, the Apostle saith, that "we have a House not made with hands, everlasting in the Heavens : " [5] that is, immortality prepared for us, wherewith we are to be clothed at the end, when we shall have risen from the dead ; and he saith, "Wherein we are not willing to be stripped, but to be clothed upon, that the mortal may be swallowed up of life." [6] If it might so be, we should so will, he saith, to become immortal, as that now that same immortality might come, and now as we are it should change us, in order that this our mortal body by life should be swallowed up, and the body should not be laid aside through death, so as at the end again to have to be recovered. Although then from evil to good things we pass, nevertheless the very passage is somewhat bitter, and hath the gall which the Jews gave to the Lord in the Passion, hath something sharp to be endured, whereby they are shown that gave Him vinegar to drink.[7] . . . For here both sweet are temporal pleasures, and bitter are temporal tribulations : but who would not drink the cup of tribulation temporal, fearing the fire of hell ; and who would not contemn the sweetness of the world, longing for the sweetness of life eternal? From hence that we may be delivered let us cry : lest perchance amidst oppressions we consent to iniquity, and truly irreparably we be swallowed up.

---

[1] *Non est græcum nomen.*   [2] John xiii. 1.

[3] Isa. liii. 2.   [4] John xxi. 18.   [5] 2 Cor. v. 1.
[6] 2 Cor. v. 4.   [7] Matt. xxvii. 34.

4. "Fixed I am in the clay of the deep, and there is no substance" (ver. 2). What called He clay? Is it those very persons that have persecuted? For out of clay man hath been made.[1] But these men by falling from righteousness have become the clay of the deep, and whosoever shall not have consented to them persecuting and desiring to draw him to iniquity, out of his clay doth make gold. For the clay of the same shall merit to be converted into a heavenly form,[2] and to be made associate of those of whom saith the Title of the Psalm, "in behalf of them that shall be changed." But at the time when these were the clay of the deep, I stuck in them: that is, they held Me, prevailed against Me, killed Me. "Fixed" then "I am in the clay of the deep, and there is no substance." What is this, "there is no substance"? Can it be that clay itself is not a substance? What is then, "fixed I am"? Can it be that Christ hath thus stuck? Or hath He stuck, and was not, as hath been said in the book of Job, "the earth delivered into the hands of the ungodly man"?[3] Was He fixed in body, because it could be held, and suffered even crucifixion? For unless with nails He had been fixed, crucified He had not been. Whence then "there is no substance"? Is that clay not a substance? But we shall understand, if it be possible, what is, "and there is no substance," if first we shall have understood what is a substance. For there is substance spoken of even of riches, as we say, he hath substance, and he hath lost substance. . . .

5. God is a sort of substance: for that which is no substance, is nothing at all. To be a substance then is to be something. Whence also in the Catholic Faith against the poisons of certain heretics thus we are builded up, so that we say, Father and Son and Holy Spirit are of one substance. What is, of one substance? For example, if gold is the Father, gold is also the Son, gold also the Holy Spirit. Whatever the Father is because He is God, the same is the Son, the same the Holy Spirit. But when He is the Father, this is not what He is. For Father He is called not in reference to Himself, but in reference to the Son: but in reference to Himself God He is called. Therefore in that He is God, by the same He is a substance. And because of the same substance the Son is, without doubt the Son also is God. But yet in that He is Father, because it is not the name of the substance, but is referred to the Son; we do not say that the Son is Father in the same manner as we say the Son is God. Thou askest what the Father is; we answer, God. Thou askest what is the Father and the Son: we answer, God.

If questioned of the Father alone, answer thou God: if questioned of both, not Gods, but God, answer thou. We do not reply as in the case of men, when thou inquirest what is father Abraham, we answer a man; the substance of him serveth for answer: thou inquirest what is his son Isaac, we answer, a man; of the same substance are Abraham and Isaac: thou inquirest what is Abraham and Isaac, we answer not man, but men. Not so in things divine. For so great in this case is the fellowship of substance, that of equality it alloweth, plurality alloweth not. If then it shall have been said to thee, when thou tellest me that the Son is the same as the Father, in fact the Son also is the Father; answer thou, according to the substance I have told thee that the Son is the same as the Father, not according to that term which is used in reference to something else. For in reference to Himself He is called God, in reference to the Father is called Son. And again, the Father in reference to Himself is called God, in reference to the Son He is called Father. The Father as He is called in reference to the Son, is not the Son: the Son as He is called in reference to the Father, is not the Father: what the Father is called in reference to Himself and the Son in reference to Himself, the same is Father and Son, that is, God. What is then, "there is no substance"? After this interpretation of substance, how shall we be able to understand this passage of the Psalm, "Fixed I am in the clay of the deep, and there is no substance"? God made man,[4] He made substance; and O that he had continued in that which God made Him! If man had continued in that which God made him, in him would not have been *fixed* He whom God begot. But moreover because through iniquity man fell from the substance wherein he was made[5] (for iniquity itself is no substance; for iniquity is not a nature which God formed, but a perverseness which man made); the Son of God came to the clay of the deep, and was fixed; and that was no substance wherein He was fixed, because in the iniquity of them He was fixed. "All things by Him were made, and without Him there was made nothing."[6] All natures by Him were made, iniquity by Him was not made, because iniquity was not made.[7] Those substances by Him were made, which praise Him. The whole creation praising God is commemorated by the three children in the furnace,[8] and from things earthly to things heavenly, or from things heavenly to things earthly reacheth the hymn of them praising God. Not that all these things have sense to praise; but

---

[1] Gen. ii. 7. [2] *Habitudinem.* [3] Job ix. 24.

[4] Gen. i. 27. [5] Gen. iii. 6. [6] John i. 3.
[7] Oxf. MSS. "was no substance."
[8] Dan. iii. [In the *Benedicite*, after Baruch, in the Apocrypha —C.]

because all things being well meditated upon, do beget praise, and the heart by considering creation is fulfilled to overflowing with a hymn to the Creator. All things do praise God, but only the things which God hath made. Do ye observe in that hymn that covetousness praiseth God? There even the serpent praiseth God, covetousness praiseth not. For all creeping things are there named in the praise of God: there are named all creeping things; but there are not there named any vices. For vices out of ourselves and out of our own will we have: and vices are not a substance. In these was fixed the Lord, when He suffered persecution: in the vice of the Jews, not in the substance of men which by Him was made.

6. "I have come into the depth of the sea, and the tempest hath made Me to sink down." Thanks to the mercy of Him who came into the depth of the sea, and vouchsafed to be swallowed by the sea whale, but was vomited forth the third day.[1] He came into the depth of the sea, in which depth we were thrust down, in which depth we had suffered shipwreck: He came thither Himself, and the tempest made Him to sink down: for there He suffered waves, those very men; tempests, the voices of men saying, "Crucify, Crucify."[2] Though Pilate said, I find not any cause in this Man why He should be killed: there prevailed the voices of them, saying, "Crucify, Crucify." The tempest increased, until He was made to sink down that had come into the depth of the sea. And the Lord suffered in the hands of the Jews that which He suffered not when upon the waters He was walking:[3] the which not only He had not suffered Himself, but had not allowed even Peter to suffer it.

7. "I have laboured, crying, hoarse have become my jaws" (ver. 3). Where was this? When was this? Let us question the Gospel. For the Passion of our Lord in this Psalm we perceive. And, indeed, that He suffered we know; that there came in waters even unto His Soul, because peoples prevailed even unto His death, we read, we believe; in the tempest that He was sunk down, because tumult prevailed to His killing, we acknowledge: but that He laboured in crying, and that His jaws were made hoarse, not only we read not, but even on the contrary we read, that He answered not to them a word, in order that there might be fulfilled that which in another Psalm hath been said, "I have become as it were a man not hearing, and having not in his mouth reproofs."[4] And that which in Isaiah hath been prophesied, "like a sheep to be sacrificed He was led, and like a lamb before one shearing Him, so He opened not His

mouth."[5] If He became like a man not hearing, and having not in His mouth reproofs, how did He labour crying, and how were His jaws made hoarse? Is it that He was even then silent, because He was hoarse with having cried so much in vain? And this indeed we know to have been His voice on the Cross out of a certain Psalm: "O God, My God, why hast Thou forsaken Me?"[6] But how great was that voice, or of how long duration, that in it His jaws should have become hoarse? Long while He cried, "Woe unto you, Scribes and Pharisees:"[7] long while He cried, "Woe unto the world because of offences."[8] And truly hoarse in a manner He cried, and therefore was not understood, when the Jews said, What is this that He saith? "Hard is this saying, who is able to hear it?"[9] We know not what He saith. He said all these words: but hoarse were His jaws to them that understood not His words. "Mine eyes have failed from hoping in My God." Far be it that this should be taken of the person of the Head: far be it that His eyes should have failed from [10] hoping in His God: in whom rather there was God reconciling the world to Himself,[11] and Who was the Word made flesh and dwelled in us, so that not only God was in Him, but also He was Himself God. Not so then: the eyes of Himself, our Head, failed not from hoping in His God: but the eyes of Him have failed in His Body, that is, in His members. This voice is of the members, this voice is of the Body, not of the Head. How then do we find it in His Body and members? . . .

8. Thus "there have been multiplied above the hairs of My head they that hate Me gratis" (ver. 4). How multiplied? So as that they might add to themselves even one out of the twelve.[12] "There have been multiplied above the hairs of My head they that hate Me for nought." With the hairs of His head He hath compared His enemies. With reason they were shorn when in the place of Calvary He was crucified.[13] Let the members accept this voice, let them learn to be hated gratis. For now, O Christian, if it must needs be that the world hate thee, why dost thou not make it hate thee gratis, in order that in the Body of thy Lord and in this Psalm sent before concerning Him, thou mayest acknowledge thy own voice? How shall it come to pass that the world hate thee gratis? If thou no wise hurtest any one, and art still hated: for this is gratis, without cause. . . .

9. "O God, Thou hast known mine improvidence" (ver. 5). Again out of the mouth of the Body. For what improvidence is there

---

[1] Matt. xii. 40.   [2] John xix. 6.   [3] Matt. xiv. 25.
[4] Ps. xxxviii. 14.

[5] Isa. liii. 7.
[7] Matt. xxiii. 13, 15, etc.
[9] John vi. 60, vii. 36, xvi. 17, 18.
[11] 2 Cor. v. 19.   [12] Matt. xxvi. 14.

[6] Ps. xxii. 1.
[8] Matt. xviii. 7.
[10] Ab.
[13] Matt. xxvii. 33.

in Christ? Is He not Himself the Virtue of God, and the Wisdom of God? Doth He call this His .improvidence, whereof the Apostle speaketh, "the foolishness of God is wiser than men"?[1] Mine improvidence, that very thing which in Me they derided that seem to themselves to be wise, Thou hast known why it was done. For what was so much like improvidence, as, when He had it in His power with one word to lay low the persecutors, to suffer Himself to be held, scourged, spit upon, buffeted, with thorns to be crowned, to the tree to be nailed? It is like improvidence, it seemeth a foolish thing; but this foolish thing excelleth all wise men. Foolish indeed it is: but even when grain falleth into the earth, if no one knoweth the custom of husbandmen, it seemeth foolish. . . . Improvidence it appeareth; but hope maketh it not to be improvidence. He then spared not Himself: because even the Father spared Him not, but delivered Him up for us all.[2] And of the Same, "Who loved me," saith the Apostle, "and delivered up Himself for me:"[3] for except a grain shall have fallen into the land so that it die, fruit, He saith, it will not yield.[4] This is the improvidence. "And my transgressions from Thee are not concealed." It is plain, clear, open, that this must be perceived to be out of the mouth of the Body. Transgressions none had Christ: He was the bearer of transgressions, but not the committer. "Are not concealed:" that is, I have confessed to Thee all my transgressions, and before my mouth Thou hast seen them in my thought, hast seen the wounds which Thou wast to heal. But where? Even in the Body, in the members: in those believers out of whom there was now cleaving to Him that member, who was confessing his sins.

10. "Let them not blush in[5] Me, that wait for Thee, O Lord, Lord of virtues" (ver. 6). Again, the voice of the Head, "Let them not blush in Me:" let it not be said to them, Where is He on whom ye were relying? Let it not be said to them, Where is He that was saying to you, "Believe ye[6] in God, and in Me believe"?[7] "Let them not blush in Me, that wait for Thee," O Lord, Lord of virtues. Let them not be confounded concerning Me, that seek Thee, O God of Israel." This also may be understood of the Body, but only if thou consider the Body of Him not one man: for in truth one man is not the Body of Him, but a small member, but the Body is made up of members. Therefore the full Body of Him is the whole Church. With reason then saith the Church, "Let them not blush in Me, that wait for Thee, O Lord, Lord of virtues." . . .

11. "For because of Thee I have sustained upbraiding, shamelessness hath covered my face" (ver. 7). No great thing is that which is spoken of in "I have sustained:" but that which is spoken of in "for Thy sake I have sustained," is. For if thou sustainest because thou hast sinned; for thine own sake thou sustainest, not for the sake of God. For to you what glory is there, saith Peter, if sinning ye are punished, and ye bear it? But if thou sustainest because thou hast kept the commandment of God, truly for the sake of God thou sustainest; and thy reward remaineth for everlasting, because for the sake of God thou hast sustained revilings.[8] For to this end He first sustained, in order that we might learn to sustain. . . . "Shamelessness hath covered my face." Shamelessness is what? Not to be confused. Lastly, it seemeth to be as it were a fault, when we say, the man is shameless. Great is the shamelessness of the man, that he doth not blush. Therefore shamelessness is a kind of folly. A Christian ought to have this shamelessness, when he cometh among men to whom Christ is an offence. If he shall have blushed because of Christ, he will be blotted out from the book of the living. Thou must needs therefore have shamelessness when Thou art reviled because of Christ; when they say, Worshipper of the Crucified, adorer of Him that died ill, venerator of Him that was slain! here if thou shalt blush thou art a dead man. For see the sentence of Him that deceiveth no one. "He that shall have been ashamed of Me before men, I will also be ashamed of him before the Angels of God."[9] Watch therefore thyself whether there be in thee shamelessness; be thou boldfaced,[10] when thou hearest a reproach concerning Christ; yea be boldfaced. Why fearest thou for thy forehead which thou hast armed with the sign of the Cross? . . .

12. "An alien I have become to My brethren, and a stranger to the sons of My mother" (ver. 8). To the sons of the Synagogue He became a stranger. . . . Why so? Why did they not acknowledge? Why did they call Him an alien? Why did they dare to say, we know not whence He is? "Because the zeal of Thine House hath eaten Me up:" that is, because I have persecuted in them their own iniquities, because I have not patiently borne those whom I have rebuked, because I have sought Thy glory in Thy House, because I have scourged them that in the Temple dealt unseemly:[11] in which place also there is quoted, "the zeal of Thine House hath eaten Me up." Hence an alien, hence a stranger; hence, we know not whence He is. They would have acknowledged

[1] 1 Cor. i. 25.   [2] Rom. viii. 32.   [3] Gal. ii. 20.
[4] John xii. 24.   [5] Or, "for Me."
[6] Oxf. mss. "ye believe."   [7] John xiv. 1.

[8] 1 Pet. ii. 20.   [9] Matt. x. 33; Luke ix. 26.
[10] *Frontosus.*   [11] John ii. 15.

whence I am, if they had acknowledged that which Thou hast commanded. For if I had found them keeping Thy commandments, the zeal of Thine House would not have eaten Me up. "And the reproaches of men reproaching Thee haven fallen upon Me." Of this testimony Paul the Apostle hath also made use (there hath been read but now the very lesson), and saith, "Whatsoever things aforetime have been written, have been written that we might be instructed." [1] . . . Why "Thee"? Is the Father reproached, and not Christ Himself? Why have "the reproaches of men reproaching Thee fallen upon Me"? Because, "he that hath known Me, hath known the Father also:"[2] because no one hath reviled Christ without reviling God: because no one honoureth the Father, except he that honoureth the Son also.[3]

13. "And I have covered in fasting My Soul, and it became to Me for a reviling" (ver. 10). His fasting was, when there fell away all they that had believed in Him; because also it was His hunger, that men should believe in Him: because also it was His thirst, when He said to the woman, I thirst, "give Me to drink:"[4] yea for her faith He was thirsting. And from the Cross when He was saying, "I thirst,"[5] He was seeking the faith of them for whom He had said, "Father, forgive them, for they know not what they do."[6] But what did those men give to drink to Him thirsty? Vinegar. Vinegar is also called *old*.[7] With reason of the old man they gave to drink, because they willed not to be new. Why willed they not to become new? Because to the title of this Psalm whereon is written, "For them that shall be changed," they belonged not. Therefore, "I have covered in fasting My Soul." Lastly, He put from Him even the gall which they offered: He chose rather to fast than to accept bitterness. For they enter not into His Body that are embittered,[8] whereof in another place a Psalm saith, "They that are embittered shall not be exalted in themselves."[9] Therefore, "I have covered in fasting My Soul: and it became to Me for a reviling." This very thing became to Me for a reviling, that I consented not to them, that is, from them I fasted. For he that consenteth not to men seducing to evil, fasteth from them; and through this fasting earneth reviling, so that he is upbraided because he consenteth not to the evil thing.

14. "And I have set sackcloth my garment" (ver. 11). Already before [10] we have said something of the sackcloth, from whence there is this, "But I, when they were troubling Me, was covering myself with sackcloth, and was humbling My Soul in fasting. I have set sackcloth for My garment:" that is, have set against them My flesh, on which to spend their rage, I have concealed My divinity. "Sackcloth," because mortal the flesh was: in order that by sin He might condemn sin in the flesh.[11] "And I have set sackcloth my garment: and I have been made to them for a parable," that is, for a derision. It is called a parable, whenever a comparison is made concerning some one, when he is evil spoken of. "So may this man perish," for example, "as that man did," is a parable: that is, a comparison and likeness in cursing. "I have been made to them," then, "for a parable."

15. "Against Me were reviling they that were sitting in the gate" (ver. 12). "In the gate" is nothing else but in public. "And against Me they were chanting,[12] they that were drinking wine." Do ye think, brethren, that this hath befallen Christ alone? Daily to Him in His members it happeneth: whenever perchance it is necessary for the servant of God to forbid excess of wine and luxuries in any village or town, where there hath not been heard the Word of God, it is not enough that they sing, nay more even against him they begin to sing, by whom they are forbidden to sing. Compare ye now His fasting and their wine.

16. "But I with My prayer with Thee,[13] O Lord" (ver. 13). But I was with Thee. But how? With Thee by praying. For when thou art evil spoken of, and knowest not what thou mayest do; when at thee are hurled reproaches, and thou findest not any way of rebuking him by whom they are hurled; nothing remaineth for thee but to pray. But remember even for that very man to pray. "But I with my prayer with Thee, O Lord. It is the time of Thy good pleasure, O God." For behold the grain is being buried, there shall spring up fruit. "It is the time of Thy good pleasure, O God." Of this time even the Prophets have spoken, whereof the Apostle maketh mention: "Behold now the time acceptable, behold now the day of salvation." [14] "It is the time of Thy good pleasure, O God. In the multitude of Thy mercy." This is the time of good pleasure, "in the multitude of Thy mercy." For if there were not a multitude of Thy mercy, what should we do for the multitude of our iniquity? "In the multitude of Thy mercy; Hearken to me in the truth of Thy Salvation." Because He hath said, "of Thy mercy," he hath added truth also: for "mercy and truth" are all the ways of the Lord.[15] Why mercy? In forgiving sins. Why truth? In fulfilling the promises.

17. "Save Thou Me from the mire, that I

---

[1] Rom. xv. 4.　　[2] John xiv. 9.　　[3] John v. 23.
[4] John iv. 7.　　[5] John xix. 28.　　[6] Luke xxiii. 34.
[7] *Vetus.*　　[8] *Amaricantes.*　　[9] Ps. lxvi. 7.
[10] Ps. xxxv., p. 82, note 11, *supra.*

[11] Rom. viii. 3.　　[12] *Psallebant.*　　[13] *Ad Te.*
[14] 2 Cor. vi. 2.　　[15] Ps. xxv. 10.

may not stick " (ver. 14). From that whereof above he had spoken, " Fixed I am in the clay of the deep, and there is no substance."[1] Furthermore, since ye have duly received the exposition of that expression, in this place there is nothing further for you to hear particularly. From hence he saith that he must be delivered, wherein before he said that he was fixed : " Save Thou Me from the mire, that I may not stick." And he explaineth this himself : " Let Me be rescued from them that hate Me." They were themselves therefore the clay wherein he had stuck. But the following perchance suggesteth itself. A little before he had said, Fixed I am ; now he saith, Save Thou Me from the mire, that I may not stick : " whereas after the meaning of what was said before he ought to have said, Save Thou Me from the mire where I had stuck, by rescuing Me, not by causing that I stick not. Therefore He had stuck in flesh, but had not stuck in spirit. He saith this, because of the infirmity of His members. Whenever perchance thou art seized by one that urgeth thee to iniquity, thy body indeed is taken, in regard to the body thou art fixed in the clay of the deep : but so long as thou consentest not, thou hast not stuck ; but if thou consentest, thou hast stuck. Let then thy prayer be in that place, in order that as thy body is now held, so thy soul may not be held, so thou mayest be free in bonds.

18. " Let not the tempest of waters drown Me " (ver. 15). But already he had been drowned. " I have come into the depth of the sea," thou hast said, and " the tempest hath drowned Me,"[1] thou hast said. It hath drowned after the flesh, let it not drown after the Spirit. They to whom was said, If they shall have persecuted you in one city, flee ye into another ;[2] had this said to them, that neither in flesh they should stick, nor in spirit. For we must not desire to stick even in flesh ; but as far as we are able we ought to avoid it. But if we shall have stuck, and shall have fallen into the hands of sinners : then in body we have stuck, we are fixed in the clay of the deep, it remaineth to entreat for the soul that we stick not, that is, that we consent not, that the tempest of water drown us not, so that we go into the deep of the clay. " Neither let the deep swallow Me, nor the pit close her mouth upon Me." What is this, brethren ? What hath he prayed against ? Great is the pit of the depth of human iniquity : every one, if he shall have fallen into it, will fall into the deep. But yet if a man being there placed confesseth his sins to his God, the pit will not shut her mouth upon him : as is written in another Psalm, " From the depths I have cried to Thee, O Lord ; Lord, hearken unto my voice."[3] But

if there is done in him that which another passage of Scripture saith, " When a sinner shall have come into the depth of evil things, he will despise,"[4] upon him the pit hath shut her mouth. Why hath she shut her mouth? Because she hath shut his mouth. He hath lost confession, really dead he is, and there is fulfilled in him that which elsewhere is spoken of, " From a dead man, as from one that is not, there perisheth confession."[5] . . .

19. " Hearken unto me, O Lord, for sweet is Thy mercy " (ver. 16). He hath given this as a reason why He ought to be hearkened unto, because sweet is the mercy of God. . . . To a man set in trouble the mercy of God must needs be sweet. Concerning this sweetness of the mercy of God see ye what in another place the Scripture saith : " Like rain in drought, so beautiful is the mercy of God in trouble."[6] That which there he saith to be " beautiful," the same he saith here to be " sweet." Not even bread would be sweet, unless hunger had preceded. Therefore even when the Lord permitteth or causeth us to be in any trouble, even then He is merciful : for He doth not withdraw nourishment, but stirreth up longing. Accordingly what saith he now, " Hearken to me, O Lord, for sweet is Thy mercy "? Now do not Thou defer hearkening, in so great trouble I am, that sweet to me is Thy mercy. For to this end Thou didst defer to succour, in order that to me that wherewith Thou didst succour might be sweet : but now no longer is there cause why Thou must defer ; my trouble hath arrived at the appointed measure of distress, let Thy mercy come to do the work of goodness. " After the multitude of Thy pities have regard unto me : " not after the multitude of my sins.

20. " Turn not away Thy face from Thy child "[7] (ver. 17). And this is a commending of humility ; " from Thy child," that is, " from Thy little one : " because now I have been rid of pride through the discipline of tribulation, " turn not away Thy face from Thy child." This is that beautiful mercy of God, whereof he spake above. For in the following verse he explaineth that whereof he spake : " For I am troubled, speedily hearken Thou unto me." What is " speedily "? Now there is no cause why Thou must defer it : I am troubled, my affliction hath gone before ; let Thy mercy follow.

21. " Give heed to my soul, and redeem her," doth need no exposition : let us see therefore what followeth. " Because of mine enemies deliver me " (ver. 18). This petition is evidently wonderful, neither briefly to be touched upon, nor hastily to be skipped over ; truly wonderful : " Because of mine enemies deliver me." What

[1] Ps. lxix. 2. [2] Matt. x. 23. [4] Prov. xviii. 3. [5] Ecclus. xvii. 28.
[3] Ps. cxxx. 1, 2. [6] Ecclus. xxxv. 20. [7] *Puero ;* E. V. " servant."

is, "Because of mine enemies deliver me "? . . .
I see no reason for this petition, "Because of
mine enemies deliver me:" unless we understand it of something else, which when I shall
have spoken by the help of the Lord, He shall
judge in you, that dwelleth in you.[1] There is a
kind of secret deliverance of holy men: this for
their own sakes is made. There is one public
and evident: this is made because of their enemies, either for their punishment, or for their
deliverance. For truly God delivered not the
brothers in the book of Maccabees from the fires
of the persecutor.[2] . . . But again the Three
Children openly were delivered from the furnace
of fire;[3] because their body also was rescued,
their safety was public. The former were in
secret crowned, the latter openly delivered: all
however saved. . . . There is then a secret deliverance, there is an open deliverance. Secret
deliverance doth belong to the soul, open deliverance to the body as well. For in secret the
soul is delivered, openly the body. Again, if so
it be, in this Psalm the voice of the Lord let us
acknowledge: to the secret deliverance doth
belong that whereof he spake above, "Give heed
to my soul, and redeem her." There remaineth
the body's deliverance: for on His arising and
ascending into the Heavens, and sending the
Holy Ghost from above, there were converted
to His faith they that at His death did rage, and
out of enemies they were made friends through
His grace, not through their righteousness.[4]
Therefore he hath continued, "Because of mine
enemies deliver me. Give heed to my soul,"
but this in secret: but "because of mine enemies deliver" even my body. For mine enemies
it will profit nothing if soul alone Thou shalt
have delivered; that they have done something,
that they have accomplished something, they
will believe. "What profit is there in my blood,
while I go down into corruption?"[5] Therefore
"give heed to my soul, and redeem her," which
Thou alone knowest: secondly also, "because
of mine enemies deliver me," that my flesh may
not see corruption.

22. "Thou knowest my reproach, and my confusion, and my shame" (ver. 19). What is reproach? What is confusion? What shame?
Reproach is that which the enemy casteth in
the teeth. Confusion is that which gnaweth the
conscience. Shame is that which causeth even
a noble brow to blush, because of the upbraiding
with a pretended crime. There is no crime;
or even if there is a crime, it doth not belong to
him, against whom it is alleged: but yet the
infirmity of the human mind ofttimes is made
ashamed even when a pretended crime is alleged;
not because it is alleged, but because it is be-

lieved. All these things are in the Body of the
Lord. For confusion in Him could not be, in
whom guilt was not found. There was alleged
as a crime against Christians, the very fact that
they were Christians. That indeed was glory:
the brave gladly received it, and so received it
as that they blushed not at all for the Lord's
name. For fearlessness had covered the face
of them, having the effrontery of Paul, saying,
"for I blush not because of the Gospel: for the
virtue of God it is for salvation to every one believing."[6] O Paul, art not thou a venerator of
the Crucified? Little it is, he saith, for me not
to blush for it: nay, therein alone I glory, wherefore the enemy thinketh me to blush. "But
from me far be it to glory, save in the Cross of
Jesus Christ, through whom to me the world is
crucified, and I to the world."[7] At such a brow
as this then reproach alone could be hurled.
For neither could there be confusion in a conscience already made whole, nor shame in a brow
so free. But when it was being alleged against
certain that they had slain Christ, deservedly
they were pricked through with evil conscience,
and to their health confounded and converted,
so that they could say, "Thou hast known my
confusion." Thou therefore, O Lord, hast known
not only my reproach but also my confusion, in
certain shame also: who, though in me they believe, publicly blush to confess me before ungodly
men, human tongue having more influence with
them than promise divine. Behold ye therefore
them: even such are commended to God, not
that so He may leave them, but that by aiding
them He may make them perfect. For a certain
man believing and wavering hath said, "I believe, O Lord, help Thou mine unbelief."[8]

23. "In Thy sight are all they that trouble Me"
(ver. 20). Why I have reproach, Thou knowest;
why confusion, Thou knowest; why shame,
Thou knowest: therefore deliver Thou me because of mine enemies, because Thou knowest
these things of me, they know not; and thus,
because they are themselves in Thy sight, not
knowing these things, they will not be able to be
either confounded or corrected, unless openly
Thou shalt have delivered me because of mine
enemies. "Reproach my heart hath expected,
and misery." What is, "hath expected"? Hath
foreseen these things as going to be, hath foretold them as going to be. For He came not
for any other purpose. If He had been unwilling to die, neither would He have willed to be
born: for the sake of resurrection He did both.
For there were two particular things known to
us among mankind, but one thing unknown.
For we knew that men were born and died:
that they rose again and lived for everlasting we

[1] Oxf. MSS. "in you also." [2] 2 Macc. vii.
[3] Dan. iii. 26. [4] Acts i. 9, ii. 41. [5] Ps. xxx. 9. [6] Rom. i. 16. [7] Gal. vi. 14. [8] Mark ix. 24.

knew not. That He might show to us that which we knew not, He took upon Him the two things which we knew. To this end therefore He came. " Reproach my heart hath expected and misery." But the misery of whom? For He expected misery, but rather of the crucifiers, rather of the persecutors, that in them should be misery, in Him mercy. For pitying the misery of them even while hanging on the Cross, He saith, " Father, forgive them, for they know not what they do."[1] What then did it profit, that I expected? That is, what did it profit that I foretold? What did it profit that I said to this end I had come? I came to fulfil that which I said, " I waited for one that together should be made sorrowful, and there was not; and men comforting, and I found not:" that is, there was none. For that which in the former verse He said, " I waited for one that together should be made sorrowful," the same is in the following verse, " and men comforting." But that which in the former verse is, " and there was not;" the same in the following verse is, " and I found not." Therefore another sentence is not added, but the former is repeated. Which sentence if we reconsider, a question may arise. For were His disciples nowise made sorrowful when He was led to the Passion, when on the tree hanged, when dead? So much were they made sorrowful, that Mary Magdalene, who first saw Him, rejoicing told them as they were mourning what she had seen.[2] The Gospel speaketh of these things: it is not our presumption, not our suspicion: it is evident that the disciples grieved, it is evident that they mourned. Strange women were weeping, when to the Passion He was being led, unto whom turning He saith, " Weep ye, but for yourselves, do not for Me."[3] . . . Peter certainly loved very much, and without hesitation threw himself to walk on the waves,[4] and at the voice of the Lord he was delivered: and though following Him when led to the Passion, with the boldness of love, yet being troubled, thrice he denied Him. Whence, except because an evil thing it seemed to him to die? For he was shunning that which he thought an evil thing. This then even in the Lord he was lamenting, which he was himself shunning. On this account even before he had said, " Far be it from Thee, O Lord, merciful be Thou to Thyself: there shall not come to pass this thing:"[5] at which time he merited to hear, " Satan;" after that he had heard, " Blessed art thou, Simon Bar-Jona." Therefore in that sorrowfulness which the Lord felt because of those for whom He prayed, " Father, forgive them, for they know not what they do:"[1] no companion He found. " And I waited for

one that together should be made sorrowful, and there was not." There was not at all. " And men comforting, and I found not." Who are men comforting? Men profiting. For they comfort us, they are the comfort of all preachers of the Truth.

24. " And they gave for My food gall, and in My thirst they gave Me vinegar to drink " (ver. 22). This was done indeed to the letter. And the Gospel declareth this to us. But we must understand, brethren, that the very fact that I found not comforters, that the very fact that I found not one that together should be made sorrowful, this was My gall, this to Me was bitter, this was vinegar: bitter because of grief, vinegar because of their old man. For we read, that to Him indeed gall was offered, as the Gospel speaketh; but for drink, not for food.[6] Nevertheless, we must so take and consider that when fulfilled, which here had been before predicted, " They gave for My food gall:" and in that very action, not only in this saying, we ought to seek for a mystery, at secret things to knock, to enter the rent veil of the Temple, to see there a Sacrament, both in what there hath been said and in what there hath been done. " They gave," He saith, " for My food gall:" not the thing itself which they gave was food, for it was drink: but " for food they gave it." Because already the Lord had taken food, and into it there had been thrown gall. But He had taken Himself pleasant food, when He ate the Passover with His disciples: therein He showed the Sacrament of His Body.[7] Unto this food so pleasant, so sweet, of the Unity of Christ, of which the Apostle maketh mention, saying, " For one bread, One Body, being many we are;"[8] unto this pleasant food who is there that addeth gall, except the gainsayers of the Gospel, like those persecutors of Christ? For less the Jews sinned in crucifying Him walking on earth, than they that despise Him sitting in Heaven. That which then the Jews did, in giving above the food which He had already taken that bitter draught to drink, the same they do that by evil living bring scandal upon the Church: the same do embittered heretics, " But let them not be exalted in their own selves."[9] They give gall after so delectable meat. But what doth the Lord? He admitteth them not to His Body. In this mystery, when they presented gall, the Lord Himself tasted, and would not drink.[6] If we did not suffer them, neither at all should we taste: but because it is necessary to suffer them, we must needs taste. But because in the members of Christ such sort cannot be, they can be tasted, received into the

1 Luke xxiii. 34.   2 John xx. 18; Mark xvi. 9.
3 Luke xxiii. 28.   4 Matt. xiv. 29.   5 Matt. xvi. 22.

6 Matt. xxvii. 34.
7 Luke xxii. 19.   The Sacrament of the Body of Christ.
8 1 Cor. x. 17.   9 Ps. lxvi. 7.

Body they cannot be. "And they gave for My food gall, and in My thirst they gave Me vinegar to drink." I was thirsting, and vinegar I received: that is, for the faith of them I longed, and I found oldness.

25. "Let the table of them be made in their own presence for a trap" (ver. 23). Like the trap which for Me they set, in giving Me such a draught, let such a trap be for them. Why then, "in their own presence"? "Let the table of them be made for a trap," would have been sufficient. They are such as know their iniquity, and in it most obstinately do persevere: in their own presence there is made a trap for them. These are they that, being too destructive, "go down into Hell alive."[1] Lastly, of persecutors what hath been said? Except that the Lord were in us, perchance alive they had swallowed us up.[2] What is alive? Consenting to them, and knowing that we ought not to consent to them. Therefore in their own presence there is made a trap, and they are not amended. Even though in their own presence there is a trap, let them not fall into it. Behold they know the trap, and thrust out foot, and bow their necks to be caught. How much better were it to turn away from the trap, to acknowledge sin, to condemn error, to be rid of bitterness, to pass over into the Body of Christ, to seek the Lord's glory! But so much prevaileth presumption of mind, that even in their own presence the trap is, and they fall into it. "Let the eyes of them be darkened, that they see not,"[3] followeth here: that whereas without benefit they have seen, it may chance to them even not to see. "Let the table of them," therefore, "be made in their own presence for a trap." It is not from one wishing, but from one prophesying: not in order that it may come to pass, but because it will come to pass. This we have often remarked, and ye ought to remember it: lest that which the prescient mind saith in the Spirit of God, it should seem with ill will to imprecate. . . . Let it then be done to them, "both for a requital and for a stumbling-block." And is this by any means unjust? It is just. Why? For it is "for a requital." For not anything would happen to them, which was not owed. "For a requital" it is done, "and for a stumbling-block:" for they are themselves a stumbling-block to themselves. "Let the eyes of them be darkened, that they see not, and the back of them alway bow Thou down" (ver. 24). This is a consequence. For they, whose eyes have been darkened that they see not, it followeth, must have their back bowed down. How so? Because when they have ceased to take knowledge of things above, they must

needs think of things below. He that well heareth, "lift up the heart," a bowed back hath not. For with stature erect he looketh for the hope laid up for him in Heaven; most especially if he send before him his treasure, whither his heart followeth.[4] But, on the other hand, they perceive not the hope of future life; already being blinded, they think of things below: and this is to have a bowed back: from which disorder the Lord delivered that woman. For Satan hath bound her eighteen years, and her that was bowed down[5] He raised up:[6] and because on the Sabbath He did it, the Jews were scandalized; suitably were they scandalized at her being raised up, themselves being bowed. "Pour forth upon them Thine anger, and let the indignation of Thine anger overtake them" (ver. 25), are plain words: but nevertheless, in "overtake them" we perceive them as it were fleeing. But whither are they to flee? Into Heaven? Thou art there. Into Hell? Thou art present. Their wings they will not take to fly straight:[7] "Let the indignation of Thine anger overtake them," let it not permit them to escape.

26. "Let the habitation of them become forsaken"[8] (ver. 26). This is now evident. For in the same manner as He hath mentioned not only a secret deliverance of His, saying, "Give heed to My soul, and redeem her;"[9] but also one open after the body, adding, "because of mine enemies deliver me:" so also to these men He foretelleth how there are to be certain secret misfortunes, whereof a little before He was speaking. . . . For the blindness of the Jews was secret vengeance: but the open was what? "Let their habitation become forsaken, and in their tabernacles let there be not any one to inhabit." There hath come to pass this thing in the very city Jerusalem, wherein they thought themselves mighty in crying against the Son of God, "Crucify, Crucify;"[10] and in prevailing because they were able to kill Him that raised dead men. How mighty to themselves, how great, they seemed! There followed afterwards the vengeance of the Lord, stormed was the city, utterly conquered the Jews, slain were I know not how many thousands of men. No one of the Jews is permitted to come thither now: where they were able to cry against the Lord, there by the Lord they are not permitted to dwell. They have lost the place of their fury: and O that even now they would know the place of their rest! What profit to them was Caiaphas in saying,[11] "If we shall have let go this man thus, there will come

[1] Ps. lv. 15.   [2] Ps. cxxiv. 1-3.   [3] Ps. lxix. 24.

[4] Matt. vi. 21.
[5] Curvatam, Ben. Most MSS. curatam, "cured."
[6] Luke xiii. 16.   [7] Ps. cxxxix. 7-9.   [8] Acts i. 20.
[9] Ps. lxix. 19.   [10] John xix. 6.
[11] Or, "What did it profit Caiaphas to say?" MSS.

the Romans, and take away from us both place and kingdom "? [1] Behold, both they did not let Him go alive, and He liveth : and there have come the Romans, and have taken from them both place and kingdom. But now we heard, when the Gospel was being read, " Jerusalem, Jerusalem, how often would I have gathered together thy sons, as a hen her chickens under her wings, and thou wouldest not? Behold, there is left to you your house forsaken." [2] . . .

27. Why so? " For Him whom Thou hast smitten they have themselves persecuted, and upon the pain of my wounds they have added " (ver. 27). How then have they sinned if they have persecuted one by God smitten? What sin is ascribed to their mind? Malice. For the thing was done in Christ which was to be. To suffer indeed He had come, and He punished him through whom He suffered. For Judas the traitor was punished, and Christ was crucified : but us He redeemed by His blood, and He punished him in the matter of his price. For he threw down the price of silver, for which by him the Lord had been sold ; [3] and he knew not the price wherewith he had himself by the Lord been redeemed.[4] This thing was done in the case of Judas. But when we see that there is a sort of measure of requital in all men, and that not any one can be suffered to rage more than he hath received power to do : how have they "added," or what is that smiting of the Lord? Without doubt He is speaking in the person of him from whom He had received a body, from whom He had taken unto Him flesh, that is in the person of mankind, of Adam himself who was smitten with the first death because of his sin.[5] Mortal therefore here are men born, as born with their punishment : to this punishment they add, whosoever do persecute men. For now here man would not have had to die, unless God had smitten him. Why then dost thou, O man, rage more than this? Is it little for a man that some time he is to die? Each one of us therefore beareth his punishment : to this punishment they would add that persecute us. This punishment is the smiting of the Lord. For the Lord smote man with the sentence : " What day ye shall have touched it," He saith, " with death ye shall die." [6] Out of this death He had taken upon Him flesh, and our old man hath been crucified together with Him.[7] By the voice of that man He hath said these words, " Him whom Thou hast smitten they have themselves persecuted, and upon the pain of My wounds they have added." Upon what pain of wounds? Upon the pain of sins they have themselves added.

For sins He hath called His wounds. But do not look to the Head, consider the Body ; according to the voice whereof hath been said by the Same in that Psalm, wherein He showed there was His voice, because in the first verse thereof He cried from the Cross, " God, My God, look upon Me, why hast Thou forsaken Me?" [8] There in continuation He saith, " Afar from My safety are the words of Mine offences." . . .

28. " Lay Thou iniquity upon their iniquity " (ver. 28). What is this? Who would not be afraid? To God is said, " Lay Thou iniquity upon their iniquity." Whence shall God lay iniquity? For hath He iniquity to lay? For we know that to be true which hath been spoken through Paul the Apostle, " What then shall we say? Is there anywise iniquity with God? Far be it." [9] Whence then, " Lay Thou iniquity upon iniquity "? How must we understand this? May the Lord be with us, that we may speak, and because of your weariness may be able to speak briefly. Their iniquity was that they killed a just Man : there was added another, that they crucified the Son of God. Their raging was as though against a man : but " if they had known, the Lord of Glory they had never crucified." [10] They with their own iniquity willed to kill as it were a man : there was laid iniquity upon their own iniquity, so that the Son of God they should crucify. Who laid this iniquity upon them? He that said, " Perchance they will reverence My Son," [11] Him I will send. For they were wont to kill servants sent to them, to demand rent and profit. He sent the Son Himself, in order that Him also they might kill. He laid iniquity upon their own iniquity. And these things did God do in wrath, or rather in just requital? For, " May it be done to them," He saith, " for a requital and for a stumblingblock." [12] They had deserved to be so blinded as not to know the Son of God. And this God did, laying iniquity upon their iniquity ; not in wounding, but in not making whole. For in like manner as thou increasest a fever, increasest a disorder, not by adding disorder, but by not relieving : so because they were of such sort as that they merited not to be healed, in their very naughtiness in a manner they advanced ; as it is said, " But evil men and wicked doers advance for the worse : " [13] and iniquity is laid upon their own iniquity. " And let them not enter in [14] Thy righteousness." This is a plain thing.

29. " Let them be blotted out from the book of the living " (ver. 29). For had they been some time written therein? Brethren, we must not so take it, as that God writeth any one in

---

[1] John xi. 48.   [2] Matt. xxiii. 37, 38.   [3] Matt. xxvii. 5.
[4] *Redemptus*, Oxf. mss.; and two in Ben. *redimendus*, " was to be redeemed." See note at the end of *Homilies on St. John*.
[5] Gen. iii. 6.   [6] Gen. ii. 17.   [7] Rom. vi. 6.

[8] Ps. xxii. 1.   [9] Rom. ix. 14.   [10] 1 Cor. ii. 8.
[11] Matt. xxi. 37.   [12] Ps. lxix. 22.   [13] 2 Tim. iii. 13.
[14] Oxf. mss. " into."

the book of life, and blotteth him out. If a man said, "What I have written I have written,"[1] concerning the title where it had been written, "King of the Jews:" doth God write any one, and blot him out? He foreknoweth, He hath predestined all before the foundation of the world that are to reign with His Son in life everlasting.[2] These He hath written down, these same the Book of Life doth contain. Lastly, in the Apocalypse, what saith the Spirit of God, when the same Scripture was speaking of the oppressions that should be from Antichrist? "There shall give consent[3] to him all they that have not been written in the book of life."[4] So then without doubt they will not consent that have been written. How then are these men blotted out from that book wherein they were never written? This hath been said according to their own hope, because they thought of themselves that they were written. What is, "let them be blotted out from the book of life"? Even to themselves let it be evident, that they were not there. By this method of speaking hath been said in another Psalm, "There shall fall from Thy side a thousand, and tens of thousands from on Thy right hand:"[5] that is, many men shall be offended, even out of that number who thought that they would sit with Thee, even out of that number who thought that they would stand at Thy right hand, being severed from the left-hand goats:[6] not that when any one hath there stood, he shall afterwards fall, or when any one with Him hath sat, he shall be cast away; but that many men were to fall into scandal, who already thought themselves to be there, that is, many that thought that they would sit with Thee, many that hoped that they would stand at the right hand, will themselves fall. So then here also they that hoped as though by the merit of their own righteousness themselves to have been written in the book of God, they to whom is said, "Search the Scriptures, wherein ye think yourselves to have life eternal:"[7] when their condemnation shall have been brought even to their own knowledge, shall be effaced from the book of the living, they shall know themselves not to be there. For the verse which followeth, explaineth what hath been said: "And with just men let them not be written." I have said then, "Let them be effaced," according to their hope: but according to Thy justice I say what?

30. "Poor and sorrowful I am" (ver. 30). Why this? Is it that we may acknowledge that through bitterness of soul this poor One doth speak evil? For He hath spoken of many things to happen to them. And as if we were saying to Him, "Why such things?" — "Nay, not so much!" He answereth, "poor and sorrowful I am." They have brought Me to want, unto this sorrow they have set Me down, therefore I say these words. It is not, however, the indignation of one cursing, but the prediction of one prophesying. For He was intending to recommend to us certain things which hereafter He saith of His poverty and His sorrow, in order that we may learn to be poor and sorrowful. For, "Blessed are the poor, for theirs is the kingdom of Heaven."[8] And, "Blessed are they that mourn, for they shall be comforted." This therefore He doth Himself before now show to us: and so, "poor and sorrowful I am." The whole Body of Him saith this. The Body of Christ in this earth is poor and sorrowful. But let Christians be rich. Truly if Christians they are, they are poor; in comparison with the riches celestial for which they hope, all their gold they count for sand. "And the health of Thy countenance, O God, hath taken Me up." Is this poor One anywise forsaken? When dost thou deign to bring near to thy table a poor man in rags? But again, this poor One the health of the countenance of God hath taken up: in His countenance He hath hidden His need. For of Him hath been said, "Thou shalt hide them in the hiding place of Thy countenance."[9] But in that countenance what riches there are would ye know? Riches here give thee this advantage, that thou mayest dine on what thou wilt, whenever thou wilt: but those riches, that thou mayest never hunger. "The health of Thy countenance, O God, hath taken Me up." For what purpose? In order that no longer I may be poor, no longer sorrowful? "I will praise the name of the Lord with a song, I will magnify Him in praise" (ver. 31). Now it hath been said, this poor One praiseth the name of the Lord with a song, he magnifieth Him in praise. When would He have ventured to sing, unless He had been refreshed from hunger? "I will magnify Him with praise." O vast riches! What jewels of God's praise hath he brought out of his inward treasures! These are my riches! "The Lord hath given, the Lord hath taken away."[10] Then miserable he hath remained? Far be it. See the riches: "As it hath pleased the Lord, so hath been done, be the name of the Lord blessed."

31. "And it shall please God:" that I shall praise Him, shall please: "above a new calf, bearing horns and hoofs." More grateful to Him shall be the sacrifice of praise than the sacrifice of a calf. "The sacrifice of praise shall glorify me."[11] "Immolate to God the sacrifice of praise."[12] So then His praise going forth from my mouth shall please God more than a great

---

[1] John xix. 22.　　　[2] Rom. viii. 29.　　　[3] E. V. "worship."
[4] Rev. xiii. 8.　　　[5] Ps. xci. 7.　　　[6] Matt. xxv. 33.
[7] John v. 39.

[8] Matt. v. 3.　　　[9] Ps. xxxi. 22.　　　[10] Job i. 21.
[11] Ps. l. 23.　　　[12] Ps. l. 14.

victim led up to His altar. . . . Therefore above this calf my praising shall please Thee, such as hereafter will be, after poverty and sorrow, in the eternal society of Angels, where neither adversary there shall be in battle to be tossed, nor sluggard from earth to be stirred up. "Let the needy see and rejoice" (ver. 32). Let them believe, and in hope be glad. Let them be more needy, in order that they may deserve to be filled: lest while they belch out pride's satiety, there be denied them the bread whereon they may healthily live. "Seek the Lord," ye needy, hunger ye and thirst; [1] for He is Himself the living bread that came down from Heaven.[2] "Seek ye the Lord, and your soul shall live." Ye seek bread, that your flesh may live: the Lord seek ye, that your soul may live.[3]

32. "For the Lord hath hearkened to the poor" (ver. 33). He hath hearkened to the poor, and He would not have hearkened to the poor, unless they were poor. Wilt thou be hearkened to? Poor be thou: let sorrow cry out from thee, and not fastidiousness. "And His fettered ones He hath not despised." Being offended at His servants, He hath put them in fetters: but them crying from the fetters He hath not despised. What are these fetters? Mortality, the corruptibleness of the flesh are the fetters wherewith we have been bound. And would ye know the weight of these fetters? Of them is said, "The body which is corrupted weigheth down the soul." [4] Whenever men in the world will to be rich, for these fetters they are seeking rags. But let the rags of the fetters suffice: seek so much as is necessary for keeping off want, but when thou seekest superfluities, thou longest to load thy fetters. In such a prison then let the fetters abide even alone. "Sufficient for the day be the evil thereof." [5] "Let there praise Him heavens and earth, sea and all things creeping in them" (ver. 34). The true riches of this poor man are these, to consider the creation, and to praise the Creator. "Let there praise Him heavens and earth, sea and all things creeping therein." And doth this creation alone praise God, when by considering of it God is praised?

33. Hear thou another thing also: "for God shall save Sion" (ver. 35). He restoreth His Church, the faithful Gentiles He doth incorporate with His Only-Begotten; He beguileth not them that believe in Him of the reward of His promise. "For God shall save Sion; and there shall be builded the cities of Juda." These same are the Churches. Let no one say, when shall it come to pass that there be builded the cities of Juda? O that thou wouldest acknowledge the Edifice, and be a living stone, that thou mightest enter into Her. Even now the cities of Juda are being built. For Juda is interpreted confession. By confession of humility there are being builded the cities of Juda: in order that there may remain without the proud, who blush to confess. "For God shall save Sion." What Sion? Hear in the following words: "and the seed of His servants shall possess Her, and they that love His name shall dwell therein" (ver. 36). . . .

PSALM LXX.[6]

1. Thanks to the "Corn of wheat," [7] because He willed to die and to be multiplied: thanks to the only Son of God, our Lord and Saviour Jesus Christ, who disdained not to undergo our death, in order that He might make us worthy of His life. Behold Him that was single until He went hence; as He said in another Psalm, "Single I am until I go hence;" [8] for He was a single corn of wheat in such sort as that He had in Himself a great fruitfulness of increase; in how many corns imitating the Passion of Him we exult, when we celebrate the nativities of the Martyrs! Many therefore members of Him, under one Head our Saviour Himself, being bound together in the bond of love and peace (as ye judge it fit that ye know, for ye have often heard), are one man: and of the same, as of one man, the voice is ofttimes heard, in the Psalms, and thus one crieth as though it were all, because all in one are one. . . .

2. There is then in this Psalm the voice of men troubled, and so indeed of Martyrs amid sufferings in peril, but relying on their own Head. Let us hear them, and speak with them out of sympathy of heart, though it be not with similarity of suffering. For they are already crowned, we are still in peril: not that such sort of persecutions do vex us as have vexed them, but worse perchance in the midsts of all kinds of so great scandals. For our own times do more abound in that woe, which the Lord cried: "Woe to the world because of scandals." [9] And, "Because iniquity hath abounded, the love of man shall wax cold." [10] For not even that holy Lot at Sodom suffered corporal persecution from any one, or had it been told him that he should not dwell there: [11] the persecution of him were the evil doings of the Sodomites. Now then that Christ sitteth in Heaven, now that He is glorified, now that necks of kings are made subject to His yoke, and their brows placed beneath His sign, now that not any one remaineth to dare openly to trample upon Christians, still, however, we groan amid instruments and singers, still those enemies of the Martyrs, because with words and

---

---

steel they have no power, with their own wantonness do persecute them. And O that we were sorrowing for Heathens alone : it would be some sort of comfort, to wait for those that not yet have been signed with the Cross of Christ ; when they should be signed, and when, by His authority attached, they should cease to be mad. We see besides men wearing on their brow the sign of Him, at the same time on that same brow wearing the shamelessness of wantonness, and on the days and celebrations of the Martyrs not exulting but insulting. And amid these things we groan, and this is our persecution, if there is in us the love which saith, "Who is weak, and I am not weak? Who is scandalized, and I burn not?"[1] Not any servant of God, then, is without persecution : and that is a true saying which the Apostle saith, "But even all men that will to live godly in Christ, shall suffer persecution."[2] . . .

3. "O God, to my aid make speed" (ver. 1). For need we have for an everlasting aid in this world. But when have we not? Now however being in tribulation, let us especially say, "O God, to my aid make speed." "Let them be confounded and fear that seek my soul." Christ is speaking : whether Head speak or whether Body speak ; He is speaking that hath said, "Why persecutest thou Me?"[3] He is speaking that hath said, "Inasmuch as ye have done it to one of the least of Mine, to Me ye have done it."[4] The voice then of this Man is known to be of the whole man, of Head and of Body : that need not often be mentioned, because it is known. "Be they confounded," he saith, "and fear that seek my soul." In another Psalm He saith, "I was looking unto the right and saw, and there was not one that would know Me : flight hath perished from Me, and there is not one to seek out My soul."[5] There of persecutors He saith, that there was not one to seek out His soul : but here, "Let them be confounded and fear that seek My soul." . . . And where is that which thou hast heard from thy Lord, "Love ye your enemies, do good to them that hate you, and pray for them that persecute you"?[6] Behold thou sufferest persecution, and cursest them from whom thou sufferest : how dost thou imitate the Passions of thy Lord that have gone before, hanging on the cross and saying, "Father, forgive them, for they know not what they do."[7] To persons saying such things the Martyr replieth and saith, thou hast set before me the Lord, saying, "Father, forgive them, for they know not what they do : " understand thou my voice also, in order that it may be thine too : for what have I said concerning mine enemies? "Let them be confounded and

fear." Already such vengeance hath been taken on the enemies of the Martyrs. That Saul that persecuted Stephen, he was confounded and feared. He was breathing out slaughters,[8] he was seeking some to drag and slay : a voice having been heard from above, "Saul, Saul, why persecutest thou Me,"[3] he was confounded and laid low, and he was raised up to obedience, that had been inflamed unto persecuting. This then the Martyrs desire for their enemies, "Let them be confounded and fear." For so long as they are not confounded and fear, they must needs defend their actions : glorious they think themselves, because they hold, because they bind, because they scourge, because they kill, because they dance, because they insult, and because of all these doings they be some time confounded and fear.[9] For if they be confounded, they will also be converted : because converted they cannot be, unless they shall have been confounded and shall have feared. Let us then wish these things to our enemies, let us wish them without fear. Behold I have said, and let me have said it with you, may all that still dance and sing and insult the Martyrs "be confounded and fear : " at last within these walls confounded may they beat their breasts !

4. "Let them be turned away backward and blush that think evil things to me" (ver. 2). At first there was the assault of them persecuting, now there hath remained the malice of them thinking. In fact, there are in the Church distinct seasons of persecutions following one another.[10] There was made an assault on the Church when kings were persecuting : and because kings had been foretold as to persecute and as to believe, when one had been fulfilled the other was to follow. There came to pass also that which was consequent ; kings believed, peace was given to the Church, the Church began to be set in the highest place of dignity, even on this earth, even in this life : but there is not wanting the roar of persecutors, they have turned their assaults into thoughts. In these thoughts, as in a bottomless pit, the devil hath been bound,[11] he roareth and breaketh not forth. For it hath been said concerning these times of the Church, "The sinner shall see, and shall be angry."[12] And shall do what? That which he did at first? Drag, bind, smite? He doeth not this. What then? "With his teeth he shall gnash, and shall pine away." And with these men the Martyr is, as it were, angry, and yet for these men the Martyr prayeth. For in like manner as he hath wished well to those men

---

[1] 2 Cor. xi. 29.   [2] 2 Tim. iii. 12.   [3] Acts ix. 4.
[4] Matt. xxv. 40.   [5] Ps. cxlii. 4.   [6] Matt. v. 44.
[7] Luke xxiii. 34.

[8] Acts vii. 58, ix. 1.
[9] Oxf. MSS. "and no more defend their doings."
[10] The reading *sequere* mentioned in Ben. is probably a mistake for *seque*, which is found at Oxford. Or it is, "follow them in their succession."
[11] *Vide* Rev. xx. 3.   [12] Ps. cxii. 10.

concerning whom he hath said, "Let them be confounded and fear that seek my soul:"[1] so also now, "Let them be turned backward, and blush, that think evil things to me." Wherefore? In order that they may not go before, but follow. For he that censureth the Christian religion, and on his own system willeth to live, willeth as it were to go before Christ, as though He indeed had erred and had been weak and infirm, because He either willed to suffer or could suffer in the hands of the Jews; but that he is a clever man for guarding against all these things; in shunning death, even in basely lying to escape death, and slaying his soul that he may live in body, he thinketh himself a man of singular and prudent measures. He goeth before in censuring Christ, in a manner he outstrippeth Christ: let him believe in Christ, and follow Christ. For that which had been desired but now for persecutors thinking evil things, the same the Lord Himself said to Peter. Now in a certain place Peter willed to go before the Lord. . . . A little before, "Blessed art thou, Simon Bar-Jona, for flesh and blood hath not revealed it to thee, but My Father which is in Heaven:" now in a moment, "Go back behind Me, Satan."[2] What is, "Go back behind Me"? Follow Me. Thou willest to go before Me, thou willest to give Me counsel, it is better that thou follow My counsel: this is, "go back," go back behind Me. He is silencing one outstripping, in order that he may go backward; and He is calling him Satan, because he willeth to go before the Lord. A little before, "blessed;" now, "Satan." Whence a little before, "blessed"? Because, "to thee," He saith, "flesh and blood hath not revealed it, but My Father which is in Heaven." Whence now, "Satan"? Because "thou savourest not," He saith, "the things which are of God, but the things which are of men." Let us then that would duly celebrate the nativities of the Martyrs, long for the imitation of the Martyrs; let us not wish to go before the Martyrs, and think ourselves to be of better understanding than they, because we shun sufferings in behalf of righteousness and faith which they shunned not. Therefore be they that think evil things, and in wantonness feed their hearts, "turned backward and blush." Let them hear from the Apostle afterwards saying, "But what fruit had ye some time in those things at which ye now blush?"

5. What followeth? "Let them be turned away forthwith blushing, that say to me, Well, well" (ver. 3). Two are the kinds of persecutors, revilers and flatterers. The tongue of the flatterer doth more persecute than the hand of the slayer: for this also the Scripture hath called

a furnace. Truly when the Scripture was speaking of persecution, it said, "Like gold in a furnace it hath proved them" (speaking of Martyrs being slain), "and as the holocaust's victim it hath received them."[3] Hear how even the tongue of flatterers is of such sort: "The proving," he saith, "of silver and of gold is fire; but a man is proved by the tongue of men praising him."[4] That is fire, this also is fire: out of both thou oughtest to go forth safe. The censurer hath broken thee, thou hast been broken in the furnace like an earthen vessel. The Word hath moulded thee, and there hath come the trial of tribulation: that which hath been formed, must needs be seasoned; if it hath been well moulded, there hath come the fire to strengthen. Whence He said in the Passion, "Dried up like a potsherd hath been My virtue."[5] For Passion and the furnace of tribulation had made Him stronger. . . .

6. And what cometh to pass when they are all turned back and blush, whether it be they that seek my soul, or they that think evil things to me, or they that with perverse and feigned benevolence with tongue would soften the stroke which they inflict, when they shall have been themselves turned away and confounded; there shall come to pass what? "Let them exult and be joyous in Thee:" not in me, not in this man or in that man; but in whom they have been made light that were darkness. "Let them exult and be joyous in Thee, all that seek Thee" (ver. 4). One thing it is to seek God, another thing to seek man. "Let them be joyous that seek Thee." They shall not be joyous then that seek themselves,[6] whom Thou hast first sought before they sought Thee. Not yet did that sheep seek the Shepherd, it had strayed from the flock, and He went down to it;[7] He sought it, and carried it back upon His shoulders. Will He despise thee, O sheep, seeking Him, who hath first sought thee despising Him and not seeking Him? Now then begin thou to seek Him that first hath sought thee, and hath carried thee back on His shoulders. Do thou that which He speaketh of, "They that are My sheep hear My voice, and follow Me."[8] If then thou seekest Him that first hath sought thee, and hast become a sheep of His, and thou hearest the voice of thy Shepherd, and followest Him; see what He showeth to thee of Himself, what of His Body, in order that as to Himself thou mayest not err, as to the Church thou mayest not err, that no one may say to thee, that is Christ which is not Christ, or that is the Church which is not the Church. For many men have said that Christ had no flesh, and that Christ hath

---

[1] Ps. lxx. 2. [2] Matt. xvi. 23.

[3] Wisd. iii. 6. [4] Prov. xxvii. 21. [5] Ps. xxii. 15.
[6] mss. Reg. *non te*, " aught but Thee." [7] Luke xv. 4.
[8] John x. 27.

not risen in His Body: do not thou follow the voices of them. Hear thou the voice of Himself the Shepherd, that was clothed with flesh, in order that He might seek lost flesh. He hath risen again, and He saith, "Handle ye and see; for a spirit hath not flesh and bones as ye see Me have."[1] He showeth Himself to thee, the voice of Him follow thou. He showeth also the Church, that no one may deceive thee by the name of Church. "It behoved," He saith, "Christ to suffer, and to rise again from the dead the third day, and that there should be preached repentance and remission of sins through all nations, beginning with Jerusalem."[2] Thou hast the voice of Thy Shepherd, do not thou follow the voice of strangers:[3] and a thief thou shalt not fear, if thou shalt have followed the voice of the Shepherd. But how shalt thou follow? If thou shalt neither have said to any man, as if it were by his own merit, Well, well: nor shalt have heard the same with joy, so that thy head be not made fat with the oil of a sinner.[4] "Let all them exult and be joyous in Thee, that seek Thee; and let them say" —let them say what, that exult? "Be the Lord alway magnified!" Let all them say this, that exult and seek Thee. What? "Be the Lord alway magnified; yea, they that love Thy salvation." Not only, "Be the Lord magnified;" but also, "alway." . . . A sinner thou art, be He magnified in order that He may call; thou confessest, be He magnified in order that He may forgive: now thou livest justly, be He magnified in order that He may direct: thou perseverest even unto the end, be He magnified in order that He may glorify. "Be the Lord," then, "alway magnified; yea, they love His saving health." For from Him they have salvation, not from themselves. The saving health of the Lord our God, is the Saviour our Lord Jesus Christ: whosoever loveth the Saviour, confesseth himself to have been made whole; whosoever confesseth himself to have been made whole, confesseth himself to have been sick.[5] Not their own saving health, as if they could save themselves of themselves: not as it were the saving health of a man, as though by him they could be saved. "Do not," he saith, "confide in princes, and in the sons of men, in whom there is no safety."[6] Why so? "Of the Lord is safety, and upon Thy people is Thy blessing."[7]

7. Behold, "Be the Lord magnified:" wilt thou never, wilt thou nowhere? In Him was something, in me nothing: but if in Him is whatsoever I am, be He, not I. But thou then what? "But I am needy and poor" (ver. 5).

He is rich, He abounding, He needing nothing. Behold my light, behold whence I am illumined; for I cry, "Thou shalt illumine my candle, O Lord."[8] What then of thee? "But I am needy and poor." I am like an orphan, my soul is like a widow destitute and desolate: help I seek, alway mine infirmity I confess. There have been forgiven me my sins, now I have begun to follow the commandments of God: still, however, I am needy and poor. Why still needy and poor? Because "I see another law in my members fighting against the law of my mind."[9] Why needy and poor? Because, "blessed are they that hunger and thirst after righteousness."[10] Still I hunger, still I thirst: my fulness hath been put off, not taken away. "O God, aid Thou me." Most suitably also Lazarus is said to be interpreted, "one aided:" that needy and poor man, that was transported into the bosom of Abraham;[11] and beareth the type of the Church, which ought alway to confess that she hath need of aid. This is true, this is godly. "I have said to the Lord, My God Thou art." Why? "For my goods Thou needest not."[12] He needeth not us, we need Him: therefore He is truly Lord. For thou art not the very true Lord of thy servant: both are men, both needing God. But if thou supposest thy servant to need thee, in order that thou mayest give him bread; thou also needest thy servant, in order that he may aid thy labours. Each one of you doth need the other. Therefore neither of you is truly lord, and neither of you truly servant. Hear thou the true Lord, of whom thou art the true servant: "I have said to the Lord, My God Thou art." Why art Thou Lord? "Because my goods Thou needest not"? But what of thee? "But I am needy and poor." Behold the needy and poor: may God feed, may God alleviate, may God aid: "O God," he saith, "aid Thou me."

8. "My helper and deliverer art Thou; O Lord, delay not." Thou art the helper and deliverer: I need succour, help Thou; entangled I am, deliver Thou. For no one will deliver from entanglings except Thee. There stand round about us the nooses of divers cares, on this side and on that we are torn as it were with thorns and brambles, we walk a narrow way, perchance we have stuck fast in the brambles: let us say to God, "Thou art my deliverer." He that showed us the narrow way,[13] hath taught us to follow it. . . .

9. What is, "delay not"? Because many men say, it is a long time till Christ comes. What then: because we say, "delay not," will He come before He hath determined to come?

[1] Luke xxiv. 39.　　　[2] Luke xxiv. 46, 47.
[3] John x. 5.　　　[4] Ps. cxli. 5.
[5] Here Oxf. MSS. repeat, "They that love Thy saving health."
[6] Ps. cxlvi. 3.　　　[7] Ps. iii. 8.
[8] Ps. xviii. 28.　　[9] Rom. vii. 23.　　[10] Matt. v. 6.
[11] Luke xvi. 23.　　[12] Ps. xvi. 2.　　[13] Matt. vii. 14.

What meaneth this prayer, "delay not"? May not Thy coming seem to me to be too long delayed. For to thee it seemeth a long time, to God it seemeth not long, to whom a thousand years are one day, or the three hours of a watch.[1] But if thou shalt not have had endurance, late for thee it will be: and when to thee it shall be late, thou wilt be diverted from Him, and wilt be like unto those that were wearied in the desert, and hastened to ask of God the pleasant things which He was reserving for them in the Land; and when there were not given on their journey the pleasant things, whereby perchance they would have been corrupted, they murmured against God, and went back in heart unto Egypt:[2] to that place whence in body they had been severed, in heart they went back. Do not thou, then, so, do not so: fear the word of the Lord, saying, "Remember Lot's wife."[3] She too being on the way, but now delivered from the Sodomites, looked back; in the place where she looked back, there she remained: she became a statue of salt, in order to season thee. For to thee she hath been given for an example, in order that thou mayest have sense, mayest not stop infatuated on the way. Observe her stopping and pass on: observe her looking back, and do thou be reaching forth unto the things before, as Paul was.[4] What is it, not to look back. "Of the things behind forgetful," he saith. Therefore thou followest, being called to the heavenly reward, whereof hereafter thou wilt glory. For the same Apostle saith, "There remaineth for me a crown of righteousness, which in that day the Lord, the just Judge, shall render to me."[5]

PSALM LXXI.[6]

1. In all the holy Scriptures the grace of God that delivereth us commendeth itself to us, in order that it may have us commended. This is sung of in this Psalm, whereof we have undertaken to speak. . . . This grace the Apostle commendeth: by this he got to have the Jews for enemies, boasting of the letter of the law and of their own justice. This then commending in the lesson which hath been read, he saith thus: "For I am the least of the Apostles, that am not worthy to be called an Apostle, because I persecuted the Church of God."[7] "But therefore mercy," he saith, "I obtained, because ignorant I did it in unbelief."[8] Then a little afterwards, "Faithful the saying is, and worthy of all acceptation, that Christ Jesus came into the world to save sinners, of whom I am first."[9]

Were there before him not any sinners? What then, was he the first then? Yea, going before all men not in time, but in evil disposition. "But therefore," he saith, "mercy I obtained," in order that in me Christ Jesus might show all long-suffering, for the imitation of those that shall believe in Him unto life eternal: that is, every sinner and unjust man, already despairing of himself, already having the mind of a gladiator,[10] so as to do whatsoever he willeth, because he must needs be condemned, may yet observe the Apostle Paul, to whom so great cruelty and so very evil a disposition was forgiven by God; and by not despairing of himself may he be turned unto God. This grace God doth commend to us in this Psalm also. . . .

2. The title then of this Psalm is, as usual, a title intimating on the threshold what is being done in the house: "To David himself for the sons of Jonadab, and for those that were first led captive." Jonadab (he is commended to us in the prophecy of Jeremiah) was a certain man, who had enjoined his sons not to drink wine, and not to dwell in houses, but in tents. But the commandment of the father the sons kept and observed, and by this earned a blessing from the Lord.[11] Now the Lord had not commanded this, but their own father. But they so received it as though it were a commandment from the Lord their God; for even though the Lord had not commanded that they should drink no wine and should dwell in tents; yet the Lord had commanded that sons should obey their father. In this case alone a son ought not to obey his father, if his father should have commanded anything contrary to the Lord his God. For indeed the father ought not to be angry, when God is preferred before him. But when a father doth command that which is not contrary to God; he must be heard as God is: because to obey one's father God hath enjoined. God then blessed the sons of Jonadab because of their obedience, and thrust them in the teeth of His disobedient people, reproaching them, because while the sons of Jonadab were obedient to their father, they obeyed not their God. But while Jeremiah was treating of these topics, he had this object in regard to the people of Israel, that they should prepare themselves to be led for captivity into Babylon, and should not hope for any other thing, but that they were to be captives. The title then of this Psalm seemeth from thence to have taken its hue, so that when he had said, "Of the sons of Jonadab;" he added, "and of them that were first led captive:" not that the sons of Jonadab were led captive, but because to them that were to be led captive there were

---

[1] Ps. xc. 4.
[2] Exod. xvi. 2; Acts vii. 39.
[3] Luke xvii. 32.
[4] Philip. iii. 13.
[5] 2 Tim. iv. 8.
[6] Lat. LXX.
[7] 1 Cor. xv. 9.
[8] 1 Tim. i. 13.
[9] 1 Tim. i. 15.

[10] *Gladiatorium animum;* i.e., of utter desperation, since a gladiator would expect to perish in one fight if not in another.
[11] Jer. xxxv. 6, etc.

opposed the sons of Jonadab, because they were obedient to their father: in order that they might understand that they had been made captive, because they were not obedient to God. It is added also that Jonadab is interpreted, "the Lord's spontaneous one." What is this, the Lord's spontaneous one? Serving God freely with the will. What is, the Lord's spontaneous one? "In me are, O God, Thy vows, which I will render of praise to Thee."[1] What is, the Lord's spontaneous one? "Voluntarily I will sacrifice to Thee."[2] For if the Apostolic teaching admonisheth a slave to serve a human master, not as though of necessity, but of good will, and by freely serving make himself in heart free; how much more must God be served with whole and full and free will, who seeth thy very will? . . . The first man made us captive, the second man hath delivered us from captivity. "For as in Adam all die, so also in Christ all shall be made alive." But in Adam they die through the flesh's nativity, in Christ they are delivered through the heart's faith. It was not in thy power not to be born of Adam: it is in thy power to believe in Christ. Howsoever much then thou shalt have willed to belong to the first man, unto captivity thou wilt belong. And what is, shalt have willed to belong? or what is, shalt belong? Already thou belongest: cry out, "Who shall deliver me from the body of this death?"[3] Let us hear then this man crying out this.

3. "O God, in Thee I have hoped, O Lord, I shall not be confounded for everlasting" (ver. 1). Already I have been confounded, but not for everlasting. For how is he not confounded, to whom is said, "What fruit had ye in these things wherein ye now blush?"[4] What then shall be done, that we may not be confounded for everlasting? "Draw near unto Him, and be ye enlightened, and your faces shall not blush."[5] Confounded ye are in Adam, withdraw from Adam, draw near unto Christ, and then ye shall not be confounded. "In Thee I have hoped, O Lord, I shall not be confounded for everlasting." If in myself I am now[6] confounded, in Thee I shall not be confounded for everlasting.

4. "In Thine own righteousness deliver me, and save me" (ver. 2). Not in mine own, but in Thine own: for if in mine own, I shall be one of those whereof he saith, "Being ignorant of God's righteousness, and their own righteousness willing to establish, to the righteousness of God they were not made subject."[7] Therefore, "in Thine own righteousness," not in mine. For mine is what? Iniquity hath gone before. And when I shall be righteous, Thine own righteousness it will be: for by righteousness given to me by Thee I shall be righteous; and it shall be so mine, as that it be Thine, that is, given to me by Thee. For I believe on Him that justifieth an ungodly man, so that my faith is counted for righteousness.[8] Even so then the righteousness shall be mine, not however as though mine own, not as though by mine own self given to myself: as they thought who through the letter made their boast, and rejected grace. . . . It is a small thing then that thou acknowledge the good thing which is in thee to be from God, unless also on that account thou exalt not thyself above him that hath not yet, who perchance when he shall have received, will outstrip thee. For when Saul was a stoner of Stephen,[9] how many were the Christians of whom he was persecutor! Nevertheless, when he was converted, all that had gone before he surpassed. Therefore say thou to God that which thou hearest in the Psalm, "In Thee I have hoped, O Lord, I shall not be confounded for everlasting: in Thine own righteousness," not in mine, "deliver me, and save me." "Incline unto me Thine ear." This also is a confession of humility. He that saith, "Incline unto me," is confessing that he is lying like a sick man laid at the feet of the Physician standing. Lastly, observe that it is a sick man that is speaking: "Incline unto me Thine ear, and save me."

5. "Be Thou unto me for a protecting God" (ver. 3). Let not the darts of the enemy reach unto me: for I am not able to protect myself. And a small thing is "protecting:" he hath added, "and for a walled place, that Thou mayest save me." "For a walled place" be Thou to me, be Thou my walled place. . . . Behold, God Himself hath become the place of thy fleeing unto, who at first was the fearful object of thy fleeing from. "For a walled place," he saith, be Thou to me, "that Thou mayest save me." I shall not be safe except in Thee: except Thou shalt have been my rest, my sickness shall not be able to be made whole. Lift me from the earth; upon Thee I will lie, in order that I may rise unto a walled place. What can be better walled? When unto that place thou shalt have fled for refuge, tell me what adversaries thou wilt dread? Who will lie in wait, and come at thee? A certain man is said from the summit of a mountain to have cried out, when an Emperor was passing by, "I speak not[10] of thee:" the other is said to have looked back and to have said, "Nor I of thee." He had despised an Emperor with glittering arms, with mighty army. From whence? From a strong place. If he was secure on a high spot of earth, how secure art thou on Him by whom heaven

---

1 Ps. lvi. 12.   2 Ps. liv. 6.   3 Rom. vii. 24.
4 Rom. vi. 21.   5 Ps. xxxiv. 5.   6 Oxf. mss. *nunc.*
7 Rom. x. 3.

8 Rom. iv. 5.   9 Acts vii. 59.   10 Or, "I care not."

and earth were made? I, if for myself I shall have chosen another place, shall not be able to be safe. Choose thou indeed, O man, if thou shalt have found one, a place better walled. There is not then a place whither to flee from Him, except we flee to Him. If thou wilt escape Him angry, flee to Him appeased. "For my firmament and my refuge Thou art." "My firmament" is what? Through Thee I am firm, and by Thee I am firm. "For my firmament and my refuge Thou art:" in order that I may be made firm by Thee, in whatever respects I shall have been made infirm in myself, I will flee for refuge unto Thee. For firm the grace of Christ maketh thee, and immovable against all temptations of the enemy. But there is there too human frailness, there is there still the first captivity, there is there too the law in the members fighting against the law of the mind, and willing to lead captive in the law of sin:[1] still the body which is corrupt presseth down the soul.[2] Howsoever firm thou be by the grace of God, so long as thou still bearest an earthly vessel, wherein the treasure of God is, something must be dreaded even from that same vessel of clay.[3] Therefore "my firmament Thou art," in order that I may be firm in this world against all temptations. But if many they are, and they trouble me: "my refuge Thou art." For I will confess mine infirmity, to the end that I may be timid like a "hare," because I am full of thorns like a "hedgehog." And as in another Psalm is said, "The rock is a refuge for the hedgehogs and the hares:"[4] but the Rock was Christ.[5]

6. "O God, deliver me from the hand of the sinner" (ver. 4). Generally, sinners, among whom is toiling he that is now to be delivered from captivity: he that now crieth, "Unhappy man I, who shall deliver me from the body of this death? The grace of God through Jesus Christ our Lord."[6] Within is a foe, that law in the members; there are without also enemies: unto what cryest thou? Unto Him, to whom hath been cried, "From my secret sins cleanse me, O Lord, and from strange sins spare Thy servant."[7] . . . But these sinners are of two kinds: there are some that have received Law, there are others that have not received: all the heathen have not received Law, all Jews and Christians have received Law. Therefore the general term is sinner; either a transgressor of the Law, if he hath received Law; or only unjust without Law, if he hath not received the Law. Of both kinds speaketh the Apostle, and saith, "They that without Law have sinned, without Law shall perish, and they that in the Law

have sinned, by the Law shall be judged."[8] But thou that amid both kinds dost groan, say to God that which thou hearest in the Psalm, "My God, deliver me from the hand of the sinner." Of what sinner? "From the hand of him that transgresseth the Law, and of the unjust man." He that transgresseth the Law is indeed also unjust; for not unjust he is not, that transgresseth the Law: but every one that transgresseth the Law is unjust, not every unjust man doth transgress the Law. For, "Where there is not a Law," saith the Apostle, "neither is there transgression."[9] They then that have not received Law, may be called unjust, transgressors they cannot be called. Both are judged after their deservings. But I that from captivity will to be delivered through Thy grace, cry to Thee, "Deliver me from the hand of the sinner." What is, from the hand of him? From the power of him, that while he is raging, he lead me not unto consenting with him; that while he lieth in wait, he persuade not to iniquity. "From the hand of the sinner and of the unjust man." . . .

7. Lastly, there followeth the reason why I say this: "for Thou art my patience" (ver. 5). Now if He is patience rightly, He is that also which followeth, "O Lord, my hope from my youth." My patience, because my hope: or rather my hope, because my patience. "Tribulation," saith the Apostle, "worketh patience, patience probation, but probation hope, but hope confoundeth not."[10] With reason in Thee I have hoped, O Lord, I shall not be confounded for everlasting. "O Lord, my hope from my youth." From thy youth is God thy hope? Is He not also from thy boyhood, and from thine infancy? Certainly, saith he. For see what followeth, that thou mayest not think that I have said this, "my hope from my youth," as if God noways profited mine infancy or my boyhood; hear what followeth: "In Thee I have been strengthened from the womb." Hear yet: "From the belly of my mother Thou art my Protector" (ver. 6). Why then, "from my youth," except it was the period from which I began to hope in Thee? For before in Thee I was not hoping, though Thou wast my Protector, that didst lead me safe unto the time, when I learned to hope in Thee. But from my youth I began in Thee to hope, from the time when Thou didst arm me against the Devil, so that in the girding of Thy host being armed with Thy faith, love, hope, and the rest of Thy gifts, I waged conflict against Thine invisible enemies, and heard from the Apostle, "There is not for us a wrestling against flesh and blood, but against principalities, and powers," etc.[11] There a young man it is that doth fight against these

---

[1] Rom. vii. 23.   [2] Wisd. ix. 15.   [3] 2 Cor. iv. 7.
[4] Ps. civ. 18.   [5] 1 Cor. x. 4.   [6] Rom. vii. 24, 25.
[7] Ps. xix. 12.

[8] Rom. ii. 12.   [9] Rom. iv. 15.   [10] Rom. v. 3-5.
[11] Eph. v. 12.

things: but though he be a young man, he falleth, unless He be the hope of Him to whom he crieth, " O Lord, my hope from my youth." " In Thee is my singing alway." Is it only from the time when I began to hope in Thee until now? Nay, but " alway." What is, " alway"? Not only in the time of faith, but also in the time of sight. For now, " So long as we are in the body we are absent from the Lord: for by faith we walk, not by sight: "[1] there will be a time when we shall see that which being not seen we believe: but when that hath been seen which we believe, we shall rejoice: but when that hath been seen which they believed not, ungodly men shall be confounded. Then will come the substance whereof there is now the hope. But, "Hope which is seen is not hope. But if that which we see not we hope for, through patience we wait for it."[2] Now then thou groanest, now unto a place of refuge thou runnest, in order that thou mayest be saved; now being in infirmity thou entreatest the Physician: what, when thou shalt have received perfect soundness also, what when thou shalt have been made " equal to the Angels of God,"[3] wilt thou then perchance forget that grace, whereby thou hast been delivered? Far be it.

8. " As it were a monster I have become unto many" (ver. 7). Here in time of hope, in time of groaning, in time of humiliation, in time of sorrow, in time of infirmity, in time of the voice from the fetters — here then what? " As it were a monster I have become unto many." Why, " As it were a monster"? Why do they insult me that think me a monster? Because I believe that which I see not. For they being happy in those things which they see, exult in drink, in wantonness, in chamberings, in covetousness, in riches, in robberies, in secular dignities, in the whitening of a mud wall, in these things they exult: but I walk in a different way, contemning those things which are present, and fearing even the prosperous things of the world, and secure in no other thing but the promises of God. And they, " Let us eat and drink, for to-morrow we die."[4] What sayest thou? Repeat it: " let us eat," he saith, " and drink." Come now, what hast thou said afterwards? " for to-morrow we die." Thou hast terrified, not led me astray. Certainly by the very thing which thou hast said afterwards, thou hast stricken me with fear to consent with thee. " For to-morrow we die," thou hast said: and there hath preceded, " Let us eat and drink." For when thou hadst said, " Let us eat and drink; " thou didst add, " for to-morrow we die." Hear the other side from me, " Yea let us fast and pray, 'for to-morrow we die.' " I keeping this way, strait and narrow,

" as it were a monster have become unto many: but Thou art a strong helper." Be Thou with me, O Lord Jesus, to say to me, faint not in the narrow way, I first have gone along it, I am the way itself,[5] I lead, in Myself I lead, unto Myself I lead home. Therefore though " a monster I have become unto many;" nevertheless I will not fear, for "Thou art a strong Helper."

9. " Let my mouth be fulfilled with praise, that with hymn I may tell of Thy glory, all the day long Thy magnificence " (ver. 8). What is " all the day long"? Without intermission. In prosperity, because Thou dost comfort: in adversity, because Thou dost correct: before I was in being, because Thou didst make; when I was in being, because Thou didst give health: when I had sinned, because Thou didst forgive; when I was converted, because Thou didst help; when I had persevered, because Thou didst crown.

10. My hope from my youth, " cast me not away in time of old age " (ver. 9). What is this time of old age? "When my strength shall fail, forsake Thou not me." Here God maketh this answer to thee, yea indeed let thy strength fail, in order that in thee mine may abide: in order that thou mayest say with the Apostle, " When I am made weak, then I am mighty."[6] Fear not, that thou be cast away in that weakness, in that old age. But why? Was not thy Lord made weak on the Cross? Did not most mighty men and fat bulls before Him, as though a man of no strength, made captive and oppressed, shake the head and say, " If Son of God He is, let Him come down from the Cross"?[7] Has he deserted because He was made weak, who preferred not to come down from the Cross, lest He should seem not to have displayed power, but to have yielded to them reviling? What did He hanging teach thee, that would not come down, but patience amid men reviling, but that thou shouldest be strong in thy God? Perchance too in His person was said, " As it were a monster I have become unto many, and Thou art a strong Helper."[8] In His person according to His weakness, not according to His power; according to that whereby He had transformed us into Himself, not according to that wherein He had Himself come down. For He became a monster unto many. And perchance the same was the old age of Him; because on account of its oldness it is not improperly called old age, and the Apostle saith, " Our old man hath been crucified together with Him."[9] If there was there our old man, old age was there; because old, old age.[10] Nevertheless, because a true saying is, "Renewed

---

[1] 2 Cor v. 6.   [2] Rom. viii. 24.   [3] Matt. xxii. 30.
[4] 1 Cor xv. 32.

[5] John xiv. 6.   [6] 2 Cor. xii. 10.   [7] Matt. xxvii. 39, 40, etc.
[8] Ps. lxxi. 6.   [9] Rom. vi. 6.
[10] [A. N. F. vol. i. p. 392, note 6. — C.]

as an eagle's shall be Thy youth;"[1] He rose Himself the third day, promised a resurrection at the end of the world. Already there hath gone before the Head, the members are to follow. Why dost thou fear lest He should forsake thee, lest He cast thee away for the time of old age, when thy strength shall have failed? Yea at that time in thee will be the strength of Him, when thy strength shall have failed.

11. Why do I say this? "For mine enemies have spoken against me, and they that were keeping watch for My soul, have taken counsel together (ver. 10): saying, God hath forsaken Him, persecute Him, and seize Him, for there is no one to deliver Him" (ver. 11). This hath been said concerning Christ. For He that with the great power of Divinity, wherein He is equal to the Father, had raised to life dead persons, on a sudden in the hands of enemies became weak, and as if having no power, was seized. When would He have been seized, except they had first said in their heart, "God hath forsaken Him?" Whence there was that voice on the Cross, "My God, My God, why hast Thou forsaken Me?"[2] So then did God forsake Christ, though "God was in Christ reconciling the world to Himself,"[3] though Christ was also God, out of the Jews indeed according to the flesh, "Who is over all things, God blessed for ever,"[4] — did God forsake Him? Far be it. But in our old man our voice it was, because our old man was crucified together with Him:[5] and of that same our old man He had taken a Body, because Mary was of Adam. Therefore the very thing which they thought, from the Cross He said, "Why hast Thou forsaken Me?"[6] Why do these men think Me left alone to their evil? What is, think Me forsaken in their evil? "For if they had known, the Lord of glory they had never crucified.[7] Persecute and seize Him." More familiarly however, brethren, let us take this of the members of Christ, and acknowledge our own voice in these words: because even He used such words in our person, not in His own power and majesty; but in that which He became for our sakes, not according to that which He was, who hath made us.

12. "O Lord, my God, be not far from me" (ver. 12). So it is, and the Lord is not far off at all. For, "The Lord is nigh unto them that have bruised the heart."[8] "My God, unto my help look Thou." "Be they confounded and fail that engage[9] my soul" (ver. 13). What hath he desired? "Be they confounded and fail." Why hath he desired it? "That engage my soul"? What is, "That engage my soul"? Engaging

as it were unto some quarrel. For they are said to be engaged that are challenged to quarrel. If then so it is, let us beware of men that engage our soul. What is, "That engage our soul"? First provoking us to withstand God, in order that in our evil things God may displease us. For when art thou right, so that to thee the God of Israel may be good, good to men right in heart?[10] When art thou right? Wilt thou hear? When in that good which thou doest, God is pleasing to thee; but in that evil which thou sufferest, God is not displeasing to thee. See ye what I have said, brethren, and be ye on your guard against men that engage your souls. For all men that deal with you in order to make you be wearied in sorrows and tribulations, have this aim, namely, that God may be displeasing to you in that which ye suffer, and there may go forth from your mouth, "What is this? For what have I done?" Now then hast thou done nothing of evil, and art thou just, He unjust? A sinner I am, thou sayest, I confess, just I call not myself. But what, sinner, hast thou by any means done so much evil as he with whom it is well? As much as Gaiuseius?[11] I know the evil doings of him, I know the iniquities of him, from which I, though a sinner, am very far; and yet I see him abounding in all good things, and I am suffering so great evil things. I do not then say, O God, "what have I done" to Thee, because I have done nothing at all of evil; but because I have not done so much as to deserve to suffer these things. Again, art thou just, He unjust? Wake up, wretched man, thy soul hath been engaged! I have not, he saith, called myself just. What then sayest thou? A sinner I am, but I did not commit so great sins, as to deserve to suffer these things. Thou sayest not then to God, just I am, and Thou art unjust: but thou sayest, unjust I am, but Thou art more unjust. Behold thy soul hath been engaged, behold now thy soul wageth war. What? Against whom? Thy soul, against God; that which hath been made against Him by whom it was made. Even because thou art in being to cry out against Him, thou art ungrateful. Return, then, to the confession of thy sickness, and beg the healing hand of the Physician. Think thou not they are happy who flourish for a time. Thou art being chastised, they are being spared: perchance for thee chastised and amended an inheritance is being kept in reserve. . . . Lastly, see what followeth, "Let them put on confusion and shame, that think evil things to me." "Confusion and shame," confusion because of a bad conscience, shame because of modesty. Let this befall them, and they will be good. . . .

---

[1] Ps. ciii. 5.
[2] Ps. xxii. 1.
[3] 2 Cor. v. 19.
[4] Rom. ix. 5.
[5] Rom. vi. 6.
[6] Matt. xxvii. 46.
[7] 1 Cor. ii. 8.
[8] Ps. xxxiv. 18.
[9] *Committentes.*
[10] Ps. lxxiii. 1.
[11] *Al.* Gaius.

13. "But I alway in Thee will hope, and will add to all Thy praise" (ver. 14). What is this? "I will add to all Thy praise," ought to move us. More perfect wilt thou make the praise of God? Is there anything to be superadded? If already that is all praise, wilt thou add anything? God was praised in all His good deeds, in every creature of His, in the whole establishment of all things, in the government and regulation of ages, in the order of seasons, in the height of Heaven, in the fruitfulness of the regions of earth, in the encircling of the sea, in every excellency of the creature everywhere brought forth, in the sons of men themselves, in the giving of the Law, in delivering His people from the captivity of the Egyptians, and all the rest of His wonderful works: not yet He had been praised for having raised up flesh unto life eternal. Be there then this praise added by the Resurrection of our Lord Jesus Christ: in order that here we may perceive His voice above all past praise: thus it is that we rightly understand this also. .∙.

14. "My mouth shall tell out Thy righteousness" (ver. 15): not mine. From thence I will add to all Thy praise: because even that I am righteous, if righteous I am, is Thy righteousness in me, not mine own: for Thou dost justify the ungodly.[1] "All the day long Thy salvation." What is, "Thy salvation"? Let no one assume to himself, that he saveth himself, "Of the Lord is Salvation."[2] Not any one by himself saveth himself, "Vain is man's salvation."[3] "All the day long Thy Salvation:" at all times. Something of adversity cometh, preach the Salvation of the Lord: something of prosperity cometh, preach the Salvation of the Lord. Do not preach in prosperity, and hold thy peace in adversity: otherwise there will not be that which hath been said, "all the day long." For all the day long is day together with its own night. Do we when we say, for example, thirty days have gone by, mention the nights also; do we not under the very term days include the nights also? In Genesis what was said? "The evening was made, and the morning was made, one day."[4] Therefore a whole day is the day together with its own night: for the night doth serve the day, not the day the night. Whatever thou doest in mortal flesh, ought to serve righteousness: whatever thou doest by the commandment of God, be it not done for the sake of the advantage of the flesh, lest day serve night. Therefore all the day long speak of the praise of God, to wit, in prosperity and in adversity; in prosperity, as though in the day time; in adversity, as though in the night time: all the day long nevertheless speak of the praise of God, so that thou mayest not have

sung to no purpose, "I will bless God at every time, alway the praise of Him is in my mouth."[5] . . .

15. Therefore, he saith, "For I have not known tradings."[6] What are these tradings? Let traders hear and change their life; and if they have been such, be not such; let them not know what they have been, let them forget; lastly, let them not approve, not praise; let them disapprove, condemn, be changed, if trading is a sin. For on this account, O thou trader, because of a certain eagerness for getting, whenever thou shalt have suffered loss, thou wilt blaspheme; and there will not be in thee that which hath been spoken of, "all the day long Thy praise." But whenever for the price of the goods which thou art selling, thou not only liest, but even falsely swearest; how in thy mouth all the day long is there the praise of God? While, if thou art a Christian, even out of thy mouth the name of God is being blasphemed, so that men say, see what sort of men are Christians! Therefore if this man for this reason speaketh the praise of God all the day long, because he hath not known tradings; let Christians amend themselves, let them not trade. But a trader saith to me, behold I bring indeed from a distant quarter merchandise unto these places, wherein there are not those things which I have brought, by which means I may gain a living: I ask but as reward for my labour, that I may sell dearer than I have bought: for whence can I live, when it hath been written, "the worker is worthy of his reward"?[7] But he is treating of lying, of false swearing. This is the fault of me, not of trading: for I should not, if I would, be unable to do without this fault. I then, the merchant, do not shift mine own fault to trading: but if I lie, it is I that lie, not the trade. For I might say, for so much I bought, but for so much I will sell; if thou pleasest, buy. For the buyer hearing this truth would not be offended, and not a whit less all men would resort to me: because they would love truth more than gain. Of this then, he saith, admonish me, that I lie not, that I forswear not; not to relinquish business whereby I maintain myself. For to what dost thou put me when thou puttest me away from this? Perchance to some craft? I will be a shoemaker, I will make shoes for men. Are not they too liars? are not they too false-swearers? Do they not, when they have contracted to make shoes for one man, when they have received money from another man, give up that which they were making, and undertake to make for another, and deceive him for whom they have promised to make speedily? Do they not often say, to-day I am about it, to-day I'll get

---

[1] Rom. iv. 5.   [2] Ps. iii. 8.   [3] Ps. lx. 11.
[4] Gen. i. 5.

[5] Ps. xxxiv. 1.   [6] E. V. "For I know not the number thereof."
[7] Luke x. 7.

them done? Secondly, in the very sewing do they not commit as many frauds? These are their doings and these are their sayings: but they are themselves evil, not the calling which they profess. All evil artificers, then, not fearing God, either for gain, or for fear of loss or want, do lie, do forswear themselves; there is no continual praise of God in them. How then dost thou withdraw me from trading? Wouldest thou that I be a farmer, and murmur against God thundering, so that, fearing hail, I consult a wizard, in order to learn what to do to protect me against the weather; so that I desire famine for the poor, in order that I may be able to sell what I have kept in store? Unto this dost thou bring me? But good farmers, thou sayest, do not such things. Nor do good traders do those things. But why, even to have sons is an evil thing, for when their head is in pain, evil and unbelieving mothers seek for impious charms and incantations? These are the sins of men, not of things. A trader might thus speak to me — Look then, O Bishop, how thou understand the tradings which thou hast read in the Psalm: lest perchance thou understand not, and yet forbid me trading. Admonish me then how I should live; if well, it shall be well with me: one thing however I know, that if I shall have been evil, it is not trading that maketh me so, but my iniquity. Whenever truth is spoken, there is nothing to be said against it.

16. Let us inquire then what he hath called tradings, which indeed he that hath not known, all the day long doth praise God. Trading[1] even in the Greek language is derived from action, and in the Latin from want of inaction: but whether it be from action or want of inaction, let us examine what it is. For they that are active traders, rely as it were upon their own action, they praise their works, they attain not to the grace of God. Therefore traders are opposed to that grace which this Psalm doth commend. For it doth commend that grace, in order that no one may boast of his own works. Because in a certain place is said, "Physicians shall not raise to life,"[2] ought men to abandon medicine? But what is this? Under this name are understood proud men, promising salvation to men, whereas "of the Lord is Salvation."[3] . . . With reason the Lord drave from the Temple them to whom He said, "It is written, My House shall be called the House of prayer, but ye have made it a house of trading;"[4] that is, boasting of your works, seeking no inaction, nor hearing the Scripture speaking against your unrest and trading, "be ye still, and see that I am the Lord."[5] . . .

17. But there is in some copies, "For I have not known literature." Where some books have "trading," there others "literature:" how they may accord is a hard matter to find out; and yet the discrepancy of interpreters perchance showeth the meaning, introduceth no error. Let us inquire then how to understand literature also, lest we offend grammarians in the same way as we did traders a little before: because a grammarian too may live honourably in his calling, and neither forswear nor lie. Let us examine then the literature which he hath not known, in whose mouth all the day long is the praise of God. There is a sort of literature of the Jews: for to them let us refer this; there we shall find what hath been said: just as when we were inquiring about traders, on the score of actions and works, we found that to be called detestable trading, which the Apostle hath branded, saying, "For being ignorant of God's righteousness, and willing to establish their own, to the righteousness of God they were not made subject."[6] . . . Just as then we found out the former charge against traders, that is men boasting of action, exalting themselves because of business which admitteth no inaction, unquiet men rather than good workmen; because good workmen are those in whom God worketh; so also we find a sort of literature among the Jews. . . . Moses wrote five books: but in the five porches encircling the pool,[7] sick men were lying, but they could not be healed. See how the letter remained, convicting the guilty, not saving the unrighteous. For in those five porches, a figure of the five books, sick men were given over rather than made whole. What then in that place did make whole a sick man? The moving of the water. When that pool was moved there went down a sick man, and there was made whole one, one[8] because of unity: whatsoever other man went down unto that same moving was not made whole. How then was there commended the unity of the Body crying from the ends of the earth? Another man was not healed, except again the pool were moved. The moving of the pool then did signify the perturbation of the people of the Jews when the Lord Jesus Christ came. For at the coming of an Angel the water in the pool was perceived to be moved. The water then encircled with five porches was the Jewish nation encircled by the Law. And in the porches the sick lay, and in the water alone when troubled and moved they were healed. The Lord came, troubled was the water; He was crucified, may He come down in order that the sick man may be made whole. What is, may He come down? May He humble Himself. Therefore whosoever ye be that

---

[1] *Negotiatio*, Lat.; πραγμάτεια, Gr.
[2] Ps. lxxxviii. 10.
[3] Ps. iii. 8.
[4] Matt. xxi. 13. E. V. "den of robbers."
[5] Ps. xlvi. 10.
[6] Rom. x. 3.
[7] John v. 2.
[8] Oxf. MSS. repeat *unus*.

love the letter without grace, in the porches ye will remain, sick ye will be, lying ill, not growing well. . . . For the same figure also it is that Eliseus at first sent a staff by his servant to raise up the dead child. There had died the son of a widow his hostess; it was reported to him, to his servant he gave his staff: go thou, he saith, lay it on the dead child. Did the prophet not know what he was doing? The servant went before, he laid the staff upon the dead, the dead arose not. "For if there had been given a law which could have made alive, surely out of the law there had been righteousness."[1] The law sent by the servant made not alive: and yet he sent his staff by the servant, who himself afterwards followed, and made alive.[2] For when that infant arose not, Eliseus came himself, now bearing the type of the Lord, who had sent before his servant with the staff, as though with the Law: he came to the child that was lying dead, he laid his limbs upon it. The one was an infant, the other a grown man: he contracted and shortened in a manner the size of his full growth, in order that he might fit the dead child. The dead then arose, when he being alive adapted himself to the dead: and the Master did that which the staff did not; and grace did that which the letter did not. They then that have remained in the staff, glory in the letter; and therefore are not made alive. But I will to glory concerning Thy grace. . . . In that same grace I glorying "literature have not known:" that is, men on the letter relying, and from grace recoiling, with whole heart I have rejected.

18. With reason there followeth, "I will enter into the power of the Lord:" not mine own, but the Lord's. For they gloried in their own power of the letter, therefore grace joined to the letter they knew not. . . . But because "the letter killeth, but the Spirit maketh alive:"[3] "I have not known literature, and I will enter into the power of the Lord." Therefore this verse following doth strengthen and perfect the sense, so as to fix it in the hearts of men, and not suffer any other interpretation to steal in from any quarter. "O Lord, I will be mindful of Thy righteousness alone" (ver. 16). Ah! "alone." Why hath he added "alone," I ask you? It would suffice to say, "I will be mindful of Thy righteousness." "alone," he saith, entirely: there of mine own I think not. "For what hast thou which thou hast not received? But if also thou hast received, why dost thou glory as if thou hast not received."[4] Thy righteousness alone doth deliver me, what is mine own alone is nought but sins. May I not glory then of my own strength, may I not remain in the letter; may I reject "literature," that is, men glorying of the letter, and on their own strength perversely, like men frantic, relying: may I reject such men, may I enter into the power of the Lord, so that when I am weak, then I may be mighty; in order that Thou in me mayest be mighty, for, "I will be mindful of Thy righteousness alone."

19. "O God, Thou hast taught me from my youth" (ver. 17). What hast thou taught me? That of Thy righteousness alone I ought to be mindful. For reviewing my past life, I see what was owing to me, and what I have received instead of that which was owing to me. There was owing punishment, there hath been paid grace: there was owing hell, there hath been given life eternal. "O God, Thou hast taught me from my youth." From the very beginning of my faith, wherewith Thou hast renewed me, Thou didst teach me that nothing had preceded in me, whence I might say that there was owing to me what Thou hast given. For who is turned to God save from iniquity? Who is redeemed save from captivity? But who can say that unjust was his captivity, when he forsook his Captain and fell off to the deserter? God is for our Captain,[5] the devil a deserter: the Captain gave a commandment, the deserter suggested guile:[6] where were thine ears between precept and deceit? was the devil better than God? Better he that revolted[7] than He that made thee? Thou didst believe what the devil promised, and didst find what God threatened. Now then out of captivity being delivered, still however in hope, not yet in substance, walking by faith, not yet by sight, "O God," he saith, "Thou hast taught me from my youth." From the time that I have been turned to Thee,[8] renewed by Thee who had been made by Thee, re-created who had been created, re-formed who had been formed: from the time that I have been converted, I have learned that no merits of mine have preceded, but that Thy grace hath come to me gratis, in order that I might be mindful of Thy righteousness alone.

20. What next after youth? For, "Thou hast taught me," he saith, "from my youth:" what after youth? For in that same first conversion of thine thou didst learn, how before conversion thou wast not just, but iniquity preceded, in order that iniquity being banished, there might succeed love: and having been renewed into a new man, only in hope, not yet in substance, thou didst learn how nothing of thy good had preceded, and by the grace of God thou wast converted to God: now perchance since the time that thou hast been converted wilt thou have anything of thine own, and on thy own

---

[1] Gal. iii. 21.   [2] 2 Kings iv. 20-36.   [3] 2 Cor. iii. 6.
[4] 1 Cor. iv. 7.

[5] *Imperator.*   [6] Gen. ii. 17, iii. 5.
[7] *Defecit; al. te infecit,* "that infected thee."
[8] [Augustin here talks like the poet Cowper, or like Wesley and Whitefield: and the fact is very instructive in connection with his doctrine of baptism. See Cowper's "Truth," line 17th from close. — C.]

strength oughtest thou to rely? Just as men are wont to say, now leave me, it was necessary for thee to show me the way; it is sufficient, I will walk in the way. And he that hath shown thee the way, "wilt thou not that I conduct thee to the place?" But thou, if thou art conceited, "let me alone, it is enough, I will walk in the way." Thou art left, and through thy weakness again thou wilt lose the way. Good were it for thee that He should have conducted thee, who first put thee in the way. But unless He too lead thee, again also thou wilt stray: say to Him then, "Conduct me, O Lord, in Thy way, and I will walk in Thy truth."[1] But thy having entered on the way, is youth, the very renewal and beginning of the faith. For before thou wast walking through thy own ways a vagabond; straying through woody places, through rough places, torn in all thy limbs, thou wast seeking a home, that is, a sort of settlement of thy spirit, where thou mightest say, it is well; and being in security mightest say it, at rest from every uneasiness, from every trial, in a word from every captivity; and thou didst not find. What shall I say? Came there to thee one to show thee the way? There came to thee the Way itself, and thou wast set therein by no merits of thine preceding, for evidently thou wast straying. What, since the time that thou hast set foot therein dost thou now direct thyself? Doth He that hath taught thee the way now leave thee? No, he saith: "Thou hast taught me from my youth; and even until now I will tell forth Thy wonderful works." For a wonderful thing is that which still Thou doest; namely, that Thou dost direct me, who in the way hast put me: and these are Thy wonderful works. What dost thou think to be the wonderful works of God? What is more wonderful among God's wonderful works, than the raising the dead? But am I by any means dead, thou sayest? Unless dead thou hadst been, there would not have been said to thee, "Rise, thou that sleepest, and arise from the dead, and Christ shall enlighten thee."[2] Dead are all unbelievers, all unrighteous men; in body they live, but in heart they are extinct. But he that raiseth a man dead according to the body, doth bring him back to see this light and to breathe this air: but he that raiseth is not himself light and air to him; he beginneth to see, as he saw before. A soul is not so resuscitated. For a soul is resuscitated by God; though even a body is resuscitated by God: but God, when He doth resuscitate a body, to the world doth bring it back: when He doth resuscitate a soul, to Himself He bringeth it back. If the air of this world be withdrawn, there dieth body: if God be withdrawn, there dieth

soul. When then God doth resuscitate a soul, unless there be with her He that hath resuscitated, she being resuscitated liveth not. For He doth not resuscitate, and then leave her to live to herself: in the same manner as Lazarus, when he was resuscitated after being four days dead, was resuscitated by the Lord's corporal presence. . . . The Lord withdrew from that same city or from that spot, did Lazarus cease to live? Not so is the soul resuscitated: God doth resuscitate her, she dieth if God shall have withdrawn. For I will speak boldly, brethren, but yet the truth. Two lives there are, one of the body, another of the soul: as the life of the body is the soul, so the life of the soul is God: in like manner as, if the soul forsake, the body dieth: so the soul dieth, if God forsake. This then is His grace, namely, that He resuscitate and be with us. Because then He doth resuscitate us from our past death, and doth renew in a manner our life, we say to Him, "O God, Thou hast taught me from my youth." But because He doth not withdraw from those whom He resuscitateth, lest when He shall have withdrawn from them they die, we say to Him, "and even until now I will tell forth Thy wonderful works:" because while Thou art with me I live, and of my soul Thou art the life, which will die if she be left to herself. Therefore while my life is present, that is, my God, "even until now," what next?

21. "And even unto oldness[3] and old age"[4] (ver. 18). These are two terms for old age, and are distinguished by the Greeks. For the gravity succeeding youth hath another name among the Greeks, and after that same gravity the last age coming on hath another name; for πρεσβύτης signifieth grave, and γέρων old. But because in the Latin language the distinction of these two terms holdeth not, both words implying old age are inserted, oldness and old age: but ye know them to be two ages. "Thou hast taught me Thy grace from my youth; and even until now;" after my youth, "I will tell forth Thy wonderful works," because Thou art with me in order that I may not die, who hast come in order that I may rise: "and even unto oldness and old age," that is, even unto my last breath, unless with me Thou shalt have been, there will not be any merit of mine; may Thy grace alway remain with me. Even one man would say this, thou, he, I; but because this voice is that of a certain great Man, that is, of the Unity itself, for it is the voice of the Church; let us investigate the youth of the Church. When Christ came, He was crucified, dead, rose again, called the Gentiles, they began to be converted, became Martyrs strong in Christ, there

---

[1] Ps. lxxxvi. 11.   [2] Eph. v. 14.   [3] *Senecta.*   [4] *Senium.*

was shed faithful blood, there arose a harvest for the Church: this is Her youth. But seasons advancing let the Church confess, let Her say, "Even until now I will tell forth Thy wonderful works." Not only in youth, when Paul, when Peter, when the first Apostles told: even in advancing age I myself, that is, Thy Unity, Thy members, Thy Body, "will tell forth Thy marvellous works." What then? "And even unto oldness and old age," I will tell forth Thy wonderful works: even until the end of the world here shall be the Church. For if She were not to be here even unto the end of the world; to whom did the Lord say, "Behold, I am with you always, even unto the consummation of the world"? Why was it necessary that these things should be spoken in the Scriptures? Because there were to be enemies of the Christian Faith who would say, "for a short time are the Christians, hereafter they shall perish, and there shall come back idols, there shall come back that which was before. How long shall be the Christians?"[1] "Even unto oldness and old age:" that is, even unto the end of the world. When thou, miserable unbeliever, dost expect Christians to pass away, thou art passing away thyself without Christians: and Christians even unto the end of the world shall endure; and as for thee with thine unbelief when thou shalt have ended thy short life, with what face wilt thou come forth to the Judge, whom while thou wast living thou didst blaspheme? Therefore "from my youth, and even until now, and even unto oldness and old age, O Lord, forsake not me." It will not be, as mine enemies say, even for a time. "Forsake not me, until I tell forth Thine arm to every generation that is yet to come." And the Arm of the Lord hath been revealed to whom?[2] The Arm of the Lord is Christ. Do not Thou then forsake me: let not them rejoice that say, "only for a set time the Christians are." May there be persons to tell forth Thine arm. To whom? "To every generation that is yet to come." If then it be to every generation that is yet to come, it will be even unto the end of the world: for when the world is ended, no longer any generation will come on.

22. "Thy power and Thy righteousness" (ver. 19). That is, that I may tell forth to every generation that is yet to come, Thine arm. And what hath Thine arm effected? This then let me tell forth, that same grace to every generation succeeding: let me say to every man that is to be born, nothing thou art by thyself, on God call thou, thine own are sins, merits are God's:[3] punishment to thee is owing, and when reward shall have come, His own gifts He will crown, not thy merits. Let me say to every

generation that is to come, out of captivity thou hast come, unto Adam thou didst belong. Let me say this to every generation that is to come, that there is no strength of mine, no righteousness of mine; but "Thy strength and Thy righteousness, O God, even unto the most high mighty works which Thou hast made." "Thy power and Thy righteousness," as far as what? even unto flesh and blood? Nay, "even unto the most high mighty works which Thou hast made." For the high places are the heavens, in the high places are the Angels, Thrones, Dominions, Principalities, Powers: to Thee they owe it that they are; to Thee they owe it that they live, to Thee they owe it that righteously they live, to Thee they owe it that blessedly they live. "Thy power and Thy righteousness," as far as what? "Even unto the most high mighty works which Thou hast made." Think not that man alone belongeth to the grace of God. What was Angel before he was made? What is Angel, if He forsake him who hath created? Therefore "Thy power and Thy justice even unto the most high mighty works which Thou hast made."

23. And man exalteth himself: and in order that he may belong to the first captivity, he heareth the serpent suggesting, "Taste, and ye shall be as Gods."[4] Men as Gods? "O God, who is like unto Thee?" Not any in the pit, not in Hell, not in earth, not in Heaven, for all things Thou hast made. Why doth the work strive with the Maker? "O God, who is like unto Thee?" But as for me, saith miserable Adam, and Adam is[5] every man, while I perversely will to be like unto Thee, behold what I have become, so that from captivity to Thee I cry out: I with whom it was well under a good king, have been made captive under my seducer; and cry out to Thee, because I have fallen from Thee. And whence have I fallen from Thee? While I perversely seek to be like unto Thee. . . .

24. Ill straying, ill presuming, doomed to die by withdrawing from the path[6] of righteousness: behold he breaketh the commandment, he hath shaken off from his neck the yoke of discipline, uplifted with high spirit he hath broken in sunder the reins of guidance: where is he now? Truly captive he crieth, "O Lord, who is like unto Thee?" I perversely willed to be like unto Thee, and I have been made like unto a beast! Under Thy dominion, under Thy commandment, I was indeed like: "But a man in honour set hath not perceived, he hath been compared to beasts without sense,

---

[1] See on Ps. xl. § 1 and note. Oxf. edition.　　　[2] Isa. liii. 1.
[3] Oxf. MSS. add, "by grace given to thee."
[4] Gen. iii. 5.
[5] Ben. "In Adam every man;" but it is noted that the MSS. omit "in."
[6] "Life," most MSS.

and hath been made like unto them." [1]   Now out of the likeness of beasts cry though late and say, "O God, who is like unto Thee?"

25. "How great troubles hast Thou shown to me, many and evil!" (ver. 20).   Deservedly, proud servant.   For thou hast willed perversely to be like thy God, who hadst been made after the image of thy Lord.[2]   Wouldest thou have it to be well with thee, when withdrawing from that good?   Truly God saith to thee, if thou withdrawest from Me, and it is well with thee, I am not thy good.   Again, if He is good, and in the highest degree good, and of Himself to Himself good, and by no foreign good thing good, and is Himself our chief good; by withdrawing from Him, what wilt thou be but evil?   Also if He is Himself our blessedness, what will there be to one withdrawing from Him, except misery?   Return thou then after misery, and say, "O Lord, who is like unto Thee?   How great troubles hast Thou shown to me, many and evil!"

26. But this was discipline; admonition, not desertion.   Lastly, giving thanks, he saith what?   "And being turned Thou hast made me alive, and from the bottomless places of the earth again Thou hast brought me back."   But when before?   What is this "again"?   Thou hast fallen from a high place, O man, disobedient slave, O thou proud against thy Lord, thou hast fallen.   There hast come to pass in thee, "every one that exalteth himself shall be humbled:" may there come to pass in thee, "every one that humbleth himself shall be exalted."[3]   Return thou from the deep.   I return, he saith, I return, I acknowledge; "O God, who is like unto Thee?   How great troubles hast Thou shown to me, many and evil! and being turned Thou hast made me alive, and from the bottomless places of the earth again Thou hast brought me back."   "We perceive," I hear.   Thou hast brought us back from the bottomless places of the earth, hast brought us back from the depth and drowning of sin.   But why "again"?   When had it already been done?   Let us go on, if perchance the latter parts of the Psalm itself do not explain to us the thing which here we do not yet perceive, namely, why he hath said "again."   Therefore let us hear: "How great troubles Thou hast shown to me, many and evil!   And being turned Thou hast made me alive, and from the bottomless places of the earth again Thou hast brought me back."   What then?   "Thou hast multiplied Thy righteousness, and being turned Thou hast comforted me, and from the bottomless places of the earth again Thou hast brought me back" (ver. 21).   Behold a second "again"!   If we labour to unravel this "again" when written once, who will be able to unravel

it when doubled?   Now "again" itself is a redoubling, and once more there is written "again."   May He be with us from whom is grace, may there be with us the arm also which we are telling forth to every generation that is to come: may He be with us Himself, and as with the key of His Cross open to us the mystery that is locked up.   For it was not to no purpose that when He was crucified the veil of the temple was rent in the midst, but to show that through His Passion the secret things of all mysteries were opened.[4]   May He then Himself be with men passing over unto Him, be the veil taken away:[5] may our Lord and Saviour Jesus Christ tell us why such a voice of the Prophet hath been sent before, "Thou hast shown to me troubles many and evil: and being turned Thou hast made me alive, and from the bottomless places of the earth again Thou hast brought me back."   Behold this is the first "again" which hath been written.   Let us see what this is, and we shall see why there is a second "again."

27. . . . Therein Christ died, wherein thou art to die: and therein Christ rose again, wherein thou art to rise again.   By His example He taught thee what thou shouldest not fear, for what thou shouldest hope.   Thou didst fear death, He died: thou didst despair of rising again, He rose again.   But thou sayest to me, He rose again, do I by any means rise again?   But He rose again in that which for thee He received of thee.   Therefore thy nature in Him hath preceded thee; and that which was taken of thee, hath gone up before thee: therein therefore thou also hast ascended.   Therefore He ascended first, and we in Him: because that flesh is of the human race. . . .   Behold one "again."   Hear of its being fulfilled from the Apostle: "If then ye have risen with Christ, the things which are above seek ye, where Christ is sitting on the right hand of God; the things which are above mind ye, not the things which are upon the earth."[6]   He then hath gone before: already we also have risen again, but still in hope.   Hear the Apostle Paul saying this same thing: "Even we ourselves groan in ourselves, looking for the adoption, the redemption of our body."   What is it then that Christ hath granted to thee?   Hear that which followeth: "For by hope we are saved: but hope which is seen is not hope.   For that which a man seeth, why doth he hope for?   But if that which we see not we hope for, through patience we wait for it."   We have been brought back therefore again from the bottomless places in hope.   Why again?   Because already Christ had gone before.   But because we shall rise again in substance, for now in hope we are living, now after faith we are

---

[1] Ps. xlix. 12.   [2] Gen. i. 27.   [3] Luke xiv. 11.   [4] Matt. xxvii. 51.   [5] 2 Cor. iii. 16.   [6] Col. iii. 1, 2.

walking; we have been brought back from the bottomless places of the earth, by believing in Him who before us hath risen again from the bottomless place of the earth. . . . Thou hast heard one "again," thou hast heard the other "again;" one "again" because of Christ going before; and the other, yet however in hope, and a thing which remaineth to be in substance. "Thou hast multiplied Thy righteousness,"[1] already in me believing, already in those that first have risen again in hope. . . . "Thou hast multiplied Thy righteousness, and being turned Thou hast comforted me:" and because of the body to rise again at the end, "even from the bottomless places of the earth again Thou hast brought me back.

28. "For I will confess to Thee in the vessels of a Psalm Thy truth" (ver. 22). The vessels of a Psalm are a Psaltery. But what is a Psaltery? An instrument of wood and strings.[2] What doth it signify? There is some difference between it and a harp: . . . there seemeth to be signified by the Psaltery the Spirit, by the harp the flesh. And because he had spoken of two bringings back of ours from the bottomless places of the earth, one after the Spirit in hope, the other after the body in substance; hear thou of these two: "For I will confess to Thee in the vessels of a Psalm Thy truth." This after the Spirit: concerning the body what? "I will psalm to Thee on a harp, Holy One of Israel."

29. Again hear this because of that same "again" and "again." "My lips shall exult when I shall psalm to Thee" (ver. 23). Because lips are wont to be spoken of both belonging to the inner and to the outward man, it is uncertain in what sense lips have been used: there followeth therefore, "And my soul which Thou hast redeemed." Therefore regarding the inward lips having been saved in hope, brought back from the bottomless places of the earth in faith and love, still however waiting for the redemption of our body,[3] we say what? Already he hath said, "And my soul which Thou hast redeemed." But lest thou shouldest think the soul alone redeemed, wherein now thou hast heard one "again," "but still," he saith; why still? "but still my tongue also:" therefore now the tongue of the body: "all day long shall meditate of Thy righteousness" (ver. 24): that is, in eternity without end. But when shall this be? Hereafter at the end of the world, at the resurrection of the body and the changing into the Angelic state. Whence is it proved that this is spoken of the end, "but still my tongue also all day long shall meditate of Thy righteousness"? "When they shall have been confounded and shall have blushed, that seek evil things for me."

When shall they be confounded, when shall they blush, save at the end of the world? For in two ways they shall be confounded, either when they shall believe in Christ, or when Christ shall have come. For so long as the Church is here, so long as grain groaneth amid chaff, so long as wheat groaneth amid tares,[4] so long as vessels of mercy groan amid vessels of wrath made for dishonour,[5] so long as lily groaneth amid thorns, there will not be wanting enemies to say, "When shall he die, and his name perish?"[6] "Behold there shall come the time when Christians shall be ended and shall be no more: as they began at a set time, so even unto a particular time they shall be." But while they are saying these things and without end[7] are dying, and while the Church is continuing preaching the Arm of the Lord[8] to every generation that is to come; there shall come Himself also at last in His glory,[9] there shall rise again all the dead, each with his cause: there shall be severed good men to the right hand, but evil men to the left, and they shall be confounded that did insult, they shall blush that did mock: and so my tongue after resurrection shall meditate of Thy righteousness, all day long of Thy praise, "when they shall have been confounded and shall have blushed, that seek evil things for me."

PSALM LXXII.[10]

1. "For Salomon" indeed this Psalm's title is fore-noted: but things are spoken of therein which could not apply to that Salomon king of Israel after the flesh, according to those things which holy Scripture speaketh concerning him: but they can most pertinently apply to the Lord Christ. Whence it is perceived, that the very word Salomon is used in a figurative sense, so that in him Christ is to be taken. For Salomon is interpreted peace-maker: and on this account such a word to Him most truly and excellently doth apply, through Whom, the Mediator, having received remission of sins, we that were enemies are reconciled to God. For "when we were enemies we were reconciled to God through the death of His Son."[11] The Same is Himself that Peace-maker. . . . Since then we have found out the true Salomon, that is, the true Peace-maker: next let us observe what the Psalm doth teach concerning Him.

2. "O God, Thy judgment to the King give Thou, and Thy justice to the King's Son" (ver. 1). The Lord Himself in the Gospel saith, "The Father judgeth not any one, but all judgment He hath given to the Son:"[12] this is then,

---

[1] Or, "justice." [2] [See p. 170, supra. — C.]
[3] Rom. viii. 23.

[4] Matt. iii. 12, xiii. 30.   [5] 2 Tim. ii. 20.   [6] Ps. xli 5.
[7] "Faith," most MSS.   [8] [See A. N. F. vol. v. 516, 520. — C.]
[9] Matt. xxv. 31.   [10] Lat. LXXI.   [11] Rom. v. 10.
[12] John v. 22.

"O God, Thy judgment to the King give Thou."
He that is King is also the Son of the King:
because God the Father also is certainly King.
Thus it hath been written, that the King made a
marriage for His Son.[1] But after the manner of
Scripture the same thing is repeated. For that
which he hath said in, "Thy judgment;" the
same he hath otherwise expressed in, "Thy justice:" and that which he hath said in, "the
King," the same he hath otherwise expressed in,
"to the King's Son." . . . But these repetitions
do much commend the divine sayings, whether
the same words, or whether in other words the
same sense be repeated: and they are mostly
found in the Psalms, and in the kind of discourse
whereby the mind's affection is to be awakened.

3. Next there followeth, "To judge Thy
people in justice, and Thy poor in judgment"
(ver. 2). For what purpose the royal Father
gave to the royal Son His judgment and His
justice is sufficiently shown when he saith, "To
judge Thy people in justice;" that is, for the
purpose of judging Thy people. Such an idiom
is found in Salomon: "The Proverbs of Salomon, son of David, to know wisdom and discipline:"[2] that is, the Proverbs of Salomon, for
the purpose of knowing wisdom and discipline.
So, "Thy judgment give Thou, to judge Thy
people:" that is, "Thy judgment" give Thou for
the purpose of judging Thy people. But that
which he saith before in, "Thy people," the
same he saith afterwards in, "Thy poor:" and
that which he saith before in, "in justice;" the
same afterward in, "in judgment:" according
to that manner of repetition. Whereby indeed
he showeth, that the people of God ought to be
poor, that is, not proud, but humble. For,
"blessed are the poor in spirit, for theirs is the
kingdom of Heaven."[3] In which poverty even
blessed Job was poor even before he had lost
those great earthly riches. Which thing for this
reason I thought should be mentioned, because
there are certain persons who are more ready to
distribute all their goods to the poor,[4] than
themselves to become the poor of God. For
they are puffed up with boasting wherein they
think their living well should be ascribed to
themselves, not to the grace of God: and
therefore now they do not even live well, however great the good works which they seem to
do. . . .

4. But seeing that he hath changed the order
of the words (though he had first said, "O
God, Thy judgment to the King give Thou, and
Thy justice to the King's Son," putting judgment
first, then justice), and hath put justice first, then
judgment, saying, "To judge Thy people in
justice, and Thy poor in judgment:" he doth
more clearly show that he hath called judgment
justice, proving that there is no difference made
by the order in which the word is placed,
because it signifieth the same thing. For it is
usual to say "wrong judgment" of that which
is unjust: but justice iniquitous or unjust we are
not wont to speak of. For if wrong and unjust it be; no longer must it be called justice.
Again, by putting down judgment and repeating
it under the name of justice, or by putting down
justice and repeating it under the name of judgment, he clearly showeth that he specially nameth
that judgment which is wont to be put instead
of justice, that is, that which cannot be understood of giving an evil judgment. For in the
place where He saith, "Judge not according to
persons, but right judgment judge ye;"[5] He
showeth that there may be a wrong judgment,
when He saith, "right judgment judge ye:"
lastly, the one He doth forbid, the other He doth
enjoin. But when without any addition He
speaketh of judgment, He would at once have
just judgment to be understood: as is that which
He saith, "Ye forsake the weightier matters of
the Law, mercy and judgment."[6] That also
which Jeremiah saith is, "making his riches
not with judgment."[7] He saith not, making his
riches by wrong or unjust judgment, or not with
judgment right or just, but not with judgment:
calling not anything judgment but what is right
and just.

5. "Let the mountains bear peace to the
people, and the hills justice" (ver. 3). The
mountains are the greater, the hills the less.
These are without doubt those which another
Psalm hath, "little with great."[8] For those
mountains did exult like rams, and those hills
like lambs of the sheep, at the departure of
Israel out of Egypt, that is, at the deliverance
of the people of God from this world's servitude. Those then that are eminent in the
Church for passing sanctity, are the mountains,
who are meet to teach other men also,[9] by so
speaking as that they may be faithfully taught,
by so living as that they may imitate them to
their profit: but the hills are they that follow the
excellence of the former by their own obedience.
Why then "the mountains peace: and the hills
justice"?[10] Would there perchance have been
no difference, even if it had been said thus,
Let the mountains bear justice to the people
and the hills peace? For to both justice, and
to both peace is necessary: and it may be that
under another name justice herself may have been
called peace. For this is true peace, not such
as unjust men make among them. Or rather

---

[1] Matt. xxii. 2.   [2] Prov. i. 1.   [3] Matt. v. 3.
[4] God's poor.

[5] John vii. 24.   [6] Matt. xxiii. 23.   [7] Jer. xvii. 11.
[8] Ps. cxiv. 4, 6.   [9] 2 Tim. ii. 2.
[10] [Coleridge has justly remarked on the feebleness of this Latin
word *justice*, as compared with our English "righteousness." — C.]

with a distinction not to be overlooked must that be understood which he saith, " the mountains peace, and the hills justice "? For men excelling in the Church ought to counsel for peace with watchful care; lest for the sake of their own distinctions by acting proudly they make schisms and dissever the bond of union. But let the hills so follow them by imitation and obedience, that they prefer Christ to them: lest being led astray by the empty authority of evil mountains (for they seem to excel), they tear themselves away from the Unity of Christ. . . .

6. Thus also most pertinently may be understood, "let the mountains bear peace to the people," namely, that we understand the peace to consist in the reconciliation whereby we are reconciled to God: for the mountains receive this for His people. . . . "Let the mountains, therefore, receive peace for the people, and the hills justice: " so that in this manner, both being at one, there may come to pass that which hath been written, " justice and peace have kissed one another." [1] But that which other copies have, "let the mountains receive peace for the people, and let the hills: " I think must be understood of all sorts of preaching of Gospel peace, whether those that go before, or those that follow after. But in these copies this followeth, " in justice He shall judge the poor of the people." But those copies are more approved of which have that which we have expounded above, " let the mountains bear peace to the people, and the hills justice." But some have, "to Thy people;" some have not to "Thy," but only "to the people."

7. " He shall judge the poor of the people, and shall save the sons of the poor" (ver. 4). The poor and the sons of the poor seem to me to be the very same, as the same city is Sion and the daughter of Sion. But if it is to be understood with a distinction, the poor we take to be the mountains, but the sons of the poor the hills: for instance, Prophets and Apostles, the poor, but the sons of them, that is, those that profit under their authority, the sons of the poor. But that which hath been said above, " shall judge; " and afterwards, "shall save; " is as it were a sort of exposition in what manner He shall judge. For to this end He shall judge, that He may save, that is, may sever from those that are to be destroyed and condemned, those to whom He giveth " salvation ready to be revealed at the " last time.[2] For by such men to Him is said, " Destroy not with ungodly men my soul: " [3] and, " Judge Thou me, O God, and sever my cause from the nation unholy." [4] We must observe also that he saith not, He shall judge the poor people, but, " the poor of the

people." For above when he had said, " to judge Thy people in justice and Thy poor in judgment," [5] the same he called the people of God as His poor, that is, only the good and those that belong to the right hand side. But because in this world those for the right and those for the left feed together, who, like lambs and goats at the last are to be put asunder; [6] the whole, as it is mingled together, he hath called by the name of the People. And because even here he putteth judgment in a good sense, that is, for the purpose of saving: therefore he saith, " He shall judge the poor of the people," that is, shall sever for salvation those that are poor among the people. " And He shall humble the false-accuser." No false-accuser can be more suitably recognised here than the devil. False accusation in his business. " Doth Job worship God gratis? " [7] But the Lord Jesus doth humble him, by His grace aiding His own, in order that they may worship God gratis, that is, may take delight in the Lord.[8] He humbled him also thus; because when in Him the devil, that is, the prince of this world, had found nothing,[9] he slew Him by the false accusations of the Jews, whom the false-accuser made use of as his vessels, working in the sons of unbelief.[10] . . .

8. "And He shall endure to the sun," or, "shall endure with the sun " (ver. 5). For thus some of our writers have thought would be more exactly translated that which in the Greek is συμπαραμενεῖ. But if in Latin it could have been expressed in one word, it must have been expressed by *compermanebit:* however, because in Latin the word cannot be expressed, in order that the sense at least might be translated, it hath been expressed by, "He shall endure with the sun." For He shall co-endure to the sun is nothing else but, " He shall endure with the sun." But what great matter is it for Him to endure with the sun, through whom all things were made, and without whom nothing was made,[11] save that this prophecy hath been sent before for the sake of those who think that the religion of the Christian name up to a particular time in this world will live, and afterwards will be no more? [12] " He shall endure " therefore " with the sun," so long as the sun riseth and setteth, that is, so long as these times revolve, there shall not be wanting the Church of God, that is, Christ's body on earth. But that which he addeth, " and before the moon, generations of generations : " he might have expressed by, and before the sun, that is, both with the sun and before the sun: which would have been understood by both with times and before times. That then which goeth before time is eternal:

---

[1] Ps. lxxxv. 10.   [2] 1 Pet. i. 5.   [3] Ps. xxvi. 9.
[4] Ps. xliii. 1.

[5] Ps. lxxii. 2.   [6] Matt. xxv. 32.   [7] Job i. 9.
[8] Ps. xxxvii. 4.   [9] John xiv. 30.   [10] Eph. ii. 2.
[11] John i. 3.   [12] See on Ps. xli. p. 128, note 9.

and that is truly to be held eternal which by no time is changed, as, " in the beginning was the Word." [1] But by the moon he hath chosen rather to intimate the waxings and wanings of things mortal. Lastly, when he had said, " before the moon," wishing in a manner to explain for what purpose he inserted the moon, " generations," he saith, " of generations."   As though he were saying, before the moon, that is, before the generations of generations which pass away in the departure and succession of things mortal, like the lunar wanings and waxings. And thus what is better to be understood by His enduring before the moon, than that He taketh precedence of all mortal things by immortality?   Which also as followeth may not impertinently be taken, that whereas now, having humbled the false-accuser, He sitteth at the right hand of the Father, this is to endure with the sun. For the brightness of the eternal glory is understood to be the Son : [2] as though the Sun were the Father, and the Brightness of Him His Son. But as these things may be spoken of the invisible Substance of the Creator, not as of that visible creation wherein are bodies celestial, of which bright bodies the sun hath the pre-eminence, from which this similitude hath been drawn : just as they are drawn even from things earthly, to wit, stone, lion, lamb, man having two sons, and the like : therefore having humbled the false-accuser, He endureth with the sun : because having vanquished the devil by the Resurrection, He sitteth at the right hand of the Father,[3] where He dieth no more, and death no longer over Him shall have dominion.[4] This too is before the moon, as though the First-born from the dead were going before the Church, which is passing on in the departure and succession of mortals. These are " the generations of generations."   Or perchance it is because generations are those whereby we are begotten mortally ; but generations of generations those whereby we are begotten again immortally. And such is the Church which He went before, in order that He might endure before the moon, being the First-born of the dead. To be sure, that which is in the Greek γενεας γενεῶν, some have interpreted, not " generations," but, " of a generation of generations : " because γενεας is of ambiguous case in Greek, and whether it be the genitive singular της γενεᾶς, that is, of the generation, or the accusative plural τὰς γενεὰς, that is, the generations, doth not clearly appear, except that deservedly that sense hath been preferred wherein, as though explaining WHAT he had called " the moon," he added in continuation, " generations of generations."

9. " And He shall come down like rain into a

fleece, and like drops distilling upon the earth " (ver. 6). He hath called to our minds and admonished us, that what was done by Gedeon the Judge, in Christ hath its end. For he asked a sign of the Lord, that a fleece laid on the floor should alone be rained upon, and the floor should be dry ; and again, the fleece alone should be dry, and the floor should be rained upon ; and so it came to pass.[5] Which thing signified, that, being as it were on a floor in the midst of the whole round world, the dry fleece was the former people Israel. The same Christ therefore Himself came down like rain upon a fleece, when yet the floor was dry : whence also He said, " I am not sent but to the sheep which were lost of the house of Israel." [6] There He chose out a Mother by whom to receive the form of a servant, wherein He was to appear to men : there the disciples, to whom He gave this same injunction, saying, " Into the way of the nations go ye not away, and into the cities of the Samaritans enter ye not : go ye first to the sheep which are lost of the house of Israel." [7] When He saith, go ye first to them, He showeth also that hereafter, when at length the floor was to be rained upon, they would go to other sheep also, which were not of the old people Israel, concerning whom He saith, " I have other sheep which are not of this fold, it behoveth Me to bring in them also, that there may be one flock and one Shepherd." [8] Hence also the Apostle : " for I say," he saith, " that Christ was a minister of the Circumcision for the truth of God, to confirm the promises of the fathers." [9] Thus rain came down upon the fleece, the floor being yet dry. But inasmuch as he continueth, " but that the nations should glorify God for His mercy : " [10] that when the time came on, that should be fulfilled which by the Prophet He saith, " a people whom I have not known hath served Me, in the hearkening of the ear it hath obeyed Me : " [11] we now see, that of the grace of Christ the nation of the Jews hath remained dry, and the whole round world through all nations is being rained upon by clouds full of Christian grace. For by another word he hath indicated the same rain, saying, " drops distilling : " no longer upon the fleece, but " upon the earth."   For what else is rain but drops distilling? But that the above nation under the name of a fleece is signified, I think is either because they were to be stripped of the authority of teaching, just as a sheep is stripped of its skin ; or because in a secret place He was hiding that same rain, which He willed not should be preached to uncircumcision, that is, be revealed to uncircumcised nations.

10. " There shall arise in His days justice

---

[1] John i. 1.   [2] Heb. i. 3.   [3] Mark xvi. 19.
[4] Rom. vi. 9.

[5] Judg. vi. 36–38.   [6] Matt. xv. 24.   [7] Matt. x. 5, 6.
[8] John x. 16.   [9] Rom. xv. 8.   [10] Rom. xv. 9.
[11] Ps. xviii. 43.

and abundance of peace, until the moon be taken away" (ver. 7). The expression *tollatur* some have interpreted by "be taken away," but others by "be exalted," translating one Greek word, which is there used, ἀνταναιρεθῇ, just as each of them thought good. But they who have said, "be removed," and they who have said, "be taken away," do not so very much differ. For by the expression, "be removed," custom doth teach us that there should be rather implied, that a thing is taken away and is no more, than that it is raised to a higher place: but "be taken away" can be understood in no other way at all, than that a thing is destroyed: that is, it is no more: but by "be exalted," only that it is raised to a higher place. Which indeed when it is put in a bad sense is wont to signify pride: as is the passage, "In thy wisdom be not exalted."[1] But in a good sense it belongeth to a more exceeding honour, as, for instance, when anything is being raised; as is, "In the nights exalt ye your hands unto holy places, and bless ye the Lord."[2] Here then if we have understood the expression, "be removed," what will be, "until the moon be removed," but that it be so dealt with that it be no more? For perchance he willed this also to be perceived, that mortality is to be no longer, "when the last enemy shall be destroyed, death:"[3] so that abundance of peace may be brought down so far as that nothing may withstand the felicity of the blessed from the infirmity of mortality: which will come to pass in that age, of which we have the faithful promise of God through Jesus Christ our Lord, concerning which it is said, "There shall arise in His days justice and abundance of peace:" until, death being utterly overcome and destroyed, all mortality be consumed. But if under the term moon, not the mortality of the flesh through which the Church is now passing, but the Church Herself in general hath been signified, which is to endure for everlasting, being delivered from this mortality, thus must be taken the expression, "There shall arise in His days justice and abundance of peace, until the moon be exalted;" as though it were said, There shall arise in His days justice, to conquer the contradiction and rebellion of the flesh, and whereby there may be made a peace so increasing and abundant, until the moon be exalted, that is, until the Church be lifted up, through the glory of the Resurrection to reign with Him, who went before Her in this glory, the firstborn of the dead, that He might sit at the right hand of the Father;[4] thus with the sun[5] enduring before the moon, in the place whereunto hereafter was to be exalted the moon also.

11. "And He shall be Lord from sea even unto sea, and from the river even unto the ends of the round world" (ver. 8): He to wit concerning whom he had said, "There shall arise in His days justice and abundance of peace, until the moon be exalted."[6] If the Church here is properly signified under the term moon, in continuation he showed how widely that same Church He was going to spread abroad, when He added, "and He shall be Lord from sea even unto sea." For the land is encircled by a great sea which is called the Ocean: from which there floweth in some small part in the midst of the lands, and maketh those seas known to us, which are frequented by ships. Again, in "from sea even unto sea" He hath said, that from any one end of the earth even unto any other end, He would be Lord, whose name and power in the whole world were to be preached and to prevail exceedingly. To which, that there might not be understood in any other manner, "from sea even unto sea:" He immediately added, "and from the river even unto the ends of the round world." Therefore that which He saith in "even unto the ends of the round world," the same He had said before in "from sea even unto sea." But in that which now He saith, "from the river," He hath evidently expressed that He willed Christ to publish at length His power from that place from whence also He began to choose His disciples, to wit from the river Jordan, where upon the Lord, on His baptism, when the Holy Ghost descended, there sounded a voice from Heaven, "This is My beloved Son."[7] From this place then His doctrine and the authority of the heavenly ministry setting out, is enlarged even unto the ends of the round world, when there is preached the Gospel of the kingdom in the whole world, for a testimony unto all nations: and then shall come the end.[8]

12. "In His presence shall fall down the Ethiopians, and His enemies shall lick the earth" (ver. 9). By the Ethiopians, as by a part the whole, He hath signified all nations, selecting that nation to mention especially by name, which is at the ends of the earth. By "in His presence shall fall down" hath been signified, shall adore Him. And because there were to be schisms in divers quarters of the world, which would be jealous of the Church Catholic spread abroad in the whole round world, and again those same schisms dividing themselves into the names of men, and by loving the men under whose authority they had been rent, opposing themselves to the glory of Christ which is throughout all lands; so when He had said, "in His presence shall fall down the Ethi-

---

[1] Ecclus. xxxii. 4; Vulgate, xxxii. 6.   [2] Ps. cxxxiv. 2.
[3] 1 Cor. xv. 26.   [4] Mark xvi. 19.   [5] Or, "abiding."

[6] Ps. lxxii. 7.   [7] Matt. iii. 17.   [8] Matt. xxiv. 14.

opians," He added, "and His enemies shall lick the earth : " that is, shall love men, so that they shall be jealous of the glory of Christ, to whom hath been said, " Be Thou exalted above the Heavens, O God, and above all the earth Thy glory." [1]   For man earned to hear, " Earth thou art, and unto earth thou shalt go." [2]   By licking this earth, that is, being delighted with the vainly talking authority of such men, by loving them, and by counting them for the most pleasing of men, they gainsay the divine sayings, whereby the Catholic Church hath been foretold, not as to be in any particular quarter of the world, as certain schisms are, but in the whole universe by bearing fruit and growing so as to attain even unto the very Ethiopians, to wit, the remotest and foulest of mankind. [3]

13. [4] " The kings of Tharsis and the isles shall offer gifts, the kings of the Arabians and of Saba shall lead [5] presents " (ver. 10).   This no longer requireth an expounder but a thinker ; yea it doth thrust itself upon the sight not only of rejoicing believers, but also of groaning unbelievers — except perchance we must inquire why there hath been said, " shall lead presents."   For there are wont to be led those things which can walk.   For could it by any means have been spoken with reference to the sacrifice of victims ?   Far be it that such " righteousness " should arise in His days.   But those gifts which have been foretold as to be led, seem to me to signify men, whom into the fellowship of the Church of Christ the authority of kings doth lead : although even persecuting kings have led gifts, knowing not what they did, in sacrificing the holy Martyrs.   " And there shall adore Him all kings of the earth, all nations shall serve Him " (ver. 11).

14. But while he is explaining the reasons why so great honour is paid Him by kings, and He is served of all nations : " because He hath delivered," he saith, " the needy man from the mighty, and the poor man, to whom was no helper " (ver. 12).   This needy and poor man is the people of men believing in Him. In this people are also kings adoring Him.   For they do not disdain to be needy and poor, that is, humbly confessing sins, and needing the glory of God [6] and the grace of God, in order that this King, Son of the King, may deliver them from the mighty one.   For this same mighty one is he who above was called the Slanderer : whom mighty to subdue men to himself, and to hold them bound in captivity, not his virtue did make, but men's sins.   The

same is himself also called strong ; therefore here mighty also.   But He that hath humbled the slanderer and hath entered into the house of the strong man to bind him and to spoil his vessels, [7] He " hath delivered the needy and the poor man."   For this neither the virtue of any one could accomplish, nor any just man, nor any Angel.   When then there was no helper, by His coming He saved them Himself.

15. But it might occur to one ; if because of sins man was held by the devil, have sins pleased Christ, who saved the needy man from the mighty?   Far be it.   But " He it is that shall spare the helpless and poor man " (ver. 13) : that is, shall remit sins to the man, humble and not trusting in his own merits, or hoping for salvation because of his own virtue, but needing the grace of his Saviour.   But when he hath added, " and the souls of the poor He shall save : " he hath recommended to our notice both the aids of grace ; both that which is for the remission of sins, when he saith, " He shall spare the poor and needy man ; " and that which doth consist in the imparting of righteousness, when he hath added, " and the souls of the poor He shall save."   For no one is meet of himself for salvation (which salvation is perfect righteousness), unless God's grace aid : because the fulness of the law is nought but love, which doth not exist in us of ourselves, but is shed abroad in our hearts through the Holy Spirit which hath been given unto us. [8]

16. " From usuries and iniquity He shall redeem the souls of them " (ver. 14).   What are these usuries but sins, which are also called debts ? [9] But I think they have been called usuries, because more of ill is found in the punishments than hath been committed -in the sins.   For, for example's sake, while a man-slayer killeth only the body of a man, but can no wise hurt the soul ; of himself both soul and body is destroyed in hell.   Because of such despisers of present commandment and deriders of future punishment hath been said, " I coming would have exacted with usuries," [10] from these usuries are redeemed the souls of the poor by that blood which hath been shed for the remission of sins.   He shall redeem, I say, from usuries, by remitting sins which owed larger punishments : but He shall redeem from iniquity, by helping them by grace even to do righteousness.   Therefore the same two things have been repeated which were said above.   For in that which is above, " He shall spare the helpless and poor man," [11] there is understood " from usuries : " but in that which there he saith, " and the souls of the poor He shall save ; " there seemeth to have been implied, " from iniquity : " so that the words " He shall

[1] Ps. cviii. 5.   [2] Gen. iii. 19.
[3] [It must be borne in mind that the Hindoos as well as the sons of Phut were so called. — C.]
[4] Oxf. MSS. add here: " Observe, brethren, that it is said in this Psalm."
[5] Vid. infra.   [6] Rom. iii. 23.

[7] Matt. xii. 29.   [8] Rom v. 5.   [9] Matt. vi. 12.
[10] Matt. xxv. 27.   [11] Ps. lxxii. 13.

redeem," are understood with both. So when He shall spare the poor and helpless man, and shall save the souls of the poor: thus "from usuries and iniquity He shall redeem the souls of them. And honourable shall be the name of Him in the presence of them." For they give honour to His name for so great benefits, and they respond that "meet and right it is"[1] to render thanks to the Lord their God. Or, as some copies have it, "and honourable is the name of them in the presence of Him:" for even if Christians seem despicable to this world, the name of them in the presence of Him is honourable, who to them hath given it, no longer remembering those names in His lips, whereby before they used to be called, when they were bound fast by the superstitions of the Gentiles, or signed with names derived from their own evil deserts, before they were Christians, which name is honourable in the presence of Him, even if it seemeth despicable to enemies.

17. "And He shall live, and there shall be given to Him of the gold of Arabia" (ver. 15). There would not have been said, "and He shall live"(for of whom could not this be said, though living for ever so brief a space of time on this earth?) unless that life were being recommended to our notice, wherein He "dieth no more, and death over Him shall have no more dominion."[2] And thus, "and He shall live," that was despised in death: for, as another Prophet saith, "there shall be taken away from the earth the life of Him."[3] But what is, "and there shall be given to Him of the gold of Arabia"? For the fact that from thence even the former Salomon received gold, in this Psalm hath been in a figure transferred unto another true Salomon, that is, the true Peace-maker. For the former did not have dominion "from the river even unto the ends of the round world."[4] Thus then hath been prophesied, that even the wise men of this world in Christ would believe. But by Arabia we understand the Gentiles; by gold wisdom, which doth as much excel among all doctrines as gold among metals. Whence hath been written, "Receive ye prudence as silver,[5] and wisdom as proved gold."[6] "And they shall pray concerning Himself alway." That which the Greek hath, περὶ αὐτοῦ, some have interpreted by "concerning Himself," some "for Himself," or "for Him." But what is, "concerning Himself," except perchance that for which we pray, saying, "Thy kingdom come"?[7] For Christ's coming shall make present to believers the kingdom of God. But how to understand "for Him" is difficult;

except that when prayer is made for the Church, for Himself prayer is made, because she is His Body. For concerning Christ and the Church hath been sent before a great Sacrament,[8] "there shall be two in one flesh." But now that which followeth, "all the day long," that is, in all time, "they shall bless Him," is sufficiently evident.

18. "And there shall be a firmament on the earth, on the tops of the mountains" (ver. 16). For, "all the promises of God in Him are Yea,"[9] that is, in Him are confirmed: because in Him hath been fulfilled whatever hath been prophesied for our salvation. For the tops of the mountains it is meet to understand as the authors of the divine Scriptures, that is, those persons through whom they were supplied: wherein He is indeed Himself the Firmament: for unto Him all things that have been divinely written are ascribed. But this He willed should be on earth; because for the sake of those that are upon earth, they were written. Whence He came also Himself upon earth, in order that He might confirm all these things, that is, in Himself might show them to have been fulfilled. "For it was necessary," He saith, "for all things to be fulfilled which were written in the Law, and the Prophets, and Psalms, concerning Me:"[10] that is, "in the tops of the mountains."[11] For so there cometh in the last times the evident Mount of the Lord, prepared on the summit of the mountains: of which here he speaketh, "in the tops of the mountains." "Highly super-exalted above Libanus shall be His fruit." Libanus we are wont to take as this world's dignity: for Libanus is a mountain bearing tall trees, and the name itself is interpreted whiteness.[12] For what marvel, if above every brilliant state of this world there is superexalted the fruit of Christ, of which fruit the lovers have contemned all secular dignities? But if in a good sense we take Libanus, because of the "cedars of Libanus which He hath planted:"[13] what other fruit must be understood, that is being exalted above this Libanus, except that whereof the Apostle speaketh when he is going to speak concerning that love of his, "yet a pre-eminent way to you I show"?[14] For this is put forward even in the first rank of divine gifts, in the place where he saith, "but the fruit of the Spirit is love:"[15] and with this are conjoined the remaining words as consequent. "And they shall flourish from the city like hay of the earth." Because city is used ambiguously, and there is not annexed of Him, or of God, for there hath not been said, "from the city" of Him, or "from the city" of God, but only "from the city:" in a good sense it is understood, in order that from the city of God,

---

[1] *Dignum et justum*, used then, as still, in the service for Holy Communion. [In all the liturgies, according to Sir William Palmer. See A. N. F. vol. vii. p. 532, note 9.—C.]
[2] Rom vi. 9.   [3] Isa. liii. 8.
[4] Ps. lxxii. 8.   [5] "And not silver," E. V.
[6] Prov. viii. 10.   [7] Matt. vi. 10.

[8] Eph. v. 32.   [9] 2 Cor. i. 20.   [10] Luke xxiv. 44.
[11] Isa. ii. 2.   [12] *Candidatio*.   [13] Ps. civ. 16.
[14] 1 Cor. xii. 31.   [15] Gal. v. 22.

that is, from the Church, they may flourish like grass; but grass bearing fruit, as is that of wheat: for even this is called grass [1] in Holy Scripture; as in Genesis [2] there is a command for the earth to bring forth every tree and every grass, and there is not added every wheat: which without doubt would not have been passed over unless under the name of grass this also were understood; and in many other passages of the Scriptures this is found. But if we must take, "and they shall flourish like the grass of the earth," in the same manner as is said, "all flesh is grass, and the glory of a man like the flower of grass:" [3] certainly then that city must be understood which doth intimate this world's society: for it was not to no purpose that Cain was the first to build a city. [4] Thus the fruit of Christ being exalted above Libanus, that is, above enduring trees and undecaying timbers, because He is the everlasting fruit, all the glory of a man according to the temporal exaltation of the world is compared to grass; for by believers and by men already hoping for life eternal temporal felicity is despised, in order that there may be fulfilled that which hath been written, "all flesh is grass, and all the glory of flesh as the flower of grass: the grass hath dried, the flower hath fallen off, but the word of the Lord doth endure for ever." There is the fruit of Him exalted above Libanus. For always flesh hath been grass, and the glory of flesh as the flower of grass: but because it was not clearly proved what felicity ought to have been chosen and preferred, the flower of grass was esteemed for a great matter: not only it was by no means despised, but it was even chiefly sought after. As if therefore at that time He shall have begun to be thus, when there is reproved and despised whatever used to flourish in the world, thus hath been said, "superexalted above Libanus shall be the fruit of Him, and they shall flourish from the city like grass of the earth:" that is, glorified above all things shall be that which is promised for everlasting, and compared to the grass of the earth shall be whatever is counted a great matter in the world.

19. "Be," therefore, "the name of Him blessed for ever: before the sun endureth the name of Him" (ver. 17). By the sun times are signified. Therefore for everlasting endureth the name of Him. For eternity doth precede times, and is not bounded by time. "And there shall be blessed in Him all the tribes of the earth." For in Him is fulfilled that which hath been promised to Abraham. "For He saith not, In seeds, as though in many; but as though in one, And to thy Seed, which is Christ." [5] But to Abraham is said, "In thy Seed shall be blessed all the tribes of the earth." [6] And not the sons of the flesh but the sons of promise are counted in the Seed. [7] "All nations shall magnify Him." As if in explanation there is repeated that which above hath been said. For because they shall be blessed in Him, they shall magnify Him; not of themselves making Him to be great, that of Himself is great, but by praising and confessing Him to be great. For thus we magnify God: thus also we say, "Hallowed be Thy name," [8] which is indeed always holy.

20. "Blessed be the Lord God of Israel, who hath done wonderful things alone" (ver. 18). Contemplating all things above spoken of, a hymn bursteth [9] forth; and the Lord God of Israel is blessed. For that is being fulfilled which hath been spoken to that barren woman, "and He that hath delivered Thee, the God of Israel, shall Himself be called of the whole earth." [10] "He doeth" Himself "marvellous things alone:" for whosoever do them, He doth Himself work in them, "who doeth wonderful things alone." "And blessed be the name of His glory [11] for everlasting, and for age of age" (ver. 19). For what else should the Latin interpreters have said, who could not have said for everlasting, and for everlasting of everlasting? For it soundeth as if one thing were meant in the expression "for everlasting," and another thing in the expression "for age:" but the Greek hath εἰς τὸν αἰῶνα, καὶ εἰς τὸν αἰῶνα τοῦ αἰῶνος, which perchance more meetly might have been rendered by, "for age, and for age of age:" so that by "for age," might have been understood as long as this age [12] endureth; but "for age of age," that which after the end of this is promised to be. "And there shall be fulfilled with the glory of Him every land: so be it, so be it." Thou hast commanded, O Lord, so it is coming to pass: so it is coming to pass, until that which began with the river, may attain fully even unto the ends of the round world.

PSALM LXXIII. [13]

1. This Psalm hath an inscription, that is, a title, "There have failed the hymns of David, the son of Jesse. [14] A Psalm [15] of Asaph himself." So many Psalms we have on the titles whereof is written the name David, nowhere there is added, "son of Jesse," except in this alone. Which we must believe hath not been done to no purpose, nor capriciously. For everywhere

1 *Fœnum.*   2 Gen. i. 11. [See p. 206, *supra.*—C.]
3 Isa. xl. 6.   4 Gen. iv. 17.
5 Gal. iii. 16.

6 Gen. xxii. 18.   7 Rom. ix. 8.   8 Matt. vi. 9.
9 Lit. "is belched."   10 Isa. liv. 5.
11 "Majesty," most MSS., Ben.   12 Or, "world."
13 Lat. LXXII.
14 This sentence in our version and in the Vulgate stands at the end of the previous Psalm. [Where it is more significant. David can prophesy no further concerning the glory that shall be revealed. See A. N. F. vol. i. p. 211, note 3.—C.]
15 Title of Psalm lxxiii.

God doth make intimations to us, and to the understanding thereof doth invite the godly study of love. What is, "there have failed the hymns of David, the son of Jesse"? Hymns are praises of God accompanied with singing: hymns are songs containing the praise of God. If there be praise, and it be not of God, it is no hymn: if there be praise, and God's praise, and it be not sung, it is no hymn. It must needs then, if it be a hymn, have these three things, both praise, and that of God, and singing. What is then, "there have failed the hymns"? There have failed the praises which are sung unto God. He seemeth to tell of a thing painful, and so to speak deplorable. For he that singeth praise, not only praiseth, but only praiseth with gladness: he that singeth praise, not only singeth, but also loveth him of whom he singeth. In praise, there is the speaking forth of one confessing; in singing, the affection of one loving. "There have failed" then "the hymns of David," he saith: and he hath added, "the son of Jesse." For David was king of Israel, son of Jesse,[1] at a certain time of the Old Testament, at which time the New Testament was therein hidden, like fruit in a root. For if thou seek fruit in a root, thou wilt not find, and yet dost thou not find any fruit in the branches, except that which hath gone forth from the root. . . . And in like manner as Christ Himself to be born after the flesh was hidden in the root, that is in the seed of the Patriarchs, and at a certain time must be revealed, as at the fruit appearing, according as it is written, "there hath flourished a shoot from the root of Jesse:"[2] so also the New Testament itself which is in Christ, in those former times was hidden, being known to the Prophets alone, and to the very few godly men, not by the manifestation of things present, but by the revelation of things future. For what meaneth it, brethren (to mention but one thing), that Abraham sending his faithful servant to espouse a wife for his only son, maketh him swear to him, and in the oath saith to him, " Put thy hand under my thigh, and swear"?[3] What was there in the thigh of Abraham, where he put his hand in swearing? What was there there, except that which even then was promised to him, "In thy seed shall be blessed all nations"?[4] Under the name of thigh, flesh is signified. From the flesh of Abraham, through Isaac and Jacob, and not to mention many names, through Mary was our Lord Jesus Christ.

2. But that the root was in the Patriarchs, how shall we show? Let us question Paul. The Gentiles now believing in Christ, and desiring as it were to boast over the Jews who crucified Christ; although also from that same people there came another wall, meeting in the corner, that is, in Christ Himself, the wall of uncircumcision, that is, of the Gentiles, coming from a different quarter: when, I say, the nations were lifting up themselves, he doth thus depress them. "For if thou," he saith, "being cut out of the natural wild olive, hast been graffed in among them, do not boast against the branches: for if thou boastest, thou dost not bear the root, but the root thee."[5] Therefore he speaketh of certain branches broken off from the root of the Patriarchs because of unbelief, and the wild olive therein graffed in, that it might be partaker of the fatness of the olive, that is, the Church coming out of the Gentiles. And who doth graff the wild olive on the olive? The olive is wont to be graffed on the wild olive; the wild olive on the olive we never saw. For whosoever may have done so will find no berries but those of the wild olive. For that which is graffed in, the same groweth, and of that kind the fruit is found. There is not found the fruit of the root but of the graft. The Apostle showing that God did this thing by His Omnipotence, namely, that the wild olive should be graffed into the root of the olive, and should not bear wild berries, but olive — ascribing it to the Omnipotence of God, the Apostle saith this, "If thou hast been cut out of the natural wild olive and against nature hast been graffed into a good[6] olive, do not boast," he saith, "against the branches."[7] . . .

3. In the time then of the Old Testament, brethren, the promises from our God to that carnal people were earthly and temporal. There was promised an earthly kingdom, there was promised that land into which they were also led, after being delivered from Egypt: by Jesus[8] son of Nave they were led into the land of promise, where also earthly Jerusalem was builded, where David reigned: they received the land, after being delivered from Egypt, by passing through the Red Sea. . . . Such were also those promises, which were not to endure, through which however were figured future promises which were to endure, so that all that course of temporal promises was a figure and a sort of prophecy of things future. Accordingly when that kingdom was failing, where reigned David, the son of Jesse, that is, one that was a man, though a Prophet, though holy, because he saw and foresaw Christ to come, of whose seed also after the flesh He was to be born: nevertheless a man, nevertheless not yet Christ, nevertheless not yet our King Son of God, but king David son of Jesse: because then that kingdom

---

[1] 1 Sam. xvi. 19. [2] Isa. xi. 1.
[3] Gen. xxiv. 2. [See p. 148, note 11, supra. — C.]
[4] Gen. xxii. 18.

[5] Rom. xi. 17, 18.
[6] Ben. notes that the word "good" is not in the MSS.; it is found at Oxford, and probably in MSS. used for earlier editions.
[7] Rom. xi. 24, 18.
[8] [i.e., Joshua the son of Nun. — C.]

was to fail, through the receiving of which kingdom at that time God was praised by carnal men; for this thing alone they esteemed a great matter, namely, that they were delivered temporally from those by whom they were being oppressed, and that they had escaped from persecuting enemies through the Red Sea, and had been led through the desert, and had found country and kingdom: for this alone they praised God, not yet perceiving the thing which God was designing beforehand and promising in these figures. In the failing therefore of those things for which the carnal people, over whom reigned that David, was praising God, "there failed the hymns of David," not the Son of God, but the "son of Jesse." . . .

4. Whose voice is the Psalm? "Of Asaph."[1] What is Asaph? As we find in interpretations from the Hebrew language into the Greek, and those again translated to us from the Greek into the Latin, Asaph is interpreted Synagogue. It is the voice therefore of the Synagogue. But when thou hast heard Synagogue, do not forthwith abhor it, as if it were the murderer of the Lord. That Synagogue was indeed the murderer of the Lord, no man doubteth it: but remember, that from the Synagogue were the rams whereof we are the sons. Whence it is said in a Psalm, "Bring ye to the Lord the sons of rams."[2] What rams are thence? Peter, John, James, Andrew, Bartholomew, and the rest of the Apostles. Hence also he too at first Saul, afterwards Paul: that is, at first proud, afterwards humble. . . . Therefore even Paul came to us from the Synagogue, and Peter and the other Apostles from the Synagogue. Therefore when thou hast heard the voice of the Synagogue, do not look to the deserving thereof, but observe the offspring. There is speaking therefore in this Psalm, the Synagogue, after the failing of the hymns of David, the son of Jesse: that is, after the failing of things temporal, through which God was wont to be praised by the carnal people. But why did these fail, except in order that others might be sought for? That there might be sought for what? Was it things which were not there? No, but things which were there being hidden in figures: not which were not yet there,[3] but which there as it were in a sort were concealed in certain secret things of mysteries. What things? "These," saith the Apostle himself, "were our figures."[4] . . .

5. It was the Synagogue therefore, that is, they that there worshipped God after a godly sort, but yet for the sake of earthly things, for the sake of these present things (for there are ungodly men who seek the blessings of present things from demons: but this people was on this account better than the Gentiles, because although it were blessings present and temporal, yet they sought them from the One God, who is the Creator of all things both spiritual and corporal). When therefore those godly men after the flesh were observing—that is that Synagogue which was made up of good men, men for the time good, not spiritual men, such as were the Prophets therein, such as were the few that understood the kingdom heavenly, eternal—that Synagogue, I say, observed what things it received from God, and what things God promised to that people, abundance of things earthly, land, peace, earthly felicity: but in all these things were figures, and they not perceiving what was there concealed in things figured, thought that God gave this for a great matter, and had nothing better to give to men loving Him and serving Him: they remarked and saw certain sinners, ungodly, blasphemers, servants of demons, sons of the Devil, living in great naughtiness and pride, yet abounding in such things earthly, temporal, for which sort of things they were serving God themselves: and there sprang up a most evil thought in the heart, which made the feet to totter, and almost slip out of God's way. And behold this thought was in the people of the Old Testament: I would it be not in our carnal brethren, when now openly there is being proclaimed the felicity of the New Testament. . . .

6. "How good is the God of Israel!" But to whom? "To men right in heart" (ver. 1). To men perverse what? Perverse He seemeth. So also in another Psalm He saith: "With a holy man holy Thou shalt be, and with the innocent man innocent Thou shalt be, and with the perverse man perverse Thou shalt be."[5] What is, perverse Thou shalt be with the perverse man? Perverse the perverse man shall think Thee. Not that by any means God is made perverse. Far be it: what He is, He is. But in like manner as the sun appeareth mild to one having clear, sound, healthy, strong eyes, but against weak eyes doth dart hard spears, so to say; the former looking at it it doth invigorate, the latter it doth torture, though not being itself changed, but the man being changed: so when thou shalt have begun to be perverse, and to thee God shall seem to be perverse, thou art changed, not He. That therefore to thee will be punishment which to good men is joy. He calling to mind this thing, saith, "How good is the God of Israel to men right in heart!"

7. But what to thee? "But my feet were almost moved" (ver. 2). When were the feet moved, except when the heart was not right?

[1] See Title of Psalm.   [2] Ps. xxix. 1, Gr. and Lat.
[3] Oxf. MSS. add, "not which," etc.
[4] 1 Cor. x. 6.
[5] Ps. xviii. 25.

Whence was the heart not right? Hear: "My steps were well nigh overthrown." What he hath meant by "almost," the same he hath meant by "well nigh:" and what he hath meant by "my feet were almost moved," the same he hath meant by "my steps were overthrown." Almost my feet were moved, almost my steps were overthrown. Moved were the feet: but whence were the feet moved and the steps overthrown? Moved were the feet to going astray, overthrown were the steps to falling: not entirely, but "almost." But what is this? Already I was going to stray, I had not gone: already I was falling, I had not fallen.

8. But why even this? "For I was jealous," he saith, "in the case of sinners, looking on the peace of sinners" (ver. 3). I observed sinners, I saw them to have peace. What peace? Temporal, transient, falling, and earthly: but yet such as I also was desiring of God. I saw them that served not God to have that which I desired in order that I might serve God: and my feet were moved, and my steps were almost overthrown. But why sinners have this, he saith briefly: "Because there is no avoidance of their death, and there is a firmament in their scourge" (ver. 4). Now I have perceived, he saith, why they have peace, and flourish on the earth; because of their death there is no avoidance, because death sure and eternal doth await them, which neither doth avoid them, nor can they avoid it, "because there is no avoidance of their death, and there is a firmament in their scourge." And there is a firmament in their scourge. For their scourge is not temporal, but firm for everlasting. Because of these evil things then which are to be to them eternal, now what? "In the labours of men they are not, and with men they shall not be scourged" (ver. 5). Doth not even the devil himself escape scourging with men, for whom nevertheless an eternal punishment is being prepared?

9. Wherefore on this account what do these men, while they are not scourged, while they labour not with men? "Therefore," he saith, "there hath holden them pride" (ver. 6). Observe these men, proud, undisciplined; observe the bull, devoted for a victim, suffered to stray at liberty; and to damage whatever he may, even up to the day of his slaughter. Now it is a good thing, brethren, that we should hear in the very words of a prophet of this bull as it were, whereof I have spoken. For thus of him the Scripture doth make mention in another place: he saith that they are, as it were, made ready as for a victim, and that they are spared for an evil liberty.[1] "Therefore," he saith, "there hath holden them pride." What is, "there hath

holden them pride"? "They have been clothed about with their iniquity and ungodliness." He hath not said, covered; but, "clothed about," on all sides covered up with their ungodliness. Deservedly miserable, they neither see nor are seen, because they are clothed about; and the inward parts of them are not seen. For whosoever could behold the inward parts of evil men, that are as it were happy for a time, whosoever could see their torturing consciences, whosoever could examine their souls racked with such mighty perturbations of desires and fears, would see them to be miserable even when they are called happy. But because "they are clothed about with their iniquity and ungodliness," they see not; but neither are they seen. The Spirit knew them, that saith these words concerning them: and we ought to examine such men with the same eye as that wherewith we know that we see, if there is taken from our eyes the covering of ungodliness. . . .

10. At first these men are being described. "There shall go forth as if out of fat their iniquity" (ver. 7). . . . A poor beggar committeth a theft; out of leanness hath gone forth the iniquity: but when a rich man aboundeth in so many things, why doth he plunder the things of others? Of the former the iniquity out of leanness, of the other out of fatness, hath gone forth. Therefore to the lean man when thou sayest, Why hast thou done this? Humbly afflicted and abject he replieth, Need hath compelled me. Why hast thou not feared God? Want was urgent. Say to a rich man, Why doest thou these things, and fearest not God?—supposing thee to be great enough to be able to say it—see if he even deigneth to hear; see if even against thyself[2] there will not go forth iniquity out of his fatness. For now they declare war with their teachers and reprovers, and become enemies of them that speak the truth, having been long accustomed to be coaxed with the words of flatterers, being of tender ear, of unsound heart. Who would say to a rich man, Thou hast ill done in robbing other men's goods? Or perchance if any man shall have dared to speak, and he is such a man as he could not withstand, what doth he reply? All that he saith is in contempt of God. Why? Because he is proud. Why? Because he is fat. Why? Because he is devoted for a victim. "They have passed over unto purpose of heart." Here within they have passed over. What is, "they have passed over"? They have crossed over the way. What is, "they have passed over"? They have exceeded the bounds of mankind, men like the rest they think not themselves. They have passed over, I say, the bounds of mankind. When thou sayest to

---

[1] Prov. vii. 22.

[2] Ed. *in teipso;* Ben. conj. and Oxf. MSS. *in teipsum.*

such a man, Thy brother this beggar is; when thou sayest to such a man, Thy brother [1] this poor man is; the same parents ye have had, Adam and Eve: do not heed thy haughtiness, do not heed the vapour unto which thou hast been elevated; although an establishment waiteth about thee, although countless gold and silver, although a marbled house doth contain thee, although fretted ceilings cover thee, thou and the poor man together have for covering that roof of the universe, the sky; but thou art different from the poor man in things not thine own, added to thee from without: thyself see in them, not them in thee. Observe thyself, how thou art in relation to the poor man; thyself, not that which thou hast. For why dost thou despise thy brother? In the bowels of your mothers ye were both naked. Forsooth, even when ye shall have departed this life, and these bodies shall have rotted, when the soul hath been breathed forth, let the bones of the rich and poor man be distinguished! I am speaking of the equality of condition, of that very lot of mankind, wherein all men are born: [2] for both here doth a man become rich, and a poor man will not alway be here: and as a rich man doth not come rich, so neither doth he depart rich; the very same is the entrance of both, and like is the departure. I add, that perchance ye will change conditions. Now everywhere the Gospel is being preached: observe a certain poor man full of sores, who was lying before the gate of a rich man,[3] and was desiring to be filled with crumbs, which used to fall from the table of the rich man; observe also that likeness [4] of thine who was clothed with purple and fine linen, and fared sumptuously every day. It chanced, I say, for that poor man to die, and to be borne by the Angels into the bosom of Abraham: but the other died and was buried; for the other's burial perchance no one cared. . . . Brethren, how great was the toil of the poor man! Of how long duration were the luxuries of the rich man! But the condition which they have received in exchange is everlasting. . . . Deservedly too late he will say, "Send Lazarus," [5] "let him tell even my brethren;" since to himself there is not granted the fruit of repentance. For it is not that repentance [6] is not given, but everlasting will be the repentance, and no salvation after repentance. Therefore these men "have passed over unto purpose of heart."

11. "They have thought and have spoken spitefulness" (ver. 8). But men do speak spitefulness even with fear: but these men how? "Iniquity on high they have spoken." Not only

they have spoken iniquity; but even openly, in the hearing of all, proudly; "I will do it;" "I will show you;" "thou shalt know with whom thou hast to do;" "I will not let thee live." Thou [7] mightest have but thought such things, not have given utterance to them! Within the chambers of thought at least the evil desire might have been confined, he might have at least restrained it within his thought. Why? Is he perchance lean? "There shall go forth as if out of fatness the iniquity of them." "Iniquity on high they have spoken."

12. "They have set against Heaven their mouth, and their tongue hath passed over above the earth"(ver. 9). For this, "hath passed over above the earth" is, they pass over all earthly things? What is it to pass over all earthly things? He doth not think of himself as a man that can die suddenly, when he is speaking; he doth menace as if he were alway to live: his thought doth transcend earthly frailty, he knoweth not with what sort of vessel he is enwrapped; he knoweth not what hath been written in another place concerning such men: "His spirit shall go forth, and he shall return unto his earth, in that day shall perish all his thoughts." [8] But these men not thinking of their last day, speak pride,[9] and unto Heaven they set their mouth, they transcend the earth. If a robber were not to think of his last day, that is, the last day of his trial, when sent to prison, nothing would be more monstrous than he: and yet he might escape. Whither dost thou flee to escape death? Certain will that day be. What is the long time which thou hast to live? How much is the long time which hath an end, even if it were a long time? To this there is added that it is nought: and the very thing which is called long time is not a long time, and is uncertain. Why doth he not think of this? Because he hath set against Heaven his mouth, and his tongue hath passed over above the earth. "And full days shall be found in them."

13. "Therefore there shall return hither My people" (ver. 10). Now Asaph himself is returning hither. For he saw these things abound to unrighteous men, he saw them abound to proud men: he is returning to God, and is beginning to inquire and discuss. But when? "When full days shall be found in them." What is "full days"? "But when there came the fulness of time, God sent His Son." [10] This is the very fulness of time, when He came to teach men that things temporal should be despised, that they should not esteem as a great matter whatever object evil men covet, that they should suffer whatever evil men fear. He became the

---

[1] The words from "this beggar," added from Oxf. mss.
[2] [See A. N. F. vol. vii. p. 151. — C.]
[3] Luke xvi. 19.   [4] Al. "father."   [5] Luke xvi. 27.
[6] Used, of course, in the lower sense. [The sense, i.e., of mere attrition. See Roman doctrine, Liguori, vol. iv. p. 245, ed. Paris, 1852. — C.]

[7] Oxf. mss. and some of Ben. "Thou proud man, thou," etc.
[8] Ps. cxlvi. 4.   [9] Oxf. and other mss. "proud things."
[10] Gal. iv. 4.

way, He recalled us to inward thought, admonished us of what should be sought of God. And see from what thought reacting upon itself, and in a manner recalling the waves of its impulse, he doth pass over unto choosing true things.

14. "And they said, How hath God known, and is there knowledge in the Most High?" (ver. 11). See through what thought they pass. Behold unjust men are happy, God doth not care for things human. Doth He indeed know what we do? See what things are being said. We are inquiring, brethren, "How hath God known," etc. (no longer let Christians say it). For how doth it appear to thee that God knoweth not, and that there is no knowledge in the Most High? He replieth, "Lo! themselves they are sinners, and in the world they have gotten abundant riches" (ver. 12). Both sinners they are, and in the world they have gotten abundant riches. He confessed that he willed not to be a sinner in order that he might have riches. A carnal soul for things visible and earthly would have sold its justice. What sort of justice is that which is retained for the sake of gold, as if gold were a more precious thing than justice herself, or as if when a man denieth the deposit of another man's goods, he to whom he denied them should suffer a greater loss, than he that denieth them to him. The former doth lose a garment, the latter fidelity. "Lo! they are themselves sinners, and in the world they have gotten abundant riches." On this account therefore God knoweth not, and on this account there is no knowledge in the Most High.

15. "And I said, therefore[1] without cause I have justified my heart" (ver. 13). In that I serve God, and have not these things; they serve him not, and they abound in these things: "therefore without cause I have justified my heart, and have washed among the innocent my hands." This without cause I have done. Where is the reward of my good life? Where is the wage of my service? I live well and am in need; and the unjust man doth abound. "And I have washed among the innocent my hands. And I have been scourged all the day long" (ver. 14). From me the scourges of God do not impart. I serve well, and I am scourged; he serveth not, and is honoured. He hath proposed to himself a great question. The soul is disturbed, the soul doth pass over things which are to pass away unto despising things earthly and to desiring things eternal. There is a passage of the soul herself in this thought; where she doth toss in a sort of tempest she will reach the harbour. And it is with her as it is with sick persons, who are less violently sick, when recovery is far off: when recovery is at hand

they are in higher fever; physicians call it the "critical[2] accession" through which they pass to health: greater fever is there, but leading to health: greater heat, but recovery is at hand. So also is this man enfevered. For these are dangerous words, brethren, offensive, and almost blasphemous, "How hath God known?" This is why I say, "and almost;" He hath not said, God hath not known: he hath not said, there is no knowledge in the Most High: but as if inquiring, hesitating, doubting. This is the same as he said a little before, "My steps were almost overthrown."[3] He doth not affirm it, but the very doubt is dangerous. Through danger he is passing to health. Hear now the health: "Therefore in vain I have justified my heart, and have washed among the innocent my hands: and I have been scourged all the day long, and my chastening was in the morning." Chastening is correction. He that is being chastened is being corrected. What is, "in the morning"? It is not deferred. That of the ungodly is being deferred, mine is not deferred: the former is too late or is not at all; mine is in the morning.

16. "If I said, I shall declare thus; behold, the generation of Thy sons I have reprobated" (ver. 15): that is, I will teach thus. How wilt thou teach? that there is no knowledge in the Most High, that God doth not know? Wilt thou propound this opinion, that without cause men live justly who do live justly; that a just man hath lost his service, because God doth more show favour to evil men, or else He doth care for no one? Wilt thou tell this, declare this? He doth restrain himself by an authority repressing him. What authority? A man wisheth some time to break out in this sentiment: but he is recalled by the Scriptures directing us alway to live well, saying, that God doth care for things human, that He maketh a distinction between a godly man and an ungodly man. Therefore this man also wishing to put forth this sentiment, doth recollect himself. And what saith he? "I have reprobated the generation of Thy sons." If I shall declare thus, the generation of just men I shall reprobate. As also some copies have it, "Behold, the generation of thy sons with which I have been in concert:" that is, with which consisting of Thy sons I have been in concert; that is, with which I have agreed, to which I have been conformed: I have been out of time with all, if so I teach. For he doth sing in concert who giveth the tune together; but he that giveth not the tune together doth not sing in concert. Am I to say something different from that which Abraham said, from that which Isaac said, from that which Jacob said, from that which the Prophets said?

---

[1] MSS. want "therefore."　　　[2] MSS. *creticam.*　　　[3] Ps. lxxiii. 2.

For all they said that God doth care for things human, am I to say that He careth not? Is there greater wisdom in me than in them? Greater understanding in me than in them? A most wholesome authority hath called back his thought from ungodliness. And what followeth? That he might not reprobate, he did what? "And I undertook to know" (ver. 16). May God be with him in order that he may know. Meanwhile, brethren, from a great fall he is being withheld, when he doth not presume that he already knoweth, but hath undertaken to know that which he knew not. For but now he was willing to appear as if knowing, and to declare that God hath no care of things human. For this hath come to be a most naughty and ungodly doctrine of unrighteous men. Know, brethren, that many men dispute and say that God careth not for things human, that by chances all things are ruled, or that our wills have been made subject to the stars, that each one is not dealt with according to his deserts, but by the necessity of his stars, — an evil doctrine, an impious doctrine. Unto these thoughts was going that man whose feet were almost moved, and whose steps were all but overthrown, into this error he was going; but because he was not in tune with the generation of the sons of God, he undertook to know, and condemned the knowledge wherein with God's just men he agreed not. And what he saith let us hear; how that he undertook to know, and was helped, and learned something, and declared it to us. "And I undertook," he saith, "to know." "In this labour is before me." Truly a great labour; to know in what manner both God doth care for things human, and it is well with evil men, and good men labour. Great is the importance of the question; therefore, "and this labour is before me." As it were there is standing in my face a sort of wall, but thou hast the voice of a Psalm, "In my God I shall pass over the wall." [1]

17. . . . And he hath done this; for he saith how long labour is before him; "until I enter into the sanctuary of God, and understand upon the last things" (ver. 17). A great thing it is, brethren: now for a long time I labour, he saith, and before my face I see a sort of insuperable labour, to know in what manner both God is just, and doth care for things human, and is not unjust because men sinning and doing wicked actions have happiness on this earth; but the godly and men serving God are wasted ofttimes in trials and in labours; a great difficulty it is to know this, but only "until I enter into the Sanctuary of God." For in the Sanctuary what is presented to thee, in order that

thou mayest solve this question? "And I understand," he saith, "upon the last things:" not present things. I, he saith, from the Sanctuary of God stretch out mine eye unto the end, I pass over present things. All that which is called the human race, all that mass of mortality is to come to the balance, is to come to the scale, thereon will be weighed the works of men. All things now a cloud doth enfold: but to God are known the merits of each severally. "And I understand," he saith, "upon the last things:" but not of myself; for before me there is labour. Whence "may I understand upon the last things"? Let me enter into the Sanctuary of God. In that place then he understood also the reason why these men now are happy.

18. To wit, "because of deceitfulness Thou hast set upon them" (ver. 18). Because deceitful they are, that is fraudulent; because deceitful they are, they suffer deceits. What is this, because fraudulent they are they suffer a fraud? They desire to play a fraud upon mankind in all their naughtinesses, they themselves also suffer a frand, in choosing earthly good things, and in forsaking the eternal. Therefore, brethren, in their very playing off a fraud they suffer a fraud. In that which but now I said, brethren, "What manner of wit [2] hath he who to gain a garment doth lose his fidelity?" hath he whose garment he hath taken suffered a fraud, or he that is smitten with so great a loss? If a garment is more precious than fidelity, the former doth suffer the greater loss: but if incomparably good faith doth surpass the whole world, the latter shall seem to have sustained the loss of a garment; but to the former is said, "What doth it profit a man if he gain the whole world, but suffer the loss of his own soul?" [3] Therefore what hath befallen them? "Because of deceitfulness Thou hast set for them: Thou didst throw them down while they were being exalted." He hath not said, Thou didst throw them down because they were lifted up: not as it were after that they were lifted up Thou didst throw them down; but in their very lifting up they were thrown down. For thus to be lifted up is already to fall.

19. "How have they become a desolation suddenly?" (ver. 19). He is wondering at them, understanding unto the last things. "They have vanished." Truly like smoke, which while it mounteth upward, doth vanish, so they have vanished. How doth he say, "They have vanished"? In the manner of one who understandeth the last things: "they have perished because of their iniquity." "Like as the dream of one rising up" (ver. 20). How have they vanished? As vanisheth the dream of one rising up.

---

[1] Ps. xviii. 29.   [2] Cor.   [3] Matt. xvi. 26.

Fancy a man in sleep to have seen himself find treasures; he is a rich man, but only until he awaketh. "Like as the dream of one rising up:" so they have vanished, like the dream of one awaking. It is sought then and it is not: there is nothing in the hands, nothing in the bed. A poor man he went to sleep, a rich man in sleep he became: had he not awoke, he were a rich man: he woke up, he found the care which he had lost while sleeping. And these men shall find the misery which they had prepared for themselves. When they shall have awoke from this life, that thing doth pass away which was grasped as if in sleep. "Like as the dream of one rising up." And that there might not be said, "What then? a small thing doth their glory seem to thee, a small thing doth their state seem to thee, small things seem to thee inscriptions, images, statues, distinctions, troops of clients?" "O Lord," he saith, "in Thy city their image [1] Thou shalt bring to nothing." . . . He hath taken away the pride of rich men, he giveth counsel.[2] As if they[3] were saying, We are rich men, thou dost forbid us to be proud, dost prohibit us from boasting of the parade of our riches: what then are we to do with these riches? Is it come to this, that there is nothing which they may do therewith? "Be they rich," he saith, "in good works; let them readily distribute, communicate."[4] And what doth this profit? "Let them treasure unto themselves a good foundation for the future, that they may lay hold of true life."[5] Where ought they to lay up treasure for themselves? In that place whereunto he set his eye, when entering into the Sanctuary of God. Let there shudder all our rich brethren, abounding in money, gold, silver, household, honours, let them shudder at that which but now hath been said, "Thou shalt bring to nothing their image." Are they not worthy to suffer these things, to wit that God bring to nothing their image in His city, because also they have themselves brought to nothing the image of God in their earthly city?

20. "Because my heart was delighted" (ver. 21). He is saying with what things he is tempted: "because my heart was delighted," he saith, "my reins also were changed." When those temporal things delighted me, my reins were changed. It may also be understood thus: "because my heart was delighted" in God, "my reins also were changed, that is, my lusts were changed, and I became wholly chaste. "My reins were changed." And hear how. "And I was brought unto nothing, and I knew not" (ver. 22). I,

the very man, who now say these things of rich men, once longed for such things: therefore " even I was brought to nothing " when my steps were almost overthrown. "And I was brought unto nothing, and I knew not." We must not therefore despair even of them, against whom I was saying such things.

21. What is, "I knew not"? "As it were a beast I became to Thee, and I am alway with Thee "(ver. 23). There is a great difference between this man and others. He became as it were a beast in longing for earthly things, when being brought to nothing he knew not things eternal: but he departed not from his God, because he did not desire these things of demons, of the devil. For this I have already brought to your notice. The voice is from the Synagogue, that is, from that people which served not idols. A beast indeed I became, when desiring from my God things earthly: but I never departed from That my God.

22. Because then, though having become a beast, I departed not from my God, there followeth, "Thou hast held the hand of my right hand." He hath not said my right hand, but " the hand of my right hand." If the hand of the right hand it is, a hand hath a hand. "The hand Thou hast held of my right hand," in order that Thou mightest conduct me. For what hath he put hand? For power. For we say that a man hath that in his hand which he hath in his power: just as the devil said to God concerning Job, "Lay to Thine hand, and take away the things which he hath."[6] What is, lay to Thine hand? Put[7] forth power. The hand of God he hath called the power of God: as hath been written in another place, "death and life are in the hands of the tongue."[8] Hath the tongue hands? But what is, in the hands of the tongue? In the power of the tongue. What is, in the power of the tongue? "Out of thy mouth thou shalt be justified, and out of thy mouth thou shalt be condemned."[9] "Thou hast held," therefore, "the hand of my right hand," the power of my right hand. What was my right hand? That I was alway with Thee. Unto the left I was holding, because I became a beast, that is, because there was an earthly concupiscence in me: but the right was mine, because I was alway with thee. Of this my right hand Thou hast held the hand, that is, hast directed the power. What power? "He gave them power to become sons of God."[10] He is beginning now to be among the sons of God, belonging to the New Testament. See in what manner the hand of his right hand was held. "In Thy will Thou hast conducted me." What is, "in thy will"? Not in my merits. What is, "in Thy

[1] Oxf. MSS. "images."
[2] [He uses the word *ferimus* in the omitted paragraph. — C.] He seems to mean, that such teaching, addressed to any one in common intercourse, would be "smiting."
[3] Oxf. MSS. "the rich."   [4] 1 Tim. vi. 18.
[5] 1 Tim. vi. 19.

[6] Job i. 11.   [7] Lit. "give."   [8] Prov. xviii. 21.
[9] Matt. xii. 37.   [10] John i. 12.

will"? Hear the apostle, who was at first a beast longing for things earthly, and living after the Old Testament. He saith what? " I that at first was a blasphemer, and persecutor, and injurious: but mercy I obtained." [1] What is, "in Thy will"? " By the grace of God I am what I am." [2] " And in [3] glory Thou hast taken me up." Now to what glory he was taken up, and in what glory, who can explain, who can say? Let us await it, because in the Resurrection it will be, in the last things it will be.

23. And he is beginning to think of that same Heavenly felicity, and to reprove himself, because he hath been a beast, and hath longed for things earthly. " For what have I in Heaven, and from Thee what have I willed upon earth?" (ver. 25). By your voice I see that ye have understood.[4] He compared with his earthly will the heavenly reward which he is to receive; he saw what was there being reserved for him; and while thinking and burning at the thought of some ineffable thing, which neither eye hath seen, nor ear heard, nor into the heart of man hath ascended,[5] he hath not said, this or that I have in Heaven, but, " what have I in Heaven?" What is that thing which I have in Heaven? What is it? How great is it? Of what sort is it? " And," since that which I have in heaven doth not pass away, "from Thee what have I willed upon earth?" [6]. . . Thou reservest, he saith, for me in Heaven riches immortal, even Thyself, and I have willed from Thee on earth that which even ungodly men have, which even evil men have, which even abandoned men have, money, gold, silver, jewels, households, which even many wicked men have: which even many profligate women have, many profligate men: these things as a great matter I have desired of my God upon earth: though my God reserveth Himself for me in Heaven!

24. " My heart and my flesh hath failed, O God of my heart" (ver. 26). This then for me in Heaven hath been reserved, " God of my heart, and my portion is my God." What is it, brethren? Let us find out our riches, let mankind choose their parts. Let us see men torn with diversity of desires: let some choose war-service, some advocacy, some divers and sundry offices of teaching, some merchandise, some farming, let them take their portions in human affairs: let the people of God cry, " my portion is my God." Not for a time "my portion;" but " my portion is my God for everlasting." Even if I alway have gold, what have I? Even if I

did not alway have God, how great a good should I have? To this is added, that He promiseth Himself to me, and He promiseth that I shall have this for everlasting. So great a thing I have, and never have it not. Great felicity: " my portion is God!" How long? " For everlasting." For behold and see after what sort He hath loved him; He hath made his heart chaste: " God of my heart, and my portion is God for everlasting." His heart hath become chaste, for nought now God is loved, from Him is not sought any other reward. He that doth seek any other reward from God, and therefore is willing to serve God, more precious doth make that which he willeth to receive, than Him from whom he willeth to receive. What then, is there no reward belonging to God? None except Himself. The reward belonging to God, is God Himself. This he loveth, this he esteemeth; if any other thing he shall have loved, the love will not be chaste. Thou art receding from the Fire immortal, thou wilt grow cold, wilt be corrupted. Do not recede. Recede not, it will be thy corruption, it will be thy fornication. Now he is returning, now he is repenting, now he is choosing repentance, now he is saying, " my portion is God." And after what sort is he delighted with that Same, whom he hath chosen for his portion.

25. " Behold, they that put themselves afar from Thee shall perish " (ver. 27). He therefore departed from God, but not far: for " I have become as it were a beast," he saith, and " I am alway with Thee." [7] But they have departed afar, because not only things earthly they have desired, but have sought them from demons and the Devil. " They that put themselves afar from Thee shall perish." And what is it, to become afar from God? " Thou hast destroyed every man that committeth fornication away from Thee." To this fornication is opposed chaste love. What is chaste love? Now the soul doth love her Bridegroom: what doth she require of Him, from Her Bridegroom whom she loveth? Perchance in like manner as women choose for themselves men either as sons-in-law or as bridegrooms: she perchance chooseth riches, and loveth his gold, and estates, and silver and cattle and horses, and household, and the like. Far be it. He doth love Him alone, for nought he doth love Him: because in Him he hath all things, for " by Him were made all things." [8]

26. But thou doest what? " But for me to cleave to God is a good thing " (ver. 28). This is whole good. Will ye have more? I grieve at your willing. Brethren, what will ye have more? Than to cleave to God nothing is better, when we shall see Him face to face.[9] But now

---

[1] 1 Tim. i. 13.   [2] 1 Cor. xv. 10.
[3] So mss.; Ben. " with."
[4] [Here there were voluntary " amens," or the like, from the people. See p. 207, *supra*. —C.]
[5] 1 Cor. ii. 9.
[6] [Here he interpolates: "I will speak as I am able, but forgive me: accept my endeavour, mine earnestness to attempt; for to explain it I have not power." —C.]

[7] Ps. lxxiii. 21.   [8] John i. 3.   [9] 1 Cor. xiii. 12.

what? For yet as a stranger I am speaking: "to cleave," he saith, "to God is a good thing:" but now in my sojourning (for not yet hath come the substance), I have "to put in God my hope." So long therefore as thou hast not yet cloven, therein put thy hope. Thou art wavering, cast forward an anchor to the land.[1] Not yet dost thou cleave by presence, cleave fast by hope. "To put in God my hope." And by doing what here wilt thou put in God thy hope? What will be thy business, but to praise Him whom thou lovest, and to make others to be fellow-lovers of Him with thee? Lo, if thou shouldest love a charioteer, wouldest thou not carry along other men to love him with thee? A lover of a charioteer whithersoever he goeth doth speak of him, in order that as well as he others also may love him. For nought are loved abandoned men, and from God is reward required in order that He may be loved? Love thou God for nought, grudge God to no one. . . . For what followeth? "In order that I may tell forth all Thy praises in the courts of the daughter of Sion." "In the courts:" for the preaching of God beside the Church is vain. A small thing it is to praise God and to tell forth all His praise. In the courts of the daughter of Sion tell thou forth. Make for unity, do not divide the people; but draw them unto one, and make them one. I have forgotten how long I have been speaking. Now the Psalm being ended, even judging by this closeness,[2] I suppose I have held a long discourse: but it doth not suffice for your zeal; ye are too impetuous.[3] O that with this impetuosity ye would seize upon the kingdom of Heaven.

PSALM LXXIV.[4]

1. This Psalm's Title is, "Of the Understanding of Asaph." Asaph in Latin is translated congregation, in Greek Synagogue. Let us see what this Synagogue hath understood. But let us understand firstly Synagogue: from thence we shall understand what the Synagogue hath understood. Every congregation is spoken of under the general name of Synagogue: one both of beasts and of men may be called a congregation; but here there is no congregation of beasts when we heard "understanding." . . . For this the Psalm's Title doth prescribe, saying, "Of the understanding of Asaph." It is therefore a certain understanding congregation whereof we are about to hear the voice. But since properly Synagogue is said of the congregation of the people of Israel, so that wheresoever we may have heard Synagogue, we are no longer

wont to understand any but the people of the Jews; let us see whether perchance the voice in this Psalm be not of that same people. But of what sort of Jews and of what sort of people of Israel? For they are not of the chaff, but perchance of the grain;[5] not of the broken branches, but perchance of those that are strengthened. "For not all that are of Israel are Israelites."[6] . . . There are therefore certain Israelites, of whom was he concerning whom was said, "Behold an Israelite indeed, in whom guile is not."[7] I do not say in the same manner as we are Israelites, for we also are the seed of Abraham. For to the Gentiles the Apostle was speaking, when he said, "Therefore the seed of Abraham ye are, heirs according to promise."[8] According to this therefore all we are Israelites, that follow the footsteps of the faith of our father Abraham. But let us understand here the voice of the Israelites in the same manner as the Apostle saith, "For I also am an Israelite, of the seed of Abraham, of the tribe of Benjamin."[9] Here therefore let us understand that whereof the Prophets have spoken, "a remnant shall be saved."[10] Of the remnant therefore saved let us hear in this place the voice; in order that there may speak that Synagogue which had received the Old Testament, and was intent upon carnal promises; and by this means it came to pass that their feet were shaken. For in another Psalm, where too the title hath Asaph, there is said what? "How good is the God of Israel to men right in heart. But my feet were almost moved."[11] And as if we were saying, whence were thy feet moved? "Well nigh," he saith, "my steps were overthrown, because I was jealous in the case of sinners, looking on the peace of sinners."[12] For while according to the promises of God belonging to the Old Testament he was looking for earthly felicity, he observed it to abound with ungodly men; that they who worshipped not God were enriched with those things which he was looking for from God: and as though without cause he had served God, his feet tottered. . . . But opportunely it hath chanced not by our own but by God's dispensation, that just now we heard out of the Gospel, that "the Law was given by Moses, Grace and Truth came by Jesus Christ."[13] For if we distinguish between the two Testaments, Old and New, there are not the same Sacraments[14] nor the same promises;[15] nevertheless, the same commandments[16] for the most part. . . . When examined they are either all found to be the same, or there are scarce any in the Gospel which have not been spoken by the Prophets.

---

[1] Oxf. mss. "Wavering, from the earth cast an anchor before thee upward."
[2] Odore, lit. "smell;" one ms. ardore, "heat;" Ben. conj. sudore.　[3] [P. 341, note 4, supra. — C.]
[4] Lat. LXXIII. Sermon to the people.

[5] Matt. iii. 12.　[6] Rom. ix. 6.　[7] John i. 47.
[8] Gal. iii. 29.　[9] Rom. xi. 1.　[10] Rom. ix. 27.
[11] Ps. lxxiii. 1, 2.　[12] Ps. lxxiii. 2.　[13] John i. 17.
[14] Sacramenta.　[15] Promissa.　[16] Præcepta.

The Commandments are the same, the Sacraments are not the same, the Promises are not the same. Let us see wherefore the commandments are the same; because according to these we ought to serve God. The Sacraments are not the same, for some Sacraments there are giving Salvation, others promising a Saviour. The Sacraments of the New Testament give Salvation, the Sacraments of the Old Testament did promise a Saviour.[1] When therefore thou hast now the things promised, why dost thou seek the things promising, having now the Saviour? . . . God through the New Testament hath taken out of the hands of His sons those things which are like the playthings of boys, in order that He might give something more useful to them growing up, on that account must He be supposed not to have given those former things Himself. He gave both Himself. But the Law itself through Moses was given, Grace and Truth came through Jesus Christ :[2] Grace because there is fulfilled through love that which by the letter was being enjoined, Truth because there is being rendered that which was promised. This thing therefore this Asaph hath understood. In a word, all things which to the Jews had been promised have been taken away. Where is their kingdom? Where the Temple? Where the Anointing? Where is Priest? Where are now the Prophets among them? From what time there came He that by the Prophets was foretold, in that nation there is now nothing of these things; now she hath lost things earthly, and not yet doth seek things Heavenly.

2. Thou shouldest not therefore hold fast to things earthly, although God doth bestow them. . . . See ye how that in fearing to lose things earthly, the Jews slew the King of Heaven. And what was done to them? They lost even those very things earthly : and in the place where they slew Christ, there they were slain : and when, being unwilling to lose the land, they slew the Giver of life, that same land being slain they lost; and at that very time when they slew Him, in order that by that very time they might be admonished of the reason wherefore they suffered these things. For when the city of the Jews was overthrown, they were celebrating the Passover, and with many thousands of men the whole nation itself had met together for the celebration of that festival.[3] In that place God (through evil men indeed, but yet Himself good; through unjust men, but Himself just and justly) did so take vengeance upon them, that there were slain many thousands of men, and the city itself was overthrown. Of this thing in this Psalm "the understanding of Asaph" doth complain, and in the very plaint the understanding as it were doth distinguish things earthly from things heavenly, doth distinguish the Old Testament from the New Testament : in order that thou mayest see through what things thou art passing, what thou shouldest look for, what to forsake, to what to cleave. Thus then he beginneth.

3. "Wherefore hast Thou repelled us, O God, unto the end?"(ver. 1). "Hast repelled unto the end," in the person of the congregation which is properly called Synagogue. "Wherefore hast Thou repelled us, O God, unto the end?" He censureth not, but inquireth "wherefore," for what purpose, because of what hast Thou done this? What hast Thou done? "Thou hast repelled us unto the end." What is, "unto the end"? Perchance even unto the end of the world. Hast Thou repelled us unto Christ, who is the End to every one believing?[4] For, "Wherefore hast Thou repelled us, O God, unto the end?" "Thy spirit[5] hath been wroth at the sheep of Thy flock." Wherefore wast Thou wroth at the sheep of Thy flock, but because to things earthly we were cleaving, and the Shepherd we knew not?

4. "Remember Thou Thy congregation, which Thou hast possessed from the beginning" (ver. 2). Can this by any means be the voice of the Gentiles? Hath He possessed the Gentiles from the beginning? Nay, but He hath possessed the seed of Abraham, the people of Israel even according to the flesh, born of the Patriarchs our fathers : of whom we have become the sons, not by coming out of their flesh, but by imitating their faith. But those, possessed by God from the beginning, what befell them? "Remember Thy congregation which Thou hast possessed from the beginning. Thou hast redeemed the rod of Thine inheritance." That same congregation of Thine, being the rod of Thine inheritance, Thou hast redeemed. This same congregation he hath called "the rod of the inheritance." Let us look back to the first thing that was done, when He willed to possess that same congregation, delivering it from Egypt, what sign He gave to Moses, when Moses said to Him, "What sign shall I give that they may believe me, that Thou hast sent me? And God saith to him, What dost thou bear in thine hand? A rod. Cast it on to the ground," etc.[6] What doth it intimate? For this was not done to no purpose. Let us inquire of the writings of God. To what did the serpent persuade man? To death.[7] Therefore death is from the serpent. If death is from the serpent, the rod in the ser-

---

[1] [Note this use of the word "Sacrament."—C.]
[2] John i. 17.
[3] See Josephus, book vi. c. 9, § 3, whence the whole number of the besieged is stated at 1,197,000, of whom 1,100,000 perished. [The coincidence of the Passover with this day of retribution is noteworthy. On Good Friday accordingly occurs a prayer for the Jews, in the Anglican Liturgy.—C.]

[4] Rom. x. 4.   [5] *Animus.*
[6] Exod. iv. 1-3.
[7] Gen. iii. 1. [See A. N. F. vol. iii. p. 63, note 12.—C.]

pent is Christ in death.[1] Therefore also when by serpents in the desert they were being bitten and being slain, the Lord commanded Moses to exalt a brazen serpent in the desert, and admonish the people that whosoever by a serpent had been bitten, should look thereupon and be made whole.[2] Thus also it was done : thus also men, bitten by serpents, were made whole of the venom by looking upon a serpent.[3] To be made whole of a serpent is a great Sacrament. What is it to be made whole of a serpent by looking upon a serpent? It is to be made whole of death by believing in one dead. And nevertheless Moses feared and fled.[4] What is it that Moses fled from that serpent? What, brethren, save that which we know to have been done in the Gospel? Christ died and the disciples feared, and withdrew from that hope wherein they had been.[5] . . . But, at that time some thousands of the Jews themselves, the crucifiers of Christ, believed : and because they had been found at hand, they so believed as that they sold all that they had, and the price of their goods before the feet of the Apostles they laid.[6] Because then this thing was hidden, and the redemption of the rod of God was to be more conspicuous in the Gentiles : he explaineth of what he saith that which he hath said, "Thou hast redeemed the rod of Thine inheritance." This he hath said not of the Gentiles in whom it was evident. But of what? "Mount Sion." Yet even Mount Sion can be otherwise understood. "That one which[7] Thou hast dwelled in the same." In the place where the People was aforetime, where the Temple was set up, where the Sacrifices were celebrated, where at that time were all those necessary things giving promise of Christ. A promise, when the thing promised is bestowed is now become superfluous. . . .

5. "Lift up Thine hand upon their pride at the end" (ver. 3). As Thou didst repel us at the end, so "lift up Thine hand upon the pride of them at the end." The pride of whom? Of those by whom Jerusalem was overthrown. But by whom was it, but by the kings of the Gentiles? Well was the hand of Him lifted up upon the pride of them at the end : for they too have now known Christ. "For the end of the Law is Christ for righteousness to every one believing."[8] How well doth he wish for them ! As if angry he is speaking, and he is seeming to speak evil :[9] and O that there would come to pass the evil which he speaketh : nay now in the name of Christ that it is coming to pass let us

rejoice. Now they holding the sceptre are being made subject to the Word of the Cross : now is coming to pass that which was foretold, "there shall adore Him all the kings of the earth, all nations shall serve Him."[10] Now on the brows of kings more precious is the sign of the Cross, than the jewel of a crown. "Lift up Thine hand upon the pride of them at the end. How great things hath the enemy of malice wrought in Thy holy places !" In those which were Thy holy places, that is, in the temple, in the priesthood, in all those sacraments which were at that time. In good sooth the enemy at that time wrought. For the Gentiles at that time who did this, were worshipping false Gods, were adoring idols, were serving demons : nevertheless they wrought many evil things on the Saints of God. When could they if they had not been permitted? But when would they have been permitted, unless those holy things, at first promised, were no longer necessary, when He that had promised was Himself holden? Therefore, "how great things hath the enemy of malice wrought in Thy holy places !"

6. "And all they have boasted, that hate Thee" (ver. 4). Observe the servants of demons, the servants of idols : such as at that time the Gentiles were, when they overthrew the temple and city of God, "and they boasted." "In the midst of Thy festival." Remember what I said, that Jerusalem was overthrown at the time when the very festival was being celebrated : at which festival they crucified the Lord. Gathered together they raged, gathered together they perished. "They have set signs, their own signs, and they have not known" (ver. 5). They had signs to place there, their standards, their eagles, their own dragons, the Roman signs ; or even their statues which at first in the temple they placed ; or perchance "their signs" are the things which they heard from the prophets of their demons. "And they have not known." Have not known what? How "thou shouldest have had no power against Me, except it had been given thee from above."[11] They knew not how that not on themselves honour was conferred, to afflict, to take, or overthrow the city, but their ungodliness was made as it were the axe of God. They were made the instrument of Him enraged, not so as to be the kingdom of Him pacified. For God doth that which a man also ofttime doth. Sometimes a man in a rage catcheth up a rod lying in the way, perchance any sort of stick, he smiteth therewith his son, and then throweth the stick into the fire and reserveth the inheritance for his son : so sometime God through evil men doth instruct good men, and through the tem-

---

[1] [In sin, which is death. The Lamb was made sin (*i.e.* a serpent) for us. 2 Cor. v. 21. — C.]
[2] Numb. xxi. 8;　　[3] John iii. 14.　　[4] Exod. iv. 3.
[5] Luke xxiv. 21.　　[6] Acts iv. 34, 35.
[7] Oxf. mss. *in quo* for *quem*.　　[8] Rom. x. 4.
[9] Or, "curse."

poral power of them that are to be condemned He worketh the discipline of them that are to be saved. For why do you suppose, brethren, that discipline was even thus inflicted upon that nation, in order that it might perish utterly? How many out of this nation did afterwards believe, how many are yet to believe? Some are chaff, others grain; over both however there cometh in the threshing-drag; but under one threshing-drag the one is broken up, the other is purged. How great a good hath God bestowed upon us by the evil of Judas the traitor! By the very ferocity of the Jews how great a good was bestowed upon believing Gentiles! Christ was slain in order that there might be on the Cross One for him to look to who had been stung by the serpent.[1] . . .

7. Now let us hasten over the verses following after the destruction of Jerusalem, for the reason that they are both evident, and it doth not please me to tarry over the punishment even of enemies. "As if in a forest of trees with axes, they have cut down the doors thereof at once; with mattock and hammer they have thrown Her down" (ver. 6). That is, conspiring together, with firm determination, "with mattock and hammer" they have thrown Her down. "They have burned with fire Thy Sanctuary, they have defiled on the ground the Tabernacle of Thy name" (ver. 7).

8. "They have said in their heart (the kindred of them is in one)"—Have said what? "Come ye, let us suppress the solemnities of the Lord from the land" (ver. 8). "Of the Lord," hath been inserted in the person of this man, that is, in the person of Asaph. For they raging would not have called Him the Lord whose temple they were overthrowing. "Come ye, let us suppress all the solemnities of the Lord from the land." What of Asaph? What understanding hath Asaph in these words? What? Doth he not profit even by the discipline accorded? Is not the mind's crookedness made straight? Overthrown were all things that were at first: nowhere is there priest, nowhere Altar of the Jews, nowhere victim, nowhere Temple. Is there then no other thing to be acknowledged which succeeded this departing? Or indeed would this promissory sign have been taken away, unless there had come that which was being promised? Let us see therefore in this place now the understanding of Asaph, let us see if he profiteth by tribulation. Observe what he saith: "Our signs we have not seen, no longer is there prophet, and us He will not know as yet" (ver. 9). Behold those Jews who say that they are not known as yet, that is, that they are yet in captivity, that not yet they are deliv-

ered, do yet expect Christ. Christ will[2] come, but He will come as Judge; the first time to call, afterwards to sever. He will come, because He hath come,[3] and that He will come is evident; but hereafter from above He will come. Before thee He was, O Israel. Thou wast bruised because thou didst stumble against Him lying down: that thou mayest not be ground to powder, observe Him coming from above. For thus it was foretold by the prophet: "Whoever shall stumble upon that stone shall be bruised, and upon whomsoever it shall have come, it shall grind him to powder."[4] He doth bruise when little, He shall grind to powder when great. Now thy signs thou seest not, now there is no prophet: and thou sayest, "and us He will not know as yet:" because yourselves know not Him as yet. "No longer is there a prophet; and us He will not know as yet."

9. "How long, O God, shall the enemy revile?" (ver. 10). Cry out as if forsaken, as if deserted: cry out like a sick man, who hast chosen rather to smite the physician than to be made whole: not as yet doth He know thee. See what He hath done, who doth not know thee as yet. For they to whom there hath been no preaching of Him, shall see; and they that have not heard shall understand: and thou sent criest out, "No longer is there a prophet, and us He will not know as yet."[5] Where is thine understanding? "The adversary doth provoke Thy name at the end."[6] For this purpose the adversary doth provoke Thy name at the end, that being provoked Thou mayest reprove, reproving Thou mayest know them at the end: or certainly, "at the end," in the sense of even unto the end.

10. "Wherefore dost Thou turn away Thine hand, and Thy right hand from the midst of Thy bosom unto the end?" (ver. 11). Again, another sign which was given to Moses. For in like manner as above from the rod was a sign, so also from the right hand now. For when that thing had been done concerning the rod, God gave a second sign: "thrust," He saith, "thine hand into thy bosom, and he thrust it: draw it forth, and he drew it forth: and it was found white,"[7] that is, unclean. For whiteness on the skin is leprosy,[8] not fairness of complexion. For the heritage of God itself, that is, His people, being cast out became unclean. But what saith He to him? Draw it back into thy bosom. He drew it back, and it was restored to its own colour. When doest Thou this, saith this Asaph? How long dost Thou alienate Thy right hand from Thy bosom, so that being with-

---

[1] Numb. xxi. 8. Oxf. MSS. "and to be healed."

[2] Oxf. MSS. "truly."
[3] Oxf. MSS. "He will come, that hath already come."
[4] Luke xx. 18; Isa. xxviii. 16.   [5] Ps. lxxiv. 9.
[6] *In finem.*   [7] Exod. iv. 6.   [8] Lev. xiii. 25.

out unclean it remaineth? Draw it back, let it return to its colour, let it acknowledge the Saviour. "Wherefore dost thou turn away Thine hand, and Thy right hand from the midst of Thy bosom unto the end?" These words he crieth, being blind, not understanding, and God doeth what He doeth. For wherefore came Christ? "Blindness in part happened unto Israel, in order that the fulness of the Gentiles might enter in, and so all Israel might be saved."[1] Therefore now, O Asaph, acknowledge that which hath gone before, in order that thou mayest at least follow, if thou wast not[2] able to go before. For not in vain came Christ, or in vain was Christ slain, or in vain did the corn fall into the ground; but it fell that it might rise manifold.[3] A serpent was lifted up in the desert, in order that it might cure of the poison him that was smitten.[4] Observe what was done. Do not think it to be a vain thing that He came: lest He find thee evil, when He shall have come a second time.

11. Asaph hath understood, because on the Title of the Psalm there is, "understanding of Asaph." And what saith he? "But God, our King before the worlds, hath wrought Salvation in the midst of the earth" (ver. 12). On the one hand we cry, "No longer is there prophet, and us He will not know as yet:"[5] but on the other hand, "our God, our King, who is before the worlds" (for He is Himself in the beginning of the Word[6] by whom were made the worlds), "hath wrought Salvation in the midst of the earth." "God therefore, our King before the worlds," hath done what? "hath wrought Salvation in the midst of the earth:" and I am yet crying as if forsaken! . . . Now the Gentiles are awake, and we are snoring, and as though God hath forsaken us, in dreams we are delirious. "He hath wrought Salvation in the midst of the earth."

12. Now therefore, O Asaph, amend thyself according to thy understanding, tell us what sort of Salvation God hath wrought in the midst of the earth. When that earthly Salvation of yours was overthrown, what did He do, what did He promise? "Thou didst confirm in Thy virtue the sea" (ver. 13). As though the nation of the Jews were as it were dry land severed from the waves, the Gentiles in their bitterness were the sea, and on all sides they washed about that land: behold, "Thou hast confirmed in Thy virtue the sea," and the land remained thirsting for Thy rain. "Thou hast confirmed in Thy virtue the sea, Thou hast broken in pieces the heads of dragons in the water." Dragons' heads, that is, demons' pride, wherewith the Gentiles were pos-

sessed, Thou hast broken in pieces upon the water: for those persons whom they were possessing, Thou by Baptism hast delivered.

13. What more after the heads of dragons? For those dragons have their chief, and he is himself the first great dragon. And concerning him what hath He done that hath wrought Salvation in the midst of the earth? Hear: "Thou hast broken the head of the dragon" (ver. 14). Of what dragon? We understand by dragons all the demons that war under the devil: what single dragon then, whose head was broken, but the devil himself ought we to understand? What with him hath He done? "Thou hast broken the head of the dragon." That is, the beginning of sin. That head is the part which received the curse, to wit that the seed of Eve should mark the head of the serpent.[7] For the Church was admonished to shun the beginning of sin. Which is that beginning of sin, like the head of a serpent? The beginning of all sin is pride.[8] There hath been broken therefore the head of the dragon, hath been broken pride diabolical. And what with him hath He done, that hath wrought Salvation in the midst of the earth? "Thou hast given him for a morsel to the Ethiopian peoples." What is this? How do I understand the Ethiopian peoples? How but by these all nations? And properly by black men: for Ethiopians are black. They are themselves called to the faith who were black; the very same indeed, so that there is said to them, "for ye were sometime darkness, but now light in the Lord."[9] . . . Thence was also that calf which the people worshipped, unbelieving, apostate, seeking the gods of the Egyptians, forsaking Him who had delivered them from the slavery of the Egyptians: whence there was enacted that great Sacrament. For when Moses was thus wroth with them worshipping and adoring the idol,[10] and, inflamed with zeal for God, was punishing temporally, in order that he might terrify them to shun death everlasting; yet the head itself of the calf he cast into the fire, and ground to powder, destroyed, strawed on the water, and gave to the people to drink: so there was enacted a great Sacrament. O anger prophetic, and mind not perturbed but enlightened! He did what? Cast it into the fire, in order that first the form itself may be obliterated; piece by piece grind it down, in order that little by little it may be consumed: cast it into the water, give to the people to drink! What is this but that the worshippers of the devil were become the body of the same? In the same manner as men confessing Christ become the Body of Christ; so that to them is said, "but ye are the Body of Christ

1 Rom. xi. 25.
2 Oxf. MSS. "wast unwilling, and wast not."
3 John xii. 24.　　4 Numb. xxi. 9.　　5 Ps. lxxiv. 9.
6 John i. 1.

7 Gen. iii. 15.　　　　　　8 Eccles. x. 13.
9 Eph. v. 8. [See p. 331, note 3, *supra.* — C.]
10 Exod. xxxii. 19.

and the members."[1]　The body of the devil was to be consumed, and that too by Israelites was to be consumed.　For out of that people were the Apostles, out of that people the first Church. . . . Thus the devil is being consumed with the loss of his members.　This was figured also in the serpent of Moses.　For the magicians did likewise, and casting down their rods they exhibited serpents : but the serpent of Moses swallowed up the rods of all those magicians.[2]　Let there be perceived therefore even now the body of the devil : this is what is coming to pass, he is being devoured by the Gentiles who have believed, he hath become meat for the Ethiopian peoples.　This again, may be perceived in, "Thou hast given him for meat to the Ethiopian peoples," how that now all men bite him.　What is, bite him ?　By reproving, blaming, accusing. Just as hath been said, by way of prohibition indeed, but yet the idea expressed : "but if ye bite and eat up one another, take heed that ye be not consumed of one another."[3]　What is, bite and eat up one another ?　Ye go to law with one another, ye detract from one another, ye heap revilings upon one another.　Observe therefore now how that with these bitings the devil is being consumed.　What man, when angry with his servant, even a heathen, would not say to him, Satan ?[4]　Behold the devil given for meat. This saith Christian, this saith Jew, this saith heathen :[4] him he worshippeth, and with him he curseth ! . . .

14. "Thou hast cleft the fountains and torrents" (ver. 15) : in order that they might flow with the stream of wisdom, might flow with the riches of the faith, might water the saltness of the Gentiles, in order that they might convert all unbelievers into the sweetness of the faith by their watering. . . . In some men the Word of God becometh a well of water springing up unto life eternal ;[5] but others hearing the Word, and not so keeping it as that they live well, yet not keeping silence with tongue, they become torrents.　For they are properly called torrents which are not perennial : for sometimes also in a secondary sense torrent is used for river : as hath been said, "with the torrent of Thy pleasures Thou shalt give them to drink."[6]　For that torrent shall not ever be dried up.　But torrents properly are those rivers named, which in summer fail, but with winter rains are flooded and run.　Thou seest therefore a man sound in faith, that will persevere even unto the end, that will not forsake God in any trial ; for the sake of the truth, not for the sake of falsehood and error, enduring all difficulties.　Whence is this man so vigorous, but because the Word hath become in

him a well of water springing up unto life eternal ?[5]　But the other receiveth the Word, he preacheth, he is not silent, he runneth : but summer proveth whether he be fountain or torrent. Nevertheless through both be the earth watered, by Him who hath wrought Salvation in the midst of the earth : let the fountains overflow, let the torrents run.

15. "Thou hast dried up the rivers of Etham" (ver. 15). . . . What is Etham ?　For the word is Hebrew.　What is Etham interpreted ?　Strong, stout.　Who is this strong and stout one, whose rivers God drieth up ?　Who but that very dragon ?　For "no one entereth into the house of a strong man that he may spoil his vessels, unless first he shall have bound fast the strong man."[7]　This is that strong man on his own virtue relying, and forsaking God : this is that strong man, who saith, "I will set my seat by the north, and I will be like the Most High."[8]　Out of that very cup of perverse strength he hath given man to drink.　Strong they willed to be, who thought that they would be Gods by means of the forbidden food.　Adam became strong, over whom was reproachfully said, "Behold, Adam hath become like one of us."[9] . . . As though they were strong, "to the righteousness of God they have not been made subject."[10]　Observe ye that a man hath put out of the way his own strength, and remained weak, needy, standing afar off, not daring even to raise his eyes to Heaven ; but smiting his breast, and saying, "O Lord, merciful be Thou to me a sinner."[11]　Now he is weak, now he confesseth his weakness, he is not strong : dry land he is, be he watered with fountains and torrents.　They are as yet strong who rely on their own virtue.　Be their rivers dried up, let there be no advancement in the doctrines of the Gentiles, of wizards, of astrologers, of magic arts : for dried up are the rivers of the strong man : "Thou hast dried up the rivers of Etham."　Let there dry up that doctrine ; let minds be flooded with the Gospel of truth.

16. "Thine own is the day and Thine own is the night" (ver. 16).　Who is ignorant of this, seeing that He hath Himself made all these things ; for by the Word were made all things ?[12] To that very One Himself who hath wrought Salvation in the midst of the earth, to Him is said, "Thine own is the night."　Something here we ought to perceive which belongeth to that very Salvation which He hath wrought in the midst of the earth.　"Thine own is the day." Who are these ?　The spiritual.　"And Thine own is the night."　Who are these ?　The carnal. . . . "Thou hast made perfect sun and

---

[1] 1 Cor. xii. 27.　　[2] Exod. vii. 12.　　[3] Gal. v. 15.
[4] [A note of the state of heathenism in our author's time. — C.]
[5] John iv. 14.　　[6] Ps. xxxvi. 8.

[7] Mark xii. 29.　　　　　[8] Isa. xiv. 13.
[9] Gen. iii. 22.　　　　　[10] Rom. x. 3.
[11] Luke xviii. 13.　　　　[12] John i. 3.

moon : " the sun, spiritual men, the moon, carnal men. As yet carnal he is, may he not be forsaken, and may he too be made perfect. The sun, as it were a wise man : the moon, as it were an unwise man : Thou hast not however forsaken. For thus it is written, "A wise man endureth as the sun, but a foolish man as the moon is changed." [1] What then? Because the sun endureth, that is, because the wise man endureth as the sun, a foolish man is changed like the moon, is one as yet carnal, as yet unwise, to be forsaken? And where is that which hath been said by the Apostle, "To the wise and unwise a debtor I am"? [2]

17. "Thou hast made all the ends of the earth" (ver. 17). . . . Behold in what manner He hath made the ends of the earth, that hath wrought Salvation in the midst of the earth. "Thou hast made all the ends of the earth. Summer and spring Thou hast made them." Men fervent in the Spirit are the summer. Thou, I say, hast made men fervent in the Spirit : Thou hast made also the novices in the Faith, they are the "spring." "Summer and Spring Thou hast made them." They shall not glory as if they have not received : "Thou hast made them."

18. "Mindful be Thou of this Thy creature" (ver. 18). Of what creature of Thine? "The enemy hath reviled the Lord." O Asaph, grieve over thine old blindness in understanding : "the enemy hath reviled the Lord." It was said to Christ in His own nation, "a sinner is this Man : we know not whence He is : " we know Moses, to him spake God ; this Man is a Samaritan.[3] "And the unwise people hath provoked Thy name." The unwise people Asaph was at that time, but not the understanding of Asaph at that time. What is said in the former Psalm? "As it were a beast I have become unto Thee, and I am alway with Thee : " [4] because He went not to the gods and idols of the Gentiles. Although he knew not, being like a beast, yet he knew again as a man. For he said, " alway I am with Thee, like a beast : " and what afterwards in that place in the same Psalm, where Asaph is? "Thou hast held the hand of my right hand, in Thy will Thou hast conducted me, and with glory Thou hast taken me up." [5] In Thy will, not in my righteousness : by Thy gift, not by my work. Therefore here also, "the enemy hath reviled the Lord : and the unwise people hath provoked Thy name." Have they all then perished? Far be it. . . . For even the Apostle Paul through unbelief had been broken, and through faith unto the root he was restored. So evidently "the unwise people provoked Thy name," when it was said, "If Son of God He is, let Him come down from the Cross." [6]

19. But what sayest thou, O Asaph, now in understanding? "Deliver not to the beasts a soul confessing to Thee" (ver. 19). . . . To what beasts, save to those the heads whereof were broken in pieces upon the water? For the same devil is called, beast, lion, and dragon. Do not, he saith, give to the Devil and his Angels a soul confessing to Thee. Let the serpent devour, if still I mind things earthly, if for things earthly I long, if still in the promises of the Old Testament, after the revealing of the New, I remain. But forasmuch as now I have laid down pride, and my own righteousness I will not acknowledge, but Thy Grace ; against me let proud beasts have no power. "The souls of Thy poor forget Thou not unto the end." Rich we were, strong we were : but Thou hast dried up the rivers of Etham : no longer we establish our own righteousness, but we acknowledge Thy Grace ; poor we are, hearken to Thy beggars. Now we do not dare to lift our eyes to Heaven, but smiting our breasts we say, "O Lord, be Thou merciful to me a sinner." [7]

20. "Have regard unto Thy Testament" [8] (ver. 20). Fulfil that which Thou hast promised : the tables we have, for the inheritance we are looking. "Have regard unto Thy Testament," not that old one : not for the sake of the land of Canaan I ask, not for the sake of the temporal subduing of enemies, not for the sake of carnal fruitfulness of sons, not for the sake of earthly riches, not for the sake of temporal welfare : "Have regard unto Thy Testament," wherein Thou hast promised the kingdom of Heaven. Now I acknowledge Thy Testament : now understanding is Asaph, no beast is Asaph, now he seeth that which was spoken of, "Behold, the days come, saith the Lord, and I will accomplish with the House of Israel and of Juda a new Testament, not after the Testament which I ordered [9] with their Fathers." [10] "Have regard unto Thy Testament : for they that have been darkened have been filled of the earth of unrighteous houses : " because they had unrighteous hearts. Our "houses" are our hearts : therein gladly dwell they that are blessed with pure heart.[11] "Have regard," therefore, "unto Thy Testament : " and let the remnant be saved : [12] for many men that give heed to earth are darkened, and filled with earth. For there hath entered into their eyes dust, and it hath blinded them, and they have become dust which the wind sweepeth from the face of the earth.[13] "They that have been darkened have been filled of the earth of unrighteous houses." For by giving heed to earth they have been darkened, concerning whom there is said in another

[1] Ecclus. xxvii. 11.   [2] Rom. i. 14.
[3] John ix. 24, 29; John viii. 48.   [4] Ps. lxxiii. 22.
[5] Ps. lxxiii. 23.   [6] Matt. xxvii. 40.

[7] Luke xviii. 13.   [8] Or, "Covenant."   [9] Disposui.
[10] Jer. xxxi. 31.   [11] Matt. v. 8.   [12] Rom. ix. 27.
[13] Ps. i. 4.

Psalm, "Let their eyes be blinded, that they see not, and their back ever bow Thou down." [1] With earth, then, "they that have been darkened have been filled, with the earth of unrighteous houses : " because they have unrighteous hearts. . . .

21. "Let not the humble man be turned away confounded " (ver. 21). For them pride hath confounded. "The needy and helpless man shall praise Thy name." Ye see, brethren, how sweet ought to be poverty : ye see that poor and helpless men belong to God, but "poor in spirit, for of them is the Kingdom of Heaven." [2] Who are the poor in spirit? The humble, men trembling at the words of God, confessing their sins, neither on their own merits, nor on their own righteousness relying. Who are the poor in spirit? They who when they do anything of good, praise God, when anything of evil, accuse themselves. "Upon whom shall rest My Spirit," saith the Prophet, "but upon the humble man, and peaceful, and trembling at My words?" [3] Now therefore Asaph hath understood, now to the earth he adhereth not, now the earthly promises out of the Old Testament he requireth not. . . .

22. "Arise, O Lord, judge Thou my cause " [4] (ver. 22). . . . Because I am not able to show my God, as if I were following an empty thing, they revile me. And not only Heathen, or Jew, or heretic ; but sometimes even a Catholic brother doth make a grimace when the promises of God are being preached, when a future resurrection is being foretold.[5] And still even he, though already washed with the water of eternal Salvation, bearing the Sacrament of Christ, perchance saith, "and what man hath yet risen again?" And, "I have not heard my father speaking out of the grave, since I buried him !" "God hath given to His servants a law for time, to which [6] let them betake themselves : for what man cometh back from beneath?" And what shall I do with such men? Shall I show them what they see not? I am not able : for not for the sake of them ought God to become visible. . . . I see not, he saith : what am I to believe? Thy soul is seen then, I suppose? Fool, thy body is seen : thy soul who doth see? Since therefore thy body alone is seen, why art thou not buried? He marvelleth that I have said, If body alone is seen, why art thou not buried? And he answereth (for he knoweth as much as this), Because I am alive. How know I that thou art alive, of whom I see not the soul? How know I? Thou wilt answer, Because I speak, because I walk, because I work. Fool, by the

operations of the body I know thee to be living, by the works of creation canst thou not know the Creator? And perchance he that saith, when I shall be dead, afterwards I shall be nothing ; hath both learned letters, and hath learned this doctrine from Epicurus, who was a sort of doting philosopher, or rather lover of folly not of wisdom, whom even the philosophers themselves have named the hog : who said that the "chief good " was pleasure of body ; this philosopher they [7] have named the hog, wallowing in carnal mire. From him perchance this lettered man hath learned to say, I shall not be, after I have died. Dried be the rivers of Etham ! Perish those doctrines of the Gentiles, flourish the plantations of Jerusalem ! Let them see what they can, in heart believe what they cannot see ! Certainly all those things which throughout the world now are seen, when God was working Salvation in the midst of the earth, when those things were being spoken of, they were not then as yet : and behold at that time they were foretold, now they are shown as fulfilled, and still the fool saith in his heart, "there is no God." [8] Woe to the perverse hearts : for so will there come to pass the things which remain, as there have come to pass the things which at that time were not, and were being foretold as to come to pass. Hath God indeed performed [9] to us all the things which He promised, and concerning the Day of Judgment alone hath He deceived us? Christ was not on the earth ; He promised, He hath performed : no virgin had conceived ; He promised, He hath performed : the precious Blood had not been shed whereby there should be effaced the handwriting of our death ; He promised, He hath performed : not yet had flesh risen again unto life eternal ; He promised, He hath performed : not yet had the Gentiles believed ; He promised, He hath performed : not yet heretics armed with the name of Christ, against Christ were warring ; He foretold, He hath performed : not yet the idols of the Gentiles from the earth had been effaced ; He foretold, He hath performed : when all these things He hath foretold and performed, concerning the Day of Judgment alone hath He lied? It will come by all means as these things came ; for even these things before they came to pass were future, and as future were first foretold, and afterwards they came to pass. It will come, my brethren. Let no one say, it will not come : or, it will come, but far off is that which will come. But to thyself it is near at hand to go hence. . . . If thou shalt have done that which the devil doth suggest, and shalt have despised that which God hath commanded ;

---

[1] Ps. lxix. 23.　　[2] Matt. v. 3.　　[3] Isa. lxvi. 2.
[4] E. V. " Thine own cause."
[5] [1 Cor. xv. 35. — C.]
[6] *Quod (tempus ?)*. Oxf. mss. *quam (legem)*.

[7] Oxf. mss. " philosopher." [Hor. *Ep.* iv. 16; and Cic. *De Officiis*, iii. 33. — C.]
[8] Ps. xiv. 1.　　[9] *Exhibuit.*

there will come the Judgment Day, and thou wilt find that true which God hath threatened, and that false which the devil hath promised. . . . "Remember Thy reproaches, those which are from the imprudent man all the day long." For still Christ is reviled: nor will there be wanting all the day long, that is, even unto the end of time, the vessels of wrath. Still is it being said, "Vain things the Christians do preach:" still is it being said, "A fond thing is the resurrection of the dead." "Remember Thy reproaches." But what reproaches, save those "which are from the imprudent man all the day long?" Doth a prudent man say this? Nay, for a prudent man is said to be one far-seeing. If a prudent man is one far-seeing, by faith he seeth afar: for with eyes scarce that before the feet is seen.

23. "Forget not the voice of them that implore Thee" (ver. 23). While they groan for and expect now that which Thou hast promised from the New Testament, and walk by that same Faith, "do Thou not forget the voice of them imploring Thee." But those still say, "Where is Thy God? Let the pride of them that hate Thee come up alway to Thee." Do not forget even their pride. Nor doth He forget: no doubt He doth either punish or amend.

PSALM LXXV.[1]

1. . . . The Title of this Psalm thus speaketh: "At the end,[2] corrupt not." What is, "corrupt not?" That which Thou hast promised, perform. But when? "At the end." To this then let the mind's eye be directed, "unto the end." Let all the things which have occurred in the way be passed over, in order that we may attain to the end. Let proud men exult because of present felicity, let them swell with honours, glitter in gold, overflow with domestics, be encircled with the services of clients: these things pass away, they pass away like a shadow. When that end shall have come, when all who now hope in the Lord are to rejoice, then to them shall come sorrow without end. When the meek shall have received that which the proud deride, then the vapouring of the proud shall be turned into mourning. Then shall there be that voice which we know in the Book of Wisdom: for they shall say at that time when they see the glory of the Saints, who, when they were in humiliation, endured them; who, when they were exalted, consented not — at that time then they shall say, "These are they whom sometime we have had in derision."[3] Where they also say, "What hath pride profited us, and the boasting of riches hath bestowed upon us what?"

All things have passed away like a shadow. Because on things corruptible they relied, their hope shall be corrupted: but our own hope at that time shall be substance. For in order that the promise of God may remain whole and sure and certain towards us, we have said out of a heart[4] of faith, "at the end corrupt not." Fear not, therefore, lest any mighty man should corrupt the promises of God. He doth not corrupt, because He is truthful; He hath no one more mighty by whom His promise may be corrupted: let us be then sure concerning the promises of God; and let us sing now from the place where the Psalm beginneth.

2. "We will confess to Thee, O Lord, we will confess to Thee, and will invoke Thy name" (ver. 1). Do not invoke, before thou confess: confess, and invoke. For Him whom thou art invoking, unto thyself thou callest. For what is it to invoke, but unto thyself to call? If He is invoked by thee, that is, if He is called to thee, unto whom doth He draw near? To a proud man He draweth not near. High indeed He is, one lifted up attaineth not unto Him. In order that we may reach all exalted objects, we raise ourselves, and if we are not able to reach them, we look for some appliances or ladders, in order that being exalted we may reach exalted objects: contrariwise God is both high, and by the lowly He is reached. It is written, "Nigh is the Lord to them that have bruised the heart."[5] The bruising of the heart is Godliness, humility. He that bruiseth himself is angry with himself. Let him make himself angry in order that he may make Him merciful; let him make himself judge, in order that he may make Him Advocate. Therefore God doth come when invoked. Unto whom doth He come? To the proud man He cometh not. . . . Take heed therefore what ye do: for if He knoweth, He is not unobservant.[6] It is better therefore that He be unobservant than known. For what is that same being unobservant, but not knowing? What is, not to know? Not to animadvert. For even as the act of one avenging animadversion is wont to be spoken of. Here one praying that He be unobservant: "Turn away Thy face from my sins."[7] What then wilt thou do if He shall have turned away His face from thee? A grievous thing it is, and to be feared, lest He forsake thee. Again, if He turn not away His face, He animadverteth. God knoweth this thing, God can do this thing, namely, both turn away face from one sinning, and not turn away from one confessing. . . . Confess therefore and invoke. For by confessing thou purgest the Temple, into which He may

1 Lat. LXXIV.   Sermon to the Commonalty.
2 In finem.   3 Wisd. v. 3.
4 4 mss. "mouth."   5 Ps xxxiv. 18.
6 Non ignoscit, "doth not forgive" (take no notice).
7 Ps. li. 9.

come, when invoked. Confess and invoke. May He turn away face from thy sins, not turn away from thee : turn away face from that which thou hast wrought,[1] not turn away from that which He hath Himself wrought.[2] For thee, as man, He hath Himself wrought, thy sins thou hast thyself wrought. . . .

3. But that there is a strengthening of the sense in repetition, by many passages of the Scriptures we are taught. Thence is that which the Lord saith, "Verily, Verily." [3] Thence in certain Psalms is, "So be it, So be it." [4] To signify the thing, one "So be it" would have been sufficient : to signify confirmation, there hath been added another "So be it." . . . Countless passages of such sort there are throughout all the Scriptures. With these it is sufficient that we have commended to your notice a way of speaking which ye may observe in all like cases : now to the substance attend : "We will confess to Thee," he saith, "and we will invoke." I have said why before invocation confession doth precede : because whom thou dost invoke, him thou dost invite. But he willeth not to come when invoked, if thou shalt have been lifted up : lifted up if thou shalt have been, thou wilt not be able to confess. And thou deniest not any things to God that He knoweth not. Therefore thy confession doth not teach Him, but it purgeth thee.

4. . . . Hear ye now the words of Christ. For these seemed not as it were to be His words,[5] "We will confess to Thee, O God, we will confess to Thee, and will invoke Thy name." Now beginneth the discourse in the person of the Head. But whether Head speaketh or whether members speak, Christ speaketh : He speaketh in the person of the Head, He speaketh in the person of the Body. But what hath been said? There shall be two in one flesh.[6] "This is a great Sacrament : " " I," he saith, "speak in Christ and in the Church." [7] And He Himself in the Gospel, "Therefore no longer two, but one flesh." [8] For in order that ye may know these in a manner to be two persons, and again one by the bond of marriage, as one He speaketh in Isaiah, and saith, "As upon a Bridegroom he hath bound upon me a mitre, and as a Bride he hath clothed me with an ornament." [9] A Bridegroom He hath called Himself in the Head, a Bride in the Body. He is speaking therefore as One, let us hear Him, and in Him let us also speak. Let us be the members of Him, in order that this voice may possibly be ours also. "I will tell forth," he saith, "all Thy marvellous things." Christ is preaching Him-

self, He is preaching Himself even in His members now existing, in order that He may guide unto Him others, and they may draw near that were not, and may be united with those members of Him, through which members of Him the Gospel hath been preached ; and there may be made one Body under one Head, in one Spirit, in one Life.

5. And he saith what? "When I shall have received," he saith, " the time,[10] I will judge justices " (ver. 2). When shall He judge justices? When He shall have received the time. Not yet is the precise time. Thanks to His mercy : He first preacheth justices, and then He judgeth justices. For if He willed to judge before He willed to preach, who would be found that should be delivered : who would meet Him that should be absolved? Now therefore is the time of preaching : "I will tell," he saith, "all Thy marvellous works." Hear Him telling, hear Him preaching : for if thou shalt have despised Him, "when I shall have received the time," He saith, "I will judge justices." I forgive, He saith, now sins to one confessing, I will not spare hereafter one despising. . . . He hath received a time as Son of Man ; He doth govern times as Son of God. Hear how as Son of Man He hath received the time of judging. He saith in the Gospel, "He hath given to Him power to execute judgment, because Son of Man He is." [11] According to His nature as Son of God, He hath never received power of judging, because He never lacked the power of judging : according to His nature as Son of Man He hath received a time, as of being born, and of suffering, as of dying, and of rising again, and of ascending, so of coming and of judging. In Him His Body also saith these words, for not without them He will judge. For He saith in the Gospel, "Ye shall sit upon twelve thrones judging the twelve tribes of Israel." [12] Therefore whole Christ saith, that is, Head and Body in the Saints, "when I shall have received the time, I will judge justices."

6. But now what? "The earth hath flowed down " (ver. 3). If the earth hath flowed down, whence hath it flowed down except by sins? Therefore also they are called delinquencies. To delinquish is as it were by a kind of liquidity [13] to slip down from the stability of firmness in virtue and righteousness. For it is through desire of lower things that every man sinneth : as he is strengthened by the love of higher things, so he falleth down and as it were melteth away by desire of lower things. This flux of things by the sins of man the merciful forgiver observing, being a merciful forgiver of

---

[1] *Fecisti.*　　　[2] *Fecit.*　　　[3] John i. 51.
[4] Ps. lxxii. 19, lxxxix. 52.
[5] Oxf. mss. "members."　　　[6] Gen. ii. 24.
[7] Eph. v. 32.　　　[8] Matt. xix. 6.　　　[9] Isa. lxi. 10.

[10] E. V. "the congregation."　　　[11] John v. 27.
[12] Matt. xix. 28.
[13] *De liquido quodam. Al. de loco quodam.* [Qu. *deliquesce* ? —C.]

sins, not yet an exactor of punishments, He observeth and saith : The earth herself indeed hath flowed down by them that dwell in her. That which followeth is an exposition, not an addition. As though thou wert saying, in what manner hath the earth flowed down? Have the foundations been withdrawn, and hath anything therein been swallowed up in a sort of gulf? What I mean by earth is all they that dwell therein. I have found, he saith, the earth sinful. And I have done what? " I have strengthened the pillars thereof." What are the pillars which He hath strengthened? Pillars He hath called the Apostles. So the Apostle Paul concerning his fellow-Apostles saith, "who seemed to be pillars." [1] And what would those pillars have been, except by Him they had been strengthened? For on occasion of a sort of earthquake even these very pillars rocked : at the Passion of the Lord all the Apostles despaired. Therefore those pillars which rocked at the Passion of the Lord, by the Resurrection were strengthened. The Beginning of the building hath cried out through the pillars thereof, and in all those pillars the Architect Himself hath cried out. For the Apostle Paul was one pillar of them when he said, "Would ye receive a proof of Him that speaketh in me — Christ?" [2] Therefore, "I," he saith, "have strengthened the pillars thereof : " I have risen again, I have shown that death is not to be feared, I have shown to them that fear, that not even the body itself doth perish in the dying. There terrified them wounds, there strengthened them scars. The Lord Jesus could have risen again without any scar : for what great matter were it for that power, to restore the frame of the body to such perfect soundness, as that no trace at all of past wound should appear? He had power whence He might make it whole even without scar : but He willed to have that whereby He might strengthen the rocking pillars.

7. We have heard now, brethren, that which day by day is not kept secret : let us hear now what He hath cried through these pillars. . . . He crieth what? " I have said to unjust men, Do not unjustly " (ver. 4). . . . But already they have done, and they are guilty : already there hath flowed down the earth, and all they that dwell therein. Pricked to the heart were they that crucified Christ,[3] they acknowledged their sin, they learned something of the Apostle, that they might not despair of the pardon of the Preacher.[4] For as Physician He had come, and therefore had not come to the whole. "For there is no need," He saith, "to the whole of a physician, but to them that are sick. I have

not come to call righteous men, but sinners to repentance." [5] Therefore, "I have said to unjust men, Do not unjustly." They heard not. For of old to us it was spoken : we heard not, we fell, were made mortal, were begotten mortal : the earth flowed down. Let them hear the Physician even now in order that they may rise, Him that came to the sick man, Him whom they would not hear when whole in order that they might not fall, let them hear when lying down in order that they may rise. . . . " I have said to unjust men, Do not unjustly ; and to the delinquent, Do not exalt your horn." There shall be exalted in you the horn of Christ, if your horn be not exalted. Your horn is of iniquity, the horn of Christ is of majesty.

8. " Be not therefore lifted up : speak not iniquity against God " (ver. 5). . . . What saith He in another Psalm? "These things thou hast done," having enumerated certain sins. "These things thou hast done," He saith, "and was silent." [6] What is, "I was silent"? He is never silent with commandment, but meanwhile He is silent with punishment : He is keeping still from vengeance, He doth not pronounce sentence against the condemned. But this man saith thus, I have done such and such things, and God hath not taken vengeance ; behold I am whole, nought of ill hath befallen me. "These things thou hast done, and I was silent : thou hast suspected iniquity, that I shall be like unto thee." What is, "that I shall be like unto thee "? Because thou art unjust, even Me thou hast deemed unjust ; as though an approver of thy misdeeds, and no adversary, no avenger thereof. And what afterwards saith He to thee? "I will convict thee, and will set thee before thine own face "? [6] What is this? Because now by sinning behind thy back thou settest thyself, seest not thyself, examinest not thyself ; I will set thee before thyself, and will bring upon thee punishment from thyself. So also here, "Speak not iniquity against God." Attend. Many men speak this iniquity ; but dare not openly, lest as blasphemers they be abhorred by godly men : in their heart they gnaw upon these things, within they feed upon such impious food ; it delighteth them to speak against God, and if they break not out with tongue, in heart they are not silent. Whence in another Psalm is said, "The fool hath said in his heart, There is no God." [7] The fool hath said, but he hath feared men : he would not say it where men might hear ; and he said it in that place where He might Himself hear concerning whom he said it. Therefore here also in this Psalm (dearly beloved attend), whereas that which He said, "Do not speak iniquity against

---

[1] Gal. ii. 9.   [2] 2 Cor. xiii. 3.   [3] Acts ii. 37.
[4] *Prædicatoris.* Some MSS. *Peccatores,* "that sinners might not despair of pardon."

[5] Matt. ix. 12, 13.   [6] Ps. l. 21.   [7] Ps. xiv. 1.

God," this He saw many men do in heart, He hath also added, "for neither from East, nor from West, nor from the deserts of the mountains (ver. 6), for God is Judge" (ver. 7). Of thine iniquities God is Judge. If God He is, everywhere He is present. Whither wilt thou take thyself away from the eyes of God, so that in some quarter thou mayest speak that which He may not hear? If from the East God judgeth, withdraw into the West, and say what thou wilt against God: if from the West, go into the East, and there speak: if from the deserts of the mountains He judgeth, go into the midst of the peoples, where thou mayest murmur to thyself. From no place judgeth He that everywhere is secret, everywhere open; whom it is allowed no one to know as He is, and whom no one is permitted not to know. Take heed what thou doest. Thou art speaking iniquity against God. "The Spirit of the Lord hath filled the round world" (another Scripture saith this), "and that which containeth all things hath knowledge of the voice: wherefore he that speaketh unjust things cannot be hid." [1] Do not therefore think God to be in places: He is with thee such an one as thou shalt have been. What if such an one as thou shalt have been? Good, is, thou shalt have been good; and evil to thee He will seem, if evil thou shalt have been; but a Helper, if good thou shalt have been; an Avenger, if evil thou shalt have been. There thou hast a Judge in thy secret place. Willing to do something of evil, from the public thou retirest into thy house, where no enemy may see; from those places of thine house which, are open and before the eyes of men, thou removest thyself into a chamber; thou fearest even in thy chamber some witness from some other quarter, thou retirest into thy heart, there thou meditatest: He is more inward than thy heart. Whithersoever therefore thou shalt have fled, there He is. From thyself whither wilt thou flee? Wilt thou not follow thyself whithersoever thou shalt flee? But since there is One more inward even than thyself, there is no place whither thou mayest flee from God angry, but to God reconciled. There is no place at all whither thou mayest flee. Wilt thou flee from Him? Flee to Him. . . . What then shall we do now? "Let us come before His face," ἐν ἐξομολογήσει, come before in confession: He shall come gentlé whom thou hadst made angry. "Neither from the deserts of the mountains, for God is Judge:" not from the East, not from the West, not from the deserts of the mountains. Wherefore? "For God is Judge." If in any place He were, He would not be God: but because God is Judge, not man, do not expect

Him out of places. His place thou wilt be, if thou art good, if after having confessed [2] thou shalt have invoked Him.

9. "One He humbleth, and another He exalteth" (ver. 7). Whom humbleth, whom exalteth this Judge? Observe these two men in the temple, and ye see whom He humbleth and whom He exalteth. "They went up into the Temple to pray," He saith, "the one a Pharisee, and the other a Publican. . . . "Verily I say unto you, that Publican went down justified more than that Pharisee: for every one that exalteth himself shall be humbled; and he that humbleth himself shall be exalted." [3] Thus hath been explained a verse of this Psalm. God the Judge doth what? "One He humbleth, and another He exalteth:" He humbleth the proud, He exalteth the humble.

10. "For the cup in the hand of the Lord of pure wine is full of mixed" (ver. 8). Justly so. "And He hath poured out of this úpon this man; nevertheless, the dreg thereof hath not been emptied; there shall drink all the sinners of earth." Let us be somewhat recruited; there is here some obscurity. . . . The first question that meeteth us is this, "of pure wine it is full of mixed." How "of pure," if "of mixed"? But when he saith, "the cup in the hand of the Lord" (to men instructed in the Church of Christ I am speaking), ye ought not indeed to paint in your heart God as it were circumscribed with a human form, lest, though the temples are shut up, ye forge images in your hearts. This cup therefore doth signify something. We will find out this. But "in the hand of the Lord," is, in the power of the Lord. For the hand of God is spoken of for the power of God. For even in reference to men ofttimes is said, in hand he hath it: that is, in his power he hath it, when he chooseth he doth it. "Of pure wine it is full of mixed." In continuation he hath himself explained: "He hath inclined," he saith, "from this unto this man; nevertheless the dreg thereof hath not been emptied." Behold how it was full of mixed wine. Let it not therefore terrify you that it is both pure and mixed: pure because of the genuineness thereof, mixed because of the dreg. What then in that place is the wine, and what the dreg? And what is, "He hath inclined from this unto this man," in such sort that the dreg thereof was not emptied?

11. Call ye to mind from whence he came to this: "one He humbleth, and another He exalteth." [4] That which was figured to us in the Gospel through two men, a Pharisee and a Publican, [5] this let us, taking in a wider sense, understand of two peoples, of Jews and of Gentiles: the

---

[1] Wisd. i. 7, 8.

[2] Oxf. mss. "being converted."   [3] Luke xviii. 10, etc.
[4] Ps. lxxv. 7.   [5] Luke xviii. 10.

people of the Jews that Pharisee was, the people of the Gentiles that Publican. . . . As those by being proud have withdrawn, so these by confessing have drawn near. The cup therefore full of pure wine in the hand of the Lord, as far as the Lord giveth me to understand,[1] . . . the cup of pure wine full of the mixed, seemeth to me to be the Law, which was given to the Jews, and all that Scripture of the Old Testament, as it is called; there are the weights of all manner of sentences. For therein the New Testament lieth concealed, as though in the dreg of corporal Sacraments. The circumcision of the flesh is a thing of great mystery,[2] and there is understood from thence the circumcision of the heart. The Temple of Jerusalem is a thing of great mystery, and there is understood from it the Body of the Lord. The land of promise[3] is understood to be the Kingdom of Heaven. The sacrifice of victims and of beasts hath a great mystery: but in all those kinds of sacrifices is understood that one Sacrifice and only victim of the Cross, the Lord, instead of all which sacrifices we have one; because even those figured these, that is, with those these were figured. That people received the Law, they received commandments just and good.[4] What is so just as, thou shalt not kill, thou shalt not commit adultery, thou shalt not steal, thou shalt not speak false testimony, honour thy father and mother, thou shalt not covet the property of thy neighbour, one God thou shalt adore, and Him alone thou shalt serve,[5] all these things belong to the wine. But those things carnal have as it were sunk down in order that they might remain with them, and there might be poured forth from thence all the spiritual understanding. But "the cup in the hand of the Lord," that is, in the power of the Lord: "of pure wine," that is, of the mere Law: "is full of mixed," that is, is together with the dreg of corporal Sacraments. And because the one He humbleth, the proud Jew, and the other He exalteth, the confessing Gentile; "He hath inclined from this unto this," that is, from the Jewish people unto the Gentile people. Hath inclined what? The Law. There hath distilled from thence a spiritual sense. "Nevertheless, the dreg thereof hath not been emptied," for all the carnal Sacraments have remained with .the Jews. "There shall drink all the sinners of the earth." Who shall drink? "All the sinners of the earth." Who are the sinners of the earth?

The Jews were indeed sinners, but proud: again, the Gentiles were sinners, but humble. All sinners shall drink, but see, who the dreg, who the wine. For those by drinking the dreg have come to nought: these by drinking the wine have been justified. I would dare to speak of them even as inebriated, and I shall not fear: and O that all ye were thus inebriated. Call to mind, "Thy cup inebriating, how passing beautiful!"[6] But why? Do ye think, my brethren, that all those who by confessing Christ even willed to die, were sober? So drunk they were, that they knew not their friends. All their kindred, who strove to divert them from the hope of Heavenly rewards by earthly allurements, were not acknowledged, were not heard by them drunken. Were they not drunken, whose heart had been changed? Were they not drunken, whose mind had been alienated from this world? "There shall drink," he saith, "all the sinners of the earth." But who shall drink the wine? Sinners shall drink, but in order that they may not remain sinners; in order that they may be justified, in order that they may not be punished.

12. "But I," for all drink, but separately I, that is, Christ with His Body, "for ever will rejoice, I will Psalm to the God of Jacob" (ver. 9): in that promise to be at the end, whereof is said, "corrupt not."[7] "And all the horns of sinners I will break, and there shall be exalted the horns of the Just" (ver. 10). This is, the one He humbleth, the other He exalteth. Sinners would not have their horns to be broken, which without doubt will be broken at the end. Thou wilt not have Him then break them, do thou to-day break them. For thou hast heard above, do not despise it: "I have said to unjust men, Do not unjustly, and to the delinquents, Do not exalt the horn."[8] When thou hast heard, do not exalt the horn, thou hast despised and hast exalted the horn: thou shalt come to the end, where there shall come to pass, "All the horns of sinners I will break, and there shall be exalted the horns of the Just." The horns of sinners are the dignities of proud men: the horns of the Just are the gifts of Christ. For by horns exultations are understood. Thou hatest on earth earthly exultation, in order that thou mayest have the heavenly. Thou lovest the earthly, He doth not admit thee to the Heavenly: and unto confusion will belong thy horn which is broken, just as unto glory it will belong, if thy horn is exalted. Now therefore there is time for making choice, then there will not be. Thou wilt not say, I will be let go and will make choice. For there have preceded the words, "I have said to the unjust." If I have not said, make ready an excuse, make ready a

---

[1] [Here he interpolates a noteworthy parenthesis; viz., "For there may be some other who may give a better interpretation, because the obscurity of the Scriptures is such that it is a difficult thing for them to produce but one interpretation. Nevertheless, whatever interpretation shall have been disclosed, it must needs accord with the rule of faith: we neither envy our elders, nor, little as we are, do we despair. What seemeth good to us I am telling Your Love, not that I may stop up your ears against others, who will perchance say something better."—C.]
[2] Sacramenti.   [3] Oxf. mss. "hath a great mystery, and."
[4] Exod. xx. 1-17.   [5] Deut. vi. 4, 5, etc.

[6] Ps. xxiii. 5.   [7] Vid. Title.   [8] Ps. lxxv. 5.

defence : but if I have said, seize first upon confession, lest thou come unto damnation ; for then confession will be too late, and there will be no defence.

PSALM LXXVI.[1]

1. The Jews are wont to glory in this Psalm which we have sung, saying, " Known in Judæa is God, in Israel great is the name of Him : " and to revile the Gentiles to whom God is not known, and to say that to themselves alone God is known ; seeing that the Prophet saith, " Known in Judæa is God." In other places therefore He is unknown. But God is known in very deed in Judæa, if they understand what is Judæa. For indeed God is not known except in Judæa. Behold even we say this, that except a person shall have been in Judæa, known to him God cannot be. But what saith the Apostle ? He that in secret is a Jew, he that is so in circumcision of the heart, not in letter but in spirit.[2] There are therefore Jews in circumcision of the flesh, and there are Jews in circumcision of the heart. Many of our holy fathers[3] had both the circumcision of the flesh, for a seal of the faith, and circumcision of the heart, for the faith itself. From these fathers these men degenerating, who now in the name do glory, and have lost their deeds ; from these fathers, I say, degenerating, they have remained Jews in flesh, in heart Heathens. For these are Jews, who are out of Abraham, from whom Isaac was born, and out of him Jacob, and out of Jacob the twelve Patriarchs, and out of the twelve Patriarchs the whole people of the Jews.[4] But they were generally called Jews for this reason, that Judah was one of the twelve sons of Jacob, a Patriarch among the twelve, and from his stock the Royalty came among the Jews. For all this people after the number of the twelve sons of Jacob, had twelve tribes. What we call tribes are as it were distinct houses and congregations of people. That people, I say, had twelve tribes, out of which twelve tribes one tribe was Judah, out of which were the kings ; and there was another tribe, Levi, out of which were the priests. But because to the priests serving the temple no land was allotted,[5] but it was necessary that among twelve tribes all the Land of promise should be shared : there having been therefore taken out one tribe of higher dignity, the tribe of Levi, which was of the priests, there would have remained eleven, unless by the adoption of the two sons of Joseph the number twelve were completed.

What this is, observe. One of the twelve sons of Jacob was Joseph. . . . This Joseph had two sons, Ephraim and Manasse. Jacob, dying, as though by will, received those his grandsons into the number of sons, and said to his son Joseph, " The rest that are born shall be to thee ; but these to me, and they shall divide the land with their brethren." [6] As yet there had not been given nor divided the land of promise, but he was speaking in the Spirit, prophesying. The two sons therefore of Joseph being added, there were made up nevertheless twelve tribes, since now there are thirteen. For instead of one tribe of Joseph, two were added, and there were made thirteen. There being taken out then the tribe of Levi, that tribe of priests which did serve the Temple, and lived by the tithes of all the rest unto whom the land was divided, there remain twelve. In these twelve was the tribe of Judah, whence the kings were. For at first from another tribe was given King Saul,[7] and he was rejected as being an evil king ; after there was given from the tribe of Judah King David, and out of him from the tribe of Judah were the Kings.[8] But Jacob had spoken of this, when he blessed his sons, " there shall not fail a prince out of Judah, nor a leader from his thighs, until there come He to whom the promise hath been made." [9] But from the tribe of Judah there came Our Lord Jesus Christ. For He is, as the Scripture saith, and as ye have but now heard, out of the seed of David born of Mary.[10] But as regardeth the Divinity of our Lord Jesus Christ, wherein He is equal with the Father, He is not only before the Jews, but also before Abraham himself ; [11] nor only before Abraham, but also before Adam ; nor only before Adam, but also before Heaven and earth and before ages : for all things by Himself were made, and without Him there was made nothing.[12] Because therefore in prophecy hath been said, " there shall not fail a prince out of Judah," etc. : [9] former times are examined, and we find that the Jews always had their kings of the tribe of Judah, and had no foreign king before that Herod who was king when the Lord was born. Thence began foreign kings, from Herod.[13] Before Herod all were of the tribe of Judah, but only until there should come He to whom the promise had been made. Therefore when the Lord Himself came, the kingdom of the Jews was overthrown, and removed from the Jews. Now they have no king ; because they will not acknowledge the true King. See now whether they must be called Jews. Now ye do see that they must not be called Jews. They have themselves with their own voice resigned that name, so that they are not worthy to be

---

[1] Lat. LXXV. Sermon to the Commonalty, wherein he disputeth against the Donatists, and treateth of vows.
[2] Rom. ii. 29.
[3] [This habit of the primitive faithful, claiming the fatherhood of Abraham and the prophets, is conspicuous in our author. — C.]
[4] Gen. xxi. 1, xxv. 26, xxix. 32, etc.   [5] Numb. xviii. 20.

[6] Gen. xlviii. 5.   [7] 1 Sam. ix. 1.   [8] 1 Sam. xvi. 12.
[9] Gen. xlix. 10.   [10] 2 Tim. ii. 8.   [11] John viii. 58.
[12] John i. 3.   [13] Luke iii. 1.

called Jews, except only in the flesh. When did they sever themselves from the name? They said, "We have no king but Cæsar."[1] O ye who are called Jews and are not, if ye have no king but Cæsar, there hath failed a Prince of Judah: there hath come then He to whom the promise hath been made. They then are more truly Jews, who have been made Christians out of Jews: the rest of the Jews, who in Christ have not believed, have deserved to lose even the very name. The true Judæa, then, is the Church of Christ, believing in that King, who hath come out of the tribe of Judah through the Virgin Mary; believing in Him of whom the Apostle was just now speaking, in writing to Timothy, "Be thou mindful that Jesus Christ hath risen from the dead, of the seed of David, after my Gospel."[2] For of Judah is David, and out of David is the Lord Jesus Christ. We believing in Christ do belong to Judah: and we acknowledge Christ. We, that with eyes have not seen, in faith do keep Him. Let not therefore the Jews revile, who are no longer Jews. They said themselves, "We have no king but Cæsar."[1] For better were it for them that their king should be Christ, of the seed of David, of the tribe of Judah. Nevertheless because Christ Himself is of the seed of David after the flesh, but God above all things blessed for ever,[3] He is Himself our King and our God; our King, inasmuch as born of the tribe of Judah, after the flesh, was Christ the Lord, the Saviour; but our God, who is before Judah, and before Heaven and earth, by whom were made all things,[4] both spiritual and corporal. For if all things by Himself were made; even Mary herself, out of whom He was born, by Himself was made. . . .

2. "Known in Judæa is God, in Israel great is the Name of Him" (ver. 1). Concerning Israel also we ought so to take it as we have concerning Judæa: as they were not the true Jews, so neither was that the true Israel. For what is Israel said to be? One seeing God. And how have they seen God, among whom He walked in the flesh; and while they supposed Him to be man, they slew Him? . . . "In Israel great is His Name." Wilt thou be Israel? Observe that man concerning whom the Lord saith, "Behold an Israelite indeed, in whom guile is not."[5] If a true Israelite is he in whom guile is not, the guileful and lying are not true Israelites. Let them not say then, that with them is God, and great is His name in Israel. Let them prove themselves Israelites, and I grant that "in Israel great is His Name."

3. "And there hath been made in peace a place for Him, and His habitation is in Sion" (ver. 2). Again, Sion is as it were the country

of the Jews; the true Sion is the Church of Christians. But the intrepretation of the Hebrew names is thus handed down to us: Judæa is interpreted confession, Israel, one seeing God. After Judæa is Israel. Wilt thou see God? First do thou confess, and then in thyself there is made a place for God; because "there hath been made in peace a place for Him." So long as then thou confessest not thy sins, in a manner thou art quarrelling with God. For how art thou not disputing with Him, who art praising that which displeaseth Him? He punisheth a thief, thou dost praise theft: He doth punish a drunken man, thou dost praise drunkenness. Thou art disputing with God, thou hast not made for Him a place in thy heart: because in peace is His place. And how dost thou begin to have peace with God? Thou beginnest with Him in confession. There is a voice of a Psalm, saying, "Begin ye to the Lord in confession."[6] What is, "Begin ye to the Lord in confession"? Begin ye to be joined to the Lord. In what manner? So that the same thing may displease you as displeaseth Him. There displeaseth Him thy evil life; if it please thyself, thou art disunited from Him; if it displease thee, through confession to Him thou art united. . . .

4. "There He hath broken the strength of bows, and the shield, and the sword, and the battle" (ver. 3). Where hath He broken? In that eternal peace, in that perfect peace. And now, my brethren, they that have rightly believed see that they ought not to rely on themselves: and all the might of their own menaces, and whatsoever is in them whetted for mischief, this they break in pieces; and whatsoever they deem of great virtue wherewith to protect themselves temporally, and the war which they were waging against God by defending their sins, all these things He hath broken there.

5. "Thou enlightening marvellously from the eternal mountains" (ver. 4). What are the eternal mountains? Those which He hath Himself made eternal; which are the great mountains, the preachers of truth. Thou dost enlighten, but from the eternal mountains: the great mountains are first to receive Thy light, and from Thy light which the mountains receive, the earth also is clothed. But those great mountains the Apostles have received, the Apostles have received as it were the first streaks of the rising light. . . . Wherefore also, in another place, a Psalm saith what? "I have lifted up mine eyes unto the mountains, whence there shall come help to me."[7] What then, in the mountains is thy hope, and from thence to thee shall there come help? Hast thou stayed at the mountains? Take heed what thou doest. There

---

[1] John xix. 15.　　[2] 2 Tim. ii. 8.　　[3] Rom. ix. 5.
[4] John i. 3.　　[5] John i. 47.　　[6] Ps. cxlvii. 7.　　[7] Ps. cxxi. 1.

is something above the mountains : above the mountains is He at whom the mountains tremble. "I have lifted up," he saith, "mine eyes unto the mountains, whence there shall come help to me." But what followeth? "My help," he saith, "is from the Lord, who hath made Heaven and earth."[1] Unto the mountains indeed I have lifted up eyes, because through the mountains to me the Scriptures were displayed : but I have my heart in Him that doth enlighten all mountains. . . .

6. "There have been troubled all the unwise in heart" (ver. 5). . . . How have they been troubled? When the Gospel is preached. And what is life eternal? And who is He that hath risen from the dead? The Athenians wondered, when the Apostle Paul spake of the resurrection of the dead, and thought that he spake but fables.[2] But because he said that there was another life which neither eye hath seen, nor ear heard, nor hath it gone up into the heart of man,[3] therefore the unwise in heart were troubled. But what hath befallen them? "They have slept their sleep, and all men of riches have found nothing in their hands." They have loved things present, and have gone to sleep in the midst of things present : and so these very present things have become to them delightful : just as he that seeth in a dream himself to have found treasure, is so long rich as he waketh not. The dream hath made him rich, waking hath made him poor. Sleep perchance hath held him slumbering on the earth, and lying on the hard ground, poor and perchance a beggar ; in sleep he hath seen himself to lie on an ivory or golden bed, and on feathers heaped up ; so long as he is sleeping, he is sleeping well, waking he hath found himself on the hard ground, whereon sleep had taken him. Such men also are these too : they have come into this life, and through temporal desires, they have as it were slumbered here ; and them riches, and vain pomps that fly away, have taken, and they have passed away : they have not understood how much of good might be done therewith. For if they had known of another life, there they would have laid up unto themselves the treasure which here was doomed to perish : like as Zacchæus, the chief of the Publicans, saw that good[4] when he received the Lord Jesus in his house, and he saith, "The half of my goods I give to the poor, and if to any man I have done any wrong, fourfold I restore."[5] This man was not in the emptiness of men dreaming, but in the faith of men awake. . . .

7. "By Thy chiding, O God of Jacob, there have slept all men that have mounted horses" (ver. 6). Who are they that have mounted horses? They that would not be numble. To sit on horseback is no sin ; but it is a sin to lift up the neck of power against God, and to deem one's self to be in some distinction. Because thou art rich, thou hast mounted ; God doth chide, and thou sleepest. Great is the anger of Him chiding, great the anger. Let your Love observe the terrible thing. Chiding hath noise, the noise is wont to make men wake. So great is the force of God chiding, that he said, "By Thy chiding, O God of Jacob, there have slept all men that have mounted horses." Behold what a sleep that Pharaoh slept who mounted horses. For he was not awake in heart, because against chiding he had his heart hardened.[6] For hardness of heart is slumber. I ask you, my brethren, how they sleep, who, while the Gospel is sounding, and the Amen, and the Hallelujah, throughout the whole world, yet will not condemn their old life, and wake up unto a new life. There was the Scripture of God in Judæa only, now throughout the whole world it is sung. In that one nation one God who made all things was spoken of, as to be adored and worshipped ; now where is He unsaid? Christ hath risen again, though derided on the Cross ; that very Cross whereon He was derided, He hath now imprinted on the brows of kings : and men yet sleep. . . .

8. "Thou art terrible, and who shall withstand Thee at that time by Thine anger?" (ver. 7). Now they sleep, and perceive not Thee angry ; but for cause that they should sleep, He was angry. Now that which sleeping they perceived not, at the end they shall perceive. For there shall appear the Judge of quick and dead. "And who shall withstand Thee at that time by Thine anger?" For now they speak that which they will, and they dispute against God and say, who are the Christians? or who is Christ? or what fools are they that believe that which they see not, and relinquish the pleasures which they see, and follow the faith of things which are not displayed to their eyes ! Ye sleep and snore,[7] ye speak against God, as much as ye are able. "How long shall sinners, O Lord, how long shall sinners glory, they answer and will speak iniquity?"[8] But when doth no one answer and no one speak, except when he turneth himself[9] against himself? . . .

9. "From Heaven Thou hast hurled judgment : the earth hath trembled, and hath rested" (ver. 8). She which now doth trouble herself, she which now speaketh, hath to fear at the end and to rest. Better had she now rested, that at the end she might have rejoiced. Rested? When? "When God arose unto judgment, that He might save all the meek in heart" (ver. 9). Who are the meek in heart? They that on

[1] Ps. cxxi. 2.   [2] Acts xvii. 18, 32.   [3] 1 Cor. ii. 9.
[4] Many omit " good."   [5] Luke xix. 8.
[6] Exod. xiv. 8.   [7] *Balatis.*   [8] Ps. xciv. 3.
[9] Oxf. MSS. " they," " themselves."

snorting horses have not mounted, but in their humility have confessed their own sins. "For the thought of a man shall confess to Thee, and the remnants of the thought shall celebrate solemnities to Thee" (ver. 10). The first is the thought, the latter are the remnants of the thought. What is the first thought? That from whence we begin, that good thought whence thou wilt begin to confess. Confession uniteth us to Christ. But now the confession itself, that is, the first thought, doth produce in us the remnants of the thought: and those very "remnants of thought shall celebrate solemnities to Thee." What is the thought which shall confess? That which condemneth the former life, that whereunto that which it was is displeasing, in order that it may be that which it was not, is itself the first thought. But because thus thou oughtest to withdraw from sins, with the first thought after having confessed to God, that it may not escape thy memory that thou hast been a sinner; in that thou hast been a sinner, thou dost celebrate solemnities to God. Furthermore it is to be understood as followeth. The first thought hath confession, and departure from the old life. But if thou shalt have forgotten from what sins thou hast been delivered, thou dost not render thanks to the Deliverer, and dost not celebrate solemnities to thy God. Behold the first confessing thought of Saul the Apostle, now Paul, who at first was Saul, when he heard a voice from Heaven! . . . He put forth the first thought of obedience: when he heard, "I am Jesus of Nazareth, whom thou persecutest," "O Lord," he saith, "what dost Thou bid me to do?"[1] This is a thought confessing: now he is calling upon the Lord, whom he persecuted. In what manner the remnants of the thought shall celebrate solemnities, in the case of Paul ye have heard, when the Apostle himself was being read: "Be thou mindful that Christ Jesus hath risen from the dead, of the seed of David, after my Gospel."[2] What is, be thou mindful? Though effaced from thy memory be the thought, whereby at first thou hast confessed: be the remnant of the thought in the memory. : . .

10. Even once was Christ sacrificed for[3] us, when we believed; then was thought; but now there are the remnants of thought, when we remember Who hath come to us, and what He hath forgiven us; by means of those very remnants of thought, that is, by means of the memory herself, He is daily so sacrificed for us,[4] as if He were daily renewing us, that hath renewed us by His first grace. For now the Lord hath renewed us in Baptism, and we have become new men,

in hope indeed rejoicing, in order that in tribulation we may be patient:[5] nevertheless, there ought not to escape from our memory that which hath been bestowed upon us. And if now thy thought is not what it was, — for the first thought was to depart from sin: but now thou dost not depart, but at that time didst depart, — be there remnants of thought, lest He who hath made whole escape from memory. . . .

11. "Vow ye, and pay to the Lord our God" (ver. 11). Let each man vow what he is able, and pay it. Do not vow and not pay: but let every man vow, and pay what he can. Be ye not slow to vow: for ye will accomplish the vows by powers not your own. Ye will fail, if on yourselves ye rely: but if on Him to whom ye vow ye rely, ye will be safe to pay. "Vow ye, and pay to the Lord our God." What ought we all in common to vow? To believe in Him, to hope from Him for life eternal, to live godly according to a measure common to all. For there is a certain measure common to all men. To commit no theft is not a thing enjoined *merely* upon one devoted to continence,[6] and not enjoined upon the married woman: to commit no adultery is enjoined upon all men: not to love wine-bibbing, whereby the soul is swallowed up, and doth corrupt in herself the Temple of God, is enjoined to all alike: not to be proud, is enjoined to all men alike: not to slay man, not to hate a brother, not to lay a plot to destroy any one, is enjoined to all in common. The whole of this we all ought to vow. There are also vows proper for individuals: one voweth to God conjugal chastity, that he will know no other woman besides his wife:[7] so also the woman, that she will know no other man besides her husband. Other men also vow, even though they have used such a marriage, that beyond this they will have no such thing, that they will neither desire nor admit the like: and these men have vowed a greater vow than the former. Others vow even virginity from the beginning of life, that they will even know no such thing as those who having experienced have relinquished: and these men have vowed the greatest vow. Others vow that their house shall be a place of entertainment for all the Saints that may come: a great vow they vow. Another voweth to relinquish all his goods to be distributed to the poor, and go into a community, into a society of the Saints: a great vow he doth vow. "Vow ye, and pay to the Lord our God." Let each one vow what he shall have willed to vow; let him give heed to this, that he pay what he hath vowed. If any man doth look back with regard to what he hath vowed to God, it

---

[1] Acts ix. 5, 6.　　[2] 2 Tim. ii. 8.
[3] *Nobis Christus immolatur;* the mss. have not *pro*, which is in the earlier editions. — *Ben.*
[4] *Nobis sic immolatur.*

[5] Rom. xii. 12.　　[6] *Castimoniali.*
[7] The wife being living, and supposing he may survive. The following case would be that of one *already* a widower.

is an evil. Some woman or other devoted to continence hath willed to marry: what hath she willed? The same as any virgin. What hath she willed? The same as her own mother. Hath she willed any evil thing? Evil certainly. Why? Because already she had vowed to the Lord her God. For what hath the apostle Paul said concerning such? Though he saith that young widows may marry if they will:[1] nevertheless he saith in a certain passage, "but more blessed she will be, if so she shall have remained, after my judgment."[2] He showeth that she is more blessed, if so she shall have remained; but nevertheless that she is not to be condemned, if she shall have willed to marry. But what saith he concerning certain who have vowed and have not paid? "Having," he saith, "judgment, because the first faith they have made void."[3] What is, "the first faith they have made void"? They have vowed, and have not paid. Let no brother therefore, when placed in a monastery, say, I shall depart from the monastery: for neither are they only that are in a monastery to attain unto the kingdom of Heaven, nor do those that are not there not belong unto God. We answer him, but they have not vowed; thou hast vowed, thou hast looked back. When the Lord was threatening them with the day of judgment, He saith what? "Remember Lot's wife."[4] To all men He spake. For what did Lot's wife? She was delivered from Sodom, and being in the way she looked back. In the place where she looked back, there she remained. For she became a statue of salt,[5] in order that by considering her men might be seasoned, might have sense, might not be infatuated, might not look back, lest by giving a bad example they should themselves remain and season others. For even now we are saying this to certain of our brethren, whom perchance we may have seen as it were weak in the good they have purposed. And wilt thou be such an one as he was? We put before them certain who have looked back. They are savourless[6] in themselves, but they season others, inasmuch as they are mentioned, in order that fearing their example they may not look back. "Vow ye, and pay." For that wife of Lot to all doth belong. A married woman hath had the will to commit adultery; from her place whither she had arrived she looked back. A widow who had vowed so to remain hath willed to marry, she hath willed the thing which was lawful to her who hath married, but to herself was not lawful, because from her place she hath looked back. There is a virgin devoted to continence,

already dedicated to God; let her have[7] also the other gifts which truly do adorn virginity itself, and without which that virginity is unclean. For what if she be uncorrupt in body and corrupt in mind? What is it that he hath said? What if no one hath touched the body, but if perchance she be drunken, be proud, be contentious, be talkative? All these things God doth condemn. If before she had vowed, she had married, she would not have been condemned: she hath chosen something better, hath overcome that which was lawful for her; she is proud, and doth commit so many things unlawful. This I say, it is lawful for her to marry before that she voweth, to be proud is never lawful. O thou virgin of God, thou hast willed not to marry, which is lawful: thou dost exalt thyself, which is not lawful. Better is a virgin humble, than a married woman humble: but better is a married woman humble, than a virgin proud. But she that looked back upon marriage is condemned, not because she hath willed to marry; but because she had already gone before, and is become the wife of Lot by looking back. Be ye not slow, that are able, whom God doth inspire to seize upon higher callings: for we do not say these things in order that ye may not vow, but in order that ye may vow and may pay. Now because we have treated of these matters, thou perchance wast willing to vow, and now art not willing to vow. But observe what the Psalm hath said to thee. It hath not said, "Vow not;" but, "Vow and pay." Because thou hast heard, "pay," wilt thou not vow? Therefore wast thou willing to vow, and not to pay? Nay, do both. One thing is done by thy profession, another thing will be perfected by the aid of God. Look to Him who doth guide thee, and thou wilt not look back to the place whence He is leading thee forth. He that guideth thee is walking before thee; the place from whence He is guiding thee is behind thee. Love Him guiding, and He doth not condemn thee looking back.[8]

12. "All they that are in the circuit of Him shall offer gifts." Who are in the circuit of Him? . . . Whatever is common to all is in the midst. Why is it said to be in the midst? Because it is at the same distance from all, and at the same proximity to all. That which is not in the middle, is as it were private. That which is public is set in the middle, in order that all they that come may use the same, may be enlightened. Let no one say, it is mine: lest he should be wanting to make his own share of that which is in the midst for all. What then is, "All

---

[1] 1 Tim. v. 14.　　[2] 1 Cor. vii. 40.　　[3] 1 Tim. v. 12.
[4] Luke xvii. 32.　　[5] Gen. xix. 26.
[6] *Fatui*.

[7] Oxf. MSS. *habeat*.
[8] [See A. N. F. vol. iv. p. 40, and General Index, *sub voce* "Marriage."—C.]

they that are in the circuit of Him shall offer gifts"? All they that understand truth to be common to all, and who do not make it as it were their own by being proud concerning it, they shall offer gifts; because they have humility: but they that make as it were their own that which is common to all, as though it were set in the middle, are endeavouring to lead men astray to a party, these shall not offer gifts. . . . "To Him terrible." Let therefore all men fear that are in the circuit of Him. For therefore they shall fear, and with trembling they shall praise; because they are in the circuit of Him, to the end that all men may attain unto Him, and He may openly meet all, and openly enlighten all. This is, to stand in awe with others.[1] When thou hast made him as it were thine own, and no longer common, thou art exalted unto pride; though it is written, "Serve ye the Lord in fear, and exult unto Him with trembling."[2] Therefore they shall offer gifts, who are in the circuit of Him. For they are humble who know truth to be common to all.

13. To whom shall they offer gifts? "To Him terrible, and to Him that taketh away the spirit of princes" (ver. 12). For the spirits of princes are proud spirits. They then are not His Spirits; for if they know anything, their own they will it to be, not public; but, that which setteth Himself forth as equal toward all men, that setteth Himself in the midst, in order that all men may take as much as they can, whatever they can; not of what is any man's, but of what is God's, and therefore of their own because they have become His. Therefore they must needs be humble: they have lost their own spirit, and they have the Spirit of God. . . . For if thou shalt have confessed thyself dust, God out of dust doth make[3] man. All they that are in the circuit of Him do offer gifts. All humble men do confess to Him, and do adore Him. "To Him terrible they offer gifts." Whence to Him terrible exult ye with trembling:[2] "and to Him that taketh away the spirit of princes:" that is, that taketh away the haughtiness of proud men. "To Him terrible among the kings of the earth." Terrible are the kings of the earth, but He is above all, that doth terrify the kings of the earth. Be thou a king of the earth, and God will be to thee terrible. How, wilt thou say, shall I be a king of the earth? Rule the earth, and thou wilt be a king of the earth. Do not therefore with desire of empire set before thine eyes exceeding wide provinces, where thou mayest spread abroad thy kingdoms; rule thou the earth which thou bearest. Hear the Apostle ruling the earth: "I do not so fight as if beating air, but I chasten my

body, and bring it into captivity, lest perchance preaching to other men, I myself become a reprobate."[4] . . .

PSALM LXXVII.[5]

1. This Psalm's lintel is thus inscribed: "Unto the end, for Idithun, a Psalm to Asaph himself." What "Unto the end" is, ye know. Idithun is interpreted "leaping over those men," Asaph is interpreted "a congregation." Here therefore there is speaking "a congregation that leapeth over," in order that it may reach the End, which is Christ Jesus.[6] . . .

2. "With my voice," he saith, "to the Lord I have cried" (ver. 1). But many men cry unto the Lord for the sake of getting riches and avoiding losses, for the safety of their friends, for the security of their house, for temporal felicity, for secular dignity, lastly, even for mere soundness of body, which is the inheritance[7] of the poor man. For such and such like things many men do cry unto the Lord; scarce one for the sake of the Lord Himself. For an easy thing it is for a man to desire anything of the Lord, and not to desire the Lord Himself; as if forsooth that which He giveth could be sweeter than Himself that giveth. Whosoever therefore doth cry unto the Lord for the sake of any other thing, is not yet one that leapeth over. . . . He doth indeed hearken to thee at the time when thou dost seek Himself, not when through Himself thou dost seek any other thing. It hath been said of some men, "They cried, and there was no one to save them; to the Lord, and He hearkened not unto them."[8] For why? Because the voice of them was not unto the Lord. This the Scripture doth express in another place, where it saith of such men, "On the Lord they have not called."[9] Unto Him they have not ceased to cry, and yet upon the Lord they have not called. What is, upon the Lord they have not called? They have not called the Lord unto themselves:[10] they have not invited the Lord to their heart, they would not have themselves inhabited by the Lord. And therefore what hath befallen them? "They have trembled with fear where fear was not." They have trembled about the loss of things present, for the reason that they were not full of Him, upon whom they have not called. They have not loved gratis, so that after the loss of temporal things they could say, "As it hath pleased the Lord, so hath been done, be the name of the Lord blessed."[11] Therefore this man saith, "My voice is unto the Lord, and He

---

[1] *Contremiscere.*　　[2] Ps. ii. 11.
[3] Or, "make thee man" (three MSS ap. Ben. *te*).

[4] 1 Cor. ix. 26, 27.
[5] Lat. LXXVI. Sermon to the Commonalty.
[6] [See p. 112, *supra.*—C.]　　[7] *Patrimonium.*
[8] Ps. xviii. 41.　　[9] Ps. xiv. 4.
[10] *In se non vocaverunt.*
[11] Job i. 21.

doth hearken unto me." Let him show us how this cometh to pass.

3. "In the day of tribulation I have sought out God" (ver. 2). Who art thou that doest this thing? In the day of thy tribulation take heed what thou seekest out. If a jail be the cause of tribulation, thou seekest to get forth from jail: if fever be the cause of tribulation, thou seekest health: if hunger be the cause of tribulation, thou seekest fulness: if losses be the cause of tribulation, thou seekest gain: if expatriation be the cause of tribulation, thou seekest the home of thy flesh. And why should I name all things, or when could I name all things? Dost thou wish to be one leaping over? In the day of thy tribulation seek out God: not through God some other thing, but out of tribulation God, that to this end God may take away tribulation, that thou mayest without anxiety cleave unto God. "In the day of my tribulation, I have sought out God:" not any other thing, but "God I have sought out." And how hast thou sought out? "With my hands in the night before Him." . . .

4. Tribulation must not be thought to be this or that in particular. For every individual that doth not yet leap over, thinketh that as yet to be no tribulation, unless it be a thing which may have befallen this life of some sad occasion: but this man, that leapeth over, doth count this whole life to be his tribulation. For so much doth he love his supernal country, that the earthly pilgrimage is of itself the greatest tribulation. For how can this life be otherwise than a tribulation, I pray you? how can that not be a tribulation, the whole whereof hath been called temptation?[1] Thou hast it written in the book of Job,[2] is not human life a temptation upon earth? Hath he said, human life is tempted upon earth? Nay, but life itself is a temptation. If therefore temptation, it must surely be a tribulation. In this tribulation therefore, that is to say in this life, this man that leapeth over hath sought out God. How? "With my hands," he saith. What is, "with my hands"? With my works. For he was not seeking any thing corporeal, so that he might find and handle something which he had lost, so that he might seek with hands coin, gold, silver, vesture, in short everything which can be held in the hands. Howbeit, even our Lord Jesus Christ Himself willed Himself to be sought after with hands, when to His doubting disciple He showed the scars.[3] . . . What then, to us belongeth not the seeking with hands? It belongeth to us, as I have said, to seek with works. When so? "In the night." What is, "in the night"? In this age. For it is night until there shine forth day

in the glorified advent of our Lord Jesus Christ. For would ye see how it is night? Unless we had here had a lantern, we should have remained in darkness. For Peter saith, "We too have more sure the prophetic discourse, whereunto ye do well to give heed, as to a lantern shining in a dark place, until day shine, and the day-star arise in your hearts."[4] There is therefore to come day after this night, meanwhile in this night a lantern is not lacking. And this is perchance what we are now doing: by explaining these passages, we are bringing in a lantern, in order that we may rejoice in this night. Which indeed ought alway to be burning in your houses. For to such men is said, "The Spirit quench ye not."[5] And as though explaining what he was saying, he continueth and saith, "Prophecy despise ye not:" that is, let the lantern alway shine in you. And even this light by comparison with a sort of ineffable day is called night. For the very life of believers by comparison with the life of unbelievers is day. . . . Night and day — day in comparison with unbelievers, night in comparison with the Angels. For the Angels have a day, which we have not yet. Already we have one that unbelievers have not: but not yet have believers that which Angels have: but they will have, at the time when they will be equal to the Angels of God, that which hath been promised to them in the Resurrection.[6] In this then which is now day and yet night; night in comparison with the future day for which we yearn, day in comparison with the past night which we have renounced: in this night then, I say, let us seek God with our hands. Let not works cease, let us seek God, be there no idle yearning. If we are in the way, let us expend our means in order that we may be able to reach the end. With hands let us seek God. . . . "With my hands in the night before Him, and I have not been deceived."

5. . . . "My soul hath refused to be comforted" (ver. 2). So great weariness did here possess me, that my soul did close the door against all comfort. Whence such weariness to him? It may be that his vineyard hath been hailed on, or his olive hath yielded no fruit, or the vintage hath been interrupted by rain. Whence the weariness to him? Hear this out of another Psalm. For therein is the voice of the same: "weariness hath bowed me down, because of sinners forsaking Thy law."[7] He saith then that he was overcome with so great weariness because of this sort of evil thing; so as that his soul refused to be comforted. Weariness had well nigh swallowed him up, and sorrow had ingulfed him altogether beyond remedy, he refuseth to be comforted. What then re-

---

[1] Or, "trial."   [2] Job vii. 1.   [3] John xx. 27.   [4] 2 Pet. i. 19.   [5] 1 Thess. v. 19.   [6] Matt. xxii. 30.   [7] Ps. cxix. 53.

mained? In the first place, see whence he is comforted. Had he not waited for one who might condole with him?[1] . . . "I have been mindful of God, and I have been delighted" (ver. 3). My hands had not wrought in vain, they had found a great comforter. While not being idle, "I have been mindful of God, and I have been delighted." God must therefore be praised, of whom this man being mindful, hath been delighted, and hath been comforted in sorrowful case, and refreshed when safety was in a manner despaired of: God must therefore be praised. In fine, because he hath been comforted, in continuation he saith, "I have babbled." In that same comfort being made mindful of God, I have been delighted, and have "babbled." What is, "I have babbled"? I have rejoiced, I have exulted in speaking. For babblers they are properly called, that by the common people are named talkative, who at the approach of joy are neither able nor willing to be silent. This man hath become such an one. And again he saith what? "And my spirit hath fainted."

6. With weariness he had pined away; by calling to mind God, he had been delighted, again in babbling he had fainted: what followeth? "All mine enemies have anticipated watches" (ver. 4). All mine enemies have kept watch over me; they have exceeded in keeping watch over me; in watching they have been beforehand with me. Where do they not lay traps? Have not mine enemies anticipated all watches? For who are these enemies, but they of whom the Apostle saith, "Ye have not wrestling against flesh and blood."[2] . . . Against the devil and his angels we are waging hostilities. Rulers of the world he hath called them, because they do themselves rule the lovers of the world. For they do not rule the world, as if they were rulers of heaven and earth: but he is calling sinners the world. . . . With the devil and his angels there is no concord. They do themselves grudge us the kingdom of Heaven. They cannot at all be appeased towards us: because "all mine enemies have anticipated watches." They have watched more to deceive than I to guard myself. For how can they have done otherwise than anticipate watches, that have set everywhere scandals, everywhere traps? Weariness doth invest the heart, we have to fear lest sorrow swallow us up: in joy to fear lest the spirit faint in babbling: "all mine enemies have anticipated watches." In fine, in the midst of that same babbling, whiles thou art speaking, and art speaking without fear, how much is oft-times found which enemies would lay hold of and censure, whereon they would even found ac-

cusation and slander — "he said so, he thought so, he spake so!" What should man do, save that which followeth? "I have been troubled, and I spake not." Therefore when he was troubled, lest in his babbling enemies anticipating watches should seek and find slanders, he spake not. . . .

7. "I have thought on ancient days" (ver. 5). Now he, as if he were one who had been beaten out of doors, hath taken refuge within: he is conversing in the secret place of his own heart. And let him declare to us what he is doing there. It is well with him. Observe what things he is thinking of, I pray you. He is within, in his own house he is thinking of ancient days. No one saith to him, thou hast spoken ill: no one saith to him, thou hast spoken much: no one saith to him, thou hast thought perversely. Thus may it be well with him, may God aid him: let him think of the ancient days, and let him tell us what he hath done in his very inner chamber, whereunto he hath arrived, over what he hath leaped, where he hath abode. "I have thought on ancient days; and of eternal years I have been mindful." What are eternal years? It is a mighty thought. See whether this thought requireth anything but great silence. Apart from all noise without, from all tumult of things human let him remain quiet within, that would think of those eternal years. Are the years wherein we are eternal, or those wherein our ancestors have been, or those wherein our posterity are to be? Far be it that they should be esteemed eternal. For what part of these years doth remain? Behold we speak and say, "in this year:" and what have we got of this year, save the one day wherein we are. For the former days of this year have already gone by, and are not to be had; but the future days have not yet come. In one day we are, and we say, in this year: nay rather say thou, to-day, if thou desirest to speak of anything present. For of the whole year what hast thou got that is present? Whatsoever thereof is past, is no longer; whatsoever thereof is future, is not yet: how then, "this year"? Amend the expression: say, to-day. Thou speakest truth, henceforth I will say, "to-day." Again observe this too, how to-day the morning hours have already past, the future hours have not yet come. This too therefore amend: say, in this hour. And of this hour what hast thou got? Some moments thereof have already gone by, those that are future have not yet come. Say, in this moment. In what moment? While I am uttering syllables, if I shall speak two syllables, the latter doth not sound until the former hath gone by: in a word, in that same one syllable, if it chance to have two letters, the latter letter doth not sound, until the former hath

[1] Ps. lxviii. 20.   [2] Eph. vi. 12.

gone by. What then have we got of these years? These years are changeable: the eternal years must be thought on, years that stand, that are not made up of days that come and depart; years whereof in another place the Scripture saith to God, "But Thou art the Self-same, and Thy years shall not fail." [1] On these years this man that leapeth over, not in babbling without, but in silence [2] hath thought.

8. "And I have meditated in the night with my heart" (ver. 6). No slanderous person seeketh for snares in his words, in his heart he hath meditated. "I babbled." Behold there is the former babbling. Watch again, that thy spirit faint not. I did not, he saith, I did not so babble as if it were abroad: in another way now. How now? "I did babble, and did search out my spirit." If he were searching the earth to find veins of gold, no one would say that he was foolish; nay, many men would call him wise, for desiring to come at gold: how great treasures hath a man within, and he diggeth not! This man was examining his spirit, and was speaking with that same his spirit, and in the very speaking he was babbling. He was questioning himself, was examining himself, was judge over himself. And he continueth; "I did search my spirit." He had to fear lest he should stay within his own spirit: for he had babbled without; and because all his enemies had anticipated watches, he found there sorrow, and his spirit fainted. He that did babble without, lo, now doth begin to babble within in safety, where being alone in secret, he is thinking on eternal years. . . .

9. And thou hast found what? "God will not repel for everlasting" (ver. 7). Weariness he had found in this life; in no place a trustworthy, in no place a fearless comfort. Unto whatsoever men he betook himself, in them he found scandal, or feared it. In no place therefore was he free from care. An evil thing it was for him to hold his peace, lest perchance he should keep silence from good words; to speak and babble without was painful to him, lest all his enemies, anticipating watches, should seek slanders in his words. Being exceedingly straitened in this life, he thought much of another life, where there is not this trial. And when is he to arrive thither? For it cannot but be evident that our suffering here is the anger of God. This thing is spoken of in Isaiah, "I will not be an avenger unto you for everlasting, nor will I be angry with you at all times." [3] . . . Will this anger of God alway abide? This man hath not found this in silence. For he saith what? "God will not repel for everlasting, and He will not add any more that it should be well-pleasing to

Him still." That is, that it should be well-pleasing to Him still to repel, and He will not add the repelling for everlasting. He must needs recall to Himself His servants, He must needs receive fugitives returning to the Lord, He must needs hearken to the voice of them that are in fetters. "Or unto the end will He cut off mercy from generation to generation?" (ver. 8).

10. "Or will God forget to be merciful?" (ver. 9). In thee, from thee unto another there is no mercy unless God bestow it on thee: and shall God Himself forget mercy? The stream runneth: shall the spring itself be dried up? "Or shall God forget to be merciful: or shall He keep back in anger His mercies?" That is, shall He be so angry, as that He will not have mercy? He will more easily keep back anger than mercy.

11. "And I said." Now leaping over himself he hath said what? "Now I have begun:" (ver. 10), when I had gone out even from myself. Here henceforth there is no danger: for even to remain in myself, was danger. "And I said, Now I have begun: this is the changing of the right hand of the Lofty One." Now the Lofty One hath begun to change me: now I have begun something wherein I am secure: now I have entered a certain palace [4] of joys, wherein no enemy is to be feared: now I have begun to be in that region, where all mine enemies do not anticipate watches. "Now I have begun: this is the changing of the right hand of the Lofty One."

12. "I have been mindful of the works of the Lord" (ver. 11). Now behold him roaming among the works of the Lord. For he was babbling without, and being made sorrowful thereby his spirit fainted: he babbled within with his own heart, and with his spirit, and having searched out that same spirit he was mindful of the eternal years, was mindful of the mercy of the Lord, how God will not repel him for everlasting; and he began now fearlessly to rejoice in His works, fearlessly to exult in the same. Let us hear now those very works, and let us too exult. But let even us leap over in our affections, and not rejoice in things temporal. For we too have our bed. Why do we not enter therein? Why do we not abide in silence? Why do we not search out our spirit? Why do we not think on the eternal years? Why do we not rejoice in the works of God? In such sort now let us hear, and let us take delight in Himself speaking, in order that when we shall have departed hence, we may do that which we used to do while He spake; if only we are making the beginning of Him whereof he spake in, "Now I have begun." To rejoice in the works of God, is to forget even

[1] Ps. cii. 27.   [2] Oxf. mss. "his own silence."
[3] Isa. lvii. 16.
[4] Al. "air."

thyself, if thou canst delight in Him alone. For what is a better thing than He? Dost thou not see that, when thou returnest to thyself, thou returnest to a worse thing? " for I shall be mindful from the beginning of Thy wonderful works.

13. "And I will meditate on all Thy works, and on Thy affections I will babble " (ver. 12). Behold the third babbling! He babbled without, when he fainted; he babbled in his spirit within, when he advanced; he babbled on the works of God, when he arrived at the place toward which he advanced. "And on Thy affections:" not on my affections. What man doth live without affections? And do ye suppose, brethren, that they who fear God, worship God, love God, have not any affections? Wilt thou indeed suppose and dare to suppose, that painting, the theatre, hunting, hawking, fishing, engage the affections, and the meditation on God doth not engage certain interior affections of its own, while we contemplate the universe, and place before our eyes the spectacle of the natural world, and therein labour to discover the Maker, and find Him nowhere unpleasing, but pleasing above[1] all things?

14. "O God, Thy way is in the Holy One " (ver. 13). He is contemplating now the works of the mercy of God around us, out of these he is babbling, and in these affections he is exulting. At first he is beginning from thence, "Thy way is in the Holy One?" What is that way of Thine which is in the Holy One? "I am," He saith, "the Way, the Truth, and the Life."[2] Return therefore, ye men, from your affections.... "Who is a great God, like our God?"[3] Gentiles have their affections regarding their gods, they adore idols, they have eyes and they see not; ears they have and they hear not; feet they have and they walk not. Why dost thou walk to a God that walketh not? I do not, he saith, worship such things, and what dost thou worship? The divinity which is there. Thou dost then worship that whereof hath been said elsewhere, "for the Gods of the nations are demons."[4] Thou dost either worship idols, or devils. Neither idols, nor devils, he saith. And what dost thou worship? The stars, sun, moon, those things celestial. How much better Him that hath made both things earthly and things celestial. "Who is a great God like our God?"

15. "Thou art the God that doest wonderful things alone " (ver. 14). Thou art indeed a great God, doing wonderful things in body, in soul; alone doing them. The deaf have heard, the blind have seen, the feeble have recovered, the dead have risen, the paralytic have been strengthened. But these miracles were at that time performed on bodies, let us see those

wrought on the soul. Sober are those that were a little before drunken, believers are those that were a little before worshippers of idols: their goods they bestow on the poor that did rob before those of others.... "Wonderful things alone." Moses too did them, but not alone: Elias too did them, even Eliseus did them, the Apostles too did them, but no one of them alone. That they might have power to do them, Thou wast with them: when Thou didst them they were not with Thee. For they were not with Thee when Thou didst them, inasmuch as Thou didst make even these very men. How "alone"? Is it perchance the Father, and not the Son? Or the Son, and not the Father? Nay, but Father and Son and Holy Ghost. For it is not three Gods but one God that doeth wonderful things alone, and even in this very leaping over. For even his leaping over and arriving at these things was a miracle of God: when he was babbling within with his own spirit, in order that he might leap over even that same spirit of his, and might delight in the works of God, he then did wonderful things himself. But God hath done what? "Thou hast made known unto the people Thy power."[5] Thence this congregation of Asaph leaping over; because He hath made known in the peoples His virtue. What virtue of His hath He made known in the peoples? "But we preach Christ crucified, ... Christ the power of God and the wisdom of God."[6] If then the virtue of God is Christ, He hath made known Christ in the peoples. Do we not yet perceive so much as this; and are we so unwise, are we lying so much below, do we so leap over nothing, as that we see not this?

16. "Thou hast redeemed in Thine arm Thy people " (ver. 15). "With Thine arm," that is, with Thy power. "And to whom hath the arm of the Lord been revealed?"[7] "Thou hast redeemed in Thine arm Thy people, the sons of Israel and of Joseph." How as if two peoples, "the sons of Israel and of Joseph"? Are not the sons of Joseph among the sons of Israel?... He hath admonished us of some distinction to be made. Let us search out our spirit, perchance God hath placed there something — God whom we ought even by night to seek with our hands, in order that we may not be deceived — perchance we shall discover even ourselves in this distinction of "sons of Israel and of Joseph." By Joseph He hath willed another people to be understood, hath willed that the people of the Gentiles be understood. Why the people of the Gentiles by Joseph? Because Joseph was sold into Egypt by his brethren.[8] That Joseph whom the brethren envied, and sold

---

[1] One ms. "through."   [2] John xiv. 6.
[3] Ps. cxiii. 5.   [4] Ps. cxxxv. 15.

[5] *Virtus.* "Virtue," Oxf. ed.   [6] 1 Cor. i. 23.
[7] Isa. liii. 1.   [8] Gen. xxxvii. 28.

him into Egypt, when sold into Egypt, toiled, was humbled; when made known and exalted, flourished, reigned. And by all these things he hath signified what? What but Christ sold by His brethren, banished from His own land, as it were into the Egypt of the Gentiles? There at first humbled, when the Martyrs were suffering persecutions: now exalted, as we see; inasmuch as there hath been fulfilled in Him, "There shall adore Him all kinds of the earth, all nations shall serve Him."[1] Therefore Joseph is the people of the Gentiles, but Israel the people of the Hebrew nation. God hath redeemed His people, "the sons of Israel and of Joseph." By means of what? By means of the corner stone,[2] wherein the two walls have been joined together.

17. And he continueth how? "The waters have seen Thee, O God, and they have feared: and the abysses have been troubled" (ver. 16). What are the waters? The peoples. What are these waters hath been asked in the Apocalypse,[3] the answer was, the peoples. There we find most clearly waters put by a figure for peoples. But above he had said, "Thou hast made known in the peoples Thy virtue."[4] With reason therefore, "the waters have seen Thee, and they have feared." They have been changed because they have feared. What are the abysses? The depths of waters. What man among the peoples is not troubled, when the conscience is smitten? Thou seekest the depth of the sea, what is deeper than human conscience? That is the depth which was troubled, when God redeemed with His arm His people. In what manner were the abysses troubled? When all men poured forth their consciences in confession.

18. In praises of God, in confessions of sins, in hymns and in songs, in prayers, "There is a multitude of the sound of waters. The clouds have uttered a voice" (ver. 17). Thence that sound of waters, thence the troubling of the abysses, because "the clouds have uttered a voice." What clouds? The preachers of the word of truth. What clouds? Those concerning which God doth menace a certain vineyard, which instead of grape had brought forth thorns, and He saith, "I will command My clouds, that they rain no rain upon it."[5] In a word, the Apostles forsaking the Jews, went to the Gentiles: in preaching Christ among all nations, "the clouds have uttered a voice." "For Thine arrows have gone through." Those same voices of the clouds He hath again called arrows. For the words of the Evangelists were arrows. For these things are allegories. For properly neither an arrow is rain, nor rain is an arrow: but yet

the word of God is both an arrow because it doth smite; and rain because it doth water. Let no one therefore any longer wonder at the troubling of the abysses, when "Thine arrows have gone through." What is, "have gone through"? They have not stopped in the ears, but they have pierced the heart. "The voice of Thy thunder is in the wheel" (ver. 18). What is this? How are we to understand it? May the Lord give aid. When boys we were wont to imagine, whenever we heard thunderings from Heaven, that carriages were going forth as it were from the stables. For thunder doth make a sort of rolling like carriages. Must we return to these boyish thoughts, in order to understand, "the voice of Thy thunder is in the wheel," as though God hath certain carriages in the clouds, and the passing along of the carriages doth raise that sound? Far be it. This is boyish, vain, trifling. What is then, "The voice of Thy thunder is in the wheel"? Thy voice rolleth. Not even this do I understand. What shall we do? Let us question Idithun himself, to see whether perchance he may himself explain what he hath said: "The voice," he saith, "of Thy thunder is in the wheel." I do not understand. I will hear what thou sayest: "Thy lightnings have appeared to the round world." Say then, I had no understanding. The round world is a wheel.[6] For the circuit of the round world is with reason called also an "orb:" whence also a small wheel is called an "orbiculus." "The voice of Thy thunder is in the wheel:" Thy "lightnings have appeared to the round world." Those clouds in a wheel have gone about the round world, have gone about with thundering and with lightning, they have shaken the abyss, with commandments they have thundered, with miracles they have lightened. "Unto every land hath gone forth the sound of them, and unto the ends of the orb the words of them."[7] "The land hath been moved and made to tremble:" that is, all men that dwell in the land. But by a figure the land itself is sea. Why? Because all nations are called by the name of sea, inasmuch as human life is bitter, and exposed to storms and tempests. Moreover if thou observe this, how men devour one another like fishes, how the stronger doth swallow up the weaker — it is then a sea, unto it the Evangelists went.

19. "Thy way is in the sea" (ver. 19). But now Thy way was in the Holy One, now "Thy way is in the sea:" because the Holy One Himself is in the sea, and with reason even did walk upon the waters of the sea.[8]

---

[1] Ps. lxxii. 11.　　　[2] Eph. ii. 20.　　　[3] Rev. xvii. 15.
[4] Ps. lxxvii. 14.　　　[5] Isa. v. 6.
[6] [No idea of a sphere, but of a plane, bounded by the encircling horizon. — C.]
[7] Ps. xix. 4.　　　[8] Matt. xiv. 25.

"Thy way is in the sea," that is, Thy Christ is preached among the Gentiles. . . . "Thy way is in the sea, and Thy paths in many waters," that is, in many peoples. "And Thy footsteps will not be known." He hath touched certain, and wonder were it if it be not those same Jews. Behold now the mercy of Christ hath been so published to the Gentiles, that "Thy way is in the sea. Thy footsteps will not be known." How so, by whom will they not be known, save by those who still say, Christ hath not yet come? Why do they say, Christ hath not yet come? Because they do not yet recognise Him walking on the sea.

20. "Thou hast led home Thy people like sheep in the hand of Moses and of Aaron" (ver. 20). Why He hath added this is somewhat difficult to discover. . . . They banished Christ; sick as they were, they would not have Him for their Saviour; but He began to be among the Gentiles, and among all nations, among many peoples. Nevertheless, a remnant of that people hath been saved. The ungrateful multitude hath remained without, even the halting breadth of Jacob's thigh.[1] For the breadth of the thigh is understood of the multitude of lineage, and among the greater part of the Israelites a certain multitude became vain and foolish, so as not to know the steps of Christ on the waters. "Thou hast led home Thy people like sheep," and they have not known Thee. Though Thou hast done such great benefits unto them, hast divided sea, hast made them pass over dry land between waters, hast drowned in the waves pursuing enemies, in the desert hast rained manna for their hunger, leading them home "by the hand of Moses and Aaron:" still they thrust Thee from them, so that in the sea was Thy Way, and Thy steps they knew not.

PSALM LXXVIII.[2]

1. This Psalm[3] doth contain the things which are said to have been done among the old people: but the new and latter people is being admonished, to beware that it be not ungrateful regarding the blessings of God, and provoke His anger against it, whereas it ought to receive His grace. . . . The Title thereof doth first move and engage our attention. For it is not without reason inscribed, "Understanding[4] of Asaph:" but it is perchance because these words require a reader who doth perceive not the voice which the surface uttereth, but some inward sense. Secondly, when about to narrate and mention all these things, which seem to need a hearer

more than an expounder: "I will open," he saith, "in parables my mouth, I will declare propositions from the beginning."[5] Who would not herein be awakened out of sleep? Who would dare to hurry over the parables and propositions, reading them as if self-evident, while by their very names they signify that they ought to be sought out with deeper view? For a parable hath on the surface thereof the similitude of something: and though it be a Greek word, it is now used as a Latin word. And it is observable, that in parables, those which are called the similitudes of things are compared with things with which we have to do. But propositions, which in Greek are called προβλήματα, are questions having something therein which is to be solved by disputation. What man then would read parables and propositions cursorily? What man would not attend while hearing these words with watchful mind, in order that by understanding he may come by the fruit thereof?

2. "Hearken ye," He saith, "My people, to My law" (ver. 1). Whom may we suppose to be here speaking, but God? For it was Himself that gave a law to His people, whom when delivered out of Egypt He gathered together, the which gathering together is properly named a Synagogue, which the word Asaph is interpreted to signify. Hath it then been said, "Understanding of Asaph," in the sense that Asaph himself hath understood; or must it be figuratively understood, in the sense that the same Synagogue, that is, the same people, hath understood, unto whom is said, "Hearken, My people, unto My law"? Why is it then that He is rebuking the same people by the mouth of the Prophet, saying, "But Israel hath not known Me, and My people hath not understood"?[6] But, in fact, there were even in that people they that understood, having the faith which was afterwards revealed, not pertaining to the letter of the law, but the grace of the Spirit. For they cannot have been without the same faith, who were able to foresee and foretell the revelation thereof that should be in Christ, inasmuch as even those old Sacraments were significants of those that should be. Had the prophets alone this faith, and not the people too? Nay indeed, but even they that faithfully heard the Prophets, were aided by the same grace in order that they might understand what they heard. But without doubt the mystery[7] of the Kingdom of Heaven was veiled in the Old Testament, which in the fulness of time should be unveiled in the New.[8] "For," saith the Apostle, "they did drink of the Spiritual Rock following them, but the Rock was

---

[1] Gen. xxxii. 32.   [2] Lat. LXXVII.
[3] Dictated A.D 415. See Ep. 169, to Evodius. — *Ben.*
[4] [*Intellectus*, Vulg.; *Eruditionis*, Jerome; Συνέσεως τῷ Ἀσάφ, Sept. — C.]

[5] Ps. lxxvii. 2.
[6] Isa. i. 3.   [7] *Sacramentum.*
[8] [*Velabatur in Veteri, quod revelaretur in Novo.* — C.]

Christ." [1]   In a mystery therefore theirs was the same meat and drink as ours, but in signification the same, not in form ; [2] because the same Christ was Himself figured to them in a Rock, manifested to us in the Flesh.   " But," he saith, " not in all of them God was well pleased." [3]   All indeed ate the same spiritual meat and drank the same spiritual drink, that is to say, signifying something spiritual : but not in all of them was God well pleased.   When, he saith, " not in all : " there were evidently there some in whom was God well pleased ; and although all the Sacraments were common, grace, which is the virtue of the Sacraments, was not common to all.   Just as in our times, now that the faith hath been revealed, which then was veiled, to all men that have been baptized in the name of the Father and of the Son and of the Holy Ghost, [4] the Laver of regeneration is common ; but the very grace whereof these same are the Sacraments, whereby the members of the Body of Christ are to reign [5] together with their Head, is not common to all.   For even heretics have the same Baptism, and false brethren too, in the communion of the Catholic name.

3. Nevertheless, neither then nor now without profit is the voice of him, saying, " Hearken ye, My people, to My law."   Which expression is remarkable in all the Scriptures, how he saith not, " hearken thou," but, " hearken ye."   For of many men a people doth consist : to which many that which followeth is spoken in the plural number.   " Incline ye your ear unto the words of My mouth."   " Hearken ye," is the same as, " Incline your ear : " and what He saith there, " My law," this He saith here in, " the words of My mouth."   For that man doth godly hearken to the law of God, and the words of His mouth, whose ear humility doth incline : not he whose neck pride doth lift up.   For whatever is poured in is received on the concave surface of humility, is shaken off from the convexity of swelling. Whence in another place, " Incline," he saith, " thine ear, and receive the words of understanding." [6]   We have been therefore sufficiently admonished to receive even this Psalm of this understanding of Asaph, [7] to receive, I say, with inclined ear, that is, with humble piety.   And it hath not been spoken of as being of Asaph himself, but to Asaph himself.   Which thing is evident by the Greek article, and is found in certain Latin copies.   These words therefore are of understanding, that is, of intelligence, which hath been given to Asaph himself : which we had better understand not as to one man, but as to

the congregation of the people of God ; whence we ought by no means to alienate ourselves. For although properly we say " Synagogue " of Jews, but " Church " of Christians, because a " Congregation " [8] is wont to be understood as rather of beasts, but a " convocation " as rather of men : yet that too we find called a Church, and it perhaps is more suitable for us [9] to say, " Save us, O Lord, our God, and congregate us from the nations, in order that we may confess to Thy Holy Nane." [10]   Neither ought we to disdain to be, nay we ought to render ineffable thanks, for that we are, the sheep of His hands, which He foresaw when He was saying, " I have other sheep which are not of this fold, them too I must lead in, that there may be one flock and one Shepherd : " [11] that is to say, by joining the faithful people of the Gentiles with the faithful people of the Israelites, concerning whom He had before said, " I have not been sent but to the sheep which have strayed of the house of Israel." [12]   For also there shall be congregated before Him all nations, and He shall sever them as a shepherd the sheep from the goats. [13]   Thus then let us hear that which hath been spoken.   " Hearken ye, My people, to My law, incline ye your ear unto the words of My mouth : " not as if addressed to Jews, but rather as if addressed to ourselves, or at least as if these words were said as well to ourselves (as to them [14]).   For when the Apostle had said, " But not in all them was God well pleased," thereby showing that there were those too in whom God was well pleased : he hath forthwith added, " For they were overthrown in the desert : " [15] secondly he hath continued, " but these things have been made our figures." . . . To us therefore more particularly these words have been sung.   Whence in this Psalm among other things there hath been said, " That another generation may know, sons who shall be born and shall arise." [16]   Moreover, if that death by serpents, and that destruction by the destroyer, and the slaying by the sword, were figures, as the Apostle evidently doth declare, inasmuch as it is manifest that all those things did happen : for he saith not, in a figure they were spoken, or, in a figure they were written, but, in a figure, he saith, they happened to them : with how much greater diligence of godliness must those punishments be shunned whereof those were the figures ? For beyond a doubt as in good things there is much more of good in that which is signified by the figure, than in the figure itself : so also in evil things very far worse are the things which are

---

[1] 1 Cor. x. 4.   [2] Specie.
[3] 1 Cor. x 5.   [4] Matt. xxviii. 19.
[5] So Oxf. mss.; Ben. " are regenerated," which makes scarcely an intelligible sense.
[6] Prov. v. 1.
[7] [He subjoins as follows: " For the word on the Title is put in the genitive case: hujus intellectûs, not hic intellectus." — C.]

[8] He takes con-gregatio as the Latin for synagogue, and expressing merely bringing together, and convocatio as Latin for ecclesia, which expresses calling.
[9] i.e., than for them.   [10] Ps. cvi. 47.
[11] John x. 16.   [12] Matt. xv. 24.   [13] Matt. xxv. 32.
[14] Oxf. mss. add quam Judæis.
[15] 1 Cor. x. 5.   [He cites to verse 12, entire. — C.]
[16] Ps. lxxviii. 6.

signified by the figures, while so great are the evil things which as figures do signify. For as the land of promise, whereunto that people was being led, is nothing in comparison with the Kingdom of Heaven, whereunto the Christian people is being led : so also those punishments which were figures, though they were so severe, are nothing in comparison with the punishments which they signify. But those which the Apostle hath called figures, the same this Psalm, as far as we are able to judge, calleth parables and propositions : not having their end in the fact of their having happened, but in those things whereunto they are referred by a reasonable comparison. Let us therefore hearken unto the law of God — us His people — and let us incline our ear unto the words of His mouth.

4. "I will open," he saith, "in parables My mouth, I will declare propositions from the beginning" (ver. 2). From what beginning he meaneth, is very evident in the words following. For it is not from the beginning, what time the Heaven and earth were made, nor what time mankind was created in the first man : but what time the congregation that was led out of Egypt ; in order that the sense may belong to Asaph, which is interpreted a congregation. But O that He that hath said, "I will open in parables My mouth," would also vouchsafe to open our understanding unto them ! For if, as He hath opened His mouth in parables, He would in like sort open the parables themselves : and as He declareth "propositions," He would declare in like sort the expositions thereof, we should not be here toiling : but now so hidden and closed are all things, that even if we are able by His aid to arrive at anything, whereon we may feed to our health, still we must eat the bread in the sweat of our face ; and pay the penalty of the ancient sentence [1] not with the labour of the body only, but also with that of the heart. Let him speak then, and let us hear the parables and propositions.

5. "How great things we have heard, and have known them, and our fathers have told them to us" (ver. 3). The Lord was speaking higher up. For of what other person could these words be thought to be, "Hearken ye, O My people, to My law"? [2] Why is it then that now on a sudden a man is speaking, for here we have the words of a man, "our fathers have told them to us." Without doubt God, now about to speak by a man's ministry, as the Apostle saith, "Will ye to receive proof of Him that is speaking in me, Christ?" [3] in His own person at first willed the words to be uttered, lest a man speaking His words should be despised as a man. For it is thus with the sayings of God which make their way to us through our bodily sense. The Creator moveth the subject creature by an invisible working ; not so that the substance is changed into anything corporal and temporal, when by means of corporal and temporal signs, whether belonging to the eyes or to the ears, as far as men are able to receive it, He would make His will to be known. For if an angel is able to use air, mist, cloud, fire, and any other natural substance or corporal species ; [4] and man to use face, tongue, hand, pen, letters, or any other significants, for the purpose of intimating the secret things of his own mind : in a word, if, though he is a man, he sendeth human messengers, and he saith to one, "Go, and he goeth ; and to another, Come, and he cometh ; and to his servant, Do this, and he doeth it ; " [5] with how much greater and more effectual power doth God, to whom as Lord all things together are subject, use both the same angel and man, in order that He may declare whatsoever pleaseth Him? . . . For those things were heard in the Old Testament which are known in the New : heard when they were being prophesied, known when they were being fulfilled. Where a promise is performed, hearing is not deceived. "And our fathers," Moses and the Prophets, "have told unto us."

6. "They have not been hidden from their sons in another generation" (ver. 4). This is our generation.wherein there hath been given to us regeneration. "Telling forth the praises of the Lord and His powers, and His wonderful works which He hath done." The order of the words is, "and our fathers have told unto us, telling forth the praises of the Lord." The Lord is praised, in order that He may be loved. For what object can be loved more to our health? "And He hath raised up a testimony in Jacob, and hath set a law in Jacob" (ver. 5). This is the beginning whereof hath been spoken above, "I will declare propositions from the beginning." [6] So then the beginning is the Old Testament, the end is the New. For fear doth prevail in the law.[7] "But the end of the law is Christ for righteousness to every one believing ; " [8] at whose bestowing "love is shed abroad in our hearts through the Holy Spirit, which hath been given to us : " [9] and love made perfect doth cast out fear,[10] inasmuch as now without the Law the righteousness of God hath been made manifest. But inasmuch as He hath a testimony by the Law and the Prophets,[11] therefore, "He hath raised up a testimony in Jacob." For even that Tabernacle which was

---

[4] [Judg. xiii. 20. This mysterious subject may be illustrated from Holy Scripture so as to justify our author's very broad statement. It throws light on Gen. iii. 1-16, and also 2 Pet. ii. 16. Compare on verse 49 of this Psalm, *infra.*—C.]
[5] Luke vii. 8.   [6] Ps. lxxviii. 2.   [7] Ps. cxi. 10.
[8] Rom. x. 4.   [9] Rom. v. 5.   [10] 1 John iv. 18.
[11] Rom. iii. 21.

---

[1] Gen. iii. 19.   [2] Ps. lxxviii. 1.   [3] 2 Cor. xiii. 3.

set up with a work so remarkable and full of such wondrous meanings, is named the Tabernacle of Testimony, wherein was the veil over the Ark of the Law, like the veil over the face of the Minister of the Law;[1] because in that dispensation there were "parables and propositions." For those things which were being preached and were coming to pass were hidden in veiled meanings, and were not seen in unveiled manifestations. But "when thou shalt have passed over unto Christ," saith the Apostle, "the veil shall be taken away."[2] For "all the promises of God in Him are yea, Amen."[3] Whosoever therefore doth cleave to Christ, hath the whole of the good which even in the letters of the Law he perceiveth not: but whosoever is an alien from Christ, doth neither perceive, nor hath. "He hath set a law in Israel." After his usual custom he is making a repetition. For "He hath raised up a testimony," is the same as, "He hath set a law," and "in Jacob," is the same as "in Israel." For as these are two names of one man, so law and testimony are two names of one thing. Is there any difference, saith some one, between "hath raised up" and "hath set"? Yea indeed, the same difference as there is between "Jacob" and "Israel:" not because they were two persons, but these same two names were bestowed upon one man for different reasons; Jacob because of supplanting, for that he grasped the foot of his brother at his birth:[4] but Israel because of the vision of God.[5] So "raised up" is one thing, "set" is another. For, "He hath raised up a testimony," as far as I can judge, hath been said because by it something has been raised up; "For without the Law," saith the Apostle, "sin was dead: but I lived sometime without the Law: but at the coming in of the commandment sin revived."[6] Behold that which hath been raised up by the testimony, which is the Law, so that what was lying hidden might appear, as he saith a little afterwards: "But sin, that it might appear sin, through a good thing hath wrought in me death."[7] But "He hath set a law," hath been said, as though it were a yoke upon sinners, whence hath been said, "For upon a just man law hath not been imposed."[8] It is a testimony then, so far forth as it doth prove anything; but a law so far forth as it doth command; though it is one and the same thing. Wherefore just as Christ is a stone, but to believers for the Head of the corner, while to unbelievers a stone of offence and a rock of scandal;[9] so the testimony of the Law to them that use not the Law lawfully,[10] is a testimony whereby sinners are to be convicted as deserving of punishment; but to them that use the same lawfully, is a testimony whereby sinners are shown unto whom they ought to flee in order to be delivered. . . .

7. "How great things," he saith, "He hath commanded our fathers, to make the same known to their sons?" (ver. 5). "That another generation may know, sons who shall be born and shall rise up, and they may tell to their sons" (ver. 6). "That they may put their hope in God, and may not forget the works of God, and may seek out His commandments" (ver. 7). "That they may not become, like their fathers, a crooked and embittering generation: a generation that hath not guided their heart, and the spirit thereof hath not been trusted with God" (ver. 8). These words do point out two peoples as it were, the one belonging to the Old Testament, the other to the New: for in that he saith, he hath implied that they received the commandments, "to make them known to their sons," but that they did not know or do them: but they received them themselves, to the end "that another generation might know," what the former knew not. "Sons who shall be born and shall arise." For they that have been born have not arisen: because they had not their heart above, but rather on the earth. For the arising is with Christ: whence hath been said, "If ye have arisen with Christ, savour ye the things which are above."[11] "And they may tell them," he saith, "to their sons, in order that they may put their hope in God." . . . "And may not forget the works of God:" that is to say, in magnifying and vaunting their own works, as though they did them themselves; while "God it is that worketh," in them that work good things, "both to will and to work according to good will."[12] "And may search out His commandments." . . . The commandments which He hath commanded. How then should they still search out, whereas they have already learned them, save that by putting their hope in God, they do then search out His commandments, in order that by them, with His aid, they may be fulfilled? And he saith why, by immediately subjoining, "and its spirit hath not been trusted with God," that is, because it had no faith, which doth obtain what the Law doth enjoin. For when the spirit of man doth work together with the Spirit of God working, then there is fulfilled that which God hath commanded: and this doth not come to pass, except by believing in Him that doth justify an ungodly man.[13] Which faith the generation crooked and embittering had not: and therefore concerning the same hath been said, "The spirit thereof hath not been trusted with God." For this hath been said much more exactly to point out the grace of

---

[1] Exod. xl. 2, 3; 2 Cor. iii. 13.
[2] 2 Cor. iii. 16.　[3] 2 Cor. i. 20.　[4] Gen. xxv. 26.
[5] Gen. xxxii. 28.　[6] Rom. vii. 8, 9.　[7] Rom. vii. 13.
[8] 1 Tim. i. 9.　[9] Ps. cxviii. 22; 1 Pet. ii. 8.
[10] 1 Tim. i. 8.

[11] Col. iii. 1.　[12] Philip. ii. 13.　[13] Rom. iv. 5.

God, which doth work not only remission of sins, but also doth make the spirit of man to work together therewith in the work of good deeds, as though he were saying, his spirit hath not believed in God. For to have the spirit trusted with God, is, not to believe that his spirit is able to do righteousness without God, but with God. For this is to believe in God: which is surely more than to believe God. For ofttimes we must believe even a man, though in him we must not believe. To believe in God therefore is this, in believing to cleave unto God who worketh good works, in order to work with Him well. . . .

8. Lastly, " The sons of Ephrem bending and shooting bows, have been turned back in the day of war" (ver. 9). Following after the law of righteousness, unto the law of righteousness they have not attained.[1] Why? Because they were not of faith. For they were that generation whereof the spirit hath not been trusted with God; but they were, so to speak, of works: because they did not, as they bended and shot their bows (which are outward actions, as of the works of the law), so guide their heart also, wherein the just man doth live by faith, which worketh by love; whereby men cleave to God, who worketh in man both to will and work according to good will.[2] For what else is bending the bow and shooting, and turning back in the day of war, but heeding and purposing in the day of hearing, and deserting in the day of temptation; flourishing arms, so to speak, beforehand, and at the hour of the action refusing to fight? But whereas he saith, " bending and shooting bows," when it would seem that he ought to have said, bending bows and shooting arrows. . . . Some Greek copies to be sure are said to have " bending and shooting with bows," so that without doubt we ought to understand arrows. But whereas by the sons of Ephrem he hath willed that there be understood the whole of that embittering generation, it is an expression signifying the whole by a part. And perhaps this part was chosen whereby to signify the whole, because from these men especially some good thing was to have been expected. . . . Although set at the left hand by his father as being the younger, Jacob nevertheless blessed with his right hand, and preferred him before his elder brother with a benediction of hidden meaning.[3] . . . For there was being figured how they were to be last that were first, and first were to be they that were last,[4] through the Saviour's coming, concerning whom hath been said, " He that is coming after me was made before me."[5] In like manner righteous Abel was preferred before the elder brother; so to Ismael Isaac; so to Esau, though born before him, his twin brother Jacob; so also Phares him-

self preceded even in birth his twin brother, who had first thrust a hand out of the womb, and had begun to be born:[6] so David was preferred before his elder brother:[7] and as the reason why all these parables and others like them preceded, not only of words but also of deeds, in like manner to the people of the Jews was preferred the Christian people, for redeeming the which as Abel by Cain,[8] so by the Jews was slain Christ. This thing was prefigured even when Jacob stretching out his hands cross-wise, with his right hand touched Ephrem standing on the left; and set him before Manasse standing on the right, whom he himself touched with the left hand.[3]

9. But what that is which he saith, " they have been turned back in the day of war," the following words do teach, wherein he hath most clearly explained this: " they have not kept," he saith, " the testament of God, and in His law they would not walk " (ver. 10). Behold what is, " they have been turned back in the day of war:" they have not kept the testament of God. When they were bending and shooting bows, they did also utter the words of most forward promise, saying, " Whatsoever things the Lord our God hath spoken we will do, and we will hear."[9] " They have been turned back in the day of war:" because the promise of obedience not hearing but temptation doth prove. But he whose spirit hath been trusted with God, keepeth hold on God, who is faithful, and " doth not suffer him to be tempted above that which he is able; but will make with the temptation a way of escape also,"[10] that he may be able to endure, and may not be turned back in the day of war. . . . Therefore these men have been thus branded: " a generation," he saith, " which hath not directed their heart."[11] It hath not been said, works, but heart. For when the heart is directed, the works are right; but when the heart is not directed, the works are not right, even though they seem to be right. And how the crooked generation hath not directed the heart, hath sufficiently been shown, when he saith, " and the spirit thereof hath not been trusted with God."[11] For God is right: and therefore by cleaving to the right, as to an immutable rule, the heart of a man can be made right, which in itself was crooked. . . .

10. " And they forgat His benefits, and the wonderful works of Him which He showed to them; before their fathers the wonderful things which He did " (ver. 11). What this is, is not a question to be negligently passed over. Concerning those very fathers he was speaking a little before, that they had been a generation crooked and embittering. . . . What fathers, inasmuch

---

[1] Rom. ix 31.   [2] Rom. i. 17; Gal. v. 6; Phil. ii. 13.
[3] Gen xlviii 14.   [4] Matt. xx. 16.   [5] John i. 27.

[6] Gen. iv. 4, xxi. 12, xxxviii. 29.   [7] 1 Sam. xvi. 12
[8] Gen. iv. 8.   [9] Exod. xix. 8.   [10] 1 Cor. x.
[11] Ps. lxxviii. 8.

as these are the very fathers, whom he would not have posterity to be like? If we shall take them to be those out of whom the others had derived their being, for example, Abraham, Isaac, Jacob, by this time they had long since fallen asleep, when God showed wonderful things in Egypt. For there followeth, "in the land of Egypt, in the plain of Thanis" (ver. 12): where it is said that God showed to them wonderful things before their fathers. Were they perchance present in spirit? For of the same the Lord saith in the Gospel, "for all do live to Him."[1] Or do we more suitably understand thereby the fathers Moses and Aaron, and the other elders who are related in the same Scripture also to have received the Spirit, of which also Moses received, in order that they might aid him in ruling and bearing the same people?[2] For why should they not have been called fathers? It is not in the same manner as God is the One Father, who doth regenerate with His Spirit those whom He doth make sons for an everlasting inheritance; but it is for the sake of honour, because of their age and kindly carefulness: just as Paul the elder saith, "Not to confound you I am writing these things, but as my dearly beloved sons I am admonishing you:"[3] though he knew of a truth that it had been said by the Lord, "Call ye no man your father on earth, for One is your Father, even God."[4] And this was not said in order that this term of human honour should be erased from our usual way of speaking: but lest the grace of God whereby we are regenerated unto eternal life, should be ascribed either to the power or even sanctity of any man. Therefore when he said, "I have begotten you;" he first said, "in Christ," and "through the Gospel;" lest that might be thought to be of him, which is of God. . . . Accordingly, the land of Egypt must be understood for a figure of this world. "The plain of Thanis" is the smooth surface of lowly commandment. For lowly commandment is the interpretation of Thanis. In this world therefore let us receive the commandment of humility, in order that in another world we may merit to receive the exaltation which He hath promised, who for our sake here became lowly.

11. For He that "did burst asunder the sea and made them go through, did confine the waters as it were in bottles" (ver. 13), in order that the water might stand up first as if it were shut in, is able by His grace to restrain the flowing and ebbing tides of carnal desires, when we renounce this world, so that all sins having been thoroughly washed away, as if they were enemies, the people of the faithful may be made to pass through by means of the Sacrament of Baptism. He that "led them home in the cloud of the day, and in the whole of the night in the illumination of fire" (ver. 14), is able also spiritually to direct goings if faith crieth to Him, "Direct Thou my goings after Thy word."[5] Of Whom in another place[6] is said, "For Himself shall make thy courses right, and shall prolong thy goings in peace"[7] through Jesus Christ our Lord, whose Sacrament in this world, as it were in the day, is manifest in the flesh, as if in a cloud; but in the Judgment it will be manifest like as in a terror by night; for then there will be a great tribulation of the world like as it were fire, and it shall shine for the just and shall burn for the unjust. "He that burst asunder the rock in the desert, and gave them water as in a great deep" (ver. 15); "and brought out water from the rock, and brought down waters like rivers" (ver. 16), is surely able upon thirsty faith to pour the gift of the Holy Spirit (the which gift the performance of that thing did spiritually signify), to pour, I say, from the Spiritual Rock that followed, which is Christ: who did stand and cry, "If any is athirst, let him come to Me:"[8] and, "he that shall have drunk of the water which I shall give, rivers of living water shall flow out of his bosom."[9] For this He spake, as is read in the Gospel,[10] to the Spirit, which they were to receive that believed in Him, unto whom like the rod drew near the wood of the Passion, in order that there might flow forth grace for believers.

12. And yet, "they," like a generation crooked and embittering, "added yet to sin against Him" (ver. 17): that is, not to believe. For this is the sin, whereof the Spirit doth convict the world, as the Lord saith, "Of sin indeed because they have not believed on Me."[11] "And they exasperated the Most High in drought," which other copies have, "in a place without water," which is a more exact translation from the Greek, and doth signify no other thing than drought. Was it in that drought of the desert, or rather in their own? For although they had drunk of the rock, they had not their bellies but their minds dry, freshening with no fruitfulness of righteousness. In that drought they ought the more faithfully to have been suppliant unto God, in order that He who had given fulness unto their jaws, might give also equity to their manners. For unto him the faithful soul doth cry, "Let mine eyes see equity."[12]

13. "And they tempted God in their hearts, in order that they might seek morsels for their souls" (ver. 18). It is one thing to ask in believing, another thing in tempting. Lastly there

---

[1] Luke xx. 38.　　[2] Numb. xi. 17.　　[3] 1 Cor. iv. 14.
[4] Matt. xxiii 9.

[5] Ps. cxix. 133.　　[6] Prov. iv. 27, LXX.
[7] These words are part of an addition in the Septuagint text.
[8] John vii. 37.　　[9] John iv. 14.　　[10] John vii. 39.
[11] John xvi. 9.　　[12] Ps. xvii. 2.

followeth, "And they slandered God, and said, Shall God be able to prepare a table in· the desert?" (ver. 19). "For He smote the rock, and the waters flowed, and torrents gushed forth : will He be able to give bread also, or to prepare a table for His people?" (ver. 20). Not believing therefore, they sought morsels for their souls. Not so the Apostle James doth enjoin a morsel to be asked for the mind, but doth admonish that it be sought by believers, not by such as tempt and slander God. "But if any one of you," he saith, "doth lack wisdom, let him ask of God, who doth give to all men abundantly, and doth not upbraid, and it shall be given to him : but let him ask in faith, nothing wavering."[1] This faith had not that generation which " had not directed their heart, and the spirit thereof had not been trusted with God."

14. "Wherefore the Lord heard, and He delayed, and fire was lighted in Jacob, and wrath went up into Israel" (ver. 21). He·hath explained what he hath called fire. He hath called anger fire : although in strict propriety fire did also burn up many men. What is therefore this that he saith, "The Lord heard, and He delayed "? Did He delay to conduct them into the land of promise, whither they were being led : which might have been done in the space of a few days, but on account of sins they must needs be wasted in the desert, where also they were wasted during forty years? And if this be so, He did then delay the people, not those very persons who tempted and slandered God : for they all perished in the desert, and their children journeyed into the land of promise. Or did He delay punishment, in order that He might first satisfy unbelieving concupiscence, lest He might be supposed to be angry, because they were asking of Him what He was not able to do? "He heard," then, "and He delayed to avenge : " and after He had done what they supposed He was not able to do, then "anger went up upon Israel."

15. Lastly, when both these things have been briefly touched, afterwards he is evidently following out the order of the narrative. "Because they believed not in God, nor hoped in His saving health " (ver. 22). For when he had told why fire was lighted in Jacob, and anger went up upon Israel, that is to say, " because they believed not in God, nor hoped in His saving health : " immediately subjoining the evident blessings for which they were ungrateful, he saith, " and He commanded the clouds above, and opened the doors of Heaven " (ver. 23). " And He rained upon them manna to eat, and gave them bread of Heaven" (ver. 24). "Bread of

angels man did eat : dainties He sent them in abundance " (ver. 25). He brought over the South Wind from Heaven, and in His virtue He led in the South West Wind " (ver. 26). " And He rained upon them fleshes like dust, and winged fowls like the sand of the sea " (ver. 27). "And they fell in the midst of their camp, around their tabernacles " (ver. 28). " And they ate and were filled exceedingly ; and their desire He brought to them : they were not deprived of their desire " (ver. 29). Behold why He had delayed. But what He had delayed let us hear. "Yet the morsel was in their mouths, and the anger of God came down upon them " (ver. 30). Behold what He had delayed. For before " He delayed : " and afterwards, " fire was lighted in Jacob and anger went up upon Israel." He had delayed therefore in order that He might first do what they had believed that He could not do, and then might bring upon them what they deserved to suffer. For if they placed their hope in God, not only would their desires of the flesh but also those of the spirit have been fulfilled. For he that . . . " opened the doors of Heaven, and rained upon them manna to eat," that He might fill the unbelieving, is not without power to give to believers Himself the true Bread from Heaven, which the manna did signify : which is indeed the food of Angels, whom being incorruptible the Word of God doth incorruptibly feed : the which in order that man might eat, He became flesh, and dwelled in us.[2] For Himself the Bread by means of the Evangelical clouds is being rained over the whole world, and, the hearts of preachers like heavenly doors, being opened, is being preached not to a murmuring and tempting synagogue, but to a Church believing and putting hope in Him. He is able also to feed the feeble faith of such as tempt not, but believe, with the signs of words uttered by the flesh and speeding through the air, as though it were fowls : not however with such as come from the north, where cold and mist do prevail, that is to say, eloquence which is pleasing to this world, but by bringing over the South Wind from Heaven ; whither, except to the earth? In order that they who are feeble in faith, by hearing things earthly may be nourished up to receive things heavenly. . . .

16. But as to unbelievers, being a crooked and embittering generation, as it were, while the morsel was yet in their mouths, "the anger of God went up upon them, and it slew among the most of them " (ver. 31) : that‚is, the most of them, or as some copies have it, " the fat ones of them," which however in the Greek copies which we had, we did not find. But if this be

---

[1] Jas. i. 5, 6.   [2] John i. 14.

the truer reading, what else must be understood by "the fat ones of them," than men mighty in pride, concerning whom is said, "their iniquity shall come forth as if out of fat"?[1] "And the elect of Israel He fettered." Even there there were elect, with whose faith the generation crooked and embittering was not mixed. But they were fettered, so that they might in no sort profit them for whom they desired that they might provide from a fatherly affection. For what is conferred by human mercy, on those with whom God is angry? Or rather hath He willed it to be understood, how that even the elect were fettered at the same time with them, in order that they who were diverse both in mind and in life, might endure sufferings with them for an example not only of righteousness, but also of patience? For we have learned that holy men were even led captive with sinners for no other reason; since in the Greek copies we read not ἐνεπόδισεν, which is "fettered;" but συνεπόδισεν, which is rather "fettered together with."

17. But the generation crooked and embittering, "in all these things sinned yet more, and they believed not in His wonderful works" (ver. 32). "And in their days failed in vanity" (ver. 33). Though they might, if they had believed, have had days in truth without failing, with Him to whom hath been said, "Thy years shall not fail."[2] Therefore, "their days failed in vanity, and their years with haste." For the whole life of mortal men is hastening, and that which seemeth to be longer is but a vapour of somewhat longer duration.

18. Nevertheless, "when he slew them they sought Him:" not for the sake of eternal life, but fearing to end the vapour too soon. There sought Him then, not indeed those whom He had slain, but they that were afraid of being slain according to the example of them. But the Scripture hath so spoken of them as if they sought God who were slain; because they were one people, and it is spoken as if of one body: "and they returned, and at dawn they came to God" (ver. 34). "And they remembered that God is their Helper, and the High God is their Redeemer" (ver. 35). But all this is for the sake of acquiring temporal good things, and for avoiding temporal evil things. For they that did seek God for the sake of temporal blessings, sought not God indeed, but things. Thus with those God is worshipped with slavish fear, not free love. Thus then God is not worshipped, for that thing is worshipped which is loved. Whence because God is found to be greater and better than all things, He must be loved more than all things, in order that He may be worshipped.

19. Lastly, here let us see the words following: "And they loved Him," he saith, "in their mouth, and in their tongue they lied unto Him" (ver. 36). "But their heart was not right with Him, and they were not counted faithful in His Testament" (ver. 37). One thing on their tongue, another thing in their heart He found, unto whom the secret things of men are naked, and without any impediment He saw what they loved rather. Therefore the heart is right with God, when it doth seek God for the sake of God. For one thing he desired of the Lord, the same he will require, that he may dwell always in the House of the Lord, and may meditate on the pleasantness of Him.[3] Unto Whom saith the heart of the faithful, I will be filled, not with the flesh-pots of the Egyptians, nor with melons and gourds, and garlick and onions, which a generation crooked and embittering did prefer even to bread celestial,[4] nor with visible manna, and those same winged fowls; but, "I will be filled, when Thy glory shall be made manifest."[5] For this is the inheritance of the New Testament, wherein they were not counted faithful; whereof however the faith even at that time, when it was veiled, was in the elect, and now, when it hath already been revealed, it is not in many that are called. "For many have been called, but few are elect."[6] Of such sort therefore was the generation crooked and embittering, even when they were seeming to seek God, loving in mouth, and in tongue lying; but in heart not right with God, while they loved rather those things, for the sake of which they required the help of God.

20. "But He is Himself merciful, and will become propitious to their sins, and He will not destroy them. And He will abound to turn away His anger, and He will not kindle all his anger" (ver. 38). By these words many men promise to themselves impunity for their iniquity from the Divine Mercy, even if they shall have persevered in being such, as that generation is described, "crooked and embittering; which hath not directed their heart, and the spirit thereof hath not been trusted with God:" with whom it is not profitable to agree. For if, to speak in their words, God will perchance not destroy no not even bad men, without doubt He will not destroy good men. Why then do we not rather choose that wherein there is no doubt? For they that lie to Him in their tongue, though their heart doth hold some other thing, do think indeed, and will, even God to be a liar, when He doth menace upon such men eternal punishment. But whilst they do not deceive Him with their lying, He doth not deceive them with

[1] Ps. lxxiii. 7.   [2] Ps. cii. 27.

[3] Ps. xxvii. 4.   [4] Exod. xvi. 3.   [5] Ps. xvii. 15, Lat.
[6] Matt. xx. 16.

speaking the truth. These words therefore of divine sayings, concerning which the crooked generation doth cajole itself, let it not make crooked like its own heart : for even when it is made crooked, they continue right.   For at first they may be understood according to that which is written in the Gospel, "that ye may be like your Father who is in the Heavens, who maketh His sun to rise upon good men and evil men, and raineth upon just men and unjust men." [1]   For who could not see, how great is the long-suffering of mercy with which He is sparing evil men? But before the Judgment, He spared them that nation in such sort, that He kindled not [2] all His anger, utterly to root it up and bring it to an end : which thing in His words and in the intercession for their sins of His servant Moses doth evidently appear, where God saith, "Let Me blot them out, and make thee into a great nation : " [3] he intercedeth, being more ready to be blotted out for them than that they should be ; knowing that he is doing this before One Merciful, who inasmuch as by no means He would blot out him, would even spare them for his sake. For let us see how greatly He spared, and doth still spare. . . . .

21. In the second place, that we may not seem to do violence to divine words, and lest in the place where there was said, "He will not destroy them," [4] we should say, "But hereafter He will destroy them : " concerning this very present Psalm let us turn to a very common phrase of the Scripture, whereby this question may be more diligently and more truly solved. Speaking of these same persons a little lower down, when He had made mention of the things which the Egyptians because of them had endured, He saith, . . . "And He led them unto the mount of His sanctification, the mount which His right hand won. And He cast out from their face the nations, and by lot distributed to them the land in the cord of distribution." [5] If any one at these words should press a question upon us, and should say, How doth he make mention of all these things as having been bestowed upon them, when the same persons were not led into the land of promise, as were delivered from Egypt, inasmuch as they were dead? What shall we reply but that they were spoken of, because they were the self-same people by means of a succession of sons? . . .

22. "And He remembered that they are flesh, a spirit [6] going and not returning " (ver. 39). Therefore calling them and pitying them through His grace, He called them back Himself, because of themselves they could not return. For how doth flesh return, " a spirit walking and not turning back," [7] while a weight of evil deserts doth weigh it down unto the lowest and far places of evil, save through the election of grace ? . . . For thus also is solved this no unimportant question, how it is written in the Proverbs, when the Scripture was speaking of the way of iniquity, " all they that walk in her shall not return." [8]   For it hath been so spoken as if all ungodly men were to be despaired of : but the Scripture did only commend grace ; for of himself man is able to walk in that way, but is not able of himself to return, except when called back by grace.

23. I say then of these crooked and embittering persons, "How often they exasperated Him in the desert, and provoked Him to wrath in the waterless place ! " (ver. 40).   "And they turned themselves and tempted God, and exasperated the Holy One of Israel " (ver. 41).   He is repeating that same unbelief of theirs, of which He had made mention above. But the reason of the repetition is, in order that there may be mentioned also the plagues which He inflicted on the Egyptians for their sakes : all which things they certainly ought to have remembered, and not to be ungrateful.   Lastly, there followeth what? "They remembered not His hands, in the day when He redeemed them from the hand of the troubler " (ver. 42).   And he beginneth to speak of what things He did to the Egyptians : " He set in Egypt His signs, and His prodigies in the plain of Thanis " (ver. 43) : " and He turned their rivers into blood, and their showers lest they should drink " (ver. 44), or rather, " the flowings of waters," as some do better understand by what is written in Greek, τὰ ὀμβρήματα, which in Latin we call *scaturigines*, waters bubbling from beneath. "He sent upon them the dog-fly, and it ate them up ; and the frog, and it destroyed them " (ver. 45).   "And He gave their fruit to the mildew, and their labours to the locust " (ver. 46).   "And He slew with hail their vineyards, and their mulberry trees with frost " (ver. 47).   "And He gave over to the hail their beasts of burden, and their possessions to the fire " (ver. 48).   "He sent upon them the anger of His indignation, indignation and anger and tribulation, a visitation through evil angels " (ver. 49).   He made a way to the course of His anger, and their beasts of burden He shut up in death " (ver. 50).   "And He smote every first-born thing in the land of Egypt, the first-fruits of their labours in the tabernacles of Cham " (ver. 51).

24. All these punishments of the Egyptians may be explained by an allegorical interpretation, according as one shall have chosen to understand them, and to compare them to the things whereunto they must be referred.   Which we too will

---

[1] Matt. v. 45.
[2] Many mss. omit " not."
[3] Exod. xxxii. 10.
[4] Ps. lxxviii. 38.
[5] Ps. lxxviii. 54, 55.
[6] Or, " breath."
[7] [Transient, and not returning. — C.]
[8] Prov. ii. 19.

endeavour to do ; and shall do it the more properly, the more we shall have been divinely aided. For to do this, those words of this Psalm do constrain us, wherein it was said, " I will open in parables my mouth, I will declare propositions from the beginning." [1] For for this cause even some things have been here spoken of, which that they befell the Egyptians at all we read not, although all their plagues are most carefully related in Exodus according to their order, so that while that which is not there mentioned we are sure hath not been mentioned in the Psalm to no purpose, and we can interpret the same only figuratively, we may at the same time understand that even the rest of the things which it is evident did happen, were done or described for the sake of some figurative meaning. For the Scripture doth so do in many passages of the prophetic sayings. . . . In the plagues therefore of the Egyptians, which are in the book which is called Exodus, where the Scripture hath been especially careful, that those things whereby they were afflicted should be all related in order, there is not found what this Psalm hath, " and He gave to the mildew their fruits." This also wherein, when he had said, " and He gave over to the hail their beasts," he hath added, " and their possession to the fire : " of the beasts slain with hail is read in Exodus ; [2] but how their possession was burned with fire, is not read at all. Although voices and fires do come together with hail, just as thunderings do commonly accompany lightnings ; nevertheless, it is not written that anything was given over to the fire that it should be burned. Lastly, the soft things which the hail could not hurt, are said not to have been smitten, that is, hurt with hard blows ; which things the locust devoured afterwards. Also that which is here spoken of, " and their mulberry trees with hoar-frost," is not in Exodus. For hoar-frost doth differ much from hail ; for in the clear winter nights the earth is made white with hoar-frost.

25. What then those things do signify, let the interpreter say as he can, let reader and hearer judge as is just. The water turned into blood seemeth to me to signify a carnal view of the causes of things. Dog-fly, are the manners of dogs,[3] who see not even their parents when first they are born. The frog is very talkative vanity. Mildew doth hurt secretly, which also some have interpreted by rust, others black mould : which evil thing to what vice is it more appropriately compared, than to what doth show itself least readily, like the trusting much in one's self? For it is a blighting air which doth work this secretly among fruits : just like in morals, secret pride, when a man thinketh himself to be some-thing, though he is nothing.[4] The locust is malice hurting with the mouth, that is, with unfaithful testimony. The hail is iniquity taking away the goods of others ; whence theft, robberies, and depredations do spring : but more by his wickedness the plunderer himself is plundered. The hoar-frost doth signify the fault wherein the love of one's neighbour by the darkness of foolishness, like as it were by the cold of night, is frozen up. But the fire, if here it is not that which is mentioned which was in the hail out of the lightning clouds, forasmuch as he hath said here, " He gave over their possession to the fire," where he implieth that a thing was burned, which by that fire we read not to have been done, — it seemeth to me, I say, to signify the savageness of wrath, whereby even man-slaying may be committed. But by the death of beasts was figured, as far as I judge, the loss of chastity. For concupiscence, whereby offspring do arise, we have in common with beasts. To have this therefore tamed and ordered, is the virtue of chastity. The death of the first-born things, is the putting off of the very justice whereby a man doth associate with mankind. But whether the figurative significations of these things be so, or whether they are better understood in another way, whom would it not move, that with ten plagues the Egyptians are smitten, and with ten commandments the tables are inscribed,[5] that thereby the people of God should be ruled? Concerning the comparing of which one with the other, inasmuch as we have spoken elsewhere, there is no need to load the exposition of this Psalm therewith : thus much we remind you, that here too, though not in the same order, yet ten plagues of the Egyptians are commemorated, forasmuch as in the place of three which are in Exodus and are not here, to wit, lice, boils, darkness ; other three are commemorated, which are not there, that is to say, mildew, hoar-frost, and fire ; not of lightning, but that whereunto their possession was given over, which is not read of in that place.

26. But it hath been clearly enough intimated, that by the judgment of God these things befell them through the instrumentality of evil angels, in this wicked world, as though it were in Egypt and in the plain of Thanis, where we ought to be humble, until there come that world, wherein we may earn to be exalted out of this humiliation. For even Egypt in the Hebrew tongue doth signify darkness or tribulations, in which tongue, Thanis,[6] as I have observed, is understood to be humble commandment. Concerning the evil angels therefore in this Psalm, while he was speaking of those very plagues, there hath been

---

[1] Ps. lxxviii. 2. [2] Exod. ix. 25.
[3] [*Obscenique canes.* Virg. *Georg.* i. 470. — C.]
[4] Gal. vi. 3.
[5] *Vid.* Sermon on the Ten Plagues and Ten Commandments.
[6] Oxf. MSS. *Taphnis.*

something inserted, which must not be passed over cursorily : " He sent upon them," he saith, " an infliction through evil angels." Now that the devil and his angels are so very evil, that for them everlasting fire is prepared, no believer is ignorant : but that there should be sent by means of them an infliction from the Lord God upon certain whom He judgeth to be deserving of this punishment, seemeth to be a hard thing to those who are little prone to consider, how the perfect justice of God doth use well even evil things. For these indeed, as far as regardeth their substance, what other person but Himself hath made? But evil He hath not made them : yet He doth use them, inasmuch as He is good, well, that is, conveniently and justly : just as on the other hand unrighteous men do use His good creatures in evil manner. God therefore doth use evil angels not only to punish evil men, as in the case of all those concerning whom the Psalm doth speak, as in the case of king Achab, whom a spirit of lying by the will of God did beguile, in order that he might fall in war : [1] but also to prove and make manifest good men, as He did in the case of Job. But as far as regardeth that corporal matter of visible elements, I suppose that thereof angels both good and evil are able to make use, according to the power given to each : just as also men good and evil do use such things, as far as they are able, according to the measure of human infirmity. For we use both earth and water, and air, and fire, not only in things necessary for our support, but also in many operations superfluous and playful, and marvellously artificial. For countless things, which are called μηχανήματα, are moulded out of these elements scientifically employed. But over these things angels have a far more extended power, both the good and the evil, though greater is that which the good have ; [2] but only so far as is commanded or permitted by the will and providence of God ; on which terms also we have it. For not even in these cases are we able to do all that we will. But in a book the most unerring we read that the devil was able even to send fire from Heaven, to burn up with wonderful and awful fierceness so great a number of the cattle of a holy man : [3] which thing no one of the faithful would dare perchance to ascribe to the devil, except it were read on the authority of Holy Scripture. But that man, being by the gift of God just and firm, and of godly knowledge, saith not, The Lord hath given, the devil hath taken away : but, " The Lord hath given, the Lord hath taken away : " [4] very well knowing that even what the devil was able to do with these elements, he would still not have done to a servant of God, except at his Lord's will and permission ; he did confound the malice of the devil, forasmuch as he knew who it was that was making use thereof to prove him. In the sons then of unbelief like as it were in his own slaves, he doth work, [5] like men with their beasts, and even therewith only so far as is permitted by the just judgment of God. But it is one thing when his power is restrained from treating even his own as he pleases, by a greater power ; another thing when to him power is given even over those who are alien from him. Just as a man with his beast, as men understand it, doeth what he will, and yet doth not indeed, if he be restrained by a greater power : but with another man's beast to do something, he doth wait until power be given from him unto whom it belongeth. In the former case the power which there was is restrained, in the latter that which there was not is conceded.

27. And if such be the case, if through evil angels God did inflict those plagues upon the Egyptians, shall we dare to say that the water also was turned into blood by means of those same angels, and that frogs were created by means of the same, the like whereunto even the magicians of Pharaoh were able to make by their enchantments ; [6] so as that evil angels stood on both sides, on the one side afflicting them, on the other side deceiving them, according to the judgment and dispensation [7] of the most just and most omnipotent God, who doth justly make use of even the naughtiness of unrighteous men ? I dare not to say so. For whence was it that the magicians of Pharaoh could by no means make lice ? [8] Was it not because even these same evil angels were not suffered to do this ? Or, to speak more truly, is not the cause hidden, and it doth exceed our powers of inquiry ? For if we shall have supposed that God wrought those things by means of evil angels, because punishments were being inflicted, and not blessings being bestowed, as though God doth inflict punishments upon no one by means of good angels, but by means of those executioners as it were of the heavenly wrath ; the consequence will be that we must believe that even Sodom was overthrown by means of evil angels, and that Abraham and Lot would seem to have entertained under their roof evil angels ; [9] the which, as being contrary to the most evident Scriptures, far be it that we should think. It is clear then that these things might have been done to men by means of good and evil angels. What should be done or when it should be done doth escape me : but Him that doeth it, it escapeth not, and him unto whom He shall have willed to reveal it. Nevertheless, as far as divine Scripture doth yield to our application thereto, on evil men that punishments are inflicted both by means of good angels, as upon

[1] 1 Kings xxii. 20.   [2] [See p. 219, n. 8, supra. — C.]
[3] Job i. 16.   [4] Job i. 21.
[5] Eph. ii. 2.   [6] Exod. viii. 7.   [7] Al. "ordinance."
[8] Exod. viii. 18, 19.   [9] Gen. xviii. 2 and xix. 1.

the Sodomites, and by means of evil angels, as upon the Egyptians, we read : but that just men with corporal penances by means of good angels are tried and proved, doth not occur to me.

28. But as far as regardeth the present passage of this Psalm, if we dare not ascribe those things which were marvellously formed out of creatures, to evil angels ; we have a thing which without doubt we can ascribe to them ; the dyings of the beasts, the dyings of the first-born, and this especially whence all these things proceeded, namely, the hardening of heart, so that they would not let go the people of God.[1]   For when God is said to make this most iniquitous and malignant obstinacy, He maketh it not by suggesting and inspiring, but by forsaking, so that they work in the sons of unbelief that which God doth duly and justly permit.[2] . . . Moreover, those evil manners which we said were signified by these corporal plagues, on account of that which was said before, " I will open in parables my mouth,"[3] are most appropriately believed by means of evil angels to have been wrought in those that are made subject to them by Divine justice.   For neither when that cometh to pass of which the apostle speaketh, " God gave them over into the lusts of their heart, that they should do things which are not convenient,"[4] can it be but that those evil angels dwell and rejoice therein, as in the matter of their own work : unto whom most justly is human naughtiness made subject, in all save those whom grace doth deliver.   " And for these things who is sufficient ? "[5]   Whence when he had said, " He sent unto them the anger of His indignation, indignation and anger and tribulation, an infliction through evil angels ; " for this which he hath added, " a way He hath made for the path of His anger "(ver. 50), whose eye, I pray, is sufficient to penetrate, so that it may understand and take in the sense lying hidden in so great a profundity?   For the path of the anger of God was that whereby He punished the ungodliness of the Egyptians with hidden justice : but for that same path He made a way, so that drawing them forth as it were from secret places by means of evil angels unto manifest offences, He most evidently inflicted punishment upon those that were most evidently ungodly.   From this power of evil angels nothing doth deliver man but the grace of God, whereof the Apostle speaketh, " Who hath delivered us from the power of darkness, and hath translated us into the kingdom of the Son of His love : "[6] of which things that people did bear the figure, when they were delivered from the power of the Egyptians, and translated into the kingdom of the land of promise flowing with milk and honey, which doth signify the sweetness of grace.

29. The Psalm proceedeth then after the commemoration of the plagues of the Egyptians (ver. 51) and saith, " And He took away like sheep His people, and He led them through like a flock in the desert " (ver. 52).   " And He led them down in hope, and they feared not, and their enemies the sea covered " (ver. 53). This cometh to pass to so much the greater good, as it is a more inward thing, wherein being delivered from the power of darkness, we are in mind translated into the Kingdom of God, and with respect to spiritual pastures we are made to become sheep of God, walking in this world as it were in a desert, inasmuch as to no one is our faith observable : whence saith the Apostle, " Your life is hidden with Christ in God."[7]   But we are being led home in hope, " For by hope we are saved."[8]   Nor ought we to fear.   For, " If God be for us, who can be against us ? "[9] And our enemies the sea hath covered, He hath effaced them in baptism by the remission of sins.

30. In the next place there followeth, " And He led them into the mountain of His sanctification " (ver. 54).   How much better into Holy Church !   " The mountain which His right hand hath gotten."   How much higher is the Church which Christ hath gotten, concerning whom has been said, " And to whom has the arm of the Lord been revealed ? "[10] (ver. 55). " And He cast forth from the face of them the nations."   And[11] from the face of His faithful. For nations in a manner are the evil spirits of Gentile errors.   " And by lot He divided unto them the land in the cord of distribution."   And in us " all things one and the same Spirit doth work, dividing severally to every one as He willeth."[12]

31. " And He made to dwell in their tabernacles the tribes of Israel."   In the tabernacles, he saith, of the Gentiles He made the tribes of Israel to dwell, which I think can better be explained spiritually, inasmuch as unto celestial glory, whence sinning angels have been cast forth and cast down, by Christ's grace we are being uplifted.   For that generation crooked and embittering, inasmuch as for these corporal blessings they put not off the coat of oldness, " Did tempt " yet, " and provoked the high God, and His testimonies they kept not (ver. 56) : and they turned them away, and they kept not the covenant, like their fathers " (ver. 57).   For under a sort of covenant and decree they said, " All things which our Lord God hath spoken we will do, and we will hear."[13]   It is a remark-

---

[1] Exod. iv. 21.   [2] Eph. ii. 2.   [3] Ps. lxxviii. 2.
[4] Rom. i. 24, 28.   [5] 2 Cor. ii. 16.   [6] Col. i. 13.

[7] Col. iii. 3.   [8] Rom. viii. 24.   [9] Rom. viii. 31.
[10] Isa. liii. 1.   [11] Oxf. mss. add, " He did cast out nations."
[12] 1 Cor. xii. 11.   [13] Exod. xix. 8.

able thing indeed which he saith, "like their fathers:" while throughout the whole text of the Psalm he was seeming to speak of the same men as it were, yet now it appeareth that the words did concern those who were already in the land of promise, and that the fathers spoken of were of those who did provoke in the desert. "They were turned," he saith, "into a crooked," or, as some copies have it, "into a perverse bow" (ver. 58). But what this is doth better appear in that which followeth, where he saith, "And unto wrath they provoked Him with their hills" (ver. 59). It doth signify that they leaped into idolatry. The bow then was perverted, not for the name of the Lord, but against the name of the Lord: who said to the same people, "Thou shalt have none other Gods but Me."[1] But by the bow He doth signify the mind's intention. This same idea, lastly, more clearly working out, "And in their graven idols," he saith, "they provoked Him to indignation."

32. "God heard, and He despised:" that is, He gave heed and took vengeance. "And unto nothing He brought Israel exceedingly" (ver. 60). For when God despised, what were they who by God's help were what they were? But doubtless he is commemorating the doing of that thing, when they were conquered by the Philistines in the time of Heli the priest, and the Ark of the Lord was taken, and with great slaughter they were laid low.[2] This it is that he speaketh of. "And He rejected the tabernacle of Selom, His tabernacle, where He dwelled among men" (ver. 61). He hath elegantly explained why He rejected His tabernacle, when he saith, "where He dwelled among men." When therefore they were not worthy for Him to dwell among, why should He not reject the tabernacle, which indeed not for Himself He had established, but for their sakes, whom now He judged unworthy for Him to dwell among. "And He gave over unto captivity their strength, and their beauty unto the hands of the enemy." The very Ark whereby they thought themselves invincible, and whereon they plumed themselves, he calleth their "virtue" and "beauty." Lastly, also afterward, when they were living ill, and boasting of the temple of the Lord, He doth terrify them by a Prophet, saying, "See ye what I have done to Selom, where was My tabernacle."[3] "And He ended with the sword His people, and His inheritance He despised" (ver. 62). "Their young men the fire devoured:" that is, wrath. "And their virgins mourned not" (ver. 63). For not even for this was there leisure, in fear of the foe. "Their priests fell by the sword, and their widows were not lamented" (ver. 64). For there fell by the

sword the sons of Heli, of one of whom the wife being widowed, and presently dying in child-birth,[4] because of the same confusion could not be mourned with the distinction of a funeral. "And the Lord was awakened as one sleeping" (ver. 65). For He seemeth to sleep, when He giveth His people into the hands of those whom He hateth, when there is said to them, "Where is thy God?"[5] "He was awakened, then, like one sleeping, like a mighty man drunken with wine." No one would dare to say this of God, save His Spirit. For he hath spoken, as it seemeth to ungodly men reviling; as if like a drunken man He sleepeth long, when He succoureth not so speedily as men think.[6]

33. "And He smote His enemies in the hinder parts" (ver. 66): those, to wit, who were rejoicing that they were able to take His Ark: for they were smitten in their back-parts.[7] Which seemeth to me to be a sign of that punishment, wherewith a man will be tortured, if he shall have looked back upon things behind; which, as saith the Apostle, he ought to value as dung.[8] For they that do so receive the Testament of God, as that they put not off from them the old vanity, are like the hostile nations, who did place the captured Ark of the Testament beside their own idols. And yet those old things even though these be unwilling do fall: for "all flesh is hay, and the glory of man as the flower of hay. The hay hath dried up, and the flower hath fallen off:"[9] but the Ark of the Lord "abideth for everlasting," to wit, the secret testament of the kingdom of Heaven, where is the eternal Word of God. But they that have loved things behind, because of these very things most justly shall be tormented. For "everlasting reproach He hath given to them." (ver. 67).

34. "And He rejected," he saith, "the tabernacle of Joseph, and the tribe of Ephraim[10] He chose not" (ver. 68). "And He chose the tribe of Judah" (ver. 69). He hath not said, He rejected the tabernacle of Reuben, who was the first-born son of Jacob;[11] nor them that follow, and precede Judah in order of birth; so that they being rejected and not chosen, the tribe of Judah was chosen. For it might have been said that they were deservedly rejected; because even in the blessing of Jacob wherewith he blessed his sons, he mentioneth their sins,[12] and deeply abhorreth them; though among them the tribe of Levi merited to be the priestly tribe, whence

---

[1] Exod. xx. 3.　　[2] 1 Sam. iv. 10, etc.　　[3] Jer. vii. 12.

[4] 1 Sam. iv. 19.　　[5] Ps. xlii. 3.　　[6] *Al.* "require."
[7] 1 Sam. v. 6.　　[8] Phil. iii. 8.　　[9] Isa. xl. 6, 7.
[10] [Jeroboam represented the house of Joseph (1 Kings xi. 28), and was offended at the removal of the Tabernacle (1 Kings viii. 4) to Jerusalem. But God overruled his rebellion in such wise, that Ephraim (as the ten tribes were called, from the pre-eminent one) carried away, and, not returning, did not, as tribes, share in the rejection of the Messiah, "the Shepherd and Stone of Israel;" thus indicated in the prophetic benediction of Jacob, Gen. xlix. 24. — C.]
[11] Gen. xlix. 3.
[12] Gen. xlix. 5.

also Moses was.[1]   Nor hath he said, He rejected the tabernacle of Benjamin, or the tribe of Benjamin He chose not, out of which a king already had begun to be ; for thence there had been chosen Saul ;[2] whence because of the very proximity of the time, when he had been rejected and refused, and David chosen,[3] this might conveniently have been said ; but yet was not said : but he hath named those especially who seemed to excel for more surpassing merits.   For Joseph fed in Egypt his father and his brethren, and having been impiously sold, because of his piety, chastity, wisdom, he was most justly exalted ;[4] and Ephraim by the blessing of his grandfather Jacob was preferred before his elder brother :[5] and yet God "rejected the tabernacle of Joseph, and the tribe of Ephraim He chose not."   In which place by these names of renowned merit, what else do we understand but that whole people with old cupidity requiring of the Lord earthly rewards, rejected and refused, but the tribe of Judah chosen not for the sake of the merits of that same Judah?   For far greater are the merits of Joseph, but by the tribe of Judah, inasmuch as thence arose Christ according to the flesh, the Scripture doth testify of the new people of Christ preferred before that old people, the Lord opening in parables His mouth.   Moreover, thence also in that which followeth, " the Mount Sion which He chose," we do better understand the Church of Christ, not worshipping God for the sake of the carnal blessings of the present time, but from afar looking for future and eternal rewards with the eyes of faith : for Sion too is interpreted a " looking out."

35. Lastly there followeth, " and He builded like as of unicorns His sanctification " (ver. 70) : or, as some interpreters have made thereof a new word, " His sanctifying."[6]   The unicorns are rightly understood to be those, whose firm hope is uplifted unto that one thing, concerning which another Psalm saith, " One thing I have sought of the Lord, this I will require."[7]   But the sanctifying of God, according to the Apostle Peter, is understood to be a holy people and a royal priesthood.[8]   But that which followeth, " in the land which He founded for everlasting : " which the Greek copies have εἰς τὸν αἰῶνα, whether it be called by us " for everlasting," or " for an age," is at the pleasure of the Latin translators ; forasmuch as it doth signify either : and therefore the latter is found in some Latin copies, the former in others.   Some also have it in the plural, that is, " for ages : ", which in the Greek copies which we have had we have not found. But which of the faithful would doubt, that the Church, even though, some going, others coming,

she doth pass out of this life in mortal manner, is yet founded for everlasting?

36. " And He chose David His servant " (ver. 71).   The tribe, I say, of Judah, for the sake of David : but David for the sake of Christ : the tribe then of Judah for the sake of Christ. At whose passing by blind men cried out, " Have pity on us, Son of David : "[9] and forthwith by His pity they received light, because true was the thing which they cried out.   This then the Apostle doth not cursorily speak of, but doth heedfully notice, writing to Timothy, " Be thou mindful, that Christ Jesus hath risen from the dead, of the seed of David," etc.[10]   Therefore the Saviour Himself, made according to the flesh of the seed of David, is figured in this passage under the name of David, the Lord opening in parables His mouth.   And let it not move us, that when he had said, " and He chose David," under which name he signified Christ, he hath added, " His servant," not His Son.   Yea even hence we may perceive, that not the substance of the Only-Begotten coeternal with the Father, but the " form of a servant " was taken of the seed of David.

37. " And He took him from the flocks of sheep, from behind the teeming sheep He received him : to feed Jacob His servant, and Israel His inheritance " (ver. 72).   This David indeed, of whose seed the flesh of Christ is, from the pastoral care of cattle was translated to the kingdom of men : but our David, Jesus Himself, from men to men, from Jews to Gentiles, was yet according to the parable from sheep to sheep taken away and translated.   For there are not now in that land " Churches of Judæa in Christ," which belonged to them of the circumcision after the recent Passion and Resurrection of our Lord, of whom saith the Apostle, " But I was unknown by face to the Churches of Judæa, which are in Christ," etc.[11]   Already from hence those Churches of the circumcised people have passed away : and thus in Judæa, which now doth exist on 'the earth, there is not now Christ.[12] He hath been removed thence, now He doth feed flocks of Gentiles.   Truly from behind teeming sheep He hath been taken thence.   For those former Churches were of such sort, as that of them it is said in the Song of Songs, " Thy teeth — are like a flock of shorn ewes going up from the washing,[13] all of which do bear twins, and a barren one is not among them."[14]   For they then laid aside like as it were fleeces the burdens of the world,[15] when before the feet of the Apostles they laid the prices of their sold goods,[16] going up from that Laver, concerning which the

---

[1] Exod. ii. 1.   [2] 1 Sam. ix. 1.   [3] 1 Sam. xvi. 1.
[4] Gen. xli. 40.   [5] Gen. xlviii. 17, 19.   [6] *Sanctificium.*
[7] Ps. xxvii. 4.   [8] 1 Pet. ii. 9.

[9] Matt. xx. 30.   [10] 2 Tim. ii. 8.
[11] Gal. i. 22, 23.   [12] [A noteworthy testimony. — C.]
[13] *Lavacro.*   [14] Song of Sol. iv. 2.
[15] Acts ii. 45.   [16] Acts iv. 34, 35.

apostle Peter doth admonish them, when they were troubled because they had shed the blood of Christ, and he saith, "Repent ye, and let each one of you be baptized in the name of the Lord Jesus Christ, and your sins shall be forgiven you." [1] But twins they begat, the works, to wit, of the two commandments of twin love, love of God, and love of one's neighbour: whence a barren one there was not among them. From behind these teeming sheep our David having been taken, doth now feed other flocks among the Gentiles, and those too "Jacob" and "Israel." For thus hath been said, "to feed Jacob His servant, and Israel His inheritance." . . . Unless perchance any one be willing to make such a distinction as this; viz. that in this time Jacob serveth; but he will be the eternal inheritance of God, at that time when he shall see God face to face, whence he hath received the name Israel. [2]

38. "And He fed them," he saith, "in the innocence of His heart" (ver. 73). What can be more innocent than He, who not only had not any sin whereby to be conquered, but even not any to conquer? "And in the understanding of His hands He led them home:" or, as some copies have it, "in the understandings of His hands." Any other man might suppose that it would have been better had it been said thus, "in innocence of hands and understanding of heart;" but He who knew better than others what He spake, preferred to join with the heart innocence, and with the hands understanding. It is for this reason, as far as I judge; because many men think themselves innocent, who do not evil things because they fear lest they should suffer if they shall have done them; but they have the will to do them, if they could with impunity. Such men may seem to have innocence of hands, but yet not that of heart. And what, I pray, or of what sort is that innocence, if of heart it is not, where man was made after the image of God? [3] But in this which he saith, "in understanding (or intelligence) of His hands He led them home," he seemeth to me to have spoken of that intelligence which He doth Himself make in believers: and so "of His hands:" for making doth belong to the hands, but in the sense wherein the hands of God may be understood; for even Christ was a Man in such sort, that He was also God. . . .

PSALM LXXIX. [4]

1. Over the title of this Psalm, being so short and so simple, I think we need not tarry. But the prophecy which here we read sent

before, we know to be evidently fulfilled. For when these things were being sung in the times of King David, nothing of such sort, by the hostility of the Gentiles, as yet had befallen the city Jerusalem, nor the Temple of God, which as yet was not even builded. For that after the death of David his son Salomon made a temple to God, who is ignorant? That is spoken of therefore as though past, which in the Spirit was seen to be future.

"O God, the Gentiles have come into Thine inheritance" (ver. 1). Under which form of expression other things which were to come to pass, are spoken of as having been done. Nor must this be wondered at, that these words are being spoken to God. For they are not being represented to Him not knowing, by whose revelation they are foreknown; but the soul is speaking with God with that affection of godliness, of which God knoweth. [5] For even the things which Angels proclaim to men, they proclaim to them that know them not; but the things which they proclaim to God, they proclaim to Him knowing, when they offer our prayers, and in ineffable manner consult the eternal Truth respecting their actions, as an immutable law. And therefore this man of God is saying to God that which he is to learn of God, like a scholar to a master, not ignorant but judging; and so either approving what he hath taught, or censuring what he hath not taught: especially because under the appearance of one praying, the Prophet is transforming into himself those who should be at the time when these things were to come to pass. [6] But in praying it is customary to declare those things to God which He hath done in taking vengeance, and for a petition to be added, that henceforth He should pity and spare. In this way here also by him the judgments are spoken of by whom they are foretold, as if they were being spoken of by those whom they befell, and the very lamentation and prayer is a prophecy.

2. "They have defiled Thy holy Temple, they have made Jerusalem for a keeping of apples." "They have made the dead bodies of Thy servants morsels for the fowls of heaven, the fleshes of Thy saints for the beasts of the earth" (ver. 2). "They have poured forth their blood like water in the circuit of Jerusalem, and there was no one to bury them" (ver. 3). If in this prophecy any one of us shall have thought that there must be understood that laying waste of Jerusalem, which was made by Titus the Roman Emperor, when already the Lord Jesus Christ, after His Resurrection and

---

[1] Acts ii. 38.   [2] Gen. xxxii. 28.   [3] Gen. i. 27.
[4] Lat. LXXVIII. Preached after the Exposition of Psalm lxxviii., as appears elsewhere.

[5] One Oxf. MS. "love thou to speak with God with affection of godliness, things of which God knoweth;" al. "For what things doth not God see?"
[6] [Compare 1 Pet. i. 12, a text which floods with light the subject of inspiration. — C.]

Ascension, was being preached among the Gentiles, it doth not occur to me how that people could now have been called the inheritance of God, as not holding to Christ, whom having rejected and slain, that people became reprobate, which not even after His Resurrection would believe in Him, and even killed His Martyrs. For out of that people Israel whosoever have believed in Christ; to whom the offer of Christ was made, and in a manner the healthful and fruitful fulfilment of the promise; concerning whom even the Lord Himself saith, "I am not sent but to the sheep which have been lost of the house of Israel,"[1] the same are they that out of them are the sons of promise; the same are counted for a seed;[2] the same do belong to the inheritance of God. From hence are Joseph that just man, and the Virgin Mary who bore Christ:[3] hence John Baptist the friend of the Bridegroom, and his parents Zacharias and Elisabeth:[4] hence Symeon the old,[5] and Anna the widow, who heard not Christ speaking by the sense of the body; but while yet an infant not speaking, by the Spirit perceived Him: hence the blessed Apostles: hence Nathanael, in whom guile was not:[6] hence the other Joseph, who himself too looked for the kingdom of God:[7] hence that so great multitude who went before and followed after His beast, saying, "Blessed is He that cometh in the name of the Lord:"[8] among whom was also that company of children, in whom He declared to have been fulfilled, "Out of the mouth of infants and sucklings Thou hast perfected praise."[9] Hence also were those after His resurrection, of whom on one day three and on another five thousand were baptized,[10] welded into one soul and one heart by the fire of love; of whom no one spoke of anything as his own, but to them all things were common.[11] Hence the holy deacons, of whom Stephen was crowned with martyrdom before the Apostles.[12] Hence so many Churches of Judæa, which were in Christ, unto whom Paul was unknown by face,[13] but known for an infamous ferocity, and more known for Christ's most merciful grace. Hence even he, according to the prophecy sent before concerning him, "a wolf ravening, in the morning carrying off, and in the evening dividing morsels;"[14] that is, first as persecutor carrying off unto death, afterwards as a preacher feeding unto life. These are they that are out of that people the inheritance of God. . . . So then even at this time a remnant through election of Grace have been saved. This remnant out of that nation doth belong to the inheritance[15]

of God: not those concerning whom a little below he saith, "But the rest have been blinded." For thus he saith. "What then? That which Israel sought, this he hath not obtained: but the election hath obtained it: but the rest have been blinded."[16] This election then, this remnant, that people of God, which God hath not cast off, is called His inheritance. But in that Israel, which hath not obtained this, in the rest that were blinded, there was no longer an inheritance of God, in reference to whom it is possible that there should be spoken, after the glorification of Christ in the Heavens, in the time of Titus the Emperor, "O God, there have come the Gentiles unto Thine inheritance," and the other things which in this Psalm seem to have been foretold concerning the destruction of both the temple and city belonging to that people.

3. Furthermore herein we ought either to perceive those things which were done by other enemies, before Christ had come in the flesh: at that time when there were even the holy prophets, when the carrying away into Babylon took place,[17] and that nation was grievously afflicted, and at the time when under Antiochus also the Maccabees, having endured horrible sufferings, were most gloriously crowned.[18] Or certainly if after the Resurrection and Ascension of the Lord the inheritance of God must be understood to be here spoken of; such things must be understood herein, as at the hands of worshippers of idols, and enemies of the name of Christ, His Church, in such a multitude of martyrs, endured. . . . This Church then, this inheritance of God, out of circumcision and uncircumcision hath been congregated, that is, out of the people of Israel, and out of the rest of the nations, by means of the Stone which the builders rejected, and which hath become for the Head of the corner,[19] in which corner as it were two walls coming from different quarters were united. "For Himself is our peace, who hath made both one, that He might build two into Himself, making peace, and might unite together[20] both in one Body unto God:"[21] in which Body we are sons of God, "crying, Abba Father."[22] Abba, on account of their language; Father, on account of ours. For Abba is the same as Father. . . .

4. But now in that which followeth, "they have made Jerusalem for a keeping of apples;" even the Church herself is rightly understood under this name, even the free Jerusalem our mother,[23] concerning whom hath been written, "many more are the sons of the forsaken, than

---

[1] Matt. xv. 24.   [2] Rom. ix. 8.   [3] Matt. i. 16.
[4] Luke i. 5.   [5] Luke ii. 25.   [6] John i. 47.
[7] John xix. 38; Luke xxiii. 51.   [8] Matt. xxi. 9.
[9] Ps. viii. 2.   [10] Acts ii. 41, iv. 4.   [11] Acts iv. 32.
[12] Acts vii. 59.   [13] Gal. i. 22.   [14] Gen. xlix. 27.
[15] One MS. "are the inheritance."

[16] Rom. xi. 7.   [17] 2 Kings xxiv. 14.   [18] 2 Macc. vii.
[19] Ps. cxviii. 22.   [20] *Coadunaret*. MSS. "might change."
[21] Eph. ii. 14, etc.   [22] Rom. viii. 15.
[23] Gal. iv. 26.

of her that hath the husband." [1] The expression, "for a keeping of apples," I think must be understood of the desertion which the wasting of persecution hath effected : that is, like a keeping of apples ; for the keeping of apples is abandoned, when the apples have passed away. And certes when through the persecuting Gentiles the Church seemed to be forsaken, unto the celestial table, like as it were many and exceeding sweet apples from the garden of the Lord, the spirits of the martyrs did pass away.

5. "They have made," he saith, "the dead bodies of Thy servants morsels for the fowls of heaven, the fleshes of Thy saints for the beasts of the earth" (ver. 2). The expression, "dead bodies," hath been repeated in "fleshes : " and the expression, "of Thy servants," hath been repeated in, "of Thy saints." This only hath been varied, "to the fowls of heaven, and to the beasts of the earth." Better have they interpreted who have written "dead," than as some have it, "mortal." For "dead" is only said of those that have died ; but mortal is a term applied even to living bodies. When then, as I have said, to their Husbandman the spirits of martyrs like apples had passed away, their dead bodies and their fleshes they set before the fowls of heaven and the beasts of the earth : as if any part of them could be lost to the resurrection, whereas out of the hidden recesses of the natural world He will renew the whole, by whom even our hairs have been numbered.[2]

6. "They have poured forth their blood like water," that is, abundantly and wantonly, "in the circuit of Jerusalem" (ver. 3). If we herein understand the earthly city Jerusalem, we perceive the shedding of their blood in the circuit thereof, whom the enemy could find outside the walls. But if we understand it of that Jerusalem, concerning whom hath been said, "many more are the sons of her that was forsaken, than of her that hath the husband," [1] the circuit thereof is throughout the universal earth. For in that lesson of the Prophet, wherein is written, "many more are the sons of her that was forsaken, than of her that hath the husband : " a little after unto the same is said, "and He that hath delivered thee, shall be called the God of Israel of the universal earth." [3] The circuit then of this Jerusalem in this Psalm must be understood as followeth : so far as at that time the Church had been expanded, bearing fruit, and growing in the universal world, when in every part thereof persecution was raging, and was making havoc of the Martyrs, whose blood was being shed like water, to the great gain of the celestial treasuries. But as to that which hath been added, "and there was

no one to bury : " it either ought not to seem to be an incredible thing that there should have been so great a panic in some places, that not any buriers at all of holy bodies came forward : or certes that unburied corpses in many places might lie long time, until being by the religious in a manner stolen [4] they were buried.

7. "We have become," he saith, "a reproach to our neighbours" (ver. 4). Therefore precious not in the sight of men, from whom this reproach was, but "precious [5] in the sight of the Lord is the death of His saints." [6] "A scoffing and derision : " or, as some have interpreted it, "a mockery to them that are in our circuit." It is a repetition of the former sentence. For that which above hath been called, "a reproach," the same hath been repeated in, "a scoffing and derision : " and that which above hath been said in, "to our neighbours," the same hath been repeated in, "to them that are in our circuit." Moreover, in reference to the earthly Jerusalem, the neighbours, and those in the circuit of that nation, are certainly understood to be other nations. But in reference to the free Jerusalem our mother,[7] there are neighbours even in the circuit of her, among whom, being her enemies, the Church dwelleth in the circuit of the round world.

8. In the second place now giving utterance to an evident prayer, whence it may be perceived that the calling to remembrance of former affliction is not by way of information but prayer ; "How long," he saith, "O Lord, wilt Thou be angry, unto the end? shall Thy jealousy burn like fire?" (ver. 5). He is evidently asking God not to be angry unto the end, that is, that this so great oppression and tribulation and devastation may not continue even unto the end ; but that He moderate His chastening, according to that which is said in another Psalm, "Thou shalt feed us with the bread of tears, and Thou shalt give us to drink of tears in measure." [8] For the, "how long, O Lord, wilt Thou be angry, unto the end?" hath been spoken in the same sense as if it had been said, Be not, O Lord, angry unto the end. And in that which followeth, "shall Thy jealousy burn like fire?" both words must be understood, both, "how long," and, "unto the end : " just as if there had been said, how long shall there burn like fire Thy jealousy unto the end? For these two words must be understood in the same manner as that word which was used a little higher up. namely, "they-have-made." For while the former sentence hath, "they have made the dead bodies of Thy servants morsels for the fowls of heaven : " [9] this

[1] Isa. liv. 1. [2] Matt. x. 30. [3] Isa. liv. 5.

[4] [" With pious sacrilege a grave I stole," Dr. Young. —C.]
[5] Oxf. MSS. rep. "precious." [6] Ps. cxvi. 15.
[7] Gal. iv. 26. [8] Ps. lxxx. 5. [9] Ps. lxxix. 2.

word the latter sentence hath not, wherein is said, " the fleshes of Thy saints for the beasts of the earth ; " but there is surely understood what the former hath, namely, " they have made."

Moreover, the anger and jealousy of God[1] are not emotions of God ; as some do charge upon the Scriptures which they do not understand :[2] but under the name of anger is to be understood the avenging of iniquity ; under the name of jealousy, the exaction of chastity ; that the soul may not despise the law of her Lord, and perish by departing in fornication from the Lord. These then in their actual operation in men's affliction are violent ; but in the disposal of God they are calm, unto whom hath been said, " But Thou, O Lord of virtues, with calmness dost judge."[3] But it is clearly enough shown by these words, that for sins these tribulations do befall men, though they be faithful : although hence may bloom the Martyrs' glory by occasion of their patience, and the yoke of discipline godly endured as the scourge of the Lord. Of this the Maccabees amid sharp tortures,[4] of this the three men amid flames innocuous,[5] of this the holy Prophets in captivity, do testify. For although paternal correction most bravely and most godly they endure, yet they do not hide the fact, that these things have befallen them for the deservings of their sins.[6] . . .

9. But that which he addeth, " Pour forth Thine anger upon the nations which have not known Thee, and upon the kingdoms which have not called upon Thy name " (ver. 6) ; this too is a prophecy, not a wish. Not in the imprecation of malevolence are these words spoken, but foreseen by the Spirit they are predicted : just as in the case of Judas the traitor, the evil things which were to befall him have been so prophesied as if they were wished. For in like manner as the prophet doth not command Christ, though in the imperative mood he giveth utterance to what he saith, " Gird Thou Thy sword about Thy thigh, O Most Mighty : in Thy beauty and in Thy goodliness, both go on, and prosperously proceed, and reign : "[7] so he doth not wish, but doth prophesy, who saith, " Pour forth Thine anger upon the nations which have not known Thee." Which in his usual way he repeateth, saying, " And upon the kingdoms which have not called upon Thy name." For nations have been repeated in kingdoms : and that they have not known Him, hath been repeated in this, that they have not called upon His name. How then must be understood, what the Lord saith in the Gospel[8] concerning stripes, " the many and the few "? if greater the anger of God

is against the nations, which have not known the Lord? For in this which he saith, " Pour forth Thine anger," with this word he hath clearly enough pointed out, how great anger he hath willed that there should be understood. Whence afterwards he saith, " Render to our neighbours seven times as much."[9] Is it not that there is a great difference between servants, who, though they know not the will of their Lord, do yet call upon His name, and those that are aliens from the family of so great a Master, who are so ignorant of God, as that they do not even call upon God? For in place of Him they call upon either idols or demons, or any creature they choose ; not the Creator, who is blessed for ever. For those persons, concerning whom he is prophesying this, he doth not even intimate to be so ignorant of the will of their God, as that still they fear the Lord Himself ; but so ignorant of the Lord Himself, that they do not even call upon Him, and that they stand forth as enemies of His name. There is a great difference then between servants not knowing the will of their God, and yet living in His family and in His house, and enemies not only setting the will against knowing the Lord Himself, but also not calling upon His name, and even in His servants fighting against it.

10. Lastly, there followeth, " For they have eaten up Jacob, and his place they have made desolate " (ver. 7). . . . How we should view " the place " of Jacob, must be understood. For rather the place of Jacob may be supposed to be that city, wherein was also the Temple, whitherunto the whole of that nation for the purpose of sacrifice and worship, and to celebrate the Passover, the Lord had commanded to assemble. For if the assemblies of Christians, letted and suppressed by persecutors, has been what the Prophet would have to be understood, it would seem that he should have said, places made desolate, not place. Still we may take the singular number as put for the plural number ; as dress for clothes, soldiery for soldiers, cattle for beasts : for many words are usually spoken in this manner, and not only in the mouths of vulgar speakers, but even in the eloquence of the most approved authorities. Nor to divine Scripture herself is this form of speech foreign. For even she hath put frog for frogs, locust for locusts,[10] and countless expressions of the like kind. But that which hath been said, " They have eaten up Jacob," the same is well understood, in that many men into their own evil-minded body, that is, into their own society, they have constrained to pass.

11. . . . He subjoineth, " Remember not our iniquities of old " (ver. 8). He saith not by-

---

[1] The anger and jealousy of God.   [2] Manichæus.
[3] Wisd. xii. 18.   [4] 2 Macc. vii. 1, 2, etc.
[5] Dan. iii. 21.   [6] Ps. cxviii. 18 ; Heb. xii. 6.
[7] Ps. xlv. 3, 4.   [8] Luke xii. 47 ; 48.

[9] Ps. lxxix. 13.   [10] Ps. lxxviii. 46.

gone, which might have even been recent; but "of old," that is, coming from parents. For to such iniquities judgment, not correction, is [1] owing. "Speedily let Thy mercies anticipate us." Anticipate, that is, at Thy judgment. For "mercy exalteth above in judgment." [2] Now there is "judgment without mercy," but to him that hath not showed mercy. But whereas he addeth, "for we have become exceeding poor:" unto this end he willeth that the mercies of God should be understood to anticipate us; that our own poverty, that is, weakness, by Him having mercy, should be aided to do His commandments, that we may not come to His judgment to be condemned.

12. Therefore there followeth, "Help us, O God, our healing [3] One" (ver. 9). By this word which he saith, "our healing One," he doth sufficiently explain what sort of poverty he hath willed to be understood, in that which he had said, "for we have become exceeding poor." For it is that very sickness, to which a healer is necessary. But while he would have us to be aided, he is neither ungrateful to grace, nor doth he take away free-will. For he that is aided, doth also of himself something. He hath added also, "for the glory of Thy Name, O Lord, deliver us:" in order that he who glorieth, not in himself, but in the Lord may glory. [4] "And merciful be Thou," he saith, "to our sins for Thy Name's sake:" not for our sake. For what else do our sins deserve, but due and condign punishments? But "merciful be Thou to our sins, for Thy Name's sake." Thus then Thou dost deliver us, that is, dost rescue us from evil things, while Thou dost both aid us to do justice, and art merciful to our sins, without which in this life we are not. For "in Thy sight shall no man living be justified." [5] But sin is iniquity. [6] And "if Thou shalt have marked iniquities, who shall stand?" [7]

13. But that which he addeth, "lest at any time they should say among the Gentiles, Where is their God?" (ver. 10) must be taken as rather for the Gentiles themselves. For to a bad end they come that have despaired of the true God, thinking that either He is not, or doth not help His own, and is not merciful to them. But this which followeth, "and that there may be known among the nations before our eyes the vengeance of the blood of Thy servants which hath been shed:" is either to be understood as of the time, when they believe in the true God that used to persecute His inheritance; because even that is vengeance, whereby is slain the fierce iniquity of them by the sword of the Word of God, concerning which hath been said, "Gird Thou

Thy sword:" [8] or when obstinate enemies at the last are punished. For the corporal ills which they suffer in this world, they may have in common with good men. There is also another kind of vengeance; that wherein the Church's enlargement and fruitfulness in this world after so great persecutions, wherein they supposed she would utterly perish, the sinner and unbeliever and enemy seeth, and is angry; "with his teeth he shall gnash, and shall pine away." [9] For who would dare to deny that even this is a most heavy punishment? But I know not whether that which he saith, "before our eyes," is taken with sufficient elegance, if by this sort of punishment we understand that which is done in the inmost recesses of the heart, and doth torment even those who blandly smile at us, while by us there cannot be seen what they suffer in the inner man. But the fact, that whether in them believing their iniquity is slain, or whether the last punishment is rendered to them persevering in their naughtiness, without difficulty of doubtfulness is understood in the saying, "that there may be known before our eyes vengeance among the nations."

14. And this indeed, as we have said, is a prophecy, not a wish. . . . And the Lord in the Gospel [10] hath set before us the widow for an example, who longing to be avenged, did intercede with the unjust judge, who at length heard her, not as being guided by justice, but overcome with weariness: but this the Lord hath set before us, to show that much more the just God will speedily make the judgment of His elect, who cry unto Him day and night. Thence is also that cry of the Martyrs under the altar of God, [11] that they may be avenged in the judgment of God. Where then is the, "Love your enemies, do good unto them that hate you, and pray for them that persecute you"? [12] Where is also the, "Not rendering evil for evil, nor cursing for cursing:" [13] and, "unto no man rendering evil for evil"? [14] . . . For when the Lord was exhorting us to love enemies, He set before us the example of our Father, who is in Heaven, "who maketh His sun to rise upon good men and evil men, and raineth upon just men and unjust men:" [15] doth He yet therefore not chasten even by temporal correction, or not condemn at the last the obstinately hardened? Let therefore an enemy be so loved as that the Lord's justice whereby he is punished displease us not, and let the justice whereby he is punished so please us, as that the joy is not at his evil but at the good Judge. But a malevolent soul is sorrowful, if his enemy by being corrected shall have escaped punishment: and

---

[1] Al. "would be."   [2] Jas. ii. 13.   [3] Salutaris.
[4] 1 Cor. i. 31.   [5] Ps. cxliii. 2.
[6] i.e., injustice. 1 John iii. 4 and v. 17.
[7] Ps. cxxx. 3.

[8] Ps. xlv. 4.   [9] Ps. cxii. 10.   [10] Luke xviii. 3.
[11] Rev. vi. 9.   [12] Matt. v. 44.   [13] 1 Pet. iii. 9.
[14] Rom. xii. 17.   [15] Matt. v. 45.

when he seeth him punished, he is so glad that he is avenged, that he is not delighted with the justice of God, whom he loveth not, but with the misery of that man whom he hateth: and when he leaveth judgment to God, he hopeth that God will hurt more than he could hurt: and when he giveth food to his hungering enemy, and drink to him thirsty, he hath an evil-minded sense of that which is written, "For thus doing thou shalt heap coals of fire upon his head." [1] . . . In such sort then under the appearance of one asking in this Psalm, future vengeance on the ungodly is prophesied of, as that we are to understand that holy men of God have loved their enemies, and have wished no one anything but good, which is godliness in this world, everlasting life in that to come; but in the punishments of evil men, they have taken pleasure not in the ills of them, but in God's good judgments; and wheresoever in the holy Scriptures we read of their hatreds against men, they were the hatreds of vices, which every man must needs hate in himself, if he loveth himself.

15. But now in that which followeth, "Let there come in before Thy sight," or, as some copies have it, " In Thy sight, the groans of the fettered:" not easily doth any one discover that the Saints were thrown into fetters by persecutors; and if this doth happen amid so great and manifold a variety of punishments, so rarely it doth happen, that it must not be believed that the prophet had chosen to allude to this especially in this verse. But, in fact, the fetters are the infirmity and the corruptibleness of the body, which do weigh down the soul. For by means of the frailty thereof, as a kind of material for certain pains and troubles, the persecutor might constrain her unto ungodliness. From these fetters the Apostle was longing to be unbound, and to be with Christ; [2] but to abide in the flesh was necessary for their sakes unto whom he was ministering the Gospel. Until then this corruptible put on incorruption, and this mortal put on immortality,[3] like as it were with fetters, the weak flesh doth let the willing spirit.[4] These fetters then not any do feel, but they that in themselves do groan being burthened, desiring to be clothed upon with the tabernacle which is from Heaven; [5] because both death is a terror, and mortal life is sorrow. In behalf of these men groaning the Prophet doth redouble his groaning, that their groaning may "come in in the sight of the Lord." They also may be understood to be fettered, who are enchained with the precepts of wisdom, the which being patiently supported are turned into ornaments: whence it hath been written, "Put thy feet into her fetters." [6] "According to the

greatness," he saith, "of Thy arm, receive Thou unto adoption the sons of them that are put to death:" [7] or, as is read in some copies, "Possess Thou sons by the death of the punished." [8] Wherein the Scripture seemeth to me to have sufficiently shown, what hath been the groan of the fettered, who for the name of Christ endured most grievous persecutions, which in this Psalm are most clearly prophesied. For being beset with divers sufferings, they used to pray for the Church, that their blood might not be without fruit to posterity; in order that the Lord's harvest might more abundantly flourish by the very means whereby enemies thought that she would perish. For "sons of them that were put to death" he hath called them who were not only not terrified by the sufferings of those that went before, but in Him for whose name they knew them to have suffered, being inflamed with their glory which did inspire them to the like, in most ample hosts they believed. Therefore he hath said, "According to the greatness of Thine arm." For so great a wonder followed in the case of Christian peoples, as they, who thought they would prevail aught by persecuting her, no wise believed would follow.

16. "Render," he saith, "to our neighbours seven times so much into their bosoms " (ver. 13). Not any evil things he is wishing, but things just he is foretelling and prophesying as to come. But in the number seven, that is, in sevenfold retribution, he would have the completeness of the punishment to be perceived, for with this number fulness is wont to be signified. Whence also there is this saying for the good, "He shall receive in this world seven times as much:" [9] which hath been put for all. "As if having nothing, and possessing all things." [10] Of neighbours he is speaking, because amongst them dwelleth the Church even unto the day of severing: for not now is made the corporal separation. "Into their bosoms," he saith, as being now in secret, so that the vengeance which is now being executed in secret in this life, hereafter may be known among the nations before our eyes. For when a man is given over to a reprobate mind, in his inward bosom he is receiving what he deserveth of future punishments. "Their reproach wherewith they have reproached Thee, O Lord." This do Thou render to them sevenfold into their bosoms, that is, in return for this reproach, most fully do Thou rebuke them in their secret places. For in this they have reproached Thy Name, thinking to efface Thee from the earth in Thy servants.

---

[1] Rom. xii. 20.   [2] Phil. i. 23.   [3] 1 Cor. xv. 54.
[4] Matt. xxvi. 41.   [5] 2 Cor. v. 4.   [6] Ecclus. vi. 24.

[7] *Mortificatorum.*
[8] *Punitorum,* but mss. ap. Ben. and Oxf. *mortificatorum.*
[9] Mark x. 30. On Matt. xix. 29 there is a var. reading " manifold," but not " sevenfold." E. V. " hundred-fold."
[10] 2 Cor. vi. 10.

17. "But we Thy people" (ver. 14), must be taken generally of all the race of godly and true Christians. "We," then, whom they thought they had power to destroy, "Thy people, and the sheep of thy flock:" in order that he that glorieth may glory in the Lord,[1] "will confess to Thee for an age." But some copies have it, "will confess to Thee for everlasting." Out of a Greek ambiguity this diversity hath arisen. For that which the Greek hath, εἰς τὸν αἰῶνα, may be interpreted both by "for everlasting," and "for an age;" but according to the context we must understand which is the better interpretation. The sense then of this passage seemeth to me to show, that we ought to say "for an age," that is, even unto the end of time. But the following verse after the manner of the Scriptures, and especially of the Psalms, is a repetition of the former with the order changed, putting that before which in the former case was after, and that after which in the former case was before. For whereas in the former case there had been said, "we will confess to Thee," instead of the same herein hath been said, "We will proclaim Thy praise." And so whereas in the former case there had been said, "for an age," instead of the same herein hath been said, "for generation and generation." For this repetition of generation doth signify perpetuity: or, as some understand it, it is because there are two generations, an old and a new. . . . But in many places of holy Scriptures we have already made known to you that confession is also put for praise: as in this passage it is, "These words ye shall say in confession, 'That the works of the Lord are very good.'"[2] And especially that which the Saviour Himself saith, who had not any sin at all, which by repentance to confess: "I confess to Thee, Father, Lord of heaven and earth, that Thou hast hid these things from the wise and prudent, and hast revealed them to babes."[3] I have said this, in order that it may be more clearly perceived how in the expression, "We will proclaim Thy praise," the same hath been repeated as had been said higher up, "We will confess to Thee."

PSALM LXXX.[4]

1. . . . If perchance things obscure demand the office of an interpreter, those things which are evident ought to require of me the office of a reader. The song here is of the Advent of the Lord and of our Saviour Jesus Christ, and of His vineyard. But the singer of the song is that Asaph, as far as doth appear, enlightened and converted, by whose name ye know the synagogue to be signified. Lastly, the title of the Psalm is: "For the end in behalf of them that shall be changed;" that is, for the better. For Christ, the end of the Law,[5] hath come on purpose that He should change men for the better. And he addeth, "a testimony to Asaph himself." A good testimony of truth. Lastly, this testimony doth confess both Christ and the vineyard; that is, Head and Body, King and people, Shepherd and flock, and the entire mystery of all Scriptures, Christ and the Church. But the title of the Psalm doth conclude with, "for the Assyrians." The Assyrians are interpreted, "men guiding." Therefore it is no longer a generation which hath not guided the heart[6] thereof, but now a generation guiding. Therefore hear we what he saith in this testimony.

2. What is, "Thou that feedest Israel, hearken, Thou that conducteth Joseph like sheep"? (ver. 1). He is being invoked to come, He is being expected until He come, He is being yearned for until He come. Therefore may He find "men guiding:" "Thou that conductest," he saith, "Joseph like sheep:" Joseph himself like sheep. Joseph himself are the sheep, and Joseph himself is a sheep. Observe Joseph; for although even the interpretation of his name doth aid us much, for it signifieth increase; and He came indeed in order that the grain given to death[7] might arise manifold;[8] that is, that the people of God might be increased. . . . "Thou that sittest upon the Cherubin." Cherubin is the seat of the glory of God, and is interpreted the fulness of knowledge. There God sitteth in the fulness of knowledge. Though we understand the Cherubin to be the exalted powers and virtues of the heavens: yet, if thou wilt, thou wilt be Cherubin.[9] For if Cherubin is the seat of God, hear what saith the Scripture: "The soul of a just man is the seat of wisdom." How, thou sayest, shall I be the fulness of knowledge? Who shall fulfil this? Thou hast the means of fulfilling it: "The fulness of the Law is love."[10] Do not run after many things, and strain thyself. The amplitude of the branches doth terrify thee: hold by the root, and of the greatness of the tree think not. Be there in thee love, and the fulness of knowledge must needs follow. For what doth he not know that knoweth love? Inasmuch as it hath been said, "God is love."[11] "Appear." For we went astray because Thou didst not appear. "Before Ephraim and Benjamin and Manasse" (ver. 2). Appear, I say, before the nation of the Jews, before the people of Israel. For there is Ephraim, there Manasses, there Benjamin. But to the interpretation let us look: Ephraim is fruit-bearing,

[1] 1 Cor. i. 31.   [2] Ecclus. xxxix. 33.   [3] Matt. xi. 25.
[4] Lat. LXXIX. A Sermon delivered to the people.

[5] Rom. x. 4.   [6] Ps. lxxviii. 8, p. 369, supra.
[7] Mortificatum.   [8] John xii. 24.
[9] See St. Macarius, Hom. 1.   [10] Rom. xiii. 10.
[11] 1 John iv. 8.

Benjamin son of right hand, Manasses one forgetful. Appear Thou then before one made fruitful, before a son of the right hand: appear Thou before one forgetful, in order that he may be no longer forgetful, but Thou mayest come into his mind that hast delivered him. . . . For weak Thou wast when it was being said, "If Son of God He is, let Him come down from the Cross."[1] Thou wast seeming to have no power: the persecutor had power over Thee: and Thou didst show this aforetime, for Jacob too himself prevailed in wrestling, a man with an angel. Would he at any time, except the angel had been willing? And man prevailed, and the angel was conquered: and victorious man holdeth the angel, and saith, "I will not let thee go, except thou shalt have blessed me."[2] A great sacrament! He both standeth conquered, and blesseth the conqueror. Conquered, because he willed it; in flesh weak, in majesty strong. . . . Having been crucified of weakness, rise Thou in power:[3] "Stir up Thy power, and come Thou, to save us."

3. "O God, convert us." For averse we have been from Thee, and except Thou convert us, we shall not be converted. "And illumine Thy face, and we shall be saved" (ver. 3). Hath He anywise a darkened face? He hath not a darkened face, but He placed before it a cloud of flesh, and as it were a veil of weakness; and when He hung on the tree, He was not thought the Same as He was after to be acknowledged when He was sitting in Heaven. For thus it hath come to pass. Christ present on the earth, and doing miracles, Asaph knew not; but when He had died, after that He rose again, and ascended into Heaven, he knew Him. He was pricked to the heart, and he may have spoken[4] also of Him this testimony which now we acknowledge in this Psalm. Thou didst cover Thy face, and we were sick: illumine Thou the same, and we shall be whole.

4. "O Lord God of virtues, how long wilt Thou be angry with the prayer of Thy servant?" (ver. 4). Now Thy servant. Thou wast angry at the prayer of Thy enemy, wilt Thou still be angry with the prayer of Thy servant? Thou hast converted us, we know Thee, and wilt Thou still be angry with the prayer of Thy servant? Thou wilt evidently be angry, in fact, as a father correcting, not as a judge condemning. In such manner evidently Thou wilt be angry, because it hath been written, "My son, drawing near unto the service of God, stand thou in righteousness and in fear, and prepare thy soul for temptation."[5] Think not that now the wrath of God hath passed away, because

thou hast been converted. The wrath of God[6] hath passed away from thee, but only so that it condemn not for everlasting. But He scourgeth, He spareth not: because He scourgeth every son whom He receiveth.[7] If thou refusest to be scourged, why dost thou desire to be received? He scourgeth every son whom He receiveth. He who did not spare even His only Son, scourgeth every one. But nevertheless, "How long wilt Thou be angry with the prayer of Thy servant?" No longer thine enemy: but, "Thou wilt be angry with the prayer of Thy servant," how long? There followeth: "Thou wilt feed us with the bread of tears, and wilt give us to drink with tears in measure" (ver. 5). What is, "in measure"? Hear the Apostle: "Faithful is God, who doth not suffer you to be tempted above that ye are able to bear."[8] The measure is, according to your powers: the measure is, that thou be instructed, not that thou be crushed.

5. "Thou hast set us for a contradiction to our neighbours" (ver. 6). Evidently this did come to pass: for out of Asaph were chosen they that should go to the Gentiles and preach Christ, and should have it said to them, "Who is this proclaimer of new demons?"[9] "Thou hast set us for a contradiction to our neighbours." For they were preaching Him who was the subject of the contradiction. Whom did they preach? That after He was dead, Christ rose again. Who would hear this? Who would know this? It is a new thing. But signs did follow, and to an incredible thing miracles gave credibility. He was contradicted, but the contradictor was conquered, and from being a contradictor was made a believer. There, however, was a great flame: there the martyrs fed with the bread of tears, and given to drink in tears, but in measure, not more than they are able to bear; in order that after the measure of tears there should follow a crown of joys. "And our enemies have sneered at us." And where are they that sneered? For a long while it was said, Who are they that worship the Dead One, that adore the Crucified? For a long while so it was said. Where is the nose of them that sneered? Now do not they that censure flee into caves, that they may not be seen? But ye see what followeth: "O Lord God of virtues, convert us, and show Thy face, and we shall be whole" (ver. 7). "A vineyard out of Egypt Thou hast brought over, Thou hast cast out the nations, and hast planted her" (ver. 8). It was done, we know. How many nations were cast out? Amorites, Cethites, Jebusites, Gergesites, and Evites: after whose expulsion and overthrow, there was led in the people deliv-

---

[1] Matt. xxvii. 40. [2] Gen. xxxii. 26. [3] 2 Cor. xiii. 4.
[4] Oxf. mss. "he spoke." [5] Ecclus. ii. 1.

[6] So Oxf. mss.; Ben. "it." [7] Heb. xii. 6.
[8] 1 Cor. x. 13. [9] Acts xvii. 18. E. V. "strange gods."

ered out of Egypt, into the land of promise. Whence the vineyard was cast out, and where she was planted, we have heard. Let us see what next was done, how she believed, how much she grew, what ground she covered.

6. "A way Thou hast made in the sight of her, and hast planted the roots of her, and she hath filled the land" (ver. 9). Would she have filled the land, unless a way had been made in the sight of her? What was the way which was made in the sight of her? "I am," He saith, "the Way, the Truth, and the Life." [1] With reason she hath filled the land. That hath now been said of this vineyard, which hath been accomplished at the last. But in the mean time what? "She hath covered the mountains with her shadow, and with her branch the cedars of God" (ver. 10). "Thou hast stretched out her boughs even unto the sea, and even unto the river her shoots" (ver. 11). This requireth the office of an expositor, that of a reader and praiser [2] doth not suffice: aid me with attention; for the mention of this vineyard in this Psalm is wont to overcloud with darkness the inattentive. . . . But nevertheless the first Jewish nation was this vine But the Jewish nation reigned as far as the sea and as far as the river. As far as the sea; it appeareth in Scripture [3] that the sea was in the vicinity thereof. And as far as the river Jordan. For on the other side of Jordan some part of the Jews was established, but within Jordan was the whole nation. Therefore, "even unto the sea and even unto the river," is the kingdom of the Jews, the kingdom of Israel: but not "from sea even unto sea, and from the river even unto the ends of the round world;" [4] this is the future perfection of the vineyard, concerning which in this place he hath foretold. When, I say, he had foretold to thee the perfection, he returneth to the beginning, out of which the perfection was made. Of the beginning wilt thou hear? "Even unto the river." Of the end wilt thou hear? "He shall have dominion from sea even unto sea:" [4] that is, "she hath filled the earth." Let us look then to the testimony of Asaph, as to what was done to the first vineyard, and what must be expected for the second vineyard, nay to the same vineyard. . . . What then, the vineyard before the sight whereof a way was made, that she should fill the earth, at first was where? "Her shadow covered the mountains." Who are the mountains? The Prophets. Why did her shadow cover them? Because darkly they spake the things which were foretold as to come. Thou hearest from the Prophets, Keep the Sabbath-day, on the eighth day circumcise a child, offer sacrifice of ram, of calf, of he-goat. Be not troubled, her shadow

doth cover the mountains of God; there will come after the shadow a manifestation. "And her shrubs the cedars of God," that is, she hath covered the cedars of God; very lofty, but of God. For the cedars are types of the proud, that must needs be overthrown. The "cedars of Lebanon," the heights of the world, this vineyard did cover in growing, and the mountains of God, all the holy Prophets and Patriarchs.

7. Then what? "Wherefore hast Thou thrown down her enclosure?" (ver. 12). Now ye see the overthrow of that nation of the Jews: already out of another Psalm ye have heard, "with axe and hammer [5] they have thrown her down." [6] When could this have been done, except her enclosure had been thrown down. What is her enclosure? Her defence. For she bore herself proudly against her planter. The servants that were sent to her and demanded a recompense, the husbandmen they scourged, beat, slew: there came also the Only Son, they said, "This is the Heir; come, let us kill Him, and our own the inheritance will be:" they killed Him, and out of the vineyard they cast Him forth. [7] When cast forth, He did more perfectly possess the place whence He was cast forth. For thus He threatens her through Isaiah, "I will throw down her enclosure." Wherefore? "For I looked that she should bring forth grapes, but she brought forth thorns." [8] I looked for fruit from thence, and I found sin. Why then dost thou ask, O Asaph, "Why hast Thou thrown down her enclosure?" For knowest thou not why? I looked that she should do judgment, and she did iniquity. Must not her enclosure needs be thrown down? And there came the Gentiles when the enclosure was thrown down, the vineyard was assailed, and the kingdom of the Jews effaced. This at first he is lamenting, but not without hope. For of directing the heart he is now speaking, that is, for the "Assyrians," for "men directing," the Psalm is. "Wherefore hast Thou thrown down her enclosure: and there pluck off her grapes all men passing along the way." What is "men passing along the way?" Men having dominion for a time.

8. "There hath laid her waste the boar from the wood" (ver. 13). In the boar from the wood what do we understand? To the Jews a swine is an abomination, and in a swine they imagine as it were the uncleanness of the Gentiles. But by the Gentiles was overthrown the nation of the Jews: but that king who overthrew, was not only an unclean swine, but was also a boar. For what is a boar but a savage swine, a furious swine? "A boar from the wood hath laid her waste." "From the wood," from

---

[1] John xiv. 6.   [2] One MS. "hearer."   [3] Numb. xxxiv. 5.   [4] Ps. lxxii. 8.

[5] *Fractorio.*   [6] Ps. lxxiv. 6.   [7] Matt. xxi. 35, etc.   [8] Isa. v. 2.

the Gentiles. For she was a vineyard, but the Gentiles were woods. But when the Gentiles believed, there was said what? "Then there shall exult all the trees of the woods." [1] "The boar from the wood hath laid her waste; and a singular wild beast hath devoured her." "A singular wild beast" is what? The very boar that laid her waste is the singular wild beast. Singular, because proud. For thus saith every proud one, It is I, it is I, and no other.

9. But with what profit is this? "O God of virtues turn Thou nevertheless" (ver. 14). Although these things have been done, "Turn Thou nevertheless." "Look from heaven and see, and visit this vineyard." "And perfect Thou her whom Thy right hand hath planted" (ver. 15). No other plant Thou, but this make Thou perfect. For she is the very seed of Abraham, she is the very seed in whom all nations shall be blessed: [2] there is the root where is borne the graffed wild olive. "Perfect Thou this vineyard which Thy right hand hath planted." But wherein doth He perfect? "And upon the Son of man, whom Thou hast strengthened to Thyself." What can be more evident? Why do ye still expect, that we should still explain to you in discourse, and should we not rather cry out with you in admiration, "Perfect Thou this vineyard which Thy right hand hath planted, and upon the Son of man" perfect her? What Son of man? Him "whom Thou hast strengthened to Thyself." A mighty stronghold: build as much as thou art able. "For other foundation no one is able to lay, except that which is laid, which is Christ Jesus." [3]

10. "Things burned with fire, and dug up, by the rebuke of Thy countenance shall perish" (ver. 16). What are the things burned with fire and dug up which shall perish from the rebuke of His countenance? Let us see and perceive what are the things burned with fire and dug up. Christ hath rebuked what? Sins: by the rebuke of His countenance sins have perished. Why then are sins burned with fire and dug up? Of all sins, two things are the cause in man, desire and fear.[4] Think, examine, question your hearts, sift your consciences, see whether there can be sins, except they be either of desire, or of fear. There is set before thee a reward to induce thee to sin, that is, a thing which delighteth thee; thou doest it, because thou desirest it. But perchance thou wilt not be allured by bribes; thou art terrified with menaces, thou doest it because thou fearest. A man would bribe thee, for example, to bear false witness. Countless cases there are, but I am setting before you the plainer cases, whereby ye may imagine the rest. Hast thou hearkened unto God, and hast thou said in thy heart, "What doth it profit a man, if he gain the whole world, but of his own soul suffer loss?"[5] I am not allured by a bribe to lose my soul[6] to gain money. He turneth himself to stir up fear within thee, he who was not able to corrupt thee with a bribe, beginneth to threaten loss, banishment, massacres, perchance, and death. Therein now, if desire prevailed not, perchance fear will prevail to make thee sin. . . . What had evil fear done? It had dug up, as it were. For love doth inflame, fear doth humble: therefore, sins of evil love, with fire were lighted: sins of evil fear were dug up. On the one hand, evil fear doth humble, and good love doth light; but in different ways respectively. For even the husbandman interceding for the tree, that it should not be cut down, saith, "I will dig about it, and will apply a basket of dung."[7] The dug trench doth signify the godly humility of one fearing, and the basket of dung the profitable squalid state of one repenting. But concerning the fire of good love the Lord saith, "Fire I have come to send into the world."[8] With which fire may the fervent in spirit burn, and they too that are inflamed with the love of God and their neighbour. And thus, as all good works are wrought by good fear and good love, so by evil fear and evil love all sins are committed. Therefore, "Things set alight with fire and dug up," to wit, all sins, "by the rebuke of Thy countenance shall perish."

11. "Let Thy hand be upon the Man of Thy right hand, and upon the Son of Man whom Thou hast strengthened Thyself" (ver. 17). "And we depart not from Thee. . . . Thou wilt quicken us, and Thy Name we will invoke" (ver. 18). Thou shalt be sweet to us, "Thou wilt quicken us." For aforetime we did love earth, not Thee: but Thou hast mortified our members which are upon the earth.[9] For the Old Testament, having earthly promises, seemeth to exhort that God should not be loved for nought, but that He should be loved because He giveth something on earth. What dost thou love, so as not to love God? Tell me. Love, if thou canst, anything which He hath not made. Look round upon the whole creation, see whether in any place thou art held with the birdlime of desire, and hindered from loving the Creator, except it be by that very thing which He hath Himself created, whom thou despisest. But why dost thou love those things, except because they are beautiful? Can they be as beautiful as He by whom they were made? Thou admirest these things, because thou seest not Him: but through those things which thou admirest, love Him whom thou seest not. Examine the creation; if of itself it is, stay therein: but if it is of Him, for no other reason is it pre-

---

[1] Ps. xcvi. 12.　　[2] Gen. xxii 18.　　[3] 1 Cor. iii. 11.
[4] All sins are either of desire or of fear.
[5] Matt. xvi. 26.　　[6] Or, "life."　　[7] Luke xiii. 8.
[8] Luke xii. 49.　　[9] Col. iii. 5.

judicial to a lover, than because it is preferred to the Creator. Why have I said this? With reference to this verse, brethren. Dead, I say, were they that did worship God that it might be well with them after the flesh: " For to be wise after the flesh is death : " [1] and dead are they that do not worship God gratis, that is, because of Himself He is good, not because He giveth such and such good things, which He giveth even to men not good. Money wilt thou have of God? Even a robber hath it. Wife, abundance of children, soundness of body, the world's dignity, observe how many evil men have. Is this all for the sake of which thou dost worship Him? Thy feet will totter,[2] thou wilt suppose thyself to worship without cause, when thou seest those things to be with them who do not worship Him. All these things, I say, He giveth even to evil men, Himself alone He reserveth for good men. "Thou wilt quicken us;" for dead we were, when to earthly things we did cleave; dead we were, when of the earthly man we did bear the image. "Thou wilt quicken us;" Thou wilt renew us, the life of the inward man Thou wilt give us. "And Thy Name we will invoke;" that is, Thee we will love. Thou to us wilt be the sweet forgiver of our sins, Thou wilt be the entire reward of the justified. "O Lord God of virtues, convert us, and show Thy face, and we shall be whole "(ver. 20).

PSALM LXXXI.[3]

1. For a Title this Psalm hath, "Unto the end for the presses, on the fifth of the Sabbath, a Psalm to Asaph himself." Into one title many mysteries are heaped together, still so that the lintel of the Psalm indicates the things within. As we have to speak of the presses, let no one expect that we shall speak of a vat, of a press, of olive baskets ; [4] because neither the Psalm hath this, and therefore it indicateth the greater mystery. . . .

No such thing did ye hear in this when it was reading. Therefore take the presses for the mystery of the Church, which is now transacting. In the presses we observe three things, pressure, and of the pressure two things, one to be laid up, the other to be thrown away. There takes place then in the press a treading, a crushing, a weight: and with these the oil strains out secretly into the vat,[5] the lees run openly down the streets.

Look intently on this great spectacle. For God ceaseth not to exhibit to us that which we may look upon with great joy, nor is the madness of the Circus to be compared with this spectacle. That belongeth to the lees, this to the oil. When therefore ye hear the blasphemers babble impudently and say that distresses abound in Christian times ; for ye know that they love to say this : and it is an old proverb, yet one that began from Christian times, " God gives no rain ; count it to the Christians ! " [6] Although it was those of old that said thus. But these now say also, " That God sends rain, count it to the Christians ! God sends no rain ; we sow not. God sends rain ; we reap not ! " And they wilfully make that an occasion of showing pride, which ought to make them more earnest in supplication, choosing rather to blaspheme than to pray.

When therefore they talk of such things, when they make such boasts, when they say these things, and say them in defiance, not with fear, but with loftiness, let them not disturb you. For suppose that pressures abound ; be thou oil. Let the lees, black with the darkness of ignorance, be insolent ; and let it, as though cast away in the streets, go gibing publicly : but do thou by thyself in thy heart, where He who seeth in secret will requite thee, strain off into the vat. . . . To name some one thing about which even they murmur who make them : How great plunderings, they say, are there in our times, how great distresses of the innocent, how great robberies of other men's goods ! Thus indeed thou takest notice of the lees, that other men's goods are seized ; to the oil thou givest no heed, that to the poor are given even men's own. The old time had no such plunderers of other men's goods : but the old time had no such givers of their own goods. . . .

2. Wherefore also " on the fifth of the sabbath "? [7] What is this? Let us go back to the first works of God, if perchance we may not there find somewhat in which we may also understand a mystery. For the sabbath is the seventh day, on which " God rested from all His works," [8] intimating the great mystery of our future resting from all our works. First of the sabbath then is called that first day, which we also call the Lord's day ; second of the sabbath, the second day ; . . . and the sabbath itself the seventh day. See ye therefore to whom this Psalm speaketh. For it seems to me that it speaketh to the baptized. For on the fifth day God from the waters created animals : on the fifth day, that

[1] Rom. viii 6.　　[2] Ps. lxxiii. 2.
[3] Lat. LXXX. A Sermon to the people of Carthage. [He makes this preface: " We have undertaken to speak to you of the present Psalm; let your quietness aid our voice, for it is somewhat worn out: the attention of the hearers, and the help of Him who bids me speak, will give it strength."—C.]
[4] Fiscinis.　　[5] Gemellarium.

[6] Duc ad Christianos; al. dicat Christianus, with other variations. The Ben. editor refers to De Civ. Dei, ii. c. 3, where a similar proverb is noticed; and Tertull. Apol. c. 40, " If the Tiber rises to the walls, if the Nile rises not upon the fields, presently the cry is, ' The Christians to the lions ! ' " and St. Cyprian to Demetrianus, speaking of the like complaints with respect to other calamities; to which may be added, St. Aug. De Civ. Dei, i. c. 1, of the sack of Rome, such a complaint being the occasion of his writing the book for its refutation. [See this series, vol. ii. p. xi., and A. N. F. vol. iii. 47.—C.]
[7] [Or, "week."—C.]　　[8] Gen. ii. 2.

is, on the " fifth of the sabbath," God said, " Let the waters bring forth creeping things of living souls." [1]　See ye, therefore, ye in whom the waters have already brought forth creeping things of living souls.　For ye belong to the presses, and in you, whom the waters have brought forth, one thing is strained out, another is thrown away.　For there are many that live not worthily of the baptism which they have received.　For how many that are baptized have chosen rather to be filling the Circus than this Basilica !　How many that are baptized are either making booths in the streets, or complaining that they are not made !

But this Psalm, " For the presses," and " on the fifth of the sabbath," is sung " unto Asaph." Asaph was a certain man called by this name, as Idithun, as Core, as other names that we find in the titles of the Psalms : yet the interpretation of this name intimates the mystery of a hidden truth.　Asaph, in fact, in Latin is interpreted " congregation."　Therefore, " For the presses, on the fifth of the sabbath," it is sung " unto Asaph," that is, for a distinguishing pressure, to the baptized, born again of water, the Psalm is sung to the Lord's congregation.　We have read the title on the lintel, and have understood what it means by these " presses."　Now if you please let us see the very house of the composition, that is, the interior of the press.　Let us enter, look in, rejoice, fear, desire, avoid.　For all these things ye are to find in this inward house, that is, in the text of the Psalm itself, when we shall have begun to read, and, with the Lord's help, to speak what He grants us.

3.　Behold yourselves, O Asaph, congregation of the Lord.　" Exult ye unto God our helper " (ver. 1).　Ye who are gathered together to-day, ye are this day the congregation of the Lord, if indeed unto you the Psalm is sung, " Exult ye unto God our helper."　Others exult unto the Circus, ye unto God : others exult unto their deceiver, do ye exult unto your helper : others exult unto their god their belly, do ye exult unto your God your helper.　" Jubilate unto the God of Jacob."　Because ye also belong to Jacob : yea, ye are Jacob, the younger people to which the elder is servant.[2]　" Jubilate unto the God of Jacob."　Whatsoever ye cannot explain in words, ye do not therefore forbear exulting : what ye shall be able to explain, cry out : what ye cannot, jubilate.　For from the abundance of joys, he that cannot find words sufficient, useth to break out into jubilating ; " Jubilate unto the God of Jacob."

4.　" Take the Psalm, and give the tabret " (ver. 2).　Both " take," and " give."　What is, " take " ? what, " give " ?　" Take the Psalm, and

give the tabret."　The Apostle Paul saith in a certain place,[3] reproving and grieving, that no one had communicated with him in the matter of giving and receiving.　What is, " in the matter of giving and receiving," but that which he hath openly set forth in another place.[4]　" If we have sowed unto you spiritual things, is it a great thing if we reap your carnal things."　And it is true that a tabret, which is made of hide, belongs to the flesh.　The Psalm, therefore, is spiritual, the tabret, carnal.　Therefore, people of God, congregation of God, " take ye the Psalm, and give the tabret : " take ye spiritual things, and give carnal.　This also is what at that blessed Martyr's table [5] we exhorted you, that receiving spiritual things ye should give carnal.　For these which are built for the time, are needful for receiving the bodies either of the living or of the dead, but in time that is passing by.　Shall we after God's judgment take up these buildings to Heaven ?　Yet without these we shall not be able to do at this time the things which belong to the possessing of Heaven.　If therefore ye are eager in getting spiritual things, be ye devout in expending carnal things.　" Take the Psalm, and give the tabret : " take our voice, return your hands.

5.　" The pleasant psaltery,[6] with the harp." I remember that we once intimated to your charity the difference of psaltery and harp.[7] . . . For heavenly is the preaching of the word of God.　But if we wait for heavenly things, let us not be sluggish in working at earthly things ; because, " the psaltery is pleasant," but, " with the harp."　The same is expressed in another way as above, " Take the Psalm, and give the tabret : " here for " Psalm," is put " psaltery," for " tabret," " harp."　Of this, however, we are admonished, that to the preaching of God's word we make answer by bodily works.

6.　" Sound the trumpet " (ver. 3).　This is, Loudly and boldly preach, be not affrighted ! as the Prophet says in a certain place, " Cry out, and lift up as with a trumpet thy voice." [8]　Sound the trumpet in the beginning of the month of the trumpet."　It was ordered, that in the beginning of the month there should be a sounding of the trumpet : and this even now the Jews do in bodily sort, after the spirit they understand it not.　For the beginning of the month, is the new moon : the new moon, is the new life.　What is the new moon ?　" If any, then, is in Christ,

---

[3] Phil. iv. 15.　　　　[4] 1 Cor. ix. 11.
[5] St. Cyprian's, who is named in § 21, note 4 ; namely, at Carthage, on the spot of his martyrdom.　" In that same place," says St. Augustin, Ser. 113, " a table was constructed to God, which is called Cyprian's table, not because Cyprian ever ate there, but because there he was offered up, and because by that very offering of his he prepared that table, not to feed or be fed on, but whereon sacrifice might be offered to God, to whom himself also was offered." — Ben.
[6] Or, " The psaltery is pleasant."
[7] [He repeats.　See Ps. xliii. 4, p. 139, supra. — C.]
[8] Isa. lviii. 1.

---

[1] Gen. i. 20.　　　　[2] Gen. xxv. 23.

he is a new creature." [1] What is, "sound the trumpet in the beginning of the month of the trumpet"? With all confidence preach ye the new life, fear not the noise of the old life.

7. "Because it is a commandment for Israel, and a judgment for the God of Jacob" (ver. 4). Where a commandment, there judgment. For, "They that have sinned in the Law, by the Law shall be judged." [2] And the very Giver of the commandment, the Lord Christ, the Word made flesh, saith, "For judgment I am come into the world, that they that see not may see, and they that see may be made blind." [3] What is, "That they that see not may see, they that see be made blind," but that the lowly be exalted, the proud thrown down? For not they that see are to be made blind, but those who to themselves seem to see are to be convicted of blindness. This is brought about in the mystery of the press, that they who see may not see, and they that see be made blind.

8. "A testimony in Joseph He made that" (ver. 5). Look you, brethren, what is it? Joseph is interpreted augmentation. Ye remember, ye know of Joseph sold into Egypt : Joseph sold into Egypt [4] is Christ passing over to the Gentiles. There Joseph after tribulations was exalted, and here Christ, after the suffering of the Martyrs, was glorified. Thenceforth to Joseph the Gentiles rather belong, and thenceforth augmentation ; because, "Many are the children of her that was desolate, rather than of her that hath the husband." [5] "He made it, till he should go out of the land of Egypt." Observe that also here the "fifth of the sabbath" is signified : when Joseph went out from the land of Egypt, that is, the people multiplied through Joseph, he was caused to pass through the Red Sea. Therefore then also the waters brought forth creeping things of living souls. [6] No other thing was it that there in figure the passage of that people through the sea foreshowed, than the passing of the Faithful through Baptism ; the apostle is witness : for "I would not have you ignorant, brethren," he said, "that our fathers were all under the cloud, and all passed through the sea, and were all baptized unto Moses in the cloud and in the sea." [7] Nothing else then the passing through the sea did signify, but the Sacrament of the baptized ; nothing else the pursuing Egyptians, but the multitude of past sins. Ye see most evident mysteries. The Egyptians press, they urge ; so then sins follow close, but no farther than to the water. Why then dost thou fear, who hast not yet come, to come to the Baptism of Christ, to pass through the Red Sea? What is "Red"? Consecrated with the

Blood of the Lord. Why fearest thou to come? The consciousness, perhaps, of some huge offences goads and tortures in thee thy mind, and says to thee that it is so great a thing thou hast committed, that thou mayest despair to have it remitted thee. Fear lest there remain anything of thy sins, if there lived any one of the Egyptians ! [8]

But when thou shalt have passed the Red Sea, when thou shalt have been led forth out of thine offences "with a mighty hand and with a strong arm," [9] thou wilt perceive mysteries that thou knowest not : since Joseph himself too, "when he came out of the land of Egypt, heard a language which he knew not." Thou shalt hear a language which thou knowest not : which they that know now hear and recognise, bearing witness and knowing. Thou shalt hear where thou oughtest to have thy heart : [10] which just now when I said many understood and answered by acclamation, the rest stood mute, because they have not heard the language which they knew not. Let them hasten, then, let them pass over, let them learn.

9. "He turned away from burdens his back" (ver. 6). Who "turned away from burdens his back," but He that cried, "Come unto Me, all ye that labour and are heavy laden"? [11] In another manner this same thing is signified. What the pursuit of the Egyptians did, the same thing do the burdens of sins. As if thou shouldest say, From what burdens? "His hands in the basket did serve." By the basket are signified servile works ; to cleanse, to manure, to carry earth, is done with a basket, [12] such works are servile : because "every one that doeth sin, is the slave of sin ;" and "if the Son shall have made you free, then will ye be free indeed." [13] Justly also are the rejected things of the world counted as baskets, but even baskets did God fill with morsels ; "Twelve baskets" [14] did He fill with morsels ; because "He chose the rejected things of this world to confound the things that were mighty." [15] But also when with the basket Joseph did serve, he then carried earth, because he did make bricks. "His hands in the basket did serve."

10. "In tribulation thou didst call on Me, and I delivered thee" (ver. 8). Let each Christian conscience recognise itself, if it have devoutly passed the Red Sea, [16] if with faith in believing and observing it hath heard a strange language which it knew not, let it recognise itself as having been heard in its tribulation. For that was a great tribulation, to be weighed

---

[1] 2 Cor. v. 17.   [2] Rom. ii. 12.   [3] John ix. 39.
[4] Oxf. MSS. repeat the words.   [5] Isa. liv. 1.
[6] Gen. i. 20.   [7] 1 Cor. x. 1, 2.

[8] Exod. xiv. 29, 30.   [9] Exod. xiii. 3; Deut. vi. 21.
[10] Matt. vi. 21, and Off. Euch.   [11] Matt. xi. 28.
[12] To this day it is common in many countries to do with a basket what we usually do with a barrow.
[13] John viii. 34–36.   [14] Matt. xiv 20.
[15] 1 Cor. i. 27.   [16] Exod. xiv. 22; 1 Cor. x. 2.

down with loads of sins. How does the conscience, lifted from the earth, rejoice. Lo, thou art baptized, thy conscience which was yesterday overladen, to-day rejoiceth thee. Thou hast been heard in tribulation, remember thy tribulation. Before thou camest to the water, what anxiety didst thou bear on thee! what fastings didst thou practise! what tribulations didst thou carry in thy heart! what inward, pious, devout prayers! Slain are thine enemies; all thy sins are blotted out. In tribulation thou didst call upon Me, and I delivered thee.

11. "I heard thee in the hidden part of the tempest." Not in a tempest of the sea, but in a tempest of the heart. "I proved thee in the water of contradiction." Truly, brethren, truly, he that was heard in the hidden part of the tempest ought to be proved in the water of contradiction. For when he hath believed, when he hath been baptized, when he hath begun to go in the way of God, when he hath striven to be strained into the vat, and hath drawn himself out from the lees that run in the street, he will have many disturbers, many insulters, many detractors, many discouragers, many that even threaten where they can, that deter, that depress. This is all the "water of contradiction." I suppose there are some here to-day, for instance, I think it likely there are some here whom their friends wished to hurry away to the circus, and to I know not what triflings of this day's festivity: perchance they have brought those persons with them to church. But whether they have brought those with them, or whether they have by them not permitted themselves to be led away to the circus, in the "water of contradiction" have they been tried. Do not then be ashamed to proclaim what thou knowest, to defend even among blasphemers what thou hast believed. . . . However much the bad that are aliens may rage, O that our own bad people would not help them!

Ye recollect what was said of Christ, that He was thus born for "the fall of many, and the rising again of many, and for a sign to be spoken against."[1] We know, we see: the sign of the Cross has been set up, and it has been spoken against. There has been speaking against the glory of the Cross: but there was a title over the Cross which was not to be corrupted. For there is a title in the Psalm,[2] "For the inscription of the title, corrupt thou not." It was a sign to be spoken against: for the Jews said, "Make it not, King of the Jews, but make it, that He said I am the King of the Jews."[3] Conquered was the contradiction; it was answered, "What I have written, I have written."

12. All this, from the beginning of the Psalm up to this verse, we have heard of the oil of the press. What remains is rather for grief and warning: for it belongs to the lees of the press, even to the end; perchance also not without a meaning in the interposition of the "Diapsalma." But even this too is profitable to hear, that he who sees himself already of the oil may rejoice; he that is in danger of running among the lees may beware. To both give heed, choose the one, fear the other.

"Hear, O My people, and I will speak, and will bear witness unto thee" (ver. 8). For it is not to a strange people, not to a people that belongs not to the press: "Judge ye," He saith, "between Me and My vineyard."[4]

13. "Israel, if thou shalt have heard Me, there shall not be in thee any new god" (ver. 9). A "new god" is one made for the time: but our God is not new, but from eternity to eternity. And our Christ is new, perchance, as Man,[5] but eternal God. For what before the beginning? And truly, "In the beginning was the Word, and the Word was with God, and the Word was God."[6] And our Christ Himself is the Word made flesh, that He might dwell in us.[7] Far be it, then, that there should be in any one a new god. A new god is either a stone or a phantom. He is not, saith one, a stone; I have a silver and a gold one. Justly did he choose to name the very costly things, who said, "The idols of the nations are silver and gold." Great are they, because they are of gold and silver; costly they are, shining they are; but yet, "Eyes they have, and see not!"[8] New are these gods. What newer than a god out of a workshop? Yea, though those now old ones spiders' webs have covered over, they that are not eternal are new. So much for the Pagans.[9] . . .

14. For if there be error in thee, Thou wilt not worship a strange god. If thou think not of a false god, thou wilt not worship a manufactured god: for "there will not" be in thee any strange god. "For I am." Why wouldest thou adore what is not? "For I am the Lord thy God" (ver. 10). Because "I am I that Am," and indeed "I Am" He saith, I that Am, over every creature: yet to thee what good have I afforded in time? "Who brought thee out of the land of Egypt." Not to that people alone is it said. For we all were brought out of the land of Egypt, we have all passed through the Red Sea; our enemies pursuing us have perished in the water. Let us not be ungrateful to our God; let us not forget God that abideth, and fabricate in ourselves a new god. "I, who led thee out of the land of Egypt," saith God. "Open wide

---

[1] Luke ii. 34.　　[2] Ps. lx. Tit.　　[3] John xix. 21.

[4] Isa. v. 3.
[5] *Recens fortè Homo, sed sempiternus Deus.* Quoted by Peter Lombard, *Sentences*, book iii. dist. 12. — Ben.
[6] John i. 1.　　[7] John i. 14.　　[8] Ps. cxv. 4, 5.
[9] [He turns to the Arians, Manichæans, and other heretics. — C.]

thy mouth, and I will fill it." Thou sufferest straitness in thyself because of the new god set up in thy heart; break the vain image, cast down from thy conscience the feigned idol: "open wide thy mouth," in confessing, in loving: "and I will fill it," because with me is the fountain of life.

15. "And My people obeyed not My voice" (ver. 11). For He would not speak these things except to His own people. For, "we know that whatsoever things the Law saith, it saith to them that are in the Law."[1] "And Israel did not listen to Me." Who? To whom? Israel to Me. O ungrateful soul! Through Me the soul, by Me the soul called, by Me brought back to hope, by Me washed from sins! "And Israel did not listen to Me!" For they are baptized and pass through the Red Sea: but on the way they murmur, gainsay, complain, are stirred with seditions, ungrateful to Him who delivered them from pursuing enemies, who leads through the dry land, through the desert, yet with food and drink, with light by night and shade by day.

16. "And I let them go according to the affections of their heart" (ver. 12). Behold the press: the orifices are open, the lees run. "And I let them go," not according to the healthfulness of My commands; but, according to the affections of their heart: I gave them up to themselves. The Apostle also saith, "God gave them up to the desires of their own hearts."[2] "I let them go according to the affection of their heart, they shall go in their own affections." There is what ye shudder at, if at least ye are straining out into the hidden vats of the Lord, if at least ye have conceived a hearty love for His storehouses, there is what ye shudder at. Some stand up for the circus, some for the amphitheatre, some for the booths in the streets, some for the theatres, some for this, some for that, some finally for their "new gods;" "they shall go in their own affections."

17. "If My people would have heard Me, if Israel would have walked in My ways" (ver. 13). For perchance that Israel saith, Behold I sin, it is manifest, I go after the affections of my own heart: but what can I do?[3] The devil doth this. Demons do this. What is the devil? Who are the demons? Certainly thine enemies. "Unto nothing all their enemies I would have brought down; and on them that oppress them I would have sent forth My hand" (ver. 14). But now what have they to do to complain of enemies? Themselves are become the worse enemies. For how? What followeth? Of enemies ye complain, yourselves, what are ye?

18. "The enemies of God have lied unto Him" (ver. 15). Dost thou renounce? I renounce.[4] And he returns to what he renounced. In fact, what things dost thou renounce, except bad deeds, diabolical deeds, deeds to be condemned of God, thefts, plunderings, perjuries, manslayings, adulteries, sacrileges, abominable rites, curious arts.[5] . . .

19. If therefore all those works "shall not possess the kingdom of God" (yea not the works, but "they that do such things;"[6] for such works there shall be none in the fire: for they shall not, while burning in that fire, be committing theft or adultery; but "they that do such things shall not possess the kingdom of God"); they shall not therefore be on the right hand, with those to whom it shall be said, "Come, ye blessed of My Father, receive the kingdom:" because, "they that do such things shall not possess the kingdom of God." If therefore on the right they shall not be, there remaineth not but that they must be on the left. To those on the left what shall He say? "Go ye into eternal fire." Because, "their time shall be for ever."

20. Explain to us, then, saith one, how those that build wood, hay, stubble, on the foundation, do not perish, but "are saved, yet so as by fire"? An obscure question indeed that, but as I am able I tell you briefly. Brethren, there are men altogether despisers of this world, to whom nothing is pleasant that flows in the course of time, they cling not by love to any earthly works, holy, chaste, continent, just, perchance even selling all their goods and distributing to the poor, or "possessing as though they possessed not, and using this world as though not using it."[7] But there are others who cling to things allowed to infirmity with a degree of affection. He robs not another of his estate, but so loves his own, that if he loses it he will be disturbed. He does not covet another's wife, but so clings to his own, so cohabits with his own, as not therein to keep the measure prescribed in the laws, for the sake of begetting children. He does not take away other men's things, but reclaims his own, and has a law-suit with his brother. For to such it is said, "Now indeed there is altogether a fault among you, because ye have law-suits with each other."[8] But these very suits he orders to be tried in the Church, not to be dragged into court, yet he says they are faults. For a Christian contends for earthly things more than becomes one to whom the kingdom of Heaven is promised. Not the whole of his heart doth he raise upward, but some part of it he draggeth on the earth. . . . Therefore if thou lovest thy possession, yet dost not for its

---

[1] Rom. iii. 19.   [2] Rom. i. 24.
[3] *Quid facio?* Perhaps, What do *I* do? *i.e.* What of it is *my* doing?

[4] He alludes to the form of interrogatory at Baptism.
[5] *Curiositatibus.* See Acts xix. 19.
[6] Gal. v. 21.   [7] 1 Cor. vii. 30, 31.   [8] 1 Cor. vi. 7.

sake commit violence, dost not for its sake bear false witness, dost not for its sake commit man-slaughter, dost not for its sake swear falsely, dost not for its sake deny Christ: in that thou wilt not for its sake do these things, thou hast Christ for a foundation. But yet because thou lovest it, and art saddened if thou losest it, upon the foundation thou hast placed, not gold, or silver, or precious stones, but wood, hay, stubble. Saved therefore thou wilt be, when that begins to burn which thou hast built, yet so as by fire. For let no one on this foundation building adul-teries, blasphemies, sacrileges, idolatries, perjuries, think he shall be "saved through fire," as though they were the "wood, hay, stubble:" but he that buildeth the love of earthly things on the foundation of the kingdom of Heaven, that is upon Christ, his love of temporal things shall be burned, and himself shall be saved through the right [1] foundation.

21. . . . "And He fed them of the fat of wheat, and from the rock with honey He satisfied them" (ver. 16). In the wilderness from the rock He brought forth water,[2] not honey. "Honey" is wisdom, holding the first place for sweetness among the viands of the heart. How many enemies of the Lord, then, that lie unto the Lord, are fed not only of the fat of wheat, but also from the rock with honey, from the wisdom of Christ? How many are delighted with His word, and with the knowledge of His sacraments, with the unfolding of His parables, how many are delighted, how many applaud with clamour! And this honey is not from any chance person, but "from the rock." But "the Rock was Christ."[3] How many, then, are satisfied with that honey, cry out, and say, It is sweet; say, Noth-ing better, nothing sweeter could be thought or said! and yet the enemies of the Lord have lied unto Him. I like not to dwell any more on matters of grief; although the Psalm endeth in terror to this purpose, yet from the end of it, I pray you, let us return to the heading: "Exult unto God our Helper." Turned unto God.[4]

PSALM LXXXII.[5]

1. This Psalm, like others similarly named, was so entitled either from the name of the man who

wrote it, or from the explanation of that same name, so as to refer in meaning to the Syna-gogue, which Asaph signifies; especially as this is intimated in the first verse. For it begins, "God stood in the synagogue of gods" (ver. 1). Far however be it from us to understand by these Gods the gods of the Gentiles, or idols, or any creature in heaven or earth except men; for a little after this verse the same Psalm relates and explains what Gods it means in whose syna-gogue God stood, where it says, "I have said, Ye are gods, and ye are all the children of the Most High: but ye shall die like men, and fall like one of the princes." In the synagogue of these children of the Most High, of whom the same Most High said by the mouth of Isaiah, "I have begotten sons and brought them up, but they despised Me,"[6] stood God. By the syna-gogue we understand the people of Israel, because synagogue is the word properly used of them, although they were also called the Church. Our congregation, on the contrary, the Apostles never called synagogue, but always Ecclesia; whether for the sake of the distinction, or because there is some difference between a congregation whence the synagogue has its name, and a con-vocation whence the Church is called Ecclesia:[7] for the word congregation (or flocking together) is used of cattle, and particularly of that kind properly called "flocks,"[8] whereas convocation (or calling together) is more of reasonable creatures, such as men are. . . . I think then that it is clear in what synagogue of gods God stood.

2. The next question is, whether we should understand the Father, or the Son, or the Holy Spirit, or the Trinity, "to have stood among the congregation of gods, and in the midst to distin-guish the gods;" because Each One is God, and the Trinity itself is One God. It is not in-deed easy to make this clear, because it cannot be denied that not a bodily but a spiritual pres-ence of God, agreeable to His nature, exists with created things in a wonderful manner, and one which but a few do understand, and that imperfectly: as to God it is said, "If I shall as-cend into heaven, Thou art there; if I shall go down into hell, Thou art there also."[9] Hence it is rightly said, that God stands in the congre-gation of men invisibly, as He fills heaven and earth, which He asserts of Himself by the Proph-et's mouth;[10] and He is not only said, but is, in a way, known to stand in those things which He hath created, as far as the human mind can conceive, if man also stands and hears Him, and rejoices greatly on account of His voice within. But I think that the Psalm intimates something that took place at a particular time, by God's

---

[1] *Idoneum.*　　[2] Exod. xvii. 6.　　[3] 1 Cor. x. 4.

[4] Possibly alluding to the last verse of Ps. lxxx. Or it may direct them to turn to God and repeat the Psalm. A similar incidental addition occurs at the end of the exposition of Ps. lxii. [After this ceremony (after the word) he adds: "Not lightly have your minds in the name of Christ been occupied with the Divine exhibitions, and raised to earnestness, not only for desiring some things, but also for shunning some things. These are the exhibitions that are useful, healthful, building up, not destroying: yea both destroying and building up, destroying 'new gods,' building up faith in the true and eternal God. Also for to-morrow we invite your love. To-morrow, they have, as we have heard, a sea in the theatre: let us have a harbour in Christ. But since the day after to-morrow, that is, the fourth of the week, we cannot meet at the 'Table of Cyprian,' because it is the festival of the holy Martyrs, to-morrow let us meet at that Table." See p. 391, *supra*.— C.]

[5] Lat. LXXXI. A Psalm for Asaph himself.

[6] Isa. i. 2.　　[7] ἐκκλησία from καλεῖν.　　[8] *Greges.*
[9] Ps. cxxxix. 8.　　[10] Jer. xxiii. 24.

standing in the congregation of gods. For that standing by which He fills heaven and earth, neither belongs peculiarly to the synagogue, nor varies from time to time. "God," therefore, "stood in the congregation of gods;" that is, He who said of Himself, "I am not sent but to the lost sheep of the house of Israel."[1] The cause too is mentioned; "but in the midst, to judge of the gods." . . .

3. "How long will ye judge unrighteously, and accept the persons of the ungodly" (ver. 2); as in another place, "How long are ye heavy in heart?"[2] Until He shall come who is the light of the heart? I have given a law, ye have resisted stubbornly: I sent Prophets, ye treated them unjustly, or slew them, or connived at those who did so. But if they are not worthy to be even spoken to, who slew the servants of God that were sent to them, ye who were silent when these things were doing, that is, ye who would imitate as if they were innocent those who then were silent, "how long will ye judge unrighteously, and accept the persons of the ungodly?" If the Heir comes even now, is He to be slain? Was He not willing for your sake to become as it were a child under guardians? Did not He for your sake hunger and thirst like one in need? Did He not cry to you, "Learn of Me, for I am meek and lowly of heart"?[3] Did He not "become poor, when He was rich, that by His poverty we might be made rich"?[4] "Give sentence," therefore, "for the fatherless[5] and the poor man, justify the humble and needy" (ver. 3). Not them who for their own sake are rich and proud, but Him who for your sake was humble and poor, believe ye to be righteous: proclaim Him righteous. But they will envy Him, and will not at all spare Him, saying, "This is the Heir, come, let us kill Him, and the inheritance shall be ours." "Deliver," then, "the poor man, and save the needy from the hands of the ungodly" (ver. 4). This is said that it might be known, that in that nation where Christ was born and put to death, those persons were not guiltless of so great a crime, who being so numerous, that, as the Gospel says, the Jews feared them, and therefore dared not lay hands on Christ, afterwards consented, and permitted Him to be slain by the malicious and envious Jewish rulers: yet if they had so willed, they would still have been feared, so that the hands of the wicked would never have prevailed against Him. For of these it is said elsewhere, "Dumb dogs, they know not how to bark." Of them too is that said, "Lo, how the righteous perisheth, and no man layeth it to heart."[6] He perished[7] as far as lay in them who would have Him to perish; for

how could He perish by dying, who in that way rather was seeking again what had perished? If then they are justly blamed and deservedly rebuked, who by their dissembling suffered such a wicked deed to be committed; how must they be blamed, or rather not only blamed, but how severely must they be condemned, who did this of design and malice?

4. To all of them, verily, what follows is most fitly suited: "They did not know nor understand, they walk on in darkness" (ver. 5). "For if even they had known, they would never have crucified the Lord of glory:"[8] and those others, if they had known, would never have consented to ask that Barabbas should be freed, and Christ should be crucified. But as the above-mentioned blindness happened in part unto Israel until the fulness of the Gentiles should come in, this blindness of that People having caused the crucifixion of Christ, "all the foundations of the earth shall be moved." So have they been moved, and shall they be moved, until the predestined fulness of the Gentiles shall come in. For at the actual death of the Lord the earth was moved, and the rocks rent.[9] And if we understand by the foundations of the earth those who are rich in the abundance of earthly possessions, it was truly foretold that they should be moved, either by wondering that lowliness, poverty, death, should be so loved and honoured in Christ, when it is to their mind great misery; or even in that themselves should love and follow it, and set at nought the vain happiness of this world. So are all the foundations of the earth moved, while they partly admire, and partly are even altered. For as without absurdity we call foundations of heaven those on whom the kingdom of heaven is built up in the persons of saints and faithful; whose first foundation is Christ Himself, born of the Virgin, of whom the Apostle says, "Other foundation can no man lay than that which is laid, which is Christ Jesus;"[10] next the Apostles and Prophets themselves, by whose authority the heavenly place is chosen,[11] that by obeying them we may be builded together with them; whence he says to the Ephesians, "Ye are built upon the foundation of Apostles and Prophets, Christ Jesus Himself being the chief corner stone."[12] . . . But the kingdom of earthly happiness is pride, to oppose which came the lowliness of Christ, rebuking those whom He wished by lowliness to make the children of the Most High, and blaming them: "I said, Ye are gods, ye are all the children of the Most High" (ver. 6). "But ye shall die like men, and fall like one of the princes" (ver. 7). Whether to those He said this, "I said, Ye are gods," and to those

[1] Matt. xv. 24. [2] Ps. iv. 2, Vulg. [3] Matt. xi. 29.
[4] 2 Cor. viii. 9. [5] *Pupillo.* [6] Isa. lvi. 10, lvii. 1.
[7] Oxf. MSS. "perisheth," "lieth."

[8] 1 Cor. ii. 8. [9] Matt. xxvii. 51. [10] 1 Cor. iii. 11.
[11] *Eligitur.* [12] Eph. ii. 20.

particularly who are unpredestined to eternal life ; and to the other, " But ye shall die like men," etc., "and shall fall like one of the princes," in this way also distinguishing the gods ; or whether He blames all together, in order to distinguish the obedient and those who received correction, " I said, Ye are gods, and ye are all the children of the Most High : " that is, to all of you I promised celestial happiness, " but ye," through the infirmity of your flesh, " shall die like men," and through haughtiness of soul, " like one of the princes," that is, the devil, shall not be exalted, but " shall fall." As if He said : Though the days of your life are so few, that ye speedily die like men, this avails not to your correction : but like the devil, whose days are many in this world, because he dies not in the flesh, ye are lifted up so that ye fall. For by devilish pride it came to pass that the perverse and blind rulers of the Jews envied the glory of Christ : by this will it came to pass, and still does, that the lowliness of Christ crucified unto death is lightly esteemed in the eyes of them who love the excellence of this world.

5. And therefore that this vice may be cured, in the person of the Prophet himself it is said, " Arise, O God, and judge the earth " (ver. 8) ; for the earth swelled high when it crucified Thee : rise from the dead, and judge the earth. " For Thou shalt destroy among all nations." What, but the earth? that is, destroying those who savour of earthly things, or destroying the feeling itself of earthly lust and pride in believers ; or separating those who do not believe, as earth to be trodden under foot and to perish. Thus by His members, whose conversation is in heaven, He judges the earth, and destroys it among all nations. But I must not omit to remark, that some copies have, " for Thou shalt inherit among all nations." This too may be understood agreeably to the sense, nor does anything prevent both meanings existing at once. His inheritance takes place by love, which in that He cultivates by His commands and gracious mercy, He destroys earthly desires.

PSALM LXXXIII.[1]

1. Of this Psalm the title is, " A song of a Psalm of Asaph." We have already often said what is the interpretation of Asaph, that is, congregation. That man, therefore, who was called Asaph, is named in representation of the congregation of God's people in the titles of many Psalms. But in Greek, congregation is called synagogue, which has come to be held for a kind of proper name for the Jewish people, that it should be called The Synagogue ; even as the Christian

people is more usually called The Church, in that it too is congregated.

2. The people of God, then, in this Psalm saith, " O God, who shall be like unto Thee ? " (ver. 1). Which I suppose to be more fitly taken of Christ, because, being made in the likeness of men,[2] He was thought by those by whom He was despised to be comparable to other men : for He was even " reckoned among the unrighteous,"[3] but for this purpose, that He might be judged. But when He shall come to judge, then shall be done what is here said, " O God, who is like unto Thee ? " For if the Psalms did not use to speak to the Lord Christ, that too would not be spoken which not one of the faithful can doubt was spoken unto Christ. " Thy throne, O God, is for ever and ever, a sceptre of righteousness is the sceptre of Thy kingdom."[4] To him therefore also now it is said, " O God, who shall be like unto Thee ? " For unto many Thou didst vouchsafe to be likened in Thy humiliation, even so far as to the robbers that were crucified with Thee : but when in glory Thou shalt come, " who shall be like unto Thee ? " . . .

3. " For lo Thine enemies have sounded, and they that hate Thee have lifted up the head " (ver. 2). He seems to me to signify the last days, when these things that are now repressed by fear are to break forth into free utterance, but quite irrational, so that it should rather be called a " sound," than speech or discourse. They will not, therefore, then begin to hate, but " they that hate Thee " will then " lift up the head." And not " heads," but " head ; " since they are to come even to that point, that they shall have that head, which " is lifted up above all that is called God, and that is worshipped ; "[5] so that in him especially is to be fulfilled, " He that exalteth himself shall be abased ; "[6] and when He to whom it is said, " Keep not silence, nor grow mild, O God," shall " slay him with the breath of His mouth, and shall destroy with the brightness of His coming."[7] " Upon Thy people they have malignantly taken counsel " (ver. 3). Or, as other copies have it, " They have cunningly devised counsel, and have devised against Thy saints." In scorn this is said. For how should they be able to hurt the nation or people of God, or His saints, who know how to say, " If God be for us, who shall be against us ? "[8]

4. " They have said, Come, and let us destroy them from a nation " (ver. 4). He has put the singular number for the plural : as it is said, " Whose is this cattle," even though the question be of a flock, and the meaning " these cattle." Lastly, other copies have " from nations," where

---

[2] Phil. ii. 7.　　　[3] Isa. liii. 12.　　　[4] Ps. xlv. 6.
[5] 2 Thess. ii. 4.　　[6] Luke xiv. 11.　　　[7] 2 Thess. ii. 8.
[8] Rom. viii. 31.

the translators have rather followed the sense than the word. " Come, and let us destroy them from a nation." This is that sound whereby they " sounded " rather than spake, since they did vainly make a noise with vain sayings. " And let it not be mentioned of the name of Israel any more." This others have expressed more plainly, " and let there not be remembrance of the name of Israel any more." Since, " let it be mentioned of the name " (*memoretur nominis*), is an unusual phrase in the Latin language ; for it is rather customary to say, " let the name be mentioned " (*memoretur nomen*) ; but the sense is the same. For he who said, " let it be mentioned of the name," translated the Greek phrase. But Israel must here be understood in fact of the seed of Abraham, to which the Apostle saith, " Therefore ye are the seed of Abraham, according to the promise heirs." [1] Not Israel according to the flesh, of which he saith, " Behold Israel after the flesh."

5. " Since they have imagined with one consent ; together against Thee have they disposed a testament " (ver. 5) : as though they could be the stronger. In fact, " a testament " is a name given in the Scriptures not only to that which is of no avail till the death of the testators, but every convenant and decree they used to call a testament. For Laban and Jacob made a testament,[2] which was certainly to have force between the living ; and such cases without number are read in the words of God. Then he begins to make mention of the enemies of Christ, under certain proper names of nations ; the interpretation of which names sufficiently indicates what he would have to be understood. For by such names are most suitably figured the enemies of the truth. " Idumæans," for instance, are interpreted either " men of blood," or " of earth." " Ismaelites," are " obedient to themselves," and therefore not to God, but to themselves. " Moab," " from the father ; " which in a bad sense has no better explanation, than by considering it so connected with the actual history, that Lot, a father, by the illicit intercourse procured by his daughter, begat him ; since it was from that very circumstance he was so named.[3] Good, however, was his father, but as " the Law is good if one use it lawfully," [4] not impurely and unlawfully. " Hagarens," proselytes, that is strangers, by which name also are signified, among the enemies of God's people, not those who become citizens, but those who persevere in a foreign and alien mind, and when an opportunity of doing harm occurs, show themselves. " Gebal," " a vain valley," that is, humble in pretence. " Amon," " an unquiet people," or " a people of sadness." " Amalech," " a people

licking ; " whence elsewhere it is said, " and his enemies shall lick the earth." [5] The " alien race," though by their very name in Latin, they sufficiently show themselves to be aliens, and for this cause of course enemies, yet in the Hebrew are called " Philistines," which is explained, " falling from drink," as of persons made drunken by worldly luxury. " Tyre " in Hebrew is called Sor ; which whether it be interpreted straitness or tribulation, must be taken in the case of these enemies of God's people in that sense, of which the Apostle speaks, " Tribulation and straitness on every soul of man that doeth evil." [6] All these are thus enumerated in the Psalms : " The tabernacles of the Edomites, Ishmaelites, Moab and the Hagarenes, Gebal, and Amon, and Amalech, and the Philistines with those who inhabit Tyre."

6. And as if to point out the cause why they are enemies of God's people, he adds, " For Assur came with them." Now Assur is often used figuratively for the devil, " who works in the children of disobedience," [7] as in his own vessels, that they may assail the people of God. " They have holpen the children of Lot," he saith : for all enemies, by the working in them of the devil, their prince, " have holpen the children of Lot," who is explained to mean " one declining." But the apostate angels are well explained as the children of declension, for by declining from truth they swerved to become followers of the devil. These are they of whom the Apostle speaks : " Ye wrestle not against flesh and blood, but against principalities and powers, and the rulers of the darkness of this world, against spiritual wickedness in high places." [8] Those invisible [9] enemies are holpen then by unbelieving men, in whom they work in order to assail the people of God.

7. Now let us see what the prophetic spirit prays may fall upon them, rather foretelling than cursing. " Do thou to them," he saith, " as unto Madian and Sisera, as unto Jabin at the brook of Kishon" (ver. 9). " They perished at Endor, they became as the dung of the earth " (ver. 10). All these, the history relates, were subdued and conquered by Israel, which then was the people of God : as was the case also with those whom he next mentions : " Make their princes like Oreb and Zeb, and Zebee and Salmana " (ver. 11). The meaning of these names is as follows : Madian is explained a perverted judgment : Sisera, shutting out of joy : Jabin, wise.[10] But in these enemies conquered by God's people is to be understood that wise man of whom the Apostle speaketh, " Where is the wise ? where is the scribe ? where is the disputer of this world ? " [11] Oreb is dryness, Zeb, wolf, Zebee, a victim, namely of the wolf ;

1 Gal. iii. 29.   2 Gen. xxxi. 44.
3 Gen. xix. 36, 37.   4 1 Tim. i. 8.

5 Ps. lxxii. 9.   6 Rom. ii. 9.   7 Eph. ii. 2.
8 Eph. vi. 12.   9 Oxf. mss. " and spiritual."
10 Judg. iv. 7, 8.   11 1 Cor. i. 20.

for he too has his victims ; Salmana, shadow of commotion. All these agree to the evils which the people of God conquer by good. Moreover Kishon, the torrent in which they were conquered, is explained, their hardness. Endor, where they perished, is explained, the Fountain of generation, but of the carnal generation namely, to which they were given up, and therefore perished, not heeding the regeneration which leadeth unto life, where they shall neither marry nor be given in marriage,[1] for they shall die no more. Rightly then it is said of these : " they became as the dung of the earth," in that nothing was produced of them but fruitfulness of the earth. As then all these were in figure conquered by the people of God, as figures, so he prays that those other enemies may be conquered in truth.

8. "All their princes, who said, Let us take to ourselves the sanctuary of God in possession " (ver. 12). This is that vain noise, with which, as said above, Thy enemies have made a murmuring. But what must be understood by " the sanctuary of God," except the temple of God ? as saith the Apostle : " For the temple of God is holy,[2] which temple ye are."[3] For what else do the enemies aim at, but to take into possession, that is, to make subject to themselves the temple of God, that it may give in to their ungodly wills ?

9. But what follows ? " My God, make them like unto a wheel " (ver. 13). This is fitly taken as meaning that they should be constant in nothing that they think ; but I think it may also be rightly explained, make them like unto a wheel, because a wheel is lifted up on the part of what is behind,[4] is thrown down on the part of what is in front ; and so it happens to all the enemies of the people of God. For this is not a wish, but a prophecy. He adds : " as the stubble in the face of the wind." By face he means presence ; for what face hath the wind, which has no bodily features, being only a motion, in that it is a kind of wave of air ? But it is put for temptation, by which light and vain hearts are hurried away.

10. This levity, by which consent is easily given to what is evil, is followed by severe torment ; therefore he proceeds : —

" Like as the fire that burneth up the wood, and as the flame that consumeth the mountains " (ver. 14) : " so shalt Thou persecute them with Thy tempest, and in Thy anger shalt disturb them " (ver. 15). Wood, he saith, for its barrenness, mountains for their loftiness ; for such are the enemies of God's people, barren of righteousness, full of pride. When he says, " fire " and " flame," he means to repeat under another term, the idea of God judging and punishing. But in saying, " with Thy tempest," he means, as he goes on to explain, " Thy anger : " and the former expression, " Thou shalt persecute," answers to, " Thou shalt disturb." We must take care, however, to understand, that the anger of God is free from any turbulent emotion ; for His anger is an expression for His just method of taking vengeance : as the law might be said to be angry when its ministers are moved to punish by its sanction.

11. " Fill their faces with shame, and they shall seek Thy name, O Lord " (ver. 16). Good and desirable is this which he prophesieth for them : and he would not prophesy thus, unless there were even in that company of the enemies of God's people, some men of such kind that this would be granted to them before the last judgment : for now they are mixed together, and this is the body of the enemies, in respect of the envy whereby they rival the people of God. And now, where they can, they make a noise and lift up their head : but severally, not universally as they will do at the end of the world, when the last judgment is about to fall. But it is the same body, even in those who out of this number shall believe and pass into another body (for the faces of these are filled with shame, that they may seek the name of the Lord), as well as in those others who persevere unto the end in the same wickedness, who are made as stubble before the wind, and are consumed like a wood and barren mountains. To these he again returns, saying, " They shall blush and be vexed for ever and ever " (ver. 17). For those are not vexed for ever and ever who seek the name of the Lord, but having respect unto the shame of their sins, they are vexed for this purpose, that they may seek the name of the Lord, through which they may be no more vexed.

12. Again, he returns to these last, who in the same company of enemies are to be made ashamed for this purpose, that they may not be ashamed for ever : and for this purpose to be destroyed in as far as they are wicked, that being made good they may be found alive for ever. For having said of them, " Let them be ashamed and perish," he instantly adds, " and let them know that Thy name is the Lord, Thou art only the Most Highest in all the earth " (ver. 18). Coming to this knowledge, let them be so confounded as to please God : let them so perish, as that they may abide. " Let them know," he says, " that Thy name is the Lord : " as if whoever else are called lords are named so not truly but by falsehood, for they rule but as servants, and compared with the true Lord are not lords ; as it is said, I Am that I Am :[5] as if those things

---

[1] Luke xx. 35.　　　[2] *Sanctum.*　　　[3] 1 Cor. iii. 17.
[4] *Ex his quæ retrò sunt extollitur, ex his quæ ante sunt dejicitur.*

[5] Exod. iii. 14.

which are made are not, compared with Him by whom they are made. He adds, "Thou only art the Most Highest in all the earth : " or, as other copies have it, " over all the earth ; " as it might be said, in all the heaven, or over all the heaven : but he used the latter word in preference, to depress the pride of earth. For earth ceaseth to be proud, that is, man ceaseth, to whom it was said, " Thou art dust ; "[1] and " why is earth and ashes proud?"[2] when he saith that the Lord is the Most Highest above all the earth, that is, that no man's thoughts avail against those " who are called according to His purpose," and of whom it is said, " If God is for us, who can be against us?"[3]

PSALM LXXXIV.[4]

1. This Psalm is entitled, " For the winepresses." And, as you observed with me, my beloved (for I saw that you attended most closely), nothing is said in its text either of any press, or wine-basket, or vat, or of any of the instruments or the building of a winepress ; nothing of this kind did we hear read ; so that it is no easy question what is the meaning of this title inscribed upon it, " for the winepresses." For certainly, if after the title it mentioned anything about such things as I enumerated, carnal persons might have believed that it was a song concerning those visible winepresses ; but as it has this title, yet says nothing afterwards of those winepresses which we know so well, I cannot doubt that there are other winepresses, which the Spirit of God intended us to look for and to understand here. Therefore, let us recall to mind what takes place in these visible winepresses, and see how this takes place spiritually in the Church. The grape hangs on the vines, and the olive on its trees. For it is for these two fruits that presses are usually made ready ; and as long as they hang on their boughs, they seem to enjoy free air ; and neither is the grape wine, nor the olive oil, before they are pressed. Thus it is with men whom God predestined before the world to be conformed to the image of His only-begotten Son,[5] who has been first and especially pressed in His Passion, as the great Cluster. Men of this kind, therefore, before they draw near to the service of God, enjoy in the world a kind of delicious liberty, like hanging grapes or olives : but as it is said, " My son, when thou drawest near to the service of God, stand in judgment and fear, and make thy soul ready for temptation : "[6] so each, as he draweth near to the service of God, findeth that he is come to the winepress ; he shall undergo tribulation, shall be crushed, shall be pressed, not that he may perish in this world, but that he may flow down into the storehouses of God. He hath the coverings of carnal desires stripped off from him, like grape-skins : for this hath taken place in him in carnal desires, of which the Apostle speaks, " Put ye off the old man, and put on the new man."[7] All this is not done but by pressure : therefore the Churches of God of this time are called winepresses.

2. But who are we who are placed in the winepresses? "Sons of Core." For this follows : " For the winepresses, to the sons of Core." The sons of Core has been explained, sons of the bald : as far as those could explain it to us, who know that language, according to their service due to God.[8] . . .

3. But being placed under pressure, we are crushed for this purpose, that for our love by which we were borne towards those worldly, secular, temporal, unstable, and perishable things, having suffered in them, in this life, torments, and tribulations of pressures, and abundance of temptations, we may begin to seek that rest which is not of this life, nor of this earth ; and the Lord becomes, as is written, " a refuge for the poor man."[9] What is, " for the poor man "? For him who is, as it were, destitute, without aid, without help, without anything on which he may rest, in earth. For to such poor men, God is present. For though men abound in money on earth, . . . they are filled more with fear than with enjoyment. For what is so uncertain as a rolling thing? It is not unfitly that money itself is stamped round, because it remains not still. Such men, therefore, though they have something, are yet poor. But those who have none of this wealth, but only desire it, are counted also among rich men who will be rejected ; for God takes account not of power, but of will. The poor then are destitute of all this world's substance, for even though it abounds around them, they know how fleeting it is ; and crying unto God, having nothing in this world with which they may delight themselves, and be held down, placed in abundant pressures and temptations, as if in winepresses, they flow down, having become oil or wine. What are these latter but good desires? For God remains their only object of desire ; now they love not earth. For they love Him who made heaven and earth ; they love Him, and are not yet with Him. Their desire is delayed, in order that it may increase ; it increases, in order that it may receive. For it is not any little thing that God will give to him who desires, nor does he need to be little exercised to be made fit to receive so great a good : not anything which He hath made will God give, but Himself who made all things. Exercise thy-

　　¹ Gen. iii. 19.　　² Ecclus. x. 9.　　³ Rom. viii. 28, 31.
⁴ Lat. LXXXIII.　⁵ Rom. viii. 29.　⁶ Ecclus. ii. 1.

⁷ Col. iii. 9, 10; Eph. iv. 22.　⁸ [See pp. 132, 140, *supra.* — C.]
⁹ Ps. ix. 9.

self to receive God : that which thou shalt have for ever, desire thou for a long time. . . .

4. Wherefore, most beloved, as each can, make vows, and perform to the Lord God [1] what each can : let no one look back, no one delight himself with his former interests, no one turn away from that which is before to that which is behind : let him run until he arrive : for we run not with the feet but with the desire. But let no one in this life say that he hath arrived. For who can be so perfect as Paul? [2] Yet he saith, "Brethren, I count not myself to have attained."

5. If therefore thou feelest the passions of this world, even when thou art happy, thou understandest now that thou art in the winepress. . . . If therefore the world smile upon thee with happiness, imagine thyself in the winepress, and say, " I found trouble and heaviness, and I did call upon the name of the Lord." [3] He said not, I found trouble, without meaning, of such a kind as was hidden : for some troubles are hidden from some in this world, who think they are happy while they are absent from God. " For as long as we are in the body," he saith, " we are absent from the Lord." [4] If thou wert absent from thy father, thou wouldest be unhappy : art thou absent from the Lord, and happy? There are then some who think it is well with them. But those who understand, that in whatever abundance of wealth and pleasures, though all things obey their beck, though nothing troublesome creep in, nothing adverse terrify, yet that they are in a bad case as long as they are absent from the Lord ; with a most keen eye these have found trouble, and grief, and have called on the name of the Lord. Such is he who sings in this Psalm. Who is he? The Body of Christ. Who is that? You, if you will : all we, if we will : for Christ's Body is one. . . .

" How lovely are Thy tabernacles, O Lord of Hosts " (ver. 1). He was in some tabernacles, that is, in winepresses : but he longed for other tabernacles, where is no pressure : in this he sighed for them, from these, he, as it were, flowed down into them by the channel of longing desire.

6. And what follows? " My soul longeth and faileth for the courts of the Lord " (ver. 2). It is not enough that it " longeth and faileth : " for what doth it fail? " For the courts of the Lord." The grape when pressed hath failed : but for what? So as to be changed into wine, and to flow into the vat, and into the rest of the storeroom, to be kept there in great quiet. Here it is longed for, there it is received : here are sighs, there joy : here prayers, there praises : here groans, there rejoicing. Those things which I

mentioned, let no one while here turn from ashamed : let no one be unwilling to suffer. There is danger, lest the grape, while it fears the winepress, should be devoured by birds or by wild beasts. . . .

7. Thou hast heard a groan in the winepress, " My soul longeth and faileth for the courts of the Lord : " hear how it holdeth out, rejoicing in hope : " My heart and my flesh have rejoiced in the living God." Here they have rejoiced for that cause. Whence cometh rejoicing, but of hope? Wherefore have they rejoiced? " In the living God." What has rejoiced in thee? " My heart and my flesh." Why have they rejoiced? " For," saith he, " the sparrow hath found her a house, and the turtle-dove a nest, where she may lay her young " (ver. 3). What is this? He had named two things, and he adds two figures of birds which answer to them : he had said that his heart rejoiced and his flesh, and to these two he made the sparrow and turtle-dove to correspond : the heart as the sparrow, the flesh as the dove. The sparrow hath found herself a home : my heart hath found itself a home. She tries her wings in the virtues of this life, in faith, and hope, and charity, by which she may fly unto her home : and when she shall have come thither, she shall remain ; and now the complaining voice of the sparrow, which is here, shall no longer be there. For it is the very complaining sparrow of whom in another Psalm he saith, " Like a sparrow alone on the housetop." [5] From the housetop he flies home. Now let him be on the housetop, treading on his carnal house : he shall have a heavenly house, a perpetual home : that sparrow shall make an end of his complaints. But to the dove he hath given young, that is, to the flesh : " the dove hath found a nest, where she may lay her young." The sparrow a home, the dove a nest, and a nest too where she may lay her young. A home is chosen as for ever, a nest is framed for a time : with the heart we think upon God, as if the sparrow flew to her home : with the flesh we do good works. For ye see how many good works are done by the flesh of the saints ; for by this we work the things we are commanded to work, by which we are helped in this life. " Break thy bread to the hungry, and bring the poor and roofless into thy house ; and if thou see one naked, clothe him : " [6] and other such things which are commanded us we work only through the flesh. . . . We speak, brethren, what ye know : how many seem to do good works without the Church? [7] how many even Pagans feed the hungry, clothe the naked, receive the

[1] Ps. lxxvi. 11.   [2] Phil. iii. 13.
[3] Ps. cxvi. 3, 4.   [4] 2 Cor. v. 6.

[5] Ps. cii. 7.   [6] Isa. lviii. 7.
[7] Ed. Ben. refers to P. Lombard, *II. Sent*. Dist. 41, where this passage is quoted on the question, "Are all the works of those who are without faith evil ?" [See A. N. F. vol. ii. p. 517, note 4.— C.]

stranger, visit the sick, comfort the prisoner? how many do this? The dove seems, as it were, to bring forth young: but finds not herself a nest. How many works may heretics do not in the Church; they place not their young in a nest. They shall be trampled on and crushed: they shall not be kept, shall not be guarded. . . . In that faith lay thy young: in that nest work thy works. For what the nests are, what that nest is, follows at once. Having said, And the dove hath found herself a nest, where she may lay her young; as if thou hadst asked, What nest? "Thy altars, O Lord of Hosts, my King and my God." What is, "My King and my God?" Thou who rulest me, who hast created me.

8. . . . "Blessed are those who dwell in Thy house" (ver. 4). . . . If thou hast thy own house, thou art poor; if God's, thou art rich. In thy own house thou wilt fear robbers; of the house of God, He is Himself the wall. Therefore "blessed are those who dwell in Thy house." They possess the heavenly Jerusalem, without constraint, without pressure, without difference and division of boundaries; all have it, and each have all. Great are those riches. Brother crowdeth not brother: there is no want there. Next, what will they do there? For among men it is necessity which is the mother of all employments. I have already said, in brief, brethren, run in your mind through any occupations, and see if it is not necessity alone which produces them. Those very eminent arts which seem so powerful in giving help to others, the art of speaking in their defence or of medicine in healing, for these are the most excellent employments in this life; take away litigants, who is there for the advocate to help? take away wounds and diseases? what is there for the physician to cure? And all those employments of ours which are required and done for our daily life, arise from necessity. To plough, to sow, to clear fallow ground, to sail; what is it which produces all these works, but necessity and want? Take away hunger, thirst, nakedness; who has need of all these things? . . . For instance, the injunction, "Break thy bread to the hungry." For whom could you break bread, if there were nobody hungry? "Take in the roofless poor into thy house."[1] What stranger is there to take in, where all live in their own country? What sick person to visit, where they enjoy perpetual health? What litigants to reconcile, where there is everlasting peace? What dead to bury, where there is eternal life? None of those honourable actions which are common to all men will then be your employment, nor any of these good works; the young swallows will then fly out of their nest.

What then? You have said already what we shall have; "Those who dwell in Thy house are blessed." Say now what they shall do, for I see not then any need to induce me to action. Even what I am now saying and arguing springs from some need. Will there be any such argument there to teach the ignorant, or remind the forgetful? Or will the Gospel be read in that country where the Word of God Itself shall be contemplated? . . . "They shall be always praising Thee." This shall be our whole duty, an unceasing Hallelujah. Think not, my brethren, that there will be any weariness there: if ye are not able to endure long here in saying this, it is because[2] some want draws you away from that enjoyment. If what is not seen gives not so much joy here, if with so much eagerness under the pressure and weakness of the flesh we praise that which we believe, how shall we praise that which we see? "When death shall be swallowed up in victory, when this mortal shall have put on immortality,"[3] no one will say, "I have been standing a long time;" no one will say, "I have fasted a long time," "I have watched a long time." For there shall be great endurance, and our immortal bodies shall be sustained in contemplation of God. And if the word which we now dispense to you keeps your weak flesh standing so long, what will be the effect of that joy? how will it change us? "For we shall be like Him, since we shall see Him as He is."[4] Being made like Him, when shall we ever faint? what shall draw us off? Brethren, we shall never be satiated with the praise of God, with the love of God. If love could fail, praise could fail. But if love be eternal, as there will there be beauty inexhaustible, fear not lest thou be not able to praise for ever Him whom thou shalt be able to love for ever. For this life let us sigh.

9. But how shall we come thither? "Happy is the man whose strength is in Thee" (ver. 5). He knew where he was, and that by reason of the frailty of his flesh he could not fly to that state of blessedness: he thought upon his own burden, as it is said elsewhere; "For the corruptible body weighs down the soul, and the earthly house depresses the understanding which has many thoughts."[5] The Spirit calls upward, the weight of the flesh calls back again downward: between the double effort to raise and to weigh down, a kind of struggle ensues: this struggle goes toward the pressure of the winepress. Hear how the Apostle describes this same struggle of the winepress, for he was himself afflicted there, there he was pressed. . . . "Miserable man that I am: who shall deliver me from the body of this death? The grace of

---

[1] Isa. lviii. 7.

[2] Oxf. MSS. "want keeps you not away."
[3] 1 Cor. xv. 54.   [4] 1 John iii. 2.   [5] Wisd. ix. 15.

God through Jesus Christ our Lord." [1] . . . "For I delight in the Law of God according to the inner man." But what shall I do? how shall I fly? how shall I arrive thither? "I see another law in my members," etc. . . . And as in the words of the Apostle, that difficulty and that almost inextricable struggle is alleviated by the addition, "The grace of God through Jesus Christ our Lord;" so here, when he sighed in the ardent longing for the house of God, and those praises of God, and when a kind of despair arose at the feeling of the burden of the body and the weight of the flesh, again he awoke to hope, and said (ver. 5), "Blessed is the man whose taking up [2] is in Thee."

10. What then does God supply by His grace to him whom He taketh hold of to lead him on? He goes on to say: "He hath placed steps [3] in his heart." . . . Where does it place steps? "In his heart, in the valley of weeping" (ver. 6). So here thou hast for a winepress the valley of weeping, the very pious tears in tribulation are the new wine of those that love. . . . They went forth "weeping," he says, "casting their seed." [4] Therefore, by the grace of God may upward steps be placed in thy heart. Rise by loving. Hence the Psalm "of degrees" is called. . . . "He hath placed steps of ascent to the place which He hath appointed" (ver. 7). Now we lament; whence proceed our lamentations, but from that place where the steps of our ascent are placed? Whence comes our lamentation, but from that cause wherefore the Apostle exclaimed that he was a wretched man, because he saw another law in his members, warring against the law in his mind? [5] And whence does this proceed? From the penalty of sin. And we thought that we could easily be righteous as it were by our own strength, before we received the command; "but when the command came, sin revived; but I died," [6] saith the Apostle. For a law was given to men, not such as could save them at once, but it was to show them in what severe sickness they were lying. . . . But when sin was made manifest by the law given, sin was but increased, for it is both sin, and against the Law; "Sin," saith he, "taking occasion by the command, wrought in me all manner of concupiscence." [7] What does he mean by "taking occasion by the law"? Having received the command, men tried as by their own strength to obey it; conquered by lust, they became guilty of transgression of this very command also. But what saith the Apostle? "Where sin abounded, grace hath much more abounded;" [8] that is, the disease increased, the medicine became of more avail. Accordingly,

my brethren, did those five porches of Solomon, in the middle of which the pool lay, heal the sick at all? The sick, says the Evangelist, lay in the five porches. [9] In the Gospel we have and read it. Those five porches are the law in the five books of Moses. For this cause the sick were brought forth from their houses that they might lie in the porches. So the law brought the sick men forth, but did not heal them: but by the blessing of God the water was disturbed, as by an Angel descending into it. At the sight of the water troubled, the one person who was able, descended and was healed. That water surrounded by the five porches, was the people of the Jews shut up in their law. The Lord came and disturbed this people, so that He Himself was slain. For if the Lord had not troubled the Jews by coming down to them, would He have been crucified? So that the troubled water signified the Passion of the Lord, which arose from His troubling the Jewish people. The sick man who believeth in this Passion, like him who descended into the troubled water, is healed thereby. He whom the Law could not heal, that is, while he lay in the porches, is healed by grace, by faith in the Passion of our Lord Jesus Christ. . . .

11. "He shall give blessing," saith he, "who gave the law." . . . Grace shall come after the law, grace itself is the blessing. And what has that grace and blessing given unto us? "They shall go from virtue to virtue." For here by grace many virtues are given. "For to one is given by the Spirit the word of wisdom, to another the word of knowledge according to the same Spirit, to another faith, to another the gift of healing, to another different kinds of tongues, to another the interpretation of tongues, to another prophecy." [10] Many virtues, but necessary for this life; and from these virtues we go on to "a virtue." To what "virtue"? To "Christ the Virtue of God and the Wisdom of God." [11] He giveth different virtues in this place, who for all the virtues which are necessary and useful in this valley of weeping shall give one virtue, Himself. For in Scripture and in many writers four virtues are described useful for life: prudence, by which we discern between good and evil; justice, by which we give each person his due, "owing no man anything," [12] but loving all men: temperance, by which we restrain lusts; fortitude, by which we bear all troubles. These virtues are now by the grace of God given unto us in the valley of weeping: from these virtues we mount unto that other virtue. And what will that be, but the virtue of the contemplation of God alone? . . . It follows in that place: "They shall go from virtue to

---

[1] Rom. vii. 24, 25.   [2] *Susceptio.*   [3] *Ascensus.*
[4] Ps. cxxxvi. 5, 6.   [5] Rom. vii. 23.   [6] Rom. vii. 9.
[7] Rom. vii. 8.   [8] Rom. v. 20.

[9] John. v. 3.   [10] 1 Cor. xii. 8-10.
[11] 1 Cor. i. 24.   [12] Rom. xiii. 8.

virtue." What virtue? That of contemplation. What is contemplation? "The God of Gods shall appear in Sion." The God of Gods, Christ of the Christians. . . . When all is finished, that mortality makes necessary, He shall appear to the pure in heart, as He is, "God with God," The Word with the Father, "by which all things were made."

12. And again, from the thought of those joys he returns to his own sighs. He sees what has come before in hope, and where he is in reality. . . . Therefore returning to the groans proper to this place, he saith, "O Lord God of virtues, hear my prayer: hearken, O God of Jacob" (ver. 8): for Jacob himself also Thou hast made Israel out of Jacob. For God appeared unto him, and he was called Israel,[1] seeing God. Hear me therefore, O God of Jacob, and make me Israel. When shall I become Israel? When the God of Gods shall appear in Sion.

13. "Behold, O God our defender. And look on the face of Thy Christ" (ver. 9). For when doth God not look upon the face of His Christ? What is this, "Look on the face of Thy Christ"? By the face we are known. What is it then, Look on the face of Thy Christ? Cause Thy Christ to become known to all. Look on the face of Thy Christ: let Christ become known to all, that we may be able to go from strength to strength, that grace may abound, since sin hath abounded.

14. "For one day in Thy courts is better than a thousand" (ver. 10). Those courts they were for which he sighed, for which he fainted. "My soul longeth and faileth for the courts of the Lord:"[2] one day there is better than a thousand days. Men long for thousands of days, and wish to live here long: let them despise these thousands of days, let them long for one day, which has neither rising nor setting: one day, an everlasting day, to which no yesterday yields, which no to-morrow presses. Let this one day be longed for by us. What have we to do with a thousand days? We go from the thousand days to one day; let us hasten to that one day,[3] as we go from strength to strength.

15. "I have chosen to be cast away in the house of the Lord, rather than to dwell in the tents of sinners" (ver. 11). For he found the valley of weeping, he found humility by which he might rise: he knoweth that if he would raise himself he shall fall, if he humble himself he shall be exalted: he hath chosen to be cast away, that he may be raised up. How many beside this tabernacle of the Lord's winepress, that is beside the Catholic Church, wishing to be lifted up, and loving their honours, refuse to see the truth. If this verse had been in their heart, would they not cast away honours, and run to the valley of weeping, and hence find in their heart the way of ascent, and hence go from virtues to virtue, placing their hope in Christ, not in some man or another? A good word is this, a word to rejoice in, a word to be chosen. He himself chose to be cast away in the house of the Lord; but He who invited him to the feast, when he chose a lower place calleth him to a higher one, and saith unto him, "Go up higher."[4] Yet he chose not but to be in the house of the Lord, in any part of it, so that he were not outside the threshold.

16. Wherefore did he choose? . . . "Because God loveth mercy and truth" (ver. 12). The Lord loveth mercy, by which He first came to my help: He loveth truth, so as to give to him that believeth what He has promised.[5] Hear in the case of the Apostle Paul, His mercy and truth, Paul who was first Saul the persecutor. He needed mercy, and he has said that it was shown towards him: "I who was before a blasphemer, and a persecutor, and injurious: but I obtained mercy, that in me Christ Jesus might show forth all longsuffering towards those who shall believe in Him unto life eternal."[6] So that, when Paul received pardon of such great crimes, no one should despair of any sins whatever being forgiven him. Lo! Thou hast Mercy. . . . Lo, we see that Paul holdeth Him a debtor, having received mercy, demanding truth. The Lord, he says, shall give back in that day. What shall He give thee back, but that which He oweth thee? How oweth He unto thee? What hast thou given Him? "Who hath first given unto Him, and it shall be restored to him again."[5] The Lord Himself hath made Himself a debtor, not by receiving, but by promising: it is not said unto Him, Restore what Thou hast received: but, Restore what Thou hast promised. He hath shown mercy unto me, he saith, that He might make me innocent: for before I was a blasphemer and injurious: but by His grace I have been made innocent. But He who first showed mercy, can He deny His debt? "He loveth mercy and truth. He will give grace and glory." What grace, but that of which the same one said: "By the grace of God I am what I am"?[7] What glory, but that of which he said, "There is laid up for me a crown of glory"?[8]

17. Therefore "the Lord will not withhold good from those who walk in innocence" (ver. 12). Why then, O men, are ye unwilling to keep innocence, except in order that ye may have good things? . . . Thou seest wealth in the hands of robbers, of the impious, the wicked,

1 Gen. xxxii. 28.   2 Ps. lxxxiv. 2.
3 Oxf. MSS. add, "let us hasten," etc.

4 Luke xiv. 10.   5 Rom. xi. 29.   6 1 Tim. i. 13, 16.
7 1 Cor. xv. 10.   8 2 Tim. iv. 8.

the base ; in the hands of scandalous and criminal men thou seest wealth : God giveth them these things on account of their fellowship in the human race, for the abundant overflowing of His goodness : who also " maketh His sun to rise upon the good and the evil, and causeth it to rain upon the righteous and upon the sinners." [1] Giveth He so much to the wicked, and keepeth nothing for thee? He keepeth something : be at ease, He who had mercy on thee when thou wast impious, doth He desert thee when thou hast become pious? He who gave to the sinner the free gift of His Son's death, what keepeth He for the saved through that death? Therefore be at ease. Hold Him a debtor, for thou hast believed in Him promising. What then remains for us here, in the winepress, in affliction, in hardship, in our present dangerous life? What remains for us, that we may arrive thither? " O Lord God of virtues, blessed is the man that putteth his hope in Thee."

PSALM LXXXV.[2]

1. . . . Its title is, " A Psalm for the end, to the sons of Core." [3] Let us understand no other end than that of which the Apostle speaks : for, " Christ is the end of the law." [4] Therefore when at the head of the title of the Psalm he placed the words, "for the end," he directed our heart to Christ. If we fix our gaze on Him, we shall not stray : for He is Himself the Truth unto which we are eager to arrive, and He Himself the Way [5] by which we run. . . .

2. The Prophet singeth to Him of the future, and useth words as it were of past time : he speaks of things future as if already done, because with God that which is future has already taken place. . . . " Lord, Thou hast been favourable unto Thy land " (ver. 1) ; as if He had already done so. " Thou hast turned away the captivity of Jacob." His ancient people of Jacob, the people of Israel, born of Abraham's seed, in the promise to become one day the heir of God. That was indeed a real people, to whom the Old Testament was given ; but in the Old Testament the New was figured : that was the figure, this the truth expressed. In that figure, by a kind of foretelling of the future, there was given to that people a certain land of promise, in a region where the people of the Jews abode ; where also is the city of Jerusalem, whose name we have all heard of. When this people had received possession of this land,

they suffered many troubles from their neighbouring enemies who surrounded them : and when they sinned against their God, they were given into captivity, not for destruction, but for discipline ; their Father not condemning, but scourging them. And after being seized on, they were set free, and many times were both made captives, and set free ; and they are now in captivity, and that for a great sin, even because they crucified their Lord. What then are we to understand them to mean by the words, " Thou hast turned away the captivity of Jacob "? . . . This Psalm hath prophesied in song. " Thou hast turned away the captivity of Jacob." To whom did it speak? To Christ ; for it said, " for the end, for the sons of Core : " for He hath turned away the captivity of Jacob. Hear Paul himself confessing : " O wretched man that I am, who shall deliver me from the body of this death?" He asked who it should be, and straightway it occurred to him, " The grace of God through Jesus Christ our Lord.[6] Of this grace of God the Prophet speaketh to our Lord Jesus Christ, " Thou hast turned away the captivity of Jacob." Attend to the captivity of Jacob, attend, and see that it is this : Thou hast turned away our captivity, not by setting us free from the barbarians, with whom we had not met, but by setting us free from bad works, from our sins, by which Satan held sway over us. For if any one has been set free from his sins, the prince of sinners hath not whence he may hold sway over him.

3. For how did He turn away the captivity of Jacob? See, how that that setting free is spiritual, see how that it is done inwardly. " Thou hast forgiven," he saith, " the iniquity of Thy people : Thou hast covered all their sins " (ver. 2). Behold how He hath turned away their captivity, in that He hath remitted iniquity : iniquity held them captive ; thy iniquity forgiven, thou art freed. Confess therefore that thou art in captivity, that thou mayest be worthy to be freed : for he that knoweth not of his enemy, how can he invoke the liberator? " Thou hast covered all their sins." What is, " Thou hast covered "? So as not to see them. How didst Thou not see them? So as not to take vengeance on them. Thou wast unwilling to see our sins : and therefore sawest Thou them not, because Thou wouldest not see them : " Thou hast covered all their sins." " Thou hast appeased all Thy anger : Thou hast turned Thyself from Thy wrathful indignation " (ver. 3).

4. And as these things are said of the future, though the sound of the words is past, it follows : " Turn us, O God of our salvation " (ver. 4).

---

[1] Matt. v. 45.　　[2] Lat. LXXXIV. A sermon to the people.
[3] [He repeats the former comment on this. See pp. 132, 400, *supra.*—C.]
[4] Rom. x. 4.　　[5] John xiv. 6.　　[6] Rom. vii. 24, 25.

That which he had just related as if it were done, how prayeth he that it may be done, except because he wished to show that he had spoken as if of the past in prophecy? But that it was not yet done which he had said was done he showeth by this, that he prayeth that it may be done: "Turn us, O God of our salvation, and turn away Thine anger from us." Didst thou not say before: "Thou hast appeased all Thy anger, Thou has turned Thyself from Thy wrathful indignation"? How then now sayest thou, "And turn away Thine anger from us"? The Prophet answereth: These things I speak of as done, because I see them about to be done: but because they are not yet done, I pray that they may come, which I have already seen.

5. "Be not angry with us for ever" (ver. 5). For by the anger of God we are subject to death, and by the anger of God we eat bread on this earth in want, and in the sweat of our face.[1] This was Adam's sentence when he sinned: and that Adam was every one of us, for "in Adam all die;"[2] the sentence passed on him hath taken effect after him on us. For we were not yet ourselves, but we were in Adam: therefore whatever happened to Adam himself took effect on us also, so that we should die: for we all were in him. . . . So far as this the sin of thy father hurts thee not, if thou hast changed thyself, even as it would not hurt thy father if he had changed himself. But that which our stock hath received unto its subjection to death, it hath derived from Adam. What hath it so derived? That frailty of the flesh, this torture of pains, this house of poverty, this chain of death, and snares of temptations; all these things we carry about in this flesh; and this is the anger of God, because it is the vengeance of God. But because it was so to be, that we should be regenerated, and by believing should be made new, and all that mortality was to be removed in our resurrection, and the whole man was to be restored in newness; "For as in Adam all die, so also in Christ shall all be made alive;"[2] seeing this the Prophet saith, "Be not angry with us for ever, nor stretch out Thy wrath from one generation to another." The first generation was mortal by Thy wrath: the second generation shall be immortal by Thy mercy. . . .

6. "O God, Thou shalt turn us again, and make us alive" (ver. 6). Not as if we ourselves of our own accord, without Thy mercy, turn unto Thee, and then Thou shalt make us alive: but so that not only our being made alive is from Thee, but our very conversion, that we may be made alive. "And Thy people shall rejoice in Thee." To their own evil they shall rejoice in themselves: to their own good they

shall rejoice in Thee. For when they wished to have joy of themselves, they found in themselves woe: but now because God is all our joy, he that will rejoice securely, let him rejoice in Him who cannot perish. For why, my brethren, will ye rejoice in silver? Either thy silver perisheth, or thou: and no one knows which first: yet this is certain, that both shall perish; which first, is uncertain. For neither can man remain here always, nor can silver remain here always: so too gold, so garments, so houses, so money, so broad lands, so, lastly, this light itself. Be not thou willing then to rejoice in these: but rejoice in that light which hath no setting: rejoice in that dawn which no yesterday precedes, which no to-morrow follows. What light is that? "I," saith He, "am the Light of the world."[3] He who saith unto thee, "I am the Light of the world," calls thee to Himself. When He calls thee, He converts thee: when He converts thee, He healeth thee: when He hath healed thee, thou shalt see thy Converter, unto whom it is said, "Show us Thy mercy, O Lord, and grant us Thy salvation" (ver. 7): Thy salvation, that is, Thy Christ.[4] Happy is he unto whom God showeth His mercy. He it is who cannot indulge in pride, unto whom God showeth His mercy. For by showing him His salvation He persuadeth him that whatever good man has, he hath not but from Him who is all our good. And when a man has seen that whatever good he has he hath not from himself, but from his God; he sees that everything which is praised in him is of the mercy of God, not of his own deserving; and seeing this, he is not proud; not being proud, he is not lifted up; not lifting himself up, he falleth not; not falling, he standeth; standing, he clingeth fast; clinging fast, he abideth; abiding, he enjoyeth, and rejoiceth in the Lord his God. He who made him shall be unto him a delight: and his delight no one spoileth, no one interrupteth, no one taketh away. . . . Therefore, what saith John in his Epistle? "Beloved, now are we the sons of God, and it doth not yet appear what we shall be."[5] Who would not rejoice, if suddenly while he was wandering abroad, ignorant of his descent, suffering want, and in a state of misery and toil, it were announced, Thou art the son of a senator: thy father enjoys an ample patrimony on your family estate; I bid thee return to thy father: how would he rejoice, if this were said to him by some one whose promise he could trust? One whom we can trust, an Apostle of Christ, hath come and said to us, Ye have a father, ye have a country, ye have an inheritance. Who is

---

[1] Gen. iii. 19. [2] 1 Cor. xv. 22.

[3] John viii. 12.
[4] [i.e., Thy *Joshua*, which is inwoven with the idea of salvation everywhere in the Old Testament (see Gen. xlix. 18), till all is fixed in Christ, the true Joshua. Matt. I. 21.— C.]
[5] 1 John iii. 2.

that father? "Beloved, we are the sons of God." [1] . . . Therefore He [2] promised us to show Himself unto us. Think, my brethren, what His beauty is. All those beautiful things which ye see, which ye love, He made. If these are beautiful, what is He Himself? If these are great, how great is He? Therefore from these things which we love here, let us the more long for Him : and despising these things, let us love Him : that by that very love we may by faith purify our hearts, and His vision, when it cometh, may find our heart purified. The light which shall be shown unto us ought to find us whole : this is the work of faith now. This is what we have spoken here : "And grant us Thy salvation : " grant us Thy Christ, that we may know Thy Christ, see Thy Christ ; not as the Jews saw Him and crucified Him, but as the Angels see Him, and rejoice.

7. "I will hearken" (ver. 8). The Prophet spoke : God spoke within in him, and the world made a noise without. Therefore, retiring for a little from the noise of the world, and turning himself back upon himself, and from himself upon Him whose voice he heard within ; sealing up his ears, as it were, against the tumultuous disquietude of this life, and against the soul weighed down by the corruptible body, and against the imagination, that through the earthly tabernacle pressing down,[3] thinketh on many things,[4] he saith, "I will hearken what the Lord God speaketh in me ; " and he heard, what? "For He shall speak peace unto His people." The voice of Christ, then, the voice of God, is peace : it calleth unto peace. Ho! it saith, whosoever are not yet in peace, love ye peace : for what can ye find better from Me than peace? What is peace? Where there is no war. What is this, where there is no war? Where there is no contradiction, where there is no resistance, nothing to oppose. Consider if we are yet there : consider if there is not now a conflict with the devil, if all the saints and faithful ones wrestle not with the prince of demons. And how do they wrestle with him whom they see not? They wrestle with their own desires, by which he suggests unto them sins : and by not consenting to what he suggests, though they are not conquered, yet they fight. Therefore there is not yet peace where there is fighting. . . . Whatever we provide for our refreshment, there again we find weariness. Art thou hungry? one asks thee : thou answerest, I am. He places food before thee for thy refreshment ; continue thou to use it, for thou hadst need of it ; yet in continuing that which thou needest for refreshment, therein findest thou weariness. By long sitting thou wast tired ; thou risest and refresh-

est thyself by walking ; continue that relief, and by much walking thou art wearied ; again thou wouldest sit down. Find me anything by which thou art refreshed, wherein if thou continue thou dost not again become weary. What peace then is that which men have here, opposed by so many troubles, desires, wants, wearinesses? This is no true, no perfect peace. What will be perfect peace? "This corruptible must put on incorruption, and this mortal must put on immortality." [5] . . . Persevere in eating much ; this itself will kill thee : persevere in fasting much, by this thou wilt die : sit continually, being resolved not to rise up, by this thou wilt die : be always walking so as never to take rest, by this thou wilt die ; watch continually, taking no sleep, by this thou wilt die ; sleep continually, never watching, thus too thou wilt die. When therefore death shall be swallowed up in victory, these things shall no longer be : there will be full and eternal peace. We shall be in a City, of which, brethren, when I speak I find it hard to leave off, especially when offences wax common. Who would not long for that City whence no friend goeth out, whither no enemy entereth,[6] where is no tempter, no seditious person, no one dividing God's people, no one wearying the Church in the service of the devil ; since the prince himself of all such is cast into eternal fire, and with him those who consent unto him, and who have no will to retire from him? There shall be peace made pure in the sons of God, all loving one another, seeing one another full of God, since God shall be all in all.[7] We shall have God as our common object of vision, God as our common possession, God as our common peace. For whatever there is which He now giveth unto us, He Himself shall be unto us instead of His gifts ; this will be full and perfect peace. This He speaketh unto His people : this it was which he would hearken unto who said, "I will hearken what the Lord God will say unto me : for He shall speak peace unto His people, and to His saints, and unto those who turn their hearts unto Him." Lo, my brethren, do ye wish that unto you should belong that peace which God uttereth? Turn your heart unto Him : not unto me, or unto that one, or unto any man. For whatever man would turn unto himself the hearts of men, he falleth with them. Which is better, that thou fall with him unto whom thou turnest thyself, or that thou stand with Him with whom thou turnest thyself? Our joy, our peace, our rest, the end of all troubles, is none but God : blessed are "they that turn their hearts unto Him."

---

[1] 1 John iii. 2.   [2] Oxf. MSS. "Therefore if He has."
[3] Oxf. MSS. *deprimente.*   [4] Wisd. ix. 15.
[5] 1 Cor. xv. 53.
[6] [This exquisite passage, adopted by Bishop Horne in his precious illustrations of the Psalter, reads in the original as follows: *unde amicus non exit, quo inimicus non intrat.*— C.]
[7] 1 Cor. xv. 28.

8. "Nevertheless, His salvation is nigh them that fear Him" (ver. 9). There were some even then who feared Him in the Jewish people. Everywhere throughout the earth idols were worshipped: devils were feared, not God: in that nation God was feared. But why was He feared? In the Old Testament He was feared, lest He should give them up to captivity, lest He should take away their land from them, lest He should destroy their vines with hail, lest He should make their wives barren, lest He should take away their children from them. For these carnal promises of God captivated their minds, which as yet were of small growth, and for these things God was feared: but He was near unto them who even for these things feared Him. The Pagan prayed for land to the devil: the Jew prayed for land to God: it was the same thing which they prayed for, but not the same to whom they prayed. The latter, though seeking what the Pagan sought, yet was distinguished from the Pagan; for He sought it of Him who had made all things. And God, who was far[1] from the Gentiles, was near[1] unto them: yet He had regard even to those who were afar off, and to those who were near, as the Apostle said: "And He came and preached peace to you who were afar off, and to them that were near."[2] Whom did He mean by those near? The Jews, because they[3] worshipped one God. Whom by those who were afar off? The Gentiles, because they had left Him by whom they were made, and worshipped things which themselves had made. For it is not in space that any one is far from God, but in affections. Thou lovest God, thou art near unto Him. Thou hatest God, thou art far off. Thou art standing in the same place, both while thou art near and far off. This it was, my brethren, which the Prophet had regard to: although he saw the mercy of God extending over all, yet he saw something especial and peculiar shown toward the Jews, and he saith, "Nevertheless, I will hearken what the Lord God shall say unto me: for He shall speak peace unto His people;" and His people shall be, not Judæa only, but it shall be gathered together out of all nations: "For He shall speak peace unto His Saints, and to those who turn their hearts unto Him," and to all who shall turn their hearts unto Him from the whole world. "Nevertheless, His salvation shall be nigh them that fear Him, that glory may dwell in our land:" that is, in that land in which the Prophet was born, greater glory shall dwell, because Christ began to be preached from thence. Thence were the Apostles, and thither first they were sent; from thence were the Prophets, there first was the Temple, there

sacrifice was made to God, there were the Patriarchs, there He Himself came of the seed of Abraham, there Christ was manifested, there Christ appeared; for from thence was the Virgin Mary who bore Christ. There He walked with His feet, there He worked miracles. Thirdly, He ascribed so great honour to that nation, that when a certain Canaanitish woman interrupted Him, praying for the healing of her daughter, He said unto her, "I am not sent but unto the lost sheep of the house of Israel."[4] Seeing this, the Prophet saith, "that glory may dwell in our land."

9. "Mercy and truth have met together" (ver. 10). "Truth in our land," in a Jewish person, "mercy" in the land of the Gentiles. For where was truth? Where the utterances of God were. Where was mercy? On those who had left their God, and turned themselves unto devils. Did He look down[5] also upon them? Yea, as if He said, Call those who are fugitives afar off, who have departed far from Me: call them, let them find Me who seek them, since they themselves would not seek Me. Therefore, "Mercy and truth have met together: righteousness and peace have kissed each other." Do righteousness, and thou shalt have peace; that righteousness and peace may kiss each other. For if thou love not righteousness, thou shalt not have peace; for those two, righteousness and peace, love one another, and kiss one another: that he who hath done righteousness may find peace kissing righteousness. They two are friends: thou perhaps willest the one, and not the other: for there is no one who wills not peace: but all will not work righteousness. Ask all men, Willest thou peace? With one mouth the whole race of man answers thee, I wish, I desire, I will, I love it. Love also righteousness: for these two, righteousness and peace, are friends; they kiss one another: if thou love not the friend of peace, peace itself will not love thee, nor come unto thee. For what great thing is it to desire peace? Every bad man longeth for peace. For peace is a good thing. But do righteousness, for righteousness and peace kiss one another, they quarrel not together. . . .

10. "Truth hath sprung out of the earth, and righteousness hath looked down from heaven" (ver. 11). "Truth hath sprung out of the earth:" Christ is born of a woman. The Son of God hath come forth of the flesh. What is truth? The Son of God. What is the earth? Flesh. Ask whence Christ was born, and thou seest that "Truth is sprung out of the earth." But the Truth which sprang out of the earth was before the earth, and by It the heaven and the earth were made: but in order that righteous-

---

[1] Oxf. MSS. "near," "nearer."   [2] Eph. ii. 17.
[3] Oxf. MSS. "who."

[4] Matt. xv. 24.   [5] *Despexit*; one MS. *dispexit*.

ness might look down from heaven, that is, in order that men might be justified by Divine grace, Truth was born of the Virgin Mary ; that He might be able to offer a sacrifice to justify them, the sacrifice of suffering, the sacrifice of the Cross. And how could He offer a sacrifice for our sins, except He died? How could He die, except He received from us that wherein He might die ; that is, unless He received from us mortal flesh, Christ could not have died : because the Word of God dieth not, Godhead dieth not, the Virtue and Wisdom of God doth not die. How should He offer a sacrifice, a healing victim, if He died not? How should He die, unless He clothed Himself with flesh? How should He put on flesh, except truth sprang out of the earth?

11. On the same passage we may mention another meaning. " Truth is sprung out of the earth : " confession from man. For thou, O man, wast a sinner. O earth, who when thou hadst sinned didst hear the sentence, " Earth thou art, and unto earth shalt thou return," [1] from thee let truth spring, that righteousness may look down from heaven. How doth truth spring from thee, whilst thou art a sinner, whilst thou art unrighteous? Confess thy sins, and truth shall spring out of thee. For if whilst thou art unrighteous, thou callest thyself just, how can truth spring out of thee? But if being unrighteous thou dost confess thyself to be so, " truth hath sprung out of the earth." . . . What " righteousness hath looked down from heaven"? It is that of God, as though He said : Let us spare this man, for he spareth not himself : let us pardon him, for he himself confesseth. He is changed so as to punish his sin : I too will change, so as to set him free.

12. " For the Lord shall give sweetness, and our land shall give her increase " (ver. 12). . . . He will give unto thee the sweetness of working righteousness, so that righteousness shall begin to delight thee, whom before unrighteousness delighted : so that thou who at first didst delight in drunkenness, shalt rejoice in sobriety : and thou who didst at first rejoice in theft, so as to take from another man what thou hadst not, shalt seek to give to him that hath not that which thou hast : and thou who didst take delight in robbing, shalt delight now in giving : thou whom shows delighted, shalt delight in prayer ; thou who didst delight in trifling and lascivious songs, shalt now delight in singing hymns to God ; in running to church, thou who at first didst run to the theatre. Whence is that sweetness born to thee, except from this, that " God giveth sweetness"? For, behold, ye see what I mean : behold, I have spoken unto you the word of God, I have

sown seed in your devout hearts, finding your souls furrowed, as it were, with the plough of confession : with devout attention ye have received the seed ; think now upon the word which ye have heard, like those who break up the clouds, lest the fowls should carry away the seed, that what is sown may be able to spring up there : and unless God rain upon it, what profits it that it is sown? This is what is meant by " our land shall give her increase." May He with His visitations, in leisure, in business, in your house, in your bed, at meal-time, in conversation, in walks, visit your hearts, when we are not by. May the rain of God come and make to sprout what is sown there : and when we are not by, and are resting quietly, or otherwise employed, may God give increase to the seeds which we have sown, that remarking afterwards your improved characters, we too may rejoice for your fruit.

13. " For righteousness shall go before him, and he shall direct his steps in the way " (ver. 14) : that righteousness, namely, which consists in confession of sins : for this is truth itself. For thou oughtest to be righteous towards thyself, and to punish thyself : for this is the beginning of man's righteousness, that thou shouldest punish thyself, who art evil, and God should make thee good. Therefore since this is the beginning of man's righteousness, this becomes a way for God, that God may come unto thee : there make for Him a way, in confession of sins. Therefore John too, when he was baptizing in the water of repentance, and would have men come to him repenting of their former deeds, spoke thus : " Prepare the way of the Lord, make His paths straight." [2] Thou didst please thyself in thy sins, O man : let that which thou wast displease thee, that thou mayest be able to become what thou wast not. Prepare the way of the Lord : let that righteousness go before, of confession of sins : He will come and visit thee, for now He hath where to place His steps, He hath whereby He may come to thee. Before thou didst confess thy sins, thou hadst shut up the way of God : there was no way by which He might come unto thee. Confess thy past life, and thou openest a way ; and Christ shall come unto thee, and " shall place His steps in the way," that He may guide thee with His own footsteps.

PSALM LXXXVI.[3]

1. No greater gift could God have given to men than in making His Word, by which He created all things, their Head, and joining them to Him as His members : that the Son of God might

---

[1] Gen. iii. 19.

[2] Matt. iii. 3.
[3] Lat. LXXXV. A sermon to the people at Carthage, delivered on the vigil of a festival, perhaps of St. Cyprian.

become also the Son of man, one God with the Father, one Man with men; so that when we speak to God in prayer for mercy, we do not separate the Son from Him; and when the Body of the Son prays, it separates not its Head from itself: and it is one Saviour of His Body, our Lord Jesus Christ, the Son of God, who both prays for us, and prays in us, and is prayed to by us. He prays for us, as our Priest; He prays in us, as our Head; He is prayed to by us, as our God. Let us therefore recognise in Him our words, and His words in us. Nor when anything is said of our Lord Jesus Christ, especially in prophecy, implying a degree of humility below the dignity of God, let us hesitate to ascribe it to Him who did not hesitate to join Himself unto us. . . . He is prayed to in the form of God, in the form of a servant He prayeth; there the Creator, here created; assuming unchanged the creature, that it might be changed, and making us with Himself one Man, Head and Body. Therefore we pray to Him, through Him, in Him; and we speak with Him, and He speaks with us; we speak in Him, He speaks in us the prayer of this Psalm, which is entitled, " A Prayer of David." For our Lord was, according to the flesh, the son of David; but according to His divine nature, the Lord of David, and his Maker. . . . Let no one then, when he hears these words, say, Christ speaketh not; nor again say, I speak not; nay rather, if he own himself to be in the Body of Christ, let him say both, Christ speaks, and I speak. Be thou unwilling to say anything without Him, and He saith nothing without thee. . . .

2. " Bow down Thine ear, O Lord, and hear me " (ver. 1). He speaks in the form of a servant: speak thou, O servant, in the form of thy Lord: " Bow down Thine ear, O Lord." He bows down His ear, if thou dost not lift up thy neck: for unto the humble He draweth near: from him that is exalted He removes afar off, except whom He Himself hath exalted from being humble. God then bows down His ear unto us. For He is above, we below: He in a high place, we in a lowly one, yet not deserted. " For while we were yet sinners, Christ died for us. For scarcely for a just man will one die: yet for a good man peradventure one would even dare to die : "[1] but our Lord died for the wicked. For no merits of ours had gone before, for which the Son of God should die: but the more, because there were no merits, was His mercy great. How sure then, how firm is the promise, by which for the righteous He keepeth His life, who for the wicked gave His own death ! " For I am poor and in misery." To the rich then He boweth not down His ear : unto the

poor and him that is in misery He boweth down His ear, that is, unto the humble, and him that confesseth, unto him that is in need of mercy: not unto him that is full, who lifteth up himself and boasteth, as if he wanted nothing, and saith, " I thank Thee that I am not as this Publican." For the rich Pharisee boasted of his merits : the poor Publican confessed his sins.[2]

3. Yet do not take what I have said, my brethren, in such a way, as if God does not hear those who have gold and silver, and a household, and farms, if they happen to be born to this estate, or hold such a rank in the world : only let them remember the Apostle's words : " Charge those who are rich in this world, that they be not highminded."[3] For those that are not high-minded are poor in God, and to the poor and needy and those in want He inclines His ear. For they know that their hope is not in gold and silver, nor in those things in which for a time they seem to abound. It is enough that riches ruin them not; it is enough that they do them no harm : for good they can do them none. What certainly profiteth is a work of mercy, done by a rich or by a poor man : by a rich man, with will and deed; by a poor man, with will alone. When therefore he is such an one as despiseth in himself everything which is wont to swell men with pride, he is one of God's poor : He inclines unto him His ear, for He knows that his heart is contrite. . . . Was it really for the merit of his poverty that the poor man was carried away by Angels,[4] or was it for the sin of his riches that the rich man was sent away to be tormented? In that poor man is signified the honour which is paid to humility, in that rich man the condemnation which awaits pride. I will prove shortly that it was not riches but pride which was tormented in that rich man. It is certain that the poor man was carried into the bosom of Abraham : of Abraham himself Scripture saith that he had here very much gold and silver, and was rich on the earth.[5] If every one that is rich is hurried away to be tormented, how could Abraham have gone before that poor man, so as to be ready to receive him when carried to his bosom? But Abraham in his riches was poor, humble, reverencing all commands, and obeying them. So true was it that he counted all those riches for nothing, that on God's command he was ready to sacrifice his son,[6] for whom he was keeping his riches. Learn therefore ye to be poor and needy, whether ye have anything in this world, or whether ye have not. . . .

4. " Preserve Thou My Soul, for I am holy " (ver. 2). I know not whether any one could say this, " I am holy," but He who was in the world without sin : He by whom all sins were not

---

[1] Rom. v. 8, 7.

[2] Luke xviii. 11-13. [3] 1 Tim. vi. 17. [4] Luke xvi. 19-24.
[5] Gen. xiii. 2. [6] Gen. xxii. 10.

committed but remitted.[1]   We own it to be His voice saying, "Preserve Thou My Soul, for I am holy ; " of course in that form of a servant which He had assumed.   For in that was flesh, in that was also a Soul.   For He was not, as some [2] have said, only Flesh and the Word : but Flesh and Soul also, and the Word, and all this, One Son of God, One Christ, One Saviour ; in the form of God equal to the Father, in the form of a servant the Head of the Church. When therefore I hear, " for I am holy," I recognise His voice : yet do I exclude my own? Surely He speaks inseparably from His body when He speaks thus.   Shall I then dare to say, " For I am holy"?   If holy as making holy, and as needing none to sanctify, I should be proud and false : but if holy as made holy, as it is written, " Be ye holy, for I am holy," [3] then the body of Christ may venture, and that one Man " crying from the end of the earth," [4] may venture with his Head, and under his Head, to say, " For I am holy."   For he hath received the grace of holiness, the grace of Baptism, and of remission of sins.[5] . . . Say unto thy God, I am holy, for Thou hast sanctified me : because I received, not because I had : because Thou gavest, not because I deserved.   For on another side thou art beginning to do an injury to our Lord Jesus Christ Himself.   For if all Christians who are faithful and have been baptized in Him have put Him on, as the Apostle saith, "As many as are baptized in Christ have put on Christ : " [6] if they have been made members of His body, and say that they are not holy, they do injury to their Head, of whom they are members, and yet not holy.   Look thou where thou art and from thy Head assume dignity.   For thou wert in darkness, "but now light in the Lord." [7]   "Ye were sometime darkness," he saith : but did ye remain darkness?   Was it for this the Enlightener came, that ye might still remain darkness, or that in Him ye might become light?   Therefore, every Christian by himself, therefore also the whole body of Christ, may say, it may cry everywhere, while it suffers tribulations, various temptations and offences, it may say, " Preserve Thou my soul, for I am holy : my God, save Thy servant, that putteth his trust in Thee." See thou, that holy man is not proud, since he putteth his trust in God.

5. " Be merciful unto me, O Lord, for I have cried unto Thee all day " (ver. 3).   Not " one day : " understand "all day" to mean continually : from the time that the body of Christ groans being in afflictions, until the end of the world, when afflictions pass away, that man groaneth and calleth upon God : and each one of us after his measure hath his part in that cry in the whole body.   Thou hast cried in thy days, and thy days have passed away : another hath come after thee, and cried in his days : and thou here, he there, another elsewhere : the body of Christ crieth all the day, its members departing and succeeding one another.   One Man it is that reaches to the end of the world : the same members of Christ cry, and some members already rest in Him, some still cry, some when we shall be at rest will cry, and after them others will cry.   It is the whole body of Christ whose voice He hears, saying, " Unto Thee have I cried all the day."   Our Head on the right hand of the Father intercedes for us : some members He recovereth, others He scourgeth, others He cleanseth, others He comforteth, others He is creating, others calling, others recalling, others correcting, others restoring.

6. " Make glad the soul of Thy servant : for unto Thee, O Lord, have I lifted up my soul " (ver. 4).   Make it glad, for unto Thee have I lifted it up.   For it was on earth, and from the earth it felt bitterness : lest it should wither away in bitterness, lest it should lose all the sweetness of Thy grace, I lifted it up unto Thee : make Thou it glad with Thyself.   For Thou alone art gladness : the whole world is full of bitterness.   Surely with reason He admonishes His members to lift up their hearts.   May they hear and do it : may they lift up unto Him what on earth is ill.   There the heart decayeth not, if it be lifted up to God.   It thou hadst corn in thy rooms below, thou wouldest take it up higher, lest it should grow rotten. Wouldest thou remove thy corn, and dost thou suffer thy heart to rot on the earth?   Thou wouldest take thy corn up higher : lift up thy heart to heaven.   And how can I, dost thou say?   What ropes are needed? what machines? what ladders?   Thy affections are the steps : thy will the way.   By loving thou mountest, by neglect thou descendest.   Standing on the earth thou art in heaven, if thou lovest God.   For the heart is not so raised as the body is raised : the body to be lifted up changes its place : the heart to be lifted up changes its will.

7. " For Thou, Lord, art good and gracious " (ver. 5). . . . Even prayers are often hindered by vain thoughts, so that the heart scarcely remains fixed on God : and it would hold itself so as to be fixed, and somehow flees from itself, and finds no frames in which it can enclose itself, no bars by which it may keep in its flights and wandering movements, and stand still to be made glad by its God.   Scarcely does one such prayer occur amongst many.   Each one might say that this happened to him, but that it happened not to others, if we did not find in the holy Scripture David praying in a certain place,

[1] *Non commissor sed dimissor.*   [2] *Apollinarians.*
[3] Lev. xix. 2.   [4] Ps. lxi. 2.   [5] 1 Cor. vi. 11.
[6] Gal. iii. 27.   [7] Eph. v. 8.

and saying, "Since I have found my heart, O Lord, so that I might pray unto Thee."[1] He said that he had found his heart, as if it were wont to flee from him, and he to follow it like a fugitive, and not be able to catch it, and to cry to God, "For my heart hath deserted me."[2] Therefore, my brethren, thinking over what he saith here, I think I see what he meaneth by "gracious." I seem to feel that for this reason he calls God gracious, because He bears with those failings of ours, and yet expects prayer from us, in order to make us perfect: and when we have given it to Him, He receives it gratefully, and listens to it, and remembers not those many prayers which we pour out unthinkingly, and accepts the one which we can scarcely find. For what man is there, my brethren, who, on being addressed by his friend, when he wishes to answer his address, sees his friend turn away from him and speak to another, who is there who would bear this? Or if you appeal to a judge, and set him up to hear you, and all at once, while you are speaking to him, pass from him, and begin to converse with your friend, who would endure this? Yet God endures the hearts of so many persons who pray and think of different things. . . . What then? Must we despair of mankind, and say that every man is already condemned into whose prayers any wandering thoughts have crept and interrupted them? If we say this, my brethren, I know not what hope remains. Therefore because there is some hope before God, because His mercy is great, let us say unto Him, "For unto Thee, O Lord, have I lifted up my soul." And how have I lifted it up? As I could, as Thou gavest me strength, as I could catch it when it fled away. . . . From infirmity I sink: heal Thou me, and I shall stand: strengthen Thou me, and I shall be strong. But until Thou do this, Thou bearest with me: "For Thou, Lord, art good and gracious, and of great mercy." That is, not only "of mercy," but "of great mercy:" for as our iniquity abounds, so also aboundeth Thy mercy. "Unto all that call upon Thee." What is it then which Scripture saith in many places: "They shall call, and I will not hear them"?[3] Yet surely Thou art merciful to all that call upon Thee; but that some call, yet call not upon Him, of whom it is said, "They have not called upon God."[4] They call, but not on God. Thou callest upon whatever thou lovest: thou callest upon whatever thou callest unto thyself, whatever thou wishest to come unto thee. Therefore if thou callest upon God for this reason, in order that money may come unto thee, that an inheritance may come unto thee, that worldly rank may come unto thee, thou callest upon those things which thou desirest may come unto thee: but thou makest God the helper of thy desires, not the listener to thy needs. God is good, if He gives what thou wishest. What if thou wishest ill, will He not then be more merciful by not giving? Then, if He gives not, then is God nothing to thee; and thou sayest, How much I have prayed, how often I have prayed, and have not been heard! Why, what didst thou ask? Perhaps that thy enemy might die. What if he at the same time were praying for thy death? He who created thee, created him also: thou art a man, he too is a man; but God is the Judge: He hears both, and He grants their prayer to neither. Thou art sad, because thou wast not heard when praying against him; be glad, because his prayer was not heard against thee. But thou sayest, I did not ask for this; I asked not for the death of my enemy, but for the life of my child; what ill did I ask? Thou askedst no ill, as thou didst think. What if "he was taken away, lest wickedness should alter his understanding."[5] But he was a sinner, thou sayest, and therefore I wished him to live, that he might be corrected. Thou wishedst him to live, that he might become better; what if God knew, that if he lived he would become worse? . . . If, therefore, thou callest on God as God, be confident thou shalt be heard: thou hast part in that verse: "And of great mercy unto all that call upon Thee." . . .

8. Think, brethren, and reflect what good things God giveth unto sinners: and learn hence what He keepeth for His own servants. To sinners who blaspheme Him every day He giveth the sky and the earth, He giveth springs, fruits, health, children, wealth, abundance: all these good things none giveth but God. He who giveth such things to sinners, what thinkest thou He keeps for His faithful ones? Is this to be believed of Him, that He who giveth such things to the bad, keepeth nothing for the good? Nay verily He doth keep, not earth, but heaven for them. Too common a thing perhaps I say when I say heaven; Himself rather, who made the heaven. Fair is heaven, but fairer is the Maker of heaven. But I see the heavens, Him I see not. Because thou hast eyes to see the heavens: a heart thou hast not yet to see the Maker of heaven: therefore came He from heaven to earth, to cleanse the heart, that He may be seen who made heaven and earth. But wait thou with full patience for salvation. By what treatment to cure thee, He knoweth: by what cutting, what burning, He knoweth. Thou hast brought sickness on thyself by sinning: He comes not only to nurse, but also to cut and to burn. Seest

[1] 2 Sam. vii. 27.　　[2] Ps. xxxviii. 10.　　[3] Prov. i. 28.
[4] Ps. liii. 4.

[5] Wisd. iv. 11.

thou not how much men suffer under the hands of physicians, when a man promises them an uncertain hope? Thou wilt be cured, says the physician: thou wilt be cured, if I cut. It is a man who speaks, and to a man that he speaks: neither is he sure who speaks, nor he who hears, for he who is speaking to the man hath not made man, and knows not perfectly what is passing in man: yet at the words of a man who knows not what is passing in man, man sooner believeth, submits his limbs, suffers himself to be bound, often without being bound is cut or burned; and receives perhaps health for a few days, even when just healed not knowing when he may die: perhaps, while being healed, dies; perhaps cannot be healed. But to whom hath God promised anything, and deceived him?

9. "Fix my prayer in Thy ears, O Lord" (ver. 6). Great earnestness of him who prays! That is, let not my prayer go out of Thine ears, fix it then in Thine ears. How did he travail that he might fix his prayer in the ears of God? Let God answer and say to us; Wouldest thou that I fix thy prayer in My ears? Fix My law in thy heart; "and attend to the voice of my prayer."

10. "In the day of my trouble I have cried unto Thee, for Thou hast heard me" (ver. 7). A little before he had said, All the day have I cried, all the day have I been troubled. Let no Christian then say that there is any day in which he is not troubled. By "all the day" we have understood the whole of time. What then, is there trouble even when it is well with us? Even so, trouble. How is there trouble? Because "as long as we are in the body we are absent from the Lord."[1] Let what will abound here, we are not yet in that country whither we are hastening to return. He to whom foreign travel is sweet, loveth not his country: if his country is sweet, travel is bitter; if travel is bitter, all the day there is trouble. When is there not trouble? When there is joy in one's country. "At Thy right hand are delights for evermore."[2] "Thou shalt fill me with joy," he saith, "with Thy countenance: that I may see the delight of the Lord."[3] There toil and groaning shall pass away: there shall be not prayer but praise; there Alleluia, there Amen, the voice in concord with Angels; there vision without failing and love without weariness. So long therefore as we are not there, ye see that we are not in that which is good. But do all things abound? If all things abound, see if thou art assured that all things perish not. But I have what I had not: more money is come to me which I had not before. Perhaps more fear too is come, which thou hadst not before: perhaps thou wast so much

the more secure as thou wast the poorer. In fine, be it that thou hast wealth, that thou hast redundance of this world's affluence, that thou hast assurance given thee that all this shall not perish; besides this, that God say unto thee, Thou shalt remain for ever in these things, they shall be for ever with thee, but My face thou shalt not see. Let none ask counsel of the flesh: ask ye counsel of the Spirit: let your heart answer you; let hope, faith, charity, which has begun to be in you, answer. If then we were to receive assurance that we should always be in affluence of worldly goods, and if God were to say to us, My face ye shall not see, would ye rejoice in these goods? Some one might perhaps choose to rejoice, and say, These things abound unto me, it is well with me, I ask no more. He hath not yet begun to be a lover of God: he hath not yet begun to sigh like one far from home. Far be it, far be it from us: let them retire, all those seductions: let them retire, those false blandishments: let them be gone, those words which they say daily unto us, "Where is thy God?" Let us pour out our soul[4] over us,[5] let us confess in tears, let us groan in confession, let us sigh in misery. Whatever is present with us besides our God, is not sweet: we would not have all things that He hath given, if He gives not Himself who gave all things.

11. "Among the gods there is none like unto Thee, O Lord" (ver. 8). What did he say? "Among the gods," etc. Let the Pagans make for themselves what gods they will; let them bring workmen in silver and in gold, furbishers, sculptors; let them make gods. What kind of gods? Having eyes, and seeing not;[6] and the other things which the Psalm mentions in what follows. But we do not worship these, he says; we do not worship them, these are symbols. What then do ye worship? Something else that is worse: for the gods of the gentiles are devils. What then? Neither, say they, do we worship devils. Ye have certainly nothing else in your temples, nothing else inspires your prophets than a devil.[7] But what do ye say? We worship Angels, we have Angels as gods. Ye know not altogether what Angels are. Angels worship the one God, and favour not men who wish to worship Angels and not God. For we find Angels of high rank[8] forbidding men to adore them, and commanding them to adore the true God.[9] But when they say Angels, suppose they mean men, since it is said, "I have said, Ye are Gods, and all the children of the Most Highest."[10] Whatever[11] man thinks to the contrary, that which was made is not like Him who made it. Except God, whatever else there is in the

---

[1] 2 Cor. v. 6. [2] Ps. xvi. 11. [3] Ps. xxvii. 4.

[4] Ps. xlii. 3, 4. [5] Super nos. [6] Ps. cxv. 5.
[7] Ps. xcvi. 5. [8] Honoratos. [9] Rev. xix. 10.
[10] Ps. lxxxii. 6. [11] Quodlibet aliud.

universe was made by God. What a difference there is between Him who made, and that which was made, who can worthily imagine? Therefore this man said, "there is none like unto Thee, O Lord : there is not one that can do as thou doest." But how much God is unlike them he said not, because it cannot be said. Let your Charity attend : God is ineffable : we more easily say what He is not than what He is. Thou thinkest of the earth ; this is not God : thou thinkest of the sea ; this is not God : of all things which are in the earth, men and animals ; this is not God : of all things which are in the sea, which fly through the air ; this is not God : whatever shines in the sky, the stars, sun and moon ; this is not God : the heaven itself ; this is not God : think of the Angels, Virtues, Powers, Archangels, Thrones, Seats, Principalities ; this is not God. What is He then? I could only tell thee, what He is not. Askest thou what He is? What "the eye hath not seen, nor the ear heard, nor hath risen up into the heart of man."[1] . . .

12. "All nations that Thou hast made shall come and worship before Thee, O Lord" (ver. 9). He has announced the Church : "All nations." If there is any nation which God hath not made, it will not worship Him : but there is no nation which God hath not made ; because God made Adam and Eve, the source of all nations, thence all nations sprang. All nations therefore hath God made. When was this said? When before Him there worshipped none but a few holy men in one people of the Hebrews, then this was said : and see now what it is which was said : "All nations that Thou hast made," etc. When these things were spoken, they were not seen, and they were believed : now that they are seen, why are they denied? "All nations that Thou hast made shall come and worship before Thee, O Lord, and shall glorify Thy Name."

13. "For Thou art great, and doing wondrous things : Thou alone art the great God" (ver. 10). Let no man call himself great. Some were to be who would call themselves great : against these it is said, "Thou alone art the great God." For what great thing is ascribed to God, when it is said that He alone is the great God? Who knows not that He is the great God? But because there were to be some who would call themselves great and make God little, against these it is said, "Thou alone art the great God." For what Thou sayest is fulfilled, not what those say who call themselves great. What hath God said by His Spirit? "All nations." What saith he, whoever he is, who calleth himself great? "Far from it : God is not worshipped in all nations : all nations have perished, Africa alone remains." This thou sayest, who callest thyself great :[2] another thing He saith who alone is the great God. What saith He, who alone is the great God? "All nations." I see what the only great God hath said : let man be silent, who is falsely great ; great only in appearance, because he disdains to be small. Who disdains to be small? He who saith this. Whoever will be great among you, said the Lord, shall be your servant.[3] If that man had wished to be the servant of his brethren, he would not have separated them from their mother : but when he wishes to be great, and wishes not to be small, as would be for his welfare, God, who resisteth the proud, and giveth grace to the humble,[4] because He alone is great, fulfilleth all things which He predicted, and contradicteth those who blaspheme. For such persons blaspheme against Christ, who say that the Church has perished from the whole world, and is left only in Africa. If thou wert to say to him, Thou wilt lose thy villa, he would perhaps scarcely keep from laying his hand upon thee : and yet he says, that Christ has lost His inheritance, redeemed by His own Blood ! See now what a wrong he does, my brethren. The Scripture says, "In a wide nation is the king's honour ; but in the domination of the people is the affliction[5] of a prince."[6] This wrong then thou dost unto Christ, to say that His people is diminished to that small number. Was it for this thou wast born, for this thou callest thyself a Christian, that thou mayest grudge Christ His glory, whose sign thou sayest that thou bearest on thy forehead, and hast lost out of thy heart? In a wide nation is the king's honour : acknowledge thy King : give Him glory, give Him a wide nation. What wide nation shall I give Him, dost thou say? Choose not to give Him from thy own heart, and thou wilt give aright. Whence am I to give? thou wilt say. Lo, give from hence : "All nations that Thou hast made shall come and worship before Thee, O Lord." Say this, confess this, and thou hast given a wide nation : for all nations in One are one : this is very oneness. For as there is a Church and Churches, and those are Churches which also are a Church, so that is a nation which was nations : formerly nations, many nations, now one nation. Why one nation? Because one faith, one hope, one charity, one expectation. Lastly, why not one nation, if one country? Our country is heavenly, our country is Jerusalem : whoever is not a citizen of it, belongs not to that nation : but whoever is a citizen of it is in that one nation of God. And this nation, from the east to the west, from the north and the sea, is extended through the four quarters of the whole world. This God saith : From the east and west, from

---

[1] 1 Cor. ii. 9.

[2] The Donatist.   [3] Matt. xx. 26.   [4] Jas. iv. 6.
[5] Contritio.   [6] Prov. xiv. 28.

the north and the sea, give glory to God. This He foretold, this He fulfilled, who alone is great. Let him therefore who would not be little cease from saying this against Him who alone is great: for there cannot be two great, God and Donatus.[1]

14. "Lead me, O Lord, in Thy way, and I will walk in Thy truth" (ver. 11). Thy way, Thy truth, Thy life, is Christ. Therefore belongeth the Body to Him, and the Body is of Him. I am the Way, and the Truth, and the Life.[2] "Lead me, O Lord, in Thy way." In what way? "And I will walk in Thy truth." It is one thing to lead to the way, another to guide in the way. Behold man everywhere poor, everywhere in need of help. Those who are beside the way are not Christians, or not yet Catholics: let them be guided to the way: but when they have been brought to the way and made Catholics in Christ, they must be guided by Him in the way itself, lest they fall.[3] Now assuredly they walk in the way. "Lead me, O Lord, in Thy way:" surely I am now in Thy way, lead me there. "And I will walk in Thy truth:" while Thou leadest I shall not err: if Thou let me go, I shall err. Pray then that He let thee not go, but lead thee even to the end. How doth He lead thee? By always admonishing, always giving thee His hand. And the arm of the Lord, to whom is it revealed?[4] For in giving His Christ He giveth His hand: in giving His Hand, He giveth His Christ. He leadeth to the way, in leading to His Christ: He leadeth in the way, by leading in His Christ, and Christ is truth. "Lead me," therefore, "O Lord, in Thy way, and I will walk in Thy truth:" in Him verily who said, "I am the Way, and the Truth, and the Life."[2] For Thou who leadest in the way and the truth, whither leadest Thou, but unto life? In Him then, unto Him Thou leadest.

15. "Let my heart be made glad, so that it may fear Thy name." There is then fear in gladness. How can there be gladness, if fear? Is not fear wont to be painful? There will hereafter be gladness without fear, now gladness with fear; for not yet is there perfect security, nor perfect gladness. If there is no gladness, we faint: if full security, we rejoice wrongly. Therefore may He both sprinkle on us gladness, and strike fear into us, that by the sweetness of gladness He may lead us to the abode of security; by giving us fear, may cause us not to rejoice wrongly, and to withdraw from the way. Therefore saith the Psalm: "Serve the Lord in fear, and rejoice unto Him with trembling:"[5] so also saith the Apostle Paul; "Work out your own salvation with fear and trembling; for it is God

that worketh in you."[6] Whatever prosperity comes then, my brethren, is rather to be feared: those things which ye think to be prosperous, are rather temptations. An inheritance cometh, there cometh wealth, there is an abundant overflow of some happiness: these are temptations: take care that they corrupt you not. Whatever prosperity also there is according to Christ, and the true love of Christ: if perhaps thou hast gained thy wife, who was of the party of Donatus: if thy sons have been made believers who were Pagans: if perhaps thou hast gained thy friend who wished to draw thee away to the theatres, and thou hast drawn him to the church: if some hostile opponent of thine who was furiously mad against thee, laying aside his fury, has become gentle, and owned God, and now barks at thee no more, but cries with thee against wickedness: these things are pleasant. For what do we rejoice for, if we do not rejoice for these things? Or what other are our joys, but these? But because tribulations also abound, and temptations, and dissensions, and schisms, and other evils,[7] without which this world cannot be, until iniquity pass away: let not that rejoicing make us secure, but let our heart be so made glad, as to fear the name of the Lord, lest it be made glad on one side, be stricken on another. Expect not security in journeying: if ever we wish for it here, it will be the birdlime of the body,[8] not the safety of the man. "Let my heart be made glad, so that it may fear Thy name."

16. "I will confess unto Thee, O Lord my God, in my whole heart, and I will glorify Thy name for ever" (ver. 12): "for great is Thy mercy toward me, and Thou hast delivered my soul from the nethermost hell" (ver. 13). Do not be angry, brethren, if I do not explain what I have said as though I were certain. For I am a man, and as much as is granted to me concerning the sacred Scriptures, so much I venture to speak: nothing of myself. Hades[9] I have not yet seen, nor have you: and there will be perhaps another way for us, and not through Hades. These things are uncertain. But because Scripture, which cannot be gainsaid, says, "Thou hast delivered my soul from the nethermost hell," we understand that there are as it were two hells, an upper one and a lower one: for how can there be a lower hell, unless because there is also an upper? The one would not be called lower, except by comparison with that upper part. It appears then, my brethren, that there is some heavenly abode of Angels: there is there a life of ineffable joys, there immortality and incorruption, there all things abiding accord-

1 [He made his little sect the whole Catholic Church. So now the Roman communion claims to be the whole Catholic communion, cutting itself off even from the Easterns. — C.]
2 John xiv. 6.   3 [See Acts xviii. 26.— C.]
4 Isa. liii. 1.   5 Ps. ii. 11.

6 Philip. ii. 12, 13.   7 Oxf. mss. "other such evils."
8 Al. "of the heart."
9 Infernum: used, as our word "hell" in the Apostles' Creed, for the place of departed spirits. [Note he has no dogma on this point, but speaks of his views as uncertain. — C.]

ing to the gift and grace of God. That part of the creation is above. If then that is above, but this earthly part, where is flesh and blood, where is corruptibleness, where is nativity and mortality, departure and succession, changeableness and inconstancy, where are fears, desires, horrors, uncertain joys, frail hope, perishable existence; I suppose that all this part cannot be compared with that heaven of which I was just now speaking; if then this part cannot be compared with that, the one is above, the other below. And whither do we go after death, unless there is a depth deeper than this depth [1] in which we are in the flesh and in this mortal state? For "the body is dead," saith the Apostle, "because of sin." [2] Therefore even here are the dead; that thou mayest not wonder because it is called *infernum*, if it abounds with the dead. For he saith not, the body is about to die: but, "the body is dead." Even now surely our body hath life: and yet compared with that body which is to be like the bodies of Angels, the body of man is found to be dead, although still having life. But again, from this *infernum*, that is from this part of Hades, there is another lower, whither the dead go: from whence God would rescue our souls, even sending thither His own Son. For it was on account of these two hells, my brethren, that the Son of God was sent, on all sides setting free. To this hell he was sent by being born, to that by dying. Therefore it is His voice in that Psalm, not according to any man's conjecture, but an Apostle explaining, when he saith, "For Thou wilt not leave my soul in hell." [3] Therefore it is here also either His voice, "Thou hast delivered my soul from the nethermost hell:" or our voice by the Lord Jesus Christ Himself: for on this account He came even unto hell, that we might not remain in hell.

17. I will mention another opinion also. For perhaps even in hell itself there is some lower part where are thrust the ungodly who have sinned most. [4] For whether in hell there were not some places where Abraham was, we cannot define sufficiently. For not yet had the Lord come to hell that He might rescue from thence the souls of all the saints who had gone before, [5] and yet Abraham was there in repose. [6] And a certain rich man when he was in torments in hell, when he saw Abraham, lifted up his eyes. He could not have seen him by lifting up his eyes, unless the one was above, the other below. And what did Abraham answer unto him, when he said, "send Lazarus." "My son," he said, "remember that thou in thy lifetime receivedst

thy good things, and likewise Lazarus evil things: but now he is at rest, but thou art tormented. And besides this," he said, "between us and you there is a great gulf fixed, so that neither can we go to you, nor can any one come from thence to us." [7] Therefore between these two hells, perhaps, in one of which the souls of the just have gotten rest, in the other the souls of the ungodly are tormented, one waiting and praying here, placed here in the body of Christ, and praying in the voice of Christ, said that God had delivered his soul from the nethermost hell, because He delivered him from such sins as might have been the means of drawing him down to the torments of the nethermost hell. . . . Some one having a troublesome cause was to be sent to prison: another comes and defends him; what does he say when he thanks him? Thou hast delivered my soul out of prison. A debtor was to be hanged up: [8] his debt is paid; he is said to be delivered from being hanged up. They were not in all these evils: but because they were in such due course towards them, [9] that unless aid had been brought, they would have been in them, they rightly say that they are delivered from thence, whither they were not suffered by their deliverers to be taken. Therefore, brethren, whether it be this or that, consider me to be herein an inquirer into the word of God, not a rash assertor. [10]

18. "O God, the transgressors of the law have arisen up against me" (ver. 14). Whom calleth he transgressors of the law? Not the Pagans, who have not received the law: for no one transgresseth that which he hath not received; the Apostle saith clearly, "For where there is no law, there is no prevarication." [11] Transgressors of the law he calls "prevaricators." Whom then do we understand, brethren? If we take this word from our Lord Himself, the transgressors of the law were the Jews. . . . They did not keep the law, and accused Christ as if He transgressed the law. And we know what the Lord suffered. Thinkest thou His Body suffers no such thing now? How can this be? "If they called the Master of the house Beelzebub, how much more those of his household? The disciple is not above his master, nor the servant above his lord." [12] The body also suffereth transgressors of the law, and they rise up against the Body of Christ. Who are the transgressors of the law? Do the Jews perchance dare to rise up against Christ? No: for it is not they that cause us much trouble. For they have not

---

[1] *Infernum inferius hoc inferno.* Lit. "a hell than this hell."
[2] Rom. viii. 10.
[3] Ps. xvi. 10.   [4] So St. Gregory on Job l. xii. § 14.
[5] St. Gregory on Job, l. xiii. §§ 48, 49.   [6] Luke xvi. 22.

[7] Luke xvi. 24-26.
[8] *Suspendendus.* The word is used of the preparation for torture, as in the *gesta Proconsularia* in the case of Felix of Aptungis, Opp. S. Aug t. ix Appendix, when Ingentius, the forger, was to be threatened with torture, *Proconsul dixit, Suspendatur.*
[9] *Quia talibus meritis agebantur.*
[10] [Note his caution and great humility. — C.]
[11] Rom. iv. 15.   [12] Matt. x. 25, 24.

yet believed: they have not yet owned their salvation. Against the Body of Christ bad Christians rise up, from whom the Body of Christ daily suffereth trouble. All schisms, all heresies, all within who live wickedly and engraft their own character on those who live well, and draw them over to their own side, and with evil communications corrupt good manners; these persons "transgressing the law rose up against Me."[1] Let every pious soul speak, let every Christian soul speak. That one which suffers not this, let it not speak. But if it is a Christian soul, it knows that it suffers evils: if it owns in itself its own sufferings, let it own herein its own voice; but if it is without suffering, let it[2] also be without the voice; but that it may not be without suffering, let it walk along the narrow way,[3] and begin to live godly in Christ: it must of necessity suffer this persecution. For "all," saith the Apostle, "who will live godly in Christ, suffer persecution."[4]

"And the synagogue of the powerful have sought after My soul." The synagogue of the powerful is the congregation of the proud. The synagogue of the powerful rose up against the Head, that is, our Lord Jesus Christ, crying and saying with one mouth, Crucify Him, crucify Him:[5] of whom it is said, "The sons of men, their teeth are spears and arrows, and their tongue a sharp sword."[6] They did not strike, but cried: by crying they struck, by crying they crucified Him. The will of those who cried was fulfilled, when the Lord was crucified: 'And they did not place Thee before their eyes." How did they not place Him before them? They did not know Him God. They should have spared him as Man: what they saw, according to this they should have walked. Suppose that He was not God, He was man: was He therefore to be slain? Spare Him a man, and own Him God.

19. "And Thou, Lord God, art One who hast compassion and merciful, longsuffering, and very pitiful, and true" (ver. 15). Wherefore longsuffering and very pitiful, and One who hast compassion? Because hanging on the Cross He said: "Father, forgive them, for they know not what they do."[7] Whom prayeth He to? for whom doth He pray? Who prayeth? Where prayeth He? The Son prays to the Father, crucified for the ungodly, in the midst of very insults, not of words but of death inflicted, hanging on the Cross; as if for this He had His hands stretched out, that thus He might pray for them, that His "prayer might be directed like incense in the sight of the

Father, and the lifting up of His hands like an evening sacrifice."[8]

20. If therefore Thou art "true," "Look upon me, and have mercy upon me: give power unto Thy servant." Because Thou art "true," "give power unto Thy servant" (ver. 16). Let the time of patience pass away, the time of judgment come. How, "give power"? The Father judgeth no man, but hath committed all judgment unto the Son.[9] He rising again will come even to earth Himself to judge: He will appear terrible who appeared despicable. He will show His power, who showed His patience; on the Cross was patience; in the judgment will be power. For He will appear as Man judging, but in glory: because "as ye saw Him go," said the Angels, "so He will come."[10] His very form shall come to judgment; therefore the ungodly also shall see Him: for they shall not see the form of God. For blessed are the pure in heart, for they shall see God.[11] . . . In the vision of the Father there is also the vision of the Son: and in the vision of the Son there is also the vision of the Father. Therefore He adds a consequence, and says: "Know ye not that I am in the Father, and the Father in Me?"[12] that is, both in Me seen the Father is seen, and in the Father seen the Son too is seen. The vision of the Father and the Son cannot be separated: where nature and substance is not separated, there vision cannot be separated. For that ye may know that the heart ought to be made ready for that place, to see the Divinity of the Father and Son and Holy Spirit, in which though not seen we believe, and by believing cleanse the heart that there may be able to be sight: the Lord Himself saith in another place, "He that hath My commands and keepeth them, he it is that loveth Me: and he that loveth Me shall be loved by My Father: and I will love him, and will manifest Myself unto him."[13] Did they not see Him, with whom He was talking? They both saw Him, and did not see Him? they saw something, they believed something: they saw Man, they believed in God. But in the Judgment they shall see the same Lord Jesus Christ as Man, together with the wicked: after the Judgment, they shall see God, apart from the wicked.

21. "And save the Son of Thine handmaid." The Lord is the Son of the handmaid. Of what handmaid? Her who when He was announced as about to be born of her, answered and said, "Behold the handmaid of the Lord: be it unto me according to Thy word."[14] He saved the Son of His handmaid, and His own Son: His own Son, in the Form of God;[15] the Son of

---

[1] 1 Cor. xv. 33.   [2] Oxf mss. "it must needs."
[3] Matt. vii. 14.   [4] 2 Tim. iii. 12.   [5] John xix. 6.
[6] Ps. lvii. 4.
[7] Luke xxiii 34.

[8] Ps. cxli. 2.   [9] John v. 22.   [10] Acts i. 11.
[11] Matt. v. 8.   [12] John xiv. 10.   [13] John xiv. 21.
[14] Luke i. 38.   [15] Philip. i. 6.

His handmaid in the form of a servant. Of the handmaid of God, therefore, the Lord was born in the form of a servant; and He said, "Save the Son of Thine handmaid." And He was saved from death, as ye know, His flesh, which was dead, being raised again. . . . And each several Christian placed in the Body of Christ may say, "Save the Son of Thine handmaid." Perhaps he cannot say, "Give power unto Thy servant:" because it was He, the Son, who received power. Yet wherefore saith He not this also? Was it not said to servants, "Ye shall sit upon twelve thrones, judging the twelve tribes of Israel"? [1] and the servants say, "Know ye not that we shall judge Angels?" [2] Each one therefore of the saints receiveth also power, and each several saint is the son of His handmaid. What if he is born of a pagan mother, and has become a Christian? How can the son of a pagan be the son of His handmaid: He is indeed the son of a pagan mother after the flesh, but the son of the Church after the Spirit.

22. "Show me a sign for good" (ver. 17). What sign, but that of the Resurrection? The Lord says: "This wicked and provoking generation seeketh after a sign; and there shall no sign be given it, but the sign of the Prophet Jonah." [3] Therefore in our Head a sign has been shown already for good; each one of us also may say, "Show me a sign for good:" because at the last trumpet, at the coming of the Lord, both "the dead shall be raised incorruptible, and we shall be changed." [4] This will be a sign for good. "That they who hate me may see it, and be ashamed." In the judgment they shall be ashamed unto their destruction, who will not now be ashamed unto their healing. Now therefore let them be ashamed: let them accuse their own ways, let them keep the good way: because none of us liveth without being ashamed, unless he first be ashamed and live anew. Now God grants them the approach of a healthy shame, if they despise not the medicine of confession: but if they will not now be ashamed, then they shall be ashamed, when "their iniquities shall convince them to their face." [5] How shall they be ashamed? When they shall say, "These are they whom we had sometimes in derision, and a parable of reproach. We fools counted their life madness: how are they numbered among the children of God! What hath pride profited us?" [6] Then shall they say this: let them say it now, and they say it to their health. For let each one turn humbly to God, and now say, What hath my pride profited me? and hear from the Apostle, "For what glory had ye in those things of which ye are now ashamed?" [7] Ye see that there is even now a wholesome shame while there is a place of penitence: but then one which will be late, useless, fruitless. . . .

23. "For Thou, Lord, hast holpen me, and comforted me." "Hast holpen me," in struggle; "and comforted me," in sorrow. For no one seeketh comfort, but he who is in misery. Would ye not be consoled? Say that ye are happy, and ye hear, "My people" (now ye answer, and I hear a murmur, as of persons who remember the Scriptures.[8] May God, who hath written this in your hearts, confirm it in your deeds. Ye see, brethren, that those who say unto you, Ye are happy, seduce you), "O My people, they that call you happy cause you to err, and disturb the way of your feet." [9] So also from the Epistle of the Apostle James: "Be afflicted, and mourn: let your laughter be turned to mourning." [10] Ye see what ye have heard read: when would such things be said unto us in the land of security? This surely is the land of offences, and temptations, and of all evils, that we may groan here, and deserve to rejoice there; here to be troubled, and there to be comforted, and to say, "For Thou hast delivered mine eyes from tears, my feet from falling: I will please the Lord in the land of the living." [11] This is the land of the dead. The land of the dead passeth, the land of the living cometh. In the land of the dead is labour, grief, fear, tribulation, temptation, groaning, sighing: here are false happy ones, true unhappy, because happiness is false, misery is true. But he that owneth himself to be in true misery, will also be in true happiness: and yet now because thou art miserable, hear the Lord saying, "Blessed are they that mourn." [12] O blessed they that mourn! Nothing is so akin to misery as mourning: nothing so remote and contrary to misery as blessedness: Thou speakest of those who mourn, and Thou callest them blessed! Understand, He saith, what I say: I call those who mourn blessed. Wherefore blessed? In hope. Wherefore mourning? In act. For they mourn in this death, in these tribulations, in their wandering: and because they own themselves to be in this misery, and mourn, they are blessed. Wherefore do they mourn? The blessed Cyprian was put to sorrow in his passion: now he is comforted with his crown; now though comforted, he was sad. For our Lord Jesus Christ still intercedeth for us: all the Martyrs who are with Him intercede for us. Their intercessions pass not away, except when our mourning is passed away: but when our mourning shall have passed away, we all with

---

[1] Matt. xix. 28.   [2] 1 Cor. vi. 3.
[3] Matt. xii. 39   [4] 1 Cor. xv. 52.
[5] Wisd. iv. 20, *deducent eos.* LXX. ἐλέγξει.
[6] Wisd. v. 3–5. 8.

[7] Rom. vi. 21.
[8] [A striking note of the manner of ancient congregations. — C.]
[9] Isa. iii. 12, Lat. and E. V. margin.
[10] Jas. iv. 9.   [11] Ps. cxvi. 8, 9.   [12] Matt. v. 4.

one voice, in one people, in one country, shall receive comfort, thousands of thousands joined with Angels playing upon harps, with choirs of heavenly powers living in one city. Who mourneth there? Who there sigheth? Who there toileth? Who there needeth? Who dieth there? Who there showeth mercy? Who breaketh bread to the hungry there, where all are satisfied with the bread of righteousness? No one saith unto thee, Receive a stranger; there no one will be a stranger to thee: all live in their own country. No one saith unto thee, Set at one thy friends disputing; in everlasting peace they enjoy the Face of God. No one saith unto thee, Visit the sick; health and immortality abide for ever. No one saith unto thee, Bury the dead; all shall be in everlasting life. Works of mercy stop, because misery is found not. And what shall we do there? Shall we perhaps sleep? If now we fight against ourselves, although we carry about a house of sleep, this flesh of ours, and keep watch with these lights, and this solemn feast gives us a mind to watch; what wakefulness shall that day give unto us! Therefore we shall be awake, we shall not sleep. What shall we do?[1] There will be no works of mercy, because there will be no misery. Perhaps there will be these necessary works which there are here now, of sowing, ploughing, cooking, grinding, weaving? None of these, for there will be no want. Thus there will be no works of mercy, because misery is past away: where there is no want nor misery, there will be neither works of necessity nor of mercy. What will be there? What business shall we have? What action? Will there be no action, because there is rest? Shall we sit there, and be torpid, and do nothing? If our love grow cold, our action will grow cold. How then will that love resting in the face of God, for whom we now long, for whom we sigh, how will it inflame us, when we shall have come to Him? He for whom while as yet we see Him not, we so sigh, how will He enlighten us, when we shall have come to Him? How will He change us? What will He make of us? What then shall we do, brethren? Let the Psalm tell us: "Blessed are they who dwell in Thy house." Why? "They shall praise Thee for ever and ever."[2] This will be our employment, praise of God. Thou lovest and praisest. Thou wilt cease to praise, if thou cease to love. But thou wilt not cease to love, because He whom thou seest is such an One as offends thee not by any weariness: He both satisfies thee, and satisfies thee not. What I say is wonderful. If I say that He satisfies thee, I am afraid lest as though satisfied thou shouldest wish to depart, as from a dinner or from a sup-

per. What then do I say? doth He not satisfy thee? I am afraid again, that if I say, He doth not satisfy thee, thou shouldest seem to be in want: and shouldest be as it were empty, and there should be in thee some void which ought to be filled. What then shall I say, except what can be said, but can hardly be thought? He both satisfies thee, and satisfies thee not: for I find both in Scripture. For while He said, "Blessed are the hungry, for they shall be filled;"[3] it is again said of Wisdom, "Those who eat Thee shall hunger again, and those who drink shall thirst again."[4] Nay, but He did not say "again," but he said, "still:" for "shall thirst again" is as if once having been filled he departed and digested, and returned to drink. So it is, "Those who eat Thee shall still hunger:' thus when they eat they hunger: and those who drink Thee, even thus when drinking, thirst. What is it, to thirst in drinking? Never to grow weary. If then there shall be that ineffable and eternal sweetness, what doth He now seek of us, brethren, but faith unfeigned, firm hope, pure charity? and man may walk in the way which the Lord hath given, may bear troubles, and receive consolations.

PSALM LXXXVII.[5]

1. The Psalm which has just been sung is short, if we look to the number of its words, but of deep interest in its thoughts.[6] . . . The subject of song and praise in that Psalm is a city, whose citizens are we, as far as we are Christians: whence we are absent, as long as we are mortal: whither we are tending: through whose approaches, undiscoverable among the brakes and thorns that entangle them, the Sovereign of the city made Himself a path[7] for us to reach it. Walking thus in Christ, and pilgrims till we arrive, and sighing as we long for a certain ineffable repose that dwells within that city, a repose of which it is promised, that "the eye of man hath never seen" such, "nor ear heard, nor hath it entered into his heart to conceive;" let us chant the song of a longing heart: for he who truly longs, thus sings within his soul, though his tongue be silent: he who does not, however he may resound in human ears, is voiceless to God. See what ardent lovers of that city were they by whom these words were composed, by whom they have been handed down to us; with how deep a feeling were they sung by those! A feeling that the love of that city created in them: that love the Spirit of God inspired; "the love

---

[3] Matt. v. 6.　　　　[4] Ecclus. xxiv. 21.
[5] Lat. LXXXVI. A discourse to the people, perhaps at Carthage, delivered the day after that on the preceding Psalm. See § 8.
[6] [For his discourse he pleads the command of a brother.—C.] Perhaps Aurelius, bishop of Carthage.—Ben.
[7] Se fecit viam.

---

[1] [See Ps. lxxxiv. p. 402, supra.—C.]　　　[2] Ps. lxxxiv. 4.

of God," he saith, "shed abroad in our hearts by the Holy Ghost, which is given unto us." Fervent with this Spirit then, let us listen to what is said of that city.

2. "Her foundations are upon the holy hills" (ver. 1). The Psalm had as yet said nothing of the city: it begins thus, and says, "Her foundations are upon the holy hills." Whose? There can be no doubt that foundations, especially among the hills, belong to some city. Thus filled with the Holy Spirit, and with many thoughts of love and longing for that city, as if after long internal meditation, that citizen bursts out, "Her foundations are upon the holy hills;" as if he had already said something concerning it. And how could he have said nothing on a subject, respecting which in his heart he had never been silent? For how could "her foundations" have been written, of which nothing had been said before? But, as I said, after long and silent travailing in contemplation of that city in his mind, crying to God, he bursts out into the ears of men thus: "Her foundations are upon the holy hills." And, supposing persons who heard to enquire of what city he spoke he adds, "the Lord loveth the gates of Sion." Behold, then, a city whose foundations are upon the holy hills, a city called Sion, whose gates the Lord loveth, as he adds, "above all the dwellings of Jacob." But what doth this mean, "her foundations on the holy hills"? What are the holy hills upon which this city is built? Another citizen tells us this more explicitly, the Apostle Paul: of this was the Prophet a citizen, of this the Apostle citizen: and they spoke to exhort the other citizens. But how are these, I mean the Prophets and Apostles, citizens? Perhaps in this sense; that they are themselves the hills, upon which are the foundations of this city, whose gates the Lord loveth. Let then another citizen state this clearly, that I may not seem to guess. Speaking to the Gentiles, and telling them how they were returning, and being, as it were, framed together into the holy structure, "built," he says, "upon the foundations of the Apostles and Prophets:" and because neither the Apostles nor Prophets, upon whom the foundations of that city rest, could stand by their own power, he adds, "Jesus Christ Himself being the head corner stone."[1] That the Gentiles, therefore, might not think they had no relation to Sion: for Sion was a certain city of this world, which bore a typical resemblance as a shadow to that Sion of which he presently speaketh, that Heavenly Jerusalem, of which the Apostle saith, "which is the mother of us all;"[2] they might not be said to bear no relation to Sion, on the ground that they did not belong to the Jewish people, he addresses them thus: "Now therefore ye are no more strangers and foreigners, but fellow citizens with the saints, and of the household of God, and are built upon the foundation of the Apostles and Prophets."[3] Thou seest the structure of so great a city: yet whereon does all that edifice repose, where does it rest, that it may never fall? "Jesus Christ Himself," he saith, "being the head corner stone."

3. . . . But that ye may know that Christ is at once the earliest and the highest foundation, the Apostle saith, "Other foundation can no man lay than is laid, which is Christ Jesus."[4] How, then, are the Prophets and Apostles foundations, and yet Christ so, than whom nothing can be higher? How, think you, save that as He is openly styled, Saint of saints, so figuratively Foundation of foundations? Thus if thou art thinking of mysteries, Christ is the Saint of saints: if of a subject flock, the Shepherd of shepherds: if of a structure, the Pillar of pillars. In material edifices, the same stone cannot be above and below: if at the bottom, it cannot be at the top: and *vice versâ:* for almost all bodies are liable to limitations in space: nor can they be everywhere or for ever; but as the Godhead is in every place, from every place symbols may be taken for It; and not being any of these things in external properties, It can be everything in figure. Is Christ a door, in the same sense as the doors we see made by carpenters? Surely not; and yet He said, "I am the door." Or a shepherd, in the same capacity as those who guard sheep? though He said, "I am the Shepherd." Both these names occur in the same passage: in the Gospel, He said, that the shepherd enters by the door: the words are, "I am the good Shepherd;" and in the same passage, "I am the door:"[5] and who is the shepherd who enters by the door? "I am the good Shepherd:" and what is the door by which Thou, Good Shepherd, enterest? How then art Thou all things? In the sense in which everything is through Me. To explain: when Paul enters by the door, does not Christ? Wherefore? Not because Paul is Christ: but since Christ is in Paul: and Paul acts through Christ. The Apostle says, "Do ye seek a proof of Christ speaking in me?"[6] When His saints and faithful disciples enter by the door, does not Christ enter by the door? How are we to prove this? Since Saul, not yet called Paul, was persecuting those very saints, when He called to him from Heaven, "Saul, Saul, why persecutest thou Me?"[7] Himself then is the foundation, and corner stone: rising from the bottom: if indeed

---

[1] Eph. ii. 20.   [2] Gal. iv. 26.   [3] Eph. ii. 19, 20.

[4] 1 Cor. iii. 11.   [5] John x. 11, 9.   [6] 2 Cor. xiii. 3.
[7] Acts ix. 4.

from the bottom: for the base of this foundation is the highest exaltation of the building: and as the support of bodily fabrics rests upon the ground, that of spiritual structures reposes on high. Were we building up ourselves upon the earth, we should lay our foundation on the lowest level: but since our edifice is a heavenly one, to Heaven our Foundation has gone before us: so that our Saviour, the corner stone, the Apostles, and mighty Prophets, the hills that bear the fabric of the city, constitute a sort of living structure. This building now cries from your hearts; that you may be built up into its fabric, the hand of God, as of an artificer, worketh even through my tongue. Nor was it without a meaning that Noah's ark was made of "square beams," [1] which were typical of the form of the Church. For what is it to be made square? Listen to the resemblance of the squared stone: like qualities should the Christian have: for in all his trials he never falls: though pushed, and, as it were, turned over, he falls not: and thus too, whichever way a square stone is turned, it stands erect. . . . In earthly cities, one thing is the structure of buildings: another thing are the citizens that dwell therein: that city is builded of its own inmates, who are themselves the blocks that form the city, for the very stones are living: "Ye also," says the Apostle, "as living stones, are built up a spiritual house,[2] words that are addressed to ourselves. Let us then pursue the contemplation of that city.

4. "The Lord loveth the gates of Sion more than all the dwellings of Jacob" (ver. 2). I have made the foregoing remarks, that ye may not imagine the gates are one thing, the foundations another. Why are the Apostles and Prophets foundations? Because their authority is the support of our weakness. Why are they gates? because through them we enter the kingdom of God: for they proclaim it to us: and while we enter by their means, we enter also through Christ, Himself being the Gate. And twelve gates of Jerusalem are spoken of,[3] and the one gate is Christ, and the twelve gates are Christ: for Christ dwells in the twelve gates, hence was twelve the number of the Apostles. There is a deep mystery in this number of twelve: "Ye shall sit," says our Saviour, "on twelve thrones, judging the twelve tribes of Israel." [4] If there are twelve thrones there, there will be no room for the judgment-seat of Paul, the thirteenth Apostle, though he says that he shall judge not men only, but even Angels; which, but the fallen Angels? "Know ye not, that we shall judge Angels," [5] he writes. The world would answer, Why dost thou boast that thou

shalt be a judge? Where will be thy throne? Our Lord spoke of twelve thrones for the twelve Apostles: one, Judas, fell, and his place being supplied by Matthias, the number of twelve thrones was made up: [6] first, then, discover room for thy judgment-seat; then threaten that thou wilt judge. Let us, therefore, reflect upon the meaning of the twelve thrones. The expression is typical of a sort of universality, as the Church was destined to prevail throughout the whole world: whence this edifice is styled a building together into Christ: and because judges come from all quarters, the twelve thrones are spoken of, just as the twelve gates, from the entering in from all sides into that city. Not only therefore have those twelve, and the Apostle Paul, a claim to the twelve thrones, but, from the universal signification, all who are to sit in judgment: in the same manner as all who enter the city, enter by one or the other of the twelve gates. There are four quarters of the globe: East, West, North, and South: and they are constantly alluded to in the Scriptures. From all those four winds; our Lord declares in the Gospel that He will call his sheep "from the four winds;" [7] therefore from all those four winds is the Church called. And how called? On every side it is called in the Trinity: no otherwise is it called than by Baptism in the name of the Father, the Son, and the Holy Ghost: four then being thrice taken, twelve are found. Knock, therefore, with all your hearts at these gates: and let Christ cry within you: "Open me the gates of righteousness." [8] For He went before us the Head: He follows Himself in His Body. . . .

5. "Very excellent things are said of thee, thou city of God" (ver. 3). He was, as it were, contemplating that city of Jerusalem on earth: for consider what city he alludes to, of which certain very excellent things are spoken. Now the earthly city has been destroyed: after suffering the enemy's rage, it fell to the earth; it is no longer what it was: it exhibited the emblem, and the shadow hath passed away. Whence then are "very excellent things spoken of thee, thou city of God"? Listen whence: "I will think upon Rahab and Babylon, with them that know Me" (ver. 4). In that city, the Prophet, in the person of God, says, "I will think upon Rahab and Babylon." Rahab belongs not to the Jewish people; [9] Babylon belongs not to the Jewish people; as is clear from the next verse: "For the Philistines [10] also, and Tyre, with the Ethiopians, were there." Deservedly then, "very excellent things are spoken of thee, thou city of God:" for not only is the Jewish nation, born of the flesh of Abraham,

[1] Gen. vi. 14, LXX.   [2] 1 Pet. ii. 5.   [6] Acts i. 15–26.   [7] Mark xiii. 27.   [8] Ps. cxviii. 19.
[3] Rev. xxi. 12.   [4] Matt. xix. 28.   [5] 1 Cor. vi. 3.   [9] Josh. ii.1, vi. 25.   [10] *Alienigenæ*, ἀλλόφυλοι.

included therein, but all nations also, some of which are named that all may be understood. "I will think," he says, "upon Rahab:" who is that harlot? That harlot in Jericho, who received the spies and conducted them out of the city by a different road: who trusted beforehand in the promise, who feared God, who was told to hang out of the window a line of scarlet thread, that is, to bear upon her forehead the sign of the blood of Christ. She was saved there, and thus represented the Church of the Gentiles: whence our Lord said to the haughty Pharisees, "Verily I say unto you, that the publicans and the harlots go into the kingdom of God before you."[1] They go before, because they do violence: they push their way by faith, and to faith a way is made, nor can any resist, since they who are violent take it by force. For it is written, "The kingdom of Heaven suffereth violence, and the violent take it by force."[2] Such was the conduct of the robber, more courageous on the cross than in the place of ambush.[3] "I will think upon Rahab and Babylon." By Babylon is meant the city of this world: as there is one holy city, Jerusalem; one unholy, Babylon: all the unholy belong to Babylon, even as all the holy to Jerusalem. But he slideth[4] from Babylon to Jerusalem. How, but by Him who justifieth the ungodly: Jerusalem is the city of the saints; Babylon of the wicked: but He cometh who justifieth the ungodly: since it is said, "I will think" not only "upon Rahab," but "upon Babylon," but with whom? "with them that know Me." . . .

6. Listen now to a deep mystery. Rahab is there through Him, through whom also is Babylon, now no longer Babylon, but beginning to be Jerusalem. The daughter is divided against her mother, and will be among the members of that queen to whom is said, "Forget thine own people, and thy father's house, so shall the king have pleasure in thy beauty."[5] For how could Babylon aspire to Jerusalem? How could Rahab reach those foundations? How could the Philistines, or Tyre, or the people of the Ethiopians? Listen to this verse, "Sion, my mother, a man shall say."[6] There is then a man who saith this: through whom all those I have mentioned make their approach. Who is this man? It tells if we hear, if we understand. It follows, as if a question had been raised, through whose aid Rahab, Babylon, the Philistines, Tyre, and the Morians, gained an entrance. Behold, through whom they come; "Sion, my mother, a man shall say; and a man was born in her, and Himself the Most High hath founded her" (ver. 5).

What, my brethren, can be clearer? Truly, because "very excellent things are spoken of thee, thou city of God." Lo, "Sion, O mother, a man shall say." What man? "He who was born in her."[7] It is then the man who was born in her, and He Himself hath founded her. Yet how can He be born in the city which He Himself founded? It had already been founded, that therein He might be born. Understand it thus, if thou canst: "Mother Sion, he shall say;" but it is "a man" that "shall say, Mother Sion; yea, a man was born in her:" and yet "he hath founded her" (not a man, but), "the Most High." As He created a mother of whom He would be born, so He founded a city in which He would be born. What hope is ours, brethren! On our behalf the Most High, who founded the city, addresses that city as a mother: and "He was born in her, and the Most High hath founded her."

7. As though it were said, How do ye know this? All of us have sung these Psalms: and Christ, Man for our sake, God before us, sings within us all. But is this much to say, "before us," of Him who was before heaven and earth and time? He then, born for our sakes a man, in that city, also founded her when He was the Most High. Yet how are we assured of this? "The Lord shall rehearse it when He writeth up the people" (ver. 6), as the following verse has it. "The Lord shall declare, when He writeth up the people, and their princes." What princes?[8] "Those who were born in her;" those princes who, born within her walls, became therein princes: for before they could become princes in her, God chose the despised things of the world to confound the strong. Was the fisherman, the publican, a prince? They were indeed princes: but because they became such in her. Princes of what kind were they? Princes come from Babylon, believing monarchs of this world, came to the city of Rome, as to the head of Babylon: they went not to the temple of the Emperor, but to the tomb of the Fisherman. Whence indeed did they rank as princes? "God chose the weak things of the world to confound the strong, and the foolish things He hath chosen, and things which are not as though they were, that things which are may be brought to nought."[9] This He doth who "from the ground raises the helpless, and from the dunghill exalts the poor."[10] For what purpose? "That He may set him with the princes, even with the princes of His people."[11] This is a mighty deed, a deep source of pleasure and exultation. Orators came later into that city, but they could

---

[1] Matt. xxi. 31.   [2] Matt. xi. 12.   [3] In fauce.
[4] Dilabitur, which would seem to mean the writer; al. derivatur, "there is a drawing off," i.e. of citizens.
[5] Ps. xlv. 10, 11.
[6] St. Augustin, Tertullian, and others read μήτηρ Σίων, for the reading of the LXX., μήτι.

[7] Or, "He who was made man in her," Qui homo factus est in ea.
[8] Et Principes is added in the text, but it has no equivalent in our version.
[9] 1 Cor. i. 26, 27.   [10] Ps. cxiii. 7.   [11] Ps. cxiii. 8.

never have done so, had not fishermen preceded them. These things are glorious indeed, but where could they take place, but in that city of God, of whom very excellent things are spoken?

8. So thus, after drawing together and mingling every source of joyous exultation, how doth he conclude? "The dwelling as of all that shall be made joyous is in Thee" (ver. 7). As if all made joyous, all rejoicing, shall dwell in that city. Amid our journeyings here we suffer bruises: our last home shall be the home of joy alone. Toil and groans shall perish: prayers pass away, hymns of praise succeed. There shall be the dwelling of the happy; no longer shall there be the groans of those that long, but the gladness of those who enjoy. For He will be present for whom we sigh: we shall be like Him, as we shall see Him as He is:[1] there it will be our whole task to praise and enjoy the presence of God: and what beyond shall we ask for, when He alone satisfies us, by whom all things were made? We shall dwell and be dwelt in; and shall be subject to Him, that God may be all in all.[2] "Blessed," then, "are they that dwell in Thy house." How blessed? Blessed in their gold, and silver, their numerous slaves, and multiplied offspring? "Blessed are they that dwell in Thy house: for ever and ever they will be praising Thee."[3] Blessed in that sole labour[4] which is rest! Let this then be the one and only object of our desire, my brethren, when we shall have reached this pass. Let us prepare ourselves to rejoice in God: to praise Him. The good works which conduct us thither, will not be needed there. I described, as far as I could, only yesterday,[5] our condition there: works of charity there will be none, where there will be no misery: thou shalt not find one in want, one naked, no one will meet you tormented with thirst, there will be no stranger, no sick to visit, no dead to bury, no disputants to set at peace. What then wilt thou find to do? Shall we plant new vines, plough, traffic, make voyages, to support the necessities of the body? Deep quiet shall be there; all toilsome work, that necessity demands, will cease: the necessity being dead, its works will perish too. What then will be our state? As far as possible, the tongue of a man thus told us. "As it were, the dwelling of all who shall be made perfect is in Thee."[6] Why does he say, "as it were '? Because there shall be such joy there as we know not here. Many pleasures do I behold here, and many rejoice in this world, some in one thing, others in another; but there is nothing to compare with that delight, but it shall be "as it were" being made joyful. For if I say joyfulness, men at once think of such

joyfulness as men use to have in wine, in feasting, in avarice, and in the world's distinctions. For men are elated by these things, and mad with a kind of joy: but "there is no joy, saith the Lord, unto the wicked."[7] There is a sort of joyfulness which the ear of man hath not heard, nor his eye seen, nor hath it entered into his heart to conceive.[8] "As it were, the dwelling of all who shall be made joyful is in Thee." Let us prepare for other delights: for a kind of shadow is what we find here, not the reality: that we may not expect to enjoy such things there as here we delight in: otherwise our self-denial will be avarice. Some persons, when invited to a rich banquet, where there are many and costly dishes yet to come on, abstain from breaking their fast: if you ask the reason, they tell you that they are fasting: which is indeed a great work, a Christian work. Yet be not hasty in praising them: examine their motives: it is their belly, not religion, that they are consulting. That their appetite may not be palled by ordinary dishes, they abstain till more delicate food is set before them. This fast then is for the gullet's sake. Fasting is undoubtedly important: it fights against the belly and the palate; but sometimes it fights for them. Thus, my brethren, if ye imagine that we shall find any such pleasures in that country to which the heavenly trumpet urges us on, and on that account abstain from present enjoyments, that ye may receive the like more plentifully there, ye imitate those I have described, who fast only for greater feasting, and abstain only for greater indulgence. Do not ye like this: prepare yourselves for a certain ineffable delight: cleanse your hearts from all earthly and secular affections. We shall see something, the sight of which will make us blessed: and that alone will suffice for us. What then? Shall we not eat? Yes: we shall eat: but that shall be our food, which will ever refresh, and never fail. "In Thee is the dwelling of all who shall be, as it were, made joyful." He has already told us how we shall be made joyful. "Blessed are they that dwell in thy house: for ever and ever they will be praising Thee."[3] Let us praise the Lord as far as we are able, but with mingled lamentations: for while we praise we long for Him, and as yet have Him not. When we have, all our sorrows will be taken from us, and nothing will remain but praise, unmixed and everlasting. Now let us pray.[9]

PSALM LXXXVIII.[10]

1. The Title of this eighty-seventh Psalm contains a fresh subject for enquiry: the words

---

[1] 1 John iii. 2.   [2] 1 Cor. xv. 28.   [3] Ps. lxxxiv. 4.
[4] *Otioso negotio.*   [5] On the former Psalm, p. 419, *supra.*
[6] *Tanquam jucundatorum omnium habitatio in te.*

[7] Isa. xlviii. 22.   [8] 1 Cor. ii. 9.
[9] *Conversi ad Dominum.* See p. 395, note 4, *supra.*
[10] Lat. LXXXVII. Dictated after the exposition of Ps. xlii. (see § 14), and perhaps after that of Ps. lxviii.

occurring here, " for Melech to respond," being nowhere else found. We have already given our opinion on the meaning of the titles *Psalmus Cantici* and *Canticum Psalmi :* [1] and the words, "sons of Core," are constantly repeated, and have often been explained : so also " to the end ; " but what comes next in this title is peculiar. For "Melech" we may translate into Latin " for the chorus," for chorus is the sense of the Hebrew word Melech.[2] . . . The Passion of our Lord is here prophesied. Now the Apostle Peter saith, " Christ also suffered for us, leaving us an example, that we should follow His steps ; " [3] this is the meaning of " to respond." The Apostle John also saith, " As Christ laid down His life for us, so ought we also to lay down our lives for the brethren ; " [4] this also is to respond. But the choir signifies concord, which consists in charity : whoever therefore in imitation of our Lord's Passion gives up his body to be burnt, if he have not charity, does not answer in the choir, and therefore it profiteth him nothing.[5] Further, as in Latin the terms Precentor and Succentor are used to denote in music the performer who sings the first part, and him who takes it up ; just so in this song of the Passion, Christ going before is followed by the choir of martyrs unto the end of gaining crowns in Heaven. This is sung by " the sons of Core," that is, the imitators of Christ's Passion : as Christ was crucified in Calvary, which is the interpretation of the Hebrew word Core.[6] This also is " the understanding of Æman the Israelite : " [7] words occurring at the end of this title. Æman is said to mean, " his brother : " for Christ deigns to make those His brethren, who understand the mystery of His Cross, and not only are not ashamed of it, but faithfully glory in it, not praising themselves for their own merits, but grateful for His grace : so that it may be said to each of them, " Behold an Israelite indeed, in whom there is no guile," [8] just as holy

Scripture says of Israel himself, that he was without guile.[9]

2. " O Lord God of my salvation, I have cried day and night before Thee " (ver. 1). Let us therefore now hear the voice of Christ singing before us in prophecy, to whom His own choir should respond either in imitation, or in thanksgiving.

" O let my prayer enter into Thy presence, incline Thine ear unto my calling" (ver. 2). For even our Lord prayed, not in the form of God, but in the form of a servant ; for in this He also suffered. He prayed both in prosperous times, that is, by " day," and in calamity, which I imagine is meant by " night." The entrance of prayer into God's presence is its acceptance : the inclination of His ear is His compassionate listening to it : for God has not such bodily members as we have. The passage is however, as usual, a repetition.[10]

3. " For my soul is filled with evils, and my life draweth nigh unto hell " (ver. 3). Dare we speak of the Soul of Christ as " filled with evils," when the passion had strength as far as it had any, only over the body? . . . The soul therefore may feel pain without the body : but without the soul the body cannot. Why therefore should we not say that the Soul of Christ was full of the evils of humanity, though not of human sins? Another Prophet says of Him, that He grieved for us : [11] and the Evangelist says, " And He took with Him Peter and the two sons of Zebedee, and began to be sorrowful and very heavy : " and our Lord Himself saith unto them of Himself, " My soul is exceeding sorrowful, even unto death." [12] The Prophet who composed this Psalm, foreseeing that this would happen, introduces Him saying, " My soul is full of evils, and My life draweth nigh unto hell." For the very same sense is here expressed in other words, as when He said, " My soul is sorrowful, even unto death." The words, " My soul is sorrowful," are like these, " My soul is full of evils : " and what follows, " even unto death," like, " my life draweth nigh unto hell." These feelings of human infirmity our Lord took upon Him, as He did the flesh of human infirmity, and the death of human flesh, not by the necessity of His condition, but by the free will of His mercy, that He might transfigure into Himself His own body, which is the Church (the head of which He deigned to be), that is, His members in His holy and faithful disciples : that if amid human temptations any one among them happened to be in sorrow and pain, he might not therefore think that he was separated from His favour :

---

[1] On Ps. xlvii. p. 160; also xlvi. p. 155, note 8.
[2] [The author here adds: " What other meaning then can we attach to the words, ' for the chorus to respond,' but this, that the choir is to make responses with the singer ? And thus we must suppose that not this only, but other Psalms were chanted, though they have received different titles, probably for the sake of variety to relieve weariness: for this Psalm was not the only one held worthy of choral responses, since it is not the only one which relates to our Lord's Passion. If indeed there is any other reason for so great a variety in the titles, by which it can be shown that all the Psalms which are distinguished in their titles are so marked, as that the title of no one of them can be fitted to another, I must confess that I could not discover it, though I tried long; and whatever I have read on the subject in the works of my predecessors has not satisfied my hopes, or, perhaps, my slowness of apprehension. I will therefore explain in allusion to what mystery the words, ' for the choir to respond,' that is, that the singer should be answered by a choir, seem to me to be used."—C.]
[3] 1 Pet. ii. 21.   [4] 1 John iii. 16.
[5] 1 Cor. xiii. 3.
[6] Matt. xxvii. 33.
[7] *Israelitæ*, vulg. *Ezrahitæ*. See also the title of the next Psalm. Ben. conjectures it may be for *Zaraite*, as Ethan and Heman are called sons of Zara, 1 Chron. ii. 6, and in 1 Kings iv. 31, where Solomon is said to be " wiser than Ethan the Ezrahite and Heman." LXX. has *Zarite*.
[8] John i. 47.

[9] Gen. xxv. 27.
[10] The words, " O let my prayer enter into Thy presence," being equivalent to, " Incline Thine ear unto my calling."
[11] Isa. liii. 4.   [12] Matt. xxvi. 37, 38.

that the body, like the chorus following its leader, might learn from its Head, that these sorrows were not sin, but proofs of human weakness. We read of the Apostle Paul, a chief member in this body, and we hear him confessing that his soul was full of such evils, when he says, that he feels "great heaviness and continual sorrow in heart for his brethren according to the flesh, who are Israelites."[1] And if we say that our Lord was sorrowful for them also at the approach of His Passion, in which they would incur the most atrocious guilt, I think we shall not speak amiss. Lastly, the very thihg said by our Saviour on the Cross, "Father, forgive them, for they know not what they do,"[2] is expressed in this Psalm below, "I am counted as one of them that go down into the pit" (ver. 4): by them who knew not what they were doing, when they imagined that He died like other men, subjected to necessity, and overcome by it. The word "pit" is used for the depth of woe or of Hell. "I have been as a man that hath no help."

4. "Free among the dead" (ver. 5). In these words our Lord's Person is most clearly shown: for who else is free among the dead but He who though in the likeness of sinful flesh is alone among sinners without sin?[3] . . . He therefore, "free among the dead," who had it in His power to lay down His life, and again to take it; from whom no one could take it, but He laid it down of His own free will; who could revive His own flesh, as a temple destroyed by them, at His will; who, when all had forsaken Him on the eve of His Passion, remained not alone, because, as He testifies, His Father forsook Him not;[4] was nevertheless by His enemies, for whom He prayed, who knew not what they did, . . . counted "as one who hath no help; like unto them that are wounded, and lie in the grave." But he adds, "Whom thou dost not yet remember:" and in these words there is to be remarked a distinction between Christ and the rest of the dead. For though He was wounded, and when dead laid in the tomb,[5] yet they who knew not what they were doing, or who He was, regarded Him as like others who had perished from their wounds, and who slept in the tomb, who are as yet out of remembrance of God, that is, whose hour of resurrection has not yet arrived. For thus the Scripture speaks of the dead as sleeping, because it wishes them to be regarded as destined to awake, that is, to rise again. But He, wounded and asleep in the tomb, awoke on the third day, and became "like a sparrow that sitteth alone on the housetop,"[6] that is, on the right hand of His Father in Heaven: and now "dieth no more, death shall

no more have dominion over Him."[7] Hence He differs widely from those whom God hath not yet remembered to cause their resurrection after this manner: for what was to go before in the Head, was kept for the Body in the end. God is then said to remember, when He does an act: then to forget, when He does it not: for neither can God forget, as He never changes, nor remember, as He can never forget. "I am counted" then, by those who know not what they do, "as a man that hath no help:" while I am "free among the dead," I am held by these men "like unto them that are wounded, and lie in the grave." Yet those very men, who account thus of Me, are further said to be "cut away from Thy hand," that is, when I was made so by them, "they were cut away from Thy hand;" they who believed Me destitute of help, are deprived of the help of Thy hand: for they, as he saith in another Psalm,[8] have digged a pit before me, and are fallen into the midst of it themselves. I prefer this interpretation to that which refers the words, "they are cut away from Thy hand," to those who sleep in the tomb, whom God hath not yet remembered: since the righteous are among the latter, of whom, even though God hath not yet called them to the resurrection, it is said, that their "souls are in the hands of God,"[9] that is, that "they dwell under the defence of the Most High; and shall abide under the shadow of the God of Heaven."[10] But it is those who are cut away from the hand of God, who believed that Christ was cut off from His hand, and thus accounting Him among the wicked, dared to slay Him.

5. "They laid Me in the lowest pit" (ver. 6), that is, the deepest pit. For so it is in the Greek. But what is the lowest pit, but the deepest woe, than which there is none more deep? Whence in another Psalm it is said, "Thou broughtest me out also of the pit of misery."[11] "In a place of darkness, and in the shadow of death," whiles they knew not what they did, they laid Him there, thus deeming of Him; they knew not Him "whom none of the princes of this world knew."[12] By the "shadow of death," I know not whether the death of the body is to be understood, or that of which it is written, "That they walked in darkness and in the land of the shadow of death, a light is risen on them,"[13] because by belief they were brought from out of the darkness and death of sin into light and life. Such an one those who knew not what they did thought our Lord, and in their ignorance accounted Him among those whom He came to help, that they might not be such themselves.

---

[1] Rom. ix. 2, 4.　　[2] Luke xxiii. 34.　　[3] Rom. viii. 3.
[4] John viii. 29.　　[5] Matt. xxvii. 50, 60.
[6] Ps. cii. 7.

[7] Rom. vi. 9.　　　[8] Ps. lvii. 7.　　　[9] Wisd. iii. 1.
[10] Ps. xci. 1. [Noteworthy as the author's view of the state of the faithful departed. — C.]
[11] Ps. xl. 3.　　[12] 1 Cor. ii. 8.　　[13] Isa. ix. 2.

6. " Thy indignation lieth hard upon Me " (ver. 7), or, as other copies have it, " Thy anger ; " or, as others, " Thy fury : " the Greek word θυμὸς having undergone different interpretations. For where the Greek copies have ὀργὴ, no translator hesitated to express it by the Latin *ira ;* but where the word is θυμὸς, most object to rendering it by *ira*, although many of the authors of the best Latin style, in their translations from Greek philosophy, have thus rendered the word in Latin. But I shall not discuss this matter further : only if I also were to suggest another term, I should think " indignation " more tolerable than " fury," this word in Latin not being applied to persons in their senses. What then does this mean, " Thy indignation lieth hard upon Me," except the belief of those, who knew not the Lord of Glory ? [1] who imagined that the anger of God was not merely roused, but lay hard upon Him, whom they dared to bring to death, and not only death, but that kind, which they regarded as the most execrable of all, namely, the death of the Cross : whence saith the Apostle, " Christ hath redeemed us from the curse of the Law, being made a curse for us : for it is written, Cursed is every one that hangeth upon a tree." [2] On this account, wishing to praise His obedience which He carried to the extreme of humility, he says, " He humbled Himself, and became obedient unto death ; " and as this seemed little, he added, " even the death of the Cross ; " [3] and with the same view, as far as I can see, he says in this Psalm, " And all thy suspensions," or, as some translate " waves," others " tossings," " Thou hast brought over Me." We also find in another Psalm, " All thy suspensions and waves are come in upon Me," [4] or, as some have translated better, " have passed over Me : " for it is δῆλθον in Greek, not εἰσῆλθον : and where both expressions are employed, " waves " and " suspensions," one cannot be used as equivalent to the other. In that passage we explained " suspensions " as threatenings, " waves " as the actual sufferings : both inflicted by God's judgment : but in that place it is said, " All have passed over Me," here, " Thou hast brought all upon Me." In the other case, that is, although some evils took place, yet, he said, all those which are here mentioned passed over ; but in this case, " Thou hast brought them upon Me." Evils pass over when they do not touch a man, as things which hang over him, or when they do touch him, as waves. But when he uses the word " suspensions," he does not say they passed over, but, " Thou hast brought them upon Me," meaning that all which impended had come to pass. All things which were predicted of His Passion impended, as long as they remained in the prophecies for future fulfilment.

7. " Thou hast put Mine acquaintance far from Me " (ver. 8). If we understand by acquaintance those whom He knew, it will be all men ; for whom knew He not ? But He calls those acquaintance, to whom He was Himself known, as far as they could know Him at that season : at least so far forth as they knew Him to be innocent, although they considered Him only as a man, not as likewise God. Although He might call the righteous whom He approved, acquaintance, as He calls the wicked unknown, to whom He was to say at the end, " I know you not." [5] In what follows, " and they have set Me for an abhorrence to themselves ; " those whom He called before " acquaintance," may be meant, as even they felt horror at the mode of that death : but it is better referred to those of whom He was speaking above as His persecutors. " I was delivered up, and did not get forth." Is this because His disciples were without, while He was being tried within ? [6] Or are we to give a deeper meaning to the words, " I cannot get forth " as signifying, " I remained hidden in My secret counsels, I showed not who I was, I did not reveal Myself, was not made manifest " ? And so it follows, —

" My eyes became weak from want " (ver. 9). For what eyes are we to understand ? If the eyes of the flesh in which He suffered, we do not read that His eyes became weak from want, that is, from hunger, in His Passion, as is often the case ; as He was betrayed after His Supper, and crucified on the same day : if the inner eyes, how were they weakened from want, in which there was a light that could never fail ? But He meant by His eyes those members in the body, of which He was Himself the head, which, as brighter and more eminent and chief above the rest, He loved. It was of this body that the Apostle was speaking, when he wrote, taking his metaphor from our own body, " If the whole body were an eye, where were the hearing ? " etc. [7] What he wished understood by these words, he has expressed more clearly, by adding, " Now ye are the body of Christ, and members in particular." [8] Wherefore as those eyes, that is, the holy Apostles, to whom not flesh and blood, but the Father which is in Heaven had revealed Him, so that Peter said, " Thou art Christ, the Son of the Living God," [9] when they saw Him betrayed, and suffering such evils, saw Him not such as they wished, as He did not come forth, did not manifest Himself in His virtue and power, but still hidden in His secrecy, [10] endured everything as a man overcome and enfeebled,

---

[1] 1 Cor. ii. 8.　　　　[2] Gal. iii. 13.
[3] Phil. ii. 8.　　　　[4] Ps. xlii. 7.

[5] Matt. vii. 23.　　[6] Matt. xxvi. 56.　　[7] 1 Cor. xii. 17–21.
[8] 1 Cor. xii. 27.　　[9] Matt. xvi. 16.
[10] *In suis interioribus.*

they became weak for want, as if their food, their Light, had been withdrawn from them.

8. He continues, "And I have called upon Thee." This indeed He did most clearly, when upon the Cross. But what follows? "All the day I have stretched forth My hands unto Thee," must be examined how it must be taken. For if in this expression we understand the tree of the Cross, how can we reconcile it with the "whole day"? Can He be said to have hung upon the Cross during the whole day, as the night is considered a part of the day? But if day, as opposed to night, was meant by this expression, even of this day, the first and no small portion had passed by at the time of His crucifixion. But if we take "day" in the same sense of time (especially as the word is used in the feminine, a gender which is restricted to that sense in Latin, although not so in Greek, as it is always used in the feminine, which I suppose to be the reason for its translation in the same gender in our own version), the knot of the question will be drawn tighter: for how can it mean for the whole space of time, if He did not even for one day stretch forth His hands on the Cross? Further, should we take the whole for a part, as Scripture sometimes uses this expression, I do not remember an instance in which the whole is taken for a part, when the word "whole" is expressly added. For in the passage of the Gospel where the Lord saith, "The Son of Man shall be three days and three nights in the heart of the earth,"[1] it is no extraordinary licence to take the whole for the part, the expression not being for three "whole" days and three whole nights: since the one intermediate day was a whole one, the other two were parts, the last being part of the first day, the first part of the last. But if the Cross is not meant here, but the prayer, which we find in the Gospel that He poured forth in the form of a servant to God the Father, where He is said to have prayed long before His Passion, and on the eve of His Passion, and also when on the Cross, we do not read anywhere that He did so throughout the whole day. Therefore by the stretched-out hands throughout the whole day, we may understand the continuation of good works in which He never ceased from exertion.

9. But as His good works profited only the predestined to eternal salvation, and not all men, nor even all those among whom they were done, he adds, "Dost thou show wonders among the dead?" (ver. 10). If we suppose this relates to those whose flesh life has left, great wonders have been wrought among the dead, inasmuch as some of them have revived:[2] and in our Lord's descent into Hell, and His ascent as the conqueror of death, a great wonder

was wrought among the dead. He refers then in these words, "Dost Thou show wonders among the dead?" to men so dead in heart, that such great works of Christ could not rouse them to the life of faith: for he does not say that wonders are not shown to them because they see them not, but because they do not profit them. For, as he says in this passage, "the whole day have I stretched forth My hands to Thee:" because He ever refers all His works to the will of His Father, constantly declaring that He came to fulfil His Father's will:[3] so also, as an unbelieving people saw the same works, another Prophet saith, "I have spread out my hands all day unto a rebellious people, that believes not, but contradicts."[4] Those then are dead, to whom wonders have not been shown, not because they saw them not, but since they lived not again through them. The following verse, "Shall physicians revive them, and shall they praise Thee?" means, that the dead shall not be revived by such means, that they may praise Thee. In the Hebrew there is said to be a different expression: giants being used where physicians are here: but the Septuagint translators, whose authority is such that they may deservedly be said to have interpreted by the inspiration of the Spirit of God owing to their wonderful agreement, conclude, not by mistake, but taking occasion from the resemblance in sound between the Hebrew words expressing these two senses, that the use of the word is an indication of the sense in which the word giants is meant to be taken. For if you suppose the proud meant by giants, of whom the Apostle saith, "Where is the wise? where is the scribe? where is the disputer of this world?"[5] there is no incongruity in calling them physicians, as if by their own unaided skill they promised the salvation of souls: against whom it is said, "Of the Lord is safety."[6] But if we take the word giant in a good sense, as it is said of our Lord, "He rejoiceth as a giant to run his course;"[7] that is Giant of giants, chief among the greatest and strongest, who in His Church excel in spiritual strength. Just as He is the Mountain of mountains; as it is written, "And it shall come to pass in the last days, that the mountain of the Lord's house shall be manifested in the top of the mountains:"[8] and the Saint of saints: there is no absurdity in styling these same great and mighty men physicians. Whence saith the Apostle, "if by any means I may provoke to emulation them which are my flesh, and might save some of them."[9] But even such physicians, even though they cure not by their own power (as not even of their

[1] Matt. xii. 40.　　[2] Matt. xxvii. 52.

[3] John vi. 38.　　[4] Isa. lxv. 2.　　[5] 1 Cor. i. 20.
[6] Ps. iv. 8.　　[7] Ps. xix. 5.　　[8] Isa. ii. 2.
[9] Rom. xi. 14.

own do those of the body), yet so far forth as by faithful ministry they assist towards salvation, can cure the living, but not raise the dead : of whom it is said, " Dost Thou show wonders among the dead?" For the grace of God, by which men's minds in a certain manner are brought to live a fresh life, so as to be able to hear the lessons of salvation from any of its ministers whatever, is most hidden and mysterious. This grace is thus spoken of in the Gospel. " No man can come to Me, except the Father which hath sent Me draw him;"[1] . . . in order to show, that the very faith by which the soul believes, and springs into fresh life from the death of its former affections, is given us by God. Whatever exertions, then, the best preachers of the word,[2] and persuaders of the truth through miracles, may make with men, just like great physicians : yet if they are dead, and through Thy grace have not a second life, " Dost Thou show wonders among the dead, or shall physicians raise them? and shall they " whom they raise " praise Thee "? For this confession declares that they live : not, as it is written elsewhere, " Thanksgiving perisheth from the dead, as from one that is not."[3]

10. " Shall one show Thy loving-kindness in the grave, or Thy faithfulness in destruction?" (ver. 11). The word " show " is of course understood as if repeated, Shall any show Thy faithfulness in destruction? Scripture loves to connect loving-kindness and faithfulness, especially in the Psalms. " Destruction " also is a repetition of " the grave," and signifies them who are in the grave, styled above " the dead," in the verse, " Dost thou show wonders among the dead?" for the body is the grave of the dead soul; whence our Lord's words in the Gospel, " Ye are like unto whited sepulchres, which indeed appear beautiful outward, but within are full of dead men's bones, and of all uncleanness. Even so ye outwardly appear righteous unto men, but within ye are full of hypocrisy and iniquity."[4]

11. " Shall thy wondrous works be known in the dark, and thy righteousness in the land where all things are forgotten?" (ver. 12), the dark answers to the land of forgetfulness : for the unbelieving are meant by the dark, as the Apostle saith, " For ye were sometimes darkness;"[5] and the land where all things are forgotten, is the man who has forgotten God; for the unbelieving soul can arrive at darkness so intense, " that the fool saith in his heart, There is no God."[6] Thus the meaning of the whole passage may thus be drawn out in its connection : " Lord, I have called upon Thee,"

amid My sufferings; " all day I have stretched forth my hands unto Thee " (ver. 13). I have never ceased to stretch forth My works to glorify, Thee. Why then do the wicked rage against Me, unless because " Thou showest not wonders among the dead"? because those wonders move them not to faith, nor can physicians restore them to life that they may praise Thee, because Thy hidden grace works not in them to draw them unto believing : because no man cometh unto Me, but whom Thou hast drawn. Shall then " Thy loving-kindness be showed in the grave "? that is, the grave of the dead soul, which lies dead beneath the body's weight : " or Thy faithfulness in destruction "? that is, in such a death as cannot believe or feel any of these things. " For how then in the darkness " of this death, that is, in the man who in forgetting Thee has lost the light of his life, " shall Thy wondrous works and Thy righteousness be known." . . .

12. But that those prayers, the blessings of which surpass all words, may be more fervent and more constant, the gift that shall last unto eternity is deferred, while transitory evils are allowed to thicken. And so it follows : " Lord, why hast Thou cast off my prayer?" (ver. 14), which may be compared with another Psalm :[7] " My God, My God, look upon me ; why hast Thou forsaken me?" The reason is made matter of question, not as if the wisdom of God were blamed as doing so without a cause ; and so here. " Lord, why hast Thou cast off my prayer?" But if this cause be attended to carefully, it will be found indicated above ; for it is with the view that the prayers of the Saints are, as it were, repelled by the delay of so great a blessing, and by the adversity they encounter in the troubles of life, that the flame, thus fanned, may burst into a brighter blaze.

13. For this purpose he briefly sketches in what follows the troubles of Christ's body. For it is not in the Head alone that they took place, since it is said to Saul too, " Why persecutest thou Me?"[8] and Paul himself, as if placed as an elect member in the same body, saith, " That I may fill up that which is behind of the afflictions of Christ in my flesh."[9] " Why then, Lord, hast Thou cast off my soul? why hidest Thou Thy face from me?"

" I am poor, and in toils from my youth up : and when lifted up, I was thrown down, and troubled " (ver. 15).

" Thy wraths went over me : Thy terrors disturbed me " (ver. 16).

" They came round about me all day like water : they compassed me about together " (ver. 17).

---

[1] John vi. 44.
[2] Ben. refers to P. Lombard, 4 Sent. Dist. 18, Hic quæritur.
[3] Ecclus. xvii. 26.　　[4] Matt. xxiii. 27, 28.
[5] Eph v. 8.　　[6] Ps. xiv. 1.

[7] Ps. xxii. 1.　　[8] Acts ix. 4.　　[9] Col. i. 24.

"A friend Thou hast put far from me : and mine acquaintance from my misery " (ver. 18). All these evils have taken place, and are happening in the limbs of Christ's body, and God turns away His face from their prayers, by not hearing as to what they wish for, since they know not that the fulfilment of their wishes would not be good for them. The Church is "poor," as she hungers and thirsts in her wanderings for that food with which she shall be filled in her own country : she is " in toils from her youth up," as the very Body of Christ saith in another Psalm, " Many a time have they overcome me from my youth." [1] And for this reason some of her members are lifted up even in this world, that in them may be the greater lowliness. Over that Body, which constitutes the unity of the Saints and the faithful, whose Head is Christ, go the wraths of God : yet abide not : since it is of the unbelieving only that it is written, that "the wrath of God abideth upon him." [2] The terrors of God disturb the weakness of the faithful, because all that can happen, even though it actually happen not, it is prudent to fear ; and sometimes these terrors so agitate the reflecting soul with the evils impending around, that they seem to flow around us on every side like water, and to encircle us in our fears. And as the Church while on pilgrimage is never free from these evils, happening as they do at one moment in one of her limbs, at another in another, he adds, "all day," signifying the continuation in time, to the end of this world. Often too, friends and acquaintances, their worldly interests at stake, in their terror forsake the Saints ; of which saith the Apostle, "all men forsook me : may it not be laid to their charge." [3] But to what purpose is all this, but that early in the morning, that is, after the night of unbelief, the prayers of this holy Body may in the light of faith prevent God, until the coming of that salvation, which we are at present saved by hoping for, not by having, while we await it with patience and faithfulness. Then the Lord will not repel our prayers, as there will no longer be anything to be sought for, but everything that has been rightly asked, will be obtained : nor will He turn His face away from us, since we shall see Him as He is : [4] nor shall we be poor, because God will be our abundance, all in all : [5] nor shall we suffer, as there will be no more weakness : nor after exaltation shall we meet with humiliation and confusion, as there will be no adversity there : nor bear even the transient wrath of God, as we shall abide in His abiding love : nor will His terrors agitate us, because His promises realized will bless us : nor

will our friend and acquaintance, being terrified, be far from us, where there will be no foe to dread.

PSALM LXXXIX.[6]

1. Understand, beloved, this Psalm, which I am about to explain, by the grace of God, of our hope in the Lord Jesus Christ, and be of good cheer, because He who promised, will fulfil all, as He has fulfilled much : for it is not our own merit, but His mercy, that gives us confidence in Him. He Himself is meant, in my belief, by " the understanding of Æthan the Israelite : " [7] which has given this Psalm its title. You see then, who is meant by Æthan : but the meaning of the word is " strong." No man in this world is strong, except in the hope of God's promises : for as to our own deservings, we are weak, in His mercy we are strong. Weak then in himself, strong in God's mercy, the Psalmist thus begins : " I will sing of Thy mercies, O Lord, for ever : with my mouth will I make known Thy truth unto all generations " (ver. 1).

2. Let my limbs, he saith, serve the Lord : I speak, but it is of Thine I speak. "With my mouth will I make known Thy truth : " if I obey not Thee, I am not Thy servant : if I speak on my own part, I am a liar. To speak then from Thee,[8] and in my own person, are two things : one mine, one Thine : Truth Thine, language mine. Let us hear then what faithfulness he maketh known, what mercies he singeth.

3. " For Thou hast said, Mercy shall be built up for ever " (ver. 2). It is this that I sing : this is Thy truth, for the making known of which my mouth serveth. In such wise Thou sayest, I build, as not to destroy : for some Thou destroyest and buildest not ; and some whom Thou destroyest Thou dost rebuild. For unless there were some who were destroyed to be rebuilt, Jeremiah would not have written, " See, I have this day set thee to throw down and to build." [9] And indeed all who formerly worshipped images and stones could not be built up in Christ, without being destroyed as to their old error. While, unless some were destroyed not to be built up, it would not be written, " He shall destroy them, and not build them up." [10] . . . In what follows, he joins these two words, mercy and faithfulness ; " For Thou hast said, Mercy shall be built up for ever : Thy truth shall be established in the Heavens : " in which mercy and truth are repeated, " for all the ways of the Lord are mercy and truth," [11] for truth in the fulfilment of promises could not be shown, unless mercy in the remission of sins preceded. Next, as many

---

[6] Lat. LXXXVIII. Delivered in the morning, on the festival of some Martyrs.
[7] See note on title of Ps. lxxxviii.
[8] Abs Te.

[1] Ps. cxxix. 1.   [2] John iii. 36.   [3] 2 Tim. iv. 16.
[4] 1 John iii. 2.   [5] 1 Cor. xv. 28.   [9] Jer. i. 10.   [10] Ps. xxviii. 5.   [11] Ps. xxv. 10.

things were promised in prophecy even to the people of Israel that came according to the flesh from the seed of Abraham, and that people was increased that the promises of God might be fulfilled in it; while yet God did not close the fountain of His goodness even to the Gentiles, whom He had placed under the rule of the Angels, while He reserved the people of Israel as His own portion: the Apostle expressly mentions the Lord's mercy and truth as referring to these two parties. For he calls Christ "a minister of the Circumcision for the truth of God, to confirm the promises made unto the fathers." [1] See how God deceived not; see how He cast not off His people, whom He foreknew. For while the Apostle is treating of the fall of the Jews, to prevent any from believing them so far disowned [2] of God, that no wheat from that floor's fanning could reach the granary, he saith, "God hath not cast away His people, whom He foreknew; for I also am an Israelite." [3] If all that nation are thorns, how am I who speak unto you wheat? So that the truth of God was fulfilled in those Israelites who believed, and one wall from the circumcision is thus brought to meet the corner stone. But this stone would not form a corner, unless it received another wall from the Gentiles: so that the former wall relates in a special manner to the truth, the latter to the mercy of God. "Now I say," says the Apostle, "that Jesus Christ was a minister of the Circumcision for the truth of God, to confirm the promise made unto the fathers: and that the Gentiles might glorify God for His mercy." [4] Justly then is it added, "Thy truth shalt Thou stablish in the Heavens:" for all those Israelites who were called to be Apostles became as Heavens which declare the glory of God: as it is written by them, "The Heavens declare the glory of God, and the firmament showeth His handywork." [5] . . . Since, although they were taken up from hence before the Church filled the whole world, yet as "their words reached to the ends of the world," we are right in supposing this which we have just read, "Thy truth shalt Thou stablish in the Heavens," fulfilled in them.

4. "Thou hast said, I have made a covenant with My chosen" (ver. 3). What covenant, but the new, by which we are renewed to a fresh inheritance, in our longing desire and love of which we sing a new song. "I have made a covenant with My chosen," saith the Psalmist: "I have sworn unto David My servant." How confidently does he speak, who understands, whose mouth serves truth! I speak without fear; since "Thou hast said." If Thou makest me fearless, because Thou hast said, how much more so dost Thou make me, when Thou hast

sworn! For the oath of God is the assurance of a promise. Man is justly forbidden to swear: [6] lest by the habit of swearing, since a man may be deceived, he fall into perjury. God alone swears securely, because He alone is infallible.

5. Let us see then what God hath sworn. "I have sworn," He saith, "to David My servant; thy seed will I establish for ever" (ver. 4). But what is the seed of David, but that of Abraham. And what is the seed of Abraham? "And to thy seed," He saith, "which is Christ." [7] But perhaps that Christ, the Head of the Church, the Saviour of the body, [8] is the seed of Abraham, and therefore of David; but we are not Abraham's seed? We are assuredly; as the Apostle saith, "And if ye be Christ's, then are ye Abraham's seed, and heirs according to the promise." [9] In this sense, then, let us take the words, brethren, "Thy seed will I stablish for ever," not only of that Flesh of Christ, born of the Virgin Mary, but also of all of us who believe in Christ, for we are limbs of that Head. This body cannot be deprived of its Head: if the Head is in glory for ever, so are the limbs, so that Christ remains entire for ever. "Thy seed will I stablish for ever: and set up thy throne to generation and generation." We suppose he saith, "for ever," because it is "to generation and generation:" since he has said above, with "my mouth will I ever be showing Thy truth to generation and generation." What is "to generation and generation"? To every generation: for the word needed not as many repetitions, as the coming and passing away of the several generations. The multiplication of generations is signified and set forth to notice by the repetition. Are possibly two generations to be understood, as ye are aware, my beloved brethren, and as I have before explained? for there is now a generation of flesh and blood: there will be a future generation in the resurrection of the dead. Christ is proclaimed here: He will be proclaimed [10] there: here He is proclaimed, that He may be believed in: there, He will be welcomed, that He may be seen. "I will set up Thy throne from one generation to another." Christ hath now a throne in us, His throne is set up in us: for unless he sate enthroned within us, He would not rule us: but if we were not ruled by Him, we should be thrown down by ourselves. He therefore sits within us, reigning over us: He sits also in another generation, which will come from the resurrection of the dead. Christ will reign for ever over His Saints. God has promised this; He hath said it: if this is not enough, God hath sworn it. As then the promise is certain, not on account of our deserv-

---

[1] Rom. xv. 8.　　[2] *Improbatos.*　　[3] Rom. xi. 1, 2.
[4] Rom. xv. 8, 9.　　[5] Ps. xix. 1.
[6] Matt. v. 34.　　[7] Gal. iii. 16.
[8] Eph. v. 23.　　[9] Gal. iii. 29.
[10] Oxf. MSS. "He is proclaimed;" and so again below.

ings, but of His pity, no one ought to be afraid in proclaiming that which he cannot doubt of. Let that strength then inspire our hearts, whence Æthan received his name, "strong in heart:" let us preach the truth of God, the utterance of God, His promises, His oath; and let us, strengthened on every side by these means, glorify God, and by bearing Him along with us, become Heavens.

6. "O Lord, the very Heavens shall praise Thy wondrous works" (ver. 5). The Heavens will not praise their own merits, but Thy wondrous works, O Lord. For in every act of mercy on the lost, of justification of the unrighteous, what do we praise but the wondrous works of God? Thou praisest Him, because the dead have risen: praise Him yet more, because the lost are redeemed. What grace, what mercy of God! Thou seest a man yesterday a whirlpool of drunkenness, to-day an ornament of sobriety: a man yesterday the sink of luxury, to-day the beauty of temperance: yesterday a blasphemer of God, to-day His praiser: yesterday the slave of the creature, to-day the worshipper of the Creator. From all these desperate states men are thus converted: let them not look at their own merits: let them become Heavens, and praise the wondrous works of Him by whom they were made Heavens. . . .

7. "For who is he among the clouds, who shall be compared unto Thee, Lord!" (ver. 6). Is this to be the praise of the Heavens, is this to be their rain? What? are the preachers confident, because "none among the clouds shall be compared unto the Lord"? Does it appear to you, brethren, a high ground of praise, that the clouds cannot be compared with their Creator? If it is taken in its literal, not in its mystical meaning, it is not so: what? are the stars that are above the clouds to be compared with the Lord? what? can the Sun, Moon, Angels, Heavens, be even compared with the Lord? Why is it then that he says, as if he meant some high praise, "For who is he among the clouds?" etc. We understand, my brethren, those clouds, as the Heavens, to be the preachers of truth; Prophets, Apostles, the announcers of the word of God. . . . If therefore the clouds are the preachers of the truth, let us first enquire why they are clouds. For the same men are Heavens and clouds: Heavens from the brightness of the truth, clouds from the hidden things of the flesh: for all clouds are obscure, owing to their mortality: and they come and go. It is on account of these very obscurities of the flesh, that is, of the clouds, that the Apostle saith, "Therefore judge nothing before the time, until the Lord come, who will bring to light the hidden things of darkness."[1] You see at this

moment what a man is saying: but what he has in his heart, you cannot see: what is forced from the cloud, you see, what is kept within the cloud, you see not. For whose eyes pierce the cloud? The clouds therefore are the preachers of the truth in the flesh. The Creator of all things Himself came in the flesh. . . . We are called clouds on account of the flesh, and we are preachers of the truth on account of the showers of the clouds: but our flesh comes in one way, His by another. We too are called sons of God, but He is the Son of God in another sense. His cloud comes from a Virgin, He is the Son from eternity, co-eternal[2] with the Father. "Who is he then among the clouds, that shall be compared unto the Lord? and what is he among the sons of God, that shall be like unto the Lord?" Let the Lord Himself say whether He can find one like unto Himself. "Whom do men say that I the Son of Man am?" Because I appear, because I am seen, because I walk among you, and perhaps at present I am become common; say, whom do men say that I the Son of Man am? Surely when they see a son of man, they see a cloud; but say, "Whom do men say that I am?" In answer they gave Him the reports of men; "Some say that Thou art John the Baptist: some Elias, and others Jeremias, or one of the prophets." Many clouds and sons of God are here mentioned: for because they were righteous and holy, as the sons of God, Jeremias, Elias, and John are called also sons of God: in their character of preachers of God, they are styled clouds. Ye have said what clouds men imagine Me to be: do ye too say, "Whom say ye that I am?" Peter replying in behalf of all, one for those who were one,[3] answered, "Thou art the Christ, the Son of the living God;"[4] not like those sons of God who are not made equal to Thee: Thou hast come in the flesh: but not as the clouds, who are not to be compared unto Thee.

8. . . . "God is very greatly to be feared in the counsel of the righteous, and to be had in dread of all them that are round about Him" (ver. 7). God is everywhere; who therefore are round about Him, who is everywhere? For if He has some round about Him, He is represented as finite on every side. Moreover, if it is truly said to God[5] and of God, "of His greatness there is no end;"[6] who remain, who are round about Him, except because He who is everywhere, chose to be born of the flesh on one spot, to dwell among one nation, in one place to be crucified, from one spot to rise again and ascend into Heaven. Where He did this, the Gentiles are round about Him. If He remained

---

[1] 1 Cor. iv. 5.

[2] *Æqualis.*   [3] *Pro unitate unus.*   [4] Matt. xvi. 13–16.
[5] Oxf. mss. "by God."   [6] Ps. cxlv. 3.

where He did these things, He would not be "great, and be had in dread of all them that are round about Him;" but since He preached when there in such a manner as to send preachers of His own name through all nations over the whole world; by working miracles among His servants, He is become "great, and to be had in dread of all them that are round about Him."

9. "O Lord God of Hosts, who is like unto Thee? Thy truth, most mighty Lord, is on every side" (ver. 8). Great is Thy power: Thou hast made Heaven and earth, and all things that in them are: but greater still is thy loving-kindness, which has shown forth Thy truth to all around Thee. For if Thou hadst been preached only on the spot where Thou didst deign to be born, to suffer, to rise again, to ascend; the truth of that promise of God would have been fulfilled, to confirm the promises made unto the fathers: but the promise, "that the Gentiles may glorify God for His mercy,"[1] would not have been fulfilled, had not that truth been explained, and diffused to those around Thee from the spot where Thou didst deign to appear. On that spot Thou didst thunder out of Thy own cloud: but to scatter rain upon the Gentiles round about, Thou hast sent other clouds. Truly in Thy power hast Thou fulfilled what Thou hast said, "Hereafter shall ye see the Son of Man sitting on the right hand of power, and coming in the clouds of Heaven."[2]

10. . . . For ye have heard, like men accustomed to the watering of the clouds of God, "Thy truth" then "is in the circuit of Thee." But when without persecutions, when without opposition, since it is said, that "He was born for a sign which shall be spoken against"?[3] Since then that nation, where Thou didst deign to be born, and to dwell, was as a land separated from the waves of the heathen, so that it appeared dry and ready for watering with rain, while the rest of the nations were as a sea in the bitterness of their sterility; what do Thy preachers who scatter Thy truth in circuit of Thee, when the waves of that sea rage furiously? "Thou rulest the power of the sea" (ver. 9). For what was the result of the sea raging thus, but the day which we are now keeping holy? It slew Martyrs, scattered seeds of blood, the harvest of the Church sprang up. Safely then let the clouds go forth: let them diffuse Thy truth in circuit of Thee, let them not fear the savage waves. "Thou rulest the power of the sea." The sea swells, buffets, and roars: but "God is faithful, who will not suffer you to be tempted beyond what ye are able:"[4] and so, "Thou stillest the waves thereof when they rise."

11. Lastly, what hast Thou done in the sea itself, to pacify its rage, and to weaken it? "Thou hast humbled the proud[5] as one that is wounded" (ver. 10). There is a certain proud serpent in the sea, of which another passage of Scripture speaks, "I will command the serpent, and he shall bite him;"[6] and again, "There is that Leviathan, whom Thou hast made to mock him,"[7] whose head He bruises above the water. "Thou," he says, "hast humbled the proud, as one that is wounded." Thou hast humbled Thyself, and the proud was humbled: for the proud held the proud ones through pride: but the great One is humbled, and by believing in Him become small. While the little one is nourished by the example of One who from greatness descended to humility, the devil has lost what he held: because the proud held only the proud. When such an example of humility was displayed before them, men learned to condemn their own pride, and to imitate the humility of God. Thus also the devil, by losing those whom he had in his power, has even himself been humbled; not chastened, but thrown prostrate. "Thou hast humbled the proud like one that is wounded." Thou hast been humbled, and hast humbled others: Thou hast been wounded, and hast wounded others: for Thy blood, as it was shed to blot the handwriting of sins,[8] could not but wound him. For what was the ground of his pride, except the bond which he held against us. This bond, this handwriting, Thou hast blotted out with Thy blood: him therefore hast Thou wounded, from whom Thou hast rescued so many victims. You must understand the devil wounded, not by the piercing of the flesh, which he has not, but by the bruising of his proud heart. "Thou hast scattered Thine enemies abroad with Thy mighty arm."

12. "The heavens are thine, the earth also is Thine" (ver. 11). From Thee, over Thy earth they rain. Thine are the heavens, by whom is preached Thy truth in circuit of Thee; "Thine is the earth," which has received Thy truth in circuit of Thee; and what has resulted from that rain? "Thou hast laid the foundation of the round world, and all that therein is." "Thou hast created the north and the seas" (ver. 12). For nothing has any power against Thee, against its Creator. The world indeed may rage through its own malice, and the perversity of its will; does it nevertheless pass over the bound laid down by the Creator, who made all things? Why then do I fear the north wind? Why do I fear the seas? In the north indeed is the devil, who said, "I will sit in the sides of the north; I

---

[1] Rom. xv. 9.
[2] Matt. xxvi. 64.
[3] Luke ii. 34.

[4] 1 Cor. x. 13.
[7] Ps. civ. 26.
[5] E. V. *Rahab.*
[8] Col. ii. 14.
[6] Amos ix. 3.

will be like the Most High; "[1] but Thou hast humbled, as one wounded, the proud one. Thus what Thou hast done in them has more force for Thy dominion, than their own will has for their wickedness. " Thou hast created the north and the seas."

13. " Thabor and Hermon shall rejoice in Thy name." Those mountains are here understood, but they have a meaning. " Thabor and Hermon shall rejoice in Thy name." Thabor, when interpreted, signifies an approaching light. But whence comes the light of which it is said, " Ye are the light of the world,"[2] unless from Him concerning whom it is written, " That was the true light, which lighteth every man coming into the world "?[3] The light then which is the light of the world comes from that light which is not kindled from any other source, so that there is no fear lest it be extinguished. The light then comes from Him, who is that candle which is not set beneath the bushel, but on a candlestick, Thabor the coming light. Hermon means his curse. Justly the light comes and is made the curse of him. Of whom but the devil, the wounded one, the proud one? Our illumination then is given from Thee ; that he is held accursed of us, who kept us in his own error and pride, is from Thee. " Thabor and Hermon, therefore, shall rejoice," not in their own merits, " but in Thy name." For they shall say, " Not unto us, Lord, not unto us, but to Thy name give the praise," on account of the raging sea : lest " the heathen say, Where is now their God? "[4]

14. " Thou hast a mighty arm " (ver. 13). Let no man arrogate anything to himself. " Thou hast a mighty arm : " by Thee we were created, by Thee we have been defended. " Thou hast a mighty arm : strong be Thy hand, and high be Thy right hand."

15. " Righteousness and judgment are the preparation of Thy seat " (ver. 14). Thy righteousness and judgment will appear in the end : they are now hidden. Of Thy righteousness it is treated in another Psalm,[5] " on the hidden things of the Son." There will then be a manifestation of Thy righteousness and judgment : some will be set on the right, others on the left hand :[6] and the unbelieving will tremble, when they see what now they mock at, and believe not : the righteous will rejoice, when they shall see what they now see not, yet believe. " Righteousness and judgment are the preparation of Thy seat : " especially in the Day of Judgment. What then now? " mercy and truth go before Thy face." I should fear the preparation of Thy seat, Thy justice, and Thy coming judgment, did not mercy and truth go before Thee : why should I at the end fear Thy righteousness, when with Thy mercy going before Thee Thou blottest out my sins, and by showing forth Thy truth fulfillest Thy promises? " Mercy and truth go before Thy face." For " all the paths of the Lord are mercy and truth."[7]

16. In all these things shall we not rejoice? or shall we contain our joy? or shall words suffice for our gladness? or shall the tongue be able to express our rejoicing? If therefore no words suffice, " Blessed is the people, O Lord, that knoweth glad shouting " (ver. 15). O blessed people ! dost thou conceive aright, dost thou understand, glad shouting? For except thou understand glad shouting, thou canst not be blessed. What do I mean by understanding glad shouting? Whether thou knowest the source of that rejoicing which is beyond words to express. For this joy is not of thyself, since " he that glorieth, let him glory in the Lord."[8] Rejoice not then in thy own pride, but in God's grace. See that that grace is such, that the tongue fails to express its greatness, and then thou understandest glad shouting. . . . O Lord, " they shall walk in the light of Thy countenance." " They shall rejoice in Thy name all the day "(ver. 16). That Thabor and Hermon shall rejoice in Thy name : all day shall they rejoice, if they will, in Thy name ; but if they will rejoice in their own name, they shall not rejoice all day : for they shall not continue in their joy, when they shall delight in themselves, and fall through pride. That they may rejoice all day, therefore, " they shall rejoice in Thy name, and in Thy righteousness shall they be exalted." Not in their own, but in Thine : lest they have a zeal of God, but not according to knowledge. For some are noted by the Apostle, that they have a zeal of God, but not according to knowledge, " being ignorant of God's righteousness, and going about to establish their own," and not rejoicing in Thy light, and thus " not submitting themselves unto the righteousness of God."[9] And why? because " they have a zeal of God, but not according to knowledge." But the people who knoweth glad shouting (for the former err from want of knowledge, but blessed is the people not that knoweth not, but that knoweth glad shouting), whence ought it to shout, whence to rejoice, but in Thy name, walking in the light of Thy countenance? And it shall deserve to be exalted, but in Thy righteousness : let every man take away altogether his own righteousness, and be humbled : the righteousness of God shall come, and he shall be exalted, " and in Thy righteousness shall they be exalted."

17. " For Thou art the glory of their strength : and in Thy good pleasure Thou shalt lift up our horns " (ver. 17) : because it has seemed good to Thee, not because we are worthy.

---

[1] Isa. xiv. 13, 14.　　[2] Matt. v. 14.　　[3] John i. 9.
[4] Ps. cxv. 1, 2.　　[5] Ps. ix. Tit.　　[6] Matt. xxv. 33.
[7] Ps. xxv. 10.　　[8] 1 Cor. i. 31.　　[9] Rom. x. 2, 3.

18. "For of the Lord is our taking up" (ver. 18). For I was moved like a heap of sand, that I might fall; and I should have fallen, had not the Lord taken me up. "For of the Lord is (our [1]) taking up: and of the Holy One of Israel our King." Himself is thy taking up, Himself thy illumination: in His light thou art safe, in His light thou walkest, in His righteousness thou art exalted. He took thee up, He guards thy weakness: He gives thee strength of Himself, not of thyself.

19. "Thou spakest sometime in vision unto Thy sons, and saidst" (ver. 19). Thou spakest in thy vision. Thou didst reveal this to Thy Prophets. For this reason Thou spakest in vision, that is, in revelation: whence Prophets were called seers. They saw something within, which they were to speak without: and secretly they heard what they preached openly.[2] Then "Thou spakest in vision unto Thy sons, and saidst, I have laid help upon One that is mighty." Ye understand Who is meant by mighty? "I have exalted One chosen out of the people." And Who is meant by chosen? One who, ye rejoice, is already exalted.

20. "I have found David My servant:" that David from David's seed: "with My holy oil have I anointed Him" (ver. 20): for it is said of Him, "God, even Thy God, hath anointed Thee with the oil of gladness above Thy fellows."[3]

21. "My hand shall hold Him fast, and My arm shall strengthen Him" (ver. 21): because there was a taking up of man; because flesh was assumed in the Virgin's womb,[4] because by Him who in the form of God is coequal with the Father, the form of a servant was taken, and He became obedient unto death, even the death of the Cross.[5]

22. "The enemy shall not be able to do him violence" (ver. 22). The enemy rages indeed: but he shall not be able to do Him violence: he is wont to hurt, but he shall not hurt. How then shall he afflict Him? he will exercise Him, but he shall not hurt Him. There shall be profit in his raging; for those against whom he rages shall be crowned in their conquering. For how is he conquered, if he rages not against us? or where is God our helper, if we fight not? The enemy therefore shall do what is in his power; but "he shall not be able to do Him violence: the son of wickedness shall not come nigh to hurt Him."

23. "I will cut in pieces His enemies before His face" (ver. 23). They are cut in pieces from their conspiracy, and in that they believe they are cut in pieces; for they believe by degrees; as when the calf's head was ground small, they will come to be the drink of God's people.

For Moses ground down the calf's head, and sprinkled it upon the water, and made the children of Israel drink it.[6] All the unbelieving are ground: they believe by degrees; and they are drunk by the people of God, and pass into Christ's body. "I will cut in pieces His foes before His face: and put to flight them that hate Him." . . .

24. "My truth also and My mercy is with Him" (ver. 24). All the paths of the Lord are mercy and truth. Remember, as much as ye can, how often these two attributes are urged upon us, that we render them back to God. For as He showed us mercy that He might blot out our sins, and truth in fulfilling His promises; so also we, walking in His path, ought to give back to Him mercy and truth; mercy, in pitying the wretched; truth, in not judging unjustly. Let not truth rob you of mercy, nor mercy hinder truth: for if through mercy you shall have judged contrary to truth, or by rigorous truth shall have forgotten mercy, you will not be walking in the path of God, where "mercy and truth meet together."[7] "And in My name shall His horn be exalted." Why should I say more? Ye are Christians, recognise Christ.

25. "I will set His hand also in the sea" (ver. 25): that is, He shall rule over the Gentiles; "and His right hand in the floods." Rivers run into the sea: avaricious men roll onwards into the bitterness of this world: yet all these kinds of men will be subject to Christ.

26. "He shall call me, Thou art My Father, and the lifter up of My salvation" (ver. 26). "And I will make Him my first-born; higher than the kings of the earth" (ver. 27). Our Martyrs, whose birthdays we are celebrating, shed their blood on account of these things, which were believed though not yet seen; how much more brave ought we to be, as we see what they believed? For they had not yet seen Christ raised on high among the kings of the earth: as yet princes were taking counsel together against the Lord and His Anointed: what follows in the same Psalm was not then fulfilled, "Be wise now therefore, O ye kings: be learned, ye that are judges of the earth."[8] Now indeed Christ has been exalted among the kings of the earth.

27. "My mercy will I keep for Him for ever: and my Testament faithful with Him" (ver. 28). On His account, the Testament is faithful: in Him the Testament is mediated: He is the Sealer, the Mediator of the Testament, the Surety of the Testament, the Witness of the Testament, the Heritage of the Testament, the Coheir of the Testament.

28. "His seed will I make to endure world without end" (ver. 29). Not only for this

---

[1] Oxf. MSS. "our." [2] 1 Sam. iii. 9-18. [3] Ps. xlv. 7.
[4] Luke i. 31. [5] Phil. ii. 6, 8. [6] Exod. xxxii. 20. [7] Ps. lxxxv. 10.
[8] Ps. ii. 2 10.

world, but unto the world without end : [1] whither His seed, which is His heritage, the seed of Abraham, which is Christ, will pass.[2] But if ye are Christ's, ye are also Abraham's seed : and if ye are destined His heirs for ever, " He will establish His seed unto world without end : and His throne as the days of Heaven." The thrones of earthly kings are as the days of the earth : different are the days of Heaven from those of earth. The days of Heaven are those years of which it is said, "Thou art the same, and Thy years shall not fail." [3] The days of the earth are soon overtaken by their successors : those which precede are shut out from us : nor do those which succeed remain : but they come that they may go, and are almost gone before they are come. Such are the days of earth. But the days of Heaven, which are also the " One day " of Heaven,[4] and the never failing years, have neither beginning nor end : nor is any day there narrowed between yesterday and to-morrow : no one there expects the future, nor loses the past : but the days of Heaven are always present, where His throne shall be for ever and ever.[5] . . .

29. This is a strong pledge of the promise of God. The sons of this David are the children of the Bridegroom ; all Christians therefore are called His sons. But it is much indeed that God promises, that if Christians, that is, " If his children forsake My law, and walk not in My judgments " (ver. 30) ; " if they profane My statutes, and keep not My commandments " (ver. 31) ; I will not spurn them, nor will I send them away from Me in perdition : but what will I do? " I will visit their offences with the rod, and their sin with scourges " (ver. 32). It is not the mercy of one that calls them only ; but also that chastises and scourges them. Let therefore thy Father's hand be upon thee, and if thou art a good son, repel not chastening ; for " what son is there, to whom his father giveth not chastening ? " [6] Let Him chasten him, so long as He takes not from him His mercy : let Him beat him when obstinate, as long as He does not disinherit him. If thou hast well understood the promises of thy Father, fear not to be scourged, but to be disinherited : " for whom the Lord loveth He chasteneth : and scourgeth every son whom He receiveth." [7] Does the sinful son spurn chastening, when he sees the only Son without sin scourged? " I will visit their offences with the rod." Thus too the Apostle threatens : " What will ye? shall I come unto

you with a rod? " [8] Let not pious sons say, if Thou art coming with a rod, come not at all. For it is better to be taught with the Father's rod, than to perish in the caresses of the robber.

30. " Nevertheless, My mercy will I not utterly take from Him " (ver. 33). From whom? From that David to whom I gave these promises, whom " I anointed with my holy oil of gladness above His fellows." [9] Do you recognise Him from whom God will not utterly take away His mercy? That no one may anxiously say, since He speaks of Christ as Him from whom He will not take away His mercy, What then will become of the sinner? Did He say anything like this, " I will not take My loving-kindness utterly from them "? " I will visit," He saith, " their offences with the rod, and their sin with scourges." Thou didst expect for thy own security, " I will not utterly take my loving-kindness from " them. And indeed this is the reading of some books, but not of the most accurate : though, where they have it, it is a reading by no means inconsistent with the real meaning. For how can it be said that He will not utterly take His mercy from Christ? Has the Saviour of the body committed aught of sin either in Heaven or in earth, " who sitteth even at the right hand of God, who also maketh intercession for us "? [10] Yet it is from Christ : but from His members, His body which is the Church. For in this sense He speaks of it as a great thing that He will not take away His mercies from Him, supposing us not to recognise the only Son, who is in the bosom of the Father ; [11] for there the Man is not counted for His Person, but the One Person is God and Man. He therefore does not utterly take His mercies from Him, when He takes not His mercy from His body, His members,[12] in which, even while He was enthroned in Heaven, He was still suffering persecutions on earth ; and when He cried from Heaven, " Saul, Saul," not why persecutest thou My servants, nor why persecutest thou My saints, nor My disciples, but, " why persecutest thou Me? " [13] As then, while no one persecuted Him when sitting in Heaven, He cried out, " Why persecutest thou Me? " when the Head recognised its limbs, and His love allowed not the Head to separate Himself from the union of the body : so, when He taketh not away His mercies from Him, it is surely that He taketh it not from us, who are His limbs and body. Yet ought we not on that account to sin not without apprehension, and perversely to assure ourselves that we shall not

---

[1] *In seculum seculi.*   [2] Gal. iii. 15, 29.
[3] Ps. cii. 27.   [4] Oxf. MSS. add "which are," etc.
[5] [Here he adds: " Let us, if you please, reserve what remains; since the Psalm is a long one, and we have yet some farther opportunity of speaking with you in Christ's name. Refresh your strength therefore: I do not mean that of your mind, for in mind I see that you are incapable of fatigue; but on account of the slaves of the soul, that your bodies may be sustained in their service, refresh yourselves for a little, and being refreshed return to your meal." — C.]
[6] Heb. xii. 7.   [7] Heb. xii. 6.

[8] 1 Cor. iv. 21.   [9] Ps. xlv. 7.
[10] Rom. viii. 34.   [11] John i. 18.
[12] *i.e* we may consider it as not said of Him at all, for though He is Man, yet being God also He would not, in His own Person, need assurance; therefore it is said of Him in His members.
[13] Acts ix. 4.

perish, be our actions what they may. For there are certain sins and certain offences, to define and discourse of which it is either impossible for me, or if it were possible, it would be too tedious for the time we have at present. For no man can say that he is without sin; for if he says so, he will lie; "if we say that we have no sin, we deceive ourselves, and the truth is not in us." [1] Each one therefore is needfully scourged for his own sins; but the mercy of God is not taken away from him, if he be a Christian. Certainly if thou committest such offences as to repel the hand of Him who chasteneth, the rod of Him who scourgeth thee, and art angry at the correction of God, and fliest from thy Father when He chasteneth thee, and wilt not suffer Him to be thy Father, because He spares thee not when thou dost sin; thou hast estranged thyself from thy heritage, He has not thrown thee off; for if thou wouldest abide being scourged, thou wouldest not abide disinherited. "Nor will I do hurt in My truth." For His mercy in setting free shall not be taken away, lest His truth in taking vengeance do harm.

31. "My covenant will I not profane, nor reject the thing that is gone out of my lips" (ver. 34). Because his sons sin, I will not on this account be found false: I have promised; I will do. Suppose they choose to sin even as past hope, and so fall into sins as to offend their Father's countenance, and deserve to be disinherited; is it not still God Himself, of whom it is said, "From these stones" He "will raise up sons to Abraham"? [2] Therefore I tell you, brethren, many Christians sin venially, [3] many are scourged and so corrected for their sin, chastened, and cured; many turn away altogether, striving with a stiff neck against the discipline of the Father, even wholly refusing God as their Father, though they have the mark of Christ, and so fall into such sins, that it can only be announced against them, "that they who do such things shall not inherit the kingdom of God." [4] Nevertheless, Christ shall not be destitute of an inheritance on their account: not for the chaff's sake shall the wheat also perish: [5] nor on account of bad fish shall nothing be cast into the vessels from that net. [6] "The Lord knows them that are His." [7] For He who predestined us before we were born, promised undoubtingly: "For whom He did predestinate, them He also called: and whom He called, them He also justified: and whom He justified, them He also glorified." [8] Let desperate sinners sin as far as they choose: let the members of Christ reply,

"If God is with us, who shall be against us?" God will not therefore do hurt in His truth, nor will He "profane His Testament." His Testament remains immovable, because in His foreknowledge He predestined His heirs; and "He will not reject the thing that is gone out of His lips."

32. Listen for thy confirmation in hope, for thy security, if thou knowest thyself to be among the members of Christ. "I have sworn once by My holiness that I will not lie unto David" (ver. 35). Dost thou wait till God swear a second time? How often is He to swear, if in one oath He is false? One oath He made for our life, who sent His Only One to die for us. "I have sworn once by My holiness, that I will not lie unto David." "His seed shall endure for ever" (ver. 36). His seed endures for ever; because the Lord knows them that are His. "And His seat is like as the sun before me:" "and as the moon perfect for evermore: and the faithful witness in heaven" (ver. 37). They are His seat, in whom He sits and reigns. But if His seat, His members also; because even our members are the seat of our head. See how all our other members sustain our head: but the head supports nothing above itself, but is itself supported by the rest of our limbs, as if the whole body of a man were the seat of his head. His seat, therefore, all in whom God reigns, "shall be like as the sun before Me," He saith: because the righteous in the kingdom of My Father "shall shine like the sun." [9] But the sun is meant in a spiritual, not a bodily sense, as that which shines from Heaven, which He maketh to rise upon the just and unjust. [10] Finally, that sun is not before men's eyes only, but even those of cattle and the smallest insects; for which of the vilest animals sees not that sun? What does he say to distinguish the sun meant here? "Like as the sun before Me." Not before men, before the flesh, before mortal animals, but "before Me, and as the moon." But what moon? one "that is perfect for evermore." For although that moon which we know becomes perfect, the next day she begins to wane, after her orb is full. "He shall be as the moon perfect for evermore," He saith. His seat shall be made perfect as the moon, but that moon is one which will be perfect for evermore. If as the sun, why also as the moon? the Scriptures usually signify by the moon the mortality of this flesh, because of its increasings and decreasings, because of its transitory nature. The moon is also interpreted as Jericho: one who was descending from Jerusalem to Jericho fell among robbers: [11] for he was descending from immortality to mortality. Similar then is the flesh to

---

[1] 1 John i. 8.　　[2] Matt. iii. 9.
[3] *Tolerabiliter.* [1 John v. 16, 17.—C.]　[4] Gal. v. 21.
[5] Matt. iii. 12.　　[6] Matt. xiii. 47.　[7] 2 Tim. ii. 19.
[8] Rom. viii. 29, 30.

[9] Matt. xiii. 43.　　[10] Matt. v. 45.　　[11] Luke x. 30.

that moon, which every month suffers increase and decrease : but that flesh of ours will be perfect in the resurrection : "and a faithful witness in heaven." Thus then, if it was our mind only that would be perfected, he would compare us only to the sun : if our body only, to the moon ; but as God will perfect us in both, in respect of the mind it is said, "like as the sun before Me," because God only seeth the mind : and "as the moon," so is the flesh : which "shall be made perfect for evermore," in the resurrection of the dead : "and a faithful witness in Heaven," because all that was asserted of the resurrection of the dead was true. I beseech you, hear this again more clearly, and remember it : for I know that some understand, while others are yet enquiring perhaps what I meant. There is no article of the Christian faith which has encountered such contradiction as that of the resurrection of the flesh. Finally, He who was born for a sign that should be spoken against,[1] resumed His own flesh after death to meet the caviller ; and He who could have so completely cured His wounds that their scars would have entirely vanished, retained those scars in His body, that He might cure the wounds of doubt in the heart. Indeed nothing has been attacked with the same pertinacious, contentious contradiction, in the Christian faith, as the resurrection of the flesh. On the immortality of the soul many Gentile philosophers have disputed at great length, and in many books they have left it written that the soul is immortal : when they come to the resurrection of the flesh, they doubt not indeed, but they most openly deny it, declaring it to be absolutely impossible that this earthly flesh can ascend to Heaven. Thus that moon shall be perfect for evermore, and shall be the faithful witness in heaven against all gainsayers.

33. These promises, so sure, so firm, so open, so unquestioned, were made concerning Christ. For although some are mysteriously veiled, yet some are so clear, that all that is obscure is easily revealed by them. Such being the case, see what follows : "But Thou hast approved and brought to nothing and forsaken Thine Anointed" (ver. 38). "Thou hast overthrown the testament of Thy servant, and profaned His holiness on the ground" (ver. 39). "Thou hast broken down all His hedges, and made His strongholds a terror" (ver. 40). . . . How is this? Thou hast promised all those things : and Thou hast brought to pass their reverse. Where are now the promises which but a little before filled us with delight? which we so joyfully applauded, which we so fearlessly made our boast of? It is as if one promised, and another

destroyed. And this is the mystery : for the words are not "another," but "Thou," Thou who didst promise, who didst even swear in condescension to human doubt, Thou hast promised this, and done thus ! Whence shall I get Thy oath, where shall I find Thy promise fulfilled? Would then God promise, or swear thus falsely? and yet why then these promises, and these acts? I answer, that He acted thus in fulfilment of those promises. But who am I, to say this? Let us see therefore whether it is the language of the Truth ; what I say will not then be without foundation. It was David to whom the fulfilment of these promises in his seed, that is, in Christ, was promised : and as they were addressed to David, men expected their completion in David. Further, lest when any Christian asserted these promises to have referred to Christ, another by applying them to David, because he described the fulfilment of all of them in David, might thus err ; He cancelled them in David, thus obliging us when we see them unfulfilled in David, to look to another quarter for their fulfilment. Thus also in the case of Esau and Jacob, we find the elder worshipped by the younger, though it is written, "The elder shall serve the younger ; "[2] so when you see it unfulfilled in those two brothers, you look for two peoples in whom to discover the completion of what God in His truth deigns to promise. "From the fruit of thy body," saith the Lord unto David, "shall I set upon thy sea."[3] He promised from his seed something for evermore : and Solomon, born to him, became master of such wisdom,[4] that the promise of God respecting the fruit of David's body was believed to have been fulfilled in him ; but Solomon fell,[5] and gave room for hoping for Christ ; that since God can neither be deceived nor deceive, He might not make His promise to rest in one who He knew would fall, but you might after the fall of Solomon look back to God, and demand His promise. Hast Thou, O Lord, deceived? Hast Thou failed to fulfil Thy promise? Dost Thou not exhibit what Thou hast sworn? Perhaps God might reply, I swore and promised : but Solomon would not persevere. What then? Didst not Thou, Lord God, know beforehand that he would not persevere? Indeed Thou didst know. Why then didst Thou promise me what should be eternal in one who would not persevere? Hast Thou not answered ; "But if his children forsake My law, and walk not in My judgments ; if they keep not My statutes, and profane My testament ; " yet My promise shall remain, and My oath shall be fulfilled : "I have sworn once in My Holiness," within, in a certain mystery, in the very spring whence the Prophets

---

[1] Luke ii. 34. [A. N. F. vol. iii. p. 525.—C].

[2] Gen. xxv. 23.　　[3] Ps. cxxxii. 11.
[4] Oxf. mss. "and such prudence."　　[5] 1 Kings xi. 1, etc.

drank, whence they burst forth to us of these things, " I have sworn once " that I will not fail David. Show forth then what Thou hast sworn, give us what Thou hast promised. The fulfilment is taken from that David, that it might not be looked for in that David : wait therefore for what I have promised.

34. Even David himself knew this. Consider his words ; " Thou hast rejected and brought him down to nothing." Where then is Thy promise? " Thou hast put off Thine anointed." This expression cheers us, among much that is sorrowful : for the promise of God is still valid ; for¹ Thou hast put off Thine Anointed, not taken Him away. See then what was the fate of that David, in whom the ignorant hoped for the fulfilment of the promises of God, in order that those promises might be more firmly relied upon for their fulfilment in another. " Thou hast put off Thine Anointed : Thou hast overthrown the testament of Thy servant." For where is the Old Testament of the Jews? where that land of promise, in which they sinned while they dwelt in it, on the overthrow of which they wandered afar? Ask you for the kingdom of the Jews ; it exists not : you ask for the altar of the Jews ; it is not : you ask for the sacrifice of the Jews ; it is not : you ask for the priesthood of the Jews ; it is not. " Thou hast overthrown the testament of Thy servant, and profaned his holiness on the earth." Thou hast shown that what they thought holy, was earthly. " Thou hast broken down all his hedges," with which Thou hast entrenched him : for how could he have been spoiled unless his hedges had been broken down? " Thou hast made his strongholds a terror." Why terror? That it should be said to the sinners, " For if God spared not the natural branches, take heed lest He also spare not thee."²

" All they that go by the way have spoiled him : " that is, all the heathen that go by the way, meaning, all who pass through this life, have spoiled Israel, have spoiled David. First of all, see his fragments in all nations : for it is of the Jews that it is said, " They shall be a portion for foxes."³ For the Scripture calls wicked, crafty, and cowardly kings, whom another's virtue terrifies, foxes. Thus when our Lord Himself was speaking of the threatening Herod, He said, " Go ye, and tell that fox."⁴ The king who fears no man, is not a fox : like that Lion of Judah, of whom it is said, " Stooping down Thou didst rise up, and didst sleep as a lion."⁵ At Thy will Thou didst stoop down, at Thy will didst rise ; because Thou wouldest, Thou didst sleep. And thus in another Psalm he says, " I⁶ slept."⁷

Was not the sentence complete, " I slept, and took rest, and rose up again, because the Lord shall uphold Me "? Why is the word *ego* added? and thus with a strong emphasis on the word I, they raged against *Me*, they troubled *Me* : but had *I* not willed, *I* had not slept. Those then concerning whom it was declared that they should be a portion for foxes, are now spoken of as follows ; " All they that go by have spoiled him : and he is become a reproach to his neighbours " (ver. 41). " Thou hast set up the right hand of his enemies, and made all his adversaries to rejoice " (ver. 42). Look at the Jews, and see all things fulfilled that were predicted. " Thou hast turned away the help of his sword." How they were used to fight few in number, and to strike down many. " Thou hast turned away the help of his sword, and Thou givest him not victory in the battle " (ver. 43). Naturally⁸ then is he conquered, naturally taken prisoner, naturally made an outcast from his kingdom, naturally scattered abroad : for he lost that land, for which he slew the Lord. " Thou hast loosed him from cleansing " (ver. 44). What is this? Amongst all the evils, this is a matter for great fear ; for howsoever God may beat, howsoever He may be wroth, howsoever He may flog and scourge, yet let Him scourge him bound, whom He is to cleanse, not " loose him from cleansing." For if He loose him from being purified, he becomes incapable of cleansing, and must be an outcast. From what cleansing then is the Jew loosed? From faith ; for by faith we live :⁹ and it is said of faith, " purifying their hearts by faith : "¹⁰ and as it is only the faith of Christ that cleanses ; by disbelief in Christ, they are loosed from purification. " Thou hast loosed him from cleansing, and cast his throne down to the ground." And so Thou hast broken it. " The days of his seat hast Thou shortened " (ver. 45). They imagined that they should reign for ever. " And covered him with confusion." All these things happened to the Jews, Christ yet not being taken away, but His advent deferred.

35. Let us therefore see whether God fulfils His promises. After these stern penalties which have been recorded as having been inflicted upon this people and kingdom, that God might not be supposed to have fulfilled His promises in it, and so not to grant another kingdom in Christ, of which kingdom there shall be no end ; the Prophet addresses Him in these words, " Lord, how long wilt Thou hide Thyself unto the end? " (ver. 46). For possibly it was not from them and to the end ; because " blindness in part is happened to Israel, until the fulness of the Gentiles be come in, and so all Israel shall

---

¹ *Non abstulisti sed distulisti.*
² Rom. xi. 21.   ³ Ps. lxiii. 10.   ⁴ Luke xiii. 32.
⁵ Gen. xlix. 9.   ⁶ *Ego.*   ⁷ Ps. iv. 8.

⁸ *Merito.*   ⁹ Gal. iii. 11.   ¹⁰ Acts xv. 9.

be saved." [1] But in the mean while " shall Thy wrath burn like fire."

36. " O remember what my substance is " (ver. 47). That David, who was placed among the Jews in the flesh, in Christ in hope, speaks; " Remember what is my substance." For not because the Jews fell away, did my substance fail : for from that people came the Virgin Mary, and from her the flesh of Christ ; that Flesh sins not, but purifies sins ; there, saith David, is my substance. " O remember what my substance is." For the root has not entirely perished ; the seed shall come to whom the promise was made, ordained by Angels in the hand of a Mediator.[2] " For Thou hast not made all the sons of men for nought " (ver. 47). Lo ! all the sons of men have gone into vanity : yet Thou hast not made them for nought. If then all went into vanity, whom Thou hast not made for nought ; hast Thou not reserved some instrument to purify them from vanity? This which Thou hast reserved to Thyself to cleanse men from vanity is Thy Holy One, in Him is my substance : for from Him are all, whom Thou hast not made for nought, purified from their own vanity. To them it is said, " O ye sons of men, how long are ye heavy in heart? Wherefore have ye such pleasure in vanity, and seek after leasing?" [3] Perhaps they might become anxious, and turn from their vanity, and when they found themselves polluted with it, might seek for purification from it : then help them, make them secure. " Know this also, that the Lord hath made wonderful His Holy One." [4] He has made His Holy One to be admired : thence He has purified all from their vanity : there, saith David, is my substance : O remember it ! " For Thou hast not made all the sons of men for nought." Thou hast therefore reserved something to purify them : and who is He whom Thou hast reserved? "What man is he that liveth, and shall not see death?" This man then who shall live and not see death, shall purify them from nothingness. For He made not all men for nought, nor can He who made them so despise His own creatures, as not to convert and purify them.

37. " What man is he that shall live, and shall not see death?" (ver. 48). For being raised from the dead He dieth no more, and death hath no more dominion over Him.[5] And as in another Psalm it is said, " Thou shalt not leave my soul in Hell, neither shalt Thou suffer Thy Holy One to see corruption," [6] the Apostolic teaching takes up this testimony, and in the Acts of the Apostles [7] thus argues against the unbelieving ; Men and brethren, we know that the patriarch David is dead and buried, and his flesh

hath seen corruption. Therefore it cannot be said of him, " neither shalt Thou suffer Thy Holy One to see corruption." Of whom then is it said? " What man is he that shall live, and shall not see death?" Perhaps there is no man such. Nay, but " who is it?" is said to make thee inquire, not despair. But perhaps there may be some man " that shall live, and shall not see death," and yet perhaps he did not speak of Christ, who died? There is no man " that shall live, and shall not see death," except Him who died for mortals. That thou mayest be assured that it is said of Him, consider the sequel ; " What man is he that liveth, and shall not see death?" Did He never die then? He did. How then shall He live, and never see death? " He shall deliver His own soul from the hands of Hell." He is spoken of alone indeed, in that He alone of all others " shall live, and shall not see death : He shall deliver His own soul from the hand of Hell," because although the rest of His faithful shall rise from the dead, and shall themselves live for evermore, without seeing death ; yet they shall not themselves deliver their own souls from the hands of Hell. He who delivers His own soul from the hands of Hell, Himself delivers those of His believers : they cannot do so of themselves. Prove that He delivers His own soul. " I have power to lay down My life, and I have power to take it again. No man taketh ' it from Me ; ' for I Myself slept, but I lay it down of Myself, and take it again," [8] because it is He Himself who delivers His own soul from the hands of Hell.

38. But in the very faith in Christ great difficulties occurred, and the heathen in their rage long said, " When shall he die, and his name perish?" On account of these then who have now long believed in Christ, but were destined to doubt for some time, these words follow, " Lord, where are Thy old loving-kindnesses?" (ver. 49). We have now acknowledged Christ our purifier, we now possess Him in whom Thy promises were to be fulfilled ; show forth in Him what Thou hast promised. It is He Himself that shall live, and not see death : Himself who delivers His own soul from the hand of Hell : and yet we are still in suffering. Thus spoke the Martyrs, whose birthdays we are celebrating. He shall live, and not see death : He delivers His soul from the hands of Hell : yet " for Thy sake we are killed all the day long : and are counted as sheep appointed to be slain." [9] " Lord, where are Thy old loving-kindnesses which Thou swarest unto David in Thy truth?"

39. " Remember, Lord, the rebuke that Thy servants have " (ver. 50). Even while Christ was living, and while He was sitting on His

---

[1] Rom. xi. 25.   [2] Gal. iii. 19.   [3] Ps. iv. 2.
[4] Ps. iv. 3.   [5] Rom. vi. 9.   [6] Ps. xvi. 10.
[7] Acts ii. 29.

[8] John x. 18; Ps. iii. 5.   [9] Ps. xliv. 22.

Father's right hand, reproaches were cast against the Christians: they long were reproached with the name of Christ. That widowed one who brought forth, and whose children were more than those of the married wife,[1] heard ill names, heard reproaches: but the Church, multiplied as she is, extending right and left, no longer remembers the reproach of her widowhood. "Remember, Lord," in the memory of whom there is abundant sweetness. "Remember," forget not. Remember what? "the rebuke that Thy servants have: and how I do bear in my bosom the rebukes of many people." I went, saith he, to preach of Thee, and I heard reproaches, and bore them in my bosom, because I was fulfilling the prophecy. "Being defamed we entreat: we are made as the filth of the earth, and are the offscouring of all things unto this day."[2] Long the Christians bore reproaches in their bosom, in their heart: nor dared resist their revilers; before, when it was a crime to answer a heathen: it is now a crime to remain a heathen. Thanks be to the Lord! He remembered our rebukes: He raised the horn of His Anointed on high, He made Him the Wonderful among the kings of the earth. Now no one insults Christians, or if he does, it is not in public: he speaks as if he were still more fearful of being heard, than anxious to be believed. "I bear in my bosom the rebukes of many people."

40. "Wherewith Thine enemies have blasphemed Thee, O Lord" (ver. 51), both Jews and Pagans. "Wherewith they have blasphemed." Wherewith have they blasphemed Thee? "With the change of Thine Anointed."[3] They objected that Christ died, and was crucified. Madmen, what is your reproach? Although there is now no one to use it: yet supposing some still remaining that so speak, what is your reproach? that Christ died? He was not destroyed, but changed. He is styled "dead" on account of the three days. Wherewith then have thine enemies blasphemed Thee? Not with the loss, not with the perdition of Thine Anointed, but with His "change." He was changed from temporal to eternal life: He was changed from the Jews to the Gentiles; He was changed from earth to heaven. Let then Thy vain enemies blaspheme Thee still for the change of Thine Anointed. Would that they may be changed: they will not in that case blaspheme the change of Christ, which displeases them, since they themselves will not be changed. "For there is no change with them, and they fear not God."[4]

41. They have blasphemed the change of Christ; but what dost thou answer? "The blessing of[5] the Lord for evermore. Amen and Amen" (ver. 52). Thanks to His mercy,[6] thanks to His grace. We express our thanks: we do not give them, nor return them, nor repay them: we express our thanks in words, while in fact we retain our sense of them.[7] He saved us for no reward, He heeded not our impieties: He searched us out when we searched not for Him, He found, redeemed, emancipated us from the bondage of the devil and the power of his wicked angels: He drew us to Him to purify us by that faith, from which He releases those enemies only who believe not, and who for that reason cannot be purified. Let those who still remain infidels say every day what they choose; day by day they shall be fewer and fewer that remain; let them revile, mock, accuse, not the death, but the change of Christ. Do they not see that, when they say these things, they fail in purpose either by believing or by dying? For their curse is temporal: but the blessing of the Lord "for evermore." To confirm that blessing is added, "Amen and Amen." This is the signature of the bond of God. Secure then of His promises, let us believe the past, recognise the present, hope for the future. Let not the enemy lead us astray from the way, that He, who gathers us like chickens under His wings, may foster us: lest we stray from His wings, and the hawk of the air carry us off while yet unfledged. For the Christian ought not to hope in himself: if he hopes to be strong, let him be reared by his mother's warmth. This is the hen who gathers her young together; whence is the reproach of our Saviour against the unbelieving Jerusalem. "Behold, your house shall be left unto you desolate."[8] Hence was it said, "Thou hast made his strongholds a terror." Since then they would not be gathered together under the wings of this hen, and have given as a warning to teach us to dread the unclean spirits that fly in the air, seeking daily what they may devour; let us gather ourselves under the wings of this hen, the divine Wisdom, since she is weakened even unto death of her chickens. Let us love our Lord God, let us love His Church: Him as a Father, Her as a Mother: Him as a Lord, Her as His Handmaid, as we are ourselves the Handmaid's sons. But this marriage is held together by a bond of great love: no man offends the one, and wins favour of the other. Let no man say, "I go indeed to the idols, I consult possessed ones and fortune-tellers: yet I abandon not God's Church; I am a Catholic." While thou holdest to thy Mother, thou hast offended thy Father. Another says, Far be it from me; I consult no sorcerer, I seek out no possessed one, I never ask advice

---

[1] Psa. liv. 1; Gal. iv. 27.   [2] 1 Cor. iv. 13.   [3] *Christi*.
[4] Ps. lv. 19.   [5] Oxf. MSS. "blessed be."

[6] Oxf. MSS. add here, "what else shall I say but."
[7] Oxf. MSS. *Rem tenemus*, while we retain possession of the (unrequited) benefit.
[8] Matt. xxiii. 38.

by sacrilegious divination, I go not to worship idols, I bow not before stones; though I am in the party of Donatus. What does it profit you not to have offended your Father, if he avenges your offended Mother? what does it serve you, if you acknowledge the Lord, honour God, preach His name, acknowledge His Son, confess that He sitteth by His right hand; while you blaspheme His Church? Does not the analogy of human marriages convince you? Suppose you have some patron, whom you court every day, whose threshold you wear with your visits, whom you daily not only salute, but even worship, to whom you pay the most loyal courtesy; if you utter one calumny against his wife, could you re-enter his house? Hold then, most beloved, hold all with one mind to God the Father, and the Church our Mother. Celebrate with temperance the birthdays of the Saints, that we may imitate those who have gone before us, and that they who pray for you may rejoice over you; that "the blessing of the Lord may abide on you for evermore. Amen and Amen."

PSALM XC.[1]

1. This Psalm is entitled, "The prayer of Moses the man of God," through whom, His man, God gave the law to His people, through whom He freed them from the house of slavery, and led them forty years through the wilderness. Moses was therefore the Minister of the Old, and the Prophet of the New Testament. For "all these things," saith the Apostle, "happened unto them for ensamples: and they are written for our admonition, unto whom the ends of the world come."[2] In accordance therefore with this dispensation which was vouchsafed to Moses, this Psalm is to be examined, as it has received its title from his prayer.

2. "Lord," he saith, "Thou hast been our refuge from one generation to another" (ver. 1): either in every generation, or in two gener-ations, the old and new: because, as I said, he was the Minister of the Testament that related to the old generation, and the Prophet of the Testament which appertained to the new. Jesus Himself, the Surety of that covenant, and the Bridegroom in the marriage which He entered into in that generation, saith, "Had ye believed Moses, ye would have believed Me: for he wrote of Me."[3] Now it is not to be be-lieved that this Psalm was entirely the compo-sition of that Moses, as it is not distinguished by any of those of his expressions[4] which are used in his songs: but the name of the great servant of God is used for the sake of some in-timation, which should direct the attention of the reader or listener. "Lord," he saith, "Thou hast been our refuge from one generation to the other."

3. He adds, how He became our refuge, since He began to be that, viz. a refuge, to us which He had not been before, not that He had not existed before He became our refuge: "Before the mountains were brought forth, or ever the earth and the world were made: and from age even unto age Thou art" (ver. 2). Thou therefore who art for ever, and before we were, and before the world was, hast become our ref-uge ever since we turned to Thee. But the ex-pression, "before the mountains," etc., seems to me to contain a particular meaning; for moun-tains are the higher parts of the earth, and if God was before even the earth were formed (or, as some books have it, from the same Greek word, "framed "[5]), since it was by Him that it was formed, what is the need of saying that He was before the mountains, or any certain parts of it, since God was not only before the earth, but before heaven and earth, and even the whole bodily and spiritual creation? But it may cer-tainly be that the whole rational creation is marked by this distinction; that while the lofti-ness of Angels is signified by the mountains, the lowliness of man is meant by the earth. And for this reason, although all the works of cre-ation are not improperly said to be either made or formed; nevertheless, if there is any propri-ety in these words, the Angels are "made;" for as they are enumerated among His heavenly works, the enumeration itself is thus concluded: "He spake the word, and they were made; He commanded, and they were created;"[6] but the earth was "formed," that man might thence be created in the body. For the Scripture uses this word, where we read, God made, or "God formed man out of the dust of the ground."[7] Before then the noblest parts of the creation (for what is higher than the rational part of the Heavenly creation) were made: before the earth was made, that Thou mightest have worshippers upon the earth; and even this is little, as all these had a beginning either in or with time; but "from age to age Thou art." It would have been better, from everlasting to everlasting: for God, who is before the ages, exists not from a certain age, nor to a certain age, which has an end, since He is without end. But it often happens in the Scripture, that the equivocal Greek word causes the Latin translator to put age for eternity and eternity for age. But he very rightly does not say, Thou wast from ages, and unto ages Thou shalt be: but puts the verb in the present, intimating that the substance of God is altogether immutable. It is not, He

---

[1] Lat. LXXXIX.   [2] 1 Cor. x. 11.   [3] John v. 46.
[4] *Literis*. [But see Delitzsch (ed. Clark), vol. iii. p. 48.—C.]   [5] *Fingeretur*.   [6] Ps. cxlviii. 5.   [7] Gen. ii. 7.

was, and Shall be, but only Is. Whence the expression, I AM THAT I AM; and, I AM "hath sent me unto you;"[1] and, "Thou shalt change them, and they shall be changed: but Thou art the same, and Thy years shall not fail."[2] Behold then the eternity that is our refuge, that we may fly thither from the mutability of time, there to remain for evermore.

4. But as our life here is exposed to numerous and great temptations, and it is to be feared lest we may be turned aside by them from that refuge, let us see what in consequence of this the prayer of the man of God seeks for. "Turn not Thou man to lowness" (ver. 3): that is, let not man, turned aside from Thy eternal and sublime things, lust for things of time, savour of earthly things. This prayer is what God has Himself enjoined us, in the Prayer, "Lead us not into temptation,"[3] He adds, "Again Thou sayest, Come again, ye children of men." As if he said, I ask of Thee what Thou hast commanded me to ask: giving glory to His grace, that "he that glorieth, in the Lord he may glory:"[4] without whose help we cannot by an exertion of our own will overcome the temptations of this life. "Turn not Thou man to lowness: again thou sayest, Turn again, ye children of men." But grant what Thou hast enjoined, by hearing the prayer[5] of him who can at least pray, and aiding the faith of the willing soul.

5. "For a thousand years in Thy sight are but as yesterday, which is past by" (ver. 4): hence we ought to turn to Thy refuge, where Thou art without any change, from the fleeting scenes around us; since however long a time may be wished for for this life, "a thousand years in Thy sight are but as yesterday:" not as to-morrow, which is to come: for all limited periods of time are reckoned as having already passed. Hence the Apostle's choice is rather to aim at what is before,[6] that is, to desire things eternal, and to forget things behind, by which temporal matters should be understood. But that no one may imagine a thousand years are reckoned by God as one day, as if with God days were so long, when this is only said in contempt of the extent of time: he adds, "and as a watch in the night:" which only lasts three hours. Nevertheless men have ventured to assert their knowledge of times, to the pretenders to which our Lord said, "It is not for you to know the times or seasons, which the Father hath put in His own power:"[7] and they allege that this period may be defined six thousand years, as of six days. Nor have they heeded the words, "are but as one day which is past by:" for, when this was uttered, not a thousand

years only had passed, and the expression, "as a watch in the night," ought to have warned them that they might not be deceived by the uncertainty of the seasons: for even if the six first days in which God finished His works seemed to give some plausibility to their opinion, six watches, which amount to eighteen hours, will not consist with that opinion.

6. Next, the man of God, or rather the Prophetic spirit, seems to be reciting some law written in the secret wisdom of God, in which He has fixed a limit to the sinful life of mortals, and determined the troubles of mortality, in the following words: "Their years are as things which are nothing worth: in the morning let it fade away like the grass" (ver. 5). The happiness therefore of the heirs of the old covenant, which they asked of the Lord their God as a great boon, attained to receive this Law in His mysterious Providence. Moses seems to be reciting it: "Their years shall be things which are esteemed as nothing." Such are those things which are not before they are come: and when come, shall soon not be: for they do not come to be here, but to be gone. "In the morning," that is, before they come, "as a heat[8] let it pass by;" but "in the evening," it means after they come, "let it fall, and be dried up, and withered" (ver. 6). It is "to fall" in death, be "dried up" in the corpse, "withered" in the dust. What is this but flesh, wherein is the accursed lust of fleshly things? "For all flesh is grass, and all the goodliness of man as the flower of the field; the grass withereth, the flower fadeth: but the word of the Lord abideth for ever."[9]

7. Making no secret that this fate is a penalty inflicted for sin, he adds at once, "For we consume away in Thy displeasure, and are troubled at Thy wrathful indignation" (ver. 7): we consume away in our weakness, and are troubled from the fear of death; for we are become weak, and yet fearful to end that weakness. "Another," saith He, "shall gird thee, and carry thee whither thou wouldest not:"[10] although not to be punished, but to be crowned, by martyrdom; and the soul of our Lord, transforming us into Himself, was sorrowful even unto death: for "the Lord's going out" is no other than in "death."

8. "Thou hast set our misdeeds before Thee" (ver. 8): that is, Thou hast not dissembled Thine anger: "and our age in the light of Thy countenance." "The light of Thy countenance" answers to "before Thee," and to "our misdeeds," as above.

9. "For all our days are failed, and in Thine anger we have failed" (ver. 9). These words

---

[1] Exod. iii. 14.   [2] Ps. cii. 26, 27.   [3] Matt. vi. 13.
[4] 1 Cor. i. 31.   [5] *Precem petentis exaudiendo.*
[6] Phil. iii. 13.   [7] Acts i. 7.

[8] [*Al.* "as an herb." — C.]
[9] Isa. xl. 6, 8.   [10] John xxi. 18.

sufficiently prove that our subjection to death is a punishment. He speaks of our days failing, either because men fail in them from loving things that pass away, or because they are reduced to so small a number; which he asserts in the following lines: "our years are spent in thought like a spider." [1] "The days of our age are threescore years and ten; and though men be so strong that they come to fourscore years, yet is more of them but labour and sorrow" (ver. 10). These words appear to express the shortness and misery of this life: since those who have reached their seventieth year are styled old men. Up to eighty, however, they appear to have some strength; but if they live beyond this, their existence is laborious through multiplied sorrows. Yet many even below the age of seventy experience an old age the most infirm and wretched: and old men have often been found to be wonderfully vigorous even beyond eighty years. It is therefore better to search for some spiritual meaning in these numbers. For the anger of God is not greater on the sins of Adam (through whom alone "sin entered into the world, and death by sin, and so death passed upon all men"),[2] because they live a much shorter time than the men of old; since even the length of their days is ridiculed in the comparison of a thousand years to yesterday that is past, and to three hours: especially since at the very time when they provoked the anger of God to send the deluge in which they perished, their life was at its longest span.

10. Moreover, seventy and eighty years equal a hundred and fifty; a number which the Psalms clearly insinuate to be a sacred one. One hundred and fifty have the same relative signification as fifteen, the latter number being composed of seven and eight together: the first of which points to the Old Testament through the observation of the Sabbath; the latter to the New, referring to the resurrection of our Lord. Hence the fifteen steps in the Temple. Hence in the Psalms, fifteen "songs of degrees." Hence the waters of the deluge overtopped the highest mountains by fifteen cubits:[3] and many other instances of the same nature. "Our years are passed in thought like a spider." We were labouring in things corruptible, corruptible works were we weaving together: which, as the Prophet Isaiah saith, by no means covered us.[4] "The days of our years are in themselves," etc. A distinction is here made between themselves and their strength:[5] "in themselves," that is, in the years or days themselves, may mean in temporal things, which are promised in the Old Testament, signified by the

number seventy; "but if" not in themselves, but "in their strength," refers not to temporal things, but to things eternal, "fourscore years," as the New Testament contains the hope of a new life and resurrection for evermore: and what is added, that if they pass this latter period,[6] "their strength is labour and sorrow," intimates that such shall be the fate of him who goes beyond this faith, and seeks for more. It may also be understood thus: because although we are established in the New Testament, which the number eighty signifies, yet still our life is one of labour and sorrow, while "we groan within ourselves, awaiting the adoption, to wit, the redemption of our body; for we are saved by hope; and if we hope for that we see not, then do we with patience wait for it." [7] This relates to the mercy of God, of which he proceeds to say, "Since thy mercy cometh over us,[8] and we shall be chastened:" for "the Lord chasteneth whom He loveth, and scourgeth every son whom He receiveth," [9] and to some mighty ones He giveth a thorn in the flesh, to buffet them, that they may not be exalted above measure through the abundance of the revelations, so that strength be made perfect in weakness.[10] Some copies read, we shall be "taught," instead of "chastened," which is equally expressive of the Divine Mercy; for no man can be taught without labour and sorrow; since strength is made perfect in weakness.

11. "For who knoweth the power of Thy wrath: and for the fear of Thee to number Thine anger?" (ver. 11). It belongs to very few men, he saith, to know the power of Thy wrath; for when Thou dost spare, Thy anger is so far heavier against most men; that we may know that labour and sorrow belong not to wrath, but rather to Thy mercy, when Thou chastenest and teachest those whom Thou lovest, to save them from the torments of eternal punishment: as it is said in another Psalm,[11] "The sinner hath provoked the Lord: He will not require it of him according to the greatness of His wrath." With this also is understood, "Who knoweth?" Such is the difficulty of finding any one who knoweth how to number Thine anger by Thy fear, that he adds this, meaning that it is to the purpose that Thou appearest to spare some, with whom Thou art more angry, that the sinner may be prospered in his path, and receive a heavier doom at the last. For when the power of human wrath hath killed the body, it hath nothing more to do: but God hath

---

[6] St. Augustin seems to refer the word *amplius* to a period beyond the eighty years. In the English version it clearly applies to the attainment of that age.

[7] Rom. viii. 23-25.

[8] *Quoniam supervenit super nos mansuetudo, et corripiemur:* the equivalent in the Prayer Book is, "so soon passeth it away, and we are gone."

[9] Heb. xii. 6.　　[10] 2 Cor. xii. 7, 9.　　[11] Ps. x. 3, Lat.

---

[1] *Sicut aranea meditabantur.*　　[2] Rom. v. 12.
[3] Gen. vii 20.　　[4] Isa. lix. 6.
[5] *Aliud est in ipsis, aliud in potentatibus.*

power both to punish here, and after the death of the body to send into Hell, and by the few who are thus taught, the vain and seductive prosperity of the wicked is judged to be greater wrath of God.[1] . . .

12. "Make Thy right hand so well known" (ver. 12). This is the reading of most of the Greek copies: not of some in Latin, which is thus, "Make Thy right hand well known to me." What is, "Thy right hand," but Thy Christ, of whom it is said, And to whom is the Arm of the Lord revealed?[2] Make Him so well known, that Thy faithful may learn in Him to ask and to hope for those things rather of Thee as rewards of their faith, which do not appear in the Old Testament, but are revealed in the New: that they may not imagine that the happiness derived from earthly and temporal blessings is to be highly esteemed, desired, or loved, and thus their feet slip,[3] when they see it in men who honour Thee not: that their steps may not give way, while they know not how to number Thine anger. Finally, in accordance with this prayer of the Man that is His,[4] He has made His Christ so well known as to show by His sufferings that not these rewards which seem so highly prized in the Old Testament, where they are shadows of things to come, but things eternal, are to be desired. The right hand of God may also be understood in this sense, as that by which He will separate His saints from the wicked: because that hand becomes well known, when it scourgeth every son whom He receiveth, and suffers him not, in greater anger, to prosper in his sins, but in His mercy scourgeth him with the left,[5] that He may place him purified on His right hand.[6] The reading of most copies, "make Thy right hand well known to me," may be referred either to Christ, or to eternal happiness: for God has not a right hand in bodily shape, as He has not that anger which is aroused into violent passion.

13. But what he addeth,[7] "and those fettered in heart in wisdom;" other copies read, "instructed," not "fettered:" the Greek verb, expressing both senses, only differing by a single syllable.[8] But since these also, as it is said, put their "feet in the fetters" of wisdom, are taught wisdom (he means the feet of the heart, not of the body), and bound by its golden chains[9] depart not from the path of God, and become not runaways from him; whichever reading we adopt, the truth in the meaning is safe. Them thus fettered, or instructed in heart in wisdom, God makes so well known in the New Testament,

that they despised all things for the Faith which the impiety of Jews and Gentiles abhorred; and allowed themselves to be deprived of those things which in the Old Testament are thought high promises by those who judge after the flesh.

14. And as when they became so well known, as to despise these things, and by setting their affections on things eternal, gave a testimony through their sufferings (whence they are called witnesses or martyrs in the Greek), they endured for a long while many bitter temporal afflictions. This man of God giveth heed to this, and the prophetic spirit under the name of Moses continues thus, "Return, O Lord, how long? and be softened concerning Thy servants" (ver. 13). These are the words of those, who, enduring many evils in that persecuting age, become known because their hearts are bound in the chain of wisdom so firmly, that not even such hardships can induce them to fly from their Lord to the good things of this world. "How long wilt Thou hide Thy face from me, O Lord?"[10] occurs in another Psalm, in unison with this sentence, "Return, O Lord, how long?" And that they who, in a most carnal spirit, ascribe to God the form of a human body, may know that the "turning away" and "turning again" of His countenance is not like those motions of our own frame, let them recollect these words from above in the same Psalm, "Thou hast set our misdeeds before Thee, and our secret sins in the light of Thy countenance." How then does he say in this passage, "Return," that God may be favourable, as if He had turned away His face in anger; when as in the former he speaks of God's anger in such a manner, as to insinuate that He had not turned away His countenance from the misdeeds and the course of life of those He was angry with, but rather had set them before Him, and in the light of His countenance? The word, "How long," belongs to righteousness beseeching, not indignant impatience. "Be softened," some have rendered by a verb, "soften." But "be softened" avoids an ambiguity; since to soften is a common verb: for he may be said to soften who pours out prayers, and he to whom they are poured out: for we say, I soften thee, and I soften toward thee.[11]

15. Next, in anticipation of future blessings, of which he speaks as already vouchsafed, he says, "We are satisfied with Thy mercy in the morning" (ver. 14). Prophecy has thus been kindled for us, in the midst of these toils and sorrows of the night, like a lamp in the darkness, until day dawn, and the Day-star arise in our hearts.[12] For blessed are the pure in heart, for they shall see God: then shall the righteous be filled with that blessing for which they hunger

---

[1] Matt. x. 28; Ps. lxxiii. 2, 3, 17.
[2] Isa. liii. 1.   [3] Ps. lxxiii. 2.   [4] *Hominis sui.*
[5] *Al.* "on the left."   [6] Matt xxv. 33.
[7] *Et compeditos corde in sapientiâ.*
[8] πεπαιδευμένους, πεπεδημένους.   [9] Ecclus. vi. 24.
[10] Ps. xiii. 1.   [11] *Deprecor te, et deprecor a te.*
[12] 2 Pet. i. 19.

and thirst now,[1] while, walking in faith, they are absent from the Lord.[2] Hence are the words, "In Thy presence is fulness of joy:"[3] and, "Early in the morning they shall stand by, and shall look up:"[4] and as other translators have said it, "We shall be satisfied with Thy mercy in the morning;" then they shall be satisfied. As he says elsewhere, "I shall be satisfied, when Thy glory shall be revealed."[5] So it is said, "Lord, show us the Father, and it sufficeth us:" and our Lord Himself answereth, "I will manifest Myself to Zion;"[6] and until this promise is fulfilled, no blessing satisfies us, or ought to do so, lest our longings should be arrested in their course, when they ought to be increased until they gain their objects. "And we rejoiced and were glad all the days of our life." Those days are days without end: they all exist together: it is thus they satisfy us: for they give not way to days succeeding: since there is nothing there which exists not yet because it has not reached us, or ceases to exist because it has passed; all are together: because there is one day only, which remains and passes not away: this is eternity itself. These are the days respecting which it is written, "What man is he that lusteth to live, and would fain see good days?"[7] These days in another passage are styled years: where unto God it is said, "But Thou art the same, and Thy years shall not fail:"[8] for these are not years that are accounted for nothing, or days that perish like a shadow: but they are days which have a real existence, the number of which he who thus spoke, "Lord, let me know mine end" (that is, after reaching what term I shall remain unchanged, and have no further blessing to crave), "and the number of my days, what it is" (what *is*, not what is not): prayed to know. He distinguishes them from the days of this life, of which he speaks as follows, "Behold, Thou hast made my days as it were a span long,"[9] which are not, because they stand not, remain not, but change in quick succession: nor is there a single hour in them in which our being is not such, but that one part of it has already passed, another is about to come, and none remains as it is. But those years and days, in which we too shall never fail, but evermore be refreshed, will never fail. Let our souls long earnestly for those days, let them thirst ardently for them, that there we may be filled, be satisfied, and say what we now say in anticipation, "We have been satisfied," etc. "We have been comforted again now, after the time that Thou hast brought us low, and for the years wherein we have seen evil" (ver. 15).

16. But now in days that are as yet evil, let us speak as follows. "Look upon Thy servants, and upon Thy works" (ver. 16). For Thy servants themselves are Thy works, not only inasmuch as they are men, but as Thy servants, that is, obedient to Thy commands. For we are His workmanship, created not merely in Adam, but in Christ Jesus, unto good works, which God hath before ordained that we should walk in them:[10] "for it is God which worketh in us both to will and to do of His good pleasure."[11] "And direct their sons:" that they may be right in heart, for to such God is bountiful; for "God is bountiful to Israel, to those that are right in heart.". . .

17. "And let the brightness of the Lord our God be upon us" (ver. 17); whence the words, "O Lord, the light of Thy countenance is marked upon us."[12] And, "Make Thou straight the works of our hands upon us:" that we may do them not for hope of earthly reward: for then they are not straight, but crooked. In many copies the Psalm goes thus far, but in some there is found an additional verse at the end, as follows, "And make straight the work of our hands." To these words the learned have prefixed a star, called an asterisk, to show that they are found in the Hebrew, or in some other Greek translations, but not in the Septuagint. The meaning of this verse, if we are to expound it, appears to me this, that all our good works are one work of love: for love is the fulfilling of the Law.[13] For as in the former verse he had said, "And the works of our hands make Thou straight upon us," here he says "work," not works, as if anxious to show, in the last verse, that all our works are one, that is, are directed with a view to one work. For then are works righteous, when they are directed to this one end: "for the end of the commandment is charity out of a pure heart, and of a good conscience, and of faith unfeigned."[14] There is therefore one work, in which are all, "faith which worketh by love:"[15] whence our Lord's words in the Gospel, "This is the work of God, that ye believe in Him whom He hath sent."[16] Since, therefore, in this Psalm, both old and new life, life both mortal and everlasting, years that are counted for nought, and years that have the fulness of loving-kindness and of true joy, that is, the penalty of the first and the reign of the Second Man, are marked so very clearly; I imagine, that the name of Moses, the man of God, became the title of the Psalm, that pious and right-minded readers of the Scriptures might gain an intimation that the Mosaic laws, in which God appears to promise only, or nearly only, earthly rewards for good works, without doubt contains under a veil some such hopes as this Psalm displays. But when any one has passed over to Christ, the

---

[1] Matt. v. 8, 6.   [2] 2 Cor. v. 6.   [3] Ps. xvi. 11.
[4] Ps. v. 3.   [5] Ps. xvii. 15.   [6] John xiv. 8, 21.
[7] Ps. xxxiv. 12.   [8] Ps. cii. 27.   [9] Ps. xxxix. 4, 5.

[10] Eph. ii. 10.   [11] Philip. ii. 13.   [12] Ps iv. 6.
[13] Rom. xiii. 10.   [14] 1 Tim. i. 5.   [15] Gal. v. 6.
[16] John vi. 29.

veil will be taken away :[1] and his eyes will be unveiled, that he may consider the wonderful things in the law of God, by the gift of Him, to whom we pray, " Open Thou mine eyes, and I shall see the wondrous things of Thy law.[2]

PSALM XCI.[3]

1. This Psalm is that from which the Devil dared to tempt our Lord Jesus Christ : let us therefore attend to it, that thus armed, we may be enabled to resist the tempter, not presuming in ourselves, but in Him who before us was tempted, that we might not be overcome when tempted. Temptation to Him was not necessary : the temptation of Christ is our learning, but if we listen to His answers to the devil, in order that, when ourselves are tempted, we may answer in like manner, we are then entering through the gate, as ye have heard it read in the Gospel. For what is to enter by the gate? To enter by Christ, who Himself said, " I am the door : "[4] and to enter through Christ, is to imitate His ways. . . . He urges us to imitate Him in those works which He could not have done had He not been made Man ; for how could He endure sufferings, unless He had become a Man? How could He otherwise have died, been crucified, been humbled? Thus then do thou, when thou sufferest the troubles of this world, which the devil, openly by men, or secretly, as in Job's case, inflicts ; be courageous, be of long suffering ; " thou shalt dwell under the defence of the Most High," as this Psalm expresses it : for if thou depart from the help of the Most High, without strength to aid thyself, thou wilt fall.

2. For many men are brave, when they are enduring persecution from men, and see them openly rage against themselves : imagining they are then imitating the sufferings of Christ, in case men openly persecute them ; but if assailed by the hidden attack of the devil, they believe they are not being crowned by Christ. Never fear when thou dost imitate Christ. For when the devil tempted our Lord, there was no man in the wilderness ; he tempted Him secretly ; but he was conquered, and conquered too when openly attacking Him. This do thou, if thou wishest to enter by the door, when the enemy secretly assails thee, when he asks for a man that he may do him some hurt by bodily troubles, by fever, by sickness, or any other bodily sufferings, like those of Job. He saw not the devil, yet he acknowledged the power of God. He knew that the devil had no power against him, unless from the Almighty Ruler of all things he received that power : the whole glory he gave to God, power to the devil he gave not. . . .

3. He then who so imitates Christ as to endure all the troubles of this world, with his hopes set upon God, that he falls into no snare, is broken down by no panic fears, he it is " who dwelleth under the defence of the Most High, who shall abide under the protection of God " (ver. 1), in the words with which the Psalm, which you have heard and sung, begins. You will recognise the words, so well known, in which the devil tempted our Lord, when we come to them. " He shall say unto the Lord, Thou art my taker up, and my refuge : my God " (ver. 2). Who speaks thus to the Lord? " He who dwelleth under the defence of the Most High : " not under his own defence. Who is this? He dwelleth under the defence of the Most High, who is not proud, like those who ate, that they might become as Gods, and lost the immortality in which they were made. For they chose to dwell under a defence of their own, not under that of the Most High : thus they listened to the suggestions of the serpent,[5] and despised the precept of God : and discovered at last that what God threatened, not what the devil promised, had come to pass in them.

4. Thus then do thou say also, " In Him will I trust. For He Himself shall deliver me " (ver. 3), not I myself. Observe whether he teaches anything but this, that all our trust be in God, none in man. Whence shall he deliver thee? " From the snare of the hunter, and from a harsh word." Deliverance from the hunter's net is indeed a great blessing : but how is deliverance from a harsh word so? Many have fallen into the hunter's net through a harsh word. What is it that I say? The devil and his angels spread their snares, as hunters do : and those who walk in Christ tread afar from those snares : for he dares not spread his net in Christ : he sets it on the verge of the way, not in the way. Let then thy way be Christ, and thou shalt not fall into the snares of the devil. . . .

But what is, " from a harsh word "? The devil has entrapped many by a harsh word : for instance, those who profess Christianity among Pagans suffer insult from the heathen : they blush when they hear reproach, and shrinking out of their path in consequence, fall into the hunter's snares. And yet what will a harsh word do to you? Nothing. Can the snares with which the enemy entraps you by means of reproaches, do nothing to you? Nets are usually spread for birds at the end of a hedge, and stones are thrown into the hedge : those stones will not harm the birds. When did any one ever hit a bird by throwing a stone into a hedge? But the bird, frightened at the harmless noise, falls into the nets ; and thus men who fear the vain reproaches of their calumniators, and who blush at unprovoked insults, fall into the snares of the hunters, and are taken captive by the devil. . . . Just as among the heathen, the Christian who fears their reproaches falls into the snare of the hunter: so among the Christians, those who endeavour to be more diligent and better than the rest, are doomed to bear insults from Christians themselves. What then doth it profit, my brother, if thou occasionally find a city in which there is no heathen? No one there insults a man because he is a Christian, for this reason, that there is no Pagan therein: but there are many Christians who lead a bad life, among whom those who are resolved to live righteously, and to be sober among the drunken, and chaste among the unchaste, and amid the consulters of astrologers sincerely to worship God, and to ask after no such things, and among spectators of frivolous shows will go only to church, suffer from those very Christians reproaches, and harsh words, when they address such a one, "Thou art the mighty, the righteous, thou art Elias, thou art Peter: thou hast come from heaven." They insult him: whichever way he turns, he hears harsh sayings on each side: and if he fears, and abandons the way of Christ, he falls into the snares of the hunters. But what is it, when he hears such words, not to swerve from the way? On hearing them, what comfort has he, which prevents his heeding them, and enables him to enter by the door? Let him say; What words am I called, who am a servant and a sinner? To my Lord Jesus they said, "Thou hast a devil."[1] You have just heard the harsh words spoken against our Lord: it was not necessary for our Lord to suffer this, but in doing so He has warned thee against harsh words, lest thou fall into the snares of the hunters.

5. "He shall defend thee between His shoulders, and thou shalt hope under His wings" (ver. 4). He says this, that thy protection may not be to thee from thyself, that thou mayest not imagine that thou canst defend thyself; He will defend thee, to deliver thee from the hunter's snare, and from an harsh word. The expression, "between His shoulders," may be understood both in front and behind: for the shoulders are about the head; but in the words, "thou shalt hope under His wings," it is clear that the protection of the wings of God expanded places thee between His shoulders, so that God's wings on this side and that have thee in the midst, where thou shalt not fear lest any one hurt thee: only be thou careful never to leave that spot, where no foe dares approach. If the hen defends her chickens beneath her wings; how much more shalt thou be safe beneath the wings

of God, even against the devil and his angels, the powers who fly about in mid air like hawks, to carry off the weak young one? For the comparison of the hen to the very Wisdom of God is not without ground; for Christ Himself, our Lord and Saviour, speaks of Himself as likened to a hen; "how often would I have gathered thy children," etc.[2] That Jerusalem would not: let us be willing. . . . If you consider other birds, brethren, you will find many that hatch their eggs, and keep their young warm: but none that weakens herself in sympathy with her chickens, as the hen does. We see swallows, sparrows, and storks outside their nests, without being able to decide whether they have young or no: but we know the hen to be a mother by the weakness of her voice, and the loosening of her feathers: she changes altogether from love for her chickens: she weakens herself because they are weak. Thus since we were weak, the Wisdom of God made Itself weak, when the Word was made flesh, and dwelt in us,[3] that we might hope under His wings.

6. "His truth shall surround thee with a shield" (ver. 5). What are "the wings," the same is "the shield:" since there are neither wings nor shield. If either were literally, how could the one be the same as the other? can wings be a shield or a shield wings? But all these expressions, indeed, are figuratively used through likenesses. If Christ were really a Stone,[4] He could not be a Lion; if a Lion,[5] He could not be a Lamb: but He is called both Lion, and Lamb,[6] and Stone, and Calf, and anything else of the sort, metaphorically, because He is neither Stone, nor Lion, nor Lamb, nor Calf, but Jesus Christ, the Saviour of all of us, for these are likenesses, not literal names. "His truth shall be thy shield," it is said: a shield to assure us that He will not confound those whose trust is in themselves with those who hope in God. One is a sinner, and the other a sinner: but suppose one that presumes upon himself is a despiser, confesses not his sins, and he will say, if my sins displeased God, He would not suffer me to live. But another dared not even raise his eyes, but beat upon his breast, saying, "God be merciful to me a sinner."[7] Both this was a sinner, and that: but the one mocked, the other mourned: the one was a despiser, the other a confessor, of his sins. But the truth of God, which respects not persons, discerns the penitent from him who denies his sin, the humble from the proud, him who presumes upon himself from him who presumes on God. "Thou shalt not be afraid for any terror by night."

7. "Nor for the arrow that flieth by day, for

---

[1] John viii. 48.

[2] Matt. xxiii. 37.
[3] John i. 14.
[4] Acts iv. 10, 11.
[5] Rev. v. 5.
[6] John i. 29.
[7] Luke xviii. 13.

the matter[1] that walketh in darkness, nor for the ruin and the devil that is in the noon-day" (ver. 6). These two clauses above correspond to the two below; "Thou shalt not fear" for "the terror by night, from the arrow that flieth by day:" both because of "the terror by night," from "the matter that walketh in darkness:" and because of "the arrow that flieth by day," from "the ruin of the devil of the noon-day." What ought to be feared by night, and what by day? When any man sins in ignorance, he sins, as it were, by night: when he sins in full knowledge, by day. The two former sins then are the lighter: the second are much heavier; but this is obscure, and will repay your attention, if, by God's blessing, I can explain it so that you may understand it. He calls the light temptation, which the ignorant yield to, "terror by night:" the light temptation, which assails men who well know, "the arrow that flieth by day." What are light temptations? Those which do not press upon us so urgently, as to overcome us, but may pass by quickly if declined. Suppose these, again, heavy ones. If the persecutor threatens, and frightens the ignorant grievously, I mean those whose faith is as yet unstable, and know not that they are Christians that they may hope for a life to come; as soon as they are alarmed with temporal ills, they imagine that Christ has forsaken them, and that they are Christians to no purpose; they are not aware that they are Christians for this reason, that they may conquer the present, and hope for the future: the matter that walketh in darkness has found and seized them. But some there are who know that they are called to a future hope; that what God has promised is not of this life, or this earth; that all these temptations must be endured, that we may receive what God hath promised us for evermore; all this they know: when however the persecutor urges them more strenuously, and plies them with threats, penalties, tortures, at length they yield, and although they are well aware of their sin, yet they fall as it were by day.

8. But why does he say, "at noon-day"? The persecution is very hot; and thus the noon signifies the excessive heat. . . . The demon that is "in the noon-day," represents the heat of a furious persecution: for these are our Lord's words, "The sun was up; and because they had no root, they withered away:" and when explaining it, He applies it to those who are offended when persecution ariseth, "Because they have not root in themselves." We are therefore right in understanding by the demon that destroyeth in the noon-day, a violent persecution. Listen, beloved, while I describe the persecution,

from which the Lord hath rescued His Church. At first, when the emperors and kings of the world imagined that they could extirpate from the earth the Christian name by persecution, they proclaimed, that any one who confessed himself a Christian, should be smitten. He who did not choose to be smitten, denied that he was a Christian, knowing the sin he was committing: the arrow that flieth by day reached him. But whoever regarded not the present life, but had a sure trust in a future one, avoided the arrow, by confessing himself a Christian; smitten in the flesh, he was liberated in the spirit: resting with God, he began peacefully to await the redemption of his body in the resurrection of the dead: he escaped from that temptation, from the arrow that flieth by day. "Whoever professes himself a Christian, let him be beheaded;" was as the arrow that flieth by day. The "devil that is in the noon-day" was not yet abroad, burning with a terrible persecution, and afflicting with great heat even the strong. For hear what followed; when the enemy saw that many were hastening to martyrdom, and that the number of fresh converts increased in proportion to that of the sufferers, they said among themselves, We shall annihilate the human race, so many thousands are there who believe in His Name; if we kill all of them, there will hardly be a survivor on earth. The sun then began to blaze, and to glow with a terrible heat. Their first edict had been, Whoever shall confess himself a Christian, let him be smitten. Their second edict was, Whoever shall have confessed himself a Christian, let him be tortured, and tortured even until he deny himself a Christian. . . . Many therefore who denied not,[2] failed amid the tortures; for they were tortured until they denied. But to those who persevered in professing Christ, what could the sword do, by killing the body at one stroke, and sending the soul to God? This was the result of protracted tortures also: yet who could be found able to resist such cruel and continued torments? Many failed: those, I believe, who presumed upon themselves, who dwelt not under the defence of the Most High, and under the shadow of the God of Heaven; who said not to the Lord, "Thou art my lifter up:" who trusted not beneath the shadow of His wings, but reposed much confidence in their own strength. They are thrown down by God, to show them that it is He that protects them, He overrules their temptations, He allows so much only to befall them, as each person can sustain.

9. Many then fell before the demon of the noon-day. Would ye know how many? He goes on, and says, "A thousand shall fall beside thee, and ten thousand at thy right hand; but it

---

[1] *Negotium.*

[2] [Under the first edict. — C.]

shall not come nigh thee " (ver. 7). To whom, brethren, but to Christ Jesus, is this said? . . . For the members, the body, and the head, are not separate from one another: the body and the head are the Church and her Saviour. How then is it said, "A thousand shall fall beside thee, and ten thousand by thy right hand "? Because they shall fall before the devil, that destroyeth at noon. It is a terrible thing, my brethren, to fall from beside Christ, from His right hand; but how shall they fall from beside Him? Why the one beside Him, the other at His right hand? Why a thousand beside Him, ten thousand at His right hand? Why a thousand beside Him? Because a thousand are fewer than the ten thousand who shall fall at His right hand. Who these are will soon be clear in Christ's name; for to some He promised that they should judge with Him, namely, to the Apostles, who left all things, and followed Him. . . . Those judges then are the heads of the Church, the perfect. To such He said, "If thou wilt be perfect, go and sell that thou hast, and give to the poor." [1] What means the expression, "if thou wilt be perfect "? it means, if thou wilt judge with Me, and not be judged. . . . Many such at that period, who had distributed their all to the poor, and already promised themselves a seat beside Christ in judgment of the nations, failed amid their torments under the blazing fire of persecution, as before the demon of the noon-day, and denied Christ. These are they who have fallen "beside" Him: when about to sit with Christ for the judgment of the world, they fell.

10. I will now explain who are they who fall on the right hand of Christ. . . . And because many have fallen from that hope of being judges, but yet many, many more from that of being on His right hand, the Psalmist thus addresses Christ, "A thousand shall fall beside Thee, and ten thousand at Thy right hand." And since there shall be many, who regarded not all these things, with whom, as it were with His own limbs, Christ is one, he adds, "But it shall not come nigh Thee." Were these words addressed to the Head alone? Surely not; surely neither (doth it come nigh) to Paul, nor Peter, nor all the Apostles, nor all the Martyrs, who failed not in their torments. What then do the words, "it shall not come nigh," mean? Why were they thus tortured? The torture came nigh the flesh, but it did not reach the region of faith. Their faith then was far beyond the reach of the terrors threatened by their torturers. Let them torture, terror will not come nigh; let them torture, but they will mock the torture, putting their trust in Him who conquered before them, that the rest might conquer. And who conquer, except they

who trust not in themselves? . . . Who will not fear? He who trusts not in himself, but in Christ. But those who trust in themselves, although they even hope to judge at the side of Christ, although they hoped they should be at His right hand, as if He said to them, "Come, ye blessed of My Father," etc.; yet the devil that is at noon overtook them, the raging heat of persecution, terrifying with violence; and many fell from the hope of the seat of judgment, of whom it is said, "A thousand shall fall beside thee;" many too fell from the hope of reward for their duties,[2] of whom it was said, "And ten thousand at thy right hand." But this downfall and devil that is at noon-day "shall not come nigh thee," that is, the Head and the body; for the Lord knows who are His.[3]

11. "Nevertheless, with thine eyes shalt thou behold, and see the reward of the ungodly " (ver. 8). What is this? Why "nevertheless"? Because the wicked were allowed to tyrannize over Thy servants, and to persecute them. Will they then have been allowed to persecute Thy servants with impunity? Not with impunity, for although Thou hast permitted them, and Thine own have thence received a brighter crown, "nevertheless," etc. For the evil which they willed, not the good they unconsciously were the agents of, will be recompensed them. All that is wanting is the eye of faith, by which we may see that they are raised for a time only, while they shall mourn for evermore; and to those into whose hands is given temporal power over the servants of God, it shall be said, "Depart into everlasting fire, prepared for the devil and his angels." [4] But if every man have but eyes in the sense in which it is said, "With thine eyes shalt thou behold," it is no unimportant thing to look upon the wicked flourishing in this life, and to have an eye to him, to consider what will become of him in the end, if he fail to reform his ways: for those who now would thunder upon others, will afterwards feel the thunderbolt themselves.

12. "For Thou, Lord, art my hope " (ver. 9). He has now come to the power which rescues him from falling by the "downfall and the devil of the noon-day." "For Thou, Lord, art my hope: Thou hast set Thy house of defence very high." What do the words "very high " mean? For many make their house of defence in God a mere refuge from temporal persecution; but the defence of God is on high, and very secret, whither thou mayest fly from the wrath to come. Within "Thou hast set thine house of defence very high. There shall no evil happen unto Thee: neither shall any plague come nigh Thy dwelling" (ver. 10).

---

[1] Matt. xix 21.

[2] *Obsequiorum.* [3] 2 Tim. ii. 19. [4] Matt. xxv. 41.

13. The Holy City is not the Church of this country only, but of the whole world as well: not that of this age only, but from Abel himself down to those who shall to the end be born and believe in Christ, the whole assembly of the Saints, belonging to one city; which city is Christ's body, of which Christ is the Head. There, too, dwell the Angels, who are our fellow-citizens: we toil, because we are as yet pilgrims: while they within that city are awaiting our arrival. Letters have reached us too from that city, apart from which we are wandering: those letters are the Scriptures, which exhort us to live well. Why do I speak of letters only? The King himself descended, and became a path to us in our wanderings: that walking in Him, we may neither stray, nor faint nor fall among robbers, nor be caught in the snares that are set near our path. This character, then, we recognise in the whole Person of Christ, together with the Church. . . . He Himself is our Head, He is God, co-equal with the Father, the Word of God, by whom all things were made:[1] but God to create, Man to renew; God to make, Man to restore. Looking upon Him, then, let us hear the Psalm. Listen, beloved. This is the teaching and doctrine of this school, which may enable you to understand, not this Psalm only, but many, if ye keep in mind this rule. Sometimes a Psalm, and all prophecy as well, in speaking of Christ, praises the Head alone, and sometimes from the Head goes to the Body, that is, the Church, and without apparently changing the Person spoken of: because the Head is not separate from the Body, and both are spoken of as one . . .

14. What then, my brethren, what is said of our Head? "For Thou, Lord, art my hope," etc. Of this we have spoken, "for He hath given His angels charge over Thee, to keep Thee in all Thy ways" (ver. 11). You heard these words but now, when the Gospel was being read; attend therefore. Our Lord, after He was baptized, fasted. Why was He baptized? That we might not scorn to be baptized. For when John said to our Lord, "Comest Thou to me to be baptized? I ought to be baptized by Thee;" and our Lord replied, "Suffer it to be so now, for thus it becometh us to fulfil all righteousness;"[2] He wished to fulfil all humility, so that He should be washed, who had no defilement. . . . Our Lord, then, was baptized, and after baptism He was tempted; He fasted forty days, a number which has, as I have often mentioned, a deep meaning. All things cannot be explained at once, lest needful time be too much taken up. After forty days He was an hungred. He could have fasted without ever feeling hunger; but then

how could He be tempted? or had He not overcome the tempter, how couldest thou learn to struggle with him? He was hungry; and then the tempter said, "If Thou be the Son of God, command that these stones be made bread." Was it a great thing for our Lord Jesus Christ to make bread out of stones, when He satisfied so many thousands with five loaves? He made bread out of nothing. For whence came that quantity of food, which could satisfy so many thousands? The sources of that bread are in the Lord's hands. This is nothing wonderful; for He Himself made out of five loaves bread enough for so many thousands,[3] who also every day out of a few seeds raises up on earth immense harvests. These are the miracles of our Lord: but from their constant operation they are disregarded. What then, my brethren, was it impossible for the Lord to create bread out of stones? He made men even out of stones, in the words of John the Baptist himself, "God is able of these stones to raise up children unto Abraham."[4] Why then did He not so? That he might teach thee how to answer the tempter, so that if thou wast reduced to any straits and the tempter suggested, if thou wast a Christian and belongedst to Christ, would He desert thee now? . . . Listen to our Lord: "Man shall not live by bread alone, but by every word that proceedeth out of the mouth of God." Dost thou think the word of God bread? If the Word of God, through which all things were made, was not bread, He would not say, "I am the bread which came down from heaven."[5] Thou hast therefore learnt to answer the tempter, when pressed with hunger.

15. What if he tempt thee in these words: If thou wast a Christian, thou wouldest do miracles, as many Christians have done? Thou, deceived by a wicked suggestion, wouldest tempt the Lord thy God, so as to say to Him, If I am a Christian, and am before Thine eyes, and Thou dost account me at all in the number of Thine own, let me also do something like the many works which Thy Saints have done. Thou hast tempted God, as if thou wert not a Christian, unless thou didst this. Many who desired such things have fallen. For that Simon the sorcerer desired such gifts of the Apostles, when he wished to buy the Holy Spirit for money.[6] He loved the power of working miracles, but loved not the imitation of humility. . . . What then, if he tempt thee thus, "work miracles"? that thou mayest not tempt God, what shouldest thou answer? What our Lord answered. The devil said to Him, "Cast Thyself down; for it is written, He shall give His Angels charge concerning Thee," etc. If Thou shalt cast Thyself down,

---

[1] John i. 3.   [2] Matt. iii. 14, 15.

[3] Matt. xiv. 17, 21.   [4] Matt. iii. 9.
[5] John vi. 41.   [6] Acts viii. 18.

Angels shall receive Thee. And it might indeed, my brethren, happen, if our Lord had cast Himself down, the attending Angels would receive our Lord's flesh; but what does He say to him? "It is written again, Thou shalt not tempt the Lord thy God." [1] Thou thinkest Me a man. For the devil came to Him with this view, that he might try whether He were the Son of God. He saw His Flesh; but His might appeared in His works: the Angels had borne witness. He saw that He was mortal, so that he might tempt Him, that by Christ's temptation the Christian might be taught. What then is written? "Thou shalt not tempt the Lord thy God." Let us not then tempt the Lord, so as to say, If we belong to Thee, let us work a miracle.

16. Let us return to the words of the Psalm. "They shall bear Thee in their hands, lest at any time Thou hurt Thy foot against a stone" (ver. 12). Christ was raised up in the hands of Angels, when He was taken up into heaven: not that, if Angels had not sustained Him, He would have fallen: but because they were attending on their King. Say not, Those who sustained Him are better than He who was sustained. Are then cattle better than men, because they sustain the weakness of men? And we ought not to speak thus either; for if the cattle withdraw their support, their riders fall. But how ought we to speak of it? For it is said even of God, "Heaven is My throne." [2] Because then heaven supports Him, and God sits thereon, is therefore heaven the better? Thus also in this Psalm we may understand it of the service of the Angels: it does not pertain to any infirmity in our Lord, but to the honour they pay, and to their service. . . . What the finger of God is, the Gospel explaineth to us; for the finger of God is the Holy Ghost. How do we prove this? Our Lord, when answering those who accused Him of casting out devils in the name of Beelzebub, saith, "If I cast out devils by the Spirit of God;" [3] and another Evangelist, in relating the same saying, saith, "If I with the finger of God cast out devils." [4] What therefore is in one stated clearly, is darkly expressed in another. Thou didst not know what was the finger of God, but another Evangelist explains it by terming it the Spirit of God. The Law then written by the finger of God was given on the fiftieth day after the slaughter of the lamb, and the Holy Ghost descended on the fiftieth day after the Passion of our Lord Jesus Christ. The Lamb was slain, the Passover was celebrated, the fifty days were completed, and the Law was given. But that Law was to cause fear, not love: but that fear might be changed into love, He who was truly righteous

was slain: of whom that lamb whom the Jews were slaying was the type. He arose from the dead: and from the day of our Lord's Passover, as from that of the slaying of the Paschal lamb, fifty days are counted; and the Holy Ghost descended, now in the fulness of love, not in the punishment of fear. [5] Why have I said this? For this then our Lord arose, and was glorified, that He might send His Holy Spirit. And I said long ago that this was so, because His head is in heaven, His feet on earth. If His head is in heaven, His feet on earth; what means our Lord's feet on earth? Our Lord's saints on earth. Who are our Lord's feet? The Apostles sent throughout the whole world. Who are our Lord's feet? All the Evangelists, in whom our Lord travelleth over all nations. . . . We need not therefore wonder that our Lord was raised up to heaven by the hands of Angels, that His foot might not dash against a stone: lest those who on earth toiled in His body, while they were travelling over the whole world might become guilty of the Law, He took from them fear, and filled them with love. Through fear Peter thrice denied Him, [6] for he had not yet received the Holy Ghost: afterwards, when he had received the Holy Spirit, he began to preach with confidence. . . . Our Lord so dealt with him, as if He said, thrice thou hast denied Me through fear: thrice confess Me through love. With that love and that charity He filled His disciples. Why? Because He hath set His house of defence very high: because when glorified He sent the Holy Ghost, He released the faithful from the guilt of the Law, that His feet might not dash against a stone.

17. "Thou [7] shalt go upon the asp and the basilisk; the lion and the dragon shalt thou tread under thy feet" (ver. 13). Ye know who the serpent is, and how the Church treadeth upon him, as she is not conquered, because she is on her guard against his cunning. And after what manner he is a lion and a dragon, I believe you know also, beloved. The lion openly rages, the dragon lies secretly in covert: the devil hath each of these forces and powers. When the Martyrs were being slain, it was the raging lion: when heretics are plotting, it is the dragon creeping beneath us. Thou hast conquered the lion; conquer also the dragon: the lion hath not crushed [8] thee, let not the dragon deceive thee. . . . A few women in the Church have bodily virginity: but the virginity of the heart all the faithful have. In the very matter of faith he feared that the heart's virginity would be corrupted by the devil: and those who have lost it, are uselessly virgins in their bodies.

---

[1] Deut. vi. 16.   [2] Isa. lxvi. 1; Acts vii. 49.
[3] Matt. xii. 28.   [4] Luke xi. 20.

[5] Acts ii. 1-4.
[6] Matt. xxvi. 69-75.   [7] On this verse, see on Ps. xl. 1.
[8] *Al.* "let not the lion crush." [Note what follows. — C.]

What does a woman who is corrupt in heart preserve in her body? Thus a Catholic married woman is before a virgin heretic. For the first is not indeed a virgin in her body, but the second has become married in her heart; and married not unto God as her husband, but unto the dragon. But what shall the Church do? The basilisk is the king of serpents, as the devil is the king of wicked spirits.

18. These are the words of God to the Church. "Because he hath set his love in me, therefore will I deliver him" (ver. 14). Not only therefore the Head, which now sits in heaven, because He hath set His house of defence very high, to which no evil shall happen, neither shall any plague come nigh His dwelling; but we also, who are toiling on earth, and are still living in temptations, whose steps are feared for, lest they fall into snares, may hear the voice of the Lord our God consoling us, and saying to us, "Because he hath set his love upon me, therefore will I deliver him: I will set him up, because he hath known my name."

19. "He shall call upon me, and I will hear him: yea, I am with him in trouble" (ver. 15). Fear not when thou art in trouble, as if the Lord were not with thee. Let faith be with thee, and God is with thee in thy trouble. There are waves on the sea, and thou art tossed in thy bark, because Christ sleepeth. Christ slept in the ship, while the men were perishing.[1] If thy faith sleep in thy heart, Christ is as it were sleeping in thy ship: because Christ dwelleth in thee through faith, when thou beginnest to be tossed, awake Christ sleeping: rouse up thy faith, and thou shalt be assured that He deserts thee not. But thou thinkest thou art forsaken, because He rescueth thee not when thou thyself dost wish. He delivered the Three Children from the fire?[2] Did He, who did this, desert the Maccabees?[3] God forbid! He delivered both of these: the first bodily, that the faithless might be confounded; the last spiritually, that the faithful might imitate them. "I will deliver him, and bring him to honour."

20. "With length of days will I satisfy him" (ver. 16). What is length of days? Eternal life. Brethren, imagine not that length of days is spoken of in the same sense as days are said to be long in summer, short in winter. Hath he such days to give us? That length is one that hath no end, eternal life, that is promised us in long days. And truly, since this sufficeth, with reason he saith, "will I satisfy him." What is long in time, if it hath an end, satisfieth us not: for that reason it should not be even called long. And if we are covetous, we ought to be covetous of eternal life: long for such a life, as hath

no end. Lo, a line in which our covetousness may be extended. Dost thou wish money without limit? Long for eternal life without limit. Dost thou wish that thy possession may have no end? Seek for eternal life. "I will show him my salvation." Nor is this, my brethren, to be briefly passed over. "I will show him my salvation:" He means, I will show him Christ Himself. Why? Was He not seen on earth? What great thing hath He to show us? But He did not appear such as we shall see Him. He appeared in that shape in which those who saw Him crucified Him: behold, those who saw Him, crucified Him: we have not seen Him, yet we have believed. They had eyes, have not we? yea, we too have the eyes of the heart: but, as yet we see through faith, not by sight. When will it be sight? When shall we, as the Apostle saith, see Him "face to face"?[4] which God promiseth us as the high reward of all our toils. Whatever thou toilest in, thou toilest for this purpose, that thou mayest see Him. Some great thing it is we are to see, since all our reward is seeing; and our Lord Jesus Christ is that very great sight. He who appeared humble, will Himself appear great, and will rejoice us, as He is even now seen of His Angels. . . . Let us love and imitate Him: let us run after his ointments, as is said in the Song of Solomon: "Because of the savour of thy good ointments, we will run after thee."[5] For He came, and gave forth a savour that filled the world. Whence was that fragrance? From heaven. Follow then towards heaven, if thou do not answer[6] falsely when it is said, "Lift up your hearts," lift up your thoughts, your love, your hope: that it may not rot upon the earth. . . . "For wherever thy treasure is, there will be thy heart also."[7]

PSALM XCII.[8]

1. . . . We are not Christians, except on account of a future life: let no one hope for present blessings, let no one promise himself the happiness of the world, because he is a Christian: but let him use the happiness he hath, as he may, in what manner he may, when he may, as far as he may. When it is present, let him give thanks for the consolation of God: when it is wanting, let him give thanks to the Divine justice. Let him always be grateful, never ungrateful: let him be grateful to his Father, who soothes and caresses him: and grateful to his Father when He chasteneth him with the scourge, and teacheth him: for He ever loveth, whether He caress or threaten: and let him say

---

[1] Matt. viii. 24, 25. [2] Dan. iii. 29, 30. [3] 2 Macc. vii.

[4] 1 Cor. xiii 12. [5] Song of Sol. i. 3.
[6] [The response to the *Sursum Corda*. See A. N. F. vol. vii. p. 543, note 7. — C.]
[7] Matt. vi. 21.
[8] Lat. XCI. A sermon to the people, preached on Saturday.

what ye have heard in the Psalm : "It is a good thing to give thanks unto the Lord ; and to sing praises unto Thy Name, Thou Most Highest" (ver. 1).

2. This Psalm is entitled, a Psalm to be sung on the Sabbath day. Lo, this day is the Sabbath, which the Jews at this period observe by a kind of bodily rest, languid and luxurious. They abstain from labours, and give themselves up to trifles ; and though God ordained the Sabbath, they spend it in actions which God forbids. Our rest is from evil works, theirs from good ; for it is better to plough than to dance. They abstain from good, but not from trifling, works. God proclaims to us a Sabbath. What sort of Sabbath? First consider, where it is. It is in the heart, within us ; for many are idle with their limbs, while they are disturbed in conscience. . . . That very joy in the tranquillity of our hope, is our Sabbath. This is the subject of praise and of song in this Psalm, how a Christian man is in the Sabbath of his own heart, that is, in the quiet, tranquillity, and serenity of his conscience, undisturbed ; hence he tells us here, whence men are wont to be disturbed, and he teaches thee to keep Sabbath in thine own heart.

3. . . . Accuse thyself, and thou receivest indulgence. Besides, many do not accuse Satan, but their fate. My fate led me, saith one : when you ask him, why did you do it? why did you sin? he replies, by my evil fate. Lest he should say, I did it ; he points to God as the source of his sin : with his tongue he blasphemes. He saith not this indeed openly as yet, but listen, and see that he saith this. You ask of him, what is fate : and he replies, evil stars. You ask, who made, who appointed the stars ; he can only answer, God. It follows, then, that whether he doth so directly or indirectly,[1] still he accuseth God, and when God punisheth sins, he maketh God the author of his own sins. It cannot be that God punishes what He hath wrought : He punisheth what thou doest, that He may set free what He hath wrought. But sometimes, setting aside everything else, they attack God directly : and when they sin, they say, God willed this ; if God had not willed it, I should not have sinned. Does He warn thee for this, that not only He may not be listened to, to keep thee from sin, but even be accused because thou dost sin? What then doth this Psalm teach us? "It is a good thing to confess[2] unto the Lord." What is to confess unto the Lord? In both cases : both in thy sins, because thou hast done them ; and in thy good works, confess unto the Lord, because He hath

done them. Then shalt thou "sing unto the Name of God, the Most Highest :" seeking the glory of God, not thine own ; His Name, not thine. For if thou seekest the Name of God, He also seeketh thy name ; but if thou hast neglected the Name of God, He also doth blot out thine. . . .

4. "To tell of Thy mercy early in the morning, and of Thy truth in the night season" (ver. 2). What is the meaning of this ; that the mercy of God is to be told us in the morning, and in the night the truth of God? The morning is, when it is well with us ; the night, the sadness of tribulation. What then did he say in brief? When thou art prosperous, rejoice in God, for it is His mercy. Now, perhaps thou wouldest say, If I rejoice in God, when I am prosperous, because it is His mercy ; what am I to do when I am in sorrow, in tribulation? It is His mercy, when I am prosperous ; is it then His cruelty, when I am in adversity? If I praise His mercy when it is well with me, am I then to exclaim against His cruelty when it is ill? No. But when it is well, praise His mercy : when ill, praise His truth : because He scourgeth sins, He is not unjust. . . . During the night Daniel confessed the truth of God : he said in his prayer, "We have sinned, and committed iniquity, and have done wickedly. O Lord, righteousness belongeth unto Thee : but unto us confusion of face."[3] He told of the truth of God during the night-season. What is it to tell of the truth of God in the night-season? Not to accuse God, because thou sufferest aught of evil : but to attribute it to thy sins, His correction : to tell of His loving-kindness early in the morning, and of His truth in the night-season. When thou *doest this*, thou dost always praise God, always confess to God, and sing unto His Name.

5. "Upon a psaltery of ten strings, with a song, and upon the harp" (ver. 3). Ye have not heard of the psaltery of ten strings for the first time : it signifies the ten commandments of the Law. But we must sing upon that psaltery, and not carry it only. For even the Jews have the Law : but they carry it : they sing not. . . . "And upon the harp." This means, in word and deed ; "with a song," in word ; "upon the harp," in work. If thou speakest words alone, thou hast, as it were, the song only, and not the harp : if thou workest, and speakest not, thou hast the harp only. On this account both speak well and do well, if thou wouldest have the song together with the harp.

6. "For Thou, Lord, hast made me glad through Thy works ; and I will rejoice in giving praise for the operations of Thy hands" (ver. 4).

---

[1] *Sive per transennam sive per cannam longam, sive per proximum.*
[2] *Confiteri.*

[3] Dan. ix. 5, 7.

Ye see what he saith. Thou hast made me living well, Thou hast formed me: if by chance I do aught of good, I will rejoice in the work of Thy hands: as the Apostle saith, "For we are His workmanship, created unto good works."[1] For unless He formed thee to good works, thou wouldest not know any works but evil. . . . Because thou canst not have truth from thy own self, it remains that thou drink it thence, whence it floweth: as if thou hast gone back from the light, thou art in darkness: as a stone glows not with its own heat, but either from the sun or fire, and if thou withdraw it from the heat, it cools: there it appears, that the heat was not its own; for it became heated either by the sun or by fire: thus thou also, if thou withdraw from God, wilt become cold; if thou approach God, thou wilt warm: as the Apostle saith "fervent in spirit."[2] Also what saith he of the light? If thou approach Him, thou wilt be in light; therefore saith the Psalm, "Look upon Him, and be lightened; and your faces shall not be ashamed."[3] Because therefore thou canst do no good, unless lightened by the light of God, and warmed by the spirit of God; when thou shalt see thyself working well, confess unto God, and say what the Apostle saith; say unto thyself, that thou be not puffed up, "For what hast thou that thou didst not receive?"[4] . . .

7. That wretched man who doeth good, and suffereth evils, seeth him, becometh disturbed, and saith, O God, the wicked, I imagine, please Thee, and Thou hatest the good, and lovest those who work iniquity. . . . The Sabbath being now lost in the inner man, and the tranquillity of his heart being shut out, and good thoughts repelled, he now beginneth to imitate him whom he seeth flourishing amid his evil deeds; and turneth himself also to evil works. But God is long-suffering, because He is eternal,[5] and he knoweth the day of His own judgment, where He weigheth all things.

8. Teaching us this, what saith he? "O Lord, how glorious are Thy works: Thy thoughts are made very deep" (ver. 5). Verily, my brethren, there is no sea so deep as these thoughts of God, who maketh the wicked flourish, and the good suffer: nothing so profound, nothing so deep: therein every unbelieving soul is wrecked, in that depth, in that profundity. Dost thou wish to cross this depth? Remove not from the wood of Christ's Cross: thou shalt not sink: hold thyself fast to Christ. What do I mean by this, hold fast to Christ? It was for this reason that He chose

to suffer on earth Himself. Ye have heard, while the prophet was being read, how He "did not turn away His back from the smiters, and His face from the spittings of men," how "He turned not His cheek from their hands;"[6] wherefore chose He to suffer all these things, but that He might console the suffering? He could have raised His flesh at the last day: but then thou wouldest not have had thy ground of hope, since thou hadst not seen Him. He deferred not His resurrection, that thou mightest not still be in doubt. Suffer then tribulation in the world with the same end as that which thou hast observed in Christ: and let not those who do evil, and flourish in this life, move thee. "Thy thoughts are very deep." Where is the thought of God? Rejoice not as the fish who is exulting in his bait: the fisherman hath not drawn his hook: the fish hath as yet the hook in his jaws. And what seemeth to thee long, is short; all these things pass over quickly. What is the long life of man to the eternity of God? Dost thou wish to be of long-suffering? Consider the eternity of God. For thou regardest thy few days, and in thy few days thou dost wish all things to be fulfilled. What things? The condemnation of all the wicked: and the crowning of all the good: dost thou wish these things to be fulfilled in thy days? God fulfilleth them in His own time. Why dost thou suffer weariness? He is eternal: He waiteth: He is of long-suffering: but thou sayest, I am not of long-suffering, because I am mortal. But thou hast it in thy power to become so: join thy heart to the eternity of God, and with Him thou shalt be eternal. . . .

9. For this reason, after saying, "Thy thoughts are very deep," he at once subjoins: "An unwise man doth not well consider this, and a fool doth not understand it" (ver. 6). What are the things which an unwise man doth not well consider, and which a fool doth not understand? "When the ungodly are green as the grass." What is, "as the grass"? They flourish when it is winter, but they will wither in the summer. Thou observest the flower of the grass? What more quickly passeth by? What is brighter? What is greener? Let not its verdure delight thee, but fear its withering. Thou hast heard of the ungodly being green as the grass: hear also of the righteous: "For lo." In the mean while, consider the ungodly; they flourish as the grass; but who are they who understand it not? The foolish and unwise. "When the ungodly are green as the grass, and all men look upon the workers of iniquity" (ver. 7). All who in their heart think not aright of God, look upon the ungodly when they are as green as grass, that

---

[1] Eph. ii. 10.   [2] Rom. xii. 11.
[3] Ps. xxxiv. 5, Bible Version.   [4] 1 Cor. iv. 7.
[5] [*Deus autem patiens est quia æternus est.* One of those felicitous maxims in which our author abounds. — C.]

[6] Isa. l. 6.

is, when they flourish for a time. Why do they look upon them? "That they may be destroyed for ever." For they regard their momentary bloom, they imitate them, and wishing to flourish with them for a time, perish for evermore : this is, "That they may be destroyed for ever."

10. "But Thou, Lord, art the Most Highest for evermore" (ver. 8). Waiting above in Thy eternity until the season of the wicked be past, and that of the just come. "For lo." Listen, brethren. Already he who speaketh (for he speaketh in our person, in the person of Christ's body, for Christ speaketh in His own body, that is, in His Church), hath joined himself unto the eternity of God : as I a little before was saying unto you, God is long-suffering and patient, and alloweth all those evil deeds which He seeth to be done by wicked men. Wherefore? because He is eternal, and seeth what He keepeth for them. Dost thou also wish to be long-suffering and patient? Join thyself to the eternity of God : together with Him wait for those things which are beneath thee : for when thy heart shall have cleaved unto the Most Highest, all mortal things will be beneath thee : say then what follows, "For lo, thine enemies shall perish." Those who now flourish, shall afterwards perish. Who are the enemies of God? Brethren, perhaps ye think those only enemies of God who blaspheme? They indeed are so, and those wicked men who neither in tongue nor in thought cease to injure God. And what do they do to the eternal, most high God? If thou strike with thy fist upon a pillar, thou art hurt : and thinkest thou that where thou strikest God with thy blasphemy, thou art not thyself broken? for thou doest nothing to God. But the enemies of God are openly blasphemers. and daily they are found hidden. Beware of such enmities of God. For the Scripture revealeth some such secret enemies of God : that because thou knowest them not in thy heart, thou mayest know in God's Scriptures, and beware of being found with them. James saith openly in his Epistle, "Know ye not that the friendship of the world is enmity with God?"[1] Thou hast heard. Dost thou wish not to be an enemy of God? Be not a friend of this world : for if thou art a friend of this world, thou wilt be an enemy of God. For as a wife cannot be an adulteress, unless she be an enemy to her own husband : so a soul which is an adulteress through its love of worldly things, cannot but be an enemy to God. It feareth, but loveth not : it feareth punishment, but is not delighted with righteousness. All lovers of the world, therefore, are enemies of God, all the curious after trifles, all consulters of diviners, astrologers, and evil spirits. Let them enter, or not enter, Churches : they are enemies of God. They may flourish for a season like grass, but

they will perish, when He beginneth to visit them, and pronounce His sentence upon all flesh. Join thyself to the Scripture of God, and say with this Psalm, "For lo, thine enemies shall perish" (ver. 9). Be not found there, where they shall perish. "And all the workers of iniquity shall be destroyed."

11. . . . "But mine horn shall be exalted like the horn of an unicorn" (ver. 10). Why did He say, "like the horn of an unicorn"? Sometimes an unicorn signifies pride, sometimes it means the lifting up of unity ; because unity is lifted up, all heresies shall perish with the enemies of God. And "mine horn shall be exalted like an unicorn." When will it be so? "And mine old age shall be in the fatness of mercy."[2] Why did he say, "my old age"? He means, my last days ; as our old age is the last season in our lives, so the whole of what the body of Christ at present suffereth in labours, in cares, in watchings, in hunger, in thirst, in stumbling-blocks, in wickednesses, in tribulations, is its youth : its old age, that is, its last days, will be in joy. And beware, beloved, that ye think not death meant also, in that he hath spoken of old age : for man groweth old in the flesh for this reason, that he may die. The old age of the Church will be white with good works, but it shall not decay through death. What the head of the old man is, that our works will be. Ye see how the head groweth old, and whiteneth, as fast as old age approacheth. Thou sometimes dost seek in the head of one who groweth old duly in his own course a black hair, yet thou findest it not : thus when our life shall have been such, that the blackness of sins may be sought, and none found, that old age is youthful, is green, and ever will be green. Ye have heard of the grass of sinners, hear ye of the old age of the righteous : "My old age shall be in the fatness of mercy."

12. "And Mine eye hath beheld on mine enemies" (ver. 11). Whom doth he call his enemies? All the workers of iniquity. Do not observe whether thy friend be wicked : let an occasion come, and then thou provest him. Thou beginnest to go contrary to his iniquity, and then thou shalt see that when he was flattering thee, he was thy enemy ; but thou hadst not yet knocked, not to raise in his heart what was not there, but that what was there might break out. "Mine eye also hath looked upon mine enemies : and mine ear shall hear his desire of the wicked that rise up against me." When? In my old age. What is, in old age? In the last times. And what shall our ear hear? Standing on the right hand, we shall hear what shall be said to them that are on the left.[3]

---

[1] Jas. iv. 4.

[2] So LXX.

[3] [The words "my desire" are not in the Hebrew: what the Hebrew implies is the patient expectation of a just judgment, by which truth shall at last be vindicated. See Rev. vi. 10. — C.]

13. The grass withereth, the flower of sinners dieth away: what of the righteous? "The righteous shall flourish like a palm tree" (ver. 12). The ungodly are green as grass; "The righteous shall flourish like a palm tree." By the palm tree he signifieth height. Possibly he had also this meaning in the palm, that in its extremities it is beautiful: so that thou mayest trace its beginning from the earth, its end in its topmost branches, wherein its whole beauty dwelleth. The rough root appeareth in the earth, the beautiful foliage toward the sky. Thy beauty too, then, shall be in the end. Thy root is fixed fast: but our root is upward. For our root is Christ, who hath ascended into heaven. Humbled, he shall be exalted; "he shall spread abroad like a cedar in Libanus." See what trees he spoke of: the righteous shall flourish like a palm-tree: and shall spread abroad like a cedar in Libanus. When the sun hath gone forth, doth the palm-tree wither? Doth the cedar die? But when the sun hath been glowing for some hours, the grass drieth up. The judgment, therefore, shall come, that sinners may wither, and the faithful flourish.

14. "Such as are planted in the house of the Lord, shall flourish in the courts of the house of our God" (ver. 12). "They shall be yet more increased in fruitful old age, and shall be quiet, that they may show it forth" (ver. 13). Such is the Sabbath, which but a little while ago I commended unto you, whence the Psalm hath its title. "They shall be quiet, that they may show it forth." Wherefore are they quiet that show it forth? The grass of sinners moveth them not: the cedar and palm-tree not even in tempests are bent. They are therefore quiet, that they may show it forth: and with reason, since at present they must show it forth even unto men who mock at it. O wretched men, who are lovers of the world! Those who are planted in the house of the Lord, show it to you: those who praise the Lord with song and lute, in word and deed, show it forth to you, and tell you. Be not seduced by the prosperity of the wicked, admire not the flower of grass: admire not those who are happy only for a season, but miserable unto eternity. . . . If ye wish to flourish like a palm-tree, and to spread abroad like a cedar in Libanus, and not to wither like grass when the sun is hot; as those who appear to flourish when the sun is absent. If then ye wish not to be as grass, but as the palm-tree and the cedar, what will ye show forth? "How true the Lord my strength is: and that there is no unrighteousness in Him." How is it there is no unrighteousness? A man committeth so great crimes; he is well, he hath sons, a plentiful house, he is full of pride, is exalted by his honours, is revenged on his enemies, and doeth

every evil deed; another man, innocent, attending to his own affairs, not robbing another's goods, doing nothing against any one, suffereth in chains, in prison, tosseth and sigheth in poverty. How is it that there is no unrighteousness in Him? Be quiet, and thou shalt know: for thou art disturbed, and in thy chamber thou dost darken thy light. The eternal God doth wish to shine upon thee: do not then make thee cloudy weather from thy own disturbed mind. Be quiet within thyself, and see what I say unto thee. Because God is eternal, because for the present He spareth the bad, bringing them to repentance: He scourgeth the good, instructing them in the way unto the kingdom of heaven: "There is no unrighteousness in Him:" fear not. . . . What, if He leaveth this man unpunished now, because he is doomed to hear, "Depart into everlasting fire." But when? when thou shalt be placed at the right hand, then shall it be said to those placed on the left, "Depart into the everlasting fire, which is prepared for the devil and his angels." Let not therefore those things move thee: Be quiet, keep Sabbath, and show "how true the Lord my strength is: and that there is no unrighteousness in Him."

PSALM XCIII.[1]

1. . . . It is entitled, "The Song of praise of David himself, on the day before the Sabbath, when the earth was founded." Remembering then what God did through all those days, when He made and ordained all things, from the first up to the sixth day (for the seventh He sanctified, because He rested on that day after all the works, which He made very good), we find that He created on the sixth day (which day is here mentioned, in that he saith, "before the Sabbath") all animals on the earth; lastly, He on that very day created man in His own likeness and image. For these days were not without reason ordained in such order, but for that ages also were to run in a like course, before we rest in God.[2] But then we rest if we do good works. As a type of this, it is written of God, "God rested on the seventh day," when He had made all His works very good.[3] For He was not wearied, so as to need rest, nor hath He now left off to work, for our Lord Christ saith openly, "My Father worketh hitherto."[4] For He saith this unto the Jews, who thought carnally of God, and understood not that God worketh in quiet, and always worketh, and is always in quiet. We also, then, whom God willed then to figure in Himself, shall have rest after all good works. . . . And because these good works are doomed

1 Lat. XCII. A sermon to the people.
2 [Compare p 103, supra.—C.]
3 Gen. i. and ii. 1-3.
4 John v. 17.

to pass away, that sixth day also, when those very good works are perfected, hath an evening; but in the Sabbath we find no evening, because our rest shall have no end: for evening is put for end. As therefore God made man in His own image on the sixth day: thus we find that our Lord Jesus Christ came into the sixth age, that man might be formed anew after the image of God. For the first period, as the first day, was from Adam until Noah: the second, as the second day, from Noah unto Abraham: the third, as the third day, from Abraham unto David: the fourth, as the fourth day, from David unto the removal to Babylon: the fifth period, as the fifth day, from the removal to Babylon unto the preaching of John. The sixth day beginneth from the preaching of John, and lasteth unto the end: and after the end of the sixth day, we reach our rest. The sixth day, therefore, is even now passing.[1] And it is now the sixth day, see what the title hath; "On the day before the Sabbath, when the earth was founded." Let us now listen to the Psalm itself: let us enquire of it, how the earth was made, whether perhaps the earth was then made: and we do not read so in Genesis. When, therefore, was the earth founded? when, unless when that which hath been but now read in the Apostle taketh place: "If," he saith, "ye are stedfast, immovable."[2] When all who believe throughout all the earth are stedfast in faith, the earth is founded: then man is made in the image of God. That sixth day in Genesis signifieth this. . . .

2. "The Lord reigneth, He is clothed with beauty; the Lord is clothed with strength, and is girded" (ver. 1). We see that He hath clothed Himself with two things: beauty and strength. But why? That He might found the earth. So it followeth, "He hath made the round world so sure, that it cannot be moved." Whence hath He made it so sure? Because He hath clothed Himself in beauty. He would not make it so sure, if He put on beauty only, and not strength also. Why therefore beauty, why strength? For He hath said both. Ye know, brethren, that when our Lord had come in the flesh, of those to whom He preached the Gospel, He pleased some, and displeased others. For the tongues of the Jews were divided against one another: "Some said, He is a good Man; others said, Nay, but He deceiveth the people."[3] Some then spoke well, others detracted from Him, tore Him, bit and insulted Him. Towards those therefore whom He pleased, "He put on beauty;" towards those whom He displeased, "He put on strength." Imitate then thy Lord, that thou mayest become His garment: be with beauty towards those whom thy good

works please: show thy strength against detractors. . . .

3. Perhaps we should enquire respecting this word also, why he said, "He is girded." Girding signifieth work: for every man then girdeth himself, when he is about to work. But wherefore did he use the word *præcinctus*, instead of *cinctus?* For he saith in another Psalm,[4] "Gird Thee with Thy sword upon Thy thigh, O Thou most mighty: the people shall fall under Thee:" using the word *accingere*, not *cingere*, nor *præcingere:* this word being applied to the act of attaching anything to the side by girding it. The sword of the Lord, wherewith He conquered the round world by killing iniquity, is the Spirit of God in the truth of the word of God. Wherefore is He said to bind His sword around His thigh? In another place, on another Psalm we have spoken in another manner of girding: but nevertheless, since it hath been mentioned, it ought not to be passed over. What is the girding on of the sword around the thigh? He meaneth the flesh by the thigh. For the Lord would not otherwise conquer the round world, unless the sword of truth came into the flesh. Why therefore is He here said to be girded in front (*præcinctus*)? He who girdeth himself before, placeth something before himself, wherewith he is girded; whence it is said, He girded Himself before with a towel, and began to wash the disciples' feet. Because He was humble when He girded Himself with a towel. He washed the feet of His own disciples. But all strength is in humility: because all pride is fragile: therefore when He was speaking of strength, he added, "He is girded:" that thou mayest remember how thy God was girded in humility, when He washed His disciples' feet.[5] . . . After He had washed their feet, again He sat down; He said unto them, "Ye call me Lord and Master: and ye say well; for so I am. If I then, your Lord and Master, have washed your feet; how ought ye also to do to one another's feet?" If therefore strength is in humility, fear not the proud. The humble are like a rock: the rock seems to lie downwards: but nevertheless it is firm. What are the proud? Like smoke: although they are lofty, they vanish. We ought therefore to ascribe our Lord's being girded to His humility, according to the mention of the Gospel, that He was girded, that He might wash His disciples' feet.

4. . . . "For He hath made the round world sure, which cannot be moved." . . . What then is the round world, "which cannot be moved"? This He would not mention specially, if there were not also a round world that can be moved. There is a round world that shall not be moved.

---

[1] [See Barnabas, A. N. F. vol. i. p. 146.—C.]
[2] 1 Cor. xv. 58.   [3] John vii. 12.   [4] Ps. xlv. 3.   [5] John xiii. 4-15.

There is a round world that shall be moved. For the good who are stedfast in the faith are the round world: that no man may say,[1] they are only in part of it; while the wicked who abide not in faith, when they have felt any tribulation, are throughout the whole world. There is therefore a round world movable: there is a world immovable: of which the Apostle speaketh. Behold, the round world movable. I ask thee, of whom speaketh the Apostle in these words, "Of whom is Hymenæus and Philetus; who concerning the truth have erred, saying that the resurrection is past already: and overthrow the faith of some?"[2] Did these belong to the round world, that shall not be moved? But they were chaff: and as he saith, "they overthrow the faith of some." . . . "Nevertheless, the foundation of God standeth sure; having his seal," — what seal hath it as its sure foundation? — "The Lord knoweth them that are His." This is the round world that shall not be moved; "The Lord knoweth them that are His." And what seal hath it? "And let every one that nameth the name of Christ depart from unrighteousness." Let him depart from unrighteousness: for he cannot depart from the unrighteous, for the chaff is mixed with the wheat until it is fanned. . . .

5. "Thy throne is established from thence, O Lord" (ver. 2). What is, "from thence"? From that time. As if he said, What is the throne of God? Where doth God sit? In His Saints. Dost thou wish to be the throne of God? Prepare a place in thy heart where He may sit. What is the throne of God, except where God dwelleth? Where doth God dwell, except in His temple? What is His temple? Is it surrounded with walls? Far from it. Perhaps this world is His temple, because it is very great, and a thing worthy to contain God. It contains not Him by whom it was made. And wherein is He contained? In the quiet soul, in the righteous soul: that is it that containeth Him. . . . He who said, "Before Abraham was, I am:"[3] not before Abraham only, but before Adam: not only before Adam, but before all the angels, before heaven and earth; since all things were made through Him: he added, lest thou, attending to the day of our Lord's nativity, mightest think He commenced from that time, "Thy throne is established, O God." But what God? "Thou art from everlasting:" for which he uses ἀπ' αἰῶνος, in the Greek version; that word being sometimes used for an age, sometimes for everlasting. Therefore, O Thou who seemest to be born "from thence," Thou art from everlasting! But let not human birth be thought of, but Divine eternity. He began then from the time of His birth; He grew:[4] ye have heard

the Gospel. He chose disciples, He replenished them, His disciples began to preach. Perhaps this is what he speaketh of in the following verse.

6. "The floods lift up their voices" (ver. 3). What are these floods, which have lift up their voices? We heard them not: neither when our Lord was born, did we hear rivers speak, nor when He was baptized, nor when He suffered; we heard not that rivers did speak. Read the Gospel, ye find not that rivers spoke. It is not enough that they spoke: "They have lift up their voice:" they have not only spoken, but bravely, mightily, in a lofty voice. What are those rivers which have spoken? . . . The Spirit itself was a mighty river, whence many rivers were filled. Of that river the Psalmist saith in another passage, "The rivers of the flood thereof shall make glad the city of God."[5] Rivers then were made to flow from the belly of the disciples, when they received the Holy Spirit: themselves were rivers, when they had received that Holy Spirit. Whence did those rivers lift their voices? wherefore did they lift them up? Because at first they feared. Peter was not yet a river, when at the question of the maid-servant he thrice denied Christ: "I do not know the man."[6] Here he lieth through fear: he lifteth not his voice as yet: he is not yet the river. But when they were filled with the Holy Spirit, the Jews sent for them, and enjoined them not to preach at all, nor to teach in the name of Jesus. . . . For when the Apostles had been dismissed from the council of the Jews, they came to their own friends, and told them what the priests and elders said unto them: but they on hearing lifted up their voices with one accord unto the Lord, and said, "Lord, it is Thou who hast made heaven and earth, and the sea, and all that in them is;"[7] and the rest which floods lifting up their voices might say, "Wonderful are the hangings of the sea" (ver. 4). For when the disciples had lifted up their voices unto Him, many believed, and many received the Holy Spirit, and many rivers instead of few began to lift up their voice. Hence there followeth, "from the voices of many waters, wonderful are the hangings of the sea;" that is, the waves of the world. When Christ had begun to be preached by so powerful voices, the sea became enraged, persecutions began to thicken. When therefore the rivers had lift up their voice, "from the voices of many waters, wonderful" were "the hangings of the sea." To be hung aloft is to be lifted up; when the sea rages, the waves are hung as from above. Let the waves hang over as they choose; let the sea roar as it chooseth; the hangings of the sea indeed are mighty, mighty are the threatenings,

---

[1] As the Donatists.　　[2] 2 Tim. ii. 17–19.　　[3] John viii. 58.　　[4] Luke ii. 40, 52.　　[5] Ps. xlvi. 4.　　[6] Matt. xxvi. 69–74.　　[7] Acts iv. 24.

mighty the persecutions ; but see what followeth :
" but yet the Lord, who dwelleth on high, is
mightier." Let therefore the sea restrain itself,
and sometime become calmed ; let peace be
granted by Christians. The sea was disturbed,
the vessel was tossed ; the vessel is the Church :
the sea, the world. The Lord came, He walked
over the sea, and calmed the waves. How did
the Lord walk over the sea? Above the heads
of those mighty foaming waves. Principalities
and kings believed ; they were subdued unto
Christ. Let us not therefore be frightened ; because " the Lord, who dwelleth on high, is
mightier."

7. " Thy testimonies, O Lord, are very surely
believed " (ver. 5). The Lord, who dwelleth
on high, is mightier than the mighty overhangings of the sea. " Thy testimonies are very
surely believed." " Thy testimonies," because
He had said beforehand, " These things I have
spoken unto you, that in Me ye might have
peace. In the world ye shall have tribulation."
. . . He added, " but be of good cheer, I have
overcome the world." [1] If then He saith, " I
have overcome the world," cling unto Him who
overcame the world, who overcame the sea.
Rejoice in Him, because the Lord, who dwelleth
on high, is mightier, and, " Thy testimonies are
very surely believed." And what is the end of
all these? " Holiness becometh Thine house, O
Lord ! " Thine house, the whole of Thine house,
not here and there : but the whole of Thine
house, throughout the whole world. Why
throughout the whole of the round world? " Because He hath set aright the round world, which
cannot be moved." [2] The Lord's house will be
strong : it will prevail throughout the whole
world : many shall fall : but that house standeth ;
many shall be disturbed, but that house shall not
be moved. Holiness becometh Thine house, O
Lord ! " For a short time only? No. " Unto
length of days."

PSALM XCIV.[3]

1. As we listened with much attention, while the
Psalm was in reading, so let us listen attentively,
while the Lord revealeth the mysteries which
He hath deigned to obscure in this passage.
For some mysteries in the Scriptures are shut up
for this reason, not that they may be denied, but
that they may be opened unto those who knock.
If therefore ye knock with affection of piety, and
sincere heartfelt love, He, who seeth from what
motives ye knock, will open unto you.[4] It is
known unto all of us (and I wish we may not be
among their number), that may murmur against

God's long-suffering, and grieve either that impious and wicked men live in this world, or that
they have great power ; and what is more, that
the bad generally have great power against the
good, and that the bad often oppress the good ;
that the wicked exult, while the good suffer ;
the evil are proud, while the good are humbled.
Observing such things in the human race (for
they abound), impatient and weak minds are perverted, as if they were good in vain ; since God
averteth, or seemeth to avert, His eyes from the
good works of the pious and faithful, and to pro-
mote the wicked in those pleasures which they
love. Weak men, therefore, imagining that they
live well in vain, are induced either to imitate the
wickedness of those whom they see flourishing :
or if either through bodily or mental weakness
they are deterred from doing wrong by a fear of
the penal laws of the world ; not because they
love justice, but, to speak more openly, fearing
the condemnation of men among men, they refrain indeed from wicked deeds, but refrain not
from wicked thoughts. And among their wicked
thoughts, the chief is the wickedness which
leadeth them impiously to imagine that God is
neglectful, and regardless of human affairs : and
that He either holdeth in equal estimation the
good and the wicked : or even, and this is a still
more pernicious notion, that He persecuteth the
good, and favoureth the wicked. He who thinketh thus, although he doth no harm to any man,
doth the greatest to himself, and is impious
against himself, and by his wickedness hurteth
not God, but slayeth himself. . . .

2. The Psalm hath this title, that is, this inscription : " A Psalm of David himself, on the
fourth day of the week." This Psalm is about
to teach patience in the sufferings of the righteous : it enjoineth patience against the prosperity of the wicked, and buildeth up patience.
This is the drift of the whole of it, from beginning to end. Wherefore then hath it such a
title, " on the fourth of the week "? The first of
the week is the Lord's day : the second, is the
second week-day, which people of the world
call the Moon's day : the third, is the third week-
day, which they term Mars' day. The fourth of
the Sabbaths therefore is the fourth week-day,
which by Pagans is styled Mercury's day, and
also by many Christians ; but I would not call it
so : and I wish they would change for the better,
and cease to do so ; for they have a phrase of
their own, which they may use. For these
terms are not of universal use : many nations
have severally different names for them : so that
the mode of speech used by the Church better
beseemeth the mouth of a Christian.[5] Yet if
custom hath induced any person to utter that

---

[1] John xvi. 33.   [2] Ps. xcvi. 10.
[3] Lat. XCIII. Delivered in another's diocese, at the request of
an assembly of bishops, as appears from the conclusion.
[4] Matt. vii. 7.

[5] [" The first day of the week," etc. — C.]

with his tongue which his heart doth disapprove, let him remember, that all those whose names the stars bear were men, and that the stars did not commence their existence in the sky, when those men began theirs, but were there long before; but on account of some mortal services rendered unto mortals, those men in their own times, because they had great power, and were eminent in this life, since they were beloved by men, not on account of eternal life, but of temporal services, received divine honours. For then men of the old world, in being deceived and wishing to deceive, pointed to the stars in heaven, to flatter those who had done them any good service in their affection for this life, saying, that that was the star of such a man, this of another; while the man who had not beheld them before, so as to see that those stars were there before the birth of the man, were deceived into a belief: and thus this vain opinion was conceived. This erroneous opinion the devil strengthened, Christ overthrew. According to our mode of speech, then, the fourth of the week is taken for the fourth day from the Lord's day. Attend, therefore, beloved, to what this title meaneth. Here is a great mystery, and a truly hidden one. . . . Let us therefore recall from the holy Scripture in Genesis, what was created on the first day; we find light: what was created on the second day; we find the firmament, which God called heaven: what was created on the third day; we find the form of earth and sea, and their separation, that all the gathering together of the waters was called sea, and all that was dry, the earth. On the fourth day, the Lord made the lights in heaven:[1] "The sun to rule the day: the moon and stars to govern the night:"[2] this was the work of the fourth day. What then is the reason that the Psalm hath taken its title from the fourth day: the Psalm in which patience is enjoined against the prosperity of the wicked, and the sufferings of the good. Thou findest the Apostle Paul speaking. "Do all things without murmurings and disputings: that ye may be blameless and harmless, the sons of God, without rebuke, in the midst of a crooked and perverse nation, among whom ye shine as lights in the world, holding forth the word of life."[3] . . .

3. Let us now attend to the Psalm. "The Lord is the God of vengeance; the God of vengence hath dealt confidently" (ver. 1). Dost thou think that He doth not punish? "The God of vengeance" punisheth. What is, "The God of vengeance"? The God of punishments. Thou murmurest surely because the bad are not punished: yet do not murmur, lest thou be among those who are punished. That man hath committed a theft, and liveth: thou murmurest against God, because he who committed a theft on thee dieth not. . . . Therefore, if thou wouldest have another correct his hand, do thou first correct thy tongue: thou wouldest have him correct his heart towards man, correct thy heart towards God; lest perchance, when thou desirest the vengeance of God, if it come, it find thee first. For He will come: He will come, and will judge those who continue in their wickedness, ungrateful for the prolongation of His mercy, for His long-suffering, treasuring up unto themselves wrath against the day of wrath, and revelation of the righteous judgment of God, who will render to every man according to his deeds:[4] because, "The Lord is the God of vengeance," therefore hath He "dealt confidently." . . . Our safety is our Saviour: in Him He would place the hope of all the needy and poor. And what saith He? "I will deal confidently in Him." What meaneth this? He will not fear, will not spare the lusts and vices of men. Truly, as a faithful physician, with the healing knife of preaching in His hand, He hath cut away all our wounded parts. Therefore such as He was prophesied and preached beforehand, such was He found. . . . How great things then did He, of whom it is said, "He taught them as one having authority," say unto them? "Woe unto you, Scribes and Pharisees, hypocrites!"[5] What great things did He say unto them, before their face? He feared no one. Why? Because He is the God of vengeance. For this reason He spared them not in words, that they might remain for Him after to spare them in judgment; because if they were unwilling to accept the healing of His word, they would afterwards incur their Judge's doom. Wherefore? Because He hath said, "The Lord is the God of vengeance, the God of vengeance hath dealt confidently;" that is, He hath spared no man in word. He who spared not in word when about to suffer, will He spare in judgment when about to judge? He who in His humility feared no man, will He fear any man in His glory? From His dealing thus confidently in time past, imagine how He will deal at the end of time. Murmur not then against God, who seemeth to spare the wicked; but be thou good, and perhaps for a season He may not spare thee the rod, that He may in the end spare thee in judgment. . . .

4. And what followed, because He dealt confidently? "Be exalted, Thou Judge of the world" (ver. 2). Because they imprisoned Him when humble, thinkest thou they will imprison Him when exalted? Because they judged Him when

---

[1] Gen. i. 3–19.   [2] Ps. cxxxvi. 8, 9.
[3] Philip. ii. 14–16.

[4] Rom. ii. 4–6.   [5] Matt. xxiii. 13, 16.

mortal, will they not be judged by Him when immortal? What then saith He? "Be exalted," Thou, who hast dealt confidently, the confidence of whose word the wicked bore not, but thought they did a glorious deed, when they seized and crucified Thee; they who ought to have seized on Thee with faith, seized Thee with persecution. Thou then who hast among the wicked dealt confidently, and hast feared no man, because Thou hast suffered, "be exalted;" that is, arise again, depart into heaven. Let the Church also bear with long-suffering what the Church's Head hath borne with long-suffering. "Be exalted, Thou Judge of the world: and reward the proud after their deserving." He will reward them, brethren. For what is this, "Be exalted, Thou Judge of the world: and reward the proud after their deserving"? This is the prophecy of one who doth predict, not the boldness of one who commandeth. Not because the Prophet said, "Be exalted, Thou Judge of the world," did Christ obey the Prophet, in arising from the dead, and ascending into heaven; but because Christ was to do this, the Prophet predicted it. He seeth Christ abased in the spirit, abased he seeth Him: fearing no man, in speech sparing no man, and he saith, "He hath dealt confidently." He seeth how confidently He hath dealt, he seeth Him arrested, crucified, humbled, he seeth Him rising from the dead, and ascending into heaven, and from thence to come in judgment of those, among whose hands He had suffered every evil: "Be exalted," he saith, "Thou Judge of the world, and reward the proud after their deserving." The proud He will thus reward, not the humble. Who are the proud? Those to whom it is little to do evil: but they even defend their own sins. For on some of those who crucified Christ, miracles were afterwards performed, when out of the number of the Jews themselves there were found believers, and the blood of Christ was given unto them. Their hands were impious, and red with the blood of Christ. He whose blood they had shed, Himself washed them. They who had persecuted His mortal body which they had seen, became part of His very body, that is, the Church. They shed their own ransom, that they might drink their own ransom. For afterwards more were converted. . . .

5. "Lord, how long shall the ungodly, how long shall the ungodly triumph?" (ver. 3). "They answer, and will speak wickedness, they all will speak that work unrighteousness" (ver. 4). What is their saying, but against God, when they say: What profiteth it us that we live thus? What wilt thou reply? Doth God truly regard our deeds? For because they live, they imagine that God knoweth not their actions. Behold, what evil happeneth unto them! If

the officers [1] knew where they were, they would arrest them; and they therefore avoid the officer's eyes, that they may escape instant apprehension; but no one can escape the eye of God, since He not only seeth within the closet, but within the recesses of the heart. Even they themselves believe that nothing can escape God: and because they do evil, and are conscious of what they have done, and see that they live while God knoweth, though they would not live if the officer discovered them; they say unto themselves, These things please God: and, in truth, if they displeased Him, as they displease kings, as they displease judges, as they displease governors, as they displease recorders,[2] yet could we escape the eye of God, as we do escape the eyes of those authorities? Therefore these things please God. . . . Some righteous man cometh, and saith, Do not commit iniquity. Wherefore? That thou mayest not die. Behold, iniquity I have committed: why do I not die? That man wrought righteousness: and he is dead: why is he dead? I have wrought iniquity: why hath not God carried me off? Behold, that man did righteously: and why hath He thus visited him? why suffereth He thus? They answer; this is the meaning of the word "answer:" for they have a reply to make; because they are spared, from the long-suffering of God, they discover an argument for their reply. He spareth them for one reason, they answer for another, because they still live. For the Apostle telleth us wherefore He spareth, he expoundeth the grounds of the long-suffering of God: "And thinkest thou this, O man, that judgest them which do such things, and doest the same, that thou shalt escape the judgment of God? Or despisest thou the riches of His goodness, and forbearance, and long-suffering; not knowing that the long-suffering of God leadeth thee to repentance?" "But thou," that is, he who answereth and saith, If I displeased God, He would not spare me, hear what he worketh for himself; hear the Apostle; "but after thy hardness and impenitent heart treasurest up into thyself wrath against the day of wrath, and revelation of the righteous judgment of God; who will render to every man according to his deeds." [3] He therefore increaseth His long-suffering, thou increasest thine iniquity. His treasure will consist in eternal mercy towards those who have not despised His mercy; but thy treasure will be discovered in wrath, and

---

[1] *Stationarius.* Soldiers, and officers of the governors, stationed in certain places through the provinces and cities, who gave information to the magistrates of notorious offences   Ex l. 1, c. *De Curios. et Stationar.* libro 12, et ex l. 31, *De Episc. et Cler.* in C. Theod. Ben. Cod. Theod. Gothof. l. vi. Tit. 29.

[2] *Commentariensibus,* masters of prisons, and notaries, whose duty it was to keep records of imprisonments and offenders, and to receive indictments. — *Ben.*

[3] Rom. ii. 5, 6.

what thou daily layest up by little and little, thou wilt find in the accumulated mass; thou layest up by the grain, but thou wilt find the whole heap. Omit not to watch thy slightest daily sins: rivers are filled from the smallest drops.

6. . . . "They have humbled Thy people, O Lord; and have troubled Thine heritage" (ver. 5). "They have murdered the widow, and the fatherless: and slain the proselyte" (ver. 6); that is, the traveller, the pilgrim: the comer from far, as the Psalmist calleth himself. Each of these expressions is too clear in meaning to make it worth while to dwell upon them.

7. "And they have said, The Lord shall not see" (ver. 7): He observeth not, regardeth not these things: He careth for other matters, He understandeth not. These are the two assertions of the wicked: one which I have just quoted, "These things hast thou done, and I held my tongue, and thou thoughtest unrighteousness, that I will be like thyself." What meaneth, "that I will be like thyself"? Thou thinkest that I see thy deeds, and that they are pleasing unto Me, because I do not punish them. There is another assertion of the wicked: because God neither regardeth these things, nor observeth that He may know how I live, God heedeth me not. Doth then God make any reckoning of me? or doth He even take account of me? or of men in general? Unhappy man! He cared for thee, that thou mightest exist: doth He not care that thou live well? Such then are the words of these last; "and yet they have said, The Lord shall not see: neither shall the God of Jacob regard it."

8. "Take heed now, ye that are unwise among the people: O ye fools, some time understand!" (ver. 8). He teacheth His people whose feet might slip: any one among them seeth the prosperity of the wicked, himself living well among the Saints of God, that is, among the number of the sons of the Church: he seeth that the wicked flourish, and work iniquity, he envieth, and is led to follow them in their actions; because he seeth that apparently it profiteth him nothing that he liveth well in humility, hoping for his reward here. For if he hopeth for it in future, he loseth it not; because the time is not yet come for him to receive it. Thou art working in a vineyard: execute thy task, and thou shalt receive thy pay. Thou wouldest not exact it from thy employer, before thy work was finished, and yet dost thou exact it from God before thou dost work? This patience is part of thy work, and thy pay dependeth upon thy work: thou who dost not choose to be patient, choosest to work less upon the vineyard: since this act of patience belongeth to thy labouring itself, which is to gain thy pay. But if thou art treacherous, take care,

lest thou shouldest not only not receive thy pay, but also suffer punishment, because thou hast chosen to be a treacherous labourer. When such a labourer beginneth to do ill, he watcheth his employer's eyes, who hired him for his vineyard, that he may loiter when his eye is turned away; but the moment his eyes are turned towards him, he worketh diligently. But God, who hired thee, averteth not His eyes: thou canst not work treacherously: the eyes of thy Master are ever upon thee: seek an opportunity to deceive Him, and loiter if thou canst. If then any of you had any such ideas, when ye saw the wicked flourishing, and if such thoughts caused your feet to slip in the path of God; to you this Psalm speaketh: but if perchance none of you be such, through you it doth address others, in these words, "Take heed now;" since they had said, "The Lord shall not see: neither shall the God of Jacob regard it." "Take heed," it saith, "now, ye that are unwise among the people: and ye fools, some time understand!" [1]

9. "He that planted the ear, shall He not hear? or He that made the eye, doth He not consider?" (ver. 9) "or He that instructeth the nations, shall He not reprove?" (ver. 10). This is what God is at present doing: He is instructing the nations: for this reason he sent His word to man throughout the world: He sent it by Angels, by Patriarchs, by Prophets, by servants, through so many heralds going before the Judge. He sent also His own Word Himself, He sent His own Son in Person: He sent the servants of His Son, and in these very servants His own Son. Throughout the world is everywhere preached the word of God. Where is it not said unto men, Abandon your former wickedness, and turn yourselves to right paths? He spareth, that ye may correct yourselves: He punished not yesterday, in order that to-day ye may live well. He teacheth the heathen, shall He not therefore reprove? will He not hear those whom He teacheth? will He not judge those to whom He hath beforehand sent and sown lessons of warning? If thou wast in a school, wouldest thou receive a task, and not repeat it? When therefore thou receivest it from thy master, thou art being taught: the Master giveth thy task into thy hands, and shall He not exact it from thee when thou comest to repeat it? or when thou hast begun to repeat it, shalt thou not be in fear of stripes? At present then we are receiving our work: afterwards we are placed before the Master, that we may give up to Him all our past tasks, that is, that we may give an account of all those things which are now being bestowed upon us. Hear the Apostle's words: "We must all appear before the judgment-seat

---

[1] [On Plutarch's "Delays of the Divine Justice," see the valuable translation of De Maistre, with that of Amyot. Paris, 1853. — C.]

of Christ," etc.[1] " It is He that teacheth man knowledge." Doth He not know, who maketh thee to know?

10. " The Lord knoweth the thoughts of man, that they are but vain " (ver. 11). For although thou knowest not the thoughts of God, that they are righteous ; " He knoweth the thoughts of man, that they are but vain." Even men have known the thoughts of God : but those to whom He hath become a friend, it is to them He showeth His counsel. Do not, brethren, despise yourselves : if ye approach the Lord with faith, ye hear the thoughts of God ; these ye are now learning, this is told you, and for this reason ye are taught, why God spareth the wicked in this life, that ye may not murmur against God, who teacheth man knowledge. " The Lord knoweth the thoughts of man, that they are but vain." Abandon therefore the thoughts of man, which are vain : that ye may take hold on the thoughts of God, which are wise. But who is he who taketh hold on the thoughts of God? He who is placed in the firmament of heaven. We have already chanted that Psalm, and have expounded this expression therein.

11. " Blessed is the man whom Thou chastenest, O Lord : and teachest him from Thy law " (ver. 12). Behold, thou hast the counsel of God, wherefore He spareth the wicked : the pit is being digged for the sinner. Thou wishest to bury him at once : the pit is as yet being dug for him : do not be in haste to bury him. What mean the words, " until the pit be digged up for the sinner "? or whom doth He mean by sinner? One man? No. Whom then? The whole race of such that are sinners? No ; them that are proud ; for he had said before, " Reward the proud after their deserving." For that publican, who would not so much as lift up his eyes to heaven, but " smote upon his breast, saying, God be merciful to me a sinner," [2] was a sinner ; but since he was not proud, and since God will render a recompense to the proud ; the pit is being dug not for him, but for them that are such, until He render a recompense to the proud. In the words then, " until the pit be digged up for the ungodly," understand the proud. Who is the proud? He who doth not by confession of his sins do penance, that he may be healed through his humility. Who is the proud? He who chooseth to arrogate to himself those few good things which he seemeth to possess, and who doth detract from the mercy of God. Who is the proud? He who although he doth ascribe unto God his good works, yet insulteth those who do not those good works, and raiseth himself above them. . . . This then is the Christian doctrine : no man doeth anything well except by His grace. A man's bad acts are his own : his good he doth of God's bounty. When he hath begun to do well, let not him ascribe it unto himself : when he hath not attributed it to himself, let him give thanks to Him from whom he hath received it. But when he doeth well, let him not insult him who doth not as he doth nor exalt himself above him : for the grace of, God is not stayed at him, so that it cannot reach another.

12. " That Thou mayest give him patience in days of malice : until the pit be digged up for the ungodly " (ver. 13). Have patience therefore every one, if thou art a Christian, in time of malice. Days of malice are those in which the ungodly appear to flourish, and the righteous to suffer ; but the suffering of the righteous is the rod of the Father, and the prosperity of the ungodly is their own snare. For because God giveth you patience in time of adversity, until the pit be digged up for the ungodly, do not think that the Angels are standing in some place with mattocks, and are digging that great pit which shall be able to contain the whole race of the ungodly ; and because ye see that the wicked are many, and say unto yourselves carnally : Truly what pit can contain so great a multitude of the wicked, such a crowd of sinners? where is a pit of such dimensions, as to contain all, dug? when finished? therefore God spareth them. This is not so : their very prosperity is the pit of the wicked : for into that shall they fall, as it were into a pitfall. Attend, brethren, for it is a great thing to know that prosperity is called a pitfall : " until the pit be digged up for the ungodly." For God spareth him whom He knoweth to be ungodly and impious, in His own hidden justice : and this very sparing of God, causeth him to be puffed up through his impunity. . . . The proud man raiseth himself up against God : God sinketh him : and he sinketh by the very act of raising himself up against God. For in another Psalm[3] he thus saith, " Thou hast cast them down, while they were being exalted." He said not, Thou hast cast them down, because they were exalted ; or, Thou hast cast them down, after they were exalted ; so that the period of their exaltation be one, of their casting down another : but in the very act of their exaltation were they cast down. For in proportion as the heart of man is proud, so doth it recede from God ; and if it recede from God, it sinketh down into the deep. On the other hand, the humble heart bringeth God unto it from heaven, so that He becometh very near unto it. Surely God is lofty, God is above all the heavens, He surpasseth all the Angels : how high must these be raised, to reach that exalted One? Do not burst thy-

---

[1] 2 Cor. v. 10 and Rom. xiv. 10.   [2] Luke xviii. 13.   [3] Ps. lxxii 18.

self by enlarging thyself; I give thee other advice, lest perchance in enlarging thyself thou burst, through pride: surely God is lofty: do thou humble thyself, and He will descend unto thee.

13. . . . Do thou rejoice beneath the scourge: because the heritage is kept for thee, "for the Lord will not cast off His people" (ver. 14). He chasteneth for a season, He condemneth not for ever: the others He spareth for a season, and will condemn them for evermore. Make thy choice: dost thou wish temporary suffering, or eternal punishment? temporal happiness, or eternal life? What doth God threaten? Eternal punishment. What doth He promise? Eternal rest. His scourging the good, is temporary: His sparing the wicked, is also temporary. "Neither will He forsake His inheritance."

14. "Until righteousness," he saith, "turn again unto judgment, and all they that have it are right in heart" (ver. 15). Listen now, and gain righteousness: for judgment thou canst not yet have. Thou shouldest gain righteousness first; but that very righteousness of thine shall turn unto judgment. The Apostles had righteousness here on earth, and bore with the wicked. But what is said unto them? "Ye shall sit on twelve thrones, judging the twelve tribes of Israel."[1] Their righteousness therefore shall turn unto judgment. For whoever is righteous in this life, is so for this reason, that he may endure evils with patience: let him suffer patiently the period of suffering, and the day of judging cometh. But why do I speak of the servants of God? The Lord Himself, who is the Judge of all living and dead, first chose to be judged, and then to judge. Those who have righteousness at present, are not yet judges. For the first thing is to have righteousness, and afterwards to judge: He first endureth the wicked, and afterwards judgeth them. Let there be righteousness now: afterwards it shall turn again unto judgment. And so long He endureth wicked men, as God doth will, as long as God's Church shall endure them, that she may be taught through their wickedness. Nevertheless, God will not cast off His people, "all such as have it are right in heart." Who are those who are right in heart? Those whose will is the will of God. He spareth sinners: thou dost wish Him at once to destroy sinners. Thy heart is crooked and thy will perverted, when thy will is one way and the will of God another. God wisheth to spare sinners: thou dost not wish sinners spared. God is of long-suffering to sinners: thou dost not wish to endure sinners. . . . Wish not to bend the will of God to thy will, but rather correct thy will to His. The will of God is like a rule: behold, suppose, thou hast twisted the rule: whence canst thou be set straight? But the rule itself continueth straight: for it is immutable. As long as the rule is straight, thou hast whither to turn thyself, and straighten thy perversity; thou hast a means of correcting what is crooked in thee. But what do men will? It is not enough that their own will is crooked; they even wish to make the will of God crooked according to their own heart, that God may do what they themselves will, when they ought to do that which God willeth. . . .

15. "Who will rise up for me against the wicked? or who will take my part against the evil doers?" (ver. 16). Many persuade us to divers evils: the serpent ceaseth not to whisper to thee to work iniquity: whichever way thou shalt turn, if perchance thou hast done well, thou seekest to live well with some one, and thou hardly findest any one; many wicked men surround thee, for there are few grains of wheat, and much chaff. This floor hath its grains of corn, but as yet they suffer. Therefore the whole mass of the wheat, when separated from the chaff, will be great: the grains are few, but when compared with the chaff, still many in themselves. When therefore the wicked cry out on every side, and say, Why livest thou thus? Art thou the only Christian? Why dost thou not do what others also do? Why dost thou not frequent the theatres, as others do? Why dost thou not use charms and amulets? Why dost thou not consult astrologers and soothsayers, even as others do? And thou crossest[2] thyself, and sayest, I am a Christian, that thou mayest repel them, whosoever they are; but the enemy presses on, urges his attacks; what is worse, by the example of Christians he choketh Christians. They toil on, in the midst of heat: the Christian soul suffereth tribulation: yet it hath power to conquer: hath it such power of itself? For this reason remark what he saith. For he answereth, What doth it profit me that I now find charms for myself, and gain a few days? I depart hence from this life, and repair unto my Lord, who shall send me into the flames; because I have preferred a few days to life eternal, He shall send me into hell. What hell? That of the eternal judgment of God. Is it really so (the enemy answereth), unless indeed thou really believest that God careth how men live? And perhaps it is not an acquaintance who speaketh thus to thee in the street, but thy wife at home, or possibly the husband to the faithful and holy wife, her deceiver. If it be the woman to her husband, she is as Eve unto him; if as the husband unto the wife, he is as the devil unto her: either she is herself as Eve unto thee, or thou art a serpent unto her. Sometimes the father would incline his thoughts to his son, and findeth him wicked, utterly depraved: he is in a fever of misery, he wavers, he seeketh how to subdue

---

[1] Matt. xix. 28.

[2] Et tu signas te.

him, he is almost drawn in, and consenteth : but may God be [1] near him. . . .

16. "If the Lord," he saith, "had not helped me : within a little my soul had dwelt in hell" (ver. 17). I had almost plunged into that pit which is preparing for sinners : that is, my soul had dwelt in hell. Because he already began to waver, and nearly to consent, he looked back unto the Lord. Suppose, for example's sake, he was insulted to tempt him to iniquity. For sometimes the wicked flock together, and insult the good ; especially if they are more in number, and if they have taken him alone, as there is often much chaff about one grain of wheat (though there will not be when the heap hath been fanned) ; he is then taken among many wicked ones, is insulted, and surrounded ; they wish to place themselves over him, they torment him and insult him for his very righteousness. A great Apostle ! say they ; Thou hast flown into heaven, as Elias did ! Men do these things, so that sometime, when he listeneth to the tongue of men, he is ashamed to be good among the wicked. Let him therefore resist the evil ; but not of his own strength, lest he become proud, and when he wishes to escape the proud, himself increase their number. . . .

17. "If I said, My foot hath slipt ; Thy mercy, O Lord, held me up" (ver. 18). See how God loveth confession. Thy foot hath slipt, and thou sayest not, my foot hath slipt ; but thou sayest thou art firm, when thou art slipping. The moment thou beginnest to slip or waver, confess thou that slip, that thou mayest not bewail thy total fall ; that He may help, so that thy soul be not in hell. God loveth confession, loveth humility. Thou hast slipped, as a man ; God helpeth thee, nevertheless : yet say, "My foot hath slipt." Why dost thou slip, and yet sayest, I am firm? "When I said, My foot hath slipt, Thy mercy, O Lord, hath held me up." Just as Peter presumed, but not in strength of his own. The Lord was seen to walk upon the sea, trampling on the heads of all the proud in this life. In walking upon the foaming waves, He figured His own course when He trampleth on the heads of the proud. The Church too doth trample upon them : for Peter is the Church Herself. Nevertheless, Peter dared not by himself walk upon the waters ; but what said he? "Lord, if it be Thou, bid me come unto Thee on the water." He in His own power, Peter by His order ; "bid me," he saith, "come unto Thee." He answered, "Come." For the Church also trampleth on the heads of the proud ; but since it is the Church, and hath human weakness, that these words might be fulfilled, "If I said, My

foot hath slipt," Peter tottered on the sea, and cried out, "Lord, save me !" [3] and so what is here put, "If I said, My foot hath slipt," is put there, "Lord, I perish." And what is here, "Thy mercy, O Lord, hath held me up," is there put, "And immediately Jesus stretched forth His hand, saying, O thou of little faith, wherefore didst thou doubt?" [4] It is wonderful how God proveth men : our very dangers render Him who rescueth us sweeter unto us. For see what followeth : because he said, "If I said, My foot hath slipt, Thy mercy, O Lord, hath held me up." The Lord hath become especially sweet unto him, in rescuing him from danger ; and thus speaking of this very sweetness of the Lord, he exclaimeth and saith, "O Lord, in the multitude of the sorrows that I had in my heart, Thy comforts have refreshed my soul" (ver. 19). Many sorrows, but many consolations : bitter wounds, and sweet remedies.

18. "Wilt Thou have anything to do with the stool of iniquity, who makest sorrow in learning?" (ver. 20). He hath said this, No wicked man sitteth with Thee, nor shalt Thou have anything to do with the stool of iniquity. And he giveth an account whereof he understandeth this, "For Thou makest sorrow in learning." For from this, because Thou hast not spared us, do I understand that Thou hast nothing to do with the stool of iniquity. Thou hast this in the Epistle of the Apostle Peter, and for this reason he hath adduced a testimony from the Scripture : "for the time is come," he saith, "that judgment must begin at the house of God ;" that is, the time is come for the judgment of those who belong to the house of God. If sons are scourged, what must the most wicked slaves expect? For which reason he added : "And if it first begin at us, what shall the end be of them that obey not the Gospel of God?" To which he added this testimony : "For if the righteous scarcely be saved, where shall the ungodly and sinner appear?" [5] How then shall the wicked be with Thee, if Thou dost not even spare Thy faithful, in order that Thou mayest exercise and teach them? [6] But as He spareth them not, for this reason, that He may teach them : he saith, "For Thou makest sorrow in learning." "Makest," that is, formest : from whence comes the word *figulus* (from *fingo*), and a potter's vessel is called fictile : not in the meaning of *fiction*, as a falsehood, but of forming so as to give anything being and some sort of form ; as before he said, "He that fabricated (*finxit*) the eye, shall He not see?" [7] Is that, "fabricated the eye" a falsehood? Nay, it is understood He fashioned the eye, made the eye. And is He not a potter when He makes men

frail, weak, earthly? Hear the Apostle: "We have this treasure in earthen vessels."[1] . . . Behold our Lord Himself, how He showeth Himself a potter.[2] Because He had made man of clay, He anointed him with clay, for whom He had not made eyes in the womb. And so when he saith, "Hast Thou anything to do," etc., he saith, out of grief makest learning for us, so that grief itself becomes our instruction. How is sorrow our learning? When He scourgeth thee who died for thee, and who doth not promise bliss in this life, and who cannot deceive, and when He giveth not here what thou seekest. What will He give? when will He give? how much will He give, who giveth not here, who here teacheth, who maketh sorrow in learning? Thy labour is here, and rest is promised thee. Thou takest thought that thou hast toil here: but take thought what sort of rest He promiseth. Canst thou conceive it? If thou couldest, thou wouldest see that thy toil here is nothing toward an equivalent. . . .

19. Attend, brethren; it is for sale.[3] What I have is for sale, saith God unto thee, buy it. What hath He for sale? I have rest for sale; buy it by thy toil. Attend, that we may be in Christ's name brave Christians: the remainder of the Psalm is but a little, let us not be weary. For how can he be strong in doing, who faileth in hearing? The Lord will help us to expound unto you the remainder. Attend then: God hath, as it were, proclaimed the kingdom of heaven for sale. Thou sayest unto Him, What is its value? The price is toil: if He were to say, its price is gold, it would not suffice to say this only, but thou wouldest seek to know how much gold; for there is a mass of gold, and half an ounce, and a pound, and the like. He said "price," that thou mightest not be at pains to inquire, how long thou shouldest find it. The price of the commodity is toil: how much toil is it? Now seek how much thou shouldest toil for it. Thou art not as yet told how great that toil is doomed to be, or how much toil is required of thee: God saith this unto thee, I show thee how great that rest will be; do thou judge with what measure of toil it should be bought.

20. . . . He promised rest: suffer trouble. He threateneth eternal fire; despise temporal pains: and while Christ doth watch, let thy heart be calmed, that thou also mayest reach the harbour. For He would not fail to prepare a harbour, who provided a vessel. "Hast Thou anything to do with the stool of iniquity, Thou who makest sorrow in learning?" He trieth us with the wicked, and by their persecution He teacheth us. By means of the malice of the wicked the good is scourged, through the slave the son is chastened:

thus is learning taught by sorrow. What God alloweth them power to do, that do wicked men, whom He spareth for a season, do.

21. For what followeth? "They will be captious against the soul of the righteous" (ver. 21). Why will they be captious? Because they can find no true ground of accusation. For how were they captious against our Lord? They made up false accusations,[4] because they could not find true ones. "And will condemn the innocent blood." Why all this taketh place, he will show in the sequel.

22. "And the Lord is become my refuge" (ver. 22), he saith. Thou wouldest not seek such a refuge, if thou wert not in danger: but thou hast therefore been in danger, that thou mightest seek for it: for He teacheth us by sorrow. He causeth me tribulation from the malice of the wicked: pricked with that tribulation, I begin to seek a refuge which I had ceased to seek for in that worldly prosperity. For who, that is always prosperous, and rejoiceth in present hopes, findeth it easy to remember God? Let the hope of this life give way, and the hope of God advance; that thou mayest say, "And the Lord is become my refuge:" may I sorrow for this end that the Lord may become my refuge! "And my God the help of my hope." For as yet the Lord is our hope, since as long as we are here, we are in hope, and not in possession. But lest we fail in hope, there is near us a provision to encourage us, and to mitigate those very evils which we suffer. For it is not said in vain, "God is faithful, who will not suffer you to be tempted above that ye are able: but will with the temptation also make a way to escape, that ye may be able to bear it:"[5] who will so put us into that furnace of tribulation, that the vessel may be hardened, but not broken. "And the Lord is become my refuge: and my God the help of my hope." Why then did He seem to thee to be as it were unjust, in that He spareth the evil? See then how the Psalm is now set right, and be thou set right together with the Psalm: for, for this reason the Psalm contained thy words. What words? "Lord, how long shall the ungodly, how long shall the ungodly triumph?"[6] The Psalm just now used thy words: use therefore thyself the Psalm's words in thy turn.

23. "And the Lord shall recompense them according to their works, and after their own malice; the Lord our God shall destroy them" (ver. 23). The words, "after their own malice," are not said without meaning. I am benefited through them: and yet it is said to be their malice, and not their benefits. For assuredly He trieth us, scourgeth us, by means of the wicked. To prepare us for what doth

---

[1] 2 Cor. iv. 7.   [2] Rom. iv. 20, 21.
[3] [He imitates the cries of one who sells, *Sub hasta.*—C.]   [4] Matt. xxvi. 59.   [5] 1 Cor. x. 13.   [6] Ps. xciv. 3.

He scourge us? Confessedly for the kingdom of heaven. "For He scourgeth every son whom He receiveth; for what son is he whom the father chasteneth not?"[1] and when God doth this, He is teaching us in order to an eternal heritage: and this learning He often giveth us by means of wicked men, through whom He trieth and perfecteth our love, which He doth will to be extended even to our enemies.[2] . . . Thus also they who persecuted the Martyrs, by persecuting them on earth, sent them into heaven: knowingly they caused them the loss of the present life, while unconsciously they were bestowing upon them the gain of a future life: but, nevertheless, unto all who persevered in their wicked hatred of the righteous, will God recompense after their own iniquities, and in their own malice will He destroy them. For as the goodness of the righteous is hurtful unto the wicked, so is the iniquity of the wicked beneficial unto the righteous. . . .

24. Let therefore the righteous bear with the ungodly; let the temporal suffering of the righteous bear with the temporal impunity of the wicked; for "the just shall live by faith."[3] For there is no righteousness of man in this life except to live by faith, "which worketh by love."[4] But if he liveth by faith, let him believe both that he will himself inherit rest after his present toil, and that they will suffer eternal torments after their present exultation. And if faith worketh by love, let him love his enemies also, and, as far as in him lies, have the will to profit them; for thus he will prevent their injuring him when they have the will. And whenever perchance they have received power to hurt and tyrannize; let him lift his heart above, where no man hurteth him, well taught and chastened in the law of God, that he may "have patience given him in the days of adversity, until the pit be digged up for the ungodly." . . .

25. This I say, brethren, that ye may profit from what ye have heard, and ruminate within yourselves: permit not yourselves to forget, not only by thinking over again upon these subjects, and discoursing upon them, but also by so living. For a good life which is led after God's commands, is like a pen, because it is heard writing in our hearts. If it were written on wax, it would easily be blotted out: write it in your hearts, in your character, and it shall never be blotted out.

PSALM XCV.[5]

1. I could wish, brethren, that we were rather listening to our father: but even this is a good thing, to obey our father. Since therefore he who deigneth to pray for us, hath ordered us, I will speak unto you, beloved, what from the present Psalm Jesus Christ our common Lord shall deign to give us. Now the title of the Psalm is "David's Song of praise." The "Song of praise" signifieth both cheerfulness, in that it is a song; and devotion, for it is praise. For what ought a man to praise more than that which pleaseth him so, that it is impossible that it can displease him? In the praising of God therefore we praise with security. There he who praiseth is safe, where he feareth not lest he be ashamed for the object of his praise. Let us therefore both praise and sing; that is, let us praise with cheerfulness and joy. But what we are about to praise, this Psalm in the following verses showeth us.

2. "O come, let us sing unto the Lord" (ver. 1). He calleth us to a great banquet of joy, not one of this world, but in the Lord. For if there were not in this life a wicked joy which is to be distinguished from a righteous joy, it would be enough to say, "Come, let us rejoice;" but he has briefly distinguished it. What is it to rejoice aright? To rejoice in the Lord. Thou shouldest piously joy in the Lord, if thou dost wish safely to trample upon the world. But what is the word, "Come"? Whence doth He call them to come, with whom he wisheth to rejoice in the Lord; except that, while they are afar, they may by coming draw nearer, by drawing nearer they may approach, and by approaching rejoice? But whence are they afar? Can a man be locally distant from Him who is everywhere? . . . It is not by place, but by being unlike Him, that a man is afar from God. What is to be unlike Him? it meaneth, a bad life, bad habits; for if by good habits we approach God, by bad habits we recede from God. . . . If therefore by unlikeness we recede from God, by likeness we approach unto God. What likeness? That after which we were created, which by sinning we had corrupted in ourselves, which we have received again through the remission of sins, which is renewed in us in the mind within, that it may be engraved a second time as if on coin, that is, the image of our God upon our soul, and that we may return to His treasures. . . .

3. "Let us make a joyful[6] noise unto God, our salvation.". . . Consider, beloved, those who make a joyful noise in any ordinary songs, as in a sort of competition of worldly joy; and ye see them while reciting the written lines bursting forth with a joy, that the tongue sufficeth not to express the measure of; how they shout, indicating by that utterance the feeling of the mind,

[1] Heb. xii. 7.　　[2] Matt. v. 44.　[See p. 455, § 12, *supra.* — C.]
[3] Rom. i. 17.　　[4] Gal v. 6.
[5] Lat. XCIV. A discourse delivered at the bidding of Aurelius bishop of Carthage, or perhaps of Valerius bishop of Hippo, and consequently either before or shortly after St. Augustin was consecrated bishop.

[6] *Jubilemus.*

which cannot in words express what is conceived in the heart. If they then in earthly joy make a joyful noise; might we not do so from heavenly joy, which truly we cannot express in words?

4. "Let us prevent His face by confession" (ver. 2). Confession hath a double meaning in Scripture. There is a confession of him who praiseth, there is that of him who groaneth. The confession of praise pertaineth to the honour of Him who is praised: the confession of groaning to the repentance of him who confesseth. For men confess when they praise God: they confess when they accuse themselves; and the tongue hath no more worthy use. Truly, I believe these to be the very vows, of which he speaketh in another Psalm: "I will pay Thee my vows, which I distinguished with my lips."[1] Nothing is more elevated than that distinguishing, nothing is so necessary both to understand and to do. How then dost thou distinguish the vows which thou payest unto God? By praising Him, by accusing thyself; because it is His mercy, to forgive us our sins. For if He chose to deal with us after our deserts, He would find cause only to condemn. "O come," he said therefore, that we may at last go back from our sins, and that He may not cast up with us our accounts for the past; but that as it were a new account may be commenced, all the bonds of our debts having been burnt. . . . The more therefore thou despairedst of thyself on account of thy iniquities, do thou confess thy sins; for so much greater is the praise of Him who forgiveth, as is the fulness of the penitent's confession more abundant. Let us not therefore imagine that we have receded from the song of praise, in understanding here that confession by which we acknowledge our transgressions: this is even a part of the song of praise; for when we confess our sins, we praise the glory of God.

5. "And make a joyful[2] noise unto Him with Psalms." We have already said what it is "to make a joyful noise:" the word is repeated, that it may be confirmed by the act: the very repetition is an exhortation. For we have not forgotten, so as to wish to be again admonished, what was said above, that we should make a joyful noise: but usually in passages of strong feeling a well-known word is repeated, not to make it more familiar, but that the very repetition may strengthen the impression made: for it is repeated that we may understand the feeling of the speaker. . . . Hear now: "For the Lord is a great God, and a great King above all gods" (ver. 3). "For the Lord will not cast off His people."[3] Praise be unto Him, and shouts of joy be unto Him! What people shall He not cast off? we have no right to make our own explanation here:

for the Apostle hath prescribed this unto us, he hath explained whereof it is said. For this was the Jewish people, the people where were the prophets, the people where were the patriarchs, the people begotten according to the flesh from the seed of Abraham; the people in which all the mysteries which promised our Saviour preceded us; the people among whom was instituted the temple, the anointing, the Priest for a figure, that when all these shadows were past, the Light itself might come; this therefore was the people of God; to it were the prophets sent, in it those who were sent were born; to it were delivered and entrusted the revelations of God. What then? is the whole of that people condemned? far be it. It is called the good olive-tree by the Apostle, for it commenced with the patriarchs. . . . This then is the tree itself: though some of its boughs have been broken, yet all have not. For if all the boughs were broken, whence is Peter? whence John? whence Thomas? whence Matthew? whence Andrew? whence are all those Apostles? whence that very Apostle Paul who was speaking to us but now, and by his own fruit bearing witness to the good olive? Were not all these of that people? Whence also those five hundred brethren to whom our Lord appeared after His resurrection?[4] Whence were so many thousands at the words of Peter (when the Apostles, filled with the Holy Spirit, spoke with the tongues of all nations[5]) converted with such zeal for the honour of God and their own accusation, that they who first shed the Lord's blood in their rage, learnt how to drink it now that they believed? And all these five thousand were so converted that they sold their own property, and laid the price of it at the Apostles' feet.[6] That which one rich man did not do, when he heard from the Lord's mouth, and sorrowfully departed from Him,[7] this so many thousands of those men by whose hands Christ had been crucified, did on a sudden. In proportion as the wound was deeper in their own hearts, with the greater eagerness did they seek for a physician. Since therefore all these were from thence, the Psalm saith of them, "For the Lord will not cast off His people." . . .

6. What doth the Psalm add? In His hand are all the corners of the earth" (ver. 4): we recognise the corner stone: the corner stone is Christ. There cannot be a corner, unless it hath united in itself two walls: they come from different sides to one corner, but they are not opposed to each other in the corner. The circumcision cometh from one side, the uncircumcision from the other; in Christ both peoples have met together: because He hath become the stone, of which it is written, "The stone

---

[1] Ps. lxvi. 13, 14.　　　[2] *Jubilemus.*
[3] Ps. xciv. 14. In the Sept. these nine words are added.
[4] 1 Cor. xv. 6.　　[5] Acts ii. 4.　　[6] Acts iv. 4, ii. 44.
[7] Matt. xix. 21, 22.

which the builders rejected, hath become the head of the corner." [1] . . .

7. " For the sea is His and He made it " (ver. 5). For the sea is this world, but God made also the sea : nor can the waves rage save only so far as to the shore, where He hath marked their bounds. There is therefore no temptation, that hath not received its measure. . . . "And His hands prepared the dry land." Be thou the dry land : thirst for the grace of God : that as a sweet shower it may come upon thee, may find in thee fruit. He alloweth not the waves to cover what He hath sown. "And His hands prepared the dry land." Hence also therefore let us shout unto the Lord.

8. "O come, let us worship, and fall down to Him ; and mourn before the Lord our Maker " (ver. 6). . . . Perhaps thou art burning with the consciousness of a fault ; blot out with tears the flame of thy sin : mourn before the Lord : fearlessly mourn before the Lord, who made thee ; for He despiseth not the work of His own hands in thee. Think not thou canst be restored by thyself. By thyself thou mayest fall off, thou canst not restore thyself : He who made thee restoreth thee. " Let us mourn before the Lord our Maker : " weep before Him, confess unto Him, prevent His face in confession. For who art thou who mournest before Him, and confessest unto Him, but one whom He created ? The thing created hath no slight confidence in Him who created it, and that in no indifferent fashion, but according to His own image and likeness.

9. " For He is the Lord our God " (ver. 7). But that we may without fear fall down and kneel before Him, what are we ? " We are the people of His pasture, and the sheep of His hand." See how elegantly he hath transposed the order of the words, and as it were not given its own attribute to each word ; that we may understand these very same to be the sheep, who are also the people. He said not, the sheep of His pasture, and the people of His hand ; which might be thought more congruous, since the sheep belong to the pasture ; but He said, " the people of His pasture." The people are therefore sheep, since he saith, " the people of His pasture : " the people themselves are sheep. . . . He praiseth these sheep also in the Song of Solomon, speaking of some perfect ones as the teeth of His Spouse the Holy Church : " Thy teeth are like a flock of sheep that are even shorn, which come up from the washing ; whereof every one beareth twins, and there is none barren." [2] What meaneth, " Thy teeth " ? These by whom thou speakest : for the teeth of the Church are those through whom she speaketh.

Of what sort are thy teeth ? " Like a flock of sheep that are shorn." Why, " that are shorn " ? Because they have laid aside the burdens of the world. Were not those sheep, of which I was a little before speaking, shorn, whom the bidding of God had shorn, when He saith, " Go and sell that thou hast, and give to the poor ; and thou shalt find treasure in heaven : and come and follow Me " ? [3] They performed this bidding : shorn they came. And because those who believe in Christ are baptized, what is there said ? " which come up from the washing ; " that is, come up from the cleansing. " Whereof every one beareth twins." What twins ? Those two commandments, wherefrom hang all the Law and the Prophets. [4]

10. Therefore, " To-day if ye will hear His voice, harden not your hearts " (ver. 8). O my people, the people of God ! God addresses His people : not only the people of His which He shall not cast off, but also all His people. For He speaketh in the corner stone [5] to each wall : that is, prophecy speaketh in Christ, both to the people of the Jews, and the people of the Gentiles. For some time ye heard His voice through Moses, and hardened your hearts. He then, when you hardened your hearts, spoke through a herald ; He now speaketh by Himself, let your hearts soften. He who used to send heralds before Him, hath now deigned to come Himself ; He here speaketh by His own mouth, He who used to speak by the mouths of the Prophets.

11. "As in the provocation, and in the day of temptation in the wilderness, where your fathers proved Me " (ver. 9). Let such be no more your fathers : imitate them not. They were your fathers, but if ye do not imitate them, they shall not be your fathers : yet as ye were born of them, they were your fathers. And if the heathen who came from the ends of the earth, in the words of Jeremias, "The Gentiles shall come unto Thee from the ends of the earth, and shall say, Surely our forefathers have inherited lies, vanity, and things wherein there is no profit : " [6] if the heathen forsook their idols, to come to the God of Israel ; ought Israel whom their own God led from Egypt through the Red Sea, [7] wherein He overwhelmed their pursuing foes ; whom He led out into the wilderness, fed with manna, [8] never took His rod from correcting them, never deprived them of the blessings of His mercy ; ought they to desert their own God, when the heathen have come unto Him ? " When your fathers tempted Me, proved Me, and saw My works. . . .

12. " Forty years long was I very near unto this generation, and said, It is a people that do

---

[1] Ps. cxviii. 22. [2] Song of Sol. iv. 2, vi. 5.

[3] Matt. xix. 21. [4] Matt. xxii. 40. [5] Eph. ii. 20. [6] Jer. xvi. 19. [7] Exod. xiv. 21, 22. [8] Exod. xvi. 13-35.

always err in their hearts; for they have not known My ways" (ver. 10). The forty years have the same meaning as the word "always." For that number forty indicates the fulness of ages, as if the ages were perfected in this number. Hence our Lord fasted forty days, forty days He was tempted in the desert,[1] and forty days He was with His disciples after His resurrection.[2] On the first forty days He showed us temptation, on the latter forty days consolation: since beyond doubt when we are tempted we are consoled. For His body, that is, the Church, must needs suffer temptations in this world: but that Comforter, who said, "Lo, I am with you alway, even unto the end of the world,"[3] is not wanting. For this was I with them forty years, to show such a race of men, which alway provoketh Me, even unto the end of the world: because by those forty years He meant to signify the whole of this world's duration.

13. . . . We began with exulting joy: but this Psalm hath ended with great fear: "Unto whom I sware in My wrath, that they should not enter into My rest" (ver. 11). It is a great thing for God to speak: how much greater for Him to swear? Thou shouldest fear a man when he sweareth, lest he do somewhat on account of his oath against his will: how much more shouldest thou fear God, when He sweareth, seeing He can swear nought rashly? He chose the act of swearing for a confirmation. And by whom doth God swear? By Himself: for He hath no greater by whom to swear.[4] By Himself He confirmeth His promises: by Himself He confirmeth His threats. Let no man say in his heart, His promise is true; His threat is false: as His promise is true, so is His threat sure. Thou oughtest to be equally assured of rest, of happiness, of eternity, of immortality, if thou hast executed His commandments; as of destruction, of the burning of eternal fire, of damnation with the devil, if thou hast despised His commandments. . . .

PSALM XCVI.[5]

1. My lord and brother Severus[6] still defers the pleasure we shall feel in his discourse, which he oweth us; for he acknowledgeth, that he is held a debtor. For all the Churches through which he hath passed, by his tongue the Lord hath gladdened: much more therefore ought that Church to be rejoiced, out of which the Lord hath propagated his preaching among the rest. But what shall we do, but obey his will? I said,

however, brethren, that he deferred, not that he defrauded us. Therefore let us keep him as a debtor bound, and release him not until he hath paid. Attend therefore, beloved: as far as the Lord alloweth, let us say somewhat of this Psalm, which indeed you already know; for the fresh mention of truth is sweet. Possibly when its title was pronounced, some heard it with wonder. For the Psalm is inscribed: "When the house was being built after the Captivity." This title having been prefixed, ye were perhaps expecting in the text of the Psalm to hear what stones were hewn from the mountains, what masses were drawn to the spot, what foundations were laid, what beams were placed on high, what columns raised. Its song is of nothing of this kind. . . . It is no such house that is in building; for behold where it is built, not in one spot, not in any particular region. For thus he beginneth: —

2. "O sing unto the Lord a new song; sing unto the Lord, all the earth"[7] (ver. 1). If all the earth singeth a new song, it is thus building while it singeth: the very act of singing is building: but only, if it singeth not the old song. The lust of the flesh singeth the old song: the love of God singeth the new. . . . Hear why it is a new song: the Lord saith, "A new commandment I give unto you, that ye love one another."[8] The whole earth then singeth a new song: there the house of God is built. All the earth is the house of God. If all the earth is the house of God,[9] he who clingeth not to all the earth, is a ruin, not a house; that old ruin whose shadow that ancient temple represented. For there what was old was destroyed, that what was new might be built up. . . . The Apostle bindeth us together into this very structure, and fasteneth us when bound together in that unity, saying, "Forbearing one another in love; endeavouring to keep the unity of the Spirit in the bond of peace."[10] Where there is this unity of Spirit, there is one stone; but one stone formed out of many. How one formed out of many? By forbearing one another in love. Therefore the house of the Lord our God is in building; it is this that is being wrought, for this are these words, for this these readings, for this the preaching of the Gospel over the whole world; as yet it is in building. This house hath increased greatly, and filled many nations: nevertheless, it hath not yet prevailed through all nations: by its increase it hath held many, and will prevail over all: and it is gainsaid by those who boast of their being of its household, and who say, it hath already lost ground. It still increaseth, still all those nations which have not yet believed are destined to believe; that no man may say,

[1] Matt. iv. 1–11.   [2] Acts i. 3.
[3] Matt. xxviii. 20.   [4] Heb. vi. 13.
[5] Lat. XCV. Delivered perhaps in the year 405, when the Donatists prevailed through the violence of the Circumcelliones.
[6] Bishop of Milevis, mentioned in the discourse of a preceding day on Ps. cxxxii. — *Ben.*

[7] 1 Chron. xvi. 23, etc.   [8] John xv. 12.
[9] Donatists.   [10] Eph. iv. 2, 3.

will that tongue believe? will the barbarians believe? what is the meaning of the Holy Spirit having appeared in the fiery tongues,[1] except that there is no tongue so hard that it cannot be softened by that fire? For we know that many barbarous nations have already believed in Christ: Christ already possesseth regions where the Roman empire hath never yet reached; what is as yet closed to those who fight with the sword, is not closed to Him who fighteth with wood. For "the Lord hath reigned from the wood."[2] Who is it who fighteth with wood? Christ. With His cross He hath vanquished kings, and fixed upon their forehead, when vanquished, that very cross; and they glory in it, for in it is their salvation. This is the work which is being wrought, thus the house increaseth, thus it is building: and that ye may know, hear the following verses of the Psalm: see them labouring upon, and constructing the house. "O sing unto the Lord all the earth."

3. "Sing unto the Lord, bless His Name: be telling good tidings of His salvation from day to day" (ver. 2). How doth the building increase? "Be telling," he saith, "good tidings of His salvation from day to day." Let it be preached from day to day; from day to day, he saith, let it be built; let My house, saith God, increase. And as if it were said by the workmen, Where dost Thou command it to be built? Where dost Thou will Thy house to increase? Choose for us some level, spacious spot, if Thou wish an ample house built Thee. Where dost Thou bid us be telling good tidings from day to day? He showeth the place: "Declare His honour unto the heathen:" His honour, not yours. O ye builders, "Declare His honour unto the heathen." Should ye choose to declare your own honour, ye shall fall: if His, ye shall be built up, while ye are building. Therefore they who choose to declare their own honour, have refused to dwell in that house; and therefore they sing not a new song with all the earth.[3] For they do not share it with the whole round world; and hence they are not building in the house, but have erected a whited wall. How sternly doth God threaten the whited wall?[4] There are innumerable testimonies of the Prophets, whence He curseth the whited wall. What is the whited wall, save hypocrisy, that is, pretence? Without it is bright, within it is dirt. ... A certain person,[5] speaking of this whited wall, said thus: "as, if in a wall which standeth alone, and is not connected with any other walls,

you make a door, whoever enters, is out of doors; so in that part which hath refused to sing the new song together with the house, but hath chosen to build a wall, and that a whited one, and not solid, what availeth it that it hath a door?" If thou enterest, thou art found to be without. For because they themselves did not enter by the door, their door also doth not admit them within. For the Lord saith, "I am the door: by Me they enter in."[6] . . . "Declare His honour unto the heathen." What is, unto the heathen? Perhaps by nations but a few are meant: and that part which hath raised the whited wall hath still somewhat to say: why are not Getulia, Numidia, Mauritania, Byzacium, nations? Provinces are nations. Let the word of God take the word from hypocrisy, from the whited wall, building up the house over the whole world. It is not enough to say, "Declare His honour unto the heathen;" that thou mayest not think any nations excepted, he addeth, "and His wonders unto all people."

4. "For the Lord is great, and cannot worthily be praised" (ver. 4). What Lord, except Jesus Christ, "is great, and cannot worthily be praised"? Ye know surely that He appeared as a Man: ye know surely that He was conceived in a woman's womb, ye know that He was born from the womb, that He was suckled, that He was carried in arms, circumcised, that a victim was offered for Him, that He grew; lastly, ye know that He was buffeted, spit upon, crowned with thorns, was crucified, died, was pierced with a spear; ye know that He suffered all these things: "He is great, and cannot worthily be praised." Despise not what is little, understand what is great. He became little, because ye were such: let Him be acknowledged great, and in Him ye shall be great. . . . For what can a small tongue say towards the praise of the Great One? By saying, Beyond praise,[7] he hath spoken, and hath given to imagination what it may conceive: as if saying, What I cannot utter, do thou reflect on; and when thou shalt have reflected, it will not be enough. What no man's thought uttereth, doth any man's tongue utter? "The Lord is great, and cannot worthily be praised." Let Him be praised, and preached: His honour declared, and His house built.

5. . . . For the spot where he wished to build the house, is itself woody, where it was said yesterday, "we found it in the wood."[8] For he was seeking that very house, when he said, "in the wood." And why is that spot woody? Men used to worship images: it is not wonderful that they fed hogs. For that son who left his father,

---

[1] Acts ii. 3
[2] Ps. xcvi. 11. Quoted as from this Psalm by Justin Martyr, *Apol.* i. 41. In *Dial. cum Tryph.* § 73, he accuses the Jews of expunging the words ἀπὸ τοῦ ξύλου. [See A. N. F. vol. i. p. 176, note 4, and vol. iii. p. 166, note 7. —C.]
[3] Donatists.   [4] Ezek. xiii. 10.
[5] St. Optatus of Milevis on *Don. Schism,* b. iii. c. 10, p. 67 (quoted in substance).

[6] John x. 9.   [7] *Laudabilis nimis.*
[8] Ps. cxxxii. 6. Hence it appears that Ps. cxxxii. had been expounded the day before.

and spent his all on harlots, living as a prodigal, used to feed hogs,[1] that is, to worship devils; and by this very superstition of the heathen, all the earth became a wood. But he who buildeth a house, rooteth up the wood; and for this reason it was said, "While the house was being built, after the captivity."[2] For men were held captive under the devil, and served devils; but they were redeemed from captivity. They could sell, but they could not redeem themselves. The Redeemer came, and gave a price; He poured forth His Blood, and bought the whole world. Ye ask what He bought? Ye see what He hath given; find out then what He bought. The Blood of Christ was the price. What is equal to this? What, but the whole world? What, but all nations? They are very ungrateful for their price, or very proud, who say that the price is so small that it bought the Africans only; or that they are so great, as that it was given for them alone. Let them not then exult, let them not be proud: He gave what He gave for the whole world. He knew what He bought, because He knew at what price He bought it. Thus because we are redeemed, the house is built after the captivity. And who are they who held us in captivity? Because they to whom it is said, "Declare His honour," are the clearers of the wood: that they may root out the wood, free the earth from captivity, and build, and raise up, by declaring the greatness of the Lord's house. How is the wood of devils cleared away, unless He who is above them all be preached? All nations then had devils for their gods: those whom they called gods, were devils, as the Apostle more openly saith, "The things which the Gentiles sacrifice, they sacrifice unto devils, and not to God."[3] Since therefore they were in captivity, because they sacrificed to devils, and on that account the whole earth had remained woody; He is declared to be great, and above all worldly praise.

6. . . . For when he had said, "He is more to be feared than all gods:" he added, "As for all the gods of the heathen, they are devils." . . . Because "all the gods of the heathen are devils." And is this all the praise of Him who cannot worthily be praised, that He is above all the gods of the heathen, which are devils? Wait, and hear what followeth: "It is the Lord that made the heavens." Not above all gods only therefore, but above all the heavens which He made, is the Lord. If he were to say, "above all gods, for the gods of the heathen are devils," and if the praise of our Lord stopped here, he had said less than we are accustomed to think of Christ; but when he said, "But it is the Lord that made the heavens;" see what dif-

ference there is between the heavens and devils: and what between the heavens and Him who made the heavens; behold how exalted is the Lord. He said not, But the Lord sitteth above the heavens; for perhaps some one else might be imagined to have made them, upon which He was enthroned: but, "It is the Lord that made the heavens." If He made the heavens, He made the Angels also: Himself made the Angels, Himself made the Apostles. The devils yielded to the Apostles: but the Apostles themselves were heavens, who bore the Lord. . . . O heavens, which He made, declare His honour unto the heathen! Let His house be built throughout the earth, let all the earth sing a new song.

7. "Confession and beauty are before Him" (ver. 6). Dost thou love beauty? Wishest thou to be beautiful? Confess! He said not, beauty and confession, but confession and beauty. Thou wast foul; confess, that thou mayest be fair: thou wast a sinner; confess, that thou mayest be righteous. Thou couldest deform thyself: thou canst not make thyself beautiful. But of what sort is our Betrothed, who hath loved one deformed, that he might make her fair? How, saith some one, loved He one deformed? "I came not," said He, "to call the righteous, but sinners."[4] Whom callest Thou? sinners, that they may remain sinners? No, saith He. And by what means will they cease to be sinners? "Confession and beauty are before Him." They honour Him by confession of their sins, they vomit the evils which they had greedily devoured; they return not to their vomit, like the unclean dog;[5] and there will then be confession and beauty: we love beauty; let us first choose confession, that beauty may follow. Again, there is one who loveth power and greatness: he wisheth to be great as the Angels are. There is a certain greatness in the Angels; and such power, that if the Angels exert it to the full, it cannot be withstood. And every man desireth the power of the Angels, but their righteousness every man loveth not. First love righteousness, and power shall follow thee. For what followeth here? "Holiness and greatness are in His sanctification." Thou wast before seeking for greatness: first love righteousness: when thou art righteous, thou shalt also be great. For if thou preposterously dost wish first to be great, thou fallest before thou canst rise: for thou dost not rise, thou art raised up. Thou risest better, if He raise thee who falleth not. For He who falleth not descendeth unto thee: thou hadst fallen: He descendeth, He hath stretched forth His hand unto thee; thou canst not rise by thy own strength, embrace the hand of Him who

---

[1] Luke xv. 12–15.   [2] Title of Psalm.   [3] 1 Cor. x. 20.   [4] Matt. ix. 13.   [5] 2 Pet. ii. 22.

descendeth, that thou mayest be raised up by the Strong One.

8. What then? If "confession and beauty are before Him: holiness and greatness in His sanctification" (ver. 7). This we declare, when we are building the house; behold, it is already declared unto the heathen; what ought the heathen to do, to whom those who have cleared away the wood have declared the Lord's honour? He now saith to the heathen themselves, "Ascribe unto the Lord, O ye kindreds of the people: ascribe unto the Lord worship and honour." Ascribe them not unto yourselves: because they also who have declared it unto you, have not declared their own, but His honour. Do ye then "ascribe unto the Lord worship and honour;" and say, "Not unto us, O Lord, not unto us: but unto Thy Name give the praise."[1] Put not your trust in man. If each of you is baptized, let him say: He baptizeth me, of whom the friend of the Bridegroom said, "He baptizeth with the Holy Ghost."[2] For when ye say this, ye ascribe unto the Lord worship and honour: "Ascribe unto the Lord worship and honour."

9. Ascribe unto the Lord glory unto His Name" (ver. 8). Not unto the name of man, not unto your own name, but unto His ascribe worship. . . . Confession is a present unto God. O heathen, if ye will enter into His courts, enter not empty. "Bring presents." What presents shall we bring with us? The sacrifice of God is a troubled spirit: a broken and a contrite heart, O God, shalt not Thou despise."[3] Enter with an humble heart into the house of God, and thou hast entered with a present. But if thou art proud, thou enterest empty. For whence wouldest thou be proud, if thou wert not empty? For if thou wast full, thou wouldest not be puffed up. How couldest thou be full? If thou wert to bring a present, which thou shouldest carry to the courts of the Lord. Let us not retain you much longer: let us run over what remaineth. Behold the house increasing: behold the edifice pervade the whole world. Rejoice, because ye have entered into the courts; rejoice, because ye are being built into the temple of God. For those who enter are themselves built up, they themselves are the house of God: He is the inhabitor, for whom the house is built over the whole world, and this "after the captivity." "Bring presents, and come into His courts."

10. "O worship the Lord in His holy court" (ver. 9): in the Catholic Church; this is His holy court. Let no man say, "Lo, here is Christ, or there. For there shall arise false prophets."[4] Say this unto them,[5] "There shall

not be left here one stone upon another, that shall not be thrown down." Ye are calling me to the whited wall; I adore my God in His holy court. "Let the whole earth be moved before His face."

11. "Tell it out among the nations, that the Lord reigneth from the wood:[6] and that it is He who hath made the round world so fast that it cannot be moved" (ver. 10). What testimonies of the building of the house of God! The clouds of heaven thunder out throughout the world that God's house is being built; and the frogs cry from the marsh,[7] We alone are Christians. What testimonies do I bring forward? That of the Psalter. I bring forward what thou singest as one deaf: open thine ears; thou singest this; thou singest with me, and thou agreest not with me; thy tongue soundeth what mine doth, and yet thine heart disagreeth with mine. Dost thou not sing this? Behold the testimonies of the whole world: "Let the whole earth be moved before His face:" and dost thou say, that thou art not moved? "Tell it out among the heathen, that the Lord hath reigned from the wood." Shall men perchance prevail here, and say they reign by wood, because they reign by means of the clubs of their bandits?[8] Reign by the Cross of Christ, if thou art to reign by wood. For this wood of thine maketh thee wooden: the wood of Christ passeth thee across the sea. Thou hearest the Psalm saying, "He hath set aright the round world, that it cannot be moved;" and thou sayest it hath not only been moved since it was made fast, but hath also decreased. Dost thou speak the truth, and the Psalmist falsehood? Do the false prophets, when they cry out, "Lo, here is Christ, and there,"[9] speak truth; and doth this Prophet lie? Brethren, against these most open words ye hear in the corners rumours like these; "such an one was a traditor," and, "such an one was a traditor."[10] What dost thou say? Are thy words, or the words of God, to be heard? For, "it is He who hath set aright the round world, that it cannot be moved." I show unto thee the round world built: bring thy present, and come into the courts of the Lord. Thou hast no presents: and on that account thou art not willing to enter. What is this? If God were to appoint unto thee a bull, goat, or ram, for a present, thou wouldest find one to bring: He hath appointed a humble heart, and thou wilt not enter; for thou findest not this in thyself, because thou art swollen with pride. "He hath set aright the round world, that it cannot be moved: and He shall judge the people right-

---

[1] Ps. cxv. 1.
[2] John i. 33, iii. 29. See his commentary on the passage, and on John i. 31.
[3] Ps. li. 17.   [4] Matt. xxiv. 23, 24.   [5] Donatists.

[6] See p. 471, note 21, *supra*.
[7] [*i.e.* so say the Donatists. — C.]
[8] Circumcelliones. [See p. 42, note 4, and also p. 470, note 5, *supra*. — C.]
[9] Matt. xxiv. 23.
[10] Cæcilianus and others, by communicating with whom they alleged the universal Church to have fallen.

eously." Then shall they mourn, who now refuse to love righteousness.

12. "Let the heavens rejoice, and let the earth be glad" (ver. 11). Let the heavens, which declare the glory of God, rejoice; let the heavens rejoice, which the Lord made; let the earth be glad, which the heavens rain upon. For the heavens are the preachers, the earth the listeners. "Let the sea be stirred up, and the fulness thereof." What sea? The world. The sea hath been stirred up, and the fulness thereof: the whole world was roused up against the Church, while it was being extended and built over all the earth. Concerning this stirring up, ye have heard in the Gospel, "They shall deliver you up to councils." [1] "The sea was stirred up: but how should the sea ever conquer Him who made it?

13. "The plains shall be joyful, and all things that are in them" (ver. 12). All the meek, all the gentle, all the righteous, are the "plains" of God. "Then shall all the trees of the woods rejoice." The trees of the woods are the heathen. Why do they rejoice? Because they were cut off from the wild olive, and engraffed into the good olive. [2] "Then shall all the trees of the woods rejoice:" because huge cedars and cypresses have been cut down, and undecaying timbers have been bought for the building of the house. They were trees of the woods; but before they were sent to the building: they were trees of the woods, but before they produced the olive.

14. "Before the face of the Lord. For He cometh, for He cometh to judge the world" (ver. 13). He came at first, and will come again. He first came in His Church in clouds. What are the clouds which bore Him? The Apostles who preached, respecting whom ye have heard, when the Epistle was being read: "We are ambassadors," he saith, "for Christ: we pray you in Christ's stead, be ye reconciled to God." [3] These are the clouds in whom He cometh, excepting His last Advent, when He will come to judge the quick and the dead. He came first in the clouds. This was His first voice which sounded forth in the Gospel: "From this time shall they see the Son of Man coming in the clouds." [4] What is, "from this time"? Will not the Lord come in later times, when all the tribes of the earth shall mourn? He first came in His own preachers, and filled the whole round world. Let us not resist His first coming, that we may not tremble at His second. "But woe to them that are with child, and that give suck in those days!" [5] Ye have heard but now in the Gospel: "Take ye heed, for ye know not at what hour He cometh." [6]

This is said figuratively. Who are those with child, and who give suck? Those who are with child, are the souls whose hope is in the world: but those who have gained what they hoped for, are meant by "they who give suck." For example: one wisheth to buy a country seat; he is with child, for his object is not gained as yet, the womb swelleth in hope: he buyeth it; he hath brought forth, he now giveth suck to what he hath bought. "Woe to them that are with child, and that give suck in those days!" Woe to those who put their hope in the world; woe to them that cling to those things which they brought forth through hope in the world. What then should the Christian do? He should use, not serve, the world. [7] What is this? Those that have as those that have not. . . . He who is without carefulness, waiteth without fear for his Lord's coming. For what sort of love is it of Christ, to fear lest He come? Brethren, are we not ashamed? We love Him, and yet we fear lest He come. Are we sure that we love Him? or do we love our sins more? Therefore let us hate our sins for their own sake, and love Him who will come to punish our sins. He will come, whether we like or not: for because He cometh not just now, it is no reason that He will not come at all. He will come, and when thou knowest not; and if He shall find thee ready, thy ignorance is no hurt to thee. "Then shall all the trees of the wood rejoice before the Lord; for He cometh:" at His first coming. And what afterwards? "For He cometh to judge the earth. And all the trees of the woods shall rejoice." He came first: and later to judge the earth: He shall find those rejoicing who believed in His first coming, "for He cometh."

15. "For with righteousness shall He judge the world:" not a part of it, for He bought not a part: He will judge the whole, for it was the whole of which He paid the price. Ye have heard the Gospel, where it saith, that when He cometh, "He shall gather together His elect from the four winds." [8] He gathereth all His elect from the four winds: therefore from the whole world. For Adam [9] himself (this I had said before) signifieth in Greek the whole world; for there are four letters, A, D, A, and M. But as the Greeks speak, the four quarters of the world have these initial letters, Ἀνατολὴ, they call the East; Δύσις, the West; Ἄρκτος, the North; Μεσημβρία, the South: thou hast the word Adam. Adam therefore hath been scattered over the whole world. He was in one place, and fell, and as in a manner broken small, [10] he filled the whole world: but the mercy of God

[1] Mark xiii. 9.   [2] Rom. xi. 17.   [3] 2 Cor. v. 20.
[4] Mark xiii. 26.   [5] Mark xiii. 17.   [6] Mark xiii. 33.

[7] 1 Cor. vii. 29-32.   [8] Mark xiii. 27.
[9] *Vid.* Tract. 9 in Johan. note 14, and Tract. 10, note 12. — *Ben.*
[10] *Quodammodo comminutus.*

gathered together the fragments from every side, and forged [1] them by the fire of love, and made one what was broken. That Artist knew how to do this; let no one despair: it is indeed a great thing, but reflect who that Artist was. He who made, restored: He who formed, re-formed. What are righteousness and truth? He will gather together His elect with Him to the judgment, but the rest He will separate one from another; for He will place some on the right, others on the left hand. But what is more just, what more true, than that they shall not expect mercy from their Judge, who have refused to act mercifully, before their Judge come? But those who chose to act with mercy, with mercy shall be judged. . . .

PSALM XCVII.[2]

1. . . . This Psalm is entitled, "A Psalm of David's, when his land was restored." Let us refer the whole to Christ, if we wish to keep the road of a right understanding: let us not depart from the corner stone,[3] lest our understanding suffer a fall: in Him let that become fixed, which wavered with unstable motion; let that rest upon Him, which before was waving to and fro in uncertainty. Whatever doubt a man hath in his mind when he heareth the Scriptures of God, let him not depart from Christ; when Christ hath been revealed to him in the words, let him then be assured that he hath understood; but before he arriveth at the understanding of Christ, let him not presume that he hath understood. "For Christ is the end of the law for righteousness to every one that believeth." [4] What doth this mean, and how are these words understood in Christ, "When his land was restored"? . . .

2. The earth restored is the resurrection of the flesh; for after His resurrection, all those things which are sung of in the Psalm were done. Let us then hear a Psalm full of joy on the restoration of the Earth. Let the Lord our God excite in us a hope and a pleasure worthy of so great a thing; may He rule our discourse, that it be fit for your hearts, that whatever joy our heart doth feel in such sights, He may bring on to our tongue, and thence conduct it into your ears, then to your heart, thence to your actions.

3. . . . "The Lord is King, let the earth be glad: yea, let the multitude of the isles be joyous" (ver. 1). It is so indeed, because the word of God hath been preached not in the continent alone, but also in those isles which lie in mid sea: even these are full of Christians, full of the servants of God. For the sea doth not retard Him who made it. Where ships can approach, cannot the words of God? The isles are filled.

But figuratively the isles may be taken for all the Churches. Why isles? Because the waves of all temptations roar around them. But as an isle may be beaten by the waves which on every side dash around it, yet cannot be broken, and rather itself doth break the advancing waves, than by them is broken: so also the Churches of God, springing up throughout the world, have suffered the persecutions of the ungodly, who roar around them on every side; and behold the isles stand fixed, and at last the sea is calmed.

4. "Clouds and darkness are round about Him: righteousness and judgment are the direction of His seat" (ver. 2). . . . The Lord Himself saith: "For judgment I am come into this world; that they which see not might see, and that they which see might be made blind." [5] They who seem unto themselves to see, who think themselves wise, who think healing not needful for them, that they may be made blind, may not understand. And that "they which see not may see;" that they who confess their blindness may obtain to be enlightened. Let there be therefore "clouds and darkness round about Him," for those who have not understood Him: for those who confess and humble themselves, "righteousness and judgment are the direction of His seat." He called those who believe in Him His seat: for from them hath He made Himself a seat, since in them Wisdom sitteth; for the Son of God is the Wisdom of God. But we have heard from another passage of Scripture a strong confirmation of this interpretation. "The soul of the righteous is the seat of Wisdom." [6] Because then they who have believed in Him have been made righteous: justified by faith, they have become His own seat: He sitteth in them, judging from them, and guiding them. . . .

5. "There shall go a fire before Him, and burn up His enemies on every side" (ver. 3). We remember having read in the Gospel, He shall say, "Depart into everlasting fire, prepared for the devil and his angels." [7] I do not think it is said of that fire. Why do I not? Because he speaketh of some fire, which shall go before Him, before He cometh to judgment. For it is said, that the fire goeth before Him, and burneth up His enemies on every side, that is, throughout the whole world. That fire will burn after His advent: this, on the contrary, will go before Him. What fire then is this? . . . Behold, we have understood the fire that goeth before Him, that is to be understood of a kind of temporal punishment of the unbelieving and ungodly: let us understand the fire, if possible, of the salvation of the redeemed also; for thus we had proposed. The Lord Himself saith:

---

[1] *Conflavit.*   [2] Lat. XCVI. A discourse to the people.
[3] Eph. ii. 20.   [4] Rom. x. 4.

[5] John ix. 39.   [6] Prov. xii. 23; 1 Cor. i. 24.
[7] Matt. xxv. 41.

"I am come to send fire on the earth : "[1] "fire" in the same way as a "sword;" as in another passage He saith, that He was not come to send peace, but a sword, upon earth.[2] The sword to divide, the fire to burn : but each salutary : for the sword of His own word hath in salutary wise separated us from evil habits. For He brought a sword, and separated every believer either from his father who believed not in Christ, or from his mother in like manner unbelieving : or at least, if we were born of Christian parents, from his ancestors. For no man among us had not either a grandsire, or great grandsire, or some ancestry among the heathen, and in that unbelief which is accursed before God. We are separated from that which we were before ; but the sword which separateth, but slayeth not, hath cut between us. In the same way the fire also : "I am come to send fire upon the earth." Believers in Him were set on fire, they received the flame of love : and for this reason when the Holy Spirit itself had been sent to the Apostles, It thus appeared : "cloven tongues, like as of fire."[3] Burning with this fire they set out on their march through the world, to burn and set on fire His enemies on every side. What enemies of His? They who forsaking the God who made them, adored the idols they had made. . . .

6. "His lightnings gave shine unto the world" (ver. 4). This is great joy. Do we not see? is it not clear? His lightnings have shined unto the whole world : His enemies have been set on fire, and burnt. All that gainsaid hath been burnt, and "His lightnings have given shine unto the world." How have they shone? That the world might at length believe. Whence were the lightnings? From the clouds. What are the clouds of God? The preachers of the truth. But thou seest a cloud, misty and dark in the sky, and it hath I know not what hidden within it. If there be lightning from the cloud, a brightness shineth forth : from that which thou didst despise, hath burst forth that which thou mayest dread. Our Lord Jesus Christ therefore sent His Apostles, as His preachers, like clouds : they were seen as men, and were despised ; as clouds appear, and are despised, until what thou wonderest at gleameth from them. For they were in the first place men encumbered with flesh, weak ; then, men of low station, unlearned, ignoble : but there was within what could lighten forth ; there was in them what could flash abroad. Peter a fisherman approached, prayed, and the dead arose.[4] His human form was a cloud, the splendour of the miracle was the lightning. So in their words, so in their deeds, when they do things to be

wondered at, and utter words to be wondered at, "His lightnings gave shine unto the world ; the earth saw it, and was afraid." Is it not true? Doth not the whole Christian world at length exclaim, Amen, afraid at the lightnings which burst forth from those clouds?

7. "The hills melted like wax at the presence of the Lord" (ver. 5). Who are the hills? The proud. Every high thing raising itself against God, at the deeds of Christ and of the Christians, trembled, yielded, and when I say, what hath been already said, "melted," a better word cannot be found. "The hills melted like wax at the presence of the Lord." Where is the elevation of powers? where the hardness of the unbelieving? The Lord was a fire unto them, they melted at His presence like wax ; so long hard, until that fire was applied. Every height hath been levelled ; it dareth not now blaspheme Christ : and though the Pagan believeth not in Him, he blasphemeth Him not ; though not as yet become a living stone, yet the hard hill hath been subdued. "At the presence of the Lord of the whole earth : " not of the Jews only, but of the Gentiles also, as the Apostle saith ; for He is not the God of the Jews alone, but of the Gentiles also.[5] He is therefore the Lord of the whole earth, the Lord Jesus Christ born in Judæa, but not born for Judæa alone, because before He was born He created all men ; and He who created, also new created, all men.

8. "The heavens have declared His righteousness : and all the people have seen His glory" (ver. 6). What heavens have declared? "The heavens declare the glory of God."[6] Who are the heavens? Those who have become His seat ; for as God sitteth in the heavens, so doth He sit in the Apostles, so doth He sit in the preachers of the Gospel. Even thou, if thou wilt, shalt be a heaven. Dost thou wish to be so? Purge from thy heart the earth. If thou hast not earthly lusts, and hast not in vain uttered the response, that thou hast "lifted up thy heart," thou shalt be a heaven.[7] "If ye be risen with Christ," saith the Apostle to believers, "set your affection on things above, not on things of the earth."[8] Thou hast begun to set thine affection upon things above, not on things upon earth ; hast thou not become a heaven? Thou carriest flesh, and in thy heart thou art already a heaven ; for thy conversation will be in heaven.[9] Being such, thou also declarest Christ ; for who of the faithful declareth not Christ? . . . Therefore the whole Church preacheth Christ, and the heavens declare His righteousness ; for all the faithful, whose care it is to gain unto God those who have not yet

---

[1] Luke xii. 49. [2] Matt. x. 34. [3] Acts ii. 3.
[4] Acts ix. 40.

[5] Rom. iii. 29. [6] Ps. xix. 1.
[7] [See on this, *Dignum*, etc., p. 332, note 1, *supra*. — C.]
[8] Col. iii. 1, 2. [9] Philip. iii. 20.

believed, and who do this from love, are heavens.
From them God thundereth forth the terror of
His judgment; and he who was unbelieving
trembleth, and is alarmed, and believeth. He
shows unto men what power Christ had throughout the world, by pleading with them, and leading them to love Christ. For how many this
day have led their friends either to some pan-
tomimist, or flute-player? Why, except from
their liking him? And do ye love Christ. For
He who conquered the world hath exhibited
such spectacles, as that no man can say that he
findeth in them cause for blame. For each
person's favourite in the theatre is often vanquished there. But no man is vanquished in
Christ: there is no reason for shame. Seize,
lead, draw, whom ye may: be without fear, ye
are leading unto Him, who displeaseth not those
who see Him; and ask ye Him to enlighten
them, that they may behold to good account.

9. "Confounded be all they that worship
carved images" (ver. 7). Hath not this come
to pass? Have they not been confounded?
Are they not daily confounded? For carved
images are images wrought by the hand. Why
are all who worship carved images confounded?
Because all people have seen His glory. All
nations now confess the glory of Christ: let
those who worship stones be ashamed. Because
those stones were dead, we have found a living
Stone; indeed those stones never lived, so that
they cannot be called even dead; but our Stone
is living, and hath ever lived with the Father,
and though He died for us, He revived, and
liveth now, and death shall no more have dominion over Him.[1] This glory of His the nations
have acknowledged; they leave the temples,
they run to the Churches. Do they still seek
to worship carved images? Have they not
chosen to forsake their idols? They have been
forsaken by their idols. "Who glory in their
idols." But there is a certain disputer who
seemeth unto himself learned, and saith, I do
not worship that stone, nor that image which is
without sense; . . . I worship not this image;
but I adore[2] what I see, and serve him whom I
see not. Who is that? Some invisible deity,
he replieth, who presideth over that image. By
giving this account of their images, they seem
to themselves able disputants, because they do
not worship idols, and yet do worship devils.
"The things," brethren, saith the Apostle,
"which the Gentiles sacrifice, they sacrifice unto
devils, and not to God; we know that an idol
is nothing: and that what the Gentiles sacrifice, they sacrifice to devils, and not to God;
and I would not that ye should have fellowship
with devils."[3] Let them not therefore excuse

themselves on this ground, that they are not devoted to insensate idols; they are rather devoted
to devils, which is more dangerous. For if they
were only worshipping idols, as they would not
help them, so they would not hurt them; but if
thou worship and serve devils, they themselves
will be thy masters. . . .

10. But observe holy men, who are like the
Angels. When thou hast found some holy man
who serveth God, if thou wish to worship him
instead of God, he forbiddeth thee: he will not
arrogate to himself the honour due to God, he
will not be unto thee as God, but be with thee
under God. Thus did the holy Apostles Paul
and Barnabas. They preached the word of God
in Lycaonia. When they had performed wonderful works in Lycaonia, the people of that
country brought victims, and wished to sacrifice
to them, calling Barnabas Jupiter, and Paul Mercury: they were not pleased. Did they perchance refuse to be sacrificed to, because they
abhorred to be compared to devils? No, but
because they shuddered at divine honour being
paid to men. Their own words show this: it is
no guess of ours; for the text of the book
goeth on to say how they were moved.[4] . . . Just
then, as good men forbade those who had
wished to worship them as gods, and wish rather
that God alone be worshipped, God alone be
adored, to God alone sacrifice be offered, not to
themselves; so also all the holy Angels seek His
glory whom they love; endeavour to impel and
to excite to the contemplation of Him all whom
they love: Him they declare to them, not themselves, since they are angels; and because they
are soldiers, they study only how to seek the
glory of their Captain; but if they have sought
their own glory, they are condemned as usurpers.[5]
Such were the devil and his angels; he claimed
for himself divine honour, and for all his demons; he filled the Pagan temples, and persuaded them to offer images and sacrifices to
himself. Was it not better to worship holy
Angels than devils? They answer: we do not
worship devils; we worship angels, as ye call
them, the powers and the ministers of the great
God. I wish ye would worship them: ye would
easily learn from themselves not to worship
them.[6] Hear an Angel teaching. He was
teaching a disciple of Christ, and showing him
many wonders in the Revelation of John: and
when some wonderful vision had been shown
him, he trembled, and fell down at the Angel's
feet; but that Angel, who sought not but the
glory of God, said, "See thou do it not; for I
am a fellow-servant of thee, and of thy brethren
the prophets."[7] What then, my brethren? Let
no man say, I fear lest the Angel may be angry

---

[1] Rom. vi. 9.   [2] i.e. fall down before.
[3] 1 Cor. viii. 4, x. 20, 21.

[4] Acts xiv. 14, 15.   [5] Tyranni.
[6] [See Origen, vol. iv. p. 544.—C.]   [7] Rev. xix. 10.

with me, if I worship him not as my God. He is then angry with thee, when thou hast chosen to worship him : for he is righteous, and loveth God. As devils are angry if they are not worshipped, so are Angels angry if they are worshipped instead of God. But lest the weak and trembling heart perchance say unto itself: If then the demons are incensed because they are not worshipped, I fear to offend them; what can even their chief the devil do unto thee? If he had any power over us, no one of us would remain. Are not daily so many things said against him by the mouth of Christians, and yet the harvest of Christians increaseth. When thou art angry with the most depraved of thy slaves, thou givest him the name, "Satan," Devil. Perhaps in this thou dost err, since thou sayest it to a man, and thy immoderate anger hurrieth thee to revile the image of God : and yet thou choosest a term thou deeply hatest, to apply to him. If he could, would he not revenge himself? But it is not allowed : and he doth so much only as is allowed him. For when he wished to tempt Job, he had to ask power to do so :[1] and he could do nothing had he not received power. Why then dost thou not fearlessly worship God, without whose will no one hurteth thee, and by whose permission thou art chastened, not overcome? For if it shall have pleased the Lord thy God to permit some man to hurt thee, or some spirit: He will chasten thee, that thou mayest cry unto Him :[2] "Confounded," therefore, "be all they that delight in vain gods : worship Him, all ye His angels." Let Pagans learn to worship God : they wish to worship Angels : let them imitate Angels, and worship Him who is worshipped by Angels. "Worship Him, all ye His angels." Let that Angel worship who was sent to Cornelius (for worshipping Him he sent Cornelius to Peter), himself Peter's fellow-servant; let him worship Christ, Peter's Lord. "Worship Him, all ye gods!"

11. "Sion heard of it, and rejoiced" (ver. 8). What did Sion hear? That all His Angels worship Him. . . . For the Church was not as yet among the Gentiles; in Judæa the Jews had some of them believed, and the very Jews who believed thought that they only belonged to Christ: the Apostles were sent to the Gentiles, Cornelius was preached to; Cornelius believed, was baptized, and they who were with Cornelius were also baptized.[3] But ye know what happened, that they might be baptized : the reader indeed hath not reached this point, but, nevertheless, some recollect; and let those who do not recollect, hear briefly from me. The Angel was sent to Cornelius : the Angel sent Cornelius

to Peter; Peter came to Cornelius. And because Cornelius and his household were Gentiles, and uncircumcised : lest they might hesitate to give the Gospel to the uncircumcised : before Cornelius and his household were baptized, the Holy Spirit came, and filled them, and they began to speak with tongues. Now the Holy Spirit had not fallen upon any one who had not been baptized : but upon these It fell before baptism. For Peter might hesitate whether he might baptize the uncircumcised : the Holy Spirit came, they began to speak with tongues ; the invisible gift was given, and took away all doubt about the visible Sacrament; they were all baptized. . . . What did Sion hear, and rejoice at? That the Gentiles also had received the word of God. One wall had come, but the corner existed not as yet. The name Sion is here peculiarly given to the Church which was in Judæa. "Sion heard of it, and rejoiced : and the daughters of Judah were glad." Thus it is written, "The apostles and brethren that were in Judæa heard." See if the daughters of Judæa rejoiced not. What did they hear? "That the Gentiles had also received the word of God." . . . Therefore, "The daughters of Judah rejoiced because of Thy judgments, O Lord." What is, because of Thy judgments? Because in any nation, and in any people, he that serveth Him is accepted of Him :[4] for He is not the God of the Jews only, but also of the Gentiles.[5]

12. See if this be not the reason for the joy of the daughters of Judah. "For Thou, Lord, art most high over all the earth" (ver. 9). Not in Judæa alone, but over Jerusalem; not over Sion only, but over all the earth. To this whole earth the judgments of God prevailed, so that it assembled its nations from every quarter : judgments with which they who have cut themselves off have no communion : they neither hear the prophecy, nor see its completion; "For Thou, Lord, art most high over all the earth : Thou art exalted far above all gods." What is "far"?[6] For it is said of Christ. What then meaneth "far," except that Thou mayest be acknowledged coequal with the Father? What meaneth, "above all gods"? Who are they? Idols have not life, have not sense : devils have life and sense ; but they are evil. What great thing is it that Christ is exalted above devils? He is exalted above devils : but neither is this very great ; the heathen gods indeed are devils,[7] but "He is far above all gods." Even men are styled gods : "I have said, Ye are gods : and ye are all the children of the Most Highest :" again it is written, "God standeth in the congregation of princes : He is a Judge among gods."[8] Jesus Christ our Lord is exalted above all : not only

---

[1] Job i. 11.   [2] Ps. cxviii. 18.   [3] Acts x. 47.

[4] Ps. xcvii. 35.   [5] Rom. iii. 29.   [6] Nimis.
[7] Ps. xcvi. 5.   [8] Ps. lxxxii 6, 1

above idols, not only above devils; but above all righteous men. Even this is not enough; above all Angels also: for whence otherwise is this, "Worship Him, all ye gods"? "Thou art far exalted above all gods."

13. What then do we all, who have assembled before Him, before Him who is exalted far above all gods? He hath given us a brief commandment, "O ye that love the Lord, see that ye hate the thing which is evil!" (ver. 10). Christ doth not deserve that with Him thou shouldest love avarice. Thou lovest Him: thou shouldest hate what He hateth. There is a man who is thine enemy, he is what thou art; ye are the work of one Creator, with the same nature: and yet if thy son were to speak unto thine enemy, and come to his house, and constantly converse with him, thou wouldest be inclined to disinherit him; because he speaketh with thine enemy. And how so? Because thou seemest to say justly, Thou art my enemy's friend, and seekest thou aught of my property? Attend then. Thou lovest Christ: avarice is Christ's foe; why speak with her? I say not, speak with her; why dost thou serve her? For Christ commandeth thee to do many things, and thou dost them not; she commandeth thee, and thou dost them. Christ commandeth thee to clothe the poor man: and thou dost it not; avarice biddeth thee defraud, and this thou dost in preference. If such be the case, if such thou art, do not very confidently promise thyself Christ's heritage. But thou sayest, I love Christ. Hence it appeareth that thou lovest what is good, if thou shalt be found to hate what is evil. . . .

14. Because then he had said above, "see that ye hate the thing which is evil," lest ye should fear to hate evil, lest he should kill thee, he addeth instantly, "The Lord preserveth the souls of His servants." Hear Him preserving the souls of His servants, and saying, "Fear not them which kill the body, but are not able to kill the soul."[1] He who hath most power against thee, slayeth the body. What hath he done unto thee? What he also did to the Lord thy God. Why lovest thou to have what Christ hath, if thou fearest to suffer what Christ did? He came to bear thy life, temporal, weak, subject unto death. Surely fear to die, if thou canst avoid dying. What thou canst not avoid through thy nature, why dost thou not undergo by faith? Let the adversary who threateneth take away from thee that life, God giveth thee another life: for He gave thee this life also, and without His will even this shall not be taken from thee; but if it be His will that it be taken from thee, He hath a life to give thee in exchange; fear not to be robbed for His sake. Art thou unwilling to put off a patched garment? He will give thee a robe of glory. What robe dost thou tell me of? "This corruptible must put on incorruption, and this mortal must put on immortality."[2] This very flesh of thine shall not perish. Thine enemy can rage as far as to thy death: he hath not power beyond, either over thy soul, or even over thy flesh; for although he scatter thy flesh about, he hindereth not the resurrection. Men were fearful for their life: and what said the Lord unto them? "The very hairs of your head are all numbered."[3] Dost thou, who losest not a single hair, fear the loss of thy life? All things are numbered with God. He who created all things, will restore all things. They were not, and they were created: they were, and shall they not be restored? . . . "He shall deliver them from the hand of the ungodly."

15. But perhaps thou wilt say, I lose this light. "There is sprung up a light for the righteous" (ver. 11). What light fearest thou thou mayest lose? fearest thou thou mayest be in darkness? Fear not thou mayest lose light; nay, fear lest while thou art guarding against the loss of this light, thou mayest lose that true light. For we see to whom that light is given which thou fearest losing, and with whom it is shared. Do the righteous only see this sun, when He maketh it rise over the just and unjust, and raineth upon the just and unjust?[4] Wicked men, robbers, the unchaste, beasts, flies, worms, see that light together with thee. What sort of light doth He keep for the righteous, who giveth this even to such as these? Deservedly the Martyrs beheld this light in faith; for they who despised this light of the sun, had some light in their eyes, which they longed for, who rejected this. Do you imagine that they were really in misery, when they walked in chains? Spacious was the prison to the faithful, light were the chains to the confessors. They who preached Christ amid their torments, had joy in the iron-chair. What light hath sprung up for the righteous? Not that which springeth up for the unrighteous; not that which He causeth to rise over the good and bad. There is a different light which springeth up to the righteous; of which light, that never rose upon themselves, the unrighteous shall in the end say, "Therefore have we erred from the way of truth, and the light of righteousness hath not shined upon us, and the sun of righteousness rose not upon us."[5] Behold, by loving this sun they have lain in the darkness of the heart. What did it profit them to have seen with their eyes this sun, and not in mind to have seen that light? Tobit was blind, but he used to teach his son the way of God. Ye know this, that Tobit warned his son, and said

---

[1] Matt x 28.

[2] 1 Cor. xv. 53.　　　[3] Matt. x. 30.　　　[4] Matt. v. 45.
[5] Wisd. v. 6.

to him, "Son, give alms of thy substance; because that alms suffer not to come into darkness."[1] Even he who was in darkness spoke thus. . . . Dost thou wish to know that light? Be true-hearted. What is, be true-hearted? Be not of a crooked heart before God, withstanding His will, and wishing to bend Him unto thee, and not to rule thyself to please Him; and thou wilt feel the joyful gladness which all the true-hearted know.

16. "Be glad, ye righteous" (ver. 12). Perhaps already the faithful hearing the word, "Be glad," are thinking of banquets, preparing cups, waiting for the season of roses; because it is said, "Be glad, ye righteous!" See what followeth, "Be glad in the Lord." Thou art waiting for the season of spring, that thou mayest be glad: thou hast the Lord for joyful gladness, the Lord is always with thee, He hath no special season; thou hast Him by night, thou hast Him by day. Be true-hearted; and thou hast ever joy from Him. For that joy which is after the fashion of the world, is not true joy. Hear the prophet Isaiah: "There is no joy, saith my God, to the wicked."[2] What the wicked call joy is not joy, such as he knew who made no account of their joy: let us believe him, brethren. He was a man, but he knew both kinds of joy. He certainly knew the joys of the cup, for he was a man, he knew the joy of the table, he knew the joys of marriage, he knew those joys worldly and luxurious. He who knew them saith with confidence, "There is no joy to the wicked, saith the Lord." But it is not man who speaks, it is the Lord. . . . But thou sayest, I see not that light which Isaiah saw. Believe, and thou shalt see it. For perhaps thou hast not the eye to see it; for it is an eye by which that beauty is discerned. For as there is an eye of the flesh, by means of which this light is seen: so there is an eye of the heart, by which that joy is perceived: perhaps that eye is wounded, dimmed, disturbed by passion, by avarice, by indulgence, by senseless lust; thine eye is disturbed: thou canst not see that light. Believe, before thou seest: thou shalt be healed, and shalt see.

17. "And confess to the remembrance of His holiness." Now made glad, now rejoicing in the Lord, confess unto Him; for unless it were His will, ye would not rejoice in Him. For the Lord Himself saith: "These things I have spoken to you: that in Me ye might have peace. But in the world ye shall have tribulation."[3] If ye are Christians, look for tribulations in this world; look not for more peaceful and better times. Brethren, ye deceive yourselves; what the Gospel doth not promise you, promise not to yourselves. Ye know what the Gospel saith;

we are speaking to Christians; we ought not to disobey the faith. The Gospel saith this, that in the last times many evils, many stumbling-blocks, many tribulations, much iniquity, shall abound; but he that shall endure unto the end, the same shall be saved.[4] "The love," it saith, "of many shall wax cold." Whosoever then hath been stedfastly fervent in spirit, as the Apostle saith, "fervent in spirit,"[5] his love shall not wax cold: because "the love of God is shed abroad in our hearts by the Holy Ghost, which is given unto us."[6] Let no man therefore promise himself what the Gospel doth not promise. Behold, happier times will come, and I am doing this, and purchasing this. It is good for thee to listen to Him who is not deceived, nor hath deceived any man, who promised thee joy not here, but in Himself; and when all here hath passed away, to hope that with Him thou wilt for ever reign; lest when thou dost wish to reign here, thou mayest neither enjoy gladness here, nor find it there.

PSALM XCVIII.[7]

1. "O sing unto the Lord a new song" (ver. 1). The new man knoweth this, the old man knoweth it not. The old man is the old life, and the new man the new life: the old life is derived from Adam, the new life is formed in Christ. But in this Psalm, the whole world is enjoined to sing a new song. More openly elsewhere the words are these: "O sing unto the Lord a new song; sing unto the Lord, all the whole earth;"[8] that they who cut themselves off from the communion of the whole earth,[9] may understand that they cannot sing the new song, because it is sung in the whole, and not in a part of it. Attend here also, and see that this is said. And when the whole earth is enjoined to sing a new song, it is meant, that peace singeth a new song. "For He hath done marvellous things." What marvellous things? Behold, the Gospel was just now being read, and we heard the marvellous things of the Lord. The only son of his mother, who was a widow, was being carried out dead: the Lord, in compassion, made them stand still; they laid him down, and the Lord said, "Young man, I say unto thee, Arise."[10] . . . "The Lord hath done marvellous things." What marvellous things? Hear: "His own right hand, and His holy arm, hath healed for Him." What is the Lord's holy Arm? Our Lord Jesus Christ. Hear Isaiah: "Who hath believed our report, and to whom is the arm of the Lord revealed?"[11] His holy arm then, and His own right hand, is

---

[1] Tobit iv. 7, 10. [2] Isa. lvii. 21. [3] John xvi. 33.

[4] Matt. xxiv. 3-13. [5] Rom. xii. 11. [6] Rom. v. 5.
[7] Lat. XCVII. A discourse to the people.
[8] Ps. xcvi. 1. [9] Donatists. [10] Luke vii. 12-14.
[11] Isa. liii. 1.

Himself. Our Lord Jesus Christ is therefore the arm of God, and the right hand of God: for this reason is it said, "hath He healed for Him." It is not said only, "His right hand hath healed the world," but "hath healed for Him." For many are healed for themselves, not for Him. Behold how many long for that bodily health, and receive it from Him: they are healed by Him, but not for Him. How are they healed by Him, and not for Him? When they have received health, they become wanton: they who when sick were chaste, when cured become adulterers: they who when in illness injured no man, on the recovery of their strength attack and crush the innocent: they are healed, but not unto Him. Who is he who is healed unto Him? He who is healed inwardly. Who is he that is healed inwardly? He who trusteth in Him, that when he shall have been healed inwardly, reformed into a new man, afterwards this mortal flesh too, which doth languish for a time, may in the end itself even recover its most perfect health. Let us therefore be healed for Him. But that we may be healed for Him, let us believe in His right hand.

2. "The Lord hath made known His salvation" (ver. 2). This very right hand, this very arm, this very salvation, is our Lord Jesus Christ, of whom it is said, "And all flesh shall see the salvation of God;"[1] of whom also that Simeon who embraced the Infant in his arms, spoke, "Lord, now lettest Thou Thy servant depart in peace; for mine eyes have seen Thy salvation."[2] "The Lord hath made known His salvation." To whom did He make it known? To a part, or to the whole? Not to any part specially. Let no man betray, no man deceive, no man say, "Lo, here is Christ, or there:"[3] the man who saith, Lo, He is here, or there, pointeth to some particular spots.. To whom "hath the Lord declared His salvation"? Hear what followeth: "His righteousness hath He openly showed in the sight of the heathen." Our Lord and Saviour Jesus Christ is the right hand of God, the arm of God, the salvation of God, and the righteousness of God.

3. "He hath remembered His mercy to Jacob, and His truth unto the house of Israel" (ver. 3). What meaneth this, "He hath remembered His mercy and truth"? He hath pitied, so that He promised; because He promised and showed His mercy, truth hath followed: mercy hath gone before promise, promise hath been fulfilled in truth. . . .

"And His truth unto the house of Israel." Who is this Israel? That ye may not perchance think of one nation of the Jews, hear what followeth: "All the ends of the world have seen the salvation of our God." It is not said, all the earth: but, "all the ends of the world:" as it is said, from one end to the other. Let no man cut this down, let no man scatter it abroad; strong is the unity of Christ. He who gave so great a price, hath bought the whole: "All the ends of the world."

4. Because they have seen, then, "Make a joyful noise unto the Lord, all ye lands" (ver. 4). Ye already know what it is to make a joyful noise. Rejoice, and speak. If ye cannot express your joy, shout ye; let the shout manifest your joy, if your speech cannot: yet let not joy be mute; let not your heart be silent respecting its God, let it not be mute concerning His gifts. If thou speakest to thyself, unto thyself art thou healed; if His right hand hath healed thee for Him, speak thou unto Him for whom thou hast been healed. "Sing, rejoice, and make melody."

5. "Make melody unto the Lord upon the harp: on the harp and with the voice of a Psalm" (ver. 5). Praise Him not with the voice only; take up works, that ye may not only sing, but work also. He who singeth and worketh, maketh melody with psaltery and upon the harp. Now see what sort of instruments are next spoken of, in figure: "With ductile trumpets also, and the sound of the pipe of horn" (ver. 6). What are ductile trumpets, and pipes of horn? Ductile trumpets are of brass: they are drawn out by hammering; if by hammering, by being beaten, ye shall be ductile trumpets, drawn out unto the praise of God, if ye improve when in tribulation: tribulation is hammering, improvement is the being drawn out. Job was a ductile trumpet, when suddenly assailed by the heaviest losses, and the death of his sons, become like a ductile trumpet by the beating of so heavy tribulation, he sounded thus: "The Lord gave, and the Lord hath taken away; blessed be the name of the Lord."[4] How did he sound? How pleasantly doth his voice sound? This ductile trumpet is still under the hammer. . . . We have heard how he was hammered; let us hear how he soundeth: let us, if it please you, hear the sweet sound of this ductile trumpet: "What! shall we receive good at the hand of God, and shall we not receive evil?" O courageous, O sweet sound! whom will not that sound awake from sleep? whom will not confidence in God awake, to march to battle fearlessly against the devil; not to struggle with his own strength, but His who proveth him. For He it is who hammereth: for the hammer could not do so of itself. . . . See how (I dare so speak, my brethren) even the Apostle was beaten with this very hammer: he saith, "there was given to me a thorn in the

---

[1] Luke iii. 6.   [2] Luke ii. 28-30.   [3] Matt. xxiv. 23.   [4] Job i. 21.

flesh, the messenger of Satan, to buffet me." [1] Behold he is under the hammer : let us hear how he speaketh of it : " For this thing," he saith, " I besought the Lord thrice, that it might depart from me. And He said unto me, My grace is sufficient for thee : for My strength is made perfect in weakness." I, saith His Maker, wish to make this trumpet perfect ; I cannot do so unless I hammer it ; in weakness is strength made perfect. Hear now the ductile trumpet itself sounding as it should : " When I am weak, then am I strong." . . .

6. The voice of the pipe of horn, what is it? The horn riseth above the flesh : in rising above the flesh it needs must be solid so as to last, and able to speak. And whence this? Because it hath surpassed the flesh. He who wisheth to be a horn trumpet, let him overcome the flesh. What meaneth this, let him overcome the flesh? Let him surpass the desires, let him conquer the lusts of the flesh. Hear the horn trumpets. . . . What meaneth this, " Set your affection on things above"? It meaneth, Rise above the flesh, think not of carnal things. They were not yet horn trumpets, to whom he now spoke thus : " I could not speak unto you, brethren, as unto spiritual, but as unto carnal, even as unto babes in Christ. I have fed you with milk, and not with meat ; for hitherto ye were not able to bear it : neither yet now are ye able. For ye are yet carnal." [2] They were not therefore horn trumpets, because they had not risen above the flesh. Horn both adhereth to the flesh, and riseth above the flesh ; and although it springeth from the flesh, yet it surpasseth it. If therefore thou art spiritual, when before thou wast carnal ; as yet thou art treading the earth in the flesh, but in spirit thou art rising into heaven ; for though we walk in the flesh, we do not war after the flesh. . . . Brethren, do not reproach brethren whom the mercy of God hath not yet converted ; know that as long as ye do this, ye savour of the flesh. That is not a trumpet which pleaseth the ears of God : the trumpet of boastfulness maketh the war fruitless. Let the horn trumpet raise thy courage against the devil ; let not the fleshly trumpet raise thy pride against thy brother. " Make a joyful noise in the sight of the Lord the King."

7. While ye are rejoicing, and delighted with the ductile trumpets, and the voice of the horn, what followeth? " Let the sea be stirred up, and the fulness thereof" (ver. 7). Brethren, when the Apostles, like ductile trumpets and horns, were preaching the truth, the sea was stirred up, its waves arose, tempests increased, persecutions of the Church took place. Whence hath the sea been stirred up? When a joyful noise was made, when Psalms of thanksgiving were being sung before God : the ears of God were pleased, the waves of the sea were raised. " Let the sea be stirred up, and the fulness thereof : the round world, and all that dwell therein." Let the sea be stirred up in its persecutions. " Let the floods clap their hands together " (ver. 8). Let the sea be aroused, and the floods clap their hands together ; persecutions arise, and the saints rejoice in God. Whence shall the floods clap their hands? What is to clap their hands? To rejoice in works. To clap hands, is to rejoice ; hands, mean works. What floods? Those whom God hath made floods, by giving them that Water, the Holy Spirit. " If any man thirst," saith He, " let him come unto Me, and drink. He that believeth on Me, out of his bosom shall flow rivers of living water." [3] These rivers clapped their hands, these rivers rejoiced in works, and blessed God. " The hills shall be joyful together."

8. " Before the Lord, for He is come ; for He is come to judge the earth " (ver. 9). "The hills" signify the great. The Lord cometh to judge the earth, and they rejoice. But there are hills, who, when the Lord is coming to judge the earth, shall tremble. There are therefore good and evil hills ; the good hills, are spiritual greatness ; the bad hills, are the swelling of pride. " Let the hills be joyful together before the Lord, for He is come ; for He is come to judge the earth." Wherefore shall He come, and how shall He come? " With righteousness shall He judge the world, and the people with equity " (ver. 10). Let the hills therefore rejoice ; for He shall not judge unrighteously. When some man is coming as a judge, to whom the conscience cannot lie open, even innocent men may tremble, if from him they expect a reward for virtue, or fear the penalty of condemnation ; when He shall come who cannot be deceived, let the hills rejoice, let them rejoice fearlessly ; they shall be enlightened by Him, not condemned ; let them rejoice, because the Lord will come to judge the world with equity ; and if the righteous hills rejoice, let the unrighteous tremble. But behold, He hath not yet come : what need is there they should tremble? Let them mend their ways, and rejoice. It is in thy power in what way thou willest to await the coming of Christ. For this reason He delayeth to come, that when He cometh He may not condemn thee. Lo, He hath not yet come : He is in heaven, thou on earth : He delayeth His coming, do not thou delay wisdom. His coming is hard to the hard of heart, soft to the pious. See therefore even now what thou art : if hard

---

[1] 2 Cor. xii. 7-10.   [2] 1 Cor. i. 12, iii. 1-4.   [3] John vii. 37-39.

of heart, thou canst soften; if thou art soft, even now rejoice that He will come. For thou art a Christian. Yea, thou sayest. I believe that thou prayest, and sayest, "Thy kingdom come." [1] Thou desirest Him to come, whose coming thou fearest. Reform thyself, that thou mayest not pray against thyself.

PSALM XCIX.[2]

1. Beloved brethren, it ought already to be known to you, as sons of the Church, and well instructed in the school of Christ through all the books of our ancient fathers, who wrote the words of God and the great things of God, that their wish was to consult for our good, who were to live at this period, believers in Christ; who, at a seasonable time came unto us, the first time, in humility; at the second, destined to come in exaltation. . . . For thus it is said in the Psalms: "Truth shall flourish out of the earth: and righteousness hath looked down from heaven." [3] Now, therefore, our whole design is, when we hear a Psalm, a Prophet, or the Law, all of which was written before our Lord Jesus Christ came in the flesh, to see Christ there, to understand Christ there. Attend therefore, beloved, to this Psalm, with me, and let us herein seek Christ; certainly He will appear to those who seek Him, who at first appeared to those who sought Him not; and He will not desert those who long for Him, who redeemed those who neglected Him. Behold, the Psalm beginneth concerning Him: of Him it is said: —

2. "The Lord is King, be the people angry" (ver. 1). For our Lord Jesus Christ began to reign, began to be preached, after He arose from the dead and ascended into heaven, after He had filled His disciples with the confidence of the Holy Spirit, that they should not fear death, which He had already killed in Himself. Our Lord Christ began then to be preached, that they who wished for salvation might believe in Him; and the peoples who worshipped idols were angry. They who worshipped what they had made were angry, because He by whom they were made was declared. He announced, in fact, through His disciples, Himself, who wished them to be converted unto Him by whom they were made, and to be turned away from those things which they had made themselves. They were angry with their Lord in behalf of their idols, they who even if they were angry with their slave on their idol's account, were to be condemned. For their slave was better than their idol: for God made their slave, the carpenter made their idol. They were so angry in their idol's behalf, that they feared not

to be angry with their Lord. But the words, "be they angry," are a prediction, not a command; for in a prophecy it is that this is said, "The Lord is King, be the people angry." Some good resulteth even from the enraged people: let them be angry, and in their anger let the Martyrs be crowned. . . . Ye heard when Jeremiah was being read before the reading of the Apostle,[4] if ye listened; ye saw therein the times in which we now live. He said, "The gods that have not made the heavens and the earth, let them perish from the earth, and from under the heaven." [5] He said not, The gods that have not made the heavens and earth, let them perish from the heaven and from the earth; because they never were in heaven: but what did he say? "Let them perish from the earth, and from under the heaven." As if, while the word earth was repeated, the repetition of the word heaven were wanting (because they never were in heaven): he repeateth the earth twice, since it is under heaven. "Let them perish from the earth, and from under the heaven," from their temples. Consider if this be not now taking place; if in a great measure it hath not already happened: for what, or how much, hath remained? The idols remained rather in the hearts of the pagans, than in the niches of the temples.

3. "He who sitteth between the cherubims:" thou dost understand, "He is King: let the earth be stirred up." . . . The Cherubim is the seat of God, as the Scripture showeth us, a certain exalted heavenly throne, which we see not; but the Word of God knoweth it, knoweth it as His own seat: and the Word of God and the Spirit of God hath Itself revealed to the servants of God where God sitteth. Not that God doth sit, as doth man; but thou, if thou dost wish that God sit in thee, if thou wilt be good, shalt be the seat of God; for thus is it written, "The soul of the righteous is the seat of wisdom." [6] For a throne is in our language called a seat. For some, conversant with the Hebrew tongue, have interpreted cherubim in the Latin language (for it is a Hebrew term) by the words, fulness of knowledge. Therefore, because God surpasseth all knowledge, He is said to sit above the fulness of knowledge. Let there be therefore in thee fulness of knowledge, and even thou shalt be the throne of God. . . . He knoweth all things: for our hairs are numbered before God.[7] But the fulness of knowledge which He willed man to know is different from this; the knowledge which He willed thee to have, pertaineth to the law of God. And who can, thou mayest perhaps say unto me, perfectly know the Law, so that he may have within himself the ful-

---

[1] Matt. vi. 10.
[2] Lat. XCVIII. A sermon to the people.   [3] Ps. lxxxv. 11.
[4] [The Lesson from the prophet, and the Epistle for the day. — C.]
[5] Jer. x. 11.   [6] Prov. xii. 23.   [7] Matt. x. 30.

ness of the knowledge of the Law, and be able to be the seat of God? Be not disturbed; it is briefly told thee what thou hast, if thou dost wish to have the fulness of knowledge, and to become the throne of God: for the Apostle saith, "Love is the fulfilling of the Law."[1] What followeth then? Thou hast lost the whole of thine excuse. Ask thine heart; see whether it hath love. If there be love there, there is the fulfilment of the Law there also; already God dwelleth in thee, thou hast become the throne of God. "Be the people angry;" what can the angry people do against him who hath become the throne of God? Thou givest heed unto them who rage against thee: Who is it that sitteth within thee, thou givest not heed. Thou art become a heaven, and fearest thou the earth? For the Scripture saith in another passage, that the Lord our God doth declare, "The heaven is My throne."[2] If therefore even thou by having the fulness of knowledge, and by having love, hast been made the throne of God, thou hast become a heaven. For this heaven which we look up to with these eyes of ours, is not very precious before God. Holy souls are the heaven of God; the minds of the Angels, and all the minds of His servants, are the heaven of God.

4. "The Lord is great in Sion, and high above all people" (ver. 2). . . . He whom I spoke to thee of as above the Cherubims, is great in Sion. Ask thou now, what is Sion? We know Sion to be the city of God. The city of Jerusalem is called Sion; and is so called according to a certain interpretation, for that Sion signifieth watching, that is, sight and contemplation; for to watch is to look forward to, or gaze upon, or strain the eyes to see. Now every soul is a Sion, if it trieth to see that light which is to be seen. For if it shall have gazed upon a light of its own, it is darkened; if upon His, it is enlightened. But, now that it is clear that Sion is the city of God; what is the city of God, but the Holy Church? For men who love one another, and who love their God who dwelleth in them, constitute a city unto God. Because a city is held together by some law; their very law is Love; and that very Love is God: for openly it is written, "God is Love."[3] He therefore who is full of Love, is full of God; and many, full of love, constitute a city full of God. That city of God is called Sion; the Church therefore is Sion. In it God is great. . . .

5. Do ye imagine, brethren, that they whose instruments re-echoed yesterday, are not angry with our fastings? But let us not be angry with them, but let us fast for them. For the Lord our God who sitteth in us hath said, He hath Himself commanded us to pray for our enemies, to pray for them that persecute us:[4] and as the Church doth this, the persecutors are almost extinct. . . . The drunken man doth not offend himself, but he offendeth the sober man. Show me a man who is at last happy in God, liveth gravely, sigheth for that everlasting peace which God hath promised him; and see that when he hath seen a man dancing to an instrument, he is more grieved for his madness, than for a man who is in a frenzy from a fever. If then we know their evils, considering that we also have been freed from those very evils, let us grieve for them; and if we grieve for them, let us pray for them; and that we may be heard, let us fast for them. For we do not keep our own fasts in their holidays. Different are the fasts which we celebrate through the days of the approaching Passover, through different seasons which are fixed for us in Christ: but through their holidays we fast for this reason, that when they are rejoicing, we may groan for them. For by their joy they excite our grief, and cause us to remember how wretched they are as yet. But since we see many freed thence, where we also have been, we ought not to despair even of them. And if they are still enraged, let us pray; and if still a particle of earth that hath remained behind be stirred up against us, let us continue in lamentation for them, that to them also God may grant understanding, and that with us they may hear those words, in which we are at this moment rejoicing.

6. All these very people, over whom Thou art great in Sion, "Let them confess unto Thy Name, which is great" (ver. 3). Thy Name was little when they were enraged: it hath become great; let them now confess. In what sense do we say, that the Name of Christ was little, before it was spread abroad to so great an extent? Because His report is meant by His Name. His Name was small; already it hath become great. What nation is there that hath not heard of the Name of Christ? Therefore let now the people confess unto Thy Name, which is great, who before were enraged with Thy little Name. Wherefore shall they confess? Because it is "wonderful and holy." Thy very Name is wonderful and holy. He is so preached as crucified, so preached as humbled, so preached as judged, that He may come exalted, that He may come living, that He may come to judge in power. He spareth at present the people who blaspheme Him, because "the long-suffering of God leadeth to repentance."[5] For He who now spareth, will not always spare: nor will He, who is now being preached that He may be feared, fail to come to judge. He will come, my brethren, He will

---

[1] Rom. xiii. 10.　　　[2] Isa. lxvi. 1.　　　[3] 1 John iv. 8.　　　[4] Matt. v. 44.　　　[5] Rom. ii. 4.

come : let us fear Him, and let us live so that we may be found on His right hand. For He will come, and will judge, so as to place some on the left hand, some on the right.[1] And He doth not act in an uncertain manner, so as to err perchance betwixt men, so that he who should be set on the right hand, be set on the left ; or that he who ought to stand on the left, by a mistake of God should stand on the right : He cannot err, so as to place the evil where He ought to set the good ; nor to place the good, where He should have set the evil. If He cannot err, we err, if we fear not ; but if we have feared in this life, we shall not then have what to fear for. " For the King's honour loveth judgment." . . .

7. "Thou hast prepared equity ; Thou hast wrought judgment and righteousness in Jacob." For we too ought to have judgment, we ought to have righteousness ; but He worketh in us judgment and righteousness, who created us in whom He might work them. How ought we too to have judgment and righteousness ? Thou hast judgment, when thou dost distinguish evil from good : and righteousness when thou followest the good, and turnest aside from the evil. By distinguishing them, thou hast judgment ; by doing, thou hast righteousness. "Eschew evil,' he saith, "and do good ; seek peace, and ensue it." [2] Thou shouldest first have judgment, then righteousness. What judgment ? That thou mayest first judge what is evil, and what is good. And what righteousness ? That thou mayest shun evil, and do good. But this thou wilt not gain from thyself ; see what he hath said, "Thou hast wrought judgment and righteousness in Jacob."

8. "O magnify the Lord our God" (ver. 5). Magnify Him truly, magnify Him well. Let us praise Him, let us magnify Him who hath wrought the very righteousness which we have ; who wrought it in us, Himself. For who but He who justified us, wrought righteousness in us ? For of Christ it is said, "who justifieth the ungodly." [3] . . . "And fall down before [4] His footstool : for He is holy." What are we to fall down before ? His footstool. What is under the feet is called a footstool, in Greek ὑποπόδιον, in Latin *Scabellum* or *Suppedaneum*. But consider, brethren, what he commandeth us to fall down before. In another passage of the Scriptures it is said, "The heaven is My throne, and the earth is My footstool." [5] Doth he then bid us worship the earth, since in another passage it is said, that it is God's footstool ? How then shall we worship the earth, when the Scripture saith openly, "Thou shalt worship the Lord thy God"? [6] Yet here it saith, "fall down

before His footstool : " and, explaining to us what His footstool is, it saith, "The earth is My footstool." I am in doubt ; I fear to worship the earth, lest He who made the heaven and the earth condemn me ; again, I fear not to worship the footstool of my Lord, because the Psalm biddeth me, "fall down before His footstool." I ask, what is His footstool ? and the Scripture telleth me, "the earth is My footstool." In hesitation I turn unto Christ, since I am herein seeking Himself : and I discover how the earth may be worshipped without impiety,[7] how His footstool may be worshipped without impiety. For He took upon Him earth from earth ; because flesh is from earth, and He received flesh from the flesh of Mary. And because He walked here in very flesh, and gave that very flesh to us to eat for our salvation ; and no one eateth that flesh, unless he hath first worshipped : we have found out in what sense such a footstool of our Lord's may be worshipped, and not only that we sin not in worshipping it, but that we sin in not worshipping. But doth the flesh give life ? Our Lord Himself, when He was speaking in praise of this same earth, said, "It is the Spirit that quickeneth, the flesh profiteth nothing." . . . But when our Lord praised it, He was speaking of His own flesh, and He had said, "Except a man eat My flesh, he shall have no life in him." [8] Some disciples of His, about seventy,[9] were offended, and said, "This is an hard saying, who can hear it ? " And they went back, and walked no more with Him. It seemed unto them hard that He said, "Except ye eat the flesh of the Son of Man, ye have no life in you : " they received it foolishly, they thought of it carnally, and imagined that the Lord would cut off parts from His body, and give unto them ; and they said, "This is a hard saying." It was they who were hard, not the saying ; for unless they had been hard, and not meek, they would have said unto themselves, He saith not this without reason, but there must be some latent mystery herein. They would have remained with Him, softened, not hard : and would have learnt that from Him which they who remained, when the others departed, learnt. For when twelve disciples had remained with Him, on their departure, these remaining followers suggested to Him, as if in grief for the death of the former, that they were offended by His words, and turned back. But He instructed them, and saith unto them, "It is the Spirit that quickeneth, but the flesh profiteth nothing ; the words that I have spoken unto you, they are spirit, and they are life." [10] Understand spiritu-

---

[1] Matt. xxv. 31–33.　　[2] Ps. xxxiv. 14.　　[3] Rom. iv. 5.
[4] *Adorate*. See p. 477, n. 2.　[5] Isa. lxvi. 1.　[6] Deut. vi. 13.

[7] 2 *Sent*. Dist. 9, c. *aliis autem*.　　　[8] John vi. 54.
[9] *Septuaginta fermè*. It is difficult to know whence this number comes, unless it is that of *the* Seventy. But they can hardly be supposed identical with these. One might think it a gloss but for the mention of " twelve."　　　[10] John vi. 63.

ally what I have said; ye are not to eat this body which ye see; nor to drink that blood which they who will crucify Me shall pour forth. I have commended unto you a certain mystery; spiritually understood, it will quicken. Although it is needful that this be visibly celebrated, yet it must be spiritually understood.[1]

9. "Moses and Aaron among His priests, and Samuel among such as call upon His Name: these called upon the Lord, and He heard them" (ver. 6). "He spake unto them out of the cloudy pillar" (ver. 7). . . . Of Moses it is not there stated that he was a priest. But if he was not this, what was he? Could he be anything greater than a priest? This Psalm declareth that he also was himself a priest: "Moses and Aaron among His priests." They therefore were the Lord's priests. Samuel is read of later in the Book of Kings: this Samuel is in David's times; for he anointed the holy David. Samuel from his infancy grew up in the temple. . . . He mentioneth these: and by these desireth us to understand all the saints. Yet why hath he here named those? Because we said that we ought here to understand Christ. Attend, holy brethren. He said above, "O magnify the Lord our God: and fall down before His footstool, for He is holy:" praising some one, that is, our Lord Jesus Christ; whose footstool is to be worshipped, because He assumed flesh, in which He was to appear before the human race; and wishing to show unto us that the ancient fathers also had preached of Him, because our Lord Jesus Christ is Himself the True Priest, he mentioned these, because God spake unto them out of the cloudy pillar. What meaneth, "out of the cloudy pillar"? He was speaking figuratively. For if He spoke in some cloud, those obscure words predicted some one unknown, yet to be manifest. This unknown one is no longer unknown; for He is known by us, our Lord Jesus Christ. . . . He who first spoke out of the cloudy pillar, hath in Person spoken unto us in His footstool; that is, on earth, when He had assumed the flesh, for which reason we worship His footstool, for He is holy. He Himself used to speak out of the cloud, which was not then understood: He hath spoken in His own footstool, and the words of His cloud have been understood. "They kept His testimonies, and the law that He gave them." . . . "Thou heardest them," he saith, "O Lord our God: Thou wast forgiving to them, O God" (ver. 8). God is not said to be forgiving toward anything but sins: when He pardoneth sins, then He forgiveth. And what had He in them to punish, so that He was forgiving in pardoning them? He was forgiving in pardoning their sins, He was also forgiving in punishing them. For what followeth? "And punishedst all their own affections." Even in punishing them Thou wast forgiving toward them: for not in remitting, but also in punishing their sins, hast Thou been forgiving. Consider, my brethren, what he hath taught us here: attend. God is angry with him whom, when he sinneth, He scourgeth not: for unto him to whom He is truly forgiving, He not only remitteth sins, that they may not injure him in a future life; but also chasteneth him, that he delight not in continual sin.

10. Come, my brethren; if we ask how these were punished, the Lord will aid me to tell you. Let us consider these three persons, Moses, Aaron, and Samuel: and how they were punished, since he said, "Thou hast punished all their own affections:" meaning those affections of theirs, which the Lord knew in their hearts, which men knew not. For they were living in the midst of the people of God, without complaint from man. But what do we say? That perhaps the early life of Moses was sinful; for he fled from Egypt, after slaying a man.[2] The early life of Aaron also was such as would displease God; for he allowed a maddened and infatuated people to make an idol to worship;[3] and an idol was made for God's people to worship. What sin did Samuel, who was given up when an infant to the temple? He passed all his life amid the holy sacraments of God: from childhood the servant of God. Nothing was ever said of Samuel, nothing by men. Perhaps God knew of somewhat there to chasten; since even what seemeth perfect unto men, unto that Perfection is still imperfect. Artists show many of their works to the unskilful; and when the unskilful have pronounced them perfect, the artists polish them still further, as they know what is still wanting to them, so that men wonder at things they had imagined already perfect having received so much additional polish. This happeneth in buildings, and in paintings, and in embroidery, and almost in every species of art. At first they judge it to be already in a manner perfect, so that their eyes desire nothing further: but the judgment of the inexperienced eye is one, and that of the rule of art another. Thus also these Saints were living before the eyes of God, as if faultless, as if perfect, as if Angels: but He who punished all their own affections, knew what was wanting in them. But He punished them not in anger, but in mercy: He punished them that He might perfect what He had begun, not to condemn what He had cast away. God therefore punished all their affections. How did He punish Samuel?

---

[1] [A clear exposition of the Catholic doctrine against the modern Roman, which was unknown to antiquity. See the treatise of Ratramn. ed. (Lat and Eng.) Oxford, 1838. — C.]

[2] Exod. ii. 12–15.   [3] Exod. xxxii. 1–4.

where is this punishment? . . . What was said unto Moses was a type, not a punishment. What punishment is death to an old man? What punishment was it, not to enter into that land, into which unworthy men entered? But what is said of Aaron? He also died an old man : his sons succeeded him in the priesthood : his son afterwards ruled in the priesthood : how did He punish Aaron also?[1] Samuel also died a holy old man, leaving his sons as his successors.[2] I seek for the punishment inflicted upon them, and according to men I find it not : but according to what I know the servants of God suffer every day, they were day by day punished. Read ye, and see the punishments, and ye also who are advanced bear the punishments. Every day they suffered from the obstinate people, every day they suffered from the ungodly livers ; and were compelled to live among those whose lives they daily censured. This was their punishment. He unto whom it is small hath not advanced far ; for the ungodliness of others tormenteth thee in proportion as thou hast departed far from thine own. . . .

11. "O magnify the Lord our God!" (ver. 9). Again we magnify Him. He who is merciful even when He striketh, how is He to be praised, how is He to be magnified? Canst thou show this unto thy son, and cannot God? For thou art not good when thou dost caress thy son, and evil when thou strikest him. Both when thou dost caress him thou art a father, and when thou strikest him, thou art his father : thou dost caress him, that he may not faint ; thou strikest him, that he may not perish. "O magnify the Lord our God, and worship Him upon His holy hill : for the Lord our God is holy." As he said above, "O magnify the Lord our God and fall down before His footstool : "[3] now we have understood what it is to worship His footstool : thus also but now after he had magnified the Lord our God, that no man might magnify Him apart from His hill, he hath also praised His hill. What is His hill? We read elsewhere concerning this hill, that a stone was cut from the hill without hands, and shattered all the kingdoms of the earth, and the stone itself increased. This is the vision of Daniel which I am relating. This stone which was cut from the hill without hands increased, and "became," he saith, "a great mountain, and filled the whole face of the earth."[4] Let us worship on that great mountain, if we desire to be heard. Heretics[5] do not worship on that mountain, because it hath filled the whole earth ; they have stuck fast on part of it, and have lost the whole. If they acknowledge the Catholic Church, they will worship on this hill with us. For we already see

how that stone that was cut from the mountain without hands hath increased, and how great tracts of earth it hath prevailed over, and unto what nations it hath extended. What is the mountain whence the stone was hewn without hands? The Jewish kingdom, in the first place ; since they worshipped one God. Thence was hewn the stone, our Lord Jesus Christ. . . . That stone then was born of the mountain without hands : it increased, and by its increase broke all the kingdoms of the earth. It hath become a great mountain, and hath filled the whole face of the earth. This is the Catholic Church, in whose communion rejoice that ye are. But they who are not in her communion, since they worship and praise God apart from this same mountain, are not heard unto eternal life ; although they may be heard unto certain temporal things. Let them not flatter themselves, because God heareth them in some things : for He heareth Pagans also in some things. Do not the Pagans cry unto God, and it raineth? Wherefore? Because He maketh His sun to rise over the good and the bad, and sendeth rain upon the just and the unjust.[6] Boast not therefore, Pagan, that when thou criest unto God, God sendeth rain, for He sendeth rain upon the just and the unjust. He hath heard thee in temporal things : He heareth thee not in things eternal, unless thou hast worshipped in His holy hill. "Worship Him upon His holy hill : for the Lord our God is holy." . . .

PSALM C.[7]

1. Ye heard the Psalm, brethren, while it was being chanted : it is short, and not obscure : as if I had given you an assurance, that ye should not fear fatigue. . . .

2. The title of this Psalm is, "A Psalm of confession." The verses are few, but big with great subjects ; may the seed bring forth within your hearts, the barn be prepared for the Lord's harvest.

3. "Jubilate," therefore, "unto the Lord, all ye lands " (ver. 1). This Psalm giveth this exhortation to us, that we jubilate unto the Lord. Nor doth it, as it were, exhort one particular corner of the earth, or one habitation or congregation of men ; but since it is aware that it hath sown blessings on every side, on every side it doth exact jubilance. Doth all the earth at this moment hear my voice? And yet the whole earth hath heard this voice. All the earth is already jubilant in the Lord ; and what is not as yet jubilant, will be so. For blessing, extending

---

[1] Numb. xx. 24–28, xxxiii. 38.   [2] 1 Sam. viii. 1, xxv. 1.
[3] Ps. xcix. 5.   [4] Dan. ii. 34, 35.   [5] Donatists.

[6] Matt. v. 45.
[7] Lat. XCIX. A sermon to the people, in which he speaketh remarkably concerning enduring evil men in the Church or in a monastery.

on every side, when the Church was commencing to spread from Jerusalem throughout all nations,[1] everywhere overturneth ungodliness, and everywhere buildeth up piety : the good are mingled with the wicked throughout all lands. Every land is full of the discontented murmurs of the wicked, and of the jubilance of the good. What then is it, "to jubilate"? For the title of the present Psalm especially maketh us give good heed to this word, for it is entitled, "A Psalm of confession." What meaneth, to jubilate with confession? It is the sentiment thus expressed in another Psalm : "Blessed is the people that understandeth jubilance." Surely that which being understood maketh blessed is something great. May therefore the Lord our God, who maketh men blessed, grant me to understand what to say, and grant you to understand what ye hear : "Blessed is the people that understandeth jubilance."[2] Let us therefore run unto this blessing, let us understand jubilance, let us not pour it forth without understanding. Of what use is it to be jubilant and obey[3] this Psalm, when it saith, "Jubilate unto the Lord, all ye lands," and not to understand what jubilance is, so that our voice only may be jubilant, our heart not so? For the understanding is the utterance of the heart.[4]

4. I am about to say what ye know. One who jubilates, uttereth not words, but it is a certain sound of joy without words : for it is the expression of a mind poured forth in joy, expressing, as far as it is able, the affection, but not compassing the feeling. A man rejoicing in his own exultation, after certain words which cannot[5] be uttered or understood, bursteth forth into sounds of exultation without words, so that it seemeth that he indeed doth rejoice with his voice itself, but as if filled with excessive joy cannot express in words the subject of that joy. . . . Those who are engaged at work in the fields are most given to jubilate ; reapers, or vintagers, or those who gather any of the fruits of the earth, delighted with the abundant produce, and rejoicing in the very richness and exuberance of the soil, sing in exultation ; and among the songs which they utter in words, they put in certain cries without words in the exultation of a rejoicing mind ; and this is what is meant by jubilating.[6] . . .

5. When then are we jubilant? When we praise that which cannot be uttered. For we observe the whole creation, the earth and the sea, and all things that therein are : we observe that each have their sources and causes, the power of production, the order of birth, the

limit of duration, the end in decease, that successive ages run on without any confusion, that the stars roll, as it seemeth, from the East to the West, and complete the courses of the years : we see how the months are measured, how the hours extend ; and in all these things a certain invisible element, I know not what, but some principle[7] of unity, which is termed spirit or soul, present in all living things, urging them to the pursuit of pleasure and the avoidance of pain, and the preservation of their own safety ; that man also hath somewhat in common with the Angels of God ; not with cattle, such as life, hearing, sight, and so forth ; but somewhat which can understand God, which peculiarly doth belong to the mind, which can distinguish justice and injustice, as the eye discerneth white from black. In all this consideration of creation, which I have run over as I could, let the soul ask itself : Who created all these things? Who made them? Who made among them thyself? . . . I have observed the whole creation, as far as I could. I have observed the bodily creation in heaven and on earth, and the spiritual in myself who am speaking, who animate my limbs, who exert voice, who move the tongue, who pronounce words, and distinguish sensations. And when can I comprehend myself in myself? How then can I comprehend what is above myself? Yet the sight of God is promised to the human heart, and a certain operation of purifying the heart is enjoined ; this is the counsel of Scripture. Provide the means of seeing what thou lovest, before thou try to see it. For unto whom is it not sweet to hear of God and His Name, except to the ungodly, who is far removed, separated from Him? . . .

6. Be therefore like Him in piety, and earnest in meditation : for "the invisible things of Him are clearly seen, being understood by the things that are made ;"[8] look upon the things that are made, admire them, seek their author. If thou art unlike, thou wilt turn back ; if like, thou wilt rejoice. And when, being like Him, thou shalt have begun to approach Him, and to feel God, the more love increaseth in thee, since God is love, thou wilt perceive somewhat which thou wast trying to say, and yet couldest not say. Before thou didst feel God, thou didst think that thou couldest express GOD ; thou beginnest to feel Him, and then feelest that what thou dost feel thou canst not express. But when thou hast herein found that what thou dost feel cannot be expressed, wilt thou be mute, wilt thou not praise God? Wilt thou then be silent in the praises of God, and wilt thou not offer up thanksgivings unto Him who hath willed to make Himself known unto thee? Thou didst

---

[1] Luke xxiv. 47.   [2] Ps. lxxxix. 15.   [3] *Al.* "not obey."
[4] See St. Greg. on Job i. 7, Oxf. Tr. vol. i. p. 73.
[5] Many mss. "which can."
[6] [Coleridge instances the habitual notes of the Swiss mountaineers, much in the same way. — C.]

[7] *Vestigium*, "trace."   [8] Rom. i. 20.

praise Him when thou wast seeking, wilt thou be silent when thou hast found Him? By no means; thou wilt not be ungrateful. Honour is due to Him, reverence is due to Him, great praise is due to Him. Consider thyself, see what thou art: earth and ashes; look who it is hath deserved to see, and What; consider who thou art, What to see, a man to see GOD! I recognise not the man's deserving, but the mercy of God. Praise therefore Him who hath mercy. . . .

7. "Serve the Lord with gladness." All servitude is full of bitterness: all who are bound to a lot of servitude both are slaves, and discontented. Fear not the servitude of that Lord: there will be no groaning there, no discontent, no indignation; no one seeketh to be sold to another master, since it is a sweet service, because we are all redeemed. Great happiness, brethren, it is, to be a slave in that great house, although in bonds. Fear not, bound slave, confess unto the Lord: ascribe thy bonds to thine own deservings; confess in thy chains, if thou art desirous they be changed into ornaments. . . . At the same time thou art slave, and free; slave, because thou art created such; free, because thou art loved by God, by whom thou wast created: yea, free indeed, because thou lovest Him by whom thou wast made. Serve not with discontent; for thy murmurs do not tend to release thee from serving, but to make thee a wicked servant. Thou art a slave of the Lord, thou art a freedman of the Lord: seek not so to be emancipated as to depart from the house of Him who frees thee. . . .

8. I will, therefore, saith he, live separate with a few good men: why should I live in common with crowds? Well: those very few good men, from what crowds have they been strained out? If however these few are all good: it is, nevertheless, a good and praiseworthy design in man, to be with such as have chosen a quiet life; distant from the bustle of the people, from noisy crowds, from the great waves of life, they are as if in harbour. Is there therefore here that joy? that jubilant gladness which is promised? Not as yet; but still groans, still the anxiety of temptations. For even the harbour hath an entrance somewhere or other; if it had not, no ship could enter it; it must therefore be open on some side: but at times on this open side the wind rusheth in; and where there are no rocks, ships dashed together shatter one another. Where then is security, if not even in harbour? And yet it must be confessed, it is true, that persons in harbour are in their degree much better off than when afloat on the main. Let them love one another, as ships in harbour, let them be bound together happily; let them not dash against one another: let absolute equality be preserved there,

constancy in love; and when perchance the wind rusheth in from the open side, let there be careful piloting there. Now what will one who perchance presideth over such places, nay, who serveth his brethren, in what are called monasteries, tell me? I will be cautious: I will admit no wicked man. How wilt thou admit no evil one? . . . Those who are about to enter, do not know themselves; how much less dost thou know them? For many have promised themselves that they were about to fulfil that holy life, which has all things in common, where no man calleth anything his own, who have one soul and one heart in God:[1] they have been put into the furnace, and have cracked. How then knowest thou him who is unknown even to himself? . . . Where then is security? Here nowhere; in this life nowhere, except solely in the hope of the promise of God. But there, when we shall reach thereunto, is complete security, when the gates are shut, and the bars of the gates of Jerusalem made fast;[2] there is truly full jubilance, and great delight. Only do not thou feel secure in praising any sort of life: "judge no man blessed before his death."[3]

9. By this means men are deceived, so that they either do not undertake, or rashly attempt, a better life; because, when they choose to praise, they praise without mention of the evil that is mixed with the good: and those who choose to blame, do so with so envious and perverse a mind, as to shut their eyes to the good, and exaggerate only the evils which either actually exist there, or are imagined. Thus it happeneth, that when any profession hath been ill, that is, incautiously, praised, if it hath invited men by its own reputation, they who betake themselves thither discover some such as they did not believe to be there; and offended by the wicked recoil from the good. Brethren, apply this teaching to your life, and hear in such a manner that ye may live. The Church of God, to speak generally, is magnified: Christians, and Christians alone, are called great, the Catholic (Church) is magnified; all love each other; each and all do all they can for one another; they give themselves up to prayers, fastings, hymns; throughout the whole world, with peaceful unanimity God is praised. Some one perhaps heareth this, who is ignorant that nothing is said of the wicked who are mingled with them; he cometh, invited by these praises, findeth bad men mixed with them, who were not mentioned to him before he came; he is offended by false Christians, he flieth from true Christians. Again, men who hate and slander them, precipitately blame them: asking, what sort of men are Christians? Who are Chris-

---

[1] Acts iv. 32. [2] Ps. cxlvii. 13.
[3] Ecclus. xi. 28. [See A. N. F. vol. vi. p. 279. — C.]

tians? Covetous men, usurers. Are not the very persons who fill the Churches on holidays the same who during the games and other spectacles fill the theatres and amphitheatres? They are drunken, gluttonous, envious, slanderers of each other. There are such, but not such only. And this slanderer in his blindness saith nothing of the good: and that praiser in his want of caution is silent about the bad. . . . Thus also in that common life of brethren, which exists in a monastery: great and holy men live therein, with daily hymns, prayers, praises of God; their occupation is reading; they labour with their own hands, and by this means support themselves;[1] they seek nothing covetously; whatever is brought in for them by pious brethren, they use with contentedness and charity; no one claimeth as his own what another hath not; all love, all forbear one another mutually. Thou hast praised them; thou hast praised; he who knoweth not what is going on within, who knoweth not how, when the wind entereth, ships even in harbour dash against one another, entereth as if in hope of security, expecting to find no man to forbear; he findeth there evil brethren, who could not have been found evil, if they had not been admitted (and they must be at first tolerated, lest they should perchance reform; nor can they easily be excluded, unless they have first been endured): and becometh himself impatient beyond endurance. Who asked me here? I thought that love was here. And irritated by the perversity of some few men, since he hath not persevered in fulfilling his vow, he becometh a deserter of so holy a design, and guilty of a vow he hath never discharged. And then, when he hath gone forth himself too, he also becometh a reproacher, and a slanderer; and records those things only (sometimes real), which he asserts that he could not have endured. But the real troubles of the wicked ought to be endured for the society of the good. The Scripture saith unto him: "Woe unto those that have lost patience."[2] And what is more, he belcheth abroad the evil savour of his indignation, as a means to deter them who are about to enter; because, when he had entered himself, he could not persevere. Of what sort are they? Envious, quarrelsome, men who forbear no man, covetous; saying, He did this there, and he did that there. Wicked one, why art thou silent about the good! Thou sayest enough of those whom thou couldest not endure: thou sayest nothing of those who endured thy wickedness. . . .

10. "O serve the Lord with gladness" (ver. 2): he addresseth you, whoever ye are who endure all things in love, and rejoice in hope. "Serve the Lord," not in the bitterness of murmuring, but in the "gladness of love." "Come before His presence with rejoicing." It is easy to rejoice outwardly: rejoice before the presence of God. Let not the tongue be too joyful: let the conscience be joyful. "Come before His presence with a song."

11. "Be ye sure that the Lord He is God" (ver. 3). Who knoweth not that the Lord, He is God? But He speaketh of the Lord, whom men thought not God: "Be ye sure that the Lord He is God." Let not that Lord become vile in your sight: ye have crucified Him, scourged Him, spit upon Him, crowned Him with thorns, clothed Him in a dress of infamy, hung Him upon the Cross, pierced Him with nails, wounded Him with a spear, placed guards at His tomb; He is God. "It is He that hath made us, and not we ourselves." It is He that hath made us: "and without Him was not anything made that was made."[3] What reason have ye for exultation, what reason have ye for pride? Another made you; the Same who made you, suffereth from you. But ye extol yourselves, and glory in yourselves, as if ye were created by yourselves. It is good for you that He who made you, make you perfect. . . . "We are His people, and the sheep of His pasture." Sheep and one sheep. These sheep are one sheep: and how loving a Shepherd we have! He left the ninety and nine, and descended to seek the one, He bringeth it back on His own shoulders[4] ransomed by His own blood. That Shepherd dieth without fear for the sheep, who on His resurrection regaineth His sheep.

12. "Enter into His gates with confession" (ver. 3). At the gates is the beginning: begin with confession. Thence is the Psalm entitled, "A Psalm of Confession:" there be joyful. Confess that ye were not made by yourselves, praise Him by whom ye were made. Let thy good come from Him, in departing from whom thou hast caused thine evil. "Enter into His gates with confession." Let the flock enter into the gates: let it not remain outside, a prey for wolves. And how is it to enter? "With confession." Let the gate, that is, the commencement for thee, be confession. Whence it is said in another Psalm, "Begin unto the Lord with confession."[5] What he there calleth "Begin," here he calleth "Gates." "Enter into His gates in confession." What? And when we have entered, shall we not still confess? Always confess Him: thou hast always what to confess for. It is hard in this life for a man to be so far changed, that no cause for censure be discoverable in him: thou must needs blame thyself, lest He who shall condemn blame thee. Therefore

---

[1] *Inde se transigunt.*   [2] Eccles. ii. 16.   [3] John i. 3.   [4] Luke xv. 4, 5.   [5] Ps. cxlvii. 7.

even when thou hast entered His courts, then also confess. When will there be no longer confession of sins? In that rest, in that likeness to the Angels. But consider what I have said: there will there be no confession of sins. I said not, there will be no confession: for there will be confession of praise. Thou wilt ever confess, that He is God, thou a creature; that He is thy Protector, thyself protected. In Him thou shalt be as it were hid.[1] "Go into His courts with hymns; and confess unto Him." Confess in the gates; and when ye have entered the courts, confess with hymns. Hymn are praises. Blame thyself, when thou art entering; when thou hast entered, praise Him. "Open me the gates of righteousness," he saith in another Psalm, "that I may go into them, and confess unto the Lord."[2] Did he say, when I have entered, I will no longer confess? Even after his entrance, he will confess. For what sins did our Lord Jesus Christ confess, when He said, "I confess unto Thee, O Father"?[3] He confessed in praising Him, not in accusing Himself. "Speak good of His Name."

13. "For the Lord is pleasant" (ver. 4). Think not that ye faint in praising Him. Your praise of Him is like food: the more ye praise Him, the more ye acquire strength, and He whom ye praise becometh the more sweet. "His mercy is everlasting." For He will not cease to be merciful, after He hath freed thee: it belongeth to His mercy to protect thee even unto eternal life. "His mercy," therefore, "is to everlasting: and His truth from generation to generation" (ver. 5). Understand by "from generation to generation," either every generation, or in two generations, the one earthly, the other heavenly. Here there is one generation which produceth mortals; another which maketh such as are everlasting. His Truth is both here, and there. Imagine not that His truth is not here, if His truth were not here, he would not say in another Psalm: "Truth is risen out of the earth;"[4] nor would Truth Itself say, Lo, I am with you alway, even unto the end of the world."[5]

PSALM CI.[6]

1. In this Psalm, we ought to seek in the whole body of it what we find in the first verse: "Mercy and judgment will I sing unto Thee, O Lord" (ver. 1). Let no man flatter himself that he will never be punished through God's mercy; for there is judgment also; and let no man who hath been changed for the better dread the Lord's judgment, seeing that mercy goeth before it. For when men judge, some-

times overcome by mercy, they act against justice; and mercy, but not justice, seemeth to be in them: while sometimes, when they wish to enforce a rigid judgment, they lose mercy. But God neither loseth the severity of judgment in the bounty of mercy, nor in judging with severity loseth the bounty of mercy. Suppose we distinguish these two, mercy and judgment, by time; for possibly, they are not placed in this order without a meaning, so that he said not "judgment and mercy," but "mercy and judgment:" so that if we distinguish them by succession in time, perhaps we find that the present is the season for mercy, the future for judgment. How is it that the season of mercy cometh first? Consider first how it is with God, that thou also mayest imitate the Father, in so far as He shall permit thee. . . . "He maketh His sun to rise on the evil and on the good, and sendeth rain on the just and on the unjust." Behold mercy. When thou seest the just and the unjust behold the same sun, enjoy the same light, drink from the same founts, satisfied with the same rain, blessed with the same fruits of the earth, inhale this air in the same way, possess equally the world's goods; think not that God is unjust, who giveth these things equally to the just and the unjust. It is the season of mercy, not as yet of judgment. For unless God spared at first through mercy, He would not find those whom He could crown through judgment. There is therefore a season for mercy, when the long-suffering of God calleth sinners to repentance.

2. Hear the Apostle distinguishing each season, and do thou also distinguish it. . . . "Thinkest thou," he saith, "O man, that judgest them that do such things, and doest the same, that thou shalt escape the judgment of God?" And as if we were to reply, Why do I commit such sins daily, and no evil occurreth unto me? he goeth on to show to him the season of mercy: "Despisest thou the riches of His goodness, and forbearance, and long-suffering?" And he did indeed despise them; but the Apostle hath made him anxious. "Not knowing," he saith, "that the goodness of God leadeth thee to repentance?"[7] Behold the season of mercy. But that he might not think this would last for ever, how did he in the next verse raise his fears? Now hear the season of judgment; thou hast heard the season of mercy, on which account, "mercy and judgment will I sing unto Thee, O Lord:" "But thou," saith the Apostle, "after thy hardness and impenitent heart, treasurest up unto thyself wrath against the day of wrath, and revelation of the righteous judgment of God, who will render to every man

---

[1] Ps. xxxi. 20.   [2] Ps. cxviii. 19.   [3] Matt. xi. 25.
[4] Ps. xv. 12.   [5] Matt. xxviii. 20.
[6] Lat. C.   A discourse to the people.

[7] 2 Rom. ii. 4.

according to his deeds." [1] Lo, "mercy and judgment." But he hath threatened concerning judgment: is therefore the judgment of God to be feared only, and not to be loved? To be feared by the wicked on account of punishment, to be loved by the good on account of the crown. Because then the Apostle hath alarmed the wicked in the testimony which I have quoted, hear where he giveth hope concerning judgment to the good. He puts forth himself, and shows in himself too the season of mercy. For unless he found a period of mercy, in what condition would judgment find him? A blasphemer, a persecutor, an injurer of others. For he thus speaketh, and praiseth the season of mercy, in which season we are now living: "I who was before," he saith, "a blasphemer, and a persecutor, and injurious: but I obtained mercy." But perhaps he only hath obtained mercy? Hear how he cheereth us: "That in me," he saith, "first, Christ Jesus might show forth all long-suffering, for a pattern to them which should hereafter believe on Him to life everlasting." [2] What meaneth, "that He might show forth all long-suffering"? That every sinner and wicked man might see that Paul received pardon, and might not despair of himself? Lo, he hath instanced himself, and thereby cheered others also. . . . But did Paul alone deserve this? For I had asserted, that as he raised our fears by the former testimony, so did he encourage us by the latter. When he said, "The Lord, the righteous Judge, shall render to me at that day:" he addeth, "and not to me only, but unto all them also that love His appearing" [3] and His kingdom. Since therefore, brethren, we have a season of mercy, let us not on that account flatter, or indulge ourselves, saying, God spareth ever. . . .

3. "I will sing to the harp, and will have understanding, in the spotless way. When Thou shalt come unto me" (ver. 2). Except in the spotless way, thou canst neither sing to the harp, nor understand. If thou dost wish to understand, sing in the spotless way, that is, work with cheerfulness before thy God. What is the spotless way? Hear what followeth: "I walked in innocence, in the midst of my house." This spotless way beginneth from innocence, and it endeth also in innocence. Why seek many words? Be innocent: and thou hast perfected righteousness. . . . But who is innocent? He who while he hurteth not another, injureth not himself. For he who hurteth himself, is not innocent. Some one saith: Lo, I have not robbed any one, I have not oppressed any one: I will live happily on my own substance, the fruits of my virtuous toil; I wish to have fine banquets, I wish to spend as much as pleaseth

me, to drink with those whom I like as much as I please; whom have I robbed, whom have I oppressed, who hath complained of me? He seemeth innocent. But if he corrupt himself, if he overthrow the temple of God within himself, why hope that he will act with mercy toward others, and spare the wretched? Can that man be merciful to others, who unto himself is cruel? The whole of righteousness, therefore, is reduced to the one word, innocence. But the lover of iniquity, hateth his own soul. When he loved iniquity, he fancied he was injuring others. But consider whether he was injuring others: "He who loveth iniquity," he saith, "hateth his own soul." [4] He therefore who wishes to injure another, first injureth himself; nor doth he walk, since there is no room. For all wickedness suffereth from narrowness: innocence alone is broad enough to walk in. "I walked in the innocence of my heart, in the midst of my house." By the middle of his house, he either signifieth the Church herself; for Christ walketh in her: or his own heart; for our inner house is our heart: as he hath explained in the above words, "in the innocence of my heart." What is the innocence of the heart? The middle of his house? Whoever hath a bad house in this, is driven out of doors. For whoever is oppressed within his heart by a bad conscience, just as any man in consequence of the overflow of a waterspout or of smoke goeth out of his house, suffereth not himself to dwell therein; so he who hath not a quiet heart, cannot happily dwell in his heart. Such men go out of themselves in the bent of their mind, and delight themselves with things without, that affect the body; they seek repose in trifles, in spectacles, in luxuries, in all evils. Wherefore do they wish themselves well without? Because it is not well with them within, so that they may rejoice in a good conscience. . . .

4. "I set no wicked thing before my eyes" (ver. 3). . . . I did love no wicked thing. And he explaineth this same wicked thing: "I hated them that do unfaithfulness." Attend, my brethren. If ye walk with Christ in the midst of His house, that is, if either in your heart ye have a good repose, or in the Church herself proceed on a good journey in the way of godliness; ye ought not to hate those unfaithful only who are without, but whomsoever also ye may have found within. Who are the unfaithful? They who hate the law of God; who hear, and do it not, are called unfaithful. Hate the doers of unfaithfulness, repel them from thee. But thou shouldest hate the unfaithful, not men: one man who is unfaithful, hath, ye see, two names, man, and unfaithful: God made him

---

[1] Rom. ii. 5, 6.　　[2] 1 Tim. i. 13, 16.　　[3] 2 Tim. iv. 8.　　[4] Ps. xi. 5.

man, he made himself unfaithful; love in him what God made, persecute in him what he made himself. For when thou shalt have persecuted his unfaithfulness, thou killest the work of man, and freest the work of God. "I hated the doers of unfaithfulness."

5. "The wicked heart hath not cleaved unto me." . . . The heart of a man, who wisheth not anything contrary to any that God wisheth, is called straight. . . . If therefore the righteous heart followeth God, the crooked heart resisteth God. Suppose something untoward happeneth to him, he crieth out, "God, what have I done unto Thee? What sin have I committed?" He wisheth himself to appear just, God unjust. What is so crooked as this? It is not enough that thou art crooked thyself: thou must think thy rule crooked also. Reform thyself, and thou findest Him straight, in departing from whom thou hast made thyself crooked. He doth justly, thou unjustly; and for this reason thou art perverse, since thou callest man just, and God unjust. What man dost thou call just? Thyself. For when thou sayest, "What have I done unto Thee?" thou thinkest thyself just. But let God answer thee: "Thou speakest truth: thou hast done nothing to Me: thou hast done all things unto thyself; for if thou hadst done anything for Me, thou wouldest have done good. For whatever is done well, is done unto Me; because it is done according to My commandment; but whatever of evil is done, is done unto thee, not unto Me; for the wicked man doth nothing except for his own sake, since it is not what I command." When ye see such men, brethren, reprove them, convince and correct them: and if ye cannot reprove or correct them, consent not to them.

6. "When the wicked man departed from me, I knew him not" (ver. 4). I approved him not, I praised him not, he pleased me not. For we find the word "to know" occasionally used in Scripture, in the sense of "to be pleased." For what is hidden from God, brethren? Doth He know the just, and doth He not know the unjust? What dost thou think of, that He doth not know? I say not, what thinkest thou; but what wilt thou ever think, that He will not have seen beforehand? God knoweth all things, then; and yet in the end, that is in judgment after mercy, He saith of some persons: "I will profess unto them, I never knew you; depart from Me, ye workers of iniquity." [1] Was there any one He did not know? But what meaneth, "I never knew you"? I acknowledge you not in My rule. For I know the rule of My righteousness: ye agree not with it, ye have turned aside from it, ye are crooked. Therefore He

said here also: "When the wicked man departed from Me, I knew him not." . . . Therefore, "when the wicked man departed from me," that is, when the wicked man was unlike me, and was unwilling to imitate my paths, was unwilling in his wickedness to live as I had proposed myself for his imitation; "I knew him not." What meaneth, "I knew him not"? Not that I was ignorant of him, but that I did not approve him.

7. "Whoso privily slandered his neighbour, him I persecuted" (ver. 5). Behold the righteous persecutor, not of the man, but of the sin. "With the proud eye, and the insatiable heart, I did not feed." What meaneth, "I did not feed with"? I did not eat in common with such. Attend, beloved; since ye are about to hear something wonderful. If he did not feed with this man, he did not eat with him; for to feed is to eat; how is it then that we find our Lord Himself eating with the proud? It was not only with those publicans and sinners, for they were humble: for they acknowledged their weakness, and asked for the physician. We find that He ate with the proud Pharisees themselves. A certain proud man had invited Him: it was the same who was displeased because a sinning woman, one of ill repute in the city, approached the feet of our Lord. . . . That Pharisee was proud: the Lord ate with him; what is it therefore that he saith? "With such an one I did not eat." How doth He enjoin unto us what He hath not done Himself? He exhorteth us to imitate Himself: we see that He ate with the proud; how doth He forbid us to eat with the proud? We indeed, brethren, for the sake of reproof, abstain from communion with our brethren, and do not eat with them, that they may be reformed? We rather eat with strangers, with Pagans, than with those who hold with us, if we have seen that they live wickedly, that they may be ashamed, and amend; as the Apostle saith, "And if any man obey not our word by this Epistle, note that man, and have no company with him, that he may be ashamed. Yet count him not as an enemy, but admonish him as a brother." [2] For the sake of healing others we usually do this; but nevertheless we often eat with many strangers and ungodly men.

8. The pious heart hath its banquets, the proud heart hath its banquets: for it was on account of the food of the proud heart, that he said, "with an insatiable heart." How is the proud heart fed? If a man is proud, he is envious: otherwise it cannot be. Pride is the mother of enviousness: it cannot but generate it, and ever coexist with it. Every proud man is, therefore, envious: if envious, he feedeth on

---

[1] Matt. vii. 23.   [2] 2 Thess. iii. 14.

the misfortunes of others. Whence the Apostle saith, "But if ye bite and devour one another, take heed that ye be not consumed of one another."[1] Ye see them, then, eating: eat not with these: fly such banquets: for they cannot satisfy themselves with rejoicing in others' evils, because their hearts are insatiable. Beware thou art not caught in their feasts by the devil's noose. . . . Just as birds feed at the trap, or fishes at the hook, they were taken, when they fed. The ungodly therefore have their own feasts, the godly also have theirs. Hear the feasts of the godly: "Blessed are they who hunger and thirst after righteousness: for they shall be filled."[2] If therefore the godly eateth the meat of righteousness, and the ungodly of pride; it is no wonder if he is insatiable in heart. He eateth the meat of iniquity: do not eat the meat of iniquity, and the proud in eye, and the insatiable in heart, eateth not with thee.

9. And whence wast thou fed? And what pleased thee, when he did not eat with thee? "Mine eyes," he saith, "were upon such as are faithful in the land, that they might sit with me" (ver. 6). That is, that with Me they might be seated.[3] In what sense are they "to sit"? "Ye shall sit on twelve thrones, judging the twelve tribes of Israel."[4] The faithful of the earth judge, for to them it is said, "Know ye not, that we shall judge angels?"[5] "Whoso walketh in a spotless way, he ministered unto me." To "Me," he saith, not to himself. For many minister the Gospel, but unto themselves; because they seek their own things, not the things of Jesus Christ.[6] . . .

10. "The proud man hath not dwelt in the midst of my house" (ver. 7). Understand this of the heart. The proud did not dwell in my heart: no such dwelt in my heart: for he hurried away from me. None but the meek and peaceful dwelt in my heart; the proud dwelt not there, for the unrighteous one dwelleth not in the heart of the righteous. Let the righteous be distant from thee, I know not how many miles and stations:[7] ye dwell together, if ye have one heart. "The proud doer hath not dwelt in the midst of my house: he that speaketh unjust things hath not directed in the sight of my eyes." This is the spotless way, where we understand when the Lord cometh unto us.

11. "In the morning I destroyed all the ungodly that were in the land. That I may root out all wicked doers from the city of the Lord" (ver. 8). This is obscure. There are then wicked doers in the city of the Lord, and they at present, seemingly, spared. Why so? Because it is the season of mercy: but that of judgment will come; for the Psalm thus began, "Of mercy and judgment will I sing unto Thee, O Lord." . . .

12. He at present spareth, He will then judge. But when will He judge? When night shall have passed away. For this reason He hath said: "In the morning." When the day shall at last have arrived, night having passed by. Why doth He spare them until the dawn? Because it was night. What meaneth, it was night? Because it was the season for mercy: He was merciful, while the hearts of men were hidden. Thou seest some one living ill; thou endurest him: for thou knowest not of what sort he will prove to be; since it is night; whether he who to-day liveth ill, to-morrow may live well; and whether he who to-day liveth well, to-morrow may be wicked. For it is night, and God endureth all men, since He is of long-suffering: He endureth them, that sinners may be converted unto Him. But they who shall not have reformed themselves in that season of mercy, shall be slain. And wherefore? That they may be scattered abroad[8] from the city of the Lord, from the fellowship of Jerusalem, from the fellowship of the Saints, from the fellowship of the Church. But when shall they be slain? "At dawn." What meaneth, "at dawn"? When night shall have passed away. Wherefore now doth he spare? Because it is the season of mercy. Why doth He not always spare? Because, "Mercy and judgment will I sing unto Thee, O Lord." Brethren, let no man flatter himself: all the doers of iniquity shall be slain; Christ shall slay them at the dawn, and shall destroy them from His city. But now while it is the time of mercy, let them hear Him. Everywhere He crieth out by the Law, by the Prophets, by the Psalms, by the Epistles, by the Gospels: see that He is not silent; that He spareth; that He granteth mercy; but beware, for the judgment will come.

PSALM CII.[9]

1. Behold, one poor man prayeth, and prayeth not in silence. We may therefore hear him, and see who he is: whether it be not perchance He, of whom the Apostle saith, "Though He was rich, yet for your sakes He became poor, that ye through His poverty might be rich."[10] If it is He, then, how is He poor? For in what sense He is rich, who seeth not? What then is richer than He, by whom riches were made, even those which are not true riches? For through Him we have even these riches, ability, memory, character, health of body, the senses,

---

[1] Gal. v. 15.   [2] Matt. v. 6.
[3] *Mecum sederent*. There was an ambiguity in *considerent*, as written
[4] Matt. xix. 28.   [5] 1 Cor. vi. 3.
[6] Philip. ii. 21.   [7] *Mansionibus*.

[8] Oxf. mss. *disperdantur*, "destroyed," as below.
[9] Lat. CI.   [10] 2 Cor. viii. 9.

and the conformation of our limbs: for when these are safe, even the poor are rich. Through Him also are those greater riches, faith, piety, justice, charity, chastity, good conduct: for no man hath these, except through Him who justifieth the ungodly. . . . Behold, how rich! In one so rich, how are we to recognise these words? "I have eaten ashes as it were bread: and mingled my drink with weeping."[1] Have these so great riches come to this? The former state is a very high one, this is a very lowly one. . . . Yet still examine whether this poor man be He; since, "The Word was made flesh, and dwelt among us."[2] Reflect also upon these words: "I am Thy servant, and the Son of Thine handmaid."[3] Observe, this handmaid, chaste, a virgin, and a mother: for there He received our poverty, when He was clothed in the form of a servant, emptying Himself; lest thou shouldest dread His riches, and in thy beggarly state shouldest not dare approach Him. There, I say, He put on the form of a servant, there He was clothed with our poverty; there He made Himself poor, and us rich. We are now drawing near to understand these things of Him: nevertheless we may not as yet rashly pronounce. . . .

2. Let him add poverty then to poverty: let Him transfigure unto Himself our humble body: let Him be our Head, we His limbs, let there be two in one flesh.[4] . . . For He hath deigned to hold even us as His limbs. The penitent also are among His limbs. For they are not shut out, nor separated from His Church: nor would He make the Church His spouse, unless by words like these: "Repent ye, for the kingdom of heaven is at hand."[5] Let us then hear what the head and the body prayeth, the bridegroom and bride, Christ and the Church,[6] both one Person; but the Word and the flesh are not both one thing; the Father and the Word are both one thing; Christ and the Church are both one Person, one perfect man in the form of His own fulness. . . . Let us hear therefore Christ, poor within us and with us, and for our sakes. For the title itself indicates the poor one. Lastly, remember that I conjectured who that poor one was: let us hear His prayer, and recognise His Person; and mistake not, when thou shalt have heard anything that cannot apply to His Head; it was for this reason that I have prefaced as I have, that whatever thou shalt hear of this description, thou mayest understand as sounding from the weakness of the body, and recognise the voice of the members in the head. The title is, "A Prayer of the afflicted, when he was tormented, and poured out his prayer before the Lord."

It is the same poor one who elsewhere saith: "From the ends of the earth will I call upon Thee, when my heart is in heaviness."[7] He is afflicted because He is also Christ; who in the Prophet's words calleth Himself both Bridegroom and Bride: "He hath bound on me the diadem as on a bridegroom, and as a bride hath adorned me with an ornament."[8] He called Himself Bridegroom, He called Himself Bride; wherefore this, unless Bridegroom applieth to the Head, Bride to the body? They are one voice then, because they are one flesh. Let us hear, and recognise ourselves in these words; and if we see that we are without, let us labour to be there.

3. "Hear my prayer, O Lord: and let my crying come unto Thee" (ver. 1). "Hear my prayer, O Lord," is the same as, "Let my crying come unto Thee:" the feeling of the suppliant is shown by the repetition. "Turn not Thy face away from me." When did God turn away His Face from His Son? when did the Father turn away His Face from Christ? But for the sake of the poverty of my members, "Turn not away Thy face from me: whatsoever day I am troubled, incline Thine ear unto me" (ver. 2). . . . Thou art in trouble this day, I am in trouble; another is in trouble to-morrow, I am in trouble; after this generation other descendants, who succeed your descendants, are in trouble, I am in trouble; down to the end of the world, whoever are in trouble in My body, I am in trouble. . . . Peter prayed, Paul prayed, the rest of the Apostles prayed; the faithful prayed in those times, the faithful prayed in the following times, the faithful prayed in the times of the Martyrs, the faithful pray in our times, the faithful will pray in the times of our descendants. "Right soon:" for I now ask that which Thou art willing to grant. I ask not earthly things, as an earthly man; but redeemed at last from my former captivity, I long for the kingdom of heaven; "Hear me right soon:" for it is only to such a longing that Thou hast said, "Even while Thou art speaking, I will say, Here I am."[9] Wherefore dost thou call? in what tribulation? in what want? O poor one, before the gate of God all-rich, in what longing dost thou beg? from what destitution dost thou ask relief? from what want dost thou knock, that it may be opened unto thee?

4. "For my days are consumed away like smoke" (ver. 3). O days! if days: for where day is heard of, light is understood. "My days," my times; wherefore, "like smoke," unless from the puffing up of pride? . . . See smoke, like pride, ascending, swelling, vanishing: deservedly therefore failing, and not stedfast. "And my

---

[1] Ps. cii. 9.　　　[2] John i. 14.　　　[3] Ps. cxvi. 16.
[4] Philip. iii. 21.　　[5] Matt. iii. 2.　　[6] Eph. iv. 15; John iii. 29.

[7] Ps. lxi. 2.　　　[8] Isa. lxi. 10.　　　[9] Isa. lviii. 9.

bones are scorched up as it were in an oven."
Both my bones, and my strength, not without
tribulation, not without burning. The bones of
the body of Christ, the strength of His body, is
it anywhere greater than in the Holy Apostles?
And yet see that the bones are scorched. "Who
is offended, and I burn not?"[1] They are brave,
faithful, able interpreters and preachers of the
word, living as they speak, speaking as they
hear; they are clearly brave, yet all who suffer
offences, are an oven to them. For there is love
there, and more so in the bones. The bones
are within all the flesh, and support all the flesh.
But if any man suffer any offence, and endanger
his soul; the bone is scorched in proportion as
it loveth. . . .

5. Look back to Adam, whence the human
race sprung. For how but from him was misery
propagated? whence but from him is this hered-
itary poverty? Let him then, who in his own
body was at one time in despair, now that he is
set in Christ's body, say with hope, "My heart
is smitten down, and withered like grass" (ver.
4). Deservedly, since all flesh is grass.[2] But
how did this happen unto thee? "Since I have
forgotten to eat my bread." For God had
given His commandment for bread. For what
is the bread of the soul? The serpent suggesting, and the woman transgressing, he touched
the forbidden fruit,[3] he forgot the commandment: his heart was smitten as it deserved,
and withered like grass, since he forgot to eat
his bread. Having forgotten to eat bread, he
drinketh poison: his heart is smitten, and withered like grass. . . . Now eat that bread which
thou hadst forgotten. But this very Bread hath
come, in whose body thou mayest remember
the voice of thy forgetfulness, and cry out in thy
poverty, so that thou mayest receive riches.
Now eat: for thou art in His body, who saith,
"I am the living bread which came down from
heaven."[4] Thou hadst forgotten to eat thy
bread; but after His crucifixion, "all the ends
of the earth shall be reminded, and be converted unto the Lord."[5] After forgetfulness,
let remembrance come, let bread be eaten from
heaven, that we may live; not manna, as they
did eat, and died;[6] that bread, of which it is
said, "Blessed are they who hunger and thirst
after righteousness."[7]

6. "For the voice of my groaning, the bones
cleave unto my flesh" (ver. 5). For many groan,
and I also groan; even for this I groan, because
they groan for a wrong cause. That man hath
lost a piece of money, he groaneth: he hath lost
faith, he groaneth not: I weigh the money and
the faith, and I find more cause for groaning for
him who groaneth not as he ought, or doth not
groan at all. He committeth fraud, and rejoiceth. With what gain, with what loss? He hath
gained money, he hath lost righteousness. For
the latter reason, he who knoweth how to groan,
groaneth; he who is near the head, who righteously clingeth to Christ's body, groaneth for
this reason. But the carnal do not groan for
this reason, and they cause themselves to be
groaned for, because they do not groan for this
reason; nor can we despise them, whether they
groan not at all, or groan for the wrong cause.
For we wish to correct them, we wish to amend
them, we wish to reform them: and when we
cannot, we groan; and when we groan, we are
not separated from them. . . .

7. "I am become like a pelican in the wilderness, and like an owl among ruined walls"
(ver. 6). Behold three birds and three places:
the pelican, the owl, and the sparrow;[8] and the
three places are severally, the wilderness, the
ruined walls, and the house-top. The pelican
in the wilderness, the owl in the ruined walls,
and the sparrow in the house-top. In the first
place we must explain, what the pelican signifieth: since it is born in a region which maketh
it unknown to us. It is born in lonely spots,
especially those of the river Nile in Egypt.
Whatever kind of bird it is, let us consider what
the Psalm intended to say of it. "It dwelleth,"
it saith, "in the wilderness." Why enquire of its
form, its limbs, its voice, its habits? As far as
the Psalm telleth thee, it is a bird that dwelleth
in solitude. The owl is a bird that loveth night.
Parietinæ, or ruins, as we call them, are walls
standing without roof, without inhabitants, these
are the habitation of the owl. And then as to
the house-top and the sparrows, ye are familiar
with them. I find, therefore, some one of
Christ's body, a preacher of the word, sympa-
thizing with the weak, seeking the gains of Christ,
mindful of his Lord to come.[9] Let us see these
three things from the office of His steward.
Hath such a man come among those who are
not Christians? He is a pelican in the wilderness. Hath he come among those who were
Christians, and have relapsed? He is an owl
in the ruined walls; for he forsaketh not even
the darkness of those who dwell in night, he
wisheth to gain even these. Hath he come
among such as are Christians dwelling in a house,
not as if they believed not, or as if they had let
go what they had believed, but walking luke-
warmly in what they believe? The sparrow
crieth unto them, not in the wilderness, because
they are Christians; nor in the ruined walls,
because they have not relapsed; but because
they are within the roof; under the roof rather,

---

[1] 2 Cor. xi. 29.　[2] Isa. xl. 6.　[3] Gen. iii. 6.
[4] John vi 41.　[5] Ps. xxii. 27.　[6] John vi. 49.
[7] Matt. v. 6.

[8] [In the next verse.—C.]　[9] Matt. xxv. 26.

because they are under the flesh. The sparrow above the flesh crieth out, husheth not up the commandments of God, nor becometh carnal, so that he be subject to the roof. "What ye hear in the ear, that preach ye on the house-tops."[1] There are three birds and three places; and one man may represent the three birds, and three men may represent severally the three birds; and the three sorts of places, are three classes of men: yet the wilderness, the ruined walls, and the house-top, are but three classes of men.

8. . . . Let us not pass over what is said, or even read, of this bird, that is, the pelican; not rashly asserting anything, but yet not passing over what has been left to be read and uttered by those who have written it. Do ye so hear, that if it be true, it may agree; if false, it may not hold. These birds are said to slay their young with blows of their beaks, and for three days to mourn them when slain by themselves in the nest: after which they say the mother wounds herself deeply, and pours forth her blood over her young,· bathed in which they recover life. This may be true, it may be false: yet if it be true, see how it agreeth with Him, who gave us life by His blood.[2] It agreeth with Him in that the mother's flesh recalleth to life her young with her blood; it agreeth well. For He calleth Himself a hen brooding over her young.[3] . . . If, then, it be so truly, this bird doth closely resemble the flesh of Christ, by whose blood we have been called to life. But how may it agree with Christ, that the bird herself slays her own young? Doth not this agree with it? "I will slay, and I will make alive: I will wound, and I will heal."[4] Would the persecutor Saul[5] have died, unless he were wounded from heaven; or would the preacher be raised up, unless by life given him from His blood? But let those who have written on the subject see to this; we ought not to allow our understanding of it to rest upon doubtful ground.[6] Let us rather recognise this bird in the wilderness; as the Psalm expresseth it, "A pelican in the solitude." I suppose that Christ born of a Virgin is here meant. He was born in loneliness, because He alone was thus born. After the nativity, we come to His Passion. . . . Born in the wilderness, because alone so born; suffering in the darkness of the Jews as it were in night, in their sin, as it were in ruins: what next? "I have watched:" and "am become even as it were a sparrow, that sitteth alone upon the house-top" (ver. 7). Thou hadst then slept amid the ruins, and hadst said, "I laid me

down, and slept."[7] What meaneth, "I slept"? Because I chose, I slept: I slept for love of night: but, "I rose again," followeth. Therefore "I watched," is here said. But after He watched, what did He? He ascended into heaven, He became as a sparrow by flying; that is, by ascending; "alone on the house-top;" that is, in heaven. He is therefore as the pelican by birth, as the owl by dying, as the sparrow by ascending again: there in the wilderness, as one alone; here in the ruined walls, as one slain by those who could not stand in the building; and here again watching and flying for our sakes alone on the house-top, He there intercedeth in our behalf.[8] For our Head is as the sparrow, His body as the turtle-dove. "For the sparrow hath found her an house." What house? In heaven, where He doth mediate for us. "And the turtle-dove a nest," the Church of God hath found a nest from the wood of His Cross, where "she may lay her young," her children.

9. "Mine enemies revile me all day, and they that praised me are sworn together against me" (ver. 8). With their mouth they praised, in their heart they were laying snares for me. Hear their praise: "Master, we know that Thou art true, and teachest the way of God in truth, neither carest Thou for any man. Is it lawful to give tribute unto Cæsar, or not?"[9] And whence this evil repute, except because I came to make sinners my members, that by repentance they may be in my body? Thence is all the calumny, thence the persecution. "Why eateth your Master with publicans and sinners? They that be whole need not a physician, but they that be sick."[10] Would that ye were aware of your sickness, that ye might seek a physician; ye would not slay Him, and through your infatuated pride perish in a false health.

10. "I have eaten ashes as it were bread: and mingled my drink with weeping" (ver. 9). Because He chose to have among His members these kinds of men, that they should be healed and set free, thence is the evil repute. Now at this day what is the character of Pagan calumny against us? what, brethren, do ye conceive they tell us? Ye corrupt discipline, and pervert the morality of the human race. Why dost thou attack us; say why? what have we done? By giving, he replieth, to men room for repentance, by promising impunity for all sins: for this reason men do evil deeds, careless of consequences, because everything is pardoned them, when they are converted. . . . And what is to become of thee, miserable man, if there shall be no harbour of impunity? If there is only licence for sinning, and no pardon for sins,

---

[1] Matt. x. 27.   [2] [See p. 285, note 8, *supra*. — C.]
[3] Matt. xxiii. 37.   [4] Deut. xxxii. 39.   [5] Acts ix. 4.
[6] [Compare the pardonable credulity of Clement, A. N. F. vol. i. p. 12, note 2; also p. 285, note 8, *supra*.— C.]

[7] Ps. iii. 5.   [8] Rom. viii. 34.
[9] Matt. xxii. 16, 17.   [10] Matt. ix. 11, 12.

where wilt thou be, whither wilt thou go? Surely even for thee did it happen, that that afflicted one ate ashes as it were bread, and mingled His drink with weeping. Doth not such a feast now please thee? But nevertheless, he replieth, men add to their sins under the hope of pardon. Nay, but they would add to them if they despaired of pardon. Dost thou not observe in what licentious cruelty gladiators live? whence this, except because, as destined for the sword and sacrifice, they choose to sate their lust, before they pour forth their blood?[1] Wouldest not thou also thus address thyself? I am already a sinner, already an unjust man, one already doomed to damnation, hope of pardon there is none: why should I not do whatever pleaseth me, although it be not lawful? why not fulfil, as far as I can, any longings I may have, if, after these, nothing but torments only be in store? Wouldest thou not thus speak unto thyself, and from this very despair become still worse? Rather than this, then, He who promiseth forgiveness, doth correct thee, saying, " As I live, saith the Lord, I have no pleasure in the death of the wicked; but that the wicked turn from his way and live."[2] . . . For in order that men might not live the worse from despair, He promised a harbour of forgiveness; again, that they might not live the worse from hope of pardon, He made the day of death uncertain: fixing both with the utmost providence, both as a refuge for the returning, and a terror to the loitering. Eat ashes as bread, and mingle thy drink with weeping; by means of this banquet thou shalt reach the table of God. Despair not; pardon hath been promised thee. Thanks be to God, he saith, because it is promised; I hold fast the promise of God. Now therefore live well. To-morrow, he replieth, I will live well. God hath promised the pardon; no one promised thee to-morrow. . . .

11. "And that because of thine indignation and wrath: because thou hast taken me up, thou hast cast me down" (ver. 10). This is thy wrath, O Lord, in Adam: that wrath in which we were all born, which cleaveth unto us by our birth; the wrath from the stock of iniquity, the wrath from the mass of sin: according to what the Apostle saith, " We also were once the children of wrath, even as others." For He saith not, the wrath of God shall come upon him: but, " abideth upon him: " because that wrath in which he was born is not taken away. . . . Man set in honour, is made in the image of God: raised up to this honour, lifted up from the dust, from the earth, he hath received a reasonable soul; by the vivacity of that very reason, he is placed before all beasts, cattle,

birds that fly, and fishes.[3] For which of these hath reason to understand? Because none of them is created in the image of God. . . . Therefore, " Because Thou hast taken me up, Thou hast cast me down: " punishment followeth me, because Thou hast given me a free choice. For if Thou hadst not given me a free choice, and for this reason didst not make me better than cattle, just condemnation would not follow me when I sinned. Thus Thou hast taken me up in giving me freedom of choice, and by Thy judgment Thou hast cast me down.

12. "My days have declined like a shadow" (ver. 11). . . . He had said above, " My days are consumed away like smoke; " and he now saith, " My days have declined like a shadow." In this shadow, day must be recognised; in this shadow, light must be discerned; lest afterward it be said in late and fruitless repentance, " What hath pride profited us? or what good hath riches with our vaunting brought us? All those things are passed away like a shadow."[4] Say at this season, all things will pass away like a shadow, and thou mayest not pass away like a shadow. " My days have declined like a shadow, and I am withered like grass." For he had said above, " my heart is smitten down, and I am withered like grass." But the grass bedewed with the Saviour's blood will flourish afresh. " I have withered like grass; " I, that is, man, after that disobedience; this I have suffered from Thy just judgment: but what art Thou?

13. For not because I have fallen, hast Thou grown old: for Thou art strong to set me free, who hast been strong to humble me. "But Thou, O Lord, endurest for ever: and Thy remembrance throughout all generations" (ver. 12). "Thy remembrance," because Thou dost not forget: " throughout all generations," forasmuch as we know the promise of life, both present and future.[5]

14. "Thou shalt arise, and have mercy upon Sion: for it is time that Thou have mercy upon her" (ver. 13). What time? " But when the fulness of time was come, God sent forth His Son, made of a woman, made under the Law." And where is Sion? " To redeem them that were under the Law."[6] First then were the Jews: for thence were the Apostles, thence those more than five hundred brethren,[7] thence that later multitude, who had but one heart and one soul toward God.[8] Therefore, " the time is come." What time? " Behold, now is the accepted time: behold, now is the day of salvation."[9] Who saith this? That Servant of God, that Builder, who said, " Ye are God's building."[10]

---

[1] [See p. 315, note 10, *supra.* — C.] [2] Ezek. xiii. 11.

[3] Gen. i. 26. [4] Wisd. v. 8, 9. [5] 1 Tim. iv. 8.
[6] Gal. iv. 4, 5. [7] 1 Cor. xv. 6. [8] Acts iv. 32.
[9] 2 Cor. vi. 2. [10] 1 Cor. iii. 9-11.

15. Here therefore what saith he? "For thy servants take pleasure in her stones" (ver. 14). In whose stones? In the stones of Sion? But there are those there that are not stones. Not stones of what? What then followeth? "and pity the dust thereof." I understand by the stones of Sion all the Prophets: there was the voice of preaching sent before, thence the ministry of the Gospel assumed, through their preaching Christ became known. Therefore thy servants have taken pleasure in the stones of Sion. But those faithless apostates from God, who offended their Creator by their evil deeds, have returned to the earth, whence they were taken. They have become dust, they have become ungodly.[1] But wait, Lord; bear with us, Lord; be long-suffering, O Lord: let not the wind rush in, and sweep away this dust from the face of the earth. Let thy servants come, let them come, let them acknowledge in the stones thy voice, let them pity the dust of Sion, let them be formed in thy image: let the dust say, lest it perish, "Remember that we are but dust."[2] This of Sion: was not that which crucified the Lord, dust? What is worse, it was dust from the ruined walls; altogether dust it was, but nevertheless it was not in vain said of this dust, "Father, forgive them." From this very dust there came a wall of so many thousands who believed, and who laid the price of their possessions at the Apostles' feet. From that dust then there arose a human nature formed[3] and beautiful. Who among the heathen acted thus? How few are there whom we admire for having done thus, compared with the many thousands of these converts? At first suddenly three, afterwards five thousand; all living in unity, all laying the price of their possessions, when they had sold them, at the Apostles' feet, that it might be distributed to each, as each had need, who had one soul and one heart toward God.[4] Who made this even of that very dust, but He who created Adam himself out of dust? This then is concerning Sion, but not in Sion only.

16. "The heathen shall fear Thy Name, O Lord; and all the kings of the earth Thy Majesty" (ver. 15). Now that Thou hast pitied Sion, now that Thy servants have taken pleasure in her stones, by acknowledging the foundation of the Apostles and Prophets; now that they have pitied her dust; so that man is formed, or rather re-formed, in life out of dust; hence preaching hath increased among the heathen: let the heathen fear Thy Name, let another wall approach also from the heathen, let the Corner Stone[5] be recognised, let the two who come from different regions, but who no longer differ in belief, meet in close union.

17. "For the Lord shall build up Sion" (ver. 16). This work is going on now. O ye living stones, run to the work of building, not to ruin. Sion is in building, beware of the ruined walls: the tower is building, the ark is in building; remember the deluge. This work is in progress now; but when Sion is built, what will happen? "And He will appear in His glory." That He might build up Sion, that He might be a foundation in Sion, He was seen by Sion, but not in His glory: "we have seen Him, and He had no form nor comeliness."[6] But truly when He shall have come with His angels to judge,[7] shall they not look then upon Him whom they have pierced?[8] and they shall be put to confusion when too late, who refused confusion in early and healthful repentance.

18. "He hath turned Him unto the prayer of the poor destitute, and despised not their desire" (ver. 17). This is going on now in the building of Sion: the builders of Sion pray, they groan: He is the one poor, because the poor are many; because the thousands among so many nations are one in Him, because He is the unity of the peace of the Church, He is one, He is many: one, through love: many, on account of His extension. Therefore we now pray, we now run: now, if any man hath used to be otherwise, and lived differently, let him eat ashes as it were bread, and mingle his drink with weeping. Now is the time, when Sion is in building: now the stones are entering into the structure: when the building is finished, and the house dedicated, why dost thou run, to ask when too late, to beg in vain, to knock to no purpose, doomed to abide without with the five foolish virgins?[9] Therefore now run.

19. "Let these things be written for those that come after" (ver. 18). When these words were written, they profited not so much those among whom they were written: for they were written to prophesy the New Testament, among men who lived according to the Old Testament. But God had both given that Old Testament, and had settled in that land of promise His own people. But since "Thy remembrance is from generation to generation," belongeth not to the ungodly, but to the righteous; "in our generation" belongeth to the Old Testament; while "in the other generation" belongeth to the New Testament; and since the New Testament announceth this that was prophesied, "Let these things be written for those that come after: and the people which shall be created, shall praise the Lord." Not the people which is created, but "the people which shall be created." What is clearer, my brethren? Here is prophesied that creation of which the Apostle saith:

---

[1] Ps. i. 4.　　　[2] Ps. ciii. 14.　　　[3] *Formata et formosa.*
[4] Acts ii. 41, iv. 32.　　　[5] Eph. ii. 20.

[6] Isa. liii. 2.　　　[7] Matt. xxv. 31.
[8] Zech. xii. 10.　　　[9] Matt. xxv. 12.

"Therefore if any man be in Christ, he is a new creature; old things are passed away; behold, all things are become new." [1] "For he hath looked down from His lofty sanctuary." He hath looked down from on high, that He might come unto the humble: from on high He hath become humble, that He might exalt the humble. . . .

20. "Out of the heaven did the Lord look down upon the earth" (ver. 19): "that He might hear the mournings of such as are in fetters, and deliver the children of such as are put to death" (ver. 20). We have found it said in another Psalm, "O let the sorrowful sighs of the fettered come before Thee;" [2] and in a passage where the voice of the martyrs was meant. Whence are the martyrs in fetters? . . . But God had bound them with these fetters, hard indeed and painful for a season, but endurable on account of His promises, unto whom it is said, "On account of the words of Thy lips, I have kept hard ways." We must indeed groan in these fetters in order to gain the mercy of God. These fetters must not be shunned, in order to gain a destructive freedom and the temporal and brief pleasure of this life, to be followed by perpetual bitterness. Accordingly Scripture,[3] that we may not refuse the fetters of wisdom, thus addresseth us: ". . . Then shall her fetters be a strong defence for thee, and her chains a robe of glory." Let the fettered therefore cry out, as long as they are in the chains of the discipline of God, in which the martyrs have been tried: the fetters shall be loosed, and they shall fly away, and these very fetters shall afterwards be turned into an ornament. This hath happened with the martyrs. For what have the persecutors effected by killing them, except that their fetters were thereby loosed, and turned into crowns? . . . The remission of sins, is the loosing. For what would it have profited Lazarus, that he came forth from the tomb, unless it were said to him, "loose him, and let him go"? [4] Himself indeed with His voice aroused him from the tomb, Himself restored his life by crying unto him, Himself overcame the mass of earth that was heaped upon the tomb, and he came forth bound hand and foot: not therefore with his own feet, but by the power of Him who drew him forth. This taketh place in the heart of the penitent: when thou hearest a man is sorry for his sins, he hath already come again to life; when thou hearest him by confessing [5] lay bare his conscience, he is already drawn forth from the tomb, but he is not as yet loosed. When is he loosed, and by whom is he loosed? "Whatsoever thou shalt loose on earth,"

He saith, "shall be loosed in Heaven." [6] Forgiveness of sins may justly be granted by the Church: but the dead man himself cannot be aroused except by the Lord crying within him; for God doth this within him. We speak to your ears: how do we know what may be going on in your hearts? But what is going on within, is not our doing, but His.[7]

21. "That the name of the Lord may be declared in Sion" (ver. 21). For at first, when the fettered were appointed unto death, the Church was oppressed: since these tribulations the Name of the Lord has been declared in Sion, with great freedom, in the Church herself. For she is Sion: not that one spot, at first proud, afterwards taken captive; but the Sion whose shadow was that Sion, which signifieth a watch-tower; because when placed in the flesh, we see into the things before us, extending ourselves not to the present which is now, but to the future. Thus it is a watch-tower: for every watcher gazes far. Places where guards are set, are termed watch-towers: these are set on rocks, on mountains, in trees, that a wider prospect may be commanded from a higher eminence. Sion therefore is a watch-tower, the Church is a watch-tower. . . . If therefore the Church be a watch-tower, the Name of the Lord is already declared there. Not the Lord's Name only is declared in that Sion, but "His praise," He saith, "in Jerusalem."

22. And how is it declared? "In the nations gathering together in one, and the kingdoms, that they may serve the Lord" (ver. 22). How is this accomplished, unless by the blood of the slain? How accomplished, but by the groans of the fettered? Those therefore who were in tribulation and humility have been heard; that in our times the Church might be in the great glory which we see her in, so that the very kingdoms which then persecuted her, now serve the Lord.

23. "She answered Him in the way of His strength" (ver. 23). . . . The preceding words show, that either "His praise," or "Jerusalem," answered: for it was said, "And His praise in Jerusalem; in the nations gathering together in one, and the kingdoms, that they may serve the Lord. *Respondit ei.*" We cannot say, "the kingdoms answered," for he would have said *responderunt. Respondit ei.* We cannot say, "the nations answered," for he would have said, *responderunt* (in the plural). Since then it is *Respondit ei*, in the singular, we look for the singular number above, and find that the words, "His praise," and "Jerusalem," are the

---

[1] 2 Cor. v. 17.   [2] Ps. lxxix. 11.
[3] Eccles. vi. 24-32.   [4] John xi. 44.
[5] [Public confession, the ancient discipline. A. N. F. vol. iii. pp. 666, 667. — C.]

[6] Matt. xv. 19.
[7] [Note this distinction between what the Church may do in restoring to communion, and what Christ only can do in cleansing the conscience. — C.]

only words in which we find it. But since it is
doubtful, whether it be " His praise," or " Jerusalem," let us expound it each way. How did
" His praise " answer Him? When they who
are called by Him thank Him. For He calleth,
we answer; not by our voice, but by our faith;
not by our tongue, but by our life. . . . From
His elect and holy men, Jerusalem also answereth Him. For Jerusalem also was called: and
the first Jerusalem refused to hear, and it was
said unto her, " Behold, thy house shall be left
unto the desolate." [1] . . . But that Jerusalem, of
whom it was written, " Sing, O barren, thou that
didst not bear," [2] " She hath answered Him."
What meaneth, " She hath answered Him "?
She despiseth Him not when He called. He
sent rain, She gave fruit.

24. " She answered Him: " but where? " in
the path of His strength." . . . The Church
therefore answered Him not in the way of weakness; because after His resurrection He called
the Church from the whole world, no longer
weak upon the cross, but strong in heaven. For
it is not the praise of the Christian faith that
they believe that Christ died, but that they
believe that He arose from the dead. Even the
Pagan believeth that He died; and maketh this
a charge against thee, that thou hast believed in
one dead. What then is thy praise? It is that
thou believest that Christ arose from the dead,
and that thou dost hope that thou shalt rise
from the dead through Christ: this is the praise
of faith. " For if thou shalt confess with thy
mouth that Jesus is the Lord, and shalt believe
in thy heart that God hath raised Him from
the dead, thou shalt be saved." [3] . . . This is the
faith of Christians. In this faith then, in which
the Church is gathered, " She hath answered
Him," She gave Him worship according to His
commandments: " in the path of His strength,"
not in the path of His weakness.

25. How she answered Him, ye have already
heard above. " In the gathering of the nations
into one." Herein she answered Him, in unity:
he who is not in unity, answereth Him not.
For He is One, the Church is unity: none but
unity answereth to Him who is One. . . . Since
some [4] were destined to say against her, She
hath existed, and no longer doth exist; " Show
me," He saith, " the shortness of my days,"
what is it, that I know not what apostates from
me murmur against me? why is it that lost men
contend that I have perished? For they surely
say this, that I have been, and no longer am:
" Show me the shortness of my days." I do not
ask from Thee about those everlasting days:
they are without end, where I shall be; it is
not those I ask of: I ask of temporal days;

show unto me my temporal days; " show me
the shortness," not the eternity, " of my days."
Declare unto me, how long I shall be in this
world: on account of those who say, " She hath
been," and is no more: on account of those
who say, The Scriptures are fulfilled, all nations
have believed, but the Church hath become
apostate, and hath perished from among all
nations. . . .

26. Seest thou not that there are still nations
among whom the Gospel hath not been preached?
Since then it is needful that what the Lord spoke
shall be fulfilled, declaring unto the Church the
shortness of my days, that this Gospel be
preached in all nations, and then that the end
may come, why is it that thou sayest that the
Church hath already perished from among all
nations, when the Gospel is being preached for
this purpose, that it may be in all nations?
Therefore the Church remaineth even unto the
end of the world, in all nations; and this is the
shortness of Her days, because all that is limited
is short; so that She may pass into eternity from
this brief existence. May heretics be lost,[5] may
that which they are lost, and may they be
found, that they may be what they are not.
Shortness of days will be unto the end of the
world: shortness for this reason, because the
whole of this season, I say not from this day
unto the end of the world, but from Adam down
to the end of the world, is a mere drop compared with eternity.

27. Let not therefore heretics flatter themselves
against me, because I said, " the shortness of my
days," as if they would not last down to the end
of the world. For what hath he added? " O
my God, take me not away in the midst of my
days " (ver. 24). Deal Thou not with me according as heretics speak. Lead me on unto the end
of the world, not only to the middle of my days;
and finish my short days, that Thou mayest
afterwards grant unto me eternal days. Wherefore then hast thou asked concerning the shortness of thy days? Wherefore? Dost thou wish
to hear? " Thy years are in the generation of
generations." This is why I asked concerning
those short days, because although my days
should endure unto the end of the world, yet
they are short in comparison of Thy days. For
" Thy years are in the generation of generations."
Wherefore doth he not say, Thy years are unto
worlds of worlds; for thus rather is eternity
usually signified in the holy Scriptures; but he
saith, " Thy years are in the generation of generations "? But what are thy years? what, but
those which do not come, and then pass away?
what, but they which come not, so as to cease
again? For every day in this season so cometh

---

[1] Matt. xxiii. 38.   [2] Isa. liv. 1; Gal. iv. 27.
[3] Rom. x. 9, 10.   [4] [i.e. the party of Donatus. — C.]

[5] Pereant.

as to cease again; every hour, every month, every year; nothing of these is stationary; before it hath come, it is to be; after it hath come, it will not be. Those everlasting years of thine, therefore, those years that are not changed, "are in the generation of generations." There is a "generation of generations;" in that shall thy years be. There is one such, and if we acknowledge it aright, we shall be in it, and the years of God shall be in us. How shall they be in us? Just as God Himself shall be in us: whence it is said, "That God may be all in all." [1] For the years of God, and God Himself, are not different: but the years of God are the eternity of God: eternity is the very substance of God, which hath nothing changeable; there nothing is past, as if it were no longer: nothing is future, as if it existed not as yet. There is nothing there but, Is: there is not there, Was, and Will be; because what was, is now no longer: and what will be, is not as yet: but whatever is there, simply Is. . . . Behold this great I AM! What is man's being to this? To this great I AM, what is man, whatever he be? Who can understand that TO BE? who can share it? who can pant, aspire, presume that he may be there? Despair not, human frailty! "I am," He saith, "the God of Abraham, and the God of Isaac, and the God of Jacob." Thou hast heard what I am in Myself: now hear what I am on thy account. This eternity then hath called us, and the Word burst forth from eternity. It is now eternity, it is now the Word, and no longer time.

28. . . . From so many generations thou wilt gather together all the holy offspring of all generations, and wilt form one generation thence: "In" this "generation of generations are Thy years," that is, that eternity will be in that generation, which is collected from all generations, and reduced into one; this shall share in Thy eternity. Other generations are born for fulfilling their times, out of which this one is regenerated for ever; though changed it shall be endued with life, it shall be fitted to bear Thee, receiving strength from Thee.

29. "Thou, Lord, in the beginning hast laid the foundation of the earth: and the Heavens are the work of Thy hands" (ver. 25). . . . God laid the foundation of the earth, we know: the heavens are the works of His hands. For do not imagine that God doth one thing with His hand, another by His word. What He doth by His word, He doth by His hand: for He hath not distinct bodily members, who said, "I Am That I Am." And perhaps His Word is His hand, assuredly His hand is His power. For inasmuch as it is said, "Let there be a firmament," [2] and there was a firmament; He is

understood to have created it by His Word; but when He said, "Let Us make man in Our image, after Our likeness;" [3] He seemeth to have created him by His hand. Hear therefore: "The heavens are the work of Thy hands." Lo, what He created by His word, He created also by His hands; because He created them through His excellence, through His power. Observe rather what He created, and seek not to know in what manner He created them. It is much to thee to understand how He created them, since He created thyself so, that thou mayest first be a servant obeying, and afterwards perhaps a friend understanding. [4]

30. "They shall perish, but Thou shalt endure" (ver. 26). The Apostle Peter saith this openly: "By the word of God the heavens were of old," etc. [5] He hath said then that the heavens have already perished by the flood: and we know that the heavens perished as far as the extent of this atmosphere of ours. For the water increased, and filled the whole of that space in which birds fly; thus perished the heavens that are near the earth; those heavens which are meant when we speak of the birds of heaven. But there are heavens of heavens higher than these in the firmament: but whether these also shall perish by fire, or those only which perished also by the flood, is a much harder question among the learned, nor can it easily, especially in a limited space of time, be explained. Let us therefore dismiss or put it off; nevertheless, let us know that these things perish, and that God endureth. . . .

31. Perhaps by the heavens we here may understand, without being far-fetched, the righteous themselves, the saints of God, abiding in whom God hath thundered in His commandments, lightened in His miracles, watered the earth with the wisdom of truth, for "The heavens have declared the glory of God." [6] But shall they perish? Shall they in any sense perish? In what sense? As a garment. [7] What is, as a garment? As to the body. For the body is the garment of the soul; since our Lord called it a garment, when He said, "Is not the life more than meat, and the body than raiment?" [8] How then doth the garment perish? "Though our outward man perish, yet the inward man is renewed day by day." [9] They then shall perish: but as to the body: "But Thou shalt endure." . . . Such heavens therefore shall perish; not, however, for ever; they shall perish, that they may be changed. Doth not the Psalm say this? Read the following: "They shall all wax old as doth a garment; and as a vesture shalt Thou

---

[1] 1 Cor. xv. 28.   [2] Gen. i. 6.

[3] Gen. i. 26.   [4] John xv. 15.
[5] 2 Pet. iii. 5, 6.   [6] Ps. xix. 7.
[7] Or, "as to the garment," *secundum vestimentum.*
[8] Matt. vi. 25.   [9] 2 Cor. iv. 16.

change them, and they shall be changed." Thou hearest of the garment, of the vesture, and dost thou understand anything but the body? We may therefore hope for the change of our bodies also, but from Him who was before us, and abideth after us. . . . "But Thou art the same, and Thy years shall not fail" (ver. 27). But what are we to those years with these beggarly years? and what are they? Yet we ought not to despair. He had already said in His great and exceeding Wisdom, "I Am That I Am;" and yet He saith to console us, "I am the God of Abraham, and the God of Isaac, and the God of Jacob:"[1] and we are Abraham's seed:[2] even we, although abject, although dust and ashes, trust in Him. We are servants: but for our sakes our Lord took the garb of a servant:[3] for us who are mortal the Immortal One deigned to die, for our sakes He showed His example of resurrection. Let us therefore hope that we may reach these lasting years, in which days are not spent in a revolution of the Sun, but what is abideth even as it is, because it alone truly Is.

32. "The children of Thy servants shall dwell there: and their seed shall stand fast for ages" (ver. 28): for the age of ages, the age of eternity, the age that abideth. But, "the children," he saith, "of Thy servants:" is it to be feared lest we be the servants of God, and our children, and not ourselves, dwell there? Or if we are the children of the servants, inasmuch as we are the Apostles' children, what are we to say? Can those children rising after have so unhappy a presumption, as to boast in their late succession, and so to venture to say, We shall be there; the Apostles will not be there? May this be far from their piety as children, from their faith as little ones, from their understanding when of age! The Apostles also will be there: rams go before, lambs follow. Wherefore then, "the children of Thy servants;" and not in brief, "Thy servants"? Both they are Thy servants, and their children are Thy servants; and the children of these, their grandsons, what are they but Thy servants? Thou wouldest include them all briefly, if Thou shouldest say, Thy servants shall dwell therein. . . . "The children of Thy servants," are the works of Thy servants; no one shall dwell there, but through his own works. What therefore meaneth, Their children shall dwell? Let no man boast that he shall dwell there, if he calleth himself God's servant, and hath not works; for none but children shall dwell there. What meaneth therefore, "The children of Thy servants shall dwell there"? Thy servants shall dwell there by their own works, Thy servants

shall dwell there through their own children. Be not therefore barren, if thou dost wish to dwell there; send before the children whom thou mayest follow, by sending them before thee, not by burying them. Let thy children lead thee to the land of promise, the land of the living, not of the dying: whilst thou art living here in this pilgrimage, let them go before thee, let them receive thee. . . .

PSALM CIII.[4]

1. . . . "Bless the Lord, O my soul! and all that is within me, His holy Name" (ver. 1). I suppose that he speaketh not of what is within the body; I do not suppose him to mean this, that our lungs and liver, and so forth, are to burst forth into the voice of blessing of the Lord. There are lungs in our breast indeed, like a kind of bellows, which send forth successive breathings, which breathing forth of the air inhaled is pressed out into voice and sound, when the words are articulated; nor can any utterance sound forth from our mouth, but what the pressed lungs have given vent to; but this is not the meaning here; all this relateth to the ears of men. God hath ears: the heart also hath a voice. A man speaketh to the things within him, that they may bless God, and saith unto them, "all that is within me bless His holy Name!" Dost thou ask the meaning of what is within thee? Thy soul itself. In saying then, "all that is within me, bless His holy Name," it only repeateth the above, "Bless the Lord, O my soul:" for the word "Bless," is understood. Cry out with thy voice, if there be a man to hear; hush thy voice, when there is no man to hear thee; there is never wanting one to hear all that is within thee. Blessing therefore hath already been uttered from our mouth, when we were chanting these very words. We sung as much as sufficed for the time, and were then silent: ought our hearts within us to be silent to the blessing of the Lord? Let the sound of our voices bless Him at intervals, alternately, let the voice of our hearts be perpetual. When thou comest to church to recite a hymn, thy voice soundeth forth the praises of God: thou hast sung as far as thou couldest, thou hast left the church; let thy soul sound the praises of God. Thou art engaged in thy daily work: let thy soul praise God. Thou art taking food; see what the Apostle saith: "Whether ye eat or drink, do all to the glory of God."[5] I venture to say; when thou sleepest, let thy soul praise the Lord. Let not thoughts of crime arouse thee, let not the contrivances of thieving arouse thee, let not arranged plans of corrupt

---

[1] Exod. iii. 6.   [2] Gal. iii. 29.   [3] Philip. ii. 7.

[4] Lat. CII. A sermon delivered on a feast of the Martyrs.
[5] 1 Cor. x. 31.

dealing arouse thee. Thy innocence even when thou art sleeping is the voice of thy soul.

2. "Bless the Lord, O my soul, and forget not all His rewards" (ver. 2). But the rewards of the Lord cannot be before thine eyes unless thy sins are before thine eyes. Let not delight in past sin be before thine eyes, but let the condemnation of sin be before thine eyes: condemnation from thee, forgiveness from God. For thus God rewardeth thee, so that thou mayest say, "How shall I reward the Lord for all His rewards unto me?"[1] This it was that the martyrs considering (whose memory we are this day celebrating), and all the saints who have despised this life, and as ye have heard in the Epistle of St. John, laid down their lives for the brethren, which is the perfection of love,[2] even as our Lord saith: "Greater love hath no man than this, that a man lay down his life for his friends:"[3] this the holy martyrs, then, considering, despised their lives here, that they might find them there, following our Lord's words when He said, "He that loveth his life, shall lose it; and he that loseth his life for My sake, shall keep it unto life eternal."[4] . . . "Forget not," he saith, "all His rewards:" not awards, but "rewards."[5] For something else was due, and what was not due hath been paid. Whence also these words: "What," he asketh, "shall I reward the Lord for all His rewards unto me?" Thou hast rewarded good with evil; He rewardeth evil with good. How hast thou, O man, rewarded thy God with evil for good? Thou who hast once been a blasphemer, and a persecutor, and injurious,[6] hast rewarded blasphemies. For what good things? First, because thou art: but a stone also is. Next, because thou livest: but a brute also liveth. What reward wilt thou give the Lord, for His having created thee above all the cattle; and above all the fowls of the air, in His image and likeness?[7] Seek not how to reward Him: give back unto Him His own image: He requireth no more; He demandeth His own coin.[8] . . .

3. Think thou, soul, of all the rewards of God, in thinking over all thy wicked deeds: for as many as are thy sins, so many are His rewards of good. And what present, what offering, what sacrifice, canst thou ever tender unto Him? . . . What wilt thou reward the Lord with? For thou wast reflecting, and couldest not find: "I will receive the cup of salvation." What? hath not the Lord Himself given the cup of salvation? Reward Him from thine own, if thou canst. I would say, No, do it not; reward Him not from thine own; God doth not will to be rewarded from thine own. If thou rewardest Him from thine own, thou rewardest sin. For all that thou hast thou hast from Him: sins only thou hast of thine own. He doth not wish to be rewarded from thine, He doth will from His own. Just as, if thou shouldest bring to a husbandman, from the land which he hath sown, an ear of wheat, thou hast rewarded him from the husbandman's own produce; if thorns, that hast offered him of thine own. Reward truth, in truth praise the Lord: if thou shalt choose to reward Him from thine own, thou wilt lie. He who speaketh a lie, speaketh of his own.[9] If he who speaketh a lie, speaketh of his own: so he who speaketh truth, speaketh of the Lord's. But what is to receive the cup of salvation, but to imitate the Passion of our Lord? . . . I will receive the cup of Christ, I will drink of our Lord's Passion. Beware that thou fail not. But, "I will call upon the Name of the Lord." They then who failed, called not upon the Lord; they presumed in their own strength. Do thou so return, as remembering that thou art returning what thou hast received. So then let thy soul bless the Lord, as not to forget all His rewards.

4. Hear ye all His rewards. "Who forgiveth all thy sin: who healeth all thine infirmities" (ver. 3). Behold His rewards. What, save punishment, was due unto the sinner? What was due to the blasphemer, but the hell of burning fire? He gave not these rewards: that thou mayest not shudder with dread: and without love fear Him. . . . But thou art a sinner. Turn again, and receive these His rewards: He "forgiveth all thy sin." . . . Yet even after remission of sins the soul herself is shaken by certain passions; still is she amid the dangers of temptation, still is she pleased with certain suggestions; with some she is not pleased, and sometimes she consenteth unto some of those with which she is pleased: she is taken. This is infirmity: but He "healeth all thine infirmities." All thine infirmities shall be healed: fear not. They are great, thou wilt say: but the Physician is greater. No infirmity cometh before the Almighty Physician as incurable: only suffer thou thyself to be healed: repel not His hands; He knoweth how to deal with thee. Be not only pleased when He cherisheth thee, but also bear with Him when He useth the knife: bear the pain of the remedy, reflecting on thy future health. . . . Thou dost not endure in uncertainty: He who promised thee health, cannot be deceived. The physician is often deceived: and promiseth health in the human body. Why is he deceived? Because he is not healing his own creature. God made thy body, God made thy soul. He knoweth how to restore what He

---

[1] Ps. cxvi. 12. [2] 1 John iii. 16.
[3] John xv. 13. [4] John xii. 25; Matt. x. 39.
[5] *Non tributiones, sed retributiones.* [6] 1 Tim. i. 13.
[7] Gen. i. 26, 27. [8] Matt. xxii. 21.

[9] John viii. 44.

hath made, He knoweth how to fashion again what He hath already fashioned: do thou only be patient beneath the Physician's hands: for He hateth one who rejects His hands. This doth not happen with the hands of a human physician. . . .

5. "Who redeemeth thy life from corruption" (ver. 4). Behold, "the body which is corrupted, weigheth down the soul."[1] The soul then hath life in a corruptible body. What sort of life? It suffereth burdens, it beareth weights. How great obstacles are there to thinking of God Himself, as it is right that men should think of God, as if interrupting us from the necessity of human corruption? how many influences recall us, how many interrupt, how many withdraw the mind when fixed on high? what a crowd of illusions, what tribes of suggestions? All this in the human heart, as it were, teemeth with the worms of human corruption. We have set forth the greatness of the disease, let us also praise the Physician. Shall not He then heal thee, who made thee such as to be in health, hadst thou chosen to keep the law of health which thou hadst received? . . . First think of thine own health. Sometimes a man is stricken in his own house, on his bed, with a more than usually manifest disorder; although this disorder too, which men dislike to contemplate, be plain; yet each man may be attacked with that sickness for which human physicians are sought, and may gasp with fever in his bed; perhaps he may wish to consider of his domestic affairs, to make some order or disposition relating to his estate or his house; at once he is recalled from such cares by the anxiety of his friends, plainly expressed around him, and he is advised to dismiss these subjects, and first to take thought for his health. This then is addressed unto thee, and to all men: if thou art not sick, think of other things: if thy very infirmity prove thee sick, first take heed of thy health. Christ is thy health: think therefore of Christ. Receive the cup of His saving Health, "who healeth all thine infirmities;" if thou shalt choose, thou shalt gain this Health. . . . For thy life hath been redeemed from corruption: rest secure now: the contract of good faith hath been entered upon; no man deceives, no man circumvents, no man oppresses, thy Redeemer. He hath here made a barter, He hath already paid the price, He hath poured forth His blood. The only Son of God, I say, hath shed His blood for us: O soul, raise thyself, thou art of so great price. . . . "He redeemeth thy life from corruption."

6. "Who crowneth thee with mercy and loving-kindness." Thou hadst perhaps begun to be in a manner proud, when thou didst hear the words, "He crowneth thee." I am then great, I have then wrestled. By whose strength? By thine, but supplied by Him. . . . He crowneth thee, because He is crowning His own gifts, not thy deservings. "I laboured more abundantly than they all," said the Apostle; but see what he addeth: "yet not I, but the grace of God which was with me."[2] . . . It·is then by His mercy that thou art crowned; in nothing be proud; ever praise the Lord; forget not all His rewards. It is a reward when thou, a sinner and an ungodly man, hast been called, that thou mayest be justified. It is a reward, when thou art raised up and guided, that thou mayest not fall. It is a reward, when strength is given thee, that thou mayest persevere unto the end. It is a reward, that even that flesh of thine by which thou wast oppressed riseth again, and that not even a hair of thy head perisheth. It is a reward, that after thy resurrection thou art crowned. It is a reward, that thou mayest praise God Himself for evermore without ceasing. . . .

7. After the battle, then, I shall be crowned; after the crown, what shall I do? "He who satisfieth thy longing with good things" (ver. 5). . . . Seek thy own good, O soul. For one thing is good to one creature, another to another, and all creatures have a certain good of their own, to the completeness and perfection of their nature. There is a difference as to what is essential to each imperfect thing, in order that it may be made perfect; seek for thy own good. "There is none good but One, that is, God."[3] The highest good is thy good. What then is wanting unto him to whom the highest good is good? For there are inferior goods, which are good to different creatures respectively. What, brethren, is good unto the cattle, save to fill the belly, to prevent want, to sleep, to indulge themselves, to exist, to be in health, to propagate? This is good to them: and within certain bounds it hath an allotted measure of good, granted by God, the Creator of all things. Dost thou seek such a good as this? God giveth also this: but do not pursue it alone. Canst thou, a coheir of Christ, rejoice in fellowship with cattle? Raise thy hope to the good of all goods. He will be thy good, by whom thou in thy kind hast been made good, and by whom all things in their kind were made good. For God made all things very good. . . .

8. When shall my longing be satisfied with good things? when, dost thou ask? "Thy youth shall be renewed as the eagle's." Dost thou then ask when thy soul is to be satisfied with good things? When thy youth shall be restored. And he addeth, as an eagle's. Something here

[1] Wisd. ix. 15.   [2] 1 Cor. xv. 10.   [3] Matt. xix. 17.

lieth hidden; what however is said of the eagle, we will not pass over silently, since it is not foreign to our purpose to understand it. Let this only be impressed upon our hearts, that it is not said without cause by the Holy Spirit. For it hath intimated unto us a sort of resurrection. And indeed the youth of the eagle is restored, but not into immortality, for a similitude hath been given, as far as it could be drawn from a thing mortal to signify a thing immortal, not to demonstrate it. The eagle is said, after it becometh overpowered with bodily age, to be incapable of taking food from the immoderate length of its beak, which is always increasing. For after the upper part of its beak, which forms a crook above the lower part, hath increased from old age to an immoderate length, the length of this increase will not allow of its opening its mouth, so as to form any interval between the lower beak and the crook above. For unless there be such an opening, it hath no power of biting like a forceps, by which to shear off what it may put within its jaws. The upper part therefore increasing, and being too far hooked over, it cannot open its mouth, and take any food. This old age doth to it, it is weighed down with the infirmity of age, and becometh too weak from want of power to eat; two causes of infirmity assaulting it, old age, and want. By a natural device, therefore, in order in some measure to restore its youth, the eagle is said to dash and strike against a rock the upper lip of its beak, by the too great increase of which the opening for eating is closed: and by thus rubbing it against the rock, it breaketh off the weight of its old beak, which impeded its taking food. It cometh to its food, and everything is restored: it will be after its old age like a young eagle; the vigour of all its limbs returneth, the lustre of its plumage, the guidance of its wings, it flieth aloft as before, a sort of resurrection taketh place in it. For this is the object of the similitude, like that of the Moon, which after waning and being apparently intercepted, again is renewed, and becometh full; and signifieth to us the resurrection; but when it is full it doth not remain so; again it waneth, that the signification may never cease. Thus also what hath here been said of the eagle: the eagle is not restored unto immortality, but we are unto eternal life; but the similitude is derived from hence, that the rock taketh away from us what hindereth us. Presume not therefore on thy strength: the firmness of the rock rubbeth off thy old age: for that Rock was Christ.[1] In Christ our youth shall be restored like that of the eagle. . . .

9. "The Lord executeth mercy and judgment for all them that are oppressed with wrong"

(ver. 6). . . . An adulterous woman is brought forward to be stoned according to the Law, but she is brought before the Lawgiver Himself. . . . Our Lord, at the time she was brought before Him, bending His Head, began writing on the earth. When He bent Himself down upon the earth, He then wrote on the earth: before He bent upon the earth, He wrote not on the earth, but on stone. The earth was now something fertile, ready to bring forth from the Lord's letters. On the stone He had written the Law, intimating the hardness of the Jews: He wrote on the earth, signifying the productiveness of Christians. Then they who were leading the adulteress came, like raging waves against a rock: but they were dashed to pieces by His answer. For He said to them, "He that is without sin among you, let him first cast a stone at her."[2] And again bending His head, He began writing on the ground. And now each man, when he asked his own conscience, came not forward. It was not a weak adulterous woman, but their own adulterate conscience, that drove them back. They wished to punish, to judge; they came to the Rock, their judges were overthrown by the Rock.[3] . . .

10. Execute mercy to[4] the wicked, not as being wicked. Do not receive the wicked, in so far forth as he is wicked: that is, do not receive him as if from inclination towards and love for his iniquity. For it is forbidden to give unto a sinner, and to receive sinners. Yet how is this, "Give unto every man that asketh of thee"? and this, "if thine enemy hunger, feed him"?[5] This is seemingly contradictory: but it is opened to those who knock in the name of Christ, and will be clear unto those who seek. "Help not a sinner:" and, "give not to the ungodly;"[6] and yet, "give unto every man that asketh of thee." But it is a sinner who asketh of me. Give, not as unto a sinner. When dost thou give as unto a sinner? When that which maketh him a sinner, pleaseth thee so that thou givest.[7] . . . Let those who give to a man who fights with wild beasts, tell me why they give? Why doth he give to this man? He loveth that in him, in which consists his greatest sin; this he feedeth, this he clotheth in him, wickedness itself, made public by all witnessing it. Why doth the man give, who giveth to actors, or to charioteers, or to courtesans? Do not these very persons give to human beings? But it is not the nature of God's work that they attend to, but the iniquity of the human work. . . . When therefore thou givest, thou givest to infamy, not to bravery. As then he who giveth to the fighter of beasts, giveth not to the

---

[1] 1 Cor. x. 4.

[2] John viii. 7.
[4] Oxf. MSS. "also to."
[6] Ecclus. xii. 4, 5, 6.
[3] Ps. cxli. 6.
[5] Rom. xii. 20.
[7] Oxf. MSS. add, "thou offendest God."

man, but to a most infamous profession; for if he were only a man, and not a fighter of beasts, thou wouldest not give; thou honourest him in vice, not nature: so on the other hand, if thou give to the righteous, if thou give to the prophet, if thou give to the disciple of Christ anything of which he is in want, without thinking that he is Christ's disciple, that he is God's minister, that he is God's steward; but art thinking in that case of some temporal advantage, for instance, that when perchance he shall be needful to thy cause, he may be bought for thee, because thou hast given him something; thou hast no more given to the righteous, if thou hast thus given, than he gave to the man, when he gave to the beast-fighter. The matter, then, most beloved, is quite open to us, and I conceive, that although it was obscure, it is now clear. It was to this that the Lord bound thee, when He said, "He who hath received the righteous man." That were enough. But as the righteous may be received with another intention, . . . He saith, "He who receiveth a righteous man in the name of a righteous man:"[1] that is, receiving him in consideration of his righteousness: . . . that is, because he is Christ's disciple, because he is a steward of the Mystery:[2] "Verily I say unto you, he shall in no wise lose his reward."[3] So understand, he who receiveth a sinner in the name of a sinner shall lose his reward.

11. . . . On this account therefore be merciful without fear, extend love even unto thine enemies: punish those who chance to belong to thy government, restrain them with affection, with charity, in regard to their eternal salvation; lest while thou sparest the flesh, the soul perish. Do this: and though thou have to endure many,[4] over whom thou canst not exercise discipline, because thou hast no lawful authority over them; bear their injuries; be without apprehension. He will show mercy unto thee if thou shalt have been merciful: thou shalt be merciful, without the injuries thou sufferest losing their punishment; "To Me belongeth vengeance, I will repay,"[5] saith the Lord.

12. "He made His ways known unto Moses" (ver. 7). . . . For the Law was given with this view, that the sick might be convinced of his infirmity, and pray for the physician. This is the hidden way of God. Thou hadst long ago heard, "Who healeth all thine infirmities." Their infirmities were as yet hidden in the sick; the five books were given to Moses: the pool was surrounded by five porches; he brought

forth the sick, that they might lie there, that they might be made known, not that they might be healed. The five porches discovered, but healed not, the sick; the pool healed when one descended, and this when it was disturbed:[6] the disturbance of the pool was in our Lord's Passion. . . . Since therefore this is a mystery there, he teacheth that the Law was given that sinners might be convinced of their sin, and call upon the Physician in order to receive grace. . . . Therefore, as I had begun to say, because this is a great mystery in the Law, that it was given with this view, that by the increase of sin, the proud might be humbled, the humbled might confess, the confessing might be healed; these are the hidden ways, which He made known to Moses, through whom He gave the Law, by which sin should abound, that grace might more abound. . . . "He hath made known His good pleasure unto the children of Israel." To all the children of Israel? To the true children of Israel; yea, to all the children of Israel. For the treacherous, the insidious, the hypocrites, are not children of Israel. And who are the children of Israel? "Behold an Israelite indeed, in whom is no guile."[7]

13. "The Lord is full of compassion and mercy: long-suffering, and of great mercy" (ver. 8). Why so long-suffering? Why so great in mercy? Men sin and live; sins are added on, life continueth: men blaspheme daily, and "He maketh His sun to rise over the good and the wicked."[8] On all sides He calleth to amendment, on all sides He calleth to repentance, He calleth by the blessings of creation, He calleth by giving time for life, He calleth through the reader, He calleth through the preacher, He calleth through the innermost thought by the rod of correction, He calleth by the mercy of consolation: "He is long-suffering, and of great mercy." But take heed lest by ill using the length of God's mercy, thou treasure up for thyself, as the Apostle saith, wrath in the day of wrath. . . . For some there are who prepare to turn, and yet put it off, and in them crieth out the raven's voice, "Cras! Cras!"[9] The raven which was sent from the ark, never returned.[10] God seeketh not procrastination in the raven's voice, but confession in the wailing of the dove. The dove, when sent forth, returned. How long, To-morrow! To-morrow!? Look to thy last morrow: since thou knowest not what is thy last morrow, let it suffice that thou hast lived up to this day a sinner. Thou hast heard, often thou art wont to hear, thou hast heard to-day also; daily thou hearest, and daily thou amendest not. . . .

14. "He will not alway be chiding: neither

---

[1] Oxf. mss. add, "shall receive a righteous man's reward."
[2] 1 Cor. iv. 1.   [3] Matt. x. 42.
[4] Oxf. mss. and 5 ap. Ben. *non inultus.* "Do this, and thou wilt not without revenge endure those unrighteous on which thou canst not exercise discipline."
[5] Deut. xxxii. 35.

[6] John v. 2-4.   [7] John i. 47.   [8] Matt. v. 45.
[9] "To-morrow! To-morrow!"   [10] Gen. viii. 7.

keepeth He His anger for ever" (ver. 9). Since it is in consequence of His anger that we live in the scourges and corruption [1] of mortality : we have this in punishment for the first sin. . . . Is it not through His anger, my brethren, that "in the sweat of thy face and in toil thou shalt eat bread, and the earth shall bear thorns and thistles unto thee "? [2] This was said to our fore-fathers. Or if our life is different from this ; if thou canst, turn unto some pleasure, where thou mayest not feel thorns. Choose what thou hast wished, whether thou art covetous or luxurious ; to name these two alone ; add a third passion, that of ambition ; how great thorns are there in the desire of honours ? in the luxury of lusts how great thorns? in the ardour of covetousness how great thorns? What troubles are there in base loves? What terrible anxieties here in this life? I omit hell. Beware lest thou even now become a hell unto thyself. The whole of this, my brethren, is the result of His anger : and when thou hast turned thyself unto works of righteous-ness, thou canst not but toil upon earth ; and toil endeth not before life endeth. We must toil on the way, that we may rejoice in our country. He therefore consoleth by His promises thy toil, thy labours, thy troubles, saying to thee, " He will not alway be chiding."

15. " He hath not dealt with us according to our sins " (ver. 10). Thanks unto God, because He hath vouchsafed this. We have not received what we were deserving of : " He hath not dealt with us according to our sins, nor rewarded us according to our wickednesses." " For as the height of heaven above the earth, so hath the Lord confirmed His mercy toward them that fear Him " (ver. 11). Observe the heaven : everywhere on every side it covereth the earth, nor is there any part of the earth not covered by the heaven. Men sin beneath heaven : they do all evil deeds beneath the heaven ; yet they are covered by the heaven. Thence is light for the eyes, thence air, thence breath, thence rain upon the earth for the sake of its fruits, thence all mercy from heaven. Take away the aid of heaven from the earth : it will fail at once. As then the protection of heaven abideth upon the earth, so doth the Lord's protection abide upon them that fear Him. Thou fearest God, His protection is above thee. But perhaps thou art scourged, and conceivest that God hath forsaken thee. God hath forsaken thee, [3] if the protection of heaven hath forsaken the earth.

16. " Look, how wide the east is from the west ; so far hath He set our sins from us " (ver. 12). They who know the Sacraments know this ; nevertheless, I only say what all may hear. [4] When sin is remitted, thy sins fall, thy grace riseth ; thy sins are as it were on the decline, thy grace which freeth thee on the rise. " Truth springeth from the earth." [5] What mean-eth this? Thy grace is born, thy sins fall, thou art in a certain manner made new. Thou shouldest look to the rising, and turn away from the setting. [6] Turn away from thy sins, turn unto the grace of God ; when thy sins fall, thou riseth and profitest. . . . One region of the heaven falleth, another riseth : but the region which is now rising will set after twelve hours. Not like this is the grace which riseth unto us : both our sins fall for ever, and grace abideth for ever.

17. " Yea, like as a father pitieth his own children, even so hath the Lord had mercy on them that fear Him " (ver. 13). Let Him be as angry as He shall will, He is our Father. But He hath scourged us, and afflicted us, and bruised us : He is our Father. Son, if thou bewailest, wail beneath thy Father ; do not so with indignation, do not so with the puffing up of pride. What thou sufferest, whence thou mournest, it is medicine, not punishment ; it is thy chastening, not thy condemnation. Do not refuse the scourge, if thou dost not wish to be refused thy heritage : do not think of what pun-ishment thou sufferest in the scourge, but what place thou hast in the Testament.

18. " For He knoweth our forming " [7] (ver. 14) : that is, our infirmity. He knoweth what He hath created, how it hath fallen, how it may be repaired, how it may be adopted, how it may be enriched. Behold, we are made of clay : " The first man is of the earth, earthy : the second man is the Lord from heaven." [8] He sent even His own Son, Him who was made the second man, Him who was God before all things. For He was second in His coming, first in His returning : He died after many, He arose before all. " He knoweth our forming." What forming? Ourselves. Why sayest thou that He knoweth? Because He hath pitied. " Remember that we are but dust." Addressing God Himself, he saith, " Remember," as if God could forget : He perceiveth, He knoweth in such a manner that He cannot forget. But what meaneth, " Remember "? Let thy mercy con-tinue towards us. Thou knowest our forming ; forget not our forming, lest we forget thy grace.

19. " Man, his days are but as grass " (ver. 15). Let man consider what he is ; let not man be proud. " His days are but as grass." Why is the grass proud, that is now flourishing, and in a very short space dried up? Why is the

---

[1] Oxf. MSS. " correction."
[2] Gen. iii 19, 18.
[3] Oxf. MSS. repeat this : " God hath forsaken thee."

[4] [Referring to the privacy with which the Sacraments were celebrated. —C.]
[5] Ps. lxxxv. 11.
[6] They looked toward the west, while they renounced Satan before Baptism, and then turned away to the east. See St. Cyril's *Catechetical Lectures*, lect. xix. Tr. p. 259.
[7] *Figmentum nostrum.*
[8] 1 Cor. xv. 47.

grass proud that flourisheth only for a brief season, until the sun be hot? It is then good for us that His mercy be upon us, and from grass make gold. "For he flourisheth as a flower of the field." The whole splendour of the human race; honour, powers, riches, pride, threats, is the flower of the grass. That house flourisheth, and that family is great, that family flourisheth; and how many flourish, and how many years do they live! Many years to thee, are but a short season unto God. God doth not count, as thou dost. Compared with the length and long life of ages, all the flower of any house is as the flower of the field. All the beauty of the year hardly lasteth for the year. Whatever there flourisheth, whatever there is warmed with heat, whatever there is beautiful, lasteth not; nay, it cannot exist for one whole year. In how brief a season do flowers pass away, and these are the beauty of the herbs! This which is so very beautiful, this quickly falleth.[1] Inasmuch then as He knoweth as a father our forming, that we are but grass, and can only flourish for a time; He sent unto us His Word, and His Word, which abideth for evermore, He hath made a brother unto the grass which abideth not. Wonder not that thou shalt be a sharer of His Eternity; He became Himself first a sharer of thy grass. Will He who assumed from thee what was lowly, deny unto thee what is exalted in respect of thee?

20. "The wind shall go over on it, it shall not be; and the place thereof shall know it no more" (ver. 16). For he is not speaking of grass, but of that for whose sake even the Word became grass. For thou art man, and on thy account the Word became man. "All flesh is grass:" "and the Word was made flesh."[2] How great then is the hope of the grass, since the Word hath been made flesh? That which abideth for evermore, hath not disdained to assume grass, that the grass might not despair of itself.

21. In thy reflections therefore on thyself, think of thy low estate, think of thy dust: be not lifted up: if thou art anything better, thou wilt be so by His Grace, thou wilt be so by His mercy. For hear what followeth: "but the mercy of the Lord endureth for ever and ever upon them that fear Him" (ver. 17). Ye who fear not Him, will be grass, and in grass, and in torment with the grass: for the flesh shall arise unto the torment. Let those who fear Him rejoice, because His mercy is upon them.

22. "And His righteousness upon children's children" (ver. 18). He speaketh of reward, "upon children's children." How many servants of God are there who have not children, how much less children's children? But He calleth our works our children; the reward of

works, our "children's children." "Even upon such as keep His covenant." Let men beware that all may not conceive what is here said to belong to themselves: let them choose, while they have the choice. "And keep in memory His commandments to do them." Thou wast already disposed to flatter thyself, and perhaps to recite to me the Psalter, which I have not by heart, or from memory to say over the whole Law. Clearly thou art better in point of memory than I, better than any righteous man who doth not know the Law word for word: but see that thou keep the commandments. But how shouldest thou keep them? Not by memory, but by life. "Such as keep in memory His commandments:" not, to recite them; but, "to do them." And now perhaps each man's soul is disturbed. Who remembereth all the commandments of God? who remembereth all the writings of God? Lo, I wish not only to hold them in my memory, but also to do them in my works: but who remembereth them all? Fear not: He burdeneth thee not: "on two commandments hang all the Law and the Prophets."[3] . . .

23. "The Lord hath prepared His throne in heaven" (ver. 19). Who but Christ hath prepared His throne in heaven? He who descended and ascended, He who died, and rose from the dead, He who lifted up to heaven the manhood He had assumed, hath Himself prepared His throne in heaven. The throne is the seat of the Judge: observe therefore ye who hear, that "He hath prepared His throne in heaven." . . . The kingdom is the Lord's, and He shall be the Governor among the people.[4] "And His kingdom shall rule over all."

24. "Bless ye the Lord, ye Angels of His, ye that are mighty in strength: ye that fulfil His word" (ver. 20). By the word of God, then, thou art not righteous, nor faithful, unless when thou dost it. "Ye that are mighty in strength, ye that fulfil His commandment, and hearken unto the voice of His words."

25. "Bless ye the Lord, all ye His hosts: ye servants of His that do His pleasure" (ver. 21). All ye angels, all ye that are mighty in strength: ye that do His word: all ye His hosts, ye servants of His that do His pleasure, do ye, ye bless the Lord. For all they who live wickedly, though their tongues be silent, by their lips do curse the Lord. What doth it profit if thy tongue singeth a hymn, while thy life breatheth sacrilege? By living ill thou hast set many tongues to blasphemy. Thy tongue is given to the hymn, the tongues of those who behold thee, to blasphemy. If then thou dost wish to bless the Lord, do His word, do His will. . . .

---

[1] Isa. xl. 6-8.　　[2] John i. 14.　　[3] Matt. xxii. 40.　　[4] Ps. xxii. 28.

26. "Bless ye the Lord, all ye works of His, in all places of His dominion" (ver. 22). Therefore in every place. Let Him not be blessed where He ruleth not: "in all places of His dominion." Let no man perchance say: I cannot praise the Lord in the East, because He hath departed unto the West; or, I cannot praise Him in the West, because He is in the East. "For neither from the east, nor from the west, nor yet from the desert hills. And why? God is the Judge."[1] He is everywhere, in such wise that everywhere He may be praised: He is in such wise on every side, that we may be joyful in Him on every side: He is in such wise blessed on every side, that on every side we may live well. . . . "In every place of His dominion: bless thou the Lord, O my soul!" The last verse is the same as the first: blessing is at the head of the Psalm, blessing at the end; from blessing we set out, to blessing let us return, in blessing let us reign.[2]

PSALM CIV.[3]

1. . . . "Bless the Lord, O my soul." Let the soul of us all, made one in Christ, say this. "O Lord my God, Thou art magnified exceedingly!" (ver. 1). Where art Thou magnified? "Confession and beauty Thou hast put on." Confess ye, that ye may be beautified, that He may put you on. "Clothed with light as a garment" (ver. 2). Clothed with His Church, because she is made "light" in Him, who before was darkness in herself, as the apostle saith: "Ye were sometime darkness, but now light in the Lord."[4] "Stretching out the heaven like a skin:" either as easily as thou dost a skin, if it be "as easily," so that thou mayest take it after the letter; or let us understand the authority of the Scriptures, spread out over the whole world, under the name of a skin; because mortality is signified in a skin,[5] but all the authority of the Divine Scriptures was dispensed unto us through mortal men, whose fame is still spreading abroad now they are dead.

2. "Who covereth with waters the upper parts thereof" (ver. 3). The upper parts of what? Of Heaven. What is Heaven? Figuratively only we said, the Divine Scripture. What are the upper parts of the Divine Scripture? The commandment of love, than which there is none more exalted.[6] But wherefore is love compared to waters? Because "the love of God is shed abroad in our hearts by the Holy Spirit who is given unto us."[7] Whence is the Spirit Himself water? because "Jesus stood and cried,

He that believeth on Me, out of his bosom shall flow rivers of living water."[8] Whence do we prove that it was said of the Spirit? Let the Evangelist himself declare, who followeth it up, and saith, "But this spake He of the Spirit, which they were to receive, who should believe on Him." "Who walketh above the wings of the winds;" that is, above the virtues of souls. What is the virtue of a soul? Love itself. But how doth He walk above it? Because the love of God toward us is greater than ours toward God.

3. "Who maketh spirits His angels, and flaming fire His ministers" (ver. 4): that is, those who are already spirits, who are spiritual, not carnal, He maketh His Angels, by sending them to preach His gospel. "And flaming fire His ministers." For unless the minister that preacheth be on fire, he enflameth not him to whom he preacheth.

4. "He hath founded the earth upon its firmness" (ver. 5). He hath founded the Church upon the firmness of the Church. What is the firmness of the Church, but the foundation of the Church. What is the foundation of the Church, but that of which the Apostle saith, "Other foundation can no man lay but that is laid, which is Christ Jesus."[9] And therefore, grounded on such a foundation, what hath she deserved to hear? "It shall not be bowed for-ever and ever." "He founded the earth on its firmness." That is, He hath founded the Church upon Christ the foundation. The Church will totter if the foundation totter; but when shall Christ totter, before whose coming unto us, and taking flesh on Him, "all things were made by Him, and without Him was not anything made;"[10] who holdeth all things by His Majesty,[11] and us by His goodness? Since Christ faileth not, "she shall not be bowed for ever and ever." Where are they[12] who say that the Church hath perished from the world, when she cannot even be bowed. . . .

5. "The deep, like a garment, is its clothing" (ver. 6). Whose? Is it perchance God's? But he had already said of His clothing, "Clothed with light as with a garment."[13] I hear of God clothed in light, and that light, if we will, are we. What is, if we will? if we are no longer darkness. Therefore if God is clothed with light, whose clothing, again, is the deep? For an immense mass of waters is called the deep. All water, all the moist nature, and the substance everywhere shed abroad through the seas, and rivers, and hidden caves, is all together called by one name, the Deep. Therefore we understand the earth, of which he said, "He hath founded the earth." Of it I believe he said, "The deep, like a gar-

---

[1] Ps. lxxv. 6, 7.   [2] One Oxf. MS. adds, "Amen."
[3] Lat. CIII. At Carthage, in his old age.
[4] Eph. v. 8.   [5] [Job xix. 26. — C.]
[6] Mark xii. 31.   [7] Rom. v. 5.

[8] John vii. 37, 38.   [9] 1 Cor. iii. 11.   [10] John i. 3.
[11] Heb. i. 3.   [12] Donatists.   [13] Ps. civ. 2.

ment is its clothing." For the water is as it were the clothing of the earth, surrounding it and covering it. . . .

6. "Above the mountains the waters shall stand:" that is, the clothing of the earth, which is the deep, so increased, that the waters stood even above the mountains. We read of this taking place in the deluge. . . . The Prophet minding to foretell future things, not to relate the past, therefore said it, because he would have it understood that the Church should be in a deluge of persecutions. For there was a time when the floods of persecutors had covered God's earth, God's Church, and had so covered it, that not even those great ones appeared, who are the mountains. For when they fled everywhere, how did they but cease to appear? And perchance of those waters is that saying, "Save me, O God, for the waters are come in even unto my soul."[1] Especially the waters which make the sea, stormy, unfruitful. For whatsoever earth the sea-water may have covered, it will not rather make it fruitful than bring it to barrenness. For there were also mountains beneath the waters, because above the mountains waters stood.[2] . . . Why were the Apostles hidden by flight? Because "above the mountains the waters stood."[2] The power of the waters was great, but how long? Hear what followeth.

7. "From Thy rebuke they shall fly" (ver. 7). And this was done, brethren; from God's rebuke the waters did fly; that is, they went back from pressing on the mountains. Now the mountains themselves stand forth, Peter and Paul: how do they tower! They who before were pressed down by persecutors, now are venerated by emperors. For the waters are fled from the rebuke of God; because "the heart of kings is in the hand of God, He hath bent it whither He would;"[3] He commanded peace to be given by them to the Christians; the authority of the Apostles sprang up and towered high. . . . The waters fled from the rebuke of God. "From the voice of Thy thunder they shall be afraid." Now who is there that would not be afraid, from the voice of God through the Apostles, the voice of God through the Scriptures, through His clouds? The sea is quieted, the waters have been made afraid, the mountains have been laid bare, the emperor hath given the order. But who would have given the order, unless God had thundered? Because God willed, they commanded, and it was done. Therefore let no one of men arrogate anything to himself.

8. "The mountains ascend, and the plains go down, into the place which Thou hast founded for them" (ver. 8). He is still speaking of waters. Let us not here understand mountains as of earth; nor plains, as of earth: but waves so great that they may be compared to mountains. The sea did sometime toss, and its waves were as mountains, which could cover those mountains the Apostles. But how long do the mountains ascend and the plains go down? They raged, and they are appeased. When they raged they were mountains: now they are appeased they are become plains: for He hath founded a place for them. There is a certain channel,[4] as it were a deep place, into which all those lately raging hearts of mortals have retired. . . . They were mountains formerly, now they are plains: yet, my brethren, even a dead calm[5] is sea. For wherefore are they not now violent? wherefore do they not rage? Wherefore do they not try, if they cannot overthrow our earth, at least to cover it? Wherefore not?

9. Hear. "Thou hast set a bound which they shall not pass over, neither shall they turn again to cover the earth" (ver. 9). What then, because now the bitterest waves have received a measure, that we must be allowed to preach such things even with freedom; because they have had their due limit assigned, because they cannot pass over the bound that is set, nor shall they return to cover the earth; what is doing in the earth itself? What workings take place therein, now that the sea hath left it bare? Although at its beach slight waves do make their noise, although Pagans still murmur round; the sound of the shores I hear, a deluge I dread not. What then; what is doing in the earth? "Who sendeth out springs in the little valleys" (ver. 10). "Thou sendest out," he saith, "springs in the little valleys." Ye know what little valleys are, lower places among the lands. For to hills and mountains, valleys and little valleys are opposed in contrary shape. Hills and mountains are swellings of the land: but valleys and little valleys, lownesses of the lands. Do not despise low places, thence flow springs. "Thou sendest out springs in the little valleys." Hear a mountain. The Apostle saith, "I laboured more than they all." A certain greatness is brought before us: yet immediately, that the waters may flow, he hath made himself a valley: "Yet not I, but the grace of God with me."[6] It is no contradiction that they who are mountains be also valleys: for as they are called mountains because of their spiritual greatness, so also valleys because of the humility of their spirit. "Not I," he saith, "but the grace of God with me." . . .

10. What is, "In the midst between the mountains the waters shall pass through"? We have heard who are the "mountains," the great Preach-

---

[1] Ps. lxix. 1.   [2] Oxf. mss. "shall stand."
[3] Prov. xxi. 1.

[4] *Meatus*, Ben. All the mss. *metus*, "a certain fear," which *may* be the true reading.
[5] *Malacia*.   [6] 1 Cor. xv. 10.

ers of the word, the exalted Angels of God, though still in mortal flesh; lofty not by their own power, but by His grace; but as far as relates to themselves, they are valleys, in their humility they send forth springs. "In the midst," he saith, "between the mountains, the waters shall pass through." Let us suppose this said thus, "In the midst between the Apostles shall pass through the preachings of the Word of Truth." What is, in the midst between the Apostles? What is called in the midst, is common. A common property, from which all alike live, is in the midst, and belongs not to me, but neither belongs it to thee, nor yet to me. . . . For if they are not in the midst, they are as it were private, they flow not for public use, and I have mine, and he has his own, it is not in the midst for both me and him to have it; but such is not the preaching of peace. . . . Therefore, brethren, let what we have said to your Love serve to this purpose, because of the springs: that they may flow from you, be ye valleys, and communicate with all that which ye have from God. Let the waters flow in the midst, envy ye no one, drink, be filled, flow forth when ye are filled. Everywhere let the common water of God have the glory, not the private falsehoods of men. . . .

11. For it follows, "All the beasts of the wood shall drink" (ver. 11). We do indeed see this also in the visible creation, that the beasts of the wood drink of springs, and of streams that run between the mountains: but now since it hath pleased God to hide His own wisdom in the figures of such things, not to take it away from earnest seekers, but to close it to them that care not, and open it to them that knock; it hath also pleased our Lord God Himself to exhort you by us to this, that in all these things which are said as if of the bodily and visible creation, we may seek something spiritually hidden, in which when found we may rejoice. The beasts of the wood, we understand the Gentiles, and Holy Scripture witnesses this in many places. . . .

12. These beasts, then, drink those waters, but passing; not staying, but passing; for all that teaching which in all this time is dispensed passeth. . . . Unless perchance your love thinketh that in that city to which it is said, "Praise the Lord, O Jerusalem, praise thy God, O Sion; for He hath made strong the bars of thy gates;"[1] when the bars are now strengthened and the city closed, whence, as we said some time since,[2] no friend goeth out, no enemy entereth;[3] that there we shall have a

book to read, or speech to be explained as it is now explained to you. Therefore is it now treated, that there it may be held fast: therefore is it now divided by syllables, that there it may be contemplated whole and entire. The Word of God will not be wanting there: but yet not by letters, not by sounds, not by books,[4] not by a reader, not by an expositor. How then? As, "In the beginning was the Word," etc.[5] For He did not so come to us as to depart from thence; because He was in this world, and the world was made by Him. Such a Word are we to contemplate. For "the God of gods shall appear in Zion."[6] But this when? After our pilgrimage, when the journey is done: if however after our journey is done we be not delivered to the Judge, that the Judge may send us to prison. But if when our journey is ended, as we hope, and wish, and endeavour, we shall have reached our Country, there shall we contemplate What we shall ever praise; nor shall That fail which is present to us, nor we, who enjoy: nor shall he be cloyed that eateth, nor shall that fail which he eateth. Great and wonderful shall be that contemplation. . . .

13. "The onagers shall take for their thirst." By onagers he meaneth some great beasts. For who knoweth not that wild asses are called onagers? He meaneth, therefore, some great untrained ones. For the Gentiles had no yoke of the Law: many nations lived after their own customs, ranging in proud boastfulness as in a wilderness. And so indeed did all the beasts, but the wild asses are put to signify the greater sort. They too shall drink for their thirst, for for them too the waters flow. Thence drinks the hare, thence the wild ass: the hare little, the wild ass great; the hare timid, the wild ass fierce: either sort drinks thence, but each for his thirst. . . . So faithfully and gently doth it flow, as at once to satisfy the wild ass, and not to alarm the hare. The sound of Tully's voice rings out, Cicero is read, it is some book, it is a dialogue of his, whether his own, or Plato's, or by whatever such writer: some hear that are unlearned, weak ones of less mind; who dareth to aspire to such a thing? It is a sound of water, and that perchance turbid, but certainly flowing so violently, that a timid animal dare not draw near and drink. To whom soundeth a Psalm, and he saith, It is too much for me? Behold now what the Psalm soundeth; certainly they are hidden mysteries, yet so it soundeth, that even children are delighted to hear, and the

---

[1] Ps. cxlvii. 12, 13.
[2] See on Ps lxxxv. 10 and on Ps. cxlvii. on ver. 13. — *Ben.*
[3] [This beautiful expression may be found in divers places in these expositions: *e g.* on Ps. xlix. ver. 15 (p. 186, *supra*), where it is of slightly different sense: also on Ps. lxxxv. ver. 9, (p. 407, *supra*), and, *infra*, on Ps. cxlviii. 13. The Latin is felicitous though varied:

Unde amicus non exit, quo inimicus non intrat. I love the familiar English: "Where no enemy ever enters, and whence no friend departs." — C.]
[4] [I suppose many Christians have said, "Shall I no more recall my Bible, and be refreshed by the recollection of these songs of our pilgrimage?" I could not think of heaven as a place where the Holy Scriptures should be forgotten. The author's idea comforts me. — C.]
[5] John i. 1.　　　　　[6] Ps. lxxxiv. 7.

unlearned come to drink, and when filled burst forth in singing. . . .

14. Then the Psalm goes on in its text, "Upon them[1] the fowls of the heaven shall inhabit" (ver. 12). . . . Upon the mountains, then, the fowls of the air shall have their habitation. We see these birds dwell upon the mountains, but many of them dwell in plains, many in valleys, many in groves, many in gardens, not all upon mountains. There are some fowls that dwell not save on the mountains. Some spiritual souls doth this name denote. Fowls are spiritual hearts, which enjoy the free air. In the clearness of heaven these birds delight, yet their feeding is on the mountains, there will they dwell. Ye know the mountains, they have been already treated of. Mountains are Prophets, mountains are Apostles, mountains are all preachers of the truth. . . .

15. But think not that those "fowls of heaven" follow their own authority; see what the Psalm saith : " From the midst of the rocks they shall give their voice." Now, if I shall say to you, Believe, for this said Cicero, this said Plato, this said Pythagoras : which of you will not laugh at me? For I shall be a bird that shall send forth my voice not from the rock. What ought each one of you to say to me? what ought he who is thus instructed to say? "If any one shall have preached unto you a gospel other than that ye have received, let him be anathema."[2] What dost thou tell me of Plato, and of Cicero, and of Virgil? Thou hast before thee the rocks of the mountains, from the midst of the rocks give me thy voice. Let them be heard, who hear from the rock : let them be heard, because also in those many rocks the One Rock is heard : for "the Rock was Christ."[3] Let them therefore be willingly heard, giving their voice from the midst of the rocks. Nothing is sweeter than such a voice of birds. They sound, and the rocks resound : they sound ; spiritual men discuss : the rocks resound, testimonies of Scripture give answer. Lo ! thence the fowls give their voice from the midst of the rocks, for they dwell on the mountains.

16. "Watering the mountains from the higher places " (ver. 13). Now if a Gentile uncircumcised man comes to us, about to believe in Christ, we give him baptism, and do not call him back to those works of the Law. And if a Jew asks us why we do that, we sound from the rock, we say, This Peter did, this Paul did : from the midst of the rocks we give our voice. But that rock, Peter himself, that great mountain, when he prayed and saw that vision, was watered from above. . . .

17. " From the fruit of Thy works shall the

earth be satisfied." What is, " From the fruit of Thy works "? Let no man glory in his own works : but " he that glorieth, let him glory in the Lord." [4] With Thy grace he is satisfied, when he is satisfied : let him not say that grace was given for his own merits. If it is called grace, " it is gratuitously given ; " if it is returned for works, wages are paid.[5] Freely therefore receive, because ungodly thou art justified.

18. " Bringing forth grass for the cattle, and green herb for the service of men " (ver. 14). This is true, I perceive ; I recognise the creation : the earth doth bring forth grass for the cattle, and green herb for the service of men. But I perceive the words, " Thou shalt not muzzle the mouth of the ox which treadeth out the corn : Doth God take care for oxen? For our sakes therefore the Scripture saith it." [6] How then doth the earth bring forth grass for the cattle? Because " the Lord hath ordained that they which preach the Gospel should live of the Gospel." He sent preachers, saying unto them, " Eat such things as are set before you of them : for the labourer is worthy of his hire." [7] . . . They give spiritual, they receive carnal things ; they give gold, they receive grass. . . . " If we have sown unto you spiritual things, is it a great matter if we shall reap your carnal things ? " [8] This the Apostle said, a preacher so laborious, so indefatigable, so well tried, that he giveth this very grass to the earth. " Nevertheless," he saith, " we have not used this power." He showeth that it is due to him, yet he received it not ; nor hath he condemned those who have received what was due. For those were to be condemned who exact what is not due, not they who accept their recompense : yet he gave up even his own recompense. Thou dost not cease to owe to another, because one hath given up his dues, otherwise thou wilt not be the watered earth which bringeth forth grass for the cattle. . . . Thou receivest spiritual things, give carnal things in return : to the soldier they are due, to the soldier thou returnest them ; thou art the paymaster[9] of Christ. " Who goeth a warfare any time at his own charges? who planteth a vineyard, and eateth not of the fruit thereof? or who feedeth a flock, and eateth not of the milk of the flock? I speak not thus, that it should be so done unto me." [10] There has been such a soldier as gave up his rations of food even to the paymaster : yet let the paymaster pay the rations. . . .

19. " That it may bring forth bread out of the earth." What bread? Christ. Out of what earth? From Peter, from Paul, from the other

---

[1] Illos.   [2] Gal. i. 9.   [3] 1 Cor. x. 4.

[4] 1 Cor. i. 31.   [5] Rom. iv. 4, 5.   [6] 1 Cor. ix. 9.
[7] Luke x. 7, 8.   [8] 1 Cor. ix. 11.
[9] Provincialis. See this series, vol. vii. p. 440, note 3.
[10] 1 Cor. ix. 7, 15.

stewards of the truth. Hear that it is from the earth: "We have," saith St. Paul, "this treasure in earthen vessels, that the excellency of the power may be of God, and not of us." [1] He is the bread who descended from heaven,[2] that He might be brought forth out of the earth, when He is preached through the flesh of His servants. The earth bringeth forth grass, that it may bring forth bread from the earth. What earth bringeth forth grass? Pious, holy nations. That bread may be brought forth out of what earth? The word of God out of the Apostles, out of the stewards of God's Sacraments, who still walk upon the earth, who still carry an earthly body.

20. "And wine maketh glad the heart of man" (ver. 15). Let no man prepare himself for intoxication; nay, let every man prepare him for intoxication. "How excellent is Thy cup which maketh inebriate!" [3] We choose not to say, Let no man be drunk. Be inebriated; yet beware, from what source. If the excellent cup of the Lord doth saturate you, your ebriety shall be seen in your works, it shall be seen in the holy love of righteousness, it shall, lastly, be seen in the estrangement of your mind, but from things earthly to heavenly. "To make him a cheerful countenance with oil." . . . What is the making the countenance cheerful with oil? The grace of God; a sort of shining for manifestation; as the Apostle saith, "The Spirit is given to every man for manifestation." [4] A certain grace which men can clearly see in men, to conciliate holy love, is termed oil, for its divine splendour; and since it appeared most excellent in Christ, the whole world loveth Him; who though while here He was scorned, is now worshipped by every nation: "For the kingdom is the Lord's, and He shall be Governor among the people." [5] For such is His grace, that many, who do not believe on Him, praise Him, and declare that they are unwilling to believe on Him, because no man can fulfil what He doth command. They who with reproaches once raged against Him, are hindered by His very praises. Yet by all is He loved, by all is He preached; because He is excellently anointed, therefore He is Christ: for He is called Christ from the Chrism or anointing which He had. Messiah in the Hebrew, Christ in the Greek, Unctus in the Latin: but He anointeth over His whole Body. All therefore who come, receive grace, that their countenances may be made glad with oil.

21. "And bread strengtheneth man's heart." What is this, brethren? As it were, he hath forced us to understand what bread he was speaking of. For while that visible bread

strengtheneth the stomach, feedeth the body, there is another bread which strengtheneth the heart, in that it is the bread of the heart. . . . There is therefore a wine that truly maketh glad the heart, and knoweth not to do aught else than to gladden the heart. But that thou mayest not imagine that this indeed should be taken of the spiritual wine, but not of that spiritual bread; He hath shown this very point, that it is also spiritual: "and bread," he saith, "strengtheneth man's heart." So understand it therefore of the bread as thou dost understand it of the wine; hunger inwardly, thirst inwardly: "Blessed are they," saith our Lord, "who hunger and thirst after righteousness; for they shall be filled." [6] That bread is righteousness, that wine is righteousness: it is truth, Christ is truth.[7] "I am," He said, "the living bread, who came down from heaven;" [8] and, "I am the Vine, and ye are the branches." [9]

22. "The trees of the plain shall be satisfied" (ver. 16): but with this grace, brought forth out of the earth. "The trees of the plain," are the lower orders of the nations. "And the cedars of Libanus which He hath planted." The cedars of Libanus, the powerful in the world, shall themselves be filled. The bread, and wine, and oil of Christ hath reached senators, nobles, kings; the trees of the plain are filled. First the humble are filled; next also the cedars of Libanus, yet those which He hath planted; pious cedars, religious faithful; for such hath He planted. For the ungodly also are cedars of Libanus; for, "The Lord shall break the cedars of Libanus." [10] For Libanus is a mountain: there are those trees, even according to the letter most long-lived and most excellent. But Libanus is interpreted, as we read in those who have written of these things, a brightness: and this brightness seemeth to belong to this world, which at present shineth and is refulgent with its pomps. There are the cedars of Libanus, which the Lord hath planted; those which the Lord hath planted shall be filled. . . .

23. "There shall the sparrows build their nests: their leader is the house of the coot" (ver. 17). Where shall the sparrows build? In the cedars of Libanus. . . . Who are the sparrows? Sparrows are birds indeed, and fowls of the air, but small fowls are wont to be called sparrows. There are therefore some spiritual ones that build in the cedars of Libanus: that is, there are certain servants of God who hear in the Gospel, "Sell all that thou hast, and give to the poor; and thou shalt have treasure in heaven; and come and follow Me." [11] . . . Let him who hath resigned many things, not be

---

[1] 2 Cor. iv. 7.   [2] John vi. 41.   [3] Ps. xxiii. 5.
[4] 1 Cor. xii. 7.   [5] Ps. xxii. 28.

[6] Matt. v. 6.   [7] John xiv. 6.
[8] John vi. 51.   [9] John xv. 5.
[10] Ps. xxix. 5.   [11] Matt. xix. 21.

proud. We know that Peter was a fisherman: what then could he give up, to follow our Lord? Or his brother Andrew, or John and James the sons of Zebedee, themselves also fishermen;[1] and yet what did they say? "Behold, we have forsaken all, and followed Thee."[2] Our Lord said not to him, Thou hast forgotten thy poverty; what hast thou resigned, that thou shouldest receive the whole world? He, my brethren, who resigned not only what he had, but also what he longed to have, resigned much. . . .

24. But although the sparrows will build in the cedars of Libanus, "the house of the coot is their leader." What is the house of the coot? The coot, as we all know, is a water bird, dwelling either among the marshes, or on the sea. It hath rarely or never a home on the shore; but in places in the midst of the waters, and thus usually in rocky islets, surrounded by the waves. We therefore understand that the rock is the fit home of the coot, it never dwelleth more securely than on the rock. On what sort of rock? One placed in the sea. And if it is beaten by the waves, yet it breaketh the waves, is not broken by them: this is the excellency of the rock in the sea. How great waves beat on our Lord Jesus Christ? The Jews dashed against Him; they were broken, He remained whole. And let every one who doth imitate Christ, so dwell in this world, that is, in this sea, where he cannot but feel storms and tempests, that he may yield to no wind, to no wave, but remain whole, while he meets them all. The home of the coot, therefore, is both strong and weak. The coot hath not a home on lofty spots; nothing is more firm and nothing more humble than that home. Sparrows build indeed in cedars, on account of actual need: but they hold that rock as their leader, which is beaten by the waves, and yet not broken; for they imitate the sufferings of Christ. . . .

25. What then followeth? "The loftiest hills are for the stags" (ver. 18). The stags are mighty, spiritual, passing in their course over all the thorny places of the thickets and woods. "He maketh my feet like harts' feet, and setteth me up on high."[3] Let them hold to the lofty hills, the lofty commandments of God; let them think on sublime subjects, let them hold those which stand forth most in the Scriptures, let them be justified in the highest: for those loftiest hills are for the stags. What of the humble beasts? what of the hare? what of the hedgehog? The hare is a small and weak animal: the hedgehog is also prickly: the one is a timid animal, the other is covered with prickles. What do the prickles signify, except sinners? He who sinneth daily, although not great sins, is covered

over with the smallest prickles. In his timidity he is a hare: in his being covered with the minutest sins, he is a hedgehog: and he cannot hold those lofty and perfect commandments. For "the loftiest hills are for the stags." What then? do these perish? No. For so "is the rock the refuge for the hedgehogs and the hares."[4] For the Lord is a refuge for the poor. Place that rock upon the land, it is a refuge for hedgehogs, and for hares: place it on the sea, it is the home of the coot. Everywhere the rock is useful. Even in the hills it is useful: for the hills without the rock's foundation would fall into the deep. . . .

26. "He appointed the Moon for certain seasons" (ver. 19). We understand spiritually the Church increasing from the smallest size, and growing old as it were from the mortality of this life; yet so, that it draweth nearer unto the Sun. I speak not of this moon visible to the eye, but of that which is signified by this name. While the Church was in the dark, while she as yet appeared not, shone not forth as yet, men were led astray, and it was said, This is the Church, here is Christ; so that "while the Moon was dark, they shot their arrows at the righteous in heart."[5] How blind is he who now, when the Moon is full, wandereth astray? "He appointed the Moon for certain seasons." For here the Church temporarily is passing away: for this subjection to death will not remain for ever: there will some time be an end of waxing and waning; it is appointed for certain seasons. "And the sun knoweth his going down." And what sun is this, but that Sun of righteousness, whom the ungodly will lament on the day of judgment never having risen for them; they who will say on that day, "Therefore we wandered from the way of truth, and the light of righteousness shone not on us, and the sun did not arise upon us."[6] That sun riseth for him who understandeth Christ. . . .

27. Nor think, brethren, that the sun ought to be worshipped by some men, because the sun doth sometimes in the Scriptures signify Christ. For such is the madness of men;[7] as if we said that a creature should be worshipped, when it is said, the sun is an emblem of Christ. Then worship the rock also, for it also is a type of Christ.[8] "He was brought as a lamb to the slaughter:"[9] worship the lamb also, since it is a type of Christ. "The Lion of the tribe of Judah hath prevailed;"[10] worship the lion also, since it signifieth Christ. Observe how numerous are the types of Christ: all these are Christ in similitude, not in essence. . . .

---

[1] Matt. iv. 18, 21.   [2] Matt. xix. 27.   [3] Ps. xviii. 33.

[4] Ps. ix. 9.   [5] Ps. xi. 2.   [6] Wisd. v. 6.
[7] [What would our author have said to the teaching of the Trent Catechism on image-worship? See A. N. F. vol. iii. p. 76. — C.]
[8] 1 Cor. x. 4.   [9] Isa. liii. 7.   [10] Rev. v. 5.

28. What then, when the sun went down, when our Lord suffered? There was a sort of darkness with the Apostles, hope failed, in those to whom He at first seemed great, and the Redeemer of all men. How so? "Thou didst make darkness, and it became night; wherein all the beasts of the forest shall move" (ver. 20). . . . Here the beasts of the forest are used in different ways: for these things are always understood in varying senses; as our Lord Himself is at one time termed a lion, at another a lamb. What is so different as a lion and a lamb? But what sort of lamb? One that could overcome the wolf, overcome the lion. He is the Rock, He the Shepherd, He the Gate. The Shepherd entereth by the gate: and He saith, "I am the good Shepherd:" and, "I am the Door of the Sheep." [1] . . . Learn thus to understand, when these things are spoken figuratively; lest perchance when ye have read that the Rock signifieth Christ,[2] ye may understand it to mean Him in every passage. In one place it meaneth one thing, another in another, just as we can only understand the meaning of a letter by seeing its position.[3] "The lion's whelps roaring after their prey, do seek their meat from God" (ver. 21). Justly then our Lord, when nigh unto His going down, the very Sun of Righteousness recognising His going down, said to His disciples, as if darkness being about to come, the lion would roam about to seek whom he might devour, that that lion could devour no man, unless with leave: "Simon," said He, "this night Satan hath desired to have you, that he may sift you as wheat. But I have prayed for thee, that thy faith fail not." [4] When Peter thrice denied,[5] was he not already between the lion's teeth? . . .

29. "The Sun hath arisen, and they get them away together, and lay them down in their dens" (ver. 22). More and more as the Sun riseth, so that Christ is recognised by the round world, and glorified therein, do the lion's whelps get them away together; those devils recede from the persecution of the Church, who instigated men to persecute the house of God, by working in the sons of unbelief.[6] Now that none of them dareth persecute the Church, "the Sun hath arisen, and they get them away together." And where are they? "And they lay them down in their dens." Their dens are the hearts of the unbelieving. How many carry lions crouching in their hearts? They burst not forth thence, they make no assault upon the pilgrim Jerusalem. Wherefore do they not so? Because the Sun is already risen, and is shining over the whole world.

30. What art thou doing, O man of God? thou, O Church of God? what art thou, O body of Christ, whose Head is in Heaven? what art thou doing, O man, His unity? "Man," he saith, "shall go forth to his work" (ver. 23). Let therefore this man work good works in the security of the peace of the Church, let him work unto the end. For sometime there will be a sort of general darkening, and a sort of assault will be made, but in the evening, that is, in the end of the world: but now the Church doth work in peace and tranquillity; for "man shall go forth to his work, and to his labour, unto the evening."

31. "O Lord, how great are made Thy works!" (ver. 24). Justly great, justly sublime! where were those works made, that are so great? what was that station where God stood, or that seat whereupon He sat, when He did those works? what was the place where He worked thus? whence did those so beautiful works proceed at the first? To take it word for word, every ordained creation, running by ordinance, beautiful by ordinance, rising by ordinance, setting by ordinance, going through all seasons by ordinance, whence hath it proceeded? whence hath the Church herself received her rise, her growth, her perfection? In what manner is she destined to a consummation in immortality? with what heralding is she preached? by what mysteries is she recommended? by what types is she concealed? by what preaching is she revealed? where hath God done these things? I see great works. "How great are made Thy works, O Lord!" I ask where He hath made them: I find not the place: but I see what followeth: "In Wisdom hast Thou made them all." All therefore Thou hast made in Christ. . . . "The earth is full of Thy creation." The earth is full of the creation of Christ. And how so? We discern how: for what was not made by the Father through the Son? Whatever walketh and doth crawl on earth, whatever doth swim in the waters, whatever flieth in the air, whatever doth revolve in heaven, how much more then the earth, the whole universe, is the work of God. But he seems to me to speak here of some new creation, of which the Apostle saith, "If any man be in Christ, he is a new creature: old things have passed away; behold, all things are become new. And all things are of God." [7] All who

---

[1] John x. 11, 7.   [2] 1 Cor. x. 4.

[3] *Circumstantia sui exponuntur.* [He adds, "If thou hast heard the first letter in the word Deus, and thinkest it must always belong to it alone, thou wilt blot it out in the word Diabolus. For the word Deus beginneth with the same letter as the word Diabolus: and nothing is so far apart, as God from the devil. Consider how utterly ignorant of things both human and divine he must be, who shall say of the letter D, it ought not to be used in the beginning of the word devil: and when thou hast asked the reason, replieth, I read that letter in the name of God. Such a man is laughed at: for he is not worthy of an argument. Do not then so childishly interpret these divine things, as if any of you were to think, from my having said above that the beasts of the forest signifies the Gentiles, while I now say that they signify devils and the angels of disobedience, that I am contradicting what I said before. For they are only figures, and wherever they occur, are explained by the context they have." — C.]

[4] Luke xxii. 31, 32.   [5] Matt. xxvi. 70, 74.   [6] Eph. ii. 2.   [7] 2 Cor. v. 17, 18.

believe in Christ, who put off the old man, and put on the new,[1] are a new creature. "The earth is full of Thy works." On one spot of the earth He was crucified, in one small spot that seed fell into the earth, and died; but brought forth great fruit. . . .

32. "The earth is full of Thy creation." Of what creation of Thine is the earth full? Of all trees and shrubs, of all animals and flocks, and of the whole of the human race; the earth is full of the creation of God. We see, know, read, recognise, praise, and in these we preach of Him; yet we are not able to praise respecting these things, as fully as our heart doth abound with praise after the beautiful contemplation of them. But we ought rather to heed that creation, of which the Apostle saith, "If any man be in Christ, he is a new creature: old things are passed away; behold, all things are become new."[2] What "old things have passed away"? In the Gentiles, all idolatry; in the Jews themselves, all that servitude unto the Law, all those sacrifices that were harbingers of the present Sacrifice. The oldness of man was then abundant; One came to renovate His own work, to melt His silver, to form His coin, and we now see the earth full of Christians believing in God, turning themselves away from their former uncleanness and idolatry, from a past hope to the hope of a new age: and behold it is not yet realized, but is already possessed in hope, and through that very hope we now sing, and say, "The earth is full of Thy creation." We do not as yet sing this in our country, nor yet in that rest which is promised, the bars of the gates of Jerusalem not being as yet made fast;[3] but still in our pilgrimage gazing upon the whole of this world, upon men who on every side are running unto the faith, fearing hell, despising death, loving eternal life, scorning the present, and filled with joy at such a spectacle, we say, "The earth is full of Thy creation."

33. . . . . "So is the great and wide sea also; wherein are things creeping innumerable, both small and great beasts" (ver. 25). He speaketh of the sea as terrible. Snares creep in this world, and surprise the careless suddenly; for who numbereth the temptations that creep? They creep, but beware, lest they snatch us away. Let us keep watch on the Wood; even in the water,[4] even on the waves, we are safe: let not Christ sleep, let not faith sleep; if He hath slept, let Him be awakened; He will command the winds; He will calm the sea;[5] the voyage will be ended, and we shall rejoice in our country. For I see in this terrible sea un-

believers still; for they dwell in barren and bitter waters: but they are both small and great. We know this: many little men of this world are still unbelievers, many great men of this world are so: there are living creatures, both small and great, in this sea. They hate the Church: the name of Christ is a burden to them: they rage not, because they are not permitted; the cruelty which cannot burst forth in deeds, is shut up within the heart. For all, whether small or great, "creeping things, both small and great," who at present grieve at the temples being shut, the altars overthrown, the images broken, the laws which make it a capital crime to sacrifice to idols; all who mourn on this account, are still in the sea. What then of us? And by what road then are we to journey unto our country? Through this very sea, but on the Wood. Fear not the danger; that wood which holdeth together the world doth bear thee up.

34. "There shall go the ships" (ver. 26). Lo, ships float upon that which alarmed you, and sink not. By ships we understand churches; they go among the storms, among the tempests of temptations, among the waves of the world, among the beasts, both small and great. Christ on the wood of His cross is the Pilot. "There shall go the ships." Let not the ships fear, let them not much mind where they float, but by Whom they are steered. "There shall go the ships." What voyage do they find tedious, when they feel that Christ is their Pilot? They will sail safely, let them sail diligently, they will reach their promised haven, they will be led to the land of rest.

35. There is also in that sea somewhat which transcends all creatures, great and small. What is this? Let us hear the Psalm: "There is that Leviathan, whom Thou hast formed to make sport of him." There are creeping things innumerable, both small and great beasts; there shall the ships go, and shall not fear, not only the creeping things innumerable, and beasts both small and great, but not even the serpent which is there; "whom Thou," he speaketh unto God, "hast made to make sport of him." This is a great mystery; and yet I am about to utter what ye already know. Ye know that a certain serpent is the enemy of the Church: ye have not seen him with the eyes of the flesh, but ye see him with the eyes of faith. . . .

36. This serpent then, our ancient enemy, glowing with rage, cunning in his wiles, is in the mighty sea. "Here is that Leviathan, whom Thou hast formed to make sport of him." Do thou now make sport of the serpent: for for this end was this serpent made. He falling by his own sin from the sublime realms of the heavens, and made devil instead of angel, received a certain region of his own in this

---

[1] Eph. iv. 22–24.   [2] 2 Cor. v. 17.   [3] Ps. cxlvii. 13.
[4] Some mss. add, "On the cross let us sail;" but this may be a gloss.
[5] Matt. viii. 24–26.

mighty and spacious sea. What thou thinkest his kingdom, is his prison. For many say: wherefore hath the devil received so great power, that he may rule in this world, and prevaileth so much, can do so much? How much prevaileth he? How much can he do? Unless by permission, he can do nothing. Do thou so act, that he may not be allowed to attack thee; or if he be allowed to tempt thee, he may depart vanquished, and may not gain thee. For he hath been allowed to tempt some holy men, servants of God: they overcame him, because they departed not from the way, they whose heel he watched, fell not. . . .

37. He then, my brethren, who doth wish to watch the serpent's head, and safely to pass this sea; for it must be that this serpent dwelleth here, and, as I had commenced saying, the devil when he fell from heaven received this region; let him watch his head, on the part of the fear of the world, and of the lusts of the world. For it is hence that he suggesteth some object of fear or of desire; he trieth thy love, or thy fear. If thou fearest hell, and lovest the kingdom of God, thou wilt watch his head. . . . "There is no power but of God." [1] What then fearest thou? Let the dragon be in the waters, let the dragon be in the sea: thou art to pass through it. He is made so as to be made sport of, he is ordained to inhabit this place, this region is given him. Thou thinkest that this habitation is a great thing for him, because thou knowest not the dwellings of the angels whence he fell: [2] what seemeth to thee his glory, is his damnation.

38. . . . What then fearest thou? Perhaps he is about to try thy flesh: it is the scourge of thy Lord, not the power of thy tempter. His wish is to injure that salvation which is promised: but he is not allowed: but that he may not be allowed, have Christ for thy Head: repel the serpent's head: consent not unto his suggestion, slip not from thy path. "There is that Leviathan, whom Thou hast made to make sport of him."

39. Dost thou wish to see how incapable he is of hurting thee, unless permitted? "These," he saith, "wait all upon Thee, that Thou mayest give them meat in due season" (ver. 27). And this serpent wisheth to devour, but he devoureth not whom he wisheth. . . . Thou hast heard what the serpent's meat is. Thou dost not wish that God give thee to be devoured by the serpent; because not the serpent's food: i.e. forsake not the Word of God. For where it is said to the serpent, "Dust thou shalt eat," it is said to the transgressor, "Dust thou art, and unto dust thou shalt return." [3] Thou dost not

wish to be the serpent's food? be not dust. How, thou repliest, shall I not be dust? If thou hast not a taste for earthly things. Hear the Apostle, that thou mayest not be dust. For the body which thou wearest is earth: but do thou refuse to be earth. What meaneth this? "Set your affection on things above, not on things on the earth." [4] If thou dost not set thy affections on earthly things, thou art not earth: if thou art not earth, thou art not devoured by the serpent, whose appointed food is earth. The Lord giveth the serpent his food when He will, what He will: but He judgeth rightly, he cannot be deceived, He giveth him not gold for earth. "When Thou hast given it them, they gather it." . . .

40. "When thou openest Thy hand, they shall all be filled with good" (ver. 28). What is it, O Lord, that Thou openest Thy hand? Christ is Thy hand. "To whom is the arm of the Lord revealed?" [5] To whom it is revealed, unto him it is opened: for revelation is opening. "When Thou openest Thy hand, they shall all be filled with good." When Thou revealest Thy Christ, "they shall all be filled with good." But they have not good from themselves; this is oftentimes proved unto them. "When Thou hidest Thy face, they are troubled" (ver. 29). Many filled with good have attributed to themselves what they had, and have wished to boast as in their own righteousnesses, and have said to themselves, I am righteous; I am great: and have become self-complacent. Unto these the Apostle speaketh: "What hast thou, that thou didst not receive?" [6] But God, wishing to prove unto man that whatever he hath he hath from Him, so that with good he may gain humility also, sometimes troubleth him; He turneth away His face from him, and he falleth into temptation; and He showeth him that his righteousness, and his walking aright, was only under His government. . . .

41. But wherefore dost Thou do this? wherefore dost Thou hide Thy face, that they may be troubled? "Thou shalt take away their breath, and they shall fail." Their breath was their pride; they boast, they attribute things to themselves, they justify themselves. Hide, therefore, Thy face, that they may be troubled: take away their breath, and let them fail; let them cry unto Thee, "Hear me, O Lord, and that soon, for my spirit waxeth faint: hide not Thy face from me." [7] "Thou shalt take away their breath, and they shall fail, and shall be turned to their dust." The man who repenteth of his sin discovereth himself, that he had not strength of himself; and doth confess unto God, saying, that he is earth and ashes. O proud one, thou

---

[1] Rom. xiii. 1.
[2] Oxf. MSS. add, "Thou admirest the dwellings of the dead where he is cast down."
[3] Gen. iii. 14; 19.

[4] Col. iii. 2.
[5] Isa. liii. 1.
[6] 1 Cor. iv. 7.
[7] Ps. cxliii. 7.

art turned to thine own dust, thy breath hath been taken away; no longer dost thou boast thyself, no longer extol thyself, no longer justify thyself; thou seest that thou art made of dust, and when the Lord turneth away His face, thou hast fallen back into thine own dust. Pray, therefore, confess thy dust and thy weakness.

42. And see what followeth : " Thou shalt send forth Thy Spirit,[1] and they shall be made " (ver. 30). Thou shalt take away their spirit, and send forth Thine own : Thou shalt take away their spirit : they shall have no spirit of their own. Are they then forsaken? " Blessed are the poor in spirit : "[2] but they are not forsaken. They refused to have a spirit of their own : they shall have the Spirit of God. Such were our Lord's words to the future martyrs :[3] " It is not ye that speak, but the Spirit of your Father which speaketh in you." Attribute not your courage to yourselves. If it is yours, He saith, and not Mine, it is obstinacy, not courage. " For we are His workmanship," saith the Apostle, " created unto good works."[4] From His Spirit we have received grace, that we may live unto righteousness : for it is He that justifieth the ungodly.[5] " Thou shalt take away their spirit, and they shall fail ; Thou shalt send forth Thy Spirit, and they shall be made : and Thou shalt renew the face of the earth : " that is, with new men, confessing themselves to have been justified, not righteous of their own power, so that the grace of God is in them. What then? When He hath taken away our spirit, we shall be turned again to our dust, beholding to our edification our weakness, that when we receive His Spirit we may be refreshed. See what followeth : " Be the glory of the Lord for ever " (ver. 31). Not thine, not mine, not his, or his ; not for a season, but " for ever." " The Lord shall rejoice in His works." Not in thine, as if they were thine : because if thy works are evil, it is through thy iniquity ; if good, it is through the grace of God. " The Lord shall rejoice in His works."

43. " Who looketh on the earth, and maketh it tremble ; who toucheth the hills, and they shall smoke " (ver. 32). O earth, thou wast exulting in thy good, to thyself thou didst ascribe thy fulness and opulence ; behold, the Lord looketh on thee, and causeth thee to tremble. May He look on thee, and make thee tremble : for the trembling of humility is better than the confidence of pride. . . . For it is God, he saith, which worketh in you. For this reason then with trembling, because God worketh in you. Because He gave, because what thou hast cometh not from thee, thou shalt work with fear and trembling, for if thou fearest not Him, He will take away what He gave. Work, therefore, with trem-

bling. Hear another Psalm : " Serve the Lord with fear, and rejoice unto Him with trembling."[6] If we must rejoice with trembling, God beholdeth us, there cometh an earthquake ; when God looketh upon us, let our hearts tremble ; then will God rest there. Hear Him in another passage : " Upon whom shall My Spirit rest? Even on him that is lowly and quiet, and who trembleth at My Word."[7]

" Who looketh on the earth, and maketh it tremble ; who toucheth the hills, and they shall smoke " (ver. 32). The hills were proud, and boastful of themselves, God had not touched them : He toucheth them, and they shall smoke. What meaneth the smoking of the hills? That they pray unto the Lord. Behold great hills, proud hills, vast hills, prayed not to God : they wished themselves to be entreated, and entreated not Him who was above them. For what powerful, arrogant, proud man is there upon the earth, who deigneth humbly to entreat God? I speak of the ungodly, not of the " cedars of Libanus, which the Lord hath planted." Every ungodly man, unhappy soul, knoweth not how to entreat God, while he wisheth himself to be entreated by men. He is a hill ; it is needful that God touch him, that he may smoke : when he hath begun to smoke, he will offer prayers unto God, as it were the sacrifice of his heart. He smoketh unto God, he then beateth his breast ; he beginneth to weep, for smoke doth elicit tears.

44. " I will sing unto the Lord in my life " (ver. 33). What will sing? Everything that is willing. Let us sing unto the Lord in our life. Our life at present is only hope ; our life will be eternity hereafter : the life of mortal life, is the hope of an everlasting life. " I will praise my God while I have my being." Since I am in Him for ever and ever, while I have my being, I will praise my God. Let us not imagine that, when we have commenced praising God in that state, we shall have any other work : our whole life will be for the praises of God. If we become weary of Him whom we praise, we may also become weary of praising. If He is ever loved, He is ever praised by us.

45. " Let my discourse be pleasing to Him : my joy shall be in the Lord " (ver. 34). What is the discourse of man unto God, save the confession of sins? Confess unto God what thou art, and thou hast discoursed with Him. Discourse unto Him, do good works, and discourse. " Wash you, make you clean," saith Isaiah.[8] What is it to discourse unto God? Unfold thyself to him who knoweth thee, that He may unfold Himself to thee who knowest not Him. Behold, it is thy discourse that pleaseth the Lord ; the offering of thy humility, the tribulation of

---

[1] Or, " breath."   [2] Matt. v. 3.   [3] Matt. x. 20.
[4] Eph. ii. 10.   [5] Rom. iv. 5.   [6] Ps. ii 11.   [7] Isa. lxvi. 2.   [8] Isa. i. 16.

thy heart, the holocaust of thy life, this pleaseth God. But what is pleasing to thyself? "My joy shall be in the Lord." This is that discoursing which I meant between God and thyself: show thyself to Him who knoweth thee, and He showeth Himself unto thee who knowest not him. Pleasing unto Him is thy confession: sweet unto thee is His grace. He hath spoken Himself unto thee. How? By the Word. What Word? Christ. . . .

46. "Let the sinners be consumed out of the earth" (ver. 35). He seemeth angry! O holy soul, which here doth sing and groan! Would that our soul were with that very soul! Would that it were coupled with it, associated, conjoined with it! It shall behold also His loving-kindness when he is angry. For who but he who is filled with charity, understandeth this? Thou tremblest, because he curseth. And who doth curse? A saint. Without doubt he is listened to. But it is said unto the saints, "Bless, and curse not." [1] What is then the sense of the words, "Let the sinners be consumed out of the earth"? Let them utterly be consumed; let their spirit be taken away, that He may send forth His own Spirit, and they may be restored. "And the ungodly, so that they be no more." In what that they be no more, save as wicked men? Let them therefore be justified, that they may no longer be ungodly. The Psalmist saw this, and was filled with joy, and repeateth the first verse of the Psalm: "Bless thou the Lord, O my soul." Let our soul bless the Lord, brethren, since He hath deigned to give unto us both understanding and the power of language, and unto you attention and earnestness in hearing. Let each, as he can recall to mind what he hath heard, by mutual conversation stir up the food ye have received, ruminate on what ye have heard, let it not descend in you into the bowels of forgetfulness. Let the treasure to be desired [2] rest upon your lips. These matters have been sought out and discovered with great labour, with great labour have they been announced and discoursed of; may our toil be fruitful unto you, and may our soul bless the Lord.

PSALM CV. [3]

1. This Psalm is the first of those to which is prefixed the word Allelujah; the meaning of which word, or rather two words, is, Praise the Lord. For this reason he beginneth with praises: "O confess unto the Lord, and call upon His Name" (ver. 1); for this confession is to be understood as praise, just as these words of our Lord, "I confess to Thee, O Father, Lord of heaven and earth." [4] For after commencing

with praise, calling upon God is wont to follow, whereunto he that prayeth doth next add [5] his longings: whence the Lord's Prayer itself hath at the commencement a very brief praise, in these words, "Our Father which art in Heaven." [6] The things prayed for, then follow. . . . This also followeth, "Tell the people what things He hath done;" [7] or rather, to translate literally from the Greek, as other Latin copies too have it, "Preach the Gospel of His works among the Gentiles." Unto whom is this addressed, save unto the Evangelists in prophecy?

2. "O sing unto Him, and play on instruments unto Him" (ver. 2). Praise Him both by word and deed; for we sing with the voice, while we play with an instrument, that is, with our hands. "Let your talking be of all His wondrous works. Be ye praised in His holy Name" (ver. 3). These two verses may without any absurdity seem paraphrases of the two words above; so that, "Let your talking be of all His wondrous works," may express the words, "O sing unto Him;" and what followeth, "be ye praised in His holy Name," may be referred to the words, "and play on instruments unto Him;" the former relating to the "good word" wherewith we sing unto Him, in which His wondrous works are told; the latter to the good work, in which sweet music is played unto Him, so that no man may wish to be praised for a good work on the score of his own power to do it. For this reason, after saying, "be ye praised," which assuredly they who work well deservedly may, he added, "in His holy Name," since "he that glorieth, let him glory in the Lord." [8] . . . This is to be praised in His holy Name. Whence we read also in another Psalm: "My soul shall be praised in the Lord: let the meek hear thereof, and be glad;" [9] which here in a sense followeth, "Let the heart of them rejoice that seek the Lord:" for thus the meek are glad, who do not rival with a bitter jealousy those whom they imitate as already workers of good.

3. "Seek the Lord, and be strengthened" [10] (ver. 4). This is very literally construed from the Greek, though it may seem not a Latin word: whence other copies have, "be ye confirmed;" others, "be ye corroborated." . . . While these words, then, "Come unto Him, and be enlightened," [11] apply to seeing; those in the text relate to doing: "Seek the Lord, and be strengthened." . . . But what meaneth, "Seek His face evermore"? I know indeed that to cling unto God is good for me; [12] but if He is always being sought, when is He found? Did he mean by "evermore," the whole of the life we live

---

[1] Rom. xii. 14.   [2] Prov. xxi. 20.
[3] Lat. CIV.   [4] Matt. xi. 25.

[5] Oxf. MSS. "the sinner doth allege."   [6] Matt. vi. 9.
[7] John xxi. 17.   [8] 1 Cor. i. 31.   [9] Ps. xxxiv. 2.
[10] *Confortamini.*   [11] Ps. xxxiv. 4.   [12] Ps. lxxiii. 27.

here, whence we become conscious that we ought thus to seek, since even when found He is still to be sought? To wit, faith hath already found Him, but hope still seeketh Him. But love hath both found Him through faith, and seeketh to have Him by sight, where He will then be found so as to satisfy us, and no longer to need our search. For unless faith discovered Him in this life, it would not be said, "Seek the Lord." Also, if when discovered by faith, He were not still to be diligently sought, it would not be said, "For if we hope for that we see not, then do we with patience wait for it." [1] . . . And truly this is the sense of the words, "Seek His face evermore;" meaning that discovery should not terminate that seeking, by which love is testified, but with the increase of love the seeking of the discovered One should increase.

4. "Remember," he saith, "His marvellous works that He hath done, His wonders, and the judgments of His mouth" (ver. 5). This passage seemeth like that, "Thou shalt say unto the children of Israel, I AM hath sent me unto you:" an expression which, in ever so small part, scarce a mind [2] taketh in. Then mentioning His own Name, He mercifully mingled in His grace towards men, saying, "I am the God of Abraham, the God of Isaac, and the God of Jacob; this is My Name for ever." [3] By which He would have it to be understood, that they whose God He declared Himself lived with Him for ever, and He said this, which might be understood even by children, that they who by the great powers of love knew how to seek His face for evermore, might according to their capacity comprehend, I AM THAT I AM.

5. Unto whom is it said, "O ye seed of Abraham His servant, ye children of Jacob, His chosen"? (ver. 6). . . . He next addeth, "He is the Lord our God: His judgments are in all the world" (ver. 7). Is He the God of the Jews only? [4] God forbid! "He is the Lord our God:" because the Church, where His judgments are preached, is in all the world. . . .

6. "He hath been alway mindful of His covenant" (ver. 8). Other copies read, "for evermore;" and this arises from the ambiguity of the Greek. But if we are to understand "alway" of this world and not of eternity, why, when he explaineth what covenant He was mindful of, doth he add, "The word that He made to a thousand generations"? Now this may be understood with a certain limitation; but he afterwards saith, "Even the covenant that He made with Abraham" (ver. 9): "and the oath that He sware unto Isaac; and appointed the same unto

Jacob for a law, and to Israel for an everlasting [5] testament" (ver. 10). But if in this passage the Old Testament is to be understood, on account of the land of Canaan; for thus the language of the Psalm runneth, "saying, Unto thee will I give the land of Canaan: the lot of your inheritance" (ver. 11): how is it to be understood as everlasting, since that earthly inheritance could not be everlasting? And for this reason it is called the Old Testament, because it is abolished by the New. But a thousand generations do not seem to signify anything eternal, since they involve an end; and yet are also too numerous for this very temporal state. For by howsoever few years a generation is limited, such as in Greek is called γενέα, whereof the shortest period some have fixed is at fifteen years, after which period man hath the power of generation; what then are those "thousand generations," not only from the time of Abraham, when that promise was made him, unto the New Testament, but from Adam himself down to the end of the world? For who would dare to say that this world should last for 15000 years? Hence it seemeth to me that we ought not to understand here the Old Testament, which it said through the prophet was to be cancelled by the New: "Behold, the days come, saith the Lord, when I will make a new covenant." [6] . . . After saying, "He hath been mindful of His covenant unto an age;" which we ought to understand as lasting for evermore, the covenant, namely, of justification and an eternal inheritance, which God hath promised to faith; he addeth, "and the Word that He commanded [7] unto a thousand generations." What meaneth "commanded"? . . . The command then was faith, that the righteous should live by faith; [8] and an eternal inheritance is set before this faith. "A thousand generations," then, are, on account of the perfect number, to be understood for all; that is, as long as generation succeedeth generation, so long is it commanded to us to live by faith. This the people of God doth observe, the sons of promise who succeed by birth, and depart by death, until every generation be finished; and this is signified by the number thousand; because the solid square of the number ten, ten times ten, and this taken ten times amounts to a thousand. "Even the covenant," he saith, "which He made with Abraham: and the oath that He sware unto Isaac; and appointed the same unto Jacob," that is, Jacob himself, "for a law." These are the very three

---

[1] Rom. viii. 25.
[2] *Rara mens.* Oxf. MSS. read "a pure mind."
[3] Exod. iii. 14, 15.   [4] Rom. iii. 29.

[5] [He adds: "Where there is no room for doubt: for the Greek has αἰώνιον, which our interpreters have never rendered by any other word than eternal; though scarce any authors in any passage have used αἰώνιος in the sense of everlasting. Unless perhaps, because they render αἰων as meaning time, in a more familiar way, they may choose to interpret αἰώνιον, not eternal, but 'for an age;' which I do not remember any one having ventured to do." Conf. Matt. xxv. 46. —C.]   [6] Jer. xxxi. 31, 32.   [7] *Mandavit.*   [8] Rom. i. 17.

patriarchs, whose God He calleth Himself in a special sense, whom the Lord also doth name in the New Testament, where He saith, "Many shall come from the east and the west, and shall sit down with Abraham, and Isaac, and Jacob, in the kingdom of heaven."[1] This is everlasting inheritance. . . .

7. He next followeth out the history well known in the truth of the holy Scriptures. "When they were in small numbers, very few, and they strangers in the land" (ver. 12) ; that is, in the land of Canaan. . . . But some copies have the words "very few, and they strangers," in the accusative case,[2] the translator having turned the Greek phrase too literally into Latin. If we were to render the whole clause in this way, we must say, "that they were very few, and they strangers ;" but the phrase, "while they were," is the meaning of the Greek ; and the verb, "to be," takes not an accusative, but a nominative after it.[3]

8. "What time as they went from one nation to another, from one kingdom to another people" (ver. 13). This is a repetition of what he had said, "from one nation to another." "He suffered no man to do them harm : but reproved even kings for their sakes" (ver. 14). "Touch not," He said, "Mine anointed, and do My prophets no harm" (ver. 15). He declareth the words of God chiding or reproving kings, that they might not harm the holy fathers, while they were small in number, very few, and they strangers in the land of Canaan. Although these words be not read in the books of that history, yet they are to be understood as either secretly spoken, as God speaketh in the hearts of men by unseen and true visions, or even as announced through an Angel. For both the king of Gerar and the king of the Egyptians were warned from Heaven not to harm Abraham,[4] and another king not to harm Isaac,[5] and others not to harm Jacob ;[6] while they were very few, and strangers, before he went over into Egypt to sojourn with his sons : which is understood to be herein mentioned. But since it occurred to ask, before they passed over and multiplied in Egypt, how so few in number, and those strangers in a foreign land, could maintain themselves : he next addeth, "He suffered no man to do them wrong," etc.

9. But it may well excite a question, in what sense they were styled (Christs, or) anointed, before there was any unction, from which this title was given to the kings.[7] . . . Whence then were those patriarchs at that time called "anointed"? For that they were prophets, we read concerning Abraham ; and certainly, what is manifestly said of him, should be understood

of them also. Are they styled "christs," because, even though secretly, yet they were already Christians? For although the flesh of Christ came from them, nevertheless Christ came before them ; for He thus answered the Jews, "Before Abraham was, I am."[8] But how could they not know Him, or not believe in Him ; since they are called prophets for this very reason, because, though somewhat darkly, they announced the Lord beforehand? Whence He saith Himself openly, "Your father Abraham desired to see My day, and he saw it, and was glad."[9] For no man was ever reconciled unto God outside of that faith which is in Christ Jesus, either before His Incarnation, or after : as it ·is most truly defined by the Apostle : "For there is one God, and one Mediator between God and men, the Man Christ Jesus."[10]

10. He then beginneth to relate how it happened that they went from one nation to another, from one kingdom to another people. "He calleth," he saith, "for a famine upon the land : and brake all the staff of bread" (ver. 16). Thus it happened that they went from one nation to another, from one kingdom to another people. But the expressions of the holy Scriptures are not to be negligently passed by. "He called," he saith, "for a famine upon the land ;" as if famine were some person, or some animated body, or some spirit that would obey Him who called. . . . Under this impression the old Romans consecrated some such deities, as the goddess Fever, and the god Paleness. Or meaneth it, as is more credible, He said there should be famine ; so that calling be the same thing as mentioning by name ; mentioning by name, as speaking ; speaking, as commanding? Nor doth the Apostle say,[11] "He calleth those things which be not, that they may be ;" but, "as though they were." For with God that hath already happened which, according to His disposition, is fixed for the future : for of Him it is elsewhere said, "He who made things to come."[12] And here when famine happened, then it is said to have been called, that is, that that which had been determined in His secret government, might be realized. Lastly, he at once expounds, how He called for the famine, saying, "He brake all the staff of bread."

11. "But He had sent a man before them" (ver. 17). What man? "Even Joseph." How did He send him? "Joseph was sold to be a bond-servant." When this happened, it was the sin of his brethren, and, nevertheless, God sent Joseph into Egypt. We should therefore meditate on this important and necessary subject, how God useth well the evil works of men, as

---

1 Matt. viii. 11.   2 *Paucissimos et incolas.*
3 LXX. ἐν τῷ εἶναι αὐτοὺς. "For we cannot say, *cum essent paucissimos*, but *cum essent paucissimi.*"
4 Gen. xii. 17-20, xx. 3.   5 Gen. xxvi. 8-11.
6 Gen. xxxii., xxxiii.   7 Ps. xlv. 8.

8 John viii. 58.   9 John viii. 56.
10 1 Tim. ii. 5.   11 Rom. iv. 17.
12 Isa. xlv. 11.

they on the other hand use ill the good works of God.

12. Next he doth relate the story, mentioning what Joseph suffered in his low estate, and how he was raised on high. "His feet they hurt in the stocks: the iron entered into his soul, until his word came" (ver. 18). That Joseph was put in irons, we do not indeed read; but we ought no ways to doubt that it was so. For some things might be passed over in that history, which nevertheless would not escape the Holy Spirit, who speaketh in these Psalms. We understand by the iron which entered into his soul, the tribulation of stern necessity; for he did not say body, but "soul." There is a somewhat similar expression in the Gospel, where Simeon saith unto Mary, "A sword shall pierce through thy own soul also." [1] That is, the Passion of the Lord, which was a fall unto many, and in which the secrets of many hearts were revealed, since their sentiments respecting the Lord were extorted from them, without doubt made His own Mother exceeding sorrowful, heavily struck with human bereavement. Now Joseph was in this tribulation, "until his word came," with which he truly interpreted dreams: whence he was introduced to the king, that unto him also he might foretell what would happen in respect to his dreams.[2] But since he said, "Until his words were heard," that we might not altogether so understand "his," that any one might think so great an event was to be ascribed unto man; he at once added, "The word of the Lord inflamed him" (ver. 19); or, as other copies have it more closely from the Greek, "The word of the Lord fired him," that he also might be reputed amongst those to whom it is said, "Receive ye praise in His holy Name." [3]

13. "The king sent and loosed him, the prince of the peoples, and let him go free" (ver. 20). The "king" is the same as "the prince of the peoples:" he "loosed" him from his bonds, "and let him go free" from his prison. "He made him lord also of his house: and ruler of all his substance" (ver. 21). "That he might inform his princes like unto himself, and teach his old men wisdom" (ver. 22). The Greek hath, "and teach his elders wisdom." Which might altogether be rendered to the letter thus; "Might inform his princes like unto himself, and make his elders wise." The word translated old men being presbyters or elders, not *gerontas*, old men: and to teach wisdom being from the Greek to *sophize*, which cannot be rendered by a single word in Latin, and is from the word *sophia*, wisdom, different from prudence, which is in Greek *phronesis*. Yet we do not read this in the high elevation of Joseph, as we read not of fetters in his low estate. But how could it happen that so great a man, the worshipper of the One True God, whilst in Egypt, should have been intent upon the nourishing of bodies, and the government of carnal matters only, and have felt no anxiety for souls, and how he could render them better? But those things are written in that history, which, according to the intention of the writer, in whom was the Holy Spirit, were judged sufficient for signifying future events in that narration.

14. "Joseph also came into Egypt, and Jacob was a stranger in the land of Ham" (ver. 23). Israel is the same with Jacob, as is Egypt with the land of Ham. Here it is very plainly shown, that the Egyptian race sprang from the seed of Cham, the son of Noah, whose first-born was Canaan. So that in those copies wherein in this passage Canaan is read, we must alter the reading. It is better construed, "was a stranger," than "dwelt," as other copies have it: which would be the same as "was an inhabitant," for it meaneth nothing different; the very same word is used in the Greek passage above, where it is said, "Very few, and they strangers in the land." Moreover, the state of an *incola* or *accola* doth not signify a native, but a stranger. Behold how "they went from one nation to another." What had been briefly proposed, hath been briefly explained in the narration. But from what kingdom they passed over to another people may well be asked. For they were not yet reigning in the land of Canaan, because the kingdom of the people of Israel had not yet been established there. How then can it be understood, except by anticipation, because the kingdom of their seed was destined there to exist?

15. Next is related what happened in Egypt. "And He increased," he saith, "His people exceedingly, and made them stronger than their enemies" (ver. 24). Even the whole of this is briefly set forth, in order that the manner in which it took place may be afterwards related. For the people of God was not made stronger than their enemies the Egyptians, at the time when their male offspring were slain, or when they were worn out with making bricks; but when by His powerful hand, by the signs and portents of the Lord their God, they became objects of fear and of honour, until the opposition of the hardened king was overcome, and the Red Sea overwhelmed the persecutor with his army.

16. "And He turned their heart so, that they hated His people, and dealt untruly with His servants" (ver. 25). Is it to be in any wise understood or believed, that God turneth man's heart to do sin? . . . For they were not good before they hated His people; but being malignant and

---

[1] Luke ii. 35.   [2] Gen. xli.   [3] Ps. cv. 3.

ungodly, they were such as would readily envy their prosperous sojourners. And so, in that He multiplied His own people, this bountiful act turned the wicked to envy. For envy is the hatred of another's prosperity. In this sense, therefore, He turned their heart, so that through envy they hated His people, and dealt untruly with His servants. It was not then by making their hearts evil, but by doing good to His people, that He turned their hearts, that were evil of their own accord, to hatred. For He did not pervert a righteous heart, but turned one perverted of its own accord to the hatred of His people, while He was to make a good use of that evil;[1] not by making them evil, but by lavishing blessings upon those, which the wicked might most readily envy.

17. The following verses, which are sung in praise of Him when Allelujah is chanted, show how He used this hatred of theirs, both for the trial of His own people, and for the glory of His Name, which is profitable for us. "He sent Moses His servant, and Aaron whom He had chosen *him*" (ver. 26). "Whom He had chosen," would be sufficient; but there is no difficulty in the addition of "him." It is a phrase of Scripture, as, "The land in which they shall dwell in it:"[2] a phrase which the divine pages are full of.

18. "He set forth in them the words of His tokens, and of His wonders in the land of Ham" (ver. 27). We ought not to understand by "the words of His tokens," words literally, words with which the tokens and wonders were worked, that is, which they uttered, that these tokens and wonders might take place. For many were performed without words, either with a rod, or with outstretched hand, or by ashes sent towards heaven. . . .

19. "He sent darkness, and made it dark" (ver. 28). This is also written among the plagues with which the Egyptians were smitten. But what followeth, is variously read in different copies. For some have, "and they provoked His words;" while others read, "and they provoked not His words;" but the reading first mentioned we have found in most; while, where the negative particle is added, we could hardly discover two copies. But perhaps the false reading has abounded owing to the easy sense; for what is easier understood than this, "They provoked His words," that is, by their contumacious rebellions? We have endeavoured to explain the other reading also according to some true sense: and this for the present occurs: "They provoked not His words," that is, in Moses and Aaron; because they most patiently

bore with a very stiffnecked people, until all things which God had determined to work by them, were fulfilled in order.

20. "He turned their waters into blood, and slew their fish" (ver. 29). "He made their land frogs, yea, even in the king's chambers" (ver. 30): as if he were to say, He turned their land into frogs. For there was so great a multitude of frogs, that this might well be said by hyperbole.

21. "He spake the word, and there came all manner of flies, and lice in all their quarters" (ver. 31). If it be asked when He spake, it was in His Word before it took place; and there it was, without time, at what time it should take place: although even then He commanded it to be done, when it was to be done, through Angels, and through his servants Moses and Aaron.

22. "He made their rains hail" (ver. 32). It is a similar expression to the former, "He made their land frogs;" except that the whole land was not actually turned into frogs, though the whole of the rain may have been turned into hail. "A burning fire in their land:" understand, "He sent."

23. "He smote their vines also and fig-trees; and brake every tree of their coasts" (ver. 33). This was done by the violence of the hail, and by lightnings; whence he spoke of the fire as "burning."

24. "He spake the word, and the locust came, and the caterpillar, of which there was no number" (ver. 34). The locusts and the caterpillars are one plague: of which the one is the parent, the other the offspring.

25. "And did eat up all the grass in their land, and devoured the fruit of the ground" (ver. 35). Even grass is fruit, as Scripture is wont to speak, which calleth even the ripe corn grass; but it wished these two things to harmonize in number with the two which it had spoken of before, that is, the locust and the caterpillar. But the whole of this doth belong to the variety of speech, which is a remedy for weariness, not to any difference of senses.

26. "He smote every first-born in their land: even the first-fruits of all their strength" (ver. 36). This is the last plague, excepting the death in the Red Sea. "The first-fruits of all their strength," I imagine to be an expression derived from the first-born of cattle. These plagues are ten in number, but they are not all mentioned, nor in the same order in which they are there read to have happened. For praisegiving is free from the law which bindeth one who is relating or composing a history. And since the Holy Spirit is the Author and Dictator, through the Prophet, of this praise; by the very same authority with which He guided him who wrote that history, he doth both mention some-

---

[1] [A felicitous exposition of the sense in which "good is brought out of evil." Compare A. N. F. vol. viii. pp. 140 and 223.—C.]
[2] Numb. xiii. 20; Lev. xviii. 3.

thing to have taken place which is not there read, and passeth over what is there read.

27. Now he addeth this also to the praises of God, that He led the Israelites out of Egypt enriched with silver and gold ; because even they were then in such a condition, that they could not as yet despise the just and due, though temporal, reward of their toils. . . . "He brought them forth also in silver and gold" (ver. 37) : this too is a Scripture idiom ; for "in silver and gold" is said for the same as if it had been said "with silver and gold : there was not one feeble person among their tribes : " in body, not in mind. This also was a great blessing of God, that in this necessity of removal there was no infirm person.

28. "Egypt was glad at their departing : for their fear fell upon them " (ver. 38) ; that is, the fear of the Hebrews upon the Egyptians. For "their fear " is not that with which the Hebrews feared, but that with which they were feared. Some one will say, how then were the Egyptians unwilling to dismiss them? why did they let them go as if they expected them to return? why did they lend them gold and silver, as to men who were to return, and to repay them, if " Egypt was glad at their departing"? But we must understand, after that final destruction of the Egyptians, and the terrible overthrow of the mighty pursuing army in the Red Sea, that the rest of the Egyptians feared lest the Hebrews should return, and with great ease crush the relics of them : illustrating what he had stated, that He made His people stronger than their enemies.

29. He now proceedeth to the divine blessings which were conferred upon them as they wandered in the desert. "He spread out a cloud to be their covering : and fire to give them light in the night season " (ver. 39). This is as clear as it is well known.

30. "They asked, and the quail came " (ver. 40). They did not desire quails, but flesh. But since the quail is flesh, and in this Psalm he speaketh not of the provocation of those who did not please God, but of the faith of the elect, the true seed of Abraham ; they are to be understood to have desired that that might come which might crush the murmurs of those who provoked. Then in the next line, " And He filled them with the bread of heaven," he has not indeed named manna, but it is obscure to none who hath read those records.

31. " He opened the rock of stone, and the waters flowed out : so that rivers ran in the dry places " (ver. 41). This fact too is understood as soon as read.

32. But in all these blessings of His, God doth commend in Abraham the merit of faith. For the Psalmist goeth on to say, " For why?

He remembered His holy promise, which He made to Abraham His servant " (ver. 42). " And He brought forth His people with joy, and His chosen with gladness " (ver. 43). What he said, " His people," he has repeated in, " His chosen." So also what he said, " with joy," he has repeated in, "with gladness." " And gave them the lands of the heathen : and they took the labours of the people in possession " (ver. 44). " The lands of the heathen," and " the labours of the people," are the same ; and the words, " He gave," are repeated in these, " they took in possession."

33. . . . " That they may keep His statutes, and seek out His law " (ver. 45). Lastly, since by the seed of Abraham he wished those to be understood here, who were truly the seed of Abraham, such as were not wanting even in that people ; as the Apostle Paul clearly showeth, when he saith, " But not in all of them was God well pleased ; " [1] for if He was not pleased with all, surely there were some in whom He was well pleased : since then this Psalm praiseth such men as this, he hath said nothing here of the iniquities and provocations and bitterness of those with whom God was not well pleased. But since not only the justice but also the mercy of Almighty God, the merciful, was shown even unto the wicked ; concerning these attributes the rest of the Psalm pursueth the praises of God. And yet both sorts were in one people : nor did the latter pollute the good with the contagion of their iniquities. For " the Lord knoweth who are His ; " [2] and if he cannot separate in this world from wicked men, yet, " let every one that nameth the name of Christ depart from iniquity." . . .

PSALM CVI.[3]

1. This Psalm also hath the title Allelujah prefixed to it : and this twice. But some say, that one Allelujah belongeth to the end of the former Psalm, the other to the beginning of this. And they assert, that all the Psalms bearing this title have Allelujah at the end, but not all at the beginning ; so that they will not allow any Psalm which hath not Allelujah at the end, to have it at the beginning ; supposing that what seemeth to belong to the commencement, really belongeth to the end of the former Psalm. But until they persuade us by some sure proofs that this is true, we will follow the general custom, which, whenever it findeth Allelujah, attributes it to the same Psalm, at the head of which it is found. For there are very few copies (and I have found this in none of the Greek copies, which I have been able to inspect) which have Allelujah at the end of the CLth Psalm ; after which there is

---

[1] 1 Cor. x. 5.　　　[2] 2 Tim. ii. 19.　　　[3] Lat. CV.

no other which belongeth to the same canon. But not even this could outweigh custom, although all the copies had it so. For it might be that, with some reference to the praise of God, the whole book of Psalms, which is said to consist of five books (for they say that the books severally end where it is written Amen, Amen), might be closed with this last Allelujah, after all that hath been sung; nor, on account of the end of the CLth Psalm, do I see that it is necessary that all the Psalms entitled Allelujah, should have Allelujah at the end. But when there is a double Allelujah at the head of a Psalm, why as our Lord sometimes once, sometimes twice over, saith Amen, in the same way Allelujah may not sometimes be used once, sometimes twice, I know not: especially, since as in this CVth, both the Allelujahs are placed after the mark by which the number of the Psalm is described, whereas the one, if it belonged to the end of the former Psalm, ought to have been placed before the number; and the Allelujah which belonged to the Psalm of this number, should have been written after the number. But perhaps even in this an ignorant habit hath prevailed, and some reason may be assigned of which we are as yet uninformed, so that the judgment of truth ought rather to be our guide than the prejudice of custom. In the mean time, before we are fully instructed in this matter, whenever we find Allelujah written, whether once or twice, after the number of the Psalm, according to the most usual custom of the Church, we will ascribe it to that Psalm to which the same number is prefixed; confessing that we both believe the mysteries of all the titles in the Psalms, and of the order of the same Psalms, to be important, and that we have not yet been able, as we wish, to penetrate them.

2. But I find these two Psalms, the CVth and CVIth so connected, that in one of them, the first, the people of God is praised in the person of the elect, of whom there is no complaint, whom I imagine to have been there in those with whom God was well pleased; [1] but in the following Psalm those are mentioned among the same people who have provoked God; though the mercy of God was not wanting even to these. . . . This Psalm therefore beginneth like the former; "Confess ye unto the Lord." But in that Psalm these words follow: "And call upon His Name:" whereas here, it is as follows, "For He is gracious, [2] and His mercy endureth for ever" (ver. 1). Wherefore in this passage a confession of sins may be understood; for after a few verses we read, "We have sinned with our fathers, we have done amiss, and dealt wickedly;" but in the words, "For He is gracious, and His mercy endureth for ever," there is chiefly the praise of God, and in His praise confession. Although when any one confesses his sins, he ought to do so with praise of God; nor is a confession of sins a pious one, unless it be without despair, and with calling upon the mercy of God. It therefore doth contain His praise, whether in words, when it calleth Him gracious and merciful, or in the feeling only, when he believeth this. . . . If that mercy be here understood, in respect of which no man can be happy without God; we may render it better, "for ever:" but if it be that mercy which is shown to the wretched, that they may either be consoled in misery, or even freed from it; it is better construed, "to the end of the world," in which there will never be wanting wretched persons to whom that mercy may be shown. Unless indeed any man ventured to say, that some mercy of God will not be wanting even to those who shall be condemned with the devil and his angels; not a mercy by which they may be freed from that condemnation, but that it may be in some degree softened for them: and that thus the mercy of God may be styled eternal, as exercised over their eternal misery. [3] . . .

3. "Who can express the mighty acts of the Lord?" (ver. 2). Full of the consideration of the Divine works, while he entreateth His mercy, "Who," he saith, "can express the mighty acts of the Lord, or make all His praises heard?" We must supply what was said above, to make the sense complete here, thus, "Who shall make all His praises heard?" that is, who is sufficient to make all His praises heard? "Shall make" them "heard," he saith; that is, cause that they be heard; showing, that the mighty acts of the Lord and His praises are so to be spoken of, that they may be preached to those who hear them. But who can make "all" heard? Is it that as the next words are, "Blessed are they that alway keep judgment, and do righteousness in every time" (ver. 3); he perhaps meant those praises of His, which are understood as His works in His commandments? "For it is God," saith the Apostle, "who worketh in you," [4] . . . since He worketh in these things in a manner that cannot be spoken. "Who will do all His praises heard?" that is, who, when he hath heard them, doth all His praises? which are the works of His commandments. As far as they are done, although all which are heard are not performed, He is to be praised, who "worketh in us both to will and to do of His good pleasure." [4] For this reason,

---

[1] 1 Cor. x. 5.
[2] "Some copies read, 'for He is gracious,' others, 'for He is sweet:' one Greek word, χρηστὸς, having been differently translated. Also in the words, 'for His mercy endureth to the end of the world;' the Greek hath εἰς τον αἰῶνα, which may be interpreted 'for ever.'"

[3] [Luke xii. 47, 48. — C.]   [4] Philip. ii. 13.

while he might have said, all His commandments, or, all the works of His commandments;
he preferred saying, " His praises." . . .

4. But unless there were some difference between judgment and righteousness, we should
not read in another Psalm, " Until righteousness
turn again unto judgment." [1]   The Scripture,
indeed, loveth to place these two words together; as, " Righteousness and judgment are
the habitation of His seat; " [2] and this, " He
shall make thy righteousness as clear as the
light, and thy judgment as the noon-day; " [3]
where there is apparently a repetition of the
same sentiment.   And perhaps on account of
the resemblance of signification one may be put
for the other, either judgment for righteousness,
or righteousness for judgment: yet, if they be
spoken of in their proper sense, I doubt not
that there is some difference; viz. that he is
said to keep judgment who judgeth rightly, but
he to do righteousness who acts righteously.
And I think that the verse, " Until righteousness
turn again unto judgment," may not absurdly be
understood in this sense: that here also those
are called blessed, who keep judgment in faith,
and do righteousness in deed. . . .

5. Next, since God justifieth, that is, maketh
men righteous, by healing them from their iniquities, a prayer followeth: " Remember me, O
Lord, according to the favour that Thou bearest
unto Thy people " (ver. 4): that is, that we
may be among those with whom Thou art well
pleased; since God is not well pleased with
them all.   " O visit me with Thy salvation."
This is the Saviour Himself, in whom sins are
forgiven, and souls healed, that they may be able
to keep judgment, and do righteousness; and
since they who here speak know such men to
be blessed, they pray for this themselves. . . .
" Visit us," then, " with Thy salvation," that is,
with Thy Christ.   " To see the felicity of Thy
chosen, and to rejoice in the gladness of Thy
people " (ver. 5): that is, visit us for this reason
with Thy salvation, that we may see the felicity
of Thy chosen, and rejoice in the gladness of
Thy people.   For " felicity " [4] some copies read
" sweetness; " as in the former passage, " For
He is gracious; " where others read, " for He is
sweet."   And it is the same word in the Greek,
as is elsewhere read, " The Lord shall show
sweetness: " [5] which some have translated
"felicity," others "bounty."   But what meaneth,
" Visit us to see the felicity of Thy chosen: "
that is, that happiness which Thou givest to
Thine elect: except that we may not remain
blind, as those unto whom it is said, " But now
ye say we see: therefore your sin remaineth." [6]

For the Lord giveth sight to the blind,[7] not by
their own merits, but in the felicity He giveth
to His chosen, which is the meaning of " the
felicity of Thy chosen: " as, the help of my
countenance, is not of myself, but is my God.[8]
And we speak of our daily bread, as ours, but
we add, Give unto us.[9] . . . " That Thou mayest be praised with Thine inheritance."   I wonder this verse hath been so interpreted in many
copies, since the Greek phrase is one and the
same in these three verses. . . . But since this
seemeth a doubtful expression, if that sense be
true according to which interpreters have preferred, " That Thou mayest be praised," the two
preceding verses also must be so understood, because, as I have said, there is one Greek expression in these three verses; so that the whole
should be thus understood, " Visit us with Thy
salvation, that Thou mayest see the felicity of
Thy chosen; " that is, visit us for this purpose,
that Thou mayest cause us to be there, and
mayest see us there; that "Thou mayest rejoice
in the gladness of Thy people," that is, that
Thou mayest be said to rejoice, since they
rejoice in Thee; that " Thou mayest be praised
with Thine inheritance," that is, mayest be
praised with it, since it may not be praised save
for Thy sake. . . .

6. But let us hear what they next confess:
" we have sinned with our fathers: we have
done amiss, and dealt wickedly " (ver. 6).   What
meaneth "with our fathers"? . . . " Our fathers,"
he saith, " regarded not Thy wonders in Egypt "
(ver. 7); and many other things also, he doth
relate of their sins.   Or is, " we have sinned
with our fathers," to be understood as meaning,
we have sinned like our fathers, that is, by
imitating their sins?   If it be so, it should be
supported by some example of this mode of
expression: which did not occur to me when
I sought on this occasion an instance of any one
saying that he had sinned, or done anything,
with another, whom he had imitated by a similar
act after a long interval of time.   What meaneth
then, " Our fathers understood not Thy wonders; " save this, they did not know what Thou
didst wish to convince them of by these miracles?
What indeed, save life eternal,[10] and a good, not
temporal, but immutable, which is waited for
only through endurance?   For this reason they
impatiently murmured, and provoked, and they
asked to be blessed with present and fugitive
blessings, " Neither were they mindful of the
greatness of Thy mercy."   He reproveth both
their understanding and memory.   Understanding there was need of, that they might meditate
unto what eternal blessings God was calling them

---

[1] Ps. xciv. 15.   [2] Ps. xcvii. 2.
[3] Ps. xxxvii. 6.   [4] *Bonitate.*
[5] Ps. lxxxv. 13.   [6] John ix. 41.

[7] Ps. cxlvi. 8.   [8] Ps. xliii. 5.   [9] Matt. vi. 11.
[10] [A *thesis* which might be maintained against the brilliant para-
dox of Warburton.—C.]

through these temporal ones; and of memory, that at least they might not forget the temporal wonders which had been wrought, and might faithfully believe, that by the same power which they had already experienced, God would free them from the persecutions of their enemies; whereas they forgot the aid which He had given them in Egypt, by means of such wonders, to crush their enemies. "And they provoked, as they went up to the sea, even to the Red Sea." [1] We ought especially to notice how the Scripture doth censure the not understanding that which ought to have been understood, and the not remembering that which ought to have been remembered; which men are unwilling to have ascribed to their own fault, for no other reason than that they may pray less, and be less humble unto God, in whose sight they should confess what they are, and might by praying for His aid, become what they are not. For it is better to accuse even the sins of ignorance and negligence, that they may be done away with, than to excuse them, so that they remain; and it is better to clear them off by calling upon God, than to clench them by provoking Him.

He addeth, that God acted not according to their unbelief. "Nevertheless," he saith, "He saved them for His Name's sake: that He might make His power to be known" (ver. 8): not on account of any deservings of their own.

7. "He rebuked the Red Sea also, and it was dried up" (ver. 9). We do not read that any voice was sent forth from Heaven to rebuke the sea; but he hath called the Divine Power by which this was effected, a rebuke: unless indeed any one may choose to say, that the sea was secretly rebuked, so that the waters might hear, and yet men could not. The power by which God acteth is very abstruse and mysterious, a power which He causeth that even things devoid of sense instantly obey at His will. "So He led them through the deeps, as through a wilderness." He calleth a multitude of waters the deeps. For some wishing to give the sense of this whole verse, have translated, "So He led them forth amid many waters." What then doth "through the deeps, as through a wilderness," mean, except that that had become as a wilderness from its dryness, where before had been the watery deeps?

8. "And He saved them from the hating ones" [2] (ver. 10). Some translators, in order to

avoid an expression unusual in Latin, have rendered the word, by a circumlocution, "And He saved them from the hand of those that hated them, and redeemed them from the hand of the enemy." What price was given in this redemption? Is it a prophecy, since this deed was a figure of Baptism, wherein we are redeemed from the hand of the devil at a great price, which price is the Blood of Christ? whence this is more consistently figured forth, not by any sea indiscriminately, but by the Red Sea; since blood hath a red colour.

9. "As for those that troubled them, the waters overwhelmed them: there was not one of them left" (ver. 11); not of all the Egyptians, but of those who pursued the departing Israelites, desirous either of taking or of killing them.

10. "Then believed they in His words" (ver. 12). The expression seemeth barely Latin, for he saith not "believed His word," [3] or "on His words," [4] but "in His words;" [5] yet it is very frequent in Scripture. "And praised praise unto Him;" such an expression as when we say, "This servitude he served," "such a life he lived." He is here alluding to that well-known hymn, commencing, "I will sing unto the Lord, for He hath triumphed gloriously: the horse and the rider hath He thrown into the sea." [6]

11. "They acted hastily: they forgot His works" (ver. 13): other copies read more intelligibly, "They hastened, they forgot His works, and would not abide His counsel." For they ought to have thought, that so great works of God towards themselves were not without a purpose, but that they invited them to some endless happiness, which was to be waited for with patience; but they hastened to make themselves happy with temporal things, which give no man true happiness, because they do not quench insatiable longing: for "whosoever," saith our Lord, "shall drink of this water, shall thirst again." [7]

12. Lastly, "And they lusted a lust in the wilderness, and they tempted God in the dry land" (ver. 14). The "dry land," or land without water, and "desert," are the same: so also are, "they lusted a lust," and, "they tempted God." The form of speech is the same as above, "they praised a praise." [8]

13. "And He gave them their desire, and sent fulness withal into their souls" (ver. 15). But He did not thus render them happy: for it was not that fulness of which it is said, "Blessed are they which do hunger and thirst after righteousness: for they shall be filled." [9] In this passage he doth not speak of the rational soul, but

---

[1] [The author says, "The copy which I was reading from, had the passage thus: And a star had been prefixed to these two last words, 'even the Red Sea:' which doth mark those readings which occur in the Hebrew, and not in the Septuagint translation. But most of the copies, whether Greek or Latin, which I have been able to inspect, read thus: 'and they provoked,' or, and this is more literally from the Greek, 'and they wrought bitterness, as they went up in the Red Sea.' . . . The word, 'went up,' is used, from the position of the land being such, that we speak of going down from the land of Canaan into Egypt, and of going up from Egypt into it." — C.]
[2] Odientium.

[3] Verbis.   [4] In verba.   [5] In verbis.
[6] Exod. xv. 1. [Compare Rev. xv. 3. — C.]
[7] John iv. 4, 13.   [8] Ps. cvi. 12.   [9] Matt. v. 6.

of the soul as giving animal life to the body; to the substance of which belong meat and drink, according to what is said in the Gospel, " Is not the soul more than meat, and the body than raiment?"[1] as if it belonged to the soul to eat, to the body to be clothed.

14. "And they angered Moses in the tents, and Aaron the saint of the Lord" (ver. 16). What angering, or, as some have more literally rendered it, what provocation,[2] he speaketh of, the following words sufficiently show.

15. "The earth opened," he saith, "and swallowed up Dathan, and covered over the congregation of Abiram" (ver. 17): "swallowed up" answereth to "covered over." Both Dathan and Abiram were equally concerned in a most sacrilegious schism.[3]

16. "And the fire was kindled in their company; the flame burnt up the sinners" (ver. 18). This word is not in Scripture usually applied to those, who, although they live righteously, and in a praiseworthy manner, are not without sin. Rather, as there is a difference between those who scorn and scorners, between men who murmur and murmurers, between men who are writing and writers, and so forth; so Scripture is wont to signify by sinners such as are very wicked, and laden with heavy loads of sins.

17. "And they made a calf in Horeb, and worshipped the graven image" (ver. 19). "Thus they changed their glory, in the similitude of a calf that eateth hay" (ver. 20). He saith not "into" the likeness, but "in" the likeness. It is such a form of speech as where he said, "and they believed in His words."[4] With great effect in truth he saith not, they changed the glory of God when they did this; as the Apostle also saith, "They changed the glory of the incorruptible God into an image made like to corruptible man:"[5] but "their glory." For God was their glory, if they would abide His counsel, and hasten not. . . .

18. "They forgat God who saved them" (ver. 21). How did He save them? "Who did so great things in Egypt: Wondrous works in the land of Ham, and fearful things in the Red Sea" (ver. 22). The things that are wondrous, are also fearful; for there is no wonder without a certain fear: although these might be called fearful, because they beat down their adversaries, and showed them what they ought to fear.

19. "So He said, He would have destroyed them" (ver. 23). Since they forgot Him who saved them, the Worker of wondrous works, and

made and worshipped a graven image, by this atrocious and incredible impiety they deserved death. "Had not Moses His chosen stood before Him in the breaking." He doth not say, that he stood in the breaking,[6] as if to break the wrath of God, but in the way of the breaking, meaning the stroke which was to strike them: that is, had he not put himself in the way for them, saying, "Yet now, if Thou wilt forgive their sin; — and if not, blot me, I pray Thee, out of Thy book." Where it is proved how greatly the intercession of the saints in behalf of others prevaileth with God. For Moses, fearless in the justice of God, which could not blot him out, implored mercy, that He would not blot out those whom He justly might. Thus he "stood before Him in the breaking, to turn away His wrathful indignation, lest He should destroy them."

20. "Yea, they thought scorn of that pleasant land" (ver. 24). But had they seen it? How then could they scorn that which they had not seen, except as the following words explain, "and believed not in His words." Indeed, unless that land which was styled the land that flowed with milk and honey,[7] signified something great, through which, as by a visible token, He was leading those who understood His wondrous works to invisible grace and the kingdom of heaven, they could not be blamed for scorning that land, whose temporal kingdom we also ought to esteem as nothing, that we may love that Jerusalem which is free, the mother of us all,[8] which is in heaven, and truly to be desired. But rather unbelief is here reproved, since they gave no credence to the words of God, who was leading them to great things through small things, and hastening to bless themselves with temporal things, which they carnally savoured of, they "abided not His counsel," as is said above.

21. "But murmured in their tents, and hearkened not unto the voice of the Lord" (ver. 25); who strongly forbade them to murmur.

22. "Then lift He up His hand against them, to overthrow them in the wilderness" (ver. 26); "to cast out their seed among the nations: and to scatter them in the lands" (ver. 27).

23. "They were initiated also unto Baalpeor;" that is, were consecrated to the Gentile idol; "and ate the offerings of the dead" (ver. 28). "Thus they provoked Him to anger with their own inventions; and destruction was multiplied among them" (ver. 29). As if He had deferred the lifting up of His hand which was to cast them down in the desert, and to cast out their seed among the nations, and to scatter them in the lands; as the Apostle saith: "And even as they did not like to retain God in their knowl-

---

[1] Matt. vi. 26.   [2] *Amaricationem.*
[3] [Numb. xvi. 1; Jude 11. Dathan and Abiram were laymen; Korah and others were Levites who presumed to exercise the higher offices of the priesthood. Numb. xvi. 9, 10. Compare 2 Chron. xxvi. 18. — C.]
[4] Ps. cvi. 12.   [5] Rom. i. 23.

[6] *Confractioni.*   [7] Exod. iii. 8.   [8] Gal. iv. 26.

edge, God gave them over to a reprobate mind, to do those things which are not convenient." [1] "'Destruction,' therefore, 'was multiplied among them,' when they were heavily punished for their heavy sins."

24. "Then stood up Phineas, and appeased Him, and the shaking ceased" (ver. 30). He hath related the whole briefly, because he is not here teaching the ignorant, but reminding those who know the history. The word "shaking" here is the same as "breaking" before. For it is one word in the Greek. Lastly, so great was their wickedness, in being consecrated to the idol, and eating the sacrifices of the dead (that is, because the Gentiles [2] sacrificed to dead men as to God), that God would not be otherwise appeased than as Phineas the Priest appeased Him, when he slew a man and a woman together whom he found in adultery. [3] If he had done this from hatred towards them, and not from love, while zeal for the house of God devoured him, it would not have been counted unto him for righteousness. . . . Christ our Lord indeed, when the New Testament was revealed, chose a milder discipline; but the threat of hell is more severe, and this we do not read of in those threatenings held out by God in His temporal government.

25. "And that was counted unto him for righteousness among all posterities for evermore" (ver. 31). God counted this unto His Priest for righteousness, not only as long as posterity shall exist, but "for evermore;" for He who knoweth the heart, knoweth how to weigh with how much love for the people that deed was done.

26. "And they angered Him at the waters of strife: so that Moses was vexed for their sakes" (ver. 32); "because they provoked his spirit, so that he spake doubtfully [4] with his lips" (ver. 33). What is spake doubtfully? As if God, who had done so great wonders before, could not cause water to flow from a rock. For he touched the rock with his rod with doubt, and thus distinguished this miracle from the rest, in which he had not doubted. He thus offended, thus deserved to hear that he should die, without entering into the land of promise. [5] For being disturbed by the murmurs of an unbelieving people, he held not fast that confidence which he ought to have held. Nevertheless, God giveth unto him, as unto His chosen, a good testimony even after his death, so that we may see that this wavering of faith was punished with this penalty only, that he was not allowed to enter that land, whither he was leading the people. . . .

27. But they of whose iniquities this Psalm speaketh, when they had entered into that temporal land of promise, "destroyed not the heathen, which the Lord commanded them" (ver. 34); "but were mingled among the heathen, and learned their works" (ver. 35). "Insomuch that they worshipped their idols, which became to them an offence" (ver. 36). Their not destroying them, but mingling with them, became to them an offence.

28. "Yea, they offered their sons and their daughters unto devils" (ver. 37); "and shed innocent blood, even the blood of their sons and of their daughters, whom they offered unto the idols of Canaan" (ver. 38). That history doth not relate that they offered their sons and daughters to devils and idols; but neither can that Psalm lie, nor the Prophets, who assert this in many passages of their rebukes. But the literature of the Gentiles is not silent respecting this custom of theirs. But what is it that followeth? "And the land was slain with bloods." We might suppose that this was a mistake of the writer, and that he had written *interfecta* for *infecta*, were it not for the goodness of God, who hath willed His Scriptures to be written in many languages; were it not that we see it written as in the text in many Greek [6] copies which we have inspected; "the land was slain with bloods." What meaneth then, "the land was slain," unless this be referred to the men who dwelt in the land, by a metaphorical expression. . . . For they themselves were slaying their own souls when they offered up their sons, and when they shed the blood of infants who were far from consent to this crime: whence it is said, "They shed innocent blood." "The land" therefore "was slain with bloods, and defiled by their works" (ver. 39), since they themselves were slain in soul, and defiled by their works; "and they went a whoring after their own inventions." By inventions are meant what the Greeks call ἐπιτηδεύματα: for this word doth occur in the Greek copies both in this and a former passage, where it is said, "They provoked Him to anger with their own inventions;" "inventions" in both instances signifying what they had initiated others in. Let no man therefore suppose inventions to mean what they had of themselves instituted, without any example before them to imitate. Whence other translators in the Latin tongue have perferred pursuits, affections, imitations, pleasures, to inventions: and the very same who here write inventions, have elsewhere written pursuits. I chose to mention this, lest the word inventions, applied to what they had not invented, but imitated from others, might raise a difficulty.

---

[1] Rom. i. 28.
[2] Oxf. mss. "They like the Gentiles."   [3] Numb. xxv. 8.
[4] *Distinxit.*   [5] Deut. xxxii. 49-52.

[6] *Infecta*, Vulgate; *interfecta* = ἐφονοκτονήθη, Sept.

29. "Therefore was the wrath of the Lord kindled against His own people" (ver. 40). Our translators have been unwilling to use the word anger, for the Greek θυμὸς; though some have used it; while others translate by "indignation" or "mind."[1] Whichever of these terms be adopted, passion doth not affect God; but the power of punishing hath assumed this name metaphorically from custom.

30. "Insomuch that He abhorred His own inheritance; and He gave them over into the hand of the heathen: and they that hated them were lords over them" (ver. 41): "and their enemies oppressed them, and they were brought low under their hands" (ver. 42). Since he hath called them the inheritance of God, it is clear that He abhorred them, and gave them over into their enemies' hands, not in order to their perdition, but for their discipline. Lastly, he saith, "Many a time did He deliver them." "But they provoked Him with their own counsels" (ver. 43). This is what he said above, "They did not abide His counsel." Now a man's counsel is pernicious to himself, when he seeketh those things which are his own only, not those which are God's.[2] In whose inheritance, which inheritance He Himself is to us, when He deigneth His presence for our enjoyment, being with the Saints, we shall suffer no straitening from the society, by our love of anything as our own possession. For that most glorious city, when it hath gained the promised inheritance, in which none shall die, none shall be born, will not contain citizens who shall individually rejoice in their own, for "God shall be all in all."[3] And whoever in this pilgrimage faithfully and earnestly doth long for this society, doth accustom himself to prefer common to private interests, by seeking not his own things, but Jesus Christ's: lest, by being wise and vigilant in his own affairs, he provoke God with his own counsel; but, hoping for what he seeth not, let him not hasten to be blessed with things visible; and, patiently waiting for that everlasting happiness which he seeth not, follow His counsel in His promises, whose aid he prayeth for in his prayers. Thus he will also become humble in his confessions; so as not to be like those, of whom it is said, "They were brought down in their wickedness."

31. Nevertheless, God, full of mercy, forsook them not. "And He saw when they were in adversity, when He heard their complaint" (ver. 44). "And He thought upon His covenant, and repented, according to the multitude of His mercies" (ver. 45). He saith, "He repented," because He changed that wherewith He seemed about to destroy them. With God indeed all things are arranged and fixed; and when He seemeth to act upon sudden motive, He doth nothing but what He foreknew that He should do from eternity; but in the temporal changes of creation, which He ruleth wonderfully, He, without any temporal change in Himself, is said to do by a sudden act of will what in the ordained causes of events He hath arranged in the unchangeableness of His most secret counsel, according to which He doth everything according to defined seasons, doing the present, and having already done the future. And who is capable of comprehending these things?[4] Let us therefore hear the Scripture, speaking high things humbly, giving food for the nourishment of children, and proposing subjects for the research of the older: that everlasting covenant "which He made with Abraham," not the old which is abolished, but the new which is hidden even in the old. "And pitied them," etc. He did that which He had covenanted, but He had foreknown that He would yield this to them when they prayed in their adversity; since even their very prayer, when it was not uttered, but was still to be uttered, undoubtedly was known unto God.

32. So "He gave them unto compassions, in in the sight of all that had taken them captive" (ver. 46). That they might not be vessels of wrath, but vessels of mercy.[5] The compassions unto which He gave them are named in the plural for this reason, I imagine, because each one hath a gift of his own from God, one in one way, another in another.[6] Come then, whosoever readest this, and dost recognise the grace of God, by which we are redeemed unto eternal life through our Lord Jesus Christ, by reading in the apostolical writings, and by searching in the Prophets, and seest the Old Testament revealed in the New, the New veiled in the Old; remember the words of our Lord Jesus Christ, where, when He driveth him out of the hearts of the faithful, He saith, "Now is the prince of this world cast out:"[7] and again of the Apostle, when he saith, "Who hath delivered us from the power of darkness, and hath translated us into the kingdom of His dear Son."[8] Meditate on these and such like things, examine also the Old Testament, and see what is sung in that Psalm, the title of which is, When the temple was being built after the captivity:[9] for there it is said, "Sing unto the Lord a new song." And, that thou mayest not think it doth refer to the Jewish people only, he saith, "Sing unto the Lord, all the whole earth: sing unto the Lord, and praise His Name: declare," or rather, "give the good news of," or, to transfer the very word

---

[1] [Compare p. 426, § 6. — C.]   [2] Philip. ii. 21.
[3] 1 Cor. xv. 28.
[4] 2 Cor. ii. 16.   [5] Rom. ix. 22, 23.   [6] 1 Cor. vii. 7.
[7] John xii. 31.   [8] Col. i. 13.
[9] See LXX. Ps. xcvi. 1.

used in the Greek, "evangelize day from day, His salvation." Here the Gospel (Evangelium) is mentioned, in which is announced the Day that came from Day, our Lord Christ, the Light from Light, the Son from the Father. This also is the meaning of His salvation : for Christ is the Salvation of God, as we have shown above.[1] . . .

33. "Deliver us, O Lord our God, and gather us from among the nations (other copies read, "from the heathen ") ; that we may give thanks unto Thy holy Name, and make our boast of Thy praise " (ver. 47). Then he hath briefly added this very praise, "Blessed be the Lord God of Israel from everlasting, and world without end "[2] (ver. 48) : by which we understand from everlasting to everlasting ; because He shall be praised without end by those of whom it is said, "Blessed are they that dwell in Thy house : they will be alway praising Thee."[3] This is the perfection of the Body of Christ on the third day, when the devils had been cast out, and cures perfected, even unto the immortality of the body itself, the everlasting reign of those who perfectly praise Him, because they perfectly love Him ; and perfectly love Him, because they behold Him face to face. For then shall be completed the prayer at the commencement of this Psalm : [4] "Remember us, O Lord, according to the favour that Thou bearest unto Thy people," etc. For from the Gentiles He doth not gather only the lost sheep of the house of Israel,[5] but also those which do not belong to that fold ; so that there is one flock, as is said, and one Shepherd. But when the Jews suppose that that prophecy belongeth to their visible kingdom, because they know not how to rejoice in the hope of good things unseen, they are about to rush into the snares of him, of whom the Lord saith, " I am come in My Father's Name, and ye receive Me not : if another shall come in his own name, him ye will receive."[6] Of whom the Apostle Paul saith : "that Man of Sin shall be revealed, the son of perdition," etc. And a little after he saith, "Then shall that Wicked be revealed, whom the Lord shall consume with the Spirit of His mouth, and shall destroy with the brightness of His coming," etc.[7] . . . Through that Apostate, through him who exalteth himself above all that is called God, or that is worshipped, it seemeth to me, that the carnal people of Israel will suppose that prophecy to be fulfilled, where it is said, "Deliver us, O Lord, and gather us from among the heathen ; " that under His guidance, before the eyes of their visible enemies, who had visibly taken them captive, they are to have visible glory. Thus they

will believe a lie, because they have not received the love of truth, that they might love not carnal, but spiritual blessings. . . . For Christ had other sheep that were not of this fold : [8] but the devil and his angels had taken captive all those sheep, both among the Israelites and the Gentiles. The power, therefore, of the devil having been cast out of them, in the sight of the evil spirits who had taken them captive, their cry in this prophecy is, that they may be saved and perfected for evermore : "Deliver us, O Lord our God, and gather us from among the heathen." Not, as the Jews imagine it, fulfilled through Antichrist, but through our Lord Christ coming in the name of His Father, "Day from day, His salvation ; " of whom it is here said, "O visit us in Thy salvation ! And let all the people say," the predestined people of the circumcision and of the uncircumcision, a holy race, an adopted people, "So be it ! So be it !"[9]

PSALM CVII.[10]

1. This Psalm commendeth unto us the mercies of God, proved in ourselves, and is therefore the sweeter to the experienced. And it is a wonder if it can be pleasing to any one, except to him who has learned in his own case, what he hears in this Psalm. Yet was it written not for any one or two, but for the people of God, and set forth that it might know itself therein as in a mirror. Its title needeth not now to be treated, for it is Halleluia, and again Halleluia. Which we have a custom of singing at a certain time in our solemnities, after an old tradition of the Church : nor is it without a sacred meaning that we sing it on particular days.[11] Halleluia we sing indeed on certain days,[12] but every day we think it. For if in this word is signified the praise of God, though not in the mouth of the flesh, yet surely in the mouth of the heart. "His praise shall ever be in my mouth."[13] But that the title hath Halleluia not once only but twice, is not peculiar to this Psalm, but the former also hath it so. And as far as appears from its text, that was sung of the people of Israel, but this is sung of the universal Church of God, spread through the whole world. Perchance, it not unfitly hath Halleluia twice, because we cry, Abba, Father. Since Abba is nothing else but Father, yet not without meaning the Apostle said, "in whom we cry, Abba, Father ; "[14] but because one wall indeed coming to the Corner Stone crieth Abba, but the other, from the other side crieth Father ; viz., in that Corner Stone,

---

[1] Above, § 5.
[2] Oxf. mss. add, " so be it ! so be it !"
[3] Ps. lxxxiv. 4.
[4] [Vers. 4, 5, p. 527, supra. — C.]
[5] Matt. xv. 24.
[6] John v. 24.
[7] 2 Thess. ii. 3–11.
[8] John x. 16.
[9] Oxf. mss. add, " Amen."
[10] Lat. CVI.
[11] [It was not used in Lent, and was a feature of the Easter solemnities. See Ps. cxi. infra. — C.]
[12] See on Ps. cxi.
[13] Ps. xxxiv. 1.
[14] Rom. viii. 15.

"who is our Peace, who hath made both one." . . .

2. "Confess unto the Lord that He is sweet, because for aye in His mercy" (ver. 1). This confess ye that He is sweet: if ye have tasted, confess. But he cannot confess, who hath not chosen to taste, for whence shall he say that that is sweet, which he knoweth not. But ye if ye have tasted how sweet the Lord is,[1] "Confess ye to the Lord that He is sweet." If ye have tasted with eagerness, break forth[2] with confession. "For aye is His mercy," that is, for ever. For here "for aye," is so put, since also in some other places of Scripture, for aye, that is, what in Greek is called εἰς αἰῶνα, is understood for ever. For His mercy is not for a time, so as not to be for ever, since for this purpose His present mercy is over men, that they may live with the Angels for ever.

3. "Let them say who are redeemed of the Lord, whom He hath redeemed from the hand of their enemies" (ver. 2). Redeemed indeed it seems was also the people of Israel from the land of Egypt, from the hand of slavery, from fruitless labours, from miry works; yet let us see whether those who say these things, are they who were freed by the Lord from Egypt. It is not so. But who are they? "Those whom He redeemed." Still one might take it also of them, as redeemed from the hand of their enemies, that is, of the Egyptians. Let them be expressed exactly who they are, for whom this Psalm would be sung. "He gathered them from the lands;" these might still be the lands of Egypt, for there are many lands even in one province. Let him speak openly. "From the east and the west, from the north and the sea" (ver. 3). Now then we understand these redeemed, in the whole circle of the earth. This people of God, freed from a great and broad Egypt, is led, as through the Red Sea,[3] that in Baptism it may make an end of its enemies. For by the sacrament as it were of the Red Sea, that is by Baptism consecrated with the Blood of Christ, the pursuing Egyptians, the sins, are washed away. . . . "But all these things happened to them in a figure, and were written for our admonition, on whom the ends of the ages have come."[4] . . .

4. "They wandered in the wilderness, in a dry place, they found not the way of a city to dwell in" (ver. 4). We have heard a wretched wandering; what of want? "Hungry and thirsty, their soul fainted in them" (ver. 5). But wherefore did it faint? for what good? For God is not cruel, but He maketh Himself known, in that it is expedient for us, that He be entreated by us fainting, and that aiding us He

be loved. And therefore after this wandering, and hunger, and thirst, "And they cried unto the Lord in their trouble, and He delivered them out of their distress" (ver. 6). And what did He for them, as they were wandering? "And He led them in the right way" (ver. 7). They found not the way of a city to dwell in, with hunger and thirst they were vexed and faint, "and He led them into the right way, that they might go into a city to dwell in." How He helped their hunger and thirst, He saith not, but even this expect ye: "Let them confess unto the Lord His mercies, and His wonders towards the children of men" (ver. 8). Tell them, ye that are experienced, to the inexperienced; ye that are already in the way, already directed towards finding the city, already at last free from hunger and thirst. "Because He hath satisfied the empty soul, and filled the hungry soul with good things" (ver. 9).

5. "Them that sit in darkness, and in the shadow of death, fast bound in beggary and iron" (ver. 10). Whence this, but that thou wast attributing things to thyself? that thou wast not owning the grace of God? that thou wast rejecting the counsel of God[5] concerning thee? For see what He addeth: "Because they rebelled against the words of the Lord through pride" (ver. 11), not knowing the righteousness of God, and wishing to establish their own,[6] "and they were bitter against the counsel of the Most High." "And their heart was brought low in labour" (ver. 12). And now fight against lust; if God cease to aid thou mayest strive, thou canst not conquer. And when thou shalt be pressed by thine evil, thy heart will be brought low in labour, so that now with humbled heart thou mayest learn to cry out, "O wretched man that I am! who shall deliver me from the body of this death?"[7] . . . Freed, thou wilt confess the mercies of the Lord. "And they cried unto the Lord when they were troubled, and He delivered them out of their distresses" (ver. 13). They were freed from the second temptation. There remains that of weariness and loathing. But first see what He did for them when freed. "And He led them out of darkness and the shadow of death, and brake their bonds asunder" (ver. 14). "Let them confess to the Lord His mercies, and His wonders to the children of men" (ver. 15). Wherefore? what difficulties hath He overcome? "Because He brake the gates of brass, and snapped the bars of iron" (ver. 16). "He took them up from the way of their iniquity, for because of their unrighteousnesses they were brought low" (ver. 17). Because they gave honour to themselves, not to God, because they were establishing their own

---

[1] 1 Pet. ii. 3.
[2] *Eructate.*
[3] Exod. xiv. 22.
[4] 1 Cor. x. 11.
[5] Luke vii. 30.
[6] Rom. x. 3.
[7] Rom. vii. 24.

righteousness, not knowing the righteousness of God,[1] they were brought low. They found that they were helpless without His aid, who were presuming on their own strength alone.

6. "Their soul abhorred all manner of meat" (ver. 18). Now they suffer satiety. They are sick of satiety. They are in danger from satiety. Unless perchance thou thinkest they could be killed with famine, but cannot with satiety. See what followeth. When he had said, "Their soul abhorred all manner of meat," lest thou shouldest think them, as it were, safe of their fulness, and not rather see that they would die of satiety : "And they came near," he saith, " even unto the gates of death." What then remaineth? That even when the word of God delighteth thee, thou account it not to thyself; nor for this be puffed up with any sort of arrogance, and having an appetite for food, proudly spurn at those who are in danger from satiety. " And they cried out unto the Lord when they were in trouble, and He delivered them out of their distresses" (ver. 19). And because it was a sickness not to be pleased, " He sent His Word, and healed them " (ver. 20). See what evil there is in satiety; see whence He delivers, to whom he crieth that loathes his food. " He sent His Word, and healed them, and snatched them," from whence? not from wandering, not from hunger, not from the difficulty of overcoming sins, but " from their corruption." It is a sort of corruption of the mind to loathe what is sweet. Therefore also of this benefit, as of the others before, " Let them confess to the Lord His mercies, and His wonders unto the sons of men " (ver. 21). " And sacrifice the sacrifice of praise " (ver. 22). For now that He may be praised, the Lord is sweet, "and let them tell out His works with gladness." Not with weariness, not with sadness, not with anxiety, not with loathing, but " with gladness."

7. . . . "They who go down on the sea in ships, doing their business on the mighty waters " (ver. 23) ; that is, amongst many peoples. For that waters are often put for peoples, the Apocalypse of John is witness, when on John's asking what those waters were, it was answered him, they are peoples. They then who do their business on mighty waters, " they have seen the works of the Lord, and His wonders in the deep " (ver. 24). For what is deeper than human hearts? hence often break forth winds; storms of sedition, and dissensions, disturb the ship. And what is done in them? God, willing that both they who steer, and they who are conveyed, should cry unto Him, " He spake, and the breath of the storm stood " (ver. 25). What is, stood? Abode, continued, still disturbeth,

long tosseth ; rageth, and passeth not away. " For He spake, and the breath of the storm stood." And what did that breath of the storm? "They go up even to the heavens," in daring; "They go down even into the deeps " (ver. 26), in fearing. "Their soul wasted in miseries." " They were disturbed, and moved like a drunken man " (ver. 27). They who sit at the helm, and they who faithfully love the ship, feel what I say. Certainly, when they speak, when they read, when they interpret, they appear wise. Woe for the storm ! "and all their wisdom," he saith, "was swallowed up." Sometimes all human counsels fail ; whichever way one turns himself, the waves roar, the storm rageth, the arms are powerless : where the prow may strike, to what wave the side may be exposed, whither the stricken ship may be allowed to drift, from what rocks she must be kept back lest she be lost, is impossible for her pilots to see. And what is left but that which follows? " And they cried out unto the Lord when they were troubled, and He delivered them from their distresses " (ver. 28). "And He commanded the storm, and it stood unto clear air " (ver. 29), " and the waves of it were still." Hear on this point the voice of a steersman, one that was in peril, was brought low, was freed. " I would not," he saith, " have you ignorant, brethren, of our distress, which befell us in Asia, that " we were pressed above strength, and above measure " (I see all his " wisdom swallowed up "), " so that we were weary," he saith, " even of life." [2] . . .

" And they were glad, because they were still, and He brought them into the haven of their desire " (ver. 30). " Let His mercies confess unto the Lord, and His wonders towards the sons of men " (ver. 31). Everywhere, without exception, let not our merits, not our strength, not our wisdom, " confess unto the Lord," but, " His mercies." Let Him be loved in every deliverance of ours, who has been invoked in every distress.

8. "And let them exalt Him in the assembly of the people, and praise Him in the seat of the elders " (ver. 32). Let them exalt, let them praise, peoples and elders, merchants and pilots. For what hath He done in this assembly? What hath He established? Whence hath He rescued it? What hath He granted it? Even as He resisted the proud, and gave grace to the humble : [3] the proud, that is, the first people of the Jews, arrogant, and extolling itself on its descent from Abraham, and because to that nation " were entrusted the oracles of God." [4] These things did not avail them unto soundness, but unto pride of heart, rather to swelling than to greatness. What then did God, resisting the

---

[1] Rom. x. 3.   [2] 2 Cor. i. 8.   [3] Jas. iv. 6.   [4] Rom. iii. 2.

proud, but giving grace to the humble ; cutting off the natural branches for their pride ; graffing in the wild olive for its humility?

" He made the rivers a wilderness " (ver. 33). Waters did run there, prophecies were in course. Seek now a prophet among the Jews ; thou findest none. For " He made the outgoings of waters to be thirst." Let them say, " Now there is no prophet more, and He will not know us any more." [1] " A fruitful land to be salt-pools " (ver. 34). Thou seekest there the faith of Christ, thou findest not : thou seekest a prophet, thou findest not : thou seekest a sacrifice, thou findest not : thou seekest a temple, thou findest none. Wherefore this? " From the wickedness of them that dwell therein." Behold how He resisteth the proud : hear how He giveth grace to the humble. " He made the wilderness to be a standing water, and the dry ground to be outgoings of waters " (ver. 35). " And He caused the hungry to dwell there " (ver. 36). Because to Him it was said, " Thou art a Priest for ever, after the order of Melchizedec." [2] For thou seekest a sacrifice among the Jews ; thou hast none after the order of Aaron. Thou seekest it after the order of Melchizedec ; thou findest it not among them, but through the whole world it is celebrated in the Church. " From the rising of the sun to the setting thereof the name of the Lord is praised." [3] . . . " And they sowed fields, and planted vineyards, and gat fruit of corn " (ver. 37) : at which that workman rejoiceth, who saith, " Not because I desire a gift, but I seek fruit." [4] " And He blessed them, and they were multiplied exceedingly, and their cattle were not diminished " (ver. 38). This standeth. For " the foundation of God standeth sure ; because the Lord knoweth them that are His." [5] They are called " beasts of burden," and " cattle," that walk simply in the Church, yet are useful ; not much learned, but full of faith. Therefore, whether spiritual or carnal, " He blessed them."

9. " And they became few, and were vexed " (ver. 39). Whence this? From athwart? Nay, from within. For that they should " become few," " They went out from us, but they were not of us." [6] But therefore he speaketh as of these, of whom he spake before, that they may be discerned with understanding ; because he speaketh as if of the same, because of the sacraments they have in common. For they belong to the people of God, though not by the virtue, yet surely by the appearance of piety : for concerning them we have heard the Apostle, " In the last times there shall come grievous times, for there shall be men lovers of themselves." [7]

The first evil is, " lovers of themselves ; " that is, as being pleased with themselves. Would that they were not pleasing to themselves, and were pleasing to God : would that they would cry out in their difficulties, and be freed from their distresses. But while they presumed greatly on themselves, " they were made few." It is manifest, brethren : all who separate themselves from unity become few. For they are many ; but in unity, while they are not parted from unity. For when the multitude of unity hath begun no more to belong to them, in heresy and schism, they are few. " And they were vexed, from distress of miseries and grief." " Contempt was poured on princes " (ver. 40). For they were rejected by the Church of God, and the more because they wished to be princes, therefore they were despised, and became salt that had lost its savour, cast out abroad, so that it is trodden under foot of men. [8] " And He led them astray in the pathless place, and not in a way." Those above in the way, those directed to a city, and finally led thither, not led astray ; but these, where there was no way, led astray. What is, " Led them astray "? God " gave them up to their own hearts' lusts." [9] For " led astray " means this, gave them up to themselves. For if thou enquire closely, it is they that lead themselves astray. . . . " And He helped the poor out of beggary " (ver. 41). What meaneth this, brethren? Princes are despised, and the poor helped. The proud are cast aside, and the humble provided for. . . . " And made him households like sheep." Thou understandest one poor man and one beggar of him concerning whom he said, " He hath helped the poor out of misery : " this poor man is now many households, this poor man is many nations ; many Churches are one Church, one nation, one household, one sheep. These are great mysteries, great types, how profound, how full of hidden meanings ; how sweetly discovered, since long hidden. Therefore, " the righteous will consider this, and rejoice : and the mouth of all wickedness shall be stopped " (ver. 42). That wickedness that doth prate against unity, and compelleth truth to be made manifest, shall be convicted, and have its mouth stopped.

10. " Who is wise? and he will consider these things ; and will understand the mercies of the Lord " (ver. 43). . . . Not his own deservings, not his own strength, not his own power ; but " the mercies of the Lord ; " who, when he was wandering and in want, led him back to the path, and fed him ; who, when he was struggling against the difficulties of his sins, and bound down with the fetters of habit, released and freed him ; who, when he loathed the Word of God,

---

[1] Ps. lxxiv. 9.　　[2] Ps. cx. 4.　　[3] Ps. cxiii. 3 and Mal. i. 10.
[4] Philip. iv. 17.　[5] 2 Tim. ii. 19.　[6] 1 John ii. 19.
[7] 2 Tim. iii. 2.

[8] Matt. v. 13.　　　　　　[9] Rom. i. 24.

and was almost dying with a kind of weariness, restored him by sending him the medicine of His Word; who, when he was endangered among the risks of shipwreck and storm, stilled the sea, and brought him into port; who, finally, placed him in that people, where He giveth grace to the humble; not in that where he resisteth the proud; and hath made him His own, that remaining within he may be multiplied, not that going out he may be minished. The righteous see this, and rejoice. "The mouth," therefore, "of all wickedness shall be stopped."

PSALM CVIII.[1]

1. I have not thought that the CVIIIth Psalm required an exposition; since I have already expounded it in the LVIIth Psalm,[2] and in the LXth, of the last divisions of which this Psalm consisteth. For the last part of the LVIIth is the first of this, as far as the verse, "Thy glory is above all the earth." Henceforth to the end, is the last part of the LXth: as the last part of the CXXXVth is the same as that of the CXVth,[3] from the verse, "The images of the heathen are but gold and silver:" as the XIVth[4] and LIIId,[5] with a few alterations in the middle, have everything the same from the beginning to the end. Whatever slight differences therefore occur in this CVIIIth Psalm, compared with those two, of parts of which it is composed, are easy to understand; just as we find in the LVIIth,[6] "I will sing and give praise; awake, O my glory:" here, "I will sing and give praise, with my glory."[7] Awake, is said there, that he may sing and give praise therewith. Also, there, "Thy mercy is great" (or, as some translate, "is lifted up") "unto the heavens;"[8] but here, "Thy mercy is great above the heavens."[9] For it is great unto the heavens, that it may be great in the heavens; and this is what he wished to express by "above the heavens." Also in the LXth, "I will rejoice, I will divide Shechem:"[10] here "I will be exalted, and will divide Shechem."[11] Where is shown what is signified in the division of Shechem, which it was prophesied should happen after the Lord's exaltation, and that this joy doth refer to that exaltation; so that He rejoiceth, because He is exalted. Whence he elsewhere saith, "Thou hast turned my heaviness into joy; Thou hast put off my sackcloth, and girded me with gladness."[12] Also there, "Ephraim, the strength of my head:"[13] but here, "Ephraim the taking up of my head."[14] But strength cometh from taking up, that is, He

maketh men strong by taking up, causing fruit in us; for the interpretation of Ephraim is, bearing fruit. But "taking up" may be understood of us, when we take up Christ; or of Christ, when He, who is Head of the Church, taketh us up. And the words, "them that trouble us," in the former Psalm,[15] are the same with "our enemies," in this.[16]

2. We are taught by this Psalm, that those titles which seem to refer to history are most rightly understood prophetically, according to the object of the composition of the Psalms. . . . And yet this Psalm is composed of the latter portions of two,[17] whose titles are different. Where it is signified that each concur in a common object, not in the surface of the history, but in the depth of prophecy, the objects of both being united in this one, the title of which is, "A Song or Psalm of David:"[18] resembling neither of the former titles, otherwise than in the word David. Since, "in many places, and in diverse manners," as the Epistle to the Hebrews saith, "God spoke in former times to the fathers through the Prophets;"[19] yet He spoke of Him whom He sent afterwards, that the words of the Prophets might be fulfilled: for "all the promises of God in Him are yea."[20]

PSALM CIX.[21]

1. Every one who faithfully readeth the Acts of the Apostles, acknowledgeth that this Psalm containeth a prophecy of Christ; for it evidently appeareth that what is here written, "let his days be few, and let another take his office," is prophesied of Judas, the betrayer of Christ. . . . For as some things are said which seem peculiarly to apply to the Apostle Peter, and yet are not clear in their meaning, unless when referred to the Church, whom he is acknowledged to have figuratively represented, on account of the primacy[22] which he bore among the Disciples; as it is written, "I will give unto thee the keys of the kingdom of heaven,"[23] and other passages of the like purport: so Judas doth represent those Jews who were enemies of Christ, who both then hated Christ, and now, in their line of succession, this species of wickedness continuing, hate Him. Of these men, and of this people, not only may what we read more openly discovered in this Psalm be conveniently understood, but also those things which are more expressly stated concerning Judas himself.

2. The Psalm, then, beginneth thus: "O God,

---

[1] Lat. CVII. Why no exposition is here given.
[2] Ps. lvii. 8-12, lx. 5-12.   [3] Ps. cxxxv. 15. cxv. 4.
[4] Ps. xiv.   [5] Ps. liii.   [6] Ps. lvii. 7, 8.
[7] Ps. cviii 1.   [8] Ps. lvii. 10.   [9] Ps. cviii. 4.
[10] Ps. lx. 6.   [11] Ps. cviii. 7.   [12] Ps. xxx. 11.
[13] Ps. lx. 7.   [14] Ps. cviii. 8.

[15] Ps. lx. 12.   [16] Ps. cviii. 13.   [17] Ps. lvii. Tit.; Ps. lx. Tit.
[18] Ps. cviii. Tit.   [19] Heb. i. 1.
[20] 2 Cor. i. 20.   [21] Lat. CVIII.
[22] [That he was *facile princeps* in the original college, nobody denies; that he had any supremacy over his brethren, all antiquity, as well as Holy Scripture, disproves. The keys were equally given to the others. See A. N. F. vol. viii. p. 601 *et seq.*—C.]
[23] Matt. xvi. 19.

be not silent as to my praise; for the mouth of the ungodly, yea, the mouth of the deceitful is opened upon me" (ver. 1). Whence it appeareth, both that the blame, which the ungodly and the deceitful is not silent of, is false, and that the praise, which God is not silent of, is true. " For God is true, but every man a liar; "[1] for no man is true, except him in whom God speaketh. But the highest praise is that of the only-begotten Son of God, in which He is proclaimed even that which He is, the only-begotten Son of God. But this did not appear, but, when His weakness appeared, lay hid, when the mouth of the ungodly and deceitful was opened upon Him; and for this reason his mouth was opened, because His virtue was concealed: and he saith, "the mouth of the deceitful was opened," because the hatred which was covered by deceit burst out into language.

3. "They have spoken against me with false tongues" (ver. 2): then chiefly when they praised him as a " good Master" with insidious adulation. Whence it is elsewhere said: "and they that praised me, are sworn together against me."[2] Next, because they burst into cries, " Crucify Him, crucify Him; "[3] he hath added, " They compassed me about also with words of hatred." They who with a treacherous tongue spoke words seemingly of love, and not of hatred, "against me," since they did this insidiously; afterwards " compassed me about with words" not of false and deceitful love, but of open " hatred, and fought against me without a cause." For as the pious love Christ for nought, so do the wicked hate Him for nought; for as truth is earnestly sought by the best men on its own account, without any advantage, external to itself, in view, so is wickedness sought by the worst men. Whence among secular authors it is said of a very bad man, " he was wicked and cruel for no object."[4]

4. "In place," saith he, " of loving me, they detracted from me" (ver. 3). There are six different acts of this class, which may, when mentioned, very easily be borne in mind; (1) to return good for evil, (2) not to return evil for evil; (3) to return good for good, (4) to return evil for evil; (5) not to return good for good, (6) to return evil for good. The two first of these belong to the good, and the first of these two is the better; the two last belong to the wicked, and the latter of the two is the worse; the two middle to a sort of middle class of persons, but the first of these borders upon the good, the latter on the bad. We should remark these things in the holy Scriptures. Our Lord Himself returneth good for evil, who " justifieth the ungodly; "[5] and who, when hanging upon the Cross, said, " Father, forgive them; for they know not what they do."[6] . . .

5. But after he had said, " in place of loving me, they detracted from me ;" what doth he add? " But I gave myself unto prayer. " He said not indeed what he prayed, but what can we better understand than for them themselves? For they were detracting greatly from Him whom they crucified, when they ridiculed Him as if He were a man, whom in their opinion they had conquered; from which Cross He said, " Father, forgive them, for they know not what they do ; " so that while they in the depth of their malignity were rendering evil for good, He in the height of His goodness was rendering good for evil. . . . The divine words then teach us by our Lord's example, that when we feel others ungrateful to us, not only in that they do not repay us with good, but even return evil for good, we should pray ; He indeed for others who were raging against Him, or in sorrow, or endangered in faith ; but we for ourselves in the first place, that we may by the mercy and aid of God conquer our own mind, by which we are borne on to the desire of revenge, when any detraction is made from us, either in our presence or our absence. . . .

6. He addeth, " Thus have they rewarded me evil for good " (ver. 4). And as if we asked, what evil? for what good? " And hatred," he saith, " for my good will." This is the sum total of their great guilt. For how could the persecutors injure Him who died of His own free-will, and not by compulsion? But this very hatred is the greatest crime of the persecutor, although it be the willing atonement of the sufferer. And he hath sufficiently explained the sense of the above words, " In place of loving me," since they owed love not as a general duty only, but in return for His love : in that he hath here added, " for my good will." This love He mentioneth in the Gospel, when He saith, " How often would I have gathered thy children together, and thou wouldest not ! "[7]

7. He then beginneth to prophesy what they should receive for this very impiety; detailing their lot in such a manner, as if he wished its realization from a desire of revenge. Some not understanding this mode of predicting the future, under the appearance of wishing evil, suppose hatred to be returned for hatred, and an evil will for an evil will, since in truth it belongeth to few to distinguish, in what way the punishment of the wicked pleaseth the accuser, who longeth to satiate his enmity ; and in how widely different a way it pleaseth the judge, who with a righteous mind punisheth sins. For the former returneth evil for evil : but the judge when he punisheth doth

---

[1] Rom. iii. 4.   [2] Ps. cii. 8.   [3] John xix. 6.
[4] Sallust. *Bell. Cat.* i.   [5] Rom. iv. 5.   [6] Luke xxiii. 34.   [7] Matt. xxiii. 37.

not return evil for evil, since he returneth justice to the unjust; and what is just, is surely good. He therefore punisheth not from delight in another's misery, which is evil for evil: but from love of justice, which is good for evil. . . .

8. "Set thou an ungodly man to be ruler over him; and let Satan stand at his right hand" (ver. 5). Though the complaint had been before concerning many, the Psalm is now speaking of one. . . . Since therefore he is here speaking of the traitor Judas, who, according to the Scripture in the Acts of the Apostles, was to be punished with the penalty due to him,[1] what meaneth, "set thou an ungodly man over him," save him whom in the next verse he mentioneth by name, when he saith, "and let Satan stand at his right hand"? He therefore who refused to be subject unto Christ, deserved this, that he should have the devil set over him, that is, that he should be subject unto the devil. . . . For this reason also it is said of those who, preferring the pleasures of this world to God, styled the people blessed who have such and such things, "their right hand is a right hand of iniquity."[2] . . .

9. "When sentence is given upon him, let him be condemned, and let his prayer be turned into sin" (ver. 6). For prayer is not righteous except through Christ, whom he sold in his atrocious sin:. but the prayer which is not made through Christ, not only cannot blot out sin, but is itself turned into sin. But it may be inquired on what occasion Judas could have so prayed, that his prayer was turned into sin. I suppose that before he betrayed the Lord, while he was thinking of betraying Him; for he could no longer pray through Christ. For after he betrayed Him, and repented of it, if he prayed through Christ, he would ask for pardon; if he asked for pardon, he would have hope; if he had hope, he would hope for mercy; if he hoped for mercy, he would not have hanged himself in despair. . . .

10. "Let his days be few" (ver. 7). By "his days," he meant the days of his apostleship, which were few; since before the Passion of our Lord, they were ended by his crime and death. And as if it were asked, What then shall become of that most sacred number twelve, within which our Lord willed, not without a meaning, to limit His twelve first Apostles? he at once addeth, "and let another take his office." As much as to say, let both himself be punished according to his desert, and let his number be filled up.

11. "Let his children be fatherless, and his wife a widow" (ver. 8). After his death, both his children were fatherless, and his wife a widow. "Let his children be vagabonds, and be carried away, and beg their bread" (ver. 9). By "vagabonds" he meaneth, uncertain whither to go,

destitute of all help. "Let them be driven from their habitations." He here explaineth what he had said above, "Let them be carried away." How all this happened to his wife and children, the following verses explain.

12. "Let the extortioner search out all his substance, and let the strangers spoil his labour" (ver. 10). "Let there be no man to help him" (ver. 11): that is, to guard his posterity; wherefore followeth, "nor to have compassion on his fatherless children"

13. But as even orphans may, without one to help them, and without a guardian, nevertheless increase amid trouble and want, and preserve their race by descent; he next saith, "Let his posterity be destroyed; and in the next generation let his name be clean put out" (ver. 12): that is, let what hath been generated by him generate no more, and quickly pass away.

14. But what is it that he next addeth? "Let the wickedness of his fathers be had in remembrance in the sight of the Lord, and let not the sin of his mother be done away" (ver. 13). Is it to be understood, that even the sins of his fathers shall be visited upon him? For upon him they are not visited, who hath been changed in Christ, and hath ceased to be the child of the wicked, by not having imitated their conduct.[3] . . . And to these words, "I will visit the sins of the fathers upon the children,"[4] is added, "who hate Me;" that is, hate Me as their fathers hated Me: so that as the effect of imitating the good is that even their own sins are blotted out, so the imitation of the wicked causeth men to suffer not their own deservings only, but those also of those whom they have imitated. . . .

15. "Let them alway be against[5] the Lord" (ver. 14). "Against the Lord," meaneth in the Lord's sight: for other translators have rendered this line, "let them be always in the sight of the Lord;" while others have rendered it, "let them be before the Lord alway;" as it is elsewhere said, "Thou hast set our misdeeds in Thy sight."[6] By "alway," he meaneth that this great crime should be without pardon, both here, and in a future life. "Let the memorial of them perish from off the earth:" that is, of his father and of his mother. By memorial of them, he meaneth, that which is preserved by successive generations: this he prophesied should perish from the earth, because both Judas himself, and his sons, who were the memorial of his father and mother, without any succeeding offspring, as it is said above, were consumed in the short space of one generation.[7] . . .

---

[1] Acts i. 20.　　　[2] Ps. cxliv. 11.

[3] Ezek. xviii. 4, 20.　[4] Exod. xx. 5.　[5] Contra.　[6] Ps. xc. 8.
[7] [Here he inquires whether Judas, in Hades, could know the condition of his family; and he replies, "It is indeed a great question, and not one to be discussed at present, because it belongeth to a labour of greater extent, whether, or to what degree, or in what manner, the spirits of the dead are aware of what is passing around us." He compares Luke xvi. 23, 28.—C.]

16. "And that, because he remembered not to act mercifully" (ver. 15); either Judas, or the people itself. But "remembered not" is better understood of the people: for if they slew Christ, they might well remember the deed in penitence, and act mercifully towards His members, whom they most perseveringly persecuted. For this reason he saith, "but persecuted the poor man and the beggar" (ver. 16). It may indeed be understood of Judas; for the Lord did not disdain to become poor, when He was rich, that we might be enriched by His poverty.[1] But how shall I understand the word "beggar," save perhaps because He said to the Samaritan woman, "Give me to drink,"[2] and on the Cross He said, "I thirst."[3] But as to what followeth, I do not see how it can be understood of our Head Himself, that is, the Saviour of His own body, whom Judas persecuted. For after saying, "He persecuted the poor man and the beggar:" he addeth, "and to slay," that is, "that he might slay Him," for some have so rendered it, "Him that was pricked at the heart." This expression is not commonly used except of the stings of past sins in the sorrows of penitence; as it is said of those who, when they had heard the Apostles after our Lord's ascension, were "pricked in heart," even they who had slain the Lord. . . .

17. The Psalm then continueth: "His delight was in cursing, and it shall happen to him" (ver. 17). Although Judas loved cursing, both in stealing from the money bag, and selling and betraying the Lord: nevertheless, that people more openly loved cursing, when they said, "His blood be on us, and on our children."[4] "He loved not blessing, therefore it shall be far from him." Such was Judas indeed, since he loved not Christ, in whom is everlasting blessing; but the Jewish people still more decidedly refused blessing, unto whom he who had been enlightened by the Lord said, "Will ye also be His disciples?"[5] "He clothed himself with cursing, like as with a raiment:" either Judas, or that people. "And it came into his bowels like water."[6] Both without, then, and within; without, like a garment; within, like water: since he hath come before the judgment-seat of Him "who hath power to destroy both body and soul in hell;"[7] the body without, the soul within. "And like oil into his bones." He showeth that he worketh evil with delight, and storeth up cursing for himself, that is, everlasting punishment; for blessing is eternal life. For at present evil deeds are his delight, flowing like water into his bowels, like oil into his bones; but it is styled cursing, because God hath appointed torments for such men.

18. "Let it be unto him as the cloak which covereth him" (ver. 18). Since he hath before spoken of the cloak, why doth he repeat it? When he said, "He clothed himself with cursing as with a raiment;" doth the raiment with which he is "covered" differ from that with which he is "clothed"? For every man is clothed with his tunic, covered with his cloak; and what is this, save boasting in iniquity, even in the sight of men? "and as the girdle," he saith, "that he is alway girded withal." Men are girded chiefly that they may be better fit for toil, that they may not be hindered by the folds of their dress. He therefore girdeth himself with curses, who designeth an evil which he hath carefully contrived, not on a sudden impulse, and who learneth in such a manner to do evil, that he is always ready to commit it.

19. "This is the work of them that slander me before the Lord" (ver. 19). He said not, "their reward," but, "their work:" for it is clear that by the clothing, covering, water, oil, and girdle, he was describing the very works by which eternal curses are procured. It is not then one Judas, but many, of whom it is said, "This is the work of them that slander me before the Lord." Although indeed the plural number might have been put for the singular; even as, when Herod died, it was said by the Angel, "They are dead which sought the young Child's life."[8] But who slander Christ more before the Lord, than they who slander the very words of the Lord, by declaring that it is not He whom the Law of the Lord and His Prophets announced beforehand? "And of those that speak evil against my soul:" by denying that He, when He had willed, could have arisen: though He saith, "I have power to lay down My life, and I have power to take it again."[9]

20. "But work Thou with me, O Lord God" (ver. 20). Some have thought "mercifully" should be understood, some have actually added it; but the best copies have the words thus: "But work Thou with me, O Lord God, for Thy Name's sake." Whence a higher sense should not be passed over, supposing the Son to have thus addressed the Father, "Deal Thou with Me," since the works of the Father and of the Son are the same. Where although we understand mercy,—for these words follow, "for sweet is Thy mercy,"—because he said not, "In me," or, "over me;" or anything of this sort: but, "work Thou with Me;" we rightly understand that the Father and Son together work mercifully towards the vessels of mercy.[10] "Work with me,"[1]

[1] 2 Cor. viii. 9.   [2] John iv. 7.   [3] John xix. 28.
[4] Matt. xxxii. 25.   [5] John ix 27.
[6] [It seems to me there is here a reference to the water of jealousy, Numb. v. 22, 23. Compare Acts i. 18. As to oil, generally a blessing, compare Ps. lv. 21; Prov. v. 3, 4. "For envy they delivered Him." Prov. xiv. 30.—C.]
[7] Matt. x. 28.

[8] Matt. ii. 20.   [9] John x. 18.
[10] Rom. ix. 23.   [1] *Fac Mecum.*

may also be understood to mean, help me. We use this expression in our daily language, when we are speaking of anything which is in our favour; "It works with us." For the Father aideth the Son, as far as the Deity aideth Man, on account of His having assumed the "form of a servant," to which Man, God, and to which "Form of a servant," the Lord too is Father. For in the "form of God," the Son needeth not aid, for He is eqally all-powerful with the Father, on which account He also is the helper of men. . . . And because when he had said, "Work Thou with me," he added, "for Thy Name's sake," he hath commended grace. For without previous deserving works, human nature was raised to such a height, that the whole in one, the Word and Flesh, that is, God and Man, was styled the Only-begotten Son of God. And this was done that that which had been lost might be sought by Him who had created it, through that which had not been lost; whence the following words, "For Thy mercy is sweet."

21. "O deliver me, for I am needy and poor" (ver. 21). Need and poverty is that weakness, through which He was crucified.[1] "And my heart is disturbed within me." This alludeth to those words which He spoke when His Passion was drawing near, "My soul is exceeding sorrowful, even unto death."[2]

22. "I go hence like a shadow that declineth" (ver. 22). By this he signified death itself. For as night comes of the shadow's declining, so death comes of mortal flesh. "And am driven away as the locusts." This I think would be more suitably understood of His members, that is, of His faithful disciples. That he might make it much plainer, he preferred writing "locusts" in the plural number: although many may be understood where the singular number is used, as in that passage, "He spake, and the locust came;"[3] but it would have been more obscure. His disciples, then, were driven away, that is, were put to flight by persecutors, either the multitude of whom He wished to be signified by the word locusts, or their passing from one place to another.

23. "My knees are weak through fasting" (ver. 23). We read, that our Lord Christ underwent a fast of forty days:[4] but had fasting so great power over Him, that His knees were weakened? Or is this more suitably understood of His members, that is, of His saints? "And my flesh is changed because of the oil;"[5] because of spiritual grace. Whence Christ was so called from the Greek word, *chrisma*, which signifies unction. But the flesh was changed

through the oil, not for the worse, but for the better, that is, rising from the dishonour of death to the glory of immortality. . . . His flesh was not yet changed. But whether the Holy Spirit be represented by water through the notion of ablution or irrigation, or by oil through that of exultation and the inflaming of charity; It doth not differ from Itself, because Its types are different. For there is a great difference between the lion and the lamb, and yet Christ is represented by both. . . .

24. "I became also a reproach unto them" (ver. 24): through the death of the Cross. "For Christ hath redeemed us from the curse of the law, being made a curse for us."[6] "They looked upon Me, and shaked their heads." Because they beheld His crucifixion, without beholding His resurrection: they saw when His knees were weakened, they saw not when His flesh was changed.

25. "Help me, O Lord my God: O save me according to Thy mercy" (ver. 25). This may be referred to the whole, both to the Head and to the body: to the Head, owing to His having taken the form of a servant; to the body, on account of the servants themselves. For He might even in them have said unto God, "Help Me:" and, "O save Me:" as in them He said unto Paul, "Why persecutest thou Me"?[7] The following words, "according to Thy mercy," describe grace given gratuitously, not according to the merit of works.

26. "And let them know how that this is Thy Hand, and that Thou, Lord, hast made it" (ver. 26). He said, "Let them know," of those for whom He even prayed while they were raging; for even those who afterwards believed in Him were among the crowd who shook their heads in mockery of Him. But let those who ascribe unto God the shape of the human body, learn in what sense God hath a hand. Let us therefore understand, that the Hand of God meaneth Christ: whence it is elsewhere said, "Unto whom is the arm of the Lord revealed?"[8] . . .

27. "Though they curse, yet bless Thou" (ver. 27). Vain therefore and false is the cursing of the sons of men, that have pleasure in vanity, and seek a lie;[9] but when God blesseth, He doth what He saith. "Let them be confounded that rise up against me." For their imagining that they have some power against Me, is the reason that they rise up against Me; but when I shall have been exalted above the heavens, and My glory shall have commenced spreading over the whole earth, they shall be confounded. "But Thy servant shall rejoice:" either on the right hand of the Father, or in His members when they rejoice, both in hope

---

1 2 Cor. xiii. 4. 2 Matt. xxvi. 38.
3 Ps. cv. 34. 4 Matt. iv. 2.
5 [Strange that our author's power of association fails to connect this with John xii 7, and so with another incident in the history of Judas, quite to his purpose. See this series, vol. vi. p. 174.—C.]

6 Gal. iii. 13. 7 Acts ix. 4.
8 Isa. liii. 1. 9 Ps. iv. 2.

among temptations, and after temptations for evermore.

28. "Let my slanderers be clothed with shame" (ver. 28) : that is, let it shame them to have slandered me. But this may also be understood as a blessing, in that they are amended. "And let them cover themselves with their own confusion, as with a double cloak;" for *diplois* is a double cloak; that is, let them be confounded both within and without : both before God and before men.

29. "As for me, I will confess greatly[1] unto the Lord with my mouth" (ver. 29). . . . Is He said to "praise among the multitude" because He is with His Church here even unto the end of the world;[2] so that we may understand by "among the multitude," that He is honoured by this very multitude? For he is said to be in the midst, unto whom the chief honour is paid. But if the heart is, as it were, that which is midmost of a man, no better construction can be put on this passage than this, I will praise Him in the hearts of many. For Christ dwelleth through faith in our hearts;[3] and therefore he saith, "with my mouth," that is, with the mouth of my body, which is the Church.

30. "For He stood at the right hand of the poor" (ver. 30). It was said of Judas, "Let Satan stand at his right hand;" since he chose to increase his riches by selling Christ; but here the Lord stood at the right hand of the poor, that the Lord Himself might be the poor man's riches. "He stood at the right hand of the poor," not to multiply the years of a life that one day must end, nor to increase his stores, nor to render him strong in the strength of the body, or secure for a time; "but," he saith, "to save my soul from the persecutors." Now the soul is rendered safe from the persecutors, if we do not consent to them unto evil; but there is no such consent to them when the Lord standeth at the right hand of the poor, that he may not give way through his very poverty, that is, weakness. This aid was given to the Body of Christ in the case of all the holy Martyrs.

PSALM CX.[4]

1. . . . This Psalm is one of those promises, surely and openly prophesying our Lord and Saviour Jesus Christ; so that we are utterly unable to doubt that Christ is announced in this Psalm, since we are now Christians, and believe the Gospel. For when our Lord and Saviour Jesus Christ asked of the Jews, whose Son they alleged Christ to be, and they had replied, "the Son of David;" He at once replied to their answer, "How then doth David in spirit call Him Lord, saying, The Lord said unto My Lord?" etc. "If then," He asked, "David in the spirit call Him Lord, how is He his son?"[5] With this verse this Psalm beginneth.

2. "The Lord said unto my Lord, Sit Thou on My right hand, until I make Thine enemies Thy footstool" (ver. 1). We ought, therefore, thoroughly to consider this question proposed to the Jews by the Lord, in the very commencement of the Psalm. For if what the Jews answered be asked of us, whether we confess or deny it; God forbid that we should deny it. If it be said to us, Is Christ the Son of David, or not? if we reply, No, we contradict the Gospel; for the Gospel of St. Matthew thus beginneth, "The book of the generation of Jesus Christ, the Son of David."[6] The Evangelist declareth, that he is writing the book of the generation of Jesus Christ, the Son of David. The Jews, then, when questioned by Christ, whose Son they believed Christ to be, rightly answered, the Son of David. The Gospel agreeth with their answer. Not only the suspicion of the Jews, but the faith of Christians, doth declare this. . . . "If then David in the spirit called Him Lord, how is He his son?" The Jews were silent at this question: they found no further reply: yet they did not seek Him as the Lord, for they did not acknowledge Him to be Himself that Son of David. But let us, brethren, both believe and declare : for, "with the heart we believe unto righteousness: but with the mouth confession is made unto salvation;"[7] let us believe, I say, and let us declare both the Son of David, and the Lord of David. Let us not be ashamed of the Son of David, lest we find the Lord of David angry with us.

3. . . . We know that Christ sitteth at the right hand of the Father, since His resurrection from the dead, and ascent into heaven. It is already done : we saw not it, but we have believed it : we have read it in the Scripture, have heard it preached, and hold it by faith. So that by the very circumstance that Christ was David's Son, He became His Lord also. For That which was born of the seed of David was so honoured, that It was also the Lord of David. Thou wonderest at this, as if the same did not happen in human affairs. For if it should happen, that the son of any private person be made a king, will he not be his father's lord? What is yet more wonderful may happen, not only that the son of a private person, by being made a king, may

[1] [He says : " The word *nimis* is used in Latin to express excess, the contrary to *parum*, which meaneth deficiency. The Greek word for *nimis* is ἄγαν : but this verse hath σφόδρα, not ἄγαν; which our translators have sometimes rendered by *nimis*, sometimes by *valdè* ('very much'). Now if *nimis* be taken as equivalent to *valdè*, it may be understood of praise : for this confession signifieth praise. For the next words are, ' and I will praise Him among the multitude.' " — C.]

[2] Matt. xxviii. 20. [3] Eph. iii. 17.

[4] Lat. CIX. A sermon to the people.

[5] Matt. xxii. 42-45. [6] Matt. i. 1. [7] Rom. x. 10.

become his father's lord; but that the son of a layman, by being made a Bishop, may become his father's father. So that in this very circumstance, that Christ took upon Him the flesh, that He died in the flesh, that He rose again in the same flesh, that in the same He ascended into Heaven, and sitteth on the right hand of His Father, in this same flesh so honoured, so brightened, so changed into a heavenly garb, He is both David's Son, and David's Lord. . . .

4. Christ, therefore, sitteth at the right hand of God, the Son is on the right hand of the Father, hidden from us. Let us believe. Two things are here said: that God said, "Sit Thou on My right hand;" and added, "until I make Thy enemies Thy footstool;" that is, beneath Thy feet. Thou dost not see Christ sitting at the right hand of the Father: yet thou canst see this, how His enemies are made His footstool. While the latter is fulfilled openly, believe the former to be fulfilled secretly. What enemies are made His footstool? Those to whom imagining vain things it is said, "Why do the heathen so furiously rage together: and why do the people imagine a vain thing?" etc.[1] . . . He therefore sitteth at the right hand of God, till His enemies be placed beneath His feet. This is going on, this is taking place: although it is accomplished by degrees, it is going on without end. For though the heathen rage, will they, taking counsel together against Christ, prevent the fulfilment of these words: "I will give thee the heathen for thine inheritance, and the utmost parts of the earth for thy possession"? . . . "Their memorial is perished with a cry;" but, "The Lord shall endure for ever:"[2] as another Psalm, but not another Spirit, saith.

5. And what followeth? "The Lord shall send the rod of Thy power out of Sion" (ver. 2). It appeareth, brethren, it most clearly appeareth, that the Prophet is not speaking of that kingdom of Christ, in which He reigneth for ever with His Father, Ruler of the things which are made through Him: for when doth not God the Word reign, who is in the beginning with God?[3] For it is said, "Now unto the King eternal, immortal, invisible, the only wise God, be honour and glory for ever and ever."[4] To what eternal King? To one invisible, incorruptible. For in this, that Christ is with the Father, invisible and incorruptible, because He is His Word, and His Power, and His Wisdom, and God with God, through whom all things were made; He is "King eternal;" but, nevertheless, that reign of temporal government, by which, through the mediation of His flesh, He called us into eternity, beginneth with Chris-

tians; but of His reign there shall be no end. His enemies therefore are made His footstool, while He is sitting on the right hand of His Father, as it is written; this is now going on, this will go on unto the end. . . .

6. When therefore He hath sent the rod of His power out of Sion: what shall happen? "Be Thou ruler, even in the midst among Thine enemies." First, "Be Thou ruler in the midst of Thine enemies:" in the midst of the raging heathen. For shall He rule "in the midst of His enemies" at a later season, when the Saints have received their reward, and the ungodly their condemnation? And what wonder if He shall then rule, when the righteous reign with Him for ever, and the ungodly burn with eternal punishments? What wonder, if He shall then? Now "in the midst of Thine enemies," now in this transition of ages, in this propagation and succession of human mortality, now while the torrent of time is gliding by, unto this is the rod of Thy power sent out of Sion, "that Thou mayest be Ruler in the midst of Thine enemies." Rule Thou, rule among Pagans, Jews, heretics, false brethren. Rule Thou, rule, O Son of David, Lord of David, rule in the midst of Pagans, Jews, heretics, false brethren. "Be Thou Ruler in the midst of Thine enemies." We understand not this verse aright, if we do not see that it is already going on. . . .

7. "With Thee the beginning on the day of Thy power" (ver. 3). What is this day of His power, when is there beginning with Him, or what beginning, or in what sense is there beginning with Him, since He is the Beginning? . . .

8. What meaneth, "With Thee is the beginning"? Suppose anything you please as the beginning. Of Christ Himself, it would rather have been said, Thou art the Beginning, than, With Thee is the beginning. For He answered to those who asked Him, "Who art Thou?" and said, "Even the same that I said unto you, the Beginning;"[5] since His Father also is the Beginning, of whom is the only-begotten Son, in which Beginning was the Word, for the Word was with God. What then, if both the Father and the Son are the beginning, are there two beginnings? God forbid! For as the Father is God, and the Son is God, but the Father and the Son are not two Gods, but one God: so is the Father Beginning and the Son Beginning, but the Father and the Son are not two, but one Beginning. "With Thee is the beginning." Then it shall appear in what sense the beginning is with Thee. Not that the beginning is not with Thee here also. For hast Thou not also said, "Behold, ye shall be scattered, every man to his own, and shall leave Me alone; but I am

[1] Ps. ii. 1, etc.   [2] Ps. ix. 7.   [3] John i. 1.
[4] 1 Tim. i. 17.   [5] John viii. 25.

not alone, because the Father is with Me"?[1] Here therefore also, the beginning is with Thee. For Thou hast said elsewhere also, "But the Father that dwelleth in Me, He doeth His works."[2] "With Thee is the beginning:" nor was the Father ever separated from Thee. But when the Beginning shall appear to be with Thee, then shall it be manifest unto all who are made like Thee; since they shall see Thee as Thou art;[3] for Philip saw Thee here, and sought the Father.[4] Then therefore shall be seen what now is believed: then shall "the beginning be with Thee" in the sight of the righteous, in the sight of saints; the ungodly being removed, that they may not see the brightness of the·Lord. . . .

9. Explain of what power thou speakest. Because here also, as is said, His power is mentioned, when the rod of His power is sent forth out of Sion, that He may be Ruler in the midst of His enemies. Of what power speakest thou, "In the splendour of the saints"? "In the splendour," he saith, "of the saints." He speaketh of that power when the saints shall be in splendour; not when still carrying about their earthly flesh, and groaning in a mortal and corruptible body. . . .

10. But this is put off, this will be granted afterwards: what is there now? "From the womb I have begotten Thee, before the morning star." What is here? If God hath a Son, hath He also a womb? Like fleshly bodies, He hath not; for He hath not a bosom either; yet it is said, "He who is in the bosom of the Father, hath declared Him."[5] But that which is the womb, is the bosom also: both bosom and womb are put for a secret place. What meaneth, "from the womb"? From what is secret, from what is hidden; from Myself, from My substance; this is the meaning of "from the womb;" for, "Who shall declare His generation?"[6] Let us then understand the Father saying unto the Son, "From My womb before the morning star have I brought Thee forth." What then meaneth, "before the morning star"? The morning star is put for the stars, as if the Scripture signified the whole from a part, and from one conspicuous star all the stars. But how were those stars created? "That they may be for signs, and for seasons, and for days, and years."[7] . . . This expression also, "before the morning star," is used both figuratively and literally, and was thus fulfilled. For the Lord was born at night from the womb of the Virgin Mary; the testimony of the shepherds doth assert this, who were "keeping watch over their flock."[8] *So David:* O Thou, my Lord, who sittest at the right hand of my Lord, whence

art Thou my Son, except because, "From the womb before the morning star I have begotten Thee"?

11. And unto what art Thou born? "The Lord hath sworn, and will not repent: Thou art a Priest for ever after the order of Melchizedec" (ver. 4). For unto this wast Thou born from the womb before the morning star, that Thou mightest be a Priest for ever after the order of Melchizedec. For in that character in which He was born of the Father, God with God, coeternal with Him who begot Him, He is not a Priest; but He is a Priest on account of the flesh which He assumed, on account of the victim which He was to offer for us received from us. "The Lord," then, "hath sworn." What then meaneth, the Lord hath sworn? Doth the Lord, who forbiddeth men to swear,[9] Himself swear? Or doth He possibly forbid man to swear chiefly on this account, that he may not fall into perjury, and for this reason the Lord may swear, since He cannot be forsworn. For man, who, through a habit of swearing, may slip into perjury, is rightly forbidden to swear: for he will be farther from perjury in proportion as he is far from swearing. For the man who sweareth, may swear truly or falsely: but he who sweareth not, cannot swear falsely; for he sweareth not at all. Why then should not the Lord swear, since the Lord's oath is the seal of ·the promise? Let Him swear by all means. What then dost thou, when thou swearest? Thou callest God to witness: this is to swear, to call God to witness; and for this reason there must be anxiety, that thou mayest not call God to witness anything false. If therefore thou by an oath dost call God to witness, why then should not God also call Himself to witness with an oath? "I live, saith the Lord," this is the Lord's oath. . . . "The Lord sware," then, that is, confirmed: "He will not repent," He will not change. What? "Thou art a Priest for ever. "For ever," for He will not repent. But Priest, in what sense? Will there be those victims, victims offered by the Patriarchs, altars of blood, and tabernacle, and those sacred emblems of the Old Covenant? God forbid! These things are already abolished; the temple being destroyed, that priesthood taken away, their victim and their sacrifice having alike disappeared, not even the Jews have these things. They see that the priesthood after the order of Aaron hath already perished, and they do not recognise the Priesthood after the order of Melchizedec. I speak unto believers. If catechumens understand not something, let them lay aside sloth, and hasten unto knowledge. It is not therefore

---

[1] John xvi. 32.   [2] John xiv. 10.   [3] 1 John iii. 2.
[4] John xiv. 8.   [5] John i. 18.   [6] Isa. liii. 8.
[7] Gen. i. 14.   [8] Luke ii. 7, 8.

[9] Matt. v. 34.

needful for me to disclose mysteries here : [1] let the Scriptures intimate to you what is the Priesthood after the order of Melchizedec.

12. "The Lord on Thy right hand" (ver. 5). The Lord had said, "Sit Thou on My right hand;" now the Lord is on His right hand, as if they changed seats. . . . That very Christ, the "Lord on Thy right hand," unto whom Thou hast sworn, and it will not repent Thee: what doth He, Priest for evermore? What doth He, who is at the right hand of God, and intercedeth for us,[2] like a priest entering into the inner places, and into the holy of holies, into the mysteries of heaven, He alone being without sin, and therefore easily purifying from sins.[3] He therefore "on Thy right hand shall wound even kings in the day of His wrath." What kings, dost thou ask? Hast thou forgotten? "The kings of the earth stood up, and the rulers took counsel together against the Lord, and against His Anointed."[4] These kings He wounded by His glory, and by the weight of His Name made kings weak, so that they had not power to effect what they wished. For they strove amain to blot out the Christian name from the earth, and could not; for "Whosoever shall fall on this stone shall be broken."[5] Kings therefore fall on this "stone of offence," and are therefore wounded, when they say, Who is Christ? I know not what Jew or what Galilean He may have been, who died, who was slain in such a manner! The stone is before thy feet, lying, so to speak, mean and humble: therefore by scorning thou dost stumble, by stumbling thou fallest, by falling thou art wounded. . . . "But on whomsoever it shall fall, it will grind him to powder."[6] When therefore any one falleth upon it, it lieth as it were low; it then woundeth: but when it shall grind him to powder, then it will come from above. See how in these two words, it shall wound him and grind him to powder: he striketh upon it, and it shall come down upon him: are distinguished the two seasons, of the humiliation and the majesty of Christ, of hidden punishment and future judgment. He will not crush, when He cometh, that man whom He doth not wound when He lieth in a contemptible appearance. . . .

13. "He shall judge among the heathen: He shall fill up what hath fallen" (ver. 6). Whoever thou art who art obstinate against Christ, thou hast raised on high a tower that must fall. It is good that thou shouldest cast thyself down, become humble, throw thyself at the feet of Him

who sitteth on the right hand of the Father, that in thee a ruin may be made to be built up. For if thou abidest in thy evil height, thou shalt be cast down when thou canst not be built up. For of such the Scripture saith in another passage: "Therefore shall He break down, and not build them up."[7] Beyond doubt he would not say *this* of some, unless there were some whom He broke down so as to build them up again. And this is going on at this time, while Christ is judging among the heathen in such a manner as to fill up what hath fallen. "He shall smite many heads over the earth." Here upon the earth in this life He shall smite many heads. He maketh them humble instead of proud; and I dare to say, my brethren, that it is more profitable to walk here humbly with the head wounded, than with the head erect to fall into the judgment of eternal death. He will smite many heads when he causeth them to fall, but He will fill them up and build them up again.

14. "He shall drink· of the brook[8] in the way, therefore shall he lift up his head" (ver. 7). Let us consider Him drinking of the brook in the way: first of all, what is the brook? the onward flow of human mortality: for as a brook is gathered together by the rain, overflows, roars, runs, and by running runs down, that is, finishes its course; so is all this course of mortality. Men are born, they live, they die, and when some die others are born, and when they die others are born, they succeed, they flock together, they depart and will not remain. What is held fast here? what doth not run? what is not on its way to the abyss as if it was gathered together from rain? For as a river suddenly drawn together from rain from the drops of showers runneth into the sea, and is seen no more, nor was it seen before it was collected from the rain; so this hidden rain is collected together from hidden sources, and floweth on; at death again it travelleth where it is hidden: this intermediate state soundeth and passeth away. Of this brook He drinketh, He hath not disdained to drink of this brook; for to drink of this brook was to Him to be born and to die. What this brook hath, is birth and death; Christ assumed this, He was born, He died. "Therefore hath He lifted up His head;" that is, because He was humble, and "became obedient unto death, even the death of the Cross: therefore God also hath highly exalted Him, and given Him a Name which is above every name; that at the Name of Jesus every knee shall bow, of things in Heaven, and things in earth, and things under the earth; and that every tongue shall confess that Jesus Christ the Lord is in the glory of God the Father."[9]

---

[1] [He says elsewhere on Ps. civ. ver. 3: "What is that which is hidden, and is not public in the Church? The Sacrament of Baptism, the Sacrament of the Eucharist. For our good works even Pagans see, but Sacraments are hidden from them." Note the implications: two Sacraments, and no public celebration of the Eucharist. See A. N. F. vol. viii. Primitive Liturgies *passim*. — C.]
[2] Rom. viii. 34.   [3] Heb. ix. 12, 14, 24.   [4] Ps. ii. 2.
[5] Matt. xxi. 44.   [6] Luke xx. 18.

[7] Ps. xxviii. 5.   [8] *De torrente*.   [9] Philip. ii. 8-11.

PSALM CXI.[1]

1. The days have come for us to sing Allelujah.[2] . . . Now these days come only to pass away, and pass away to come, again, and typify the day which does not come and pass away, because it is neither preceded by yesterday to cause it to come, nor pressed upon by the morrow to cause it to pass. . . . For as these days succeed in regular season, with a joyful cheerfulness, the past days of Lent, whereby the misery of this life before the Resurrection of the Lord's body is signified ; so that day which after the Resurrection shall be given to the full body of the Lord, that is, to the holy Church, when all the troubles and sorrows of this life have been shut out, shall succeed with perpetual bliss. But this life demandeth from us self-restraint, that although groaning and weighed down with our toil and struggles, and desiring to be clothed upon with our house which is from heaven,[3] we may refrain from secular pleasures : and this is signified by the number of forty, which was the period of the fasts of Moses, and Elias,[4] and our Lord Himself. . . . But by the number fifty after our Lord's resurrection, during which season we sing Allelujah, not the term and passing away of a certain season is signified, but that blessed eternity ; because the *denary*[5] added to forty signifieth the reward paid to the faithful who toil in this life, which our Father hath prepared an equal share of for the first and for the last. Let us therefore hear the heart of the people of God full of divine praises. He representeth in this Psalm some one exulting in happy joyfulness, he prefigureth the people whose hearts are overflowing with the love of God, that is, the body of Christ, freed from all evil.

2. "I will make confession unto Thee, O Lord," he saith, "with my whole heart" (ver. 1). Confession is not always confession of sins, but the praise of God is poured forth in the devotion of confession. The former mourneth, the latter rejoiceth : the former showeth the wound to the physician, the latter giveth thanks for health. The latter confession signifieth some one, not merely freed from every evil, but even separate from all the ill-disposed. And for this reason let us consider the place where he confesseth unto the Lord with all his heart. "In the counsel," he saith, "of the upright, and in the congregation : " I suppose, of those who shall "sit upon the twelve thrones, judging the twelve tribes of Israel."[6] For there will be no longer an unjust man among them, the thefts of no Judas are allowed, no Simon Magus is baptized, wishing to buy the Spirit, whilst he

designeth to sell it ;[7] no coppersmith like Alexander doth many evil deeds,[8] no man covered with sheep's clothing creepeth in with feigned fraternity ; such as those among whom the Church must now groan, and such as she must then shut out, when all the righteous shall be gathered together.

"These are the great works of the Lord, sought out unto all His wills " (ver. 2) : through which mercy forsaketh none who confesseth, no man's wickedness is unpunished.[9] . . . Let man choose for himself what he listeth : the works of the Lord are not so constituted, that the creature, having free discretion allowed him, should transcend the will of the Creator, even though he act contrary to His will. God willeth not that thou shouldest sin ; for He forbiddeth it : yet if thou hast sinned, imagine not that the man hath done what he willed, and that hath happened to God which He willed not. For as He would that man would not sin, so would He spare the sinner, that he may return and live ; He so willeth finally to punish him who persisteth in his sin, that the rebellious cannot escape the power of justice. Thus whatever choice thou hast made, the Almighty will not be at a loss to fulfil His will concerning thee.

3. "Confession and glorious deeds are His work " (ver. 3). What is a more glorious deed than to justify the ungodly ? But perhaps the work of man preventeth that glorious work of God, so that when he hath confessed his sins, he deserveth to be justified. . . . This is the glorious work of the Lord : for he loveth most, to whom most is forgiven.[10] This is the glorious work of the Lord : for "where sin abounded, there did grace much more abound." [11] But perhaps a man would deserve justification from works. "Not," saith he, "of works, lest any man boast. For we are His workmanship, created in Christ Jesus unto good works " [12] For a man worketh not righteousness save he be justified : but by "believing on Him that justifieth the ungodly," [13] he beginneth with faith ; that good may not by preceding show what he hath deserved, but by following what he hath received. . . .

4. "He hath made His wonderful works to be remembered " (ver. 4) : by abasing this man, exalting that. Reserving unusual miracles for a fit season, that thus human weakness, intent upon novelty, may remember them, although His daily miracles be greater. He created so many trees throughout the whole earth, and no one wondereth : He dried up one with a word, and the hearts of mortals were thunderstruck.[14] For that miracle, which hath not through its frequency

---

[1] Lat. CX. A sermon to the people at the Paschal festival.
[2] [See Ps. cvii. p. 532, *supra.* — C.]   [3] 2 Cor. v. 2.
[4] Exod. xxxiv. 28; 1 Kings xix. 8.   [5] Matt. xx. 10.
[6] Matt. xix. 28.

[7] Acts viii. 13, 18, 19.   [8] 2 Tim. iv. 14.   [9] Heb. xii. 6.
[10] Luke vii. 42-48.   [11] Rom. v. 20.   [12] Eph. ii. 9, 10.
[13] Rom. iv. 5.   [14] Matt. xxi. 19, 20.

become common, will cling most firmly to the heart. But of what use were the miracles, save that He might be feared? What too would fear profit, unless "the gracious and merciful Lord" gave "meat unto them that fear Him"? (ver. 5). meat that doth not spoil, "bread that cometh down from heaven," [1] which He gave to no deservings of ours. For "Christ died for the ungodly." [2] No one then would give such food, save a gracious and merciful Lord. But if He gave so much to this life, if the sinner who was to be justified received the Word made flesh; what shall he receive when glorified in a future world? For, "He shall ever be mindful of His covenant." Nor hath He who hath given a pledge, given the whole.

5. "He shall show His people the power of His works" (ver. 6). Let not the holy Israelites, who have left all their possessions and have followed Him, be saddened; let them not be sorrowful and say, "Who then can be saved?" For "it is easier for a camel to go through the eye of a needle, than for a rich man to enter into the kingdom of God." For "with men these things are impossible, but with God all things are possible." [3] "That He may give them the heritage of the heathen." For they went to the heathen, and enjoined the rich of this world "not to be high-minded, nor to trust in uncertain riches, but in the living God," [4] to whom that is easy which is difficult for men. For thus many were called, thus the heritage of the heathen has been occupied, thus it hath happened, that even many who have not abandoned all their possessions in this life in order to follow Him, have despised even life itself for the sake of confessing His Name; and like camels humbling themselves to bear the burden of troubles, have entered as it were through a needle's eye, through the piercing straits of suffering. He hath wrought these effects, unto whom all things are possible.

6. "The works of His hands are verity and judgment" (ver. 7). Let verity be held by those who are judged here. Martyrs are here sentenced, and brought to the judgment-seat, that they may judge not only those by whom they have been judged, but even give judgment on angels, [5] against whom was their struggle here, even when they seemed to be judged by men. Let not tribulation, distress, famine, nakedness, the sword, separate from Christ. For "all His commandments are true;" [6] He deceiveth not, He giveth us what He promised. Yet we should not expect here what He promised; we should not hope for it: but "they stand fast for ever and ever, and are done in truth and equity" (ver. 8). It is equitable and just that we should

labour here and repose there; since "He sent redemption unto His people" (ver. 9). But from what are they redeemed, save from the captivity of this pilgrimage? Let not therefore rest be sought, save in the heavenly country. God indeed gave the carnal Israelites an earthly Jerusalem, "which is in bondage with her children:" but this is the Old Covenant, pertaining unto the old man. But they who there understood the figure, even then were heirs of the New Covenant; for "Jerusalem which is above is free, which is our everlasting mother in heaven." [7] But that transitory promises were given in that Old Testament is proved by the fact itself: however, "He hath commended His covenant for ever." But what, but the New? Whosoever dost wish to be heir of this, deceive not thyself, and think not of a land flowing with milk and honey, nor of pleasant farms, nor of gardens abounding in fruits and shade: desire not how to gain anything of this sort, such as the eye of covetousness is wont to lust for. For since "covetousness is the root of all evils," [8] it must be cut off, that it may be consumed here; not be put off, that it may be satisfied there. First escape punishments, avoid hell; before thou longest for a God who promiseth, beware of one who threateneth. For "holy and reverend is His Name."

7. . . . . "The fear of the Lord," therefore, "is the beginning of wisdom." "Understanding is good" (ver. 10). Who gainsayeth? But to understand, and not to do, is dangerous. It is "good," therefore, "to those that do thereafter." Nor let it lift up the mind unto pride; for, "the praise of Him," the fear of whom is the beginning of wisdom, "endureth for ever:" and this will be the reward, this the end, this the everlasting station and abode. There are found the true commandments, made fast for ever and ever; here is the very heritage of the New Covenant commanded for ever. "One thing," he saith, "I have desired of the Lord, which I will require: even that I may dwell in the house of the Lord all the days of my life." [9] For, "blessed are they that dwell in the house" of the Lord: "they will be alway praising" [10] Him; for "His praise endureth for ever."

PSALM CXII. [11]

1. I believe, brethren, that ye remarked and committed to memory the title of this Psalm. "The conversion," he saith, "of Haggai and Zechariah." These prophets were not as yet in existence, when these verses were sung. [12] . . .

---

[1] John vi. 27, 51.　　[2] Rom. v. 6.　　[3] Matt xix. 24-26.
[4] 1 Tim. vi. 17.　　[5] 1 Cor. vi. 3.　　[6] Rom. viii. 35.

[7] Gal. iv. 25, 26.　　[8] 1 Tim. vi. 10.　　[9] Ps. xxvii. 4.
[10] Ps. lxxxiv. 4.
[11] Lat. CXI. A discourse to the people.
[12] [He argues from the relations of these prophets to the building of the second temple. — C.]

But both, the one within a year after the other, began to prophesy that which seemeth to pertain to the restoration of the temple, as was foretold so long before.[1] . . . "For the temple of God is holy, which temple ye are." [2] Whoever therefore converteth himself to the work of this building together, and to the hope of a firm and holy edifice, like a living stone from the miserable ruin of this world, understandeth the title of the Psalm, understandeth "the conversion of Haggai and Zechariah." Let him therefore chant the following verses, not so much with the voice of his tongue as of his life. For the completion of the building will be that ineffable peace of wisdom, the "beginning" of which is the "fear of the Lord:" let him therefore, whom this conversion buildeth together, begin thence.

2. "Blessed is the man that feareth the Lord: he will have great delight in His commandments" (ver. 1). God, who alone judgeth both truthfully and mercifully, will see how far he obeyeth His commandments: since "the life of man on earth is a temptation," [3] as holy Job saith. But "He who judgeth us is the Lord." [4] . . . He therefore will see how far each man profiteth in His commandments; yet he who loveth the peace of this building together, shall have great delight in them; nor ought he to despair, since there is "peace on earth for men of good will." [5]

3. Next follows, "His seed shall be mighty upon earth" (ver. 2). The Apostle witnesseth, that the works of mercy are the seed of the future harvest, when he saith, "Let us not be weary in well doing, for in due season we shall reap;" [6] and again, "But this I say, He which soweth sparingly, shall reap also sparingly." [7] But what, brethren, is more mighty than that not only Zacchæus should buy the kingdom of Heaven by the half of his goods,[8] but even the widow for two mites,[9] and that each should possess an equal share there? What is more mighty, than that the same kingdom should be worth treasures to the rich man, and a cup of cold water to the poor? . . . "Glory and riches shall be in his house" (ver. 3). For his house is his heart; where, with the praise of God, he liveth in greater riches with the hope of eternal life, than with men flattering, in palaces of marble, with splendidly adorned ceilings, with the fear of everlasting death. "For his righteousness endureth for ever:" this is his glory, there are his riches. While the other's purple, and fine linen, and grand banquets, even when present, are passing away; and when they have come to an end, the burning tongue shall cry out,

longing for a drop of water from the finger's end.[10]

4. "Unto the right-hearted there ariseth up light in the darkness" (ver. 4). Justly do the godly direct their heart unto their God, justly do they walk with their God, preferring His will to themselves; and having no proud presumption in their own. For they remember that they were some time in darkness, but are now light in the Lord.[11] "Merciful, pitying, and just is the Lord God." It delighteth us that He is "merciful and pitying," but it perhaps terrifieth us that the Lord God is "just." Fear not, despair not at all, happy man, who fearest the Lord, and hast great delight in His commandments; be thou sweet, be merciful and lend. For the Lord is just in this manner, that He judgeth without mercy him who hath not shown mercy; [12] but, "Sweet is the man who is merciful and lendeth" (ver. 5): God will not spew him out of His mouth as if he were not sweet. "Forgive," He saith, "and ye shall be forgiven; give, and it shall be given unto you." [13] Whilst thou forgivest that thou mayest be forgiven, thou art merciful; whilst thou givest that it may be given unto thee, thou lendest. For though all be called generally mercy where another is assisted in his distress, yet there is a difference where thou spendest neither money, nor the toil of bodily labour, but by forgiving what each man hath sinned against thee, thou gainest free pardon for thine own sins also. . . . He who is unwilling to give to the poor, seeketh riches; listen to what is written, "Thou shalt have treasure in heaven." [14] Thou wilt not then lose honour by forgiving: for it is a very laudable triumph to conquer anger: wilt not grow poor by giving; for a heavenly treasure is a more safe possession. The former verse, "Riches and plenteousness shall be in his house," was pregnant with this verse.

5. He therefore who doth these things, "shall guide his words with discretion." His deeds themselves are the words whereby he shall be defended at the Judgment; which shall not be without mercy unto him, since he hath himself shown mercy. "For he shall never be moved" (ver. 6): he who, called to the right hand, shall hear these words, "Come, ye blessed of My Father, inherit the kingdom prepared for you from the foundation of the world." For no works of theirs, save works of mercy, are there mentioned. He therefore shall hear, "Come, ye blessed of My Father;" for, "the generation of the right ones shall be blessed." Thus, "the righteous shall be had in everlasting remembrance." "He will not be afraid of any evil hearing; for his heart standeth fast and believeth

1 Ezra i. 5; Hagg. i ; Zech. i.　　2 1 Cor. iii. 17.
3 Job vii. 1.　　　　　　　　　　　4 1 Cor. iv. 4.
5 Luke ii. 14.　　6 Gal. vi. 9.　　7 2 Cor. ix. 6.
8 Luke xix. 8.　　9 Mark xii. 42.

10 Luke xvi. 24.　　11 Eph. v. 8.　　12 Jas. ii. 13.
13 Luke vi. 37, 38.　　14 Matt. xix. 21.

in the Lord " (ver. 7). Such as the words which he will hear addressed to those on the left hand, " Depart into everlasting fire, prepared for the devil and his angels." [1] He therefore who seeketh here not his own things, but those of Jesus Christ,[2] most patiently endureth sufferings, waiteth for the promises with faith. Nor is he broken down by any temptations : " His heart is established, and will not shrink, until he see beyond his enemies " (ver. 8). His enemies wished to see good things here, and when invisible blessings were promised them, used to say, " Who will show us any good ? " [3] Let our heart therefore be established, and shrink not, until we see beyond our enemies. For they wish to see good things of men in the land of the dying ; we trust to see the good things of the Lord in the land of the living.[4]

6. But it is a great thing to have the heart established, and not to be moved, while they rejoice who love what they see, and mock at him who hopeth for what he seeth not ; " what the Lord hath prepared for them that love Him." [5] How great is the value of this which is not seen, and it is bought for so much as each man is able to give for it. On this account he also " dispersed abroad, and gave to the poor " (ver. 9) : he saw not, yet he kept buying ; but He was storing up the treasure in heaven, who deigned to hunger and thirst in the poor on earth. It is no wonder then if " his righteousness remaineth for ever : " He who created the ages being his guardian. " His horn," whose humility was scorned by the proud, " shall be exalted with honour."

7. " The ungodly shall see it, and he shall be angered " (ver. 10) : this is that late and fruitless repentance. For with whom rather than himself is he " angered," when he shall say, " Our pride, what hath it profited us ? the boastfulness of our riches, what hath it given us ? " [6] seeing the horn of him exalted with honour, who " dispersed abroad, and gave to the poor." " He shall gnash with his teeth, and consume away : " for " there shall be weeping and gnashing of teeth." For he will no more bring forth leaves and bloom, as would happen if he had repented in season : but he will then repent, when " the desire of the ungodly shall perish," no consolation succeeding. " The desire of the ungodly shall perish," when " all things shall pass away like a shadow," [7] when the flower shall fall down on the withering of the grass. " But the word of the Lord that endureth for ever," [8] as it is mocked by the vanity of the falsely happy, so will laugh at the perdition of the same when truly miserable.

PSALM CXIII.[9]

1. . . . When ye hear sung in the Psalms, " Praise the Lord, ye children " (ver. 1) ; imagine not that that exhortation pertaineth not unto you, because having already passed the youth of the body, ye are either blooming in the prime of manhood, or growing gray with the honours of old age : for unto all of you the Apostle saith, " Brethren, be not children in understanding ; howbeit, in malice be ye children, but in understanding be men." [10] What malice in particular, save pride ? For it is pride that, presuming in false greatness, suffereth not man to walk along the narrow path, and to enter by the narrow gate ; but the child easily entereth through the narrow entrance ; and thus no man, save as a child, entereth into the kingdom of heaven. " Praise the Name of the Lord." . . . Let Him therefore be alway proclaimed : " Blessed be the Name of the Lord, from this time forth for evermore " (ver. 2). Let Him be proclaimed everywhere : " From the rising up of the sun unto the going down of the same, praise ye the Name of the Lord " (ver. 3).

2. If any of the holy children who praise the Name of the Lord were to ask of me and say to me, " for evermore " I understand to mean unto all eternity : but why " from this," and why is not the Name of the Lord blessed before this, and before all ages? I will answer the infant, who asketh not in contumacy. Unto you it is said, masters and children, unto you it is said, " Praise the Name of the Lord ; blessed be the Name of the Lord : " let the Name of the Lord be blessed, " from this," that is, from the moment ye speak these words. For ye begin to praise, but praise ye without end. . . . Or, since in this passage he seemeth to signify rather humility than childhood, the contrary of which is the vain and false greatness of pride ; and for this reason none but children praise the Lord, since the proud know not how to praise Him ; let your old age be childlike, and your childhood like old age ; that is, that neither may your wisdom be with pride, nor your humility without wisdom, that ye may " praise the Lord from this for evermore." Wherever the Church of Christ is diffused in her childlike saints, " Praise ye the Name of the Lord ; " that is, " from the rising up of the sun unto the going down of the same."

3. " The Lord is high above all heathen " (ver. 4). The heathen are men : what wonder if the Lord be above all men ? They see with their eyes those whom they worship high above themselves to shine in heaven, the sun and moon and stars, creatures which they serve while they

[1] Matt. xxv. 34, 41.						[2] Philip. ii. 21.
[3] Ps. iv. 6.
[4] Ps. xxvii. 13.
[5] 1 Cor. ii. 9.
[6] Wisd. v. 8.
[7] Wisd. v. 8, 9.
[8] Isa. xl. 8.

[9] Lat. CXII. A discourse to the people.
[10] 1 Cor. xiv. 20; Matt. xviii. 3.

neglect the Creator. But not only " is the Lord high above all heathen ; " but " His glory " also " is above the heavens." The heavens look up unto Him above themselves ; and the humble have Him together with them, who do not worship the heavens instead of Him, though placed in the flesh beneath the heavens.

4. " Who is like unto the Lord our God, that hath His dwelling so high ; and yet beholdeth the humble ? " (ver. 5). Any one would think that He dwelleth in the lofty heavens, whence He may behold the humble things on earth ; but " He beholdeth the humble things that are in heaven and earth " (ver. 6): what then is His high dwelling, whence He beholdeth the humble things that are in heaven and earth? Are the humble things He beholdeth His own high dwelling itself? For He thus exalteth the humble, so as not to make them proud. He therefore both dwelleth in those whom He raiseth high, and maketh them heaven for Himself, that is, His own abode ; and by seeing them not proud, but constantly subject to Himself, He beholdeth even in heaven itself these very humble things, in whom raised on high He dwelleth. For the Spirit thus speaketh through Isaiah : " Thus saith the Highest that dwelleth on high, that inhabiteth eternity ; the Lord Most High, dwelling in the holy." He hath expounded what He meant by dwelling on high, by the more full expression, " dwelling in the holy." . . .

5. And he hath moved us also to enquire whether the Lord our God beholdeth the same humble things in heaven and in earth : or different humble things in heaven to what He beholdeth on earth. . . . But if the Lord our God beholdeth other humble things in heaven to what He doth on earth ; I suppose that He already beholdeth in heaven those whom He hath called, and in whom He dwelleth ; while on earth He beholdeth those whom He is now calling, that He may dwell in them. For He hath the one with Him musing on heavenly things, the others He is waking, while they yet dream things earthly. But since it is difficult to call even those humble, who have not as yet submitted their necks in piety to the gracious yoke of Christ, since the divine writings throughout the whole Psalm warn us to understand holy by the word humble ; there is also another interpretation, which, Beloved, ye may consider with me. I believe that those are now meant by heavens who shall sit upon twelve thrones, and shall judge with the Lord ; [1] and under the name of the earth, the rest of the multitude of the blessed, who shall be set on the right hand, that through works of mercy they may be praised and received into everlasting habitations by those whom

they have made friends to themselves from the mammon of unrighteousness in this mortal life.[2] . . .

6. " He taketh up the destitute out of the dust, and lifteth the poor out of the mire " (ver. 7) ; " that He may set Him with the princes, even with the princes of His people " (ver. 8). Let not then the heads of the exalted disdain to be humble, beneath the Lord's right hand. For though the faithful steward of the Lord's money be placed together with the princes of the people of God, although he be destined to sit on the twelve seats, and even to judge angels ; [1] yet he is taken up destitute from the dust, and lifted from out of the mire. Was not he possibly lifted up from the mire, who " served divers lusts and pleasures " ? . . .

7. What then, brethren, if we have already heard of those humble things which are in heaven, lifted up from the mire, that they might be set with the princes of the people ; have we by consequence heard nothing of the humble things which the Lord beholdeth on the earth? For those friends who will judge with their Lord are fewer, while those whom they receive into everlasting habitations are more in number. For although the whole of a heap of corn compared with the separate chaff may seem to contain few in number ; yet considered by itself, it is abundant. . . . The Church then speaketh thus in that sense, wherein she seemeth to bear no offspring among those crowds who have not given up all things, that they might follow the Lord, and might sit upon the twelve thrones.[1] But how many in the same crowd, who make unto themselves friends of the mammon of unrighteousness,[2] shall stand on the right hand through works of mercy? He not only then lifteth up from the mire him whom He is to place with the princes of His people ; but also, " Maketh the barren woman to keep house, and to be a joyful mother of children " (ver. 9) : He who dwelleth on high, and beholdeth the humble things that are in heaven and earth, the seed of Abraham like the stars of heaven, holiness set on high in heavenly habitations ; and like the sand on the sea shore, a merciful and countless multitude gathered together from the harmful waves, and the bitterness of impiety.

PSALM CXIV.[3]

1. The river Jordan, when they were entering across it into the land of promise, when touched by the feet of the priests who bore the Ark, stood still from above with bridled stream, while it flowed down from below, where it ran on into the sea, until the whole people passed over, the

---

[1] Matt. xix. 28.   [2] Luke xvi. 9.   [3] Lat. CXIII.

priests standing on the dry ground.[1] We know these things, but yet we should not imagine in this Psalm, to which we have now answered by chanting Allelujah, that it is the purpose of the Holy Spirit, that while we call to mind those deeds of the past, we should not consider things like unto them yet to take place. For "these things," as the Apostle saith, "happened unto them for ensamples."[2]

2. "When Israel came out of Egypt, and the house of Jacob from among the strange people" (ver. 1), "Judah was His sanctuary, and Israel His dominion" (ver. 2) ; "the sea saw that and fled, Jordan was driven back" (ver. 3). Think not that past deeds are related unto us, but rather that the future is predicted ; since, while those miracles also were going on in that people, things present indeed were happening, but not without an intimation of things future. . . . Some things he has related differently to what we have learnt and read there : that he might not truly be thought to be repeating past acts rather than to be prophesying future things. For in the first place, we read not that the Jordan was driven back, but that it stood still on the side nearest the source of its streams, while the people were passing through ; next, we read not of the mountains and hills skipping : all which he hath added, and repeated. For after saying, "The sea saw that, and fled ; Jordan was driven back : " he added, " The mountains skipped like rams, and the little hills like young sheep" (ver. 4) : and then asketh, " What aileth thee, O thou sea, that thou fleddest : and thou, Jordan, that thou wast driven back ? " (ver. 5). "Ye mountains, that ye skipped like rams ; and ye little hills, like young sheep ? " (ver. 6).

3. Let us therefore consider what we are taught here ; since both those deeds were typical of us, and these words exhort us to recognise ourselves. For if we hold with a firm heart the grace of God which hath been given us, we are Israel, the seed of Abraham : unto us the Apostle saith, " Therefore are ye the seed of Abraham."[3] . . . Let therefore no Christian consider himself alien to the name of Israel. For we are joined in the corner stone with those among the Jews who believed, among whom we find the Apostles chief. Hence our Lord in another passage saith, "And other sheep I have, which are not of this fold ; them also I must bring, that there may be one fold and one Shepherd."[4] The Christian people then is rather Israel, and the same is preferably the house of Jacob ; for Israel and Jacob are the same. But that multitude of Jews, which was deservedly reprobated for its perfidy, for the pleasures of the flesh sold their birthright, so that they belonged not to Jacob, but rather to

Esau. For ye know that it was said with this hidden meaning, "That the elder shall serve the younger."[5]

4. But Egypt, since it is said to mean affliction, or one who afflicteth, or one who oppresseth, is often used for an emblem of this world ; from which we must spiritually withdraw, that we may not be bearing the yoke with unbelievers.[6] For thus each one becometh a fit citizen of the heavenly Jerusalem, when he hath first renounced this world ; just as that people could not be led into the land of promise, save first they had departed from Egypt. But as they did not depart thence, until freed by Divine help ; so no man is turned away in heart from this world, unless aided by the gift of the Divine mercy. For what was there once prefigured, the same is fulfilled in every faithful one in the daily travailings of the Church, in this end of the world, in this, as the blessed John writeth, last time.[7] Hear the Apostle the teacher of the Gentiles, thus instructing us : " I would not, brethren, that ye should be ignorant, how that all our fathers were under the cloud, and all passed through the sea ; and were all baptized unto Moses in the cloud and in the sea, and did all eat the same spiritual meat, and did all drink the same spiritual drink ; for they drank of that spiritual rock that followed them, and that rock was Christ. But with many of them God was not well pleased, for they were overthrown in the wilderness. Now these things were our examples."[8] What more do ye wish, most beloved brethren? For it is surely clear, not from human conjecture, but from the declaration of an Apostle, that is, of God and our Lord : for God spoke in them, and though from clouds of flesh, yet it was God who thundered : surely then it is clear by so great testimony that all these things which were done in figure, are now fulfilled in our salvation ; because then the future was predicted, now the past is read, and the present observed.

5. Hear what is even more wonderful, that the hidden and veiled mysteries of the ancient books are in some degree revealed by the ancient books. For Micah the prophet speaketh thus. "According to the days of thy coming out of Egypt will I show unto him marvellous things, etc.[9] . . . In this Psalm, therefore, although the wonderful spirit of prophecy doth look into the future, yet it seemeth, as it were, to be merely detailing to the past. "Judah," he saith, "was His sanctuary : the sea saw that and fled : " "was," "saw," and "fled," are words of the past tense ; and "Jordan was driven back, and the mountains skipped, and the earth trembled," in like manner have a past expression, without, however, any difficulty in understanding by them the

---

[1] Josh iii. 15-17.　　　　　　[2] 1 Cor. x. 11.
[3] Gal. iii. 29; Rom. iv. 10, etc.　　[4] John x. 16.
[5] Gen xxv. 33, 23.　　[6] 2 Cor. vi. 14.　　[7] 1 John ii. 18.
[8] 1 Cor. x. 1-6.　　[9] Micah vii. 15-19.

future. . . . For though it was so long after the departure of that people from Egypt, and so long before these seasons of the Church, that he sang what I have quoted; nevertheless, he witnesseth that he is foretelling the future without any question. "According to the days," he saith, "of thy coming out of the land of Egypt will I show unto him marvellous things." "The nations shall see and be confounded." This is what is here said, "The sea saw that, and fled:" for if in this passage, through words of the past tense the future is secretly revealed, as is the case; who would venture to explain the words, "shall see and be confounded," of past events? And a little lower down he [1] alludeth more clearly than light itself to those very enemies of ours, who followed us flying, that they might slay us, that is, our sins, which are overwhelmed and extinguished in Baptism, just as the Egyptians were drowned in the sea, saying, since "He retaineth not His anger for ever, because He is of good will and merciful, He will turn again, He will have compassion upon us, He will drown our iniquities: and Thou wilt cast all their sins into the depths of the sea."

6. What is it, most beloved? ye who know yourselves to be Israelites according to Abraham's seed, ye who are of the house of Jacob, heirs according to promise, know that even ye have gone forth from Egypt, since ye have renounced this world; that ye have gone forth from a foreign people, since by the confession of piety, ye have separated yourselves from the blasphemies of the Gentiles. For it is not your tongue, but a foreign one, which knoweth not how to praise God, to whom ye sing Allelujah. For "Judah" hath become "His sanctuary" in you; for "he is not a Jew which is one outwardly; neither is that circumcision, which is outward in the flesh; but he is a Jew which is one inwardly, and by circumcision of the heart." [2] Examine then your hearts, if faith hath circumcised them, if confession hath cleansed them; in you "Judah" hath become "His sanctuary," in you "Israel" hath become "His dominion." For "He gave" unto you "the power to become the sons of God." [3] . . .

7. But I would not that ye should seek without yourselves, how the Jordan was turned back, I would not ye should augur anything evil. For the Lord chideth those who have "turned" their "back" unto Him, "and not their face." [4] And whoever forsaketh the source of his being, and turneth away from his Creator; as a river into the sea, he glides into the bitter wickedness of this world. It is therefore good for him that he turn back, and that God whom he had set behind his back, may be before his face as he

returneth; and that the sea of this world, which he had set before his face, when he was gliding on towards it, may become behind him; and that he may so forget what is behind him, that he may "reach forward to what is before him;" [5] which is profitable for him when once converted. . . .

8. "Tremble, thou earth, at the presence of the Lord, at the presence of the God of Jacob" (ver. 7). What meaneth, "at the presence of the Lord," save at the presence of Him who said, "Lo, I am with you alway, even unto the end of the world." [6] For the earth trembled; but because it had remained slothful, it was made to tremble, so that it might be more firmly fixed at the presence of the Lord.

9. "Who turned the hard rock into standing waters, and the flint stone into springing wells" (ver. 8). For He melted Himself, and what may be called His hardness to water those who believe on Him, that He might in them become "a fountain of water gushing forth unto everlasting life;" [7] because formerly, when He was not known, He seemed hard. Hence they who said, "This is an hard saying, who can bear it?" [8] were confounded, and waited not until He should flow and stream upon them when the Scriptures were revealed. The rock, that hardness, was turned into pools of water, that stone into fountains of waters, when on His resurrection, "He expounded unto them, commencing with Moses and all the prophets, how Christ ought to suffer thus;" [9] and sent the Holy Ghost, of whom He said, "If any man thirst, let him come unto Me, and drink." [10]

PSALM CXV.[11]

1. "Not unto us, O Lord, not unto us, but unto Thy Name give the praise" (ver. 1). For that grace of the water that gushed from the rock ("now that rock was Christ" [12]), was not given on the score of works that had gone before, but of His mercy "that justifieth the ungodly." [13] For "Christ died for sinners," [14] that men might not seek any glory of their own, but in the Lord's Name.

2. "For Thy loving mercy, and for Thy truth's sake" (ver. 2). Observe how often these two qualities, loving mercy and truth, are joined together in the holy Scriptures. For in His loving mercy He called sinners, and in His truth He judgeth those who when called refused to come. "That the heathen may not say, Where is now their God?" For at the last, His loving mercy and truth will shine forth, when "the sign of the Son of man shall appear

---

[1] [i.e. Micah. See vii. 19. — C.]   [2] Rom. ii. 28, 29.
[3] John i. 12.   [4] Jer. ii. 27.

[5] Philip. iii. 13.   [6] Matt. xxviii. 30.   [7] John iv. 14.
[8] John vi. 60.   [9] Luke xxiv. 26, 27. [10] John vii. 37.
[11] Lat. CXIII.   [12] 1 Cor. x. 4.   [13] Rom. iv. 5.
[14] Rom. v. 6. [In Sept. and Vulg. this Psalm is joined with Ps. cxiv. — C.]

in heaven, and then shall all tribes of the earth cry woe ; " [1] nor shall they then say, " Where is their God?" when He is no longer preached unto them to be believed in, but displayed before them to be trembled at.

3. " As for our God, He is in heaven above " (ver. 3). Not in heaven, where they see the sun and moon, works of God which they adore, but " in heaven above," which overpasseth all heavenly and earthly bodies. Nor is our God in heaven in such a sense, as to dread a fall that should deprive Him of His throne, if heaven were withdrawn from under Him. " In heaven and earth He hath made whatsoever pleased Him." Nor doth He stand in need of His own works, as if He had place in them where He might abide ; but endureth in His own eternity, wherein He abideth and hath done whatsoever pleased Him, both in heaven and earth ; for they did not support Him, as a condition of their being created by Him : since, unless they had been created, they could not have supported Him. Therefore, in whatsoever He Himself dwelleth, He, so to speak, containeth this as in need of Himself, He is not contained by this as if He needed it. Or it may be thus understood : " In heaven and in earth He hath done whatsoever pleased Him," whether among the higher or the lower orders of His people, He hath made His grace His free gift, that no man may boast in the merits of his own works. . . .

4. " Their idols," he saith, " are silver and gold, even the work of men's hands " (ver. 4). That is, although we cannot display our God to your carnal eyes, whom ye ought to recognise through his works ; yet be not seduced by your vain pretences, because ye can point with the finger to, the objects of your worship. For it were much worthier for you not to have what to point to, than that your hearts' blindness should be displayed in what is exhibited to these eyes by you : for what do ye exhibit, save gold and silver? They have indeed both bronze, and wood, and earthenware idols, and of different materials of this description ; but the Holy Spirit preferred mentioning the more precious material, because when every man hath blushed for that which he sets more by, he is much more easily turned away from the worship of meaner objects. For it is said in another passage of Scripture concerning the worshippers of images, " Saying to a stock, Thou art my father ; and to a stone, Thou hast brought me forth." [2] But lest that man who speaketh thus not to a stone or stock, but to gold and silver, seem wiser to himself ; let him look this way, let him turn hitherwards the ear of his heart : " The idols of the Gentiles are gold and silver." Nothing mean and con-

temptible is here mentioned : and indeed to that mind which is not earth, both gold and silver is earth, but more beautiful and brilliant, more solid and firm. Employ not then the hands of men, to create a false Deity out of that metal which a true God hath created ; nay, a false man, whom thou mayest worship for a true God. . . .

5. " For they have mouths, and speak not : eyes have they, and see not " (ver. 5). " They have ears, and hear not : noses have they, and smell not " (ver. 6). " They have hands, and handle not ; feet have they, and walk not ; neither cry they through their throat " (ver. 7). Even their artist therefore surpasseth them, since he had the faculty of moulding them by the motion and functions of his limbs : though thou wouldest be ashamed to worship that artist. Even thou surpassest them, though thou hast not made these things, since thou doest what they cannot do. Even a beast doth excel them ; for unto this it is added, " neither cry they through their throat." For after he had said above, " they have mouths, and speak not ; " what need was there, after he had enumerated the limbs from head to feet, to repeat what he had said of their crying through their throat ; unless, I suppose, because we perceive that what he mentioned of the other members, was common to men and beasts? For they see, and hear, and smell, and walk, and some, apes for instance, handle with hands. But what he had said of the mouth, is peculiar to men : since beasts do not speak. But that no one might refer what hath been said to the works of human members alone, and prefer men only to the gods of the heathen ; after all this he added these words, " neither cry they through their throat : " which again is common to men and cattle. . . . How much better then do mice and serpents, and other animals of like sort, judge of the idols of the heathen, so to speak, for they regard not the human figure in them when they see not the human life. For this reason they usually build nests in them, and unless they are deterred by human movements, they seek for themselves no safer habitations. A man then moveth himself, that he may frighten away a living beast from his own god ; and yet worshippeth that god who cannot move himself, as if he were powerful, from whom he drove away one better than the object of his worship. . . . Even the dead surpasseth a deity who neither liveth nor hath lived. . . .

6. But they seem to themselves to have a purer religion, who say, I neither worship an idol, nor a devil ; but in the bodily image I behold an emblem [3] of that which I am bound to

---

[1] Matt. xxiv. 30.   [2] Jer. ii. 27.   [3] [The pretext of all image-worship. — C.]

worship. . . . They presume to reply, that they worship not the bodies themselves, but the deities which preside over the government of them. One sentence of the Apostle, therefore, testifieth to their punishment and condemnation ; "Who," he saith, " have changed the truth of God into a lie, and worshipped and served the creature more than the Creator, who is blessed for ever." [1] For in the former part of this sentence he condemned idols ; in the latter, the account they give of their idols : for by designating images wrought by an artificer by the names of the works of God's creation, they change the truth of God into a lie ; while, by considering these works themselves as deities, and worshipping them as such, they serve the creature more than the Creator, who is blessed for ever. . . .

7. But, it will be said, we also have very many instruments and vessels made of materials or metal of this description for the purpose of celebrating the Sacraments, which being consecrated by these ministrations are called holy, in honour of Him who is thus worshipped for our salvation : and what indeed are these very instruments or vessels, but the work of men's hands? But have they mouth, and yet speak not? have they eyes, and see not? do we pray unto them, because through them we pray to God? This is the chief cause of this insane profanity, that the figure resembling the living person, which induces men to worship it, hath more influence in the minds of these miserable persons, than the evident fact that it is not living, so that it ought to be despised by the living.[2]

8. The result that ensueth is that described in the next verse : " They that make them are like unto them, and so are all such as put their trust in them " (ver. 8). Let them therefore see with open eyes, and worship with shut and dead understandings, idols that neither see nor live. "But the house of Israel hath hoped in the Lord " (ver. 9). " For hope that is seen is not hope ; for what a man seeth, why doth he yet hope for? But if we hope for that we see not, then do we with patience wait for it." [3] But that this patience may endure to the end, " He is their helper and defender." Do perhaps spiritual persons (by whom carnal minds are built up in " the spirit of meekness," [4] because they pray as higher for lower minds) already see, and is that already to them reality which to the lower is hope? It is not so. For even " the house of Aaron hath hope in the Lord " (ver. 10). Therefore, that they also may stretch forward perseveringly towards those things which are before them, and may run perseveringly, until

they may apprehend that for which they are apprehended,[5] and may know even as they are known,[6] " He is their helper and defender." For both " fear the Lord, and have hoped in the Lord : He is their helper and defender " (ver. 11).

9. For we do not by our deservings prevent the mercy of God ; but, " The Lord hath been mindful of us, and hath blessed us. He hath blessed the house of Israel, He hath blessed the house of Aaron " (ver. 12). But in blessing both of these, " He hath blessed all that fear the Lord " (ver. 13). Dost thou ask, who are meant by both of these? He answereth, " both small and great." That is, the house of Israel with the house of Aaron, those who among that nation believed in Jesus the Saviour. . . . For in the character of those who out of that nation believed, it is said, " Except the Lord of Sabaoth had left us a seed, we had been as Sodoma, and been made like unto Gomorrha." [7] Seed, because when it has been scattered over the earth, it multiplied.

10. For the great ones, of the house of Aaron, have said, " May the Lord increase you more and more, you and your children " (ver. 14). And thus it hath happened. For children that have been raised even from the stones have flocked unto Abraham : [8] sheep which were not of this fold, have flocked unto him, that there might be one flock, and one shepherd ; [9] the faith of all nations was added, and the number grew, not only of wise priests, but of obedient peoples ; the Lord increasing not only their fathers more and more, who in Christ might show the way to the rest who should imitate them, but also their children, who should follow their fathers' pious footsteps.

11. Therefore the Prophet saith unto these great and small, the mountains and the little hills, the rams and the young sheep, what followeth : " Ye are the blessed of the Lord, who made heaven and earth " (ver. 15). As if he should say, Ye are the blessed of the Lord, who made the heaven in the great, earth in the small : not this visible heaven, studded with luminaries which are objects to these eyes. For " The heaven of heavens is the Lord's " (ver. 16) ; who hath elevated the minds of some saints to such a height, that they became teachable by no man, but by God Himself ; in comparison of which heaven, whatever is discerned with carnal eyes is to be called earth ; which " He hath given to the children of men ; " that when it is contemplated, whether in that region which illumineth above, as that which is called heaven, or in that which is illumined beneath, which is properly called earth (since in comparison with that which is called heaven of heaven, the whole,

[1] Rom. i. 25.
[2] [Compare the gross misstatements and bad reasoning of the Trent Catechism. A. N. F. vol. iii. p. 76. — C.]
[3] Rom. viii. 24, 25.　　　　[4] Gal. vi. 1.

[5] Philip. iii. 12–14.　　[6] 1 Cor. xiii. 12.　　[7] Rom. ix. 29.
[8] Matt. iii. 9.　　[9] John x. 1–16, 28, 29.

as we have said, is earth ;) the whole therefore of this earth He hath given to the children of men, that by the consideration of it, as far as they can, they may conceive of the Creator, whom with their yet weak hearts they cannot see without that aid to their conception.

12. . . . But nevertheless since they derive the truth and richness of wisdom, not from man nor through man, but through God Himself, they have received little ones who shall be heaven, that they may know that they are heaven of heaven ; as yet however earth, unto which they say, " I have planted, Apollos watered, but God gave the increase." [1] For to those very sons of men whom He made heaven, He who knoweth how to provide for the earth through heaven, hath given earth upon which they work. May they therefore abide, heaven and earth, in their God, who made them, and let them live from Him, confessing unto Him, and praising Him ; for if they choose to live from themselves, they shall die, as it is written, " From the dead, as though he were not, confession ceaseth." [2] But, " The dead praise not Thee, O Lord, neither all they that go down into silence " (ver. 17). For the Scripture in another passage proclaimeth, " The sinner, when he cometh into the abyss of wickednesses, scorneth." [3] " But we, who live, will praise the Lord, from this time forth for evermore " (ver. 18).

PSALM CXVI.[4]

1. " I have loved, since the Lord will hear the voice of my prayer " (ver. 1). Let the soul that is sojourning in absence from the Lord sing thus, let that sheep which had strayed sing thus, let that son who had " died and returned to life," who had " been lost and was found ; " [5] let our soul sing thus, brethren, and most beloved sons. Let us be taught, and let us abide, and let us sing thus with the Saints : " I have loved : since the Lord will hear the voice of my prayer." Is this a reason for having loved, that the Lord will hear the voice of my prayer? and do we not rather love, because He hath heard, or that He may hear? What then meaneth, " I have loved, since the Lord will hear"? Doth he, because hope is wont to inflame love, say that he hath loved, since he hath hoped that God will listen to the voice of his prayer?

2. But whence hath he hoped for this? Since, he saith, " He hath inclined His ear unto me : and in my days I have called upon Him " (ver. 2). I loved, therefore, because He will hear ; He will hear, " because He hath inclined His ear unto me." But whence knowest thou, O human soul, that God hath inclined His ear unto thee, except thou sayest, " I have believed "? These three things, therefore, " abide, faith, hope, charity : " [6] because thou hast believed, thou hast hoped ; because thou hast hoped, thou hast loved. . . .

3. And what are thy days, since thou hast said, " In my days I have called upon Him "? Are they those perchance, in which " the fulness of time came," and " God sent His Son," [7] who had already said, " In an acceptable time have I heard thee, and in a day of salvation have I helped thee "? [8] . . . I may rather call my days the days of my misery, the days of my mortality, the days according to Adam, full of toil and sweat, the days according to the ancient corruption.   " For I lying, stuck fast in the deep mire," [9] in another Psalm also have cried out, " Behold, Thou hast made my days old ; " [10] in these days of mine have I called upon Thee. For my days are different from the days of my Lord.   I call those my days, which by my own daring I have made for myself, whereby I have forsaken Him : and, since He reigneth everywhere, and is all-powerful, and holdeth all things, I have deserved prison ; that is, I have received the darkness of ignorance, and the bonds of mortality. . . . For in these days of mine, " The snares of death compassed me round about, and the pains of hell gat hold upon me " (ver. 3) : pains that would not have overtaken me, had I not wandered from Thee. But now they have overtaken me ; but I found them not, while I was rejoicing in the prosperity of the world, in which the snares of hell deceive the more.

4. But after " I too found trouble and heaviness, I called upon the Name of the Lord " (ver. 4).   For trouble and profitable sorrow I did not feel ; trouble, wherein He giveth aid, unto whom it is said, " O be Thou our help in trouble : and vain is the help of man." [11]   For I thought I might rejoice and exult in the vain help of man ; but when I had heard from my Lord, " Blessed are they that mourn, for they shall be comforted : " [12] I did not wait until I should lose those temporal blessings in which I rejoiced, and should then mourn : but I gave heed to that very misery of mine which caused me to rejoice in such things, which I both feared to lose, and yet could not retain ; I gave heed to it firmly and courageously, and I saw that I was not only agonized by the adversities of this world, but even bound by its good fortune ; and thus " I found the trouble and heaviness " which had escaped me, " and called upon the Name of the Lord ; O Lord, I beseech Thee, deliver my

---

[1] 1 Cor. iii. 6.   [2] Ecclus. xvii. 26.   [3] Prov. xviii. 3, LXX.
[4] Lat. CXV. A sermon to the common people.
[5] Luke xv. 6, 24.

[6] 1 Cor. xiii. 13.   [7] Gal. iv. 4.   [8] Isa. xlix. 8.
[9] Ps. lxix. 2.   [10] Ps. xxxix. 5.   [11] Ps. lx. 11.
[12] Matt. v. 4.

soul." Let then the holy people of God say, " I called upon the Name of the Lord : " and let the remainder of the heathen hear, who do not as yet call upon the Name of the Lord ; let them hear and seek, that they may discover trouble and heaviness, and may call upon the Name of the Lord, and be saved. . . .

5. "Gracious is the Lord, and righteous ; yea, our God is merciful " (ver. 5). He is gracious, righteous, and merciful. Gracious in the first place, because He hath inclined His ear unto me ; and I knew not that the ear of God had approached my lips, till I was aroused by those beautiful feet, that I might call upon the Lord's Name : for who hath called upon Him, save he whom He first called? Hence therefore He is in the first place "gracious ; " but "righteous," because He scourgeth ; and again, "merciful," because He receiveth ; for " He scourgeth every son whom He receiveth ; " nor ought it to be so bitter to me that He scourgeth, as sweet that He receiveth. For how should not "The Lord, who keepeth little ones " (ver. 6), scourge those whom, when of mature age, He seeketh to be heirs ; " for what son is he whom the father chasteneth not? "[1] "I was in misery, and He helped me." He helped me, because I was in misery ; for the pain which the physician causeth by his knife is not penal, but salutary.

6. "Turn again then unto thy rest, O my soul ; for the Lord hath done good to thee " (ver. 7) : not for thy deservings, or through thy strength ; but because the Lord hath done good to thee. "Since," he saith, " He hath delivered my soul from death" (ver. 8). It is wonderful, most beloved brethren, that, after he had said that his soul should turn unto rest, since the Lord had rewarded him ; he added, since " He hath delivered my soul from death." Did it turn unto rest, because it was delivered from death? Is not rest more usually said of death? What is the action of him whose life is rest, and death disquietude? Such then ought to be the action of the soul, as may tend to a quiet security, not one that may increase restless toil ; since He hath delivered it from death, who, pitying it, said, " Come unto Me, all ye that labour and are heavy laden, and I will give you rest," etc.[2] Meek therefore and humble, following, so to speak, Christ as its path, should the action of the soul be that tendeth towards repose ; nevertheless, not slothful and supine ; that it may finish its course, as it is written, " In quietness make perfect thy works."[3] "Thou hast delivered my soul from death, mine eyes from tears, and my feet from falling." Whoever feeleth the chain of this flesh, chanteth these things as fulfilled in hope towards himself. For it is truly said,

" I was in misery, and He delivered me ; " but the Apostle saith this also truly, that we are saved by hope.[4] And that we are delivered from death, is well said to be already fulfilled, so that we may understand the death of unbelievers, of whom he saith, "Leave the dead to bury their dead."[5] . . . He will then clear our eyes of tears, when He shall save our feet from falling. For there will then be no slipping of our feet as they walk, when there will be no sliding of the weak flesh. But now, however firm our path, which is Christ, be ; yet since we place flesh, which we are enjoined to subdue, beneath us ; in the very work of chastening and subduing it, it is a great thing not to fall : but not to slip in the flesh, who can attain? "I shall please in the sight of the Lord, in the land of the living " (ver. 9). . . . We "labour" indeed now, because we are awaiting "the redemption of our body :"[6] but, "when death shall have been swallowed up in victory, and this corruptible shall have put on incorruption, and this mortal immortality ; "[7] then there will be no weeping, because there will be no falling ; and no falling, because no corruption. And therefore we shall then no longer labour to please, but we shall be entirely pleasing in the sight of the Lord, in the land of the living.

7. . . . "I believed," saith he, " and therefore did I speak. But I was sorely brought down " (ver. 10). For he suffered many tribulations, for the sake of the word which he faithfully held, faithfully preached ; and he was sorely brought down ; as they feared who loved the praise of men better than that of God. But what meaneth, "But I"? He should rather say, I believed, and therefore I have spoken, and I was sorely brought down : why did he add, "But I," save because a man may be sorely brought down by those who oppose the truth, the truth itself cannot, which he believeth and speaketh? Whence also the Apostle, when he was speaking of his chain, saith, "the word of God is not bound."[8] So this man also, since there is one person of the holy witnesses, that is, of the Martyrs of God, saith, "I believed, and therefore will I speak." "But I ; " not that which I believed, not the word which I have delivered ; "but I was sorely brought down."

8. "I said in my trance, All men are liars " (ver. 11). By trance he meaneth fear, which when persecutors threaten, and when the sufferings of torture or death impend, human weakness suffereth. For this we understand, because in this Psalm the voice of Martyrs is heard. For trance is used in another sense also, when the mind is not beside itself by fear, but is possessed by some inspiration of revelation. "But I said

[1] Heb. xii. 6, 7.   [2] Matt. xi. 28–30.   [3] Ecclus. iii. 19.

[4] Rom. viii. 24.   [5] Matt. viii. 22.   [6] Rom. viii. 23.
[7] 1 Cor. xv. 53, 54.   [8] 2 Tim. ii. 9.

in my haste, All men are liars." In consternation he hath had regard to his infirmity, and hath seen that he ought not to presume on himself; for as far as pertaineth to the man himself, he is a liar, but by the grace of God he is made true; lest yielding to the pressure of his enemies he might not speak what he had believed, but might deny it; even as it happened to Peter, since he had trusted in himself, and was to be taught that we ought not to trust in man. And if every one ought not to trust in man, surely not in himself; because he is a man. Rightly therefore in his fear did he perceive that every man was a liar; since they also whom no fear robs of their presence of mind, so that they never lie by yielding to the persecutors, are such by the gifts of God, not by their own strength. . . .

9. "What," he asketh, "what reward shall I give unto the Lord, for all the benefits that He hath returned unto me?" (ver. 12). He saith not, for all the benefits that He hath done unto me; but, "for all the benefits that He hath returned unto me." What deeds then on the man's part had preceded, that all the benefits of God were not said to be given, but returned? What had preceded, on the man's part, save sins? God therefore repayeth good for evil, whilst unto Him men repay evil for good; for such was the return of those who said, "This is the heir: come, let us kill him."[1]

10. But this man seeketh what he may return unto the Lord, and findeth not, save out of those things which the Lord Himself returneth. "I will receive," he saith, "the cup of salvation, and call upon the Name of the Lord" (ver. 13). "My vows will I render to the Lord, before all His people" (ver. 14). Who hath given thee the cup of salvation, which when thou takest, and callest upon the Name of the Lord, thou shalt return unto Him a reward for all that He hath returned unto thee? Who, save He who saith, "Are ye able to drink the cup that I shall drink of?"[2] Who hath given unto thee to imitate His sufferings, save He who hath suffered before for thee? And therefore, "Right dear in the sight of the Lord is the death of His Saints" (ver. 15). He purchased it by His Blood, which He first shed for the salvation of slaves, that they might not hesitate to shed their blood for the Lord's Name; which, nevertheless, would be profitable for their own interests, not for those of the Lord.

11. Let therefore the slave purchased at so great a price confess his condition, and say, "Behold, O Lord, how that I am Thy servant: "I am Thy servant, and the son of Thine handmaid" (ver. 16). . . . This, therefore, is the son of the heavenly Jerusalem, which is above,

the free mother of us all.[3] And free indeed from sin she is, but the handmaid of righteousness; to whose sons still pilgrims it is said, "Ye have been called unto liberty;"[4] and again he maketh them servants, when he saith, "but by love serve one another." . . . Let therefore that servant say unto God, Many call themselves martyrs, many Thy servants, because they hold Thy Name in various heresies and errors; but since they are beside Thy Church, they are not the children of Thy handmaid. But "I am Thy servant, and the son of Thine handmaid." "Thou hast broken my bonds asunder."

12. "I will offer to Thee the sacrifice of praise" (ver. 17). For I have not found any deserts of mine, since Thou hast broken my bonds asunder; I therefore owe Thee the sacrifice of praise; because, although I will boast that I am Thy servant, and the son of Thy handmaid, I will glory not in myself, but in Thee, my Lord, who hast broken asunder my bonds, that when I return from my desertion, I may again be bound unto Thee.

13. "I will pay my vows unto the Lord" (ver. 18). What vows wilt thou pay? What victims hast thou vowed? what burnt-offerings, what holocausts? Dost thou refer to what thou hast said a little before, "I will receive the cup of salvation, and will call upon the Name of the Lord;" and, "I will offer to Thee the sacrifice of thanksgiving"? and indeed whosoever well considereth what he is vowing to the Lord, and what vows he is paying, let him vow himself, let him pay himself as a vow: this is exacted, this is due. On looking at the coin, the Lord saith, "Render unto Cæsar the things which are Cæsar's, and unto God the things which are God's:"[5] his own image is rendered unto Cæsar: let His image be rendered unto God.

14. "In the courts," he saith, "of the Lord's house" (ver. 19). What is the Lord's house, the same is the Lord's handmaid: and what is God's house, save all His people? It therefore followeth, "In the sight of all His people." And now he more openly nameth his mother herself. For what else is His people, but what followeth, "In the midst of thee, O Jerusalem"? For than that which is returned grateful, if it be returned from peace, and in peace. But they who are not sons of this handmaid, have loved war rather than peace. . . .

PSALM CXVII.[6]

1. "O praise the Lord, all ye heathen: praise Him, all ye nations" (ver. 1). These are the courts of the Lord's house, this all His people,

---

[1] Matt. xxi. 38.   [2] Matt. xx. 22. [He omits ver. 14.—C.]

[3] Gal. iv. 26.   [4] Gal. v. 13.   [5] Matt. xxii. 21.
[6] Lat. CXVI. A sermon to the people.

this the true Jerusalem. Let those rather listen who have refused to be the children of this city, since they have cut themselves off from the communion of all nations.[1] " For His merciful kindness is ever more and more towards us : and the truth of the Lord endureth for ever " (ver. 2). These are those two things, loving-kindness and truth, which in the CXVth Psalm I admonished you should be committed to memory. But " the merciful kindness of the Lord is ever more and more towards us," since the furious tongues of hostile nations have yielded to His Name, through which we have been freed : " and the truth of the Lord endureth for ever," whether in those things which He promised to the righteous, or in those which He hath threatened to the ungodly.

PSALM CXVIII.[2]

1. . . . We are taught in this Psalm, when we chaunt Allelujah, which meaneth, Praise the Lord, that we should, when we hear the words, " Confess unto the Lord " (ver. 1), praise the Lord. The praise of God could not be expressed in fewer words than these, " For He is good." I see not what can be more solemn than this brevity, since goodness is so peculiarly the quality of God, that the Son of God Himself when addressed by some one as " Good Master," by one, namely, who beholding His flesh, and comprehending not the fulness of His divine nature, considered Him as man only, replied, " Why callest thou Me good? There is none good but one, that is, God."[3] And what is this but to say, If thou wishest to call Me good, recognise Me as God? But since it is addressed, in revelation of things to come, to a people freed from all toil and wandering in pilgrimage, and from all admixture with the wicked, which freedom was given it through the grace of God, who not only doth not evil for evil, but even returneth good for evil ; it is most appropriately added, " Because His mercy endureth for ever."

2. " Let Israel now confess that He is good, and that His mercy endureth for ever " (ver. 2). " Let the house of Aaron now confess that His mercy endureth for ever " (ver. 3). " Yea, let all now that fear the Lord confess that His mercy endureth for ever " (ver. 4). Ye remember, I suppose, most beloved, what is the house of Israel, what is the house of Aaron, and that both are those that fear the Lord. For they are " the little and the great,"[4] who have already in another Psalm been happily introduced into your hearts : in the number of whom all of us should rejoice that we are joined together, in His grace who is good, and whose mercy endureth for ever ; since they were listened to who said, " May the

Lord increase you more and more, you and your children ; "[5] that the host of the Gentiles might be added to the Israelites who believed in Christ, of the number of whom are the Apostles our fathers, for the exaltation of the perfect and the obedience of the little children ; that all of us when made one in Christ, made one flock under one Shepherd, and the body of that Head, like one man, may say, " I called upon the Lord in trouble, and the Lord heard me at large " (ver. 5). The narrow straits of our tribulation are limited : but the large way whereby we pass along hath no end. " Who shall lay anything to the charge of God's elect? "[6]

3. " The Lord is my helper ; I will not fear what man doeth unto me " (ver. 6). But are men, then, the only enemies that the Church hath? What is a man devoted to flesh and blood, save flesh and blood? But the Apostle saith, " We wrestle not against flesh and blood, but against," . . . he saith, " spiritual wickedness in high places ; "[7] that is, the devil and his angels ; that devil whom elsewhere he calleth " the prince of the power of the air."[8] Hear therefore what followeth : " The Lord is my helper : therefore shall I despise mine enemies " (ver. 7). From what class soever my enemies may arise, whether from the number of evil men, or from the number of evil angels ; in the Lord's help, unto whom we chant the confession of praise, unto whom we sing Allelujah, they shall be despised.

4. But, when my enemies have been brought to contempt, let not my friend present himself unto me as a good man, so as to bid me repose my hope in himself : for " It is better to trust in the Lord, than to put any confidence in man " (ver. 8). Nor let any one, who may in a certain sense be styled a good angel, be regarded by myself as one in whom I ought to put my trust : for " no one is good, save God alone ; "[9] and when a man or an angel appear to aid us, when they do this of sincere affection, He doth it through them, who made them good after their measure. " It is " therefore " better to trust in the Lord, than to put any confidence in princes " (ver. 9). For angels also are called princes, even as we read in Daniel, " Michael, your prince."[10]

5. " All nations compassed me round about, but in the Name of the Lord have I taken vengeance on them " (ver. 10). " They kept me in on every side, they kept me in, I say, on every side ; but in the Name of the Lord have I taken vengeance on them " (ver. 11). He signifieth the toils and the victory of the Church ; but, as if the question were asked how she could have overcome so great evils, he look-

---

[1] Donatists.　　[2] Lat. CXVII.　　[3] Mark x. 17, 18.
[4] Ps. cxv. 12, 13.

[5] Ps. cxv. 14.　　[6] Rom. viii. 33.　　[7] Eph. vi. 12.
[8] Eph. ii. 2.　　[9] Mark x. 18.　　[10] Dan. xii. 1.

eth back to the example, and declareth what she had first suffered in her Head, by adding what followeth, "They kept me in on every side:" and the words, "All nations," are with reason not repeated here, because this was the act of the Jews alone. There that very religious nation (which is the body of Christ, and in behalf of which was done all that was done in mortal form with immortal power, by that inward divinity, through the outward flesh), suffered from persecutors, of whose race that flesh was assumed and hung upon the cross.

6. "They came about me as bees do a hive, and burned up even as the fire among the thorns: and in the Name of the Lord have I taken vengeance on them" (ver. 12). Here then the order of the words corresponds with the order of events. For we rightly understand that our Lord Himself, the Head of the Church, was surrounded by persecutors, even as bees surround a hive. For the Holy Spirit is speaking with mystic subtlety of what was done by those who knew not what they did. For bees make honey in the hives: while our Lord's persecutors, unconscious as they were, rendered Him sweeter unto us even by His very Passion; so that we may taste and see how sweet is the Lord,[1] "Who died for our sins, and arose for our justification."[2] But what followeth, "and burned up even as the fire among the thorns," is better understood of His Body, that is, of a people spread abroad, whom all nations compassed about, since it was gathered together from all nations. They consumed this sinful flesh, and the grievous piercings of this mortal life, in the flame of persecution. "Taken vengeance on them:" either because they themselves, that wickedness, which in them persecuted the righteous, having been extinguished, were joined with the people of Christ; or because the rest of them, who have at this time scorned the mercy of Him who calleth them, will at the end feel the truth of Him who judgeth them.

7. "I have been driven on like a heap of sand, so that I was falling, but the Lord upheld me" (ver. 13). For though there were a great multitude of believers, that might be compared to the countless sand, and brought into one communion as into one heap; yet "what is man, save Thou be mindful of Him?"[3] He said not, the multitude of the Gentiles could not surpass the abundance of my host, but, "the Lord," he saith, "hath upheld me." The persecution of the Gentiles succeeded not in pushing forward, to its overthrow, the host of the faithful dwelling together in the unity of the faith.

8. "The Lord is my strength and my praise, and is become my salvation" (ver. 14). Who then fall, when they are pushed, save they who choose to be their own strength and their own praise? For no man falleth in the contest, except he whose strength and praise faileth. He therefore whose strength and praise is the Lord, falleth no more than the Lord falleth. And for this reason He hath become their salvation; not that He hath become anything which He was not before, but because they, when they believed on Him, became what they were not before, and then He began to be salvation unto them when turned towards Him, which He was not to them when turned away from Himself.

9. "The voice of joy and health is in the dwellings of the righteous" (ver. 15); where they who raged against their bodies thought there was the voice of sorrow and destruction. For they did not know the inward joy of the saints in their future hope. Whence the Apostle also saith, "As sorrowful, yet alway rejoicing;"[4] and again, "And not only so, but we glory in tribulations also."[5]

10. "The right hand of the Lord hath brought mighty things to pass" (ver. 16). What mighty things? saith he. "The right hand of the Lord," he saith, "hath exalted me." It is a mighty thing to exalt the humble, to deify the mortal, to bring perfection out of infirmity, glory from subjection, victory from suffering, to give help, to raise from trouble; that the true salvation of God might be laid open to the afflicted, and the salvation of men might remain of no avail to the persecutors. These are great things: but what art thou surprised at? hear what he repeateth: "The right hand of the Lord hath brought mighty things to pass."

11. "I shall not die, but live, and declare the works of the Lord" (ver. 17). But they, while they were dealing havoc and death on every side, thought that the Church of Christ was dying. Behold, he now declareth the works of the Lord. Everywhere Christ is the glory of the blessed Martyrs. By being beaten He conquered those who struck Him; by being patient of torments, the tormentors;[6] by loving, those who raged against Him.

12. Nevertheless, let him point out to us, why the body of Christ, the holy Church, the people of adoption, suffered such indignities. "The Lord," he saith, "hath chastened and corrected me, but He hath not given me over unto death" (ver. 18). Let not then the boastful wicked imagine that aught hath been permitted to their power: they would not have that power, were it not given them from above. Oft doth the father of a family command his sons to be corrected by the most worthless slaves; though he designeth the heritage for the former, fetters for the latter.

---

[1] Ps. xxxiv. 8.   [2] Rom. iv. 25.   [3] Ps. viii. 4.
[4] 2 Cor. vi. 10.   [5] Rom. v. 3.
[6] MSS. *facientes*. Edd. *impatientes*.

What is that heritage? Is it of gold, or silver, or jewels, or farms, or pleasant estates? Consider how we enter into it: and learn what it is.

13. "Open me," he saith, "the gates of righteousness" (ver. 19). Behold, we have heard of the gates. What is within? "That I may," he saith, "go into them, and give thanks unto the Lord." This is the confession of praise full of wonder, "even unto the house of God, in the voice of joy and confession of praise, among such as keep holiday:"[1] this is the everlasting bliss of the righteous, whereby they are blessed who dwell in the Lord's house, praising Him for evermore.[2]

14. But consider how the gates of righteousness are entered into. "These are the gates of the Lord" he saith, "the righteous shall enter into them" (ver. 20). At least let no wicked man enter there, that Jerusalem which receiveth not one uncircumcised, where it is said, "Without are dogs."[3] Be it enough, that in my long pilgrimage "I have had my habitation among the tents of Kedar:"[4] I endured even unto the end the intercourse of the wicked, but "these are the gates of the Lord: the righteous shall enter into them."

15. "I will confess unto Thee, O Lord, for Thou hast heard me, and art become my salvation" (ver. 21). How often is that confession proved to be one of praise, that doth not point out wounds to the physician, but giveth thanks for the health it hath received. But the Physician Himself is the Salvation.

16. But who is this whom we speak of? "The Stone which the builders rejected" (ver. 22); for, "It hath become the head Stone of the corner;" to "make in Himself of twain one new man, so making peace; and that He might reconcile both unto God in one body;"[5] circumcision, to wit, and uncircumcision.

17. "By the Lord was it made unto it" (ver. 23): that is, it is made into the head stone of the corner by the Lord. For although He would not have become this, had He not suffered: yet He became not this through those from whom He suffered. For they who were building, refused Him: but in the edifice which the Lord was secretly raising, that was made the head stone of the corner which they rejected. "And it is marvellous in our eyes:" in the eyes of the inner man, in the eyes of those that believe, those that hope, those that love; not in the carnal eyes of those who, through scorning Him as if He were a man, rejected Him.

18. "This is the day which the Lord hath made" (ver. 24). This man remembereth that he had said in former Psalms, "Since He hath inclined His ear unto me, therefore will I call upon

Him as long as I live;"[6] making mention of his old days; whence he now saith, "This is the day which the Lord hath made;" that is, wherein He hath given me Salvation. This is the day whereof He said, "In an acceptable time have I heard thee, and in a day of Salvation have I helped thee;"[7] that is, a day wherein He, the Mediator, hath become the head Stone of the corner. "Let us rejoice," therefore, "and be glad in Him."

19. "Save me now, O Lord: prosper Thou well my way, O Lord" (ver. 25). Because it is the day of Salvation, "save me:" because we, returning from a long pilgrimage, are separated from those who hated peace, with whom we were peaceful, and who, when we spoke to them, made war upon us without a cause; "prosper well our way" as we return, since Thou hast become our Way.

20. "Blessed be He that cometh in the Name of the Lord" (ver. 26). Cursed, therefore, is he that cometh in his own name; as He saith in the Gospel: "if another shall come in his own name, him ye will receive."[8] "We have blessed you out of the house of God." I believe that these are the words of the great to the little, of those great ones, to wit, who in spirit commune with God the Word, who is with God, as they may in this life; and yet temper their discourse for the sake of the little ones, so that they may sincerely say what the Apostle saith: "For whether we be beside ourselves, it is to God: or whether we be sober, it is for your cause. For the love of Christ constraineth us."[9] They bless the little children from the inner house of the Lord, where that praise faileth not age after age: consider therefore what they proclaim from thence.[10]

21. "God is the Lord, who hath showed us light" (ver. 27). That Lord, who came in the Lord's Name, whom the builders refused, and who became the head Stone of the corner,[11] that "Mediator between God and man, Jesus Christ,"[12] is God, He is equal with the Father, He hath showed us light, that we might understand what we believed, and declare it to you who understand it not as yet, but already believe it. But that ye also may understand, "Declare a holy day in full assemblies, even unto the horns of the altar;" that is, even unto the inner house of God, from which we have blessed you, where are the high places of the altar. "Declare a holy day," not in a slothful manner, but "in full assemblies" (ver. 28). For this is the voice of joyfulness among those that keep holy day, who

---

[1] Ps. xlii. 4. [2] Ps. lxxxiv. 4. [3] Rev. xxii. 15.
[4] Ps. cxx. 5. [5] Eph. ii. 15, 16.

[6] Ps. cxiv. 2. [7] Isa. xlix. 8. [8] John v. 43.
[9] 2 Cor. v. 13, 14.
[10] [Contrary to all his habitual usage, our author fails to note just here what is written in St. Matt. xxi. 15, 16, concerning this Paschal Psalm, and the hosannas of children in the temple. — C.]
[11] Matt. xxi. 9, 42. [12] 1 Tim. ii. 5.

walk " in the place of the wonderful tabernacle, even unto the house of God." [1] For if there be there the spiritual sacrifice, the everlasting sacrifice of praise, both the Priest is everlasting, and the peaceful mind of the righteous an everlasting altar. . . .

22. And what shall we sing there, save His praises? What else shall we say there, save, "Thou art my God, and I will confess unto Thee; Thou art my God, and I will praise Thee. I will confess unto Thee, for Thou hast heard me, and art become my Salvation." We will not say these things in loud words; but the love that abideth in Him of itself crieth out in these words, and these words are love itself. Thus, as he began with praise, so he endeth: "Confess unto the Lord, for He is gracious, and His mercy endureth for ever" (ver. 29). With this the Psalm commenceth, with this it endeth; since, as from the commencement which we have left behind, so in the end, whither we are returning, there is not anything that can more profitably please us, than the praise of God, and Allelujah evermore.

PSALM CXIX.[2]

Aleph.

1. From its commencement, dearly beloved, doth this great Psalm exhort us unto bliss, which there is no one who desireth not. . . . And therefore this is the lesson which he teacheth, who saith, "Blessed are those that are undefiled in the way, who walk in the law of the Lord" (ver. 1). As much as to say, I know what thou wishest, thou art seeking bliss: if then thou wouldest be blessed, be undefiled. For the former all desire, the latter fear: yet without it, what all wish cannot be attained. But where will any one be undefiled, save in the way? In what way, save in the law of the Lord? . . .

---

[1] Ps. xlii. 4.
[2] Lat. CXVIII. [The author says: "Preface.—I have expounded all the rest of the Psalms, which we know the Book of the Psalms containeth, which by the custom of the Church is styled the Psalter, partly by preaching among the people, partly by dictations, as well as I, by the Lord's help, was able: but I put off the CXIXth Psalm, as well on account of its well-known length, as on account of its depth being fathomable by few. And when my brethren deeply regretted that the exposition of this Psalm alone, so far as pertaineth to the Psalms of the same volume, was wanting to my works, and strongly pressed me to pay this debt, I yielded not to them, though they long entreated and solicited me; because as often as I began to reflect upon it, it always exceeded the utmost stretch of my powers. For in proportion as it seemeth more open, so much the more deep doth it appear to me; so that I cannot show how deep it is. For in others, which are understood with difficulty, although the sense lie hid in obscurity, yet the obscurity itself appeareth; but in this, not even this is the case; since it is superficially such, that it seemeth not to need an expositor, but only a reader and listener. And now that at length I approach its interpretation, I am utterly ignorant what I can achieve in it: nevertheless, I hope that God will aid me with His Presence, that I may effect something. For thus He hath done in all those which, though at first they seemed to me difficult, and almost impracticable, I have succeeded in adequately expounding. But I decided to do this by means of sermons, which might be delivered among the people, such as the Greeks term ὁμιλίαι. For this is, I think, more equitable, that the assemblies of the Church be not defrauded of the comprehension of this Psalm, by the singing of which, as much as by that of others, they are wont to be charmed. But let the preface end here: we must now speak of the Psalm itself, to which we have thought it right to make this Preface."—C.]

2. Listen now to what he addeth: "Blessed are they that keep His testimonies, and seek Him with their whole heart" (ver. 2). No other class of the blessed seemeth to me to be mentioned in these words, than that which has been already spoken of. For to examine into the testimonies of the Lord, and to seek Him with all the heart, this is to be undefiled in the way, this is to walk in the law of the Lord. He then goeth on to say, "For they who do wickedness, shall not walk in His ways" (ver. 3). And yet we know that the workers of wickedness do search the testimonies of the Lord for this reason, that they prefer being learned to being righteous: we know that others also search the testimonies of the Lord, not because they are already living well, but that they may know how they ought to live. Such then do not as yet walk undefiled in the law of the Lord, and for this reason are not as yet blessed. . . .

3. It is written, and is read, and is true, in this Psalm, that "They who do wickedness, walk not in His ways" (ver. 3). But we must endeavour, with the help of God, " in " whose " hand are both we and our words," [3] that what is rightly said, by not being rightly understood, may not confuse the reader or hearer. For we must beware, lest all the Saints, whose words these are, " If we say that we have no sin, we deceive ourselves, and the truth is not in us;" [4] may either not be thought to walk in the ways of the Lord, since sin is wickedness, and "they who do wickedness, walk not in His ways;" or, because it is not doubtful that they walk in the ways of the Lord, may be thought to have no sin, which is beyond doubt false. For it is not said merely for the sake of avoiding arrogance and pride. Otherwise it would not be added, "And the truth is not in us;" but it would be said, Humility is not in us: especially because the following words throw a clearer light on the meaning, and remove all the causes of doubt. For when the blessed John had said this, he added, " If we confess our sins, He is faithful and just to forgive us our sins, and to cleanse us from all unrighteousness." [5] . . .

4. What meaneth, "Thou hast charged that we shall keep Thy commandments too much"? (ver. 4). Is it, "Thou hast charged too much"? or, "to keep too much"? Whichever of these we understand, the sense seems contrary to that memorable and noble sentiment which the Greeks praise in their wise men, and which the Latins agree in praising. "Do nothing too much." [6] . . . But the Latin language some-

---

[3] Wisd. vii. 16.　　[4] 1 John i. 8, 9.　　[5] 1 John i. 9.
[6] Terence, Andria, v. 34. "This Greek sentiment does not contain a word answering to that which is here read: for there, ἄγαν is used, which is nimis; but here σφόδρα, which is equivalent to valdè, very much. But sometimes, as we have said, we find nimis used, and use it ourselves, for what means valdè."—The Author.

times uses the word *nimis* in such a sense, that we find it in the holy Scripture, and employ it in our discourses, as signifying, very much. In this passage, " Thou hast charged that we keep Thy commandments too much," we simply understand very much, if we understand rightly; and if we say to any very dear friend, I love you too much, we do not wish to be understood to mean more than is fitting, but very much.

5. " O that," he saith, " my ways were made so direct, that I might keep Thy statutes " (ver. 5). Thou indeed hast charged: O that I could realize what thou hast charged. When thou hearest, " O that," recognise the words of one wishing; and having recognised the expression of a wish, lay aside the pride of presumption. For who saith that he desireth what he hath in such a manner in his power, that without need of any help he can do it? Therefore if man desireth what God chargeth, God must be prayed to grant Himself what He enjoineth. . . .

6. " So shall I not be confounded, while I have respect unto all Thy commandments " (ver. 6). We ought to look upon the commandments of God, whether when they are read, or when they are recalled to memory, as a looking-glass, as the Apostle James saith.[1] This man wisheth himself to be such, that he may regard as in a mirror the commandments of God, and may not be confounded; because he chooses not merely to be a hearer of them, but a doer. On this account he desireth that his ways may be made direct to keep the statutes of God. How to be made direct, save by the grace of God? Otherwise he will find in the law of God not a source of rejoicing, but of confusion, if he hath chosen to look into commandments, which he doth not.

7. " I will confess unto Thee," he saith, " O Lord, in the directing of my heart; in that I shall have learned the judgments of Thy righteousness " (ver. 7). This is not the confession of sins, but of praise; as He also saith in whom there was no sin, " I will confess unto Thee, O Father, Lord of heaven and earth; "[2] and as it is written in the Book of Ecclesiasticus, " Thus shalt thou say in confession, of all the works of God, that they are very good."[3] " I will confess unto Thee," he saith, " in the directing of my heart." Indeed, if my ways are made straight, I will confess unto Thee, since Thou hast done it, and this is Thy praise, and not mine. . . .

8. Next he addeth: " I will keep Thy ordinances " (ver. 8). . . . But what is it that followeth? " O forsake me not even exceedingly!"

or, as some copies have it, " even too much," instead of, " even exceedingly."[4] But since God had left the world to the desert of sins, He would have forsaken it " even exceedingly," if so powerful a cure had not supported it, that is, the grace of God through our Lord Jesus Christ; but now, according to this prayer of the body of Christ, He forsook it not " even exceedingly; " for, " God was in Christ, reconciling the world unto Himself."[5] . . .

Beth.

9. " Wherewithal shall a young man correct his way? even by keeping Thy words " (ver. 9). He questioneth himself, and answereth himself. " Wherewithal?" So far it is a question: next cometh the answer, " even by keeping Thy words." But in this place the keeping of the words of God, must be understood as the obeying His commandments in deed: for they are kept in memory in vain, if they are not kept in life also. But what is meant by " young man " here? For he might have said, wherewithal shall any one (*homo*) correct his way? or, wherewithal shall a man (*vir*) correct his way? which is usually put by the Scriptures in such a way, that the whole human race is understood. . . . But in this passage he saith neither any one, nor a man, but, " a young man." Is then an old man to be despaired of? or doth an old man correct his way by any other means than by ruling himself after God's word? Or is it perhaps an admonition at what age we ought chiefly to correct our way; according to what is elsewhere written, " My son, gather instruction from thy youth up: so shalt thou find wisdom till thy gray hairs."[6] There is another mode of interpreting it, by recognising in the expression the younger son in the Gospel,[7] who returned to himself, and said, " I will arise and go to my father."[8] Wherewithal did he correct his way, save by ruling himself after the words of God, which he desired as one longing for his father's bread. . . .

10. " With my whole heart," he saith, " have I sought thee; O repel me not from Thy commandments " (ver. 10). Behold, he prayeth that he may be aided to keep the words of God, wherewith he had said that the young man corrected his way. For this is the meaning of the words, " O repel me not from Thy commandments: " for what is it to be repelled of God, save not to be aided? For human infirmity is not equal to obeying His righteous and exalted commandments, unless His love doth prevent

---

[1] Jas. i. 23–25.
[2] Matt. xi. 25.
[3] Ecclus. xxxix. 15, 16.

[4] " For the same Greek word is here too, namely, σφόδρα: as though he wished himself to be forsaken of God, but not ' even exceedingly.' " — *The author.*
[5] 2 Cor. v. 19.   [6] Ecclus. vi. 18.
[7] Luke xv. 12, etc.
[8] Luke xv. 18.

and aid. But those whom He aideth not, these He is justly said to repel. . . .

11. "Thy words have I hid within my heart, that I may not sin against Thee" (ver. 11). He at once sought the Divine aid, lest the words of God might be hidden without fruit in his heart, unless works of righteousness followed. For after saying this, he added, "Blessed art Thou, O Lord, teach me Thy righteousnesses." (ver. 12). "Teach me," he saith, as they learn who do them ; not as they who merely remember them, that they may have somewhat to speak of. Why then doth he say, "Teach me Thy righteousnesses," save because he wisheth to learn them by deeds, not by speaking or retaining them in his memory? Since then, as it is read in another Psalm, "He shall give blessing, who gave the law ; " [1] therefore, "Blessed art Thou, O Lord," he saith, "O teach me Thy righteousness." For because I have hidden Thy words in my heart, that I may not sin against Thee, Thou hast given a law ; give also the blessing of Thy grace, that by doing right I may learn what Thou by teaching hast commanded. . . .

12. "With my lips have I been telling of all the judgments of Thy mouth " (ver. 13) ; that is, I have kept silent nothing of Thy judgments, which Thou didst will should become known to me through Thy words, but I have been telling of all of them without exception with my lips. This he seemeth to me to signify, since he saith not, all Thy judgments, but, "all the judgments of Thy mouth ; " that is, which Thou hast revealed unto me : that by His mouth we may understand His word, which He hath discovered unto us in many revelations of the Saints, and in the two Testaments ; all which judgments the Church ceaseth not to declare at all times with her lips.

13. "I have had as great delight in the way of Thy testimonies, as in all manner of riches" (ver. 14). We understand that there is no more speedy, no more sure, no shorter, no higher way of the testimonies of God than Christ, "in whom are hid all the treasures of wisdom and knowledge." [2] Thence he saith that he hath had as great delight in this way, as in all riches. Those are the testimonies, by which He deigneth to prove unto us how much He loveth us. [3] . . .

14. "I will talk of Thy commandments, and have respect unto Thy ways " [4] (ver. 15). And thus the Church doth exercise herself in the commandments of God, by speaking in the copious disputations of the learned against all the enemies of the Christian and Catholic faith ; which are fruitful to those who compose them, if nothing but the ways of the Lord is regarded in them ; but "All the ways of the Lord are," as it is written, "mercy and truth ; " [5] the fulness of which both is found in Christ. Through this sweet exercise is gained also what he subjoineth : "My meditation shall be in Thy statutes, and I will not forget Thy word " (ver. 16). "My meditation " shall be therein, that I may not forget them. Thus the blessed man in the first Psalm "shall meditate in the law " of the Lord "day and night." [6] . . .

Gimel.

15. He had said, "Wherewithal shall a young man cleanse his way? Even by keeping Thy words." Behold he now more openly asketh aid that he may do this : "Reward," he saith, "Thy servant : let me live, and keep Thy word " (ver. 17). . . . It is this reward that he asketh, who saith, "Reward Thy servant." For there are four modes of reward : either (1) evil for evil, as God will reward everlasting fire to the unrighteous ; or (2) good for good, as He will reward an everlasting kingdom to the righteous ; or (3) good for evil, as Christ by grace justifieth the ungodly ; or (4) evil for good, as Judas and the Jews through their wickedness persecuted Christ. Of these four modes of reward, the first two belong to justice, whereby evil is rewarded for evil, good for good ; the third to mercy, whereby good is rewarded for evil ; the fourth God knoweth not, for to none doth He reward evil for good. But that which I have placed third in order, is in the first instance necessary : for unless God rewarded good for evil, there would be none to whom He could reward good for good. . . .

16. Nowhere then let human pride raise itself up : God giveth good rewards unto His own gifts. . . .

17. "Open Thou mine eyes, and I will consider wondrous things of Thy law " (ver. 18). What he addeth, "I am a lodger upon earth " (ver. 19) : or, as some copies read, "I am a sojourner upon earth, O hide not Thy commandments from me," hath the same meaning. . . .

18. Here an important question ariseth respecting the soul. For the words, I am a sojourner, or lodger, or stranger upon earth, [7] cannot seem to have been said in reference to the body, since the body derives its origin from

---

[1] Ps. lxxxiv. 6. "The rain also," etc.
[2] Col. ii. 3.   [3] Rom. v. 8, 9; John xiv. 6; Rom. viii. 32.
[4] [He says: "The Greek word is, ἀδολεσχήσω, which the Latin translators have rendered sometimes by ' talking,' sometimes by ' being exercised in: ' and these seem different from one anoth r: but if the exercise of the understanding be understood, with a certain delight in uttering, they are connected with one another, and one thing, in a manner, is made up of both, so that talking is not foreign to this sort of exercise." — C.]

[5] Ps. xxvi. 9.   [6] Ps. xxv. 10.
[7] [He says: "The Greek word πάροικος is variously rendered by our translators, incola, inquilinus, or advena. Lodgers (inquilini) who have no house of their own, dwell in another man's; but sojourners (incolæ), or strangers (advenæ), are spoken of as foreigners (adventitii)." — C.]

the earth. But in this most profound question I dare not define anything. For if it might justly have been said in respect of the soul (which God forbid we should suppose derived from the earth), "I am a lodger," or "stranger upon earth;" or in reference to the whole man, since he was at one time an inhabitant of Paradise, where he who spake these words was not; or, what is more free from all controversy, if it be not every man who could say this, but one to whom an everlasting country hath been promised in heaven: this I know, "that the life of man on earth is a temptation;"[1] and that "there is a heavy yoke upon the sons of Adam."[2] But it pleaseth me more to discuss the question in accordance with this construction, that we say we are tenants or strangers upon earth, because we have found our country above, whence we have received a pledge, and where when we have arrived we shall never depart.[3] . . .

19. Those whose conversation[4] is in heaven, as far as they abide here conversant, are in truth strangers. Let them pray therefore that the commandments of God may not be hidden from them, whereby they may be freed from this temporary sojourn, by loving God, with whom they will be for evermore; and by loving their neighbour, that he may be there where they also themselves will be.

20. But what is loved by loving, if love itself be not loved? Whence by consequence that stranger upon earth, after praying that the commandments of God might not be hidden from him, wherein love is enjoined either solely or principally; declareth that he desireth to have a love for love itself, saying, "My soul hath coveted to have a desire alway after Thy judgments" (ver. 20). This coveting is worthy of praise, not of condemnation. . . .

21. But he saith not, "coveteth," only; but, "My soul hath coveted to desire Thy judgments." For there is no obstacle to possessing the judgments of God, save that they are not desired, while love hath no warmth toward winning them, though their light is so clear and shining. . . .

22. "Thou hast rebuked the proud: and cursed are they that do err from Thy commandments" (ver. 21). For the proud err from the commandments of God. For it is one thing not to fulfil the commandments of God through infirmity or ignorance; another to err from them through pride; as they have done, who have begotten us in our mortal state unto these evils. . . . But consider now, after saying, "Thou hast rebuked the proud," he saith not, Cursed are they that have erred from Thy commandments; so that only that sin of the first men should

come into the mind; but he saith, "Cursed are they that do err." For it was needful that all might be terrified by that example, that they might not err from the divine commandments, and by loving righteousness in all time, recover in the toil of this world, what we lost in the pleasure of Paradise.

23. "O turn from me shame and rebuke; for I have sought out Thy testimonies" (ver. 22). Testimonies are called in Greek μαρτύρια, which word we now use for the Latin word: whence those who on account of their testimony to Christ have been brought low by various sufferings, and have contended unto death for the truth, are not called *testes*, but by the Greek term Martyrs.[5] Since then ye hear in this term one more familiar and grateful, let us take these words as if it were said, "O turn from me shame and rebuke; because I have sought out Thy martyrdoms." When the body of Christ speaketh thus, doth it consider it any punishment to hear rebuke and shame from the ungodly and the proud, since it rather reacheth the crown by this means? Why then doth it pray that it should be removed from it as something heavy and insupportable, save because, as I said, it prayeth for its very enemies, to whom it seeth it is destructive, to cast the holy name of Christ as a reproach to Christians. . . . For my enemies, whom Thou enjoinest to be loved by me, who more and more die and are lost, when they despise Thy martyrdoms and accuse them in me, will indeed be recalled to life and be found, if they reverence Thy martyrdoms in me. Thus it hath happened: this we see. Behold, martyrdom in the name of Christ, both with men and in this world, is not only not a disgrace, but a great ornament: behold, not only in the sight of the Lord, but in the sight of men, "precious is the death of His Saints;"[6] behold, His martyrs are not only not despised, but honoured with great distinctions. . . .

24. "Princes also did sit and speak against me: but Thy servant is exercised in Thy statutes" (ver. 23). Thou who desirest to know what sort of exercise this was, understand what he hath added, "For Thy testimonies are my meditation, and Thy statutes are my counsellors" (ver. 24). Remember what I have above instructed you, that testimonies are acts of martyrdom. Remember that among the statutes of the Lord there is none more difficult and more worthy of admiration, than that every man should love his enemies.[7] Thus then the body of Christ was exercised, so that it meditated on the acts of martyrdom that testified of Him, and loved those from whom, while they rebuked and despised the Church for these very martyrdoms, she suffered persecutions. . . .

---

[1] Job vii. 1.   [2] Ecclus. xl. 1.
[3] [Here follows a homily, accordingly. — C.]
[4] Citizenship. Philip. iii. 19, 20.

[5] Either word means "witnesses."
[6] Ps. cxvi. 15.   [7] Matt. v. 44.

Daleth.

25. "My soul cleaveth to the pavement: O quicken Thou me according to Thy word" (ver. 25). What meaneth, "My soul cleaveth to the pavement, O quicken Thou me according to Thy word"? . . . If we look upon the whole world as one great house, we see that the heavens represent its vaulting, the earth therefore will be its pavement. He wisheth thereforeto be rescued from earthly things, and to say with the Apostle, "Our conversation[1] is in heaven." To cling therefore to earthly things is the soul's death; the contrary of which evil, life is prayed for, when he saith, "O quicken Thou me."

26. . . . The body itself also, because it is of the earth, is reasonably understood by the word pavement; since, because it is still corruptible and weigheth down the soul,[2] we justly groan while in it, and say unto God, "O quicken Thou me." For we shall not be without our bodies when we shall be for evermore with the Lord;[3] but then, because they will not be corruptible, nor will they weigh down our souls, if we view it strictly, we shall not cleave unto them, but they rather unto us, and we unto God. . . .

27. For what he was by himself, he confesseth in the following words: "I have acknowledged my ways, and Thou heardest me" (ver. 26). Some copies indeed read, "Thy ways:" but more, and the best Greek, read "my ways," that is, evil ways. For he seemeth to me to say this; I have confessed my sins, and Thou hast heard me; that is, so that Thou wouldest remit them. "O teach me Thy statutes." I have acknowledged my ways: Thou hast blotted them out: teach me Thine. So teach me, that I may act; not merely that I may know how I ought to act. For as it is said of the Lord, that He knew not sin,[4] and it is understood, that He did no sin; so also he ought truly to be said to know righteousness, who doeth it. This is the prayer of one who is improving. . . .

28. Finally he addeth, "Intimate to me the way of Thy righteousness" (ver. 27); or, as some copies have it, "instruct me;" which is expressed more closely from the Greek, "Make me to understand the way of Thy righteousnesses; so shall I be exercised in Thy wondrous things." These higher commandments, which he desireth to understand by edification, he calleth the wondrous things of God. There are then some righteousnesses of God so wondrous, that human weakness may be believed incapable of fulfilling them by those who have not tried. Whence the Psalmist, struggling and wearied with the difficulty of obeying them, saith, "My soul hath slumbered for very heaviness: O stab-

lish Thou me with Thy word!" (ver. 28). What meaneth, hath slumbered? save that he hath cooled in the hope which he had entertained of being able to reach them. But, he addeth, "Stablish Thou me with Thy word:" that I may not by slumbering fall away from those duties which I feel that I have already attained: stablish Thou me therefore in those words of Thine that I already hold, that I may be able to reach unto others through edification.

29. "Take Thou from me the way of iniquity" (ver. 29). And since the law of works hath entered in, that sin might abound;[5] he addeth, "And pity me according to Thy law." By what law, save by the law of faith? Hear the Apostle: "Where is boasting then? It is excluded. By what law? Of works. Nay: but by the law of faith."[6] This is the law of faith, whereby we believe and pray that it may be granted us through grace; that we may effect that which we cannot fulfil through ourselves; that we may not, ignorant of God's righteousness, and going about to establish our own, fail to submit ourselves unto the righteousness of God.[7]

30. But after he had said, "And pity me according to Thy law;" he mentioneth some of those blessings which he hath already obtained, that he may ask others that he hath not yet gained. For he saith, "I have chosen the way of truth: and Thy judgments I have not forgotten" (ver. 30). "I have stuck unto Thy testimonies: O Lord, confound me not" (ver. 31): may I persevere in striving toward the point whereunto I am running: may I arrive whither I am running! So then "it is not of him that willeth, nor of him that runneth, but of God that showeth mercy."[8] He next saith, "I will run the way of Thy commandments, when Thou hast widened my heart" (ver. 32). I could not run hadst Thou not widened my heart. The sense of the words, "I have chosen the way of truth, and Thy judgments I have not forgotten: I have stuck unto Thy testimonies," is clearly explained in this verse. For this running is along the way of the commandments of God. And because he doth allege unto the Lord rather His blessings than his own deservings; as if it were said unto him, How hast thou run that way, by choosing, and by not forgetting the judgments of God, and by sticking to His testimonies? Couldest thou do these things by thyself? I could not, he replieth. It is not therefore through my own will, as though it needed no aid of Thine; but because "Thou has widened my heart." The widening of the heart is the delight we take in righteousness. This is the gift of God, the effect of which is, that we are not straitened in His commandments through

---

[1] Citizenship. Philip. iii. 20.　　[2] Wisd. ix. 15.
[3] 1 Thess. iv. 17.
[4] 2 Cor. v. 21.

[5] Rom. v. 20.　　[6] Rom. iii. 27.　　[7] Rom. x. 3.
[8] Rom. ix. 16.

the fear of punishment, but widened through love, and the delight we have in righteousness. . . .

He.

31. In this great Psalm there cometh next in order that which, with the Lord's help, we must consider and treat of. "Set a law for me, O Lord, the way of Thy statutes, and I shall seek it alway" (ver. 33). . . .

32. Why doth this man still pray for a law to be laid down for him; which, if it had not been laid down for him, he could not have run the way of God's commandments in the breadth of his heart? But since one speaketh who is growing in grace, and who knoweth that it is God's gift that he profiteth in grace; what else doth he pray, when he prayeth that a law may be laid down for him, save that he may profit more and more? As, if thou holdest a full cup, and givest it to a thirsty man; he both exhausts it by drinking it, and prayeth for it by still longing for it. . . .

33. But what meaneth, "Evermore"? . . . Doth "evermore" mean as long as we live here, because we progress in grace so long; but after this life, he who was in a good course of improvement here, is made perfect there? . . . Here the law of God is examined into, as long as we progress in it, both by knowing it and by loving it: but there its fulness abideth for our enjoyment, not for our examination. Thus also is this spoken, "Seek His face evermore." [1] Where, evermore, save here? For we shall not there also seek the face of God, when "we shall see face to face." [2] Or if that which is loved without a change of affection is rightly said to be sought after, and our only object is, that it be not lost, we shall indeed evermore seek the law of God, that is, the truth of God: for in this very Psalm it is said, "And Thy law is the truth." [3] It is now sought, that it may be held fast; it will then be held fast that it may not be lost. . . .

34. "Give me understanding, and I shall search Thy law, yea, I shall keep it with my whole heart" (ver. 34). For when each man hath searched the law, and searched its deep things, in which its whole meaning doth consist; he ought indeed to love God with all his heart, with all his soul, with all his mind; and his neighbour as himself. "For on these two commandments hang all the Law and the Prophets." [4] This he seemeth to have promised, when he said, "Yea, I shall keep it with my whole heart."

35. But since he hath no power to do even this, save he be aided by Him who commandeth him to do what He commandeth, "Make me,"

he addeth, "to go in the path of Thy commandments, for therein is my desire" (ver. 35). My desire is powerless, unless Thou Thyself makest me to go where I desire. And this is surely the very path, that is, the path of God's commandments, which he had already said that he had run, when his heart was enlarged by the Lord. And this he calleth a "path," because "the way is narrow which leadeth unto life;" [5] and since it is narrow, we cannot run therein save with a heart enlarged. . . .

36. He next saith, "Incline mine heart unto Thy testimonies, and not to covetousness" (ver. 36). This then he prayeth, that he may profit in the will itself. [6] . . . But the Apostle saith, "Avarice is a root of all evils." [7] But in the Greek, whence these words have been rendered into our tongue, the word used by the Apostle is not πλεονεξία, which occurs in this passage of the Psalms; but φιλαργυρία, by which is signified "love of money." But the Apostle must be understood to have meant genus by species when he used this word, that is, to have meant avarice universally and generally by love of money, which is truly the root of all evils. [8] . . . If therefore our heart be not inclined to covetousness, we fear God only for God's sake, so that He is the only reward of our serving Him. Let us love Him in Himself, let us love Him in ourselves, Him in our neighbours whom we love as ourselves, whether they have Him, or in order that they may have Him. . . .

37. The next words in the Psalm which we have undertaken to expound are, "O turn away mine eyes, lest they behold vanity: and quicken Thou me in Thy way" (ver. 37). Vanity and truth are directly contrary to one another. The desires of this world are vanity: but Christ, who freeth us from the world, is truth. He is the way, too, wherein this man wisheth to be quickened, for He is also the life: "I am the way, the truth, and the life," [9] are His own words.

38. . . . He prayeth that those eyes wherewith we consider on what account we do what we do, may be turned away that they behold not vanity; that is, that he may not look to vanity, as his motive, when he doeth anything good. In this vanity the first place is held by the love of men's praise, on account of which many great deeds have been wrought by those who are styled great in this world, and who have been much praised in heathen states, seeking glory not with God, but among men, and on account of this

---

[1] Ps. cv. 4.　　　[2] 1 Cor. xiii. 12.　　　[3] Ps. cxix. 142.
[4] Matt. xxii. 37-40.

[5] Matt. vii. 14.
[6] [He says: "He useth here a Greek expression, from which covetousness generally may be understood, whereby every man seeketh more than is enough: for the word πλέον meaneth *more*, and ἕξις signifieth *having*, being derived from the verb to have. It is therefore termed πλεονεξία, from having too much: a word which the Latin translators in this passage have variously rendered by emolument, utility, and avarice, which last is best."—C.]
[7] 1 Tim. vi. 10.　　　[8] Gen. iii. 5.　　　[9] John xiv. 6.

living in appearance prudently, courageously, temperately, and righteously; and when they have reached this they have reached their reward: vain men, and vain reward.[1] . . . Moreover, if it be a vain thing to do good works for the sake of men's praises, how much more vain for the sake of getting money, or increasing it, or retaining it, and any other temporal advantage, which cometh unto us from without? Since "all things are vanity: what is man's abundance, with all his toil, wherein he laboureth under the sun?"[2] For our temporal welfare itself finally we ought not to do our good works, but rather for the sake of that everlasting welfare which we hope for, where we may enjoy an unchangeable good, which we shall have from God, nay, what God Himself is unto us. For if God's Saints were to do good works for the sake of this temporal welfare, never would the martyrs of Christ achieve a good work of confession in the loss of this same welfare. . . .

39. "O stablish Thy word in Thy servant, that I may fear Thee" (ver. 38). And what else is this than, Grant unto me that I may do according to what Thou sayest? For the word of God is not stablished in those who remove it in themselves by acting contrary to it; but it is stablished in those in whom it is immoveable. God therefore stablisheth His word, that they may fear Him, in those unto whom He giveth the spirit of the fear of Him; not that fear of which the Apostle saith, "Ye have not received the spirit of bondage again to fear;"[3] for "perfect love casteth out" this "fear,"[4] but that fear which the Prophet calleth "the spirit of the fear of the Lord;"[5] that fear which "is pure, and endureth for ever;"[6] that fear which feareth to offend Him whom it loveth.

40. "Take away my reproach which I have suspected, for Thy judgments are sweet" (ver. 39). Who is he who suspected his own reproach, and who doth not know his own reproach better than that of his neighbour? For a man may rather suspect another's than his own; since he knoweth not that which he suspecteth; but in each one's own reproach there is not suspicion for him, but knowledge, wherein conscience speaketh. What then mean the words, "the rebuke which I have suspected"? The meaning of them must be derived from the former verse; since as long as a man doth not turn away his eyes lest they behold vanity, he suspecteth in others what is going on in himself; so that he believeth another to worship God, or do good works, from the same motive as himself. For men can see what we do, but with a view to what end we act, is hidden. . . .

41. "Behold, I have coveted Thy commandments: O quicken Thou me in Thy righteousness" (ver. 40). Behold, I have coveted to love Thee with all my heart, and with all my soul, and with all my mind, and my neighbour as myself, but, "O quicken Thou me" not in my own, but "in Thy righteousness," that is, fill me with that love which I have longed for. Aid me that I may do that which Thou chargest me: Thyself give what Thou dost command. "O quicken Thou me in Thy righteousness:" for in myself I had that which would cause my death: but I find not save in Thee whence I may live. Christ is Thy righteousness, "Who of God is made unto us wisdom," etc.[7] And in Him I find Thy commandments, which I have coveted, that in Thy righteousness, that is, in Him, Thou mayest quicken me. For the Word Himself is God; and "the Word was made flesh,"[8] that He Himself also might be my neighbour.

Vau.

42. "And let Thy loving mercy come also unto us, O Lord" (ver. 41). This sentence seems annexed to the foregoing: for he doth not say, Let it come unto me, but, "*And* let it come unto me." . . . What then doth he here pray for, save that through His loving mercy who commanded, he may perform the commandments which he hath coveted? For he explaineth in some degree what he meant by adding, "even Thy salvation, according to Thy word:" that is, according to Thy promise. Whence the Apostle desireth us to be understood as the children of promise:[9] that we may not imagine that what we are is our own work, but refer the whole to the grace of God. . . . Christ Himself is the Salvation of God, so that the whole body of Christ may say, "By the grace of God I am what I am."[10]

43. "And so shall I make answer," he saith, "to them that reproach me with the word" (ver. 42). It is doubtful whether it be "reproach me with a word;" or, "I will answer with a word;" but either signifieth Christ. They to whom Christ crucified is a stumbling-block or foolishness,[11] reproach us with Him; ignorant that "the Word was made flesh, and dwelt in us;"[8] the Word which "was in the beginning," and "was with God, and was God."[12] But although they may not reproach us with the Word which is unknown unto them, because His Divinity is not known unto those by whom His weakness on the Cross is despised; let us nevertheless make answer of the Word, and let us not be terrified or confounded by their reproaches. For "if they had known" the Word, "they

---

[1] Matt. vi. 1. [2] Eccles. i. 2, 3. [3] Rom. viii. 15.
[4] 1 John iv. 18. [5] Isa. xi. 2. [6] Ps. xix. 9.

[7] 1 Cor. i. 30, 31. [8] John i. 14.
[9] Rom. ix. 8. [10] 1 Cor. xv. 10.
[11] 1 Cor. i. 23. [12] John i. 1.

would never have crucified the Lord of glory." [1] . . . Therefore, when the Psalmist had said, "I will make answer unto them that reproach me with the word : " he at once addeth, "For my trust is in Thy words," which meaneth exactly, in Thy promises.

44. "O take not the word of Thy truth away out of my mouth even exceedingly" (ver. 43). He saith, out of my mouth, because the unity of the body is speaking, among whose members those also are counted who failed at the hour by denying, but by penitence afterwards came again to life, or even, by renewing their confession, received the palm of martyrdom, which they had lost. The word of truth, therefore, was not "even exceedingly," or, as some copies have it, even every way, that is not altogether taken from the mouth of Peter, in whom was the type of the Church ; because although he denied for the hour, being disturbed with fear, yet by weeping he was restored,[2] and by confessing was afterwards crowned. The whole body of Christ therefore speaketh. . . . Next followeth, "for I have hoped in Thy judgments." Or, as some have more strictly rendered it from the Greek, "I have hoped more ; "[3] a word which, although compounded in a somewhat unusual way, yet answers the necessary purpose of conveying the truth in a translation. . . . Behold the saints and the humble in heart when they have trusted in Thee, have not failed in persecutions : behold also those who from trusting in themselves have failed, and nevertheless have belonged to the Very Body, have wept when they became known unto themselves, and have found Thy grace a more solid support, because they have lost their own pride.

45. "So shall I alway keep Thy law" (ver. 44) : that is, if Thou wilt not take the word of Thy truth out of my mouth. "Yea, unto age, and age of age : " he showeth what he meant by "alway." For sometimes by "alway" is meant, as long as we live here ; but this is not, "unto age, and age of age."[4] For it is better thus translated than as some copies have, "to eternity, and to age of age," since they could not say, and to eternity of eternity. That law therefore should be understood, of which the Apostle saith, "Love is the fulfilling of the law."[5] For this will be kept by the saints, from whose mouth the word of truth is not taken, that is, by the Church of Christ Herself, not only during this world, that is, until this world is ended ; but for another also which is styled, "world without end."[6] . . .

46. "And I walked at liberty : for I sought

Thy precepts " (ver. 45). . . . "And I walked at liberty." Here the copulative conjunction, "and," is not used as a connecting particle ; for he doth not say, and I will walk, as he had said, "and I will keep Thy commandments for ever and ever : " or if this latter verse be in the optative mood, and may I keep Thy law ; he doth not add, And may I walk at liberty, as if he had desired and prayed for both of these things ; but he saith, "And I walked at liberty." If this conjunction were not used here, and if the sentence were introduced free from any such connection with what preceded, "I walked at liberty," the reader would never be induced by anything unusual in the mode of speech to think he should seek for some hidden sense. Doubtless, then, he wished what he hath not said to be understood, that is, that his prayers had been heard ; and he then added what he had become : as if he were to say, When I prayed for these things, Thou heardest me, "And I walked at liberty ; " and so with the remaining expressions which he hath added to the same purpose.

47. . . . Whence after he had said, "And I walked at liberty," he subjoined the reason, "For I sought out Thy commandments." Some copies have not "commandments" but "testimonies : " but we find "commandments" in most, and especially in the Greek ; and who would hesitate rather to believe this tongue, as prior to our own,[7] and that from which these Psalms have been rendered into Latin? If then we wish to know how he sought out these commandments, or how they ought to be sought out, let us consider what our good Master, who both taught and gave them, saith : "Ask, and it shall be given you."[8] And a little lower, "If ye then," He saith, "being evil, know how to give good gifts unto your children, how much more shall your Father which is in Heaven give good things to them that ask Him."[9] Where He evidently showeth, that the words He had spoken, seek, ask, knock, belong only to earnestness in asking, that is, in praying. Moreover, another Evangelist saith not, He will give good things to them that ask Him ; which may be understood in many ways, either as earthly or spiritual blessings ; but has excluded other interpretations, and very carefully expressed what our Lord wished us to pray earnestly and instantly for, in these words : "How much more shall your heavenly Father give the Holy Spirit to them that ask Him."[10] . . .

48. "I spoke of Thy testimonies also," he saith, "before kings, and I was not ashamed" (ver. 46) : as one who had sought and had

---

[1] 1 Cor. ii. 8.　　　　　[2] Matt. xxvi. 70-75.
[3] *Supersperavi.* Gr. ἐπήλπισα ; literally, as he takes it, "overhoped."
[4] The phrase *in sæculum sæculi* is that which we usually render "world without end," or, "for ever and ever."
[5] Rom. xiii. 10.　　　　　[6] Lit. "age of age."

[7] [A noteworthy tribute to the Septuagint as compared with the Vulgate. — C.]
[8] Matt. vii. 7.　　　　　[9] Matt. vii. 11.
[10] Luke xi. 13. [The sevenfold gifts. — C.]

received grace to answer those who reproached him with the word, and the promise that the word of truth should not be taken from his mouth. Struggling for this truth even unto death, not even before kings was he ashamed to speak of it. For testimonies, whereof he doth avow that he was speaking, are in Greek styled μαρτύρια, a word which we now employ instead of the Latin. The name of "Martyrs," unto whom Jesus foretold, that they should confess Him even before kings,[1] is derived hence.

49. "And I meditated," he saith, "on Thy commandments, which I have loved" (ver. 47). "My hands also have I lifted up unto Thy commandments, which I have loved" (ver. 48); or, as some copies read, "which I have loved exceedingly," or "too much," or "vehemently," as they have chosen to render the Greek word σφόδρα. He then loved the commandments of God because he walked at liberty; that is, through the Holy Spirit, through whom love itself is shed abroad,[2] and enlargeth the hearts of the faithful. But he loved, both in thought and in acts. With a view to thought, he saith, "And I meditated:" as to action, "My hands also have I lifted up." But to both sentences he hath annexed the words, "which I have loved:" for "the end of the commandment is love out of a pure heart."[3] . . . The following words, "And my study was in Thy statutes," relate to both. This expression most of the translators have preferred to this, "I rejoiced in," or "I talked of," a version which some have given from the Greek ἠδολέσχουν. For he who keepeth the commandments of God, which he loveth, both in thought and in works taking delight in them, is exercised with joy, and with a certain abundance of speech, in the judgments of God.

Zain.

50. "O remember Thy word unto Thy servant, wherein Thou hast given me hope" (ver. 49). Is forgetfulness incident to God, as it is to man? Why then is it said unto Him, "O remember"? Although in other passages of holy Scripture this very word is used, as, "Why hast Thou forgotten me?"[4] and, "Wherefore forgettest Thou our misery?"[5] . . . These expressions are borrowed from moral discourses on human affections; although God doth these things according to a fixed dispensation, with no failing memory, nor with an understanding obscured, nor with a will changed. When therefore it is said unto Him, "O remember," the desire of him who prayeth is displayed, because he asketh for what was promised; God is not admonished, as if the promise had escaped from His mind.

"O remember," he saith, "Thy word unto Thy servant:" that is, fulfil Thy promise to Thy servant. "Wherein Thou hast given me hope:" that is, in Thy Word, since Thou hast promised, Thou hast caused me to hope.

51. "The same is my comfort in my humiliation" (ver. 50). Namely, that hope which is given to the humble, as the Scripture saith: "God resisteth the proud, but giveth grace unto the humble."[6] Whence also our Lord Himself saith with His own lips, "For whosoever exalteth himself shall be abased; and he that humbleth himself shall be exalted."[7] We well understand here that humiliation also, not whereby each man humbleth himself by confessing his sins, and by not arrogating righteousness to himself; but when each man is humbled by some tribulation or mortification which his pride deserved; or when he is exercised and proved by endurance;[8] whence a little after this Psalm saith, "Before I was troubled, I went wrong." . . . And the Lord Jesus, when He foretold that this humiliation would be brought upon His disciples by their persecutors, did not leave them without a hope; but gave them one, whereby they might find comfort, in these words: "In your patience shall ye possess your souls;" and declared even of their very bodies, which might be put to death by their enemies, and seemingly be utterly annihilated, that not a hair of their heads should perish.[9] This hope was given to Christ's Body, that is, to the Church, that it might be a comfort to Her in her humiliation. . . . This hope He gave in the prayer which He taught us, where He enjoined us to say, "Lead us not into temptation:"[10] for He in a manner implicitly promised that He would give to His disciples in their danger that which He taught them to ask for in their prayers. And indeed this Psalm is rather to be understood to speak of this hope: "For Thy word hath quickened me." Which they have rendered more closely who have put not "word," but "utterance." For the Greek has λόγιον, which is "utterance;" not λόγος, which is "word."

52. The next verse is, "The proud dealt exceeding wickedly: yet have I not shrinked from Thy law" (ver. 51). By the proud he wished to be understood the persecutors of the pious; and he therefore added, "yet have I not shrinked from Thy laws," because the persecution of the proud attempted to force him to do this. He saith that they dealt "exceeding wickedly," because they were not only wicked themselves, but even tried to make the godly wicked. In this humiliation, that is, in this tribulation, that hope comforted him which was given in the word of God, who promised aid, that the faith

---

[1] Matt. x. 18.   [2] Rom. v. 5.   [3] 1 Tim. i. 5.
[4] Ps. xlii. 9.   [5] Ps. xliv. 24.

[6] Jas. iv. 6 and 1 Pet. v. 5.   [7] Luke xiv. 11 and xviii. 14.
[8] Ecclus. ii. 4, 5.   [9] Luke xxi. 17, 18.   [10] Matt. vi. 13.

of the Martyrs might not faint; and who by the presence of His Spirit gave strength to them in their toils, that they might escape from the snare of the fowlers.[1] . . .

53. "For I was mindful of Thy judgments from the beginning of the world, O Lord, and received comfort" (ver. 52); or, as other copies have it, "and I was exhorted," that is, I received exhortation. For either might be rendered for the Greek παρεκλήθην. "From the beginning of the world," that is, from the birth of the human race, "I was mindful of Thy judgments" upon the vessels of wrath, which are fitted unto perdition: "and I received comfort," since through these also hast Thou shown the riches of Thy glory on the vessels of Thy mercy.[2]

54. "Weariness hath held me; for the ungodly that forsake Thy law" (ver. 53). "Thy statutes have been my songs in the house of my pilgrimage" (ver. 54). This is the low estate, in the house of mortality, of the man who sojourneth away from Paradise and the Jerusalem above, whence one going down to Jericho fell among robbers; but, in consequence of the deed of mercy which was done him by that Samaritan,[3] the statutes of God became his song in the house of his pilgrimage; although he was weary for the ungodly that forsook the law of God, since he was compelled to converse with them for a season in this life, until the floor be threshed. But these two verses may be adapted to the two clauses of the preceding verse, respectively.

55. "I have thought upon Thy Name, O Lord, in the night-season, and have kept Thy law" (ver. 55). Night is that low estate wherein is the trouble of mortality; night is in the proud who deal exceeding wickedly; night is the fear for the ungodly who forsake the law of the Lord; night is, lastly, the house of this pilgrimage, "until the Lord come, and bring to light the hidden things of darkness, and will make manifest the counsels of the hearts, and then shall every man have praise of God."[4] In this night, therefore, man ought to remember the Name of the Lord; "So that he who glorieth, may glory in the Lord."[5]

56. Considering this, he addeth, "This was made unto me, because I sought out Thy righteousnesses" (ver. 56). "Thy" righteousnesses, whereby Thou dost justify the ungodly; not mine, which never make me godly, but proud. For this man was not one of those who, "ignorant of God's righteousness, and going about to establish their own righteousness, have not submitted themselves unto the righteousness of God."[6] Others have better interpreted these righteousnesses, as those whereby men are justified for nought through God's grace, though

by themselves they cannot be righteous, "justifications."[7] But what meaneth, "This was made unto me"? What is "This"? It is perhaps the law? as he had said, "and I have kept Thy law;" to which he subjoins, "This was made unto me," meaning, "This was made my law." We must therefore enquire first what was thus made unto him, next in what manner, whatever it may have been, was made unto him. "This," he saith, "was made unto me:" not "This law," for the Greek, as I have said, refuseth this sense. Perhaps then, "This night:" since the preceding sentence stands thus: "I have thought upon Thy Name, O Lord, in the night-season:" and the next words are, "This was made unto me:" since then it is not the law, it must truly be the night which is thus spoken of. What then meaneth, "I had the night-season: for I have sought out Thy righteousnesses"? Rather light had come unto him than night, since he sought out the righteousnesses of God. And it is thus rightly understood, "It was made unto me," as if it were said, It became night for my sake, that is, that it might profit me. For that low estate of mortality is not absurdly understood as night, where the hearts of mortals are hid to one another, so that from such darkness innumerable and heavy temptations arise. . . .

Cheth.

57. Let us hear what followeth: "I have promised to keep Thy law." What meaneth, "My portion, O Lord: I have promised to keep Thy law" (ver. 57); save because the Lord will be each man's portion then, when he hath kept His law? Consider therefore what he subjoineth: "I entreated Thy face, with my whole heart:" and saying in what manner he prayed: "O be merciful," he saith, "unto me, according to Thy word" (ver. 58). And as if he had been heard and aided by Him whom he prayed unto, "I thought," he saith, "on mine own ways, and turned away my feet unto Thy testimonies" (ver. 59). That is, I turned them away from mine own ways, which displeased me, that they might follow Thy testimonies, and there might find a path. For most of the copies have not, "Because I thought," as is read in some; but only, "I thought." But what is here written, "and I turned away my feet:" some read, "Because I thought, Thou also hast turned away my feet:" that this may rather be ascribed to the grace of God, according to the Apostle's words, "For it is God who worketh in us."[8] . . .

---

[7] [He says: "Since the Greek hath not δικαιόσυναι, that is, acts of righteousness; but δικαιώματα, acts of justification. . . . For the Greek words whence these Latin words have been translated, sufficiently declare that it could not have been said of the law, for the word law is in Greek of the masculine gender, and the feminine pronoun is used in the Greek text as well."—C.]

[8] Philip. ii. 13.

[1] Ps. cxxiv. 2.   [2] Rom. ix. 22, 23.   [3] Luke x. 30, 37.
[4] 1 Cor. iv. 5.   [5] 1 Cor. i. 31.   [6] Rom. x. 3.

58. Lastly, when he had received this blessing of grace, he saith, "I was ready, and was not disturbed, that I may keep Thy commandments" (ver. 60). Which some have rendered, "to keeping Thy commandments," some "that I should keep," others "to keep," the Greek being τοῦ φυλάξασθαι.

59. But in what manner he was ready to keep the divine commandments, he hath added, in these words: "The bands of the ungodly have surrounded me: but I have not forgotten Thy law" (ver. 61). "The bands of the ungodly" are the hindrances of our enemies, whether spiritual, as the devil and his angels, or carnal, the children of disobedience, in whom the devil worketh.[1] For this word *peccatorum* is not from *peccata*, "sins;" but from *peccatores*, "sinners." Therefore when they threaten evils, with which to alarm the righteous, that they may not suffer for the law of God, they, so to speak, entangle them with bands, with a strong and tough cord of their own. For "they draw iniquity like a long rope,"[2] and thus endeavour to entangle the holy, and sometimes are allowed so to do.

60. "At midnight," he saith, "I rise to give thanks unto Thee: because of Thy righteous judgments" (ver. 62). This very fact, that the bands of the ungodly surround the righteous, is one of the righteous judgments of God. On which account the Apostle Peter saith, "The time is come when judgment must begin at the house of the Lord."[3] For he saith this of the persecutions which the Church suffered, when the bands of the ungodly surrounded them. I suppose, therefore, that by "midnight" we should understand the heavier seasons of tribulation. In which he said, "I arose:" since He did not so afflict him, as to cast him down; but tried him, so that he arose, that is, that through this very tribulation he might advance unto a bolder confession.

61. For I imagine that what followeth, "I am a companion of all them that fear Thee, and keep Thy commandments" (ver. 63), doth relate to the Head Himself, as it is in the Epistle which is inscribed to the Hebrews: "Both He that sanctifieth and they who are sanctified are all of one: for which cause He is not ashamed to call them brethren."[4] . . . Therefore Jesus Himself speaketh in this prophecy: some things in His Members and in the Unity of His Body, as if in one man diffused over the whole world, and growing up in succession throughout the roll of ages: and some things in Himself our Head. And on this account, that since He became the companion of His brethren, God of men, the Immortal of the mortal, for this reason the seed fell upon the earth, that by its death it might produce much fruit; he next addeth concerning this very fruit, "The earth, O Lord, is full of Thy mercy" (ver. 64). And whence this, save when the ungodly is justified? That we may make progress in the knowledge of this grace, he addeth, "O teach me Thy righteousnesses!"

Teth.

62. "Thou hast dealt in sweetness with Thy servant: according unto Thy word;" or rather, "according unto Thine utterance" (ver. 65). The Greek word χρηστότης hath been variously rendered by our translators by the words "sweetness" and "goodness." But since sweetness may exist also in evil, since all unlawful and unclean things afford pleasure, and it may also exist in that carnal pleasure which is permitted; we ought to understand the word "sweetness," which the Greeks termed χρηστότης, of spiritual blessings: for on this account our translators have preferred to term it "goodness." I think therefore that nothing else is meant by the words, "Thou hast dealt in sweetness with Thy servant," than this, Thou hast made me feel delight in that which is good. For when that which is good delighteth, it is a great gift of God. But when the good work which the law commandeth is done from a fear of punishment, not from a delight in righteousness, when God is dreaded, not loved; it is the act of a slave, not of a freeman.[5]

63. "O learn me sweetness, and understanding, and knowledge," he saith, "for I have believed Thy commandments" (ver. 66). He prayeth these things may be increased and perfected. For they who said, "Lord, increase our faith,"[6] had faith. And as long as we live in this world, these are the words of those who are making progress. But he addeth, "understanding," or, as most copies read, "discipline." Now the word discipline, for which the Greeks use παιδεία, is employed in Scripture, where instruction through tribulation is to be understood: according to the words, "Whom the Lord loveth He disciplineth, and scourgeth every son whom He receiveth."[7] In the literature of the Church this is usually called discipline. For this word, παιδεία,[8] is used in the Greek in the Epistle to the Hebrews, where the Latin translator saith, "No *discipline* for the present seemeth to be joyous, but grievous," etc.[9] He therefore toward whom the Lord dealeth in sweetness, that is, he in whom He mercifully inspires delight in that which is good, ought to pray instantly, that this gift may be so increased unto him, that he may not only despise all other delights in comparison with it, but also that he may endure any amount of suf-

---

[1] Eph. ii. 2.   [2] Isa. v. 18.   [3] 1 Pet. iv. 17.
[4] Heb. ii. 11, 14.

[5] John viii. 35; 1 John iv. 18.   [6] Luke xvii. 5.
[7] Heb. xii. 6.
[8] [See *Clement*, A. N. F. vol. ii. p. 213.]
[9] Heb. xii. 11.

ferings for its sake. Thus is discipline health-fully added to sweetness. This discipline ought not to be desired, and prayed for, for a small measure of grace and goodness, that is, holy love; but for so great, as may not be extin-guished by the weight of the chastening : . . . so much in fact as to enable him to endure with the utmost patience the discipline. In the third place is mentioned knowledge ; since, if knowl-edge in its greatness outstrips the increase of love, it doth not edify, but " puffeth up." [1] . . .

64. But in that he saith, not, Give unto me ; but, " O learn me ; " how is the sweetness taught, if it be not given? Since many know what doth not delight them, and find no sweetness in things of which they have knowledge. For sweetness cannot be learnt, unless it please. Also discipline, which signifieth the tribulation which chasteneth, is learnt by receiving ; that is, not by hearing, or reading, or thinking, but by feeling. . . .

65. He addeth, " for I have believed Thy com-mandments," and herein we may justly enquire, why he said not, I obeyed, rather than, I believed. For commandments are one thing, promises an-other. We undertake to obey commandments, that we may deserve to receive promises. We therefore believe promises, obey command-ments. . . . Teach me therefore sweetness by inspiring charity, teach me discipline by giv-ing patience, teach me knowledge by enlighten-ing my understanding : " for I have believed Thy commandments." I have believed that Thou who art God, and who givest unto man whence Thou mayest cause him to do what Thou com-mandest, hast commanded these things.

66. " Before I was humbled, I went wrong ; wherefore I have kept Thy word " (ver. 67) ; or, as some have it more closely, " Thy utter-ance," that is, lest I should be humbled again. This is better referred to that humiliation which took place in Adam, in whom the whole human creature, as it were, being corrupted at the root, as it refused to be subject to truth, " was made subject to vanity." [2] Which it was profitable to the vessels of mercy to feel, that by throwing down pride, obedience might be loved, and misery perish, never again to return.

67. " Sweet art Thou, O Lord ; " or, as many have it, " Sweet art Thou, even Thou, O Lord " (ver. 68). Some also, " Sweet art Thou," or, " Good art Thou : " as we have before treated of this word : " and in Thy sweetness teach me Thy statutes." He truly desireth to do the righteousnesses of God, since he desireth to learn them in His sweetness from Him unto whom he hath said, " Sweet art Thou, O Lord."

68. Next he saith, " The iniquity of the proud hath been multiplied upon me " (ver. 69) : of

those, that is, whom it profited not that human nature was humbled after it went wrong. " But I will search Thy commandments with my whole heart." Howsoever, he saith, iniquity shall abound, love shall not grow cold in me.[3] He, as it were, saith this, who in His sweetness learneth the righteousnesses of God. For in proportion as the commandments of Him who aideth us are the more sweet, so much the more doth he who loveth Him search after them, that he may perform them when known, and may learn them by doing them ; because they are more per-fectly understood when they are performed.

69. " Their heart is curdled as milk " (ver. 70). Whose, save the proud, whose iniquity he hath said hath been multiplied upon him? But he wisheth it to be understood by this word, and in this passage, that their heart hath become hard. It is used also in a good sense,[4] and is under-stood to mean, full of grace : for this word, some have also interpreted " curdled." . . .

70. " It is good for me that Thou hast humbled me : that I might learn Thy righteousnesses " (ver. 71). He hath said something kindred to this above. For by the fruit itself he showeth that it was a good thing for him to be humbled ; but in the former passage he hath stated the cause also, in that he had felt beforehand that humiliation which resulted from his punishment, when he went wrong. But in these words, " Wherefore have I kept Thy word : " and again in these, " That I might learn Thy righteous-nesses : " he seemeth to me to have signified, that to know these is the same thing as to keep them, to keep them the same thing as to know them. For Christ knew what He reproved ; and yet He reproved sin, though it is said of Him that " He knew not sin." [5] He knew therefore by a kind of knowledge, and again He knew not by a kind of ignorance. Thus also many learn the righteousnesses of God, and learn them not. For they know them in a certain way ; and again do not know them from a kind of igno-rance, since they do them not. In this sense the Psalmist therefore is to be understood to have said, That I might learn Thy righteous-nesses," meaning that kind of knowledge where-by they are performed.

71. But that this is not gained, save through love, wherein he who doeth them hath delight, on which account it is said, " In Thy sweetness teach me Thy righteousnesses : " the following verse showeth, wherein he saith, " The law of Thy mouth is better unto me than thousands of gold and silver " (ver. 72) : so that love loveth the law of God more than avarice loveth thousands of gold and silver.

---

[1] 1 Cor. viii. 1.   [2] Gen. iii. 17, etc.; Rom. viii. 20.

[3] Matt. xxiv. 12.
[4] Ps. lxviii. 15.   " A hill that is cheesed, a rich hill."
[5] 2 Cor. v. 21.

Jod.

72. . . . "Thy hands have made me, and fashioned me" (ver. 73). The hands of God are the power of God. Or if the plural number moveth them, since it is not said, Thy hand, but, "Thy hands;" let them understand by the hands of God the power and wisdom of God, both of which titles are given to one Christ,[1] who is also understood under the figure, Arm of the Lord.[2] Or let them understand by the hands of God, the Son and the Holy Spirit; since the Holy Spirit worketh conjointly with the Father and the Son: whence saith the Apostle, "But all these worketh that one and the self-same Spirit:"[3] he said, "one and the self-same;" lest as many spirits as works might be imagined, not that the Spirit worketh without the Father and the Son. It is easy therefore to see how the hands of God are to be understood: provided, at the same time, that He be not denied to do those things through His Word which He doth by His hands: nor be considered not to do those things with His hands, which He doth through His word. . . . But is this said in respect of Adam? from whom since all men were propagated, what man, since Adam was made, may not say that he himself also was made by reason of procreation and generation from Adam? Or may it rightly be said, in this sense, "Thy hands have made me, and fashioned me," namely, that every man is born even of his parents not without the work of God, God creating, they generating? Since, if the creative[4] power of God be withdrawn from things, they perish: nor is anything at all, either of the world's elements, or of parents, or of seeds, produced, if God doth not create it. . . .

73. The Greek version hath a more concise expression for our, "Give me understanding," συνέτισόν με, expressing "give understanding" by the single word συνέτισον, which the Latin cannot do; as if one could not say, Heal me; and it were necessary to say, Give me health, as it is here said, "Give me understanding;" or, make me whole, as here it may be said, make me intelligent. This indeed an Angel could do: for he said to Daniel, "I am come to give thee understanding;"[5] and this word is in the Greek, as it is here also, συνέτισαί σε; as if the Latin translator were to render θεραπεῦσαί σε by sanitatem dare tibi. For the Latin interpreter would not make a circumlocution by saying, to give thee understanding, if, as we say from health, "to heal thee," so one could say from intellect, "to intellectuate thee." But if an Angel could

do this, what reason is there that this man should pray that this be done for him by God? Is it because God had commanded the Angel to do it? Just so: for Christ is understood to have given this command to the Angel.[6] . . .

74. "That I may learn Thy commandments." Since Thou, saith he, hast formed me, do Thou new form me; that that may be done in Christ's Body, which the Apostle speaks of, "Be transformed by the renewing of your mind."[7]

75. "They that fear Thee," he saith, "will see me, and be glad" (ver. 74) : or, as other copies have it, "will be joyful: because I have hoped in Thy word:" that is, in the things which Thou hast promised, that they may be the sons of promise, the seed of Abraham, in whom all nations are blessed.[8] Who are they who fear God, and whom will they see and be glad, because he hath put his trust in the word of God? Whether it be the body of Christ, that is, the Church, whose words these are through Christ, or within it, and concerning it, these are as it were the words of Christ concerning Himself; are not they themselves among those who fear God? . . . The same persons, who see the Church and are glad, are the Church. But why said he not, They who fear Thee see me, and are glad: whereas he hath written, "fear Thee," in the present tense; while the verbs "shall see," and shall "be glad," are futures? Is it because in the present state there is fear, as long as "man's life is a temptation upon earth;"[9] but the gladness which he desired to be understood, will be then, when "the righteous shall shine in the kingdom of their Father like the sun."[10] . . .

76. "I know," she saith, "O Lord, that Thy judgments are righteous, and that in Thy truth Thou hast humbled me" (ver. 75). "O let Thy merciful kindness be my comfort, according to Thy word unto Thy servant" (ver. 76). Mercy and truth are so spoken of in the Divine Word, that, while they are found in many passages, especially in the Psalms, it is also so read in one place, "All the paths of the Lord are mercy and truth."[11] And here indeed he hath placed truth first, whereby we are humbled unto death, by the judgment of Him whose judgments are righteousness: next mercy, whereby we are renewed unto life, by the promise of Him whose blessing is His grace. For this reason he saith, "according to Thy word unto Thy servant:" that is, according to that which Thou hast promised unto Thy servant. Whether therefore it be regeneration whereby we are here adopted among the sons of God, or faith and hope and charity, which three are built up in us, although they

---

[1] 1 Cor. i. 24.
[2] Isa. liii. 1. "Where it is read, 'And unto whom hath the arm of the Lord been revealed?'"
[3] 1 Cor. xii. 11.　　[4] *Operatoria*.　　[5] Dan. x. 14.

[6] Dan. viii. 15, 16.　　[7] Rom. xii. 2.
[8] Gen. xii. 3 and xxvi. 4.
[9] Job vii. 1. [Here our author reasons against the idea of unconditional election to eternal life. — C.]
[10] Matt. xiii. 43.　　[11] Ps. xxv. 10.

come from the mercy of God; nevertheless, in this stormy and troublesome life they are the consolations of the miserable, not the joys of the blessed.

77. But since those things are destined to happen after and through these, he next saith, "O let Thy loving mercies come upon me, and I shall live" (ver. 77). For then indeed I shall truly live, when I shall not be able to fear lest I die. This is styled life absolutely and without any addition; nor is any life save that which is everlasting and blessed understood, as though it alone were to be called life, compared with which that which we now lead ought rather to be called death than life: according to those words in the Gospel, "If thou wilt enter into life, keep the commandments." [1] . . .

78. He then goeth on as follows: "Let the proud be confounded, for they have unrighteously practised iniquity against me: but I will be occupied in Thy commandments" (ver. 78). Behold, what he saith, the meditation of the law of God, or rather, his meditation the law of God.

79. "Let such as fear Thee," he saith, "and have known Thy testimonies, be turned unto me" [2] (ver. 79). But who is he who saith this? For no mortal will venture to say this, or if he say it, should be listened to. Indeed, it is He who above also hath interposed His own words, saying, "I am a partaker with all them that fear Thee." Because He was made sharer in our mortal state, that we might also become partakers in His Divine Nature, we became sharers in One unto life, He a sharer in many unto death. He it is unto whom they that fear God turn, and who know the testimonies of God, so long before predicted of Him through the Prophets, a little before displayed in His presence through miracles.

80. "O let my heart," he saith, "be unspotted in Thy righteousnesses, that I be not ashamed" (ver. 80). He returneth to the words of His body, that is, His holy people, and now prayeth that his heart may be made unspotted, that is, the heart of His members; "in the righteousnesses of God," not in their own strength: for He hath prayed for this, not presumed upon it. In the words he hath added, "that I be not ashamed," there is a resemblance to some of the earlier verses of this Psalm.[3] Whereas there, in the words, "O that," he signifieth a wish, he hath here expressed himself in the more open words of one praying: "O let my heart be sound:" so that in neither of these two sentences, each of which is one and the same, there

is found the boldness of one who trusteth in his own free will against grace. While he saith there, "so shall I not be confounded:" he saith here, "that I be not ashamed." The heart then of the members and the body of Christ is made unspotted, through the grace of God, by means of the very Head of that Body, that is, through Jesus Christ our Lord, by the "laver of regeneration," [4] wherein all our past sins have been blotted out; through the aid of the Spirit, whereby we lust against the flesh, that we be not overcome in our fight; [5] through the efficacy of the Lord's Prayer, wherein we say, "Forgive us our trespasses." [6] Thus regeneration having been given to us, our conflict having been aided, prayer having been poured forth, our heart is made unspotted, so that we be not ashamed.[7]

Caph.

81. "My soul hath failed for Thy salvation: and I have hoped because of Thy word" (ver. 81). It is not every failing that should be supposed to be blameable or deserving punishment: there is also a failing that is laudable or desirable. . . . For it is said of a good failing: "My soul hath a desire and failing to enter into the courts of the Lord." [8] So also here he saith not, faileth away from Thy salvation, but "faileth for Thy salvation," that is, towards Thy salvation. This losing ground is therefore good: for it doth indicate a longing after good, not as yet indeed gained, but most eagerly and earnestly desired. But who saith this, save the chosen generation, the royal priesthood, the holy nation, the peculiar people,[9] longing for Christ from the origin of the human race even unto the end of this world, in the persons of those who, each in his own time, have lived, are living, or are to live here? . . . The first seasons of the Church, therefore, had Saints, before the Virgin's delivery, who desired the advent of His Incarnation: but these times, since He hath ascended into heaven, have Saints who desire His manifestation to judge the quick and the dead. . . . "And I have hoped because of Thy word:" that is, of Thy promise; a hope which causeth us to await with patience that which is not seen by those who believe. Here also the Greek hath the word ἐπήλπισα, which some of our translators have preferred rendering by, "hoped-more;" since beyond doubt it will be greater than can be described.

82. "Mine eyes," he saith, "have failed for Thy word, saying, O when wilt Thou comfort me?" (ver. 82). Behold that praiseworthy and blessed failing, in the eyes again, but his inner eyes, not arising from infirmity of mind, but from the strength of his longing for the promise of God: for this he saith, "for Thy

---

[1] Matt. xix. 17.
[2] [He says: "In some copies, both Greek and Latin, we have found *convertantur mihi*, which I consider to mean just the same as if it were, *ad me*."—C.]
[3] See vers. 5, 6.

[4] Tit. iii. 5.　　[5] Gal. v. 17.　　[6] Matt. vi. 12.
[7] Luke vi. 37, 38.　　[8] Ps. lxxxiv. 2.　　[9] 1 Pet. ii. 9.

word." But in what sense can such eyes say, "When wilt Thou comfort me?" save when we pray and groan with such earnestness and ardent expectation? For the tongue, not the eyes, is wont to speak: but in some sense the voice of the eyes is the longing of prayer. But in the words, "When wilt Thou comfort me?" he showeth that he endureth as it were delay. Whence is this also, "How long, Lord, wilt Thou punish me?"[1] And this is done either that the happiness may be the sweeter when deferred, or this is the sentiment of those who long, since the space of time, which may be short to Him who cometh to their aid, is tedious to the loving. But God knoweth what He doth and when, for He "hath ordered all things in measure and number and weight."[2]

83. But when spiritual desires burn, carnal desires without doubt cool: on this account followeth, "Since I am become like a bottle in the frost, I do not forget Thy righteousnesses" (ver. 83). Truly he desireth this mortal flesh to be understood by the bottle, the heavenly blessing by the frost, whereby the lusts of the flesh as it were by the binding of the frost become sluggish; and hence it ariseth that the righteousnesses of God do not slip from the memory, as long as we do not meditate apart from them; since what the Apostle saith is brought to pass: "Make not provision for the flesh, to fulfil the lusts thereof."[3] "And I do not forget Thy righteousness:" that is, I forget them not, because I have become such. For the fervour of lust hath cooled, that the memory of love might glow.

84. "How many are the days of Thy servant? when wilt Thou be avenged of them that persecute me?" (ver. 84). In the Apocalypse,[4] these are the words of the Martyrs, and long-suffering is enjoined them until the number of their brethren be fulfilled. The body of Christ then is asking concerning its days, what they are to be in this world, and that no man might suppose that the Church would cease to exist here before the end of the world came, and that some time would elapse in this world, while the Church was now no more on earth; therefore, when he had enquired concerning the days, he added also respecting the judgment, showing indeed that the Church would exist on earth until the judgment, when vengeance shall fall upon Her persecutors. But if any one wonder why he should ask that question, to which when asked by the disciples, their Master replied, "It is not for you to know the times and the seasons;"[5] why should we not believe that in this passage of the Psalm it was prophesied that they should ask this very question, and that the words of the Church,

which were so long before uttered here, were fulfilled in their question?

85. In what followeth: "The wicked have told me pleasant tales: but not like Thy law, O Lord" (ver. 85): the Latin translators have endeavoured to render the Greek ἀδολεσχίας, which cannot be expressed in one Latin word, so that some have rendered it "delights," and others "fablings," so that we must understand to be meant some kind of compositions, but in discourse of a nature to give pleasure. Both secular literature, and the Jewish book entitled Deuterosis,[6] containing besides the canon of divine Scripture thousands of tales, comprise these in their different sects and professions; the vain and wandering loquacity of heretics holds them also. All these he wished to be considered as wicked, by whom he saith that ἀδολεσχίαι were related to him, that is, compositions which gave pleasure solely in their style: "But not," he addeth, "as Thy law, O Lord;" because truth, not words, pleases me therein.[7]

86. Lastly, he addeth, "All Thy commandments are truth: they have persecuted me unjustly; O be Thou my help" (ver. 86). And the whole sense dependeth upon the foregoing: "How many are the days of Thy servant: when wilt Thou be avenged of them that persecute me?"[8] For that they may persecute me, they have related to me these pleasant tales; but I have preferred Thy law to them, which on that account hath pleased me more, because all Thy commandments are true; not as in their discourses, where vanity aboundeth. And for this reason "they have persecuted me falsely," because in me they have persecuted nothing save the truth. Therefore help Thou me, that I may struggle for the truth even unto death; because this is at once Thy commandment, and therefore it is also the truth.

87. When the Church acted thus, She suffered what he hath added, "They had almost made an end of me upon earth" (ver. 87): a great slaughter of martyrs having been made, while they confess and preach the truth. But since it is not in vain said, "O help Thou me;" he addeth, "But I forsook not Thy commandments."

88. And that She might persevere unto the end, "O quicken me," he saith, "after Thy loving mercy: and so shall I keep the testimonies of Thy mouth" (ver. 88); where the Greek hath Μαρτύρια. This was not to be passed over in silence, on account of that sweetest name of Martyrs, who beyond doubt when so great cruelty of the persecutors was raging, that the Church

---

[1] Ps. vi. 3　　[2] Wisd. xi. 18.　　[3] Rom. xiii. 14.
[4] Rev. vi. 10, 11.　　[5] Acts i. 7.

[6] The Mishna. δευτέρωσις is used, however, by St. Jerome for tradition in general. See on Isa. lix. 12-15, in Catal. on Papias, and elsewhere; cf. Ecclus. xliii. 1, LXX.
[7] [Modern voracity for novel-reading is here rebuked. — C.]
[8] Ps. cxix. 84.

was almost made an end of upon earth, would never have kept the testimonies of God, unless that had been vouchsafed them which is here spoken of, "O quicken me after Thy loving-kindness." For they were quickened, lest by loving life, they should deny the life, and by denying it, should lose it: and thus they who for life refused to forsake the truth, lived by dying for the truth.

Lamed.

89. The man who speaketh in this Psalm, as if he were tired of human mutability, whence this life is full of temptations, among his tribulations, on account of which he had above said, "The wicked have persecuted me;"[1] and, "They have almost made an end of me upon earth"[2] (ver. 89); burning with longings for the heavenly Jerusalem; looked up to the realms above, and said, "O Lord, Thy word endureth for ever in heaven;" that is, among Thy Angels who serve everlastingly in Thine armies, without desertion.

90. But the next verse, after heaven, pertaineth consequently to earth. For this is one verse of the eight which relate to this letter. For eight verses are appended to each of these Hebrew letters,[3] until this long Psalm be ended. "Thy truth also remaineth from one generation to the other: Thou hast laid the foundation of the earth, and it abideth" (ver. 90). Beholding therefore the earth next after heaven with the gaze of a faithful mind, he findeth in it generations which are not in heaven, and saith, "Thy truth remaineth from one generation to the other:" signifying all generations by this expression, from which the Truth of God was never absent in His saints, at one time fewer, at one time more in number, according as the times happened or shall happen to vary; or wishing two particular generations to be understood, one pertaining to the Law and the Prophets, another to the Gospel. . . .

91. "Day continueth according to Thy ordinance" (ver. 91). For all these things are day: "and this is the day which the Lord hath made: let us rejoice and be glad in it:"[4] and "let us walk honestly as in the day."[5] "For all things serve Thee." He said all things of some: "all" which belong to this day "serve Thee." For the ungodly of whom it is said, "I have compared thy mother unto the night,"[6] do not serve Thee.

92. He then looketh back towards the source of this earth's deliverance, which caused it to abide when founded; and addeth, "If my delight had not been in Thy law, I should perchance have perished in my humiliation" (ver. 92). This is the law of faith, not a vain faith, but that

which worketh through love.[7] Through this grace is gained, which maketh men courageous in temporal tribulation, that they may not perish in the humiliation of mortality.

93. "I will never forget," he saith, "Thy righteousnesses, for with them Thou hast quickened me" (ver. 93). Behold how it was that he did not perish in his humiliation. For, save God quickeneth, what is man, who can indeed kill, but cannot quicken himself? ·

94. He next addeth: "I am Thine: O save me, for I have sought Thy righteousnesses" (ver. 94). We must not understand lightly the words, "I am Thine." For what is not His?[8] Why then is it that the Psalmist hath commended himself unto God somewhat in a more familiar sense, in these words, "I am Thine: O save me;" save because he wished it to be understood that he had desired to be his own only to his harm, which is the first and the greatest evil of disobedience? and as if he should say, I wished to be my own, and I lost myself: "I am Thine," he saith, "O save me, for I have sought Thy righteousnesses;" not my own inclinations, whereby I was my own, but "Thy righteousnesses," that I might now be Thine.

95. "The ungodly," he saith, "have awaited me that they might destroy me; but I have understood Thy testimonies" (ver. 95). What meaneth, "that they might destroy me"? Did he then fear that he should perish altogether at the death of his body? God forbid! and what meaneth, "have awaited me," save that he should consent with them unto iniquity? For then they would destroy him. And he hath said why he hath not perished: "I understood Thy testimonies." The Greek word, Μαρτύρια, soundeth more familiarly to the ears of the Church. For though they should slay me not consenting unto them, yet while I confessed Thy testimonies (martyria) I should not perish; but they who, that they might destroy me, were waiting till I should consent unto them, tortured me even when I did confess them. Yet he did not leave that which he had understood, looking on it and seeing an end without end, if only he should persevere unto the end.

96. Lastly, he next saith, "I have seen an end of all consummation: but Thy commandment is exceeding broad" (ver. 96). For he had entered into the sanctuary of God, and had understood the end.[9] Now "all consummation" appeareth to me in this place to signify, the striving even unto death for the truth,[10] and the endurance of every evil for the true and chief good: the end of which consummation is to excel in the kingdom of Christ, which hath no end; and there to have without death, without pain, and

---

1 Ps. cxix. 86.　　2 Ps. cxix. 87　　3 Apices.
4 Ps. cxviii. 24.　　5 Rom. xiii. 13.　　6 Hosea iv. 5, LXX.
7 Gal. v. 6.　　8 Is. xxiv. 1.　　9 Ps. lxxiii. 17.
10 Ecclus. iv. 28.

with great honour, life, acquired by the death of this life, and by sorrows and reproaches. But in what he hath added, "Thy commandment is exceeding broad;" I understand only love. For what would it have profited him, whatever death impended over him, in the midst of whatsoever torment, to confess those testimonies, if love were not in the confessor? . . . Broad therefore is the commandment of charity, that twofold commandment, whereby we are enjoined to love God and our neighbour. But what is broader than that, " on " which " hang all the Law and the Prophets "? [1]

Mem.

97. We have frequently admonished you, that love was to be understood by that praiseworthy breadth, by means of which, while we do the commandments of God, we feel no straitness. On this account also after saying above in this great Psalm, "Thy commandment is exceeding broad : " [2] in the following verse he showeth wherefore it is broad : "what love have I unto Thy law, O Lord !" (ver. 97). Love is therefore the breadth of the commandment. For how can it be that what God commandeth to be loved, be loved, and yet the commandment itself be not loved? For this itself is the law ; " in all the day," he saith, "is my study in it." Behold how I have loved it, that in the whole day my study is in it; or rather, as the Greek hath it, "all the day long," which more fully expresses the continuance of meditation. Now that is to be understood through all time ; which is, for ever. By such love lust is driven out : lust, which repeatedly opposeth our performing the commandments of the law, when " the flesh lusteth against the spirit : " [3] against which the spirit lusting, ought so to love the law of God, that it be its study during the whole day. . . .

98. And he then addeth : " Thou hast made me to understand Thy commandment above mine enemies ; for it is ever with me " (ver. 98). For " they have indeed a zeal of God, but not according to knowledge," etc.[4] But the Psalmist, who understandeth the commandment of God above these his enemies, wishes to be found with the Apostle, " not having " his " own righteousness, which is of the law, but that which is of the faith of Christ, which is of God ; " [5] not that the Law which his enemies read is not of God, but because they do not understand it, like him who understandeth it above his enemies, by clinging to the Stone upon which they stumbled. For "Christ is the end of the law," etc.,[6] " that they may be justified freely through His grace ; " [7] not like those who imagine that they obey the law of

their own strength, and are therefore, though by God's law, yet still endeavouring to set up their own righteousness ; but as the son of promise, who hungering and athirst after it,[8] by seeking, by asking, by knocking,[9] as it were begs it of the Father, that being adopted he may receive it through His only-begotten Son. . . . His enemies sought from the same commandment temporal rewards ; and therefore it was not unto them for ever, as it was unto this man. For they who have translated " for ever " have rendered better than they who have written " for an age," since at the end of time there can be no longer a commandment of the law. . . .

99. But what meaneth the following verse, " I have more understanding than my teachers "? (ver. 99). Who is he who had more understanding than all his teachers? Who, I ask, is he, who dareth to prefer himself in understanding above all the Prophets, who not only by speaking taught with so excellent authority those who lived with them, but also their posterity by writing? . . . What is here said, could not have been spoken in Solomon's person. . . . I recognise plainly Him who had more understanding than His teachers, since when He was a boy of twelve years of age, Jesus remained behind in Jerusalem, and was found by His parents after three days' space, " sitting in the temple among the doctors, hearing them and asking them questions." [10] The Son Himself hath said, " As My Father hath taught Me, I speak these things." [11] It is very difficult to understand this of the Person of the Word ; unless we can comprehend that it is the same thing for the Son to be taught as to be begotten of the Father. . . . " He took upon Himself the form of a servant ; " [12] for when He had assumed this form, men of more advanced age might think Him fit to be taught as a boy ; but He whom the Father taught, had more understanding than all His teachers. " For Thy testimonies," He saith, " are my study." For this reason He had more understanding than all His teachers, because He studied the testimonies of God, which, as concerning Himself, He knew better than they, when He spoke these words : " Ye sent unto John, and he bare witness unto the truth. But I receive not testimony from man," etc.[13]

100. But these teachers may be understood very reasonably to be those aged men, of whom he presently saith, " I am wiser than mine elders " (ver. 100). And this seemeth to me to be repeated here thus, that that age of His which is well known to us in the Gospel might be called to our remembrance ; the age of boyhood, during which He was sitting among the aged, understanding more than all His teachers. For the

[1] Matt. xxii. 37-40. [2] Ps. cxix. 96. [3] Gal. v. 17.
[4] Rom. x. 2, 3. [5] Philip. iii. 9. [6] Rom. x. 4.
[7] Rom. iii. 24.

[8] Matt. v. 6. [9] Matt. vii. 7. [10] Luke ii. 42-46.
[11] John viii. 28. [12] Philip. ii. 7. [13] John v. 33-36.

smaller and the greater in age are wont to be termed younger and elder, although neither of them hath arrived at or approached old age; although if we are concerned to seek in the Gospel the express term, elders, more than whom He understood, we find it when the Scribes and Pharisees said unto Him, "Why do Thy disciples transgress the tradition of the elders? for they wash not their hands when they eat bread."[1] Behold the transgression of the tradition of the elders is objected to Him. But He who was wiser than His elders, let us hear what answer He made them. "Why do ye also, He asked, "transgress the commandment of God by your tradition?"[2] . . .

101. But what cometh next, doth not seem to apply to the Head, but to the Body: "I have refrained my feet from every evil way, that I may keep Thy words" (ver. 101). For that Head of ours, the Saviour of the Body Himself, could not be borne by carnal lust into any evil way, so that it should be needful for Him to refrain His feet, as though they would go thither of their own accord; which we do, when we refrain our evil desires, which He had not, that they may not follow evil ways. For thus we are able to keep the word of God, if we "go not after our evil lusts,"[3] so that they attain unto the evils desired; but rather curb them with the spirit which lusteth against the flesh,[4] that they may not drag us away, seduced and overthrown, through evil ways.

102. "I have not shrunk," he saith, "from Thy judgments: for Thou hast laid down a law for me" (ver. 102). He hath stated what made him fear, so that he refrained his feet from every evil way. . . . Thou, more inward than my inmost self, Thou hast laid down a law within my heart by Thy Spirit, as it were by Thy fingers, that I might not fear it as a slave without love, but might love it with a chaste fear as a son, and fear it with a chaste love.

103. Consider then what followeth: "O how sweet are Thy words unto my throat!" (ver. 103). Or, as it is more literally rendered from the Greek, "Thy utterances, above honey and the honeycomb unto my mouth." This is that sweetness which the Lord giveth, "So that the earth yield her increase:"[5] that we do good truly in a good spirit, that is, not from the dread of carnal evil, but from the gladness of spiritual good. Some copies indeed do not read "honeycomb:" but the majority do. Now the open teaching of wisdom is like unto honey; but that is like the comb which is squeezed from the more recondite mysteries, as if from cells of wax, by the mouth of the teacher, as if he were

chewing it: but it is sweet to the mouth of the heart, not to the mouth of the flesh.

104. But what mean the words, "Through Thy commandments I get understanding"? (ver. 104). For the expressions, I have understood Thy commandments: and, "I get understanding through Thy commandments," are different. Something else then he signifieth that he hath understood from the commandments of God: that is, as far as I can see, he saith, that by obeying God's commandments he hath arrived at the comprehension of those things which he had longed to know. . . . These then are the words of the spiritual members of Christ, "Through Thy commandments I get understanding." For the body of Christ rightly saith these words in those, to whom, while they keep the commandments, a richer knowledge of wisdom is given on account of this very keeping of the commandments. "Therefore," he addeth, "I hate all evil ways." For it is needful that the love of righteousness should hate all iniquity: that love, which is so much the stronger, in proportion as the sweetness of a higher wisdom doth inspire it, a wisdom given unto him who obeyeth God, and getteth understanding from His commandments.

Nun.

105. "Thy word is a lantern unto my feet, and a light unto my paths" (ver. 105). The word "lantern" appears in the word "light;" "my feet" are also repeated in "my paths." What then meaneth "Thy Word"?[6] Is it He who was in the beginning God with God, that is, the Word by whom all things were made? It is not thus. For that Word is a light, but is not a lantern. For a lantern is a creature, not a creator; and it is lighted by participation of an unchangeable light. . . . For no creature, howsoever rational and intellectual, is lighted by itself, but is lighted by participation of eternal Truth: although sometimes day is spoken of, not meaning the Lord, but that "day which the Lord hath made,"[7] and on account of which it is said, "Come unto Him, and be lightened."[8] On account of which participation, inasmuch as the Mediator Himself became Man, He is styled lantern in the Apocalypse.[9] But this sense is a solitary one; for it cannot be divinely spoken of any of the saints, nor in any wise lawfully said of any, "The Word was made flesh,"[10] save of the "one Mediator between God and men."[11] Since therefore the only-begotten Word, coequal with the Father, is styled a light; and man when enlightened by the Word is also called a light, who is styled also a lantern, as John, as the Apostles; and since no man of these is the Word, and that Word by whom they were enlightened is not a lan-

---

1 Matt. xv. 2.   2 Matt. xv. 3.
3 Ecclus. xviii. 30.   4 Gal. v. 17.
5 Ps. lxxxv. 12.

6 John i. 1.   7 Ps. cxviii. 24.   8 Ps. xxxiv. 5.
9 Rev. xxi. 23.   10 John i. 14.   11 1 Tim. ii. 5.

tern ; what is this word, which is thus called a light and a lantern at the same time, save we understand the word which was sent unto the Prophets, or which was preached through the Apostles ; not Christ the Word, but the word of Christ, of which it is written, " Faith cometh by hearing, and hearing by the word of God " ? ¹   For the Apostle Peter also, comparing the prophetical word to a lantern, saith, " whereunto ye do well that ye take heed, as unto a lantern, that shineth in a dark place." ²   What, therefore, he here saith, " Thy word " is the word which is contained in all the holy Scriptures.

106. " I have sworn, and am stedfastly purposed to keep Thy righteous judgments " (ver. 106) : as one who walked aright in the light of that lantern, and kept to straight paths. For he calleth what he hath determined by a sacrament, an oath ; because the mind ought to be so fixed in keeping the righteous judgments of God, that its determination should be in the place of an oath. Now the righteous judgments of God are kept by faith ; when, under the righteous judgment of God, neither any good work is believed to be fruitless, nor any sin unpunished ; but, because the body of Christ hath suffered many most grievous evils for this faith, he saith, " I was humbled above measure " (ver. 107).   He doth not say, I have humbled myself, so that we must needs understand that humiliation which is commanded ; but he saith, " I was humbled above-measure ; " that is, suffered a very heavy persecution, because he swore and was stedfasly purposed to keep the righteous judgments of God. And, lest in such trouble faith herself might faint he addeth, " Quicken me, O Lord, according to Thy word : " that is, according to Thy promise. For the word of the promises of God is a lantern to the feet, and a light to the paths.   Thus also above, in the humiliation of pesecution, he prayed that God would quicken him.³ . . .

107. " Make the freewill offerings of my mouth well pleasing, O Lord " (ver. 108) : that is, let them please Thee ; do not reject, but approve them.   By the freewill offerings of the mouth are well understood the sacrifices of praise, offered up in the confession of love, not from the fear of necessity ; whence it is said, " a freewill offering will I offer Thee." ⁴   But what doth he add ? " and teach me Thy judgments " ?   Had he not himself said above, " From Thy judgments I have not swerved " ?   How could he have done thus, if he knew them not ?   Moreover, if he knew them, in what sense doth he here say, " and teach me Thy judgments " ?   Is it as in a former passage, " Thou hast dealt in sweetness with Thy servant : " presently after which we find, " teach me sweetness " ?   This passage we

explained as the words of one who was gaining in grace, and praying that he might receive in addition to what he had received.

108. " My soul is alway in Thy hand " (ver. 109).   Some copies read, " in my hand : " but most, " in Thy hand ; " and this latter is indeed easy.   For " the souls of the righteous are in God's hand : ⁵ in whose hand are both we and our words." ⁶   " And I do not forget Thy law : " as if his memory were aided to remember God's law by the hands of Him in whose hands is his soul.   But how the words, " My soul is in my hands," can be understood, I know not.   For these are the words of the righteous, not of the ungodly ; of one who is returning to the Father, not departing from the Father.⁷ . . .   Is it perhaps said, " My soul is in my hands," in this sense, as if he offered it to God to be quickened ?   Whence in another passage it is said, " Unto Thee, O Lord, have I lifted up my soul." ⁸   Since here too he had said above, " Quicken Thou me."

109. " The ungodly," he saith, " have laid a snare for me : but yet I swerved not from Thy commandments " (ver. 110).   Whence this, unless because his soul is in the hands of God, or in his own hands is offered to God to be quickened ?

110. " Thy testimonies have I gained in heritage for ever " (ver. 111).   Some wishing to express in one word what is put in one word in the Greek, have translated it *hereditavi*.   Which although it might be Latin, yet would rather signify one who gave an inheritance than one who received it, *hereditavi* being like *ditavi*.   Better, therefore, the whole sense is conveyed in two words, whether we say, " I have possessed in heritage," or, " I have gotten in heritage : " not gotten heritage, but " gotten in heritage." If it be asked, what he gained in heritage, he replieth, " Thy testimonies."   What doth he wish to be understood, save that he might become a witness of God, and confess His testimonies, that is, that he might become a Martyr of God, and might declare His testimonies, as the Martyrs do, was a gift bestowed upon him by the Father, of whom he is heir ? . . . But even their wish was prepared by the Lord.   For this reason he saith he hath gained them in heritage, and this " for ever ; " because they have not in them the temporal glory of men who seek vain things, but the eternal glory of those who suffer for a short season, and who reign without end.   Whence the next words, " Because they are the very joy of my heart : " although the affliction of the body, yet the very joy of the heart.

111. He then addeth : " I have applied my heart to fulfil Thy righteousness for ever, for my

---

¹ Rom. x. 17.   ² 2 Pet. i. 19.   ³ Ps. cxix. 87, 88.
⁴ Ps. liv. 6.

⁵ Wisd. iii. 1.   ⁶ Wisd. vii. 16.   ⁷ Luke xv. 12, 24.
⁸ Ps. xxv. 1.

reward" (ver. 112). He who saith, "I have applied my heart," had before said, "Incline my heart unto Thy testimonies:"[1] so that we may understand that it is at once a divine gift, and an act of free will. But are we to fulfil the righteousnesses of God for ever? Those works which we perform in regard to the need of our neighbours, cannot be everlasting, any more than their need; but if we do not do them from love, there is no righteousness; if we do them from love, that love is everlasting, and an ever-lasting reward is in store for it.

Samech.

112. "I have hated the unrighteous; and Thy law have I loved" (ver. 113). He saith not, I hate the wicked, and love the righteous; or, I hate iniquity, and love Thy law; but, after saying, "I have hated the unrighteous," he explains why, by adding, "and Thy law have I loved;" to show, that he did not hate human nature in unrighteous men, but their unrighteousness, whereby they are foes to the law, which he loveth.

113. He next addeth: "Thou art my helper and my taker up" (ver. 114): "my helper," to do good works: "my taker up," to escape evil ones. In the next words, "I have hoped more on Thy word," he speaketh as a son of promise.

114. But what is the meaning of the following verse: "Away from me, ye wicked, and I will search the commandments of my God"? (ver. 115). For he saith not, I will perform; but, "I will search." In order, therefore, that he may diligently and perfectly learn that law, he bids the wicked depart from him, and even forci-bly driveth them away from his company. For the wicked exercise us in the fulfilment of the commandments, but lead us away from searching into them; not only when they persecute, or wish to litigate with us; but even when they court us, and honour us, and yet expect us to occupy ourselves in aiding their own vicious and busy desire, and to bestow our time upon them; or at least harass the weak, and compel them to bring their causes before us: to whom we dare not say, "Man, who made me a judge or a divider over you?"[2] For the Apostle instituted ecclesiastical judges of such causes, forbidding Christians to contend in the forum.[3] . . . Cer-tainly, on account of those who carry on law suits pertinaciously with one another, and, when they harass the good, scorn our judgments, and cause us to lose the time that should be employed upon things divine; surely, I say, on account of these men we also may exclaim in these words of the Body of Christ, "Away from me, ye wicked! and I will search the commandments of my God."

115. "O stablish me according to Thy word and I shall live: and let me not be disappointed of my hope" (ver. 116). He who had before said, "Thou art my taker up," prayeth that he may be more and more borne up, and be led unto that, for the sake of which he endureth so many troubles; trusting that he may there live in a truer sense, than in these dreams of human affairs. For it is said of the future, "and I shall live," as if we did not live in this dead body. While "we await the redemption of our body, we are saved by hope, and hoping for that we see not, we await with patience."[4] But hope disappointeth not, if the love of God be spread abroad in our hearts through the Holy Spirit which is given unto us:[5] And, as though it were answered him in silence, Thou dost not wish to be disappointed of thy hope? Cease not to meditate upon My righteousnesses: and, feeling that this meditation is usually hindered by the weaknesses of the soul, "Help me," he saith, "and I shall be safe; yea, I will meditate in Thy righteousnesses always" (ver. 117).

116. "Thou hast scorned all," or, as it seems more closely translated from the Greek, "Thou hast brought to nought all them that depart from Thy righteousnesses: for their thought is unrighteous" (ver. 118). For this reason he exclaimed, "Help Thou me, and I shall be safe; yea, I will meditate in Thy righteousnesses al-ways:" because God bringeth to nought all those who depart from His righteousnesses. But why do they depart? Because "their thought is," he saith, "unrighteous." They advance in that direction, while they depart from God. All deeds, good or bad, proceed from the thoughts: in his thoughts every man is innocent, in his thoughts every man is guilty. . . .

117. The next words in the Psalm are, "I have counted," or "thought," or "esteemed, all the ungodly of the earth as transgressors" (ver. 119). In the Latin version many different ren-derings are given of the Greek ἐλογισάμην; but this passage hath a deep meaning. For the fol-lowing words, "Therefore have I ever loved Thy testimonies:" make it far more profound. For the Apostle saith, "The law worketh wrath;" and, explaining these words, he ad-deth, "For where no law is, there is no trans-gression:"[6] thereby showing that not all are transgressors. For all have not the law. That all have not the law, he declareth more explicit-ly in another passage, "as many as have sinned without law, shall also perish without law."[7] What then meaneth, "I have held all the un-godly of the earth as transgressors"? "As trans-gressors;" or rather "transgressing," for the Greek saith, παραβαίνοντας, not παραβάτας. . . .

[1] Ps. cxix. 36.　　　[2] Luke xii. 14.　　　[3] 1 Cor. vi. 1-6.

[4] Rom. viii. 23-25.　　　[5] Rom. v. 5.
[6] Rom. iv. 15.　　　[7] Rom. ii. 12.

"The law entered that sin might abound." But since all sins are remitted through grace, not only those which are committed without the law, but those also which are committed in the law; he addeth, "But where sin abounded, grace did much more abound." [1] . . . But, indeed, when the Apostle said, "As many as have sinned without law, shall perish without law," he was speaking of that law which God gave to His people Israel through Moses His servant. . . . For some even Catholic expositors, from a want of sufficient heedfulness, have pronounced contrary to the truth, that those who have sinned without the law perish; and that those who have sinned in the law, are only judged, and do not perish, as if they should be considered destined to be cleansed by means of transitory punishments, as he of whom it is said, "he himself shall be saved, yet so as by fire." [2] . . . The Psalmist also hath subjoined: "Therefore I loved Thy testimonies." [3] As if he should say: Since the law, whether given in paradise, or implanted by nature, or promulgated in writing, hath made all the sinners of the earth transgressors; "Therefore I loved Thy testimonies," which are in Thy law, of Thy grace; so that not my but Thy righteousness is in me. For the law profiteth unto this end, that it send us forward unto grace. For not only because it testifieth towards the manifestation of the righteousness of God, which is without the law; but also in this very point that it rendereth men transgressors, so that the letter even slayeth, it driveth us to fly unto the quickening Spirit, through whom the whole of our sins may be blotted out, and the love of righteous deeds be inspired. [4] . . .

118. The grace of God, then, being known, which alone freeth from transgression, which is committed through knowledge of the law, he saith, in prayer, "Fix with nails my flesh in Thy fear" (ver. 120). For this some Latin interpreters have literally rendered the Greek καθή-λωσον, which that language has expressed in one word. Some have preferred to render by the word *confige*, without adding *clavis;* and while they thus desire to construe one Latin by one Greek word, have failed to express the full meaning of the Greek καθήλωσον, because in *confige* nails are not mentioned, but καθήλωσον cannot be taken but of nails, nor can "fix with nails" be expressed without using two words in Latin. . . . Hath he added, "For I have feared Thy judgments"? What meaneth, "Fix me in Thy fear: for I have feared"? If he had already feared, or if he was now fearing, why did he still

pray God to crucify his flesh in His fear? Did he wish so much additional fear imparted to him as would suffice for crucifying his flesh, that is, his carnal lusts and affections; as though he should say, Perfect in me the fear of Thee; for I have feared Thy judgments? But there is here even a higher sense, which must, as far as God alloweth, be derived from searching the recesses of this Scripture : that is, in the chaste fear of Thee, which abideth from age to age, let my carnal desires be quenched; [5] "For I have feared Thy judgments," when the law, which could not give me righteousness, threatened me punishment. . . . For the inclination to sin liveth, and it then appeareth in deed, when impunity may be hoped for. But when punishment is considered sure to follow, it liveth latently : nevertheless it liveth. For it would rather it were lawful to sin, and it grieveth that what the law forbiddeth, is not lawful; because it is not spiritually delighted with the blessing of the law, but carnally feareth the evil which it threateneth. [6] But that love, which casteth out this fear, feareth with a chaste fear to sin, although no punishment follow; because it doth not even judge that impunity will follow, since from love of righteousness it considereth the very sin itself a punishment. With such a fear the flesh is crucified; since carnal delights, which are forbidden rather than avoided by the letter of the law, are overcome by the delight in spiritual blessings, and also when the victory is perfected are destroyed.

Ain.

119. "I have dealt judgment and righteousness; O give me not over unto mine oppressors" [7] (ver. 121). It is not wonderful that he should have dealt judgment and righteousness, since he had above prayed for a chaste fear from God, whereby to fix with nails his flesh, that is, his carnal lusts, which are wont to hinder our judgment from being right. But although in our customary speech judgment is either right or wrong, whence it is said unto men in the Gospel, "Judge not according to the persons, but judge righteous judgment : " [8] nevertheless in this passage judgment is used as though, if it were not righteous, it ought not to be called judgment; otherwise it would not be enough to say, "I have dealt judgment," but it would be said, I have dealt righteous judgment. . . .

---

[1] Rom. v. 20.
[2] [A fundamental objection to the doctrine of purgatory. — C.]
[3] [The author adds: "Some copies read 'always,' some do not. If it be correct, it must be understood to mean, during our present life on earth." — C.]
[4] 2 Cor. iii. 6.

[5] Ps. xix. 9.
[6] [Hence "attrition" is not sufficient to obtain remission. — C.]
[7] [The author says: "For some copies read, to them that persecute me: the Greek words τοῖς ἀντιδικοῦσι being variously interpreted by the Latin *nocentibus, persequentibus*, and *calumniantibus*. I wonder, however, that I have never met with the version *adversantibus* in any of the copies which I have read, since there is no doubt that the Greek ἀντίδικος is the same as the Latin *adversarius*. While he prays therefore that he may not be given up to his adversaries by the Lord, what doth he pray, save what we pray, when we say, 'Lead us not into temptation'?" — C.]
[8] John vii. 24.

120. Whoso therefore in the chaste fear of God hath his flesh crucified, and corrupted by no carnal allurement, dealeth judgment and the work of righteousness, ought to pray that he may not be given up to his adversaries; that is, that he may not, through his dread of suffering evils, yield unto his adversaries to do evil. For he receiveth power of endurance, which guardeth him from being overcome with pain, from Him from whom he receiveth the victory over lust, which preventeth his being seduced by pleasure.[1]

121. He next saith, "Take off Thy servant to that which is good, that the proud calumniate me not" (ver. 122). They drive me on, that I may fall into evil; do Thou take me off to that which is good. They who rendered these words by the Latin, *calumnientur*, have followed a Greek expression, not commonly used in Latin. Have the words, Let not the proud calumniate me, the same force, as, Let them "not succeed in calumniating me"?

122. . . . To prefigure His Cross, Moses by the merciful command of God raised aloft on a pole the image of a serpent in the desert, that the likeness of sinful flesh which must be crucified in Christ might be prefigured.[2] By gazing upon this healing Cross, we cast out all the poison of the scandals of the proud: the Cross, which the Psalmist intently looking upon, saith, "My eyes have failed for Thy salvation, and for the words of Thy righteousness" (ver. 123). For God made Christ Himself "to be sin for us, on account of the likeness of sinful flesh, that we may be made the righteousness of God in Him."[3] For His utterance[4] of the righteousness of God he therefore saith that his eyes have failed, from gazing ardently and eagerly, while, remembering human infirmity, he longeth for divine grace in Christ.

123. In connection with this he goes on to say, "O deal with Thy servant according to Thy loving mercy" (ver. 124); not according to my righteousness. "And teach me," he saith, "Thy righteousnesses;" those beyond doubt, whereby God rendereth men righteous, not they themselves.

124. "I am Thy servant. O grant me understanding, that I may know Thy testimonies" (ver. 125). This petition must never be intermitted. For it sufficeth not to have received understanding, and to have learnt the testimonies of God, unless it be evermore received, and evermore in a manner quaffed from the fountain of eternal light. For the testimonies of God are the better and the better known, the more understanding a man attaineth to.

125. "It is time," he saith, "for the Lord to lay to His hand" (ver. 126). For this is the reading of most copies: not as some have, "O Lord." Now what is this, save the grace which was revealed in Christ at its own time? Of which season the Apostle saith, "But when the fulness of time was come, God sent His Son."[5] . . . But wherefore is it that, seemingly anxious to show the Lord that it was time to lay to His hand, he hath subjoined, "They have scattered Thy law;" as if it were the season for the Lord to act, because the proud scattered His law. For what meaneth this? In the wickedness of transgression, they have not guarded its integrity. It was needful therefore that the Law should be given to the proud and those presuming in the freedom of their own will, after a transgression of which whosoever were contrite and humbled, might run no longer by the Law, but by faith, to aiding grace. When the Law therefore was scattered, it was time that mercy should be sent through the only-begotten Son of God.

126. "Therefore," he saith, "I love Thy commandments above gold and topaz" (ver. 127). Grace hath this object, that the commandments, which could not be fulfilled by fear, may be fulfilled by love. . . . Therefore, they are above gold and topaz stones. For this is read in another Psalm also, "Above gold and exceeding precious stones."[6] For topaz is a stone considered very precious. But they not understanding the hidden grace which was in the Old Testament, screened as it were by the veil[7] (this was signified when they were unable to gaze upon the face of Moses), endeavoured to obey the commandments of God for the sake of an earthly and carnal reward, but could not obey them; because they did not love them, but something else. Whence these were not the works of the willing, but rather the burdens of the unwilling. But when the commandments are loved for their own sake "above gold and exceeding precious stones," all earthly reward compared with the commandments themselves is vile; nor are any other goods of man comparable in any respect with those goods whereby man himself is made good.

127. "Therefore," he saith, "was I made straight unto all Thy commandments" (ver. 128). I was made straight, doubtless, because I loved them; and I clung by love to them, which were straight, that I might also myself become straight. Then what he addeth, naturally follows: "and every unrighteous way I utterly abhor." For how could it be that he who loved the straight could do aught save abhor an unrighteous way? For as, if he loved gold and precious stones, he would abhor all that might bring loss of such property: thus, since he loved the command-

---

[1] Ps. lxxxv. 12, lxii. 5.　　[2] John iii. 14.
[3] Rom. viii. 3; 2 Cor. v. 21.
[4] *Eloquium.*

[5] Gal. iv. 4.　　[6] Ps. xix. 10.
[7] Exod. xxxiv. 33–35; 2 Cor. iii. 13–15.

ments of God, he abhorred the path of iniquity, as one of the most savage rocks in the sailor's track, whereon he must needs suffer shipwreck of things so precious. That this may not be his lot, he who saileth on the wood of the Cross with the divine commandments as his freight, steereth far from thence.

Pe.

128. "Thy testimonies are wonderful: therefore hath my soul searched them" (ver. 129). Who counteth, even by their kinds, the testimonies of God? Heaven and earth, His visible and invisible works, declare in some manner the testimony of His goodness and greatness; and the very ordinary and accustomed course of nature, whereby the seasons are rapidly revolved, in all things after their kinds, however temporal and perishable, however held cheap through our constant experience of them, give, if a pious thinker give heed to them, a testimony to the Creator. But which of these is not wonderful, if we measure each not by its habitual presence, but by reason? But if we venture to bring all nature within the comprehensive view of one act of contemplation, doth not that take place in us which the prophet describeth, "I considered Thy works, and trembled"?[1] Yet the Psalmist was not terrified in his wonder at creation, but rather said that this was the reason that he ought to search it, because it was wonderful. For after saying, "Thy testimonies are wonderful," he addeth, "therefore hath my soul searched them;" as if he had become more curious from the difficulty of thoroughly searching them. For the more abstruse are the causes of anything, the more wonderful it is. . . .

129. "When thy word goeth forth," he saith, "it giveth light, and maketh His little ones to understand" (ver. 130). What is the little one save the humble and weak? Be not proud therefore, presume not in thine own strength, which is nought; and thou wilt understand why a good law was given by a good God, though it cannot give life. For it was given for this end, that it might make thee a little one instead of great, that it might show that thou hadst not strength to do the law of thine own power: and that thus, wanting aid and destitute, thou mightest fly unto grace, saying, "Have mercy upon me, O Lord, for I am weak."[2] . . . Let all be little ones, and let all the world be guilty before Thee: because "by the deeds of the Law there shall no flesh be justified" in Thy sight; "for by the Law is the knowledge of sin," etc.[3] These are Thy wonderful testimonies, which the soul of this little one hath searched; and hath therefore found, because he became humbled and a little one. For who doth Thy commandments as they ought to be done, that is, by "faith which worketh through love,"[4] save love itself be shed abroad in his heart through the Holy Spirit?[5]

130. This is confessed by this little one; "I opened my mouth," he saith, "and drew in the spirit: for I longed for Thy commandments" (ver. 131). What did he long for, save to obey the divine commandments? But there was no possibility of the weak doing hard things, the little one great things: he opened his mouth, confessing that he could not do them of himself: and drew in power to do them: he opened his mouth, by seeking, asking, knocking:[6] and athirst drank in the good Spirit, which enabled him to do what he could not do by himself, "the commandment holy and just and good."[7] Not that they themselves who "are led by the Spirit of God,"[8] do nothing; but that they may not do nothing good, they are moved to act by the good Spirit. For so much the more is every man made a good son, in proportion as the good Spirit is given unto Him by the Father in a greater measure.

131. He still prayeth. He hath opened his mouth, and drawn in the Spirit; but he still knocketh in prayer unto the Father, and seeketh: he drinketh, but the more sweet he findeth it, the more eagerly doth he thirst. Hear the words of him in his thirst. "O look Thou upon me," he saith, "and be merciful unto me: according to the judgment of those that love Thy Name" (ver. 132): that is, according to the judgment Thou has dealt unto all who love Thy Name; since Thou hast first loved them, to cause them to love Thee. For thus saith the Apostle John, "We love God, because He first loved us."[9]

132. See what the Psalmist next most openly saith: "Order my steps after Thy word: and so shall no wickedness have dominion over me" (ver. 133). Where what else doth he say than this, Make me upright and free according to Thy promise. But so much the more as the love of God reigneth in every man, so much the less hath wickedness dominion over him. What else then doth he seek than that by the gift of God he may love God? For by loving God he loveth himself, so that he may healthily love his neighbour also as himself: on which commandments hang all the Law and the Prophets.[10] What then doth he pray, save that God may cause the fulfilment by His help of those commandments which He imposeth by His bidding?

133. But what meaneth this that he saith, "O deliver me from the calumnies of men: so shall I keep Thy commandments"? (ver. 134). . . .

---

[1] Hab. iii. 2.　　[2] Ps. vi. 2.　　[3] Rom. iii. 19-21.

[4] Gal. v. 6.　　[5] Rom. v. 5.　　[6] Matt. vii. 7.
[7] Rom. vii. 12.　　[8] Rom. viii. 14.　　[9] 1 John iv. 19.
[10] Matt. xxii. 37-40.

Did not the holy people of God much the more gloriously keep the commandments among these very calumnies, when they were at their hottest in the midst of tribulations, when they yielded not to their persecutors to commit impieties? But, in truth, the meaning of these words is this : Do Thou, by pouring upon me Thy Spirit, guard me from being overcome by the terrors of human calumny, and from being drawn over to their evil deeds away from Thy commandments. For if Thou hast thus dealt with me, that is, if Thou hast in this manner delivered me by the gift of patience from their calumnies, so that I fear not the false charges they prefer against me ; among those very calumnies I will keep Thy commandments.

134. " Show the light of Thy countenance on Thy servant, and teach me thy statutes " (ver. 135) : that is, manifest Thy presence, by succouring and aiding me. " And teach me Thy righteousnesses." Teach me to work them : as it is more plainly expressed elsewhere, " Teach me to do Thy will." [1] For they who hear, although they retain in their memories what they hear, are by no means to be considered to have learnt, unless they do. For it is the word of Truth : " Every man that hath heard and hath learned of the Father, cometh unto Me." [2] He therefore who obeyeth not in deed, that is, who cometh not, hath not learnt.

135. " My eyes have descended streams of waters, because they have not kept Thy law " (ver. 136) : that is, my eyes. For in some copies there is this reading, " Because I have not kept Thy law, streams of waters " therefore " descended," that is, floods of tears.[3] . . .

Tsadze.

136. Thus, then, as if giving a reason why he had cause to weep much, and to mourn deeply for his sin, he saith, " Righteous art Thou, O Lord, and true is Thy judgment " (ver. 137). " Thou hast commanded Thy testimonies, righteousness, and Thy truth exceedingly " (ver. 138). This righteousness of God and righteous judgment and truth, is to be feared by every sinner : for thereby all who are condemned are condemned of God ; nor is there one who can righteously complain against the righteous God of his own damnation. Therefore the tears of the penitent are needful ; since if his impenitent heart were condemned, he would be most justly condemned. He indeed calleth the testimonies of God righteousness : for He proveth himself righteous by giving righteous command-

ments. And this is truth also, that God may become known by such testimonies.

137. But what is it that followeth : " My zeal hath caused me to pine " (ver. 139) ; or, as other copies read, Thy zeal? Others have also, " The zeal of Thy house :" and, " hath eaten me up," instead of, " hath caused me to pine." This, as it seems to me, has been considered as an emendation to be introduced from another Psalm, where it is written, " The zeal of Thy house hath eaten me up : " [4] a text quoted also, as we know, in the Gospel. The two words, however, " hath caused me to pine," and " hath eaten me up," are somewhat like. But the words, " my zeal," which most of the copies read, occasion no dispute : for what wonder is it if every man pineth away from his own zeal? The words read in other copies, " Thy zeal," signify a man zealous for God, not for himself : but there is no difficulty in using " my " in the same sense. . . . The Psalmist's jealousy is therefore also to be understood in a good sense : for he addeth the cause, and saith, " Because mine enemies have forgotten Thy words." . . .

138. Then considering with himself with what a flame of love he burned for the commandments of God : " Fiery," saith he, " is Thy word exceedingly, and Thy servant hath loved it " (ver. 140). Justly jealous was he of the impenitent heart in His enemies, who had forgotten God's word ; for he endeavoured to bring them unto that which he himself most ardently loved.

139. " I am young, and of no reputation ; yet do I not forget Thy righteousnesses : " not as my enemies, who " have forgotten Thy words " (ver. 141). The younger seems to grieve for those older than himself who had forgotten the righteousnesses of God, while he himself had not forgotten. For what meaneth, " I am young, yet do I not forget "? save this, Those older than me have forgotten. For the Greek word is νεώτερος, the same as that used in the words above, " Wherewithal shall a young man cleanse his way ? " [5] This is a comparative, and is therefore well understood in its relation to some one older. Let us therefore here recognise the two nations, who were striving even in Rebecca's womb ; when it was said to her, not from works, but of Him that calleth, " The elder shall serve the younger." [6] But the younger saith here that he is of no reputation : for this reason he hath become greater : since " behold, they that were first are last, and they that were last first." [7]

140. It is no wonder that they have forgotten the words of God, who have chosen to set up their own righteousness, ignorant of the righteousness of God ; [8] but he, the younger, hath not

---

[1] Ps. cxliii. 10.
[2] John vi. 45.
[3] [He adds : " There are copies which do not read ' descended,' but ' overpassed,' meaning that he said hyperbolically, that in weeping he had overpast streams of waters, that is, by weeping more than the waters flow in their streams." — C.]

[4] Ps. lxix. 9; John ii. 17.
[5] Ps. cxix. 9.
[6] Gen. xxv. 22, 23; Rom. ix. 12, 13.
[7] Matt. xx. 16.
[8] Rom. x. 3.

forgotten, for he hath not wished to have a righteousness of his own, but that of God, of which he now also saith, "Thy righteousness is an everlasting righteousness, and Thy law is the truth" (ver. 142). For how is not the law truth, through which came the knowledge of sin, and that which giveth testimony of the righteousness of God? For thus the Apostle saith: "The righteousness of God is manifested, being witnessed by the Law and the Prophets." [1]

141. On account of this law the younger suffered persecution from the elder, so that the younger saith what followeth: "Trouble and hardship have taken hold upon me: yet is my meditation in Thy commandments" (ver. 143). Let them rage, let them persecute; as long as the commandments of God be not abandoned, and, after those commandments, let even those who rage be loved.

142. "Thy testimonies are righteousness unto everlasting: O grant me understanding, and I shall live" (ver. 144). This younger one prayeth for understanding; which if he had not, he would not be "wiser than the aged;"[2] but he prayeth for it in trouble and hardships, that he may thereby understand how contemptible is all that his persecuting enemies can take from him, by whom he saith he hath been despised. Therefore he hath said, "and I shall live:" because if trouble and heaviness reached such a pitch, that his life should be terminated by the hands of his persecuting enemies, he will live for ever, who preferreth to temporal things, righteousness which remaineth for evermore. This righteousness in trouble and hardship are the *Martyria Dei*, that is, the testimonies of God, for which Martyrs have been crowned.

Koph.

143. . . . He who singeth this Psalm, mentioneth such a prayer of his own: "I have called with my whole heart; hear me, O Lord!" (ver. 145). For to what end his cry profiteth, he addeth: "I will search out Thy righteousnesses." For this purpose then he hath called with his whole heart, and hath longed that this might be given him by the Lord listening unto him, that he may search out His righteousnesses. . . .

144. "I have called, save me" (ver. 146); or as some copies, both Greek and Latin, have it, "I have called to Thee." But what is, "I have called to Thee," save that by calling I have invoked Thee? But when he had said, "save me;" what did he add? "And I will keep Thy testimonies:" that is, that I may not, through infirmity, deny Thee. For the health of the soul causeth that to be done which it is known to be our duty to do, and thus in striving even to the death of the body, if the extremity of temptation demand this in defence of the truth of the divine testimonies: but where there is not health of the soul, weakness yieldeth, and truth is deserted. . . .

145. "I have prevented in midnight," he saith, "and have cried: In Thy words have I trusted" (ver. 147). If we refer this to each of the faithful, and to the literal character of the act; it oft happeneth that the love of God is awake in that hour of the night, and, the love of prayer strongly urging us, the time of prayer, which is wont to be after the crowing of the cock, is not awaited, but prevented. But if we understand night of the whole of this world's duration; we indeed cry unto God at midnight, and prevent the fulness of time in which He will restore us what He hath promised, as is elsewhere read, "Let us prevent His presence with confession." [3] Although if we choose to understand the unripe season of this night, before the fulness of time had come,[4] that is, the ripe season when Christ should be manifested in the flesh; neither was the Church then silent, but preventing this fulness of time, in prophecy cried out, and trusted in the words of God, who was able to do what He promised, that in the seed of Abraham all nations should be blessed.[5]

146. The Church saith also what followeth, "Mine eyes have prevented the morning watch, that I might meditate on Thy words" (ver. 148). Let us suppose the morning to mean the season when "a light arose for them that sat in the shadow of death;"[6] did not the eyes of the Church prevent this morning watch, in those Saints who before were on earth, because they foresaw beforehand that this would come to pass, so that they meditated on the words of God, which then were, and announced these things to be destined in the Law and the Prophets?

147. "Hear my voice, O Lord, according to Thy loving-mercy; and quicken Thou me according to Thy judgment" (ver. 149). For first God according to His loving-mercy taketh away punishment from sinners, and will give them life afterwards, when righteous, according to His judgment; for it is not without a meaning that it is said unto Him, "My song shall be of mercy and judgment: unto Thee, O Lord;"[7] in this order of the terms: although the season of mercy itself be not without judgment, whereof the Apostle saith, "If we would judge ourselves, we should not be judged of the Lord."[8] . . . And the final season of judgment shall not be without mercy, since as the Psalm saith, "He crowneth thee with mercy and loving-kindness." But "judgment shall be without mercy," but "unto those" on the left, "who have not dealt mercy."[9]

---

[1] Rom. iii. 20, 21.   [2] Ps. cxix. 100.

[3] Ps. xcv. 2.   [4] Gal. iv. 4.   [5] Gen. xii. 3 and xxii. 18.
[6] Isa. ix. 2.   [7] Ps. ci. 1.   [8] 1 Cor. xi. 31.
[9] Jas. ii. 13.

148. "They draw nigh, that of malice persecute me : " or, as some copies read, "maliciously" (ver. 150). Then they that persecute draw nigh, when they go the length of torturing and destroying the flesh : whence the twenty-first Psalm, wherein the Lord's Passion is prophesied, saith, "O go not from me, for trouble is hard at hand ; " [1] where those things are spoken of which He suffered when His Passion was not imminent upon Him, but actually realized. "And are far from Thy law." The nearer they drew to the persecuting the righteous, so much the farther were they from righteousness. But what harm did they do unto those, to whom they drew near by persecution ; since the approach of their Lord is nearer unto their souls, by whom they no wise are forsaken?

149. Lastly, it followeth, "Thou art nigh at hand, O Lord, and all Thy ways are truth " (ver. 151). Even in their troubles, it hath been a wonted confession of the saints, to ascribe truth unto God, because they suffer them not undeservedly. So did Queen Esther,[2] so did holy Daniel,[3] so did the three men in the furnace,[4] so do other associates in their sanctity confess. But it may be asked, in what sense it is here said, "All Thy ways are truth ; " since in another Psalm it is read, "All the ways of the Lord are mercy and truth."[5] But towards the saints, All the ways of the Lord are at once mercy and truth : since He aideth them even in judgment, and thus mercy is not wanting ; and in having mercy upon them, He performeth that which He hath promised, so that truth is not wanting. But towards all, both those whom He freeth, and those whom He condemneth, all the ways of the Lord are mercy and truth ; because where He doth not show mercy, the truth of His vengeance is displayed. For He freeth many who have not deserved, but He condemneth none who hath not deserved it.

150. "From the beginning I have known," he saith, "as concerning Thy testimonies, that Thou hast grounded them for ever "[6] (ver. 152). . . . . What are these testimonies, save those wherein God hath declared that He will give an everlasting kingdom unto His sons? And since He hath declared that He will give this in His only-begotten Son, he said that the testimonies themselves were grounded for ever. For that which God hath promised through them, was everlasting. And for this reason the words, "Thou hast grounded them," are rightly thus understood, because they are shown to be true in Christ.[7] Whence then did the Psalmist know this in the beginning, save because the Church speaketh, which was not wanting to the earth from the commencement of the human race, the first-fruits whereof was the holy Abel, himself sacrificed in testimony of the future blood of the Mediator that should be shed by a wicked brother?[8] For this also was at the beginning, "They two shall be one flesh : "[9] which great mystery the Apostle Paul expounding, saith, "I speak concerning Christ and the Church."[10]

Resch.

151. Let no man, set in Christ's body, imagine these words to be alien from himself, since in truth it is the whole body of Christ placed in this humble state that speaketh : "O consider my humiliation, and deliver me : for I forget not Thy law " (ver. 153). In this place we cannot understand any law of God so suitably, as that whereby it is immutably determined that "every one that exalteth himself, shall be abased ; and every one that humbleth himself, shall be exalted."[11]

152. "Avenge Thou," he saith, "my cause, and deliver me " (ver. 154). The former sentence is here almost repeated. And what is there said, "For I do not forget Thy law," agreeth with what we read here, "Quicken me, according to Thy word." For these words are the law of God, which he hath not forgot, so that he hath abased himself, and will therefore be exalted. But the words, "Quicken me," pertain to this very exaltation ; for the exaltation of the saints is everlasting life.

153. "Health," he saith, "is far from the ungodly : for they regard not Thy righteousnesses " (ver. 155). This separateth thee, that what they have not done, thou hast done, that is, thou hast regarded the righteousnesses of God. But "what hast thou that thou hast not received? "[12] Art thou not he who a little before didst say, "I will keep Thy righteousnesses "? Thou therefore hast received from Him, unto whom thou didst call, the power to keep them. He therefore doth Himself separate thee from those from whom health is far, because they have not regarded the righteousnesses of God.

154. This he saw himself also. For I should not see it, save I saw it in Him, save I were in Him. For these are the words of the Body of Christ, whose members we are. He saw this, I say, and at once added, "Great are Thy mercies, O Lord " (ver. 156). Even our seeking out Thy righteousnesses, then, cometh of Thy

---

[1] Ps. xxii. 11.   [2] Esth. xiv. 6, 7.   [3] Dan. ix. 4, 16.
[4] Song of 3 Chil. 2-10.   [5] Ps. xxv. 10.
[6] [Here the author says: "The Greek word καταρχὰς hath been variously rendered by the Latin translators by *ab initio, initio,* and *in initiis.* Those who rendered it in the plural, have followed the Greek phrase. But it is more usual in the Latin tongue to express the idea conveyed by καταρχὰς, which in Greek is used in the plural or adverbially, by the words *ab initio,* or *initio ;* just as with us, when we say, Otherwise I do this (*alias hoc facio*), we seem to be using the plural of the feminine gender, whereas the word is an adverb, and signifies, at another time." — C.]

[7] 1 Cor. iii. 11.   [8] Gen. iv. 8.   [9] Gen. ii. 24.
[10] Eph. v. 32.   [11] Luke xiv. 11 and xviii. 14.
[12] 1 Cor. iv. 7.

mercies. " Quicken me according to Thy judgment." For I know that Thy judgments will not be upon me without Thy mercy.

155. " Many there are that trouble me, and persecute me ; yet do I not swerve from Thy testimonies" (ver. 157). This hath been realized : we know it, we recollect it, we acknowledge it. The whole earth has been crimsoned by the blood of Martyrs ; heaven is flowery with the crowns of Martyrs, the Churches are adorned with the memorials of Martyrs, seasons distinguished by the birthdays of Martyrs, cures more frequent[1] by the merits of Martyrs. Whence this, save because that hath been fulfilled which was prophesied[2] of that Man who hath been spread abroad around the whole world. We recognise this, and render thanks to the Lord our God. For thou, man, thou hast thyself said in another Psalm, " If the Lord Himself had not been on our side, they would have swallowed us up quick."[3] Behold the reason why thou hast not swerved from His testimonies, and hast won the palm of thy heavenly calling amid the hands of the many who persecuted and troubled thee.

156. " I have seen," he saith, " the foolish, and I pined " (ver. 158) : or, as other copies read, " I have seen them that keep not covenant : " this is the reading of most. But who are they who have not kept covenant, save they who have swerved from the testimonies of God, not bearing the tribulation of their many persecutors ? Now this is the covenant, that he who shall have conquered shall be crowned. They who, not bearing persecution, have by denial swerved from the testimonies of God, have not kept the covenant. These then the Psalmist saw, and pined, for he loved them. For that jealousy is good, springing from love, not from envy. He addeth in what respect they had failed to keep the covenant, " Because they kept not Thy word." For this they denied in their tribulations.

157. And he commendeth himself as differing from them, and saith, " Behold, how I have loved Thy commandments " (ver. 159). He saith not, I have not denied Thy words or testimonies, as the Martyrs were urged to do, and, when they refused, suffered intolerable torments : but he said this wherein is the fruit of all sufferings ; for, " if I give up my body to be burned, and have not charity, it profiteth me nothing."[4] The Psalmist, praising this virtue, saith, " Behold, how I have loved Thy commandments." Then he asketh his reward, " O Lord, quicken me, according to Thy mercy." These put me to death, do Thou quicken me. But if a reward be asked of mercy, which justice is bound to give ; how much greater is that mercy, which enabled

him to gain the victory, on account of which the reward was sought for ?

158. " The beginning," he saith, " of Thy words is truth ; all the judgments of Thy righteousness endure for evermore " (ver. 160). From truth, he saith, Thy words do proceed, and they are therefore truthful, and deceive no man, for in them life is announced to the righteous, punishment to the ungodly. These are the everlasting judgments of God's righteousness.

Schin.

159. We know what persecutions the body of Christ, that is, the holy Church, suffered from the kings of the earth. Let us therefore here also recognise the words of the Church : " Princes have persecuted me without a cause : and my heart hath stood in awe of Thee " (ver. 161). For how had the Christians injured the kingdoms of the earth, although their King promised them the kingdom of heaven? How, I ask, had they injured the kingdoms of earth? Did their King forbid His soldiers to pay and to render due service to the kings of the earth? Saith He not to the Jews who were striving to calumniate Him, " Render unto Cæsar the things that are Cæsar's, and unto God the things that are God's "?[5] Did He not even in His own Person pay tribute from the mouth of a fish?[6] Did not His forerunner, when the soldiers of this kingdom were seeking what they ought to do for their everlasting salvation, instead of replying, Loose your belts, throw away your arms, desert your king, that ye may wage war for the Lord, answer, " Do violence to no man : neither accuse any falsely : and be content with your wages "?[7] Did not one of His soldiers, His most beloved companion,[8] say to his fellow soldiers, the provincials,[9] so to speak, of Christ, " Let every soul be subject unto the higher powers "?[10] Does he not enjoin the Church to pray for even kings themselves?[11] How then have the Christians offended against them? What due have they not rendered? in what have not Christians obeyed the monarchs of earth? The kings of the earth therefore have persecuted the Christians without a cause. They too had their threatening words : I banish, I proscribe, I slay, I torture with claws, I burn with fires, I expose to beasts, I tear the limbs piecemeal.[12] But heed what he hath subjoined : " And my heart hath stood in awe of Thy word." My heart hath stood in awe of these words,[13] " Fear not them that kill the body," etc. I have scorned man who persecuteth me, and have overcome the devil that would seduce me.

---

[1] *Crebrescunt sanitates. De Civ. De.* xxii. 8. [Vol. ii. p. 484, this series. The miracles of post-apostolic times are not matter of faith. But see Newman's *Fleury*, Oxford, 1842.—C.]
[2] [In this verse.—C.] [3] Ps. cxxiv. 2, 3. [4] 1 Cor. xiii. 3.

[5] Matt. xxii. 21. [6] Matt. xvii. 24–26. [7] Luke iii. 14.
[8] *Comes* (count or earl), a title of honour in the Imperial Court.
[9] See on Ps. xci. and on Ps. civ. [10] Also Rom. xiii. 1, 7, 8.
[11] 1 Tim. ii. 1, 2. [12] [See A. N. F. vol. p. viii. 682.—C.]
[13] Matt. x. 28.

160. Then follows, "I am as glad of Thy word as one that findeth great spoils" (ver. 162). By the same words he conquered, of which he stood in awe. For spoils are stripped from the conquered; as he was overcome and despoiled of whom it is said in the Gospel, "except he first bind the strong man."[1] But many spoils were found, when, admiring the endurance of the Martyrs, even the persecutors believed; and they who had plotted to injure our King by the injury of His soldiers, were gained over by Him in addition. Whoever therefore standeth in awe of the words of God, fearing lest he be overcome in the contest, rejoiceth as conqueror in the same words.

161. "As for iniquity, I hate and abhor it; but Thy law have I loved" (ver. 163). That awe, therefore, of His word did not create hatred of those words, but maintained his love unimpaired. For the words of God are no other than the law of God. Far be it therefore that love perish through fear, where fear is chaste. Thus fathers are at once feared and loved by affectionate sons; thus doth the chaste wife at once fear her husband, lest she be forsaken by him, and loveth him, that she may enjoy his love. If then the human father and the human husband desire at once to be feared and loved; much more doth our Father who is in heaven,[2] and that Bridegroom, "beautiful beyond the sons of men,"[3] not in the flesh, but in goodness. For by whom is the law of God loved, save by those by whom God is loved? And what that is severe hath the father's law to good sons?[4] Let the Father's judgments therefore be praised even in the scourge, if His promises be loved in the reward.

162. Such was, assuredly, the conduct of the Psalmist, who saith, "Seven times a day do I praise Thee, because of Thy righteous judgments" (ver. 164). The words "seven times a day," signify "evermore." For this number is wont to be a symbol of universality; because after six days of the divine work of creation, a seventh of rest was added;[5] and all times roll on through a revolving cycle of seven days. For no other reason it was said, "a just man falleth seven times, and riseth up again:"[6] that is, the just man perisheth not, though brought low in every way, yet not induced to transgress, otherwise he will not be just. For the words, "falleth seven times," are employed to express every kind of tribulation, whereby man is cast down in the sight of men: and the words, "riseth up again," signify that he profiteth from all these tribulations. The following sentence in this passage sufficiently illustrates the foregoing words: for it follows, "but the wicked shall fall into mischief." Not to be deprived of strength in

any evils, is therefore the falling seven times, and the rising again of the just man. Justly hath the Church then praised God seven times in a day for His righteous judgments; because, when it was time that judgment should begin at the house of God,[7] she did not faint in all her tribulations, but was glorified with the crowns of Martyrs.

163. "Great is the peace," he saith, "that they have who love Thy law: and there is no offence to them" (ver. 165). Doth this mean that the law itself is not an offence to them that love it, or that there is no offence from any source unto them that love the law? But both senses are rightly understood. For he who loveth the law of God, honoureth in it even what he doth not understand; and what seemeth to him to sound absurd, he judgeth rather that he doth not understand, and that there is some great meaning hidden: thus the law of God is not an offence to him. . . .

164. "I have waited," he saith, "for Thy saving health, O Lord, and have loved Thy commandments" (ver. 166). For what would it have profited the righteous of old to have loved the commandments of God, save Christ, who is the saving health of God, had freed them; by the gift of whose Spirit also they were able to love the commandments of God? If therefore they who loved God's commandments, waited for His saving health; how much more necessary was Jesus, that is, the saving Health of God, for the salvation of those that did not love His commandments? This prophecy may suit also the Saints of the period since the revelation of grace, and the preaching of the Gospel, for they that love God's commandments look for Christ, that "when Christ, our life, shall appear, we may then "appear with Him in glory."[8]

165. "My soul hath kept Thy testimonies, and I have loved them exceedingly:" or, as some copies read, "hath loved them," understanding, "my soul" (ver. 167). The testimonies of God are kept, while they are not denied. This is the office of Martyrs, for testimonies are called Martyria in Greek. But since it profiteth nothing, even to be burnt with flames without charity,[9] he addeth, "and I have loved them exceedingly." . . . For he who loveth, keepeth them in the Spirit of truth and faithfulness. But generally, while the commandments of God are kept, they against whose will they are kept become our foes: then, indeed, His testimonies also must be kept courageously, lest they be denied when the enemy persecuteth. After the Psalmist, then, had declared that he had done both these things, he ascribeth unto God his having been enabled to do so, by adding, "because all my ways are

[1] Matt. xii 29.　　　[2] Matt. vi. 9.　　　[3] Ps. xlv. 2.
[4] Heb. xii. 6.　　　[5] Gen. ii. 2.　　　[6] Prov. xxiv. 16.

[7] 1 Pet. iv. 17.　　　[8] Col. iii. 4.　　　[9] 1 Cor. xiii. 3.

in Thy sight." He saith therefore, "I have kept Thy commandments and Thy testimonies; because all my ways are in Thy sight" (ver. 168). As much as to say, Hadst Thou turned away Thy face from me, I should have been confounded, nor could I keep Thy commandments and testimonies. "I have kept them," then, because "all my ways are in Thy sight." With a look favouring and aiding man, he meant it to be understood that God seeth his ways: according to the prayer, "O hide not Thou Thy face from me."[1] . . .

Tau.

166. Let us now hear the words of one praying: since we know who is praying, and we recognise ourselves, if we be not reprobate, among the members of this one praying. "Let my prayer come near in Thy sight, O Lord" (ver. 169): for, "The Lord is nigh unto them that are of a contrite heart."[2] "Give me understanding, according to Thy word." He claimeth a promise. For he saith, "according to Thy word," which is to say, according to Thy promise. For the Lord promised this when He said, "I will inform thee."[3]

167. "Let my request come before Thy presence, O Lord: deliver me, according to Thy word" (ver. 170). He repeateth what he hath asked. For his former words, "Let my prayer come near in Thy presence, O Lord:" are like unto what he saith, "Let my request come before Thy presence, O Lord:" and the words, "Give me understanding according to Thy word," agree with these, "Deliver me according to Thy word." For by receiving understanding he is delivered, who of himself through want of understanding is deceived.

168. "My lips shall burst forth praise: when Thou hast taught me Thy righteousnesses" (ver. 171). We know how God teacheth those who are docile unto God. For every one who hath heard from the Father and hath learned, comes unto Him "who justifieth the ungodly:"[4] so that he may keep the righteousnesses of God not only by retaining them in his memory, but also by doing them. Thus doth he who glorieth, glory not in himself, but in the Lord,[5] and burst forth praise.

169. But as he hath now learned, and praised God his Teacher, he next wisheth to teach. "Yea, my tongue shall declare Thy word: for all Thy commandments are righteousness" (ver. 172). When he saith that he will declare these things, he becometh a minister of the word. For though God teach within, nevertheless "faith cometh from hearing: and how do they hear without a preacher?"[6] For, because "God

giveth the increase,"[7] is no reason why we need not plant and water.

170. "Let Thy hand be stretched forth (*fiat*, be made) to save me, for I have chosen Thy commandments" (ver. 173). That I might not fear, and that not only might my heart hold fast, but my tongue also utter Thy words: "I have chosen Thy commandments," and have stifled fear with love. Let Thy hand therefore be stretched forth, to save me from another's hand. Thus God saved the Martyrs, when He permitted them not to be slain in their souls: for "vain is the safety of man "[8] in the flesh. The words, "Let Thy hand be made," may also be taken to mean Christ the Hand of God. . . . Certainly where we read the following words, "I have longed for Thy salvation, O Lord" (ver. 174): even if all our foes be reluctant, let Christ the Salvation of God occur to us: the righteous men of old confess that they longed for Him, the Church longed for His destined coming from His mother's womb, the Church longeth for His coming at His Father's right hand. Subjoined to this sentence are the words, "And Thy law is my meditation:" for the Law giveth testimony unto Christ.

171. But in this faith, though the heathen rage furiously, and the people imagine a vain thing:[9] though the flesh be slain while it preacheth Thee: "My soul shall live, and shall praise Thee: and Thy judgments shall help me" (ver. 175). These are those judgments, which it was time should begin at the house of the Lord.[10] But "they will help me," he saith. And who cannot see how much the blood of the Church hath aided the Church? how great a harvest hath risen in the whole world from that sowing?

172. At last he openeth himself completely, and showeth what person was speaking throughout the whole Psalm. "I have gone astray," he saith, "like a sheep that is lost: O seek[11] Thy servant, for I do not forget Thy commandments" (ver. 176). Let the lost sheep be sought, let the lost sheep be quickened, for whose sake its Shepherd left the ninety and nine in the wilderness,[12] and while seeking it, was torn by Jewish thorns. But it is still being sought, let it still be sought, partly found let it still be sought. For as to that company, among whom the Psalmist saith, "I do not forget Thy commandments," it hath been found; but through those who choose the commandments of God,

---

[1] Ps. xxvii. 9. [2] Ps. xxxiv. 18. [3] Ps. xxxii. 8.
[4] John vi. 45; Rom. iv. 5. [5] 1 Cor. i. 31.
[6] Rom. x. 17, 14.

[7] 1 Cor. iii. 7.
[8] Ps. lx. 11.
[9] Ps. ii. 1.
[10] 1 Pet. iv. 17.
[11] [He says: "Some copies have not "seek," but "quicken." For there is a difference only of one syllable between the corresponding Greek words ζῆσον and ζήτησον: whence the Greek copies themselves derive the variation."—C.]
[12] Matt. xviii. 12, 13.

gather them together, love them, it is still sought, and by means of the blood of its Shepherd shed and sprinkled abroad, it is found in all nations.[1]

PSALM CXX.[2]

1. The Psalm which we have just heard chanted, and have responded to with our voices, is short, and very profitable. Ye will not long toil in hearing, nor will ye toil fruitlessly in working. For it is, according to the title prefixed to it, "A song of degrees."[3] Degrees are either of ascent or of descent. But degrees, as they are used in this Psalm, are of ascending. . . . There are therefore both those who ascend and those who descend on that ladder.[4] Who are they that ascend? They who progress towards the understanding of things spiritual. Who are they that descend? They who, although, as far as men may, they enjoy the comprehension of things spiritual: nevertheless, descend unto the infants, to say to them such things as they can receive, so that, after being nourished with milk, they may become fitted and strong enough to take spiritual meat. . . .

2. When therefore a man hath commenced thus to order his ascent; to speak more plainly, when a Christian hath begun to think of spiritual amendment, he beginneth to suffer the tongues of adversaries. Whoever hath not yet suffered from them, hath not yet made progress; whoever suffereth them not, doth not even endeavour to improve. Doth he wish to know what we mean? Let him at the same time experience what is reported of us. Let him begin to improve, let him begin to wish to ascend, to wish to despise earthly, fragile, temporal objects, to hold worldly happiness for nothing, to think of God alone, not to rejoice in gain, not to pine at losses, to wish even to sell all his substance, and distribute it among the poor, and to follow Christ; let us see how he suffereth the tongues of detractors and of constant opponents, and — a still greater peril — of pretended counsellors, who lead him astray from

salvation. . . . He then, who will ascend, first of all prayeth God against these very tongues: for he saith, "When I was in trouble, I called on the Lord; and He heard me" (ver. 1). Why did He hear him? That He might now place him at the steps of ascent.

3. "Deliver my soul, O Lord, from unrighteous lips, and from a deceitful tongue" (ver. 2). What is a deceitful tongue? A treacherous tongue, one that hath the semblance of counsel, and the bane of real mischief. Such are those who say, And wilt thou do this, that nobody doth? Wilt thou be the only Christian? . . . Some deter by dissuasion, others discourage yet more by their praise. For since such is the life that hath for some time been diffused over the world, so great is the authority of Christ, that not even a pagan ventureth to blame Christ.[5] He who cannot be censured is read. They cannot contradict Christ, they cannot contradict the Gospel, Christ cannot be censured; the deceitful tongue turneth itself to praise as an hindrance. If thou praisest, exhort. Why dost thou discourage with thy praise? . . . Thou turnest thyself to another mode of dissuasion, that by false praise thou mayest turn me away from true praise;[6] nay, that by praising Christ thou mayest keep me away from Christ, saying, What is this? Behold these men have done this: thou, perhaps, wilt not be able: thou beginnest to ascend, thou fallest. It seemeth to warn thee: it is the serpent, it is the deceitful tongue, it hath poison. Pray against it, if thou wishest to ascend.

4. And thy Lord saith unto thee, "What shall be given thee, or what shall be set before thee, against the deceitful tongue?" (ver. 3). What shall be given thee, that is, as a weapon to oppose to the deceitful tongue, to guard thyself against the deceitful tongue? "Or what shall be set before thee?" He asketh to try thee: for He will answer His own question. For He answers following up his own inquiry, "even sharp arrows of the Mighty One, with coals that desolate, or that lay waste" (ver. 4). They that desolate, or that lay waste (for it is variously written in different copies), are the same, because by laying waste, as ye may observe, they easily lead unto desolation. What are these coals? First, beloved brethren, understand what are arrows. The "sharp arrows of the Mighty One," are the words of God. . . . What then are the "coals that lay waste?" It is not enough to plead with words against a deceitful tongue and unrighteous lips: it is not enough to plead with words; we must plead with examples also. . . . The word coals, then, is used to express the examples of many sinners converted to the Lord. Thou

---

[1] [He adds: "As far as I have been able, as far as I have been aided by the Lord, I have treated throughout, and expounded, this great Psalm, — a task which more able and learned expositors have performed or will perform better; nevertheless, my services were not to be withheld from it on that account, when my brethren earnestly required it of me, to whom I owed this office. That I have said nothing of the Hebrew alphabet, in which every eight verses are ranged under a particular letter, and the whole Psalm arranged in this manner, let no one wonder, since I found nothing that related especially to this Psalm: for it is not the only one which hath these letters. Let those who cannot find it in the Latin and Greek versions, since it is not adopted there, know that every set of eight verses in the Hebrew copies beginneth with that letter which is prefixed to them; as is indicated to us by those who are acquainted with the Hebrew tongue. This is done with much more care than our writers have shown in their Latin or Punic compositions of Psalms which they style *abecedarii*. For they do not begin all the verses down to the close of a period, but the first only with the same letter which they prefix to it." It was the counsel of the learned general editor to drop this Psalm entirely. For the sake of preserving the symmetry of the work, I have retained as much as I could. — C.]

[2] Lat. CXIX.   [3] In Greek it is written ἀναβαθμῶν.
[4] Gen. xxviii. 12.

[5] [Noteworthy. — C.]
[6] [The stratagem of those who glorify Jesus as a man, to deny His true character as Christ. — C.]

hearest men wonder, and say, I knew that man, how addicted he was to drinking, what a villain, what a lover of the circus, or of the amphitheatre, what a cheat: now how he serveth God, how innocent he hath become! Wonder not; he is a live coal. Thou rejoicest that he is alive, whom thou wast mourning as dead. But when thou praisest the living, if thou knowest how to praise, apply him to the dead, that he may be inflamed; whosoever is still slow to follow God, apply to him the coal which was extinguished, and have the arrow of God's word, and the coal that layeth waste, that thou mayest meet the deceitful tongue and the lying lips.

5. "Alas, that my sojourning is become far off!" (ver. 5). It hath departed far from Thee: my pilgrimage hath become a far one. I have not yet reached that country, where I shall live with no wicked person; I have not yet reached that company of Angels, where I shall not fear offences. But why am I not as yet there? Because sojourning is pilgrimage. He is called a sojourner who dwells in a foreign land, not in his own country. And when is it far off? Sometimes, my brethren, when a man goeth abroad, he liveth among better persons, than he would perhaps live with in his own country: but it is not thus, when we go afar from that heavenly Jerusalem. For a man changeth his country, and this foreign sojourn is sometimes good for him; in travelling he findeth faithful friends, whom he could not find in his own country. He had enemies, so that he was driven from his country; and when he travelled, he found what he had not in his country. Such is not that country Jerusalem, where all are good: whoever travelleth away from thence, is among the evil; nor can he depart from the wicked, save when he shall return to the company of Angels, so as to be where he was before he travelled. There all are righteous and holy, who enjoy the word of God without reading, without letters: for what is written to us through pages,[1] they perceive there through the Face of God. What a country! A great country indeed, and wretched are the wanderers from that country.

6. But what he saith, "My pilgrimage hath been made distant," are the words of those, that is, of the Church herself, who toileth on this earth. It is her voice, which crieth out from the ends of the earth in another Psalm, saying, "From the ends of the earth have I cried unto Thee.[2] . . . Where then doth he groan, and among whom doth he dwell? "I have had my habitation among the tents of Kedar." Since this is a Hebrew word, beyond doubt ye have not understood it. What meaneth, "I have

had my habitation among the tents of Kedar"? "Kedar," as far as we remember of the interpretation of Hebrew words, signifieth darkness. "Kedar" rendered into Latin is called *tenebræ*. Now ye know that Abraham had two sons, whom indeed the Apostle mentioneth,[3] and declareth them to have been types of the two covenants. . . . Ishmael therefore was in darkness, Isaac in light. Whoever here also seek earthly felicity in the Church, from God, shall belong to Ishmael. These are the very persons who gainsay the spiritual ones who are progressing, and detract from them, and have deceitful tongues and unrighteous lips. Against these the Psalmist, when ascending, prayed, and hot coals that lay waste, and swift and sharp arrows of the Mighty One, were given him for his defence. For among these he still liveth, until the whole floor be winnowed: he therefore said, "I have dwelt among the tents of Kedar." The tents of Ishmael are called those of Kedar. Thus the book of Genesis hath it: thus it hath, that Kedar belongeth unto Ishmael.[4] Isaac therefore is with Ishmael: that is, they who belong unto Isaac, live among those who belong unto Ishmael.[5] These wish to rise above, those wish to press them downwards: these wish to fly unto God, those endeavour to pluck their wings. . . .

7. "My soul hath wandered much" (ver. 6). Lest thou shouldest understand bodily wandering, he hath said that the soul wandered. The body wandereth in places, the soul wandereth in its affections. If thou love the earth, thou wanderest from God: if thou lovest God, thou risest unto God. Let us be exercised in the love of God, and of our neighbour, that we may return unto charity. If we fall towards the earth, we wither and decay. But one descended unto this one who had fallen, in order that he might arise. Speaking of the time of his wandering, he said that he wandered in the tents of Kedar. Wherefore? Because "my soul hath wandered much." He wandereth there where he ascendeth. He wandereth not in the body, he riseth not in the body. But wherein doth he ascend? "The ascent," he saith, "is in the heart."[6]

8. "With them that hated peace, I was peaceful" (ver. 7). But howsoever ye may hear, most beloved brethren, ye will not be able to prove how truly ye sing, unless ye have begun to do that which ye sing. How much soever I say this, in whatsoever ways I may expound it, in whatsoever words I may turn it, it entereth not into the heart of him in whom its operation is not. Begin to act, and see what we speak. Then tears flow forth at each word, then the Psalm is sung, and the heart doeth what is sung in the Psalm. . . .

---

[1] [See p. 512, note 4, *supra.*—C.] [2] Ps. lxi. 2.

[3] Gal. iv. 22, etc.   [4] Gen. xxv. 13.   [5] Gal. iv. 29.
[6] Ps. lxxxiv. 5.

Who are they who hate peace? They who tear asunder unity. For had they not hated peace, they would have abode in unity. But they separated themselves, forsooth on this account, that they might be righteous, that they might not have the ungodly mixed with them. These words are either ours or theirs: decide whose. The Catholic Church saith, Unity must not be lost, the Church of God must not be cut off.[1] God will judge afterwards of the wicked and the good. . . . This we also say: Love ye peace, love ye Christ. For if they love peace, they love Christ. When therefore we say, Love ye peace, we say this, Love ye Christ. Wherefore? For the Apostle saith of Christ, "He is our peace, who hath made both one."[2] If Christ is therefore peace, because He hath made both one: why have ye made two of one? How then are ye peace-makers, if, when Christ maketh one of two, ye make two of one? But since we say these things, we are peace-makers with them that hate peace; and yet they who hate peace, when we spake to them, made war on us for nought.

PSALM CXXI.[3]

1. . . . Let them "lift up their eyes to the hills, whence cometh their help" (ver. 1). What meaneth, The hills have been lightened? The Sun of righteousness hath already risen, the Gospel hath been already preached by the Apostles, the Scriptures have been preached, all the mysteries have been laid open, the veil hath been rent, the secret place of the temple hath been revealed: let them now at length lift their eyes up to the hills, whence their help cometh. . . . "Of His fulness have all we received,"[4] he saith. Thy help therefore is from Him, of whose fulness the hills received, not from the hills;[5] towards which,[6] nevertheless, save thou lift thine eyes through the Scriptures, thou wilt not approach, so as to be lighted by Him.[7]

2. Sing therefore what followeth; if thou wish to hear how thou mayest most securely set thy feet on the steps, so that thou mayest not be fatigued in that ascent, nor stumble and fall: pray in these words: "Suffer not my foot to be moved!" (ver. 3). Whereby are feet moved; whereby

was the foot of him who was in Paradise moved? But first consider whereby the feet of him who was among the Angels were moved: who when his feet were moved fell, and from an Angel became a devil: for when his feet were moved he fell. Seek whereby he fell: he fell through pride. Nothing then moveth the feet, save pride: nothing moveth the feet to a fall, save pride. Charity moveth them to walk and to improve and to ascend; pride moveth them to fall. . . . Rightly therefore the Psalmist, hearing how he may ascend and may not fall, prayeth unto God that he may profit from the vale of misery, and may not fail in the swelling of pride, in these words, "Suffer not my feet to be moved!" And He replieth unto him, "Let him that keepeth thee not sleep." Attend, my beloved. It is as if one thought were expressed in two sentences; the man while ascending and singing "the song of degrees," saith, "Suffer not my foot to be moved:" and it is as if God answered, Thou sayest unto Me, Let not my feet be moved: say also, "Let Him that keepeth thee not sleep," and thy foot shall not be moved.

3. Choose for thyself Him, who will neither sleep nor slumber, and thy foot shall not be moved. God is never asleep: if thou dost wish to have a keeper who never sleepeth, choose God for thy keeper. "Suffer not my feet to be moved," thou sayest: well, very well: but He also saith unto thee, "Let not him that keepeth thee slumber." Thou perhaps wast about to turn thyself unto men as thy keepers, and to say, whom shall I find who will not sleep? what man will not slumber? whom do I find? whither shall I go? whither shall I return? The Psalmist telleth thee: "He that keepeth Israel, shall neither slumber nor sleep" (ver. 4). Dost thou wish to have a keeper who neither slumbereth nor sleepeth? Behold, "He that keepeth Israel shall neither slumber nor sleep:" for Christ keepeth Israel. Be thou then Israel. What meaneth Israel? It is interpreted, Seeing God. And how is God seen? First by faith: afterwards by sight. If thou canst not as yet see Him by sight, see Him by faith. . . . Who is there, who will neither slumber nor sleep? when thou seekest among men, thou art deceived; thou wilt never find one. Trust not then in any man: every man slumbereth, and will sleep. When doth he slumber? When he beareth the flesh of weakness. When will he sleep? When he is dead. Trust not then in man. A mortal may slumber, he sleepeth in death. Seek not a keeper among men.

4. And who, thou askest, shall help me, save He who slumbereth not, nor sleepeth? Hear what followeth: "The Lord Himself is thy keeper" (ver. 5). It is not therefore man, that slumbereth and sleepeth, but the Lord, that

[1] [Unity on Nicene Constitutions, not those of the Decretals. Augustin himself, to maintain unity, refused communion with the See of Rome, and died in that position. — C.]

[2] Eph. ii. 14.

[3] Lat. CXX. A sermon to the people on the day of St. Crispina.

[4] John i. 16.

[5] Here some earlier editions, as quoted by Ben., add, "Christ, the Son of the supreme Father, is therefore our salvation, and our help, and with the same Father He is God Almighty, and with Him ever abiding in respect of that He is. To those mountains, therefore, which I have mentioned, if thou lift not up thine eyes." There are several other additions in the commentary on his Psalm, which however seem scarcely worthy of St. Augustin, and for which no MS. authority is given.

[6] Al. "by which thou wilt not be admonished"

[7] [Familiarity with Scripture is the Catholic principle, here everywhere presupposed. — C.]

keepeth thee. How doth He keep thee? "The Lord is thy defence upon the hand of thy right hand." . . . It seemeth to me to have a hidden sense: otherwise he would have simply said, without qualification, "The Lord will keep thee," without adding, "on thy right hand." For how? Doth God keep our right hand, and not our left? Did He not create the whole of us? Did not He who made our right hand, make our left hand also? Finally, if it pleased Him to speak of the right hand alone, why said He, "on the hand of thy right hand," and not at once "upon thy right hand"? Why should He say this, unless He were keeping somewhat here hidden for us to arrive at by knocking? For He would either say, "The Lord shall keep thee," and add no more; or if He would add the right hand, "The Lord shall keep thee upon thy right hand;" or at least, as He added "hand," He would say, "The Lord shall keep thee upon thy hand, even thy right hand," [1] not "upon the hand of thy right hand." . . .

5. I ask you, how ye interpret what is said in the Gospel, "Let not your left hand know what your right hand doeth"? [2] For if ye understand this, ye will discover what is your right hand, and what is your left: at the same time ye will also understand that God made both hands, the left and the right; yet the left ought not to know what the right doeth. By our left hand is meant all that we have in a temporal way; by our right hand is meant, whatever our Lord promiseth us that is immutable and eternal. But if He who will give everlasting life, Himself also consoleth our present life by these temporal blessings, He hath Himself made our right hand and our left. . . .

6. Let us now come to this verse of the Psalm: "The Lord is thy defence upon the hand of thy right hand" (ver. 5). By hand he meaneth power. How do we prove this? Because the power of God also is styled the hand of God. . . . Whereof John saith, "He gave unto them power to become the sons of God." [3] Whence hast thou received this power? "To them," he saith, "that believe in His Name." If then thou believest, this very power is given thee, to be among the sons of God. But to be among the sons of God, is to belong to the right hand. Thy faith therefore is the hand of thy right hand: that is, the power that is given thee, to be among the sons of God, is the hand of thy right hand. . . .

7. "May the Lord shield thee upon the hand of thy right hand" (ver. 6). I have said, and I believe ye have recognised it. For had ye not recognised it, and that from the Scriptures, ye would not signify your understanding of it by your voices. [4] Since then ye have understood, brethren, consider what followeth; wherefore the Lord shieldeth thee "upon the hand of thy right hand," that is, in thy faith, wherein we have received "power to become the sons of God," and to be on His right hand: wherefore should God shield us? On account of offences. Whence come offences? Offences are to be feared from two quarters, for there are two precepts upon which the whole Law hangeth and the Prophets, the love of God and of our neighbour. [5] The Church is loved for the sake of our neighbour, but God for the sake of God. Of God, is understood the sun figuratively: of the Church, is understood the moon figuratively. Whoever can err, so as to think otherwise of God than he ought, believing not the Father and the Son and the Holy Ghost to be of one Substance, has been deceived by the cunning of heretics, chiefly of the Arians. If he hath believed anything less in the Son or in the Holy Spirit than in the Father, he hath suffered an offence in God; he is scorched by the sun. Whoever again believeth that the Church existeth in one province only, [6] and not that she is diffused over the whole world, and whoso believeth them that say, "Lo here," and "Lo there, is Christ," [7] as ye but now heard when the Gospel was being read; since He who gave so great a price, purchased the whole world: he is offended, so to speak, in his neighbour, and is burnt by the moon. Whoever therefore erreth in the very Substance of Truth, is burnt by the sun, and is burnt through the day; because he erreth in Wisdom itself. . . . God therefore hath made one sun, which riseth upon the good and the evil, that sun which the good and the evil see; but that Sun is another one, not created, not born, through whom all things were made; [8] where is the intelligence of the Immutable Truth: of this the ungodly say, "the Sun rose not upon us." [9] Whosoever erreth not in Wisdom itself, is not burnt by the sun. Whosoever erreth not in the Church, and in the Lord's Flesh, and in those things which were done for us in time, is not burnt by the moon. But every man although he believeth in Christ, erreth either in this or that respect, unless what is here prayed for, "The Lord is thy defence upon the hand of

---

[1] *Manum dexteram.*   [2] Matt. vi. 3.   [3] John i. 12.

[4] [See p. 418, note 8, *supra.*—C.]   [5] Matt. xxii. 37-40.
[6] Donatists. [So in the Roman province, as asserted by the modern dogma of the Trent schism. A. N. F. vol. viii. p. 643.—C.]
[7] Matt. xxiv. 23.   [8] Nicene Creed.
[9] Wisd. v. 6.   Here old editions add: "of this Sun Father Athanasius, the Bishop, hath thus beautifully spoken. 'The Son of God,' he saith, 'is of the Father alone, neither made, nor created, but begotten;'" whence Possevinus, Torrensis, and Bellarmine have quoted St. Augustin as assigning the Athanasian Creed to St. Athanasius. But Petavius, *Theol. Dogm. de Trin.* l. vii. c. 8, note 7, says the words have been foisted into St. Augustin, and in fact they are not in any of our mss. nor in the editions of Amsterdam, of Erasmus, and of Louvain.—*Ben.* Some other additions are mentioned in the Benedictine notes on this Psalm, but they seem of later date than St. Augustin.

thy right hand," is realized in him. He goeth on to say, "So that the sun shall not burn thee by day, nor the moon by night" (ver. 6). Thy defence, therefore, is upon the hand of thy right hand for this reason, that the sun may not burn thee by day, nor the moon by night. Understand hence, brethren, that it is spoken figuratively. For, in truth, if we think of the visible sun, it burneth by day: doth the moon burn by night? But what is burning? Offence. Hear the Apostle's words: "Who is weak, and I am not weak? who is offended, and I burn not?"[1]

8. "For the Lord shall preserve thee from all evil" (ver. 7). From offences in the sun, from offences in the moon, from all evil shall He preserve thee, who is thy defence upon the hand of thy right hand, who will not sleep nor slumber. And for what reason? Because we are amid temptations: "The Lord shall preserve thee from all evil. The Lord preserve thy soul:" even thy very soul. "The Lord preserve thy going out and thy coming in, from this time forth for evermore" (ver. 8). Not thy body; for the Martyrs were consumed in the body: but "the Lord preserve thy soul;" for the Martyrs yielded not up their souls. The persecutors raged against Crispina,[2] whose birthday we are to-day celebrating; they were raging against a rich and delicate woman: but she was strong, for the Lord was her defence upon the hand of her right hand. He was her Keeper. Is there any one in Africa, my brethren, who knoweth her not? For she was most illustrious, noble in birth, abounding in wealth: but all these things were in her left hand, beneath her head. An enemy advanced to strike her head, and the left hand was presented to him, which was under her head. Her head was above, the right hand embraced her from above.[3] . . .

PSALM CXXII.[4]

1. As impure love inflames the mind, and summons the soul destined to perish to lust for earthly things, and to follow what is perishable, and precipitates it into lowest places, and sinks it into the abyss; so holy love raiseth us to heavenly things, and inflames us to what is eternal, and excites the soul to those things which do not pass away nor die, and from the abyss of hell raiseth it to heaven. Yet all love hath a power of its own, nor can love in the soul

of the lover be idle; it must needs draw it on. But dost thou wish to know of what sort love is? See whither it leadeth. . . .

2. This Psalm is a "Song of degrees;"[5] as we have often said to you, for these degrees[6] are not of descent, but of ascent. He therefore longeth to ascend. And whither doth he wish to ascend, save into heaven? What meaneth, into heaven? Doth he wish to ascend that he may be with the sun, moon, and stars? Far be it! But there is in heaven the eternal Jerusalem, where are our fellow-citizens, the Angels: we are wanderers on earth from these our fellow-citizens. We sigh in our pilgrimage; we shall rejoice in the city. But we find companions in this pilgrimage, who have already seen this city herself; who summon us to run towards her. At these he also rejoiceth, who saith, "I rejoiced in them who said unto me, We will go into the house of the Lord" (ver. 1). . . .

3. "Our feet were standing in the courts of Jerusalem" (ver. 2). . . . Consider what thou wilt be there; and although thou art as yet on the road, place this before thine eyes, as if thou wert already standing, as if thou wert already rejoicing without ceasing among the Angels; as if that which is written were realized in thee: "Blessed are they that dwell in Thy house; they will be alway praising Thee."[7] "Our feet stood in the courts of Jerusalem." What Jerusalem? This earthly Jerusalem also is wont to be called by the name: though this Jerusalem is but the shadow of that. And what great thing is it to stand in this Jerusalem, since this Jerusalem hath not been able to stand, but hath been turned into a ruin? Doth then the Holy Spirit pronounce this, out of the kindled heart of the loving Psalmist, as a great thing? Is not it that Jerusalem, unto whom the Lord said, "O Jerusalem, Jerusalem, thou that killest the Prophets," etc.[8] What great thing then did he desire; to stand among those who slew the Prophets, and stoned them that were sent unto them? God forbid that he should think of that Jerusalem, who so loveth, who so burneth, who so longeth to reach that Jerusalem, "our Mother,"[9] of which the Apostle saith, that She is "eternal in the Heavens."[10]

4. "Jerusalem that is being built as a city" (ver. 3). Brethren, when David was uttering these words, that city had been finished, it was not being built. It is some city he speaketh of, therefore, which is now being built, unto which living stones run in faith, of whom Peter saith, "Ye also, as lively stones, are built up a spiritual house;"[11] that is, the holy temple of God. What meaneth, ye are built up as lively stones? Thou

---

[1] 2 Cor. xi. 29.   [2] St. Crispina.
[3] Song of Sol. ii. 6. [He thus concludes: "Although the Psalm is short, yet our exposition and discourse on it hath been long. Imagine, my brethren, that owing to the birthday of the blessed Crispina I have invited you, and have been immoderate in protracting the banquet. Might not this have happened to you, if any military officer had invited you, and compel you to drink at his table without measure? May it be lawful for us to do this in a sacred exposition, that ye may be inebriated and satisfied to the full."—C.]
[4] Lat. CXXI. A discourse to the common people.

[5] See on Ps. xxxix. p. 112, and on Ps. cxx. p. 589.
[6] Or, "steps."   [7] Ps. lxxxiv. 4.   [8] Matt. xxiii. 37.
[9] Gal. iv. 26.   [10] 2 Cor. v. 1.   [11] 1 Pet. ii. 5.

livest, if thou believest : but if thou believest, thou art made a temple of God ; for the Apostle Paul saith, "The temple of God is holy, which temple are ye." [1] This city is therefore now in building ; stones are cut down from the hills by the hands of those who preach truth, they are squared that they may enter into an everlasting structure. There are still many stones in the hands of the Builder : let them not fall from His hands, that they may be built perfect into the structure of the temple. This, then, is the "Jerusalem that is being built as a city :" Christ is its foundation. The Apostle Paul saith, "Other foundation can no man lay than that is laid, which is Christ Jesus." [2] When a foundation is laid on earth, the walls are built above, and the weight of the walls tends towards the lowest parts, because the foundation is laid at the bottom. But if our foundation be in heaven, let us be built towards heaven. Bodies have built the edifice of this basilica, [3] the ample size of which ye see ; and since bodies have built it, they placed the foundation lowest : but since we are spiritually built, our foundation is placed at the highest point. Let us therefore run thither, where we may be built. . . . But what Jerusalem do I speak of? Is it that, he asketh, which ye see standing, raised on the structure of its walls? No ; but the "Jerusalem which is being built as a city." Why not, a city, instead of, "as a city ;" save because those walls, so built in Jerusalem, were a visible city, as it is by all called a city, literally ; but this is being built "as a city," for they who enter it are like living stones ; for they are not literally stones? Just as they are called stones, and yet are not so : so the city styled "as a city," is not a city ; for he said, "is being built." For by the word building, he meant to be understood the structure, and cohesion of bodies and walls. For a city [4] is properly understood of the men that inhabit there. But in saying "is building," he showed us that he meant a town. And since a spiritual building hath some resemblance to a bodily building, therefore it "is building as a city."

5. But let the following words remove all doubt that we ought not to understand carnally the words, "Whose partaking is in the same." [5] . . . What meaneth, "the same"? What is ever in the same state ; not what is now in one state, now in another. What then is, "the same," save that which is? What is that which is? That which is everlasting. . . . Behold "The Same : I AM THAT I AM, I AM." Thou canst not understand ; it is much to understand, it is much to apprehend. Remember what He,

whom thou canst not comprehend, became for thee. Remember the flesh of Christ, towards which thou wast raised when sick, and when left half dead from the wounds of robbers, that thou mightest be brought to the Inn, and there mightest be cured. [6] Let us therefore run unto the Lord's house, and reach the city where our feet may stand ; the city "that is building as a city : whose partaking is in The Same." . . .

6. That city "which partaketh in the same," partaketh in its stability : justly therefore, since he is made a sharer in its stability, saith he who runneth thither. For all things there stand where nought passeth by. Dost thou too wish to stand there and not to pass by? Run thither. Nobody hath "the same" from himself. . . .

7. "For thither the tribes went up " (ver. 4). We were asking whither he ascendeth who hath fallen ; for we said, it is the voice of a man who is ascending, of the Church rising. Can we tell whither it ascendeth? whither it goeth? whither it is raised? "Thither," he saith, "the tribes went up." Whither? To "partaking in the Same." But what are the tribes? Many know, many know not. For if we use the word "curies" in its proper sense, we understand nothing, save the "curies" which exist in each particular city, whence the terms "curiales" and "decuriones," that is, the citizens of a curia or a decuria ;' and ye know that each city hath such curies. But there are, or were at one time, curies of the people in those cities, and one city hath many curies, as Rome hath thirty-five curies of the people. [7] These are called tribes. The people of Israel had twelve of these, according to the sons of Jacob.

8. There were twelve tribes of the people of Israel : but there were good, and there were bad among them. For how evil were those tribes which crucified our Lord ! How good those who recognised the Lord ! Those tribes then who crucified the Lord, were tribes of the devil. When therefore he here said, "For thither the tribes go up ;" that thou mightest not understand all the tribes, he added, "even the tribes of the Lord." . . . What are the tribes of the Lord? "A testimony unto Israel." Hear, brethren, what this meaneth. "A testimony to Israel :" that is, whereby it may be known that it is truly Israel. . . . He is such in whom there is no guile. And what did the Lord say, when He saw Nathanael? "Behold an Israelite indeed, in whom is no guile." [8] If therefore he is a true Israelite, in whom there is no guile, those tribes go up to Jerusalem, in whom there is no guile.

---

[1] 1 Cor. iii. 17.   [2] 1 Cor. iii. 11.
[3] [Note this proof of the costly Christian architecture of this age. The *Basilica*, however, was originally an imperial court turned into a church. — C.]
[4] *Civitas*.   [5] *In id ipsum*.

[6] Luke x. 30, 34.
[7] Thirty, according to Liv. i. 13, Cic. *De Rep.* ii. 8; thirty-five afterwards, according to Sext. Pomp. in v. *Curia*, who seems to confound them with the "Tribes." See Pollet, *Hist. For. Rom.* in *Poleni Supplem.* t. i. p. 516.
[8] John i. 47.

. . . Wherefore do they go up? "To confess unto Thy Name, O Lord." It could not be more nobly expressed. As pride presumeth, so doth humility confess. As he is a presumer, who wishes to appear what he is not, so is he a confessor, who does not wish that to be seen which himself is, and loves That which He is. To this therefore do Israelites go up, in whom is no guile, because they are truly Israelites, because in them is the testimony of Israel.

9. "For there were seated seats for judgment" (ver. 5). This is a wonderful riddle, a wonderful question, if it be not understood. He calleth those seats, which the Greeks call thrones. The Greeks call chairs thrones, as a term of honour. Therefore, my brethren, it is not wonderful if even we should sit on seats, or chairs; but that these seats themselves should sit, when shall we be able to understand this? As if some one should say: let stools or chairs sit here. We sit on chairs, we sit on seats, we sit on stools; the seats themselves sit not. What then meaneth this, "For there were seated seats for judgment"? . . . If therefore heaven be the seat of God, and the Apostles are heaven; they themselves are become the seat of God, the throne of God. It is said in another passage:[1] "The soul of the righteous is the throne of wisdom." A great truth, a great truth, is declared; the throne of wisdom is the soul of the righteous; that is, wisdom sitteth in the soul of the righteous as it were in her chair, in her throne, and thence judgeth whatsoever she judgeth. There were therefore thrones of wisdom, and therefore the Lord said unto them, "Ye shall sit upon twelve thrones, judging the twelve tribes of Israel."[2] So they also shall sit upon twelve seats, and they are themselves the seats of God; for of them it is said, "For there were seated seats." Who sat? "Seats." And who are the seats? They of whom it is said, "The soul of the righteous is the seat of wisdom." Who are the seats? The heavens. Who are the heavens? Heaven. What is heaven? That of which the Lord saith, "Heaven is My seat."[3] The righteous then themselves are the seats; and have seats; and seats shall be seated in that Jerusalem. For what purpose? "For judgment." Ye shall sit, He saith, on twelve thrones, O ye thrones, judging the twelve tribes of Israel. Judging whom? Those who are below on earth. Who will judge? They who have become heaven. But they who shall be judged, will be divided into two bodies: one will be on the right hand, the other on the left. . . .

10. He at once addeth, as unto the seats them-selves, "Enquire ye the things that are for the peace of Jerusalem" (ver. 6). O ye seats, who now sit unto judgment, and are made the seats of the Lord who judgeth (since they who judge, enquire; they who are judged, are enquired of), "Enquire ye," he saith, "the things that are for the peace of Jerusalem." What will they find by asking? That some have done deeds of charity, that others have not. Those whom they shall find to have done deeds of charity, they will summon them unto Jerusalem; for these deeds are "for the peace of Jerusalem." Love is a powerful thing, my brethren, love is a pow-erful thing. Do ye wish to see how powerful a thing love is? . . . If charity be destitute of means, so that it cannot find what to bestow upon the poor, let it love: let it give "one cup of cold water;"[4] as much shall be laid to its account, as to Zaccheus who gave half his patrimony to the poor.[5] Wherefore this? The one gave so little, the other so much, and shall so much be imputed to the former? Just so much. For though his resources are unequal, his charity is not unequal.

11. . . . "And plenteousness," he addeth, "for them that love thee." He addresses Jerusalem herself, They have plenteousness who love her. Plenteousness after want: here they are desti-tute, there they are affluent; here they are weak, there they are strong; here they want, there they are rich. How have they become rich? Because they gave here what they received from God for a season, and received there what God will afterwards pay back for evermore. Here, my brethren, even rich men are poor. It is a good thing for a rich man to acknowledge him-self poor: for if he think himself full, that is mere puffing, not plenteousness. Let him own himself empty, that he may be filled. What hath he? Gold. What hath he not yet? Ever-lasting life. Let him consider what he hath, and see what he hath not. Brethren, of that which he hath, let him give, that he may receive what he hath not; let him purchase out of that which he hath, that which he hath not, "and plen-teousness for them that love thee."

12. "Peace be in thy strength" (ver. 7). O Jerusalem, O city, who art being built as a city, whose partaking is in "The Same:" "Peace be in thy strength:" peace be in thy love; for thy strength is thy love. Hear the Song of songs: "Love is strong as death."[6] A great saying that, brethren, "Love is strong as death." The strength of charity could not be expressed in grander terms than these, "Love is strong as death."[6] For who resisteth death, my brethren? Consider, my brethren. Fire, waves, the sword, are resisted: we resist principalities, we resist

---

1 [See p. 475, note 6. References there do not satisfy the Oxford editor, and here he puts a mark of inquiry; thus, " —?"—C.]
2 Matt. xix. 28.   3 Isa. lxvi. 1.

4 Matt. x. 42.   5 Luke xix. 8.   6 Cant. viii. 6.

kings; death cometh alone, who resisteth it? There is nought more powerful than it. Charity therefore is compared with its strength, in the words, "Love is strong as death." And since this love slayeth what we have been, that we may be what we were not; love createth a sort of death in us. This death he had died who said, "The world is crucified unto me, and I unto the world:"[1] this death they had died unto whom he said, "Ye are dead, and your life is hid with Christ in God."[2] Love is strong as death. . . .

13. Thus as he was here speaking of charity, he addeth, "For my brethren and companions' sake, I spoke peace of thee" (ver. 8). O Jerusalem, thou city whose partaking is in The SAME, I in this life and on this earth, I poor, he saith, I a stranger and groaning, not as yet enjoying to the full thy peace, and preaching thy peace; preach it not for my own sake, as the heretics, who seeking their own glory, say, Peace be with you: and have not the peace which they preach to the people. For if they had peace, they would not tear asunder unity. "I," he saith, "spoke peace of thee." But wherefore? "For my brethren and companions' sake:" not for my own honour, not for my own money, not for my life; for, "To me to live is Christ, and to die is gain." But, "I spoke peace of thee, for my brethren and companions' sakes." For he wished to depart, and to be with Christ: but, since he must preach these things to his companions and his brethren, to abide in the flesh, he addeth, is more needful for you.[3]

14. "Because of the house of the Lord my God, I have sought good things for thee" (ver. 9). Not on my own account have sought good things, for then I should not seek for thee, but for myself; and so should I not have them, because I should not seek them for thee; but, "Because of the house of the Lord my God," because of the Church, because of the Saints, because of the pilgrims; because of the poor, that they may go up; because we say to them, we will go into the house of the Lord: because of the house of the Lord my God itself, I have sought good things for Thee. These long and needful words gather ye, brethren, eat them, drink them, and grow strong, run, and seize.

PSALM CXXIII.[4]

1. . . . Let this singer ascend; and let this man sing from the heart of each of you, and let each of you be this man, for when each of you saith this, since ye are all one in Christ, one man saith this; and saith not, "Unto Thee, O Lord, have" we "lift up" our "eyes;" but, "Unto Thee, O Lord, have I lift up mine eyes" (ver. 1). Ye ought indeed to imagine that every one of you is speaking; but that One in an especial sense speaketh, who is also spread abroad over the whole world. . . .

What maketh the heart of a Christian heavy? Because he is a pilgrim, and longeth for his country. If thy heart be heavy on this score, although thou hast been prosperous in the world, still thou dost groan: and if all things combine to render thee prosperous, and this world smile upon thee on every side, thou nevertheless groanest, because thou seest that thou art set in a pilgrimage; and feelest that thou hast indeed happiness in the eyes of fools, but not as yet after the promise of Christ: this thou seekest with groans, this thou seekest with longings, and by longing ascendest, and while thou ascendest dost sing the Song of Degrees.

2. . . . Where then are the ladders? For we behold so great an interval between heaven and earth, there is so wide a separation, and so great a space of regions between: we wish to climb thither, we see no ladder; do we deceive ourselves, because we sing the Song of Degrees, that is, the Song of ascent? We ascend unto heaven, if we think of God, who hath made ascending steps in the heart. What is to ascend in heart? To advance towards God. As every man who faileth, doth not descend, but falleth: so every one who profiteth doth ascend: but if he so profit, as to avoid pride: if he so ascend as not to fall: but if while he profiteth he become proud, in ascending he again falleth. But that he may not be proud, what ought he to do? Let him lift up his eyes unto Him who dwelleth in heaven, let him not heed himself. . . .

3. If, my brethren, we understand by heaven the firmament which we see with our bodily eyes, we shall indeed so err, as to imagine that we cannot ascend thither without ladders, or some scaling machines: but if we ascend spiritually, we ought to understand heaven spiritually: if the ascent be in affection, heaven is in righteousness. What is then the heaven of God? All holy souls, all righteous souls. For the Apostles also, although they were on earth in the flesh, were heaven; for the Lord, enthroned in them, traversed the whole world. He then dwelleth in heaven. How? . . . How long are they the temple according to faith? As long as Christ dwelleth in them through faith; as the Apostle saith, "That Christ may dwell in your hearts through faith." But they are already heaven in whom God already dwelleth visibly, who see Him face to face; all the holy Apostles, all the holy Virtues, Powers, Thrones, Lordships, that heavenly Jerusalem, wanderers from whence we groan, and for which we pray with longing; and there God dwelleth. Thither hath the Psalmist

---

[1] Gal. vi. 14. [2] Col. iii. 3. [3] Philip. i. 21, 23, 24.
[4] Lat. CXXII. [On " Degrees," see p. 593, *supra*. — C.]

lifted up his faith, thither he riseth in affection, with longing hopes : and this very longing causeth the soul to purge off[1] the filth of sins, and to be cleansed from every stain, that itself also may become heaven ; because it hath lifted up its eyes unto Him who dwelleth in heaven. For if we have determined that that heaven which we see with our bodily eyes is the dwelling of God, the dwelling of God will pass away ; for " heaven and earth will pass away."[2] Then, before God created heaven and earth, where did He dwell? But some one saith : and before God made the Saints, where did He dwell? God dwelt in Himself, he dwelt with Himself, and God is with Himself. And when He deigneth to dwell in the Saints, the Saints are not the house of God in such wise, as that God should fall when it is withdrawn. For we dwell in a house in one way, in another way God dwelleth in the Saints. Thou dwellest in a house : if it be withdrawn, thou fallest : but God so dwelleth in the Saints, that if He should Himself depart, they fall. . . .

4. What then followeth, since he hath said, "Unto Thee do I lift up mine eyes "? (ver. 2). How hast thou lifted up thine eyes? "Behold, even as the eyes of servants look unto the hand of their masters, and as the eyes of a maiden unto the hand of her mistress : even so our eyes wait upon the Lord our God, until He have mercy upon us." We are both servants, and a hand-maiden : He is both our Master and our Mistress. What do these words mean? What do these similitudes mean? It is not wonderful if we are servants, and He our Master ; but it is wonderful if we are a maiden, and He our Mistress. But not even our being a maiden is wonderful ; for we are the Church : nor is it wonderful that He is our Mistress ; for He is the Power and the Wisdom of God. . . . When therefore thou hearest Christ, lift up thine eyes to the hands of thy Master ; when thou hearest the Power of God and the Wisdom of God, lift up thine eyes to the hands of thy Mistress ; for thou art both servant and handmaiden ; servant, for thou art a people ;[3] handmaiden,[4] for thou art the Church. But this maiden hath found great dignity with God ; she hath been made a wife. But until she come unto those spiritual embraces, where she may without apprehension enjoy Him whom she hath loved, and for whom she hath sighed in this tedious pilgrimage, she is betrothed : and hath received a mighty pledge, the blood of the Spouse for whom she sigheth without fear. Nor is it said unto her, Do not love ; as it is sometimes said to any betrothed virgin, not as yet married : and is justly said, Do not love ; when thou hast become a wife, then love : it is rightly said, because it is a pre-

cipitate and preposterous thing, and not a chaste desire, to love one whom she knoweth not whether she shall marry. For it may happen that one man may be betrothed to her, and another man marry her. But as there is no one else who can be preferred to Christ, let her love without apprehension : and before she is joined unto Him, let her love, and sigh from a distance and from her far pilgrimage. . . .

5. " For we have been much filled with contempt " (ver. 3). All that will live piously according to Christ, must needs suffer reproof,[5] must needs be despised by those who do not choose to live piously, all whose happiness is earthly. They are derided who call that happiness which they cannot see with their eyes, and it is said to them, What believest thou, madman? Dost thou see what thou believest? Hath any one returned from the world below, and reported to thee what is going on there? Behold I see and enjoy what I love. Thou art scorned, because thou dost hope for what thou seest not ; and he who seemeth to hold what he seeth, scorneth thee. Consider well if he doth really hold it. . . . I have my house, he hath boasted himself. Thou askest, what house of his own? That which my father left me. And whence did he derive this house? My grandfather left it him. Go back even to his great grandfather, then to his great grandfather's father, and he can no longer tell their names. Art thou not rather terrified by this thought, that thou seest many have passed through this house, and that none of them hath carried it away with him to his everlasting home? Thy father left it : he passed through it : thus thou also wilt pass by. If therefore thou hast a mere passing stay in thy house, it is an inn for passing guests, not an habitation for permanent abode. Yet since we hope for those things which are to come, and sigh for future happiness, and since it hath not yet appeared what we shall be, although we are already " sons of God ; "[6] for " our life is hidden with Christ in God : "[7] " we are utterly despised," by those who seek or enjoy happiness in this world.

6. " Our soul is filled exceedingly ; a reproach to the wealthy, and a contempt to the proud " (ver. 4). We were asking who were " the wealthy : " he hath expounded to thee, in that he hath said, " the proud." " Reproach " and " contempt " are the same : and " wealthy " is the same with " proud." It is a repetition of the sentence, " a reproach to the wealthy, and a contempt to the proud." Why are the proud wealthy? Because they wish to be happy here. Why? since they themselves too are miserable, are they wealthy? But perhaps when they are

---

[1] *Desudare.*   [2] Matt. xxiv. 35.   [3] *Populus* (masc.).
[4] *Ecclesia* (fem.).

[5] 2 Tim. iii. 12.   [6] 1 John iii. 2.   [7] Col. iii. 3.

miserable, they do not mock us. Listen, my beloved. Then perchance they mock when they are happy, when they boast themselves in the pomp of their riches! when they boast themselves in the inflated state of false honours: then they mock us, and seem to say, Behold, it is well with me: I enjoy the good things before me: let those who promise what they cannot show depart from me: what I see, I hold; what I see, I enjoy; may I fare well in this life. Be thou more secure; for Christ hath risen again, and hath taught thee what He will give in another life: be assured that He giveth it. But that man mocketh thee, because he holdeth what he hath. Bear with his mockeries, and thou wilt laugh at his groans: for afterwards there will come a season when these very persons will say, "This was he whom we had sometimes in derision." [1] . . .

7. To this we must add, that sometimes those also who are beneath the scourge of temporal unhappiness, mock us. . . . Did not the robber [2] mock, who was crucified with our crucified Lord? If therefore they who are not wealthy mock us, why doth the Psalm say, "A reproach to the wealthy"? If we carefully sift the matter, even these (the unfortunate) are wealthy. How are they wealthy? Yea; for if they were not wealthy, they would not be proud. For one man is wealthy in money, and proud on that score: another is wealthy in honours, and is proud on that account: another imagines himself wealthy in righteousness, and hence his pride, which is worse. They who seem not to be wealthy in money, seem to themselves to be wealthy in righteousness towards God; and when calamity overtakes them, they justify themselves, accuse God, and say, What wrong have I been guilty of, or, what have I done? Thou repliest: Look back, call to mind thy sins, see if thou hast done nothing. He is somewhat touched in conscience, and returneth to himself, and thinketh of his evil deeds; and when he hath thought of his evil deeds, not even then doth he choose to confess that he deserves his sufferings; but saith, Behold, I have clearly done many things; but I see that many have done worse, and suffer no evil. He is righteous against God. He also therefore is wealthy: he hath his breast puffed out with righteousness; since God seemeth to him to do ill, and he seemeth to himself to suffer unjustly. And if thou gavest him a vessel to pilot, he would be shipwrecked with it: yet he wishes to deprive God of the government of this world, and himself to hold the helm of Creation, and to distribute among all men pains and pleasures, punishments and rewards. Miserable soul! yet why do ye wonder? He is wealthy, but wealthy in iniquity, wealthy in malignity; but is more wealthy in iniquity, in proportion as he seemeth to himself to be wealthy in righteousness.

8. But a Christian ought not to be wealthy, but ought to acknowledge himself poor; and if he hath riches, he ought to know that they are not true riches, so that he may desire others. . . . And what is the wealth of our righteousness? How much soever righteousness there may be in us, it is a sort of dew compared to that fountain: [3] compared to that plenteousness it is as a few drops, which may soften our life, and relax our hard iniquity. Let us only desire to be filled with the full fountain of righteousness, let us long to be filled with that abundant richness, of which it is said in the Psalm, "They shall be satisfied with the plenteousness of Thy house: and Thou shalt give them drink out of the torrent of Thy pleasure." [4] But while we are here, let us understand ourselves to be destitute and in want; not only in respect of those riches which are not the true riches, but of salvation itself. And when we are whole, let us understand that we are weak. For as long as this body hungers and thirsts, as long as this body is weary with watching, weary with standing, weary with walking, weary with sitting, weary with eating; whithersoever it turneth itself for a relief from weariness, there it discovereth another source of fatigue: there is therefore no perfect soundness, not even in the body itself. Those riches are then not riches, but beggary; for the more they abound, the more doth destitution and avarice increase. . . . Let then our whole hunger, our whole thirst, be for true riches, and true health, and true righteousness. What are true riches? That heavenly abode in Jerusalem. For who is called rich on this earth? When a rich man is praised, what is meant? He is very rich: nothing is wanting to him. That surely is the praise of him that praiseth the other: for it is not this, when it is said, He wants nothing. Consider if he really want nothing. If he desires nothing, he wants nothing: but if he still desires more than what he hath, his riches have increased in such wise, that his wants have increased also. But in that City there will be true riches, because there will be nothing wanting to us there; for we shall not be in need of anything, and there will be true health. . . .

PSALM CXXIV.[5]

1. Ye already well know, dearest brethren, that a "Song of Degrees," is a song of our ascent: and that this ascent is not effected by

---

[1] Wisd. v. 3.   [2] Luke xxiii. 39.

[3] [What would our author have said of the merits of canonized "saints" applied to the remission of sins and purgatorial pains? — C.]
[4] Ps. xxxvi. 8.   [5] Lat. CXXIII. A sermon to the people.

the feet of the body, but by the affections of the heart. This we have repeatedly reminded you of: and we need not repeat it too often, that there may be room for saying what hath not yet been said. This Psalm, therefore, which ye have now heard sung for you,[1] is inscribed, "A Song of Degrees." This is its title. They sing therefore while ascending: and sometimes as it were one man singeth, sometimes as it were many; because many are one, since Christ is One, and in Christ the members of Christ constitute one with Christ, and the Head of all these members is in heaven. But although the body toileth on earth, it is not cut off from its Head; for the Head looketh down from above, and regardeth the body.[2] . . . Whether therefore one or many sing; many men are one man, because it is unity; and Christ, as we have said, is One, and all Christians are members of Christ.

2. . . . Certain members indeed of that body of which we also are, which can sing in truth, have gone before us. And this the holy Martyrs have sung: for they have already escaped, and are with Christ in joy about to receive at last incorruptible bodies, the very same which were at first corruptible, wherein they have suffered pains; of the same there will be made for them ornaments of righteousness. Therefore whether they in reality, or we in hope, joining our affections with their crowns, and longing for such a life as we have not here, and shall never gain unless we have longed for it here, let us all sing together, and say, "If the Lord Himself had not been in us." . . .

3. "If the Lord Himself had not been in us, now may Israel say" (ver. 1). . . . When? "When men rose up against us" (ver. 2). Marvel not: they have been subdued: for they were men; but the Lord was in us, man was not in us: for men rose up against us. Nevertheless men would crush other men, unless in those men who could not be crushed, there were not man, but the Lord. For what could men do to you, while ye rejoiced, and sang, and securely held everlasting bliss? what could men do to you when they rose against you, if the Lord had not been on your side? what could they do? "Perchance they had swallowed us up quick" (ver. 3). "Swallowed us up:"[3] they would not first have slain us, and so have swallowed us up. O inhuman, O cruel men! The Church swalloweth not thus.[4] To Peter it was said, "Kill and eat:"[5] not, Swallow quick. Because no man entereth into the body of the Church, save he be slain first.[6] What he was dieth, that he may be what he was not. Otherwise, he who is not slain, and is not eaten

by the Church, may be in the visible number of the people: but he cannot be in the number of the people which is known to God, whereof the Apostle saith, "The Lord knoweth who are His,"[7] save he be eaten; and eaten he cannot be, save he first be slain. The Pagan cometh, still in him idolatry liveth; he must be grafted among the members of Christ: that he may be engrafted, he must needs be eaten; but he cannot be eaten by the Church, save first he be slain. Let him renounce the world, then is he slain; let him believe in God, then is he eaten. . . . But they in whom the Lord is, are slain and die not. But they who consent[8] and live, are swallowed quick, when swallowed up they die. But they who have suffered, and have not yielded to tribulations, rejoice and say, "If the Lord had not been in us," etc.

4. . . . "When their fury was enraged upon us." They are now in anger, they now openly rage: "perchance the water had drowned us" (ver. 4). By water he meaneth ungodly nations: and we shall see what sort of water in the following verses. Whoever had consented unto them, water would have overwhelmed him. For he would die by the death of the Egyptians, he would not pass through after the example of the Israelites. For ye know, brethren, that the people of Israel passed through the water, by which the Egyptians were overwhelmed.[9] But what sort of water is this? It is a torrent, it flows with violence, but it will pass by. . . . Hence He, our Head, first drinketh, of whom it is said in the Psalms, "He shall drink of the torrent in the way: therefore shall He lift up His head." For our Head is already exalted, because He drank of the torrent by the way; for our Lord hath suffered. If therefore our Head hath been already raised up, why doth the body fear the torrent? Without doubt, because the Head hath been raised, the body also will say hereafter, "Our soul hath passed over the torrent. Perhaps our soul hath passed over the water without substance" (ver. 5). Behold, what sort of water he was speaking of, "The water perchance had overwhelmed us." But what meaneth, "without substance"?

5. In the first place, what meaneth,[10] "Per-

---

[1] ["*Unto* you," in Oxford ed., which is not necessarily the sense of the original: *quem nunc vobis cantatum audistis.* — C.]

[2] Acts ix. 4.   [3] [*i.e.*, alive: *vivos absorbuissent.* — C]

[4] [Compare Ps. xxxv. 25, p. 86, *supra.* — C.]

[5] Acts x. 13.   [6] [" Ye are dead," Col. iii. 3. — C.]

[7] 2 Tim. ii. 19.   [8] [*i e.*, to sacrifice to idols. — C.]

[9] Exod. xiv. 22-29.

[10] Gesenius, *Monum. Phœn.* p. 390, thinks both may be from the first root, signifying "difficulty;" or the latter possibly = רָֽאָ, רָֽא "let one see." [Our author says: "The Latin interpreters have thus rendered as far as they were able the Greek word ἀοα. For thus the Greek copies have it; ἀοα: and as it is an expression of doubt, it is rendered by an expression of doubt, the word 'perchance' (*fortasse*): but this is not the exact sense. We may express this Greek word by one not so Latin in its use, but adapted to your comprehension. The Punic word, *iar*, I mean not that which signifieth a wood, but the expression of doubt, is the Greek ἀρα. This the Latins may or usually do express by *Putas:* as in this instance, Dost thou think (*putas*) I have escaped this? If we say, Perchance I have escaped, ye see that it hath not this meaning: but the word, Thinkest thou, is commonly used: but not in Latin in this sense. Although I may use it, when expounding to you; for I often use words that are not Latin,

chance our soul hath passed over"? (ver. 5). Understand however the meaning to be this: "*Thinkest thou* our soul hath passed over?" and why do they say, "Thinkest thou"? Because the greatness of the danger maketh it hardly credible that he hath escaped. They have endured a great death: they have been in great dangers; they have been so much oppressed, that they almost gave consent while alive, and were all but swallowed up alive: now therefore that they have escaped, now that they are secure, but still remember the danger, the great danger, say, "Thinkest thou our soul hath passed over the water without substance?"

6. What is the water without substance, save the water of sins without substance? For sins have not substance: they have destitution, not substance; they have want, not substance. In that water without substance, the younger son lost the whole of his substance. . . . Dost thou wish to see how the water is without substance? Take away with thee to the world below what thou hast acquired: what wilt thou do? Thou hast acquired gold: thou hast lost thy faith: after a few days thou leavest this life; thou canst not take away with thee the gold thou hast acquired by the loss of thy good faith; thy heart, destitute of faith, goeth forth into punishment — thy heart, which if full of faith, would go forth unto a crown. Behold, what thou hast done is nothing: and thou hast offended God for nothing.

7. Men hear that common proverb; and the proverbs of God slumber in them. What proverb? "Better in hand than in hope."[1] Unhappy man, what hast thou in hand? Thou sayest, "Better in hand." Hold it so as not to lose it, and then say, "Better in hand." But if thou holdest it not, why dost thou not hold fast that which thou canst not lose? What then hast thou in hand? Gold. Keep it in hand, therefore: if thou hast it in hand, let it not be taken away without thy consent. But if through gold also thou art carried where thou wishest not, and if a more powerful robber seeketh thee, because he findeth thee a less powerful robber; if a stronger eagle pursue thee, because thou hast carried off a hare before him: the lesser was thy prey, thou wilt be a prey unto the greater. Men see not these things in human affairs: by so much avarice are they blinded. . . .

8. Let them escape the water without substance, and say, "Blessed be the Lord, who hath not given us over for a prey unto their teeth" (ver. 6). For the hunters were following, and had placed a bait in their trap. What bait? The sweetness of this life, so that each man for the sake of the

sweetness of this life may thrust his head into iniquity, and be caught in the trap. Not they, in whom the Lord was, they who say, "If the Lord Himself had not been in us;" they have not been taken in the trap. Let the Lord be in thee, and thou wilt not be taken in the trap.

9. "Our soul is escaped, even as a bird out of the snare of the fowlers" (ver. 7). Because the Lord was in the soul itself, therefore hath that soul escaped, even as a bird out of the snare of the fowler. Why like a bird? Because it had fallen heedlessly, like a bird; and it could say afterwards, God will forgive me. Unstable bird, rather set thy feet firm upon the rock: go not into the trap. Thou wilt be taken, consumed, crushed. Let the Lord be in thee, and He will deliver thee from greater threats, from the snare of the fowlers. As if thou wert to see a bird about to fall into a snare, thou makest a greater noise that it may fly away from the net; so also, when perhaps some even of the Martyrs were stretching out their neck after the enjoyment of this life, the Lord, who was in them, made the noise of hell, and the bird was delivered from the snare of the fowlers. The snare was the sweetness of this life: they were not entangled in the snare, and were slain; by their slaughter the net was broken; no longer did the sweetness of this life remain, that they might again be entangled by it, but it was crushed. Was the bird also crushed? Far be it! for it was not in the snare: "The snare is broken, and we are delivered."

10. . . . "Our help standeth in the Name of the Lord, who hath made heaven and earth" (ver. 8). For if this were not our help, the snare would not indeed remain for ever; but when the bird was once taken, it would be crushed. For this life will pass away; and they who shall have been taken in by its pleasures, and through these pleasures have offended God, will pass away with this life. For the snare will be broken; be ye assured of this: all the sweetness of this present life will no longer exist, when the lot assigned to it hath been fulfilled; but we must not be enthralled by it, so that when the net is broken, thou mayest then rejoice and say, "The snare is broken, and we are delivered." But lest thou think that thou canst do this of thy own strength, consider whose work thy deliverance is (for if thou art proud, thou fallest into the snare), and say, "Our help standeth in the Name of the Lord, who hath made heaven and earth." . . .

PSALM CXXV.[2]

1. This Psalm, belonging to the number of the Songs of Degrees, teacheth us, while we as-

---

that ye may understand. But in Scripture this could not be used, because it was not Latin; and as Latin failed, that was used for it which had not this meaning." — C.]

[1] *Malo quod teneo, quam quod spero.* [Eng. "A bird in the hand," etc. — C.]

[2] Lat. CXXIV. A discourse to the people.

cend and raise our minds unto the Lord our
God in loving charity and piety, not to fix our
gaze upon men who are prosperous in this world,
with a happiness that is false and unstable, and
altogether seductive ; where they cherish nothing save pride, and their heart freezeth up against
God, and is made hard against the shower of
His grace, so that it beareth not fruit. . . .

2. "They that put their trust in the Lord
shall be even as the mount Sion : they shall not
be removed for ever " (ver. 1).

3. Who are these? "They shall stand fast
for ever, who dwell in Jerusalem " (ver. 2). If
we understand this earthly Jerusalem, all who
dwelt therein have been excluded by wars and
by the destruction of the city : thou now seekest
a Jew in the city of Jerusalem, and findest him
not. Why then will " they that dwell in Jerusalem not be moved for ever," save because there
is another Jerusalem, of which ye are wont to
hear much? She is our mother, for whom we
sigh and groan in this pilgrimage, that we may
return unto her. . . . They then who dwell
therein " shall never be moved." But they who
dwelt in that earthly Jerusalem, have been
moved ; first in heart, afterwards by exile.
When they were moved in heart and fell, then
they crucified the King of the heavenly Jerusalem herself ; they were already spiritually without, and shut out of doors their very King.
For they cast Him out without their city, and
crucified Him without.[1] He too cast them out
of His city, that is, of the everlasting Jerusalem,
the Mother of us all, who is in Heaven.

4. What is this Jerusalem? He briefly describes it. "The mountains stand around Jerusalem " (ver. 2). Is it anything great, that we
are in a city surrounded by mountains? Is this
the whole of our happiness, that we shall have a
city which mountains surround? Do we not
know what mountains are? or what are mountains save swellings of the earth? Different
then from these are those mountains that we
love, lofty mountains, preachers of truth, whether
Angels, or Apostles, or Prophets. They stand
around Jerusalem ; they surround her, and, as it
were, form a wall for her. Of these lovely and
delightful mountains Scripture constantly speaketh. . . . They are the mountains of whom we
sing : " I lifted up mine eyes unto the mountains, from whence my help shall come : "[2] because in this life we have help from the holy
Scriptures.[3] And through the mountains that
receive peace, the little hills received righteousness : for what saith he of the mountains themselves? He said not, they have peace from them-

selves, or they make peace, or generate peace ;
but, they receive peace. The Lord is the source,
whence they receive peace. So therefore lift up
thine eyes to the mountains for the sake of
peace, that thy help may come from the Lord,
who hath made heaven and earth. Again, the
Holy Spirit mentioning these mountains saith
this : " Thou dost light them wonderfully from
Thy everlasting mountains."[4] He said not, the
mountains light them : but, Thou lightest them
from Thy everlasting mountains : through those
mountains whom Thou hast willed to be everlasting, preaching the Gospel, Thou lighting
them, not the mountains. Such then are the
" mountains that stand around Jerusalem."

5. And that ye may know what sort of mountains these be that stand around Jerusalem ;
where Scripture hath mentioned good mountains, very rarely, and hardly, and perhaps never,
doth it fail instantly to mention the Lord also,
or allude to Him at the same moment, that our
hopes rest not in the mountains. . . . Lest thou
again shouldest tarry in the mountains, he at
once addeth, " Even so the Lord standeth round
about His people : " that thy hope might not lie
in the mountains, but in Him who lighteth the
mountains.[5] For when He dwelleth in the
mountains, that is, in the Saints, He Himself is
round about His people ; and He hath Himself
walled His people with a spiritual fortification,
that it may not be moved for evermore. But
when Scripture speaketh of evil mountains, it
addeth not the Lord unto them. Such mountains, we have already told you often, signify
certain mighty, but evil, souls. For ye are not
to suppose, brethren, that heresies could be produced through any little souls. None save great
men have been the authors of heresies ; but in
proportion as they were mighty, so were they
evil, mountains. For they were not such mountains as would receive peace, that the hills might
receive righteousness ; but they received dissension from their father the devil. There were
therefore mountains : beware thou fly not to
such mountains. For men will come, and say
unto thee, There is a great hero, there is a great
man ! How great was that Donatus ! How
great is Maximian ! and a certain Photinus, what
a great man he was ! And Arius too, how illustrious he was ! All these I have mentioned are
mountains, but mountains that cause shipwreck.[6] . . .

6. But love such mountains, in whom the
Lord is. Then do those very mountains love
thee, if thou hast not placed hope in them.[5] See,
brethren, what the mountains of God are.
Thence they are so called in another passage :
"Thy righteousness is like the mountains of

---

[1] John xix. 17, 18.   [2] Ps. cxxi. 1, 2.
[3] [Observe in our author *passim* this implication that the laity
as well as the clergy were filled with the knowledge and comfort of
the Scriptures. — C.]

[4] Ps lxxvi. 4.   [5] [Evidence against saint-worship. — C.]
[6] [So Jude 16. — C.]   Vinc. Lir. *Common.* §§ 17-20.

God."[1] Not their righteousness, but "Thy righteousness." Hear that great mountain the Apostle. "That I may be found in Him, not having mine own righteousness, which is of the law, but that which is through the faith of Christ."[2] But they who have chosen to be mountains through their own righteousness, as certain Jews or Pharisees their rulers, are thus blamed: "Being ignorant of God's righteousness, and going about to establish their own righteousness, they have not submitted themselves unto the righteousness of God."[3] But they who have submitted themselves are exalted in such a manner as to be humble. In that they are great, they are mountains; in that they submit themselves unto God, they are valleys: and in that they have the capacity of piety, they receive the plenteousness of peace, and transmit the copious irrigation to the hills, only beware, at present, what mountains thou lovest. If thou wish to be loved by good mountains, place not thy trust even in good mountains. For how great a mountain was Paul? where is one like him found? We speak of the greatness of men. Can any one readily be found of so great grace? Nevertheless, he feared lest that bird should place trust in him: and what doth he say: "Was Paul crucified for you?"[4] But lift up your eyes unto the mountains, whence help may come unto you: for, "I have planted, Apollos hath watered:" but, your help cometh from the Lord, who hath made Heaven and earth; for, "God gave the increase."[5] "The mountains," therefore, "stand around Jerusalem." But as "the mountains stand around Jerusalem, even so standeth the Lord round about His people, from this time forth for evermore." If therefore the mountains stand around Jerusalem, and the Lord standeth round about His people, the Lord bindeth His people into one bond of love and peace, so that they who trust in the Lord, like the mount Sion, may not be moved for evermore: and this is, "from this time forth for evermore."

7. "For the Lord will not leave the rod of the ungodly upon the lot of the righteous, lest the righteous put forth their hands unto wickedness" (ver. 3). At present indeed the righteous suffer in some measure, and at present the unrighteous sometimes tyrannize over the righteous. In what ways? Sometimes the unrighteous arrive at worldly honours: when they have arrived at them, and have been made either judges or kings; for God doth this for the discipline of His folk, for the discipline of His people; the honour due to their power must needs be shown them. For thus hath God ordained His Church, that every power ordained in the world may have honour, and sometimes from those who are better than those in power. For the sake of illustration I take one instance; hence calculate the grades of all powers. The primary and every day relation of authority between man and man is that between master and slave. Almost all houses have a power of this sort. There are masters, there are also slaves; these are different names, but men and men are equal names.[6] And what saith the Apostle, teaching that slaves are subject to their masters? "Servants, be obedient to them that are your masters according to the flesh:" for there is a Master according to the Spirit. He is the true and everlasting Master; but those temporal masters are for a time only. When thou walkest in the way, when thou livest in this life, Christ doth not wish to make thee proud. It hath been thy lot to become a Christian, and to have a man for thy master: thou wast not made a Christian, that thou mightest disdain to be a servant. For when by Christ's command thou servest a man, thou servest not the man, but Him who commanded thee. He saith this also: "Servants, be obedient to them that are your masters according to the flesh."[7] Behold, he hath not made men free from being servants, but good servants from bad servants. How much do the rich owe to Christ, who orders their house for them! so that if thou hast had an unbelieving servant, suppose Christ convert him, and say not to him, Leave thy master, thou hast now known Him who is thy true Master: he perhaps is ungodly and unjust, thou art now faithful and righteous: it is unworthy that a righteous and faithful man should serve an unjust and unbelieving master. He spoke not thus unto him, but rather, Serve him: and to confirm the servant, added, Serve as I served; I before thee served the unjust. . . . If the Lord of heaven and earth, through whom all things were created, served the unworthy, asked mercy for His furious persecutors, and, as it were, showed Himself as their Physician at His Advent (for physicians also, better both in art and health, serve the sick): how much more ought not a man to disdain, with his whole mind, and his whole good will, with his whole love to serve even a bad master! Behold, a better serveth an inferior, but for a season. Understand what I have said of the master and slave, to be true also of powers and kings, of all the exalted stations of this world. For sometimes they are good powers, and fear God; sometimes they fear not God. Julian was an infidel Emperor, an apostate, a wicked man, an idolater; Christian soldiers served an infidel Emperor; when they came to the cause of Christ, they acknowledged Him only who was in

---

[1] Ps. xxxvi. 6.　　[2] Philip. iii. 9.　　[3] Rom. x. 3.
[4] 1 Cor. i. 13.　　[5] 1 Cor. iii. 6.

[6] [The Epistle to Philemon is here reflected. See A. N. F. vol. viii. p. 782, note 1, and p. 784; also vol. vii. p. 425. — C.]
[7] Eph. vi. 5.

heaven. If he called upon them at any time to worship idols, to offer incense ; they preferred God to him : but whenever he commanded them to deploy into line, to march against this or that nation, they at once obeyed. They distinguished their everlasting from their temporal master ; and yet they were, for the sake of their everlasting Master, submissive to their temporal master.

8. But will it be thus always, that the ungodly have power over the righteous? It will not be so. The rod of the ungodly is felt for a season upon the lot of the righteous ; but it is not left there, it will not be there for ever. A time will come, when Christ, appearing in his glory, shall gather all nations before Him.[1] And thou wilt see there many slaves among the sheep, and many masters among the goats ; and again many masters among the sheep, many slaves among the goats. For all slaves are not good — do not infer this from the consolation we have given to servants — nor are all masters evil, because we have thus repressed the pride of masters. There are good masters who believe, and there are evil : there are good servants who believe, and there are evil. But as long as good servants serve evil masters, let them endure for a season. " For God will not leave the rod of the ungodly upon the lot of the righteous." Why will He not? " Lest the righteous put forth their hand unto wickedness : " that the righteous may endure for a season the domination of the ungodly, and may understand that this is not for ever, but may prepare themselves to possess their everlasting heritage. . . .

9. And he therefore addeth, " Do well, O Lord, unto those that are good and true of heart " (ver. 4). They who are right in heart, of whom I was speaking a little before, — they who follow the will of God, not their own will, — reflect upon this. But they who wish to follow God, allow Him to go before, and themselves to follow ; not themselves to go before, and Him to follow ; and in all things they find Him good, whether chastening, or consoling, or exercising, or crowning, or cleansing, or enlightening ; as the Apostle saith, " We know that all things work together for good to them that love God." [2]

10. Whence the Psalmist at once addeth : " As for such as turn aside, the Lord shall lead them forth unto strangling with the workers of unrighteousness " (ver. 5) : that is, those whose deeds they have imitated ; because they took delight in their present pleasures, and did not believe in their punishments to come. What then shall they have, who are righteous in heart, and who turn not back? Let us now come to the heritage itself, brethren, for we are sons.

What shall we possess? What is our heritage? what is our country : what is it called? Peace. In this we salute you, this we announce to you, this the mountains receive, and the little hills receive as righteousness.[3] Peace is Christ : " for He is our peace, who hath made both one, and hath broken down the middle wall of partition between us." [4] Since we are sons, we shall have an inheritance. And what shall this inheritance be called, but peace? And consider that they who love not peace are disinherited. Now they who divide unity, love not peace. Peace is the possession of the pious, the possession of heirs. And who are heirs? Sons. . . . Since then Christ the Son of God is peace, He therefore came to gather together His own, and to separate them from the wicked. From what wicked men? From those who hate Jerusalem, who hate peace, who wish to tear unity asunder, who believe not peace, who preach a false peace to the people, and have it not. To whom answer is made, when they say,[5] " Peace be with you," " And with thy spirit : " but they speak falsely, and they hear falsely. Unto whom do they say, Peace be with you? To those whom they separate from the peace of the whole earth. And unto whom is it said, " And with thy spirit "? To those who embrace dissensions, and who hate peace. For if peace were in their spirit, would they not love unity, and leave dissensions? Speaking then false words, they hear false words. Let us speak true words, and hear true words. Let us be Israel, and let us embrace peace ; for Jerusalem is a vision of peace, and we are Israel, " and peace is upon Israel."

PSALM CXXVI.[6]

1. . . . How man had come into captivity, let us ask the Apostle Paul. . . . For he saith : " For we know that the Law is spiritual, but I am carnal, sold under sin." [7] Behold whence we became captives ; because we were sold under sin. Who sold us? We ourselves, who consented to the seducer. We could sell ourselves ; we could not redeem ourselves. We sold ourselves by consent of sin, we are redeemed in the faith of righteousness. For innocent blood was given for us, that we might be redeemed. Whatsoever blood he shed in persecuting the righteous, what kind of blood did he shed? Righteous men's blood, indeed, he shed ; they were Prophets, righteous men, our fathers, and Martyrs. Whose blood he shed, yet all coming of the offspring of sin. One blood he shed of Him who was not justified,[8] but born righteous : by shedding that blood, he lost those whom he held. For they

---

[1] Matt. xxv. 32, 33.   [2] Rom. viii. 28.

[3] Ps. lxxii. 3.   [4] Eph. ii. 14.   [5] [In the Liturgy. — C.]
[6] Lat. CXXV. A song of degrees. A sermon to the people.
[7] Rom. vii. 14.   [8] Or, " made righteous."

for whom innocent blood was given were redeemed, and, turned back from their captivity, they sing this Psalm.

2. "When the Lord turned back the captivity of Sion, we became as those that are comforted" (ver. 1). He meant by this to say, we became joyful. When? "When the Lord turned back the captivity of Sion." What is Sion? Jerusalem, the same is also the eternal Sion. How is Sion eternal, how is Sion captive? In angels eternal, in men captive. For not all the citizens of that city are captives, but those who are away from thence, they are captives. Man was a citizen of Jerusalem, but sold under sin he became a pilgrim. Of his progeny was born the human race, and the captivity of Sion filled all lands. And how is this captivity of Sion a shadow of that Jerusalem? The shadow of that Sion, which was granted to the Jews, in an image, in a figure, was in captivity in Babylonia, and after seventy years that people turned back to its own city.[1] . . . But when all time is past, then we return to our country, as after seventy years that people returned from the Babylonish captivity, for Babylon is this world; since Babylon is interpreted "confusion." . . . So then this whole life of human affairs is confusion, which belongeth not unto God. In this confusion, in this Babylonish land, Sion is held captive. But "the Lord hath turned back the captivity of Sion." "And we became," he saith, "as those that are comforted." That is, we rejoiced as receiving consolation. Consolation is not save for the unhappy, consolation is not save for them that groan, that mourn. Wherefore, "as those that are comforted," except because we are still mourning? We mourn for our present lot, we are comforted in hope: when the present is passed by, of our mourning will come everlasting joy, when there will be no need of consolation, because we shall be wounded with no distress. But wherefore saith he "as" those that are comforted, and saith not comforted? This word "as," is not always put for likeness: when we say "As," it sometimes refers to the actual case, sometimes to likeness: here it is with reference to the actual case. . . . Walk therefore in Christ, and sing rejoicing, sing as one that is comforted; because He went before thee who hath commanded thee to follow Him.

3. "Then was our mouth filled with joy, and our tongue with exultation" (ver. 2). That mouth, brethren, which we have in our body, how is it "filled with joy"? It useth not to be "filled," save with meat, or drink, or some such thing put into the mouth. Sometimes our mouth is filled; and it is more that we say to your holiness,[2] when we have our mouth full, we cannot speak. But we have a mouth within, that is,

in the heart, whence whatsoever proceedeth, if it is evil, defileth us, if it is good, cleanseth us. For concerning this very mouth ye heard when the Gospel was read. For the Jews reproached the Lord, because His disciples ate with unwashen hands.[3] They reproached who had cleanness without; and within were full of stains. They reproached, whose righteousness was only in the eyes of men. But the Lord sought our inward cleanness, which if we have, the outside must needs be clean also. "Cleanse," He saith, "the inside," and "the outside shall be clean also."[4] . . .

4. But let us return to what was just now read from the Gospel, relating to the verse before us, "Our mouth was filled with joy, and our tongue with delight:" for we are inquiring what mouth and what tongue. Listen, beloved brethren. The Lord was scoffed at, because His disciples ate with unwashed hands. The Lord answered them as was fitting, and said unto the crowds whom He had called unto Him, "Hear ye all, and understand: not that which goeth into the mouth defileth a man; but that which cometh out of the mouth, this defileth a man."[5] What is this? when He said, what goeth into the mouth, He meant only the mouth of the body. For meat goeth in, and meats defile not a man; because, "All things are clean to the clean;" and, "every creature of God is good, and none to be refused, if it be received with thanksgiving."[6] . . .

5. Guard the mouth of thy heart from evil, and thou wilt be innocent: the tongue of thy body will be innocent, thy hands will be innocent; even thy feet will be innocent, thy eyes, thy ears, will be innocent; all thy members will serve under righteousness, because a righteous commander hath thy heart. "Then shall they say among the heathen, the Lord hath done great things for them."

6. "Yea, the Lord hath done great things for us already, whereof we rejoice" (ver. 3). Consider, my brethren, if Sion doth not at present say this among the heathen, throughout the whole world; consider if men are not running unto the Church. In the whole world our redemption is received; Amen is answered. The dwellers in Jerusalem, therefore, captive, destined to return, pilgrims, sighing for their country, speak thus among the heathen. What do they say? "The Lord hath done great things for us, whereof we rejoice." Have they done anything for themselves? They have done ill with themselves, for they have sold themselves under sin. The Redeemer came, and did the good things for them.

7. "Turn our captivity, O Lord, as the torrents in the south" (ver. 4). Consider, my

---

[1] Jer. xxv. 11, xxix. 10.
[2] [A bishop seems to have been present.—C.]

[3] Matt. xv. 1, etc.
[5] Matt. xv. 10, 11.

[4] Matt. xxiii. 26.
[6] 1 Tim. iv. 4.

brethren, what this meaneth. . . . As torrents are turned in the south, so turn our captivity. In a certain passage Scripture saith, in admonishing us concerning good works, "Thy sins also shall melt away, even as the ice in fair warm weather." [1] Our sins therefore bound us. How? As the cold bindeth the water that it run not. Bound with the frost of our sins, we have frozen. But the south wind is a warm wind: when the south wind blows, the ice melts, and the torrents are filled. Now winter streams are called torrents; for filled with sudden rains they run with great force. We had therefore become frozen in captivity; our sins bound us: the south wind the Holy Spirit hath blown: our sins are forgiven us, we are released from the frost of iniquity; as the ice in fair weather, our sins are melted. Let us run unto our country, as the torrents in the south. . . .

8. For the next words are, "They that sow in tears, shall reap in joy" (ver. 5). In this life, which is full of tears, let us sow. What shall we sow? Good works. Works of mercy are our seeds: of which seeds the Apostle saith, "Let us not be weary in well doing; for in due season we shall reap if we faint not." [2] Speaking therefore of almsgiving itself, what saith he? "This I say; he that soweth sparingly, shall reap also sparingly." [3] He therefore who soweth plentifully, shall reap plentifully: he who soweth sparingly, shall reap also sparingly: and he that soweth nothing, shall reap nothing. Why do ye long for ample estates, where ye may sow plentifully? There is not a wider field on which ye can sow than Christ, who hath willed that we should sow in Himself. Your soil is the Church; sow as much as ye can. But thou hast not enough to do this. Hast thou the will? [4] As what thou hadst would be nothing, if thou hadst not a good will; so do not despond, because thou hast not, if thou hast a good will. For what dost thou sow? Mercy. And what wilt thou reap? Peace. Said the Angels, Peace on earth unto rich men? No, but, "Peace on earth unto men of a good will." [5] Zacchæus had a strong will, Zacchæus had great charity. [6] . . . Did then that widow who cast her two farthings into the treasury, sow little? Nay, as much as Zacchæus. For she had narrower means, but an equal will. She gave her two mites [7] with as good a will as Zacchæus gave the half of his patrimony. If thou consider what they gave, thou wilt find their gifts different; if thou look to the source, thou wilt find them equal; she gave whatever she had, and he gave what he had. . . . But if they are beggars whose profession is asking alms, in trouble they also have what to

bestow upon one another. God hath not so forsaken them, but that they have wherein they may be tried by their bestowing of alms. This man cannot walk; he who can walk, lendeth his feet to the lame; he who seeth, lendeth his eyes to the blind; and he who is young and sound, lendeth his strength to the old or the infirm, he carrieth him: the one is poor, the other is rich.

9. Sometimes also the rich man is found to be poor, and something is bestowed upon him by the poor. Somebody cometh to a river, so much the more delicate as he is more rich; he cannot pass over: if he were to pass over with bare limbs, he would catch cold, would be ill, would die: a poor man more active in body cometh up: he carries the rich man over; he giveth alms unto the rich. Think not therefore those only poor, who have not money. . . . Thus love ye, thus be ye affectioned unto one another. Attend not solely to yourselves: but to those who are in want around you. But because these things take place in this life with troubles and cares, faint not. Ye sow in tears, ye shall reap in joy.

10. How, my brethren? When the farmer goeth forth with the plough, carrying seed, is not the wind sometimes keen, and doth not the shower sometimes deter him? He looketh to the sky, seeth it lowering, shivers with cold, nevertheless goeth forth, and soweth. For he feareth lest while he is observing the foul weather, and awaiting sunshine, the time may pass away, and he may not find anything to reap. Put not off, my brethren; sow in wintry weather, sow good works, even while ye weep; for, "They that sow in tears, shall reap in joy." They sow their seed, good will, and good works. "They went on their way and wept, casting their seed" (ver. 6). Why did they weep? Because they were among the miserable, and were themselves miserable. It is better, my brethren, that no man should be miserable, than that thou shouldest do alms. . . . Nevertheless, as long as there are objects for its exercise, let us not fail amid those troubles to sow our seed. Although we sow in tears, yet shall we reap in joy. For in that resurrection of the dead, each man shall receive his own sheaves, that is, the produce of his seed, the crown of joys and of delight. Then will there be a joyous triumph, when we shall laugh at death, wherein we groaned before: then shall they say to death, "O death, where is thy strife? O death, where is thy sting?" [8] But why do they now rejoice? Because "they bring their sheaves with them."

11. In this Psalm we have chiefly exhorted you to do deeds of alms, because it is thence that we ascend; and ye see that he who ascend-

---

[1] Ecclus iii. 17.   [2] Gal. vi. 9.   [3] 2 Cor. ix. 6.
[4] Oxf. mss. "have a good will."   [5] Luke ii. 14.
[6] Luke xix. 8.   [7] Luke xxi. 1–4.

[8] 1 Cor. xv. 55.

eth, singeth the song of steps. Remember: do not love to descend, instead of to ascend, but reflect upon your ascent: because he who descended from Jerusalem to Jericho fell among thieves.[1] . . . The Samaritan as He passed by slighted us not: He healed us, He raised us upon His beast, upon His flesh; He led us to the inn, that is, the Church; He entrusted us to the host, that is, to the Apostle; He gave two pence, whereby we might be healed,[2] the love of God, and the love of our neighbour. The Apostle spent more; for, though it was allowed unto all the Apostles to receive, as Christ's soldiers, pay from Christ's subjects,[3] that Apostle, nevertheless, toiled with his own hands, and excused the subjects the maintenance owing to him.[4] All this hath already happened: if we have descended, and have been wounded; let us ascend, let us sing, and make progress, in order that we may arrive.

PSALM CXXVII.[5]

1. Among all the Songs entitled the Song of degrees, this Psalm hath a further addition in the title, that it is "Solomon's." For thus it is entitled, "A Song of degrees of Solomon. It hath therefore aroused our attention, and caused us to enquire the reason of this addition, " of Solomon." For it is needless to repeat explanations of the other words, Song of degrees. . . . Solomon was in his time David's son, a great man, through whom many holy precepts and healthful admonitions and divine mysteries have been wrought by the Holy Spirit in the Scriptures. Solomon himself was a lover of women, and was rejected by God: and this lust was so great a snare unto him, that he was induced by women even to sacrifice to idols,[6] as Scripture witnesseth concerning him. But if, by his fall what was delivered through him were blotted out, it would be judged that he had himself delivered these precepts, and not that they were delivered through him. The mercy of God, therefore, and His Spirit, excellently wrought that whatever of good was declared through Solomon, might be attributed unto God; and the man's sin, unto the man. What marvel that Solomon fell among God's people? Did not Adam fall in Paradise? Did not an angel fall from heaven, and become the devil? We are thereby taught, that no hope must be placed in any among men. . . . The name of Solomon is interpreted to mean peacemaker: now Christ is the True Peacemaker, of whom the Apostle saith, " He is our Peace, who hath made both one."[7] . . .

Since, therefore, He is the true Solomon; for that Solomon was the figure of this Peace maker, when he built the temple; that thou mayest not think he who built the house unto God was the true Solomon, Scripture showing unto thee another Solomon, thus commences this Psalm: " Except the Lord build the house, their labour is but lost that build it " (ver. 1). The Lord, therefore, buildeth the house, the Lord Jesus Christ buildeth His own house. Many toil in building: but, except He build, " their labour is but lost that build it." Who are they who toil in building it? All who preach the word of God in the Church, the ministers of God's mysteries. We are all running, we are all toiling, we are all building now; and before us others have run, toiled, and built: but " except the Lord build, their labour is but lost." Thus the Apostles seeing some fall bewailed these men, in that they had laboured in vain for them.[8] We, therefore, speak without, He buildeth within. We can observe with what attention ye hear us; He alone who knoweth your thoughts, knoweth what ye think. He Himself buildeth, He Himself admonisheth, He Himself openeth the understanding, He Himself kindleth your understanding unto faith; nevertheless, we also toil like workmen; but, " except the Lord build," etc.

2. But that which is the house of God is also a city. For the house of God is the people of God; for the house of God is the temple of God. . . . This is Jerusalem: she hath guards: as she hath builders, labouring at her building up, so also hath she guards. To this guardianship these words of the Apostle relate: " I fear, lest by any means your minds should be corrupted from the simplicity which is in Christ." [9] He was guarding the Church. He kept watch, to the utmost of his power, over those over whom he was set. The Bishops also do this. For a higher place was for this reason given the Bishops, that they might be themselves the superintendents and as it were the guardians of the people. For the Greek word *Episcopus*, and the vernacular Superintendent, are the same; for the Bishop superintends, in that he looks over. As a higher place is assigned to the vinedresser in the charge of the vineyard, so also to the Bishops a more exalted station is alloted. And a perilous account is rendered of this high station, except we stand here with a heart that causeth us to stand beneath your feet in humility, and pray for you, that He who knoweth your minds may be Himself your keeper. Since we can see you both coming in and going out; but we are so unable to see what are the thoughts of your hearts, that we cannot even see what ye do in your houses.

---

[1] Luke x. 30. [2] Luke x. 35, 37.
[3] *Provincialibus.* 1 Cor. iv. 2.
[4] 1 Thess. ii. 7, 9; 2 Thess. iii. 8, 9.
[5] Lat. CXXVI. A sermon to the common people.
[6] 1 Kings xi. 7, 8. [7] Eph. ii. 14.
[8] Gal. iv. 10, 11. [9] 2 Cor. xi. 3.

How then can we guard you? As men: as far as we are able, as far as we have received power. And because we guard you like men, and cannot guard you perfectly, shall ye therefore remain without a keeper? Far be it! For where is He of whom it is said, "Except the Lord keep the city, the watchman waketh but in vain?" (ver. 1). We are watchful on our guard, but vain in our watchfulness, except He who seeth your thoughts guard you. He keepeth guard while ye are awake, He keepeth guard also whilst ye are asleep. For He hath once slept on the Cross, and hath risen again; He no longer sleepeth. Be ye Israel: for "the Keeper of Israel neither sleepeth nor slumbereth."[1] Yea, brethren, if we wish to be kept beneath the shadow of God's wings, let us be Israel. For we guard you in our office of stewards; but we wish to be guarded together with you. We are as it were shepherds unto you; but beneath that Shepherd we are fellow-sheep with you. We are as it were your teachers from this station; but beneath Him, the One Master, we are schoolfellows with you in this school.

3. If we wish to be guarded by Him who was humbled for our sakes, and who was exalted to keep us, let us be humble. Let no one assume anything unto himself. No man hath any good, except he hath received it from Him who alone is good. But he who chooseth to arrogate wisdom unto himself, is a fool. Let him be humble, that wisdom may come, and may enlighten him. But if, before wisdom cometh unto him, he imagine that he is wise; he riseth before light, and walketh in darkness. What doth he hear in this Psalm? "It is but lost labour that ye haste to rise up before dawn" (ver. 2). What meaneth this? If ye arise before light ariseth, ye must needs lose your labour, because ye will be in the dark. Our light, Christ, hath arisen; it is good for thee to rise after Christ, not to rise before Christ. Who rise before Christ? They who choose to prefer themselves to Christ. And who are they who wish to prefer themselves to Christ? They who wish to be exalted here, where He was humble. Let them, therefore, be humble here, if they wish to be exalted there, where Christ is exalted. . . . The Lord recalled the sons of Zebedee to humility, and said unto them, "Are ye able to drink of the cup that I shall drink of?"[2] I came to be humble: and are ye wishing to be exalted before Me? The way I go, do ye follow, He saith. For if ye choose to go this way where I do not go, your labour is lost, in rising before dawn. Peter too had risen before the light, when he wished to give the Lord advice, deterring Him from suffering for us. . . . But what did our Lord do? He caused

him to rise after the Light: "Get thee behind Me, Satan."[3] He was Satan, because he wished to rise before Light. "Get thee behind Me:" that I may precede, thou mayest follow: where I go, there thou mayest go; and mayest not wish to lead Me, where thou wouldest go. . . .

4. And as if thou shouldest say, When shall we rise? we are ordered now to sit: when will be our rising? When the Lord's was. Look unto Him, who went before thee: for if thou heedest not Him, "it is lost labour for thee to rise before dawn." When was He raised? When He had died. Hope therefore for thine uplifting after thy death: have hope in the resurrection of the dead, because He rose again and ascended. But where did He sleep? On the Cross. When He slept on the Cross, He bore a sign, yea, He fulfilled what had been signified in Adam: for when Adam was asleep, a rib was drawn from him, and Eve was created;[4] so also while the Lord slept on the Cross, His side was transfixed with a spear, and the Sacraments flowed forth,[5] whence the Church was born. For the Church the Lord's Bride was created from His side, as Eve was created from the side of Adam. But as she was made from his side no otherwise than while sleeping, so the Church was created from His side no otherwise than while dying. If therefore He rose not from the dead save when He had died, dost thou hope for exaltation save after this life? But that this Psalm might teach thee, in case thou shouldest ask, When shall I rise? perhaps before I have sat down? he addeth, "When He hath given His beloved sleep" (ver. 3). God giveth this when His beloved have fallen asleep; then His beloved, that is, Christ's, shall rise. For all indeed shall rise, but not as His beloved. There is a resurrection of all the dead; but what saith the Apostle? "We shall all rise, but we shall not all be changed."[6] They rise unto punishment: we rise as our Lord rose, that we may follow our Head, if we are members of Him. . . . Hope for such a resurrection; and for the sake of this be a Christian, not for the sake of this world's happiness. For if thou wish to be a Christian for the sake of this world's happiness, since He thy Light sought not worldly happiness; thou art wishing to rise before the light; thou must needs continue in darkness. Be changed, follow thy Light; rise where[7] He rose again: first sit down, and thus rise, "when He giveth His beloved sleep."

5. As if thou shouldest ask again, who are the beloved? "Lo, children, the reward of the fruit of the womb, are an heritage of the Lord"[8]

---

[1] Ps. cxxi. 4.   [2] Matt. xx. 21, 22.

[3] Matt. xvi. 23.   [4] Gen. ii. 21, 22.   [5] John xix. 34.
[6] 1 Cor. xv. 51.
[7] So Oxf. MSS. *qua resurrexit.* Ben. *quare surrexit.*
[8] Perhaps he intends to read it, "Lo, children, the heritage of the Lord, is the reward of the fruit of the womb;" making *filii* vocative.

(ver. 3). Since he saith, "fruit of the womb," these children have been born in travail. There is a certain woman, in whom what was said unto Eve, "in sorrow shalt thou bring forth children," is shown after a spiritual manner. The Church beareth children, the Bride of Christ; and if she beareth them, she travaileth of them. In figure of her, Eve was called also "the Mother of all living."[1] He who said, "My little children, of whom I travail in birth again, until Christ be formed in you,"[2] was amongst the members of her who travaileth. But she travailed not in vain, nor brought forth in vain: there will be a holy seed at the resurrection of the dead: the righteous who are at present scattered over the whole world shall abound. The Church groaneth for them, the Church travaileth of them; but in that resurrection of the dead, the offspring of the Church shall appear, pain and groaning shall pass away. . . .

6. "Like as the arrows in the hand of the mighty one, even so are the children of those that are shot out" (ver. 4). Whence hath sprung this heritage, brethren? Whence hath sprung so numerous a heritage? Some have been shot out from the Lord's hand, as arrows, and have gone far, and have filled the whole earth, whence the Saints spring. For this is the heritage whereof it is said, "Desire of Me, and I shall give thee the heathen for thine inheritance, and the uttermost parts of the earth for thy possession."[3] And how doth this possession extend and increase unto the world's uttermost parts? Because, "like as the arrows in the hand of the mighty one," etc. Arrows are shot forth from the bow, and the stronger the arm which hath sent it forth, the farther flieth the arrow. But what is stronger than the darting of the Lord? From His bow He sendeth forth His Apostles: there could not be a spot left where an arrow shot by so strong an arm would not reach; it hath reached unto the uttermost parts of the earth. The reason it went no farther was, that there were no more of the human race beyond. For He hath such strength, that even if there were a spot beyond, whither the arrow could fly, He would dart the arrow thither. Such are the children of those who are shot forth as they that are shot forth.[4] . . .

7. Perhaps the Apostles themselves are styled the sons of those who have been shaken out, the sons of the Prophets. For the Prophets comprised closed and covered mysteries: they were shaken, that they might come forth thence manifestly. . . . Except the prophecy involved were sifted with diligence, would the concealed meanings come forth unto us? All these mean-

ings were therefore closed before the Lord's advent. The Lord came, and shook out these hidden meanings, and they were made manifest; the Prophets were shaken out, and the Apostles were born. Since then they were born of the Prophets who had been shaken out, the Apostles are sons of those that were shaken out. They, placed as the arrows in the hand of the giant, have reached the uttermost parts of the earth. . . . The Apostles the sons of the Prophets have been like as the arrows in the hand of a mighty one. If He is mighty, He hath shaken them out with a mighty hand; if He hath shaken them out with a mighty hand, they whom He hath shaken forth have arrived even at the uttermost parts of the earth.

8. "Blessed is the man who hath filled his desire from them" (ver. 5). Well, my brethren, who filleth his desire from them? Who loveth not the world. He who is filled with the desire of the world, hath no room for that to enter which they have preached. Pour forth what thou carriest, and become fit for that which thou hast not. That is, thou desirest riches: thou canst not fill thy desire from them: thou desirest honours upon earth, thou desirest those things which God hath given even unto beasts of burden, that is, temporal pleasure, bodily health, and the like; thou wilt not fulfil thy desire from them. . . . "He shall not be ashamed, when he speaketh with his enemies in the gate." Brethren, let us speak in the gate, that is, let all know what we speak. For he who chooseth not to speak in the gate, wisheth what he speaketh to be hidden, and perhaps wisheth it to be hidden for this reason, that it is evil. If he be confident, let him speak in the gate; as it is said of Wisdom, "She crieth at the gates, at the entry of the city."[5] As long as they hold unto righteousness in innocency, they shall not be ashamed: this is to preach at the gate. And who is he who preacheth at the gate? He who preacheth in Christ; because Christ is the gate whereby we enter into that city.[6] . . . They, therefore, who speak against Christ, are without the gate; because they seek their own honours, not those of Christ. But he who preacheth in the gate, seeketh Christ's honour, not his own: and, therefore, he who preacheth in the gate, saith, Trust not in me; for ye will not enter through me, but through the gate. While they who wish men to trust in themselves, wish them not to enter through the gate: it is no marvel if the gate be closed against them, and if they vainly knock for it to be opened.[7]

---

[1] Gen. iii. 16, 20. [2] Gal. iv. 19. [3] Ps. ii. 8.
[4] [Al. "shaken forth."—C.]

[5] Prov. viii. 3.
[6] John x. 9.
[7] [He concludes by asking their prayers, and promising to preach the next day on "the Gospel of the Dove." Tract iv. on St. John i. 31, 32, § 16, vol. vii. p. 31, this series; and compare Tractates v. and vi. This reference is from ed. Oxford.—C.]

PSALM CXXVIII.[1]

1. Felix the Martyr,[2] truly Felix, i.e. "Happy" both in his name and his crown, whose birthday this is, despised the world. Was he, because he feared the Lord, thence happy, thence blessed, because his wife was as a fruitful vine upon the earth, and his children stood around his table? All these blessings he hath perfectly, but in the Body of Him who is here described; and, because he understood them in this sense, he scorned things present, that he might receive things future. Ye are aware, brethren, that he suffered not the death that other martyrs suffered. For he confessed, and was set aside for torments; on another day his body was discovered lifeless. They had closed the prison to his body, not to his spirit. The executioners found him gone; when they were preparing to torture, they spent their rage for nought. He was lying dead, without sense to them, that he might not be tortured; with sense with God, that he might be crowned. Whence was he also happy, brethren, not only in name, but in the reward of everlasting life, if he loved these things.

2. "Blessed are all they that fear the Lord, and walk in His ways" (ver. 1). He speaketh to many; but since these many are one in Christ, in the next words he speaketh in the singular: "For thou shalt eat the labours of thy fruits." . . . When I speak of Christians in the plural, I understand one in the One Christ. Ye are therefore many, and ye are one; we are many, and we are one. How are we many, and yet one? Because we cling unto Him whose members we are; and since our Head is in heaven, that His members may follow. . . . Let us therefore so hear this Psalm, as considering it to be spoken of Christ: and all of us who cling unto the Body of Christ, and have been made members of Christ, walk in the ways of the Lord; and let us fear the Lord with a chaste fear, with a fear that abideth for ever. . . .

3. "Thou shalt eat the labours of thy fruits" (ver. 2). And ye, O thou, ye many who are One, "Thou shalt eat of the labours of thy fruits." He seemeth to speak perversely to those who understand not: for he should have said, thou shalt eat the fruit of thy labours. For many eat the fruit of their labours. They labour in the vineyard; they eat not the toil itself; but what ariseth from their labour they eat. They labour about trees that bear fruit: who would eat labours? But the fruit of these labours, the produce of these trees; it is this that delighteth the husbandman. What

meaneth, "Thou shalt eat the labours of thy fruits"? At present we have toils: the fruits will come afterwards. But since their labours themselves are not without joy, on account of the hope whereof we have a little before spoken, "Rejoicing in hope, patient in tribulation;"[3] at present those very labours delight us, and make us joyful in hope. If therefore our toil has been what could be eaten, and could also delight us; what will be the fruit of our labour when eaten? "They who went weeping on their way, scattering their seed,"[4] did eat their labours; with how much greater pleasure will they eat the fruits of their labours, who "shall come again with joy, bearing their sheaves with them"? . . . "Blessed art thou, and well shall it be with thee." "Blessed art thou," is of the present: "well shall it be with thee," is of the future. When thou eatest the labours of thy fruits, "blessed art thou;" when thou hast reached the fruit of thy labours, "well shall it be with thee." What hath he said? For if it be well with thee, thou wilt be happy: and if thou wilt be happy, thou wilt also have all well with thee. But there is a difference between hope and attainment. If hope be so sweet, how much sweeter will reality be?

4. Let us now come to the words, "Thy wife" (ver. 3): it is said unto Christ. His wife, therefore, is the Church: His Church, His wife, we ourselves are. "As a fruitful vineyard." But in whom is the vineyard fruitful? For we see many barren ones entering those walls; we see that many intemperate, usurious persons, slave dealers, enter these walls, and such as resort to fortune-tellers, go to enchanters and enchantresses when they have a headache. Is this the fruitfulness of the vine? Is this the fecundity of the wife? It is not. These are thorns, but the vineyard is not everywhere thorny. It hath a certain fruitfulness, and is a fruitful vine; but in whom? "Upon the sides of thy house." Not all are called the sides of the house. For I ask what are the sides. What shall I say? Are they walls, strong stones, as it were? If he were speaking of this bodily tenement, we should perhaps understand this by sides. We mean by the sides of the house, those who cling unto Christ. . . .

5. "Thy children." The wife and the children are the same. In these carnal marriages and wedlocks, the wife is one, the children other: in the Church, she who is the wife, is the children also. For the Apostles belonged to the Church, and were among the members of the Church. They were therefore in His wife, and were His wife according to their own portion which they held in His members. Why then is

---

[1] Lat. CXXVII A sermon to the people, on the day of St. Felix the Martyr. [I have transposed the first paragraph. — C.]
[2] He is said to have suffered martyrdom at Thinissa, or Thimisa, not far from Hippo, on the 6th of November. — Ben. (Mart. Rom. has Tuneti.)

it said concerning them, "When the Bridegroom shall be taken from them, then shall the children of the Bridegroom fast"?[1] She who is the wife, then, is the children also. I speak a wonderful thing, my brethren. In the words of the Lord, we find the Church to be both His brethren, and His sisters, and His mother.[2] . . . For Mary was among the sides of His House, and His relatives coming of the kindred of the Virgin Mary, who believed on Him, were among the sides of His House ; not in respect of their carnal consanguinity, but inasmuch as they heard the Word of God, and obeyed it. . . . He added ; "For whosoever shall do the will of My Father which is in heaven, the same is My brother, and sister, and mother."[3] "Brother," perhaps, on account of the male sex whom the Church hath : "sister," on account of the women whom Christ hath here in His members. How "mother," save that Christ Himself is in those Christians, whom the Church daily bringeth forth Christians through baptism? In those therefore in whom thou understandest the wife, in them thou understandest the mother, in them the children.

6. . . . Such children ought therefore to be "around" the Lord's "table, like olive-branches."[4] A complete Vine it is, a great bliss : who would now refuse to be there? When thou seest any blasphemer have a wife, children, grandchildren, and thyself perchance without them, envy them not ; discern that the promise hath been fulfilled in thee also, but spiritually. If therefore we have, why have we? Because we fear the Lord. "Lo, thus shall the man be blessed that feareth the Lord" (ver. 4). He is the man, who is also the men ; and the men are one man ; because many are one, because Christ is One.

7. "The Lord from out of Sion bless thee : and mayest thou see the good things that are of Jerusalem" (ver. 5). Even to the birds was it said, "Be fruitful and multiply."[5] Dost thou wish to hold as a great blessing what was given unto birds? Who can be ignorant, that it was given indeed by the voice of God? But use these goods, if thou receive them ; and rather think how thou mayest nourish those who have been born, than that others may be born. For it is not happiness to have children, but to have good ones. Labour in the task of nourishing them, if they be born ; but if they be not born, give thanks unto God. . . . Thy children are infants : thou dost caress the infants : the infants caress thee : do they abide thus? But thou wishest they may grow, thou wishest that their age may increase. But consider that when one age cometh, another dieth. When boyhood cometh, infancy dieth ; when youth cometh,

boyhood dieth : when manhood cometh, youth dieth ; when old age cometh, manhood dieth : when death cometh, all age dieth. As many successions of ages as thou wishest for, so many deaths of ages dost thou wish for. These things therefore "are" not. Finally, are children born unto thee to share life with thee on earth, or rather to shut thee out and to succeed thee? Rejoicest thou in those born to exclude thee? Boys when born speak somewhat like this to their parents : "Now then, begin to think of removing hence, let us too play our parts on the stage." For the whole life of temptation in the human race is a stage play ;[6] for it is said, "Every man living is altogether vanity."[7] Nevertheless, if we rejoice in children who will succeed us ; how much must we rejoice in children with whom we shall remain, and in that Father for whom we are born, who will not die, but that we may evermore live with Him? These are the good things of Jerusalem : for they "are." And how long shall I see the good things of Jerusalem? "All thy life long." If thy life be for ever, thou wilt see the good things of Jerusalem for evermore. . . .

8. For, "if in this life only," saith the Apostle, "we have hope in Christ, we are of all men most miserable."[8] For what reason were the Martyrs condemned to beasts? What is that good? Can it be declared? by what means, or what tongue can tell it? or what ears can hear it? That indeed, "Neither ear hath heard, nor hath it entered into man's heart : "[9] only let us love, only let us grow in grace : ye see, then, that battles are not wanting, and that we fight with our lusts. We fight outwardly with unbelieving and disobedient men ; we fight inwardly with carnal suggestions and perturbations : we everywhere as yet fight. . . . What sort of peace then is this? One from Jerusalem, for Jerusalem is interpreted, A vision of Peace. Thus then "mayest thou see the good things that are of Jerusalem," and that, "all thy life long — and mayest thou see," not only thy children, but, "thy children's children." What meaneth, Thy children? Thy works which thou here dost. Who are thy children's children? The fruits of thy works. Thou givest alms : these are thy children : for the sake of thine alms thou receivest everlasting life, these are thy children's children. "Mayest thou see thy children's children ; " and there shall be "peace upon Israel" (ver. 6), the last words of the Psalm. . . .

PSALM CXXIX.[10]

1. The Psalm which we have sung is short : but as it is written in the Gospel of Zacchæus

---

[1] Matt. ix. 15.   [2] Matt. xii. 46, etc.   [3] Matt. xii. 48–50.
[4] Ps. cxxxviii. 3.   [5] Gen. i. 22.

[6] [A text illustrated by our great English dramatist. — C.]
[7] Ps. xxxix. 5.   [8] 1 Cor. xv. 19.   [9] 1 Cor. ii. 9.
[10] Lat. CXXVIII. A sermon to the people.

that he was "little of stature," [1] but mighty in works; as it is written of that widow who cast two mites into the treasury, little was the money, but great was her charity; [2] thus also this Psalm, if thou count the words, is short; if thou weigh the sentiments, is great. . . . Let the Spirit of God speak, let It speak to us, let It sing to us; whether we wish or wish not to dance, let It sing. For as he who danceth, moveth his limbs to the time; so they who dance according to the commandment of God, in their works obey the sound. What therefore saith the Lord in the Gospel to those who refuse to do this? "We have piped unto you, and ye have not danced: we have mourned unto you, and ye have not lamented." [3] Let Him therefore sing; we trust in God's mercy, for there will be those by whom He consoleth us. For they who are obstinate, continuing in wickedness, although they hear the Word of God, by their offences daily disturb the Church. Of such this Psalm speaketh; for thus it beginneth.

2. "Many a time have they fought against me from my youth up" (ver. 1). The Church speaketh of those whom She endureth: and as if it were asked, "Is it now?" The Church is of ancient birth: since saints have been so called, the Church hath been on earth. At one time the Church was in Abel only, and he was fought against by his wicked and lost brother Cain.[4] At one time the Church was in Enoch alone: and he was translated from the unright-eous.[5] At one time the Church was in the house of Noah alone, and endured all who perished by the flood, and the ark alone swam upon the waves, and escaped to shore.[6] At one time the Church was in Abraham alone, and we know what he endured from the wicked. The Church was in his brother's son, Lot, alone, and in his house, in Sodom, and he endured the iniquities and perversities of Sodom, until God freed him from amidst them.[7] The Church also began to exist in the people of Israel: She endured Pharaoh and the Egyptians. The number of the saints began to be also in the Church, that is, in the people of Israel; Moses and the rest of the saints endured the wicked Jews, the peo-ple of Israel. We come unto our Lord Jesus Christ: the Gospel was preached in the Psalms.[8] . . . For this reason, lest the Church wonder now, or lest any one wonder in the Church, who wisheth to be a good member of the Church, let him hear the Church herself his Mother say-ing to him, Marvel not at these things, my son: "Many a time have they fought against me from my youth up."

3. "Now may Israel say." She now seemeth to be speaking of herself: for she seemed not to have commenced herself, but to have answered. But to whom hath she replied? To them that think and say, How great evils do we endure, how great are the scandals that every day thick-en, as the wicked enter into the Church, and we have to endure them? But let the Church reply through some, that is, through the voice of the stronger, let her reply to the complaints of the weak, and let the stable confirm the unstable, and the full-grown infant, and let the Church say, "Many a time have they vexed me from my youth up" (ver. 2). Let the Church say this: let her not fear it. For what is the meaning of this addition, "From my youth up," after the words, "Many a time have they fought against me"? At present the old age of the Church is assailed: but let her not fear. Hath she then failed to arrive at old age, because they have not ceased to fight against her from her youth up? have they been able to blot her out? Let Israel comfort herself, let the Church console herself with past examples. Why have they fought against me? "For they could not prevail against me."

4. "Upon my back have sinners built; they have done their iniquity afar off" (ver. 3). Why have they fought against me? Because "they could not prevail upon me." What is this? They could not build upon me. I con-sented not with them unto sin. For every wicked man persecuteth the good on this ac-count, because the good man consenteth not with him to evil. Suppose he do some evil, and the Bishop censure him not, the Bishop is a good man: suppose the Bishop censure him, the Bishop is a bad man. Suppose he carry off any-thing, let the man robbed be silent, he is a good man: let him only speak and rebuke, even though he doth not reclaim his goods, he is every-thing bad. He is bad then who blameth the robber, and he is good who robbeth! . . . Heed not that such an one speaketh to thee: it is a wicked man through whom It speaketh to thee; but the word of God, that speaketh to thee, is not wicked.[9] Accuse God: accuse Him, if thou canst!

5. Thou accusest a man of avarice, and he accuseth God on the ground that He made gold. Be not covetous. And God, thou repliest, should not make gold. This now remaineth, because thou canst not restrain thine evil deeds, thou accusest the good works of God: the Creator and Architect of the world displeaseth thee. He ought not to make the sun either; for many con-tend concerning the lights of their windows, and

---

[1] Luke xix. 2–9. [2] Mark xii 42, 44. [3] Matt. xi. 17.
[4] Gen. iv. 8. [5] Gen. v. 24. [6] Gen. vi.-viii.
[7] Gen. xiii.-xx. [8] Ps. xl. 5. [Heb. iv. 2. — C.]

[9] Oxf. MSS. "Heed not through whom It speaketh to thee, but take heed that it is That which speaketh to thee. He is evil through whom It speaketh to thee, but the Word of God that speaketh to thee is not evil."

drag each other before courts of law. O if we could restrain our vices! for all things are good, because a good God made all things: and His works praise Him, when their goodness is considered by him who hath the spirit of considering them, the spirit of piety and wisdom.[1] . . .

6. Lend not money at interest. Thou accusest Scripture which saith, "He that hath not given his money upon usury."[2] I wrote not this: it went not forth first from my mouth: hear God. He replieth: let not the clergy lend upon usury. Perchance he who speaketh to thee, lendeth not at interest: but if he do so lend, suppose that he doth so lend; doth He who speaketh through him lend at interest? If he doth what he enjoineth thee, and thou dost it not; thou wilt go into the flame, he into the kingdom. If he doth not what he enjoineth thee, and equally with thee doth evil deeds, and preaches duties which he doth not; ye will both equally go into the flames. The hay will burn; but "the word of the Lord abideth for evermore."[3] . . .

7. "The righteous Lord shall hew the necks of the sinners" (ver. 4). . . . Which of us doth not fix his eyes upon the earth, like the Publican, and say, "Lord, be merciful unto me a sinner"?[4] If therefore all are sinners, and none is found without sin; all must fear the sword that hangs above their neck, because "the righteous Lord shall hew the necks of the sinners." I do not imagine, my brethren, of all sinners; but in the member which He striketh, He marks what sinners He striketh. For it is not said, The righteous Lord will hew the hands of the sinners; or their feet; but because proud sinners were meant to be understood, and all proud men carry lofty necks, and not only do evil deeds, but even refuse to acknowledge them to be such, and when they are rebuked, justify themselves:[5] . . . as it is written in Job (he was speaking of an ungodly sinner), "he runneth against God, even upon his neck, upon the thick bosses of his bucklers;"[6] so he here nameth the neck, because it is thus thou exaltest thyself, and dost not fix thine eyes upon the ground, and beat thy breast. Thou shouldest cry unto Him, as it is cried in another Psalm, "I said, Lord, be merciful unto me, for I have sinned against Thee."[7] Since thou dost not choose to say this, but justifiest thy deeds against the Word of God; what followeth in Scripture cometh upon thee: the righteous Lord shall hew the necks of sinners.

8. "Let them be confounded and turned backward, as many as have evil will at Sion"

(ver. 5). They who hate Sion, hate the Church: Sion is the Church. And they who hypocritically enter into the Church, hate the Church. They who refuse to keep the Word of God, hate the Church: "Upon my back have they built:" what will the Church do, save endure the burden even unto the end?

9. But what saith he of them? The next words are, "Let them be even as the grass of the house tops: that withereth before it be plucked up" (ver. 6). The grass of the house tops is that which groweth on house tops, on a tiled roof: it is seen on high, and hath not a root. How much better would it be if it grew lower, and how much more joyfully would it bloom? As it is, it riseth higher to a quicker withering. It hath not yet been plucked up, yet hath it withered: not yet have they received sentence from the judgment of God, and already they have not the sap of bloom. Observe their works, and see that they have withered. . . . The reapers will come, but they fill not their sheaves from these. For the reapers will come, and will gather the wheat into the barn, and will bind the tares together, and cast them into the fire. Thus also is the grass of the house tops cleared off, and whatever is plucked from it, is thrown into the fire; because it had withered even before it was plucked up. The reaper filleth not his hands thence. His next words are, "Whereof the reaper filleth not his hand; neither he that bindeth up the sheaves his bosom" (ver. 7). And, "the reapers are the angels,"[8] the Lord saith.

10. "So that they who go by say not so much as, The blessing of the Lord be upon you: we have blessed you in the name of the Lord" (ver. 8). For ye know, brethren, when men pass by others at work, it is customary to address them, "The blessing of the Lord be upon you."[9] And this was especially the custom in the Jewish nation. No one passed by and saw any one doing any work in the field, or in the vineyard, or in harvest, or anything of the sort; it was not lawful to pass by without a blessing. . . . Who are the passers by? They who have already passed hence to their country through this road, that is, through this life: the Apostles were passers by in this life, the Prophets were passers by. Whom did the Prophets and Apostles bless? Those in whom they saw the root of charity? But those whom they found lifted on high on their house tops, and proud in the bosses of their bucklers, they declared against these what they were doomed to become, but they gave them no blessing. Ye therefore who read in the Scriptures, find all those wicked men whom the

---

[1] Song of Three Children, ver. 35, etc.   [2] Ps. xv. 5.
[3] Isa. xl. 8. [On this subject see p. 99, note 2, *supra*. But it is well to study this and other Fathers *passim* on this most perplexing matter. Comp. Acts xv. 28, 29; Deut. xxiii. 20; Matt. xxv. 27. — C.]
[4] Luke xviii. 13.
[5] Oxf. mss. add, "I did not this, but the stars."
[6] Job xv. 26.   [7] Ps. xli. 4.

[8] Matt. xiii. 39.
[9] [Note this Christian usage of the fifth century. — C.]

Church beareth, who are declared cursed, pertain unto Antichrist, pertain unto the devil, pertain to the chaff, pertain to the tares. . . . But they who say, None save God sanctifieth, nor is any man good save by the gift of God; they bless in the name of the Lord, not in their own name: because they are the friends of the bridegroom,[1] they refuse to be adulterers of the bride.

PSALM CXXX.[2]

1. "Out of the deep have I called unto Thee, O Lord: Lord, hear my voice" (ver. 1). Jonas cried from the deep; from the whale's belly.[3] He was not only beneath the waves, but also in the entrails of the beast; nevertheless, those waves and that body prevented not his prayer from reaching God, and the beast's belly could not contain the voice of his prayer. It penetrated all things, it burst through all things, it reached the ears of God: if indeed we ought to say that, bursting through all things, it reached the ears of God, since the ears of God were in the heart of him who prayed. For where hath not he God present, whose voice is faithful? Nevertheless, we also ought to understand from what deep we cry unto the Lord. For this mortal life is our deep. Whoever hath understood himself to be in the deep, crieth out, groaneth, sigheth, until he be delivered from the deep, and come unto Him who sitteth above all the deeps. . . . For they are very deep in the deep, who do not even cry from the deep. The Scripture saith, "When the wicked hath reached the depth of evils, he despiseth."[4] Now consider, brethren, what sort of deep that is, where God is despised. When each man seeth himself overwhelmed with daily sins, pressed down by heaps and weights, so to speak, of iniquities: if it be said unto him, Pray unto God, he laughs. In what manner? He first saith, If crimes were displeasing unto God, should I live? If God regarded human affairs, considering the great crimes which I have committed, should I not only live, but be prosperous? For this is wont to happen to those who are far in the deep, and are prosperous in their iniquities: and they are the more plunged in the deep, in proportion as they seem to be more happy; for a deceitful happiness is itself a greater unhappiness. . . .

2. "Lord, hear my voice. O let Thine ears consider well the voice of my complaint" (ver. 2). Whence doth he cry? From the deep. Who is it then who crieth? A sinner. And with what hope doth he cry? Because He who came to absolve from sins, gave hope even to the sinner down in the deep. What therefore

followeth after these words: "If Thou, Lord, wilt be extreme to mark what is amiss, O Lord, who may abide it?" (ver. 3). So, he hath disclosed from what deep he cried out. For he crieth beneath the weights and billows of his iniquities. . . . He said not, I may not abide it: but, "who may abide it?" For he saw that nigh the whole of human life on every side was ever bayed at by its sins, that all consciences were accused by their thoughts, that a clean heart trusting in its own righteousness could not be found.

3. But wherefore is there hope? "For there is propitiation with Thee" (ver. 4). And what is this propitiation, except sacrifice? And what is sacrifice, save that which hath been offered for us? The pouring forth of innocent blood blotted out all the sins of the guilty: so great a price paid down redeemed all captives from the hand of the enemy who captured them. "With Thee," then, "there is propitiation." For if there were not mercy with Thee, if Thou chosest to be Judge only, and didst refuse to be merciful, Thou wouldest mark all our iniquities, and search after them. Who could abide this? Who could stand before Thee, and say, I am innocent? Who could stand in Thy judgment? There is therefore one hope: "for the sake of Thy law have I borne Thee, O Lord." What law? That which made men guilty. For a "law, holy, just, and good,"[5] was given to the Jews; but its effect was to make them guilty. A law was not given that could give life,[6] but which might show his sins to the sinner. For the sinner had forgotten himself, and saw not himself; the law was given him, that he might see himself. The law made him guilty, the Lawgiver freed him: for the Lawgiver is the Supreme Power.[7] . . . There is therefore a law of the mercy of God, a law of the propitiation of God.[8] The one was a law of fear, the other is a law of love. The law of love giveth forgiveness to sins, blotteth out the past, warneth concerning the future; forsaketh not its companion by the way, becometh a companion to him whom it leadeth on the way. But it is needful to agree with the adversary, whilst thou art with him in the way.[9] For the Word of God is thine adversary, as long as thou dost not agree with it. But thou agreest, when it has begun to be thy delight to do what God's Word commandeth. Then he who was thine adversary becometh thy friend: so, when the way is finished, there will be none to deliver thee to the Judge. Therefore, "For the sake of Thy law I have waited for Thee, O Lord," because thou hast condescended to bring in a law of mercy, to forgive me all my sins, to give me for the future warnings that I may not offend. . . . "For the

---

1 John iii. 29.
2 Lat. CXXIX. A song of degrees. A sermon to the people.
3 Jonah ii. 2.   4 Prov. xviii. 3.

5 Rom. vii. 12.   6 Gal. iii. 21.   7 *Imperator.*
8 [Note (*Greek*) Luke xviii. 13. — C.]   9 Matt. v. 25.

sake," therefore, " of " this " law I have waited for Thee, O Lord." I have waited until Thou mayest come and free me from all need, for in my very need Thou hast not forsaken the law of mercy. . . . "My soul hath waited for Thy word." . . .

4. We therefore trust without fear on the word of Him who cannot deceive. "My soul hath trusted in the Lord, from the morning watch even unto night" (ver. 5). This morning watch is the end of night. We must therefore understand it so that we may not suppose we are to trust in the Lord for one day only. What do you conceive to be the sense, then, brethren? The words mean this: that the Lord, through whom our sins have been remitted, arose from the dead at the morning watch, so that we may hope that what went before in the Lord will take place in us. For our sins have been already forgiven: but we have not yet risen again: if we have not risen again, not as yet hath that taken place in us which went before in our Head. What went before in our Head? Because the flesh of that Head rose again; did the Spirit of that Head die? What had died in Him, rose again. Now He arose on the third day; and the Lord as it were thus speaketh to us: What ye have seen in Me, hope for in yourselves; that is, because I have risen from the dead, ye also shall rise again.

5. But there are who say, Behold, the Lord hath risen again; but must I hope on that account that I also may rise again? Certainly, on that account: for the Lord rose again in that which He assumed from thee. For He would not rise again, save He had died; and He could not have died, except He bore the flesh. What did the Lord assume from thee? The flesh. What was He that came Himself? The Word of God, who was before all things, through whom all things were made. But that He might receive something from thee, "The Word became flesh, and dwelt among us." [1] He received from thee, what He might offer for thee; as the priest receiveth from thee, what he may offer for thee, when thou wishest to appease God for thy sins. It hath already been done, it hath been done thus. Our Priest received from us what He might offer for us: for He received flesh from us, in the flesh itself He was made a victim, He was made a holocaust, He was made a sacrifice. In the Passion He was made a sacrifice; in the Resurrection He renewed that which was slain, and offered it as His first-fruits unto God, and saith unto thee, All that is thine is now consecrated: since such first-fruits have been offered unto God from thee; hope therefore that that will take place in thyself which went before in thy first-fruits.

6. Since He then rose with the morning watch,

our soul began to hope from hence: and how far? " Even unto night;" until we die; for all our carnal death is as it were sleep. . . .

7. And he returns to this, " From the morning watch let Israel hope in the Lord." Not only " let Israel hope," but " from the morning watch let Israel hope." Do I then blame the hope of the world, when it is placed in the Lord? No; but there is another hope belonging to Israel. Let not Israel hope for riches as his highest good, not for health of body, not for abundance of earthly things: he will indeed have to suffer tribulation here, if it should be his lot to suffer any troubles for the sake of the truth. . . .

8. "For with the Lord there is mercy, and with Him is plenteous redemption" (ver. 7). Admirable! This could not have been better said in its own place, on account of the words, " From the morning watch." Wherefore? Because the Lord rose again from the morning watch; and the body ought to hope for that which went before in the Head. But, lest this thought should be suggested: The Head might rise again, because It was not weighed down with sins, there was no sin in Him; what shall we do? Shall we hope for such a resurrection, as went before in the Lord, whilst we are weighed down by our sins? But see what followeth: "And He shall redeem Israel from all his sins" (ver. 8). Though therefore he was weighed down with his sins, the mercy of God is present to him. For this reason, He went before without sin, that He may blot out the sins of those that follow Him. Trust not in yourselves, but trust from the morning watch. . . .

PSALM CXXXI. [2]

1. In this Psalm, the humility of one that is a servant of God and faithful is commended unto us, by whose voice it is sung; which is the whole body of Christ. [3] For we have often warned you, beloved, that it ought not to be received as the voice of one man singing, but of all who are in Christ's Body. And since all are in His Body, as it were one man speaketh: and he is one who also is many. . . . Now he prayeth in the temple of God, who prayeth in the peace of the Church, in the unity of Christ's Body; which Body of Christ consisteth of many who believe in the whole world: and therefore he who prayeth in the temple, is heard. For he prayeth in the spirit and in truth, [4] who prayeth in the peace of the Church; not in that temple, wherein was the figure. . . .

2. "Lord, my heart is not lifted up" (ver. 1). He hath offered a sacrifice. Whence do we

[1] John i. 1, 3, 14.

[2] Lat. CXXX. A sermon to the common people.
[3] [On this principle the *Magnificat* and the *Nunc dimittis* are perpetuated as the ceaseless song of the Church. — C.]
[4] John iv. 21–24.

prove that he hath offered a sacrifice? Because humility of heart is a sacrifice. . . . If there is no sacrifice, there is no Priest. But if we have a High Priest in Heaven, who intercedeth with the Father for us (for He hath entered into the Holy of Holies, within the veil), . . . we are safe, for we have a Priest; let us offer our sacrifice there. Let us consider what sacrifice we ought to offer; for God is not pleased with burnt-offerings, as ye have heard in the Psalm. But in that place he next showeth what he offereth: "The sacrifice of God is a troubled spirit: a broken and a contrite heart, O God, shalt Thou not despise.[1]

3. "Lord, my heart was not lifted up, neither were mine eyes raised on high" (ver. 1); "I have not exercised myself in great matters, nor in wonderful things which are too high for me" (ver. 2). Let this be more plainly spoken and heard. I have not been proud: I have not wished to be known among men as for wondrous powers; nor have I sought anything beyond my strength, whereby I might boast myself among the ignorant. As that Simon the sorcerer wished to advance into wonders above himself, on that account the power of the Apostles more pleased him, than the righteousness of Christians. . . . What is above my strength, he saith, I have not sought; I have not stretched myself out there, I have not chosen to be magnified there. How deeply this self-exaltation in the abundance of graces is to be feared, that no man may pride himself in the gift of God, but may rather preserve humility, and may do what is written: "The greater thou art, the more humble thyself, and thou shalt find favour before the Lord:"[2] how deeply pride in God's gift should be feared, we must again and again impress upon you. . . .

4. "If I had not lowly thoughts, but have lifted up my soul, as one taken from his mother's breast, such the reward for my soul" (ver. 2). He seemeth as it were to have bound himself by a curse: . . . as though he had been going to say, Let it so happen to me. "As one taken away from his mother's breast, may be my soul's reward." Ye know that the Apostle saith to some weak brethren, "I have fed you with milk, and not with meat; for hitherto ye were not able to bear it, neither yet now are ye able."[3] There are weak persons who are not fit for strong meat; they wish to grasp at that which they cannot receive: and if they ever do receive, or seem to themselves to receive what they have not received, they are puffed up thereby, and become proud thereupon; they seem to themselves wise men. Now this happeneth to all heretics; who since they were animal and carnal, by defending their depraved opinions, which they could not

see to be false, were shut out of the Catholic Church. . . .

5. Another opinion indeed hath been entertained, and another sense in these words. . . . It has been evidently explained, my brethren, where God would have us to be humble, where lofty. Humble, in order to provide against pride; lofty, to take in wisdom. Feed upon milk, that thou mayest be nourished; be nourished, so that thou mayest grow; grow, so that thou mayest eat bread. But when thou hast begun to eat bread, thou wilt be weaned, that is, thou wilt no longer have need of milk, but of solid food. This he seemeth to have meant: "If I had not lowly thoughts, but have lifted up my soul:" that is, if I was not an infant in mind, I was in wickedness. In this sense, he said before, "Lord, my heart was not lifted up, nor mine eyes raised on high: I do not exercise myself in great matters, nor in wonderful things above me." Behold, in wickedness I am an infant. But since I am not an infant in understanding, "If I had not lowly thoughts, but have lifted up my soul," may that reward be mine which is given unto the infant that is weaned from his mother, that I may at length be able to eat bread.

6. This interpretation, also, brethren, displeaseth me not, since it doth not militate against the faith. Yet I cannot but remark that it is not only said, "As one taken away from milk, such may be my soul's reward;" but with this addition, "As one taken away from milk when upon his mother's breast, such may be my soul's reward." Here there is somewhat that induces me to consider it a curse. For it is not an infant, but a grown child that is taken away from milk; he who is weak in his earliest infancy, which is his true infancy, is upon his mother's breast: if perchance he hath been taken away from the milk, he perisheth. It is not without a reason then that it is added, "Upon his mother's breast." For all may be weaned by growing. He who groweth, and is thus taken away from milk, it is good for him; but hurtful for him who is still upon his mother's breast. We must therefore beware, my brethren, and be fearful, lest any one be taken away from milk before his time. . . . Let him not therefore wish to lift up his soul, when perchance he is not fit to take meat, but let him fulfil the commandments of humility. He hath wherein he may exercise himself: let him believe in Christ, that he may understand Christ. He cannot see the Word, he cannot understand the equality of the Word with the Father, he cannot as yet see the equality of the Holy Spirit with the Father and the Word; let him believe this, and suck it. He is safe, because, when he hath grown, he will eat, which he could not do before he grew by suck-

ing: and he hath a point to stretch towards. Seek not out the things that are too hard for thee, and search not the things that are above thy strength; that is, things which thou art not as yet fit to understand. And what am I to do? thou repliest. Shall I remain thus? "But what things the Lord hath commanded thee, think thereupon always."[1] What hath the Lord commanded thee? Do works of mercy, part not with the peace of the Church, place not thy trust in man, tempt not God by longing for miracles. . . .

7. For if ye be not exalted, if ye raise not your heart on high, if ye tread not in great matters that are too high for you, but preserve humility, God will reveal unto you what ye are otherwise minded in.[2] But if ye choose to defend this very thing, which ye are otherwise minded about, and with pertinacity assert it, and against the peace of the Church; this curse which he hath described is entailed upon you; when ye are upon your mother's breast, and are removed away from the milk, ye shall die of hunger apart from your mother's breast. But if ye continue in Catholic peace, if perchance ye are in anything otherwise minded than ye ought to be, God will reveal it to you, if ye be humble. Wherefore? Because "God resisteth the proud, and giveth grace unto the humble."[3]

8. This Psalm therefore concludeth to this purpose: "O Israel, trust in the Lord, from this time forth and even unto eternity"[4] (ver. 3). But the word *seculum* doth not always mean this world, but sometimes eternity; since eternity is understood in two ways; until eternity, that is, either evermore without end, or until we arrive at eternity. How then is it to be understood here? Until we arrive at eternity, let us trust in the Lord God; because when we have reached eternity, there will be no longer hope, but the thing itself will be ours.

PSALM CXXXII.[5]

1. It was right indeed, most beloved, that we should rather hear our Brother,[6] my colleague, when present before all of us. And just now he refused not, but put us off; for he extorted from me that he might now listen to me, on the condition that I also may listen to him, for in charity itself we are all listening unto Him, who is our One Master in heaven. Attend therefore to the Psalm, entitled A Song of Degrees; considerably longer than the rest under the same title. Let us not therefore linger, save

where necessity shall compel us: that we may, if the Lord permit, explain the whole. For ye also ought not to hear everything as men untaught; ye ought in some degree to aid us from your past listenings, so that it may not be needful that everything should be declared to you as though new.[7]

2. "Lord, remember David, and all his meekness" (ver. 1). David according to the truth of history was one man, king of Israel, son of Jesse. He was indeed meek, as the Divine Scriptures themselves mark and command him, and so meek that he did not even render evil for evil to his persecutor Saul. He preserved towards him so great humility, that he acknowledged him a king, and himself a dog: and answered the king not proudly nor rudely, though he was more powerful in God; but he rather endeavoured to appease him by humility, than to provoke him by pride. Saul was even given into his power, and this by the Lord God, that he might do to him what he listed: but since he was not commanded to slay him, but had it only placed in his power (now a man is permitted to use his power), he rather turned towards mercy what God gave him. . . . The humility of David is therefore commended, the meekness of David is commended; and it is said to God, "Lord, remember David, and all his meekness." For what purpose? "How he sware unto the Lord, and vowed a vow unto the Almighty God of Jacob" (ver. 2). Therefore remember for this, that he may fulfil what he hath promised. David himself vowed as though he had it in his power, and he prayeth God to fulfil his vow: there is devotion in the vow, but there is humility in the prayer. Let no one presume to think he fulfilled by his own strength what he hath vowed. He who exhorteth thee to vow, Himself aideth thee to fulfil. Let us therefore see what he vowed, and hence we comprehend how David should be understood in a figure. "David" is interpreted, "Strong of hand," for he was a great warrior. Trusting indeed in the Lord his God, he despatched all wars, he laid low all his enemies, God helping him, according to the dispensation of that kingdom; prefiguring nevertheless some One strong of hand to destroy His enemies, the devil and his angels. These enemies the Church warreth against, and conquereth. . . . What then doth he mean, "How he sware," etc.? Let us see what vow is this. We can offer God nothing more pleasing than to swear.[8] Now to swear is to promise firmly.[9]

---

[1] Ecclus. iii. 22.   [2] Philip. iii. 15.
[3] Jas iv. 6 and 1 Pet. v. 5.
[4] [He adds: "The Greek words, ἀπὸ τοῦ νῦν καὶ ἕως τοῦ αἰῶνος, are rendered in the Latin, *ex hoc nunc et usque in seculum*." — C.]
[5] Lat. CXXXI. A sermon to the common people.
[6] Ed. Ben. supposes this to be Severus, Bishop of Milevis; and refers to Exp of Ps. xcvi. § 1, p. 470, *supra*.

[7] [On this principle, I have been forced to sacrifice many repetitions excellent in themselves. — C.]
[8] Ben. thinks these words are repeated by mistake from above, in some MSS.; but they are also in our copies, and come in very much after the manner of St. Augustin.
[9] [This sufficiently modifies and expounds what he means. — C.]

Consider this vow, that is, with what ardour he vowed what he vowed, with what love, with what longing; nevertheless, he prayeth the Lord to fulfil it in these words, "O Lord, remember David, and all his meekness." In this temper he vowed his vow, and there should be a house of God : " I will not come within the tabernacle of mine house, nor climb up into my bed " (ver. 3). "I will not suffer mine eyes to sleep, nor mine eyelids to slumber " (ver. 4). This seemeth not enough ; he adds, " Neither the temples of my head to take any rest, until I find out a place for the Lord ; an habitation for the God of Jacob " (ver. 5). Where did he seek a place for the Lord? If he was meek, he sought it in himself. For how is one a place for the Lord? Hear the Prophet : " Upon whom shall My Spirit rest? Even upon him that is poor and of a contrite spirit, and trembleth at My words." [1] Dost thou wish to be a place for the Lord? Be thou poor in spirit, and contrite, and trembling at the word of God, and thou wilt thyself be made what thou seekest. For if what thou seekest be not realized in thyself, what doth it profit thee in another. . . .

3. How many thousands believed, my brethren, when they laid down the price of their possessions at the Apostles' feet ! But what saith Scripture of them? Surely they are become a temple of God ; not only each respectively a temple of God, but also all a temple of God together. They have therefore become a place for the Lord. And that ye may know that one place is made for the Lord in all, Scripture saith, They were of one heart and one soul toward God.[2] But many, so as not to make a place for the Lord, seek their own things, love their own things, delight in their own power, are greedy for their private interests. Whereas he who wisheth to make a place for the Lord, should rejoice not in his private, but the common good. . . .

4. Let us therefore, brethren, abstain from the possession of private property ; or from the love of it, if we may not from its possession ; and we make a place for the Lord. It is too much for me, saith some one. But consider who thou art, who art about to make a place for the Lord. If any senator wished to be entertained at your house, I say not senator, the deputy of some great man of this world, and should say, something offends me in thy house ; though thou shouldest love it, thou wouldest remove it, nevertheless, lest thou shouldest offend him, whose friendship thou wast courting. And what doth man's friendship profit thee? . . . Desire the friendship of Christ without fear : He wishes to be entertained at thy house ; make room for Him. What is, make room for Him? Love not

thyself, love Him. If thou love thyself, thou shuttest the door against Him ; if thou love Him, thou openest unto Him : and if thou open and He enter, thou shalt not be lost by loving thyself, but shalt find thyself with Him who loveth thee. . . .

5. "Lo, we heard of the same at Ephrata " (ver. 6). What? A place for the Lord. "We heard of it at Ephrata : and found it in the plains of the forests." [3] Did he hear it where he found it? or did he hear it in one place, find it in another? Let us therefore enquire what Ephrata is, where he heard it ; let us also enquire what mean the plains of the forests, where he found it. Ephrata, a Hebrew word, is rendered in Latin by *Speculum*,[4] as the translators of Hebrew words in the Scriptures have handed down to us, that we might understand them. They have translated from Hebrew into Greek, and from Greek we have versions into Latin. For there have been who watched in the Scriptures. If therefore Ephrata meaneth a mirror, that house which was found in the woodland plains, was heard of in a mirror. A mirror hath an image : all prophecy is an image of things future. The future house of God, therefore, was declared in the image of prophecy. "We have found it in the plains of the forests." What are the "plains of the forests"?[5] *Saltus* is not here used in its common sense, as a plot of ground of so many hundred acres ;[6] *saltus* properly signifies a spot as yet untilled and woody. For some copies read, in the plains of the wood. What then were the woodland plains, save nations yet untilled? what were they, save regions yet covered with the thorns of idolatry? Thus, though there were thorns of idolatry there, still we find a place for the Lord there, a tabernacle for the God of Jacob. What was declared in the image to the Jews, was manifested in the faith of the Gentiles.

6. "We will go into His tabernacles " (ver. 7). Whose? Those of the Lord God of Jacob. They who enter to dwell therein, are the very same who enter that they may be dwelt in. Thou enterest into thy house, that thou mayest dwell therein ; into the house of God, that thou mayest be dwelt in. For the Lord is better, and when He hath begun to dwell in thee, He will make thee happy. For if thou be not dwelt in by Him, thou wilt be miserable. That son who said, " Father, give me the portion of the goods," etc.,[7] wished to be his own master. It was well kept in his father's hands, that it might not be wasted with harlots. He received it, it was given into his own power ; going to a far country,

---

[1] Isa. lxvi. 2.   [2] Acts iv. 4, 32, 35.

[3] Oxf. MSS add these words: " We hear those things in Ephrata, we find them in the woodland plains." [Note 1 Kings vi. 7. — C.]
[4] Mirror.   [5] *Saltuum*.
[6] Centuriarum — then 200 acres. See Isid. *Etym*. xv. c. 15, § 7.
[7] Luke xv. 12-20.

he squandered it all with harlots. At length he suffered hunger, he remembered his father; he returned, that he might be satisfied with bread. Enter therefore, that thou mayest be dwelt in; and mayest be not thine own, so to speak, but His: "We will go into His tabernacles. We will worship on the spot where His feet stood." Whose feet? The Lord's, or those of the house of the Lord itself? For that is the Lord's house, wherein he saith He ought to be worshipped. Beside His house, the Lord heareth not unto eternal life; for he belongeth to God's house, who hath in charity been built in with living stones. But he who hath not charity, falleth; and while he falls, the house stands. . . .

7. But if ye incline to understand it of the house itself, where the feet of that house have stood; let thy feet stand in Christ. They will then stand, if thou shalt persevere in Christ. For what is said of the devil? "He was a murderer from the beginning, and stood not in the truth." [1] The feet of the devil therefore stood not. Also what saith he of the proud? "O let not the foot of pride come against me; and let not the hand of the ungodly cast me down. There are they fallen, all that work wickedness: they are cast down, and were not able to stand." [2] That then is the house of God, whose feet stand. Whence John rejoicing, saith: what? "He that hath the bride is the bridegroom: but the friend of the bridegroom standeth and heareth him." If he stand not, he heareth him not. Justly he standeth, because "he rejoiceth on account of the bridegroom's voice." Now therefore ye see why they fell, who rejoice because of their own voice.[3] That friend of the Bridegroom said, "The same is He which baptizeth." [4] Some say, We baptize: rejoicing in their own voice, they could not stand; and belong not to that house of which it is said, "where His feet stood."

8. "Arise, O Lord, into Thy resting place" (ver. 8). He saith unto the Lord sleeping, "Arise." Ye know already who slept, and who rose again. . . . "Thou, and the ark of Thy sanctification:" that is, Arise, that the ark of Thy sanctification, which Thou hast sanctified, may arise also. He is our Head; His ark is His Church: He arose first, the Church will arise also. The body would not dare to promise itself resurrection, save the Head arose first. The Body of Christ, that was born of Mary, hath been understood by some to be the ark of sanctification; so that the words mean, Arise with Thy Body, that they who believe not may handle.

9. "Let Thy priests be clothed with righteousness, and let Thy saints sing with joyfulness" (ver. 9). When Thou risest from the dead, and goest unto Thy Father, let that royal Priesthood be clothed with faith, since "the righteous liveth by faith;" [5] and, receiving the pledge of the Holy Spirit, let the members rejoice in the hope of resurrection, which went before in the Head: for to them the Apostle saith, "Rejoicing in hope." [6]

10. "For Thy servant David's sake, turn not away the face of Thine Anointed" (ver. 10). These words are addressed unto God the Father. "For Thy servant David's sake, turn not away the face of Thine Anointed." The Lord was crucified in Judæa; He was crucified by the Jews; harassed by them, He slept. He arose to judge those among whose savage hands He slept: and He saith elsewhere, "Raise Thou Me up again, and I shall reward them." [7] He both hath rewarded them, and will reward them. The Jews well know themselves how great were their sufferings after the Lord's death. They were all expelled from the very city, where they slew Him. What then? have all perished even from the root of David and from the tribe of Judah? No: for some of that stock believed, and in fact many thousands of men of that stock believed, and this after the Lord's resurrection. They raged and crucified Him: and afterwards began to see miracles wrought in the Name of Him Crucified; and they trembled still more that His Name should have so much power, since when in their hands He seemed unable to work any; and pricked at heart, at length believing that there was some hidden divinity in Him whom they had believed like other men, and asking counsel of the Apostles, they were answered, "Repent, and be baptized every one of you in the Name of our Lord Jesus Christ." [8] Since then Christ arose to judge those by whom He had been crucified, and turned away His Presence from the Jews, turning His Presence towards the Gentiles; God is, as it seemeth, besought in behalf of the remnant of Israel; and it is said unto Him, "For Thy servant David's sake, turn not away the presence of Thine Anointed." If the chaff be condemned, let the wheat be gathered together. May the remnant be saved, as Isaiah saith, "And the remnant hath" clearly "been saved:" [9] for out of them were the twelve Apostles, out of them more than five hundred brethren, to whom the Lord showed Himself after His Resurrection: [10] out of their number were so many thousands baptized,[11] who laid the price of their possessions at the Apostles' feet. Thus then was fulfilled the prayer here made to God: "For Thy servant David's sake, turn not away the presence of Thine Anointed."

[1] John viii. 44.   [2] Ps. xxxvi. 11, 12.   [3] Donatists.
[4] John i. 33.

[5] Rom. i. 17.   [6] Rom. xii. 12.   [7] Ps. xli. 10.
[8] Acts ii. 38.   [9] Isa. x. 21, 22.   [10] 1 Cor. xv. 6.
[11] Acts ii. 41.

11. "The Lord hath made a faithful oath unto David, and He shall not repent "(ver. 11). What meaneth, "hath made an oath"? Hath confirmed a promise through Himself. What meaneth, "He shall not repent"? He will not change. For God suffereth not the pain of repentance, nor is He deceived in any matter, so that He would wish to correct that wherein He hath erred. But as when a man repents of anything, he wisheth to change what he hath done; thus where thou hearest that God repenteth, look for an actual change. God doth it differently from thee, although He calleth it by the name of repentance; for thou dost it, because thou hadst erred; while He doth it, because He avengeth, or freeth. He changed Saul's kingdom, when He repented, as it is said: and in the very passage where the Scripture saith, "It repented Him;" it is said a little after, "for He is not a man that He should repent."[1] When therefore He changeth His works through His immutable counsel, He is said to repent on account of this very change, not of His counsel, but of His work. But He promised this so as not to change it. Just as this passage also saith: "The Lord sware, and will not repent, Thou art a Priest for ever after the order of Melchizedec;"[2] so also since this was promised so that it should not be changed, because it must needs happen and be permanent; he saith, "The Lord hath made a faithful oath unto David, and He shall not repent; Of the fruit of thy body shall I set upon thy seat." He might have said, "of the fruit of thy loins," wherefore did He choose to say, "Of the fruit of thy body"? Had He said that also, it would have been true; but He chose to say with a further meaning, *Ex fructu ventris*, because Christ was born of a woman without the man.

12. What then? "The Lord hath made a faithful oath unto David, and He shall not shrink from it; Of the fruit of thy body shall I set upon thy seat. If thy children will keep My covenant and My testimonies that I shall learn them, their children also shall sit upon thy seat for evermore" (ver. 12). If thy children keep My covenant, their children also shall sit for evermore. The parents establish a desert on behalf of their children. What if his children should keep the covenant, and their children should not keep it? Why is the happiness of the children promised in relation to their parents' deservings? For what saith He, "If thy children will keep My covenant, their children also shall sit for evermore"—He saith not, if thy children keep My covenant, they shall sit upon thy seat; and if their children

keep My covenant, they also shall sit upon thy seat: but he saith, "If thy children keep My covenant, their children also shall sit upon thy seat for evermore"—except because He here wished their fruit to be understood by their children? "If thy children," He saith, "will keep My covenant, and if thy children keep My testimonies that I shall learn them; their children also shall sit upon thy seat:" that is, this will be their fruit, that they sit upon thy seat. For in this life, brethren, do all of us who labour in Christ, all of us who tremble at His words, who in any way endeavour to execute His will, and groan while we pray His help that we may fulfil what He commandeth; do we already sit in those seats of bliss which are promised us? No: but holding His commandments, we hope this will come to pass. This hope is spoken of under the figure of sons; because sons are the hope of man living in this life, sons are his fruit. For this reason also men, when excusing their avarice, allege that they are reserving for their children what they hoard up; and, unwilling to give to the destitute, excuse themselves under the name of piety, because their children are their hope. For all men who live according to this world, declare it to be their hope, to be fathers of children they may leave behind them. Thus then He describes hope generally under the name of children, and saith, "If thy children will keep My covenant and My testimonies that I shall learn them, their children also shall sit upon thy seat for evermore:" that is, they shall have such fruits, that their hope shall not deceive them, that they may come there where they hope to come. At present therefore they are as fathers, men of hope for the future; but when they have attained what they hope, they are children; because they have brought forth and produced in their works that which they gain. And this is preserved unto them for the future,[3] because futurity[4] itself commonly signifieth children.

13. Or if thou understand actual men to be meant by children, the words, "If thy children will keep My covenant and My testimonies that I shall teach them," may mean, "If thy children will keep My covenant and testimonies that I shall teach them, and their children also;" that is, if they too keep My covenant; so that here thou must make a slight pause, and then infer that "they shall sit upon thy seat for evermore;" that is, both thy children and their children, but all if they keep My covenant. What then, if they keep it not? Hath the promise of God failed? No: but it is said and promised for this reason, that God foresaw: what, save that

they would believe? But that no man should as it were threaten God's promises, and prefer to place in his own power the fulfilment of what God promised: for this reason he saith, "He made an oath:" whereby he showeth that it will without doubt take place. How then hath He said here, "If they will keep My covenant"? Glory not in the promises, and leave out thy failing to keep the covenant. Then wilt thou be the son of David, if thou shalt keep the covenant; but if thou dost not keep it, thou wilt not be David's son. God promised to the sons of David. Say not, I am David's son if thou degenerate. If the Jews, who were born of this very stock, say not this (nay, they say it, but they are under a delusion. For the Lord saith openly, "If ye were Abraham's children, ye would do the works of Abraham."[1] He thereby denied them to be children, because they did not the works), how do we call ourselves David's children, who are not of his race according to the flesh? It follows then that we are not children, save by imitating his faith, save by worshipping God, as he worshipped. If therefore what thou hopest not through descent, thou wilt not endeavour to obtain by works; how shall the sitting upon David's seat be fulfilled in thee? And if it shall not be fulfilled in thee, thinkest thou that it shall not be fulfilled at all? And how hath He found it in the woodland tracts? and how did His feet stand? Whatsoever then thou mayest be, that house will stand.

14. "For the Lord hath chosen Sion to be an habitation for Himself" (ver. 13). Sion is the Church Herself; She is also that Jerusalem unto whose peace we are running, who is in pilgrimage not in the Angels, but in us, who in her better part waiteth for the part that will return; whence letters have come unto us, which are every day read. This city is that very Sion, whom the Lord hath chosen.

15. "This shall be My rest for ever" (ver. 14). These are the words of God. "My rest:" I rest there. How greatly doth God love us, brethren, since, because we rest, He saith that He also resteth! For He is not sometimes Himself disturbed, nor doth He rest as we do; but He saith that He resteth there, because we shall have rest in Him. "Here will I dwell: for I have a delight therein."

16. "I will bless her widow with blessings, and will satisfy her poor with bread" (ver. 15). Every soul that is aware that it is bereft of all help, save of God alone, is widowed. For how doth the Apostle describe a widow? "She that is a widow indeed and desolate, trusteth in God."[2] He was speaking of those whom we all call Widows in the Church. He saith, "She that liveth in pleasure, is dead while she liveth;" and he numbereth her not among the widows. But in describing true widows, what saith he? "She that is a widow indeed and desolate, trusteth in God, and continueth in supplications and prayers night and day." Here he addeth, "but she that liveth in pleasure, is dead while she liveth." What then makes a widow? That she hath no aid from any other source, save from God alone. They that have husbands, take pride in the protection of their husbands: widows seem desolate, and their aid is a stronger one. The whole Church therefore is one widow, whether in men or in women, in married men or married women, in young men or in old, or in virgins: the whole Church is one widow, desolate in this world, if she feel this, if she is aware of her widowhood: for then is help at hand for her. Do ye not recognise this widow in the Gospel, my brethren, when the Lord declared "that men ought always to pray and not to faint"? "There was in a city a judge," He said, "which feared not God, neither regarded man. And there was a widow in that city; and she came unto him day by day, saying, Avenge me of mine adversary." The widow, by daily importunity, prevailed with him: for the judge said within himself, "Though I fear not God, neither regard man, yet because this woman troubleth me, I will avenge her."[3] If the wicked judge heard the widow, that he might not be molested; heareth not God His Church, whom He exhorteth to pray?

17. Also, "I will satisfy her poor with bread;" what meaneth this, brethren? Let us be poor, and we shall then be satisfied. Many who trust in the world, and are proud, are Christians; they worship Christ, but are not satisfied; for they have been satisfied, and abound in their pride. Of such it is said, "Our soul is filled with the scornful reproof of the wealthy, and with the despitefulness of the proud:"[4] these have abundance, and therefore eat, but are not satisfied. And what is said of them in the Psalm? "All such as be fat upon the earth have eaten and worshipped."[5] They worship Christ, they venerate Christ, they pray unto Christ; but they are not satisfied with His wisdom and righteousness. Wherefore? Because they are not poor. For the poor, that is the humble in heart, the more they hunger, the more they eat; and the more empty they are of the world, the more hungry they are. He who is full refuseth whatsoever thou wilt give him, because he is full. Give me one who hungereth; give me one of whom it is said, "Blessed are they that hunger and thirst after righteousness, for they shall be filled:"[6]

---

[1] John viii. 39.   [2] 1 Tim. v. 5, 6.   [3] Luke xviii. 1-8.   [4] Ps. cxxiii. 4.   [5] Ps. xxii. 29.   [6] Matt. v. 6.

and these will be the poor of whom he hath just said, "And will satisfy her poor with bread." For in the very Psalm where it is said, "All such as be fat upon the earth have eaten and worshipped;" this is said of the poor also, and exactly in the same manner as in this Psalm, "The poor shall eat, and be satisfied: they that seek after the Lord shall praise Him." [1] Where it is said, "All such as be fat upon earth have eaten and worshipped:" it is said, "the poor shall eat, and be satisfied." Why, when the rich are said to have worshipped, are they not said to be satisfied; yet when the poor are mentioned, they are said to be satisfied? And whence are they satisfied? What is the nature, brethren, of this satisfying? God Himself is their bread. The bread came down upon the earth, that He might become milk unto us; and said to His own, "I am the Living Bread which came down from heaven." [2] Hence these words in the Psalm, "The poor shall eat, and be satisfied." From what source shall they be satisfied? Hear what followeth: "And they that seek after the Lord shall praise Him."

18. Be ye therefore poor, be ye among the members of that widow, let your help be solely in God alone. Money is nought; not thence will ye have aid. Many have been cast headlong down for money's sake, many have perished on account of money; many for the sake of their riches have been marked out by plunderers; they would have been safe, had they not had what made men hunt for them. Many have presumed in their more powerful friends: they in whom they presumed have fallen, and have involved in their ruin those who trusted in them. Look back upon the instances to be seen in the human race. Is it anything singular that I am telling you? We speak these things not only from these Scriptures; read them in the whole world. Take heed that ye presume not in money, in a friend, in the honour and the boasting of the world. Take away all these things: but if thou hast them, thank God if thou despisest them. But if thou art puffed up by them; think not when thou wilt be the prey of men; already art thou the Devil's prey. But if thou hast not trusted in these things, thou wilt be among the members of that widow, who is the Church, of whom it is said, "I will bless her widow with blessings;" thou wilt also be poor, and one of those of whom it is said, "And will satisfy her poor with bread."

19. Sometimes, however, and we must not pass over this without mention, thou findest a poor man proud, and a rich man humble: we daily endure such persons. Thou hearest a poor man groaning beneath a rich man, and when the more powerful rich man presseth upon him, then thou seest him humble: sometimes not even then, but even then proud; whence thou seest what he would have been, had he any property. God's poor one is therefore poor in spirit, not in his purse. Sometimes a man goeth forth having a full house, rich lands, many estates, much gold and silver; he knoweth that he must not trust in these, he humbleth himself before God, he doth good with them; thus his heart is raised unto God, so that he is aware that not only do riches themselves profit him nothing, but that they even impede his feet, save He rule them, and aid them: and he is counted among the poor who are satisfied with bread. Thou findest another a proud beggar, or not proud only because he hath nothing, nevertheless seeking whereby he may be puffed up. God doth not heed the means a man hath, but the wish he hath, and judgeth him according to his wish for temporal blessings, not according to the means which it is not his lot to have. Whence the Apostle saith of the rich, "Charge them that are rich in this world, that they be not highminded, nor trust in uncertain riches, but in the living God, who giveth us richly all things to enjoy." What therefore should they do with their riches? He goeth on to say: "That they be rich in good works, ready to distribute, willing to communicate." And see that they are poor in this world: "Laying up in store for themselves," he addeth, "a good foundation against the time to come, that they may lay hold on eternal life." [3] When they have laid hold of eternal life, then will they be rich; but since they have it not as yet, they should know that they are poor. Thus it is that God counteth among His poor all the humble in heart, who are established in that twofold charity, [4] whatever they may have in this world — among His poor, whom He satisfieth with bread.

20. "I will clothe her priests with salvation, and her saints shall rejoice and sing" (ver. 16). We are now at the end of the Psalm; attend for a short space, Beloved. "I will clothe her priests with salvation, and her saints shall rejoice and sing." Who is our salvation, save our Christ? What meaneth, therefore, "I will clothe her priests with salvation"? "As many of you as have been baptized into Christ, have put on Christ." [5] "And her saints shall rejoice and sing." Whence shall they rejoice and sing? Because they have been clothed with salvation: not in themselves. For they have become light, but in the Lord; for they were darkness before. [6] Therefore he hath added, "There will I raise up the horn of David" (ver. 17): this will be David's height, that trust be put in Christ. For horn signifieth height: and what sort of height?

---

[1] Ps. xxii. 29, 26.   [2] John vi. 51.

[3] 1 Tim. vi. 17-19.   [4] Matt. xxii. 37-39.   [5] Gal. iii. 27.
[6] Eph. v. 8.

Not carnal. Therefore, while all the bones are wrapped up in flesh, the horn goeth beyond the flesh. Spiritual altitude is a horn. But what is spiritual loftiness, save to trust in Christ? not to say, It is my work, I baptize;[1] but, "He it is who baptizeth."[2] There is the horn of David: and that ye may know that there is the horn of David, heed what followeth: "I have ordained a lantern for mine Anointed." What is a lantern? Ye already know the Lord's words concerning John: "He was a burning and a shining light."[3] And what saith John? "He it is who baptizeth." Herein therefore shall the saints rejoice, herein the priests shall rejoice: because all that is good in themselves, is not of themselves, but of Him who hath the power of baptizing. Fearlessly therefore doth every one who hath received baptism come unto His temple; because it is not man's, but His who made the horn of David to flourish.

21. "Upon Him shall My sanctification flourish" (ver. 18). Upon whom? Upon Mine Anointed. For when He saith, "Mine anointed," it is the voice of the Father, who saith, "I will bless her widow with blessings, and will satisfy her poor with bread. I will clothe her priests with salvation, and her saints shall rejoice and sing." He who saith, "There will I raise up the horn of David," is God. He Himself saith, "I have ordained a lantern for Mine Anointed," because Christ is both ours and the Father's: He is our Christ, when He saveth us and ruleth us, as He is also our Lord: He is the Son of the Father, but both our Christ and the Father's. For if He were not the Father's Christ, it would not be said above, "For Thy servant David's sake, turn not Thou away the presence of Thine Anointed." "Upon Him shall My sanctification flourish." It flourisheth upon Christ. Let none of men assume this to himself, that he himself sanctifieth: otherwise it will not be true, "Upon Him shall My sanctification flourish." The glory of sanctification shall flourish. The sanctification of Christ therefore in Christ Himself, is the power of the sanctification of God in Christ. In that he saith, "shall flourish," he refers to His glory: for when trees flourish, then are they beautiful. Sanctification therefore is in Baptism: thence it flourisheth, and is brightened. Why hath the world yielded to this beauty? Because it flourisheth in Christ; for, put it in man's power, and how doth it then flourish? since "all flesh in grass, and all the goodliness thereof as the flower of the grass."

PSALM CXXXIII.[4]

1. This is a short Psalm, but one well known and quoted. "Behold, how good and how pleasant is it, that brethren should dwell together in unity" (ver. 1). So sweet is that sound, that even they who know not the Psalter, sing that verse. . . .

2. For these same words of the Psalter, this sweet sound, that honeyed melody, as well of the mind as of the hymn, did even beget the Monasteries. By this sound were stirred up the brethren who longed to dwell together. This verse was their trumpet. It sounded through the whole earth, and they who had been divided, were gathered together. The summons of God, the summons of the Holy Spirit, the summons of the Prophets, were not heard in Judah, yet were heard through the whole world. They were deaf to that sound, amid whom it was sung; they were found with their ears open, of whom it was said, "They shall see him, who were not told of him; they shall understand who heard not."[5] Yet, most beloved, if we reflect, the very blessing hath sprung from that wall[6] of circumcision. For have all the Jews perished? and whence were the Apostles, the sons of the Prophets, the sons of the exiles?[7] He speaks as to them who know. Whence those five hundred, who saw the Lord after His resurrection, whom the Apostle Paul commemorates?[8] Whence those hundred and twenty,[9] who were together in one place after the resurrection of the Lord, and His ascension into heaven, on whom when gathered into one place the Holy Spirit descended on the day of Pentecost, sent down from heaven, sent, even as He was promised?[10] All were from thence, and they first dwelt together in unity; who sold all they had, and laid the price of their goods at the Apostles' feet, as is read in the Acts of the Apostles.[11] And distribution was made to each one as he had need,[12] and none called anything his own, but they had all things common. And what is "together in unity"? They had, he says, one mind and one heart God-wards.[13] So they were the first who heard, Behold how good and how pleasant is it, that brethren dwell together. They were the first to hear, but heard it not alone. . . .

3. From the words of this Psalm was taken the name of Monks, that no one may reproach you who are Catholics by reason of the name. When you with justice reproach heretics by reason of the Circelliones,[14] that they may be

---

[1] Donatists.　　[2] John i. 33.　　[3] John v. 35.
[4] Lat. CXXXII. A public discourse, in which he defends the Monks against the Donatists.

[5] Isa. lxv. 1.
[6] Alluding to the two walls, Jewish and Gentile, meeting in the corner. See on Ps. lix. § 5, p. 243, and on Ps. xcv. § 6, p. 468.
[7] Ps. cxxvii. 4. *Excussi*, a literal translation of the Greek LXX. ἐκτετιναγμένοι. This translation of the ambiguous Hebrew root נַעַר which means to shake out, or expel, and נַעַר a young man, is preferred by the LXX. to the "young men" of our version. St. Augustin's interpretation see on Ps. cxxvii. § 7, p. 608.
[8] 1 Cor. xv. 6.　　[9] Acts i. 15.
[10] Acts ii. 1-4.　　[11] Acts iv. 34, 35.　　[12] Acts ii. 45.
[13] Acts iv. 32.
[14] The Circumcelliones were a wandering kind of Anchorites, who lived under no rule, and were guilty of various irregularities, and who

saved by shame, they reproach you on the score of the Monks. . . .

4. Moreover, beloved, there are they who are false Monks, and we know men of this kind; but the pious brotherhood is not annulled, because of them who profess to be what they are not. There are false Monks, as there are false men among the Clergy, and among the faithful.[1] . . .

5. Since the Psalm says, "Behold, how good and how pleasant is it, that brethren should dwell together in one," why then should we not call Monks so? for *Monos*[2] is one. Not one in any manner, for a man in a crowd is one, but though he can be called one along with others, he cannot be *Monos*, that is, alone, for *Monos* means "one alone." They then who thus live together as to make one man, so that they really possess what is written, "one mind and one heart,"[3] many bodies, but not many minds; many bodies, but not many hearts; can rightly be called *Monos*, that is, one alone.[4] . . .

6. Let the Psalm tell us what they are like. "As the ointment on the head, which descended to the beard, to Aaron's beard, which descended to the fringe of his garment" (ver. 2). What was Aaron? A priest. Who is a priest, except that one Priest, who entered into the Holy of Holies? Who is that priest, save Him, who was at once Victim and Priest? save Him who when he found nothing clean in the world to offer, offered Himself? The ointment is on his head, because Christ is one whole with the Church, but the ointment comes from the head. Our Head is Christ crucified and buried; He rose again, and ascended into heaven; and the Holy Spirit came from the head. Whither? To the beard. The beard signifies the courageous; the beard distinguishes the grown men, the earnest, the active, the vigorous. So that when we describe such, we say, he is a bearded man. Thus that ointment descended first upon the Apostles, descended upon those who bore the first assaults of the world, and therefore the Holy Spirit descended on them. For they who first began to dwell together in unity, suffered persecution, but because the ointment descended

to the beard, they suffered, but were not conquered. . . .

7. "As the dew of Hermon, which fell upon the hills of Sion" (ver. 3). He would have it understood, my brethren, that it is of God's grace that brethren dwell together in unity. . . .

8. But ye should know what Hermon is. It is a mountain far distant from Jerusalem, that is, from Sion. And so it is strange that he says thus: As the dew of Hermon, which fell upon the mountains of Sion, since mount Hermon is far distant from Jerusalem, for it is said to be over Jordan. Let us then seek out some interpretation of Hermon. The word is Hebrew, and we learn its meaning from them who know that language. Hermon is said to mean, a light set on a high place. For from Christ comes the dew. No light is set on a high place, save Christ. How is He set on high? First on the cross, afterwards in heaven. Set on high on the cross when He was humbled; humbled, but His humiliation could not but be high. The ministry of man grew less and less, as was signified in John; the ministry of God in our Lord Jesus Christ increased, as was shown at their birth. The former was born, as the tradition of the Church shows, on the 24th of June, when the days begin to shorten. The Lord was born on the 25th of December, when the days begin to lengthen. Here John himself confessing, "He must increase, but I must decrease."[5] And the passion of each shows this. The Lord was exalted on the cross; John was diminished by beheading. Thus the light set on high is Christ, whence is the dew of Hermon. . . . But if he have the dew of Hermon, which fell on the hill of Sion, he is quiet, peaceable, humble, submissive, pouring forth prayer in place of murmuring. For murmurers are admirably described in a certain passage of the Scriptures, "The heart of a fool is as the wheel of a cart."[6] What is the meaning of "the heart of a fool is as the wheel of a cart"? It carries hay, and creaks. The wheel of a cart cannot cease from creaking. Thus there are many brethren, who do not dwell together, save in the body. But who are they who dwell together? They of whom it is said, "And they had one mind and one heart towards God."[3]

9. "Because there the Lord commanded blessing." Where did He command it? Among the brethren who dwell together. There He enjoined blessing, there they who dwell with one heart bless God. For thou blessest not God in division of heart. . . . Art thou straitened on earth? Depart, have thy habitation in heaven. How shall I, a man clothed in flesh, enslaved to the flesh, thou wilt say, have my habitation in heaven. First go in heart, whither thou wouldest

were censured by the forty-second Canon of the Council of Trullo. Confer also Papias: St. Jerome, *Ep.* 22, § 34; Hunneric's *Edict. Vict. Vitens.* lib. 3. A number of these, in Africa, took up the cause of Donatus in a fanatical manner, and perpetrated various acts of violence under pretence of religion, robbing and beating whom they would, sending threatening notices, etc., and sometimes seeking death, or even committing suicide under the name of Martyrdom. See on Ps. xi. p. 42, note 4, on Ps. lv. p. 218, note 1, on Ps. xcvi. p. 473, note 8, and S. Optatus. b. iii. c. iv. p. 59, where a historical account is given. Ducange refers to St. Augustin, *Ep.* 48, 50, 61, 68; *Contra Parmenian,* b. i. cap. 11; *Contra Crescon.* b. iii. c. 42, 47; *Collat. Carthag.* 3, cap. 174, 281; Possidius, *Life of St. Augustin,* c. 10, 11; *Auctor Prædestinati,* b. i. hæres 69, etc. Also *Cod. Theod. Cen.* 52, *De Hæreticis,* but doubtfully as to its application. [See Gibbon, *D. and F.* cap. xxi. note 157, ed. Milman. — C.]

[1] [See A. N. F. vol. vi. p. 279. — C.]
[2] μόνος, Gr.   [3] Acts iv. 32.
[4] [The institution has perished even in many parts of unreformed Europe, only because of the intolerable evils of their corrupt and degenerate condition. — C.]

[5] John iii. 30.   [6] Ecclus. xxxiii. 5.

follow in the body. Do not hear, "Lift up your hearts," with a deaf ear. Keep thy heart lifted up, and no one will straiten thee in heaven.

PSALM CXXXIV.[1]

1. "Behold, now, bless ye the Lord, all ye servants of the Lord " (ver. 1), "who stand in the house of the Lord, in the courts of the house of our God " (ver. 2). Why has he added, " in the courts"? Courts mean the wider spaces of a house. He who stands in the courts is not straitened, is not confined, in some fashion is enlarged. Remain in this enlargement, and thou canst love thy enemy, because thou lovest not things in which an enemy could straiten thee. How canst thou be understood to stand in the courts? Stand in charity, and thou standest in the courts. Breadth lies in charity, straitness in hatred.

2. " Lift up your hands by night in the sanctuary, and bless the Lord " (ver. 2). It is easy to bless by day. What is " by day "? In prosperity. For night is a sad thing, day a cheerful. When it is well with thee, thou dost bless the Lord. Thy son was sick, and he is made whole, thou dost bless the Lord. Thy son was sick, perchance thou hast sought an astrologer, a soothsayer, perchance a curse against the Lord has come, not from thy tongue, but from thy deeds, from thy deeds and thy life. Boast not, because thou blessest with thy tongue, if thou cursest with thy life. Wherefore bless ye the Lord. When? By night. When did Job bless? When it was a sad night. All was taken away which he possessed ; the children for whom his goods were stored were taken away. How sad was his night! Let us however see whether he blesseth not in the night. "The Lord gave, the Lord hath taken away ; it is as the Lord willed ; blessed be the name of the Lord."[2] And black was the night. . . .

3. "The Lord out of Zion bless thee, who made heaven and earth " (ver. 3). He exhorts many to bless, and Himself blesseth one, because He maketh one out of many, since " it is good and pleasant for brethren to dwell together in one."[3] It is a plural number, brethren, and yet singular, to dwell together in one. Let none of you say, It cometh not to me. Knowest thou of whom he speaks, " the Lord bless thee out of Zion." He blessed one. Be one,[4] and the blessing cometh to thee.

PSALM CXXXV.[5]

1. Very pleasant ought it be to us, and we should rejoice because it is pleasant, to which this Psalm exhorteth us. For it says, " Praise the name of the Lord " (ver. 1). And it forthwith appends the reason, why it is just to praise the name of the Lord. " Praise the Lord, ye servants." What more just? what more worthy? what more thankful? . . . For if He teaches His own servants who have deserved well of Him, the preachers of His Word, the rulers of His Church, the worshippers of His name, the obeyers of His command, that in their own conscience they should possess the sweetness of their life, lest they be corrupted by the praise or disheartened by the reproach of men ; how much the more is He above all, the unchangeable One, who teacheth these things, neither the greater if thou praisest, or the less if thou reproachest. . . . For ye will do nothing out of place, by praising your Lord, as servants. And if ye were to be for ever only servants, ye ought to praise the Lord ; how much more ought ye servants to praise the Lord, that ye may hereafter gain the privilege of sons?

2. . . . Therefore, "Ye who stand in the house of the Lord, in the courts of the house of our God, praise the Lord" (ver. 2). Be thankful ; ye were without, and ye stand within. Since then ye stand, is it a small thing for you to think where He should be praised, who raised you when you were cast down, and caused you to stand in His house, to know Him, and to praise Him? Is it a small thing, that we stand in the house of the Lord? . . . If one thinks of this, and is not unthankful, he will utterly despise himself in comparison with the love of his Lord, who hath done so great things for him. And since he hath nothing wherewith to repay God for so great benefits, what remains for him but to give Him thanks, not to repay Him? It belongs to the very act of thanksgiving, to " receive the cup of the Lord, and to call upon His name."[6] For what can the servant repay the Lord for all that He hath given him?[7]

3. What reason shall I give why you should praise Him? " Because the Lord is good " (ver. 3). Briefly in one word is here explained the praise of the Lord our God. " The Lord is good ; " good, not in the same manner as the things which He here made are good. For God made all things very good ;[8] not only good, but also very good. He made the sky and earth, and all things which are in them good, and He made them very good. If He made all these things good, of what sort is He who made them? . . .

4. How far can we speak of His goodness? Who can conceive in his heart, or apprehend how good the Lord is? Let us however return to ourselves, and in us recognise Him, and praise

---

[1] Lat. CXXXIII.   [2] Job i. 21.
[3] Ps. cxxxiii. 1.   [4] *Unum.*
[5] Lat. CXXXIV. A discourse to the people.

[6] Ps. cxvi. 13.   [7] Ps. cxvi. 12.   [8] Gen. i. 31.

the Maker in His works, because we are not fit to contemplate Him Himself. And in hope that we may be able to contemplate Him, when our heart hath been purified by faith, that hereafter it may rejoice in the Truth; now as He cannot be seen by us, let us look at His works, that we may not live without praising Him. So I [1] have said, "Praise the Lord, for He is good; sing praises unto His Name, for He is sweet. . . . He is Mediator, and thereupon is sweet. What is sweeter than angels' food? How can God not be sweet, since man ate angels' food? For men and angels live not on different meat. That is truth, that is wisdom, that is the goodness of God, but thou canst not enjoy it in like wise with the angels. . . . That man might eat angels' food, the Creator of the angels was made man.[2] If ye taste, sing praises; if ye have tasted how sweet the Lord is, sing praises; if that which ye have tasted has a good savour, praise it; who is so unthankful to cook or purveyor, as not to return thanks by praising what he tastes, if he be pleased by any food. If we are not silent on such occasions, shall we be silent concerning Him, who has given us all things? . . .

5. "For the Lord hath chosen Jacob to Himself, Israel for His own possession" (ver. 4). . . . Let not Jacob therefore extol himself, let him not boast himself, or ascribe it to his own merits. He was known before, predestinated before, elected before, not elected for his own merits, but found out, and gifted with life by the grace of God. So with all the Gentiles; for how did the wild-olive deserve, that it should be grafted in, from the bitterness of its berries, the barrenness of its wildness? It was the wood of the wilderness, not of the Lord's field, and yet He of His mercy grafted the wild-olive into the (true) olive. But up to this time the wild-olive was not grafted in.

6. . . . "Because," says he, "I know that the Lord is great, and our God is above all gods" (ver. 5). If we should say to him, we ask thee, explain to us His greatness; would he not perchance answer us, He whom I see is not so very great, if He be able to be expounded by me. Let him then return to His works, and tell us. Let him hold in his conscience the greatness of God, which he has seen, which he has committed to our faith, whither he could not lead our eyes, and enumerate some of the things which the Lord hath done here; that unto us, who cannot see His greatness as he can, He may become sweet through the works of His which we can comprehend. . . .

7. "All whatsoever the Lord willed, He made in the heaven, and in the earth, in the sea, and in all its deep places" (ver. 6). Who can comprehend these things? Who can enumerate the works of the Lord in the heaven and earth, in the sea, and in all deep places? Yet if we cannot comprehend them all, we should believe and hold them without question, because whatever creature is in heaven, whatever is in earth, whatever is in the sea and in all deep places, has been made by the Lord. . . .

8. "Raising the clouds from the ends of the earth" (ver. 7). We see these works of God in His creation. For the clouds come from the ends of the earth to the midst thereof, and rain; thou scannest not whence they arise. Hence the prophet signifies this, from "the ends of the earth," whether it be from the bottom, or from the circumference of the ends of the earth, whencesoever He wills He raises the clouds, only from the earth. "He hath made lightnings into rain." For lightnings without rain would frighten thee, and bestow nothing on thee. "He maketh lightnings unto rain." It lightens, and thou tremblest; it rains, thou rejoicest. "He hath made lightnings unto rain." He who terrified thee, Himself causest that thou shouldest rejoice. "Who bringeth the winds out of His treasures," their causes are hidden, thou knowest not whence they come. When the wind blows, thou feelest it; why it blows, or from what treasure of His wisdom it is brought forth, thou knowest not;[3] yet thou owest to God the worship of faith, for it would not blow unless He had bidden who made it, unless He had brought it forth who created it.

9. We see therefore these things in that work of His; we praise, we marvel at, we bless God; let us see what He has done among men for His people. "Who smote the first-born of Egypt" (ver. 8). But withal those divine doings are told which thou mightest love, those are not told which thou mightest fear. Attend, and see that also when He is angry, He doeth what He willeth. "From man even unto beast. He sent signs and wonders into the midst of thee, O Egypt!" (ver. 9). Ye know, ye have read what the hand of the Lord did by Moses in Egypt, to crush and cast down the proud Egyptians, "on Pharaoh and on all his servants." Little did He in Egypt: what did He after His people was led out thence? "Who smote many nations" (ver. 10), who possessed that land, which God willed to give His people. "And slew mighty kings, Sehon king of the Amorites, and Og the king of Bashan, and all the kingdoms of Canaan" (ver. 11). All these things which the Psalm records simply, do we read likewise in others of the Lord's books, and there the hand of the Lord is great. When thou seest

---

[1] "He hath said," Oxf. MSS.　　[2] Ps. lxxviii. 25.　　[3] John iii. 8.

what has been done to the wicked, take heed lest it be done to thee. . . . But when the good man sees what the wicked has suffered, let him cleanse himself from all iniquity, lest he fall into a like punishment, a like chastisement. Then ye have thoroughly understood these things. What did God then? He drove out the wicked, "And he gave their land for an inheritance, even an inheritance to Israel His servant" (ver. 12).

10. Then follows the loud cry of His praise. "Thy Name, O Lord, is for ever and ever" (ver. 13), after all these things which Thou hast done. For what do I see that Thou hast done? I behold Thy creation which Thou hast made in heaven, I behold this lower part, where we dwell, and here I see Thy gifts of clouds, and winds, and rain. I regard Thy people; Thou leddest them from the house of bondage, and didst signs and wonders upon their enemies. Thou punishedst those who caused them trouble, Thou dravest the wicked from their land, Thou killedst their kings, Thou gavest their land to Thy people: I have seen all these things, and filled with joy have said, "Lord, Thy Name is for ever and ever." . . .

11. All these things then did God overthrow, in the body at that time, when our fathers were led out of the land of Egypt, in the spirit now. Nor does His Hand cease until the end. Therefore deem not that these mighty deeds of God were then finished and have ceased. "Thy Name, O Lord," he says, "is for ever."[1] That is, Thy loving-kindness ceaseth not, Thy hand ceaseth not for ever from doing these things, which then Thou didst afore declare in a figure. "But they are written for our admonition, on whom the end of the ages is come."[2] One generation and another generation; the generation by which we are made the faithful, and are born again by baptism; the generation by which we shall rise again from the dead, and shall live with the Angels for ever. Thy Memorial, O Lord, is above this generation, and above that; for neither doth He now forget to call us, nor then will He forget to crown us.

12. "The Lord hath judged His people, and will be called upon among His servants" (ver. 14). Already hath He judged the people. Save the final judgment, the people of the Jews is judged. What is "judged"? The just are taken away, the unjust are left. But if I lie, or am thought to lie, because I have said, it is already judged, hear the Lord saying, "I have come for judgment into this world, that they who see not may see, and they who see may be made blind."[3] The proud are made blind, the lowly are enlightened. Therefore, "He hath judged His people." Isaiah spake the judgment. "And

now, thou house of Jacob, come ye, let us walk in the light of the Lord."[4] This is a small matter; but what follows? "For He hath put away His people, the house of Israel." The house of Jacob is the house of Israel; for he who is Jacob, the same is Israel. . . . Therefore God had judged His people, by separating the evil and the good; that is to say, "He shall be called upon among His servants." By whom? By the Gentiles. For how vast are the nations who have come in by faith. How many farms and desert places now come in to us? They come thence no one can tell how numerously; they would believe. We say to them, What will ye? They answer, To know the glory of God. Believe, my brethren, that we wonder and rejoice at such a claim of these rustic people. They come I know not whither, roused up by I know not whom. How shall I say, I know not by whom? I know indeed by whom, because He says, "No one cometh to Me, save whom the Father draweth."[5] They come suddenly from the woods, the desert, the most distant and lofty mountains, to the Church; and many of them, nay, near all hold this language, so that we see of a truth that God teacheth them within.[6] The prophecy of Scripture is fulfilled, when it says, "And they shall all be taught of God."[7] We say to them, What do ye long for? And they answer, To see the glory of God.[8] "For all have sinned, and come short of the glory of God."[9] They believe, they are sanctified, they will to have clergy ordained for them. Is it not fulfilled, "and He will be called upon among His servants"?

13. Lastly, after all that arrangement and dispensation, the Spirit of God turns itself to reproaching and ridiculing those idols, which are now ridiculed by their very worshippers. "The idols of the Gentiles are silver and gold" (ver. 15). As God made all these things, who made whatever He would in heaven and earth, what can anything that man maketh be, but an object of ridicule, not adoration? Was He perchance about to speak of "the idols of the Gentiles," that we might despise them all? was He about to speak of the idols of the heathen, stones and wood, plaster and pottery? I say not these, they are mean materials. I speak of that which they specially love, that which they specially honour. "The idols of the Gentiles are silver and gold, the work of men's hands." Surely it is gold, surely it is silver: because silver glitters, and gold glitters, have they therefore eyes, or do they see? . . . But as these things are senseless, why make ye men of silver and gold to be gods? See ye not that the gods which ye make see not?

---

[1] Ps. cxxxv. 13.　　[2] 1 Cor. x. 11.　　[3] John ix. 39.

[4] Isa. ii. 5.　　　　[5] John vi. 44.
[6] [These *rustics* are the *pagani* living in hamlets; he thus notes the rarity of Paganism in cities. — C.]
[7] Isa. liv. 13.　　　[8] John vi. 45.　　　[9] Rom. iii. 23.

"They have a mouth, and will not speak; they have eyes, and will not see" (ver. 16); "they have ears, and will not hear; neither is there any breath in their mouth" (ver. 17); "they have nostrils, and will not smell; they have hands, and will not work; they have feet, and will not walk." All these things could the carpenter, the silversmith, the goldsmith make, both eyes, and ears, and nostrils, and mouth, and hands, and feet, but he could give neither sight to the eyes, nor hearing to the ears, nor speech to the mouth, nor smell to the nostrils, nor motion to the hands, or going to the feet.

14. And man, thou laughest doubtless at what thou hast made, if thou knowest by whom thou art made. But of them who know not, what is said? "All they who make them, and all they who trust in them, are like them" (ver. 18). And ye believe, brethren, that there is a likeness to these idols expressed not in their flesh, but in their inner man. For "they have ears, and hear not." God calls to them indeed, "He who hath ears to hear, let him hear."[1] They have eyes, and see not, for they have the eyes of the body, and not the eyes of faith. Lastly, this prophecy is fulfilled among all the nations. . . . Is it not fulfilled? Is it not seen, as it is written? And they who remain have eyes, and see not; have nostrils, and smell not. They perceive not that savour. "We are a good savour of Christ,"[2] as the apostle says everywhere. What profiteth it, that they have nostrils, and smell not that so sweet savour of Christ? Truly it is done in them, and truly it is said of them, "All they who make them," etc.

15. But daily do men believe through the miracles of Christ our Lord; daily the eyes of the blind, the ears of the deaf are opened, the nostrils of the senseless are breathed into, the tongues of the dumb are loosed, the hands of the palsied are strengthened, the feet of the lame are guided; sons of Abraham are raised up of these stones,[3] to all of whom be it said, "Bless the Lord, ye house of Israel" (ver. 19). All are sons of Abraham; and if sons of Abraham are raised up from these stones, it is plain that they are rather the house of Israel who belong to the house of Israel, the seed of Abraham, not by the flesh, but by faith. But even granting that it is said of that house, and the people of Israel is meant, from thence did the Apostles and thousands of the circumcised believe? "Bless the Lord, ye house of Aaron. Bless the Lord, ye house of Levi" (ver. 20). Bless the Lord, ye nations, this is, the "house of Israel" generally; bless Him, ye leaders, this is, the "house of Aaron;" bless Him, ye servants, this is, the "house of Levi." What of the other nations? "Ye that fear the Lord, bless the Lord."

16. Let us also with one voice say what follows: "Blessed be the Lord out of Zion, who dwelleth in Jerusalem" (ver. 21). Out of Zion is Jerusalem too. Zion is "watching," Jerusalem the "vision of peace." In what Jerusalem will He dwell now? In that which has fallen? Nay, but in that which is our mother, which is in the heavens, of which it is said, "The desolate hath more children than she which hath a husband."[4] For now the Lord is from Zion, because we watch when He will come; now as long as we live in hope, we are in Zion. When our way is ended, we shall dwell in that city which will never fall, because the Lord dwelleth in her, and keepeth her, which is the vision of peace, the eternal Jerusalem; for the praise of which, my brethren, language sufficeth not; where we shall find no enemy, either within the Church or without the Church, neither in our flesh, nor in our thoughts. For "death shall be swallowed up in victory,"[5] and we shall be free to see God in eternal peace, being made citizens of Jerusalem, the city of God.

PSALM CXXXVI.[6]

1. "Give thanks unto the Lord, for He is good, for His mercy endureth for ever" (ver. 1). This Psalm contains the praise of God, and all its verses finish in the same way. Wherefore although many things are related here in praise of God, yet His mercy is most commended;[7] for without this plain commendation, he, whom the Holy Spirit used to utter this Psalm, would have no verse be ended. Although after the judgment, by which at the end of the world the quick and the dead must be judged, the just being sent into life eternal, the unjust into everlasting fire,[8] there will not afterwards be those, whom God will have mercy on, yet rightly may His future mercy be understood to be for ever, which He bestows on His saints and faithful ones, not because they will be miserable for ever, and therefore will need His mercy for ever, but because that very blessedness, which He mercifully bestows on the miserable, that they cease to be miserable, and begin to be happy, will have no end, and therefore "His mercy is for ever." For that we shall be just from being unjust, whole from being unsound, alive from being dead, immortal from being mortal, happy from being wretched, is of His mercy. But this that we

---

[1] Matt. xi. 15.   [2] 2 Cor. ii. 15.   [3] Matt. iii. 9.

[4] Isa. liv. 1; Gal. iv. 27.   [5] 1 Cor. xv. 54.
[6] Lat. CXXXV.
[7] [He says: "I remember, in the hundred and sixth Psalm, which begins in the same way, because the manuscript which I read had not 'for ever,' but, 'for ages' (*in sæculum*), 'His mercy,' that I enquired what we had better understand. For, in the Greek language, it is written, εἰς τὸν αἰῶνα, which may be interpreted, 'for ages' and (*in æternum*) 'for ever.' But it would be tedious to renew the enquiries I made as best I could in that place. But in this Psalm the same manuscript has not 'for ages,' which most have, but, 'for ever His mercy.'"—C.]
[8] Matt. xxv. 46.

shall be, will be for ever, and therefore "His mercy is for ever." Wherefore, "give thanks to the Lord;" that is, praise the Lord by giving thanks, "for He is good:" nor is it any temporal good you will gain from this confession, for, "His mercy endureth for ever;" that is, the benefit which He bestows mercifully upon you, is for ever.[1]

2. Then follows, "Give thanks to the God of gods, for His mercy endureth for ever" (ver. 2). "Give thanks to the Lord of lords, for His mercy endureth for ever" (ver. 3). We may well enquire, Who are these gods and lords, of whom He who is the true God is God and Lord? And we find written in another Psalm, that even men are called gods.[2] The Lord even takes note of this testimony in the Gospel, saying, "Is it not written in your Law, I have said, Ye are gods?"[3] . . . It is not therefore because they are all good, but because "the word of God came to them," that they were called gods. For were it because they are all good, He would not thus distinguish between them. He saith, "He judgeth between the gods." Then follows, "How long do ye judge iniquity!"[4] and the rest, which He says certainly not to all, but to some, because He saith it in distinguishing, and yet He distinguisheth between the gods.

3. But it is asked, If men are called gods to whom the word of the Lord came, are the Angels to be called gods, when the greatest reward which is promised to just and holy men is the being equal to Angels? In the Scriptures I know not whether it can, at least easily, be found, that the Angels are openly called gods; but when it had been said of the Lord God, "He is terrible, above all gods," he adds, as by way of exposition why he says this, "for the gods of the heathen are devils,"[5] that we might understand what had been expressed in the Hebrew, "the gods of the Gentiles are idols," meaning rather the devils which dwell in the idols.[6] For as regards images, which in Greek are called idols, a name we now use in Latin, they have eyes and see not, and all the other things which are said of them, because they are utterly without sense; wherefore they cannot be frightened, for nothing which has no sense can be frightened. How then can it be said of the Lord, "He is terrible above all gods, because the gods of the Gentiles are idols," if the devils which may be terrified are not understood to be in these images. Whence also the Apostle says, "We know that an idol is nothing."[7] This refers to its earthy

senseless material. But that no one may think, that there is no living and sentient nature, which delights in the Gentile sacrifices, he adds, "But what the Gentiles sacrifice, they sacrifice to devils, and not to God: I would not have you partakers with devils."[8] If therefore we never find in the divine words that the holy Angels are called gods, I think the best reason is, that men may not be induced by the name to pay that ministry and service of religion (which in Greek is called λειτουργία or λατρία) to the holy Angels, which neither would they have paid by man at all, save to that God, who is the God of themselves and men.[9] Hence they are much more correctly called Angels, which in Latin is *Nuntii*, that by the name of their function, not their substance, we may plainly understand that they would have us worship the God, whom they announce. The whole then of that question the Apostle has briefly expounded, when he says, "For though there be who are called gods, whether in heaven or in earth, as there are gods many and lords many; yet we have one God the Father, from whom are all, and we in Him; and one Lord Jesus Christ, by whom are all things, and we by Him."[10]

4. Let us therefore "give thanks to the God of gods, and the Lord of lords, for His mercy," etc. "Who alone did wonderful things" (ver. 4). As at the last part of every verse, it is written, "For His mercy endureth for ever," so we must understand at the beginning of each, though it be not written, "Give thanks." Which indeed in the Greek is very plain. It would be so in Latin, if our translators had been able to make use of that expression. Which indeed they could have done in this verse, if they had said, "To Him who doeth[11] wonderful things." For where we have, "who did wonderful things," the Greek has τῷ ποιήσαντι, where we must necessarily understand, "give thanks." And I would they had added the pronoun, and said to Him, "who did," or to Him "who doeth," or to Him "who made sure;" because then one might easily understand, "let us give thanks." For now it is so obscurely rendered, that he who either knows not or cares not to examine a Greek manuscript may think, "who made the heavens, who made sure the earth, who made the luminaries, for His mercy endureth for ever,"[12] has been so said, because He did these things for this reason, "because His mercy endureth for ever:" whereas they, whom He has freed from misery, belong to His Mercy: but not that we should believe that

---

[1] [He adds: "The expression, 'for He is good,' in the Greek is ἀγαθός; not as in the hundred and sixth Psalm, for there 'He is good,' in Greek is χρηστός. And so some have expounded the former, 'Since He is sweet.' For ἀγαθός is not good anyhow, but good most excellently." — C.]

[2] Ps. lxxxii. 1, vi. 7. [3] John x. 34. [4] Ps. lxxxii. 2.
[5] Ps. xcvi. 4 seq. [6] *Simulacrum;* εἰδωλον.
[7] 1 Cor. viii. 4.

[8] 1 Cor. x. 20.
[9] [The Roman dogma makes a *verbal* distinction as to worship of angels and saints, to meet the case as our author puts it here. But the vulgar cannot so distinguish; and everywhere, *practically,* this *latria* is offered. See Pius IX., the bull *Ineffabilis.* — C.]
[10] 1 Cor. viii. 5, 6. [11] *Facienti mirabilia.*
[12] Ps. cxxxvi. 5.

He makes sky, earth, and luminaries, of His Mercy; since they are marks of His Goodness, who created all things very good.[1] For He created all things, that they might have their being;[2] but it is the work of His Mercy, to cleanse us from our sins, and deliver us from everlasting misery. And so the Psalm thus addresses us, "Give thanks unto the God of gods, give thanks unto the Lord of lords." Give thanks to Him, "who alone doeth great wonders;" give thanks to Him, "who by His wisdom made the heavens;" give thanks to Him, "who stretched out the earth above the waters;" give thanks to Him, "who alone made great lights." But why we are to praise, he setteth down at the end of all the verses, "for His mercy endureth for ever."

5. But what meaneth, "who alone doeth great wonders"? Is it because many wonderful things He hath done by means of angels and men? Some wonderful things there are which God doeth alone, and these he enumerates, saying, "who by His wisdom made the heavens" (ver. 5), "who stretched out the earth above the waters" (ver. 6), "who alone made great lights" (ver. 7). For this reason did he add "alone" in this verse also, because the other wonders which he is about to tell of, God did by means of man. For having said, "who alone made great lights," he goes on to explain what these are, "the sun to rule the day" (ver. 8), "the moon and stars to govern the night" (ver. 9); then he begins to tell the wonders which He did by means of angels and men: "who smote Egypt with their first-born" (ver. 10), and the rest. The whole creation then God manifestly made, not by means of any creature, but "alone;" and of this creation he hath mentioned certain more eminent parts, that they might make us think on the whole; the heavens we can understand,[3] and the earth we see. And as there are visible heavens too, by mentioning the lights in them, he has bid us look on the whole body of the heavens as made by Him.

6. However, whether by what he saith, "who made the heavens in understanding," or, as others have rendered it, "in intelligence," he meant to signify, the heavens we can understand, or that He in His understanding or intelligence, that is, in His wisdom made the heavens (as it is elsewhere written, "in wisdom hast Thou made them all"[4]), implying thereby the only-begotten Word, may be a question. But if it be so, that we are to understand that "God by His wisdom made the heavens," why saith He this only of the heavens, whereas God made all things by the same wisdom? It is that it needed only to be expressed there, so that in the rest it might be understood without being written. How then

could it be "alone," if "in understanding" or "in intelligence" means "by His wisdom," that is, by the only-begotten Word? Is it that, inasmuch as the Trinity is not three Gods, but one God, he states that God made these things alone, because He made not creation by means of any creature?

7. But what is, "who laid out the earth above the waters"? For it is a difficult question, because the earth seemeth to be the heavier, so that it should be believed not so much to be borne on the waters, as to bear the waters. And that we may not seem contentiously to maintain our Scriptures against those who think that they have discovered these matters on sure principles, we have a second interpretation to give, that the earth which is inhabited by men, and contains the living creatures of the earth, is "laid out above the waters" because it stands out above the waters which surround it. For when we speak of a city on the sea being built "above the waters," it is not meant that the sea is under it in the same way as the waters are under the chambers of caverns, or under ships sailing over them; but it is said to be "above" the sea, because it stands up above the sea below it.

8. But if these words further signify something else which more closely concerns us, God "by His wisdom made the heavens," that is, His saints, spiritual men, to whom He has given not only to believe, but also to understand things divine; those who cannot yet attain to this, and only hold their faith firmly, as being beneath the heavens, are figured by the name of earth. And because they abide with unshaken belief upon the baptism they have received, therefore it is said, "He laid out the earth above the waters." Further, since it is written of our Lord Jesus Christ, that "in Him are hid all the treasures of wisdom and knowledge,"[5] and that these two, wisdom and knowledge, differ somewhat from one another is testified by other utterances of Scripture, especially in the words of holy Job,[6] where both are in a manner defined; not unsuitably then do we understand wisdom to consist in the knowledge and love of That which ever is and abideth unchangeable, which is God. For where he saith, "piety[7] is wisdom," in Greek is θεοσέβεια, and to express the whole of this in Latin, we may call it worship of God.[8] But to depart from evil, which he calls knowledge, what else is it but to walk cautiously and heedfully "in the midst of a crooked and perverse generation,"[9] in the night, as it were, of this world, that each one by keeping himself from iniquity may avoid being confounded with the darkness, distinguished by the light of his proper gift. . . .

9. "Who brought out Israel from the midst

---

[1] Gen. i. 31. [2] Wisd. i. 14. [3] Intelligibiles cœlos. [4] Ps. civ. 24. [5] Col. ii. 3. [6] [Job xxviii. 28. — C.] [7] Pietas, Vulg. [8] Dei cultus. [9] Philip. ii. 15.

of them" (ver. 11). He brought out also His saints and faithful ones from the midst of the wicked. " With a mighty Hand and stretched-out Arm" (ver. 12). What more powerful, what more out-stretched, than that of which is said, " To whom is the Arm of the Lord revealed? " [1] " Who divided the Red Sea in two parts " (ver. 13). He divided also in such wise, that the same baptism should be to some unto life, to others unto death. "And brought out Israel through the midst of it" (ver. 14). So too He brings out His renewed people through the laver of regeneration. " And overthrew Pharaoh and his power in the Red Sea" (ver. 15). He quickly destroyeth both the sin of His people and the guilt thereof by baptism. "Who led His people through the wilderness" (ver. 16). Us too He leadeth through the drought and barrenness of this world, that we perish not therein. " Who smote great kings" (ver. 17), " and slew famous kings" (ver. 18). From us too He smites and slays the deadly powers of the devil. "Sehon king of the Amorites" (ver. 19), an " useless shoot," or " fiery temptation," for so is Sehon interpreted : the king of " them who cause bitterness," for such is the meaning of Amorites. "And Og, the king of Basan" (ver. 20). The " heaper-together," such is the meaning of Og, and, king of " confusion," which Basan signifies. For what else doth the devil heap together but confusion? "And gave away their land for an heritage" (ver. 21), "even an heritage unto Israel His servant " (ver. 22). For He giveth them, whom once the devil owned, for an heritage to the seed of Abraham, that is, Christ. " Who remembered us in our low estate " (ver. 23), "and redeemed us from our enemies " (ver. 24) by the Blood of His only-begotten Son. "Who giveth food to all flesh " (ver. 25), that is, to the whole race of mankind, not Israelites only, but Gentiles too; and of this Food is said, " My Flesh is meat indeed." " Give thanks unto the God of Heaven" (ver 26). " Give thanks unto the Lord of lords " (ver. 27). For what he here says, " the God of Heaven," I suppose that he meant to express in other words what He had before said, "the God of gods." For what there he subjoined, he has here also repeated. "Give thanks unto the Lord of lords." " But to us there is but one God," etc., "and one Lord Jesus Christ, by whom are all things, and we by Him ; " [2] to whom we confess that " His mercy endureth for ever."

PSALM CXXXVII.[3]

1. . . . But to-day we have sung, " By the waters of Babylon we sat down and wept, when we remembered Sion " (ver. 1). . . .

2. Observe " the waters of Babylon." " The waters of Babylon " are all things which here are loved, and pass away. One man, for example, loveth to practise husbandry, to grow rich thereby, to employ his mind therein, thence to gain pleasure : let him observe the issue, and see that what he hath loved is not a foundation of Jerusalem, but a stream of Babylon. Another saith, It is a grand thing to be a soldier : all husbandmen fear those who are soldiers. . . .

3. But then other citizens of the holy Jerusalem, understanding their captivity, mark how the natural wishes and the various lusts of men hurry and drag them hither and thither, and drive them into the sea ; they see this, and they throw not themselves into the waters of Babylon, but "sit down and weep," either for those who are being carried away by them, or themselves whose deserts have placed them in Babylon, but sitting, that is, humbling themselves. O holy Sion, where all stands firm and nothing flows ! Who hath thrown us headlong into this? Why have we left thy Founder and thy society? Behold, placed where all things are flowing and gliding away, scarce one, if he can grasp the tree, shall be snatched from the stream and escape. Humbling ourselves then in our captivity, let us " sit by the waters of Babylon," let us not dare to plunge ourselves in those streams, nor to be proud and lifted up in the evil and sadness of our captivity, but let us sit, and so weep. Let us sit " by " the waters, not beneath the waters, of Babylon ; such be our humility, that it overwhelm us not. Sit " by " the waters, not " in " the waters, not " under " the waters ; but yet sit, in humble fashion, talk not as thou wouldest in Jerusalem. . . .

4. For many weep with the weeping of Babylon, because they rejoice also with the joy of Babylon. When men rejoice at gains and weep at losses, both are of Babylon. Thou oughtest to weep, but in the remembrance of Sion. If thou weepest in the remembrance of Sion, thou oughtest to weep even when it is well with thee in Babylon. . . .

5. " On the willows in the midst thereof we hung up our instruments of music " (ver. 2). The citizens of Jerusalem have their " instruments of music," God's Scriptures, God's commands, God's promises, meditation on the life to come ; but while they are dwelling " in Babylon," they " hang up their instruments." Willows are unfruitful trees, and here so placed, that no good whatever can be understood of them : elsewhere perhaps there may. Here understand barren trees, growing by the waters of Babylon. These trees are watered by the waters of Babylon, and bring forth no fruit ; just as there are men greedy, covetous, barren in good works, citizens of Babylon in such wise, that they are even trees of that region ; they are

---

[1] Isa. liii. 1. [2] 1 Cor. viii. 5, 6.
[3] Lat. CXXXVI. A sermon to the people.

fed there by these pleasures of transitory things, as though watered by "the waters of Babylon." Thou seekest fruit of them, and nowhere findest it. . . . Therefore by deferring to apply the Scriptures to them, "we hang up our instruments of music upon the willows." For we hold them not worthy to carry our instruments. We do not therefore insert our instruments into them and bind them to them, but defer to use them, and so hang them up. For the willows are the unfruitful trees of Babylon, fed by temporal pleasures, as by the "waters of Babylon."

6. "For there they that led us captive demanded of us words of songs, and they that led us away, an hymn" (ver. 3). They demanded of us words of songs and an hymn, who led us captive. . . . We are tempted by the delights of earthly things, and we struggle daily with the suggestions of unlawful pleasures; scarce do we breathe freely even in prayer: we understand that we are captives. But who led us captive? what men? what race? what king? If we are redeemed, we once were captives. Who hath redeemed us? Christ. From whom hath He redeemed us? From the devil. The devil then and his angels led us captive: and they would not lead us, unless we consented. . . .

7. "Those" then "who have led us captive," the devil and his angels, when have they spoken unto us: "Sing us one of the songs of Sion"? What answer we? Babylon beareth thee, Babylon containeth thee, Babylon nourisheth thee, Babylon speaks by thy mouth, thou knowest not to take in save what glitters for the present, thou knowest not how to meditate on things of eternity, thou takest not in what thou askest. "How shall we sing the Lord's song in a strange land?" (ver. 4). Truly, brethren, so it is. Begin to wish to preach the truth in such measure as ye know it, and see how needful it is for you to endure such mockers, persecutors of the truth, full of falsehood. Reply to them, when they ask of you what they cannot take in, and say in full confidence of your holy song, "How shall we sing the Lord's song in a strange land!"

8. But take heed how thou dwellest among them, O people of God, O body of Christ, O high-born band of wanderers (for thy home is not here, but elsewhere), lest when thou lovest them, strivest for their friendship, and fearest to displease such men, Babylon begin to delight thee and thou forget Jerusalem. In fear then of this, see what the Psalmist subjoins, see what follows. "If I forget thee, O Jerusalem" (ver. 5), amid the speeches of those who hold me captive, amid the speeches of treacherous men, amid the speeches of men who ask with ill intent, asking, yet unwilling to learn. . . . What then? "If I forget thee, O Jerusalem, let my right hand forget me."

9. "Let my tongue cleave to my jaws, if I remember not thee" (ver. 6). That is, let me be dumb, he saith, if I remember not thee. For what word, what sound doth he utter, who uttereth not songs of Sion? That is our tongue, the song of Jerusalem. The song of the love of this world is a strange tongue, a barbarous tongue, which we have learnt in our captivity. Dumb then will he be to God, who forgetteth Jerusalem. And it is not enough to remember: for her enemies too remember her, desiring to overthrow her. "What is that city?" say they; "who are the Christians? what sort of men are the Christians? would they were not Christians." Now the captive band hath conquered its capturers; still they murmur, and rage, and desire to slay the holy city that dwells as a stranger among them. Not enough then is it to remember: take heed how thou rememberest. For some things we remember in hate, some in love. And so, when he had said, "If I forget thee, O Jerusalem," etc., he added at once, "if I prefer not Jerusalem in the height of my joy." For there is the height of joy where we enjoy God, where we are safe of united brotherhood, and the union of citizenship. There no tempter shall assail us, no one be able so much as to urge us on to any allurement: there nought will delight us but good: there all want will die, there perfect bliss will dawn on us.

10. Then he turneth to God in prayer against the enemies of that city. "Remember, O Lord, the children of Edom" (ver. 7). Edom is the same who is also called Esau: for ye heard just now the words of the Apostle read, "Jacob have I loved, but Esau have I hated."[1] . . . Esau then signifieth all the carnal, Jacob all the spiritual. . . . All carnal persons are enemies to spiritual persons, for all such, desiring present things, persecute those whom they see to long for things eternal. Against these the Psalmist, looking back to Jerusalem, and beseeching God that he may be delivered from captivity, saith — what? "Remember, O Lord, the children of Edom." Deliver us from carnal men, from those who imitate Esau, who are elder brethren, yet enemies. They were first-born, but the last-born have won the pre-eminence, for the lust of the flesh hath cast down the former, the contempt of lust hath lifted up the latter. The other live, and envy, and persecute. "In the day of Jerusalem." The day of Jerusalem, wherein it was tried, wherein it was held captive, or the day of Jerusalem's happiness, wherein it is freed, wherein it reaches its goal, wherein it is made partaker of eternity? "Remember," saith he, "O Lord," forget not those "who said, Rase it, rase it, even to the foundation thereof." Remember then, it

---

[1] Rom. ix. 13.

means, that day wherein they willed to overthrow Jerusalem. For how great persecutions hath the Church suffered! How did the children of Edom, that is, carnal men, servants of the devil and his angels, who worshipped stocks and stones, and followed the lusts of the flesh, how did they say, "Extirpate the Christians, destroy the Christians, let not one remain, overthrow them even to the foundation!" Have not these things been said? And when they were said, the persecutors were rejected, the martyrs crowned. . . .

11. Then he turneth himself to her, "O daughter of Babylon, unhappy;" unhappy in thy very exulting, thy presumption, thine enmity; "unhappy daughter of Babylon!" (ver. 8). The city is called both Babylon, and daughter of Babylon: just as they speak of "Jerusalem" and "the daughter of Jerusalem," "Sion" and "the daughter of Sion," "the Church" and "the daughter of the Church." As it succeedeth the other, it is called "daughter;" as it is preferred before the other, it is called "mother." There was a former Babylon; did the people remain in it? Because it succeedeth to Babylon, it is called daughter of Babylon. O daughter of Babylon, "unhappy" thou! . . .

12. "Happy shall he be that repayeth thee, as thou hast served us." What repayment meaneth he? Herewith the Psalm closeth, "Happy, that taketh and dasheth thy little ones against the rock" (ver. 9). Her he calleth unhappy, but him happy who payeth her as she hath served us. Do we ask, what reward? This is the repayment. For what hath that Babylon done to us? We have already sung in another Psalm, "The words of the wicked have prevailed against us." [1] For when we were born, the confusion of this world found us, and choked us while yet infants with the empty notions of divers errors. The infant that is born destined to be a citizen of Jerusalem, and in God's predestination already a citizen, but meanwhile a prisoner for a time, when learneth he to love ought, save what his parents have whispered into his ears? They teach him and train him in avarice, robbery, daily lying, the worship of divers idols and devils, the unlawful remedies of enchantments and amulets. What shall one yet an infant do, a tender soul, observing what its elders do, save follow that which it seeth them doing. Babylon then has persecuted us when little, but God hath given us when grown up knowledge of ourselves, that we should not follow the errors of our parents. . . . How shall they repay her? As she hath served us. Let her little ones be choked in turn: yea let her little ones in turn be dashed, and die. What are the little ones of Babylon?

Evil desires at their birth. For there are, who have to fight with inveterate lusts. When lust is born, before evil habit giveth it strength against thee, when lust is little, by no means let it gain the strength of evil habit; when it is little, dash it. But thou fearest, lest though dashed it die not; "Dash it against the Rock; and that Rock is Christ." [2]

13. Brethren, let not your instruments of music rest in your work: sing one to another songs of Sion. Readily have ye heard; the more readily do what ye have heard, if ye wish not to be willows of Babylon fed by its streams, and bringing no fruit. But sigh for the everlasting Jerusalem: whither your hope goeth before, let your life follow; there we shall be with Christ. Christ now is our Head; now He ruleth us from above; in that city He will fold us to Himself; we shall be equal to the Angels of God. We should not dare to imagine this of ourselves, did not the Truth promise it. This then desire, brethren, this day and night think on. Howsoever the world shine happily on you, presume not, parley not willingly with your lusts. Is it a grown-up enemy? let it be slain upon the Rock. Is it a little enemy? let it be dashed against the Rock. Slay the grown-up ones on the Rock, and dash the little ones against the Rock. Let the Rock conquer. Be built upon the Rock, if ye desire not to be swept away either by the stream, or the winds, or the rain. If ye wish to be armed against temptations in this world, let longing for the everlasting Jerusalem grow and be strengthened in your hearts. Your captivity will pass away, your happiness will come; the last enemy shall be destroyed, and we shall triumph with our King, without death.

PSALM CXXXVIII. [3]

1. The title of this Psalm is brief and simple, and need not detain us; since we know whose resemblance David wore, and since in him we recognise ourselves also, for we too are members of that Body. The whole title is, "To David himself." Let us see then, what is to David himself. The title of the Psalm is wont to tell us what is treated of within it: but in this, since the title informs us not of this, but tells us only to Whom it is chanted, the first verse tells us what is treated of in the whole Psalm, "I will confess to Thee." This confession then let us hear. But first I remind you, that the term confession in Scripture, when we speak of confession to God, is used in two senses, of sin, and of praise. But confession of sin all know, confession of praise few attend to. So well known is confession of sin, that, wherever in Scripture we hear the words, "I will confess to Thee, O Lord," or,

---

[1] Ps. lxv. 3.　　　　[2] 1 Cor. x. 4.　　　[3] Lat. CXXXVII.

"we will confess to Thee," forthwith, through habitually understanding in this way, our hands hurry to beating our breast : so entirely are men wont not to understand confession to be of aught, save of sin. But was then our Lord Jesus Christ Himself too a sinner, who saith in the Gospel, "I confess to Thee, Father, Lord of heaven and earth"?[1] He goeth on to say what He confesseth, that we might understand His confession to be of praise, not of sin, "I confess to Thee, Father, Lord of heaven and earth, because Thou hast hid these things from the wise and prudent, and hast revealed them unto babes." He praised the Father, he praised God, because He despiseth not the humble, but the proud. And such confession are we now going to hear, of praise of God, of thanksgiving. "With my whole heart." My whole heart I lay upon the altar of Thy praise, an whole burnt-offering[2] of praise I offer to Thee. . . . "I will confess to Thee, O Lord, with my whole heart : for Thou hast heard the words of my mouth" (ver. 1). What mouth, save my heart? For there have we the voice which God heareth, which ear of man knoweth not at all. We have then a mouth within, there do we ask, thence do we ask, and if we have prepared a lodging or an house for God, there do we speak, there are we heard. "For He is not far from every one of us, for in Him we live, and move, and have our being."[3] Nought maketh thee far off from God, save sin only. Cast down the middle wall of sin, and thou art with Him whom thou askest.

2. "And before the Angels will I sing unto Thee." Not before men will I sing, but before the Angels. My song is my joy ; but my joy in things below is before men, my joy in things above before the Angels. For the wicked knoweth not the joy of the just : "There is no joy, saith my God, to the wicked."[4] The wicked rejoiceth in his tavern, the martyr in his chain. In what did that holy Crispina rejoice, whose festival is kept to-day? She rejoiced when she was being seized, when she was being carried before the judge, when she was being put into prison, when she was being brought forth bound, when she was being lifted up on the scaffold,[5] when she was being heard, when she was being condemned : in all these things she rejoiced ; and the wretches thought her wretched, when she was rejoicing before the Angels.

3. "I will worship toward Thy holy Temple" (ver. 2). What holy Temple? That where we shall dwell, where we shall worship. For we hasten that we may adore. Our heart is pregnant and cometh to the birth, and seeketh where it may bring forth. What is the place where God is to be worshipped? . . . "The Temple of God is holy," saith the Apostle, "which Temple ye are."[6] But assuredly, as is manifest, God dwelleth in the Angels. Therefore when our joy, being in spiritual things, not in earthly, taketh up a song to God, to sing before the Angels, that very assembly of Angels is the Temple of God, we worship toward God's Temple. There is a Church below, there is a Church above also ; the Church below, in all the faithful ; the Church above, in all the Angels. But the God of Angels came down to the Church below, and Angels ministered to Him on earth,[7] while He ministered to us ; for, "I came not," saith He, "to be ministered unto, but to minister."[8] . . . The Lord of Angels died for man. Therefore, "I will worship toward Thy holy Temple ; " I mean, not the temple made with hands, but that which Thou hast made for Thyself.

4. "And I will confess to Thy Name in Thy mercy and Thy truth." . . . These also which Thou hast given to me, do I according to my power give to Thee in return : mercy, in aiding others ; truth, in judging. By these God aideth us, by these we win God's favour. Rightly, therefore, "All the ways of the Lord are mercy and truth." No other ways are there whereby He can come to us, no other whereby we can come to Him. "For Thou hast magnified Thy holy Name over everything." What sort of thanksgiving is this, brethren? He hath magnified His holy Name over Abraham. Of Abraham was born Isaac ; over that house God was magnified ; then Jacob ; God was magnified, who said, "I am the God of Abraham, and the God of Isaac, and the God of Jacob." Then came his twelve sons. The name of the Lord was magnified over Israel. Then came the Virgin Mary. Then Christ our Lord, "dying for our sins, rising again for our justification,"[9] filling the faithful with His Holy Spirit, sending forth men to proclaim throughout the Gentiles, "Repent ye," etc.[10] Behold, "He hath magnified His holy Name above all things."

5. "In what day soever I call upon Thee, do Thou quickly hear me" (ver. 3). Wherefore, "quickly"? Because Thou hast said, "While yet thou art speaking I will say, Lo, here I am."[11] Wherefore, "quickly"? Because now I seek not earthly happiness, I have learnt holy longings from the New Testament. I seek not earth, nor earthly abundance, nor temporal health, nor the overthrow of my enemies, nor riches, nor rank : nought of these do I seek :

---

[1] *Confiteor Tibi.* Matt. xi. 25.
[2] [He adds: "A whole burnt offering is a sacrifice where the whole is burnt, for the Greek word ὅλον, (*holocaustum*, Lat.) meaneth ' whole.' " — C.]
[3] Acts xvii. 27, 28.   [4] Isa. xlviii. 22, lvii. 21.
[5] *Catasta.*

[6] 1 Cor. iii. 17.   [7] Matt. iv. 11.   [8] Matt. xx. 28.
[9] Rom. iv. 25.   [10] Matt. iii. 2.   [11] Isa. lviii. 9.

therefore "quickly hear me." Since Thou hast taught me what to seek, grant what I seek. . . .

6. Let us see then what he seeketh, with what right he hath said, "quickly hear me." For what seekest thou, that thou shouldest quickly be heard? "Thou shalt multiply me." In many ways may multiplication be understood. . . . For men are multiplied in their soul with cares: a man seemeth to be multiplied in soul, in whom vices even are multiplied. That is the multiplication of want, not of fulness. What then dost thou desire, thou who hast said, "quickly hear me," and hast withdrawn thyself entirely from the body, from every earthly thing, from every earthly desire, so as to say to God, "Thou shalt multiply me in my soul"? Explain yet further what thou desirest. Thou shalt multiply me, saith he, in my soul "with virtue." . . .

7. "Let all the kings of the earth confess to Thee, O Lord" (ver. 4). So shall it be, and so it is, and that daily; and it is shown that it was not said in vain, save that it was future. But neither let them, when they confess to Thee, when they praise Thee, desire earthly things of Thee. For what shall the kings of the earth desire? Have they not already sovereignty? Whatever more a man desire on earth, sovereignty is the highest point of his desire. What more can he desire? It must needs be some loftier eminence. But perhaps the loftier it is, the more dangerous. And therefore the more exalted kings are in earthly eminence, the more ought they to humble themselves before God. What do they do? "Because they have heard all the words of Thy mouth." In a certain nation were hidden the Law and the Prophets, "all the words of Thy mouth:" in the Jewish nation alone were "all the words of Thy mouth," the nation which the Apostle praiseth, saying, "What advantage hath the Jew? Much every way; chiefly because that unto them were committed the oracles of God." These were the words of God.[1] . . . What meant Gideon's fleece? It is like the nation of the Jews in the midst of the world, which had the grace of sacraments, not indeed openly manifested, but hidden in a cloud, or in a veil, like the dew in the fleece.[2] The time came when the dew was to be manifested in the floor; it was manifested, no longer hidden. Christ alone is the sweetness of dew: Him alone thou recognisest not in Scripture, for whom Scripture was written. But yet, "they have heard all the words of thy mouth."

8. "And let them sing in the paths of the Lord, that great is the glory of the Lord" (ver. 5). Let all the kings of the earth sing in the paths of the Lord. In what paths? Those that are spoken of above, "in Thy mercy and Thy truth." Let not then the kings of the earth be proud, let them be humble. Then let them sing in the ways of the Lord, if they be humble: let them love, and they shall sing. We know travellers that sing; they sing, and hasten to reach the end of their journey. There are evil songs, such as belong to the old man; to the new man belongeth a new song. Let then the kings of the earth too walk in Thy paths, let them walk and sing in Thy paths. Sing what? that "great is the glory of the Lord," not of kings.

9. See how he willed that kings should sing on their way, humbly bearing the Lord, not lifting themselves up against the Lord. For if they lift themselves up, what follows? "For the Lord is high, and hath respect unto the lowly" (ver. 6). Do kings then desire that He have respect unto them? Let them be humble. What then? if they lift themselves up to pride, can they escape His eyes? Lest perchance, because thou hast heard, "He hath respect unto the lowly," thou choose to be proud, and say in thy soul, God hath respect unto the lowly, He hath not respect unto me, I will do what I will. O foolish one! wouldest thou say this, if thou knewest what thou oughtest to love? Behold, even if God willeth not to see thee, dost thou not fear this very thing, that He willeth not to see thee? . . . The lofty then, it seemeth, He hath not respect unto, for it is the lowly He respecteth. "The lofty"—what? "He considereth from afar." What then gaineth the proud? To be seen from afar, not to escape being seen. And think not that thou must needs be safe on that account, for that He seeth less clearly, who seeth thee from afar. For thou indeed seest not clearly, what thou seest from afar; God, although He see thee from afar, seeth thee perfectly, yet is He not with thee. This thou gainest, not that thou art less perfectly seen, but that thou art not with Him by whom thou art seen. But what doth the lowly gain? "The Lord is nigh unto them that are of a contrite heart." Let the proud then lift himself up as much as he will, certainly God dwelleth on high, God is in heaven: wishest thou that He come nigh to thee? Humble thyself. For the higher will He be above thee, the more thou liftest thyself up.

10. "If I walk in the midst of tribulation, Thou shalt revive me" (ver. 7). True it is: whatsoever tribulation thou art in, confess, call on Him; He freeth thee, He reviveth thee. . . . Love the other life, and thou shalt see that this life is tribulation, whatever prosperity it shine with, whatever delights it abound and overflow with; since not yet have we that joy most safe and free from all temptation, which God reserveth for us in the end, without doubt it is

[1] Rom. iii. 1, 2.   [2] Judg. vi. 37, 39.

tribulation. Let us understand then what tribulation he meaneth here too, brethren. Not as though he said, "If perchance there shall any tribulation have befallen me, Thou shalt free me therefrom." But how saith he? "If I walk," etc.; that is, otherwise Thou wilt not revive me, unless I walk in the midst of tribulation.

11. "Thou hast stretched forth Thine hand over the wrath of mine enemies, and Thy right hand hath made me safe." Let mine enemies rage: what can they do? They can take my money, strip, proscribe, banish me; afflict me with grief and tortures; at last, if they be allowed, even kill me: can they do aught more? But over that which mine enemies can do, Thou hast stretched forth Thine hand. For mine enemies cannot separate me from Thee: but Thou avengest me the more, the more Thou as yet delayest. . . . Yet not to make me despair; for it follows, "and Thy right hand hath made me safe."

12. "Thou, Lord, shalt recompense for me" (ver. 8). I recompense not: Thou shalt recompense. Let mine enemies rage their full: Thou shalt recompense what I cannot. . . . "Dearly beloved, avenge not yourselves," saith the Apostle, "but rather give place unto wrath; for it is written, Vengeance is Mine, I will repay, saith the Lord."[1] There is here another sense not to be neglected, perhaps even to be preferred. "Lord" Christ, "Thou shalt repay for me." For I, if I repay, have seized; Thou hast paid what Thou hast not seized. Lord, Thou shalt "repay for me." Behold Him repaying for us. They came to Him, who exacted tribute:[2] they used to demand as tribute a didrachma, that is, two drachmas for one man; they came to the Lord to pay tribute; or rather, not to Him, but to His disciples, and they said to them, "Doth not your Master pay tribute?" They came and told Him. He saith unto Peter, "lest we should offend them, go thou to the sea, and cast an hook, and take up the fish that first cometh up: and when thou hast opened his mouth, thou shalt find a stater:[3] that take, and give for Me and thee." The first that riseth from the sea, is the First-begotten from the dead. In His mouth we find two didrachmas, that is, four drachmas: in His mouth we find the four Gospels. By those four drachmas we are free from the claims of this world, by the four Evangelists we remain no longer debtors; for there the debt of all our sins is paid. He then hath repaid for us, thanks to His mercy. He owed nothing: He repaid not for Himself: He repaid for us. . . .

13. "Lord, Thy mercy is for everlasting." . . . Not for a time only do I desire to be freed.

"Thy mercy is for everlasting," wherewith Thou hast freed the martyrs, and so hast quickly taken them from this life. "Despise not Thou the works of Thine own hands." I say not, Lord, "despise not the works of my hands:" of mine own works I boast not. "I sought," indeed, "the Lord with my hands in the night season before Him, and have not been deceived;" but yet I praise not the works of mine own hands; I fear lest, when Thou shalt look into them, Thou find more sins in them than deserts. Behold in me Thy Work, not mine: for mine if Thou seest, Thou condemnest; Thine, if Thou seest, Thou crownest. For whatever good works there be of mine, from Thee are they to me; and so they are more Thine than mine.[4] Therefore whether in regard that we are men, or in regard that we have been changed and justified from our iniquity, Lord, "despise not Thou the works of Thine own hands."

PSALM CXXXIX.[5]

1. . . . Our Lord Jesus Christ speaketh in the Prophets, sometimes in His own Name, sometimes in ours, because He maketh Himself one with us; as it is said, "they twain shall be one flesh." Wherefore also the Lord saith in the Gospel, speaking of marriage, "therefore they are no more twain, but one flesh." One flesh, because of our mortality He took flesh; not one divinity, for He is the Creator, we the creature. Whatsoever then our Lord speaketh in the person of the Flesh He took upon Him, belongeth both to that Head which hath already ascended into heaven, and to those members which still toil in their earthly wandering. Let us hear then our Lord Jesus Christ speaking in prophecy. For the Psalms were sung long before the Lord was born of Mary, yet not before He was Lord: for from everlasting He was the Creator of all things, but in time He was born of His creature. Let us believe that Godhead, and, so far as we can, understand Him to be equal to the Father. But that Godhead equal to the Father, was made partaker of our mortal nature, not of His own store, but of ours; that we too might be made partakers of His Divine Nature, not of our store, but of His.

2. "Lord, Thou hast tried me, and known me" (ver. 1). Let the Lord Jesus Christ Himself say this; let Him too say, "Lord," to the Father. For His Father is not His Lord, save because He hath deigned to be born according

---

[1] Rom. xii. 19.   [2] Matt. xvii. 24-26.
[3] That is, two didrachmas.

[4] Eph. ii. 8-10.
[5] Lat. CXXXVIII. Sermon to the people. [The author says: "We had prepared us a short Psalm, and had desired the reader to chant it; but he, through confusion at the time, as it seems, has substituted another for it. We have chosen to follow the will of God in the reader's mistake, rather than our own will by keeping our purpose." — C.]

to the flesh. He is Father of the God, Lord of the Man. Wouldest thou know to whom He is Father? To the coequal Son. The Apostle saith, "Who, being in the form of God, thought it not robbery to be equal with God." [1] To this "Form" God is Father, the "Form" equal to Himself, the only-begotten Son, begotten of His Substance. But forasmuch as for our sakes, that we might be re-made, and made partakers of His Divine Nature, being renewed unto life eternal, He was made partaker of our mortal nature, what saith the Apostle of Him? He saith, "yet He emptied Himself, and took upon Him the form of a servant, and was made in the likeness of men, and was found in fashion as a man." He was in the Form of God, equal to the Father; He took upon Him the form of a servant, so as therein to be less than the Father. . . .

3. "Thou hast known My down-sitting and Mine up-rising" (ver. 2). What here is "down-sitting," what "up-rising"? He who sitteth, humbleth himself. The Lord then "sat" in His Passion, "up-rose" in His Resurrection. "Thou," he saith, hast known this; that is, Thou hast willed, Thou hast approved; according to Thy will was it done. But if thou choosest to take the words of the Head in the person of the Body : man sitteth when he humbleth himself in penitence, he riseth up when his sins are forgiven, and he is lifted up to the hope of everlasting life. Lift not up yourselves, unless ye have first been humbled. For many wish to rise before they have sat down, they wish to appear righteous, before they have confessed that they are sinners. . . .

4. "Thou hast understood my thoughts from afar; Thou hast tracked out my path and my limit" (ver. 3) ; "and all my ways Thou hast seen beforehand" (ver. 4). What is, "from afar"? While I am yet in my pilgrimage, before I reach that, my true country, Thou hast known my thoughts. . . . The younger son went into a far country. After his toil and suffering and tribulation and want, he thought on his father, and desired to return, and said, "I will arise, and go to my father." "I will arise," said he, for before he had sat. Here then thou mayest recognise him saying, "Thou hast known my down-sitting and up-rising." I sat, in want ; I arose, in longing for Thy Bread. "Thou hast understood my thoughts from afar." For far indeed had I gone ; but where is not He whom I had left? Wherefore the Lord saith in the Gospel, that his father met him as he was coming. Truly ; for "he had understood his thoughts from afar." "My path," he saith ; what, but a bad path, the path he had walked to

leave his father? . . . What is, "my path"? that by which I have gone. What is, "my limit"? that whereunto I have reached. "Thou hast tracked out my path and my limit." That limit of mine, far distant as it was, was not far from Thine eyes. Far had I gone, and yet Thou wast there. "And all my ways Thou hast seen beforehand." He said not, "hast seen," but, "hast seen beforehand." Before I went by them, before I walked in them, Thou didst see them beforehand ; and Thou didst permit me in toil to go my own ways, that, if I desired not to toil, I might return into Thy ways. "For there is no deceit in my tongue." [2] What meant he by this? Lo, I confess to Thee, I have walked in my own way, I am become far from Thee, I have departed from Thee, with whom it was well with me, and to my good it was ill with me without Thee. . . .

5. "Behold Thou, Lord, hast known all my last doings, and the ancient ones" (ver. 5). Thou hast known my latest doings, when I fed swine ; Thou hast known my ancient doings, when I asked of Thee my portion of goods. Ancient doings were the beginnings to me of latest ills : ancient sin, when we fell ; latest punishment, when we came into this toilsome and dangerous mortality. And would that this may be "latest" to us ; it will be, if now we will to return. For there is another "latest" for certain wicked ones, to whom it shall be said, "Go ye into everlasting fire." [3] . . . "Thou hast fashioned me, and hast laid Thine hand upon me." "Fashioned me," where? In this mortality ; now, to the toils whereunto we all are born. For none is born, but God has fashioned him in his mother's womb ; nor is there any creature, whereof God is not the Fashioner. But "Thou hast fashioned me " in this toil, "and laid Thine hand upon me," Thine avenging hand, putting down the proud. For thus healthfully hath He cast down the proud, that He may lift him up humble.

6. "Thy skill hath displayed itself wonderfully in me : it hath waxed mighty : I shall not be able to attain unto it" (ver. 6). Listen now and hear somewhat, which is obscure indeed, yet bringeth no small pleasure in the understanding thereof. Moses, the holy servant of God, with whom God spake by a cloud, for, speaking after human fashion, He must needs speak to His servant through some work of His hands which He assumed, . . . longed and desired to see the true appearance of God, and said to God, who was conversing with him, "If now I have found grace in Thy sight, show me Thyself." [4] When this he desired vehemently, and would extort from God in that sort of friendly

familiarity, if we may so speak, wherewith God deigned to treat him, that he might see His Glory and His Face, in such wise as we ·can speak of God's Face, He said unto him, "Thou canst not see My Face; for no one hath seen My Face, and lived;"[1] but I will place thee in a clift of the rock, and will pass by, and will set My hand upon thee; and when I have passed by, thou shalt see My back parts. And from these words there ariseth another enigma, that is, an obscure figure of the truth. "When I have passed by," saith God, "thou shalt see My back parts;" as though He hath on one side His face, on another His back. Far be it from us to have any such thoughts of that Majesty! For whoso hath such thoughts of God, what advantageth it him that the temples are closed? He is building an idol in his own heart. In these words then are mighty mysteries. . . . They who raged against the Lord, whom they saw, now seek counsel how they may be saved; and it is said to them, "Repent, and be baptized every one of you in the Name of Jesus Christ, and your sins shall be forgiven you."[2] Behold, they saw the back parts of Him, whose face they could not see. For His Hand was upon their eyes, not for ever, but while He passed by. After He had passed He took away His Hand from their eyes. When the hand was taken from their eyes, they say to the disciples, "What shall we do?" At first they are fierce, afterwards loving; at first angry, afterwards fearful; at first hard, then pleasant; at first blind, then enlightened. . . .

7. Behold thou findest that the runaway in a far country cannot escape His eyes, from whom he fleeth. And whither can he go now, whose "limit is tracked out"? Behold, what saith he? "Whither shall I go from Thy Spirit?" (ver. 7). Who can in the world flee from that Spirit, with whom the world is filled?[3] "And whither shall I flee from Thy Face?" He seeketh a place whither to flee from the wrath of God. What place will shelter God's runaway? Men who shelter runaways, ask them from whom they have fled; and when they find any one a slave of some master less powerful than themselves, him they shelter as it were without any fear, saying in their hearts, "he hath not a master by whom he can be tracked out." But when they are told of a powerful master, they either shelter not, or they shelter with great fear, because even a powerful man can be deceived. Where is God not? Who can deceive God? Whom doth not God see? From whom doth not God demand His runaway? Whither then shall that runaway go from the Face of God? He turneth him hither and thither, as though seeking a spot to flee to.

8. "If I go up," saith he, "to heaven, Thou art there: if I go down to Hades, Thou art present" (ver. 8). At length, miserable runaway, thou hast learnt, that by no means canst thou make thyself far from Him, from whom thou hast wished to remove far away. Behold, He is everywhere; thou, whither wilt thou go? He hath found counsel, and that inspired by Him, who now deigneth to recall him. . . . If by sinning I go down to the depths of wickednesses, and spurn to confess, saying, "Who seeth me" (for "in Hades who shall confess to Thee?"[4]) there also Thou art present, to punish. Whither then shall I go that I may flee from Thy presence, that is, not find Thee angry? This plan he found: So will I flee, saith he, from Thy Face, so will I flee from Thy Spirit; from Thy avenging Spirit, Thy avenging Face thus will I flee. How? "If I take again my wings right forward, and abide in the utmost parts of the sea" (ver. 9). So can I flee from Thy Face. If he will flee to the utmost part of the sea from the Face of God, will not He from whom he fleeth be there? . . . For what are "the utmost parts of the sea," but the end of the world?· Thither let us now flee in hope and longing, with the wings of twofold love; let us have no rest, save in "the utmost parts of the sea." For if elsewhere we wish for rest, we shall be hurled headlong into the sea. Let us fly even to the ends of the sea, let us bear ourselves aloft on the wings of twofold love; meanwhile let us flee to God in hope, and in faithful hope let us meditate on that "end of the sea."

9. Now listen who may bring us thither. The very same One whose face in wrath we wish to flee from. For what followeth? "Even thither shall Thy hand conduct me, and Thy right hand lead me" (ver. 10). This let us meditate on, beloved brethren, let this be our hope, this our consolation. Let us take again through love the wings we lost through lust. For lust was the lime of our wings, it dashed us down from the freedom of our sky, that is, the free breezes of the Spirit of God. Thence dashed down we lost our wings, and were, so to speak, imprisoned in the power of the fowler; thence "He" redeemed us with His Blood, whom we fled from to be caught. He maketh us wings of His commandments; we raise them aloft now free from lime. . . . Needs then must we have wings, and needs must He conduct us, for He is our Helper. We have free-will; but even with that free-will what can we do, unless He help us who commandeth us?

10. And considering the length of the way, what said he to himself? "And I said, Peradventure the darkness shall overwhelm me" (ver.

---

[1] Exod. xxxiii. 20.   [2] Acts ii. 38.   [3] Wisd. i. 7.   [4] Ps. vi. 5.

11). Lo, now I have believed in Christ, now am I wafted aloft on the wings of twofold love. . . . Regarding the length of the way, I said to myself, " And the night was light in my delight." The night was made to me light, because in the night I despaired of being able to cross so great a sea, to surmount so long a journey, to reach the utmost parts by persevering to the end. Thanks to Him who sought me when a runaway, who smote my back with strokes of the scourge, who by calling me re-called me from destruction, who made my night light. For it is night so long as we are passing through this life. How was the night made light? Because Christ came down into the night. . . .

11. " For darkness shall not be darkened by Thee " (ver. 12). Do not thou then darken thy darkness ; God darkeneth it not, but enlighteneth it yet more ; for to Him is said in another Psalm, " Thou, Lord, shalt light my candle : my God shall enlighten my darkness." [1] But who are they who " darken their darkness," which God darkeneth not? Evil men, perverse men ; when they sin, verily they are darkness ; when they confess not their sins which they have committed, but go on to defend them, they " darken their darkness." Wherefore even if thou hast sinned, thou art in darkness, but by confessing thy darkness thou shalt obtain to have thy darkness lightened ; by defending thy darkness, thou shalt " darken thy darkness." And where wilt thou escape from double darkness, who wast in difficulty in single darkness? . . . Let us not " darken our darkness " by defending our sins, and " the night shall be light in our delight."

12. " And night shall be lightened as the day." " Night, as the day." " Day " to us is worldly prosperity, night adversity in this world : but, if we learn that it is by the desert of our sins that we suffer adversities, and our Father's scourges are sweet to us, that the Judge's sentence may not be bitter to us, so shall we find the darkness of this night to be, as it were, the light of this night. . . . But when Christ our Lord has come, and has dwelt in the soul by faith, and promised other light, and inspired and given patience, and warned a man not to delight in prosperity or to be crushed by adversity, the man, being faithful, begins to treat this world with indifference ; not to be lifted up when prosperity befalls him, nor crushed when adversity, but in all things to praise God, not only when he aboundeth, but also when he loseth ; not only when he is in health, but also when he is sick.[2] . . . " As is His darkness, so is also His light." His darkness overwhelms me not, because His light lifts me not up.

13. " For Thou, O Lord, hast possessed my reins " (ver. 13). The Possessor is within ; He occupieth not only the heart, but also the reins ; not only the thoughts, but also the delights : He then possesseth that whence I should feel delight at any light in this world : He occupieth my reins : I know not delight, save from the inward light of His Wisdom. What then? Dost thou not delight that thy affairs are very prosperous, times fortunate to thee? dost thou not delight in honour, in riches, in thy family? " I do not," saith he. Wherefore? Because " Thou hast possessed my reins, O Lord ; Thou hast taken me up from my mother's womb." While I was in my mother's womb, I did not regard with indifference the darkness of that night and the light of that night. . . . Now, having been taken up from the womb of that our mother, we look on them with indifference, and say, " As is His darkness, so is also His light." Neither doth earthly prosperity make us happy, nor earthly adversity wretched. We must maintain righteousness, love faith, hope in God, love God, love our neighbours also. After these toils we shall have unfailing light, day without setting. Fleeting is all the light and darkness of this night.

14. " I will confess to Thee, O Lord, for terribly hast Thou been made wonderful : wondrous are Thy works, and my soul knoweth it right well " (ver. 14). Aforetime " Thy knowledge was made wonderful from me, it had waxed great, nor could I attain unto it." From me then " it had waxed great." Whence doth " my soul " now " know right well," save because the " night is light in my delight? " save because Thy grace hath come unto me, and enlightened my darkness? save because Thou hast possessed my reins? save because Thou hast taken me up from my mother's womb?

15. " My bone is not hid from Thee, which Thou hast made in secret " (ver. 15). " His bone," he saith. What the people call *ossum*, is in Latin called *os*. This is the word in the Greek.[3] For we might think the word *os* is here the one which makes in the plural *ora*, not *os* (short), which makes *ossa*. He saith then, I have a certain bone (*ossum*) in secret. For this word let us prefer to use ; better is it that scholars find fault with us, than that the people understand us not. " There is then," saith he, " a certain bone of mine, within, hidden ; Thou hast made within a bone for me in secret, yet is it not hidden from Thee. In secret hast Thou made it, but hast Thou therefore hidden it from Thyself? This my bone made by Thee in secret men see not, men know not : Thou knowest, who hast made. What " bone " then meaneth he, brethren? Let us seek it, it is " in secret." But because as Christians we are speaking in the Name of the

---

[1] Ps. xviii. 28.   [2] Ps. xxxiv. 1.   [3] Gr. ὀστοῦν.

Lord to Christians, now we find what bone is of this kind. It is a sort of inward strength; for strength and fortitude are understood to be in the bones. There is then a sort of inward strength of the soul, wherein it is not broken. Whatever tortures, whatever tribulations, whatever adversities rage around, that which God hath made strong in secret in us, cannot be broken, yieldeth not. For by God is made a certain strength of patience, of which is said in another Psalm, " But my soul shall be subjected to God, for of Him is my patience." [1] . . . Wherein dost thou glory? " In tribulations, knowing that tribulation worketh patience." [2] See how that strength is fashioned within in his heart : " because the love of God is shed abroad in our hearts by the Holy Ghost which is given unto us." So is fashioned and made strong that hidden bone, that it maketh us even to glory in tribulations. But to men we seem wretched, because that which we have within is hidden from them. " And my substance is in the lower parts of the earth." Behold, in flesh is my substance, yet have I a bone within, which Thou hast fashioned, such as to cause me never to yield to any persecutions of this lower region, where still my substance is. For what great matter is it, if an Angel be brave? This is a great matter, if flesh is brave. And whence is flesh brave, whence is an earthen vessel brave, save because in it is made a bone in secret?

16. . . . " Thine eyes did see Mine imperfect one, and in Thy book shall all be written " (ver. 16), not only the perfect, but also the imperfect. Let not the imperfect fear, only let them advance. Nor yet, because I have said, " let them not fear," let them love their imperfection, and remain there, where they are found. Let them advance, as far as in them lieth. Daily let them add, daily let them approach; yet let them not fall back from the Body of the Lord : that, compacted in one Body and among these members, they may be counted worthy to have that said of them. " By day shall they wander, and none among them." " The Day" was yet on earth, even our Lord Jesus Christ. Whence He said, " Walk while ye have the day." [3] But " by day shall " His imperfect ones " wander." They too thought that our Lord Jesus Christ was only man, that He had not within Him the hidden Godhead, that He was not secretly God, but that He was that only which was seen : this they too thought. . . . But what is, " In the day they shall wander "? Shall they perish? Where then is, " In Thy book shall all be written "? When then did they " wander in the day "? When they understood not the Lord set upon earth. And what followeth? " But to

me Thy friends are made very honourable, O God " (ver. 17) ; those very ones, who " wandered in the day, and none was in them," became Thy friends, and were made very honourable to me. That bone was made in them in secret after the resurrection of the Lord, and they suffered for His Name, at whose death they had been amazed. " Mightily strengthened were their chieftainships." They became Apostles, they became leaders of the Church, they became rams leading their flocks, " mightily strengthened."

17. " I will number them, and they shall be multiplied above the sand " (ver. 18). By means of them, who " wandered in the day," lo ! there has been born all this great multitude, which now is like the sand innumerable, save by God. For He said, " they shall be multiplied above the sand," and yet He had said, " I will number them." The very same who are numbered, " shall be multiplied above the sand." For by Him is the sand numbered, by whom " the very hairs of our head are numbered." [4] " I have risen, and yet am I with Thee." Already have I suffered, saith He, already have I been buried ; lo ! I have risen, and not yet do they understand that I am with them. " Yet am I with Thee," that is, not yet with them, for not yet do they recognise Me. For thus do we read in the Gospel, that after the resurrection of our Lord Jesus Christ, when He appeared to them, they did not at once know Him. There is another meaning also : " I have risen, and yet am I with Thee," as though He would signify this present time, wherein He is as yet hidden at the right hand of the Father, before He is revealed in the brightness, wherein He shall come to judge the quick and the dead.

18. And then He telleth what meanwhile, during this whole time when He already has risen, and remaineth still with the Father, He suffereth by the intermixture of sinners in His Body, the Church, and by the separation of heretics. " If Thou, O God, shalt slay the sinners (since Thou shalt say in Thy thought, Depart from Me, ye men of blood), they shall receive in vanity their cities " (ver. 19, 20). The words seem to be connected in this order ; " If Thou, O God, shalt slay the sinners, they shall receive in vanity their cities." Thus are sinners slain, because, " having their understandings darkened, they are alienated from the life of God." [5] For on account of elation they lose confession, and so they are slain, and in them is fulfilled what Scripture saith, " Confession perisheth from the dead, as from one that is not." [6] And so " they receive in vanity their cities," that is, their vain peoples, who follow

---

[1] Ps. lxii. 5.　　[2] Rom. iv. 5.　　[3] John xii. 35.　　[4] Matt. x. 30.　　[5] Eph. iv. 18.　　[6] Ecclus. xvii. 28.

their vanity; when, puffed up by the name of righteousness, they [1] persuade men to burst the bond of unity, and blindly and ignorantly follow them, as being more righteous. . . . But now the Body of Christ, the Church, saith, Why do the proud speak falsely against me, as though I were stained by other men's sins, and so, by separating themselves, "receive in vanity their cities"? "Have not I hated those who hated Thee, Lord?" (ver. 21). Why do those who are worse themselves require of me to separate myself in body as well as spirit from the wicked, so as to root up the wheat, together with the tares, before the time of harvest, that before the time of winnowing I lose my power of enduring the chaff; that before all the different sorts of fishes are brought to the end of the world, as to the shore, to be separated, I tear the nets of peace and unity? Are the sacraments which I receive, those of evil men? Do I, by consent, communicate in their life and deeds? . . . But where is, "Love your enemies"? Is it because He said "yours," not "God's"? "Do good to them that hate you." [2] He saith not, "who hate God." So he followeth the pattern, and saith, "Have not I hated those who hated Thee, Lord?" He saith not, "Who have hated me." "And at Thine enemies did I waste away." "Thine," he said, not "mine." But those who hate us and are enemies unto us, only because we serve Him, what else do they but hate Him, and are His enemies. Ought we then to love such enemies as these? Or do not they suffer persecution for God's sake, to whom it is said, "Pray for them that persecute you"? Observe then what followeth. "With a perfect hatred did I hate them" (ver. 22). What is, "with a perfect hatred"? I hated in them their iniquities, I loved Thy creation. This it is to hate with a perfect hatred, that neither on account of the vices thou hate the men, nor on account of the men love the vices. For see what he addeth, "They became mine enemies." Not only as God's enemies, but as his own too doth he now describe them. How then will he fulfil in them both his own saying, "Have not I hated those that hated Thee, Lord," and the Lord's command, "Love your enemies"? How will he fulfil this, save with that "perfect hatred," that he hate in them that they are wicked, and love that they are men? For in the time even of the Old Testament, when the carnal people was restrained by visible punishments, how did Moses, the servant of God, who by understanding belonged to the New Testament, how did he hate sinners when he prayed for them, or how did he not hate them when he slew them, save that he "hated them with a perfect

hatred"? For with such perfection did he hate the iniquity which he punished, as to love the manhood for which he prayed.

19. Since then the Body of Christ is in the end to be severed in body also from the unholy and wicked, but now meanwhile groaneth among them, what doeth the "love of Christ among the daughters, as the lily among thorns"? [3] What are her words? what her conscience? what is the "appearance of the king's daughter within"? [4] Lo, hear what she saith. "Prove me, O God, and know my heart" (ver. 23). Do Thou, O God, Thou prove me, Thou know; not man, not an heretic, who neither knoweth how to prove, nor can know my heart, whereas Thou provest, and knowest that I consent not to the deeds of the wicked, while they think that I can be defiled by the sins of others; so that, while I in my long wandering do what I mourn in another Psalm, that is, while I "labour for peace among them that hate peace," [5] until I come to that Vision of peace, which is called Jerusalem, "which is the mother of us all," the city "eternal in the heavens;" they, contending, and falsely accusing and separating themselves, may "receive," not, evidently, in eternity, but "in vanity, their cities." Why this? Observe what followeth.

20. "And see," saith he, "if there be any way of wickedness in me, and lead me in the way everlasting" (ver. 24). "Search," he saith, "my paths," that is, my counsels and thoughts. What else saith he, but "lead me in Christ"? For who is "the way everlasting," save He that is the life everlasting? For everlasting is He who said, "I am the Way, and the Truth, and the Life." [6] If then thou findest anything in my way which displeaseth Thine eyes, since my way is mortal, do Thou "lead me in the way everlasting," wherein is no iniquity; for even "if any man sin, we have an Advocate with the Father, Jesus Christ the righteous; and He is the propitiation for our sins;" [7] He is "the Way everlasting" without sin; He is the Life everlasting without punishment.

21. These are great mysteries, brethren. How doth the Spirit of God speak with us? how doth it make us delights in this night? What is this, we ask you, brethren, whence are they sweeter, the darker they are? He mixeth us our potion after His love, in certain wondrous ways. He maketh His own sayings wondrous, so that while we were speaking what ye already knew, yet forasmuch as it was dug out of passages which seemed obscure, the knowledge itself seemed to be made new. Did ye not know, brethren, that the wicked are to be tolerated in the Church, and schisms not to be made? Did

---

[1] Donatists.   [2] Matt. v. 44.   [3] Cant. ii. 2.   [4] Ps. xlv. 13.   [5] Ps. cxx. 7.
[6] John xiv. 6.   [7] 1 John ii. 1, 2.

ye not already know, that within those nets which hold both good and bad fishes, we must abide even to the shore, nor must the nets be burst, because on the shore the good shall be separated into vessels, and the bad thrown away? Ye know this already; but these verses of this Psalm ye did not understand: that which ye did not understand is explained; that which ye knew has been renewed.

PSALM CXL.[1]

1. Our Lords have bidden me, brethren, and in them the Lord of all, to bring this Psalm to your understanding, so far as God giveth me to. May He help your prayers, that I may say those things which I ought to say, ye to hear, that to all of us the Word of God may be profitable. For all it doth not profit, for "all have not faith." [2] . . .

2. What this Psalm containeth, I believe that ye perceived when it was being chanted; for therein the Church of Christ, set in the midst of the wicked, complaineth and groaneth, and poureth out prayer to God. For her voice is in every such prophecy the voice of one in need and want, not yet satisfied, "hungering and thirsting after righteousness," [3] for whom a certain fulness in the end hath been promised, and is reserved. . . .

3. "To the end, a Psalm to David himself." No other end mayest thou look to, than is laid down for thee by the Apostle himself. For "Christ is the end." [4] . . . He was of the seed of David, not after His Godhead, whereby He is the Creator of David, but after the flesh; therefore He deigned to be called David in prophecy: look to this "end," for the Psalm is chanted "to David Himself;" hear the voice of His Body; be in His Body. Let the voice which thou hast heard be thine, and pray, and say what followeth.

4. "Deliver me, O Lord, from the wicked man" (ver. 1). Not from one only, but from the class; not from the vessels only, but from their prince himself, that is, the devil. Why "from man," if he meaneth from the devil? Because he too is called a man in a figure.[5] . . . Now then being made light, not in ourselves, but in the Lord,[6] let us pray not only against darkness, that is, against sinners, whom still the devil possesseth, but also against their prince, the devil himself, who worketh in the children of disobedience. "Deliver me from the unrighteous man." The same as "from the wicked man." For he called him wicked because unrighteous,

lest perchance thou shouldest think that any unrighteous man could be a good man. For many unrighteous men seem to be harmless; they are not fierce, are not savage, do not persecute nor oppress; yet are they unrighteous, because, following some other habit, they are luxurious, drunkards, given to pleasure. . . . Wicked then is every unrighteous man, who must needs be harmful, whether he be gentle or fierce. Whoever falls in his way, whoever is taken by his snares, will find how harmful is that which he thought harmless. For, brethren, even thorns prick not with their roots. Pull up thorns from the ground, handle their roots, and see whether thou feelest pain. Yet that in the upgrowth which causeth thee pain, proceeded from that root. Let not then men please you who seem gentle and kind, yet are lovers of carnal pleasure, followers of polluted lusts, let them not please you. Though as yet they seem gentle, they are roots of thorns. . . . And so, my brethren, body of Christ, members of Christ groaning among such wicked men, whomsoever ye find hurrying headlong into evil lusts and deadly pleasures, at once chide, at once punish, at once burn. Let the root be burnt, and there remaineth not whence the thorn may grow up. If ye cannot, be sure that ye will have them as enemies. They may be silent, they may hide their enmity, but they cannot love you. But since they cannot love you, and since they who hate you must needs seek your harm, let not your tongue and heart be slow to say to God, "Deliver me, O Lord, from the unrighteous man."

5. "Who have imagined unrighteousnesses in their heart" (ver. 2). . . . From them free me, from them let Thy hand be most powerful to deliver me. For easy is it to avoid open enmities, easy is it to turn aside from an enemy declared and manifest, while iniquity is in his lips as well as his heart; he is a troublesome enemy, he is secret, he is with difficulty avoided, who beareth good things in his lips, while in his heart he concealeth evil things. "All the day long did they make war." What is, "war"? They made for me what I was to fight against all the day. For from thence, from such hearts as these, ariseth all that the Christian fighteth against. Be it sedition, be it schism, be it heresy, be it turbulent opposition, it springeth not save from these imaginings which were concealed, and while they spake good words with their lips, "all the day long did they make war." Ye hear words of peace, yet making war departeth not from their thoughts. For the words, "all the day long," signify without intermission, throughout the whole time. "They have sharpened their tongues like serpents" (ver. 3). If still thou seekest to make out the man, behold a comparison. In the serpent above all beasts is

---

[1] Lat. CXXXIX. Sermon to the people, in the presence of an assembly of bishops.
[2] 1 Thess. iii. 2. [3] Matt. v. 6. [4] Rom. x. 4.
[5] Matt. xiii. 24–28. [6] Eph. v. 8.

there cunning and craft to hurt; for therefore does it creep.[1] It hath not even feet, so that its footsteps when it cometh may be heard. In its progress it draweth itself, as it were, gently along, yet not straightly. Thus then do they creep and crawl to hurt, having poison hidden even under a gentle touch. And so it followeth, "the poison of asps is under their lips." Behold, it is "under" their lips, that we may perceive one thing under their lips, another in their lips. . . .

6. "Preserve me, O Lord, from the hand of the sinner, from unrighteous men deliver me" (ver. 4). Here they wear their real colours, they are known; here we have no need to understand, but to act: we have need to pray, not to ask who they are. But how thou shouldest pray against such men, he explaineth in what followeth. For many pray unskilfully against wicked men. "Who have imagined," saith he, "to trip up my steps." Thus far it may be understood carnally. Every one has enemies, who seek to cheat him in trade, to rob him of money, where they are engaged together in business; every one has some neighbour his enemy, who deviseth how to bring mischief upon his family, to injure in some way his property: and surely he deviseth this by deceit, by fraud, by devilish devices he endeavoureth to accomplish this: no one can doubt it. Yet not for these reasons are they to be guarded against, but lest they lay in wait for thee and draw thee to themselves, that is, separate thee from the Body of Christ, and make thee of their body. For as Christ is the Head of the good, so is the devil their head. What is, "to trip up my steps"? Not as though thou shouldest be deceived in the business thou hast with him, or he cheat thee in a case which thou hast with him in the law courts. He hath "tripped up thy steps," if he have hindered thee in the way of God; so that what thou didst direct aright may stumble, or fall from the way, or fall in the way, or draw back from the way, or stop on the way, or go back to the place from whence it had come. Whatsoever hath done this to thee, hath tripped thee up, hath deceived thee. Against such snares as these pray thou, lest thou lose thy heavenly inheritance, lest thou lose Christ thy Joint-heir, for thou art destined to live for ever with Him, who hath made thee an heir. For thou art made an heir, not by one whom thou art to succeed after his death, but One together with whom thou art to live for ever.

7. "The proud have hidden a trap for me" (ver. 5). He hath briefly described the whole body of the devil, when he saith, "the proud." Hence is it that for the most part they call themselves righteous when they are unrighteous.

Hence is it that nothing is so grievous to them as to confess their sins. They are men who, being falsely righteous, must needs envy the truly righteous. For none envieth another in that which he wisheth not either to be or to seem. . . . Hence come all allurings and trippings up of others. This the devil first wished, when falling himself he envied man who stood. . . .

8. But those "proud ones have hidden a trap for me;" they have sought to trip up my steps. And what have they done? "And have stretched out cords as traps." What cords? The word is well known in holy Scripture, and elsewhere we find what "cords" signify. For "each one is holden with the cords of his sins,"[2] saith Scripture. And Esaias saith openly, "Woe to them that draw sin like a long rope."[3] And why is it called a "cord"? Because every sinner who persevereth in his sins, addeth sin to sin; and when he ought to amend, by accusing his sins to amend, by defending he doubleth what by confession he might have removed, and often seeketh to fortify himself by other sins, on account of the sins he hath already committed. . . . But these their sins they "spread" for the righteous, when they persuade them to do the evils which they themselves do. Therefore he said, "they spread cords and traps;" that is, by their sins they desired to overthrow me. And where did they this? "Beside the paths have they laid a stumbling-block for me:" not in the paths," but, "beside the paths." Thy "paths" are the commandments of God. They have "laid stumbling-blocks beside the paths;" do not thou withdraw out of the paths, and thou wilt not rush upon stumbling-blocks. Yet will I not that thou shouldest say, "God should prevent them from laying stumbling-blocks beside my paths, and then they would not lay them." Nay, rather, God permitted them to "lay stumbling-blocks beside thy paths," that thou shouldest not leave the paths.

9. And what remaineth? what remedy amid such ills, in such temptations, such dangers? "I said unto the Lord, Thou art my God" (ver. 6). Loud is the voice of prayer, it exciteth confidence. Is He not the God of the others? Of whom is not He God, who is the true God? Yet is He specially theirs, who enjoy Him, who serve Him, who willingly submit to Him. For the wicked too, though unwillingly, are subject to Him. . . . "Hear with Thine ears the voice of my prayer." He did not say, "Hear with Thine ears my prayer;" but, as though expressing more plainly the affection of his heart, "*the voice* of my prayer," the life of my prayer, the soul of my prayer, not that which soundeth in my words, but that which giveth life to my words. For all

---

[1] *Serpit.*   [2] Prov. v. 22.   [3] Isa. v. 18.

other noises without life may be called sounds, but not words. Words belong to those that have souls, to the living. But how many pray to God, yet have neither perception of God, nor right thoughts concerning God ! These may have the sound of prayer, the voice they cannot, for there is no life in them. This was the voice of the prayer of one who was alive, forasmuch as he understood that God was his God, saw by Whom he was freed, perceived from whom he was freed.

10. Commending this to the ears of God, let him say, " Lord, Lord." Thou Lord-Lord, that is, most truly Lord, not like unto the lords-men, not like the lords who buy with money-bags, but the Lord who buyeth with His Blood. " Lord, Lord, Thou strength of my health " (ver. 7), that is, who givest strength to my health. What is the meaning of " strength of my health " ? He complained of the stumbling-blocks and snares of sinners, of wicked men, vessels of the devil, that barked around him and laid snares around him, of the proud that envy the righteous. But He forthwith added a comfort, " He that shall endure unto the end, the same shall be saved." This he observed and feared, and, distressed at the abundance of iniquities, turned himself to hope. Verily I shall be saved, if I endure unto the end : but endurance, so as to win salvation, pertaineth unto strength ; Thou art " the strength of my salvation ; " Thou makest me to endure, that I may attain salvation. . . . Toiling then in this warfare, he looked back to the grace of God ; and because already he had begun to be heated and parched, he found, as it were, a shade, whereunder to live. " Thou hast overshadowed my head in the day of battle : " that is, in the heat, lest I be heated, lest I be parched.

11. " Deliver me not over, O Lord, by my own longing to the sinner" (ver. 8). Behold to what end Thy overshadowing shall avail for me, that I suffer not heat from myself. And what could that " sinner " do to me, rage as he would ? For wicked men raged against the martyrs, dragged them away, bound them with chains, shut them up in prisons, slew them with the sword, exposed them to wild beasts, consumed them with fire : all this they did ; yet did not God deliver them over to the sinners, because they were not delivered over by their own longing. This then pray with all thy might, that God " delivered thee not over by thine own longing to the sinner." For thou by thine own longing givest place to the devil. For lo, the devil hath set before thee gain, invited thee to dishonesty ; thou canst not have the gain, unless thou commit the dishonesty : the gain is the bait, dishonesty the snare : do thou so look on the bait, that thou see the snare also ; for thou canst not obtain the gain, unless thou commit the dishonesty ; and if thou commit the dishonesty, thou

wilt be caught. . . . Hence is thine head overshadowed in the day of battle. For longing causeth heat, but the overshadowing of the Lord tempers longing, that we may be able to bridle that whereby we were being hurried away, that we be not so heated as to be drawn to the snare. " They have thought against me ; leave me not, lest perchance they be exalted." Thou hast in another place, " They that oppress me will exult if I be moved." [1] Such are they, because such is the devil also himself. . . .

12. " The head of their going about, the toil of their own lips shall cover them " (ver. 9). Me, he saith, the shadow of Thy wings shall cover : for, " Thou hast covered me in the day of battle." Them what shall cover ? " The head of their going about ; " that is, pride. What is, " their going about " ? How they go about and stand not, how they go in the circle of error, where is journeying without end. He who goeth in a straight line, beginneth from some point, endeth at some point : he who goeth in a circle, never endeth. That is the toil of the wicked, which is set forth yet more plainly in another Psalm, " The wicked walk in a circle." [2] But " the head of their going about " is pride, for pride is the beginning of every sin. But whence is pride " the toil of their own lips " ? Every proud man is false, and every false man is a liar. Men toil in speaking falsehood ; for truth they could speak with entire facility. For he toileth, who maketh what he saith : he who wisheth to speak the truth, toileth not, for truth herself speaketh without toil. . . .

13. " Coals of fire shall fall upon them upon earth, and Thou shalt cast them down " (ver. 10). What is, " upon earth " ? Here, even in this life, here " coals of fire shall fall upon them." What are, " coals of fire " ? We know these coals. Are they different from those of which we are about to speak ? For these I see avail for punishment, those that I am about to speak of, for salvation. For we have spoken of certain coals, when man was seeking aid against a treacherous tongue. . . . The examples of the " coals " are added to the wound of the arrows (for I need not fear to say " the wound," when the Spouse herself saith, " I am wounded with love " [3]), and then the hay is consumed, and so they are called " devouring coals." The hay is devoured, but the gold is purified, and the man exchanges death for life, and begins to be himself too a burning coal ; such a coal as was the Apostle, " who before was a blasphemer and a persecutor and injurious," a coal black and extinguished ; but when he had obtained mercy, he was set on fire from heaven, the voice of Christ set him on fire, all the blackness in him

---

perished, he began to be fervent in spirit, to set others on fire with that wherewith he was set on fire himself. . . .

14. "A man full of words shall not be guided upon earth" (ver. 11). "A man full of words" loveth lies. For what pleasure hath he, save in speaking? He careth not what he speaketh, so long as he speaks. It cannot be that he will be guided. What then ought the servant of God to do, who is kindled with these "coals," and himself made a coal of salvation, what should he do? He should wish rather to hear than to speak; as it is written, "Let every man be swift to hear, slow to speak."[1] And if it may be so, let him desire this, not to be obliged to speak and talk and teach. . . . I can quickly tell you wherein each one may prove himself, not by never speaking, but by requiring a case where it is his duty to speak; let him be glad to be silent, in will, let him speak to teach, when he must. For when must thou needs speak and teach? When thou meetest with one ignorant, when thou meetest with one unlearned. If it delight thee always to teach, thou wishest always to have some ignorant one to teach. . . . "Evil shall hunt the unrighteous man to destruction." Evils come, and he standeth not; therefore said he, "they shall hunt him to destruction." For many good men, many righteous men evils have befallen, evils have, as it were, found them. Therefore when the evil pursued the good, that is, our martyrs, when they seized them, they "hunted" them, but not "to destruction." For the flesh was pressed down, the spirit was crowned; the spirit was cast out from the body, yet was nought done to the flesh which might hinder it for the future. Let the flesh be burned, scourged, mangled; is it therefore withdrawn from its Creator, because it is given into the hands of its persecutor? Will not He who created it from nothing, re-make it better than it was?

15. "I know that the Lord will maintain the right of the needy" (ver. 12). This "needy" one is not "full of words;" for he that is full of words, wisheth to abound, knoweth not to hunger. He is "needy" of whom it is said, "Blessed are they which do hunger and thirst after righteousness, for they shall be filled."[2] They groan among the stumbling-blocks of the wicked, they pray to their Head, "to be delivered from the wicked man. "And the cause of the poor." These then are they whose cause the Lord will not neglect; although now they suffer hardships, their glory shall appear, when their Head appeareth. For to such while placed here it is said, "Ye are dead, and your life is hid with Christ in God."[3] So then we are poor,

our life is hid; let us cry to Him that is our Bread.[4] . . .

16. "But the just shall confess to Thy Name" (ver. 13). Both when Thou shalt plead their cause, and when Thou shalt maintain their right, they "shall confess to Thy Name;" nought shall they attribute to their own merits, all they shall attribute to nought save to Thy mercy. . . . Therefore see what followeth, see wherewith he concludeth. "The upright shall dwell with Thy Countenance." For ill was it with them in their own countenance; well will it be with them with Thy Countenance. For when they loved their own countenance, "In the sweat of their countenance did they eat bread."[5] Thy Countenance shall come to them with abundance to satisfy them. Nought more shall they seek, for nought better have they; no more shall they abandon Thee, nor be abandoned by Thee. For after His Resurrection, what was said of the Lord? "Thou shalt fill me with joy with Thy Countenance."[6] Without His Countenance He would not give us joy. For this do we cleanse our countenance, that we may rejoice in His Countenance.[7] . . . Because too, "blessed are the poor in heart, for they shall see God;"[8] He gave the Form of Man both to good and evil, the Form of God He preserved for the pure and good, that we may rejoice in Him, and it may be well with us for ever with His Countenance.

PSALM CXLI.[9]

1. . . . The Psalm which we have just sung is in many parts somewhat obscure. When by the help of the Lord what has been said shall begin to be expounded and explained, ye will see that ye are hearing things which ye knew already. But for this cause are they said in manifold ways, that variety of expression may remove all weariness of the truth. . . .

2. "Lord, I have cried unto Thee, hear Thou me" (ver. 1). This we all can say. This not I alone say: whole Christ saith it. But it is said rather in the name of the Body: for He too, when He was here and bore our flesh, prayed; and when He prayed, drops of blood streamed down from His whole Body. So is it written in the Gospel: "Jesus prayed earnestly, and His sweat was as it were great drops of blood."[10] What is this flowing of sweat from His whole Body, but the suffering of martyrs from the whole Church? "Listen unto the voice of my prayer, while I cry unto Thee." Thou thoughtest the business of crying already finished, when thou saidst, "I have cried unto Thee." Thou hast cried; yet think not thyself

---

[1] Jas. i. 19.   [2] Matt. v. 6.   [3] Col. iii. 3.

[4] John vi. 51.   [5] Gen. iii. 19.   [6] Ps. xvi. 12.
[7] 1 John iii. 2.   [8] Matt. v. 8.
[9] Lat. CXL. Sermon to the people.   [10] Luke xxii. 44.

safe. If tribulation be finished, crying is finished: but if tribulation remain for the Church, for the Body of Christ, even to the end of the world, let it not only say, "I have cried unto Thee," but also, "Listen unto the voice of my prayer."

3. "Let my prayer be set forth in Thy sight as incense, and the lifting up of my hands an evening sacrifice" (ver. 2). That this is wont to be understood of the Head Himself, every Christian acknowledgeth. For when the day was now sinking towards evening, the Lord upon the Cross "laid down His life to take it again,"[1] did not lose it against His will. Still we too are figured there. For what of Him hung upon the tree, save what He took of us? And how can it be that the Father should leave and abandon His only begotten Son, especially when He is one God with Him? Yet, fixing our weakness upon the Cross, where, as the Apostle saith, "our old man is crucified with Him,"[2] He cried out in the voice of that our "old man," "Why hast Thou forsaken Me?"[3] That then is the "evening sacrifice," the Passion of the Lord, the Cross of the Lord, the offering of a salutary Victim, the whole burnt-offering acceptable to God. That "evening sacrifice" produced, in His Resurrection, a morning offering. Prayer then, purely directed from a faithful heart, riseth like incense from a hallowed altar. Nought is more delightful than the odour of the Lord: such odour let all have who believe.

4. . . . "Set, O Lord, a watch before my mouth, and a door of restraint around my lips" (ver. 3). He said not a barrier of restraint, but "a door of restraint." A door is opened as well as shut. If then it be a "door," let it be both opened and shut; opened, to confession of sin; closed, to excusing sin. So will it be a "door of restraint," not of ruin. For what doth this "door of restraint" profit us? What doth Christ pray in the name of His Body? "That Thou turn not aside My heart to wicked words" (ver. 4). What is, "My heart"? The heart of My Church; the heart, that is, of My Body. . . .

5. But when thine heart hath not been turned aside, O member of Christ, when thy heart hath not been turned aside "to wicked words, to making excuses in sins, with men that work in iniquity," thou shalt also not unite with their elect. For this followeth, "And I will not unite with their elect." Who are "their elect"? Those who justify themselves. Who are their elect? Those "who trust in themselves that they are righteous, and despise others," as the Pharisee said in the temple, "Lord, I thank Thee that I am not as other men are."[4] Who are their elect? "This Man, if He were a

prophet, would know what manner of woman this is that touched His feet."[5] Here thou recognisest the words of that other Pharisee, who invited our Lord to his house; when the woman of that city, who was a sinner, came and approached His Feet. . . .

For even this woman herself, "if her heart had turned aside to wicked words," would not have lacked wherewith to defend her sins. Do not women daily, her equals in defilement, but not her equals in confession, harlots, adulteresses, doers of shameful deeds, defend their sins? If they have not been seen, they deny them: if they have been caught and convicted, or have done their deeds openly, they defend them. And how easy is their defence, how ready, yet how headlong; how common, yet how blasphemous! "Had God not willed it, I had not done it: God willed it: fortune willed it: fate willed it." . . . These are the defences of "the elect" of this world. But let the members of Christ, the Body of Christ, say, let Christ say in the name of His Body, "Turn not Thou aside, My Heart, to wicked words," etc., "and I will not unite with their elect." . . .

6. "With men that work wickedness." What wickedness? Let me mention some sinful wickedness of theirs. Let me tell you one open sinful wickedness, which they acknowledge. They say, it is better for a man to be an usurer than a husbandman. Thou askest the reason, and they assign one. . . . He vexeth the members of Christ, who cleanseth the earth with a furrow: he vexeth the members of Christ, who pulleth grass from the earth: he vexeth the members of Christ, who plucketh an apple from a tree. To avoid committing their imaginary murders in the farm, he committeth real murders in usury. He dealeth no bread to the needy. See whether there can be greater unrighteousness than this righteousness.[6] He dealeth not bread to the hungry. Thou askest, wherefore? Lest the beggar receive the life which is in the bread, which they call a member of God, the substance of God, and bind it in flesh. What then do ye? why do ye eat? Have ye not flesh? Yes; but we, they say, forasmuch as we are enlightened by faith in Manes,[7] by our prayers and our Psalms, forasmuch as we are elect, we cleanse thereby that bread, and transmit it into the treasure-house of the heavens. Such are the elect, that they are not to be saved by God, but saviours of God. And this is Christ, they say, crucified in the whole universe. I received in the Gospel Christ a Saviour, but ye are in your books the saviours of Christ. Plainly ye are blasphemers of Christ, and therefore not to be saved by

---

[1] John x. 17. [2] Rom. vi. 6.
[3] Ps. xxii. 1; Matt. xxvii. 46. [4] Luke xviii. 11.

[5] Luke vii. 39. [6] i.e. as they consider it.
[7] [See *Confessions*, vol. i. p. 76, note 8, this series; also A. N. F. vol. vi. p. 175. — C.]

Christ. Therefore lest a crumb be given to the hungry, and in the crumb a member of Christ suffer, is the hungry to die of hunger? False mercy to a crumb causeth true murder of a man. But who are their elect? "Turn not thou aside, my heart, to wicked words, and I will not unite with their elect."

7. "The righteous One shall amend me in mercy, and convict me" (ver. 5). Behold the sinner confessing. He desireth to be amended in mercy, rather than praised deceitfully. . . . "Shall convict me," but "in mercy:" shall convict, yet hateth not: yea, shall all the more convict, because He hateth not. And why doth he therefore give thanks? Because, "rebuke a wise man, and he will love thee."[1] "The righteous One shall amend me." Because He persecuteth thee? God forbid. He requireth rather amending himself, who amendeth in hate. Wherefore then doth He amend? "In mercy. And shall convict me." Wherein? "In mercy. For the oil of a sinner shall not enrich my head." My head shall not grow by flattery. Undue praise is flattery: undue praise of a flatterer is "the oil of a sinner." Therefore men too, when they have mocked any one with false praise, say, "I have anointed his head." Love then to be "convicted by the righteous One in mercy;" love not to be praised by a sinner in mockery. Have oil in yourselves, and ye shall not seek the "oil of a sinner."[2] . . .

8. Thou sayest to me, What am I doing? I am beset with flatterers; they cease not to besiege me; they praise in me what I would not, that praise in me what I hold in little esteem; what I hold dear they blame in me; flatterers, treacherous, deceivers. For instance, "Gaius-eius[3] is a great man, great, learned, wise; but why is he a Christian? For great is his learning, great his reading, great his wisdom." If great is his wisdom, approve of his being a Christian; if great his learning, learnedly hath he chosen. In fine, what thou revilest, that pleaseth him whom thou praisest. But what? That praise sweeteneth not: it is "the oil of a sinner." Yet ceaseth he not to speak so. Let him not therewith "fatten thy head;" that is, rejoice not in such things; agree not to such things; consent not to such things; rejoice not in such things; and then, if he have applied to thee the oil of flattery, yet hath thy head remained as it was, it has not been puffed up, it hath not swollen. . . . "For still shall My word be well-pleasing to

them." Wait awhile: now they revile Me, saith Christ. In the early times of the Christians, the Christians were blamed on all sides. Wait as yet; and "My word shall be well-pleasing to them." The time shall come when they shall conquer thousands of men, who shall beat their breasts, and say, "Forgive us our debts, as we forgive our debtors." Even now, how many remain who blush to beat their breasts? Let them then blame us: let us bear it. Let them blame; let them hate, accuse, detract; "still shall My word be well-pleasing to them;" the time shall come when My word shall please them. . . . O wordy defence of iniquity! Verily now whole nations say this, and the thunder of nations beating their breasts ceaseth not. Rightly do the clouds thunder, wherein now God dwelleth. Where is now that wordiness, where that boasting, "I am righteous; nought of ill have I done"? Verily, when thou hast contemplated in Holy Scripture the law of righteousness, how far soever thou hast advanced, thou shalt find thyself a sinner.· . . . What sort of man am I now speaking of, brethren? I speak of him who worshippeth God alone, who confesseth Christ, who knoweth the Father and the Son and the Holy Ghost to be one God; who committeth not fornication against Him; who worshippeth not devils; who seeketh him not aid from the devil; who holdeth the Catholic Church; whom no one complaineth of as cheating; under whose oppression no weak neighbour groaneth; who assaileth not another's wife; who is content with his own, or even without his own, in such wise as is lawful, and as Apostolical discipline permitteth, with consent of both,[4] or when she is not yet married. Even he who is such as this, is yet overtaken in such things as I have mentioned. For all these daily sins then what is our hope, save to say with humble heart in the Lord's Prayer, while we defend not our sins, but confess them, "Forgive us our debts, as we forgive our debtors;"[5] and to "have an Advocate with the Father, Jesus Christ the righteous," that He may be "the propitiation for our sins"?[6] See what followeth: "their judges have been swallowed up beside the Rock" (ver. 6). What is, "swallowed up beside the Rock? That Rock was Christ.[7] They have been swallowed up beside the Rock." "Beside," that is, compared, as judges, as mighty, powerful, learned: they are called "their judges," as judging about morals, and laying down their opinions. This Aristotle said. Set him beside the Rock, and he is swallowed up. Who is Aristotle? let him hear, "Christ hath said," and he trembleth among the dead. This Pythagoras said, that Plato said. Set them beside the Rock, compare their authority to the authority

---

[1] Prov. ix. 8.　　　[2] Matt. xxv. 4, etc.
[3] This is probably taken from Tertullian, *Apol.* c. 3: "What when the generality run upon an hatred of this name with eyes so closed, that, in bearing favourable testimony to any one, they mingle with it the reproach of the name. 'A good man Caius Seius, only he is a Christian.' So another, 'I marvel that that wise man Lucius Titius hath suddenly become a Christian.' No one reflected whether Caius be not therefore good and Lucius wise, because a Christian, or therefore a Christian because wise and good." [See A. N. F. vol. iii. p. 20. — C.]

[4] 1 Cor. vii. 5.　　　[5] Matt. vi. 12.
[6] 1 John ii. 1, 2.　　　[7] 1 Cor. x. 4.

of the Gospel, compare the proud to the Crucified. Say we to them, "Ye have written your
words in the hearts of the proud; He hath
planted His Cross in the hearts [1] of kings: finally,
He died, and rose again; ye are dead, and
I will not ask how ye rise again." So "their
judges have been swallowed up beside" that
"Rock." So long do their words seem somewhat, till they are compared with the Rock.
Therefore if any of them be found to have said
what Christ too hath said, we congratulate him,
but we follow him not. But he came before
Christ. If any man speak what is true, is he
therefore before the Truth itself? Regard Christ,
O man, not when He came to thee, but when
He made thee. The sick man too might say,
"But I took to my bed before the physician
came to me." Why, for that very reason has
He come last, because thou first has sickened.

9. "They shall hear My Words, for they
have prevailed." My Words have prevailed
over their words. They have spoken clever
things, I true things. To praise one who talketh well is one thing, to praise One who speaketh
truth is another. "They shall hear My Words,
for they have prevailed." How have they prevailed? Who of them has been taken offering
sacrifice, when such things were forbidden by
the law, and has not denied it? Who of them
has been taken worshipping an idol, and has not
exclaimed, "I did it not," and feared lest he
should be convicted? Such servants hath the
devil. But how have the Words of the Lord
prevailed? "Behold, I send you forth as sheep
in the midst of wolves. Fear not those who kill
the body," etc.[2] He gave them fear, He suggested hope, He kindled love. "Fear not
death," He saith. Do ye fear death? I die
first. Fear ye, lest a hair of your head perish?
I first rise again in the flesh uninjured. Rightly
have ye heard His Words, for they have prevailed. They spake, and were slain; they fell,
and yet stood. And what was the result of so
many deaths of martyrs, save that those words
prevailed, and the earth being, so to speak, watered by the blood of Christ's witnesses, the
cross of the Church shot up everywhere? How
have they "prevailed"? We have said already,
when they were preached by men who feared
not. Feared not what? Neither banishment,
nor losses, nor death, nor crucifixion: for it was
not death alone that they did not fear; but even
crucifixion, a death than which none was thought
more accursed. It the Lord endured, that His
disciples might not only not fear death, but not
even that kind of death. When then these
things are said by men that fear not, they have
prevailed.

10. What then have all those deaths of the
martyrs accomplished? Listen: "As the fatness of the earth is spread over the earth, our
bones have been scattered beside the pit" (ver.
7). "The bones" of the martyrs, that is, the
bodies of the witnesses of Christ. The martyrs were slain, and they who slew them seemed
to prevail. They prevailed by persecution, that
the words of Christ might prevail by preaching.
And what was the result of the deaths of the
saints? What meaneth, "the fatness of the
earth is spread over the earth"? We know
that everything that is refuse is the fatness of
the earth. The things which are, as it were,
contemptible to men, enrich the earth. . . .
"Precious in the sight of the Lord is the death
of His saints."[3] As it is contemptible to the
world, so is it precious to the husbandman.
For he knoweth the use thereof, and its rich
juice; he knoweth what he desireth, what he
seeketh, whence the fertile crop ariseth; but
this world despiseth it. Know ye not that
"God hath chosen the contemptible things of
the world, and those which are not, like as those
which are, that the things which are may be
brought to nought"?[4] From the dunghill was
Peter lifted up, and Paul; when they were put
to death, they were despised: now, the earth
having been enriched by them, and the cross
of the Church springing up, behold, all that is
noble and chief in the world, even the emperor
himself, cometh to Rome, and whither does he
hasten? to the temple of the emperor, or the
memorial of the fisherman?

11. "For unto Thee, Lord, are mine eyes;
in Thee have I hoped, take not Thou away my
life" (ver. 8). For they were tortured in persecutions, and many failed. It occurreth to
him that many have failed, many have been
in hazard, and as it were in the midst of the
tribulation of persecution is sent forth the voice
of one praying; "For unto Thee, Lord, are
mine eyes:" I care not what they threaten who
stand around, "unto Thee, Lord, are mine eyes."
More do I fix mine eye on Thy promises than
on their threats. I know what Thou hast suffered for me, what Thou hast promised me.

12. "Keep me from the trap which they have
laid for me" (ver. 9). What was the trap?
"If thou consentest, I spare thee." In the trap
was set the bait of the present life; if the bird
love this bait, it falleth into the trap: but if the
bird be able to say, "The day of man have I
not desired: Thou knowest:"[5] "He shall pluck
his feet out of the net," etc.[6] Two things he
hath mentioned to be distinguished the one
from the other: the trap he said was set by
persecutors; the stumbling-blocks came from

---

[1] "On the foreheads," MSS.   [2] Matt. x. 16, 28.

[3] Ps. cxvi. 15.   [4] 1 Cor. i. 27, 28
[5] Jer. xvii. 16.   [6] Ps. xxv. 15.

those who have consented and apostatised : and from both he desires to be guarded. On the one side they threaten and rage, on the other consent and fall : I fear lest the one be such, that I fear him ; the other such, that I imitate him. "This I do to thee, if thou consent not." "Keep me from the trap," etc. "Behold, thy brother hath already consented." "And from the stumbling-blocks," etc.

13. "Sinners shall fall into his nets" (ver. 10). Not all sinners : certain sinners, who are so great sinners, as to love this life to such a degree as to prefer it to everlasting life, "shall fall into his trap." But what sayest thou ? Shall they that are such, thinkest thou, fall into his nets ? what of Thy disciples, O Christ ? Behold, when persecution was raging, when they all "left Thee alone, and went every one to his own : "[1] lo ! they who were closest to Thee, in Thy trial and persecution, when Thine enemies demanded Thee to be crucified, abandoned Thee. And that bold one, who had promised Thee that he would go with Thee even unto death, heard from the Physician what was being done in him, the sick man. For being in a fever, he had said he was whole ; but the Lord touched the vein of his heart. Then came the trial ; then came the test ; then came the accusation ; and now, questioned not by some great power, but by a humble slave, and that a woman, questioned by a handmaid, he yielded ; he denied thrice. . . . "He wept bitterly," it saith. Not yet was he fitted to suffer. To him was said, "Thou shalt follow Me afterwards."[2] Hereafter he was to be firm, having been strengthened by the Lord's Resurrection. Not yet then was it time that those "bones" should be "scattered beside the pit." For see how many failed, even to those who first hung on His mouth ; even they failed. Wherefore ? "I am alone, until I pass over : " for this followeth in the Psalm. . . .

14. Pascha, as they say who know, and who have explained to us what to read, meaneth "Passover." When then the Lord's Passion was about to come, the Evangelist, as though he would use this very word, saith, "When the hour was come that Jesus should *pass over* to the Father."[3] We hear then of Pascha in this verse, "I am alone, until I pass over." After Pascha I shall no longer be alone, after passing-over I shall no longer be alone. Many shall imitate Me, many shall follow Me. And if afterward they shall follow, what shall be the case now ? "I am alone, until I pass over." What is it that the Lord saith in this Psalm, "I am alone, until I pass over "? What is it that we have expounded ? If we have understood it,

listen to His own words in the Gospel. "Except a corn of wheat fall into the ground and die, it abideth alone ; but if it die, it beareth much fruit."[4] . . . Therefore He was alone before He was put to death. . . . So far was any from dying for the Name, that is, for confessing the Name of Christ, before that Corn of wheat fell into the ground, that even John, who was slain just before Him, being given by a wicked king to a dancing woman, was not put to death because he confessed Christ. Of course he might have been put to death for this, and that by many. If for another reason he was put to death by one man, how much more might he have been put to death by those very men, who put Christ to death ? For John gave testimony to Christ. They who heard Christ, wished to slay Him ; the man who gave testimony to Him they slew not. . . . He is not slain by the Jews who gave free testimony to Christ, whom the Jews slew ; he is slain by Herod, because he said to him, "It is not lawful for thee to have thy brother's wife."[5] For his brother had not died without issue.[6] For the law of truth, for equity, for righteousness' sake, he did die : therefore is he a saint, therefore a martyr ; but yet he died not for that Name whereby we are Christians, wherefore, save that the saying might be fulfilled, "I am alone, until I pass over."

PSALM CXLII.[7]

1. . . . "With my voice have I cried unto the Lord " (ver. 1). It were enough to say, "with voice : " not for nothing perhaps has "my " been added. For many cry unto the Lord, not with their own voice, but with the voice of their body. Let the "inner man " then, in whom "Christ" hath begun to "dwell by faith,"[8] cry unto the Lord, not with the din of his lips, but with the affection of his heart. God heareth not, where man heareth : unless this criest with the voice of lungs and side and tongue, man heareth thee not : thy thought is thy cry to the Lord. "With my voice have I prayed unto the Lord." What he meant by, " I have cried," he explained when he said, " I have prayed." For they too who blaspheme, cry unto the Lord. In the former part he set down his crying, in the latter he explained what it was. As though it were demanded, With what cry hast thou cried unto the Lord ? Unto the Lord, saith he, I have prayed. My cry is my prayer, not reviling, not murmuring, not blaspheming.

2. " I will pour out before Him my prayer" (ver. 2). What is, "before Him "? In His sight. What is, in His sight ? Where He seeth. But where doth He not see ? For so do we say,

---

[1] John xvi. 32.   [2] John xiii. 36.   [3] John xiii. 1.

[4] John xii. 24, 32.   [5] Matt. xiv. 4.   [6] [Matt. xxii. 24.—C.]
[7] Lat. CXLI.   Sermon to the people.   [8] Eph. iii. 17.

'where He seeth,' as though somewhere He seeth not. But in this assemblage of bodily substances men too see, animals too see: He seeth where man seeth not. For thy thoughts no man seeth, but God seeth. There then pour out thy prayer, where He alone seeth, who rewardeth. For the Lord Jesus Christ bade thee pray in secret: but if thou knowest what "thy closet" is, and cleansest it, there thou prayest to God. "But thou," saith He, "when thou prayest, enter into thy closet, and shut the door, and pray to thy Father in secret, and He who seeth in secret shall reward thee." [1] If men are to reward thee, pour out thy prayer before men: if God is to reward thee, pour out thy prayer before Him; and close the door, lest the tempter enter. Therefore the Apostle, because it is in our power to shut the door, the door of our hearts, not of our walls, for in it is our "closet," — because it is in our power to shut this door, saith, "neither give place to the devil." [2] But what is to "shut the door"? This door hath as it were two leaves, desire and fear. Either thou desireth something earthly, and he enters by this; or thou fearest something earthly, and he enters by that. Close then the door of fear and desire against the devil, open it to Christ. How dost thou open these folding doors to Christ? By desiring the kingdom of heaven, by fearing the fire of hell. By desire of this world the devil entereth, by desire of eternal life Christ entereth; by fear of temporal punishment the devil entereth, by fear of everlasting fire Christ entereth. . . .

3. "My tribulation I will proclaim in His sight." There is a repetition, both in the two preceding sentences, and in these which follow: the sentiments are two, but both twice expressed. . . . For, "in His sight," is the same as "before Him;" "I will proclaim my tribulation," is the same as, "I will pour out my prayer." When doest thou this? Being set in the midst of persecution, he saith, "while my spirit failed from me" (ver. 3). Wherefore hath thy spirit failed, O martyr, set in tribulation? That I may not claim my strength as mine own, that I may know that Another worketh in me the goodness I have. And men perhaps have heard that my spirit hath failed within me, and have despaired of me, and have said, "we have taken him captive, we have overpowered him;" "and Thou hast known my paths." They thought me cast down, Thou didst see me standing upright. They who persecuted me and had seized me, thought my feet entangled, "but their feet were entangled, and they fell, but we are risen, and stand upright." [3] For mine eyes are ever unto the Lord, for He shall pluck

my feet out of the net." [4] I have persevered in walking, for "he that shall persevere unto the end, the same shall be saved." [5] They thought me overpowered, but I continued walking. Where did I walk? In paths which they saw not, who thought me prisoner, in the paths of Thy righteousness, in the paths of Thy commandments. . . . For every path is a way, but not every way is a path. Why then are those ways called paths, save because they are narrow? Broad is the way of the wicked, narrow the way of the righteous. That which is "the way" is also "the ways," just as "the Church" is also "the Churches," the "heaven" also the "heavens:" they are spoken of in the plural, they are spoken of also in the singular. On account of the unity of the Church it is one Church; "My dove is one, she is the only one of her mother." [6] On account of the congregation of brethren in various places there are many Churches. "The Churches of Judæa which are in Christ rejoiced," saith Paul,[7] "and they glorified God in me." Thus he spake of Churches; and of one Church he thus speaketh, "Give none offence, neither to the Jews, nor to the Gentiles, nor to the Church of God." . . .

4. "In this way, wherein I was walking, they hid a trap for me." This "way wherein I was walking," is Christ; there have they laid a trap for me, who persecute me in Christ, for Christ's Name's sake. There then "have they hid for me a trap." What in me do they hate, what in me do they persecute? That I am a Christian. . . . For the heretics too wish to hide a stumbling-block for us in the Name of Christ, and are themselves deceived. What they think that they put in the way, they put outside the way, for they themselves are outside the way. They cannot set a trap where themselves are not. . . . The Pagan thinketh to put a stumbling-block in the way, when he saith to me, "Thou worshippest a crucified God." He findeth fault with the Cross of Christ, which he understandeth not. He thinketh that he setteth in Christ, what he setteth near the way. I will not depart from Christ, so shall I not fall from the way into the trap. Let him mock at Christ crucified, let me see the Cross of Christ on the foreheads of kings. What he laugheth at, therein am I saved. Nought is prouder than a sick man, who laugheth at his own medicine. If he laughed not at it, he would take it, and be healed. The Cross is the sign of humility, but he through excess of pride acknowledgeth not that whereby may be healed the swelling of his soul. But if I acknowledge, I am walking in the way. So far am I from blushing at the Cross, that in no secret place do I keep the Cross of Christ, but bear it on my

---

[1] Matt. vi. 6.　　[2] Eph. iv. 27.　　[3] Ps. xx. 8.

[4] Ps. xxv. 15.　　[5] Matt. x. 22.　　[6] Cant. vi. 8.
[7] Gal. i. 22, 23.

forehead. Many sacraments we receive, one in one way another in another : some as ye know we receive with the mouth, some we receive over the whole body. But because the forehead is the seat of the blush of shame, He who said, "Whosoever shall be ashamed of Me before men, of him will I be ashamed before My Father which is in heaven," [1] set, so to speak, that very ignominy which the Pagans mock at, in the seat of our shame. Thou hearest a man assail a shameless man and say, "He hath no forehead." What is, "He hath no forehead"? He hath no shame. Let me not have a bare forehead, let the Cross of my Lord cover it. . . .

5. "I considered upon the right hand, and saw" (ver. 4). He considered upon the right hand, and saw : whoso considereth upon the left hand, is blinded. What is to consider on the right hand? Where they will be to whom shall be said, "Come, ye blessed of My Father," etc.,[2] . . . He goeth on to say, "and there was none that knew me." For when thou fearest all things, who knoweth what thou regardest, whether thou directest thine eyes to the right hand or to the left? If, in bearing, thou seekest the praise of men, thou hast regarded the left : if, in bearing, thou seekest the promises of God, thou hast regarded the right hand. Hast thou regarded the right hand, thou shalt see : hast thou regarded the left hand, thou shalt be blinded. But even when thou seest on the right hand, there will be none to know thee. For who comforteth thee save the Lord? "Flight hath perished from me." He speaketh as though he were hemmed in. Let the persecutors rejoice over him ; he is overpowered, he is taken, he is hemmed in, he is conquered. "Flight hath perished" from him who fleeth not. But he who fleeth not, suffereth whatever he can for Christ : that is, he fleeth not in soul. For in body it is lawful to flee ; it is allowed, it is permitted ; for the Lord saith, "When they persecute you in one city, flee to another." [3] He then who fleeth not in soul, from him "flight hath perished." But it maketh a difference why he fleeth not ; whether because he is hemmed in, because he is caught, or because he is brave. For both from him that is caught flight hath perished, and from him that is brave flight hath perished. What flight then is to be avoided? what flight shall we allow to perish from us? That whereof the Lord speaketh in the Gospel, "The Good Shepherd layeth down his life for the sheep. But he that is an hireling, and not the shepherd, when he seeth the wolf coming, fleeth." When he seeth the ravager, why fleeth he? "Because he careth not for the sheep." [4] . . . In two ways a man's life is sought, either by his persecutors or by his lovers.[5]

So then "there is none to seek my life," he said of them ; verily they persecute my life, and they seek not my life. But if they seek my life, they will find it clinging to Thee : and if they know to seek it, they know also to imitate it.

6. "Unto thee have I cried, O Lord : I have said, Thou art my hope" (ver. 5). When I endured, when I was in tribulation, "I said, Thou art my hope." My hope here, therefore I endure. But "my portion," not here, but "in the land of the living." God giveth a portion in the land of the living ; but not something from Himself without Himself. What will He give to one that loveth Him, save Himself?

7. "Give heed unto my prayer, for much have I been humbled" (ver. 6). Humbled by persecutors, humbled in confession. He humbleth himself out of the sight of man : he is humbled by enemies in their sight. Therefore is he lifted up by Him both visibly and invisibly. Invisibly are the martyrs already lifted up ; visibly shall they be lifted up, "when this corruptible shall have put on incorruption" in the resurrection of the dead ; when this very part of him, against which alone her persecutors could rage, shall be renewed. "Fear not them that kill the body, but cannot kill the soul." [6] And what perisheth? what kill they? . . . Why then art thou anxious about the rest of thy members, when thou shalt not lose even a hair? [7] "Deliver me from them that persecute me." From whom thinkest thou that he prayeth to be delivered? From men who persecuted him? Is it so? are merely men our enemies? We have other enemies, invisible, who persecute us in another way. Man persecuteth, that he may slay the body ; another persecuteth, that he ensnare the soul.[8] . . . There are then other enemies of ours too, from whom we ought to pray God to deliver us, lest they lead us astray, either by crushing us with troubles of this world, or alluring us by its enticements. Who are these enemies? Let us see whether they are plainly described by any servant of the Lord, by any soldier, now perfected, who hath engaged with them. Hear the Apostle saying, "We wrestle not against flesh and blood : " [9] as though he would say, Turn not your hatred against men ; think not them your enemies ; think not that it is by their hostility you are being bruised ; these men whom ye fear are flesh and blood. . . . "For they are strengthened over me." Who said, "they are strengthened over me"? The Body of Christ crieth out ; it is the voice of the Church ; the members of Christ cry out, "Much hath the number of sinners increased." "Because iniquity hath abounded, the love of many waxeth cold." [10]

8. "Bring forth my soul out of prison, that

---

[1] Luke ix. 26.   [2] Matt. xxv. 34, 41.   [3] Matt. x. 23.
[4] John x. 11, etc.   [5] [i.e. "who seek to save it." — C.]

[6] Matt. x. 28.   [7] [Luke xxi. 18. — C.]   [8] Eph. ii. 2.
[9] Eph. vi. 12.   [10] Matt. xxiv. 12.

it may confess to Thy Name" (ver. 7). This "prison" has been variously understood by former writers. And perhaps it is the prison which is called in the title, "the cave." For the title of this Psalm runneth thus: "Of understanding to David himself, a prayer when he was in the cave." That which is the cave, the same is also the prison. Two things have we set before us to understand, but when we have understood one, both will be understood. A man's deserts make a prison. For in one dwelling place one man finds a house, another a prison. . . . To some then it has seemed that the "cave" and "prison" are this world; and this the Church prayeth, that it may be brought out of prison, that is, from this world, from under the sun, where all is vanity.[1] Beyond this world then God promiseth that we shall be in some sort of rest; therefore perhaps do we cry concerning this place, "Bring my soul out of prison." Our soul by faith and hope is in Christ; "Your life is hid with Christ in God." But our body is in this prison, in this world. . . . But some have said, that this prison and cave is this body, so that this is the meaning of, "Bring my soul out of prison." But this interpretation too is somewhat at fault. For what great thing is it to say, "Bring my soul out of prison," bring my soul out of the body? Do not the souls of robbers and wicked men go forth from the body, and go into worse punishment than here they have endured? What great request then is this, "Bring my soul out of prison," when, sooner or later, it must needs come forth? Perhaps the righteous saith, "Let me die now; bring forth my soul from this prison of the body." If he be too hasty, he hath not love. He ought indeed to long for and desire, as the Apostle saith, "having a desire to be dissolved and to be with Christ, which is far better." But where is love? Therefore it followeth, "but to abide in the flesh is needful for you." Let God then lead us forth from the body, when He will. Our body too might be said to be a prison, not because that is a prison which God hath made, but because it is under punishment and liable to death. For there are two things to be considered in our body, God's workmanship, and the punishment it has deserved. . . . Perhaps then he meant by, "Bring my soul out of prison," bring my soul out of corruption. If thus we understand it, it is no blasphemy, the meaning is consistent. Lastly, brethren, as I think, he meant this; "Bring my soul out of prison," bring it out of straitness. For to one who rejoiceth, even a prison is wide; to one in sorrow, a field is strait. Therefore prayeth he to be brought out of straitness. For though

in hope he have enlargement, yet in reality at at present he is straitened. . . . It is not the body that weigheth down the soul, but the corruptible body. It is not the body then that maketh the prison, but the corruption. "Bring my soul out of prison, that it may give thanks to Thy Name." Now the words which follow seem to come from the Head, our Lord Jesus Christ. And they are the same as yesterday's last words. Yesterday's last words, if ye remember, were, "I am alone, until I pass over." And here what are the last words? "The righteous shall sustain me, until thou recompense me."

PSALM CXLIII.[2]

1. . . . The title of the Psalm is, "To David himself, when his son was pursuing him." We know from the Books of Kings[3] that this happened: . . . but we must recognise here another David, truly "strong in hand," which is the explanation of David, even our Lord Jesus Christ. For all those events of past time were figures of things to come. Let us seek then in this Psalm our Lord and Saviour Jesus Christ, announcing Himself beforehand in His prophecy, and foretelling what should happen at this time by things which were done long ago. For He Himself foretold Himself in the Prophets: for He is the Word of God. Nor did they say ought of this kind, save when filled with the Word of God. They announced then Christ, being filled with Christ,[4] they went before Him about to come, and He deserted not them going before. . . .

2. Let then our Lord speak; let Christ with us, whole Christ, speak. "Lord, hear my prayer, receive with Thine ears my entreaty" (ver. 1). "Hear" and "receive with ears" are the same thing. It is repetition, it is confirmation. "In Thy truth hear me, in Thy righteousness." Take it not without emphasis when it is said, "in Thy righteousness." For it is a commendation of grace, that none of us think his righteousness his own. For this is the righteousness of God, which God hath given thee to possess. For what saith the Apostle of them, who would boast of their own righteousness? Speaking of the Jews, he saith, "they have a zeal of God, but not according to knowledge."[5] . . . Thou art perverse, because thou imputest what thou hast done ill to God, what well to thyself: thou wilt be right, when thou imputest what thou hast done ill to thyself, what well to God. . . . Behold, "in Thy righteousness hear me." For when I look upon myself, nought else do I find mine own, save sin.

3. "And enter not into judgment with Thy servant" (ver. 2). Who are willing to enter into judgment with Him, save they who, "being

---

[1] Eccles. i. 2, etc.

[2] Lat. CXLII. A sermon to the people.　　[3] 2 Sam. xv.
[4] [1 Pet. i. 10, 11, 12.—C.]　　[5] Rom. x. 2.

ignorant of the righteousness of God, go about to establish their own?" "Wherefore have we fasted, and Thou hast not seen; wherefore have we afflicted our souls, and Thou takest no knowledge?"[1] As though they would say, "We have done what Thou hast commanded, wherefore dost Thou not render to us what Thou hast promised?" God answereth thee: I will give to thee to receive what I have promised: I have given thee that thou shouldest do that whereby thou mayest receive. Finally, to such proud ones the Prophet speaketh; "Wherefore will ye plead with Me? ye have all transgressed against Me, saith the Lord."[2] Why will ye enter into judgment with Me, and recount your own righteousnesses? . . . "For before Thee every one living shall not be justified." "Every one living;" living, that is, here, living in the flesh, living in expectation of death; born a man; deriving his life of man; sprung from Adam, a living Adam; every one thus living may perhaps be justified before himself, but not before Thee. How before himself? By pleasing himself, displeasing Thee. Enter not then into judgment with me, O Lord my God. How straight soever I seem to myself, Thou bringest forth a standard from Thy store-house, Thou fittest me to it, and I am found crooked. Well is it said, "with Thy servant." It is unworthy of Thee to enter into judgment with Thy servant, or even with Thy friend.[3] . . . What of the Apostles themselves? . . . That ye may perceive it at once, they learnt to pray what we pray: to them was given the pattern of prayer by the heavenly Counsellor. "After this manner," saith He, "pray ye."[4] And having set down certain things first, He laid down this too to be said by the leaders of the sheep, the chief members of the Shepherd and Gatherer[5] of the one flock; even they learnt to say, "Forgive us our debts."[6] They said not, "Thanks be to Thee, who hast forgiven us our debts, as we too forgive our debtors," but, "Forgive, as we forgive." But surely the faithful prayed then, surely the Apostles prayed then, for this Lord's Prayer was given rather to the faithful. If those debts only were meant which are forgiven by Baptism, it would befit catechumens rather to say, "Forgive us our debts." Let the Apostles then say, yea let them say, "Forgive us our debts." And when it is said to them, "Wherefore say ye this? what are your debts?" let them answer, "for in Thy sight every one living shall not be justified."

4. "For the enemy hath persecuted my soul: he hath humbled my life on the earth" (ver. 3). Here we speak, here our Head speaketh for us. Manifestly both the devil persecuted the Soul of Christ and Judas the Soul of his Master: and now too the same devil remaineth to persecute the Body of Christ, and one Judas succeedeth another. There lacketh not then of whom the Body too may say, "For the enemy hath persecuted my soul." For what doth each one who persecuteth us endeavour save to make us abandon our heavenly hope, and savour of the earth, yield to our persecutor, and love earthly things? "They have laid me in dark places, as the dead of the world." This ye hear more readily from the Head; this ye perceive more readily in the Head. For He died indeed for us, yet was He not one of the "dead of the world." For who are the "dead of the world"? And how was not He one of the "dead of the world"? "The dead of the world" are those who have died of their own desert, receiving the reward of iniquity, deriving death from the sin transmitted to them; according as it is said, "For I was conceived in iniquity."[7] . . . In dying, saith He, I do the will of My Father, but I am not deserving of death. Nought have I done wherefore I should die, yet is it Mine own doing that I die, that by the death of an innocent One, they may be freed who had wherefore they should die. "They set me in places," as though in Hades, as though in the tomb, as though in His very Passion, "as the dead of the world."[8]

5. "And My Spirit within me," saith He, "suffered weariness" (ver. 4). Remember, "My soul is exceeding sorrowful, even unto death."[9] Here we see one voice. Do we not see plainly the transition from the Head to the members, from the members to the Head? . . .

6. But we too were there. He goes to the members. "I have called to mind the days of old" (ver. 5). Did He "call to mind the days of old," by whom every day was made? No, but the body speaketh, each one who has been justified by His grace, who dwelleth in Him in love and devout humility, speaketh and saith, "I have meditated upon all Thy works:" plainly because Thou hast made all things good, and nothing would have stood fast, which was not established by Thee. Thy creation is made a spectacle unto me: I have sought in the work the Artificer, in all that is made the Maker. Wherefore this, to what purpose this, save that he might understand, that whatever there was of good in himself was made by Him. . . . Look back then upon the Framer of thy life, the Author of thy substance, of thy righteousness, and of thy salvation: "meditate upon the works of His hands," for the righteousness too which is in thee, thou wilt find to pertain to His hand. Hear the Apostle teaching thee this, "not of works," he saith, "lest any should boast." Have

---

[1] Isa. lviii. 3.　　　　[2] Jer. ii. 29.　　　　[3] Matt. v. 40.
[4] Matt. vi 9.
[5] *Congregatoris*; mss. *Congregatores*, The gatherers.
[6] Matt. vi. 12.

[7] Ps. li. 5.　　　　[8] Ps. xxxviii. 4, 5.　　　　[9] Matt. xxvi. 38.

we no good works? Plainly we have: but see what follows; "for we are His workmanship,"[1] saith he. "We are His workmanship:" perhaps in thus speaking of workmanship, he meant to mention the nature whereby we are men? Evidently not: he was speaking of works. But let us not make conjectures; let the text go on, "for we are His workmanship, created in Christ Jesus unto good works." Think not then that thou thyself doest anything, save in so far as thou art evil. . . . "Work out your own salvation," saith the Apostle, "with fear and trembling."[2] If we do work out our own salvation, wherefore with fear, wherefore with trembling, when what we work is in our own power? Hear wherefore with fear and trembling: "for it is God that worketh in you both to will and to do, of His good pleasure." Therefore "with fear and trembling," that it may delight our Maker to work in the lowly valley. . . .

7. "I stretched forth," saith he, "my hands to Thee: my soul is as a land without water to Thee" (ver. 6). Rain upon me, saith he, to bring forth from me good fruit. "For the Lord shall give sweetness, that our land may give her fruit."[3] "I have stretched forth my hands to Thee; my soul is as a land without water," not to me, but "to Thee." I can thirst for Thee, I cannot water myself.

8. "Speedily hear me, Lord" (ver. 7). For what need of delay to inflame my thirst, when already I thirst so eagerly? Thou didst delay the rain, that I might drink and imbibe, not reject, Thy inflowing. If then Thou didst for this cause delay, now give; for, "my spirit hath failed." Let Thy Spirit fill me. This is the reason why Thou shouldest speedily hear me. I am now become "poor in spirit," make Thou me "blessed in the kingdom of heaven."[4] For he in whom his own spirit liveth, is proud, is puffed up with his own spirit against God. . . .

9. "Turn not Thou away Thy Face from me." Thou didst turn it away from me when proud. For once I was full, and in my fulness I was puffed up. Once "in my fulness I said, I shall never be moved." "I said in my fulness, I shall not be moved," knowing not Thy Righteousness, and establishing mine own; but "Thou, Lord, in Thy Will hast afforded strength to my beauty." "I said in my fulness, I shall not be moved," but from Thee came whatever fulness I had. And to prove to me that it was from Thee, "Thou didst turn away Thy Face from me, and I was troubled."[5] After this trouble, whereinto I was cast, because Thou didst turn away Thy Face, after the weariness of my spirit, after my heart was troubled within me, because Thou didst turn away Thy Face, then

became I "like a land without water to Thee: turn not Thou away Thy Face." Thou turnedst it away from me when proud; give it back to me now I am humble. Because, if Thou turn it away, "I shall be like to them that go down into the pit." What is, "that go down into the pit"? When the sinner has come into the depth of sins, he will show contempt. They "go down into the pit," who lose even confession; against which is said, "Let not the pit close her mouth over me."[6] This depth Scripture calleth mostly "a pit," into which depth when a sinner hath come, "he showeth contempt." What is, "he showeth contempt"? He no longer believeth in Providence, or if he do believe, he thinketh that he has no longer aught to do with it. . . .

10. "Make me to hear in the morning Thy mercy, for in Thee have I hoped" (ver. 8). Behold, I am in the night, yet "in Thee have I hoped," until the iniquity of the night pass away. "For we have," as Peter saith, "a more sure word of prophecy, whereunto ye do well that ye take heed, as unto a light that shineth in a dark place, until the day dawn, and the day-star arise in your hearts." "Morning" then he calleth the time after the end of the world, when we shall see what in this world we believe. But what here, until the morning come? For it is not enough to hope for the morning; we must do somewhat. Why do somewhat? God is to be sought with the hands in the night. What is, "with the hands"? By good works. Since then we must thus hope for the morning, and bear this night, and persevere in this patience until the day dawn, what meanwhile must we do here? lest perchance thou think that thou wilt do aught of thyself, whereby thou mayest earn to be brought to the morning. "Make known to me, O Lord, the way wherein I must walk." Therefore did He kindle the lamp of prophecy, therefore did He send the Lord in the vessel,[7] as it were, of the flesh, who should even say, "My strength is dried up like a potsherd."[8] Walk by prophecy, walk by the lamp of future things predicted, walk by the word of God. . . .

11. "Deliver me from mine enemies, O Lord, for unto Thee have I fled for refuge" (ver. 9). I who once fled from Thee, now flee to Thee. For Adam fled from the Face of God, and hid himself among the trees of Paradise, so that of him was said in the Book of Job, "As a servant that fleeth from his Lord, and findeth a shadow."[9] He fled from the Face of his Lord, and found a shadow. Woe to him, if he continue in the shade, lest it be said afterward, "All things are passed away like a shadow."[10] The rulers of

---

[1] Eph. ii. 9, 10. [2] Philip. ii. 12, 13. [3] Ps. lxxxv. 12.
[4] Matt. v. 3. [5] Ps. xxx. 6, 7.

[6] Ps. lxix. 15. [7] *Testâ.* [8] Ps. xxii. 15.
[9] Job vii. 2, LXX. [10] Wisd. v. 9.

this world, of this darkness, the rulers of the wicked; against these ye wrestle. Great is your conflict, not to see your enemies, and yet to conquer. Against the rulers of this world, of this darkness, the devil, that is, and his angels; not the rulers of that world, whereof is said, "the world was made by Him," but that world whereof is said, "the world knew Him not."[1] "For unto Thee have I fled for refuge." . . . Whither should I flee? "Whither shall I go from Thy Spirit?"[2]

12. "Teach me to do Thy will, for Thou art my God" (ver. 10). Glorious confession! glorious rule! "For Thou," saith he, "art my God." To another will I hasten to be re-made, if by another I was made. Thou art my all, "for Thou art my God." Shall I seek a father to get an inheritance? "Thou art my God," not only the Giver of mine inheritance, but mine Inheritance itself. "The Lord is the portion of mine inheritance."[3] Shall I seek a patron, to obtain redemption? "Thou art my God." Lastly, having been created, do I desire to be re-created? "Thou art my God," my Creator, who hast created me by Thy Word, and re-created me by Thy Word. "Teach Thou me:" for it cannot be that Thou art my God, and yet I am to be mine own master. See how grace is commended to us. This hold fast, this drink in, this let none drive out of your hearts, lest ye have "a zeal, of God, but not according to knowledge."[4] Say then this: "Thy good Spirit," not my bad one, "Thy good Spirit shall lead me into the right land." For my bad spirit hath led me into a crooked land. And what have I deserved? What can be reckoned as my good works without Thy aid, through which I might obtain and be worthy to be led by Thy Spirit into the right land?

13. Listen, then, with all your power, to the commendation of Grace, whereby ye are saved without price. "For Thy Name's sake, O Lord, Thou shalt quicken me in Thy righteousness" (ver. 11); not in mine own: not because I have deserved, but because Thou hast mercy. For were I to show mine own desert, nought should I deserve of Thee, save punishment. Thou hast pruned off from me mine own merits; Thou hast grafted in Thine own gifts. "Thou shalt bring forth my soul out of tribulation." "And in thy mercy shalt bring mine enemies to destruction: and thou shalt destroy all them that afflict my soul; for I am Thy servant" (ver. 12).

PSALM CXLIV.[5]

1. The title of this Psalm is brief in number of words, but heavy in the weight of its myste-

ries. "To David himself against Goliath." This battle was fought in the time of our fathers, and ye, beloved, remember it with me from Holy Scripture. . . . David put five stones in his scrip, he hurled but one. The five Books were chosen, but unity conquered. Then, having smitten and overthrown him, he took the enemy's sword, and with it cut off his head. This our David also did, He overthrew the devil with his own weapons: and when his great ones, whom he had in his power, by means of whom he slew other souls, believe, they turn their tongues against the devil, and so Goliath's head is cut off with his own sword.

2. "Blessed be the Lord my God, who teacheth my hands for battle, my fingers for war" (ver. 1). These are our words, if we be the Body of Christ. It seems a repetition of sentiment; "our hands for battle," and "our fingers for war," are the same. Or is there some difference between "hands" and "fingers"? Certainly both hands and fingers work. Not then without reason do we take "fingers" as put for "hands." But still in the "fingers" we recognise the division of operation, yet still a sort of unity. Behold that grace! the Apostle saith,[6] To one, this; to another, that; "there are diversities of operations; all these worketh one and the self-same Spirit;" there is the root of unity. With these "fingers" then the Body of Christ fighteth, going forth to "war," going forth to "battle." . . . By works of Mercy our enemy is conquered, and we could not have works of mercy unless we had charity, and charity we could have none unless we received it by the Holy Ghost; He then "teacheth our hands for battle, and our fingers for war:" to Him rightfully do we say, "My Mercy," from whom we have also that we are merciful: "for he shall have judgment without mercy, that hath showed no mercy."[7]

3. My Mercy and my Refuge, my Upholder and my Deliverer" (ver. 2). Much toileth this combatant, having his flesh lusting against his spirit. Keep what thou hast. Then shalt thou have in full what thou wishest, when "death shall have been swallowed up in victory;"[8] when this mortal body has been raised, and is changed into the condition of the angels, and rises aloft to a heavenly quality. . . . There is life, there are good days, where nought lusteth against the spirit, where it is not said, "Fight," but "Rejoice." But who is he that lusteth for these days? Every man certainly saith, "I do." Hear what followeth. I see that thou art toiling, I see that thou art engaged in battle, and in danger; hear what followeth: . . . "Depart from evil, and do good:" let not the poor first weep under thee, that the poor may rejoice

---

[1] John i. 10. [2] Ps. cxxxix. 7. [3] Ps. xvi. 5.
[4] Rom. x. 2. [5] Lat. CXLIII. Sermon to the people.

[6] 1 Cor. xii. 8, etc. [7] Jas. ii. 13. [8] 1 Cor. xv. 54.

through thee. For what reward, since now thou art fighting? "Seek peace, and ensue it." Learn and say, "My Mercy and my Refuge, mine Upholder and my Deliverer, my Protector:" "mine Upholder," lest I fall; "my Deliverer," lest I stick; "my Protector," lest I be stricken. In all these things, in all my toil, in all my battles, in all my difficulties, in Him have I hoped, "who subdueth my people under me." Behold, our Head speaketh together with us.

4. "Lord, what is man, that Thou hast become known unto him?" (ver. 3). All is included in "that Thou hast become known unto him." "Or the son of man, that Thou valuest him?" Thou valuest him, that is, Thou makest him of such importance, Thou countest him of such price, Thou knowest under what Thou placest him, over what Thou placest him. For valuing is considering the price of a thing. How greatly did He value man, who for him shed the blood of His only-begotten Son! For God valueth not man in the same way as one man valueth another: he, when he findeth a slave for sale, giveth a higher price for a horse than for a man. Consider how greatly He valued thee, that thou mayest be able to say, "If God be for us, who can be against us?" And how greatly did He value thee, "who spared not His own Son"? "How shall He not also with Him freely give us all things?"[1] He who giveth this food to the combatant, what keepeth He in store for the conqueror? . . .

5. "Man is made like unto vanity: his days pass away like a shadow" (ver. 4). What vanity? Time, which passeth on, and floweth by. For this "vanity" is said in comparison of the Truth, which ever abideth, and never faileth: for it too is a work of His Hand, in its degree. "For," as it is written, "God filled the earth with His good things."[2] What is "His"? That accord with Him. But all these things, being earthly, fleeting, transitory, if they be compared to that Truth, where it is said, "I Am That I Am,"[3] all this which passeth away is called "vanity." For through time it vanisheth, like smoke into the air. And why should I say more than that which the Apostle James said, willing to bring down proud men to humility, "What is," saith he, "your life? It is even a vapour, which appeareth for a little time, and then vanisheth away."[4] . . . Work then, though it be in the night, with thine hands, that is, by good works seek God, before the day come which shall gladden thee, lest the day come which shall sadden thee. For see how safely thou workest, who art not left by Him whom thou seekest; "that thy Father which seeth in secret may reward thee openly."[5] . . .

6. "Lord, bow Thy heavens, and come

down: touch the mountains, and they shall smoke" (ver. 5). "Flash Thy lightning, and Thou shalt scatter them; send forth Thine arrows, and Thou shalt confound them" (ver. 6). "Send forth Thy Hand from above, and deliver me, and draw me out of many waters" (ver. 7). The Body of Christ, the humble David, full of grace, relying on God, fighting in this world, calleth for the help of God. What are "heavens bowed down"? Apostles humbled. For those "heavens declare the glory of God;" and of these heavens declaring the glory of God it is presently said, "There is neither speech nor language, but their voices are heard among them," etc.[6] When then these heavens sent forth their voices through all lands, and did wonderful things, while the Lord flashed and thundered from them by miracles and commandments, the gods were thought to have come down from heaven to men. For certain of the Gentiles, thinking this, desired even to sacrifice to them. . . . But they commended to these the Lord Jesus Christ, humbling themselves, that God might be praised; because "the heavens" were "bowed," that "God" might "come down." . . . "Touch the mountains, and they shall smoke." So long as they are not touched, they seem to themselves great: they are now about to say, "Great art Thou, O Lord:"[7] the mountains also are about to say, "Thou only art the Most Highest over all the earth."[8]

7. But there are some that conspire, that "gather themselves together against the Lord, and against His Christ."[9] They have come together, they have conspired. "Flash forth Thy lightnings, and Thou shalt scatter them." Abound with Thy miracles, and their conspiracy shall be broken. . . . "Send forth Thine arrows, and Thou shalt confound them." Let the unsound be wounded, that, being well wounded, they may be made sound; and let them say, being set now in the Church, in the Body of Christ, let them say with the Church, "I am wounded with Love."[10] "Send forth Thine Hand from on high." What afterward? What in the end? How conquereth the Body of Christ? By heavenly aid. "For the Lord Himself shall come with the voice of the Archangel, and with the trump of God shall He descend from heaven,"[11] Himself the Saviour of the body, the Hand of God. What is, "Out of many waters"? From many peoples. What peoples? Aliens, unbelievers, whether assailing us from without, or laying snares within. Take me out of many waters, in which Thou didst discipline me, in which Thou didst roll me, to free me from my filth. This is the "water of contradiction."[12] . . . "From the hand of strange

---

[1] Rom. viii. 31, 32. [2] Ecclus. xvi. 29. [3] Exod. iii. 14.
[4] Jas. iv. 14. [5] Matt. vi. 4.

[6] Ps. xix. 1, 3, 4.   [7] Ps. xlviii. 1.   [8] Ps. lxxxiii. 18.
[9] Ps. ii. 2.   [10] Cant. ii. 5, LXX.
[11] 1 Thess. iv. 16.   [12] Numb. xx. 13.

children." Hear, brethren, among whom we are, among whom we live, from whom we long to be delivered. "Whose mouth hath spoken vanity" (ver. 8). All of you to-day, if ye had not gathered yourselves together to these divine shows[1] of the word of God, and were not at this hour engaged in them, how great vanities would ye be hearing! "whose mouth hath spoken vanity:" when, in short, would they, speaking vanity, hear you speaking vanity? "And their right hand is a right hand of iniquity." What doest thou among them with thy pastoral scrip with five stones in it? Say it to me in another form: that same law which thou hast signified by five stones, signify in some other way also. " I will sing a new song unto Thee, O God" (ver. 9). "A new song" is of grace; "a new song" is of the new man; "a new song" is of the New Testament. But lest thou shouldest think that grace departeth from the law, whereas rather by grace the law is fulfilled, "upon a psaltery of ten strings will I sing unto Thee." Upon the law of ten commandments: therein may I sing to Thee; therein may I rejoice to Thee; therein may " I sing to Thee a new song;" for, "Love is the fulfilling of the law."[2] But they who have not love may carry the psaltery, sing they cannot. Contradiction cannot make my psaltery to be silent.

8. "Who giveth salvation to kings, who redeemeth David His servant" (ver. 10). Ye know who David is; be yourselves David. Whence "redeemeth He David His servant"? Whence redeemeth He Christ? Whence redeemeth He the Body of Christ? " From the sword of ill intent deliver me." "From the sword" is not sufficient; he addeth, "of ill intent." Without doubt there is a sword of good intent. What is the sword of good intent? That whereof the Lord saith, "I came not to send peace on earth, but a sword."[3] For He was about to separate believers from unbelievers, sons from parents, and to sever all other ties, while the sword cut off what was diseased, but healed the members of Christ. Of good intent then is the sword twice sharpened, powerful with both edges, the Old and New Testaments, with the narration of the past and the promise of the future. That then is the sword of good intent: but the other is of ill intent, wherewith they talk vanity, for that is of good intent, wherewith God speaketh verity. For truly " the sons of men have teeth which are spears and arrows, and their tongue is a sharp sword."[4] "From" this " sword deliver me " (ver. 11). "And take me out of the hand of strange children, whose mouth hath spoken vanity:" just as before. And that which followeth, " their right hand is a right hand of iniquity," the same he had set down

before also, when he called them "many waters." For lest thou shouldest think that the " many waters " were good waters, he explained them by the " sword of ill intent."

9. "Whose sons are like young vines firmly planted in their youth" (ver. 12). He wisheth to recount their happiness. Observe, ye sons of light, sons of peace: observe, ye sons of the Church, members of Christ; observe whom he calleth " strangers," whom he calleth " strange children," whom he calleth " waters of contradiction," whom he calleth a " sword of ill intent." Observe, I beseech you, for among them ye are in peril, among their tongues ye fight against the desires of your flesh, among their tongues, set in the hand of the devil wherewith he fighteth.[5] . . . What vanity hath their mouth spoken, and how is their right hand a right hand of iniquity? "Their daughters are fitted and adorned after the similitude of a temple." " Their garners are full, bursting out from one store to another: their sheep are fruitful, multiplying in their streets " (ver. 13) : " their oxen are fat : their hedge is not broken down, nor their road, nor is their crying in their streets " (ver. 14). Is not this then happiness? I ask the sons of the kingdom of heaven, I ask the offspring of everlasting resurrection, I ask the body of Christ, the members of Christ, the temple of God. Is not this then happiness, to have sons safe, daughters beautiful, garners full, cattle abundant, no downfall, I say not of a wall, but not even of a hedge, no tumult and clamour in the streets, but quiet, peace, abundance, plenty of all things in their houses and in their cities? Is not this then happiness? or ought the righteous to shun it? or findest thou not the house of the righteous too abounding with all these things, full of this happiness? Did not Abraham's house abound with gold, silver, children, servants, cattle? What say we? is not this happiness? Be it so, still it is on the left hand. What is, on the left hand? Temporal, mortal, bodily. I desire not that thou shun it, but that thou think it not to be on the right hand. . . . For what ought they to have set on the right hand? God, eternity, the years of God which fail not, whereof is said, " and Thy years shall not fail."[6] There should be the right hand, there should be our longing. Let us use the left for the time, let us long for the right for eternity. "If riches increase, set not your heart upon them."[7] . . .

10. "They have called the people blessed who have these things" (ver. 15). O men that speak vanity! They have lost the true right hand, wicked and perverse, they have put on the benefits of God inversely. O wicked ones, O speakers of vanity, O strange children!

[1] Spectacula.　　[2] Rom. xiii. 10.
[3] Matt. x. 34.　　[4] Ps. lvii. 4.
[5] Eph. vi. 12.　　[6] Ps. cii. 27.　　[7] Ps. lxii. 10.

What was on the left hand, they have set on the right. What dost thou, David? What dost thou, Body of Christ? What do ye, members of Christ? What do ye, not strange children, but children of God? . . . What say ye? Say ye with us, "Blessed is the people whose Lord is their God."

PSALM CXLV.[1]

1. . . . The title is, "Praise, to David himself." Praise to Christ Himself. And since He is called David, who came to us of the seed of David, yet He was our King, ruling us, and bringing us into His kingdom, therefore "Praise to David himself" is understood to mean, Praise to Christ Himself. Christ according to the flesh is David, because He is the Son of David: but according to His Divine Nature He is the Creator of David, and Lord of David. "I will exalt Thee, my God, my King; and I will bless Thy Name for the age, and age upon age" (ver. 1). Ye see that the praise of God is here begun, and this praise is carried on even to the end of the Psalm. . . . Now then begin to praise, if thou intendest to praise for ever. He who will not praise in this transitory "age," will be silent when "age upon age" has come. But lest any one should in any otherwise also understand what he saith, "I will praise Thy Name for the age," and should seek another age, wherein to praise, he saith, "Every day will I bless Thee" (ver. 2). Praise then and bless the Lord thy God every day, that when single days have passed, and there has come one day without end, thou mayest go from praise to praise, as "from strength to strength."[2] No day shall pass by, wherein I bless Thee not. And it is no wonder, if in thy day of joy thou bless the Lord. What if perchance some day of sorrow hath dawned on thee, as is natural in the circumstances of our mortal nature, as there is abundance of offences, as temptations are multiplied; what, if something sad befall thee, a man; wilt thou cease to praise God? wilt thou cease to bless thy Creator? If thou cease, thou hast lied in saying, "every day," etc. But if thou cease not, although it seem to thee to be ill with thee in the day of thy sorrow, yet in thy God it shall be well with thee. . . .

2. "Great is the Lord, and very much to be praised" (ver. 3). How much was he about to say? what terms was he about to seek? How vast a conception hath he included in the one word, "very much"? Imagine what thou wilt, for how can that be imagined, which cannot be contained? "He is very much to be praised. And of His Greatness there is no end;" therefore said he "very much:" lest perchance thou begin to wish to praise, and think that thou canst reach the end of His praises, whose Greatness can have no end. Think not then that He, whose Greatness has no end, can ever be enough praised by thee. Is it not then better that as He has no end, so neither should thy praise have end? His Greatness is without end; let thy praise also be without end. . . .

3. For how great things besides has His boundless Goodness and illimitable Greatness made, which we do not know! When we lift the gaze of our eyes even to the heaven, and then recall it from sun, moon, and stars to the earth, and there is all this space where our sight can wander; beyond the heavens who can extend the eyesight of his mind, not to say of his flesh? So far then as His works are known to us, let us praise Him through His works.[3] "Generation and generation shall praise Thy works" (ver. 4). Every generation shall praise Thy works. For perhaps every generation is meant by "generation and generation." . . . Did he perchance mean to imply two generations by that repetition? For we are in this generation sons of God, we shall be in another generation sons of the Resurrection. Scripture hath called us "sons of the Resurrection;" the Resurrection itself it hath called Regeneration. "In the regeneration," it saith, "when the Son of Man shall be seated in His Majesty."[4] So also in another place: "For they shall not marry, nor be given in marriage, for they are the sons of the Resurrection."[5] Therefore "generation and generation shall praise Thy works. . . . And they shall tell out Thine excellence." For neither shall they praise Thy works, save in order to "tell out Thine excellence." Boys at school are set to praise, and all such things are set before them to be praised, as God hath wrought: a mortal is set to praise the sun, the sky, the earth; to come to even lesser things, to praise a rose, or a laurel; all these are works of God: they are set, they are undertaken, they are praised: the works are lauded, of the Worker they are silent. I desire in the works to praise the Creator: I love not a thankless praiser. Dost thou praise what He hath made, and art silent of Him who made? In that which thou seest, what is it that thou praisest? The form, the usefulness, some virtue, some power in the things. If beauty delight thee, what is more beautiful than the Maker? If usefulness be praised, what more useful than He who made all things? If excellence be praised, what more excellent than He by whom all things were made? . . .

4. "They shall speak of the magnificence of the glory of Thy Holiness, and shall record Thy

---

[1] Lat. CXLIV.   Sermon to the people.   [2] Ps. lxxxiv. 7.   [3] Rom. i. 20.   [4] Matt. xix. 28.   [5] Luke xx. 35, 36.

wondrous deeds" (ver. 5). "And the excellence of Thy fearful works shall they speak of: and Thy greatness, they shall relate it" (ver. 6). "The remembrance of the abundance of Thy sweetness they shall pour forth" (ver. 7) : none but Thine. See whether this man, meditating on Thy works, hath turned aside from the Worker to the work : see whether he hath sunk from Him who made, to the things which He made. Of the things which He hath made, he hath made a step up to Him, not a descent from Him to them. For if thou love these more than Him, thou wilt not have Him. And what profit is it to thee to overflow with the works, if the Worker leave thee? Truly thou shouldest love them ; but love Him more, and love them for His sake. For He doth not hold out promises, without holding out threats also : if He held out no promises, there would be no encouragement ; if He held out no threats, there would be no correction. They that praise Thee therefore shall "speak" also "of the excellence of Thy terrible deeds;" the excellence of that work of Thy hands which punisheth and administereth discipline, they shall speak of, they shall not be silent : for they shall not proclaim Thine everlasting kingdom, and be silent about Thine everlasting fire. For the praise of God, setting thee in the way, ought to show thee both what thou shouldest love, and what thou shouldest fear ; what thou shouldest seek, and what thou shouldest shun ; what thou shouldest choose, and what thou shouldest avoid. The time of choice is now, the time of receiving will be hereafter. Let then the excellence of Thy terrible things be told. Unlimited as it is, though "of Thy greatness there is no end," they shall not be silent about it. How shall they recount it, if there is no end of it? They shall recount it when they praise it ; and because there is no end of it, so of His praise also there shall be no end.[1]

5. "The remembrance of the abundance of Thy sweetness they shall pour forth." O happy feasts ! What shall they eat, who thus shall "pour forth" ! . . . So eat, that thou mayest pour forth again ; so receive, that thou mayest give. Thou eatest, when thou learnest ; thou pourest forth again, when thou teachest : thou eatest, when thou hearest ; thou pourest forth again, when thou preachest ; but that thou pourest forth, which thou hast first eaten. Finally, that most eager feaster John, to whom the very table of the Lord sufficed not, unless he leaned on the Lord's breast, and of his inmost heart drank in divine secrets ; what did he pour forth? "In the beginning was the Word, and the Word was with God."[2] How is it that it

sufficeth not to say, "Thy remembrance ;" or, "the remembrance of Thine abundance"? Because, what availeth it if it be abundant, yet not sweet? So also it is annoying if it be sweet but too little.

6. . . . By "pouring forth" this, His preachers "shall exult in His righteousness," not in their own. What then hast Thou done unto us, O Lord, whom we praise, that we should be, that we should praise, that we should "exult in Thy righteousness," that we should "utter forth the remembrance of the abundance of Thy sweetness"? Let us tell it, and, as we tell, let us praise.

7. "Merciful and pitiful is the Lord ; long-suffering, and very merciful" (ver. 8). "Sweet is the Lord to all, and His compassions reach into all His works" (ver. 9). Were He not such as this, there would be no seeking to recover us. Consider thyself : what didst thou deserve, O sinner? Despiser of God, what didst thou deserve? See if aught occur to thee but penalty, if aught occur to thee but punishment. Thou seest then what was due to thee, and what He hath given, who gave gratis. There was given pardon to the sinner ; there was given the spirit of justification ; there was given charity and love, wherein thou mayest do all good works ; and beyond this, He will give thee also life everlasting, and fellowship with the angels : all of His mercy. . . . Hear the Scripture : "I will not the death of a sinner, but rather that he should turn, and live."[3] By these words of God, he is brought back to hope ; but there is another snare to be feared, lest through this very hope he sin the more. What then didst thou also say, thou who through hope sinnest yet more? "Whensoever I turn, God will forgive me all ; I will do whatsoever I will." Say not then, "To-morrow I will turn, to-morrow I will please God ; and all to-day's and yesterday's deeds shall be forgiven me." Thou sayest true : God hath promised pardon to thy conversion ; He hath not promised a to-morrow to thy delay.[4]

8. "Sweet is the Lord to all, and His compassions are over all His works." Why then doth He condemn? why doth He scourge? Are not they whom He condemneth, whom He scourgeth, His works? Plainly they are. And wilt thou know how "His compassions are over all His works"? Thence is that long-suffering, whereby "He maketh His sun to rise on the evil and on the good."[5] Are not "His compassions over all His works, who sendeth rain upon the just and upon the unjust"? In His long-suffering He waiteth for the sinner, saying, "Turn ye to Me, and I will turn to you."[6] Are

---

[1] Ps. lxxxiv. 4.   [2] John i. 1.

[3] Ezek. xxxiii. 11.
[4] Ecclus. v. 7.   [5] Matt. v. 45.   [6] Zech. i. 3.

not "His compassions over all His works"? And when He saith, "Go ye into everlasting fire, prepared for the devil and his angels,"[1] this is not His compassion, but His severity. His compassion is given to His works: His severity is not over His works, but over thy works. Lastly, if thou remove thine own evil works, and there remain in thee nought but His work, His compassion will not leave thee: but if thou leavest not thy works, there will be severity over thy works, not over His works.

9. "Let all Thy works, O Lord, confess to Thee, and let Thy saints bless Thee" (ver 10). How so? Is not the earth His work? Are not the trees His work? Cattle, beasts, fish, fowl, are not they His works? Plainly they too are. And how shall these too confess to Him? I see indeed in the angels that His works confess to Him, for the angels are His works: and men are His works; and when men confess to Him, His works confess to Him; but have trees and stones the voice of confession? Yes, verily; "let all" His "works confess to" Him. What sayest thou? even the earth and the trees? . . . But there ariseth the same question in regard of praise, as in regard of confession. For if earth and all things devoid of sensation therefore cannot confess, because they have no voice to confess with; neither will they be able to praise, because they have no voice to proclaim with. But do not those Three Children enumerate all things, as they walked amid the harmless flames, who had leisure not only not to fear, but even to praise God? They say to all things, heavenly and earthly, "Bless ye the Lord, praise Him, and magnify Him for ever."[2] Behold how they praise. Let none think that the dumb stone or dumb animal hath reason wherewith to comprehend God. They who have thought this, have erred far from the truth. God hath ordered everything, and made everything: to some He hath given sense and understanding and immortality, as to the angels; to some He hath given sense and understanding with mortality, as to man; to some He hath given bodily sense, yet gave them not understanding, or immortality, as to cattle: to some He hath given neither sense, nor understanding, nor immortality, as to herbs, trees, stones: yet even these cannot be wanting in their kind, and by certain degrees He hath ordered His creation, from earth up to heaven, from visible to invisible, from mortal to immortal. This framework of creation, this most perfectly ordered beauty, ascending from lowest to highest, descending from highest to lowest, never broken, but tempered together of things unlike, all praiseth God. Wherefore then doth all praise God? Because when thou considerest

it, and seest its beauty, thou in it praisest God. The beauty of the earth is a kind of voice of the dumb earth. . . . And this which thou hast found in it, is the very voice of its confession, that thou praise the Creator. When thou hast thought on the universal beauty of this world, doth not its very beauty as it were with one voice answer thee, "I made not myself, God made me"?

10. For when Thy saints bless Thee, what say they? "They shall tell the glory of Thy kingdom, and talk of Thy Power" (ver. 11). How powerful is God, who hath made the earth! how powerful is God, who hath filled the earth with good things! how powerful is God, who hath given to the animals each its own life! how powerful is God, who hath given different seeds to the womb of the earth, that they might make to spring up such various shoots, such beautiful trees! how powerful, how great is God! Do thou ask, creation answereth, and by its answer, as by the confession of the creature, thou, O saint of God, blessest God, and "talkest of His power."

11. "That they may make known to the sons of men Thy power, and the glory of the greatness of the beauty of Thy kingdom" (ver 12). Thy saints then commend "the glory of the greatness of the beauty of Thy kingdom," the glory of the greatness of its beauty. There is a certain "greatness of the beauty of Thy kingdom:" that is, Thy kingdom hath beauty, and great beauty. Since whatever hath beauty, hath beauty from Thee, how great beauty hath Thy whole kingdom! Let not the kingdom frighten us: it hath beauty also, wherewith to delight us. For what is that beauty, which the saints shall hereafter enjoy, to whom it shall be said, "Come, ye blessed of My Father, enjoy the kingdom"?[3] Whence shall they come? whither shall they come? Behold, brethren, and, if ye can, as far as ye can, think of the beauty of that kingdom which is to come; whence our prayer saith, "Thy kingdom come." For that kingdom we desire may come, that kingdom the saints proclaim to be coming. Observe this world: it is beautiful. How beautiful are earth, sea, air, heavens, stars. Do not all these frighten him who considereth them? Is not the beauty of them so conspicuous, that it seemeth as though nothing more beautiful could be found? And here, in this beauty, in this fairness almost unspeakable, here worm and mice and all creeping things of the earth live with thee, they live with thee in all this beauty. How great is the beauty of that kingdom where none but angels live with Thee! There is a greatness of a certain beauty; let it be loved before it is seen, that when it is seen, it may be retained.

---

[1] Matt. xxv. 41.　　　[2] Song of Three Children, 29, etc.　　　[3] Matt. xxv. 34.

12. "Thy kingdom." What kingdom mean I? "a kingdom of all ages." For the kingdom of this age too hath its own beauty, but there is not in it that greatness of beauty, such as in the "kingdom of all ages." "And Thy dominion is in every generation and generation" (ver. 13). This is the repetition we noticed, signifying either every generation, or the generation which will be after this generation. "Faithful is the Lord in His words, and holy in all His works." [1] "Faithful is the Lord in His words:" for what hath He promised that He hath not given? "Faithful is the Lord in His words." Hereto there are certain things which He hath promised, and hath not given; but let Him be believed from the things which He hath given. We might well believe Him, if He only spake: He willed not that we should believe Him speaking, but that we should have His Scriptures in our hands: . . . as though a kind of bond of God's, which all who pass by might read, and might keep to the path of its promise. And how great things hath He already paid in accordance with that bond! Do men hesitate to believe Him concerning the Resurrection of the dead and the Life to come, which alone now remaineth to be paid, when, if He come to reckon with the unbelievers, the unbelievers must blush? If God say to thee, "Thou hast My bond: I have promised judgment, the separation of good and bad, everlasting life for the faithful, and wilt thou not believe? There in My bond read all that I have promised, reckon with me: verily even by counting up what I have paid, thou canst believe that I shall pay what still I owe. In that bond thou hast My only-begotten Son promised, "Whom I spared not, but gave Him up for you all:" [2] reckon this then among what is paid. Read the bond: I promised therein that I would give by My Son the earnest of the Holy Spirit: reckon that as paid. I promised therein the blood and the crowns of the glorious Martyrs; let the White Mass [3] remind you that My debt has been paid. . . . He setteth before the eyes of all His payment of His debts: some He hath paid in the time of our ancestors, which we saw not: some He hath paid in our times, which they saw not; throughout all generations He hath paid what was written. And what remaineth? Do men not believe Him, when He hath paid all this? What remaineth? Behold thou hast reckoned: all this He hath

paid: is He become unfaithful for the few things which remain? God forbid! Wherefore? Because "the Lord is faithful in His words, and holy in all His works."

13. "The Lord strengtheneth all that are falling" (ver. 14). But who are "all that are falling"? All indeed fall in a general sense, but he meaneth those who fall in a particular way. For many fall from Him, many also fall from their own imaginations. If they had evil imaginations, they fall from them, and "God strengthened all that are falling." They who lose anything in this world, yet are holy, are as it were dishonoured in this world, from rich become poor, from honoured of low estate, yet are they God's saints; they are, as it were, falling. But "God strengtheneth." For "the just falleth seven times, and riseth again; but the wicked shall be weakened in evils." [4] When evils befall the wicked, they are weakened thereby; when evils befall the righteous, "the Lord strengtheneth all that are falling." . . . "And lifteth up all those that have been cast down:" all, that is, who belong to him; for "God resisteth the proud." [5]

14. "The eyes of all hope upon Thee, and Thou givest them food in due season" (ver. 15). Just as when thou refreshest a sick man in due season, when he ought to receive, then Thou givest, and what he ought to receive, that Thou givest. Sometimes then men long, and he giveth not: he who tendeth, knoweth the time to give. Wherefore say I this, brethren? Lest any one be faint, if perchance he hath not been heard, when making some righteous request of God. For when he maketh any unrighteous request, he is heard to his punishment: but when making some righteous request of God, if perchance he have not been heard, let him not be down-hearted, let him not faint, let his eyes wait for the food, which He giveth in due season. When He giveth not, He therefore giveth not, lest that which He giveth do harm. [6] . . . "Thou givest them meat in due season."

15. "Thou openest Thine Hand, and fillest every living thing with blessing" (ver. 16). Though sometimes Thou givest not, yet "in due season" Thou givest: Thou delayest, not deniest, and that in due season." "Righteous is the Lord in all His ways, and holy in all His works" (ver. 17). Both when He smiteth and when He healeth, He is righteous, and in Him unrighteousness is not. Finally, all His saints, when set in the midst of tribulation, have first praised His righteousness, and so sought His blessings. They first have said, "What Thou doest is righteous." So did Daniel ask, and other holy men: "Righteous are Thy judgments: rightly have we

---

[1] This verse is not contained in the English version.
[2] Rom. viii. 32.
[3] This sermon appears from this to have been preached in the Basilica of the "White Mass." The Roman Martyrology, Aug. 24, has, "at Carthage, of the 300 holy martyrs, who, in the reign of Valerius and Gallienus, first suffered manifold torments, and at last were thrown into a burning lime-pit, and won a glorious crown of martyrdom. Hence they had the name of 'The White Mass.'" There was a Basilica in memory of them at Utica. Serm. 306 of St. Aug. is on their festival. See also Prud. *Peristeph.* 13; Ruinart, pp. 199, 518.

[4] Prov. xxiv. 16.   [5] Jas. iv. 6.   [6] 2 Cor. xii. 7.

suffered : deservedly have we suffered." They laid not unrighteousness to God, they laid not to Him injustice and folly.   First they praised Him scourging, and so they felt Him feeding.

16. "The Lord is nigh unto all that call upon Him " (ver. 18).   Where then is that, " Then shall they call upon Me, and I will not hear them "?[1]   See then what follows : "all who call upon Him in truth."   For many call upon Him, but not in truth.   They seek something else from Him, but seek not Himself.   Why lovest thou God?   " Because He hath made me whole." That is clear : it was He that made thee so. For from none else cometh health, save Him. " Because He gave me," saith another, " a rich wife, whereas I before had nothing, and one that obeyeth me."   This too He gave : thou sayest true.   " He gave me," saith another, " sons many and good, He gave me a household, He gave me all good things."   Dost thou love Him for this? . . . Therefore if God is good, who hath given thee what thou hast, how much more blessed wilt thou be when He hath given thee Himself!   Thou hast desired all these things of Him : I beseech thee desire of Him Himself also.   For these things are not truly sweeter than He is, nor in any way are they to be compared to Him.   He then who preferreth God Himself to all the things which he has received, whereat he rejoiceth, to the things he has received, he " calleth upon God in truth." . . .

17. " He will perform the will of them that fear Him " (ver. 19).   He will perform it, He will perform it : though He perform it not at once, yet He will perform it.   Certainly if therefore thou fearest God, that thou mayest do His will, behold even He in a manner ministereth to thee ; He doeth thy will.   " And He shall hear their prayer, and save them."   Thou seest that for this purpose the Physician hears, that He may save.   When?   Hear the Apostle telling thee.   " For we are saved in hope : but hope which is seen is not hope : but if what we see not we hope for, then do we with patience wait for it :[2] " the salvation," that is, which Peter calleth " ready to be revealed in the last time."[3]

18. "The Lord guardeth all that love Him, and all sinners He will destroy" (ver. 20). Thou seest that there is severity with Him, with whom is so great sweetness.   He will save all that hope in Him, all the faithful, all that fear Him, all that call upon Him in truth : " and all sinners He will destroy."   What " all sinners," save those who persevere in sin ; who dare to blame God, not themselves ; who daily argue against God ; who despair of pardon for their sins, and from this very despair heap up their sins ; or who perversely promise themselves

pardon, and through this very promise depart not from their sins and impiety?   The time will come for all these to be separated, and for the two divisions to be made of them, one on the right hand, the other on the left ; and for the righteous to receive the everlasting Kingdom, the wicked to go into everlasting fire.   Since this is so, and we have heard the blessing of the Lord, the works of the Lord, the wondrous things of the Lord, the mercies of the Lord, the severity of the Lord, His Providence over all His works, the confession of all His works ; observe how He concludeth in His praise, " My mouth shall speak the praise of the Lord, and let all flesh bless His holy Name for ever and ever " (ver. 21).

PSALM CXLVI.[4]

1. . . . Behold the Psalm soundeth ; it is the voice of some one (and that some one are ye, if ye will), of some one encouraging his soul to praise God, and saying to himself, " Praise the Lord, O my soul " (ver. 1).   For sometimes in the tribulations and temptations of this present life, whether we will or no, our soul is troubled ; of which troubling he speaketh in another Psalm.[5]   But to remove this troubling, he suggesteth joy ; not as yet in reality, but in hope ; and saith to it when troubled and anxious, sad and sorrowing, " Hope in God, for I will yet confess to Him." . . .

2. But who saith it, and to whom saith he it? What shall we say, brethren?   Is it the flesh that saith, " Praise thou the Lord, O my soul "? And can the flesh suggest good counsel to the soul?   However much the flesh be conquered, and subjected as a servant to us through strength which the Lord imparteth, that it serve us entirely as a bond slave, enough for us that it hinder us not. . . . For the body, inasmuch as it is the body, is even beneath the soul ; and every soul, however vile, is found more excellent than the most excellent body.   And let not this seem to you to be wonderful, that even any vile and sinful soul is better than any great and most surpassing body.   It is better, not in deserts, but in nature.   The soul indeed is sinful, is stained with certain defilements of lusts ; yet gold, though rusted, is better than the most polished lead.   Let your mind then run over every part of creation, and ye will see that what we are saying is not incredible, that a soul, however blameable, is yet more praiseworthy than a praiseworthy body.   There are two things, a soul and a body.   The soul I chide, the body I praise : the soul I chide, because it is sinful ; the body I praise, because it is sound.   Yet it is in its own kind that I praise the soul, and in its own kind

---

[1] Prov. i. 28.   [2] Rom. viii. 24.   [3] 1 Pet. i. 5.   [4] Lat. CXLV. Sermon to the people.   [5] Ps. xlii. 14, 15.

that I blame the soul : and so in its own kind I praise the body, or blame it. If you ask me which is better, what I have blamed or what I have praised, wondrous is the answer thou wilt receive. . . . So you speak of the best horse and the worst man : yet thou preferrest the man thou findest fault with to the horse thou praisest. . . . The nature of the soul is more excellent than the nature of the body : it surpasseth it by far, it is a thing spiritual, incorporeal, akin to the substance of God. It is somewhat invisible, it ruleth the body, moveth the limbs, guideth the senses, prepareth thoughts, putteth forth actions, taketh in images of countless things ; who is there, in short, beloved brethren, who may suffice for the praises of the soul? And yet such is the grace given to it, that this man saith, " Praise the Lord, O my soul." . . . It is not the flesh that saith it. Let the body be angel-like, still it is inferior to the soul, it cannot give advice to its superior. The flesh when duly obedient is the handmaid of the soul : the soul rules, the body obeys ; the soul commands, the body performs ; how then can the flesh give this advice to the soul? Is it then perchance the soul herself, who saith to herself, and in a manner commandeth herself, and exhorteth and asketh herself? For through certain passions in one part of her nature she wavered ; but in another part, which they call the reasonable mind, the wisdom whereby she thinks, clinging to God, and now sighing towards Him, she perceives that certain inferior parts of her are troubled by worldly emotions, and by a certain excitement of earthly desires, betake them to outward things, leaving God who is within ; so she recalleth herself from things outward to inward, from lower to higher, and says, " Praise the Lord, O my soul." . . . The soul itself giveth itself counsel from the light of God by the reasonable mind, whereby it conceiveth the wisdom fixed in the everlasting nature of its Author. It readeth there of somewhat to be feared, to be praised, to be loved, to be longed for, and sought after : as yet it graspeth it not, it comprehendeth it not ; it is, as it were, dazzled with brightness ; it has not strength to abide there. Therefore it gathers itself, as it were, into a sound state, and saith, " Praise the Lord, O my soul." . . . And then the soul, weighed down, as it were, and unable to stand up as is fitting, answereth the mind, " I will praise the Lord in my life " (ver. 2). What is, " in my life "? Because now I am in my death. Therefore first encourage thyself, and say, " Praise the Lord, O my soul." Thy soul answereth thee, I do praise so far as I can, slightly, poorly, weakly. Wherefore? Because, " while we are in the body, we are absent from the Lord." [1] . . .

---

[1] 2 Cor. v. 6.

3. " In my life." Now what has it? It might answer thee, " My death." Whence, " My death "? because I am absent from the Lord. For if to cling to Him is life, to depart from Him is death. But what comforteth thee? Hope. Now thou livest in hope : in hope praise, in hope sing. Thy death is from the sadness of this life, thou livest in hope of a future life. And how wilt thou praise thy Lord? " I will sing unto my God, as long as I have my being." What sort of praise is this, " I will sing unto my God as long as I have being "? Behold, my brethren, what sort of being this will be ; where there will be everlasting praise, there will be also everlasting being. Behold, now thou hast being : dost thou sing unto God as long as thou hast being? Behold, thou wast singing, and hast turned thyself away to some business, thou singest no longer, yet thou hast being : thou hast being, yet thou singest not. It may be also thy desire turneth thee to somewhat ; not only dost thou not sing, but thou even offendest His ears, yet thou hast being. What praise will that be, when thou praisest as long as thou hast being? But what meaneth, " as long as I have being "? Will there be any time when he will not be? Nay, rather, that " long " will be everlasting, and therefore it will be truly " long." For whatever hath end in time, however prolonged it is, is yet not " long." . . .

4. " Put not your trust in princes " (ver. 3). Brethren, here we receive a mighty task ; it is a voice from heaven, from above it soundeth to us. For now through some kind of weakness the soul of man, whensoever it is in tribulation here, despaireth of God, and chooseth to rely on man. Let it be said to one when set in some affliction, " There is a great man, by whom thou mayest be set free ; " he smileth, he rejoiceth, he is lifted up. But if it is said to him, " God freeth thee," he is chilled, so to speak, by despair. The aid of a mortal is promised, and thou rejoicest ; the aid of the Immortal is promised, and art thou sad? It is promised thee that thou shalt be freed by one who needeth to be freed with thee, and thou exultest, as at some great aid : thou art promised that Liberator, who needeth none to free Him, and thou despairest, as though it were but a fable. Woe to such thoughts : they wander far ; truly there is sad and great death in them. Approach, begin to long, begin to seek and to know Him by whom thou wast made. For He will not leave His work, if He be not left by His work.

5. . . . " His breath shall go forth, and he shall return to his earth : in that day shall all his thoughts perish " (ver. 4). Where is swelling? where is pride? where is boasting? But perhaps he will have passed to a good place, if indeed he have passed. For I know not whither he who

spake thus hath passed. For he spake in pride; and I know not whither such men pass, save that I look into another Psalm, and see that their passage is an evil one. "I beheld the wicked lifted up above the cedars of Libanus, and I passed by, and, lo, he was not; and I sought him, and his place was not found."[1] The good man, who passed by, and found not the wicked, reached a place where the wicked is not. Wherefore, brethren, let us all listen: brethren, beloved of God, let us all listen; in whatsoever tribulation, in whatsoever longing for the heavenly gift, "let us not trust in princes, nor in sons of men, in whom is no salvation." All this is mortal, fleeting, perishable.

What then must we do, if we are not to hope in sons of men, nor in princes? What must we do? "Blessed is he whose Helper is the God of Jacob" (ver. 5): not this man or that man; not this angel or that angel; but, "blessed is he whose Helper is the God of Jacob:" for to Jacob also so great an Helper was He, that of Jacob He made him Israel. O mighty help! now he is Israel, "seeing God." While then thou art placed here, and a wanderer not yet seeing God, if thou hast the God of Jacob for thy Helper, from Jacob thou wilt become Israel, and wilt be "seeing God," and all toil and all groans shall come to an end, gnawing cares shall cease, happy praises shall succeed. "Blessed is he whose Helper is the God of Jacob;" of this Jacob. Wherefore is he happy? Meanwhile, while yet groaning in this life, "his hope is in the Lord his God." . . . Who is this, "Lord his God"? . . . "To us there is one God, the Father, of whom are all things, and one Lord Jesus Christ, through whom are all things."[2] Therefore let Him be thy hope, even the Lord thy God; in Him let thy hope be. His hope too is in the lord his god, who worshippeth Saturn; his hope is in the lord his god, who worshippeth Neptune or Mercury; yea more, I add, who worshippeth his belly, of whom is said, "whose god is their belly."[3] The one is the god of the one, the other of the other. Who is this "blessed" one? for "his hope is in the Lord his God." But who is He? "Who made heaven and earth, the sea, and all that is in them" (ver. 6). My brethren, we have a great God; let us bless His holy Name, that He hath deigned to make us His possession. As yet thou seest not God; thou canst not fully love what as yet thou seest not. All that thou seest, He hath made. Thou admirest the world; why not the Maker of the world? Thou lookest up to the heavens, and art amazed: thou considerest the whole earth, and tremblest; when canst thou contain in thy thought the vastness

of the sea? Look at the countless number of the stars, look at all the many kind of seeds, all the different sorts of animals, all that swimmeth in the water, creepeth on the earth, flieth in the sky, hovereth in the air; how great are all these, how beautiful, how fair, how amazing! Behold, He who made all these, is thy God. Put thy hope in Him, that thou mayest be happy. "His hope is in the Lord his God." Observe, my brethren, the mighty God, the good God, who maketh all these things. . . . If he mentioned these things only, perhaps thou wouldest answer me, "God, who made heaven and earth and sea, is a great God: but doth He think of me?" It would be said to thee, "He made thee." How so? am I heaven, or am I earth, or am I sea? Surely it is plain; I am neither heaven, nor earth, nor sea: yet I am on earth. At least thou grantest me this, that thou art on earth. Hear then, that God made not only heaven and earth and sea: for He "made heaven and earth and sea, and all that is in them." If then He made all that is in them, He made thee also. It is too little to say, thee; the sparrow, the locust, the worm, none of these did He not make, and He careth for all. His care refers not to His commandment, for this commandment He gave to man alone. . . . As regards then the tenor of the commandment, "God doth not take care for oxen:"[4] as regards His providential care of the universe, whereby He created all things, and ruleth the world, "Thou, Lord, shalt save both man and beast." Here perhaps some one may say to me, "God careth not for oxen," comes from the New Testament: "Thou, Lord, shalt save both man and beast," is from the Old Testament. There are some who find fault, and say, that these two Testaments agree not with one another. . . . Let us hear the Lord Himself, the Chief and Master of the Apostles: "Consider," saith He, "the fowls of the air; they sow not, neither do they reap, nor gather into barns, and your heavenly Father feedeth them."[5] Therefore even beside men, these animals are objects of care to God, to be fed, not to receive a law. As far then as regards giving a law, "God careth not for oxen:" as regards creating, feeding, governing, ruling, all things have to do with God. "Are not two sparrows sold for one farthing?" saith our Lord Jesus Christ, "and one of them shall not fall to the ground without the will of your Father: how much better are ye than they."[6] Perhaps thou sayest, God counteth me not in this great multitude. There follows here a wondrous passage in the Gospel: "the hairs of your head are all numbered."[7]

6. Who keepeth truth for ever." What "truth for ever"? what "truth" doth He "keep,"

[1] Ps. xxxvii. 35, 36.   [2] 1 Cor. viii. 6.   [3] Philip. iii. 19.

[4] 1 Cor. ix. 9.   [5] Matt. vi. 26.
[6] Matt. x. 29.   [7] Matt. x. 30.

and wherein doth "He keep it for ever"? "Who executeth judgment for them that suffer wrong" (ver. 7). He avengeth them that suffer wrong. There cometh at once to thee the voice of the Apostle: "now therefore there is altogether a fault among you, that ye go to law one with another: why do ye not rather suffer wrong?"[1] He urged thee not to suffer annoyance, but to suffer wrong: for not every annoyance is wrong. For whatever thou sufferest lawfully is not a wrong; lest perchance thou shouldest say, I also am among those who have suffered wrong, for I have suffered such a thing in such a place, and such a thing for such a reason. Consider whether thou hast suffered a wrong. Robbers suffer many things, but they suffer no wrong. Wicked men, evil doers, housebreakers, adulterers, seducers, all these suffer many evils, yet is there no wrong. It is one thing to suffer wrong; it is another to suffer tribulation, or penalty, or annoyance, or punishment. Consider where thou art; see what thou hast done; see why thou art suffering; and then thou seest what thou art suffering. Right and wrong are contraries. Right is what is just. For not all that is called right, is right. What if a man lay down for you unjust right? nor indeed is it to be called right, if it is unjust. That is true right, which is also just. Consider what thou hast done, not what thou art suffering. If thou hast done right, thou art suffering wrong; if thou hast done wrong, thou art suffering right. . . .

7. "Who giveth food to the hungry." Behold, from thee I look for nothing: "God giveth food to the hungry." Who are "the hungry"? All. What is, all? To all things that have life, to all men He giveth food: doth He not reserve some food for His beloved? If they have another kind of hunger, they have also another kind of food. Let us first enquire what their hunger is, and then we shall find their food. "Blessed are they that hunger and thirst after righteousness, for they shall be filled."[2] We ought to be God's hungry ones. . . . "The Lord looseth them that are fettered; the Lord lifteth up them that are dashed down; the Lord maketh wise them that are blind" (ver. 8). Perfectly hath he by this last sentence explained to us all the preceding ones: lest perchance, when he had said, "the Lord looseth them that are fettered," we should refer it to those fettered ones, who for some crime are bound in irons by their masters: and in that he said, "He lifteth up them that are dashed down," there should occur to our minds some one stumbling or falling, or thrown from a horse. There is another kind of fall, there are other kinds of fetters, just as there

is other darkness and other light. Whereas he said, "He maketh the blind wise;" he would not say, He enlightened the blind, lest thou shouldest understand this also in reference to the flesh, as the man was enlightened by the Lord, when He anointed his eyes with clay made with spittle, and so healed him: that thou mightest not look for anything of this sort, when He is speaking of spiritual things, he pointeth to a sort of light of wisdom, wherewith the blind are enlightened. Therefore in the same way as the blind are enlightened with the light of wisdom, so are the fettered set free, and those who are dashed down are lifted up. Whereby then have we been fettered? whereby dashed down? Our body was once an ornament to us: now, we have sinned, and thereby have had fetters put on us. What are our fetters? Our mortality. . . . "The Lord loveth the righteous." And who are the "righteous"? How far are they righteous now? Just as thou hast; "the Lord guardeth proselytes" (ver. 9). "Proselytes" are strangers. Every Church of the Gentiles is a stranger. For it cometh in to the Fathers, not sprung of their flesh, but their daughter by imitating them. Yet the Lord, not any man, guardeth them. "The orphan and widow He will take up." Let none think that He taketh up the orphan for his inheritance, or the widow for any business of hers. True, God doth help them; and in all the duties of the human race, he doeth a good work, who taketh care of an orphan, who abandoneth not a widow: but in a certain way we are all orphans, not because our Father is dead, but because He is absent.[3] . . .

8. "And the way of sinners He shall root out." What is, "the way of sinners"? To mock at these things which we say. "Who is an orphan, who a widow? What kingdom of heaven, what punishment of hell is there? These are fables of the Christians. To what I see, to that will I live: "let us eat and drink, for to-morrow we die."[4] Beware lest such men persuade you of aught: let them not enter through your ears into your heart; let them find thorns in your ears: let him, who seeketh to enter thus, go away pierced: for "evil communications corrupt good manners."[5] But here perhaps thou wilt say, "Wherefore then are they prosperous? Behold, they worship not God, and commit every kind of evil daily: yet they abound in those things, through want of which I toil." Be not envious against sinners. What they receive, thou seest; what is in store for them, seest thou not? . . . Wilt thou not believe even the Lord thy God, who saith, "Broad and spacious is the way that leadeth to destruction, and many there be that walk by it"?[6] This "way the Lord will root out."

---

[1] 1 Cor. vi. 7.   [2] Matt. v. 6.

[3] [But compare (Greek) John xiv. 18. — C.]
[4] 1 Cor. xv. 32.   [5] 1 Cor. xv. 33.   [6] Matt. vii. 13.

And, when "the way of sinners" has been "rooted out," what remaineth for us? "Come, ye blessed of My father, enjoy the Kingdom;"[1] "The Lord shall reign for ever" (ver. 10). "O Sion, thy God" shall reign for ever; surely thy God will not reign without thee. "For generation and generation." He hath said it twice, because he could not say it for ever. And think not that eternity is bounded by finite words. The word eternity consists of four syllables; in itself it is without end. It could not be commended to thee, save thus, "for generation and generation." Too little hath he said: if he spoke it all day long, it were too narrow: if he spoke it all his life, must he not at length hold his peace? Love eternity: without end shalt thou reign, if Christ be thine End, with whom thou shalt reign for ever and ever. Amen.

PSALM CXLVII.[2]

1. It is said to us, "Praise the Lord" (ver. 1). This is said to all nations, not to us alone. And these words, sounded forth through separate places by the Readers, each Church heareth separately; but the one same Voice of God proclaimeth unto all, that we praise Him. And as though we asked wherefore we ought to praise the Lord, behold what reason he hath brought forward: "Praise the Lord," he saith, "for a Psalm is good." Is this all the reward of them that praise? . . . The "Psalm" is praise of God. This then he saith, "Praise the Lord, for it is good to praise the Lord." Let us not thus pass over the praise of the Lord. It is spoken, and hath passed: it is done, and we are silent: we have praised, and then rested; we have sung, and then rested. We go forth to some business which awaits us, and when other employments have found us, shall the praise of God cease in us? Not so: thy tongue praiseth but for a while, let thy life ever praise. Thus then "a Psalm is good."

2. For a "Psalm" is a song, not any kind of song, but a song to a psaltery. A psaltery is a kind of instrument of music, like the lyre and the harp, and such kinds of instruments, which were invented for music. He therefore who singeth Psalms, not only singeth with his voice, but with a certain instrument besides, which is called a psaltery, he accompanieth his voice with his hands. Wilt thou then sing a Psalm? Let not thy voice alone sound the praises of God; but let thy works also be in harmony with thy voice. . . . To please then the ear, sing with thy voice; but with thy heart be not silent, with thy life be not still. Thou devisest no fraud in thy heart: thou singest a Psalm to

God. When thou eatest and drinkest, sing a Psalm: not by intermingling sweet sounds suited to the ear, but by eating and drinking moderately, frugally, temperately: for thus saith the Apostle, "whether ye eat or drink, or whatever ye do, do all to the glory of God."[3] . . . If by immoderate voracity thou exceedest the due bounds of nature, and gluttest thyself in excess of wine, however great praises of God thy tongue sound, yet thy life blasphemeth Him. After food and drink thou liest down to sleep: in thy bed neither commit any pollution, nor go beyond the license given by the law of God: let thy marriage bed be kept chaste with thy wife: and if thou desire to beget children, yet let there not be unbridled sensuality of lust: in thy bed give honour to thy wife,[4] for ye are both members of Christ, both made by Him, both renewed by His Blood: so doing thou praisest God, nor will thy praise be altogether silent. What, when sleep has come over thee? Let not an evil conscience rouse thee from rest: so doth the innocence of thy sleep praise God. . . .

3. "Let praises be pleasant to our God." How? If He be praised by our good lives. Hear that then praise will be pleasant to Him. In another place it is said, "Praise is not seemly in the mouth of a sinner."[5] If then in the mouth of a sinner praise is not seemly, neither is it pleasant, for that only is pleasant which is seemly. . . . For praise may be pleasant to a man, when he heareth one praising with neat and clever sentiments, and with a sweet voice; but "let praise be pleasant to our God," whose ears are open not to the mouth, but to the heart; not to the tongue, but to the life of him that praiseth.

4. Who is "our God," that praise should be pleasant to Him? He maketh Himself sweet to us, He commendeth Himself to us; thanks to His condescension. . . . "But God commendeth His love to us" . . . "in that, while we were yet sinners, Christ died for us."[6] . . . Let us see whether it be the commendation which the Apostle speaketh of, that Christ died for the sinners and ungodly: "the Lord who buildeth up Jerusalem, and gathereth the dispersions of Israel" (ver. 2). For the people of Jerusalem are the people of Israel. It is Jerusalem "eternal in the heavens," whereof the Angels are citizens also. . . . All the citizens then of that city, through "seeing God," rejoice in that great and wide and heavenly city; they gaze upon God Himself. But we are wanderers from that city, driven out by sin, that we should not remain there; weighed down by mortality, that we should not return thither. God looked back on our wandering, and He

---

[1] Matt. xxv. 34.
[2] Lat. CXLVI. Sermon to the people of Carthage.

[3] 1 Cor. x. 31.
[5] Ecclus. xv. 9.

[4] 1 Pet. iii. 7.
[6] Rom. v. 8.

who "buildeth up Jerusalem," restored the part that had fallen. How restored He the part that had fallen? . . . He sent then to our captive estate His Son as a Redeemer. Take with Thee, said He, a bag, bear therein the price of the captives. For He put on Him our mortal flesh, and therein was the Blood, by the shedding of which we were to be redeemed. With that Blood He "gathered the dispersions of Israel." And if He gathered them that before were dispersed, how must we strive that they be gathered who now are dispersed? If the dispersed have been gathered, that in the Hand of the Builder they might be fashioned into the building, how should they be gathered who through disquiet have fallen from the Hand of the Builder? Behold whom we praise; behold to whom we owe praise all our life long.

5. How doth He gather? What doeth He in order to gather? "Who healeth the bruised in heart" (ver. 3). Behold the way in which the dispersions of Israel are gathered, by the healing of the bruised in heart. They who are not of a bruised heart, are not healed. What is to bruise the heart? Let it be known, brethren, let it be done, that ye may be able to be healed. For it is told in many other places of Scripture; . . . "the sacrifice of God is a troubled spirit, a bruised and contrite heart God will not despise." He healeth then the bruised in heart, for He draweth nigh unto them to heal them; as is said in another place, "the Lord is nigh unto them who have bruised their heart." [1] Who are they that have "bruised their heart"? The humble. Who are they that have not "bruised their heart"? The proud. The bruised heart shall be healed, the puffed up heart shall be dashed down. For for this purpose perhaps is it dashed down, that being bruised it may be healed. Let not our heart then, brethren, desire to be set upright, before it be upright. It is ill for that to be uplifted which is not first corrected. . . .

6. What are the means whereby He "bindeth up their bruises"? Just as physicians bind up fractures. For sometimes (observe this, beloved; it is well known to those who have observed it, or have heard it from physicians), sometimes when limbs are sound, but are crooked and distorted, physicians break them in order to set them straight, and make a new wound, because the soundness which was distorted was amiss. . . .

7. What are these means whereby He bindeth? The sacraments of this present life, whereby in the mean time we obtain our comfort: and all the words we speak to you, words which sound and pass away, all that is done in the Church in this present time, are the means whereby "He bindeth up our bruises." For just as, when the limb has become perfectly sound, the physician taketh off the bandage; so in our own city Jerusalem, when we shall have been made equal to the Angels, think ye that we shall receive there, what we have received here? Will it be needful then that the Gospel be read to us, that our faith may abide? or that hands be laid upon us by any Bishop? All these are means of binding up fractures; when we have attained perfect soundness, they will be taken off; but we should never attain it, if they were not bound up.

8. "Who telleth the number of the stars, and calleth them all by their names" (ver. 4). What great matter is it for God to "tell the number of the stars"! Men even have endeavoured to do this; whether they have been able to achieve it, is their concern; they would not however attempt it, did they not think that they should achieve it. Let us leave alone what they can do, and how far they have attained; for God I think it no great matter to count all the stars. Or doth He perhaps go over the number, lest He should forget it? Is it any great thing for God to number the stars, by whom "the very hairs of your head are numbered"? [2] The stars are certain lights in the Church comforting our night; all — of whom the Apostle saith, "In the midst of a crooked and perverse generation, among whom ye shine as lights in the world, holding the Word of life." [3] These stars God counteth; all who shall reign with Him, all who are to be gathered into the Body of His only-begotten Son, He hath counted, and still counteth them. Whoso is unworthy, is not even counted. Many too have believed, or rather may, with a kind of shadowy appearance of faith, have attached themselves to His people: yet He knoweth what He counteth, what He winnoweth away. For so great is the height of the Gospel, that it hath come to pass as was said, "I have declared, and have spoken: they are multiplied above number:" [4] there are then among the people certain supernumeraries, so to speak. What do I mean by supernumeraries? More than will be there. Within these walls are more than will be in the kingdom of God, in the heavenly Jerusalem; these are above the number. Let each one of you consider whether he shineth in darkness, whether he refuseth to be led astray by the dark iniquity of the world; if he be not led astray, nor conquered, he will be, as it were, a star, which God already numbereth. "And calling them all by their names," he saith. Herein is our whole reward. We have certain names with God; that God may

[1] Ps. xxxiv. 18.   [2] Matt. x. 30.   [3] Philip. ii. 15.   [4] Ps. xl. 5.

know our names, this we ought to wish, for this to act, for this to busy ourselves, as far as we are able; not to rejoice in other things, not even in certain spiritual gifts. . . . When the disciples returned from their mission exulting, and saying, " Lord, even the devils are subject unto us in Thy Name " [1] — then He (knowing that many would say, "have we not in Thy Name cast out devils?" to whom He should say, "I know you not ") said, " In this rejoice not, that the devils are subject unto you; but rather rejoice, because your names are written in heaven." [2]

9. " Great is our Lord " (ver. 5). The Psalmist is filled with joy, he hath poured out his words wonderfully: yet somewhat he was unable to speak, and how availed he to think on it? "And great is His power, and of His understanding is no numbering " He who " numbereth the stars," Himself cannot be numbered. Who can expound this? who can worthily even imagine what is meant by, "and of His understanding is no number"? . . . Whatsoever then that is infinite this world containeth, though it be infinite to man, yet is not to God: too little is it to say, to God: even by the angels it is numbered. His understanding surpasses all calculators; it cannot be counted by us. Numbers themselves who numbereth? What than is there with God? wherewith made He all things, and where made He all things, to whom it is said, " Thou hast arrayed all things in measure, number, and weight"? [3] Or who can number, or measure, or weigh, measure and number and weight themselves, wherein God hath ordered all things? Therefore, "of His understanding is no number." Let human voices be hushed, human thoughts still: let them not stretch themselves out to incomprehensible things, as though they could comprehend them, but as though they were to partake of them, for partakers we shall be. . . . Partakers then we shall be: let none doubt it: Scripture saith it. And of what shall we be partakers, as though these were parts in God, as though God were divided into parts? Who then can explain how many become partakers of one single substance? Require not then that which I think ye see cannot fitly be said: but return to the healing of the Saviour, bruise your heart. He will guide it, He will bind it up where it is broken, He will make it perfectly sound; and then those things will not be impossible with us, which now are impossible. For it is good that he confess weakness, who desireth to attain to the divine nature.

10. " The Lord taketh up the gentle " (ver. 6). For example; thou understandest not, thou failest to understand, canst not attain: honour

God's Scripture, honour God's Word, though it be not plain: in reverence wait for understanding. Be not wanton to accuse either the obscurity or seeming contradiction of Scripture. There is nothing in it contradictory: somewhat there is which is obscure, not in order that it may be denied thee, but that it may exercise him that shall afterward receive it. When then it is obscure, that is the Physician's doing, that thou mayest knock. He willed that thou shouldest be exercised in knocking; He willed it, that He might open to thee when thou knockest. By knocking thou shalt be exercised; exercised, thou shalt be enlarged; enlarged, thou shalt contain what is given. Be not then indignant for that it is shut; be mild, be gentle. Kick not against what is dark, nor say, It were better said, if it were said thus. For how canst thou thus say, or judge how it is expedient it be said? It is said as it is expedient it be said. Let not the sick man seek to amend his remedies: the Physician knoweth how to temper them: believe Him who careth for thee. Therefore what cometh next? . . . " The Lord taketh up the gentle, but humbleth the sinners even to the ground," he intended a certain sort of sinners to be understood, from the gentleness mentioned first. By sinners then in this place, we understand the fierce, and those who are not gentle. Wherefore doth He " humble them even to the earth "? They carp at objects of understanding, they shall perceive only things earthly. [4]

11. " Begin to the Lord in confession " (ver. 7). Begin with this, if thou wouldest arrive at a clear understanding of the truth. If thou wilt be brought from the road of faith to the profession of the reality, "begin in confession." First accuse thyself: accuse thyself, praise God. . . . What after confession? Let good works follow. " Sing unto our God upon the harp." What is, "Upon the harp"? As I have already explained, just like the Psalm upon the psaltery, so also is the " harp:" not with voice only, but with works.

12. . . . " Who covereth the heaven with clouds, who prepareth rain for the earth " (ver. 8). Now thou art alarmed, because thou canst not see the heaven: when it hath rained thou shalt gather fruit, and shalt see clear sky. Perhaps our God hath done this. For had we not the obscurity of Scripture as an occasion, we should not say to you those things wherein ye rejoice. This then perhaps is the rain whereat ye rejoice. It would not be possible for it to be expressed to you by our tongue, were it not that God covereth with clouds of figures the heaven of the Scriptures. For this purpose willed He that the words of the Prophets should

---

[1] Luke x. 17. [2] Luke x. 20. [3] Wisd. xi. 20.

[4] [See this series, vol. iv. p. 364. Here is a digression upon men " not gentle, " — the Manichees. — C.]

be obscure, that the servants of God might afterwards have that by interpreting which they might flow over the ears and hearts of men, that they might receive from the clouds of God the fatness of spiritual joy. "Who maketh grass to grow upon the mountains, and herb for the service of men." Behold the fruit of the rain. "Who maketh," saith he, "grass to grow upon the mountains." Doth it not also grow upon the low ground? Yes, but it is a great thing that it groweth "on the mountains." . . . For nothing could be more barren than the hard mountains. "And herb for the service of men." What "service"? Listen to Paul himself. "And ourselves," saith he, "your servants for Jesus Christ's sake."[1] He who said, "If we have sown unto you spiritual things, is it a great thing if we reap your carnal things?" yet said, that he was a "servant." For we are your servants, brethren. Let none of us speak of himself, as though he were greater than you. We shall be greater if we are more humble. "But whosoever will be great among you" (it is the Lord's saying), "shall be your servant."[2] Paul the Apostle, indeed, living by his own labour, refused even to receive "the grass of the mountains;" he chose to want; nevertheless, the mountains gave "grass." Because he chose not to receive, ought the mountains therefore not to give, and so to remain barren? Fruit is due to the rain, food is due to the servant, as the Lord saith, "Eat such things as they give you:" and that they should not think that they gave aught of their own, He added, "for the labourer is worthy of his hire."[3]

13. . . . Just now has been read, "Give to every one that asketh of thee;"[4] and in another place Scripture[5] saith, "Let alms sweat in thy hand, till thou findest a righteous man to whom to give it." One there is who seeketh thee, another thou oughtest to seek. Leave not indeed him who seeketh thee empty, for, "give to every one that asketh of thee;" yet still there is another whom thou oughtest to seek; "find a righteous man to whom to give it." Ye will never do this, unless ye have somewhat set aside from your substance, each what pleaseth him according to the needs of his family, as a sort of debt to be paid to the treasury. If Christ have not a state[6] of His own, neither hath He a treasury.[7] . . . Cut off then and prune off some fixed[8] sum either from thy yearly profits or

thy daily gains, else thou seemest as it were to give of thy capital, and thy hand must needs hesitate, when thou puttest it forth to that which thou hast not vowed. Cut off some part of thy income; a tenth if thou choosest, though that is but little. For it is said that the Pharisees gave a tenth; "I fast twice in the week, I give tithes of all that I possess."[9] And what saith the Lord? "Except your righteousness exceed the righteousness of the Scribes and Pharisees, ye shall not enter into the kingdom of heaven."[10] He whose righteousness thou oughtest to exceed, giveth a tenth: thou givest not even a thousandth. How wilt thou surpass him whom thou matchest not? "Who prepareth rain for the earth."

14. "And giveth unto the cattle their food" (ver. 9). These are the cattle he meaneth, even God's flocks. God defraudeth not His flock of their food through men, for whose "service He maketh the grass to grow." "And to the young of the ravens that call upon Him." Shall we perchance think this, that the ravens call upon God to give them their food? Think not that the unreasoning creature calls upon God: no creature knows how to call upon God, save the reasonable alone. Consider it as spoken in a figure, lest thou think, as some evil men say, that the souls of men migrate into cattle, dogs, swine, ravens. Give this no place in your hearts or in your faith. The soul of man is made after the image of God: He will not give His image to dog or swine. Who are "the young of the ravens"? The Israelites used to say that they alone were righteous, because to them the Law had been given: all other men of every nation they used to call sinners. And in truth all nations were given up to sin, to idolatry, to the worship of stones and stocks: but did they continue so? Although the ravens themselves, our fathers, did not, yet we, "the young of the ravens," do call upon God.[11] . . . For "the young of the ravens," who seemed to worship the images of their forefathers, have advanced, and turned to God. And now thou hearest "the young of the ravens" calling upon the one God. What then? Sayest thou to "the young of the ravens," "hast thou left thy father?" Plainly I have, saith he; for he is a raven who calls not upon God. I, "the young of the raven," do call upon God.

15. "In the power of an horse He will not take pleasure" (ver. 10). The power "of an horse" is pride. For the horse seemeth adapted as it were to bear a man aloft, that he may be more uplifted as he goes. And in truth he has a neck which typifieth a sort of pride. Let not men exalt themselves upon their worth, let them

---

[1] 2 Cor. iv. 5.   [2] Matt. xx. 26.
[3] Luke x. 7, 8.   [4] Luke vi 30.
[5] The Benedictine editors were unable to identify this text.
[6] Rempublicam.
[7] Fiscus. [The author says: "For know ye what fiscus means? Fiscus is a bag, and from the same source come also the words fiscella and fiscina. Think not that fiscus is a kind of dragon, because men are alarmed when they hear of the collector of the fiscus: the fiscus is the public purse. The Lord had one here on earth when he had the bag: and the bag was entrusted to Judas."— C.]
[8] Aliquid fixum; other MSS. fisco, which suits the context better; "prune off somewhat for the treasury," i e. Christ's treasury.

[9] Luke xviii. 12.   [10] Matt. v. 20.   [11] 1 Pet. i. 18.

not think themselves uplifted by their distinctions ; let them beware lest they be thrown by an untamed horse.[1] . . . " Nor in the tabernacle of a man will He delight." For the tabernacle of the Lord is the Holy Church spread throughout the whole world. Heretics, separating themselves from the Church's tabernacles, have set up tabernacles for themselves. For if perchance it be the lot of any, who is good and pious, who confesseth his own weakness, who is " the young of a raven that calleth on God," not to enjoy worldly distinction, he goeth not out of the Church, he setteth not up for himself a tent outside the Church, wherein God will not delight. But what saith he ? " I have chosen to be cast away in the house of God, rather than to dwell in the tents of sinners." [2]

16. But what addeth he ? " The Lord will delight in them that fear Him, and in them that hope in His mercy " (ver. 11). A robber is feared, and a wild beast is feared, and an unjust and powerful man is much feared. " The Lord will delight in them that hope in His mercy." Behold, Judas, who betrayed our Lord, feared, but he did not hope in His mercy. . . . It is well indeed that thou hast feared, but only if thou trustedst in His mercy, whom thou hast feared. He in despair " went and hanged himself." In such wise then fear the Lord, that thou trust in His mercy. . . .

17. " Praise in unison, O Jerusalem, thy God " (ver. 12). Abiding yet in captivity, they behold those flocks, or rather, the one flock of all its citizens, gathered from all sides into that city ; they see the joy of the mass, now after threshings and winnowings placed in the garner, fearing nothing, suffering no toil nor trouble ; and, as yet abiding here, in the midst of the threshing they send forward their joy of hope, and pant for it, joining as it were their hearts to the Angels of God, and to that people which shall abide with them in joy for ever. For what wilt thou then do, O Jerusalem ? Surely toil and groaning will pass away. What wilt thou do ? wilt thou plough, or sow, or plant vines, or make voyages, or trade ? What wilt thou do ? Will it still be thy duty to be engaged in the works thou now doest, good though they are, and spring from mercy ? Consider thy numbers, consider on all sides thy company : see whether any hungers, for thee to give bread to ; see whether any thirsts, for thee to give a cup of cold water to ; see whether any is a stranger, for thee to take in ; see whether any is sick, for thee to visit ; see whether any is at strife, for thee to reconcile him ; see whether any is dying, for thee to bury him. What then wilt thou do ? " Praise in unison, O Jerusalem, thy God." Be-

hold, this is thy business. As is wont to be said in inscriptions, " Use it and be happy." [3]

18. Be ye Jerusalem ; remember of whom it is said, " Lord, in Thy city their image Thou shalt bring to nought." [4] These are they who now rejoice in such pomps ; among them are they who have not come hither to-day because there is a show. To whom is it a gift ? [5] to whom is it a loss ? or why is it a gift ? why is it a loss ? For not they only who exhibit such shows are smitten with loss, but with much greater loss are they smitten who delight in gazing on them. The former have their chest drained of its gold, the latter have their breast robbed of the riches of righteousness. Most of the exhibiters of shows have to mourn for selling their estates ; how ought the sinners to mourn, for losing their souls ! Was it then for this that the Lord cried out on the Lord's Day, " Watch ye," that to-day men should watch in this way. I beseech you, ye citizens of Jerusalem, I beseech you by the peace of Jerusalem, by the Redeemer, the Builder, the Ruler of Jerusalem, that ye address your prayers to God for them. May they see, may they feel, that they are trifling ; and, intent as they are on the sights which please them, may at length look on themselves, and be displeased. For in many we rejoice that this has already been done : and once we too sat there and were mad : and how many think we now sit there, who shall yet be, not only Christians, but also Bishops ! From what is past, we conjecture what is to be : from what has already been done, we announce beforehand what God will do. Let your prayers be wakeful, ye groan not for nothing. Certainly they who have already escaped, praying for those who are still in danger, because they too having been among those in danger, are heard ; and God shall drag His people out of the captivity of Babylon ; by all means He shall redeem and deliver them, and the number of the saints who bear the image of God shall be perfected. . . . " Praise in unison," because thou consistest of many : " praise," because thou hast been made one.[6] " We being many," saith the Apostle, " are one in Christ." [7] As then we are many, " we praise in unison ; " as we are one, we " praise." The same are many and one, because He in whom they are one [6] is ever One.[8]

19. Wherefore, saith this Jerusalem, do I praise in unison the Lord, and, as Sion, praise my God ? Jerusalem is the same as Sion. For different reasons has it the two names. Jerusalem meaneth

---

[1] Ps. xx. 7.   [2] Ps. lxxxiv. 10.

[3] *Utere felix.* This and other like expr-ssions seem, from Morcelli, *Opera Epigraphica*, vol. i. p. 415, to have been usual in inscriptions upon cups and like works of art, probably when given as presents.
[4] Ps. lxxiii. 20.
[5] A play on the double meaning of the word *munus*, which, meaning literally " a gift," is also used in a special sense for " as how of gladiators."
[6] *Unum.*   [7] 1 Cor. x. 17.   [8] *Unus.*

" visions of peace ; " Sion meaneth " watching." [1]
See whether these words do not sound like
sights ; [2] that the Gentiles may not think that they
have sights and we have none. Sometimes after
the theatre or amphitheatre breaks up, when the
crowd of lost ones begins to be vomited forth
from that den, sometimes, retaining in their
minds images of their vain amusements, and
feeding their memory with things not only useless but even hurtful, rejoicing in them as if they
were sweet, while they are really deadly ; they
see often, it may be, the servants of God pass
by, they recognise them by their garb or head-
dress, or they know them by sight, [3] and they say
to one another, or inwardly, " Wretched people,
how much they lose !" Brethren, let us return
their good will (for they do mean it well) with
prayers to the Lord. They wish us well ; but
" he that loveth iniquity, hateth his own soul." [4]
If he hateth his own soul, how shall he love my
soul? Yet with a perverse, and empty, and vain
good will, if indeed it may be called good will,
they grieve that we lose what they love : let us
pray that they lose not what we love. Behold
of what character that Jerusalem is to be which
he exhorteth to praise, or rather foreseeth will
praise. For the praises of that city, when we
shall see and love and praise, will not need to be
urged on and stirred up by the voice of prophecy ; but the Prophets now say this, to drink in
as far as while they remain in this flesh they can,
the future joys of the blessed, and then giving
them forth into our ears, to arouse in us love of
that city. Let us burn with longing, let us not
be slothful in spirit. " Praise thy God, O Sion."

20. He saith, " He hath made strong the bars
of thy gates " (ver. 13). The making bars
strong is not for open gates, but shut ones,
wherefore most manuscripts read, " He hath
made strong the bolts [5] of thy gates." Observe,
beloved. He biddeth Jerusalem when closed in
to praise the Lord. We praise in unison now,
we praise now ; but it is amid offences. Many
where we wish not, enter in : many though we
wish it not, go out : therefore offences are frequent. " And because iniquity hath abounded,"
saith the Truth," the love of many waxeth cold : " [6]
because men come in whom we cannot discern,
because men go out whom we cannot retain.
Wherefore is this? Because not yet is there perfection, not yet is there the bliss that shall be.
Wherefore is this? Because as yet it is the
threshing-floor, not yet the garner. What therefore will be then, save no fear that aught of this
kind will happen? He said not only, He hath
set, but, " He hath made strong the bars of thy

gates." Let none go out, let none come in.
Let none go out, we rejoice : let none come in,
we fear. Nay, fear not this : when thou hast
entered it will be said : only be thou in the number of virgins, who carried their oil with them. . . .

21. " He hath blessed thy children within
thee." Who? He " who hath set peace as thy
borders." How ye all exult ! [7] Love peace, my
brethren. Greatly are we delighted, when the
love of peace crieth from your hearts. How
greatly doth it delight you ! I had said nothing : I had explained nothing : I but read the
verse, and ye shouted. What was it that shouted
in you? The love of peace. . . . O children
of the kingdom, O citizens of Jerusalem, in Jerusalem is the vision of peace : and all who love
peace are blest in her, and they enter in, when
the doors are being shut, and the bars made
strong. This, which when but named ye so love
and esteem, this follow after, this long for : this
love in your home, in your business, in your
wives, in your sons, in your slaves, in your
friends, in your enemies. . . .

22. What ye cried out a while ago at the very
mention of peace, ye cried from longing : your
cry was from thirst, not from fulness ; for there
will be perfect righteousness where will be perfect peace. Now we hunger and thirst after
righteousness. " They shall be filled." [8] How
shall they be filled? When we have arrived at
peace. Therefore when he had said, " Who hath
set peace for thy borders," because there is fulness and no want, he added at once, " and filleth
thee with the fat of wheat " (ver. 14). . . .

23. " Who sendeth forth His Word to the
earth " (ver. 15). Behold, on earth we toil,
weary, fainting, sluggish, cold : when should we
be raised up to the fat of wheat that satisfieth,
did not He send His Word to the earth, whereby
we were weighed down, to the earth, whereby we
were hindered from returning? He sent His
Word, He deserted us not even in the wilderness,
He rained manna from heaven. " Who sendeth
forth His Word to the earth ; " and to earth His
Word came. How? or what is His Word?
" Even unto swiftness His Word runneth." He
said not, " His Word is swift," but, " His Word
runneth even unto swiftness." Let us understand, my brethren : He could not have chosen
a better word. He who is hot grows hot by
heat, he who is cold grows cold by cold, he who
is swift becometh swift by swiftness. . . . To
what degree then doth it run? " Even to swiftness." Increase as much as you will the swiftness of the Word, and say, It is as swift as this
or that, as birds, as the winds, as the Angels ;
is any of these as great as swiftness itself, " even
unto swiftness "? What is swiftness itself, breth-

---

[1] Speculatio.   [2] Spectacula.
[3] There is better reading in some MSS.: forte for fronte, " or
they happen to know them."
[4] Ps. xi. 5.   [5] Seras.   [6] Matt. xxiv. 12.

[7] [Here were applauses. The Donatists were warlike. — C.]
[8] Matt. v. 6.

ren? It is everywhere; it is not in part. This belongeth to the Word of God, not to be in part, to be everywhere by Himself the Word, whereby He is "the Power of God and the Wisdom of God,"[1] before He had taken flesh upon Him. If we think of God in the Form of God, the Word equal to the Father, this is the Wisdom of God, of which is said, "It reacheth from one end to the other mightily."[2] What mighty speed! "It reacheth from one end to the other mightily." . . .

24. We then are burdened by the sluggishness of this cold body, and the bonds of this earthly and corruptible life; have we no hope of receiving "the Word," which "runneth even unto swiftness"? or hath abandoned us, though by the body we are depressed to the lowest depths? Did not He predestinate us, before we were born in this mortal and sluggish body? He then, who predestinated us, gave snow to the earth, even ourselves. For now let us come to those somewhat obscure verses of the Psalm, let those entanglements begin to be unrolled. Behold, we are sluggish on this earth, and are as it were frozen here. And just as happens to the flakes of snow, for they freeze above, then fall down; so as love groweth cold, human nature falleth down to this earth, and involved in a sluggish body becometh like snow. But in that snow are predestined sons of God. For, "He giveth snow like wool" (ver. 16). What is "like wool"? It meaneth, of the snow which He hath given, of these, who are as yet slow in spirit and cold, whom He hath predestinated, He is about to make somewhat. For wool is the material of a garment: when we see wool, we look on it as a sort of preparation for a garment. Therefore since He hath predestinated these, who at present are cold and creep on earth, and as yet glow not with the spirit of love (for as yet He speaketh of predestination), God hath given these as a sort of wool: He is about to make of them a garment. Rightly did the "raiment" of Christ "shine" on the mountain, "like snow."[3] The raiment of Christ did shine like snow, as though of that snow a garment had already been made: of which wool, that is, of the snow which He gave like wool, they being as yet predestined, were sluggish: but wait, see what followeth. Since He gave them as wool, a garment is made of them. For as the Church is called the Body of Christ, so is the Church also called the garment of Christ: hence cometh that which is said by the Apostle, "that He might present it to Himself a glorious Church, not having spot or wrinkle."[4] Let Him then present unto Himself a glorious Church, not having spot or wrinkle; let Him make Himself a garment of that wool, which He had predestinated in the snow. While men are yet unbelieving, and cold, and sluggish, let Him make a garment of this wool. That it may be washed from spots, let it be cleansed by faith: that it may have no wrinkle, let it be stretched out upon the cross. . . .

25. "He scattereth mist like ashes." "He scattereth," saith the Psalmist, "mist like ashes." Who? He "who giveth snow like wool." For whom He predestined, He calleth to repentance; for "whom He predestined, them He also called." But "ashes" are connected with repentance. Hear Him calling to repentance, when He upbraided certain cities, saying, "Woe unto thee, Chorazin! woe unto thee, Bethsaida! for if the mighty works which have been done in you had been done in Tyre and Sidon, they had long ago repented in dust and ashes."[5] Therefore, "He scattereth mist like ashes." What is, "He scattereth mist like ashes"? When a man is called to learn about God, and it is said to him, "Receive the truth;" he beginneth to wish to receive the Truth, but is not able; he seeth that He is under a sort of darkness, which before he saw not. . . . Wander not in the mist, follow in faith. But forasmuch as thou endeavourest to see and art not able, repent of thy sins, for mist is scattered like ashes. Repent thee now of having been obstinate against God, repent of having followed thine own evil ways. Thou hast come into this state where it is difficult for thee to see the vision of bliss, and the mist will be healthful to thee, which God scattereth like ashes. Thou thyself art as yet a mist, but like ashes. For they that are penitent, as yet roll themselves in ashes, my brethren, testifying, as it were, that they are like it, saying unto God, "I am ashes." For a certain Scripture saith, "I have despised myself, and wasted away, I have reckoned myself earth and ashes."[6] This is the humility of the penitent. When Abraham speaketh to his God, and wisheth the burning of Sodom to be disclosed to him, he saith, "I am but earth and ashes."[7] How hath this humility ever been found in great and holy men!

26. "Who sendeth His crystal like morsels of bread" (ver. 17). We need not spend our toil again in saying what crystal is. We have already said it, and I do not think that ye, beloved, have forgotten it. What is then, "He sendeth His crystal like morsels of bread"? What is "crystal"? It is very hard, it is very tightly congealed; it can not, like snow, be easily melted. Snow, hardened by many years' duration, and by the succession of ages, is called "crystal," and this "He send-

---

[1] 1 Cor. i. 24.　　　[2] Wisd. viii. 1.
[3] Matt. xvii. 2.　　　[4] Eph. v. 27.

[5] Matt. xi. 21.　　[6] Job xxx. 19, Vulg.　　[7] Gen. xviii. 27.

eth like morsels of bread." What meaneth this? They were too hard, no longer fit to be compared to snow, but to crystal; but they too are predestinated and called, and some of them even so as to feed others, to be useful to others also. And what need is there to enumerate many, whom we happen to know, this one and that one? Every one when he thinks can recall to mind how hardened and obstinate some of those whom he knows have been, how they have struggled against the truth; yet now they preach the truth, they have been made morsels of bread. Who is that one Bread? "We being many," saith the Apostle, "are one Body in Christ;" [1] he saith also, "we being many are one Bread and one Body." [2] If then the whole Body of Christ is one Bread, the members of Christ are morsels of Bread. Of some that are hard He maketh members of Himself, and useful for feeding others. . . . Behold, the Apostle Paul was a crystal, hard, resisting the truth, crying out against the Gospel, hardening himself, as it were, against the sun. . . . Since then he was crystal, he appeared clear and white, but he was hard and very cold. How was he bright and white? "An Hebrew of the Hebrews; as touching the law, a Pharisee." Behold the brightness of crystal. Now hear the hardness of crystal. "As touching zeal, persecuting the Church" [3] of Christ. Among the stoners of the holy martyr Stephen, was he, hard, perhaps harder than all. "For he kept the raiment of all who were stoning," [4] so that he stoned by the hands of all.

27. Thus then we see "the snow, the mist, the crystal:" it is good that He blow and thaw them. For if He blow not, if He Himself thaw not the hardness of this ice, "in the face of His cold who shall stand?" He abandoneth a sinner, behold, He calleth him not; behold, He openeth not his perception; behold, He poureth not in grace; let the man thaw himself, if he can, from the ice of folly. He cannot. Wherefore can he not? "In the face of His cold who shall stand?" Behold him then growing harder, and saying, "O wretched man that I am! who shall deliver me from the body of this death?" Behold, I am growing cold, behold, I am growing hard, what heat shall thaw me that I may run? "Who shall deliver me from the body of this death?" "In the face of His cold who shall stand?" And who shall free himself, if God abandon him? Who is it that freeth? "The grace of God, through Jesus Christ our Lord." [5] Are we then to despair? God forbid. For it goeth on, "He shall send out His Word, and melt them" (ver. 18). Let not then the snow despair, nor the mist, nor the crystal. For of the snow, as of wool, a garment is being made.

That mist findeth safety in repentance: for, "whom He predestinated, them He also called." But even though they be the very hardest among the predestinated, though they have been for a long time hardening, and are become crystal, they will not be hard to the mercy of God. "He shall send out His Word, and melt them." What is "melt"? Understand not "melt" in an ill sense: it meaneth, He shall liquefy, He shall thaw them. For they are hard through pride. Rightly is pride called also dulness: for whatever is dull, is also cold. . . . Despair not even of the crystal. Hear a saying of the crystal. "Who before was a blasphemer, and a persecutor, and injurious." [6] But wherefore doth God melt the crystal? That the snow despair not of itself. For he saith, "For this cause I obtained mercy, that in me first Jesus Christ might show forth all long-suffering, for a pattern to them that hereafter should believe on Him unto eternal life." [7] God then calleth unto the Gentiles, "Be melted, O crystal; come, ye snows." "His Spirit shall blow, and the waters shall flow." Lo, the "crystal" and the "snows" are melted, they turn into water, "let them that thirst, come and drink." [8] Saul, hard as crystal, persecuted Stephen unto death; Paul, now in the living water,[9] calleth the Gentiles to the Fount. . . .

28. "Announcing His Word unto Jacob, His Righteousnesses and Judgments unto Israel" (ver. 19). What "Righteousnesses," what "Judgments"? Because whatever mankind had suffered here before, when it was "snow" and "mist" and "crystal," it suffered for the deserts of its pride and uplifting against God. Let us go back to the origin of our fall, and see that most truly is it sung in the Psalm, "Before I was troubled I went wrong." [10] But he who says, "Before I was troubled I went wrong," saith also, "It is good for me that Thou hast humbled me, that I may learn Thy Righteousnesses." [11] These righteousnesses Jacob learnt from God, who made him to wrestle with an Angel; under the guise of which Angel, God Himself wrestled with him. He held Him, he exerted violence to hold Him, he prevailed to hold Him: He caused Himself to be held, in mercy, not in weakness. Jacob therefore wrestled, and prevailed: he held Him, and when he seemed to have conquered Him, asked to be blessed of Him.[12] How did he understand with Whom he had wrestled, Whom he had held? Wherefore did he wrestle violently, and hold Him? Because "the kingdom of heaven suffereth violence, and the violent take it by force." [13] Wherefore then did he wrestle? Because it is with toil. Wherefore do we with

---

[1] Rom. xii. 5.   [2] 1 Cor. x. 17.   [3] Philip. iii. 5, 6.
[4] Acts xxii. 20.   [5] Rom. vii. 24, 25.

[6] 1 Tim. i. 13.   [7] 1 Tim. i. 16.   [8] John vii. 37.
[9] John iv. 14.   [10] Ps. cxix. 67.   [11] Ps. cxix. 71.
[12] Gen. xxxii. 24, etc.   [13] Matt. xi. 12.

difficulty hold, what we so easily lose? Lest, easily getting back what we have lost, we learn to lose that which we hold. Let man have toil to hold: he will hold firmly, what he has only held after toil. These His judgments therefore God manifested to Jacob and Israel. . . .

29. "He hath not done so to the whole race" (ver. 20). Let none deceive you: it is not announced to any nation, this judgment of God; namely, how the righteous and the unrighteous suffer, how all suffer for their deserts, how the righteous themselves are freed by the grace of God, not in their own merits. This is not announced to the whole race, but only to Jacob, only to Israel. What then do we, if He hath not announced it to the whole race, but only to Jacob, only to Israel? Where will we be? In Jacob. "He hath not manifested His judgments to them." To whom? To all nations. How then are the "snows" called, when the crystal is melted? How are the nations called, now Paul is justified? How, save to be in Jacob? The wild olive is cut off from its stock, to be grafted into the olive: now they belong to the olive, no longer ought they to be called nations,[1] but one nation in Christ, the nation of Jacob, the nation of Israel . . . What is Israel? "Seeing God." Where shall he see God? In peace. What peace? The peace of Jerusalem; for, saith he, "He hath set peace for thy borders." There shall we praise: there shall we all be one, in One, unto One: for then, though many, we shall not be scattered.

PSALM CXLVIII.[2]

1. The subject of our meditation in this present life should be the praises of God; for the everlasting exaltation of our life hereafter will be the praise of God, and none can become fit for the life hereafter, who hath not practised himself for it now. So then now we praise God, but we pray to Him too. Our praise is marked by joy, our prayer by groans. . . . On account of these two seasons, one, that which now is in the temptations and tribulations of this life, the other, that which is to be hereafter in everlasting rest and exultation; we have established also the celebration of two seasons, that before Easter and that after Easter. That which is before Easter signifieth tribulation, in which we now are; that which we are now keeping after Easter, signifieth the bliss in which we shall hereafter be. The celebration then which we keep before Easter is what we do now: by that which we keep after Easter we signify what as yet we have not. Therefore we employ that time in fastings and prayer, this present time we spend in praises, and relax our fast. This is the Halle-

luia which we sing, which, as you know, meaneth (in Latin), Praise ye the Lord. Therefore that period is before the Lord's Resurrection, this, after His Resurrection: by which time is signified the future hope which as yet we have not: for what we represent after the Lord's Resurrection, we shall have after our own. For in our Head both are figured, both are set forth. The Baptism of the Lord setteth forth to us this present life of trial, for in it we must toil, be harassed, and, at last, die; but the Resurrection and Glorification of the Lord setteth forth to us the life which we are to have hereafter, when He shall come to recompense due rewards, evil to the evil, good to the good. And now indeed all the evil men sing with us, Halleluia; but, if they persevere in their wickedness, they may utter with their lips the song of our life hereafter; but the life itself, which will then be in the reality which now is typified, they cannot obtain, because they would not practise it before it came, and lay hold on what was to come.

2. "Halleluia." "Praise the Lord," thou sayest to thy neighbour, he to thee: when all are exhorting each other, all are doing what they exhort others to do. But praise with your whole selves: that is, let not your tongue and voice alone praise God, but your conscience also, your life, your deeds. For now, when we are gathered together in the Church, we praise: when we go forth each to his own business, we seem to cease to praise God. Let a man not cease to live well, and then he ever praiseth God. . . . It is impossible for a man's acts to be evil, whose thoughts are good. For acts issue from thought: nor can a man do anything or move his limbs to do aught, unless the bidding of his thought precede: just as in all things which ye see done throughout the provinces, whatsoever the Emperor biddeth goeth forth from the inner part of his palace throughout the whole Roman Empire.[3] How great commotion is caused at one bidding by the Emperor as he sits in his palace! He but moveth his lips, when he speaketh: the whole province is moved, when what he speaketh is being executed. So in each single man too, the Emperor is within, his seat is in the heart. If he be good and biddeth good things, good things are done: if he be bad and biddeth evil things, evil things are done. When Christ sitteth there, what can He bid, but what is good? When the devil is the occupant, what can he bid, but evil? But God hath willed that it should be in thy choice for whom thou wilt prepare room, for God, or for the devil: when thou hast prepared it, he who is occupant will also rule. Therefore, brethren, attend not only to the sound; when ye praise God, praise with

---

[1] *Gentes.*   [2] Lat. CXLVIII.   Sermon to the people.

[3] [A striking illustration of (the Christmas morning Lesson, Anglican) Luke ii. 1. — C.]

your whole selves : let your voice, your life, your deeds, all sing.

3. "Praise ye the Lord from heaven" (ver. 1). As though he had found things in heaven holding their peace in the praise of the Lord, he exhorteth them to arise and praise. Never have things in heaven held their peace in the praises of their Creator, never have things on earth ceased to praise God. But it is manifest that there are certain things which have breath to praise God in that disposition wherein God pleaseth them. For no one praiseth aught, save what pleaseth him. And there are other things which have not breath of life and understanding to praise God, but yet, because they also are good, and duly arranged in their proper order, and form part of the beauty of the universe, which God created, though they themselves with voice and heart praise not God, yet when they are considered by those who have understanding, God is praised in them ; and, as God is praised in them, they themselves too in a manner praise God.[1] . . .

4. "Praise ye the Lord from heaven : praise Him in the high places."[2] First he saith, "from heaven," then from earth ; for it is God that is praised, who made heaven and earth. All in heaven is calm and peaceful ; there is ever joy, no death, no sickness, no vexation ; there the blessed ever praise God ; but we are still below : yet, when we think how God is praised there, let us have our heart there, and let us not hear to no purpose, "Lift up your hearts." Let us lift up our heart above, that it become not corrupted on earth : for we take pleasure in what the Angels do there. We do it now in hope : hereafter we shall in reality, when we have come thither. "Praise Him" then "in the high places."

5. "Praise Him, all ye angels of His, praise Him, all His powers" (ver. 2). "Praise Him, sun and moon ; praise Him, all ye stars and light" (ver. 3). "Praise Him, ye heaven of heavens, and waters that are above the heavens" (ver. 4). "Let them praise the Name of the Lord" (ver. 5). When can he unfold all in his enumeration? Yet he hath in a manner touched upon them all summarily, and included all things in heaven praising their Creator. And as though it were said to him, "Why do they praise Him? what hath He conferred on them, that they should praise Him?" he goeth on, "for He spake, and they were made ; He commanded, and they were created." No wonder if the works praise the Worker, no wonder if the things that are made praise the Maker, no wonder if

creation praise its Creator. In this Christ also is mentioned, though we seem not to have heard His Name. . . . By what were they made? By the Word?[3] How doth he show in this Psalm, that all things were made by the Word? "He spake, and they were made ; He commanded, and they were created." No one speaketh, no one commandeth, save by word.

6. "He hath established them for the age, and for age upon age" (ver. 6). All things in heaven, all things above, all powers and angels, a certain city on high, good, holy, blessed ; from whence because we are wanderers, we are wretched ; whither because we are to return, we are blessed in hope ; whither when we shall have returned, we shall be blessed indeed ; "He hath given them a law which shall not pass away." What sort of command, think ye, have things in heaven and the holy angels received? What sort of command hath God given them? What, but that they praise Him? Blessed are they whose business is to praise God ! They plough not, they sow not, they grind not, they cook not ; for these are works of necessity, and there is no necessity there. They steal not, they plunder not, they commit no adultery ; for these are works of iniquity, and there is no iniquity there. They break not bread for the hungry, they clothe not the naked, they take not in the stranger, they visit not the sick, they set not at one the contentious, they bury not the dead ; for these are works of mercy, and there there is no misery, for mercy to be shown to. O blessed they ! Think we that we too shall be like this? Ah ! let us sigh, let us groan in sighing. And what are we, that we should be there? mortal, outcast, abject, earth and ashes ! But He, who hath promised, is almighty. . . .

7. Let him then turn himself to things on earth too, since he hath already spoken the praises of things in heaven. "Praise ye the Lord from the earth" (ver. 7). For wherewith began he before? "Praise ye the Lord from heaven : " and he went through things in heaven : now hear of things on earth. "Dragons and all abysses." "Abysses" are depths of water : all the seas, and this atmosphere of clouds, pertain to the "abyss." Where there are clouds, where there are storms, where there is rain, lightning, thunder, hail, snow, and all that God willeth should be done above the earth, by this moist and misty atmosphere, all this he hath mentioned under the name of earth, because it is very changeable and mortal ; unless ye think that it raineth from above the stars.[4] All these things happen here, close to the earth. Sometimes even men are on the tops of mountains, and see the clouds beneath them, and often it raineth :

---

[1] [*Homo Naturæ minister et interpres.* — *Bacon.* The "Hymn of the Three Children" was in his mind: it became very early one of the hymns of the Church. — C.]
[2] [*In excelsis.* — C.]

[3] John i. 1, 2.   [4] [See A. N. F. vol. vii. p. 57. — C.]

and all commotions which arise from the disturbance of the atmosphere, those who watch carefully see that they happen here, in this lower part of the universe. . . . Thou seest then what kind all these things are, changeable, troublous, fearful, corruptible : yet they have their place, they have their rank, they too in their degree fill up the beauty of the universe, and so they praise the Lord. He turns then to them, as though He would exhort them too, or us, that by considering them we may praise the Lord. "Dragons" live about the water, come out from caverns, fly through the air; the air is set in motion by them : "dragons" are a huge kind of living creatures, greater there are not upon the earth. Therefore with them he beginneth, "Dragons and all abysses." There are caves of hidden waters, whence springs and streams come forth : some come forth to flow over the earth, some flow secretly beneath; and all this kind, all this damp nature of waters, together with the sea and this lower air, are called abyss, or "abysses," where dragons live and praise God. What? Think we that the dragons form choirs, and praise God? Far from it. But do ye, when ye consider the dragons, regard the Maker of the dragon, the Creator of the dragon : then, when ye admire the dragons, and say, "Great is the Lord who made these," then the dragons praise God by your voices.

8. "Fire, hail, snow, ice, wind of storms, which do His word" (ver. 8). Wherefore added he here, "which do His word"? Many foolish men, unable to contemplate and discern creation, in its several places and rank, performing its movements at the nod and commandment of God, think that God doth indeed rule all things above, but things below He despiseth, casteth aside, abandoneth, so that He neither careth for them, nor guideth, nor ruleth them; but that they are ruled by chance, how they can, as they can : and they are influenced by what they say sometimes to one another : *e.g.* "If it were God that gave rain, would He rain into the sea? What sort of Providence," they say, "is this? Getulia is thirsty, and it rains into the sea." They think that they handle the matter cleverly. One should say to them, "Getulia does at all events thirst, thou dost not even thirst." For good were it for thee to say to God, "My soul hath thirsted for Thee."[1] For he that thus argueth is already satisfied; he thinketh himself learned, he is not willing to learn, therefore he thirsteth not. For if he thirsted, he would be willing to learn, and he would find that everything happeneth upon earth by God's Providence, and he would wonder at the arrangement of even the limbs of a flea. Attend, beloved. Who hath arranged the limbs

of a flea and a gnat, that they should have their proper order, life, motion? Consider one little creature, even the very smallest, whatever thou wilt. If thou considerest the order of its limbs, and the animation of life whereby it moveth; how doth it shun death, love life, seek pleasures, avoid pain, exert divers senses, vigorously use movements suitable to itself! Who gave its sting to the gnat, for it to suck blood with? How narrow is the pipe whereby it sucketh! Who arranged all this? who made all this? Thou art amazed at the smallest things; praise Him that is great. Hold then this, my brethren, let none shake you from your faith or from sound doctrine. He who made the Angel in heaven, the Same also made the worm upon earth : the Angel in heaven to dwell in heaven, the worm upon earth to abide on earth. He made not the Angel to creep in the mud, nor the worm to move in heaven. He hath assigned dwellers to their different abodes; incorruption He assigned to incorruptible abodes, corruptible things to corruptible abodes. Observe the whole, praise the whole. He then who ordered the limbs of the worm, doth He not govern the clouds? And wherefore raineth He into the sea? As though there are not in the sea things which are nourished by rain; as though He made not fishes therein, as though He made not living creatures therein. Observe how the fishes run to sweet water. And wherefore, saith he, doth He give rain to the fishes, and sometimes giveth not rain to me? That thou mayest consider that thou art in a desert region, and in a pilgrimage of life; that so this present life may grow bitter to thee, that thou mayest long for the life to come : or else that thou mayest be scourged, punished, amended. And how well doth He assign their properties to regions. Behold, since we have spoken of Getulia, He raineth here nearly every year, and giveth corn every year; here the corn cannot be kept, it soon rotteth, because it is given every year; there, because it is given seldom, both much is given, and it can be kept for long. But dost thou perchance think that God there deserteth man, or that they do not there after their own manner of rejoicing both praise and glorify God? Take a Getulian from his country, and set him amid our pleasant trees; he will wish to flee away, and return to his bare Getulia. To all places then, regions, seasons, God hath assigned and arranged what fits them. Who could unfold it? Yet they who have eyes see many things therein : when seen, they please; pleasing, they are praised; not they really, but He who made them; thus shall all things praise God.

9. It was in thought of this that the spirit of the Prophet added the words, "which do His word." Think not then that these things are moved by chance, which in every motion of theirs

---

[1] Ps. cxliii. 6; Ps. lxiii. 1; Matt. v. 6.

obey God. Whither God willeth, thither the fire spreads, thither the cloud hurries, whether it carry in it rain, or snow, or hail. And wherefore doth the lightning sometimes strike the mountain, yet strikes not the robber? . . . Perhaps He yet seeketh the robber's conversion, and therefore is the mountain which feareth not smitten, that the man who feareth may be changed. Thou also sometimes, when maintaining discipline, smitest the ground to terrify a child. Sometimes too He smiteth a man, whom He will. But thou sayest to me, Behold, He smiteth the more innocent, and passeth over the more guilty. Wonder not; death, whencesoever it come, is good to the good man. And whence dost thou know what punishment is reserved in secret for that more guilty man, if he be unwilling to be converted? Would not they rather be scorched by lightning, to whom it shall be said in the end, "Depart into everlasting fire"?[1] The needful thing is, that thou be guileless. Why so? Is it an evil thing to die by shipwreck, and a good thing to die by fever? Whether he die in this way or in that, ask what sort of man he is who dieth; ask whither he will go after death, not how he is to depart from life. . . . Whatever then happeneth here contrary to our wish, thou wilt know that it happeneth not, save by the will of God, by His providence, by His ordering, by His nod, by His laws: and if we understand not why anything is done, let us grant to His providence that it is not done without reason: so shall we not be blasphemers. For when we begin to argue concerning the works of God, "why is this?" "why is that?" and, "He ought not to have done this," "He did this ill;" where is the praise of God? Thou hast lost thy Halleluia. Regard all things in such wise as to please God and praise the Creator. For if thou wert to happen to enter the workshop of a smith, thou wouldest not dare to find fault with his bellows, his anvils, his hammers. But take an ignorant man, who knows not for what purpose each thing is, and he findeth fault with all. But if he have not the skill of the workman, and have but the reasoning power of a man, what saith he to himself? Not without reason are the bellows placed here: the workman knoweth wherefore, though I know not. In the shop he dareth not to find fault with the smith, yet in the universe he dareth to find fault with God. Therefore just as "fire, hail, snow, ice, wind of storms, which do His word," so all things in nature, which seem to foolish persons to be made at random, simply "do His word," because they are not made save by His command.

10. Then he mentioneth, that they may praise the Lord, "mountains and hills, fruitful trees and all cedars" (ver. 9): "beasts and all cattle, creeping things, and winged fowls" (ver. 10). Then he goeth to men; "kings of the earth and all people, princes and all judges of the earth" (ver. 11): "young men and maidens, old men and young, let them praise the Name of the Lord" (ver. 12). Ended is the praise from heaven, ended is the praise from earth. "For His Name only is exalted" (ver. 13). Let no man seek to exalt his own name. Wilt thou be exalted? Subject thyself to Him who cannot be humbled. "His confession is in earth and heaven" (ver. 14). What is "His confession"? Is it the confession wherewith He confesseth? No, but that whereby all things confess Him, all things cry aloud: the beauty of all things is in a manner their voice, whereby they praise God. The heaven crieth out to God, "Thou madest me, not I myself." Earth crieth out, "Thou createdst me, not I myself." How do they cry out? When thou regardest them, and findest this out, they cry out by thy voice, they cry out by thy regard. Regard the heavens, it is beautiful: observe the earth, it is beautiful: both together are very beautiful. He made them, He ruleth them, by His nod they are swayed, He ordereth their seasons, He reneweth their movements, by Himself He reneweth them. All these things then praise Him, whether in stillness or in motion, whether from earth below or from heaven above, whether in their old state or in their renewal. When thou seest all these things, and rejoicest, and art lifted up to the Maker, and gazest on "His invisible things understood by the things which are made,"[2] "His confession is in earth and heaven:" that is, thou confesseth to Him from things on earth, thou confesseth to Him from things in heaven. And since He made all things, and nought is better than He, whatsoever He made is less than He, and whatsoever in these things pleaseth thee, is less than He. Let not then what He hath made so please thee, as to withdraw thee from Him who made: if thou lovest what He made, love much more Him who made. If the things which He hath made are beautiful, how much more beautiful is He who made them. "And He shall exalt the horn of His people." Behold what Haggai and Zachariah prophesied. Now the "horn of His people" is humble in afflictions, in tribulations, in temptations, in beating of the breast; when will He "exalt the horn of His people"? When the Lord hath come, and our Sun is risen, not the sun which is seen with the eye, and "riseth upon the good and the evil,"[3] but That whereof is said, To you that hear God, "the Sun of Righteousness shall rise, and healing in

---

[1] Matt. xxv. 41. [2] Rom. i. 20. [3] Matt. v. 45.

His wings;" [1] and of whom the proud and wicked shall hereafter say, "The light of righteousness hath not shined unto us, and the sun of righteousness rose not upon us." [2] This shall be our summer. Now during the winter weather the fruits appear not on the stock; thou observest, so to say, dead trees during the winter. He who cannot see truly, thinketh the vine dead; perhaps there is one near it which is really dead; both are alike during winter; the one is alive, the other is dead, but both the life and death are hidden: summer advanceth; then the life of the one shineth brightly, the death of the other is manifested: the splendour of leaves, the abundance of fruit, cometh forth, the vine is clothed in outward appearance from what it hath in its stock. Therefore, brethren, now we are the same as other men: just as they are born, eat, drink, are clothed, pass their life, so also do the saints. Sometimes the very truth deceiveth men, and they say, "Lo, he hath begun to be a Christian: hath he lost his headache?" or, "because he is a Christian, what gaineth he from me?" O dead vine, thou observest near thee a vine that is bare indeed in winter, yet not dead. Summer will come, the Lord will come, our Splendour, that was hidden in the stock, and then "He shall exalt the horn of His people," after the captivity wherein we live in this mortal life. . . .

11. "An hymn to all His Saints." Know ye what an hymn is? It is a song with praise of God. If thou praisest God and singest not, thou utterest no hymn: if thou singest and praisest not God, thou utterest no hymn: if thou praisest aught else, which pertaineth not to the praise of God, although thou singest and praisest, thou utterest no hymn. An hymn then containeth these three things, song, and praise, and that of God. Praise then of God in song is called an hymn. What then meaneth, "An hymn to all His Saints"? Let His Saints receive an hymn: let His Saints utter an hymn: for this is what they are to receive in the end, an everlasting hymn. . . .

PSALM CXLIX. [3]

1. Let us praise the Lord both in voice, and in understanding, and in good works; and, as this Psalm exhorteth, let us sing unto Him a new song. It beginneth: "Sing ye to the Lord a new song. His praise is in the Church of the Saints" (ver. 1). The old man hath an old song, the new man a new song. The Old Testament is an old song, the New Testament a new song. In the Old Testament are temporal and earthly promises. Whoso loveth earthly

things singeth an old song: let him that desireth to sing a new song, love the things of eternity. Love itself is new and eternal; therefore is it ever new, because it never groweth old. . . . And this song is of peace, this song is of charity. Whoso severeth himself from the union of the saints, singeth not a new song; for he hath followed old strife, not new charity. In new charity what is there? Peace, the bond of an holy society, a spiritual union, a building of living stones. Where is this? Not in one place, but throughout the whole world. This is said in another Psalm, "Sing unto the Lord, all the earth." [4] From this is understood, that he who singeth not with the whole earth, singeth an old song, whatever words proceed out of his mouth. . . . We have already said, brethren, that all the earth singeth a new song. He who singeth not with the whole earth a new song, let him sing what he will, let his tongue sound forth Halleluia, let him utter it all day and all night, my ears are not so much bent to hear the voice of the singer, but I seek the deeds of the doer. For I ask, and say, "What is it that thou singest?" He answereth, "Halleluia." What is "Halleluia"? "Praise ye the Lord." Come, let us praise the Lord together. If thou praisest the Lord, and I praise the Lord, why are we at variance? Charity praiseth the Lord, discord blasphemeth the Lord." . . .

2. The field of the Lord is the world, not Africa. It is not with the Lord's field, as it is without these fields of ours, where Getulia bears sixty or an hundred fold, Numidia only ten fold: everywhere fruit is borne to Him, both an hundred fold, and sixty fold, and thirty fold: only do thou choose what thou wilt be, if thou thinkest to belong to the Lord's Cross. "The Church" then "of the saints" is the Catholic Church. The Church of the saints is not the Church of heretics. The Church of the saints is that which God first prefigured before it was seen, and then set forth that it might be seen. The Church of the saints was heretofore in writings, now it is in nations: the Church of the saints was heretofore only read of, now it is both read of and seen. When it was only read of, it was believed; now it is seen, and is spoken against. His praise is in the "children of the kingdom," that is, "the Church of the saints."

3. "Let Israel rejoice in Him who made Him" (ver. 2). What is, "Israel"? "Seeing God." He who seeth God, rejoiceth in Him by whom he was made. What is it then, brethren? we have said that we belong to the Church of the saints: do we already see God? and how are we Israel, if we see not? There is one

---

[1] Mal. iv. 2.   [2] Wisd. v. 6
[3] Lat. CXLIX. Sermon to the people.   [4] Ps. xcvi. 1.

kind of sight belonging to this present time; there will be another belonging to the time hereafter: the sight which now is, is by faith; the sight which is to be will be in reality. If we believe, we see; if we love, we see: see what? God. Ask John: "God is love;"[1] let us bless His holy Name, and rejoice in God by rejoicing in love. Whoso hath love, why send we him afar to see God? Let him regard his own conscience, and there he seeth God. . . . "And let the sons of Sion exult in their King." The sons of the Church are Israel. For Sion indeed was one city, which fell: amid its ruins certain saints dwelt after the flesh: but the true Sion, the true Jerusalem (for Sion and Jerusalem are one), is "eternal in the heavens,"[2] and is "our mother."[3] She it is that hath given us birth, she is the Church of the saints, she hath nourished us, she, who is in part a pilgrim, in part abiding in the heavens. In the part which abideth in heaven is the bliss of angels, in the part which wandereth in this world is the hope of the righteous. Of the former is said, "Glory to God in the highest;" of the latter, "and on earth peace to men of good will."[4] Let those then who, being in this life, groan, and long for their country, run by love, not by bodily feet; let them seek not ships but wings, let them lay hold on the two wings of love. What are the two wings of love? The love of God, and of our neighbour. For now we are pilgrims, we sigh, we groan. There has come to us a letter from our country: we read it to you. "And the sons of Sion shall exult in their King." The Son of God, who made us, was made one of us: and He rules us as our King, because He is our Creator, who made us. But He by whom we were made is the same as He by whom we are ruled, and we are Christians because He is Christ. He is called Christ from Chrism, that is, Anointing. . . . Give to the Priest somewhat to offer. What could man find which he could give as a clean victim? What victim? what clean thing can a sinner offer? O unrighteous, O sinful man, whatever thou offerest is unclean, and somewhat that is clean must be offered for thee. . . . Let then the Priest that is clean offer Himself, and cleanse thee. This is what Christ did. He found in man nothing clean for Him to offer for man: He offered Himself as a clean Victim. Happy Victim, true Victim, spotless Offering. He offered not then what we gave Him; yea rather, He offered what He took of us, and offered it clean. For of us He took flesh, and this He offered. But where took He it? In the womb of the Virgin Mary, that He might offer it clean for us unclean. He

is our King, He is our Priest, in Him let us rejoice.

4. "Let them praise His Name in chorus" (ver. 3). What meaneth "chorus"? Many know what a "chorus" is: nay, as we are speaking in a town, almost all know. A "chorus" is the union of singers. If we sing "in chorus," let us sing in concord. If any one's voice is out of harmony in a chorus of singers, it offendeth the ear, and throweth the chorus into confusion. If the voice of one echoing discordantly troubleth the harmony of them who sing, how doth the discord of heresy throw into confusion the harmony of them who praise. The whole world is now the chorus of Christ. The chorus of Christ soundeth harmoniously from east to west.[5] "Let them sing a psalm unto Him with timbrel and psaltery." Wherefore taketh he to him the "timbrel and psaltery"? That not the voice alone may praise, but the works too. When timbrel and psaltery are taken, the hands harmonize with the voice. So too do thou, whensoever thou singest "Halleluia," deal forth thy bread to the hungry, clothe the naked, take in the stranger: then doth not only thy voice sound, but thy hand soundeth in harmony with it, for thy deeds agree with thy words. Thou hast taken to thee an instrument, and thy fingers agree with thy tongue. Nor must we keep back the mystical meaning of the "timbrel and psaltery." On the timbrel leather is stretched, on the psaltery gut is stretched; on either instrument the flesh is crucified. How well did he "sing a psalm on timbrel and psaltery," who said, "the world is crucified unto me, and I unto the world"?[6] This psaltery or timbrel He wishes thee to take up, who loveth a new song, who teacheth thee, saying to thee, "Whosoever willeth to be My disciple, let him deny himself, and take up his cross, and follow Me."[7] Let him not set down his psaltery, let him not set down his timbrel, let him stretch himself out on the wood, and be dried from the lust of the flesh. The more the strings are stretched, the more sharply do they sound. The Apostle Paul then, in order that his psaltery might sound sharply, what said he? "Stretching forth unto those things which are before," etc.[8] He stretched himself: Christ touched him; and the sweetness of truth sounded.

5. "For the Lord hath dealt kindly among His people" (ver. 4). What dealing so kindly, as to die for the ungodly? What dealing so kindly, as with righteous Blood to blot out the handwriting against the sinner? What dealing so kindly, as to say, "I regard not what ye were, be ye now what ye were not"? He dealeth kindly in converting him that was turned away, in aiding

---

[1] 1 John iv. 16. [2] 2 Cor. v. 1.
[3] Gal. iv. 26. [4] Luke ii. 14.
[5] Ps. cxiii. 3. [6] Gal. vi. 14.
[7] Matt. xvi. 24. [8] Philip. iii. 13

him that is fighting, in crowning the conqueror. "And the meek He shall lift up in salvation." For the proud too are lifted up, but not in salvation : the meek are lifted in salvation, the proud in death : that is, the proud lift up themselves, and God humbleth them : the meek humble themselves, and God lifteth them up.

6. "The saints shall exult in glory" (ver. 5). I would say somewhat important about the glory of the saints. For there is no one who loveth not glory. But the glory of fools, popular glory as it is called, hath snares to deceive, so that a man, influenced by the praises of vain men, shall be willing to live in such fashion as to be spoken of by men, whosoever they be, in whatsoever way. Hence it is that men, rendered mad, and puffed up with pride, empty within, without swollen, are willing ever to ruin their fortunes by bestowing them on stage-players, actors, men who fight with wild beasts, charioteers. What sums they give, what sums they spend ! They lavish the powers not only of their patrimony, but of their minds too. They scorn the poor, because the people shouteth not that the poor should be given to, but the people do shout that the fighter with wild beasts be given to. When then no shout is raised to them, they refuse to spend ; when madmen shout to them, they are mad too : nay, all are mad, both performer, and spectator, and the giver. This mad glory is blamed by the Lord, is offensive in the eyes of the Almighty. . . . Thou choosest to clothe the fighter with wild beasts, who may be beaten, and make thee blush : Christ is never conquered ; He hath conquered the devil, He hath conquered for thee, and to thee, and in thee ; such a conqueror as this thou choosest not to clothe. Wherefore? Because there is less shouting, less madness about it. They then who delight in such glory, have an empty conscience. Just as they drain their chests, to send garments as presents, so do they empty their conscience, so as to have nothing precious therein.

7. But the saints who "exult in glory," no need is there for us to say how they exult : just hear the verse of the Psalm which followeth : "The saints shall exult in glory, they shall rejoice in their beds : " not in theatres, or amphitheatres, or circuses, or follies, or market places, but "in their chambers." What is, "in their chambers"? In their hearts.[1] Hear the Apostle Paul exulting in his closet : "For this is our glory, the testimony of our conscience."[2] On the other hand, there is reason to fear lest any be pleasing to himself, and so seem to be proud, and boast of his conscience. For every one ought to exult with fear, for that wherein he exulteth is God's gift, not his own desert. For there be many that please themselves, and think themselves righteous ; and there is another passage which goeth against them, which saith, "Who shall boast that he hath a clean heart, and that he is pure from sin ? "[3] There is then, so to speak, a limit to glorying in our conscience, namely, to know that thy faith is sincere, thy hope sure, thy love without dissimulation. "The exultations of God are in their mouths" (ver. 6). In such wise shall they "rejoice in their closets," as not to attribute to themselves that they are good, but praise Him from whom they have what they are, by whom they are called to attain to what they are not, and from whom they hope for perfection, to whom they give thanks, because He hath begun.

8. "And swords[4] sharpened on both sides in their hands." This sort of weapon contains a great mystical meaning, in that it is sharp on both sides. By "swords sharpened on both sides," we understand the Word of the Lord :[5] it is one sword, but therefore are they called many, because there are many mouths and many tongues of the saints. How is it two edged? It speaks of things temporal, it speaks also of things eternal. In both cases it proveth what it saith, and him whom it strikes, it severeth from the world. Is not this the sword whereof the Lord said, "I am not come to send peace upon earth, but a sword"?[6] Observe how He came to divide, how He came to sever. He divideth the saints, He divideth the ungodly, He severeth from thee that which hindereth thee. The son willeth to serve God, the father willeth not : the sword cometh, the Word of God cometh, and severeth the son from the father. . . . Wherefore then is it in their hands, not in their tongues? "And swords," it saith, "sharpened on both sides in their hands." By "in their hands," he meaneth in power. They received then the word of God in power, to speak where they would, to whom they would, neither to fear power, nor to despise poverty. For they had in their hands a sword ; where they would they brandished it, handled it, smote with it : and all this was in the power of the preachers. For if the Word be not in their hands, why is it written, "The Word of the Lord was put in the hand of the Prophet Haggai"?[7] Surely, brethren, God set not His Word in His fingers. What is meant by, "was put in his hand"? It was put into his power to preach the Word of the

---

[1] [There is a play here on the word *cubile*, which was used of a box in the theatre. *Cubile* oftens means a small apartment, and this is our author's idea. Matt. vi. 6. Elsewhere he speaks of the "closet" as the heart. I vary the text accordingly. — C.]

[2] 2 Cor. i. 12.

[3] Prov. xx. 9.

[4] *Frameæ*. [He says: "That is called a sword which is commonly called *spata*. For there are swords sharpened only on one side, which are called *machæræ*. But these *frameæ* are also called *romphææ* and *spatæ*." — C.]

[5] Heb. iv. 12.   [6] Matt. x. 34.   [7] Hag. i. 1, marg.

Lord. Lastly, we can understand these "hands" in another way also. For they who spake had the word of God in their tongues, they who wrote, in their hands.

9. Now, brethren, ye see the saints armed: observe the slaughter, observe their glorious battles. For if there be a commander, there must be soldiers; if soldiers, an enemy; if a warfare, a victory. What have these done who had in their hands swords sharpened on both sides? "To do vengeance on the nations." See whether vengeance have not been done on the nations. Daily is it done: we do it ourselves by speaking. Observe how the nations of Babylon are slain. She is repaid twofold: for so is it written of her, "repay her double for what she hath done." [1] How is she repaid double? The saints wage war, they draw their "swords twice sharpened;" thence come defeats, slaughters, severances: how is she repaid double? When she had power to persecute the Christians, she slew the flesh indeed, but she crushed not God: now she is repaid double, for the Pagans are extinguished and the idols are broken. . . . And lest thou shouldest think that men are really smitten with the sword, blood really shed, wounds made in the flesh, he goeth on and explaineth, "upbraidings among the peoples." What is "upbraidings"? Reproof. Let the "sword twice sharpened" go forth from you, delay not. Say to thy friend, if yet thou hast one [2] left to whom to say it, "What kind of man art thou, who hast abandoned Him by whom thou wast made, and worshippest what He made? Better is the Workman, than that which He worketh." When he beginneth to blush, when he beginneth to feel compunction, thou hast made a wound with thy sword, it hath reached the heart, he is about to die, that he may live.

10. "That they may bind their kings in fetters, and their nobles in bonds of iron" (ver. 8). "To execute upon them the judgment written" (ver. 9). The kings of the Gentiles are to be bound in fetters, "and their nobles in fetters," and that "of iron.". . . For these verses which we are beginning to explain are obscure. For for this purpose God willed to set down some of His verses obscurely, not that anything new should be dug out of them, but that what was already well known, might be made new by being obscurely set forth. We know that kings have been made Christians; we know that the nobles of the Gentiles have been made Christians. They are being made so at this day; they have been, they shall be; the "swords twice sharpened" are not idle in the hands of the saints. How then do we understand their being bound in fet-

ters and chains of iron? Ye know, beloved and learned brethren (learned I call you, for ye have been nourished in the Church, and are accustomed to hear God's Word read), [3] that "God hath chosen the weak things of the world to confound the strong, and the foolish things of the world hath God chosen to confound the wise, and things which are not, just as things which are, that the things which are may be brought to nought." [4] . . . It is said by the Lord, "If thou wilt be perfect, go sell all that thou hast, and give to the poor, and come, follow Me, and thou shalt have treasure in heaven." [5] Many of the nobles did this, but they ceased to be nobles of the Gentiles, they chose rather to be poor in this world, noble in Christ. But many retain their former nobility, retain their royal powers, and yet are Christians. These are, as it were, "in fetters and in bonds of iron." How so? they received fetters, to keep them from going to things unlawful, the "fetters of wisdom," [6] the fetters of the Word of God. Wherefore then are they bonds of iron and not bonds of gold? They are iron so long as they fear: let them love, and they shall be golden. Observe, beloved, what I say. Ye have heard just now the Apostle John, "There is no fear in love, but perfect love casteth out fear, because fear hath torment." [7] This is the bond of iron. And yet unless a man begin through fear to worship God, he will not attain to love. "The fear of the Lord is the beginning of wisdom." [8] The beginning then is bonds of iron, the end a collar of gold. For it is said of wisdom, "a collar of gold around thy neck." [9] . . . There cometh to us a man powerful in this world, his wife offendeth him, and perhaps hath desired another man's wife who is more beautiful, or another woman who is richer, he wisheth to put away the one he hath, yet he doeth it not. He heareth the words of the servant of God, he heareth the Prophet, he heareth the Apostle, and he doeth it not; he is told by one in whose hands is a "sword twice sharpened," "Thou shalt not do it: it is not lawful for thee: God alloweth thee not to put away thy wife, "save for the cause of fornication." [10] He heareth this, he feareth, and doeth it not. . . . Listen, young men; the bonds are of iron, seek not to set your feet within them; if ye do, ye shall be bound more tightly with fetters. Such fetters the hands of the Bishop make strong for you. Do not men who are thus fettered fly to the Church, and are here loosed? Men do fly hither, desiring to be rid of their wives: here they are more tightly bound: no man looseth these fetters. "What God joined together, let not man put asunder." [11] But these bonds are

---

[1] Rev. xviii. 6.   [2] [*i.e.*, a heathen one. — C.]

[3] [Noteworthy. — C.]   [4] 1 Cor. i. 26, etc.   [5] Matt. xix. 21.
[6] Ecclus. vi. 25.   [7] 1 John iv. 18.   [8] Ps. cxi. 10.
[9] Ecclus. vi. 24.   [10] Matt. v. 32.   [11] Matt. xix. 6.

hard. Who but knows it? This hardness the Apostles grieved at, and said, " If this be the case with a wife, it is not good to marry." [1] If the bonds be of iron, it is not good to set our feet within them. And the Lord said, " All men cannot receive this saying, but let him that can receive it, receive it." [2] " Art thou bound unto a wife? seek not to be freed," for thou art bound with bonds of iron. " Art thou free from a wife, seek not a wife ; " bind not thyself with bonds of iron.

11. " To do in them the judgment that is written." This is the judgment which the saints do throughout all nations. Wherefore "written"? Because these things were before written, and now are fulfilled. Behold now they are being done : erst they were read, and were not done. And he hath concluded thus, " this glory have all His saints." Throughout the whole world, throughout entire nations, this the saints do, thus are they glorified, thus do they " exalt God with their mouths," thus do they " rejoice in their beds," thus do they " exult in their glory," thus are they " lifted up in salvation," thus do they " sing a new song," thus in heart and voice and life they say Halleluia. Amen.

PSALM CL.[3]

1. Although the arrangement of the Psalms, which seems to me to contain the secret of a mighty mystery, hath not yet been revealed unto me, yet, by the fact that they in all amount to one hundred and fifty, they suggest somewhat even to us, who have not as yet pierced with the eye of our mind the depth of their entire arrangement, whereon we may without being over-bold, so far as God giveth, be able to speak. Firstly, the number fifteen, whereof it is a multiple ; this number fifteen, I say, signifieth the agreement of the two Testaments. For in the former is observed the Sabbath, which signifieth rest ; in the latter the Lord's Day, which signifieth resurrection. The Sabbath is the seventh day, but the Lord's Day, coming after the seventh, must needs be the eighth, and is also to be reckoned the first. For it is called the first day of the week,[4] and so from it are reckoned the second, third, fourth, and so on to the seventh day of the week, which is the Sabbath. But from Lord's Day to Lord's Day is eight days, wherein is declared the revelation of the New Testament, which in the Old was as it were veiled under earthly promises. Further, seven and eight make fifteen. Of the same number too are the Psalms which are called " of the steps," because that was the number of the steps of the Temple. Further too, the number fifty

in itself also containeth a great mystery.[5] For it consisteth of a week of weeks, with the addition of one as an eighth to complete the number of fifty. For seven times seven make forty-nine, whereto one is added to make fifty. And this number fifty is of so great meaning, that it was after the completion of that number of days from the Lord's Resurrection, that, on the fiftieth day exactly, the Holy Spirit came upon those who were gathered together in Christ. And this Holy Spirit is in Scripture especially spoken of by the number seven, whether in Isaiah or in the Apocalypse, where the seven Spirits of God are most directly mentioned, on account of the sevenfold operation of one and the self-same Spirit.[6] And this sevenfold operation is mentioned in Isaiah.[7] . . . Hence also the Holy Spirit is spoken of under the number seven. But this period of fifty the Lord divided into forty and ten : for on the fortieth day after His Resurrection He ascended into heaven, and then after ten days were completed He sent the Holy Spirit : under the number forty setting forth to us the period of temporal sojourn in this world. For the number four prevaileth in forty ; and the world and the year have each four parts ; and by the addition of the number ten, as a sort of reward added for the fulfilment of the law in good works, eternity itself is figured. This fifty the number one hundred and fifty containeth three times, as though it were multiplied by the Trinity. Wherefore for this reason too we make out that this number of the Psalm is not unsuitable.[8]

2. Now in that some have believed that the Psalms are divided into five books, they have been led by the fact, that so often at the end of Psalms are the words, " so be it, so be it." But when I endeavoured to make out the principle of this division, I was not able ; for neither are the five parts equal one to another, neither in quantity of contents, nor yet even in number of Psalms, so as for each to contain thirty. And if each book end with, " so be it, so be it," we may reasonably ask, why the fifth and last book hath not the same conclusion. We however, following the authority of canonical Scripture, where it is said, " For it is written in the book of Psalms," [9] know that there is but one book of Psalms. And I see indeed how this can be true,

---

[1] Matt. xix. 10.
[2] Matt. xix. 11, 12.
[3] Lat. CL.
[4] Una Sabbati.

[5] [Sea p. 181, note 12, *supra*. — C.]
[6] Rev. i. 20.   [7] Isa. xi. 2.
[8] [He adds: " For in the number of the fishes too which were caught in the nets which were let down after the Resurrection, by the adding of three to one hundred and fifty, we seem to have a kind of suggestion given us, into how many parts that number ought to be divided, namely, that it should contain three fifties. Though there is another account too of that number of fishes, one much more deep and pleasing, namely, that we arrive at that same number, by setting down seventeen in a column, and adding all the numbers from one to seventeen together. But in the number *ten* is signified the Law, in *seven*, Grace: for nought fulfilleth the Law save ' Love (Rom. v. 5) by the Holy Spirit,' who is set forth under the number *seven*." — C.]
[9] Acts i. 20.

and yet the other be true also, without contravening it. For it may be that there was some custom in Hebrew literature, whereby that is called one book which yet consists of more than one, just as of many churches one church consisteth, and of many heavens one heaven,[1] . . . and one land of many lands. For it is our everyday habit to say, "the globe[2] of the earth," and "the globe of the lands." And when it is said, "It is written in the book of Psalms," though the customary way of speaking is such that he seem to have wished to suggest that there is but one book, yet to this it may be answered, that the words mean "in a book of the Psalms," that is, "in any one of those five books." And this is in common language so unprecedented, or at least so rare, that we are only convinced that the twelve Prophets made one book, because we read in like manner, "As it is written in the book of the Prophets."[3] There are some too who call all the canonical Scriptures together one book,[4] because they agree in a very wondrous and divine unity. . . .

3. Whichever then of these is understood, this book, in its parts of fifty Psalms each, gives an answer important and very worthy of consideration. For it seems to me not without significance, that the fiftieth is of penitence, the hundredth of mercy and judgment, the hundred and fiftieth of the praise of God in His saints. For thus do we advance to an everlasting life of happiness, first by condemning our own sins, then by living aright, that, having condemned our ill life, and lived a good life, we may attain to everlasting life. Our predestination is not wrought in ourselves, but in secret with Him, in His foreknowledge.[5] But we are called by the preaching of repentance. We are justified in the calling of mercy and fear of judgment. He feareth not judgment, who hath previously attained salvation. Being called, we renounce the devil by repentance, that we may not continue under his yoke: being justified, we are healed by mercy, that we may not fear judgment: being glorified, we pass into everlasting life, where we praise God without end. . . . The verse wherewith this Psalm concludeth is the voice of life everlasting.

4. "Praise the Lord in His saints," that is, in those whom He hath glorified: "praise Him in the firmament of His power" (ver. 1). "Praise Him in His deeds of strength;" or, as others have explained it, "in His deeds of power: praise Him according to the multitude of His greatness" (ver. 2). All these His saints are ; as

the Apostle saith, "But we may be the righteousness of God in Him."[6] If then they be the righteousness of God, which He hath wrought in them, why are they not also the strength of Christ which He hath wrought in them, that they should rise again from the dead? For in Christ's resurrection, "strength" is especially set forth to us, for in His Passion was weakness, as the Apostle saith.[7] And well doth it say, "the firmament of His power." For it is the "firmament of His power" that He "dieth no more, death hath no more dominion over Him."[8] Why should not they also be called "the works of" God's "strength," which He hath done in them : yea rather, they themselves are the works of His strength ; just as it is said, "We are the righteousness of God in Him." For what more powerful than that He should reign for ever, with all His enemies put under His feet? Why should not they also be "the multitude of His greatness"? not that whereby He is great, but whereby He hath made them great, many as they are, that is, thousands of thousands. Just as righteousness too is understood in two ways, that whereby He is righteous, and that which He worketh in us, so as to make us His righteousness. These same saints are signified by all the musical instruments in succession, to praise God in. For what the Psalmist began with, saying, "Praise the Lord in His saints," that he carrieth out, signifying in various ways these same saints of His.

5. "Praise Him in the sound of the trumpet" (ver. 3) : on account of the surpassing clearness of note of their praise. "Praise Him in the psaltery and harp." The psaltery praiseth God from things above, the harp praiseth God from things below; I mean, from things in heaven, and things in earth, as He who made heaven and earth. We have already in another Psalm,[9] explained that the psaltery hath that board, whereon the series of strings rests that it may give a better sound, above, whereas the harp has it below. "Praise Him in the timbrel and choir" (ver. 4). The "timbrel" praiseth God when the flesh is now changed, so that there is in it no weakness of earthly corruption. For the timbrel is made of leather dried and strengthened. The "choir" praiseth God when society made peaceful praiseth Him. "Praise Him on the strings and organ." Both psaltery and harp, which have been mentioned above, have strings. But "organ" is a general name for all instruments of music, although usage has now obtained that those are specially called organ which are inflated with bellows : but I do not think that this kind is meant here.[10] For

---

[1] Ps. cxxi. 2; Gen. i. 8.
[2] *Orbem terræ*, and *orbem terrarum*. [But by *orbis terræ* does he mean "globe"? See p. 365, note 6, *supra.* — C.]
[3] Acts vii. 42.
[4] Ps. xl. 8. [*i.e.* the Bible. In the Middle Ages called rather "the Holy Library." — C.]
[5] Rom. viii. 30. [See p. 231, *supra.* — C.]

[6] 2 Cor. v. 21.   [7] 2 Cor. xiii. 4; Philip. iii. 10.
[8] Rom. vi. 9.   [9] See vol. i. p. 312.
[10] [See p. 229, note 1, *supra.* — C.]

since organ is a Greek word, applied generally, as I have said, to all musical instruments, this instrument, to which bellows are applied, is called by the Greeks by another name: but it being called organ is rather a Latin and conversational usage. When then he saith, "on the strings and organ," he seemeth to me to have intended to signify some instrument which hath strings. For it is not psalteries and harps only that have strings: but, because in the psaltery and harp, on account of the sound from things below and things above, somewhat has been found which can be understood after this distinction, he hath suggested to us to seek some other meaning in the strings themselves: for they too are flesh, but flesh now set free from corruption. And to those, it may be, he added the organ, to signify that they sound not each separately, but sound together in most harmonious diversity, just as they are arranged in a musical instrument. For even then the saints of God will have their differences, accordant, not discordant, that is, agreeing, not disagreeing, just as sweetest harmony arises from sounds differing indeed, but not opposed to one another.

6. "Praise Him on the well-sounding cymbals, praise Him on cymbals of jubilation" (ver. 5). Cymbals touch one another in order to sound, and therefore are by some compared to our lips. But I think it better to understand that God is in a manner praised on the cymbal, when each is honoured by his neighbour, not by himself, and then honouring one another, they give praise to God. But lest any should understand such cymbals as sound without life, therefore I think he added, "on cymbals of jubilation." For "jubilation," that is, unspeakable praise, proceedeth not, save from life. Nor do I think that I should pass over what musicians say, that there are three kinds of sounds, by voice, by breath, by striking: by voice, uttered by throat and windpipe, when man singeth without any instrument; by breath, as by pipe, or anything of that sort: by striking, as by harp, or anything of that kind. None then of these kinds is omitted here: for there is voice in the choir, breath in the trumpet, striking in the harp, representing mind, spirit, body,[1] but by similitudes, not in the proper sense of the words. When then he proposed, "Praise God in His saints," to whom said he this, save to themselves? And in whom are they to praise God, save in themselves? For ye, saith he, are "His saints;" ye are "His strength," but that which He wrought in you; ye are "His mighty works, and the multitude of His greatness," which He hath wrought and set forth in you. Ye are "trumpet, psaltery, harp, timbrel, choir, strings, and organ, cymbals of jubilation sounding well," because sounding in harmony. All these are ye: let nought that is vile, nought that is transitory, nought that is ludicrous, be here thought of. And since to savour of the flesh is death, "let every spirit praise the Lord" (ver. 6).

PRAYER OF ST. AUGUSTIN.

Which he was wont to use after his Sermons and Lectures.

TURN we to the Lord God, the Father Almighty, and with pure hearts offer to Him, so far as our meanness can, great and true thanks, with all our hearts praying His exceeding kindness, that of His good pleasure He would deign to hear our prayers, that by His Power He would drive out the enemy from our deeds and thoughts, that He would increase our faith, guide our understandings, give us spiritual thoughts, and lead us to His bliss, through Jesus Christ His Son our Lord, who liveth and reigneth with Him, in the Unity of the Holy Spirit, one God, for ever and ever. Amen.

---

[1] [The tripartite nature of man recognised. See A. N. F. vol. iii. p. 474.—C.]

INDEXES

INDEX OF SUBJECTS.